Strangers at the Bedside

OTHER BOOKS BY DAVID J. ROTHMAN

STRANGERS AT THE BEDSIDE

A History of How Law and Bioethics Transformed Medical Decision Making

DAVID J. ROTHMAN

BasicBooks
A Division of HarperCollins*Publishers*

Library of Congress Cataloging-in-Publication Data
Rothman, David J.
    Strangers at the bedside : a history of how law
and bioethics transformed medical decision
making / David J. Rothman
        p. cm.
    Includes bibliographical references and index.
    ISBN 0-465-08209-2
    1. Medicine—United States—Decision
making—History.   2. Medicine—Research—
United States—Decision making—History.   3.
Medical ethics—United States—History. I. Title.
R723.5.R67   1991
610'.72—dc20   90-55598
                                                   CIP

To J.R.
For Doing Good

CONTENTS

ACKNOWLEDGMENTS

IN the course of research and writing, I received significant assistance from a number of individuals, and I am pleased to be able to acknowledge their contributions. I was fortunate enough to have exceptional guides to the world of medicine, and although they will dissent from some of the things said here, my debt to them is great. All on the faculty of the Columbia College of Physicians and Surgeons, they are: Henrik Bendixen, John Driscoll, Norman Kahn, Michael Katz, Edgar Leifer, Jay Meltzer, Harold Neu, and Keith Reemtsma. The two people most responsible for my joining the faculty, Thomas Morris and Donald Tapley, taught me all that they could about navigating in strange waters.

A grant from the National Endowment for the Humanities freed me from other responsibilities, and Daniel Jones (program officer for grant RO-21349-06) was particularly helpful. The Samuel and May Rudin Foundation provided matching funds as part of its ongoing support of the program at the Center for the Study of Society and Medicine. Neither foundation is responsible for the views expressed here, which, of course, means that in no way did they attempt to influence the direction or course of the research.

I have benefited, as have so many other researchers, from the knowledgeable staff of the National Archives, the National Institutes of

ACKNOWLEDGMENTS

Health, the New York Academy of Medicine, and from the guidance of Richard Wolfe at the Countway Library of Medicine of Harvard University. I am also indebted to Daniel Fox and Ronald Bayer for their many valuable suggestions for strengthening the manuscript, and to Harold Edgar as well, although he remains convinced that historians' arguments cannot stand up to grueling cross-examination.

The idea for this book came as I prepared to deliver the University Lecture to the Columbia community, and in subsequent years, I had the opportunity to share ideas with colleagues at the University of Virginia (courtesy of John Fletcher), the University of California Medical School, San Francisco (Gunther Reisse), Cornell University (Sander Gilman), the University of Kansas Medical School (William Bartholome), and the University of Texas (William Winslade). A presentation to the annual meeting of the American Association for the History of Medicine and to the Smith Kline Beecham meeting on Controversies in Infectious Diseases (courtesy of Harold Neu) were also stimulating occasions.

Discussions with colleagues at the Center for the Study of Society and Medicine, Sherry Brandt-Rauf, Stephen Hilgartner, and Stephanie Kiceluk, helped me formulate and clarify my ideas. I benefited greatly from Robert Zussman's review of the manuscript and from his forthcoming work on medical decision making in adult intensive care units. Probably no one is more relieved at the appearance of this book than Nancy Lundebjerg, a most talented administrator in charge of the Center.

Martin Kessler, president of Basic Books, made certain that the upheavals that can sweep through publishing did not affect this book, and I am grateful to him for his confidence. My editor, Susan Rabiner, prodded and pushed the way excellent editors do, and unfailingly looked after the manuscript, and me.

Finally, I relish having one more occasion to recognize my ongoing obligations to Sheila Rothman. Her work on the history of patienthood (which is at the core of the National Endowment for the Humanities grant that we shared) will appear shortly, and again I was able to

ACKNOWLEDGMENTS

benefit from her knowledge, scholarly standards, and editorial skills. And this time, our children not only tolerated our shop talk but joined in, Matthew drawing on his experiences in photographing emergency medical care in New York City, Micol, on her personal interest in what it means to be a doctor. Put simply, they make it all worthwhile.

INTRODUCTION

Making the Invisible Visible

B EGINNING in the mid-1960s, the practice of medicine in the United States underwent a most remarkable—and thoroughly controversial—transformation. Although the changes have altered almost every aspect of the relationship between doctor and patient—indeed, between medicine and society—the essence can be succinctly summarized: the discretion that the profession once enjoyed has been increasingly circumscribed, with an almost bewildering number of parties and procedures participating in medical decision making. As late as 1969, the philosopher Hans Jonas could assert that "the physician is obligated to the patient and to no one else. . . . We may speak of a sacred trust; strictly by its terms, the doctor is, as it were, alone with his patient and God."[1] But even as he wrote, the image of a physician alone with a patient was being supplanted by one of an examining room so crowded that the physician had difficulty squeezing in and of a patient surrounded by strangers.

Well into the post–World War II period, decisions at the bedside were the almost exclusive concern of the individual physician, even when they raised fundamental ethical and social issues. It was mainly doctors who wrote and read about the morality of withholding a course of antibiotics and letting pneumonia serve as the old man's best friend, of considering a newborn with grave birth defects a "stillbirth" and sparing the parents the agony of choice and the burden of care, of experimenting on the institutionalized retarded to learn more about hepatitis, or of giving one patient and not another access to the iron lung when the machine was in short supply. Moreover, it was usually the individual physician who decided these matters at the bedside or in the privacy of the hospital room, without formal discussions with patients, their families, or even with colleagues, and certainly without drawing the attention of journalists, judges, or professional philosophers. And they made their decisions on a case-by-case basis, responding to the particular circumstances as they saw fit, reluctant by both training and practice to formulate or adhere to guidelines or rules.

By the mid-1970s, both the style and the substance of medical decision making had changed. The authority that an individual physician had once exercised covertly was now subject to debate and review by colleagues and laypeople. Let the physician design a research protocol to deliver an experimental treatment, and in the room, by federal mandate, was an institutional review board composed of other physicians, lawyers, and community representatives to make certain that the potential benefits to the subject-patient outweighed the risks. Let the physician attempt to allocate a scarce resource, like a donor heart, and in the room were federal and state legislators and administrators to help set standards of equity and justice. Let the physician decide to withdraw or terminate life-sustaining treatment from an incompetent patient, and in the room were state judges to rule, in advance, on the legality of these actions. Such a decision might also bring into the room a hospital ethics committee staffed by an unusual cadre of commentators, the bioethicists, who stood ready to replace bedside ethics with armchair ethics, to draw on philosophers' first principles, not on the accumulated experience of medical practice.

Were all these participants not company enough, the physician in the ordinary circumstances of daily practice often encountered a new type of patient, particularly among young and better educated men, and even more frequently, women, who had assimilated a new message: rather than comply dutifully with your doctor's orders, be "alert to your responsibility in the relationship, just as you would in any other adult relationship where you are purchasing services."[2] In the 1950s,

2

popular health care guides had carried such titles as "What to Do Until the Doctor Comes." The updated version might well be called: "What to Do After the Doctor Comes."

Without putting too fine a point on it, the critical period of change was 1966 to 1976. The transformation began when in 1966 a Harvard Medical School professor, Henry Beecher, exposed abuses in human experimentation. Then, in 1973, Congress, under the leadership of senators Walter Mondale and Edward Kennedy, established a national commission to explore medical ethics. The period closed with the New Jersey Supreme Court ordering doctors to yield to parental requests to remove twenty-two-year-old Karen Ann Quinlan from a respirator. The impact of these events, most generally framed, was to make the invisible visible. Outsiders to medicine—that is, lawyers, judges, legislators, and academics—penetrated its every nook and cranny, in the process giving medicine an exceptional prominence on the public agenda and making it the subject of popular discourse. This glare of the spotlight transformed medical decision making, shaping not merely the external conditions under which medicine would be practiced (something that the state, through the regulation of licensure, had always done), but the very substance of medical practice—the decisions that physicians made at the bedside.

The change was first manifested and implemented through a new commitment to collective, as against individual, decision making. There were standing committees to ensure that a researcher who would experiment with human subjects was not making a self-serving calculus of risks and benefits, and standing committees to review whether the physician who would withdraw treatment from a gravely ill newborn or, for that matter, from a terminally ill adult, was not idiosyncratic in his or her calculus of medical futility or judgment about a life not worth living. Second, a new formality came to characterize decision making. Written documentation was replacing word-of-mouth orders (or pencil notations to be erased later), as in the case of coding a patient DNR (do not resuscitate) so that if his heart stopped, the team would not make every last effort (through chemical and electrical stimulation) to revive him. This formality transformed the medical chart from an essentially private means of communication among doctors to a public piece of evidence that documented what the doctor had told, and heard from, the patient. Third, in a more subtle but no less critical

3

fashion, outsiders now framed the normative principles that were to guide the doctor–patient relationship. The critical pronouncements no longer originated in medical texts but in judicial decisions, bioethical treatises, and legislative resolutions. Outsiders, not doctors, defined the moral codes that were to guide physician behavior.

The causes and consequences of these extraordinary changes are the core concerns of this book. How did it happen that physicians, who had once ruled uncontested over their domain, came to confront committees, forms, general principles, and active patients? What were the roots of the idea, not very long ago unheard of, that "there is need to involve not only the medical profession, but lawyers, sociologists, moralists, and society at large" in the effort to resolve "complicated [medical] issues," for "the solutions will come only if society is willing to support the formal investigation by physicians, lawyers, sociologists and moralists"?[3] Why did this line become repeated so often and in such a variety of contexts as to become almost a truism? In a phrase, what brought new rules and new players to medicine?

In answering these questions, it will often be useful to contrast the perspectives and goals of physicians and nonphysicians, or outsiders as I call them. The designations are obviously broad, and for some purposes no doubt too broad. Medical specialists have often differed on policy issues from general practitioners, as anyone familiar with the history of the American Medical Association recognizes. And from 1966 to 1976, physicians were divided (albeit not evenly) among themselves on many of the substantive matters explored in this book. In almost every instance, it was physicians who assumed the role of whistle-blowers and invited outsiders in. For example, Henry Beecher, a physician, exposed the abuse of discretion by individual researchers, and physicians such as Raymond Duff and William Bartholome lifted the curtain that surrounded neonatal decision making. But that said, in the debates over ruling medicine, the great majority of physicians who went on record, including the whistle-blowers, were deeply troubled about a loss of doctors' authority at the bedside and the expanded prerogatives of outsiders. The changes that came to medicine generally came over the strenuous objections of doctors, giving the entire process an adversarial quality.

On the other side, the outsiders who entered medicine ranged from lawyers to legislators to religion and philosophy professors. Although one would not have anticipated prior agreement among them on most subjects, they shared a goal of bringing new rules to medicine. Whether drawing on a tradition of predictability (in the law) or of first principles (in philosophy or religion), they joined together to create a new formality and impose it on medicine, insisting on guidelines, regulations, and collective decision making. They concurred on the need to reduce physicians' discretion and enhance patients' autonomy.

Given such disparate views and intentions, a twofold classification of doctors and outsiders makes sense. Although it can mask important distinctions, it helps us capture and explain the essence of a decade-long conflict. It conveys an image of a relatively well drawn battle line—which fits with the contours of the events.

I am also comfortable maintaining an insider–outsider distinction because in 1983 I became Professor of Social Medicine at Columbia's College of Physicians and Surgeons, even as I continued as professor of history in the university. My mandate from the medical school was to bring the methods and materials of the humanities and social sciences into its research and teaching curriculum. In a very personal way, then, I crossed the boundary and entered the world of medicine, in the process coming to appreciate just how different a world it is.

My assignment has been both exciting and difficult. Medicine has its own language, and it was disconcerting, almost humiliating, to arrive and listen to a group of twenty-six-year-olds carry on a conversation I could barely understand. "Dropping a crit," "flipping t waves," and "running v tach" were actions whose significance I neither recognized nor appreciated. Medicine also has its own brand of shoptalk; as I describe later, a first exposure to the "interesting case"—almost certain to involve devastating disease for the patient and many unknowns for the physician—was, even for someone who had investigated institutions for the retarded and prisons, emotionally draining and often too painful to share, at least with nonphysicians. But these experiences taught me firsthand that illness is highly segregated in this society, as are those who treat it.

I was struck again and again by the vast ignorance of colleagues and friends about the world of medicine. Although I was accustomed to exploring institutions that were sealed off from the general public, I had not imagined that hospitals belonged in this category. I was frequently asked questions that revealed a startling degree of distance and unfamiliarity: "Is an operating room really a theater, with rows of seats going up?" (No) "Do surgeons bring tape decks with them?" (Sometimes) "What do you wear on rounds?" (A suit, not a white coat)— and on and on, as though my questioners had never been inside a hospital or spoken to a doctor outside of an examining room. Of course, they had read all about respirators, transplants, and other high-technology interventions. But what they lacked was a feel for the enterprise, a sense of the actors and the routines. To judge from their reactions, I was a throwback to the anthropologists of the 1920s, an explorer of foreign parts, as though 168th Street in northern Manhattan was at one with the South Seas.

In truth, I sometimes shared this sensation. Surprise was, and remains, a constant feature of going on rounds. At one of my first sessions, I was startled to hear a resident inform a senior physician, just before we entered a patient's room, that the patient had "died" yesterday, but after having had his medications adjusted, was doing much better. Later that morning she related that another patient was making good progress: he had not "died" even once, and she was confident about his prospects. Surely I was on a magic island if death was reversible and resurrection commonplace. And even after I learned that to "die" was to suffer a cardiac arrest and undergo resuscitation, not all of the sense of mystery disappeared.

I was also unprepared for the grueling and continuous pace of medical practice, a pace that helps isolate physicians in their own universe. The day starts early (seven o'clock meetings are not uncommon), and ends late; one female physician confessed to me that she considered herself only part-time because family responsibilities (raising three children) allowed her to work only a forty-hour week. And time not devoted to practice or teaching is often spent keeping pace with the latest research findings in the medical journals; nothing is more common on rounds than for attending physicians or house staff to cite a recent article on the advantages and disadvantages of a particular drug or procedure. The physicians are alert to numbers, and findings from random clinical trials carry critical authority. But numbers alone do not rule, which brings us back to the issues at hand in the control of medicine.

Perhaps the most remarkable feature of clinical decision making is the extraordinary reliance on a case-by-case approach. No two patients, after all, are exactly alike; symptoms do not appear in the same pattern in the course of disease, and the results of tests do not always fall unambiguously into one category or another. Thus, medicine is as much art as science, and the clinical anecdote becomes highly relevant to treatment decisions. Because of uncertainty, clinicians value experience highly and are prepared to make decisions on the basis of a trial of one—that is, a patient treated some ten years ago whose case resembles the one today and who improved on a particular regimen. It is this resort to the anecdote that gives physicians the air of artists, even of magicians. In the face of confusing and contradictory symptoms, physicians can pull from a hat some case from the past and make their recommendation, often leading to the patient's recovery, albeit a baffling one.

Physicians, as I have learned, frequently bring this case-by-case approach into the consideration of social and ethical issues. Offer them a principle to consider (for example, that patients have the right to know their diagnosis), and they will often come up with a case (drawn from experience) that they believe undercuts and thereby negates the principle (for instance, the seeming inappropriateness of informing a seventy-five-year-old woman about to go off to her grandchild's wedding that she has an inoperable and slow-growing brain tumor). Describe a case in the ethics of decision making at the end of life that occurred at another hospital, and the physicians initially will try to obviate the problem by claiming that those doctors made egregious errors in their treatment (for example, this patient should never have needed a respirator in the first place). It is as though their ability to resolve the incident at hand absolves them of the need to formulate or respect general principles. If they can cite a case in which the proposed rule does not hold, then they have ostensibly discredited not only the rule but the search for rules. In short, clinicians start with the case at hand, and if they have their way, stop with the case at hand.

Outsiders from various disciplines seem far more prepared to seek out the general principle in deciding social and ethical questions. A legal, as opposed to medical, mind-set is much more likely to search for the rule that should be imposed on a particular case than to see how the case can be resolved without it. Those trained in history or in other disciplines in the humanities and social sciences share this orientation. The end point is not the individual case but the light it can shed on general phenomena. In history this often prompts an impatience with biography, at least to the degree that it invokes the details of one person's life that are irrelevant to the larger social or political context. Medicine, by contrast, is closer to biography than to history, or to put this point in medicine's language, to the case history. Most of what physicians write for lay audiences, whether it is a neurologist on aphasia or a surgeon on transplants, follows this pattern—focusing on the one exciting case, or a series of cases, and letting the one instance represent all.

Clinicians appear to be as uncomfortable with sociological analyses of the collective aspects of medical decision making and the structural underpinnings of medical institutions as they are with the humanists' search for general principles. Consider, for example, the case of infants who are being treated even when the overwhelming majority of physicians and nurses do not believe treatment should continue. Tell the head of a neonatal unit that such practices persist not because of some error or breakdown in communication but because of a collective ethos that is protreatment; explain that this structural element, not the particulars of each case, is probably shaping the treatment decision, and you probably will hear a firm denial that such a process could occur. The very idea that some underlying mechanisms might constrain or dictate action is altogether alien to a perspective that insists that each case is, and must be, considered on its own merits.[4]

This perspective is transmitted from one generation of physicians to the other, not in so many words but in the very organization of medical school education. In clinical teaching the case approach is sacrosanct, and anyone who would bring social and ethical issues into the curriculum must adopt the same style. To begin with the general (What does "patient autonomy" mean?) and then move down to the particular (What are the implications for terminating treatment?) is to lose one's audience at the outset. Rather, one must start with the particular, with the specifics of a case and hope (distractions fielded) that one gets to

8

the general point. In fact, many medical schools long resisted the formal teaching of ethics, not because they believed that ethics could not be taught, but because it had to be taught at the bedside, by starting with the individual case. This type of approach, which I call *bedside ethics*, essentially meant teaching by example, by role modeling, by students taking cues from practicing physicians. Students were not to learn ethics by studying principles but by watching senior physicians resolve individual situations and then doing likewise. It is as though medical decision making begins and ends (or more precisely, should begin and end) with the dyad of the doctor and the patient alone in the examining room.

These biographical details and disciplinary outlooks help explain my approach in this book. They suggest, first, how alien rules are to medical decision making and how dogged and persistent an effort to alter this orientation would have to be. Second, although a doctor–outsider distinction may seem rudimentary, both scholarship and experience have persuaded me how real and powerful it is—so much so that in some ways this book represents my attempt to understand why a medical school would ask me (and the requests now extend, obviously, to many others) to cross over and enter its domain.

Perhaps most important, these observations make clear that from the start my own predilection strongly favored bringing rules to medicine. What I did not, however, fully appreciate at the outset was that by 1983 many of the critical battles had already been fought and a number of victories won. Thus, I immediately became a member of the institutional review board to oversee the conduct of human experimentation; I helped the medical director of the neonatal unit organize a bioethics committee, on which I took a seat; I helped a team of physicians who were conducting in vitro fertilization set up guidelines; and I sat with the heart transplant team as they pondered procedures for selecting recipients. Of course, I and the other committee members encountered resistance from colleagues. But it soon became apparent to me that what was needed most was not an insistence on bringing rules to medicine but a careful analysis of how the transformation in medical decision making had occurred.

• • •

The causes of this sweeping transformation are as far-reaching as its implications. To understand the origins and outcomes of the disputes over ruling medicine requires tracing developments within both medicine and society, a reckoning that takes into account physician behavior and more diffuse public attitudes. For in many ways, the conflicts come down to an erosion in trust, to a decline in the deference given to doctors and to their professional judgments. To grapple with such delicate and elusive sentiments as trust and deference requires scrutinizing both sides of a relationship—what doctors did and what outsiders did—to make traditional ties and procedures seem inadequate and obsolete.

Surprisingly, the story opens in the laboratory, not the examining room. A series of exposés of practices in human experimentation revealed a stark conflict of interest between clinical investigators and human subjects, between researchers' ambitions and patients' well-being. This perception undercut an older confidence in the exercise of medical discretion and gave the regulation of clinical research a special prominence on the public agenda. The ethics of experimentation attracted the concern not only of those within medicine (particularly at the National Institutes of Health and the Food and Drug Administration), but an array of outsiders, most notably politicians and academics (law professors, philosophers, and sociologists), who had previously paid scant attention to medical issues. In fact, the agitation over human experimentation quickly became linked to the rights movements that were gaining strength in the 1960s, largely because the great majority of research subjects were minorities, drawn from the ranks of the poor, the mentally disabled, and the incarcerated. This linkage ensured that the rights of research subjects (or, conversely, the felt need to restrict the discretion of the researcher) would not only capture but hold public attention.

The result was an entirely new system of governance for human experimentation. Federal regulations required mechanisms for collective decision making, thereby abridging the once considerable freedom of the investigator. No less important, human experimentation gave an entirely new weight to the idea of consent, to making certain that the subject understood the nature of the experiment and voluntarily agreed to participate. This unprecedented reliance on the mechanism of consent reflected not so much an abstract commitment to the importance of the principle of consent as a deeply felt need to protect vulnerable individuals from single-minded, overeager investigators.

Attitudes and practices initially formulated to cope with laboratory practices, quickly, if unpredictably, spread to bedside practices, and understanding the dynamics will take us through the second half of this book. The analysis begins with the altered social position of medicine in the post–World War II decades, with the fact that the doctor became a stranger and the hospital a strange place. As the social distance between doctor and patient, and between hospital and community, enlarged, a sense of trust eroded. When one could no longer assume that the physician shared the same set of values as the patient, it seemed vital to devise and implement new mechanisms, preferably formal or even rigid, to further patients' particular wishes. It became appropriate to post on hospital walls a copy of the Patient Bill of Rights, as though the facility were a factory and its users, rank-and-file labor. Even more notably, as doctor and hospital moved apart from patient and community, the practical wisdom that the practitioner had accumulated over years of clinical experience seemed less impressive and relevant than the wisdom that the philosopher or lawyer had accumulated through the study of first principles. In effect, bedside ethics gave way to bioethics.

The impact of these structural changes was intensified and propelled forward by a series of extraordinary innovations in medical practice. Almost immediately upon the heels of the exposés in human experimentation came the breakthrough in organ transplantation, first with kidneys and then most dramatically, in 1968, with hearts. Transplantation appeared to put the physician, like the researcher, in a position of conflict of interest with the patient. Taking a heart from one desperately ill patient to give to another raised the frightening prospect that a physician eager to save one life might sacrifice another. Transplantation also raised troubling questions about how best to distribute scarce resources—conventional wisdom on triage was no help—and prompted a Harvard committee, made up mostly of physicians, to attempt, unilaterally, to redefine the criterion for death by making the brain, not the heart, the determining organ. Every one of these issues swelled the ranks of outsiders who became concerned with medicine, to the point that Congress created a national commission—dominated by lay, not medical, members—to explore, first, the ethics of human experimentation and, later, all of medical ethics. And every one of these issues made it seem all the more necessary to bring collective and formal procedures to medical decision making, reinforcing the growing sense that medical decisions should not be left to the discretion of individual physicians.

The story culminated in a newborn nursery and an adult intensive care unit: Beginning with the death of a retarded newborn at the Johns Hopkins University Hospital because his parents refused to permit life-saving surgery and reaching it apogee in the case of Karen Ann Quinlan, perhaps the most famous patient in recent medical history, the license to decide questions of life and death shifted from the profession to the polity, from the hidden recesses of the hospital intensive care unit and one of medicine's best-guarded secrets to the open courtroom and everyday conversation. After Quinlan, medical decision making became the province of a collection of strangers, with judges, lawyers, ethicists, and legislators joining doctors at their patients' bedside.

As would be expected, these developments have generated many polemics, evenly divided between laypeople denouncing medical arrogance for not letting Grandma die a peaceful and quick death, and physicians complaining that the new rules undercut the delivery of good medical care and force them to badger dying patients with unnecessary questions. Consumer newsletters urge patients to assert themselves, and medical newsletters run banner headlines proclaiming that "OUTSIDERS SHOULD STAY OUT OF MEDICINE." Nostalgia mixes with anger and recriminations: Where is yesterday's family doctor? Where is yesterday's grateful patient?

The changes have also produced a more substantial body of analysis, most of it focusing on medical economics and medical technologies. Ostensibly, new rules came to medicine because care was too expensive and physicians too powerful. That both these considerations are important is beyond dispute; some regulatory measures were bound to be imposed on medicine when the bill for national health care skyrocketed from $19 billion in 1960 to $275 billion by 1980 (and on to $365 billion and 10 percent of the gross national product by 1985). It is not surprising to find the federal government—in an effort to control Medicare costs—empowering review committees to disallow reimbursements for unnecessary, long hospital stays, and to find corporations—attempting to limit expenditures on fringe benefits—insisting on the right to review recommendations to treat an employee. By the same token, technological advances have been so heady that many outsiders have deep fears (and fantasies) about their abuse. When respirators and dialysis machines could keep the dying alive for weeks, months, or years, there was bound to be widespread concern about medicine doing more than anyone might want it to do.

But neither economics nor technology required so basic a reordering of the balance between doctor and patient. There is no iron clad formula dictating what percentage of resources an advanced industrial society should devote to health care; and were the totality of the story cost containment, there would have been no reason to create oversight committees for research or to formalize DNR procedures. So too, had other considerations not intervened, one could imagine trusting the expert in the technology to determine the appropriate use of the technology. Why not let those who understand the mechanics of respiration decide when to connect or disconnect the respirator? Why not let those who are able to defy death be the ones to define death? In short, costs and technology are highly relevant to the new posture toward medicine and medical decision making, but they alone cannot explain it. Indeed, an erosion of trust may well have been a precondition for economic and technological regulation. It was because doctors were strangers that they could not be trusted with the respirator. It was because hospitals were strange institutions that their costs and practices had to be monitored.

To present the history of a change is inevitably to raise questions on the merits of the change. Was the cure worse than the disease? Did bringing new rules to medicine prove more mischievous than helpful? In the following pages I frame initial answers to these questions—although perhaps not as directly and unequivocally as some might hope. Still, to understand the elements that propelled the movement forward is to come away, I believe, convinced of its necessity and validity, albeit with significant qualifications and concerns.

One final caution: The history traced here is an ongoing one, and judgments about intended and unintended consequences are bound to be premature. The field of medicine is now buffeted by the winds of change—let one issue float up, and it is immediately blown away by yet another issue. For a time, all that anyone wanted to talk about were the new federal reimbursement formulas ("Is There Life after DRGs?" was the title of one lecture). Then the concern shifted to quality control (Can patient care and hospital budgets survive interns getting a full night's sleep?), and then focused on the treatment of AIDS (What degree of risk should a physician be required to accept? How far should AIDS patients be allowed to go in choosing their own drug regimens?). Each issue prompted the call for new rules, committees, and guidelines, and each has brought still more participants (from data retrieval specialists to AIDS activists) into medicine. Thus, it is much too early to offer final verdicts, but not too early to remember just how recently medicine and medical decision making became so central a subject in public and policy discourse. I can only hope, as do many other historians, that an analysis of the origins of a change can help us—doctors, patients, and citizens alike—to direct and enhance the change.

CHAPTER 1

The Nobility of the Material

CHANGE began with a whistle-blower and a scandal.

In June 1966, Henry Beecher, Dorr Professor of Research in Anesthesia at Harvard Medical School, published in the *New England Journal of Medicine (NEJM)* his analysis of "Ethics and Clinical Research" and thereby joined the ranks of such noted muckrakers as Harriet Beecher Stowe, Upton Sinclair, and Rachael Carson.[1] As has so often happened in the course of American history, a publication like *Uncle Tom's Cabin*, *The Jungle*, or *Silent Spring* will expose a secret—whether it be the violation of the slave family, the contamination of food, or the poisoning of the environment—so compellingly as to transform public attitudes and policy. Beecher's article fits in this tradition. Its devastating indictment of research ethics helped inspire the movement that brought a new set of rules and a new set of players to medical decision making.[2]

The piece was short, barely six double-columned pages, and the writing terse and technical, primarily aimed at a professional, not a lay, audience. Beecher tried (not altogether successfully) to maintain a tone of detachment, as though this were a scientific paper like any other. "I want to be very sure," he insisted, "that I have squeezed out of it all emotion, value judgments, and so on."[3] Even so, its publication created a furor both inside and outside the medical profession.

At its heart were capsule descriptions of twenty-two examples of investigators who had risked "the health or the life of their subjects" without informing them of the dangers or obtaining their permission. No citations to the original publications or names of the researchers appeared. Beecher did give the editors of the *NEJM* a fully annotated copy, and they vouched for its accuracy; he steadfastly refused all subsequent requests for references. Publicly, he declared that his intention was not to single out individuals but to "call attention to widespread practices." Privately, he conceded that a colleague from the Harvard Law School had advised him that to name names might open the individuals to lawsuits or criminal prosecution.[4]

The research protocols that made up Beecher's roll of dishonor seemed flagrant in their disregard of the welfare of the human subjects. Example 2 constituted the purposeful withholding of penicillin from servicemen with streptococcal infections in order to study alternative means for preventing complications. The men were totally unaware of the fact that they were part of an experiment, let alone at risk of contracting rheumatic fever, which twenty-five of them did. Example 16 involved the feeding of live hepatitis viruses to residents of a state institution for the retarded in order to study the etiology of the disease and attempt to create a protective vaccine against it. In example 17, physicians injected live cancer cells into twenty-two elderly and senile hospitalized patients without telling them that the cells were cancerous, in order to study the body's immunological responses. Example 19 involved researchers who inserted a special needle into the left atrium of the heart of subjects, some with cardiac disease and others normal, in order to study the functioning of the heart. In example 22, researchers inserted a catheter into the bladder of twenty-six newborns less than forty-eight hours old and then took a series of X rays of the bladders filling and voiding in order to study the process. "Fortunately," noted Beecher, "no infection followed the catheterization. What the results of the extensive x-ray exposure may be, no one can yet say."

Beecher's most significant, and predictably most controversial, conclusion was that "unethical or questionably ethical procedures are not uncommon" among researchers—that is, a disregard for the rights of human subjects was widespread. Although he did not provide footnotes, Beecher declared that "the troubling practices" came from "leading medical schools, university hospitals, private hospitals, governmental military departments . . . governmental institutes (the National Institutes of Health), Veterans Administration Hospitals and industry." In short, "the basis for the charges is broad." Moreover, without attempting any numerical estimate of just how endemic the practices were among researchers, Beecher reported how dismayingly easy it had been for him to compile his list. An initial list of seventeen examples had been easily expanded to fifty (and winnowed down to twenty-two for publication). He had also examined 100 consecutive studies that were reported on in 1964 "in an excellent journal; 12 of these seemed unethical." He concluded, "If only one quarter of them is truly unethical, this still indicates the existence of a serious problem."

At a time when the media were not yet scouring medical journals for stories, Beecher's charges captured an extraordinary amount of public attention. Accounts of the *NEJM* article appeared in the leading newspapers and weeklies, which was precisely what he had intended. A circumspect whistle-blower, he had published his findings first in a medical journal without naming names; but at the same time, he had informed influential publications (including the *New York Times*, the *Wall Street Journal*, *Time*, and *Newsweek*) that his piece was forthcoming. The press reported the experiments in great detail, and reporters, readers, and public officials alike expressed dismay and incredulity as they pondered what had led respectable scientists to commit such acts. How could researchers have injected cancer cells into hospitalized senile people or fed hepatitis viruses to institutionalized retarded children? In short order, the National Institutes of Health (NIH), the major funder of research in the country, was getting letters from legislators asking what corrective actions it intended to take.[5]

Beecher, as he fully expected, infuriated many of his colleagues, and they responded angrily and defensively. Some, like Thomas Chalmers at Harvard, insisted that he had grossly exaggerated the problem, taking a few instances and magnifying them out of proportion.[6] The more popular objection (which can still be heard among investigators today) was that he had unfairly assessed 1950s practices in terms of the moral standards of a later era. To these critics, the investigators that Beecher had singled out were pioneers, working before standards were set for human investigation, before it was considered necessary to inform subjects about the research and obtain their formal consent to participation. The enterprise of human investigation was so novel that research ethics had been necessarily primitive and underdeveloped.

However popular—and, on the surface, appealing—that retort is, it not only fails to address the disjuncture between public expectations and researchers' behavior but is woefully short on historical perspective. If the activity was so new and the state of ethics so crude, why did outsiders shudder as they read about the experiments? However tempting it might be to short-circuit the history, neither human experimentation nor the ethics of it was a recent invention. Still, Beecher's critics were not altogether misguided: there was something substantially different about the post–World War II laboratories and investigators. If researchers were not as morally naïve as their defenders would suggest, they occupied a very special position in time. They had inherited a unique legacy, bequeathed to them by the World War II experience.

Thus, for many reasons, it is important that we trace, however briefly, this history, particularly in its most recent phases. In no other way can we understand how investigators could have designed and conducted the trials that made up Beecher's roster. And in no other way can we understand the gap between the investigators' behavior and public expectation, a gap that would produce not only wariness and distrust but also new mechanisms for governing clinical research. These attitudes and mechanisms spread, more quickly than might have been anticipated, from the laboratory to the examining room. A reluctance to trust researchers to protect the well-being of their subjects soon turned into an unwillingness to trust physicians to protect the well-being of their patients. In the new rules for research were the origins of the new rules for medicine.

Until World War II, the research enterprise was typically small-scale and intimate, guided by an ethic consistent with community expectations.[7] Most research was a cottage industry: a few physicians, working alone, carried out experiments on themselves, their families, and their immediate neighbors. Moreover, the research was almost always therapeutic in intent; that is, the subjects stood to benefit directly if the experiments were successful. Under these circumstances, the ethics of human investigation did not command much attention; a few scientists, like Claude Bernard and Louis Pasteur, set forth especially thoughtful and elegant analyses. But for the most part, the small scale and potentially therapeutic character of the research seemed protection enough, and researchers were left to their own conscience, with almost no effort to police them. To be sure, not everyone's behavior matched the standard or lived up to expectations. By the 1890s, and even more frequently in the opening decades of the twentieth century, some investigators could not resist experimenting on unknown and unknowing populations, particularly inmates of orphanages and state schools for the retarded. But at least before World War II such practices were relatively infrequent.

The idea of judging the usefulness of a particular medication by actual results goes back to a school of Greek and Roman empiricists, but we know little about how they made their judgments and whether they actually conducted experiments on human beings. The medieval Arab medical treatises, building on classical texts, reflect an appreciation of the need for human experiments, but again the record is thin on practice. Scholars like the renowned Islamic scientist and philosopher Avicenna (980–1037) recommended that a drug be applied to two different cases to measure its efficacy, and he also insisted that "the experimentation must be done with the human body, for testing a drug on a lion or a horse might not prove anything about its effect on man." However, he offered no guidance about how or on whom such experiments should be conducted.[8]

If earlier practices remain obscure, a number of ethical maxims about experimentation do survive. Maimonides (1125–1204), a noted Jewish physician and philosopher, counseled colleagues always to treat patients as ends in themselves, not as means for learning new truths. A fuller treatment of research ethics came from the English philosopher and scientist Roger Bacon (1214–1292). He excused the inconsistencies in therapeutic practices among contemporary physicians on the following grounds: "It is exceedingly difficult and dangerous to perform operations on the human body, wherefore it is more difficult to work in that science than in any other. . . . The operative and practical sciences which do their work on insensate bodies can multiply their experiments till they get rid of deficiency and errors, but a physician cannot do this because of the nobility of the material in which he works; for that body demands that no error be made in operating upon

it, and so experience [the experimental method] is so difficult in medicine."[9] To Bacon the trade-off was worth making: the human body
was so noble a material that therapeutics would have to suffer deficiencies and errors.

Human experimentation made its first significant impact on medical
knowledge in the eighteenth century, primarily through the work of
the English physician Edward Jenner, and his research on a vaccination
against smallpox exemplifies both the style and technique that would
predominate for the next 150 years. Observing that farmhands who
contracted the pox from swine or cows seemed to be immune to the
more virulent smallpox, Jenner set out to retrieve material from their
pustules, inject that into another person, and see whether the recipient
could then resist challenges from small amounts of smallpox materials.
In November 1789 he carried out his first experiment, inoculating his
oldest son, then about a year old, with swinepox. Although the child
suffered no ill effects, the smallpox material he then received did produce an irritation, indicating that he was not immune to the disease.[10]

Jenner subsequently decided to work with cowpox material. In his
most famous and successful experiment, he vaccinated an eight-year-
old boy with it, a week later challenged him with smallpox material,
and noted that he evinced no reaction. No record exists on the interaction between Jenner and his subject save Jenner's bare account: "The
more accurately to observe the progress of the infection, I selected a
healthy boy, about eight years old, for the purpose of inoculation for
the cow-pox. The matter . . . was inserted . . . into the arm of the boy
by means of two incisions."[11] Whether the boy was a willing or unwilling subject, how much he understood of the experiment, what kind
of risk–benefit calculation he might have made, or whether his parents
simply ordered him to put out his arm to please Mr. Jenner remains
unknown. Clearly, Jenner did the choosing, but do note the odd change
in style from the active "I selected" to the passive "the matter was . . .
inserted." All we can tell for certain is that the boy was from the
neighborhood, that Jenner was a man of standing, that he chose the
boy for the experiment, and that smallpox was a dreaded disease. Still,
some degree of trust probably existed between researcher and subject,
or subject's parents. This was not an interaction between strangers, and
Jenner would have been accountable had anything untoward happened.

Word of Jenner's success spread quickly, and in September 1799 he received a letter from a physician in Vienna who had managed to obtain some vaccine for his own use. His first subject, he told Jenner, was "the son of a physician in this town." Then, encouraged by his initial success, he reported, "I did not hesitate to inoculate . . . my eldest boy, and ten days afterwards my second boy." In this same spirit, Dr. Benjamin Waterhouse, professor of medicine at Harvard, learned of Jenner's work and vaccinated seven of his children; then, in order to test for the efficacy of the procedure, he exposed three of them to the disease at Boston's Smallpox Hospital, with no ill effects. Here again, colleagues and family were the first to share in the risks and benefits of research.[12]

Even in the premodern era, neighbors and relations were not the only subjects of research. Legends tell of ancient and medieval rulers who tested the efficacy of poison potions on condemned prisoners and released those who survived. Much better documented is the example of Lady Mary Wortley Montagu, wife of the British ambassador to Turkey, who learned about Turkish successes in inoculating patients with small amounts of the smallpox material to provide immunity. Eager to convince English physicians to adopt the procedure, she persuaded King George I to run a trial by pardoning any condemned inmate at the Newgate Prison who agreed to the inoculation. In August 1721, six volunteers were inoculated; they developed local lesions but no serious illness, and all were released. As science went, the trial was hardly satisfactory and the ethics were no better—the choice between death or enrollment in the experiment was not a freely made one. But such ventures remained the exception.[13]

For most of the nineteenth century, research continued on a small scale, with individual physicians trying out one or another remedy or procedure on a handful of persons. Experimentation still began at home, on the body of the investigator or on neighbors or relatives. One European physician, Johann Jorg, swallowed varying doses of seventeen different drugs in order to analyze their effects; another, James Simpson, searching for an anesthesia superior to ether, inhaled chloroform and awoke to find himself lying flat on the floor.[14] In what is surely the most extraordinary moment in nineteenth-century human experiments, Dr. William Beaumont conducted his famous studies on "The

Physiology of Digestion" on the healed stomach wound of Alexis St. Martin. There was a signed agreement between them, though not so much a consent form (as some historians have suggested) as an apprenticeship contract; but even this form testified to the need for investigators to obtain the agreement of their subjects. St. Martin bound himself for a term of one year to "serve, abide, and continue with the said William Beaumont . . . [as] his covenant servant"; and in return for board, lodging, and $150 a year, he agreed "to assist and promote by all means in his power such philosophical or medical experiments as the said William shall direct or cause to be made on or in the stomach of him."[15]

The most brilliant researcher of the century, Louis Pasteur, demonstrates even more vividly just how sensitive investigators could be to the dilemmas inherent in human experimentation. As he conducted laboratory and animal research to find an antidote to rabies, he worried about the time when it would be necessary to test the results on people. In fall 1884 he wrote to a patron deeply interested in his work: "I have already several cases of dogs immunized after rabic bites. I take two dogs: I have them bitten by a mad dog. I vaccinate the one and I leave the other without treatment. The latter dies of rabies: the former withstands it." Nevertheless, Pasteur continued, "I have not yet dared to attempt anything on man, in spite of my confidence in the result. . . . I must wait first till I have got a whole crowd of successful results on animals. . . . But, however I should multiply my cases of protection of dogs, I think that my hand will shake when I have to go on to man."[16]

The fateful moment came some nine months later when there appeared at his laboratory door a mother with her nine-year-old son, Joseph Meister, who two days earlier had been bitten fourteen times by what was probably a mad dog. Pasteur agonized over the decision as to whether to conduct what would be the first human trial of his rabies inoculation; he consulted with two medical colleagues and had them examine the boy. Finally, he reported, on the grounds that "the death of the child appeared inevitable, I resolved, though not without great anxiety, to try the method which had proved consistently successful on the dogs." By all accounts, Pasteur passed several harrowing weeks as he oversaw the administration of twelve inoculations to the boy. ("Your father," Madam Pasteur wrote her children, "has had another bad night; he is dreading the last inoculations on the child. And yet there can be no drawing back now.") By mid-August, Pasteur relaxed, "confident of the future health of Joseph Meister" and the validity of his findings.[17] The extraordinary caution with which Pasteur approached human experimentation, even when it might save a life, was a standard that not all of his successors would maintain.[18]

The most significant formulation of research ethics in the nineteenth century was the work of Claude Bernard, professor of medicine at the College of France. Bernard conducted pioneering research in physiology, discovering, among other things, the essential role of glycogen in fueling muscle movement. In addition, he composed an exceptionally astute treatise on the methods of experimentation, including the ethics of experimentation. Fully cognizant of and generally comfortable with the traditions in human experimentation—"morals do not forbid making experiments on one's neighbor or one's self"—Bernard set down the maxim that he believed should guide practices: "The principle of medical and surgical morality," he wrote in 1865, "consists in never performing on man an experiment which might be harmful to him to any extent, even though the result might be highly advantageous to science, i.e., to the health of others." To be sure, Bernard did allow some exceptions; he sanctioned experimentation on dying patients, including feeding a condemned woman larvae of intestinal worms without her knowledge to learn whether the worms developed in her intestines after her death. "As experiments of this kind are of great interest to science and can be conclusive only on man, they seem to be wholly permissible when they involve no suffering or harm to the subject of the experiment." But Bernard made eminently clear that scientific progress did not justify violating the well-being of any individual.[19]

Bernard's writing is so celebrated today—his maxims have undoubtedly been repeated more often in the past 20 years than in the prior 100—that it is particularly important to affirm that he was not unique among contemporaries in voicing or acting on such sentiments. Let one obscure example suffice. In 1866, J. H. Salisbury, an American professor of physiology, was eager to test a theory that linked malarial fever to vapors arising from stagnant pools, swamps, and humid low grounds. (He was correct in associating such settings with malaria; his mistake was making vapors, rather than mosquitoes, the agent that spread the disease.) Accordingly, he filled six tin boxes with "decidedly malarious dying prairie bog, transported them to a district some five miles away from the malaria area, and placed them on the sill of an open second-story window of the bedroom of two young men." He instructed them to keep the box on the sill and the window open. On the twelfth and fourteenth days of the experiment one and then the other of the men came down with the fever; Salisbury repeated the experiment a second time with three more young men, and two of them contracted the fever. Although he wanted very much to continue, he stopped his research: "On account of . . . the difficulty of obtaining the consent of parties for experiments, I have been unable to conduct this part of the examination further." Clearly, the neighbors were convinced that the odors from his box caused malaria, and they would no longer consent to put themselves at risk—a judgment that Salisbury understood and did not attempt to subvert.[20]

In fact, by the nineteenth century, common law recognized both the vital role of human experimentation and the need for physicians to obtain patients' consent. As one English commentator explained in 1830: "By experiments we are not . . . speaking of the wild and dangerous practices of rash and ignorant practitioners . . . but of deliberate acts of men from considerable knowledge and undoubted talent, differing from those prescribed by the ordinary rules of practice, for which they have good reason . . . to believe will attend to the benefit of the patient, although the novelty of the undertaking does not leave the result altogether free of doubt." The researcher who had consent was "answerable neither in damages to the individual, nor on a criminal proceeding. But if the practitioner performs his experiment without giving such information to, and obtaining the consent of his patient, he is liable to compensate in damages any injury which may arise from his adopting a new method of treatment."[21] In short, the law distinguished carefully between quackery and innovation; and so long as the investigator had obtained the agreement of the subject, research was a legitimate, protected activity.

With the new understanding of germ theory in the 1890s and the growing professionalization of medical training and research in the 1900s, the sheer amount of human experimentation increased. Clinical trials of new therapeutic agents became much more frequent, even before the 1935 introduction of sulfonamides. Over this period, the intimate link between investigators and subjects weakened, although the relatively small scale and essentially therapeutic character of the research continued.

Subjects were now more likely to be a group of patients in a particular hospital rather than neighbors or kin. Physicians administered a new drug to a group of sick patients and compared their rates of recovery with past rates among similar patients or with those of other patients who did not have the drug. (Random and blind clinical trials, wherein a variety of patient characteristics are carefully matched and where researchers are purposely kept ignorant of which patient receives a new drug, were still in the future.) Thus, in Germany physicians tested antidiphtheria serum on thirty hospitalized patients and reported that only six died, compared to the previous year at the same hospital when twenty-one or thirty-two died.[22] In Canada, Banting and Best experimented with insulin therapy on diabetic patients who faced imminent death, and took recovery as clear proof of the treatment's efficacy.[23] So too, Minot and Murphy tested the value of a liver preparation against pernicious anemia by administering it to forty-five patients in remission, who all remained healthy so long as they took the treatment. The normal relapse rate was one-third, and three patients who stopped treatment on their own accord relapsed.[24] It is doubtful that many of these subjects received full information about the nature of the trial or formally consented to participate. But they probably were willing subjects, ready to gamble, even if they understood neither the odds nor the nature of the game, since the research had therapeutic potential and they were in acute distress or danger.

As medicine became more scientific, some researchers did skirt the boundaries of ethical behavior in experimentation and started elevating medical progress over the subject's welfare. But often as not, hostile public reactions made clear that they were perilously close to violating the norms. Probably the most famous experiment in this zone of ambiguity was the yellow fever work of the American army surgeon Walter Reed. In some ways, he demonstrated a genuine sensitivity to the ethics of experimentation; in other ways, he anticipated all too clearly the abuses that were to follow.

Reed's goal was to identify the source of transmission of yellow fever, which was taking a terrible toll among North and South Americans. When he began his experiments, mosquitoes had been identified as crucial to the transmission, but their precise role was still unclear. "Personally," Reed wrote from Cuba, "I feel that only can experimentation on human beings serve to clear the field for further effective work."[25] In time-honored tradition, members of the research team first subjected themselves to the mosquito bites; but it soon became apparent that larger numbers of volunteers were needed, and the team adopted a pull-them-off-the-road approach. No sooner was the decision made to use volunteers than a soldier happened by. "You still fooling with mosquitoes?" he asked one of the doctors. "Yes," the doctor replied. "Will you take a bite?" "Sure, I ain't scared of 'em," responded the man. And with this feeble effort to inform a subject about the nature of the experiment, "the first indubitable case of yellow fever . . . to be produced experimentally" occurred.[26]

As Reed's project came to rely on growing numbers of human subjects, its procedures became more formal. After two of the team's members died of yellow fever from purposeful bites, the rest, who had not yet contracted the disease, including Reed himself, decided "not to tempt fate by trying any more [infections] upon ourselves. . . . We felt we had been called upon to accomplish such work as did not justify our taking risks which then seemed really unnecessary." Instead, Reed asked American servicemen to volunteer, which some did. He also recruited Spanish workers, drawing up a contract with them: "The undersigned understands perfectly well that in the case of the development of yellow fever in him, that he endangers his life to a certain extent but it being entirely impossible for him to avoid the infection during his stay on this island he prefers to take the chance of contracting it intentionally in the belief that he will receive . . . the greatest care and most skillful medical service." Volunteers received $100 in gold, and those who actually contracted yellow fever received a bonus of an additional $100, which, in the event of their death, went to their heirs.[27]

Reed's contract was traditional in its effort to justify the research by citing benefits for the subjects—better to be sick under Reed's care than left to one's own devices. But the contract was also innovative, in that intimacy gave way to a formal arrangement that provided an enticement to undertake a hazardous assignment, and the explanation in subtle ways distorted the risks and benefits of the experiment. Yellow fever endangered life only "to a certain extent"; the likelihood that the disease might prove fatal was unmentioned. So too, the probability of contracting yellow fever outside of the experiment was presented as an absolute certainty, an exaggeration to promote subject recruitment.

Although the press had no knowledge of the contract, it did keep an eye on the research, prepared to render judgments about appropriate risks and benefits. Just how uneasy journalists were with nontherapeutic research protocols is evident from the headlines that local Cuban newspapers ran about Reed's work. "HORRIBLE IF TRUE!" declared one of them, and the accompanying story reported on "a rumor . . . so horrible" about Spanish immigrants being shut up at night in special quarters into which "are released a large number of mosquitos who have bitten individuals suffering from yellow fever. . . . If the workman is taken sick and dies the experiment has demonstrated its effectiveness." Such research, the article concluded, constituted "the most monstrous case of humanitarian . . . savagery which we have been witness to." Even more notable, after Reed and his team, but not all other investigators, were convinced that the mosquito was the agent that transmitted yellow fever, some of Reed's colleagues wanted to continue the experiments in order to identify the dangerous insect strains more precisely. An article in the *Washington Post* took them to task, urging that the human experiments be halted because it would be unconscionable to continue putting people at risk now that "all are agreed that the mosquito does the business."[28] In sum, Reed was at once candid and self-serving, and the public had little difficulty distinguishing between the two.

Some human experiments in the pre–World War II period did cross the boundaries of acceptable ethics and might well have been included on Beecher's list. A number of researchers in the United States and elsewhere could not resist using incompetent and institutionalized populations for their studies. So captive and compliant a group of people seemed ideal, from a purely experimental perspective, for testing new treatments. The Russian physician V. V. Smidovich (publishing in 1901 under the pseudonym Vikenty Veeressayev) cited more than a dozen experiments, mostly conducted in Germany, in which unknowing patients were inoculated with microorganisms of syphilis and gonor-rhea.[29] When George Sternberg, the surgeon general of the United States in 1895 (and a collaborator with Walter Reed), wanted to test the efficacy of a preparation that might immunize against or treat smallpox, he ran experiments "upon unvaccinated children in some of the orphan asylums in . . . Brooklyn."[30] Dr. Joseph Stokes, of the Department of Pediatrics at the University of Pennsylvania School of Medicine, and two colleagues analyzed the effects of "intramuscular vaccination of human beings . . . with active virus of human influenza" by experimenting on the residents of two large state institutions for the retarded.[31]

The work of Hideyop Noguchi is another notable case in point. An associate member of the Rockefeller Institute for Medical Research, Noguchi investigated the ability of a substance he called "luetin," an extract from the causative agent of syphilis, to diagnose syphilis. Just as Clemens von Pirquet had demonstrated in 1907 that the injection of a small amount of tuberculin into the skin could indicate a tubercular condition, Noguchi hoped to prove that an injection of a small amount of luetin could indicate a syphilitic condition. After carrying out animal experiments that demonstrated to his satisfaction that luetin could not transmit the disease, he moved to human experimentation. With the cooperation of fifteen New York physicians, Noguchi tested some 400 subjects, mostly inmates in mental hospitals and orphan asylums and patients in public hospitals. Two hundred fifty-four of them were syphilitic; the remainder, his "various controls," included 456 normal children and 190 adults and children suffering from such diseases as tuberculosis and pneumonia. Before administering luetin to these subjects, Noguchi and some of the physicians did first test the material on themselves, with no ill effects. But no one, including Noguchi, informed the subjects about the experiment or obtained their permission to do the tests.[32]

Noguchi did have his justifications: First, the test was safe, as shown by his own participation. Second, it ostensibly was therapeutic, in that it might detect hidden cases of syphilis among the subjects. But the arguments were patently weak and certainly did not ward off a strong outcry, at least from some quarters of the public. The antivivisection-ists, in particular, saw in this research a confirmation of their fear that a disregard for the welfare of animals would inevitably engender a disregard for the welfare of humans. Under the title "What Vivisection Invariably Leads To," one pamphleteer asked, "Are the helpless people in our hospitals and asylums to be treated as so much material for scientific experimentation, irrespective of age or consent?" And if the research was so risk-free, asked a leader of the movement, "might not the Rockefeller Institute have secured any number of volunteers by the offer of a gratuity of twenty or thirty dollars?" The press soon joined in. The *New York Times* ran the story under the banner, "THIS OUTRAGE SHOULD BE PUNISHED"; and the president of the Society for the Prevention of Cruelty to Children wanted to see criminal charges brought against Noguchi. U.S. Senator Jacob Gallinger of New Hampshire, an antivivisectionist sympathizer, called for a commission to investigate practices in New York hospitals and to enact legislation that would punish investigators who conducted such experiments. So too, the Committee on Protection of Medical Research of the American Medical Association asked editors of medical journals to examine papers submitted for publication, imploring them, "In any case of diagnosis or treatment when the procedure is novel or might be objected to, let the fact be stated that the patient or his family were fully aware of and consented to the plan."[33]

In the end, neither Noguchi's research nor the other experiments on the retarded or the mentally ill produced prosecutions, corrective legislation, or new professional review policies. Violations were too few; nontherapeutic research on captive populations was still the exception. And when the public learned about such incidents, objections quickly arose, reflecting a widely shared sense of what was fair and unfair in human experimentation. Had these norms held sway even as the methods of research changed, Beecher might not have been compelled to write his article.

CHAPTER 2

Research at War

THE transforming event in the conduct of human experimentation in the United States, the moment when it lost its intimate and directly therapeutic character, was World War II. Between 1941 and 1945 practically every aspect of American research with human subjects changed. For one, a cottage industry turned into a national program. What were once occasional, ad hoc efforts by individual practitioners now became well-coordinated, extensive, federally funded team ventures. For another, medical experiments that once had the aim of benefiting their subjects were now frequently superceded by experiments designed to benefit others—specifically, soldiers on the battlefront. For still another, researchers and subjects were more likely to be strangers to each other, with no necessary sense of shared purpose or objective. Finally, and perhaps most important, the common understanding that experimentation required the agreement of the subjects—however casual the request or general the approval—was often superceded by a sense of urgency that overrode the issue of consent.

The fact that all these characteristics first appeared in wartime, as a critical part in the battle against totalitarianism, helped ensure that they would not provoke public opposition. Neither the growing distance between researcher and subject nor the inattention to principles of consent sparked critiques or expressions of distrust. To the contrary, all these characteristics were viewed as a necessary and admirable element in the home-front effort. Later we will discuss the impact of the German atrocities, but well into the 1960s, the American research community considered the Nuremberg findings, and the Nuremberg Code, irrelevant to its own work.

In the summer of 1941, President Franklin Roosevelt created the Office of Scientific Research and Development (OSRD) to oversee the work of two parallel committees, one devoted to weapons research, the other to medical research. The need for a Committee on Medical Research (CMR) had been apparent for well over a year. The government had been sponsoring weapons research through a central agency that coordinated the work of researchers all over the country, but the chiefs of the military services could not agree on how to organize the medical research wing and lacked guiding precedents. They finally decided to establish one master agency to supervise the two activities, and thus began what Dr. Chester Keefer, one of the mainstays of the CMR, later described as "a novel experiment in American medicine, for planned and coordinated medical research had never been essayed on such a scale."[1]

Over the course of World War II the CMR recommended some 600 research proposals, many of them involving human subjects, to the OSRD for funding. The OSRD, in turn, contracted with investigators at some 135 universities, hospitals, research institutes, and industrial firms to conduct the investigations. The accomplishments of the CMR effort required two volumes to summarize (the title, *Advances in Military Medicine*, does not do justice to the scope of the investigations), and the list of publications that resulted from its grants takes up seventy-five pages. All told, the CMR expended some $25 million (a sum that pales in comparison to what the National Institutes of Health eventually spent in the 1960s), but at the time it was extraordinary.[2] In fact, the work of the CMR was so important that it supplied not only the organizational model but the intellectual justification for creating in the postwar period the National Institutes of Health. The CMR came to represent the promise of what coordinated, well-funded efforts could accomplish for scientific progress—what medical research could do for the betterment of humanity.

The health problems that confronted American soldiers and threatened to undermine their combat efficiency (and combat efficiency was the criterion) were obvious to the CMR staff, who sought quick, effective solutions. They wanted not so much to support basic research but to achieve immediate clinical payoffs. The major concerns were dysentery, influenza, malaria (in the Pacific theater), wounds, venereal diseases, and physical hardships (for example, sleep deprivation, exposure to frigid temperatures). Creating effective antidotes required skill, luck, and numerous trials with human subjects, and the CMR staff oversaw the effort with extraordinary diligence. Because it was wartime, the agency underwrote protocols that in a later day (and an earlier one as well) would have produced considerable protest. But its directors deftly managed the problem. Knowing just when to proceed aggressively or cautiously, they enhanced both the scientific and social reputation of medical research.

One primary CMR target was dysentery. Battlefront conditions did not allow for standard hygienic procedures against contaminated water and food or contagion from other carriers, and dysentery was especially debilitating to a fighting corps. No effective inoculations or antidotes existed, and the CMR wanted researchers to move ahead vigorously on both fronts. Outbreaks of the disease in so many different environments made it likely that a variety of bacteria caused the infection, and hence a vaccine would have to be effective against a great number of potentially dangerous organisms. To make matters still worse, the organisms themselves were known to be highly toxic. This meant, noted one researcher, that "inoculation . . . in adequate amounts [to create immunity] may induce such severe local and general reactions as to make general application among troops impractical."[3]

Even before facing up to these formidable problems, investigators had to find a research site. Since animal experiments would yield only limited information, sooner or later the researchers would need a setting in which to test a vaccine or an antidote on humans. The obvious location was the least satisfactory—drugs could not be evaluated in the field, on soldiers at the battlefront. The preparations might be too toxic, and besides, side effects and efficacy could not be measured under gunfire. A substitute setting would have to be found, and it did not take researchers long to identify one. Stuart Mudd, one of the leading researchers on this project for the CMR, suggested the order of things: First, "specific prophylactis by properly chosen antigenic fractions should be thoroughly explored in the laboratory." Then the agents should be tested in "institutions such as asylums," where dysentery was often rampant. This was precisely the order followed— research first on animals, then on orphans in asylums and on the retarded in institutions.[4]

No researcher and no one at CMR ever commented on the irony that to simulate the filth and lack of hygiene at the battlefront one only had to go to caretaker institutions. Rather, the fact was accepted and reported matter-of-factly: "In certain civilian institutions," noted the CMR summary volume, "where outbreaks of dysentery are not uncommon, opportunities have been furnished to observe the effect of the vaccines under approximately field conditions." Indeed, researchers scored points with the CMR for being able to get into institutions. Thus, a CMR official praised one investigator because "he has . . . access to various state institutions where facilities for study of dysentery are unexcelled."[5]

Among the most important subjects for the dysentery research were boys and girls between the ages of thirteen and seventeen in the Ohio Soldiers and Sailors Orphanage. CMR contract 293 went to doctors Merlin Cooper and B. K. Rachford of the Cincinnati Children's Hospital to attempt to immunize the children against dysentery with "killed suspensions of various types of shigella group of bacteria." The team injected different suspensions in different ways, some subcutaneously, some intramuscularly, and some intravenously; it also mixed the dysentery vaccine with the standard typhoid vaccine to learn whether the combination enhanced efficacy. All the experiments carried serious side effects, with the intravenous injections causing the most severe reactions. On 12 March 1943, ten boys were injected with ten million dysentery bacteria: "The systematic reaction," reported the team, "was profound and began within less than 30 minutes. It was essentially the same in all of the boys. The skin was pale and ashy grey in color. The blood pressure was not altered but the temperature sky-rocketed to 105°F and up in spite of measures to counteract the rise. Severe pounding headache and a constricting type of backache were almost universal complaints. The bulbar conjunctivae were hyperemic. Rapidly, nausea, vomiting and watery diarrhea ensued. Fever persisted for 24 hours and when it subsided the subjects were exhausted. By the second day all had recovered." The ten boys had an average maximum temperature of 104.6 degrees.[6]

Although the boys did appear to have built up an immunity against dysentery (measured not by direct challenge but by laboratory tests on their blood), the severity of their reaction ruled out the vaccine. The researchers then considered whether substituting subcutaneous for intravenous injections would, in their language, "hit the target." They experimented with injecting enough inoculant to give the subjects a very sore arm, "with the thought that an inflammatory reaction might break a barrier and permit a little antigen to trickle through the blood stream toward the target." To this end, they took several boys in whom "the dosage was increased cautiously until it appeared that systematic reaction, local reaction, or both were limiting factors."[7] Then, with the dose level established, they inoculated another group of ten boys subcutaneously with the vaccine, but the subjects still averaged fevers of 102 degrees, which was too severe a reaction to permit general use.

The team also tested a potential vaccine by injecting it subcutaneously in a group of girls at the Home. They experienced less swelling on their arms than did the boys, but their systemic responses were just as extreme: "Nausea, abdominal pain, headache, vomiting and on one occasion, diarrhea were observed. In one girl the reaction was unusually severe. . . . This subject became nauseated 3 hours after the injection and vomited repeatedly during the ensuing 17 hours." Although the project could not produce a safe vaccine, the researchers remained optimistic, noting that they had used very high dosages in order to make certain that they were getting substantial responses. Their final report explained that among the children at the asylum "many reactions should be classified as severe. However, there is no evidence to warrant the inference that successful immunization of human beings cannot be accomplished with dosages of vaccine too low to yield severe reactions. In these experiments dosage was purposefully raised as high as was considered safe in order to facilitate technically the measurements of heterologous immunity."[8] In other words, they had elevated the dosages to demonstrate the potency of the agent, whatever the side effects on the children.

Residents at other custodial institutions, particularly for the mentally retarded, also served as subjects for dysentery vaccine experimentation. Researchers considered them less-than-ideal candidates, not because they were incapable of giving consent but because the researchers did not know whether the condition of retardation altered reactions to the vaccine. Nevertheless, CMR-sponsored dysentery projects were conducted at the Dixon (Illinois) Institution for the Retarded and at the New Jersey State Colony for the Feeble-Minded.[9] So too, investigators evaluated the efficacy of sulfonamide preparations against dysentery by using ward patients at public hospitals for their subjects, with no information conveyed or consents obtained. Once again, the research carried significant dangers to the subjects, for the drugs under investigation could cause extensive kidney damage.[10] Indeed, James Watt, of the U.S. Public Health Service, and Sam Cumins, a resident in medicine and pathology at the Shreveport (Louisiana) Charity Hospital, published (in the widely read *Public Health Reports*) findings that included 6 deaths among 238 cases of sulfonamide-treated patients in their protocols. Although the death rate appeared lower among treated than nontreated populations, there is no indication that the subjects or their relatives had any idea that they were part of an experiment— and a risky one at that. Here is but one example:

Case 3— Twenty-month-old colored female admitted with a history of severe diarrhea. The culture was positive. . . . The patient was treated with sulfamethazine and 3 days later the temperature and clinical findings showed definite improvement. However, at the end of this time the temperature began to rise. Sulfonamide was discontinued as urinary findings indicated definite kidney damage. The patient's fever remained at a high level. Progressive toxicity ensued with oliguria. The patient died on the eighth hospital day. Death due to toxic nephritis presumably resulting from the sulfonamide used. The colon showed healing ulcerations of the mucosa.[11]

This research project, like the others, did not produce an effective vaccine or antidote. The preparations were either too potent or too weak to do any good. That most of the subjects were the institution-alized retarded or that consent was ignored did not seem to create problems, at least to judge by the silence both in the CMR and in the press. The overarching consideration was that dysentery was such a peril to the fighting soldiers that researchers on the home front had to do everything to eradicate it.

Probably the most pressing medical problem that the CMR faced right after Pearl Harbor was malaria, "an enemy even more to be feared than the Japanese."[12] Not only was the disease debilitating and deadly, but the Japanese controlled the supply of quinine, one of the few known effective antidotes. Chemists had discovered the antimalarial actions of pentaquine, but the complications, including stomach pains and diminished mental competence, were unacceptable. The CMR leaders hoped that further research would establish an effective dosage with fewer side effects or that researchers might uncover new and less toxic therapeutic agents.

Malaria, unlike dysentery, seldom occurred in the United States, so researchers had no ready sites for drug trials. After testing antidotes on animals, they would next have to transmit the disease to human subjects and then measure the efficacy of their interventions. But where were they to find subjects to participate in such protocols? The answer, with no one dissenting, was the state mental hospitals and prisons.

Dr. Alf Alving of the University of Chicago, under CMR grant 450, organized a sixty-bed clinical unit for drug testing at the Manteno (Illinois) State Hospital. The subjects were psychotic, back-ward patients whom researchers purposely infected with malaria through blood transfusions and then gave experimental antimalarial therapies. Alving's reports made no mention of any effort to obtain their consent, but the very choice of psychotic inmates demonstrates how irrelevant such concerns were. He did hire a psychiatrist to spend "between four and six hours a week discussing the psychiatric aspects of the patients we deal with at Manteno." But the assignment was to explain the subjects to the researchers, not to interpret the experiment for the subjects.[13]

Dr. Alving and other investigators relied still more heavily on prisoners to meet their research needs. Through the cooperation of the commissioner of corrections of Illinois and the warden at the Stateville penitentiary (better known as Joliet), reported Dr. Alving, "one entire floor of the prison hospital and a portion of a second floor have been turned over to the University of Chicago to carry out malarial research. Approximately 500 inmates have volunteered to act as subjects." Some were infected via mosquito bites (a mode of transmission that was more dangerous than blood transfusion) and then given pentaquine, a "promising" drug regimen. Researchers then correlated the severity of the malaria challenge (moderate, severe, extraordinarily severe), with the drug regimen, relapse rate, and side effects, which included nausea, vomiting, changes in the heartbeat rhythm (depression of T waves), fever, and blackouts. In the course of these trials, one prisoner died, suffering a heart attack after several bouts of high fever. The researchers insisted the death was unrelated to the malaria experiments, but worried about attracting other volunteers. However, the incident had no adverse impact. "We heard through the grapevine," Dr. Alving reported to Washington, "that there was considerable argument for a day or two. The end result, however, was quite astonishing. We have had quite a number of new volunteers who were converted to the worth-whileness of experimental work."[14]

Whether these prisoners were truly capable of volunteering for the experiments was not broached by the researchers, the CMR, prison officials, or the press. Almost all the commentary was congratulatory, praising the wonderful contributions that the inmates were making to the war effort. Press releases from Washington lauded the inmates' willingness to volunteer and without a promise of reward, "accept full responsibility for any ill effects, aware of the risk and discomfort . . . and knowing, too, that . . . there is a real hazard involved." Furthermore, they said, "these one-time enemies to society appreciate to the fullest extent just how completely this is everybody's war."[15]

The CMR also supported a major research effort to create a vaccine against influenza. Although not as threatening as malaria, respiratory ailments were "the cause of the greatest amount of disability" among soldiers, and of all the infections, influenza was the most feared. It not only had the highest mortality rate, but could again reach the catastrophic epidemic levels of 1919. As the CMR reported, the "memory of the great pandemic of influenza that occurred toward the end of World War I and realization of its disastrous effects stimulated, at the very beginning of mobilization, the investigation of all possible methods for the control of this disease."[16]

One team, under the direction of Dr. Werner Henle of the University of Pennsylvania Medical School and Philadelphia's Children's Hospital, conducted extensive research on vaccines against influenza A and B. His bimonthly reports to the CMR described his progress in preparing the inoculant and the arrangements made to test them on several hundred residents both at the nearby state facility for the retarded (Pennhurst) and the correctional center for young offenders. The protocols typically involved administering the vaccine to the residents and then three or six months later purposely infecting them with influenza (by fitting an aviation oxygen mask over their face and having them inhale a preparation of the virus for four minutes). The team also infected control groups with the virus, but not the vaccine, in order to compare the different rates of infection. As was to be expected with influenza, those who contracted the disease suffered fever (up to 104 degrees), aches, and pains.[17] Although the vaccines often did provide protection, they were not always free of side effects. As with the malaria preparations, researchers experimented with different preparations. One group of women residents at Pennhurst were injected with an influenza vaccine in a mineral oil base, and many of them developed nodules at the injection site that persisted for six to eighteen months; one had such a severe abscess as to require surgery.[18]

A second team working on influenza vaccines was led by Dr. Jonas Salk, who would later develop the first antipolio vaccine. This group took its human subjects from among the residents of Michigan's Ypsilanti State Hospital and followed essentially the same design as the Henle team: inoculate a group (for example, the "102 male residents of a single ward . . . [who] ranged in age from 20 to 70 years") with the vaccine and later challenge them with the virus; select a comparable group of residents for controls and infect them with the virus without the benefit of the vaccine.[19] The reports from the Salk team, published in such prestigious publications as the *Journal of Clinical Investigation*, accurately identified the subjects, and the researchers fully described the findings: "In the unvaccinated group, 11, or 41%, . . . had temperatures of 100 or more and 6, or 22%, had temperatures of 101 or above. In the 69 vaccinated individuals, 7, or 10%, had temperatures between 100 and 100.9."[20]

Pleased with these preliminary results, Salk and his team turned the entire Ypsilanti Hospital, with its 2,000 residents, into a research site, adding as well the 5,700 patients at the nearby Eloise Hospital and Infirmary. Half received the vaccine, and the other half a placebo. Blood analysis indicated immunities among the inoculated, but the best evidence of efficacy came a year later when, by chance, an epidemic of influenza broke out at Ypsilanti. To the researchers' satisfaction, those inoculated had a significantly lower incidence of the disease.

After these successes, the Office of the Surgeon General of the U.S. Army arranged for the vaccine to be tested on enrollees in the Army Specialized Training Program at eight universities and a ninth unit made up of students from five New York medical and dental colleges. "With the approval of the appropriate authorities," but with no mention of what the subjects were told about the experiment, the teams inoculated 6,263 men and injected 6,211 others with a placebo. Able to keep close track of them for follow-up studies, the researchers learned that 7 percent of the controls, as compared to only 2 percent of the inoculated, had contracted influenza within a year. The research begun on the institutionalized mentally ill and continued on recruits and students produced the desired result: an effective influenza vaccine.[21]

It was not just the success or failure of any single experiment, however, that gave CMR in particular and medical research in general such a favorable standing with the public during World War II. Closely associated with these enterprises were the efficient production and distribution of penicillin (many people mistakenly credited the war effort with the discovery of penicillin), and the CMR deserves much of the praise. Its staff helped develop and allocate the "miracle drug," promoting not only cures but morale on the war front and the home front.

It was the CMR that met the challenge posed by the renowned British pathologist Howard Florey during his visit to the United States in the summer of 1941 and his demonstration on the antibacterial properties of the penicillin mold. The problem was how to produce sufficient penicillin without sacrificing its potency. Under CMR superintendence, private drug companies began the cumbersome manufacturing process. By December 1942 enough of the drug was available to test it on 90 cases, and by December 1943, 700 cases. Thus, what might have been the most devastating medical problem confronting the armed services—death from wound infections—turned out to be altogether manageable. By June 1944 enough penicillin was available to treat all the wounded in the Normandy invasion.

The system devised by the CMR between 1942 and 1944 was successful in meeting military needs and collecting data on efficacy. Most of the drug went to ten general and military hospitals where a specially trained medical officer supervised its use and reported on outcomes. Lesser amounts went to twelve hospitals to test for efficacy against gonorrhea. (This was probably the source of the widely repeated but apocryphal tale of a medical officer who administered his only vial of penicillin to the soldier who was "wounded" in the brothel, not to the one wounded in the battlefield, because the brothel victim would return sooner to the front lines). Although the CMR records are silent on what, if anything, patients were told before receiving penicillin, the early trials typically involved the gravely ill who had failed on other therapies. Thus, in April 1943 a small group of battle casualties who had contracted osteomyelitis were being cared for without success at the Bushnell General Hospital in Brigham, Utah. A bacteriologist at the hospital wrote Chester Keefer about his own futile attempts to make enough penicillin to treat the men; Keefer then arranged to send him a limited supply of the drug from his own stores. The soldiers underwent a "remarkable" recovery, and the efficacy of penicillin against this type of infection was established.[22]

The CMR also kept some reserves of the drug to dispense on a case-by-case basis for civilian use. Any physician who believed that his patient required penicillin was to send full details of the case to the CMR, and Keefer then evaluated the request. His criterion was straightforward: he allotted the drug to patients with a deadly disease who demonstrated no satisfactory response to alternative therapies and for whom there was reason to believe penicillin might prove effective. Thus, patients with staphylococcal meningitis or puerperal fever received the drug, whereas those with tuberculosis or leukemia did not. Word of pencillin's effectiveness spread, and newspaper stories all over the country heralded the miracles that the drug performed—in one town it saved a dying child, in another, an almost moribund woman who had just given birth. Medical research became identified with miracles, and medical researchers with miracle makers.

• • •

Whenever the wartime research goals raised issues that might have aroused public opposition, the CMR directors handled the situation skillfully and delicately. They recognized the limits of CMR's maneuverability, thereby maintaining an almost perfect record of support. Two examples amply demonstrate their techniques, one involving research into the effects of hardship conditions on combatants, the other involving efforts to find a cure for gonorrhea.

Of all the research that the CMR supported, none fit more closely with wartime needs than survival under hardship conditions. The Nazi investigations produced some of the most horrific experiments conducted on concentration camp inmates and testified to at Nuremberg. The CMR, in this instance, did not violate the dignity or the rights of subjects. Where one might have expected the greatest disparity between war goals and protection of human subjects, none occurred.

The medical issues were as obvious as they were unexplored: If a group of sailors were shipwrecked and ended up on a raft with a limited supply of water, ought they to supplement their supply by drinking some amount of salt water? What ration kit would provide soldiers in very hot (or cold) climates with an optimum nutritional balance? How did heat (or cold or altitude) affect the performance of physical tasks? The subjects for CMR-sponsored research on such topics came from the ranks of conscientious objectors (COs) who believed that by enrolling as subjects, they were not primarily serving the military machine but humanity, that they were contributing to an effort not to destroy but to save lives. For this research, investigators did not use inmates of mental hospitals or institutions for the retarded, probably not for ethical reasons but because the experiments required competent and cooperative subjects. Since the measure of the effects of heat and nutrition would be performance, they wanted subjects capable of carrying out routine tasks under normal conditions.

The COs were formally under the jurisdiction of the Selective Service Administration, which in 1943 decided to allow them to volunteer for research work, either as subjects or as laboratory assistants. COs were also affiliated with a national service organization, generally, the American Friends (Quakers), the Mennonites, or the National Service Board for Religious Objectors. Hence, an investigator who wanted to use a CO in his research first had to approach the CMR and then contact both the Selective Service Administration and the CO's particular service organization. He had to compose two very different letters, one to the CMR explaining how the research would further the war effort and another to the CO's organization explaining how it would promote the well-being of humanity—and most researchers proved adept at fulfilling the dual assignment. The process was cumbersome but well worth the bother. With trained personnel so scarce, well-educated and diligent COs not only contributed to the project as cooperative subjects but as skilled assistants and administrators. The net effect of all these procedures was to put the survival research under the closest scrutiny, with government agencies, private organizations, and the subjects themselves fully informed about the experiments. The process also protected the COs from coercion, for a request for assistance went to the service organization, not directly to the individual, and the CO had to come forward and express his willingness to volunteer.

Those who did volunteer drank various mixtures of saltwater and fresh water and then had their weight checked and urine analyzed. (The findings confirmed the Ancient Mariner's view that sea water was of no benefit.) They subsisted on 500 grams a day, some with water alone, others with different foodstuffs. (Here the lesson was to stock lifeboat kits not with the standard chocolate and biscuits but with more easily digested glucose and fat.) Others sat on rooftops exposed to wind and frigid temperatures and then had their physiological responses measured; or sat in sweltering rooms, became dehydrated, and then performed simple tasks to test their efficiency; or sat in low-pressure chambers, simulating conditions at different altitudes and then underwent psychological and physiological testing. The research proceeded smoothly: the investigators pleaded for more COs, the Selective Service sought assurances that the COs were not getting off too lightly, and the COs completed their assignments and even remained with the teams afterward, satisfied that they had respected their scruples and served their nation.[23]

With even greater attention to the potential for public opposition, the CMR researchers sought a prevention and cure for gonorrhea. However intense the pressure for results, the CMR would not risk a scandal. It conducted a remarkably thorough and sensitive discussion of the ethics of research and adopted procedures that satisfied the principles of voluntary and informed consent. Indeed, the gonorrhea protocols contradict blanket assertions that in the 1940s and 1950s investigators were working in an ethical vacuum.

Everyone in the CMR and in the Surgeon General's Office recognized the threat of gonorrhea to military efficiency. In February 1943, Dr. J. Earle Moore, the chairman of the Subcommittee on Venereal Diseases for the National Research Council, informed the CMR that each year 350,000 military personnel were likely to contract fresh infections of gonorrhea. He noted, "Assuming an average loss of time of 20 days per infected man (the actual figure for Army in recent years to 1941 was 35–45 days, for Navy 10–15 days), this will account for 7,000,000 lost man days per year, the equivalent of putting out of action for a full year the entire strength of two full armored divisions or of ten aircraft carriers." Thomas Parran, the surgeon general, noted that gonorrhea not only weakened the armed services but also "represented a serious threat to the health and efficiency of our defense workers."[24] The problem, in short, was nothing to smirk about.

Nor was the problem easy to resolve. As of 1942 no one had been able to induce gonorrhea in animals, and therefore all the testing of preventives and cures would require human subjects. (That penicillin was soon to resolve the issue could not, of course, be known.) Investigators were eager to tackle the assignment but questioned the ethical, legal, and political implications. In October 1942, Dr. Moore informed Dr. Richards, the chairman of the CMR, that he had recently received a letter from Dr. Charles Carpenter, of the University of Rochester School of Medicine, who wanted to "work out a human experiment on the chemical prophylaxis of gonorrhea. He has asked me to supply him with a statement that in my opinion such human experimentation is desirable. . . . I have pointed out to Dr. Carpenter that I could not make such a statement without the approval of higher authority. May I ask you to supply me with the attitude of the Committee on Medical Research toward human experimentation in general, and toward the particular problem of human experimentation in the chemical prophylaxis of gonorrhea."[25]

Richards promised to bring the question immediately to the full committee: "In the meantime I have confidence that the Committee will support me in the statement that human experimentation is not only desirable, but necessary in the study of many of the problems of war medicine which confront us. When any risks are involved, volunteers only should be utilized as subjects, and these only after the risks have been fully explained and after signed statements have been obtained which shall prove that the volunteer offered his services with full knowledge and that claims for damages will be waived. An accurate record should be kept of the terms in which the risks involved were described." As for gonorrhea research, the CMR would have to rely on "the judgment of the Responsible Investigator, supplemented by the judgment of the committee in whose field the investigator is proceeding." Three weeks later Richards informed Moore that the CMR fully endorsed his position on human experimentation; all legal responsibility for damages rested with the investigator and his institution, but "arrangements can be made whereby both he and the Institution can be protected by insurance."[26]

Thus encouraged, Dr. Carpenter, and several other investigators as well, submitted grants to the CMR for gonorrhea research on human subjects. The protocols were elaborate and sophisticated both in terms of scientific method and protection of human subjects. In order to study the efficacy of oral and topical preventive treatments, Carpenter intended to divide volunteers into three categories: one group would take sulfonamide compounds by mouth and then be exposed to the infection; a second would be exposed to the infection, after which topical agents would be applied to the genital tract; a third would serve as controls, infected but not given any oral or topical protection. Carpenter proposed to conduct the research on prisoners, for they offered the advantage of being under complete control during the necessary observation period and out of contact with women. He informed the CMR that negotiations were already under way with prison officials in Georgia.

The CMR carefully reviewed the proposal in and out of house. The referees approved of the science and many, like Dr. R. E. Dyer, the director of the National Institutes of Health, expressly approved of the ethics: "The outline of methods to be employed seems adequate to insure a definite answer and to safeguard the volunteers."[27] But some reviewers were apprehensive about possible legal repercussions. The head of the American Medical Association (AMA), for example, was concerned that an unscrupulous lawyer might learn about the project, bring suit, and try to discredit all medical research. Taking such possibilities seriously, the CMR heads set out to make certain that every contingency had been considered and to marshal full support.

To these ends, it sponsored a day-long meeting on 29 December 1942 that brought together representatives from the military services, state health departments, and interested researchers. The group not only reviewed the protocols and explored potential legal liabilities (for example, might a state law against maiming oneself be invoked against the volunteers?) but also scrutinized a "Proposed Plan of Procedure in the Study of Chemical Prophylaxis in Human Volunteers among Prison Inmates," which was to guide all the researchers.

The proposed plan specified precisely which prisoners would be ineligible to volunteer (for instance, those who were chronically ill, had a history of rheumatic fever, or had negative reactions to sulfonamides). It also specified the protocol for transmitting the infection: a nonsulfonamide-resistant strain with a low thermal death point was to be applied for five minutes. The proposed plan also included a two-page, single-spaced "Statement of Explanation of the Experiment and Its Risks to Tentative Volunteers"—in effect, a consent form:[28]

> The study which we plan to carry on here, and for which we have asked your cooperation, is concerned with gonorrhea. You may also know this disease as the 'clap,' 'strain,' or the 'running ranges.' Some of you have had the infection at some time in the past and you know it did not make you seriously sick. Recently a simple, dependable treatment has been discovered which consists of a drug taken in the form of pills.

> What we propose to try now is to develop certain methods of *preventing* the disease. . . . Gonorrhea causes a great loss of time in the Army and Navy. . . . It is not possible to use animals for this purpose because they are not susceptible to gonorrhea. Therefore, we are calling on you for your cooperation. This is one way in which you can specifically help in the war effort. The benefits will not be limited to the armed forces . . . and it is very likely that you and your families might later profit from them.

In the first place, I want to assure you that so far as we are able to discover, there is no reason to expect any injury from this treatment, but one cannot predict with positiveness that the result in all cases will be the same. . . .

Most patients with gonorrhea can be cured within 5 to 10 days with modern treatment without experiencing discomforts or complications. A few patients with gonorrhea do not respond to modern treatment methods (probably less than 1 in 10). These patients can usually be cured by older methods, which, however, require more time to get results. A few of the patients who are treated by these older methods develop certain complications in the lower genital tract which, in most instances, are ultimately cured. In very rare instances patients treated by the older methods develop complications which involve the joints, the eyes, and other organs.

A very small percentage of patients treated by modern methods experience discomfort while taking the medication. This may consist of a tired sensation or a slight headache, but these symptoms never become serious if the patient is observed daily by the physician. Fever, skin rash, nausea, and vomiting rarely occur but do disappear rapidly when the treatment is stopped. Other reactions have been reported which involved the blood, joints, kidneys, liver, and nervous system, but these reactions have been so rare that the possibility of their occurrence is extremely remote.

Before we can accept you as part of our group, it is necessary to obtain written permission from you.

Although the document exaggerated the potential benefit of the research to the subjects and too blatantly tried to persuade them to make their contribution to the war effort, it noted the potential complications and accurately assessed the research risks. In all, it satisfied the need to inform and protect human subjects.

The CMR staff continued to move circumspectly, reviewing the proposed research with city and state health officers, prison officials, heads of major research organizations, and legal advisors. Overwhelming support for the investigations emerged, and the consensus was that using prisoners was the only feasible and acceptable option. As Dr. Moore told Dr. Richards, civilians would not have submitted to the sexual isolation and medical supervision for the necessary six months, military personnel could not have been kept from active duty for so long, and "inmates of institutions for the feeble-minded or insane" could not have been used because it would have been "clearly undesirable to subject to any experimental procedure persons incapable of providing voluntary consent."[29] A few reviewers, like Frank Jewett, the president of the National Academy of Science, questioned whether prisoners were capable of giving voluntary consent to an experiment, but most others were persuaded that the benefits of the research outweighed whatever doubts anyone might have.[30] Thomas Parran summed up the prevailing view: "The utilization of human subjects who voluntarily submit themselves to experimentation may properly be compared to the research which enabled Doctor Walter Reed and his co-workers to discover the method of transmission of yellow fever."[31]

The aftermath of these deliberations was not as interesting as the deliberations themselves. The CMR staff voted to support the research; but then, to be certain that the protocols violated no state laws, they proposed using prisoners in federal penitentiaries. James Bennett, the director of the federal system, was eager to cooperate and to help enroll subjects. "We cannot obligate the government," he informed Dr. Moore, "insofar as reduction of sentence for those who volunteer is concerned. It is believed, however, that the U.S. Board of Parole would be willing to give each subject . . . due credit and consideration for his willingness to serve his country in this manner when he becomes eligible for parole." The administrative hurdles cleared, a major project began at the U.S. penitentiary at Terre Haute, Indiana, but the investigators soon terminated it because "not any of the exposure techniques employed proved capable of producing disease with a consistency considered to be adequate for a study of experimental prophylaxis."[32] Shortly thereafter, the curative role of penicillin was established, obviating the need for additional research.

At first glance, the record of human experimentation during World War II constitutes a curious mixture of high-handedness and forethought. The research into dysentery, malaria, and influenza revealed a pervasive disregard of the rights of subjects—a willingness to experiment on the mentally retarded, the mentally ill, prisoners, ward patients, soldiers, and medical students without concern for obtaining consent. Yet, research into survival under hardship conditions and into gonorrhea was marked by formal and carefully considered protocols that informed potential subjects about the risks of participation.

Behind these differences lies the evaluation of the CMR administrators and researchers about the likely response to specific investigations. When they sensed the possibility of an adverse public reaction, they behaved cautiously. Giving gonorrhea to prisoners might have raised a storm of protest from a variety of sources, some objecting to prisoners injuring themselves, others objecting to efforts to protect the promiscuous from the consequences of their immorality; since the protocol might, therefore, have ended up on the front page of a newspaper or in a courtroom, the CMR directors were scrupulous about building a scientific consensus on the importance of the project and protecting the rights of the volunteers. As a result of these calculations and actions, the research community secured public acceptance of a new kind of medical research and human experimentation.

Most of the time, however, the CMR and the research community were confident that their work would not be questioned—that their research on dysentery, malaria, and influenza using incompetent and incarcerated subjects would pass community scrutiny. Why, then, did officials who understood the need to make subjects' participation informed and voluntary in occasional cases find it so easy to disregard the requirements in most other cases? How could they say in the case of gonorrhea that it was "clearly undesirable to subject to any experimental procedures persons incapable of providing voluntary consent," and then go ahead and do precisely that in the case of dysentery and malaria?

The answer begins with an appreciation of the fact that the first widespread use of human subjects in medical research occurred under wartime conditions. First, a sense of urgency pervaded the laboratories. Time was of the essence when combat soldiers were under the immediate threat of disease. A campaign mentality inevitably affected not only the theaters of war but the theaters of research, justifying every shortcut or elimination of time-consuming procedures. The presumption was full speed ahead, *except* where negative fallout was most likely.

But why were informing a subject about an experiment and obtaining consent defined as time-consuming, instead of necessary, measures? Because, in the second instance, wartime conditions brought a reliance on such procedures as the draft, forced military duty, and assignment to combat—and these new facts of life inevitably affected the mind-set of researchers. Every day thousands of men were forced to face death, whether or not they understood the campaign, the strategy, or the cause. Since these investigations were integral to the military effort, the rules of the battlefield seemed to apply to the laboratory. Researchers were no more obliged to obtain the permission of their subjects than the Selective Service was to obtain the permission of civilians to become soldiers. One part of the war machine conscripted a soldier, another part conscripted an experimental subject, and the same principles held for both.

Moreover, the use of mentally incompetent people as research subjects seemed to be in accord with popular expectations of sacrifices to be made on the home front. All citizens were—or were supposed to be—contributing to the war effort, even at great personal cost and inconvenience. By this standard, it was reasonable to expect the mentally ill and retarded to make their contributions too, albeit involuntary ones. It was ever so easy to believe that if these handicapped individuals could somehow have understood the nature of the request, if they could have had a momentary flash of competence and been asked whether they wished to join the experiment and further the war effort, they would have agreed. Hence, to enroll them in research was not to violate their rights but to exercise a substituted judgment: Were they competent, they would have volunteered for the project.

It requires little historical imagination to recognize the appeal of this line of argument in a society mobilized for war. Since the mentally ill and retarded had the same stake as all other citizens in an Allied victory, it seemed altogether appropriate that they be called on to perform whatever services they could. And at a time when the social value attached to consent had so frequently to give way before the necessity of conscription and obedience to orders, there was little reason for medical researchers to worry about using incompetent human subjects. Some people were ordered to face bullets and storm a hill; others were told to take an injection and test a vaccine. No one ever said that war was fair, or that it should be fairer for the incompetent than the competent.

To make this same point in traditional philosophical terms, wartime inevitably promotes teleological, as opposed to deontological, positions. The greatest good for the greatest number is the most compelling precept to justify sending some men to be killed so that others may live—and this ethic has little difficulty in defending the use of the institutionalized retarded or mentally ill for experimentation. Of course, the investigations were to be scientifically sound, and to have passed all the appropriate animal tests; but these criteria met, it appeared acceptable to test the interventions on humans, including those unable to give consent.

In sum, the lessons that the medical researchers learned in their first extensive use of human subjects was that ends certainly did justify means; that in wartime the effort to conquer disease entitled them to choose the martyrs to scientific progress. They learned, too, that the public would accept such decisions, and that so long as the researchers were attentive to potential areas of dispute, the support for research was considerable. All of this constituted an intellectual legacy that researchers would not forget, even when peacetime conditions returned.

CHAPTER 3

The Gilded Age of Research

THE twenty years between the close of World War II and the appearance of Henry Beecher's exposé witnessed an extraordinary expansion of human experimentation in medical research. Long after peace returned, many of the investigators continued to follow wartime rules. Utilitarian justifications that had flourished under conditions of combat and conscription persisted, and principles of consent and voluntary participation were often disregarded. This was, to borrow a phrase from American political history, the Gilded Age of research, the triumph of laissez-faire in the laboratory. Yet between 1945 and 1965 very few investigators or their funders took note of the changed circumstances. The thrust of public policy was not to check the discretion of the experimenter but to free up the resources that would expand the scope and opportunity for research.

The driving force in post–World War II research, including both intellectual direction and financial support, was provided by the National Institutes of Health. Created in 1930 as an outgrowth of the research laboratory of the U.S. Public Health Service, the NIH did not assume its extraordinary prominence until 1946.[1] When the Committee on Medical Research, along with the other wartime organizations, was about to be phased out, many scientists and political leaders (but not all) found the prospect of the federal government abdicating its

51

research role simply unthinkable.[2] So vital an activity could not be permitted to regress to the prewar condition of limited and haphazard support by private foundations and universities.[3]

It was not difficult to make the case for transforming the NIH into the peacetime CMR. In the fall of 1945, Vannevar Bush, the director of the Office of Scientific Research and Development, laid out plans for a Program for Postwar Scientific Research in a report entitled "Science, the Endless Frontier." Bush first listed the achievements of medical research over the past two hundred years and then noted the "spectacular" record during World War II. He recounted the victories over smallpox, typhoid, tetanus, yellow fever, and infectious diseases, noting first the discovery of the sulfa drugs and then, of course, penicillin. Medicine, he insisted, was on the verge of its most heroic explorations, and at such a moment it would be foolhardy to close off the "frontiers" of science by ending federal support.

To judge by congressional reactions as well as press comments, Bush's appeal struck a responsive chord. Although disputes broke out about the appropriate division of authority between the government and the investigator, and among the various federal agencies, there was significant agreement on the need for a federal investment in research.[4] "World medicine," noted one editorial, "appears to be approaching the threshold of a brilliant new era of discovery in which some of mankind's most dreaded diseases may be wiped out." And the proof of the assertion was in the "miracle drug"—penicillin. It unleashed the imagination of both the general public and the research community, so that no prediction of progress, however grandiose, seemed fanciful. In the fall of 1945, Alexander Fleming, who had discovered the antibacterial properties of the penicillin-producing mold, toured the United States, received a hero's welcome, and delivered the same exhilarating message: "We are only at the beginning of this great study.... We can certainly expect to do much toward reducing the sum total of human suffering."[5] Political figures echoed his refrain: "We have found the cause of a number of epidemic diseases and have practically conquered them," declared Louisiana's Senator Joseph Ransdell. "May we not expect the same kind of success against the so-called degenerative diseases if we work hard enough?"[6] And his heady optimism bore directly on the prospects for a strengthened NIH, for Ransdell was one of the Senate's strongest supporters of the new program. The press, too, invoked the wartime experience and the benefits of penicillin to buttress the case for an expanded NIH. "This seems to be the golden age of chemotherapy," commented the *New York Times*. "It is sad to realize that had it not been for the war, penicillin might not yet have been placed in the hands of physicians, and that we need something more than the natural curiosity of the research scientist to speed discovery that means so much to mankind."[7]

If the general well-being of humanity was not reason enough to justify federal support of research, then national self-interest was. In 1945, unlike 1919, there was little sense that the Allies had won a war to end all wars; hence, those concerned with defense strategies, like Secretary of the Navy James Forrestal, strongly endorsed expansion of the NIH. The United States, he argued, had been foolish not to fund medical research between the two wars and dared not repeat the error.[8] "A future aggressor," concurred editorial writers, "will move even more swiftly than Hitler did. Two oceans will not give us time to establish another OSRD. Continuous systematic research is an evident necessity. It may be regarded as a kind of military insurance."[9]

Thus, in 1945, the lesson learned from both the battlefield and the laboratory was to reorganize the NIH along the lines of the CMR and fund it generously—in effect, involve an army of investigators from universities and hospitals in the war against disease and await the impressive results. With World War II just behind and with medical research so closely linked to national security, discussions about federal research policy inevitably invoked war metaphors: Given the high stakes, the campaign was to be an all-out battle against disease. Researchers reinforced and reflected this attitude: With the potential for incredible breakthroughs so great, all—and one means *all*—methods of investigation were legitimate.

The results of this mandate were apparent first in the spectacular growth of the NIH. Congress gave the NIH not only the responsibility but the budgetary resources to expand on the work of the CMR. In 1945 the appropriation to NIH was approximately $700,000. By 1955 the figure had climbed to $36 million; by 1965, $436 million; and by 1970, $1.5 billion, a sum that allowed it to award some 11,000 grants, about one-third requiring experiments on humans. As a result of this largess, NIH was able both to run an extramural program like the CMR had done, making grants to outside investigators, and to administer an internal, intramural research program of its own. In 1953, NIH opened its Clinical Research Center, in which investigators appointed to its own staff coordinated patient treatment with medical research. Those who worked at the Bethesda site during the "halcyon days" of the 1950s, to quote the NIH deputy director during that period, J. D. Rall, were overwhelmed by the "awesome immensity of the place and diversity of research interests."[10] Indeed, the scope and significance of NIH operations were such that through the 1980s, practically every chairman of a basic science department in major American medical schools was at some point in his career an NIH fellow or NIH grant recipient.

The Clinical Center was a 500-bed research hospital that admitted patients on referral when their disease fit with the particular investigatory interests of one of the seven NIH institutes. The focus was mainly, but not exclusively, on chronic diseases, including arteriosclerosis, rheumatoid arthritis, leukemia, and schizophrenia. Every patient admitted was part of a formal research study—a research subject—but the NIH, at least before 1965, never put the matter quite so baldly. Instead, it blurred the lines between research and therapy. The Clinical Center, as its patient brochures and handbooks explained, would "benefit all people by adding to our storehouse of knowledge . . . [and] at the same time . . . provide the best possible medical and nursing care." The center's "team of experts [was] working for your better health and for new knowledge." The facility also admitted a group of volunteers drawn from religious and service organizations to serve as normal controls in some of the projects. The NIH materials hastened to assure them, as they did the patients, that their well-being came first: "The normal control is not 'experimented upon' without regard to his individual welfare. . . . The welfare of the patient takes precedence over every other consideration."[11]

The Clinical Center, however, instituted almost no formal procedures or mechanisms to ensure that patients' best interests were not sacrificed to the researchers' own agendas. The center did not, in the first instance, educate patients to be alert to possible conflicts of interest or to question the researcher closely about the protocol. The material that specifically addressed "The Patient's Part in Research at the Clinical Center" invoked the ethos of the traditional doctor–patient therapeutic relationship and essentially asked the patient to trust the researcher: "Just like the family doctor, the physician in the Clinical Center has a professional and moral obligation to do everything possible to benefit the patient. . . . The primary purpose of the Clinical Center is medical research in the interest of humanity, and this purpose is achieved at no sacrifice of benefit to the individual." That an NIH researcher was many things but assuredly *not* a family physician, or that the well-being of humanity and the well-being of a patient might diverge, were issues the NIH would not confront.

The Clinical Center set neither formal requirements to protect human subjects nor clear standards for its investigators to follow in making certain that subjects were well informed about the research protocols. As a result, the hallmark of the investigator–subject relationship was its casualness, with disclosure of risks and benefits, side effects and possible complications, even basic information on what procedures would be performed, left completely to the discretion of the individual investigator.[12] Thus, patients at the National Heart Institute were asked to sign a general consent form before undergoing surgery; but, as its director, Donald Fredrickson, later observed, explaining the procedures to the patients was "by no means universal." One reason for the omission, Fredrickson explained, was that researchers were convinced their protocols involved no significant risk to the patient; in their view, since the experiments did not depart markedly from standard practice and represented only a minor variant on major therapeutic or diagnostic interventions, the details were too trivial to justify disclosure. But Fredrickson added a second consideration, without noting the inherent contradiction between the two points: the investigators feared that discussing the research aspects in detail would "unduly alarm the patient and hinder his reasonable evaluation of procedures important to his welfare." Thus, the cardiac surgery service had its patients sign only a standard surgical consent form, even though, as Fredrickson conceded, the procedures might be anything but standard. For example, "during the surgery, research procedures are sometimes performed, such as . . . application of tiny metal clips to the heart for post-operative measurements, etc." So too, on the diagnostic cardiology unit: "Neither the details of all measurements or procedures carried out during catheterization nor a complete recital of each specific hazard is given the average patient."[13] The conclusion seems inescapable that it was not so much the subjects' well-being but the researchers' needs that kept the communication between them to a minimum.

Moreover, NIH investigators were not obliged by internal rules or their own sense of propriety to consult with colleagues in order to make certain that their evaluation of risks was not biased by an eagerness to do the research. They were not required to obtain another investigator's opinion, let alone approval, on whether the protocol was truly nothing more than a minor deviation from standard practice. To be sure, NIH did have a Medical Board Committee composed of representatives of each of the institutes and the Clinical Center staff, and NIH officials maintained that "any nonstandard, potentially hazardous procedure, or any involving normal subjects receives appropriate group consideration before it is undertaken." However, as one deputy director explained, "It is not necessary to present each project to any single central group." Investigators who wanted a consultation on whether their protocol involved "potential hazard to the life or well-being of the patient" had the option of seeking the advice of the Medical Board Committee; but if the investigators believed that their protocols were not hazardous, they were free to proceed. The choice was the investigator's alone and so, not surprisingly, the board was rarely consulted. Nor were informal consultations a regular practice. The Heart Institute, for example, had been without a director from 1953 to 1961. The result, according to Fredrickson, was "a sense of 'hopelessness' on the part of the Clinical Associates and some lack of dispassionate review of the conduct of some of the more routine aspects of research and clinical care."[14]

Researchers at the other NIH institutes were equally casual. Patients might receive a general description of the protocols, but the specifics were not often spelled out. Some investigators asked for a signature on a general release form; others noted in the chart that they had discussed the issues with the patient. NIH, however, had no fixed methods or requirements to make certain that the subject received an explanation of the procedures, indicated an understanding of them, and voluntarily consented to participate. Dr. Robert Cohen, the director of clinical investigations for the National Institute of Mental Health, reported that "in only a small percentage" of cases did patients sign a specific consent form, and even then, "the negative aspects of therapy" were not usually stipulated and recorded on the forms. His counterpart at the National Cancer Institute noted that some colleagues followed a formal procedure and others an informal one, and that they could not agree among themselves about either the style or the substance of the investigator–subject communication.[15] Thus, the Cancer Institute had no uniform policy about consent other than a general understanding that the researcher should somehow obtain it.

Peer review of NIH research protocols followed this same pattern. Officially, patient care at the Clinical Center was the joint responsibility of clinicians and researchers, and institute directors contended that consultations between them at the bedside or in committees ensured high-quality medical care and research. Ostensibly, colleagues were judging the scientific value and ethical soundness of each other's work. However, no regulations existed to ensure a timely or effective implementation. In some institutes, group consideration of research proposals took place at ward rounds conducted by the chief of service; in others, the branch chiefs and the scientific director of the institute met to discuss a particular project. But such sessions were unscheduled and infrequent, and in the absence of a formal system, everyone conceded that some research could slip through the cracks. When the clinical director of the Cancer Institute was asked, "Is it possible for a physician on the staff to do a procedure that is essentially new or different before it has been reviewed either by group consideration or by the service head?" he responded "that it is possible, that it is unlikely, and that it is assumed that senior investigators will discuss continually with their immediate superiors their current research efforts."[16] NIH officials in the 1950s clearly were unready to acknowledge that assumptions and practice might well diverge, or that explicit guidelines and procedures might seal the cracks. Left to themselves, they were ready to let the researchers handle decision making.

This policy reflected, first, a faith at the Clinical Center that the researcher–subject relationship was identical to the doctor–patient relationship.[17] In medical investigations, as in medical therapy, the well-being of patients (even if they were now subjects), was paramount.

Holding to such a premise, the Clinical Center directors unhesitatingly transferred the discretion that the physician enjoyed in the examining room directly to the investigator in the laboratory. In fact, the only time that NIH required formal review and approval of a human experimentation protocol by its Medical Board Committee was with research involving normal volunteers. NIH treated normal subjects differently precisely because they did not fit into the traditional doctor–patient relationship. Since the subjects were not sick, the researcher could not invoke a clinical model of responsibility, and NIH here—but only here—thought it necessary to go beyond a trust in the investigator's judgment.

Second, the Clinical Center assumed that researchers who were concerned about the ethics of a particular protocol would on their own initiative consult with colleagues. Peer review, however ad hoc, would provide the necessary checks; professionals would be self-regulating. The alternative—to insist on precise explanations to patients and to obtain their formal consent—seemed but an empty ritual to the NIH research community. Laypeople had neither the scientific knowledge nor emotional capability, especially when they were acutely ill, to understand protocols. "The usual patient," as one of the directors put it, wants "to avoid the necessity of grappling with painful facts related to his own welfare. He prefers (and in a real sense he has no other choice) to depend on an overriding faith that the physician and institution will safeguard his interests above any other consideration." At the Clinical Center particularly, he continued, "patients feel that they have . . . gained an opportunity that is open to relatively few."[18] These patients were not about to question or oppose the physician's judgment. The patient was to trust the physician, whether in the guise of researcher or therapist, and that was the sum of the matter.

At least some NIH chiefs recognized that other, very different considerations accounted for the softness of the procedures—namely, an enormous intellectual and emotional investment in research and the shared conviction that the laboratory would yield up answers to the great mysteries of disease. Since the researcher, not the clinician, controlled the NIH structure and occupied the positions of leadership in its hierarchy, the absence of regulations reflected researchers' preferences to keep their laboratory work unfettered. "At NIH," observed Dr. Phillipe Cardon (a psychiatrist, not a bench researcher), "taking care of patients is not by and large considered to be as challenging, important, or rewarding as is doing a clinical experiment. . . . If we were more interested in taking care of patients than in research, we wouldn't be here. It is unrealistic to expect most very good investigators also to be very good physicians (or vice versa)." Cardon himself was not overly concerned about the implications of this fact, for he, at least, trusted the researcher to "judge the relative values of right and wrong" and abide by the appropriate limits in "putting patients 'in jeopardy' for the public good." Still, he asked, "In clinical research, is the means utilized justified by the ends?"[19] His own answer seemed to be a qualified yes, provided that the peril was not too great and the potential public benefit considerable.

Raising the issue as Cardon did at once enlightened and troubled some of his NIH colleagues. "We are on the defensive," responded one of them, "because, whether we like it or not, we have in some senses utilized the concept of the end justifies the means." Each of us here, observed another, knows that "it is easy to get carried away with the importance of one's own research." Still others conceded that researchers had a "special angle of vision" (others might say a self-interest) that could lead them to minimize the risks of an experiment to the subject when the benefits to humanity seemed extraordinary. These worries, however, did not dictate NIH policy. Rather, a confidence in the ultimate value of research fostered and justified a hands-off policy that left investigators with the sole discretion to determine risks and benefits. The final word went to one institute director who concluded: "Society would be in peril if we did not do clinical research."[20]

The NIH was so committed to this position that it would not devise procedures or guidelines to govern the extensive extramural research that it supported. By 1965 the NIH extramural program was the single most important source of research grants for universities and medical schools, by NIH estimates supporting "between 1,500 and 2,000 research projects which, by their titles, indicate presumptive experimentation involving man." Nevertheless, grant provisions included no stipulations about the conduct of human experimentation, and NIH internal memoranda noted that it treated applications "for clinical research the same as for other research." NIH staff did find that many investigators, "without formal requirements for such information . . . may describe . . . local practices concerning the provision for informed consent, and other matters relating to professional ethical considerations." Reviewers, too, on their own initiative would "often deliberate ethical questions in relation to grants." However, such submissions were voluntary and the discussions random. "There is little attempt," NIH officials reported, "to develop consensus as to what clinical research practices should be, or even to define what is the nature of the ethical issues at stake."[21]

The universities made little effort to fill the gap. In 1960, Dr. Louis Welt, of the University of North Carolina School of Medicine, one of the handful of people then interested in the ethics of human experimentation, asked some eighty university departments of medicine about their practices and guidelines. He reported that of the sixty-six responding departments "only eight have a procedural document and only 24 have or favor a committee to review problems in human experimentation."[22] Shortly thereafter, a newly established Law–Medicine Research Institute at Boston University conducted a similar survey and confirmed Welt's findings. Only nine of fifty-two departments of medicine had a formal procedure for approving research involving human subjects, and only five more indicated that they favored this approach or planned to institute such procedures. Twenty-two departments did have a peer-review committee, but with merely an advisory role.[23]

Both of these surveys revealed a widespread conviction that ethical considerations in research were best left to the judgment of the investigators. They were in the best position to calculate the risks and benefits to the subjects, to share information they thought appropriate, and ultimately to decide whether the subjects were voluntarily and knowingly agreeing to participate in the experiment. The medical research community, noted the Boston University survey, has "a general skepticism toward the development of ethical guidelines, codes, or sets of procedures concerning the conduct of research." Welt not only reached the same conclusion but agreed with it: "A committee cannot take responsibility. . . . This must always be in the hands of the individual investigators." Consultations with colleagues could be useful, but "responsibilities return to their rightful place in the minds and hearts of the investigators."[24]

Granted, no profession invites regulation, and individuals, whether they work at the bench or the desk, prefer to be left alone on the assumption that they will behave ethically. Medical researchers and their institutions (from the NIH to almost all university medical schools and teaching hospitals), however, viewed the investigator's prerogative as sacrosanct, and that fact requires explanation. Perhaps any highly motivated group would have reacted in this same fashion, magnifying the importance of their own work so as to minimize the sacrifices that others would have to make for it, but few commentators called them to task. No less puzzling, in the immediate postwar decades, this delegation of authority to the researcher did not spark significant opposition or debate from outside medicine. Neither Congress nor the academy nor the media urged that human experimentation be subjected to the oversight of committees or be responsive to formal principles and codes defining the rights of subjects.[25]

The response to human experimentation might well have been otherwise. After all, the Nuremberg tribunal in 1945 and 1946 cast a shadow over the entire field of human experimentation. Revelations about the atrocities that the Nazis committed—for instance, putting subjects to death through prolonged immersion in subfreezing water to learn the limits of bodily endurance or castrating them in order to study the effects of X rays on the genitals—might have sparked a commitment in the United States to a more rigorous regulation of research. So too, the American research effort during the war may have raised questions and spurred closer oversight. Some might have suggested that Americans had come close to following the dictum, proclaimed by Hitler in 1942, that "as a matter of principle, if it is in the interest of the state, human experiments were to be permitted," that it was unacceptable for "someone in a concentration camp or prison to be totally untouched by the war, while German soldiers had to suffer the unbearable." This was, in fact, the line of argument that the defense attorney for the Nazi doctors pursued at the Nuremberg trial. With the research on American prisoners at question, he asked that the court "not overlook the fact that particularly during the last years, even outside Germany, medical experiments were performed on human beings who undoubtedly did not volunteer for these experiments."[26]

The Nuremberg Code, the set of standards on ethical research that emerged from the tribunal, might have served as a model, even if a slightly flawed one, for American guidelines. Its provisions certainly were relevant to some types of medical research that had been (and still were) under way in the United States. The opening provision of the Nuremberg Code declared: "The voluntary consent of the human subject is absolutely essential. This means that the person involved should have legal capacity to give consent." By this principle, the mentally disabled were not suitable subjects for research—a principle that American researchers did not follow. Moreover, the Code insisted that the research subject "should be so situated as to be able to exercise free power of choice," which rendered questionable the American practice of using prisoners as research subjects. The Nuremberg Code also declared that human subjects "should have sufficient knowledge and comprehension of the elements of the subject matter involved as to make an understanding and enlightened decision." Thus, American practices notwithstanding, persons mentally disabled by illness or retardation were not to be enrolled.

Yet, with a few exceptions, none of these issues received sustained analysis in the United States in the immediate postwar period. Neither the horrors described at the Nuremberg trial nor the ethical principles that emerged from it had a significant impact on the American research establishment. The trial itself did not receive extensive press coverage. Over 1945 and 1946 fewer than a dozen articles appeared in the *New York Times* on the Nazi research; the indictment of forty-two doctors in the fall of 1946 was a page-five story and the opening of the trial, a page-nine story.[27] (The announcement of the guilty verdict in August 1947 was a front-page story, but the execution of seven of the defendants a year later was again relegated to the back pages.) Over the next fifteen years only a handful of articles in either medical or popular journals took up Nuremberg.

In part, this silence may have represented a postwar eagerness to repress the memory of the atrocities. But more important, the events described at Nuremberg were not perceived by researchers or commentators to be directly relevant to the American scene. The violations had been the work of Nazis, not doctors; the guilty parties were Hitler's henchmen, not scientists. Francis Moore, a professor of surgery at Harvard Medical School and a pioneer in kidney transplantation, was especially sensitive to ethical issues in experimentation and was ahead of most of his colleagues in recognizing the dilemmas in human experimentation. But even as he decried the German atrocities, he distanced science and non-Germans from them. The "horrible nightmares of Dachau and Belsen will ever stand in the conscience of all men," he told a symposium on drug research in 1960. But the lesson had to remain "most especially in the conscience of Germans"; further, "the tragedy of this intentional suffering and torture can never be erased, but one of the ironic tragedies of the human experimentation by the German 'scientists' was that no good science of any sort came from any of this work."[28]

Madness, not medicine, was implicated at Nuremberg. Few people noticed that many of the German perpetrators were university-trained and university-appointed researchers or that many of them possessed first-rate medical credentials and had pursued notable careers. Instead, the prevailing view was that they were Nazis first and last; by definition, nothing they did, and no code drawn up in response to them, was relevant to the United States.[29]

Other articles that addressed the Nuremberg trial drew from it not the lesson that the state should regulate experimentation but quite the reverse—that the state should not interfere with medicine. Nuremberg became a stick with which to beat the idea of "socialized medicine," not the occasion to oversee research.[30] The logic of the argument was that the atrocities were the result of government interference in the conduct of research (and here, the distinction between the Nazi government and all other governments was lost). Science was pure—it was politics that was corrupting. Hence, state control over medicine through regulations that intruded in the private relationship between doctor and patient or investigator and subject were likely to pervert medicine.

Even an incident notorious enough to capture headlines and expose the unregulated character of human experimentation had a minimal impact on the mood of benign neglect. In 1962, when Senator Estes Kefauver was winding up a long and only modestly successful campaign to regulate drug company prices, the thalidomide scandal broke.

The drug, widely prescribed in Europe for pregnant women at risk for spontaneous abortion or premature delivery, was in the process of being evaluated for safety by the Food and Drug Administration (FDA). One official, Francis Kelsey, dissatisfied with the quality of the European test results, delayed approval, and in the interim the link between thalidomide and birth defects (typically, warped or missing limbs) became established. Although a major catastrophe had been averted, some 20,000 Americans, of whom 3,750 were of childbearing age and 624 were reported as pregnant, had already taken thalidomide on an experimental basis, that is, as part of the drug company protocols. However, the precise number of recipients was unknown and their identification incomplete, mostly because the companies and the prescribing physicians who were conducting the trials kept very sloppy records. Kefauver took full advantage of the scandal to clinch the case for greater regulation, and as a direct result, Congress empowered the FDA to test drugs not only for safety (an authority it had held since 1938) but for efficacy as well.

In the course of the hearings and debates on the bill, the senators learned, to the amazement of some of them, that patients who had received experimental drugs in these clinical trials did not always know that they were participating in an experiment. Many of the subjects who had taken thalidomide had had no idea that they were part of a drug trial and had not given their consent. New York's Senator Jacob Javits, profoundly disturbed by this situation, proposed an amendment to the Kefauver bill that would have compelled the secretary of Health, Education and Welfare (HEW) to issue regulations that "no such [experimental] drug may be administered to any human being in any clinical investigation unless . . . that human being has been appropriately advised that such drug has not been determined to be safe in use for human beings."[31] One might have thought that the desirability and fairness of such a regulation were indisputable; surely subjects in an experiment should be told that a drug is not demonstrably safe and asked whether they wish to take it. Yet the debates that followed were anything but mild, and the Javits amendment did not survive for long in its original form. As late as 1962, even so elementary a protection of human subjects could not win approval, and the reasons clarify why regulating medical research appeared unacceptable.

Javits cogently argued his case. He assured colleagues that he was not opposed to human experimentation and fully appreciated its critical role in medical progress ("I feel deeply that some risks must be assumed"). Nevertheless, "experimentation must not be conducted in a blind way, without people giving their consent. . . . [Otherwise,] where is the dignity, the responsibility, and the freedom of the individual?" These arguments notwithstanding, Javits recognized that the amendment was running into trouble, and attempted to salvage it by changing the language from the secretary "shall" to the secretary "may" issue such regulations; in its weakened form, intervention became discretionary, not obligatory, and allowed for as many exceptions as the secretary might wish. Javits also made clear that his proposal would affect only the administration of drugs whose safety was not known; he was not asking that patients be informed about all drugs physicians prescribed for them.[32]

Nevertheless, Javits could not persuade his colleagues to impose so elementary a requirement on researchers. First, the senators responded with extreme caution because they consistently confused experimentation with therapy and the investigator with the physician. And just as this blurring of the lines committed the NIH to a hands-off policy, so it undercut a regulatory response from Congress. Senators feared that compelling physicians to inform a patient about an experimental drug would also compel them to inform a patient about a diagnosis that was fatal; in order to get patients to take the new drug, the doctor would have to tell them that they were suffering from a life-threatening illness. For example, Colorado's Senator John Carroll, claimed to be generally sympathetic to the Javits amendment: "I believe that under normal circumstances, when a man . . . goes to a doctor, that man has a right to know if he is to be given untested medicine. . . . I firmly believe every human being has a right to know whether he is being treated with experimental medicine . . . that he is to be used as a guinea pig." Why, then, oppose the amendment? Because with a "strict, mandatory, prenotification requirement, we might prevent the doctor from helping his patients in times of extreme emergency." Or as Mississippi's Senator James Eastland insisted: "It might be an experimental drug, a single injection of which would provide him with a chance to live." The debate even slipped over into the case of the coma patient, in the process revealing the senators' inability to distinguish between the competent and the incompetent patient, and between an emergency and a nonemergency situation. Thus, one senator objected to the proposal because it would keep a comatose patient from getting potentially life-saving drugs: "How could he be notified that an experimental drug is being used?"[33]

In the Senate, as in the Clinical Center and countless university hospitals as well, the ethos of the examining room cloaked the activities of the laboratory, and the trust accorded the physician encompassed the researcher. Lawmakers were no more able than NIH officials to distinguish the human subject from the patient, so that efforts to regulate experimentation—however reasonable—were translated into attempts to regulate therapy, which were still considered unnecessary and intrusive. For any change to occur, it would first be necessary to differentiate the researcher from the doctor and the laboratory from the examining room.

Moreover, the confusion of experimentation with therapy reflected an extraordinary optimism about the prospects of innovation. The hearings may have been deeply affected by thalidomide, but when it came to regulating research, the senators saw every new drug as a potential penicillin. They hesitated to intervene in research because they assumed that experiments were likely to prove successful and the drugs under investigation would turn out to be therapeutic wonders. Through the course of the debate the senators frequently posed their hypothetical cases about experimental drugs in terms of the new, miraculous injection, the life-saving pill, the prescription that would revive the near-dead. They measured the impact of regulation not by calculating risks but by exaggerating benefits. Fantasies, not nightmare cases, ruled: the researcher who had a miracle cure for a deadly disease or who could awaken the comatose patient ought not to be burdened or bridled with administrative regulations.

Starting from such premises, it is small wonder that Congress proved unwilling to say cleanly and simply that researchers must obtain the permission of their subjects before conducting drug experiments. The Javits amendment finally emerged in the legislation as a request to the secretary of HEW to promulgate regulations so that investigators dispensing experimental drugs would obtain the consent of their subjects "except where they deem it not feasible or, in their best professional judgment, contrary to the best interests of such human beings."[34] The qualifications took the heart out of the resolution, granting investigators broad discretion to decide when such vague considerations as feasibility or best interest were being served.

Between 1945 and 1965 an occasional academic conference or organization attempted a sophisticated analysis of the issues in human experimentation—the deliberations of the Law–Medicine Research Institute at Boston University are one such example. The more typical approach, however, is exemplified by the National Society for Medical Research (NSMR). Founded to counter the campaigns of antivivisectionists, the NSMR, in 1959, for the first time devoted a conference to "Clinical Research—Legal and Ethical Aspects." Persuaded that "the law has not kept pace with modern medical developments," the conference attendees produced several useful analyses, including one on the weaknesses of the Nuremberg Code and another on the value of peer review in human experimentation. But the most notable characteristic of the 1959 conference—indeed, of much of the literature on ethics and human experimentation between 1945 and 1965—was its calmness. The discussions made the problems seem more conceptual than actual, more academically interesting than pressing. There was no sense of crisis, of lives at stake, or of trusts violated, and no hint of scandal. When Dr. Louis Welt discussed the difficulty of obtaining a noncoerced consent, the group he focused on was medical students, not prisoners or the mentally disabled. When a colleague reviewed human experimentation at the NIH Clinical Center, he found its guiding principles altogether adequate (requiring "only slight modification in light of experience") and made no comment about actual practices.[35]

When discussants glimpsed a conflict of interest between the researcher and the subject, or between the principle of the greatest good for the greatest number and the rights of the individual, they grew distinctly uncomfortable and moved either to smooth over differences or to make certain that the research enterprise was not seriously hampered. Thus, the NSMR's 1959 conference report made the ordering of priorities clear: "The standards for health research on human subjects should recognize the imperative need for testing new procedures, materials and drugs on human subjects as essential to the public interest. The protection of personal rights of individuals . . . can co-exist with the public necessity to use people—sick or well—as subjects for health research." The primary goal was testing new procedures, and the rights of individuals would coexist with it. The conference report did declare that experiments on minors or on the incompetent should have the approval of parents or guardians and should "also significantly benefit or may reasonably benefit the individual." But, probably aware of how far World War II practices had departed from this standard, the authors added a critical qualification: "There may perhaps be justification in the absence of this requirement in a national emergency or for an experiment of utmost importance. Here, the availability of certain persons, not able to consent personally, may constitute a strategic resource in terms of time or location not otherwise obtainable." Although the report conceded that "the Nazis hid behind this rationalization . . . [and] such justifications should not even be considered except in the most dire circumstances," still it gave retrospective approval to the wartime researchers and prospective approval to investigators on the brink of findings of "utmost importance."[36]

In this same spirit, several international medical organizations in the postwar decades published guidelines for human experimentation, expanding on the Nuremberg Code. Most of these efforts, however, did not involve American groups; and with the exception of a few researchers who made this a field of special study, the codes captured little attention in the United States and had minimal impact on institutional practices.[37] The American Medical Association (AMA), which spoke for the interests of general practitioners, rather than specialists or medical investigators, did frame a research code, but the stipulations were vague and lacked any reference to means of enforcement. The code required the voluntary consent of the human subject but said nothing about what information researchers should impart; who, if anyone, should monitor the process; or what the ethics were of conducting research on incompetent subjects, such as the institutionalized mentally disabled. The code did condemn experiments on prisoners, expressing explicit "disapproval of the participation in scientific experiments of persons convicted of murder, rape, arson, kidnapping, treason or other heinous crimes."[38] But its aim was to protect public safety, not inmates' rights. The AMA believed that parole boards were treating prisoner-volunteers too generously, giving them early release as a reward for assuming medical risks, and thus returning hardened criminals to the streets too quickly.[39]

In all, American researchers in the immediate post–World War II period ran their laboratories free of external constraints. The autonomy they enjoyed in conducting human experiments was limited only by their individual consciences, not by their colleagues, their funders, their universities, or any other private or public body. How the investigators exercised this discretion, the record they compiled, became the focus of Henry Beecher's analysis. What we find there is a case study of the dangers of leaving medical science on its own.

CHAPTER 4

The Doctor as Whistle-blower

THE career of Henry Beecher provided few clues that he would be the one to expose in most compelling fashion how the researchers in the post–World War II decades abused their discretion. Unlike many whistle-blowers, Beecher stood at the top of his profession. Although the family name is a famous one in American history—his kin included Harriet Beecher Stowe, the "little lady" that Lincoln credited with bringing on the Civil War, and Henry Ward Beecher, the minister who was exceptionally influential until being disgraced by an adulterous affair— Henry's branch had not prospered. He grew up in Kansas in very modest circumstances and graduated from the University of Kansas. Talented and ambitious, he worked his way through Harvard Medical School, trained in general medicine, and then joined the Harvard faculty and the staff of the Massachusetts General Hospital (MGH). Beecher was so highly regarded that when in the late 1930s Harvard and the MGH sought to professionalize the field of anesthesiology, they gave him the assignment. He did a masterful job, coming to hold the Dorr Professorship of Research in Anesthesia and to chair the department.[1]

What prompted Beecher to analyze the conduct of human experiments and to go public with his findings? Anesthesiologists do have a reputation for being the fifth column within medicine. Beecher belonged to the specialty that daily watches colleagues perform in the operating room and then discusses their relative strengths and weaknesses. He was also something of a maverick who delighted in controversy and conflict. In 1954, for example, he was senior author of "A Study of the Deaths Associated with Anesthesia and Surgery," a paper framed in highly judgmental terms. Its purpose was to determine "the extent of the responsibility which must be borne by anesthesia for failure in the total care of the surgical patient." Others would have called this an investigation of comparative mortality with anesthetic agents. The major finding was that the use of the new and very popular anesthetic agent curare was associated with a significantly higher death rate, and Beecher hoped, again in contentious fashion, that "the study itself, by directing attention to these matters, would lead to sharper criticism of existing practices with improvement in them," which it did.[2]

Beecher's concern for research ethics also drew on his personal experiences. He was both a committed investigator and one who was fully prepared to use his laboratory skills to promote societal ends. His major interest in the 1940s and 1950s was the effects of drugs on pain, performance, and perceptions, a field which he pioneered. Given the obvious military relevance of the subject, Beecher worked closely with the U.S. Army during World War II and continued the collaboration into the opening years of the cold war. He explored such questions as which narcotic was best administered to wounded soldiers in combat, and he also alerted the military to the importance of what he called "the second great power of anesthesia," that is, its potential as a truth-telling serum. In short, Beecher learned firsthand about research in the service of society and in the process may have become sensitive to how slippery a slope he was on.

The most important consideration, however, was Beecher's commitment to good science, that is, to well-designed and properly constructed research protocols. He was among the first to insist on the need for controls in drug experiments, convinced that in no other way could the investigator eliminate the placebo effect and accurately measure the efficacy of a new drug. Beecher's most lasting contribution as a researcher was to establish how the very act of taking a drug, whatever its potency, led some patients to improve; he calculated that "of the average pain relief produced by a large dose of morphine treating severe pain, nearly half must be attributed to a placebo." Hence, if the outcomes for one group taking a medication were not compared to outcomes for a similar group taking a placebo, the efficacy of a drug could not be known. "The scientist as well as the physician," insisted Beecher in 1959, "is confronted with a bewildering array of new agents launched with claims sometimes too eagerly accepted by a compassionate physician trying to help a patient in trouble. The properly controlled, quantitative approach holds the only real hope for dealing with the oncoming flood of new drugs."[3] Thus, Beecher's sharpest fear was that research of dubious ethicality might impugn the legitimacy of experimentation, discrediting the prime force bringing progress to medicine. Bad ethics would undercut the pursuit of good science, and the result would be widespread ignorance and old-fashioned quackery.[4]

When Beecher first addressed research ethics in the late 1950s, only a handful of others shared his concern, and not until the mid-1960s did his ideas capture widespread attention. The breakthrough occurred in March 1965 at a conference on drug research at Brook Lodge, Wisconsin, sponsored by the Upjohn pharmaceutical company. Beecher delivered a paper on the ethics of clinical research, which went beyond discussions of general principles to cite specific cases. Although he did not name individual investigators, he discussed specific research protocols, all published, whose ethics disturbed him. His use of real cases caught the media's attention, and both the *New York Times* and the *Wall Street Journal* ran lengthy accounts of his talk.[5] Colleagues, too, evinced an unusual interest in his remarks, by no means all of it friendly or favorable. "I really was subjected to a most humiliating experience," Beecher told a friend about the aftermath of the Brook Lodge meeting. In particular, he reported, Dr. Thomas Chalmers and Dr. David Rutstein, both colleagues at the Harvard Medical School, "called a press conference to refute what I said without finding out whether or not I could be present. They made prepared statements and the meeting was terminated before I had an opportunity to do so. Chalmers charged me with being an irresponsible exaggerator. Rutstein stood up there with him and did not dissent."[6] Beecher seemed somewhat surprised by so agitated a response, but he immediately moved to defend his position and, judging by the way he threw himself into the task, relished the opportunity.

Beecher's strategy was to turn the Brook Lodge presentation into a professional journal article that documented the ethical dilemmas in human experimentation by describing actual research protocols. He had no trouble accumulating some fifty examples of what he considered investigations of dubious ethicality, and in August 1965, he submitted the article (again without footnotes to the cases) to the *Journal of the American Medical Association (JAMA)*. In a covering letter he told the editor, John Talbott, that the manuscript represented "about ten years of as careful thought as I am capable of doing. It has been read by a great many individuals, including the president of the Massachusetts Medical Society, who, though appalled by the information, agree that it should be published, and the sooner the better. I do hope you will find this suitable for publication in the Journal . . . the finest place for it to appear, in my view. It is rather long. I do not believe it can be shortened significantly and carry the same message, which so urgently needs to be disseminated." After Talbott responded that he was sending it out for review, Beecher wrote again to emphasize how important it was that *JAMA* publish the piece: "Last year I gave an oral presentation at a closed medical meeting and the reverberations from that are still continuing. . . . Unquestionably the shoe pinched a lot of feet."[7]

In October, Talbott rejected the article, informing Beecher that neither of two reviewers favored publication. One insisted that "the story could be told in twenty-five per cent of the space, illustrated by ten items with references rather than forty-eight items without references." The other found it so "poorly organized [that] frankly, I was surprised that a thoughtful physician of Doctor Beecher's stature expected you to review this manuscript. Should the decision be to revise, I would be interested in seeing the revision provided it is well prepared and eliminates nine-tenths of the examples." Apparently not eager to get involved in publishing so controversial a piece, Talbott noted that Beecher had twice expressed an unwillingness to make substantial deletions and did not give Beecher the option of changing his mind or making revisions. He thought it best to have Beecher "start afresh with another editorial board."[8]

Beecher then turned to the *New England Journal of Medicine (NEJM)*. He submitted a slightly revised and fully annotated copy, and Dr. Joseph Garland and two of his assistants (the "brain trust," he called them) reviewed it case by case; they recommended omitting about half the protocols, apparently not so much for reasons of space but because they did not find all the examples equally compelling. Some author–editor give-and-take went on, but Beecher accepted their recommendations and was not unhappy to have the piece, in his view, "understate the problem."[9]

Conscious that the *NEJM* did not enjoy the *JAMA*'s circulation, Beecher notified the press about its forthcoming publication and at the same time warned John Knowles, the head of the MGH, that "a considerable amount of controversy" might ensue. "I have no doubt that I shall come in for some very heavy criticism. For the sake of the Hospital, I have tried to make certain that the material is as thoughtful, as accurate and as unexaggerated as possible."[10]

Beecher's indictment was powerful, arousing, as classic exposés do, a sense of disbelief that such practices had continued for so long without either scrutiny or sanction. A sample of three conveys the style of the twenty-two.

Example 16. This study was directed toward determining the period of infectivity of infectious hepatitis. Artificial induction of hepatitis was carried out in an institution for mentally defective children in which a mild form of hepatitis was endemic. . . . A resolution adopted by the World Medical Association states explicitly: "Under no circumstances is a doctor permitted to do anything which would weaken the physical or mental resistance of a human being except from strictly therapeutic or prophylactic indications imposed in the interest of the patient." There is no right to risk an injury to 1 person for the benefit of others.

Example 17. Live cancer cells were injected into 22 human subjects as part of a study of immunity to cancer. According to a recent review, the subjects (hospitalized patients) were "merely told they would be receiving 'some cells'— . . . the word cancer was entirely omitted."

Example 19. During bronchoscopy a special needle was inserted through a bronchus into the left atrium of the heart. This was done in an unspecified number of subjects, both with cardiac disease and with normal hearts. The technique was a new approach whose hazards were at the beginning quite unknown. The subjects with normal hearts were used, not for their possible benefit but for that of patients in general.[11]

The investigations that made up Beecher's roster of dishonor differed in methods and goals. The researchers in some explored physiologic responses (as in example 19); in others, they attempted to learn more about a disease (examples 16 and 17); in still others, they tested new drugs (example 4) or withheld a drug of known efficacy to test an alternative (example 1). All the examples, however, endangered the health and well-being of subjects without their knowledge or approval. Only two of the original fifty protocols, Beecher reported, so much as mentioned obtaining consent, and he doubted that even they had gone very far in that direction: "Ordinary patients will not knowingly risk their health or their life for the sake of 'science.' Every experienced clinician knows this. When such risks are taken and a considerable number of patients are involved, it may be assumed that informed consent has not been obtained in all cases." Perhaps, he was later asked, the investigators had actually obtained consent but neglected to mention it in their publications? Beecher found it fanciful to believe (as in example 1) that a group of soldiers with strep throat would knowingly participate in an experiment in which they would be denied penicillin and face the risk of contracting rheumatic fever: "I have worked on the ward of a large hospital for 35 years, [and] I know perfectly well that ward patients will not . . . volunteer for any such use of themselves for experimental purposes when the hazard may be permanent injury or death."[12]

Beecher's cases did not represent only a few bizarre examples; rather, his catalogue described how mainstream investigators in the period from 1945 to 1965 exercised their broad discretion. This fact emerges from a review of the original publications from which Beecher took his twenty-two examples—the first such review since the *NEJM* editors accepted the article for publication. (See Appendix A for complete citations to the twenty-two cases.)

Comparing the original twenty-two articles with Beecher's published account makes clear in the first instance that the strength of Beecher's indictment does not emanate from its methodological sophistication or scientific character. The selection was impressionistic, even arbitrary, not part of a random survey or systematic inquiry. Beecher himself considered the cases to be no more than apt examples, protocols that he knew about or had discovered as he read the *Journal of Clinical*

Investigation or the *NEJM*. Not surprisingly, then, the list of twenty-two has many idiosyncrasies: fully half of the studies involved research into cardiovascular physiology (examples 6 through 13 and 19 through 21), and two of the studies (examples 15 and 19) were carried out in England. But however haphazard the selection process, Beecher was singling out mainstream science—indeed, science on the frontier. To judge by such criteria as each researcher's professional affiliation, the sources of funding, and the journal of publication, these were typically protocols from leading investigators in leading institutions, working on some of the most important questions in medicine. Beecher was describing the clinical ethics of elite researchers, those already in or destined to be in positions of authority.

Beecher's twenty-two examples were current, all drawn from the immediate postwar period. One of the papers appeared in 1948, thirteen appeared between 1950 and 1959, and eight between 1960 and 1965. The journals were prestigious: six of the papers appeared in the *NEJM* (examples 1, 4 through 6, 14, and 16), five in the *Journal of Clinical Investigation* (examples 8, 10, 13, 15, 20), two in the *JAMA* (examples 2 and 9), and two in *Circulation* (examples 19 and 20). The funders of the research (which numbered more than twenty-two, since some projects received multiple support) included the U.S. military (the surgeon general's office or the Armed Forces Epidemiology Board), five projects; the National Institutes of Health, five projects; drug companies (including Merck and Parke, Davis and Company), three projects; private foundations, eight projects; and other federal offices (including the U.S. Public Health Service and the Atomic Energy Commission), three projects. Clearly, this was not research in tiny labs carried out by eccentric physicians.

Perhaps most telling were the auspices under which the research projects were conducted. Thirteen of the twenty-two examples came from university medical school clinics and laboratories: Case Western Reserve University (examples 1 and 2); the University of California Center for Health Sciences, Los Angeles (example 5); Harvard Medical School and its affiliated hospitals, including Peter Bent Brigham Hospital and Children's Hospital (examples 6, 9, 13, and 19); the University of Pennsylvania (example 7); Georgetown and George Washington Universities (example 8); Ohio State University (example 12); New

York University (example 16); Northwestern University (example 18); and Emory and Duke Universities (example 21). Three of the projects were conducted at the Clinical Center of the NIH (examples 10, 11, and 20).

The credentials of the principal investigators were one more indication of their importance. The younger ones were often research fellows, some in medicine (Case Western Reserve, example 1), others in surgery (Harvard, example 6); or postdoctoral or exchange fellows (NIH, examples 7 and 14). In two cases the more senior people were professors (NYU, example 16; Cornell, example 17). Among the junior researchers, a number were beginning to make their mark in the world of research and later went on to illustrious careers, becoming national leaders in medicine, chairmen of major departments, and winners of major awards, often for the very research that Beecher had cited.

Dr. Saul Krugman conducted the research described in Beecher's example 16, the purposeful infection with hepatitis of residents at the Willowbrook State School for the Retarded. After his Willowbrook investigations of 1956 through 1972, Dr. Krugman became the chairman of the pediatrics department at New York University and the winner, in 1972, of the Markle Foundation's John Russell Award. The citation praised Krugman for demonstrating how clinical research ought to be done. In 1983, Dr. Krugman also won the Lasker Prize, probably the highest award given for research in this country, just a notch below the Nobel Prize.

Dr. Chester Southam was the investigator in Beecher's example 17. An associate professor of medicine at the Cornell University Medical School and the chief of the section on clinical virology at the Sloan-Kettering Institute for Cancer Research, he was in charge of the research involving the injection of cancer cells into elderly and senile patients. In 1967, Dr. Southam was elected vice-president of the American Association for Cancer Research, and in 1968 he became its president.[13]

Examples 10 and 11, studies in heart physiology on patients at the NIH Clinical Center, involving "a mercury-filled resistance gauge sutured to the surface of the left ventricle" and "simultaneous catheterization of both ventricles," were conducted in 1957 and 1960 by Dr. Eugene Braunwald, then a researcher in cardiology at the NIH. (Dr.

Braunwald's is the only name to appear three times on the Beecher roll—principal investigator in these two cases, and one of the four authors of the paper in example 20.) In 1967, Dr. Braunwald won the Outstanding Service Award of the Public Health Service and in 1972, the Research Achievement Award of the American Heart Association. In 1972 he became Hersey Professor and chairman of the Department of Medicine at Peter Bent Brigham Hospital, Harvard Medical School, and he later headed the Department of Medicine at Beth Israel Hospital as well.

How is the behavior of these investigators to be understood? It will not suffice to claim that they were simply less moral or trustworthy than their colleagues. They were too well supported, too integral to the research establishment, and, ultimately, too much honored to characterize as aberrant or deviant. The idea that these particular experiments raised complicated ethical issues beyond the state of the field is no more persuasive. In practically every one of the twenty-two cases, it was self-evident that the subjects would not benefit directly from the research and might even be harmed. Neither Krugman's retarded subjects nor Southam's senile ones nor Braunwald's cardiac ones would have been better off for having participated in the protocols.

It also seems too narrow an explanation to place all the blame on raw personal ambition—the desire to get grants, win promotions, capture the prize. Undoubtedly, these considerations motivated some of the researchers, and Beecher himself, although he did not address the question directly, suggested this motivation. He stressed in particular the new and massive infusion of research funds through the NIH and the intensified research ethos in the postwar period. "Medical schools and university hospitals are increasingly dominated by investigators," he observed. "Every young man knows that he will never be promoted to a tenure post . . . unless he has proved himself as an investigator," and this at a time when "medical science has shown how valuable human experimentation can be in solving problems of disease and its treatment."[14] However valid his point, it does not explain why the research community evinced no difficulty with these protocols, why no scientist who read Krugman's publications in the 1950s protested, and why no department that reviewed the work of these researchers with-held promotion on the grounds of unethical behavior.

A better entry point for understanding how investigators and their colleagues justified these protocols is the impact of the World War II experience, because the exceptional protocol of the pre-1940 period became normative. Clinical research had come of age when medical progress, measured by antidotes against malaria, dysentery, and influenza, was the prime consideration, and traditional ethical notions about consent and voluntary participation in experimentation seemed far less relevant. A generation of researchers were trained to perform, accomplish, and deliver cures—to be heroes in the laboratory, like soldiers on the battlefield. If researchers created effective vaccines, diagnostic tests, or miracle drugs like penicillin, no one would question their methods or techniques.

This orientation survived into the postwar years, not simply because a license granted is not easily revoked, but because the laboratory achievements were so remarkable. Having been given extraordinary leeway, the researchers delivered extraordinary products: an array of antibiotics, including a cure for tuberculosis; a variety of drugs for treating cardiac abnormalities; a new understanding of hepatitis. Given this record, who would want to rein in such talent and creativity, to intrude and regulate behavior inside the laboratory? Surely not a senate committee that was investigating a drug scandal, let alone the NIH, whose extramural grants were funding the research. How much wiser to trust to the researcher and await one breakthrough after another.

Most of the researchers in Beecher's protocols were the heirs to this wartime tradition, although they had not actually participated in the war effort or held Committee on Medical Research (CMR) contracts. Of the thirty-two American investigators, only eight had been born before 1920 (of whom four had seen military service); of the twenty-four others, seventeen were born between 1921 and 1929, and seven between 1931 and 1934. They were, in other words, the products of medical and scientific training in the immediate postwar period, trained to think in utilitarian terms and ready to achieve the greatest good for the greatest number.

It is no coincidence that this cohort of investigators took as their research subjects persons who were in one sense or another devalued and marginal: they were either retarded, institutionalized, senile, alcoholic, or poor, or they were military recruits, cannon fodder for battles in a war against disease. These social characteristics at once reflected and promoted a utilitarian calculus among researchers, encouraging them to make the same judgments in the 1950s and early 1960s as their predecessors had made in the 1940s.

Beecher had relied on the logic of the situation—the patients' presumed unwillingness to put themselves at jeopardy—to argue that the researchers had not actually obtained consent from their subjects. Had he scrutinized the types of patients enrolled in the protocols more closely, he could have clinched his point, for in practically every instance, they lacked either the opportunity or the ability to exercise choice. The research subjects in examples 1 and 2 were soldiers in the armed forces; in example 3, charity patients; in examples 4 and 16, the mentally retarded; in examples 6 and 22, children or newborns; in examples 9 and 17, the very elderly; in example 12, the terminally ill; in examples 13 and 15, chronic alcoholics with advanced cases of cirrhosis. The subjects in examples 8, 10, 11, and 20 were patients in the Clinical Center, where, as we have noted, patients were generally not informed about the research procedures that accompanied treatment interventions. In fact, these four examples (involving catheterization and strain-gauge studies) were the very ones that Donald Fredrickson had cited, when he headed the Clinical Center's Heart Institute, to demonstrate that NIH patients were kept ignorant of protocols.

The incompetence of many of these subjects had enabled the researchers to assert all the more confidently their right to exercise discretion and to substitute their own judgment. Because the subjects could not understand the intricacies of a scientific protocol, the investigators felt justified in taking matters into their own hands. To Chester Southam, it was unnecessary to offer explanations to elderly and senile patients about injections of cancer cells because they would become frightened and because he knew, supposedly, that no danger existed. Some of this calculation may have reflected the laboratory version of the old clinical saw that a minor operation is an operation being performed on someone else. But Southam and other investigators were convinced that their procedures, however daring or invasive, actually carried little risk. (Little risk, but some: When Southam was later asked why, if the procedure was so harmless, had he not injected the cancer cells into his own skin, he replied that there were too few skilled cancer researchers around.) So too, Eugene Braunwald may have reasoned that it was unnecessary to obtain the permission of Clinical Center patients to insert a strain gauge on cardiac vessels or to measure cardiac functioning with a catheter because he reckoned the risks to be minimal.[15] And in this spirit, Saul Krugman reasoned that feeding live hepatitis viruses to Willowbrook residents was acceptable not only because the disease was already endemic there but because he considered the Willowbrook strain of the virus to be mild, posing no threat to the well-being of the children.[16]

After minimizing the question of risks, the researchers confidently asserted that the potential benefits were enormous. Southam conducted his experiments in the belief that the reactions of an already debilitated patient to foreign cancer cells would cast new light on the immunological system and bring him close to a cure for cancer. Was Southam an unethical researcher? Hardly, in his view. He aimed to become one of humanity's great benefactors. Behind Krugman's Willowbrook research was a conviction that he could do more good for more people if he could conquer hepatitis. Was Krugman taking advantage of the institutionalized retarded? Hardly. Whatever vaccines he produced would protect them against a disease to which they were particularly exposed. So too, Braunwald was undoubtedly convinced that his studies would be of enormous gain to all heart patients, which turned out to be correct. Was Braunwald ignoring the rights of the desperately sick at the Clinical Center? No, for the more he learned about cardiovascular functioning, the better those patients would be served.

A powerful exposé is often more able to identify a problem than to propose effective or imaginative solutions, and Beecher's contribution was no exception. He was too committed a researcher to so much as dally with the thought of abolishing human experimentation and was even reluctant to regulate it in ways that might hamper its operation. He was exceptionally ambivalent about the implications of his own findings and, at least initially, very reluctant to use them as basis for new departures. First, Beecher doubted the ability of a formal code of ethics to shape researchers' behavior. He did not believe "that very many 'rules' can be laid down to govern experimentation in man. In most cases these are more likely to do harm than good. Rules are not going to curb the unscrupulous."[17] Second, he was skeptical of the value of making the consent process itself more elaborate and trusting informed patients to look after their own best interest. After all, patients were too inclined to accede to physicians' requests, with or without well-intentioned explanations.

At the same time, however, Beecher, as much as any single figure, undercut the assumptions that were so critical to the hands-off policy at NIH and elsewhere: that the physician and the investigator were one and the same, and that the trust patients afforded to doctors should be extended to researchers. In one of his first major discussions of research ethics, an article in *JAMA* in 1959 on "Experimentation in Man," Beecher painstakingly differentiated between the two roles, subverting the idea that the ethical tradition in medicine was sufficient to produce ethical behavior in research. The two activities were "different in their procedures, in their aims, and in their immediate ends." The physician's exclusive concern was with the well-being of one particular patient; his ethical obligations were clear and uncomplicated (or at least relatively so): to do all in his power to advance the well-being of the patient. The investigator, on the other hand, was in a much more complicated position. His aim was to advance knowledge that would benefit society; his overriding allegiance was to his protocol, to a class of patients, if you will, not to the individual subjects in his protocol.

Beecher feared that a commitment to the general good as against the individual good might easily legitimate ethically dubious research, and he feared such a prospect especially because of the lessons of Nuremberg, which he was among the first to explicate. Perhaps he was conscious of the atrocities because of his earlier work with the army; in his papers are copies of then-classified German research reports, mostly dealing with the effects of exposure, which he may have evaluated, at the army's request, for their scientific value. Whatever the reason, he insisted: "Any classification of human experimentation as 'for the good of society' is to be viewed with distaste, even alarm. Undoubtedly all sound work has this as its ultimate aim, but such high-flown expressions . . . have been used within recent memory as cover for outrageous acts. . . . There is no justification here for risking an injury to an individual for the possible benefit to other people. . . . Such a rule would open the door wide to perversions of practice, even such as were inflicted by Nazi doctors on concentration-camp prisoners. . . . The individual must not be subordinated to the community. The community exists for man."[18]

On a less profound level, Beecher also distinguished the researcher from the physician by outlook and ambition. Doctors might let monetary concerns guide their actions, making treatment decisions in order to increase their incomes, but such behavior was immediately recognized as patently unethical. Investigators, however, were caught up in a system of promotions and grant getting that so emphasized research results as to obfuscate research ethics. The physician who lined his pockets at his patients' expense was condemned, whereas the researcher who produced new findings by disregarding the rights of his subjects might well win scientific prizes. Researchers knew they had to publish in order not to perish by being denied academic advancement and government funding; everyone recognized that tenure came only to those who proved themselves superb investigators, whatever their ethics. This environment nullified a concept of identity of interest between researcher and subject.

Yet the power of this critique notwithstanding, Beecher wavered, reluctant to recommend new rules or methods of regulation. He did have a short list of dos and don'ts for investigators: no use of prisoners of war for research, extreme caution about conducting research on laboratory personnel or medical students (who might feel obliged to consent because of their positions), but an allowance to do research on prisoners and volunteers if they gave consent. Beecher was also prepared to implement some type of "group decision supported by a proper consultive body," although he offered no details on how it might be organized or administered. But his final word on the researchers who conducted the twenty-two protocols was a variation on the theme of "they knew not what they did." He noted, with more rhetorical flourish than evidence or accuracy, that their "thoughtlessness and carelessness, not a willful disregard of the patient's rights, account for most of the cases encountered." Armed with such a formulation, he comfortably asserted that "calling attention ... will help to correct abuses present." He maintained such an old-fashioned faith in the integrity of the individual researcher that, after weighing all the alternatives, he concluded: "The more reliable safeguard [is] provided by the presence of an intelligent, informed, conscientious, compassionate, responsible investigator."[19]

In the end, Beecher's responses highlight the strengths and weaknesses of the insider's exposé. Without his courage, the movement to set new rules for human experimentation would have proceeded on a much slower track. Few others had the scientific knowledge and ethical sensibilities to call into question medical researchers' ethics. But at the same time, with such knowledge and sensibility came both forgiveness (investigators know not what they do) and paternalism (subjects can never understand what investigators do). Left to Beecher, the reaction to the scandals would have been an appeal to professional trust and responsibility, as though consciousness-raising could solve the problem.

CHAPTER 5

New Rules for the Laboratory

EVEN the most sensational exposé will not necessarily spark fundamental alterations in public attitudes or policy. Media attention is fickle and the competition for front-page coverage or a few minutes on the evening news so intense that even egregious scandals may fade from attention. Further, countless ways exist for those in authority to explain problems away, from blaming a few bad apples to assuring everyone that the deficiencies have already been corrected. But not all exposés disappear without a trace. They may affect those so high in power as to generate critical changes (Watergate) or reveal conditions so substandard as to shock the conscience (a hellhole of an institution for the retarded), or describe conditions so frightening in their implications as to rivet attention (images of a silent spring). Human experimentation had elements in common with all of these, helping to ensure that its scandals would produce structural change.

A number of investigators certainly attempted to minimize the problem. Some insisted, as we have seen, that Henry Beecher's cases were aberrations; although no one dared to make the point so bluntly, other researchers undoubtedly believed it proper to trade off the rights of highly marginal groups for the sake of scientific progress, to keep the World War II model operational and out of mothballs. After all, strictly utilitarian principles could justify the experiments of a Saul Krugman; the retarded, it could be argued, did not have all that much to lose when compared to the societal gains if the research produced a vaccine against hepatitis. And Beecher himself exemplified how difficult it was to break out of an older, hands-off model of maintaining a faith in the integrity of the investigator and minimizing the implications of a conflict of interest with the subject. Nevertheless, the scandals deeply affected public attitudes and brought an unprecedented degree of regulation and oversight to the laboratory.

The exposés had an especially critical impact on the leadership of the National Institutes of Health (NIH), by far the most important source of funds for clinical research, and the Food and Drug Administration (FDA), responsible for overseeing the testing and licensure of all new drugs. These agencies were exquisitely alert to congressional pressures: let public opinion be mobilized, and they might be hauled in to testify at hearings, criticized and embarrassed for failures to keep investigators in check, and left to suffer the consequences of budget cuts. Calculating in a most self-protective and painstaking manner the repercussions that would follow when public officials read articles about abuses in human experimentation and editorial writers questioned the wisdom of a continued trust in the individual researcher, they moved quickly to contain the crisis. Given the potential negative fallout, the price of inaction was unacceptably high. Thus, the fact that authority was centralized in bodies that were at once subordinate to Congress and superordinate to the research community assured that the scandals would alter practice. Indeed, this circumstance explains why the regulation of human experimentation came first and most extensively to the United States, rather than other industrialized countries.

To be sure, the leaders of the NIH and (to a lesser, but still important, degree) the FDA were integral to the medical research community. These were not outsiders or newcomers to clinical research, and they were not likely to adopt either far-reaching or consistently intrusive measures. Nevertheless, their need to act meant that this exposé would not capture headlines in today's newspaper and be forgotten tomorrow.

The NIH leaders initially concerned themselves with research ethics after the Kefauver hearings in 1962 disclosed that physicians were administering experimental drugs without informing patients. James

Shannon, then the head of the NIH, immediately requested Robert B. Livingston, the associate chief of the Division of Research Facilities and Resources, to investigate the "moral and ethical aspects of clinical investigation." Since the overwhelming sentiment in the Senate debate on the resolutions proposed by Kefauver and Javits was to leave research unfettered, the Livingston Report, delivered in November 1964, was under little external pressure to recommend a change in the laissez-faire policy. The authors of the report recognized that "there is no generally accepted professional code relating to the conduct of clinical research" and expressed "a mounting concern . . . over the possible repercussions of untoward events . . . [because] highly consequential risks are being taken by individuals and institutions as well as NIH." But they did not urge the adoption of stricter regulations. "There was strong resistance," recalled one of the participants, "on attempting to set forth any guidelines or restraints or policies in this area." The report's framers concluded that "whatever the NIH might do by way of designing a code or stipulating standards for acceptable clinical research would be likely to inhibit, delay, or distort the carrying out of clinical research," rendering any such efforts unacceptable.[1]

The Livingston Report was not to be the last word, for even before Beecher's article, disturbing incidents had continued to surface. The case that received the greatest publicity and most disturbed the NIH was Chester Southam's cancer research on senile and demented patients, begun in 1963. The attention was so great that within two years the research was the object not only of extensive press coverage but of a lawsuit and a disciplinary hearing for Southam before the New York State Board of Regents. Almost all the publicity was hostile, and none of it was lost on the NIH. "It made all of us aware," one official confessed, "of the inadequacy of our guidelines and procedures and it clearly brought to the fore the basic issue that in the setting in which the patient is involved in an experimental effort, the judgment of the investigator is not sufficient as a basis for reaching a conclusion concerning the ethical and moral set of questions in that relationship."[2]

Just as the ripple effects of Southam's research were being felt, Beecher's well-publicized 1965 lecture and then his 1966 *NEJM* article revealed that Southam's insensitivity to the ethics of experimentation was not idiosyncratic. Again, the NIH had to consider the implications of this publicity for its own functioning. At least one congressman asked NIH officials how they intended to respond to Beecher's charges, and the associate director for the extramural programs hastened to assure him that the findings "as might be expected have aroused considerable interest, alarm, and apprehension." Although "there are instances in the article which are either cited out of context, incomplete, or with certain mitigating circumstances omitted," still at NIH "constructive steps have already been taken to prevent such occurrences in research supported by the Public Health Service."[3]

However, a congressman's letter was only the most visible sign of NIH's vulnerability (or sensitivity) to political and legal pressure. Any Washington official who hoped to survive in office understood the need to react defensively—to have a policy prepared so that when criticism mounted, he or she would be able to say that yes, a problem had existed, but procedures were already in place to resolve it. The NIH director, James Shannon, readily conceded that one of his responsibilities, even if only a minor one, was "keeping the Government out of trouble." And his advisors concurred. It would be nothing less than suicidal to believe, as one of them put it, that "what a scientist does within his own institution is of no concern to the PHS." An ad hoc group appointed by Shannon to consider NIH policies reported back to him that if cases involving researchers' disregard of subjects' welfare came to court, the service "would look pretty bad by not having any system or any procedure whereby we could be even aware of whether there was a problem of this kind being created by the use of our funds."[4]

More than bureaucratic survival was at stake, though. The NIH response represented not just self-protection against potential legal and political repercussions but a reckoning with the substantive issues involved, an understanding of the causes behind the behavior of the individual researchers. By the mid-1960s it had become apparent to the NIH leadership that an incident like Chester Southam's protocol could be multiplied to twenty-two (to read Beecher) or to an even larger number by those familiar with the state of research at its own Clinical Center or other leading university and hospital laboratories. As a result of the exposés, the NIH leadership, as well as a number of individual researchers, also came to believe that a conflict of interest marked the interaction of investigator and subject: what was in the best interests of the one was not in the best interests of the other. The bedrock principle of medical ethics—that the physician acted only to promote the well-being of the patient—did not hold in the laboratory. (Later we will trace the implications of the discovery that this principle no longer held in the examining room either.) The doctor–patient relationship could no longer serve as the model for the investigator–subject relationship.

This conclusion moved Shannon and others at the NIH to alter its policies. Clinical research, they now recognized, "departs from the conventional patient–physician relationship, where the patient's good has been substituted for by the need to develop new knowledge, that the physician is no longer in the same relationship that he is in the conventional medical setting and indeed may not be in a position to develop a purely or a wholly objective assessment of the moral nature or the ethical nature of the act which he proposes to perform."[5] The researchers' aims, in other words, will distort their ethical judgments. The intrinsic nature of their quest renders them morally suspect. This postulate accepted, in February 1966 and then in revised form in July 1966, the NIH promulgated, through its parent body, the U.S. Public Health Service (PHS), guidelines covering all federally funded research involving human experimentation.

The regulators moved very carefully, aware that they were in unexplored and dangerous territory. "This policy," explained Dr. William Stewart, the surgeon general, "seeks to avoid the danger of direct Federal intervention, case by case, on the one hand, and the dangers inherent in decisions by an individual scientist on the other." The 1 July 1966 order decentralized the regulatory apparatus, assigning "responsibility to the institution receiving the grant for obtaining and keeping documentary evidence of informed patient consent." It then mandated "review of the judgment of the investigator by a committee of institutional associates not directly associated with the project"; and finally, it defined (albeit quite broadly) the standards that were to guide the committee: "This review must address itself to the rights and welfare of the individual, the methods used to obtain informed consent, and the risks and potential benefits of the investigation." As Stewart explained: "What we wanted was an assurance from [the grant-receiving institutions] that they had a mechanism set up that reviewed the potential benefit and risk of the investigation to be undertaken, and that reviewed the method that was used to obtain informed consent. And we thought that this should be done by somebody besides the investigator himself—a group. We thought this group might consist of a variety of people, and left it up to the institutions to decide." Stewart proudly stated: "We have resisted the temptation toward rigidity; for example, we have not prescribed the composition of the review groups nor tried to develop detailed procedures applicable to all situations. . . . Certainly this is not a perfect instrument. But . . . this action has introduced an important element of public policy review in the biomedical research process."[6]

Thus, for the first time and in direct response to the abuses of discretion, decisions that had traditionally been left to the individual conscience of physicians were brought under collective surveillance. Federal regulations, a compulsory system of peer review, assurances by universities and hospitals that they were monitoring the research, specific criteria that investigators had to satisfy, and a list of proscribed activities replaced the reliance on the researchers' goodwill and ethical sensibilities.

The new rules were neither as intrusive as some investigators feared nor as protective as some advocates preferred. At their core was the superintendence of the peer-review committee, known as the institutional review board (IRB), through which fellow researchers approved the investigator's procedures. With the creation of the IRB, clinical investigators could no longer decide unilaterally on the ethics of their research, but had to answer formally to colleagues operating under federal guidelines. Thus, the events in and around 1966 accomplished what the Nuremberg tribunal had not: to move medical experimentation into the public domain and to make apparent the consequences of leaving decisions about clinical research exclusively to the individual investigator.

For all the novelty of the response, policy changes designed and implemented by insiders had distinct limitations. For one, the NIH leadership did not at first insist on including in the collective decision-making process those who were outsiders to the world of research. The agency's 1966 policies still allowed scientists to review scientists to determine whether human subjects were adequately informed and protected. Given the NIH views on conflict of interest, the regulations did require that members of the review committee should have "no vested interest in the specific project involved." But they were vague about other criteria, stipulating that members should have "not only the scientific competence to comprehend the scientific content . . . but also other competencies pertinent to the judgments that need to be made." Accordingly, through the 1960s, most institutions restricted membership on the IRB to fellow investigators, and only a few included outsiders (most of whom were lawyers and clergymen) on the committee.

Second, and even more important, the NIH response focused more on the review process than the consent process. The agency did recognize the importance of the principle of consent, changing the title of its Clinical Center manual from *Group Consideration of Clinical Research Procedures* (1953) to *Group Consideration and Informed Consent in Clinical Research* (1967). And it did set forth guidelines for the researcher that cited the need to obtain "informed consent." But the NIH retained an investigator's skepticism about the ultimate value of the procedure, a position that was widely shared in the research community. As a Harvard colleague of Beecher's put it in responding to an early draft of his article: "Should informed consent be required? No! For the simple reason that it is not possible. Should any consent be required? Yes! Any teaching and research hospital must clearly identify itself as such . . . to the patient upon admission. . . . The fact that the patient is requesting admission to this hospital represents tacit consent. How do we interpret tacit consent? Not as a license but as a *trust*. This adds, not subtracts, responsibility."[7]

In keeping with this orientation, the internal memorandum enclosed with the new NIH Clinical Center manual read: "While there is general agreement that informed consent must be obtained, there is also the reservation that it is not possible to convey all the information to the subject or patient upon which he can make an intelligent decision. There is a strong feeling that the protection of the subject is best achieved by group consideration and peer judgment." Moreover, the NIH was not yet prepared or able to be very specific about what phrases like "informed consent" meant in practice. "Many of these key terms," conceded Eugene Confrey, the NIH director of research grants, "lack rigorous definition or are incompletely defined for purposes of general application." But the root of the difficulty was that NIH officials had trouble grasping the full implications of what it meant to obtain consent. The NIH publication explaining to "normal volunteers" at the Clinical Center that participation in the research was truly voluntary, declared: "You will be asked to sign a statement in which you indicate that you understand the project and agree to participate in it. If you find your assigned project to be intolerable, you may withdraw from it." Suggesting that the only grounds for withdrawal was the intolerability of the project was hardly the way to educate subjects to their freedom of choice.[8]

In effect, the NIH leadership was unwilling to abandon altogether the notion that doctors should protect patients and to substitute instead a thoroughgoing commitment to the idea of subjects protecting themselves. The 1966 guidelines were innovative, but only to a point. The NIH heads still looked to the professional to ensure the well-being of the layperson, and forced to reckon with the inadequacy of trusting to one professional, they opted to empower a group of professionals. The goal was to insure that harm was not done to the subjects, not to see that the subjects were given every opportunity and incentive to express their own wishes.[9]

FDA officials were also forced to grapple with the problems raised by human experimentation in clinical research. With a self-definition that included a commitment not only to sound scientific research (like the NIH) but to consumer protection as well, the FDA leadership did attempt to expand the prerogatives of the consumer—in this context, the human subject. Rather than emulate the NIH precedent and invigorate peer review, they looked to give new meaning and import to the process of consent.

In the immediate aftermath of the 1962 Kefauver hearings and the passage of the watered-down version of the Javits amendment, the FDA required investigators to obtain the consent of patients taking experimental drugs, but for the next several years, the precise nature of the obligation was unclear. By statute, investigators were not required to obtain consent when they found it "not feasible" or "not in the best interest of the subject"; and despite a number of efforts to have the FDA clarify the meaning of these terms (including an effort by Beecher), the agency steadfastly refused. Francis Kelsey, celebrated for holding back approval on thalidomide and now chief of the FDA Investigation Drug Branch, was prepared to say publicly that these clauses were meant to be applied narrowly for truly exceptional circumstances. But when Beecher, in 1965, asked the FDA's commissioner to confirm this position, he would only say: "The basic rule is that patient consent must be obtained except where a conscientious professional judgment is made that this is not feasible or is contrary to the best interest of the patient. It is my present opinion that it is not possible to go beyond this generalization at this time."[10]

In 1966, however, in the wake of the reactions set off by Beecher's article and the publicity given particularly to the cancer research of Chester Southam, the FDA shifted positions. On 30 August 1966, FDA officials issued a "Statement on Policy Concerning Consent for the Use of Investigational New Drugs on Humans," not only defining all the terms in the 1962 law but setting down what William Curran, one of the most astute students of NIH and FDA policies, described as "comprehensive rules regarding patient consent in clinical drug trials."

In the first instance, the FDA moved to close, albeit not eliminate, the loopholes. Distinguishing between therapeutic and nontherapeutic research (in accord with various international codes like the 1964 Helsinki Declaration and the arguments of critics like Beecher), it now prohibited all nontherapeutic research except where the subjects gave consent. When the research involved "patients under treatment" and had therapeutic potential, consent was to be obtained, except in what the FDA policymakers now frankly labeled the "exceptional cases," where consent was not feasible or in the patient's best interest. The FDA staff tried to define these terms more exactly. "Not feasible" meant that the doctor could not communicate with the patient (the example was a comatose patient) and "not in the best interest" meant that consent would "seriously affect the patient's disease status" (the example was the physician not wanting to divulge a diagnosis of cancer). In addition, the FDA, unlike the NIH, spelled out the meaning of *consent*. To give consent, the person had to have the ability to exercise choice and had to receive a "fair explanation" of the procedure, including an understanding of the experiment's purpose and duration, "all inconveniences and hazards reasonably to be expected," the nature of a controlled trial (and the possibility of going on a placebo), and any existing alternative forms of therapy available.[11]

The FDA regulations unquestionably represent a new stage in the balance of authority between researcher and subject. The blanket insistence on consent for all nontherapeutic research would have not only prohibited many of the World War II experiments but also eliminated most of the cases on Beecher's roll. The FDA's definitions of consent went well beyond the vague NIH stipulations, imparting real significance to the process. Nevertheless, ambiguities and irresolution remained. The FDA still confused research and treatment, and its clauses governing therapeutic investigations left a good deal of discretion to the doctor-researcher. Despite the insistence that consent was to be waived only in exceptional cases, the FDA allowed investigators to determine which cases these were. It was still up to them to determine the course of action for the incompetent patient or to decide when to withhold a diagnosis from the competent patient.

All these qualifications notwithstanding, the rules for human experimentation had changed, and the movement would continue and accelerate, with authority shifting from inside to outside the profession, from physicians to a very different group of actors. The NIH directors glimpsed this future. As they revised the agency's regulations, they predicted that the principles governing human experimentation (and, we may add, eventually all of medicine) were about to take new directions, the "consequence of increased attention to the problem by lawyers, physicians, psychologists, sociologists, and philosophers."[12]

Human experimentation did attract the critical attention of these professionals, almost all of whom rejected outright the utilitarian calculus adopted by the researchers. But the reasons for this rejection are not self-evident; indeed, it is easier to account for the investigators' pursuit of truth and fame than to understand why the others took so different an approach, why they did not accept the investigators' explanations and welcome the sacrifices made by a marginal, and by definition unprotesting, minority. But this was not the position adopted. Outsiders crossed over into medicine to correct what they perceived as wrongs, unwilling to accept the potential social benefit and trade off the individual interest. In short, they found harm where investigators perceived the opportunity for progress. Understanding the many reasons underlying this essential difference in outlook takes us through the rest of the book, for attitudes toward human experimentation were intertwined with attitudes toward physicians and hospitals—and then became inseparable from attitudes toward new medical procedures and technologies. Nevertheless, several points warrant immediate exploration.

First, the recognition by Beecher, as well as Shannon and others at NIH, that the traditional ethics of medicine no longer held in the laboratory and that a fundamental conflict of interest characterized the relationship between the researcher and the subject had an extraordinary impact on those outside of medicine. In fact, an appreciation of these very postulates brought philosophers, lawyers, and social scientists to a concern with medicine. Because the traditional precepts of medical ethics seemed inadequate to the problems posed by human experimentation, and because the hallowed maxims of "do no harm" and "act only in the interest of the patient," borne of a therapeutic context, did not appear to protect the subject in an experimental context, it became necessary to look to a different tradition and source for guiding principles. And this is precisely what the nonphysicians began to do, at first hesitantly and with apparent humility, later, in a more aggressive and confrontational style.

Two examples give the full flavor of the change. The topic of human experimentation initially brought to medicine Princeton University's professor Paul Ramsey, a philosopher who would exert a powerful influence over the development of the field of bioethics. In his own terms, Ramsey applied Christian ethics to contemporary issues, as evidenced in his previous books, *Christian Ethics and the Sit-In* and *War and the Christian Conscience: How Shall Modern War Be Conducted Justly?* Invited to lecture at the Yale Divinity School on medical ethics in 1968–69, he prepared for the assignment by spending a year at the Georgetown Medical School. As he later explained in *The Patient as Person*, the book that emerged from the lectures, the assignment was intimidating: "When first I had the temerity to undertake some study of ethical issues in medical practice, my resolve was to venture no comment at all—relevant or irrelevant—upon these matters until I informed myself concerning how physicians and medical investigators themselves discuss and analyze the decisions they face." He found their discussions "remarkable," convinced that no other profession "comes close to medicine in its concern to inculcate, transmit, and keep in constant repair its standards governing the conduct of its members."[13]

Nevertheless, Ramsey did not keep silent for very long, for he concluded that medicine could not be left to its own devices. Ethical problems in medicine, he declared, "are by no means technical problems on which only the expert (in this case the physician) can have an opinion," and his first case in point was human experimentation. Having read Beecher closely and having studied some of the protocols (particularly Krugman's hepatitis research), he was persuaded that the principle of the sanctity and dignity of human life was now under challenge. Raise this principle at a gathering of physicians, Ramsey observed, and one would be greeted by a counterprinciple: "It is immoral not to do research (or this experiment must be done despite its necessary deception of human beings)." His fear was that "the next step may be for someone to say that medical advancement is hampered because our 'society' makes an absolute of the inviolability of the individual. This raises the specter of a medical and scientific community freed from the shackles of that cultural norm, and proceeding on a basis of an ethos all its own."[14]

The force that drove medicine down this path was the investigators' thirst for more information, a thirst so overwhelming that it could violate the sanctity of the person. "I do not believe," insisted Ramsey, "that either the codes of medical ethics or the physicians who have undertaken to comment on them . . . will suffice to withstand the omnivorous appetite of scientific research . . . that has momentum and a life of its own."[15] In effect, Ramsey perceived, as others were starting to as well, an unavoidable conflict of interest. The goals of the researcher did not coincide with the well-being of the subject; human experimentation pitted the interests of society against the interests of the individual. In essence, the utilitarian calculus put every human (subject) at risk.

How was this threat to be countered? Ramsey had two general strategies. The first was to bring medicine directly into the public arena. We can no longer "go on assuming that what can be done has to be done or should be, without uncovering the ethical principles we mean to abide by. These questions are now completely in the public forum, no longer the province of scientific experts alone." Second, and more specifically, Ramsey embraced the idea of consent. It was to human ex-

perimentation what a system of checks a
authority, that is, the necessary limitati
"Man's capacity to become joint adventi
the consensual relationship possible; m
joint adventurer even in a good cause
Ramsey concluded: "The medical pr
that the personal integrity of physici
is good enough to experiment upon ⌐
short, human subjects, not investigators, woui⌐
protect their own interests.

These same concerns sparked the interest of other outsiders to medicine. In November 1967 and September 1968, *Daedalus* ran conferences devoted to the "Ethical Aspects of Experimentation with Human
Subjects," the first time this broadly interdisciplinary publication had
explored a medical matter in such depth.[17] Of the fifteen contributors
to the issue that emerged from these meetings, six came from the health
sciences (including Henry Beecher); the others represented a variety of
specialties: five from law (including Guido Calabresi and Paul Freund)
and one each from anthropology (Margaret Mead), sociology (Talcott
Parsons), philosophy (Hans Jonas), and law and psychiatry (Jay Katz).
Of course, some of these authors had already demonstrated a keen
interest in bringing their disciplinary insights to medicine (most notably Talcott Parsons and Jay Katz). But most were just entering a field
in which they would do outstanding work (Paul Freund, Guido Calabresi, and Hans Jonas, for example).

It was disconcerting to be among the first to cross over from one's
home discipline to medicine; and it is doubtful, now that the route has
been so well laid out, that anyone today would be as circumspect as Hans
Jonas, a professor of philosophy at the New School for Social Research,
was in describing his initiation. Reporting "a state of great humility," he
declared: "When I was first asked to comment 'philosophically' on the
subject of human experimentation, I had all the hesitation natural to a
layman in the face of matters on which experts of the highest competence
have had their say."[18] But he, like Ramsey, was convinced that the issues
were intriguing and disturbing enough to require sustained philosophical
analysis and, ultimately, new first principles.

Jonas's starting point was the inherent conflict between the noble

ining knowledge and the moral obligation to the subjects
He, too, contrasted the social good with the personal
in the language of the laboratory, the need for an adequate
size and the degradation implicit in making a person "a passive
merely to be acted on," against the welfare of the individual.
ejecting the notion that society could command the subject's "sacrifice" under the terms of the social contract, and not completely satisfied
with any method for resolving the conflict ("We have to live with the
ambiguity, the treacherous impurity of everything human"), Jonas
joined the ranks of those coming to rely primarily on the process of
consent. Indeed, for him consent served not only as the justification of
an individual's participation in an experiment but as a method for
ranking those who should be asked to become research subjects. Those
most capable of giving consent—the best educated with the greatest
degree of choice—should be the first asked; hence, on Jonas's list,
research scientists were at the top and prisoners at the bottom. He
conceded that this principle of "descending order" might hamper experimentation and slow progress, but the danger to society from a
disease was less than the danger of "the erosion of those moral values
whose loss, possibly caused by too ruthless a pursuit of scientific progress, would make its most dazzling triumphs not worth having."[19] Thus,
Jonas and Ramsey arrived at the same conclusion: the only escape,
however incomplete, from the dilemmas in experimentation was
through a revitalization of the principle of consent. Human subjects
had to become their own protectors.

The approach drawn from philosophers' first principles fit neatly
with the approach emerging from reformers' social principles. In this
coincidence of vision one finds some of the reasons why, beginning in
the 1960s, the public identified not with researchers and the triumphs
they might bring forth from their laboratories (as had been true during the 1940s and 1950s), but with the subjects of the experiments
and the harms they might suffer in the laboratory. The change in perspective mirrored a grander reorientation in social thought, one that
now looked more to securing personal rights than communal goods, to
enhancing the prerogatives of the individual, not the collective. The
political culture of the 1960s fostered an extraordinary identification

with the underdog and the minority, as evidenced by the fact that the tactics of the civil rights movement became the model for others to emulate. Just as these activists used a language of rights to counter discrimination, so too did advocates for women, children, gays, and students. It may not have been apparent or even correct to think that all of these groups actually constituted minorities (were women really a minority?) or in any conventional meaning of the term possessed rights (in what sense does a child have a right against a parent?). But those were quibbles that could not be allowed to interfere with the goal of reform. This same mind-set framed the experience of subjects in clinical research. As Beecher's protocols amply demonstrated, the subjects were drawn disproportionately from among the poor, the physically or mentally handicapped, the elderly, and the incarcerated. The result was an identification with the retarded and the senile in their vulnerability to exploitation, not with the investigators and the prospect for a vaccine against hepatitis or a cure for cancer.

This orientation fostered a distrust of constituted authorities and medical researchers became one group among many to feel the impact of the new skepticism toward the exercise of paternalism and the loss of trust in discretionary authority. "The list of those who have suffered this loss," I had occasion to write in the 1970s, "is as lengthy as it is revealing: college presidents and deans, high school principals and teachers, husbands and parents, psychiatrists, doctors, research scientists, and obviously, prison wardens, social workers, hospital superintendents, and mental hospital superintendents."[20] The momentum of change did not, however, merely consume one institution after another. *Research scientists* appeared on the list because of specific, powerful reasons for curbing the authority of the investigator—reasons that Beecher, Shannon, Ramsey, and Jonas, each in his own way, had supplied. The original purpose behind the grant of discretion, which had emerged in the Progressive Era, was that it would allow professionals, and others like parents and husbands, the opportunity to fulfill benevolent designs, to substitute their greater knowledge for that of their patients, students, children, or spouses. But now it seemed that discretion served self-interest—that deans acted in the best interests of the university, not its students; that husbands furthered their own needs, not those of their wives; that wardens looked to the needs of the prison, not the inmates. In this same fashion, investigators pursued their own goals—career advancement, discovery, prizes, and fame— while disregarding the risks to their subjects. It was a zero-sum game in or out of the laboratory. If the investigator was to win, the subject might well have to lose.

Moreover, the scandals and the way they were interpreted in terms of conflict of interest made it vital not only to import a language of rights into medicine but to bring formality and clearcut guidelines to procedures that had been casual and open-ended. In the realm of social welfare, it seemed best to define entitlements precisely rather than have the welfare mother trust to the discretion of the social worker; in treating juvenile delinquents, it seemed best to expand procedural protections instead of relying on the benevolence of a juvenile court judge or warden. And in this same spirit, in human experimentation it seemed best to establish an exacting review mechanism and a formal consent process rather than rely for protection on the conscience of the individual researcher. In sum, all these movements presumed a warfare between "them" and "us," in which self-serving motives were cloaked in the language of benevolence, and majorities took every occasion to exploit minorities. In such a combative world, one had to depend on rules, not sentiment, to secure fairness.

One last consideration helps tie all these movements together: the importance of events that converged in 1966 and signaled the heightened level of social conflict. This year witnessed the transformation of the civil rights movement from one that could dream, in Martin Luther King's eloquent words, about "a beautiful symphony of brotherhood" in which all of God's children joined hands to celebrate freedom, to one that designated "black power" as the only way to wrest control from an oppressive white ruling class. This year also witnessed the first defeat that the civil rights movement suffered in Congress, a defeat on a socially far-reaching question, relevant nationwide: open housing. And 1966 was the year that Beecher's *NEJM* article appeared and set off its many repercussions. Social change is too gradual a process to fit neatly onto a calendar (and social historians are prone to talk about generations and eras, not days and weeks), but 1966 has a special relevance to this story and makes connections among the various parts all the more secure.

CHAPTER 6

Bedside Ethics

HOWEVER appropriate it appeared to restructure the relationship between medical researchers and human subjects, to reduce the discretionary authority of the investigator by expanding the formal authority of peers (through institutional review board oversight) and the role of the subjects themselves (through a new emphasis on informed consent), it was by no means obvious that such changes were relevant to the doctor–patient relationship. Although exposés had revealed the conflict of interest between investigators and subjects and undermined the sense of trust between them, the therapeutic encounter, at least on the face it, entailed none of these problems. The treating physician seemingly had no concern apart from the care and cure of the patient; even as NIH officials and other critics of research practices came to recognize that the bedrock principle of medical ethics—the doctor as advocate for his or her patients—did not fit with human experimentation, they did not doubt that it held in medicine itself. The physician was different from the researcher, Hans Jonas insisted: "He is not the agent of society, nor of the interests of medical science . . . or future sufferers from the same disease."[1] The doctor's only agenda was the patient's well-being.

In fact, physicians shared a powerful tradition of ethical discourse that went back to Hippocrates and continued through modern times. It was at once high-minded, generous, and even heroic, yet remarkably insular and self-serving too. Physicians almost exclusively defined the problems and arrived at the resolutions, giving the deliberations a self-contained quality. Thus, any effort to bring a new set of rules to medicine, to introduce into the world of therapy the procedures that narrowed the prerogatives of the investigator, would bear a heavy burden of justification: it was one thing to regulate researchers, quite another to interfere with practicing doctors. Furthermore, any such effort was certain to provoke extraordinary resistance and hostility. Physicians, accustomed to making their own rules, were certain to find external intervention altogether unnecessary and frankly insulting. If medical ethics was to confront other traditions in ethics, whether religious or more systematically philosophical, the meeting was likely to be adversarial. Medical ethics was not lay ethics—or "bioethics," to use the more popular and current label.

From the classical age onward, the most distinguishing characteristic of medical ethics was the extent to which it was monopolized by practicing physicians, not by formal philosophers, with the minor qualification that sometimes, as in the case of a Maimonides, one person fit both categories. Physicians typically wrote the texts and, no less important, read them. As late as the 1950s, the noted psychiatrist Karl Menninger aptly commented: "With the one stellar exception of Catholic moralists, there is a strange blind spot about the ethics of health and medicine in almost all ethical literature. Volume after volume in general ethics and in religious treatises on morality will cover almost every conceivable phase of personal and social ethics *except medicine and health*." And one of the first contemporary philosophers to break with this tradition, Joseph Fletcher, agreed with Menninger that "it is a matter for wonder that the philosophers have had so little to say about the physician and his medical arts."[2]

Medical ethics as conceptualized and written by physicians had a very practical bent, concerned not as much with discerning first principles as with formulating maxims for practice. Predictably, too, the definition of what constituted an ethical problem and the choice of solutions reflected the vantage point of the doctor, not the patient—for example, what the physicians' rights and responsibilities were and how they should behave toward patients and, no less important, colleagues.

To many contemporary readers, these tracts seem most remarkable for elevating medical etiquette over medical ethics, for moving ever so nimbly from high-minded injunctions—do no harm—to professionally self-serving propositions—do not slander a fellow doctor or pay social visits to his patients or contradict him in front of his patients. In this literature, coveting a colleague's patients appeared a more serious breach than coveting his wife. But the distinction between etiquette and ethics hardly mattered to the tracts' authors or to the audience of practicing physicians. These were not exercises in philosophical discourse but manuals for practitioners who were intent on doing equally well by their patients and their practice.

Although etiquette dominated, it would be a mistake to dismiss all the tracts as business manuals on the theme of how to win patients and influence colleagues. The writings in medical ethics spelled out a series of obligations for physicians that required them to act not only responsibly but virtuously, to ignore self-interest in the pursuit of the patient's welfare. To limit the examples to the United States, Benjamin Rush, the celebrated Philadelphia physician and signer of the Declaration of Independence, in 1801 delivered a series of lectures on the "vices and virtues" of the physician in which he set down the most rigorous standards for physician behavior. The virtuous physician was abstemious, even ascetic: "The nature of his profession renders the theatre, the turf, the chase, and even a convivial table in a sickly season, improper places of relaxation to him. . . . Many lives have been lost, by the want of punctual and regular attention to the varying symptoms of diseases; but still more have been sacrificed by the criminal preference, which has been given by physicians to ease, convivial company, or public amusements and pursuits, to the care of their patients."[3] (Perhaps here one finds the roots of a tradition of physician isolation; however, Rush was anything but isolated from his society.) Moreover, Rush's ideal physician was not pecuniary minded; recognizing an ongoing obligation to the poor, he would never refuse to treat patients because of poverty, or exploit their vulnerability. Indeed, the virtuous physician was heroic: should a plague strike a community, the physician was obliged to stay and treat the ill, even at the risk of death.

A century later, Dr. Richard Cabot, a professor at the Harvard Medical School, both expanded the range of issues that belonged to medical ethics (such as fee splitting) and gave unconventional answers to conventional questions (favoring the use of birth control through contraception and always telling patients the truth). Hence, physician-dominated medical ethics was much more than a low-minded enterprise, although it did often lack intellectual rigor. The presumption was that students learned ethics not in the classroom but on the wards by emulating their teachers, by having senior attending physicians serve as role models for their juniors. "I know of no medical school in which professional ethics is now systematically taught," Cabot wrote in the mid-1920s, and the situation remained essentially unchanged through the 1950s.[4]

Just how confident physicians were about the integrity of medical ethics, and how jealously they kept it as their own special preserve, is demonstrated by the pronouncements of the American Medical Association (AMA). In the 1930s, for example, the AMA appealed to a timeless and physician-dominated medical ethics to justify its opposition to a variety of proposed policies, including national health insurance, group practice, and physician advertising. "Medical economics," declared the AMA policymakers, "has always rested fundamentally on medical ethics," whose principles were universal, not varying by time (ancient or modern) or place (Europe or the United States) or type of government (monarchy or republic). "Such continuous persistence through so wide a diversity of environments," they argued, "seems to prove that judged by the 'survival test,' medical ethics has demonstrated its essential social soundness." The reason for this astonishing record was that the ethic was based on empirical experience: "Each new rule or custom was tested in actual practice" and then judged in terms of how well it supported the "close personal relationship of the sick person and his trained medical adviser," and how well it "promoted the health of patients, as measured by morbidity and mortality statistics." In this way, AMA leaders explained, "ethics thus becomes an integral part of the practice of medicine. Anything that aids in the fight on disease is 'good'; whatever delays recovery or injures health is 'bad.' " And with a confidence that tipped over into arrogance, they concluded: "This development and treatment of medical ethics gains much greater significance when compared with the development of ethics in society as a whole." Unlike ethics in general, where one school

of thought did battle with another, medical ethics had been spared
"metaphysical or philosophic controversies."

All this added up to a dogged insistence that medical ethics should
be left entirely to medicine, which also meant that health policy should
be left entirely to medicine. For example, since "the close personal
relationship of the sick person and his trained medical adviser" was
an essential element in the ethic, public interference with medicine
through health insurance or through the sponsorship of group practice
was wrong. Indeed, any effort by outsiders to rewrite or violate these
centuries-old precepts would both subvert sound medical practice and,
even more drastically, subvert the social order, for "ethical rules and
customs are among the most important of the stabilizing elements in
society."[5] In sum, medical ethics belonged to doctors, and outsiders
had no right to intrude.

These claims did not go entirely uncontested. Catholic theologians,
for example, had their own vigorous tradition of analyzing medical
ethics, although the impact of their analyses and recommendations was
restricted to those within the Catholic fold. Publications like the *Linacre
Quarterly* were replete with articles applying Catholic dogma to medical
questions. For example, a number of Catholic ethicists debated whether
it was permissible, in the event of a tubal pregnancy, to remove the
fetus—in effect, killing it—in order to save the mother's life, or whether
one had to leave the fetus in place, despite the fact that a failure to
intervene would cause the death of the mother and the fetus as well.
(Most commentators opted for intervention, distinguishing between direct and indirect harm; death to the fetus was morally acceptable, provided it was the indirect result of treating the tubal defect.)[6] The
Catholic tradition in medical ethics was actually powerful enough to
inspire critics of its own. The journalist Paul Blanshard, for example,
wrote a blistering attack on the authority that Catholic priests ostensibly exercised over Catholic doctors and nurses in their professional
lives. But whatever its internal strength, the Catholic example exerted
little influence over medicine more generally and did not inspire non-
Catholics to make medical ethics a central intellectual concern.[7]

One of the first efforts to break the physician monopoly and explore
issues of medical ethics was Joseph Fletcher's 1954 book, *Morals and
Medicine.* Fletcher's route into this field, like Paul Ramsey's later, was

through Protestant religious ethics, not formal academic philosophy. Fletcher's aim, however, was not to apply religiously based doctrines to medical practice, but to analyze, very self-consciously, ethical issues "from the patient's point of view." He took his guiding premise from outside of medicine, insisting that individuals, in order to act as responsible moral beings, had to have the freedom and the knowledge to make choices; otherwise, he contended, "we are not responsible; we are not moral agents or personal beings." Brought into medicine, this principle meant that patients kept ignorant and rendered passive by their doctor were not moral agents but puppets in a puppet show, "and there is no moral quality in a Punch and Judy show."[8] Hence, Fletcher argued that physicians were obligated to tell patients the truth about a diagnosis and condition, not in order to satisfy a professional medical creed or legal requirement, but because patients had to be able to exercise choice.

This same assumption guided Fletcher's positions in the area of reproduction and led him to a fundamental disagreement with Catholic doctrines. In his view, contraception, artificial insemination, and sterilization were not "unnatural acts" but procedures that enhanced individual choice. Contraception "gives patients a means whereby they may become persons and not merely bodies." Artificial insemination was a method that kept the accidents of nature (sterility) from overruling "human self-determination." Fletcher also wanted to leave decisions about sterilization to the individual because "moral responsibility requires such choices to be personal decisions rather than natural necessities." He even approved of active euthanasia, since the alternative, "to prolong life uselessly, while the personal qualities of freedom, knowledge, self-possession and control, and responsibility are sacrificed is to attack the moral status of a person."[9]

Although the subject matter that Fletcher explored was relatively traditional—the ethics of reproduction and euthanasia had a long history in Catholic literature—his approach was not. Fletcher moved the discussion away from the privileges of the physicians or the requirements of religious creeds to the prerogatives of the patient, and in 1954 such a formulation was highly original. Perhaps too original, for his work did not immediately stimulate a different kind of dialogue in medical ethics. For another decade at least, the book remained an odd contribution, not, as it now appears, the beginnings of a new departure. To bring outsiders into medical decision making, to have philosophers take a place at the bedside, in effect to substitute bioethics for medical ethics would require far more than one man adopting a new approach. It would demand nothing less than a revolution in public attitudes toward medical practitioners and medical institutions, a revolution marked by a decline in trust in the doctor, and, concomitantly, in the relevance, the fairness, and the wisdom of beside ethics.

Such a revolution in attitudes is precisely what occurred between 1966 and 1976. The new rules for the laboratory permeated the examining room, circumscribing the discretionary authority of the individual physician. The doctor–patient relationship was molded on the form of the researcher–subject; in therapy, as in experimentation, formal and informal mechanisms of control and a new language of patients' rights assumed unprecedented importance. The change at first affected not so much the context of medical practice, such as licensure requirements or reimbursement schedules (that would come later), but the content of medical practice—treatment decisions made at the bedside for a particular patient. Jonas's image of the doctor alone in the examining room with the patient (and with God) gave way to the image of an examining room with hospital committee members, lawyers, bioethicists, and accountants virtually crowding out the doctor.

From the vantage point of the 1950s, the transformation would have appeared startling and unexpected. In the 1950s, after all, therapeutics had assumed unprecedented efficacy, eliminating the most deadly and crippling infectious diseases (before AIDS, one would have said all deadly infectious diseases), including polio and tuberculosis, and making notable advances against such chronic diseases as cancer and heart disease. Given this remarkable progress, one might have anticipated a golden age of doctor–patient relationships. And even the fact that other professions in the 1960s were being challenged by expressions of individual rights might not have weakened the strong bond of trust that had existed between doctors and patients. But that was not to be the case. To paraphrase the title of a 1970s collection of essays on health care, medicine was doing better, but patients were feeling worse.

Physicians themselves, as would be expected, were acutely sensitive to these changes. A few of them, as we shall see, helped inspire the movement, serving as guides in introducing outsiders to the new issues; in fact, the transformation in the ruling of medicine probably would not have progressed so rapidly or thoroughly without their assistance. But the majority, expressing themselves in the editorial columns of medical publications and from witness chairs in congressional hearings, displayed a barely disguised disdain and hostility. They inveighed against the new regulatory schemes and the empowerment of lay bodies and boards, and when they suffered defeat, took the losses badly.

How are we to understand this decline of trust, this sense that the physician, like the researcher, does not share a common interest with the patient? Why did the language of rights and the politics of a rights movement enter health care, challenging the exercise of medical discretion? Why were the traditions of medical ethics not seen as sufficient to the doctor–patient relationship? As with any broad change, the causes are multiple. The precipitous rise in physicians' income in the post–1945 period, particularly in the post–Medicare period, helped foster a belief that doctors had become more concerned with their pocketbooks than their patients. The enactment of Medicare and Medicaid instigated some of the first systematic efforts to measure quality of care, and these measurements revealed such substantial variations in physician practices (most notably, in the frequency of surgery) as to suggest that greed and ignorance were more endemic in the profession than had been imagined. In light of these findings, critics then began to analyze the weaknesses in licensure requirements and to look even more closely at the failure of the profession to discipline errant members.[10] However important these elements were in undermining a sense of trust between doctor and patient, a still more fundamental consideration first widened the breach. In the post–World War II period, a social process that had been under way for some time reached its culmination: the doctor turned into a stranger, and the hospital became a strange institution. Doctors became a group apart from their patients and from their society as well, encapsulated in a very isolated and isolating universe. The familiarity that had once characterized the doctor–patient relationship gave way to distance, making the interactions between the two far more official than intimate. By the same token, the links that had tied doctors to their communities—whether through club life, economic investments, or civic activities—were replaced by professional isolation and exclusivity. Finally, the bonds of neighborhood and ethnicity that had once made a hospital a familiar place for its patients were practically severed, giving to the institution an alien and frightening atmosphere. In sum, a three fold break occurred that severed the bonds between doctor and patient, doctor and community, and hospital and patient and community.

This enlarged social distance in large part explains why new rules and new players came into medicine and why bioethics came to replace medical ethics. Physicians who were strangers could not be trusted to exercise discretion over weighty matters of life and death; hence, a growing contingent insisted that the norms about sharing information change so that physicians would be compelled to tell patients the truth, no matter how grim the diagnosis. Physicians could not be left to decide unilaterally about terminating or withdrawing treatment; hence, a growing contingent insisted that a practice of making pencil marks on nursing charts should be replaced with a formal code that required the explicit approval of the patient and consultations among physicians. Indeed, suspicion toward physicians ran so high that the practice began of relying on third parties, the clinical bioethicist or hospital ethics committees, to protect and strengthen the patient's role in decision making.

It is not romanticizing the past practice of medicine to observe that in the pre–World War II period, physicians were more closely connected both to their patients and their community.[11] So broad a generalization inevitably does an injustice to the diversity of social class and region, but during the late nineteenth and early twentieth centuries, practically all aspects of health care worked to strengthen the ties between the medical and lay worlds. Whatever suspicion the public had toward the medical profession and its institutions (which was especially acute before 1910) did not foment a distrust of one's own physician or hospital. The exercise of medical discretion seemed less a conspiracy to maintain professional hegemony over the patient than a confident expression of beneficence, that is, the physician being willing and able to spare the patient the burden of choice or the direct confrontation with death.

When contemporary observers, like Jay Katz, a professor of psychiatry and law at Yale, portray the traditional doctor–patient relationship as "silent," their angle of vision is too narrow. Katz, for example, bases his characterization almost exclusively on normative statements, the prescriptions set down by codes of ethics or commencement-day speakers, that physicians not divulge a grim diagnosis.[12] But a wider view of the historical record amply demonstrates that doctors could be silent with their patients about a diagnosis precisely because they had not been silent with them over the years. The interactions at a time of medical crisis built on a prior history. The element of trust was strong enough to legitimate medical paternalism.

The physicians' incentives to maintain close links with patients came not so much from an abstract commitment to a principle of good doctoring but from the exigencies of maintaining a day-to-day practice. A physician had few ways of attracting or keeping patients except by establishing personal ties with them and their neighbors. Doctors might occasionally be able to rest on their credentials or expertise. By the 1920s and 1930s a medical degree from Johns Hopkins or the Columbia College of Physicians and Surgeons carried weight, and some physicians had mastered a procedure (such as thoracic surgery) that most others had not. But given the limited number of diagnostic tools (of which reading an electrocardiogram or X ray was probably the most demanding) and therapeutic interventions available, physicians had difficulties distinguishing themselves from each other on purely professional grounds.[13]

In fact, professional criteria were of such limited relevance that a huge body of medical writing warned laypeople against quackery. Undoubtedly, some of this effort was self-serving and promotional, motivated as much by professional envy as patient well-being. But some of it was genuinely altruistic, presuming with good reason that an absence of professional credentials made patients susceptible to the blandishments of charlatans. However well-intentioned, the cautionary advice tended to be negative and dispiriting: do not trust those who promise cures—those who, in effect, tell patients what they most want to hear.

On the more positive side, the medical and popular writings emphasized the primacy of personal compatibility: Choose a physician as you would choose a friend. When it fell to the renowned physician Oliver Wendell Holmes to address the graduating class of the Bellevue

Medical School in 1871, he spent most of his talk instructing them on how to get along with their patients: Be prompt in keeping appointments; never let your face mirror the gravity of the disease; resort to such stock favorites as, "You have a 'spinal irritation," if you wanted to disguise a diagnosis; and never forget that "we had one physician in our city whose smile was commonly reckoned as being worth five thousand dollars a year to him." Holmes also set down the principles by which patients should select their doctors, making his lead one: "Choose a man who is personally agreeable, for a daily visit from an intelligent, amiable, pleasant, sympathetic person will cost you no more than one from a sloven or a boor."[14] And all this advice, of course, came from the professor of anatomy at Harvard who ranked among the earliest physicians to appreciate the value of clinical trials to test efficacy of treatments. Some sixty years later a Yale professor of medicine comfortably reiterated the same advice: In choosing a physician, the prospective patient should engage the doctor in conversation; "if he spoke well on general matters the chances were that he was also intelligent in his practice."[15] This type of advice, of course, had the unintended effect of making it all the more difficult to distinguish quackery from professional medicine. As one historian of medicine has put it, "We can hardly overestimate the importance of the psychological aspects of the medical art, but it is true that psychological needs could also be largely satisfied by quacks."[16]

Patients were likely to follow such subjective and personal judgments, allowing similarities in religion, ethnic group, and socioeconomic background to guide their choice. In an era when major eastern and midwestern cities were divided into ghetto enclaves, immigrants tended to select their doctors along ethnic and religious lines. Catholics turned to Catholic doctors, Jews to Jewish doctors—a fact that, incidentally, provided incentives for members of each group to become doctors. These patterns are borne out not only by anecdotal evidence (would that some archives included the papers of neighborhood doctors along with those of the medical pioneers), but, as we shall soon see, by the structure and functioning of sectarian hospitals.

By the same token, the well-to-do were likely to use the services of equally well-to-do doctors. And rural residents were generally served medically (when they were served at all) by someone with some sympathy or at least understanding of their way of life.[17] Indeed, there was nothing unreasonable or naïve about these choices and strategies. Probably the most important attribute of physicians was their own character and the nature of their relationships with patients. In selecting a doctor, personal style, education, religion, and family background were criteria as useful as any.

Strengthening these tendencies and reflecting their importance was the fact that the great majority of doctor–patient encounters took place in the patient's home, not in an office or a hospital. One survey of 8,758 families (in eighteen states) from 1928 to 1931 reported an average of 526 physician-care visits per 1,000 people, and 294 (or 56 percent) of them involved one or more house calls.[18] In other words, more than half of patients who saw a doctor, saw him in their own home. Another survey of the period, examining physician practice patterns, revealed that a little over one-third of all their contacts with patients came through house calls, again demonstrating the centrality of the home in medical encounters.[19]

Although one cannot be certain of all the psychological and social implications of house calls, and descriptions are usually so sentimental as to arouse skepticism, on these occasions doctors were likely to gain greater insight into the patient's needs, and patients may well have become more trusting of doctors. Francis Peabody, a professor of medicine at Harvard in the 1920s, was being more than romantic in noting: "When the general practitioner goes into the home of a patient, he may know the whole background of the family life from past experience; but even when he comes as a stranger he has every opportunity to find out what manner of man his patient is, and what kind of circumstances makes his life. . . . What is spoken of as a 'clinical picture' is not just a photograph of a sick man in bed; it is an impressionistic painting of the patient surrounded by his home, his work, his relations, his friends, his joys, sorrows, hopes, and fears."[20] Or as one son recalled about a day when he accompanied his physician-father on rounds: "We spent the rest of the afternoon climbing up and down stairs and in and out of his patients' houses. I can remember being impressed by the consistently warm welcomes he received. Always he was offered tea, cakes or cookies by people anxious to hear what he had to say and grateful for his presence. And my father—he seemed to know everyone's friends and relatives. He was full of reminiscences which he and his patients shared. Every visit was an occasion for warm conversation in addition to the medical treatments. I can remember feeling proud of him, envious ('how come we didn't know him this way?'), and very tired."[21]

A recurring image in physicians' autobiographical accounts is the ride through town on the way to pay a house call. Lewis Thomas has straightforwardly described the frequency of these trips: "My father spent his hours on the road. In the early morning he made rounds at the local hospital. . . . Later in the morning, and through the afternoon, he made his house calls."[22] Others have embellished the rides with allusions to a royal tour: "The family physician, dressed in his frock coat and silk hat, driving a beautiful pair of dapple gray horses, came majestically down the avenue, when it seemed as if the whole neighborhood ceased activity to pay homage to the honored gentleman and his procession; he was their advisor, counselor and friend. . . . His human understanding seemed to draw him so near to the heart of the family."[23]

Some commentators invoke the image of Norman Rockwell–like general practitioners making house calls as the pretext for celebrating the golden age of the past when patients trusted doctors and neither lawyers nor government officials were around to pester them. But others take the image as a departure point for historical debunking: "In the United States by the early 1900s," insists one historian, "it appeared that general practice was moribund if not dead. While the role of the family doctor as advisor and counsellor was idealized . . . the archetypical family physician . . . had largely disappeared in 1915. Out-patient departments of city hospitals provided general services for the indigent masses. The American middle class was already going directly to specialists."[24] But the obituary is premature, certainly for the middle class and even for many among the poor.

It is true that through the 1930s, specialization was on the increase, and outgoing presidents of local medical societies frequently delivered valedictories on "The Passing of the Family Doctor." Prominent medical educators and prestigious national commissions also complained that the specialist was changing medicine for the worse. "In the trend toward specialism," Francis Peabody insisted, "the pendulum is swinging too far."[25] So too, in 1932 the authors of the *Report of the Commission on Medical Education*, appointed by the Association of American Medical Colleges, found that "specialism has developed beyond the actual needs in the larger community. . . . There is great need of a wider appreciation on the part of the public as well as the profession of the important function of non-specialized practice."[26]

Yet, despite the complaints, specialization was far from overtaking general practice. A 1928-to-1931 survey of health care delivery reported that 81 percent of patient visits still were to general practitioners; only a minority of encounters (19 percent) occurred with specialists. The proportion of specialists to general physicians also remained relatively low; as late as 1940, the overwhelming majority (some 70 percent) of physicians were in general practice.[27] Moreover, specialization in its initial appearance was not equivalent to specialization later. Of all medical specialists, 30 percent were in pediatrics or obstetrics-gynecology, and another 40 percent, in surgery.[28] If by the hegemony of the specialist one means physicians with great technical competence in one special area whose patients overwhelmingly come through referral from another physician and for one particular procedure, then the specialist was not at the center of American medicine before World War II. Neither pediatricians nor obstetricians-gynecologists fit this pattern, and the social consequences of the separation of surgery from general medicine can be (and undoubtedly were) grossly exaggerated.

To be sure, these changes did take away patient dollars from general practitioners—the pediatrician captured the young patient, the ob-gyn practitioners the female patient, and the surgeons the operative cases—and many of the complaints undoubtedly were inspired by this fact. As the outgoing president of the Michigan State Medical Society lamented in 1930: "I know of but one condition for which the family doctor has no competition, and that is making the emergency night call." Otherwise, "he is apologetically informed that father was injured at the factory recently and of course the factory doctor took care of him, that Sammy recently had his tonsils out by a tonsillectomist, and that when daughter contracted pneumonia of course they wanted the best and therefore employed an internist, and mother's last baby was delivered by her obstetrician."[29] But the general practitioner was still alive and well, and the specialists were hardly such devotees of research or masters of arcane procedures as to be removed from sustained contact with individual patients.

Surveys of particular communities in the pre–World War II period demonstrate the staying power of the family physician. In his survey of *The Health of Regionville*, for example, sociologist Earl Koos soon learned that physicians were well-integrated and prestigious in the community; one informant put Doctor X high on the list of the most influential townspeople and explained: "He's one of the best-educated men in town, and makes good money—drives a good car, belongs to the Rotary, and so forth." Koos also discovered that 80 percent of his class 1 households ("the successful people of Regionville") and 70 percent of the class 2 ones ("the wage-earners") had a family doctor. When he asked families how they chose their doctor, they most often cited a general reputation in the community (people speaking well of the doctor), a recommendation of a friend or relative, or a long history of treatment by the doctor. A considerable number of respondents also remarked that their choice reflected the fact that they "had come to know the doctor socially." Although Koos regretted the fact that social criteria outweighed expertise in guiding the choices ("It is perhaps a sad commentary . . . that more sensitive criteria were not available, or at least not employed, in the selection of the professional person"), his data made clear how outside the mainstream his own predilections were.[30]

The lower classes certainly experienced a different kind of medical care, but even here a significant degree of familiarity between doctors and patients existed. The poor were neither so completely dependent on public services (the inpatient beds or the outpatient dispensaries of municipal hospitals) nor so thoroughly distanced from private practitioners as has often been assumed. It is true that those deep in poverty almost always ended up in a hospital-almshouse or its clinic. (The especially "worthy" cases or "interesting" cases would make it onto the wards of a voluntary or university hospital.) But poverty was typically a transitory, rather than a fixed and permanent, state. The poor moved back and forth across the line, with their exact position at a given time fixed by the condition of the local economy, the health of the breadwinner, and the number in the household who were working.

And it was their exact position at a time of illness that helped determine the type of medical care they received.

The most precise account of this process comes from a 1938 study by Gladys Swackhamer of 365 lower-class families (81 percent had incomes under $2,000 a year) living in three New York neighborhoods, the lower East Side (heavily Jewish and Italian), the Chelsea district (polyglot, composed of east Europeans, Greeks, and others), and East Harlem (predominately Italian, with some east Europeans). Half of the families relied on both private and public medical resources, close to 30 percent used only public, and 20 percent used only private. The pattern was not complicated. If the money was at hand, the family would often choose a fee-for-service practitioner, not a clinic or agency physician, to treat the acute case that did not respond to family remedies or to the treatment recommended by the local druggist. On the other hand, should the acute case turn chronic or a chronic condition develop (including pregnancy), the patient was likely to seek care at a clinic. But if clinic treatment proved ineffective and the ailment became more bothersome or interfered with an ability to work, then the patient might return to a private doctor. Accordingly, Mr. and Mrs. K took their sick baby to the baby health clinic, but when improvement was slow in coming, they turned to a nearby private physician recommended by friends. Meanwhile, Mrs. K became pregnant and went for prenatal care to a nearby public maternity hospital; but when she became ill during her pregnancy, she went to Mr. K's family doctor, who had treated him since childhood.[31]

This does not mean that the poor had a stable relationship with a physician and could, when asked, name a family physician. Although more than two-thirds of these families had seen a private practitioner over the past twelve months, only one-third reported having a family doctor. In fact, this finding of the Swackhamer study generated the most commentary; the *New York Times*, for example, ran several stories lamenting the disappearance of the family doctor.[32] But the results of the study were more complex than this: First, one-third of a lower-class population did name a family doctor. Second, even though most of the poor had no ongoing relationship with one doctor, they were remarkably consistent in choosing a neighborhood doctor and relying on friends for referrals. When asked how they came to select their private physicians, 58 percent of the families answered that they followed the recommendations of relatives or friends; another 8 percent cited the physical proximity of the physician; and 7 percent, a personal tie to the physician (through business, religion, or language). Thus the majority of the poor did not have *a* doctor, but they had doctors who were integral to their communities.

To view these findings from the physician's perspective, neighborhood reputation counted most in terms of maintaining a following. The critical elements in building a practice were not degrees, specialty certification, hospital affiliation, or special skills. To attract and hold patients, physicians had to be sensitive, caring, able to listen, committed, and responsive to crises—not because they were saintly, but because the marketplace required it. The incentives put a premium on intimacy, and involvement with the community. In a very real sense it paid to listen to patients, so that they would not only come back but also send their friends and relatives.

The pace of medical practice also strengthened the personal ties between physician and patient. The number and power of diagnostic tools were so limited that the physician had to rely essentially on the case history. The patient's report of symptoms, the way the pain moved along the arm or the frequency of a stomach upset, were often the best guides the doctor had to the problem. One reason why medical educators and leaders worried so much about the disappearance of the family physician was because in the absence of diagnostic technologies, they put a premium on knowing the patient's constitution and family history. Information on what illnesses the patient had previously experienced—or those that the patient's parents or siblings had experienced—were vital clues to diagnosing the patient's current ailment. As Holmes explained in his *Medical Essays*: "The young man knows his patient, but the old man knows his patient's family, dead and alive, up and down for generations. He can tell beforehand what diseases their unborn children will be subject to, what they will die of if they live long enough."[33] So too, the novelist George Eliot has a character remark in *Janet's Repentance* that "it's no trifle at her time of life to part with a doctor who knows her constitution."[34] And well into the 1930s physicians continued to insist that "the family medical adviser with his knowledge of personal habits, familial tendencies and environmental conditions" would understand the "special meaning" of the symptoms of fatigue, impaired appetite, cough, dizziness, and headaches.[35]

In all, a personal knowledge of the patient had a diagnostic and therapeutic importance in medicine that is almost impossible to appreciate today. The knowledge was so complete that as two students of doctor-patient relations have observed, office records "were rarely kept, being considered unnecessary by the solo practitioner who knew, and had no trouble remembering the patient, family and their illnesses without taking notes."[36] These circumstances also help to explain why there were so few voices even in the 1920s or 1930s stressing the need to humanize medical care. Medical care was essentially composed of the human touch, and there was no need for educators or critics to promote the obvious.

Physicians were also more closely connected to their community and well integrated into the fabric of social life. One of the more suggestive indicators of this relationship may be found in literary depictions of physicians. Without minimizing the variety of descriptions in late nineteenth- and early twentieth-century texts—in some the doctor is demonic; in others, incompetent—it is notable that the narratives give physicians many roles distinct from that of professional healer.[37] Doctors can be neighbors, lovers, and friends—they come to tea and stay to flirt. They move quite freely outside the hospital setting and without a white coat or stethoscope. In other words, physicians did not inhabit a world unto themselves.

The most compelling sketch of a late nineteenth-century physician is Lydgate in George Eliot's *Middlemarch*, and although the novel is English, Eliot's portrayal was not idiosyncratic to her side of the Atlantic. The fact of Lydgate being a doctor was essential to the narrative; but he is a fully drawn character, found more often in the drawing room than in his fever hospital. Eliot frequently remarked on the low state of medicine and medical practices, which was certainly as true in the United States as in England. But Lydgate takes his profession seriously, vehemently objecting when his wife, Rosamond, wishes that he had chosen a calling that commanded more respect: " 'It is the grandest profession in the world, Rosamond,' said Lydgate gravely. 'And to say that you love me without loving the medical man in me, is the same sort of thing as to say that you like eating a peach but don't like its flavour.' " The novel, however, focuses on Lydgate the person, not the doctor. Rosamond is initially attracted to him not because of his profession but because of his relatively high birth, a fact "which distinguished him from all Middlemarch admirers, and presented marriage as a prospect of rising in rank and . . . [having] nothing to do with vulgar people." And his failings have to do with his "arrogant conceit," which is displayed far more often toward his fellow practitioners than toward his patients, and in the "commonness . . . [of] the complexion of his prejudices. . . . That distinction of mind which belonged to his intellectual ardor did not penetrate his feeling and judgment about furniture, or women, or the desirability of its being known (without his telling) that he was better born than other country surgeons."[38] In short, his virtues were those of his profession at its best (his intellectual ardor), and his faults were those of ordinary people (boring prejudices)—and such an ordering of virtue and vice, as we shall see, will not often be found in the post–1945 literature.

What was true of Eliot's Lydgate held for Anton Chekhov's Dr. Astrov in *Uncle Vanya*. "I've worked too hard," he explains in his first appearance on stage: "I'm on my feet from morning to night, I don't know what rest is. . . . During all the time you've known me, I haven't had a single free day. . . . In the third week of Lent, I went to Malitskoye, there was an epidemic . . . typhus . . . In the huts people lay on the floor in rows. . . . Filth, stench, smoke . . . I was on the move all day, didn't sit down or have a morsel of food, and when I got home they still wouldn't let me rest." But it is Astrov the misguided lover, not the doctor, who is at the core of the plot. He rejects the advances of the woman who loves him, and he proceeds to make a fool of himself in pursuit of one who does not. Over the course of the events, Astrov becomes more and more pathetic, and the strengths that remain relate to his doctoring: "Just think what sort of life that doctor has! . . . Impassable mud on the roads, frosts, snowstorms, vast distances, uncouth, primitive people, poverty and disease all around him—it would be hard for a man working and struggling day after day in such an atmosphere to keep himself sober and pure." His weaknesses are those of a man forced to live his life in what he describes as a suffocating, insipid, and vulgar atmosphere, who becomes fascinated with the idle rich and is brought to ruin by them. His closing lines to Elena Andreyevna, his temptress, capture this duality and tension well: " 'You came here with your husband, and every one of us who had been working, bustling about trying to create something, had to drop his work and occupy himself with nothing but you and your husband's gout the entire summer. Both of you—he and you—have infected us with your idleness. I was infatuated with you, and have done nothing for a whole month; meanwhile people have been sick. . . . I'm convinced that if you had stayed, the devastation would have been enormous.' "[39]

In the end, both Lydgate and Astrov are fully developed characters— doctors and lovers; indeed, better doctors than lovers—which is what gives *Middlemarch* and *Uncle Vanya* their story lines. These physicians are altogether part of the social life of their communities, in no way isolated or cut off. The narrative takes place in the drawing room, not in the hospital; the exchanges are between friends and lovers, not between doctor and patient. That the men are doctors is not incidental to the works, but this fact does not overwhelm or determine their every response.

By the 1930s this dictum was losing some of its strength. The conflict at the center of one of that decade's most popular dramas about physicians, Sidney Kingsley's *Doctors in White*, went to this very point. Laura, the would-be wife of the young doctor George Ferguson, pleads with him to have a life outside of medicine: "The important man, George, is the man who knows how to live," something her physician-father and Ferguson's mentor apparently never learned. "They have no outside interests at all. They're flat—they're colorless. They're not men—they're caricatures!" Ferguson, however, rejects her plea and the romance breaks up. This kind of scenario, however, was unusual in literary or dramatic depictions of physicians. At least before the 1950s, doctors were more generally portrayed as individuals, not as caricatures of single-minded professionals.[40]

Undoubtedly the most widely read book on American medicine in the pre–World War II period was Sinclair Lewis's *Arrowsmith*. The hero, Dr. Martin Arrowsmith, does give up everything, including wife and children, to flee to the Vermont woods and pursue his career. But this act represented the single-mindedness of the researcher, not of the practicing physician; Arrowsmith was rejecting an overbearing scientific establishment, what Lewis's guide in these matters, Paul de Kruif, called the "barrack spirit." The earlier chapters of the novel celebrate the country family doctor, De Kruif's "splendid old type of general practitioner," who was assuredly not detached from the life of the community.[41]

Reading a very different kind of text, the autobiographies of pre–World War II American doctors, also demonstrates how little distance separated doctor, patient, and community. Although physician autobiographies began appearing in the nineteenth century, a whole spate were published in the 1920s and 1930s, inspired by the same impulse: to set down an experience that seemed destined to disappear, that is, being a family doctor. Sensing that medicine was on the brink of change, these physicians wanted to preserve a record of the demands, limitations, and rewards of their profession, as reflected in such titles as *The Horse and Buggy Doctor* and *Castor Oil and Quinine*. As one writer explained, his family persuaded him to write his autobiography because "there should be a record of the old country doctor by one of the species." Another wrote: "I have been a family doctor for over thirty years. . . . My story might be called a 'case history' in defense of the family doctor. . . . The family doctor is indispensible to the community and the nation."[42]

Given such goals, the genre does not make for very interesting reading. The autobiographies are anecdotal, the stories seem trivial, and the sorts of questions one would have wanted these doctors to address (such as how they coped with therapeutic helplessness) are missing. Instead, we read about the woman who did not admit to being pregnant but who in fact was; or about the family that called doctors out at night, always exaggerated their illnesses, and never paid their bills; or about how a doctor rode through a storm (or blizzard or hurricane) to deliver a baby or mend a leg or minister to a feverish child. But the triviality is precisely the point: being a family doctor meant to work on this scale of things, to be involved with obscure people and minor events. These are not tales of heroic interventions or brilliant solutions to puzzling symptoms, but of physicians whose professional lives were intimately connected with their neighbors and community. Their visions were local; they thought small, and their victories and losses had less to do with the power of medications and more to do with the fit of personalities. They took pride in being doctors who were "capable of instantaneous automatic adjustment to every shade of human nature," rather than masters of diagnosis, treatment, or surgery.

If Lydgate and Astrov frequented the drawing rooms of the better sort, their American counterparts frequented the club rooms of their communities and mixed regularly with the local elite. Dr. Frederick Loomis's memoir of his 1920s and 1930s obstetrics practice, *Consultation Room*, described the traditional Wednesday at the country club: "The Locker rooms are filled with the bankers and the lawyers and the doctors and the brokers." In Loomis's "locker alley" were some of his "closest friends," including the president of the bank and a leading lawyer. "Each week, I looked forward eagerly to my association with these and other men at the club. My days and nights were necessarily spent with women—sick ones—and, much as I like my work, it is a pleasant contrast to step into another world, the world of men."[43] Indeed, doctors may well have been in the locker rooms as much for business as for pleasure. At a time when social relationships were essential to building and maintaining a practice, physicians, no matter how skilled or well trained, could not dare to adopt a posture of aloofness. "A physician is judged by the company he keeps," Dr. D. W. Cathell advised young practitioners (in a book so aptly entitled *The Physician Himself and What He Should Add to His Scientific Acquirements*). "Avoid associating with those who are 'under a cloud,' or are notoriously deficient, or whose hopes and ambitions are blighted. Let your associations be as far as possible with professional brethren and other people of genuine worth."[44]

The intimate and familiar manner in which doctor and patient interacted casts in a very different light some traditional physician practices toward patients, especially on the matter of truth telling. Although physicians undoubtedly differed in the degree to which they shared information with patients or sought their permission before carrying out procedures (some historians would have physicians sharing this responsibility in the early nineteenth century, whereas others date it to the 1970s), there is no question but that the ethic of medicine, from Hippocrates onward, was to have physicians keep bad news to themselves—to be the purveyors of hope, not doom. Oliver Wendell Holmes echoed this traditional wisdom when he counseled those about to enter the profession: "Your patient has no more right to all the truth you know than he has to all the medicine in your saddlebags. . . . He should get only just so much as is good for him. . . . It is a terrible thing to take away hope, every earthly hope, from a fellow creature."[45]

Behind this advice, however, was a confidence that the physician could measure out just what degree of information was good for the patient. This medical tradition was borne not only of paternalism and the relative emptiness of the doctors' saddlebags, but of a confidence that doctors were capable of substituting their judgment for that of their patients, able to spare them pain because they intuited their patients' wishes. Because they knew their patients' families "dead and alive, up and down for generations," Holmes concluded, physicians knew not only what the patients would die of if they lived long enough, but also "whether they had better live at all or remain unrealized possibilities, as belonging to a stock not worth being perpetuated."[46] Since they shared their patients' religious or class or ethnic perspective, since they had been in their patients' homes and spent time with them over the course of various illnesses, physicians were comfortable making decisions on behalf of the patients.

Well into the twentieth century, patients entering a hospital did not confront a strange or alienating environment. For one, they often entered their own ethnic institutions, and to be a patient at a St. Vincent's or a Beth Israel, a Mt. Sinai or a Sisters of Mercy, was to be in familiar surroundings at a time of crisis. By 1930, for example, there were some 640 Catholic hospitals in the United States (one-seventh of all nongovernmental hospitals), and the Catholic Hospital Association (CHA) took pride in the fact that "there was available one bed . . . for every 231.2 of the Catholic population," compared to a ratio double that for the general population.[47] In New York City from 1925 to 1945, 60 percent of the fifty-eight general hospitals had religious sponsorship (most of them Catholic or Jewish); moving westward (where one might have imagined the ethnic impact to be lower), Cincinnati in 1925 had nine general hospitals, of which four were sponsored by

Protestant groups (chiefly Methodists), two by Catholics, and one by Jews. That year, 308 Catholic patients in Cincinnati had to enter a hospital, and 165 of them (54 percent) chose one of the three Catholic hospitals; so too, 54 of the 71 Jewish patients (76 percent) entered the Jewish hospital. (Among Protestants, the figures were lower, for those in the majority did not experience the same incentives.) To be sure, Catholic and Jewish hospitals served more than Catholic and Jewish patients—the CHA estimated that 49 percent of its patients were non-Catholic—and not every member of an ethnic or religious group patronized the group's own hospitals. But a majority of Catholics did use the group's hospitals, and the figures may even have been slightly higher among Jews.[48]

There were many reasons why religious and ethnic communities built and frequented their own hospitals. They were, for example, self-consciously offering a gift to American society, paying tribute and demonstrating allegiance to American values. Immediate self-interest operated as well. For minorities, each hospital represented a place in which the group's members could learn and practice medicine, and in an era when prejudice against Jewish and Catholic applicants to medical schools and residency programs at major hospitals was widespread, this opportunity was critical. The sectarian hospital, then, was an investment in professional careers for those who might otherwise be excluded from medicine, which meant, of course, that in these hospitals the sick were most likely to be treated by fellow ethnics or coreligionists, that patients and doctors would share language, traditions, and values.

The mission of the sectarian hospitals also strengthened the bonds of trust between patient and institution. In explaining what differentiated Catholic hospitals from other hospitals, staff members emphasized meeting the human, as well as medical, needs of their patients. Their regard for the patient's spiritual welfare prompted them to look beyond the mere treatment of disease to a more general well-being. Only on their wards would nursing sisters comfort patients and make certain that priests would always be available to give extreme unction. Only on their walls would patients find the crucifix along with paintings that expressed "the deepest Catholic piety." As one Catholic physician explained, it was not enough to prescribe a medication and ignore the person; the patient could not be effectively treated "as though he were nothing but a 'curiously developed lump of matter.'" Or as another Catholic clergyman insisted, "The sweet influence of religion has ever been the means of dispelling the nervous gloom of the patient, so dangerous to his physical recovery."[49]

This same orientation pervaded Jewish institutions. Beth Israel Hospital, for example, was founded in 1900 on New York's lower East Side, first, to meet "the great necessity of having a hospital convenient to the crowded tenement district of this part of the city; second, to have a hospital that should be conducted on strictly orthodox principles in its kitchen as well as in other respects."[50] Only in a Jewish hospital would the patient be certain to find kosher food on his tray and be able to join a group in daily prayer. And only in a Jewish hospital would a Yiddish-speaking patient be assured that in a time of grave illness the doctor would know the right language and phrases with which to provide comfort.

Many of the attributes of the sectarian hospitals reappeared in the numerous small voluntary and proprietary hospitals that served local communities. The typical community hospital had less than 100 beds and was likely to be class and race specific, that is, serving the well-to-do in well-to-do neighborhoods, and the lower classes in lower-class neighborhoods. Whatever social inequalities were fostered, such arrangements helped make the institutions familiar and comfortable to their patients, and accordingly, patients sought them out. In 1933, for example, 89 percent of the patients in hospitals in the borough of Queens were from Queens, and 88 percent of all patients in Brooklyn's hospitals were Brooklyn residents. (The figure for the Bronx was 85 percent and for Staten Island, 98 percent; only in Manhattan did the percentage drop to 62 percent.) Moreover, community hospitals were generally staffed by neighborhood doctors—attending privileges were not difficult to obtain—making them more a part of the local community than the scientific community.[51]

With homogeneity and intimacy such major considerations, the idea of a "surplus bed" did not carry the meaning that it now has. Hospital and state administrators were alert to occupancy rates, but their degree of anxiety was not great. Over the 1920s and 1930s the larger voluntary general hospitals typically had occupancy rates of 60 percent of capacity, about 10 percent below the standard proposed in the health policy literature of the time. But the fact that voluntary hospitals did not attain the standard caused no alarm. In part, this attitude reflected an absence of pressure from third-party payers—federal bureaucrats did not insist that hospital administrators become more efficient in using beds. But the complacency also testified to a definition of the hospital bed as a resource that should be open in advance of need, as opposed to always in use. The CHA was more proud of the number of beds it had available to meet unexpected need than it was concerned about a relatively low occupancy rate (57.5 percent), precisely because a Catholic who suddenly required a bed should have a bed lest he or she end up in another denomination's institution. Hospital beds were not interchangeable: a Protestant hospital bed was not suitable for a Catholic or a Jew; a bed 100 miles away was not suitable for a neighbor.[52]

The longer length of patient stays also reduced the strangeness of the institution. In the 1920s the average stay (excluding newborns) in general hospitals was a little over eleven days in private hospitals, and when patients remained in a hospital for weeks rather than days, a patient subculture flourished. Patients became guides for each other, most dramatically, perhaps, in chronic-care facilities, but in acute-care hospitals as well. Their conversations served effectively to introduce and explicate the hospital to newcomers—all the more effectively when the conversations were between fellow ethnics or members of the same social class and neighborhood. The longer stays also gave physicians greater opportunities to talk with patients, and although the evidence is largely anecdotal, they may well have done so.[53]

In sum, the doctor and patient occupied the same social space. The critical element in their relationship was not silence but a shared outlook. Under these circumstances, the degree of mutual trust was great enough to keep strangers away from the bedside, and to give bedside ethics standing not only with the profession but with the lay public.

CHAPTER 7

The Doctor as Stranger

PRACTICALLY every development in medicine in the post–World War II period distanced the physician and the hospital from the patient and the community, disrupting personal connections and severing bonds of trust. Whatever the index—whether ties of friendship, religion, ethnicity, or intellectual activity—the results highlight a sharp division between the lay world and the medical world. By the 1960s the two had moved so far apart that one could have asked a lay audience about the last time they spoke to a physician and had their clothes on, and they would have been unable to remember an occasion. By the same token, if one had asked physicians about their social contacts outside the profession, they would have been hard pressed to come up with examples. The separation from the hospital has become so extreme that columnist Meg Greenfield, in a 1986 commentary entitled "The Land of the Hospital," announced that she had "just come back from a foreign place worth reporting on . . . a universe, really of its own," where she felt like "a tourist in an unfathomable, dangerous land."[1] In a spate of recent medical self-help books writers have advised patients to prepare to enter a hospital as though they were going on a trek in Nepal—take food and organize family and friends to provide necessary help. It has even been suggested that patients hang up school diplomas and pictures of their children to make certain that the chieftains of this exotic place know that they are valued persons in the outside world.

Some results of such changes are well recognized and endlessly discussed. One staple of both family magazines and medical journals is the complaint that physicians have lost their ability to relate to patients, that they have neither the desire nor the time to communicate with them. But however familiar some aspects of this subject may be, it is important to analyze the transformation closely, for not all of its causes and, even more important, not all of its implications have been recognized.

To read some of the critiques, one would think the problem is mostly a matter of educating medical students by emphasizing communication skills (so doctors learn better how to interview and how to listen) and incorporating the humanities into the curriculum (on the theory that studying the classics will increase empathy). But however worthwhile these efforts, a reliance on the education of the future practitioner as the vehicle for change minimizes the structural barriers to recasting the doctor–patient relationship. The organization and delivery of medical care almost guarantees that at a time of crisis patients will be treated by strangers in a strange environment. This circumstance has transformed many patients' behavior, encouraging a style closer to that of a wary consumer than a grateful supplicant. Moreover, this distancing helps explain why a cadre of outsiders felt compelled to enter the medical arena and promote a commitment to a more formal and collective type of medical decision making, including regulatory guidelines and committee oversight.

The first and most obvious of the structural changes that distanced patients from doctors in the post-1945 decades was the disappearance of the house call. By the early 1960s, home visits represented less than one percent of doctor–patient contacts.[2] Surprisingly, the demise of the house call is a relatively unexplored phenomenon, but it reflects a combination of professional and technological considerations. By bringing the patient to the office and hospital, physicians increased their own efficiency and incomes, enabling them to examine many more patients in much less time. The change also served to give patients quicker access to medical technologies (at first, X-ray and electrocardiogram machines; later, computerized scanners and magnetic imagers). But whatever the reason, the effect was to remove patients from familiar surroundings and deprive the doctor of a firsthand knowledge of the patients' environment. In both symbolic and real terms, doctors and patients moved apart.

This distance was further enlarged as medical specialization and sub-specialization transformed the profession in the post–World War II years. The fears of the 1930s became the realities of the 1950s and 1960s; only 20 percent of physicians now identified themselves as general practitioners, and occasional efforts to increase the pool through training programs in community medicine or family medicine showed few results. Not only were doctors now trained so intensely in the functioning of a particular organ or system that they might well lose sight of the patient's presence, but specialization meant that patients and doctors were not likely to have met before the onset of the illness, let alone to have developed a relationship. Unable to predict which organ would become the site of disease, patients had no way of anticipating whether they would require the services of a cardiologist or neurologist, and thus had no way of knowing the physician across the desk in a time of crisis. Even those with a primary physician could not be certain that the doctor would be able to follow them into the hospital; since admitting privileges to tertiary-care medical centers were often very restricted, the odds were that as the stakes in illness mounted and decisions became more critical, the patient was more likely to be in a strange setting surrounded by strangers.[3]

As specialization took hold, both the hospital and the patient also gave unprecedented weight to merit in the selection of a physician. Although an "old boy" network survived in some settings or specialties, medicine has come astonishingly close to being a meritocracy. In few other fields is sheer talent as likely to be rewarded with prestigious appointments. In most contexts, of course, such a finding would be cause for celebration, but here one must take note of an altogether unintended but significant consequence: rules of merit can foster anonymity. Doctors who gain their positions through merit might or might not share their patient's religious persuasion, ethnic identity, or social values. The triumph of the most qualified has helped make the doctor into a stranger.

After the 1950s, even sectarian hospitals no longer relied on such criteria as religion or ethnicity to select most of the house staff and senior physicians. Put another way, choice by merit accelerated the process by which the ethnic hospital lost its special relationship to its patients. It became increasingly difficult to define what was Presbyterian about Presbyterian Hospital or Jewish about Mt. Sinai Hospital, and the answer could not be found in the characteristics of either the patients or the attending physicians. (Catholic hospitals have withstood this trend to a degree, but they barely resemble their predecessors of the 1930s, which were dominated by the nursing sisters.) The trustees of Montefiore Hospital in New York, for example, celebrated the hospital's 100th anniversary in 1985 by amending its charter and eliminating the provision that a majority of its board had to be Jewish. Although the revision paid homage to the scientific ideal of universalism, it also reflected the decline of the ethnic character of the hospital. The few management tactics that attempt to keep some traditions alive—chaplains going around the wards or the opportunity to order kosher food—while not trivial, hardly reduce the impersonal atmosphere of the hospital. The ethnic hospital survives in name only. It is now in all senses a public space, with the same personal ties to its patients that a busy midtown hotel has to its guests.[4]

By the same token, demographic trends in major urban areas have disrupted the ties between patients and hospitals. Many of the voluntary hospitals, when first founded, served the residents of their immediate neighborhood. But then many residents moved to the suburbs, and few, if any, of the original constituents for the hospital remained to use its services. They were replaced by groups with very different backgrounds, identifications, and languages. If, for example, they were Hispanic, they often found the hospital even more mysterious because the staff spoke only English.

In much the same way, the hospital as a neighborhood institution almost disappeared. In New York City, for example, between 1963 and 1978, thirty-five hospitals closed; and they were, typically, smaller facilities that served a special section of the population. As the authors of one report concluded: "The communities for which these institutions had been established—generally comprising either the educated and affluent or immigrants of a single particular ethnic group—had vanished in a massive turnover of population."[5] The same process has affected smaller communities. Since the 1970s many rural and small-town hospitals have closed, reflecting mounting costs, inefficiencies of size, and patients' preference for hospitals staffed by specialists and equipped with advanced technologies.[6] The trade-off, of course, is that seriously ill patients must travel to a distant regional hospital to be cared for by strangers.

Not only the anonymity of the doctor and the hospital but the new style of medical practice have made it nearly impossible to maintain a personal and intimate link between the patient and the health care providers. Even if doctor and patient had common backgrounds or values, they might never discover it, for the pace and rhythm of contemporary medical practice erect extraordinary barriers between them. As the seriousness of the illness mounts, and the patient is more likely to be in a hospital than a physician's office, the time available to doctors to spend with one particular patient declines. Neither house staff nor attending physicians can linger at the bedside, not because they are uncaring or poorly trained, but because the external pressures to move on to the next case are overwhelming. Compared with the pre–World War II period, the patient population in major medical centers has become more seriously ill. This increased severity of disease reflects a shortened length of patient stay—usually achieved by curtailing the period of in-hospital recuperation and recovery—and a closer scrutiny over patient admissions to make certain that they really need a hospital bed. Whether the driving force is the need to cut costs or to spare the patient days in so alien an environment or to reduce the likelihood of iatrogenic complications, the result has been to transform the practice of hospital medicine.

On the wards, doctors typically scramble from crisis to crisis. No sooner do they stabilize a patient and get her on the road to recovery, than she is discharged and the next acutely ill patient takes the bed. House staff, who actually do most of the scrambling, often devise ingenious strategies to keep a recuperating patient in bed, not as a favor to the patient but as a way of reducing their workload. But ploys, like lining up an additional test, do not work for very long, for as clever as house staff might be, hospital administrators are not far behind. So physicians soon are again performing intake exams, diagnosing symp-

toms, devising a treatment plan, and responding to emergencies, knowing that the moment they rescue one patient, the cycle will inevitably
begin again.

If doctors do not as a rule linger around the bedside, it is also
because the methods of diagnosis and treatment require both frequent
and split-second interventions. Take, for example, the pace of cardiac
care. By the late 1960s the entire treatment pattern had changed:
Patients underwent a battery of exceptionally intrusive and time-
consuming diagnostic tests, including the insertion of an arterial catheter in order to measure blood pressure, with the continuing need to
check the line to make certain no infection developed. New drug therapies required scrupulous monitoring, typically, checking the blood
pressure every fifteen minutes and then adjusting the dosage. Thus, the
opportunity for the physician to develop or sustain a relationship with
the patient has become one of the casualties of a more powerful medical arsenal.

Furthermore, pausing by the bedside has come closer to being, di-
agnostically speaking, an indulgence, for the patient is frequently far
less interesting and less revealing about his symptoms than the technology. In the 1930s, conversation with patients was inseparable from
diagnosis and treatment, and thus it was not necessary to emphasize
the need to talk with them. Three decades later such conversations were
add-ons—something physicians ought to do as a moral, not medical,
obligation. Not surprisingly, as the pressure of time mounted and the
limits of energy were reached, such conversations were among the first
things to drop away.

All the while, of course, the hospital had become the prime, almost
exclusive, setting for treating serious illness, bringing with it isolation
from family and friends which hospital policies only exacerbated. The
most compelling critique of this change came from Dr. Elisabeth
Kübler-Ross, one of the first physicians to make dying her specialty.
"I remember as a child the death of a farmer," she wrote in her 1969
bestseller, *On Death and Dying*. "He asked simply to die at home, a
wish that was granted without questioning. He called in his children,
arranged his affairs and asked his friends to visit him once more, to
bid good-bye to them." By contrast, we now "don't allow children to
visit their dying parents in the hospitals," and the patient himself un-

dergoes a kind of torture: "He may cry for rest, peace and dignity, but he will get infusions, transfusions, a heart machine, or tracheostomy." The loneliest, and cruelest, setting was the intensive care unit. Kübler-Ross recounts the frustration and agony of an elderly man allowed only a five-minute visit every hour with his desperately ill wife in the ICU. "Was that the way he was to say good-bye to his wife of almost fifty years?" Kübler-Ross well understood that "there are administrative rules and laws" and "too many visitors in such a unit would be intolerable—if not for the patients, maybe for the sensitive equipment?" But surely, some way had to be found to reduce the distance between hospital, patient, and family.[7]

However important these structural considerations, they are not the totality of the story. To understand the separation of the medical and nonmedical worlds, one must also reckon with changes in the patterns of recruitment to medicine and training in medicine in the post–World War II period. For here too lie elements that have promoted the insularity of physicians and their separation from the nonmedical world. In very dramatic fashion these changes undermined the patient's confidence in the exercise of physician discretion. It made sense in an earlier era to trust to the wisdom of the doctor, knowing that his decisions would be informed not only by his greater experience—he had been there many times before—but by the ethics of the community, which he too shared. But in the postwar decades this confidence eroded. The doctors' decisions, like the researchers', seemed likely to reflect their own or their subspecialty's idiosyncratic judgments.

The process that encapsulates physicians in their own universe begins surprisingly early in their lives. A study in the 1950s of six successive classes of medical students at the University of Pennsylvania revealed that just over half the students were already considering a medical career by the time they were thirteen; if their fathers were physicians, the percentage climbed to three-quarters.[8] High school administrators and faculty (to say nothing of classmates) had little difficulty identifying which students would enter medicine. Frank Boyden, for many years the headmaster at Deerfield Academy, was convinced "that medicine stands out among all careers as being the one that schoolboys select early and with a manifest clarity of preference." And physician autobiographies confirm his point. "I cannot remember a time in my youth," recalled one doctor, "when I did not want to be a doctor."[9]

As applicants to college and as entering freshmen, the premeds identified themselves quickly—far more quickly, for example, than law students. In one comparative study, 44 percent of medical students had their minds made up about their careers before entering college; among the law students the figure was 15 percent. By the beginning of their junior year, three-quarters of those who would go on to medical school had decided on their careers, compared to one-third of law students. (Medical students, one observer quipped, decide to go to medical school just about when they get out of diapers, whereas law students decide the week before the semester begins.)[10] In the classroom, premeds stand as a group apart, already following a different work routine; three times as many premedical as prelaw students (49 percent as against 18 percent) reported finding a "great deal" of competition in college.[11] So if medical schools required a particular course (say, basic chemistry), many colleges offered a variant for nonpremed students (like chemistry for poets), who were reluctant to compete with the premeds. The premed student, noted one graduate, "narrows his horizons, intensifies his efforts in physics, chemistry, and biology and limits the amount of his general cultural baggage during precisely the three or four years that offer the last chance of a liberal education."[12]

Once in medical school, most medical students face time demands—to say nothing of the substance of the curriculum—that further separate them from their peers. By comparison to law, business, or graduate school in the arts and sciences, the daily class schedule and the academic terms are very long; and the medical campus is often distant from the other parts of the university, so even those inclined to mix with other graduate students are unable to do so. The isolation only increases during the years of residency and fellowship training. Time not spent on the wards is usually spent catching up on sleep. Thus, when physicians earn the requisite degrees and pass the national and specialty board exams, they have spent some fifteen years since high school on the training track, most of this time, segregated in a medical world.

• • •

The stuff of medicine is also isolating. To deal on a daily basis with injury, pain, disfigurement, and death is to be set apart from others. Modern society has constructed exceptionally sturdy boundaries around illness, confining it to the hospital and making it the nearly exclusive preserve of the medical profession. In effect, the hospital does for illness what the insane asylum intended to do for mental illness: enclose it in its own special territory. To be sure, this process is not new, but it has surely accelerated over the last several decades. The two great rites of passage, birth and death, have both moved into the hospital, the first by the 1920s, the second by the 1950s. The isolation of disease is certainly not complete, however. Epidemics, whether Legionnaires' disease or AIDS, rivet public attention; chronic illness is more likely to be treated in the community; and bookstore owners devote more space than ever before to self-help books explaining everything one wants to know about heart disease, diabetes, and cancer. Nevertheless, serious disease is not the substance of everyday discourse, and in more ways than might be at first recognized, this phenomenon cuts doctors off from others.

Physicians' shoptalk is not so much boring as it is filled with tales that would strike outsiders as tragic and gruesome, stories that no one else would want to hear around a dinner table, or for that matter, anywhere else. Let one personal experience clarify the point. No sooner did I join a medical school faculty than I met with the chairman and chief of service of various clinical departments (pediatrics, medicine, and so on) to explore what interest each department might have in social medicine. The sessions were informal, but much of these first conversations turned on "interesting cases," which typically involved descriptions of devastating illnesses. As each chairman told his tale, I recalled how my grandparents, whenever they heard about a case of severe disease, would chant some ritual incantation to protect their family from experiencing such a calamity. At first I thought these stories were an initiation ritual—was a historian trained to do archival work up to the stuff of medicine? But I slowly learned that this was not a rite of passage but a sharing of anecdotes and gossip; they assumed that because I was part of the faculty, I, too, would be fascinated by the shoptalk. Then, in turn, when friends asked about these meetings, I would share the stories; but as I watched their faces get tense and drawn, I learned to put aside the question and change the subject. The substance of medicine, I was learning, was easiest talked about with medical people, not because of its technical or dry qualities, but because of its scariness in exposing the frailty of human beings and the dimensions of suffering.

Recent accounts by medical school graduates of their initiation into medicine reiterate this experience. Melvin Konner's description of *Becoming a Doctor* after a career in anthropology opens with compelling images of a journey "no less exotic . . . [or] devoid of drama and palpable danger" than fieldwork. More relevant still is his emphasis on the violent aspects of medicine. The first case he relates is about Madeline, a trauma victim, who has multiple stab wounds to the chest. In order to insert a tube and facilitate her breathing, the resident anesthetized an area between two ribs under her shoulder blade. Telling the others "matter of factly" to hold down the now naked, "writhing and yelling" woman, he inserted a scalpel deep into the chest wall; and "Madeline practically leaped off the stretcher when the blade went in, screaming and writhing deliriously."[13] In effect, Konner chooses to introduce the layperson to medicine through a scene that violates ordinary conventions, describing acts that in another context would be defined as torture, and in any context, as gruesome.

Whether the isolation of physicians is self-imposed or socially imposed, the results are apparent in a variety of contexts. Physicians are notable for their lack of political involvement, particularly given their high status and incomes. Because the American Medical Association has been so vocal a lobby, one tends to forget just how removed most doctors are from politics. Questionnaires distributed to the 1959 and 1963 Harvard Medical School classes, for example, revealed that only 4 to 6 percent of the students intended to be politically active.[14] That they, and other physicians, meant what they said is evident if one looks at the number of physicians in high office or active at the state and municipal levels—probably less than 100 if one excludes agencies dealing directly with matters of health or research policy.

In fact, medical practice seems to leave very little room for any other activity. Physicians report an average workweek of fifty-four hours, not including time spent reading professional journals or educational activities. Almost 30 percent spend over sixty hours a week at work,

136

roughly 8:00 A.M. to 6:00 P.M., six days a week. Their hobbies are remarkably few, and their range of interests narrow. One sample of physicians reported spending less than three hours a week in cultural activities and less than four hours a week on family outings.[15]

This life-style helps explain why studies of physicians' family life take titles like Lane Gerber's *Married to Their Careers*. And professional norms reaffirm this outlook, expecting that medicine will not merely dominate but monopolize the practitioner's life, to the exclusion of both family and community. For example, in an address to colleagues, the president of the American College of Cardiology declared that "television, vacations, country clubs, automobiles, household gadgets, travel, movies, races, cards, house hunting, fishing, swimming, concerts, politics, civic committees, and night clubs" all are "distractions . . . [that] leave little time for medicine. . . . To the master cardiologists, the study of cardiology is the only pleasure." That his statement was not ironic or idiosyncratic is evident in the values that medical house staff everywhere are expected to adopt. As one first-year pediatric resident put it: "One of the things you learn from all the work and all the time put in at school and then the hospital is that you can't be very involved with other kinds of interests. Oh you can dabble a little, but that's all. . . . It's as if a person can't be a good doctor and a good wife or mother at the same time." And such an attitude inevitably drove doctor and patient further apart. In the words of another resident: "Sometimes all this emphasis on working constantly seems to lead to a kind of bitterness . . . toward those in society. . . . It is like all of those people are outsiders. They are really not like us. They really don't understand the kind of hours and pressures and all of the other things that happen."[16]

The validity of the lament that doctors and patients inhabit very different worlds is confirmed as well by recent popular literature. The social distance between doctor and patient finds an interesting confirmation in the disappearance of physicians from the pages of modern literature, or more precisely, their disappearance as individuals without a white coat on. The immediate post–World War II novels and stories frequently depicted doctors in hospitals and in examining rooms, but seldom in other contexts. Painters, professors, writers, lawyers, basketball players, sportswriters, soft-drink salespeople, business tycoons, journalists, farmers, and carpenters all have served as heroes or heroines, lovers, or dinner guests. But rarely doctors. A few exceptions aside, writers did not—and for the most part still do not—casually bring a doctor onto their pages. The days when the suitors could be physicians, as in *Middlemarch* or *Uncle Vanya*, have passed, apparently because the physician requires too much introduction and demands too much of a spotlight (as though the reader would ask, Why is a doctor at this party?). The physician is too distant from the writer's imagination, too alien from both the writer's and the readers' world, to fit comfortably in the dining room or the bedroom.

Sometimes, if illness or hospitalization is not integral to the story, a character who becomes a doctor disappears altogether. A 1984 novel by Alice Adams, *Superior Women*, purports to trace the lives of five Radcliffe women from college days through middle age. Actually, it traces only four of them: the fifth, Janet Marr—Jewish, aggressive, and least integrated into the circle—decides to go to medical school, and with that, drops out of the book. Another of the group, Megan Greene, meets up with a young doctor she had known as an undergraduate (the common ploy authors use to bring a doctor into the plot). The two "discuss his work at Columbia-Presbyterian. He tells her a couple of grizzly medical jokes. Of his colleagues there he says, 'A really great bunch of guys.' . . . Their conversation is in fact so sketchy, so impersonal that for a moment Megan crazily wonders if he is really sure who she is." We, in turn, may wonder why connecting a doctor to the rest of humanity seems beyond the reach of the author.[17]

Nathan Zuckerman, on the other hand, in Philip Roth's novel *The Anatomy Lesson* fantasizes about becoming a doctor as a way of alleviating the pains of body and soul. By good fortune, his college roommate, Bobby Freytag, is a physician on the faculty of the University of Chicago (how else would Zuckerman know a doctor personally?). Zuckerman turns to him for advice, only to hear, of course, that forty-year-olds should forget about going to medical school. But Zuckerman does not give up easily. He visits Freytag and envies him, as his German name promises, his freedom, that is, the freedom to become wholly immersed in one's work. " *This is life. With real teeth in it,*' exclaims Zuckerman." No holds are barred: "What the doctor wanted to know the patient told him. Nobody's secret a scandal or a disgrace— everything revealed and everything at stake. And always the enemy was wicked and real." And just how wicked emerges in the patients' diseases: a woman whose face has been half eaten away by cancer, and another who must have her larynx removed. "Another catastrophe— every moment, behind every wall, *right next door*, the worst ordeals that anyone could imagine, pain that was ruthless and inescapably real, crying and suffering truly worthy of all a man's defiance." Zuckerman thrives on it all.

Yet, the practice of medicine emerges as too exotic, too apart from the life that others lead. To read *The Anatomy Lesson* is to learn why most laypeople are content to let doctors take care of disease. The hospital is fantastic, filled with unlimited material for the novelist (or for that matter, the anthropologist), but not a place anyone else would want to frequent. And not coincidentally, neither Bobby nor any of the other physicians come alive except with their white coats on. The interns struck Zuckerman as "artless, innocent children. It was as though, leaving the platform with their medical-school diplomas, they'd taken a wrong turn and fallen back headlong into the second grade." All we learn of Bobby is that he is divorced and has a disobedient son and a grief-stricken, almost crazed father. Of Bobby's colleagues, we meet only one, and he, an emergency room doctor named Walsh, lacks the right stuff to fight disease "day after day . . . over the long haul." "You've got to watch them die without falling apart," he observes. "I can't do that."[18] To be a doctor, then, is to pursue an all-encompassing and worthy calling, but those who respond to it remain shadowy. Medicine is heroic but its knights obscure.

If not obscure, then disconnected. Dr. Solomon, the orthopedic surgeon in C. E. Poverman's 1981 novel, *Solomon's Daughter*, cannot relate to either of his children, Rose or Nick. Medicine is apparently the right profession for a writer to assign to a father who is deeply caring but incapable of reaching out. Nick, as his psychiatrist explains to Solomon, is one of those children "who have given up trying to reach anyone because they feel it won't do any good. They feel they can't make themselves understood or get any real response." Rose, after a wretched marriage, nearly kills herself in an automobile accident and is left severely damaged mentally and physically. Solomon does all he can for her, including performing a futile operation, but she is beyond the reach of either his talents or his love. Dr. Solomon is responsible and caring, but intimacy in his relationships goes beyond his ability—which may well represent the contemporary view of the physician.[19]

The most favorable depiction of a physician in popular literature takes as its hero a doctor of the 1920s and 1930s with a very odd practice. Dr. Wilbur Larch, in John Irving's *Cider House Rules*, is founder and superintendent of the St. Cloud orphanage in Maine, and his practice consists of delivering wanted babies and aborting—illegally—unwanted ones. Larch is by contrast all that a modern doctor is not, bearing even less resemblance to his successors than Mr. Chips would to a grant-driven researcher in a high-powered university. There is nothing conventional—or contemporary—about Larch. He loves his orphans, particularly Homer Wells, and does all in his power to give them a real home; he is equally passionate about the wisdom and ethics of not bringing more orphans into this world. He is not in office or hospital practice but in charge of an asylum; and he is an ether addict. When he selects Homer Wells to be his successor, he trains him as an apprentice (forget about medical schools) and designs an elaborate fraud to get Wells certified as a doctor and appointed as his successor. Larch's purpose in all this is to make certain that love, and not a rigid adherence to rules, will guide Homer's actions and his institution. Thus, when we finally have a doctor as the hero, he is unreal, a throwback to an earlier time—not someone who unites all that is so conflicted in modern medicine, but someone who represents all that modern medicine appears to have lost. Larch is an appealing, even captivating, character but in all ways irrelevant.[20]

Medicine has never lacked critics. As the historian John Burnham noted in a 1982 article aptly entitled "American Medicine's Golden Age: What Happened to It?" there is a venerable tradition of denigrating doctors that stretches from Aristophanes to Molière, and on to Ivan Illich.[21] But as a sense of doctors as strangers and hospitals as strange places permeated American society, the thrust of the critique changed, and so did the implications for public policy.

From the 1930s through the 1950s, most of the attacks on medicine were inspired by shortcomings in the system of health care delivery, particularly because medical care was often beyond the reach of the poor and increasingly placed a heavy financial burden on the middle class, especially the elderly. To critics, like journalist Richard Carter, problems began with the fact that the AMA was a powerful trade lobby and the doctor, a rapacious businessman. The opening pages of his 1958 book, *The Doctor Business*, tell about an accident in which a young boy fell into a well; after volunteers worked unstintingly for twenty-four hours to dig him out, his parents took him to a local doctor, who proceeded to bill $1,500 for his services. A public outcry followed (one U.S. senator spoke of "the outrage in my soul"), and even the AMA disassociated itself ("Not one doctor in a thousand would have charged a fee"). Pointing to this story, Carter criticized the "fee-based relations" between doctor and patient, concluding that "without presuming to tell a single M.D. how to care for a single appendix, the public can upgrade medicine from the bazaar."[22]

This type of faultfinding persisted well into the 1960s. In *The Troubled Calling*, another journalist, Selig Greenberg, described the doctor's position in terms of "the clash between the priestly nature of his vocation and the economic considerations of his career." Wondering why "such a profound discontent and unease hang over the American medical scene at the very time of medicine's greatest triumphs," Greenberg concluded that the public's hostility rested, perhaps unfairly, on an image of the doctor in his Cadillac and his wife in a mink coat. "Medicine has infinitely more to give people than they are actually getting . . . numerous health care needs remain unmet in the richest country in the world. . . . The profession's clinging to a grossly outdated concept of rugged individualism has a great deal to do with the prevailing climate of unrest."[23]

A very different critique characterized the late 1960s and 1970s, inspired not by economics but by distance and distrust, not by considerations of cost but of sentiment. To be sure, even earlier there had been numerous complaints about the unfeeling specialist or busy doctor, but they had never before reached the pitch of these protests or served as the basis for new organizations. The distinctions between the two sources of discontent emerged in the formation of the Society for Health and Human Values. They appeared even more vividly in the approach of the women's rights movement, a movement that at once fed on and reinforced a sense of separation—the doctor as stranger, indeed as male stranger.

The origins of the Society for Health and Human Values, as reconstructed by Daniel Fox, were in the early 1960s, when a small group of clergy concerned with medical ministries constituted themselves as the Committee on Medical Education and Theology. The issues that most worried them were "depersonalization," the "centrality of mechanical biology," and the "teaching of mechanistic medicine." Their goal was somehow to counter these trends through changes in medical education. Although ad hoc, unfunded, and imprecise in its aims, the committee signaled the emergence of a new concern. In 1968, the group expanded, becoming more secular than religious; it changed its name to the Committee on Health and Human Values, and its ranks came to include such physicians as Edmund Pellegrino, who had a sophisticated and abiding interest in these issues.

Not surprisingly, in light of its goals, the committee, at its 1968 meeting, addressed the specific problems emerging in human experimentation and it soon received a grant to examine how academic institutions reviewed such research. But even more central to its mission was the establishment of an institute that would "identify explicitly the human values that are lacking or inadequately represented in the study and practice of medicine and to begin to remedy this deficit." This formulation, in Fox's view, represented a kind of "doctor-bashing"; a tone of adversariness was apparent, as it would be in the introduction of bioethics. But in a larger framework, the committee was attempting to reintegrate medicine's values with societal values, to use the humanities to reduce the insularity and isolation of the medical world. Its methods and strategies were too nebulous to boast of any rapid accomplishments, but its program testified to both the growing recognition of the severity of the problem and the sources of energy that would be devoted to resolving it.[24]

Using a very different language and approach, the new feminism challenged social practices in the physician's office. They redefined doctor-patient relationships that had once seemed natural and appropriate (the good patient as compliant) as part of a larger male design to keep women powerless, and at the same time, as part of a professional design to keep all laypeople powerless. Feminist scholars and advocates denounced both the inherited politics of gender and the politics of the professions, so that the issue of men dominating women was inseparable from doctors dominating patients. Medicine, in fact, was a sitting target, first, because its ranks were almost exclusively male, and at least in obstetrics and gynecology, all the patients were female. Second, the medical establishment had been expansive in its reach, medicalizing phenomena that had once been outside the doctor's ken, capturing for its own professional territory the area of reproduction, childbirth, and sexuality. To the feminists and their supporters (like Illich), these matters ought to have remained in the lay world, particularly with the women in that world.

Feminist scholars explored the history of medicine not to celebrate great discoveries or to trace the scientific progress of the profession but to analyze the dynamics by which male doctors had excluded women and enlarged their own domain. The articles and books were passionate, even bitter, as they described physicians' opposition to women's education (on the grounds that their frail bodies could not tolerate the strain), the exclusion of women from medical schools (on the assumption that they were not sufficiently dedicated to or temperamentally suited for medicine), and the insistence that women's proper place was in the private sphere (in the belief that anatomy dictated destiny, that God had fashioned a uterus and then built the woman around it). Feminist researchers then went on to explore more generally the medicalization of American society. When doctors expelled midwives from the delivery room, or when doctors replaced women as the authors of popular child-rearing tracts, the change spoke to a reduced role not only for women but for all laypeople. When male doctors discriminated against women physicians, they were minimizing the role of sympathy against science in the profession, and thereby encouraging an impersonal and distant style of medical practice.

Feminists presented these same points to a wider public in such best-selling books as *Our Bodies, Ourselves*, originally published in 1971. Their primary target was gynecologists, but the onslaught extended to all (male) doctors, and the prescriptions were not gender specific. Take, for example, its summary paragraph on doctors: "The image and myth of the doctor as humanitarian, which has been so assiduously sold to the American public for the last fifty years, is out of date. If there ever were such doctors, they are mostly all gone now. . . . Most men in practice today most closely resemble the American businessman: repressed, compulsive, and more interested in money (and the disease process) than in people." Ascribing most of the blame to medical education and medical recruitment, the authors of *Our Bodies, Ourselves* complained that "medical students are usually very carefully selected by men who are attempting to reproduce themselves, and usually succeed. After four years of training they have almost invariably become . . . even more detached and mechanistic than they were to start with. As a group they are also more immature emotionally and sexually than their peers or the rest of the population. . . . Most doctors finishing their training are in late adolescence, psychologically speaking." The concluding advice to women—really, to all patients—followed logically on the critique: "We want you to be more alert to your responsibility in the relationship, just as you would in any other adult relationship where you are purchasing services."[25] The rules for patients had changed: docile obedience was to give way to wary consumerism. Thus, if kept waiting, a patient should take her business elsewhere; if denied information, she should find another source. The adage "never trust a stranger" now expanded to "never trust a doctor."

One final piece of evidence confirms just how widely shared this judgment was becoming in the post-1965 period, namely, the mounting sense of crisis around malpractice litigation. The apparent increase in litigation (record-keeping methods varied so greatly from state to state that firm conclusions on actual increases were difficult to reach) spurred a 1969 congressional study (chaired by Connecticut's Senator Abraham Ribicoff) of what role the federal government might play in resolving the problem. Then, two years later, President Richard Nixon appointed a HEW commission to study the causes and issue recommendations, and the AMA also organized a survey. Although these various committees noted that American society was becoming more litigious generally, they agreed that one critical element in the rise of malpractice suits was the breakdown of the doctor–patient relationship. The overwhelming majority of suits were filed against specialists, not general practitioners, because here the distance between physician and patient was greatest. Thus, it was experts in malpractice law, not consumer activists, who counseled doctors: "When the physician–patient rapport remains at a high level of trust and confidence, most patients will ride out a bad result, but when that rapport is inadequate in the beginning or is permitted to deteriorate in route, a suit is likely to follow."[26] Not only were patients distrustful of strangers, they were ready to sue them.

No one document better illustrates how new social attitudes and practices redefined both the concept of the good patient and the obligations of health care professionals and institutions than the Patient Bill of Rights, promulgated first by the Joint Commission on the Accreditation of Hospitals (JCAH) in 1970 and formally adopted by the American Hospital Association (AHA) in 1973. The initial inspiration for the document came, fittingly enough, from the National Welfare Rights Organization (NWRO). Dedicated to bringing a rights orientation into areas dominated by concepts of charity and worthiness, its leaders devoted most of their energy to making relief and welfare policies responsive to a concept of entitlement. But the NWRO also focused on other institutions that affected the lives of the poor, including public schools, and most important in our context, voluntary and public hospitals. Recognizing that the hospital system was essentially two-track, with the poor typically consigned to twelve-bed wards, treated by medical students and house staff, and, apparently, disproportionately experimented on by investigators, the NWRO attempted to impose a rights model on hospitals. In 1970, it presented a list of twenty-six proposals to the JCAH, and after negotiations, the JCAH incorporated a number of them into the preamble to that group's "Accreditation Manual." This preamble was the only document composed by health care professionals that *Our Bodies, Ourselves* reprinted and credited.[27]

As befit its origins with the NWRO, the preamble first addressed issues that particularly affected the poor. First, "no person should be denied impartial access to treatment . . . on the basis of . . . race, color, creed, national origin, or the nature of the source of payment." In this same spirit, all patients had a right to privacy, including the right not to be interviewed without their consent by "representatives of agencies not connected with the hospital," that is, welfare agencies. A patient's right to privacy also meant a respect for "the privacy of his body," and so, regardless of source of payment, the patient should be examined "shield[ed] . . . from the views of others" and should be made a part of clinical training programs (for medical students) only voluntarily. These points made, the preamble framers then addressed concerns that affected all patients, whatever their social or economic status. The process of defining rights moved across tracks, from concerns more relevant to the poor to concerns relevant to everyone. Thus, the document continued: "The patient has the right to receive . . . adequate information concerning the nature and extent of his medical problem, the planned course of treatment, and prognosis." In brief, all patients had the right to be told the truth about their medical condition.

The preamble served as the basis for the 1972 Patient Bill of Rights, adopted by the AHA after a three-year discussion by a committee that included not only the trustees of the association but four outsiders representing consumer organizations. The first of the twelve points in this bill of rights was a general statement of the right to "considerate and respectful care," and then the document addressed the most central concern, patient consent. It enlarged on the JCAH standard for truth telling by insisting that explanations be given in ways that "the patient can reasonably be expected to understand," and spelled out, in language reminiscent of the FDA stipulations, the requirements for obtaining consent both in treatment and experimentation. Its remaining points emphasized the patient's right to privacy and to a "reasonable" degree of continuity of care.

To be sure, the document disappointed a number of patients' rights activists.[28] They were quick to note that rights would not be achieved when they were handed down from on high by the medical establishment. Willard Gaylin, a psychiatrist who at that moment was helping to organize the Hastings Institute of Society, Ethics and the Life Sciences, charged that the process amounted to "the thief lecturing his victim on self-protection."[29] Others observed that none of these documents (or the variants on them that particular hospitals adopted) included any procedures for enforcement or for levying penalties, and still others criticized them because the stipulations on truth telling allowed a major exception: when doctors believed that bad news would be harmful to the patient, they were to convey it to the family. Indeed, the provisions on consent generally appeared to be self-serving restatements of legal precedents intended to reduce the frequency of patient dissatisfaction with physicians, and thereby, the frequency of malpractice suits.[30]

But these objections notwithstanding, the preamble and bill of rights had both symbolic and real importance, affecting attitudes and practices of both doctors and patients. The position on truth telling, for example, at once acknowledged the need for physicians to follow a new standard and promoted its realization. When the 1960s began, almost all physicians (90 percent in one study) reported that their "usual policy" was not to tell patients about a finding of cancer. By the close of the 1970s, an equal percentage reported that they usually did tell patients such a diagnosis.[31] Practice may not have always conformed to stated principles, but there is no doubt that, given traditional mores, a small revolution had been effected.

Thus the Patient Bill of Rights reflected the new ideological orientation that was making the concept of rights so powerful throughout American society. Leading national professional organizations, responding to external pressures, were now adopting the language and concepts of rights to delineate medical obligations. Behind the transformation lay, first, the recognition that the social distancing of doctor from patient and hospital from community rendered obsolete inherited maxims and practices. But to understand this reorientation fully, we must continue our story, for the transformation in medical decision making also reflected a series of developments taking place in medicine itself. We must return again to the 1960s, this time to examine the impact of the extraordinary innovations in the science and practice of organ transplantation.

CHAPTER 8

Life Through Death

T HE scandals in human experimentation and the broader, but no less potent, sense of the doctor as stranger first introduced new players and new rules to the once insular field of medicine. But however important these initial changes, they were only the opening forays. In the 1960s, medical procedures and technologies, especially in the area of organ transplantation, posed questions that appeared to some physicians—and to even more nonphysicians—to go beyond the fundamental principles of medical ethics or the expertise of the doctor and to require societal intervention. One advance after another framed questions that seemed to demand resolution in the public arena, not the doctor's office. Put another way, these issues combined to take medical ethics (and, to a degree, medical decision making) out of the hands of the doctor and empower a new group of lay participants.

No sooner does one mention medical procedures and technologies than a cloud of clichés threatens to descend on the subject. By now it is common for television documentaries or talk-debate shows to open with the observation that medical technology has forced agonizing choices upon us, that technology has created hard questions for which there are no right answers. But shrouded within this mist are a series of critical developments that should be highlighted. For one, it was not medical technology alone that was responsible for the change but the fact that the technology appeared at a special time, when Americans' long-lived romance with machines was weakening, indeed, when Americans' trust in physicians was weakening. For another, the technology came in special ways that were neither inevitable nor predictable, challenging the inherited precepts of medical ethics not only by an initial scarcity but by compelling doctors to make unusual trade-offs and choices. As we shall soon see, the fact that organ transplantation was the test case (as against, say, artificial organ replacement) engendered a whole series of novel dilemmas. For still another, despite the lament that there are no right answers, the more critical point is that an entirely new group of people, whether in government, the law, or the academy, were ready to pose the questions and even attempt to answer them. Finally, these developments provoked a fascinating split within medicine itself. Some doctors followed Beecher's example, alerting outsiders as well as insiders to the problems at hand. Others, the larger contingent by far, complained bitterly about the efforts to trespass on their domain, attempting by one or another strategy to rebuild their fences. For the most part, the effort was futile, but it did lend a combative tone to the entire enterprise.

The first of the technological developments that called into question the sovereignty of physicians over medical ethics and decision making involved kidney dialysis, one of the earliest and most successful of life-saving interventions. The question that the dialysis machines posed was perfectly framed to rivet both professional and lay attention. In formal terms, How was access to the technology to be determined? In its more popular version, Who gave out the seats in the only lifeboat? The answer was, not necessarily the ship's captain.

The issue captured nationwide attention in 1962, courtesy of an extraordinary piece of reporting by Shana Alexander in *Life* magazine. Two years earlier, Dr. Belding Scribner of the University of Washington Medical School in Seattle had made the breakthrough that transformed kidney dialysis from a short-term to a long-term treatment. Techniques had existed since World War II to treat an acute episode of kidney failure; William Kolff, in the Netherlands under German occupation, had devised a way to filter a patient's blood through a cellophane tubing, thereby cleansing it of impurities. The difficulty was that in order to undertake the process, a surgeon had to cut into an artery and vein to divert the flow of blood through the cleansing filter and then back to the body again—and sooner, rather than later, the patient exhausted available blood vessels. In the case of a traumatic and temporary injury to the kidneys, this mode of dialysis could tide a patient over until the organ recovered. But if the problem was chronic kidney failure, the process was useless.

In 1960, Dr. Scribner designed a permanent indwelling shunt that allowed the patient to be connected to the dialysis machine, plugged in as it were, in a matter of minutes and without a new surgical procedure. Now patients with chronic end-stage kidney disease could be kept alive with the machine performing the function of the kidneys. But the machines were in very short supply, with far fewer available than the number of patients who could benefit from them. Thus arose the decision Alexander explored in her article: who would live and who would die.

To answer the question about allocation of this scarce resource, the Seattle physicians asked the county medical society to appoint a lay committee of seven "quite ordinary people" to determine "life or death." Alexander sat in on their meetings and described their procedures and responses. The physicians at the hospital initially screened out all kidney patients not medically or psychiatrically suited for the procedure. They also made some "rather arbitrary decisions," such as ruling out children and anyone over forty-five years of age; even so, the number of claimants was still too high. The committee itself decided to limit access to residents of the state of Washington on the dubious grounds that state tax dollars had supported the research, but four candidates still remained for each place. So to select the fortunate patients, the committee relied heavily on family considerations, giving preference to heads of households with a wife and children to support. It also attempted to weigh the contribution each of the candidates would make to the community—If we give you life, what will you do for us?—invoking criteria of a conventional middle-class sort: church membership, scout work, and the like.

As fascinating as it is to reconstruct how the Seattle committee did its job, the most critical feature for our purposes is that a group of physicians, in unprecedented fashion, turned over to a lay committee life-or-death decisions prospectively and on a case-by-case basis. A prerogative that had once been the exclusive preserve of the doctor was delegated to community representatives. Why did the physicians make this extraordinary grant of power? In part, a lay committee would protect the doctors from political fallout, from charges of doing each other favors (as when the wife of a fellow physician fell ill and needed dialysis) or from abusing their authority. In part, too, a lay committee seemed preferable to a lottery or to a first-come, first-served rule. In this sense, the committee was a symbolic representation of the hope (or faith?) that a scarce resource could be distributed without abdicating all ethical responsibility, that life and death were not arbitrary, that the "good" people should first be spared suffering. The committee's assignment was daunting, but the alternative of a random process, of letting chance rule, seemed worse.

Most important, physicians turned to a lay committee because they realized that the traditional medical ethic of each doctor doing everything possible to enhance the well-being of the particular patient could not operate in these circumstances. It was apparent to the physicians that the decision was unresolvable if each advocated the well-being of an individual patient and urged that he or she be given access to the machine. Hence, it seemed preferable to empower a lay committee rather than compel doctors to abdicate their responsibilities. Rather than have physicians give first allegiance to the functioning of the system as a whole, the Seattle group turned to outsiders for help.

In making this choice, the committee transmitted a message, as Alexander accurately noted: the "acceptance of the principle that all segments of society, not just the medical fraternity, should share the burden of choice as to which patients to treat and which to let die. Otherwise society would be forcing the doctors alone to play God."[1] No matter how idiosyncratic the dialysis experience, the inevitable conclusion to be drawn from it was that experts in kidney functioning were not experts in judging the comparative value of lives. The result was that a once exclusive prerogative of the doctor was becoming socialized. A lay committee—by physicians' invitation, to be sure—had entered the examining room.

Even with this innovation, the Seattle experience did not sit well with Americans. That anyone, whether doctors or a group of laypeople, should be playing God was unseemly—and all the more so as word got out on how such committees reached their decisions. There was a patent unfairness to preferring the married over the single, the employed over the unemployed, or churchgoers over nonchurchgoers; it seemed positively un-American to reward conformists over nonconformists—or as the authors of a highly critical law review article remarked, for the Pacific Northwest to be so inhospitable toward a Henry David Thoreau with kidney trouble. Thus, the Seattle experience taught a second lesson: committees, whatever their makeup, would not necessarily resolve difficult choices. One might well need to construct principles or guidelines to make certain that medical decision making represented more than the accumulated prejudices of a handful of people, whether their training was medical or not.*

As with dialysis, physicians found the principles of traditional medical ethics inadequate to cope with the innovations in transplantation. The problems that the new techniques of kidney transplantation posed about maiming the healthy, allocating scarce resources, and defining death led a core of physicians again to bring outsiders into medicine's territory.

Although the thought of transplanting a major organ from one person or animal to another has ancient roots, and sporadic attempts to carry it out had occurred in the nineteenth and early twentieth centuries, not until the late 1940s did the procedure become more than a fantasy. The first experiments were with the kidney, for this organ was paired (making donation possible without the donor incurring great risk), and the surgical techniques were relatively simple (in contrast, for example, to transplanting a liver). The chief barrier to success was the immune system, which reacted to the new organ as though it were a foreign body and tried to reject it. In 1954 surgeons at Boston's Peter Bent Brigham Hospital successfully transplanted a kidney from one identical twin to another, thereby demonstrating that when im-

*A third lesson emerged from the experience, one worth noting briefly because of its staying power and controversial character: problems of scarce medical resources can be resolved by money. Congress eventually underwrote the costs of care for all patients with end-stage kidney disease, the first time a specific patient group received open-ended funding; and with funds available, the proliferation of dialysis machines and centers followed quickly. But as we shall see, not all allocation decisions are resolvable in this fashion, and it is debatable whether the federal budget will support such programs again.

munological responses were minimized (because of the twin's genetic similarity), the procedure was feasible. But the lifesaving feat did not point the way to controlling rejection in cases where recipients and donors were unrelated.

Investigators experimented with a number of procedures to reduce the immune response without leaving the body helpless to fight off infections. After initial failures (including the use of massive doses of X rays), they identified several chemotherapeutic agents that inhibited rejection without completely crippling the body's ability to combat disease. The number of kidney transplants then rose, and so did the success rates. In 1963 and 1964, a total of 222 kidney transplants were performed, and about half of the recipients were alive one year after the operation. Patients who received kidneys from relatives had the best chance of success (12-month survival rates for 4 out of 5 identical twins, 31 out of 45 siblings, but only 9 of 29 unrelated donors, which was about the same success ratio for those receiving kidneys from cadavers). Still, everyone recognized that more sophisticated chemical agents would soon make the procedure even more effective.[2]

In its experimental phase, kidney transplantation, particularly involving cadaver organs, raised ethical issues relatively easy to resolve. Although the death rates for the first recipients were high (most dying within a few months after the procedure), the surgeons persisted, and no one faulted them, for all the patients were on the verge of death and had no alternatives—dialysis for chronic patients was still in the future. In the 1960s, even unusual variations in transplantation research did not create significant controversy. When Dr. Keith Reemtsma, then at Tulane, put a chimpanzee kidney into a patient dying of kidney disease, there were practically no public protests and only a few raised eyebrows at the NIH. So too, Thomas Starzl, then a surgeon at the University of Colorado Medical School, solicited kidney donations from prison inmates for transplantation; when a few physicians, informally, took him to task, Starzl stopped the practice. Had kidney transplantation had to undergo scrutiny only as an experiment, it would have fitted neatly under the emerging codes governing research.[3]

As transplantation moved from experiment to therapy, however, a whole series of novel questions had to be addressed. Once again, as with dialysis, the bedrock principle of medical ethics—namely, physicians as the uncompromising advocates for their patients—did not resolve the questions at hand. A physician determined to give his or her patient the best of care faced a series of dilemmas once transplantation became a treatment option.

These dilemmas were laid out with special clarity at a three-day conference in 1966, under the auspices of the CIBA Foundation, which explored "Ethics in Medical Progress, With Special Reference to Transplantation." The conference attendees were almost all physicians, except for one lawyer and one minister; in 1966 a medical conference on ethics was still largely an internal affair. But a recognition of the limits of traditional medical ethics did prompt the participants to call for wider counsel from those who had not before played a role in medical decision making. Michael Woodruff, a transplant surgeon at the University of Edinburgh and the organizer of the conference, made this point in his opening remarks: "This symposium was planned because of the growing realization that progress in medicine brings in its train ethical problems which are the concern not only of practicing doctors but of the whole community, and which are unlikely to be solved without intensive study of an interdisciplinary kind."[4]

The first of the ethical problems that Woodruff identified was that transplant surgeons would be removing a healthy organ from a would-be donor, and such an operation might well constitute maiming a patient, a purposeful infliction of harm. Whatever the benefit to the recipient, the removal of a kidney posed an immediate danger to the donor (the anesthesia itself, to say nothing of the surgery, carried a low but real risk), as well as a long-term one—for the remaining kidney might become diseased. Some of the physicians responded that donating a kidney was the same as dashing into a burning building to rescue a trapped child; but the contention was quickly rebutted, because the would-be rescuer, unlike the kidney donor, was not directly harming himself. His aim was to bring out the child and have both of them escape—any ensuing injury would be an indirect and unintended result of his action. But in transplantation, the injury was inseparable from the act, the essence of the donation itself.[5] Woodruff wondered whether the ethical dilemma was resolved in light of the fact that the risks of living with only one kidney were low. But others countered that a maiming was no less a maiming if the injury inflicted was relatively minor. Besides, whatever the risks, medical ethics would seem to preclude a physician from carrying out such a procedure. "As physicians motivated and educated to make sick people well, we make a basic qualitative shift in our aims when we risk the health of a well person, no matter how pure our motives."[6]

The fact that the donor consented to the procedure did not obviate the difficulties. The scandals around human experimentation made all the conference participants acutely aware of the need for donor consent, but they were not convinced that the consent could be truly voluntary. Did a twin who was asked to give one of her kidneys to her dying sister make a noncoerced choice? Was she truly free to say no? And what about taking a kidney from a minor? Could a parent agree to the donation on behalf of the child? (Physicians at the Brigham hospital had already faced this dilemma and had requested and received court approval for the donation.)[7] Until now, physicians had been confident that a patient's consent to a therapeutic intervention was little more than a technicality, for doctors would not perform a procedure against the patient's best interest. But in transplantation, the premise did not hold. In strictly medical terms, losing a healthy kidney could not advance the patient's well-being.

Second, as the CIBA participants recognized, this new form of therapy, like dialysis before it, posed in stark and unavoidable terms the problem of triage, of allocating scarce resources among a pool of would-be beneficiaries. Rationing was certainly not new to medicine, and it was widely recognized both within and outside the profession that not all who required services received them. But the rationing that went on was covert, unacknowledged, and most important, external to the doctor's office. If the poor did not receive the same care as the rich, it was not the physician who made the choice or necessarily had any firsthand awareness of the problem. (Indeed, many physicians insisted, justifiably, that they reduced their fees for low-income patients and contributed their fair share of charity work.) Transplantation, however, placed the problem of rationing directly into the doctors' hands. Now physicians, not some impersonal social force or government agency, would have to select the patient who would receive the benefit of life-saving medical technology, and neither they nor anyone else had much experience in making such choices. Even triage under battlefield conditions was of little relevance. Physicians there passed over the hopeless case or the minor one so as to treat those who would most benefit from medical intervention; transplantation (and dialysis, as well) forced a choice among *all* those who would most benefit from intervention. Moreover, the physician who remained a staunch advocate for his or her patient rendered any choice among patients impossible, and the result was a stalemate. Forceful advocacy, in other words, did not solve the dilemma but exacerbated it.

Finally, the CIBA conference addressed an issue that transplantation framed in a most dramatic way: the definition of death. The issue needed to be confronted in order to increase the efficacy of the transplant procedure; if physicians continued to mark death by the stoppage of the heart, they maximized the potential for damage, for kidneys deprived of blood even for a short time deteriorated. As we shall see, the need to define death also arose from causes independent of transplantation, namely, the new artificial respirators. "Many people," noted Woodruff, "are now maintained in a sort of twilight state by the use of machines which do the work of their lung or their heart while they are completely unconscious. . . . Many of these people will never resume an independent existence away from the machines, but they can't stay on the machines for ever and ever. . . . One has to decide therefore when to switch off the machines."[8] But the decision was still more complex in transplantation. In the case of general organ failure, physicians at the bedside reached a decision that they believed represented the wishes of the patient. The transplant surgeon, however, appeared to be in a conflicted situation—possibly more concerned about the well-being of the organ recipient than the potential organ donor. In short, transplantation put the physician in the position of having to confront not only the difficult question of when life is over, but the even more excruciating question of when life is over for one patient when another may benefit.

The transformation that began with kidney dialysis and transplantation accelerated dramatically with heart transplantation. Not only did the medical marvels of this procedure capture the public's imagination in a way that no postwar innovation had, but so did its ethical and social implications. After heart transplantation, there was no keeping medical ethics or medical decision making exclusively a physician's prerogative.

With ample justification, 1968 was labeled the "year of the heart transplant." The first operation was performed by South Africa's Dr. Christiaan Barnard in December 1967. Although the recipient, Louis Washkansky, lived only eighteen days, Barnard immediately took his place alongside Charles Lindbergh, John Glenn, and other pioneering heroes. Within a short time a number of American surgeons, including Adrian Kantrowitz and Norman Shumway, performed transplants. In fact, the initial enthusiasm for the procedure was so overwhelming that in 1968, surgeons performed 108 transplants and in November alone, 26 transplants.

Francis Moore, a professor of surgery at Harvard and Peter Bent Brigham Hospital and an exceptionally articulate and socially aware physician, immediately recognized the implications of heart transplantation for medical ethics. In the early 1960s Moore had written at length and with insight about the ethics of kidney transplants. (His 1965 book, *Give and Take*, remains one of the best histories of kidney transplantations.)[9] Now, in the late 1960s, he was convinced that heart transplantation gave an unprecedented popularity, even panache, to the field. And like a climber who learns that others—and amateurs at that—have discovered his favorite route, Moore fretted about the impact that outsiders might have. Heart transplantation, he noted, "has brought a new set of ideas and perplexities to the general public. A surprising number of eminent people, who appear to be surprised, shocked, and startled into public statements by heart transplants, have actually been silent, apathetic, and as uninvolved as distant spectators during the extremely critical years of kidney transplantation in the United States." Moore trusted that they would study this earlier experience, especially what he and others had said about it, for otherwise, "listeners and readers must likewise be sentenced to a long series of statements by newcomers as they gradually become aware of the problems that others have faced and solved for many years."[10]

Moore's expectation that newcomers would respect and appreciate that doctors had been there first was fanciful. Heart transplantation did raise many of the same questions as kidney transplantation, but the fact that it was now hearts meant that concerns about conflict of interest, the definition of death, and allocation of the scarce organs commanded wider attention and made it seem more obvious that the questions were too fraught with social and political consequences to allow doctors to monopolize the discussion. From 1968 to 1970 the ranks of those ready to influence medical decision making increased dramatically, and the popular press, academic journals, and the *Congressional Record* all reflected the change.

Again, it was not a medical procedure or technology that was the decisive consideration but the widespread sense that older rules of medicine no longer were sufficient to guide decisions. Heart transplantation made it apparent that an ethic of advocating for one's patient and doing no harm were not sufficient to the task of knowing when to terminate care for one patient so another might live. One Oregon physician, writing in the *Journal of the American Medical Association,* declared that "the people, law, and medicine must come into some comfortable and realistic rapprochement on the moral, ethical, legal, humanistic, and economic aspects of this problem," precisely because transplantation involves the interests of "two individuals, the donor and the recipient."[11] Another physician, a neurosurgeon, went even further, urging in a *New England Journal of Medicine* article that his colleagues do the almost unthinkable, that is, adopt the mind-set of lawyers in order to resolve what appeared "at least on the surface to be a conflict of interest." Attorneys "can remain the best of friends . . . and yet fight each other relentlessly in the courtroom on their respective client's behalf." In this spirit, physicians should take sides, one protecting his patient's welfare (the potential donor) even as his colleague (representing the recipient) clamored for the organ. "This state of mind," he conceded, "is foreign to the physician's make-up, since he has always worked with his colleagues for a common cause." But transplantation compelled physicians to recognize "a conflict of interest, acknowledge its existence," and adopt a new outlook.[12]

Those outside, as well as inside, medicine fully appreciated the strains that transplantation placed on the conventional doctor–patient relationship. Even as the popular press devoted pages to Barnard's first transplant, it pondered the potential for conflict of interest. "Can I ever be certain," *Newsweek* reported one woman as saying, "that doctors would do everything possible to save my life if I had a nasty accident or a terrible disease, that they would not be influenced by what I could contribute to another person?"[13] In effect, heart transplantation helped to equate the physician with the researcher and the patient with the subject. No one—neither doctor nor patient—could be confident that the patient's best interest would be the sole or even central concern. The doctor at the bedside might be thinking about benefits to humanity—by perfecting the heart transplant procedure— or about benefits to the patient in the next room who needed a new heart, but not necessarily about the desperate patient before him.

Heart transplantation also required exquisite calculations on allocating scarce medical resources, a predicament that encouraged lay involvement in medical decision making. Questions of allocations obviously had a social component: Was it in the public interest to devote enormous resources to a procedure that would benefit only a handful of individuals? And whatever the answer, it was evident to many observers that the profession would have to be far more open and sharing about the decision. "The public has acquired the right to be informed of our activities," declared Dr. Rene Menguy, chairman of the department of surgery at the University of Chicago School of Medicine. "There is no place in our own society for taxation without representation, and for the simple reason that the American public has supported our efforts . . . it has acquired the right to be informed of our activities. Whether we like it or not the transplantation of a human heart, like a space launch at Cape Kennedy, now belongs to the public domain."[14] For heart transplantation to flourish, the legislature had to be allowed into the examining room.

Finally, whatever ambiguities about the definition of death could be skirted with kidney transplantation or with mechanical respirators had to be confronted directly when the heart was the organ at issue.[15] Even as late as 1968, neither the use of cadaver kidney transplants nor the dependence on mechanical respirators was sufficient to make brain death a public issue. To be sure, the number of patients using artificial breathing devices in intensive care units had increased, and so had those in a kind of limbo between life and death—not alive, because they were in a coma and incapable of breathing of their own; but not dead, because their heart and lungs, albeit with mechanical assistance, continued to function. But the question of what should be done was not yet of general concern (and would not be until 1976, when Karen Ann Quinlan's parents asked to have her removed from a respirator). The issue remained relatively obscure because doctors, inside the closed world of the intensive care units, turned off the machines when they believed the patient's death was imminent and irreversible. "Very few hospitals," reported a committee of neurologists in 1969, "had any regulations on the matter of discontinuing the mechanical aids to respiration and circulation. No one has encountered any medicolegal difficulties. Very few have sought legal opinions."[16] The intensive care units were a private domain, whatever the formal definition of death, and doctors exercised their discretion.

Heart transplantation, however, a far more public act, forced a clear-cut consideration of the validity of a brain-death standard. Once doctors transplanted a beating heart from donor to recipient—and the feat was celebrated in the media—the need to redefine death was readily apparent. The heart to be transplanted, remarked one noted surgeon, "should be removed and implanted in the recipient patient as close as possible to the moment when death of the donor can be established. This fact makes transplantation surgery more dramatic, and gives rise to much more emotional thinking and discussion than any other field of surgery has done."[17]

The first systematic effort at redefinition took place at Harvard, for reasons that return us to Henry Beecher. His concern for the ethics of experimentation had prompted Harvard to establish a Standing Committee on Human Studies, in essence a research review committee, with Beecher as its chairman. Since Beecher was an anesthesiologist, he had daily experience with respirators and intensive care units, and his surgeon colleagues at the Massachusetts General Hospital, especially Dr. Joseph Murray, had led the way in kidney transplantation. (Murray later won the Nobel Prize in Medicine for his work in this area.) All these elements encouraged him in October 1967 to suggest to Robert Ebert, the dean of the Harvard Medical School, that the Committee on Human Studies broaden its concerns to redefine death: "Both Dr. Murray and I think the time has come for a further consideration of the definition of death. Every major hospital has patients stacked up wait-ing for suitable donors."[18] Ebert thought the idea a good one, but it took Barnard's transplant feat to have him appoint such a committee. "With its pioneering interest in organ transplantation," Ebert told prospective committee members, "I believe the faculty of the Harvard Medical School is better equipped to elucidate this area than any other single group."[19]

The committee, which became known as the Harvard Brain Death Committee, deliberated from January through August 1968, and its final report, published in *JAMA*, represents an important transition in the history of who shall rule medicine.[20] On the one hand, the com-mittee was sensitive to many of the legal and ethical implications of its assignment, taking the still unusual step of including among its mem-bers nonphysicians. Not only were all the appropriate medical special-ties represented—medicine, anesthesiology, and neurosurgery (for its work with electroencephalographic [EEG] machines), but so was law, in the person of health law professor William Curran. Beecher also asked Professor George Williams of the Harvard Divinity School to join the committee, but Williams suggested instead "not a church his-torian who instinctively looks to the past, but rather a professional ethicist," someone "primarily oriented to the present and the future." Williams recommended his colleague Ralph Potter, who had already written on abortion and "whose special ethical field right now is the problem of the just war in the atomic age."[21] Beecher followed his advice and the committee had both a lawyer and a philosopher. At the same time, the committee's approach remained traditional in the sense that its members supported prerogatives for medicine that were in the process of being challenged, attempting, unsuccessfully, to make the definition of death a strictly medical concern. In the end, the Harvard report did not so much resolve the questions around brain death as propel them into the public domain.

The committee worked smoothly and quickly. Its members agreed from the outset that irreversible coma should be "a new criterion for death," and without much difficulty they defined the procedures that should establish the condition: two flat EEG readings from a patient not on barbiturates who displayed no reflex activity. The committee was quick, indeed too quick, to presume a broad social consensus on the desirability of a brain-death definition. The members concluded that at a time when "the improvements in resuscitative and support measures . . . [produce] an individual whose heart continues to beat but whose brain is irreversibly damaged," everyone was likely to agree that new criteria for terminating treatment were desirable. "The burden is great on patients who suffer permanent loss of intellect, on their families, on the hospitals, and on those in need of hospital beds already occupied by these comatose patients." Surely what was best for society—like making hospital beds more available—was best for the individual. The committee was also very concerned with transplant patients. "An issue of secondary but by no means minor importance," read the introduction to an early draft of the report, "is that with increased experience and knowledge and development in transplantation, there is great need for tissues and organs of, among others, the patient whose cerebrum has been hopelessly destroyed in order to restore those who are salvageable."[22]

Finally, the committee insisted that defining the concept of death and formally pronouncing death were the exclusive privilege of doctors: "The patient's condition can be determined only by a physician. When the patient is hopelessly damaged as defined above, the family and all colleagues who have participated in major decisions concerning the patient, and all nurses involved, should be so informed. Death is to be declared and *then* the respirator turned off. The decision to do this and the responsibility for it are to be taken by the physician-in-charge, in consultation with one or more physicians who have been directly involved in the case. It is unsound and undesirable to force the family to make the decision." The committee gave short shrift to potential religious objections and even to the role of law. "If this [brain death] position is adopted by the medical community," the members declared, "it can form the basis for change in the current legal concept of death. No statutory change in the law should be necessary since the law treats this question essentially as one of fact to be determined by physicians."[23] In effect, the committee presumed that because a doctor pronounced a particular patient to be dead, therefore doctors automatically were the ones who should define the standard of death.

The Harvard Brain Death Committee had many supporters among doctors. Medical journals endorsed its recommendations both because its case for brain death was well substantiated and they shared its readiness to maintain physician authority.[24] As one *JAMA* editorial noted: "In the resolution of whatever differences there are between medical and legal definitions of death, it seems clear that physicians rather than barristers must be the ones to establish the rules. . . . Lawyers and judges are not biologists, nor are they often 'in at the death.' They would doubtless be glad to follow the leader."[25]

And yet, the Harvard committee members sensed that the group's effort to control the definition of death might not succeed. The report did, after all, urge the physician in charge of the patient to consult with other colleagues—something not ordinarily required in pronouncing death—because it might be helpful in "providing an important degree of protection against later questions which might be raised." The committee also recognized that the patient's family might want to have a say in the decision to discontinue the respirator and firmly advised that "it is unsound and undesirable to force the family to make the decision." But even this formulation suggested a more complicated reality than the committee would admit. If the physician was first to pronounce the patient dead and then to turn off the machine, then the family's intervention was not merely unsound but absurd. To debate the role of the family was to recognize on some level that a finding of brain death involved more than strictly medical criteria; no matter what the committee said, this pronouncement of death was not like all other pronouncements of death. The committee might well wish to assert its authority, but the family, like the bar and the pulpit, would not necessarily abdicate responsibility.

Hence, the Harvard report immediately sparked criticism and opposition. A number of medical colleagues took Beecher himself to task, arguing that his eagerness to facilitate transplantation violated the very maxims he had set forth to govern human experimentation, namely, that worthwhile ends do not justify unethical means. When Ebert had reviewed an early draft, he counseled Beecher to modify the introductory language on transplantation. "The connotation of this statement is unfortunate, for it suggests that you wish to redefine death in order to make viable organs more readily available to persons requiring transplants. Immediately the reader thinks how this principle might be abused. . . . Would it not be better to state the problem, and indicate that obsolete criteria for the definition of death can lead to controversy in obtaining organs for transplantation?"[26] Beecher and the rest of the committee agreed, and adopted more guarded language: "The decision to declare the person dead, and then to turn off the respirator [should] be made by physicians not involved in any later effort to transplant organs or tissue from the deceased individual. This is advisable in order to avoid any appearance of self-interest by the physicians involved."[27] But even so, the suspicion remained that brain death was a tactic that would sacrifice the well-being of some patients for that of others.

Still more controversial outside of the profession was the committee's readiness to have physicians unilaterally define the moment of death. Just how problematic the position was is apparent from the extensive media coverage of the issue; if this had simply been a doctor's prerogative, one would not have seen articles on "When Is Death?" become commonplace in magazines like *Reader's Digest* and "thanatology" become a headline word in *Time*.[28] And at least some physicians found this attention altogether proper. A lengthy editorial in the *Annals of Internal Medicine*, entitled "When Do We Let the Patient Die?" declared: "The public is becoming much more aware and wants to know, and indeed should know, about these problems; after all, they not only are the final arbiters of the moral standards operative in our society— they are the patients."[29]

The brain-death issue galvanized more than a diffuse public discussion. Particular groups, especially religious ones, insisted on having their say. The Harvard committee blurred facts (this patient is dead) and values (this is the proper definition of death), but others scrupulously maintained the distinction. Thus, one Protestant ethicist argued that only religious leaders could "dispel our myths about life and death"; and if he was ready in this instance to put religion at the service of medicine "by disspiritualizing the heart from its poetic and romantic mythicization and shattering the superstition which surrounds the life–death threshold," the price that medicine had to pay in return was to abandon "the 'hands-off' attitude that seeks to guard the autonomy of the medical profession to deal in an isolated fashion with the great social ethical issues."[30] By the same token, Orthodox Jewish spokesmen objected to the definition because their tenets made the heart, not the brain, the seat of life. Catholic leaders feared that the state, following the physicians' lead, would soon be passing other legislation about life and death—here it involved the comatose; next it might affect the fetus. In response to such sentiments, hospitals began to hold joint clergy–physician meetings on brain death, recognizing that the question of when a person is dead "not only concerns physicians, but philosophers, theologians, moralists, lawmakers, judges, in fact—everyone."[31]

Heart transplantation brought into the public domain not only issues about medical resources and definitions of life and death, but the ability of medicine to keep its own house in order. Too much of a circus atmosphere surrounded the first transplant procedures, and physicians seemed to be more intent on celebrity status than on advancing the welfare of their patients. "There has never been anything like it in medical annals," Dr. Irvine Page, president of the American Heart Association, told a specially convened National Congress on Medical Ethics of the AMA. The frantic hunt for publicity among surgeons, with Barnard as the leading case in point; the instant reporting of results to the press; the neglect in presenting findings to scientific publications; and the readiness to ignore considerations of patient privacy and confidentiality all led Page to conclude, "I fear the public has gotten a view of medicine which will further downgrade its intellectual and compassionate aspects."[32]

Moreover, observers inside and outside medicine were convinced that surgeons had joined a "me-too brigade." Heart transplantation was moving too rapidly, and the outcomes did not justify the frequency of the procedure. The mortality rates were very high (only 9 of the first 100 patients given a heart were still alive as of June 1969),[33] and the major cause of failure, the body's rejection of the organ, was not well understood. In January 1968 the readers of the *New York Times* learned from medical correspondent Howard Rusk of an "international epidemic of cardiac transplants," which made it "practically impossible . . . for the average television viewer to get out of the operating room or the cardiac clinic." Worse yet, he continued, neither the viewer nor the surgeon belonged there, for "the technological advances and surgical techniques have completely outstripped the basic immunological knowledge needed to prevent rejection."[34] A few months later, the Board of Medicine of the National Academy of Sciences declared that heart transplantation should be considered an experimental procedure, "a scientific exploration of the unknown," and urged that only inter-disciplinary teams under rigorous research protocols—not simply technically proficient surgeons—should do the procedure and publish "systematic observation," not press releases.[35] Then in June 1968, editors of the leading British medical journal, *Lancet*, insisted that "too much was attempted too soon." Furthermore, they contended, "the story of the past months . . . is not one that the profession round the world can look upon with ease. It was not only the too-ready-acclamation in the papers, on television. . . . Surgical skill and ambition clearly ran some way ahead of the advice about the control of rejection and infection that immunologists and pathologists could confidently give."[36] By the winter of 1968, what might well be called a moratorium set in. Never officially acknowledged as such, the moratorium represented an almost complete about-face, with the number of transplants dropping sharply for almost all of the teams (with the exception of Norman Shumway's exemplary group at Stanford).

All these pronouncements and decisions were reported blow by blow in the popular press, and in Washington as well. As sociologists Renee Fox and Judy Swazey noted at the time, "Debates about the pros and cons of cardiac transplantation have taken place as much on the pages of daily newspapers as within the medical profession."[37] *Time, Newsweek*, and the *Nation* followed the story carefully, frequently running their accounts under such headlines as "WERE TRANSPLANTS PREMATURE?" and "TOO MUCH, TOO FAST?" They reported on the National Academy of Sciences resolution, the negative remarks of Page, the call by a group of physicians for a transplant moratorium, and a conference of "physicians, lawyers and theologians . . . to discuss the legal, ethical and practical aspects of transplants." They also kept a box score: *Time* noted in December 1968, the one-year anniversary, that among recipients "another death is being reported almost daily."[38]

That the events around transplantation swelled the ranks of outsiders ready to look over the physician's shoulder was apparent to the profession, who reacted very defensively. Whatever their views toward transplantation, physicians wanted to keep medical decisions in medical hands. Their pleas and comments reveal just how powerful the antipathy was to laypeople telling physicians what to do. As critical as Irvine Page was of the transplant circus, he was equally apprehensive about the "plethora of committees, task forces, and the like discussing transplantation. It would be surprising if they discovered anything new." Page worried, too, about a reliance on legislation to solve such problems as defining death or deciding just how long the life of a desperately ill patient must be prolonged: "There is a grave error in equating the amount of health legislation passed, the good of the patient, and the ethical behavior of the physician! . . . We must not overdo a good thing as may happen as legislation begins to replace conscience. The physician cannot dispose of his responsibility by abdication."[39] Writing in *JAMA*, Dr. Lyman Brewer also lamented the "carnival atmosphere around the performance of a surgical operation," and he fully appreciated that the procedure raised many ethical questions, particularly which patients should receive the "seldom available transplant." Nevertheless, he insisted: "This is a problem that should be solved by clinicians and not lay groups. . . . The medical profession control circumstances under which cardiac transplants are performed. Rigid laws passed by the legislature, rules laid down by legal and clerical boards or other groups, might becloud rather than clear the atmosphere. . . . The sine qua non of the practice of medicine is the integrity of the physician and the surgeon in treating the patient. Without it, filling-in of forms and reports to comply with rigid rules and to justify the operative procedure is meaningless."[40]

To Brewer, as to Page, rules and laws were inevitably rigid, futile, and detrimental to the doctor–patient relationship. No matter how inadequate the profession's initial response to transplantation, outside intervention would only make matters worse. Or as Dr. Michael DeBakey, who would soon take his place among the ranks of transplant surgeons, put it: "The moral, ethical, legal, and psychologic implications of human cardiac transplantation will undoubtedly be more far-reaching than anticipated from the present brief experience. . . . Should medical scientists abrogate their responsibility to their patients and to society to resolve such issues when they arise, they can expect restrictions to be prescribed from without."[41] Which, of course, is precisely what came to pass.

CHAPTER 9

Commissioning Ethics

In 1968, the U.S. Congress joined the growing ranks of those interested in medical ethics and decision making. The controversies moved from professional journals and conferences into Washington committee rooms, and despite the opposition and delaying tactics of physicians, in 1973 Congress created a national commission charged with recommending policies for human experimentation, and then in 1978 appointed a successor commission to examine almost every pressing issue in medical ethics. The commission idea was first fueled by the controversy surrounding heart transplantation; it then gathered momentum from a more general concern with new medical technologies, and finally became a reality in the wake of recurring scandals in human experimentation. In each instance, whether the case at hand was cardiac surgery or innovations in genetics and behavior modification, outsiders came to believe that the medical profession was incapable of self-regulation. As a result, the transformation we have been tracing became all the more anchored. As late as 1966, physicians had a monopoly over medical ethics; less than a decade later, laypeople, dominating a national commission, were setting the ethical standards. Medical decision making had become everybody's business.

In February 1968, three months after Christiaan Barnard's surgical feat, Walter Mondale, then a senator from Minnesota, introduced a bill to establish a Commission on Health Science and Society to assess and report on the ethical, legal, social, and political implications of biomedical advances. Mondale was struck by the novel questions that transplantation raised and the limited relevance of traditional medical ethics. As he explained in opening the subcommittee hearing on his resolution: "The scientific breakthroughs of the last few months were current highlights in a dazzling half century of truly unprecedented advance in the medical and biological sciences. . . . These advances and others yet to come raised grave and fundamental ethical and legal questions for our society—who shall live and who shall die; how long shall life be preserved and how shall it be altered; who shall make decisions; how shall society be prepared." Mondale urged the establishment of a national commission to serve as a forum in which not only doctors and biomedical researchers but lay representatives would explore these issues together. "Some professional must understand that society has a stake in what he is doing, and that society must know not only what he is doing, but the implications of his efforts." Oklahoma's Senator Fred Harris, who chaired the subcommittee and carried a populist's distrust of the expert, shared Mondale's concerns. "These matters," he declared, "ought to be talked about in the open by people from various backgrounds with various viewpoints—theological as well as medical, legal as well as sociological and psychological."[1]

To many physicians and investigators, particularly those working on the frontiers of their disciplines, the prospect of a federally sponsored national commission was, to understate the point, dismaying. Even those who did not object to bringing a few representatives from law or philosophy onto medicine's turf, to have them join a physician-dominated committee, thought it exceptionally meddlesome to have Congress organize a Commission on Health Science and Society, allot a few places on it to doctors, make the majority laypeople, and then have the group frame recommendations binding the profession. Given the size of the NIH research budget, Mondale was able to persuade some physicians to testify (albeit without great enthusiasm) in favor of such a commission. But much more impressive was the unbending opposition to the proposal. In 1968 the leaders of medicine fought doggedly to maintain their authority over all medical matters, in the process educating Mondale and others to the fact that whatever influence outsiders would exert would have to be wrested away from the profession.

The hearings opened with lukewarm endorsements from the first witnesses, who, fittingly enough, were all transplant surgeons—John Najarian, Adrian Kantrowitz, and later, Norman Shumway. They enthusiastically told the subcommittee to increase federal investments in research, and only then went on to allow, in vague terms, that the ethical and social questions surrounding transplantation made a commission appropriate. "I think no longer must that portion of our society cloak itself in an aura of mystique about medicine," conceded Najarian. "For a long time I think justifiably we had to. We worked more or less by a pinch of this, a pinch of that, and so as a result it was just as well to remain some sort of pseudo deity. . . . But today . . . we have accumulated scientific knowledge to the point that we stand on firm ground." He believed that a commission would do well to standardize a definition of brain death; but, he warned, it had to be very careful not to disrupt the mainstream work of science or interfere with the ongoing research at the leading institutions: "As far as the general ethical questions are concerned, I think . . . if these transplant operations are carried out in the university atmosphere, you are in the milieu here I think of the best social conscience you can have." University medical schools and hospitals, he noted, were already establishing their own review committees "and should be left to these devices, and . . . not be imposed [on] by the Federal Government. . . . However . . . if these operations are to be performed outside of teaching centers . . . then there may be some external needs for imposing certain restrictions."[2] In other words, a commission might well be needed to superintend the minor league players, but it had little relevance to the major leaguers. Norman Shumway, for his part, grudgingly allowed that "transplantation of the heart, fortunately or unfortunately, cannot be done without public notice and public support. . . . We are at the threshold of a wondrous new era in medicine, and doctors will need help to realize fully its potential."[3] But the priorities should be clear: the commission should assist physicians, not coerce them.

The qualifications and hesitations disappeared when laypeople or an unusual physician like Beecher testified. To them it seemed self-evident that in some fashion or another, public input had to shape the direction of medicine. Beecher's testimony in support of a commission drew on the lessons he had learned in human experimentation: Laypeople must bring their own ethical rules to medicine because "science is not the highest value under which all other orders of values have to be subordinated. . . . Science must be inserted into the order of values."[4] The Reverend Kenneth Vaux from the Institute of Religion at the Texas Medical Center shared these convictions, making his point by quoting J. Robert Oppenheimer's aphorism: "What is technically sweet, though irresistible, is not necessarily good." Everett Mendelsohn, a historian of science at Harvard who had served on its brain-death committee, staked out the commission's territory by distinguishing, as others had begun to do, the technical component in health care from the social component: "On this social component, the physician's judgment . . . is no more informed than that of the layman, or the social scientist whose view is based on his other knowledge of the social needs that a society may have."[5] And Jerald Braver, the dean of the University of Chicago Divinity School, happily anticipated that the commission would help ensure that "research in the health sciences not be conducted as if it is divorced from society and totally independent or autonomous."[6] In sum, to all these witnesses it was time to bring new rules to medicine.[7]

However strong this presumption appeared to Mondale and his supporters, it was far from accepted truth among many of the leading medical practitioners and researchers. The one witness who most vigorously contradicted their claims was Christiaan Barnard. His opposition was unqualified, almost nasty, perhaps reflecting the fact that he came from a country in which the doctor's authority was still unchallenged, or that he was not dependent on Congress or NIH for his funding. Barnard testified on Friday afternoon, March 8, just three months after his first transplant, and the media attention was ample proof of how thoroughly transplantation had captured the public imagination. ("May I say to you," Mondale noted, "this is . . . an indication of your significance in modern society—when you consider how crowded this room is with press and television at five o'clock on a Friday afternoon in Washington.") Such pleasantries brought the Senator little in return. Barnard led off with a brief description of the transplantation at Capetown and then immediately declared his all-out opposition to a public and nonmedical commission. To Mondale's intention of creating something more than a hospital-based committee of doctors, Barnard responded, "I must say that I think you are seeing ghosts where there are no ghosts. If I am in competition with my colleagues of this country, which I am not . . . then I would welcome such a commission, because it would put the doctors [in the United States] . . . so far behind me, and hamper the group of doctors so much that I will go so far ahead that they will never catch up with me."[8]

Mondale and his committee colleagues tried to get Barnard to concede that physicians did require guidance on some questions, but Barnard would not yield an inch: "It has been said," he observed, "that we now need a new definition for death . . . and we should have other people to tell us when we should say a patient is dead. I do not see why this is necessary. Doctors are called in every day in hospitals to certify that a patient is dead. . . . That doctor is often a very junior doctor—an intern—and he comes, he examines the patient, and establishes that the patient is dead. . . . In the case of a transplant of an organ, this decision is made by an expert team of doctors. . . . So why do we have to have new definitions for death, or commissions to tell us when we should say that a patient is dead. We as doctors have done that for many, many years." As for help in allocating a scarce resource: "This decision should be made by the doctors—because they have made the same decision in the past." He was asked, Since surgeons everywhere have waiting lists for operations, how do they determine who goes to the top of the list? "By deciding which patient needs it most," he replied.[9] When pushed by Connecticut's Senator Abraham Ribicoff on whether he truly believed that "doctors only should decide among the multiplicity of patients," Barnard responded: "A lot of these problems that you are seeing today, and a lot of people are mentioning today, these problems the doctors have had to handle for many years. These are not new problems. You cannot tell me one single new problem in our heart transplantation that we have not had for many years." When Ribicoff countered that for a physician to decide who lived and who died was new, and that it was debatable whether doctors should make that determination alone, Barnard answered: "I do not think the public is qualified to make the decision. . . . You cannot have control over these things. You must leave it in the people's hands who are capable of doing it."[10]

Reluctant to have this celebrity so unequivocally oppose his proposal, Mondale took a turn: "We have the ethical questions of when is a person dead, who gives the vital organ to whom, who decides when there are many who will die, but only a few can be saved. . . . Don't you believe that these issues could be profitably studied by a sophisticated and responsible commission composed of the finest men in the medical fields, health administrators, responsible theologians, attorneys and other persons?" Barnard gave an unqualified no: "Senator, by wanting to set up a commission, you must have one of two reasons. Either you are seeing new problems, or you are not satisfied with the way the doctors have handled the problems in the past. That is the only reason you can ask for a new commission." Mondale ended the questioning, and Barnard left with his opposition unqualified: "If we [in South Africa] could have done this without a commission to control and to give us guidance—do you feel it is necessary in this country to have some commission to guide your doctors and your scientists? I feel that if you do this, it will be an insult to your doctors and what is more, it would put progress back a lot."[11]

Considering that a Senate subcommittee usually enjoys broad latitude in inviting testimony, the depth of the opposition to the commission indicates just how hostile medical opinion was. Mondale was effusive in introducing Dr. Owen Wangensteen, who from 1930 to 1967 directed the department of surgery at the University of Minnesota Hospital; however, Dr. Wangensteen was anything but effusive about the commission. The thought that theologians might pronounce on medical questions raised for him the specter of Puritan ministers thundering against the practice of smallpox vaccination. Wangensteen's greatest fear was not that ethical questions would be ignored but that medical innovators would be "manacled by well-intentioned but meddlesome intruders." He told the committee, "I would urge you with all the strength I can muster, to leave this subject to conscionable people in the profession who are struggling valiantly to advance medicine."[12] Mondale, ever persistent, asked, "Don't you think there are nondoctors, persons not in the medical profession, who could bring to this problem useful insights, or do you think it ought to be left exclusively

173

to the medical profession?" To which Wangensteen replied: "The fellow who holds the apple can peel it best. . . . If you are thinking of theologians, lawyers, philosophers, and others to give some direction here . . . I cannot see how they could help. I would leave these decisions to the responsible people doing the work."[13]

This was also the position that Jesse Edwards, the president of the American Heart Association, defended. The public was too emotional to be involved in this type of inquiry, and a commission, he feared, might prematurely restrict transplant surgery. The Heart Association leadership was sensitive to the need to draw up guidelines and included on the organization's committee a number of nonphysicians. But for Congress to enter this field and empower a lay body to superintend medicine would bring disastrous results. Concluded Edwards: "The one thing we would want to avoid would be getting into a technical situation which would make it easy for restrictive legislation."[14]

However unyielding the opposition, Mondale and his supporters were convinced that this battle had to be fought and won. As they surveyed the territory, transplantation was only the lead issue, at the top of a burgeoning list of concerns whose resolution appeared to them to require more than the insights of physicians. Indeed, many of the developments that worried them seemed to have less to do with doctoring (in the old-fashioned sense) and much more to do with machines and research. It was not the physician at the bedside but the technician at the dial and the investigator at the bench that appeared, at least to those outside medicine, to demand new players setting down new rules.

Hence, the Mondale hearings moved from transplantation to two other innovations—genetic engineering and behavior control, where the breakthroughs were yet to come, but the potential social and ethical consequences already seemed scary. Transplantation, after all, remained a procedure whose sole purpose was to benefit the patient, and considerations of equity drove the debate. Genetic engineering and behavior control, whatever their therapeutic potential, raised apocalyptic visions of George Orwell's *1984*, with political misuse and social control of the most egregious sort. "The transplantation of human organs," explained Mondale, "already has raised such serious public questions as who shall live and who shall die. But coming techniques of genetic intervention and behavior control will bring profound moral, legal, ethical, and social questions for a society which one day will have the power to shape the bodies and minds of its citizens."[15]

Nevertheless, the geneticists and the psychiatrists who testified were as antagonistic to the idea of a commission as the surgeons. Again, what seemed apparent and beyond dispute to the senators was irrelevant or even mischievous to these witnesses. Mondale's remarks were studded with references to "the terror of a brave new world" and "the terror of nuclear holocaust." But the researchers were certain that all this was fantasy, and government's primary obligation was to fund their research and stay out of the way.

Just how far apart the two sides were emerged in the testimony of Dr. Arthur Kornberg, winner of the 1959 Nobel Prize for his work in the biochemistry of DNA. Kornberg, in his own terms, had synthesized a DNA copy of a simple virus with six genes, and the replication had the full genetic activity of natural DNA. To laypeople, however, Kornberg had "created life in a test tube." He recognized that the media preferred to use an attention-grabbing word like *creation*, as opposed to *synthesis*, and that people were startled to learn not only that "genetics or heredity was simply chemistry" but also that genetic engineering was now a "prospect." And Kornberg could appreciate that "this prospect fascinates people. It also frightens them and I can understand why it does." But for the foreseeable future, the difficulty, he believed, was "not too much but too little knowledge. I see no ethical or moral problems that are different in kind or quantity that face us today with this new knowledge of genes and gene action." Kornberg desperately wanted Congress to devote the resources necessary "to exploit the opportunities to expand our knowledge," but beyond that, it should not intervene.

The Mondale committee, however, was not so complacent. Senator Ribicoff immediately asked, "Do you see this work of yours leading to the creation of a master race?" "Oh no," responded Kornberg. "This is so very remote." "What about the legal and ethical questions that do arise from genetics," Ribicoff continued. "Who makes the decision of who uses it, with what people?" Kornberg found the question sophomoric. "I really do not have the capacity to answer some of the questions that are not well-defined and still so distant. I have learned from experience it is more meaningful for me to focus on problems that confront me directly. What confronts us is a great opportunity to exploit openings . . . for understanding the chemical basis of the human organism." Ribicoff, still dissatisfied, persisted. "Is science amoral? Does science concern itself with the ethical, social and human consequences of its acts and its achievements? . . . At what stage does the scientist become concerned with the good as well as just the success of the work that he is doing?" Kornberg had little more to add: "I can only repeat that many of the dire consequences of genetic research are still remote."[16]

Mondale brought the questioning back to the commission. Addressing both Kornberg and fellow geneticist Joshua Lederberg (who had also testified), Mondale noted that both had demonstrated a "great interest" in reviewing their "financial problems—but a great reluctance for review of the social problems that might flow from the research." Continued Mondale, "I find your reluctance to take that second step . . . to be a little bit mystifying." Kornberg impatiently explained that this was the first time he had ever testified before Congress and that it was "an arena for which, as scientists, we are not trained, and for which we have no natural affinity." Indeed, it was not just a matter of taste but of priorities, and in lines that Mondale would not forget, Kornberg declared: "There are absolutely no scientific rewards, no enlargement of scientific skills that accrue from involvement in public issues. . . . The biochemist who deals with molecules cannot afford any time away from them. Today I am not in the laboratory. I do not know what is going on at the bench. Tomorrow I will be less able to cope with the identity and behavior of molecules. . . . If the research worker were to become a public figure, it would destroy him as a scientist." A commission would only serve to thwart or distract the scientist, and all to the aim of tilting at windmills. "This concern [over] our creating little men in test tubes, and a super race, is really not so relevant today."[17]

The commission proposal fared somewhat better when the committee turned to the last of its major concerns, behavior control. The committee learned from Dr. Seymour Ketty, a professor of psychiatry at Harvard Medical School, about the advances in biochemistry and physiology of the brain that were bringing a new dimension to the study of behavior and emotions. Ketty reported that electrodes placed in the brain of animals could stimulate rage or aggression, and "when similar techniques have been applied to man during neurosurgical operations, reports have been obtained of . . . recollections of the past, blocking of thought, as well as emotional changes such as anxiety, fear, friendliness or happiness."[18] David Krech, a professor of psychology at the University of California at Berkeley, told the committee about drugs that seem to be able to improve the memories and problem-solving abilities of laboratory animals. The senators took this information as one more item that belonged on the commission's agenda. The group would have to explore the implications of an ability to manipulate behavior by techniques that would alter moods or heighten intellectual capacities; they would even have to consider whether it would be possible to put a pill into a reservoir and turn an entire community into . . . political slaves? supermen? great thinkers? working drones?

Ketty, like the other investigators, thought the concerns—and the commission enterprise—premature at best. If the Orwellian fantasy was to be realized, it would arrive through a political, not a scientific, route: "Manipulation of the brain by any of the biological techniques which could be developed in the foreseeable future would involve such drastic invasions of privacy, integrity, and the inalienable rights of the individual that in their application behavioral control would already have been achieved even if the electrodes carried no current and the pill were a placebo." Krech, on the other hand, was far more enthusiastic about the commission: "Neither the medicine man nor scientist is better equipped to deal with the question of ethics and values and social good . . . than is any other thoughtful and concerned man. The brain researcher . . . has neither the requisite wisdom nor experience nor knowledge to say to society: 'Don't worry your unscientific heads about this; I will save society (from me!).' " It was to Krech, not Ketty, that Mondale remarked, "I am most appreciative for this very fine testimony."[19]

Mondale's 1968 proposal to establish a National Commission on Health Science and Society did not win immediate passage for a variety of reasons. For one, the Nixon administration was unwilling to support the creation of a forum that would give liberals like Mondale, Harris, and Ribicoff the opportunity to play farsighted policy analysts, or for that matter, to create a forum that would rival the executive department's own committees and review structures in the Department of Health, Education and Welfare. For another, the proposal itself was much too broadly drawn, and no one could precisely define its assignment. Was this commission to review and make recommendations on all of transplantation, genetics, behavior modification, and human experimentation and do so in a one-year period? Several witnesses also suggested that the most pressing problem facing American medicine was not the implications of future technologies but the immediate problem of getting minorities access to current technologies. (The report of the Kerner Commission had just been released, and its image of America as two nations—one rich, the other poor—highlighted the inequities in health care delivery. Whites had a life of expectancy of 71 years; nonwhites, 64 years. Whites had an infant mortality rate of 16 deaths per 1,000 births; nonwhites, 25 deaths.)[20] Mondale recognized the need to examine access to medical care, and he suggested that the commission would take on this task as well, thereby making its mandate even more impossible to fulfill.

The most important cause of initial failure, however, was that Mondale had not anticipated the depth of the opposition. What he defined as a "measly little study commission," physicians and researchers defined as a major battle in the war to rule medicine. Looking back, Mondale was frankly bitter about their opposition: "All we have said is, 'Let's have a public study commission.' . . . But the reaction has been fantastic. In 1968, they bootlegged Christiaan Barnard down here to tell us why this would put South Africa ahead of the United States in medical science. He said, 'You will have a politician in every surgical room.' The major portion of the American public bought what he said. . . . They got Doctor Kornberg in here, who is a great scientist, and what did he say? . . . The biochemist who deals with molecules cannot afford any time away from them. . . . In other words, he asked us, 'Why are you wasting my time here?' . . . I sense an almost psychopathic objection to the public process, a fear that if the public gets involved, it is going to be anti-science, going to be hostile and unsupportive." Mondale concluded: "I have a feeling that medicine does not want to explain its case partly because they went through the period [of the 1950s] . . . in a preferred status, like the FBI. I think we are at a point now where American medicine has to explain itself."[21]

The roots of the divide went much deeper than a 1950s mind-set, though. The gap between a Mondale on the one side and a Kornberg on the other was well nigh unbridgeable. Starting from diametrically opposed premises, they reached contradictory conclusions, talking past each other, without the slightest appreciation of the alternative position. And in this separation one finds yet another impetus to the movement to bring new rules to medicine, and another reason for its eventual success.

The controversy did not come down in any simple sense to a dispute over technologies. Christiaan Barnard did have a point when he argued that the technologies did not pose social or ethical challenges; physicians had been trusted before to make difficult decisions, and public policy willing, they could be trusted again. But a number of outsiders found this response unacceptable, in part, for the reasons we have already explored—the scandals in human experimentation, the social distancing of the physician, and the inadequacies of traditional medical ethics. The Mondale hearings, however, added still another consideration: the feats made possible by medical technologies had transferred medicine from the category of the helping profession to the category of engineering. The image of the physician that ran through the testimony was not of a person holding the patient's hand at the bedside but of someone turning the machine's dials in an intensive care unit. The focus of the hearings was not the doctor–patient relationship—no one made a single reference to this subject or to allied ones like truth telling—or the mounting cost of medical care—no one mentioned the percentage of the GNP going to health care. Rather, the primary concern was with the potential misuse of the technology—framed by the assortment of anxieties and ambivalent feelings that technology raised in other, nonmedical settings. It was somewhat paradoxical, and not a little unfair, but just as medicine became technological, the medical establishment brought upon itself all the distrust that technology in the late 1960s and 1970s generated. Just when doctors and investigators could promise "better living through chemistry," the slogan had become suspect, even the object of derision.

Thus, those who wished to circumscribe the autonomy of the medical profession gained strength not because medical technology in some inevitable way demanded it, but because social definitions of technology demanded it. There was nothing automatic or inevitable about the presumption that when a respirator ventilated a patient, a federal commission was needed to explore the ethics of medicine, or that an ethics committee or a philosopher had to be present on the hospital floor. Rather, because a machine ventilated the patient, outsiders thought such interventions legitimate and necessary.

Keenly aware of these attitudes, Mondale often commented during the hearings that "this society is in a constant race to keep up with advancing technologies, understand them, and see that they are put to constructive use. We have been too late, too secret, and too superficial in too many cases. One of the results is the terror of automation-produced unemployment. Another is the terror of nuclear holocaust. . . . Our experience with the atom teaches us that we must look closely at the implications of what we do." It seemed to him self-evident that "when a scientist unravels a technique for engineering future generations [note "engineering," not "curing" or "helping," future generations], that is not a matter solely for the scientist's interest. It fundamentally . . . affects mankind—perhaps in a more searching sense than the atomic bomb."[22] Fred Harris took his cautionary text on technology from the environment: "Wouldn't it have been far wiser of us to have thought about the consequences of detergents long before we put them on the market, and messed up all our streams with the effluent?"[23] By the same token, "the highway planners were . . . moving that traffic, it is true, but they forget about the people." It would not be the experts, the insiders, who would make cities "more liveable, more rewarding," but outsiders.[24] And in this same fashion, Abraham Ribicoff likened medical technology to nuclear technology: Would doctors Kornberg, Lederberg, and Barnard later have doubts and be "soul-searching" about the wisdom of their research like those scientists "who were involved in the creation of the atomic bomb and hydrogen bomb? . . . I have been personally struck by the traumatic effect that the consequences of atomic research and atomic bombs, and hydrogen bombs, have had upon so many pure scientists, brilliant scientists, who worked in this field. And you get the feeling that many of them felt that when they see the consequences of their discoveries maybe they wish they were a plumber or a truck driver." Ribicoff came away from the hearings convinced that "society does have a concern with the great breakthroughs that are taking place." He concluded, "I think it is well that people worry about them now instead of both scientists and society in general waking up with a guilty conscience 20 years after the event."[25]

However obvious and persuasive the analogies seemed to Mondale, Harris, and Ribicoff, they seemed irrelevant and misleading to the physicians and researchers who testified. What outsiders defined as technological, they saw as therapeutic; they were not engineers but doctors, and to inhibit their enterprise was to set back the development of life-saving interventions for desperately ill patients. Heart surgeon Adrian Kantrowitz told the committee that although others puzzled over "the question of whether experimental heart surgery contains ethical, moral, social, legal, economic, and political problems of a quality or magnitude ever before encountered," he sorted through them easily. "The ethics of heart transplantation . . . are, first of all, the ethics of medicine, the ethics of reverence for human life. . . . The ethical problem can be summarized in a few words: can the patient survive by any other known means? . . . The process is no different from . . . deciding whether a patient is an appropriate candidate for some new drug. Will anything else probably help the patient?"[26] One did not need a commission—or a committee of philosophers, lawyers, and clergymen—to answer such questions.

Those in genetics and psychiatry were no less confident about the therapeutic character of their work. They would not be second-guessing themselves twenty years later, for they were creating agents of cure, not of destruction. They were not in the business of genetic *engineering* or behavior *control* but of treatment, and once the general public grasped the distinction, its anxiety would be reduced and it would stop peering over doctors' shoulders. Thus, when Senator Ribicoff asked Arthur Kornberg whether his research might promote a master race, Kornberg responded that his aim was "to relieve a good deal of suffering and distress . . . correcting well-known diseases that plague people." As for a master race, he replied, "I would like to be part of 'a master race' relieved of some of the scourges that have plagued people for centuries."[27] If Kornberg preferred staying in his laboratory to appearing at a hearing in Washington, it was not only because he found testifying uncongenial but because he thought the questions miscast.

Once again, as in the case of human experimentation, insiders and outsiders had contradictory perspectives. To the one view, technology was threatening to outdistance social values, and laypeople had to join with scientists—knowledgeable, but not wise—to ponder the implications of their research. In light of the history of technology in the twentieth century, surely this was a most necessary and reasonable proposal. But to the other view, the public was, once again, misconstruing the work of the physician-scientist. At best, a national commission would take the researchers away from their laboratories for a number of days; at worst, it would tie investigators' hands and retard scientific progress. Thus, each side found its own propositions axiomatic, and its opponents perverse for resisting the obvious merits of the arguments.

Although Walter Mondale's hopes for a commission fell through in 1968, he did not abandon the idea. In 1969, Senator Harris's Subcommittee on Government Research was dissolved, and Mondale failed to become chairman of the Subcommittee on Health.[28] In 1971 and then again in 1973, he reintroduced the resolutions, finally reaping victory in 1974, with the creation of the National Commission for the Protection of Human Subjects of Biomedical and Behavioral Research. What accounts for both the persistence and the accomplishment? Why did the initial stalemate give way to the creation of a commission that, even if it was not as powerful as its first supporters would have preferred, assuredly gave a new weight and legitimacy to the role of outsiders in medicine?

First, there is no discounting Mondale's disgust with the 1968 testimony and the attitude of medicine's representatives. The hostility of Christiaan Barnard and Arthur Kornberg not only provoked his anger but reinforced his sense that researchers could not be trusted to keep their house in order. Moreover, support for a national commission broadened from 1968 to 1973 as scandals recurred in human experimentation, each one eroding the degree of trust between investigators and the public. Undoubtedly, the most disturbing incident was the Tuskegee research of the U.S. Public Health Service (PHS). From the mid-1930s into the early 1970s, its investigators had been visiting Macon County, Alabama, to examine, but not to treat, a group of blacks who were suffering from secondary syphilis. The press, on a tip from one of the researchers, finally blew the whistle, and subsequent investigations made clear just how sorry the behavior of the PHS was. Whatever rationalizations it could muster for not treating blacks in the 1930s (when treatment was of questionable efficacy and very complicated to administer), it could hardly defend instructing draft boards not to conscript the subjects for fear that they might receive treatment in the army; and worse, it could not justify its unwillingness to give the subjects a trial of penicillin after 1945. The PHS leaders' lame excuse was that with the advent of antibiotics, no one would ever again be able to trace the long-term effects of syphilis.[29]

Only a shade less notorious than Tuskegee were the experiments conducted at the University of Cincinnati General Hospital. The investigators, funded by the Department of Defense, applied whole and partial body radiation to patients with terminal cancer. The hospital claimed that the investigators had obtained the patients' consent and that the primary goal of the research was therapeutic. But critics insisted that the real purpose was to provide the Department of Defense with data that might protect the combat effectiveness of military troops who might be exposed to radiation. In fact, over the fifteen years that the experiments continued, therapeutic results were minimal, and the university never provided any documentation, such as signed forms, that consent had been obtained. Most damaging of all, the Cincinnati subjects closely resembled the Tuskegee ones: indigent, black, and with no more than a grade-school education. It was difficult to avoid the conclusion that once again investigators had chosen the underprivileged to be martyrs for scientific knowledge.[30]

Given the persistent interest of senators like Mondale, Jacob Javits, and Edward Kennedy in the regulation of biomedical research and practices, and the exposés in human experimentation, the opening months of 1973 witnessed an extraordinary burst of congressional bills and hearings. Senator Mondale reintroduced his resolution to establish a national advisory commission, Senators Javits and Hubert Humphrey reintroduced their bill to regulate human experimentation more closely, and they supported legislation that would place "an increased emphasis on the ethical, social, legal, and moral implications of advances in biomedical research and technology" in the education of health care professionals.[31] All of these bills became the occasion in the winter and spring of 1973 for Senator Kennedy to conduct hearings on the "Quality of Health Care—Human Experimentation."[32] Because of the recurrent scandals, human experimentation was most likely to rivet public attention and justify an increased surveillance and regulation of the laboratory. But the target was broader: really, all of medicine. The hearings' ultimate goal was to demonstrate that no wing of the medical profession could be trusted to keep its house in order—that medicine required a new kind of collective oversight. As Mondale put it: "Normally this committee finds itself at war with the medical profession over economics. But in this case we find ourselves at odds with the academic medical community, which says 'Leave us alone. Stay off our campuses. Send us the money but don't come in and see how we do our experimenting.' "[33]

Kennedy, more artfully than Mondale earlier, structured the hearings to demonstrate the need for outside intervention. The thrust of the opening testimony was to substantiate that physicians as well as researchers abused professional discretion; that the ethical and social dilemmas confronting medicine were not just futuristic but here and now; and finally, that all Americans, not just the poor and the institutionalized, were affected by these problems. "Human experimentation," announced Kennedy in his first statement, "is part of the routine practice of medicine." An absence of vigorous oversight, "coupled with the most unlimited freedom of action which physicians have in the treatment of their patients," allowed dangerous practices, including the premature use of unproven and untested drugs and procedures. "The question," insisted Kennedy, "is whether or not we can tolerate a system where the individual physician is the sole determinant of the safety of an experimental procedure. After all, it is the patients who must live the consequences of that decision."[34]

The case in point was the misuse of two drugs with contraceptive effects, Depo-Provera and DES (diethylstilbestrol). Both had been approved by the FDA for treatment purposes (Depo-Provera for the treatment of advanced cancers of the uterus and endometriosis, DES to prevent miscarriage), but neither was approved as a contraceptive. Once the FDA licensed a drug for one purpose, however, physicians were free to prescribe it for other purposes, and a parade of witnesses reported that many doctors were not only dispensing Depo-Provera and DES as contraceptives but failing to inform patients about potential side effects or obtain their consent.[35] The Senate committee learned that doctors at one Tennessee clinic injected a group of welfare mothers with Depo-Provera without explaining that it had caused breast cancer in a breed of dogs. Also, some fifteen university health clinics prescribed DES to women students as a "morning after" pill, without telling them of its cancer-causing potential for them and for their future children. As one witness declared, in precisely the terms that Kennedy wanted to hear, "Whether the subjects are prisoners, college students, military personnel or poor people, they share a common sense of captivity and the use of any drugs on them must be regulated with paramount regard for their well-being."[36]

Were these incidents not enough, there were still other examples wherein the poor in particular were the hapless victims of medical research and, indeed, medical practice. In 1972, Mexican American women who had gone to a clinic in San Antonio for contraceptives unknowingly became subjects in an experiment to identify whether the side effects of contraceptive pills were physiological or psychological; half the women were given contraceptive pills, the other half, placebos, in order to allow the investigators to match reported side effects with the active agent or the placebo. The problem, of course, was that the placebo group might well become pregnant, which ten of them promptly did. The experiment itself and the failure of the medical society to discipline the doctors involved not only confirmed the idea that "poor minority people" were particularly liable to be abused but also demonstrated, yet again, the inability of the profession to police its own members.

The hearings then moved from relatively ordinary concerns such as contraception to the extraordinary—to the use of psychosurgery to treat, in the words of its foremost advocate, Dr. Orlando Andy, a neurosurgeon at the University of Mississippi Medical Center, "aggressive, uncontrollable, violent, and hyperactive behavior which does not respond to various other medical forms of therapy." Kennedy first had the head of the National Institute of Mental Health (NIMH) establish that psychosurgery was an experimental procedure, and that the NIMH had no authority over a private doctor who wanted to practice it. The senator then made his point with Dr. Andy himself:

Q: Basically, then, you make an independent judgment whether to move ahead on this kind of operation?

A: Yes. The final decision is always mine in terms of whether or not an operation will or will not be done.

Q: Do you have any board or panel that continues to review the various bases for the psychosurgery in which you have been involved?

A: No. We don't have a board of supervisors or investigators or peer review type of activity over what we are doing.[37]

This was a surgeon ready to tamper with the human brain to control antisocial behavior, and no one—no peer group or federal regulatory body—was in a position to regulate him.

Next, after a brief discussion on genetic engineering, the hearings turned to experimentation in prison. Kennedy here aimed to demonstrate that prisoners in state penitentiaries and city jails were guinea pigs for medical researchers. In light of the impressive organization of rights groups and their important courtroom victories in the late 1960s and early 1970s, Kennedy was eager to define unbounded medical discretion as a problem in minority rights. "During the course of these hearings," he noted, "we have heard that those who have borne the principal brunt of research—whether it is drugs or even experimental surgery—have been the more disadvantaged people within our society; have been the institutionalized, the poor, and minority members."[38] The coalition, then, that would bring new rules to medicine would be composed of both ordinary citizens and rights activists, or in political terms, the center and the left.

That prisons were laboratories unto themselves was easily documented. Jessica Mitford, who had just published her exposé on the subject, recounted how pharmaceutical companies were altogether dependent on prisoners for testing new drugs, but the sums paid to them were "a pittance"—about a dollar a day, which was enough to attract many recruits because the dollar "represents riches when viewed in terms of prison pay scales."[39] Other witnesses made clear that the FDA was not kept informed on what transpired in prisons, or for that matter in jails, where pretrial detainees were also recruited for tests.

The unmistakable lesson that emerged from every aspect of the hearing was that outsiders had to regulate the medical and biomedical research community. Bernard Barber, a Columbia University sociologist, reporting on an extensive survey of existing practices, concluded that peer review was totally inadequate to the task of supervising research: "There has been no sign of the kind of intensive, imaginative, coordinated, persisting action with regard to the ethics of experimentation that the biomedical research profession has displayed in advancing the cause of medical research and therapy." Considerations of science still took precedence over considerations of ethics. Jay Katz, fresh from his service as chairman on the task force to examine the Tuskegee events, was also convinced that effective oversight would not come from inside medicine: "The research community has made no concerted effort either to impose any meaningful self-regulation on its practices or to discuss in any scholarly depth the permissible limits of human research. Therefore, I submit, regulation has to come from elsewhere."[40]

Others, too, like Willard Gaylin, the president of the Hastings Institute, were not at all hopeful that the professional associations, like the AMA, would be able to develop or enforce necessary safeguards. "These institutions," observed Gaylin, "were originally designed as protective guilds, and they still function primarily in that sense. . . . I suspect that they will always be more concerned with the protection of the rights of their constituents than with the public per se." He, for one, was eager to empower the patient: "Patient-consumers must no longer trust exclusively the benevolence of the professional. But basic decisions must be returned to the hands of the patient population whose health and future will be affected. . . . We should all share in the decision making."[41] Still others, like Alexander Capron at the University of Pennsylvania Law School, argued strongly on behalf of a greatly expanded federal role. "I do not share the view of the researchers who have expressed alarm and dismay over this growing scrutiny . . . by 'meddlesome intruders,' " declared Capron. "The objective of the 'outsiders,' like that of the biomedical scientists, is to reduce human suffering—a goal which requires not only the advance of knowledge through experimentation but also the protection of the experimental subjects."[42]

The legislative proposal that emerged from the Kennedy hearings called for the creation of a National Commission for the Protection of Human Subjects. Its eleven members were to be chosen from among "the general public and from individuals in the fields of medicine, law, ethics, theology, biological science, physical science, social science, philosophy, humanities, health administration, government, and public affairs." The very length of the roster as well as the stipulation that no more than five of the members could be researchers made clear just how critical the principle of external oversight had become. Kennedy repeatedly emphasized this point: Policy had to emanate "not just from the medical profession, but from ethicists, the theologians, philosophers and many other disciplines." Bernard Barber predicted, altogether accurately, that the commission "would transform a fundamental moral problem from a condition of relative professional neglect and occasional journalistic scandal to a condition of continuing public and professional visibility and legitimacy. . . . For the proper regulation of the powerful professions of modern society, we need a combination of insiders and outsiders, of professionals and citizens."[43]

The give-and-take of politics did not allow for the precise type of commission that Kennedy and his supporters envisioned. Although their version passed the Senate intact, the House enacted a variant proposal, and the resulting conference committee weakened the body. The commission became temporary, rather than permanent, and advisory (to the secretary of HEW), without any enforcement powers of its own.

Even in its reduced state, however, the commission represented a critical departure. First, it made apparent that the monopoly of the medical profession in medical ethics was over. The issues were now public and national—the province of an extraordinary variety of outsiders. Second, it gave an institutional expression to this change, because the commission provided a forum for outsiders that would command attention from both the media and public officials. The commission members had a national audience, and so did those who testified before them. Finally, although the commission was not permanent and was charged to investigate not all of medicine but only human experimentation, it had a vital and continuing presence. When its mandate was about to expire in 1978, Kennedy was able to transform it into the President's Commission for the Study of Ethical Problems in Medicine and give it the scope that Mondale had urged a decade before. By 1978, of course, the role of outsiders was much more firmly established. Bioethics was a field, would-be bioethicists had career lines to follow, and the notion that medical ethics belonged exclusively to medicine had been forgotten by most everyone, except for a cadre of older physicians and a handful of historians.

CHAPTER 10

No One to Trust

THE movement to bring new rules to medicine did not stop at the biomedical frontiers. Beginning in the early 1970s, the most elemental aspects of medicine—decisions on birth and death, on what lives were or were not worth living—became the center of public debate and controversy. Traditionally, these questions had been at the essence of bedside ethics, the exclusive preserve of doctors: they decided whether a newborn's deficits were so grave or an elderly patient's prognosis so poor that he or she would be better off untreated. But now, wearing a white coat was not a prerequisite—or, it seemed, even a qualification—for resolving these predicaments. Outsiders first superintended the work of physicians in the laboratory and then ultimately in the infant nursery and adult intensive care unit.

Although the progression from issue to issue seemed logical, even inevitable, the reality was more complex, and each shift was bitterly contested at every point. As in human experimentation, one again finds whistle-blowers and scandals, contentiousness and rancor, a deep mistrust among many physicians of inflexible rules that would interfere with their ability to make case-by-case decisions and a no less profound dissatisfaction among many laypeople with the exercise of medical discretion. In fact, resolving the conflicts in neonatal nurseries prompted still more outsiders to cross over into medicine. In human experimentation, two parties were at odds—the researcher and the subject. In the neonatal unit, three parties interacted—the doctor, the parent(s), and the infant—and the shadow of the state loomed larger here than elsewhere. In sorting out the best locus for decision making, some wanted to preserve a traditional physician hegemony, but most others were prepared to invoke parental and third-party input, albeit for very different reasons. Some believed that parents and third parties must participate if doctors were going to be able to terminate treatment; others saw in third parties the only protection against the conspiracy of doctors and parents to discriminate against the handicapped newborn. Still others saw in third parties the only way for parents to realize their choices against a doctor. Small wonder, then, that many commentators, unable to decide where to put their trust, opted to make medical decision making more collective and more responsive to outsiders. And small wonder that the judgment calls in the neonatal nursery became the focus of academic and popular discourse, and eventually legislative and judicial regulation.

Although there is something artificial about selecting a single starting point for this analysis, the case of the Johns Hopkins baby stands out. In 1969 a baby suffering from a digestive abnormality was born in a community hospital at Virginia's Eastern Shore. The infant was transferred immediately to the Johns Hopkins University Hospital, and his doctors discovered an intestinal blockage, a problem readily correctable through surgery. But the baby was also mentally retarded because of Down's syndrome. Upon being told of the situation, the parents refused to give permission for the surgery, and the hospital complied with their wishes. The infant was moved to a corner of the nursery, and over a period of fifteen days, starved to death.[1]

In the opinion of several physicians at Johns Hopkins, the case was not all that unusual. It was common knowledge, at least within the profession, that many infants born with spina bifida—a condition in which the spinal column is exposed and underdeveloped, causing paralysis, incontinence, and, frequently, mental retardation—never left the delivery room; the chart entry read "stillbirth." (When it later became the practice to intervene aggressively with spina bifida infants, the number of "stillbirths" went down almost to zero.) The Hopkins staff also believed that recourse to the courts was a waste of time because judges would always uphold the parents' desires.

Nevertheless, the baby's death deeply affected the resident who had pulled the feeding lines (William Bartholome), the chief resident (Norman Fost), and the chief of service (Robert Cooke, himself the father of two handicapped children). Indeed, they were so disturbed by the course of events that they took the issue outside the hospital. With assistance from members of the Kennedy family, whose concern for the treatment of the mentally retarded was exemplified in the work of the Joseph P. Kennedy Foundation, they oversaw the making of a short film about the incident, with a ten-minute segment devoted to the case and then a fifteen-minute panel discussion on the ethical principles involved.

The film opened with a close-up of a newborn baby crying lustily; included a sequence in which a couple, backs to the camera, discussed their preferences with the physician; and closed with a long shot of the bassinet at the far end of the nursery. It was extraordinarily moving— and misleading. A viewer would presume that the newborn shown on camera was *the* very baby, that the couple were the real parents, and what was being filmed was the short, unhappy life and death of the baby—not a re-creation made several years later. The credits only hinted that it was a re-creation, for the point of the film was to arouse indignation, which it certainly did.[2]

It was first shown in October 1971, at a three-day symposium on "Human Rights, Retardation, and Research," which the Kennedy Foundation sponsored. Although the conference covered a good deal of ground—from the "Ethics of New Technologies in Beginning Life" to "Why Should People Care, How Should People Care?"—and the conferees were exceptionally diverse—Mother Teresa was there, as were Elie Wiesel, James Watson, and B. F. Skinner—the Johns Hopkins incident became the lead story. The press had been invited to a special preview of the film, and journalists wrote about it extensively and provocatively.[3] Newspaper headlines were variations on the theme of "MDS WATCH AS SICK BABY STARVES." Shortly afterward, the ten-minute segment was shown on national television, and viewers as well as readers responded with indignation. Letters to the editor called the physicians' behavior "unspeakable" and "shocking."[4] Bags of mail came to Bartholome and Cooke. Almost all of the correspondents condemned the refusal to carry out the surgery, and many of them made analogies to the Nazis. Johns Hopkins was "something out of the bowels of Dachau" and its policies reminiscent of "Adolf Hitler's program." Said one correspondent: "We condemn Nazi Germany for what they did to exterminate the Jews. Is this country any better?"[5]

The level of indignation was so intense that the Johns Hopkins incident became the occasion to organize new forums to promote the analysis and discussion of ethical issues in medical decision making. Right before the opening of the Kennedy symposium, Georgetown University announced the creation of an institute that would join biology with ethics in what was now being called "bioethics."[6] "A determined effort has to be made," declared Georgetown's President Robert Henle, "to bring to bear on these human problems all the traditional wisdoms of our religions and our philosophy." With a $1.35 million grant from the Kennedy Foundation, the new institute aimed to "put theologians next to doctors." André Hellegers, an obstetrician-gynecologist, was appointed head of the institute; and not surprisingly, the illustrative cases had to do with disabilities, mental retardation, and medical care at birth. As Edward Kennedy declared, in a line he would be repeating in other contexts: "These problems should not be left to the politician and to the medical profession, or wholly to the theologian." Sargent Shriver made the same observation more aggressively: "I'd be happy to see one of the ethicists blast one of the doctors for doing something wrong."[7]

Bringing outsiders into medicine seemed ever so necessary to the three Johns Hopkins physicians as well. Bartholome responded to many of those who questioned him about the case that the "solution will come only if society is willing to support the formal investigation by physicians, lawyers, sociologists and moralists of these complicated issues."[8] The Johns Hopkins Hospital directors sought to counter the negative publicity by announcing, one week after the film's showing, that it was establishing a review board composed of a pediatrician, a surgeon, a psychiatrist, a clergyman, and a lawyer to advise on difficult ethical cases—and again the illustrative case was how to respond when parents of a retarded infant refused to allow life-saving surgery.[9]

The incident soon faded from the press, and for the moment, ethics institutes and hospital review boards remained the exception. But the

Johns Hopkins baby framed the first debates about life and death in the infant nursery, and the case's centrality gave both the discussions and the policies that emerged from them a very special emotional, as well as intellectual, cast.

It was physicians who first diligently pursued the implications of the case, attempting to achieve their own consensus. Within a year of the Kennedy forum, the prestigious Ross Conference on Pediatric Research, which previously had focused almost exclusively on scientific concerns (from endocrine dysfunction to the use of radioisotopes), devoted its deliberations to the "Ethical Dilemmas in Current Obstetric and Newborn Care." Just as the 1966 CIBA Foundation conference had helped raise considerations of ethics in transplantation, so the 1972 Ross Conference highlighted ethics in newborn nurseries. Because this meeting, like CIBA's, was an initial foray into the territory, most of the participants were physicians (twenty-two of the twenty-nine), but medicine was not as insular as it had been. Joining the physicians were a clergyman, a lawyer, and two of the new breed of bioethicists, Joseph Fletcher, now recognized for his pioneering work, and Robert Veatch, an associate at the Hastings Institute of Society, Ethics, and the Life Sciences.[10]

The two keynote speeches made abundantly clear that the departure point for this conference, like CIBA's, was the recognition that the inherited maxims of medical ethics were not sufficient to resolve the ethical questions at hand. Robert Willson, the chairman of obstetrics and gynecology at the University of Michigan School of Medicine, observed that "the obstetrician-gynecologist of the past was less often forced to make decisions which were contrary to his personal and professional code of ethics than is his contemporary counterpart." William Zuelzer, a pediatrician at Wayne State University, elaborated the point: "Until quite recently the very questions we are here to ask were taboo in a society whose medical ethic has not changed since Hippocrates. Our unconditional commitment to the preservation of life posed no moral or ecological problems." But this essential principle was no longer adequate to determine whether to "preserve life against nature's apparent intentions simply because we have the gadgetry that allows us to do so." Concluded Zuelzer, "Clearly, we are about to cast off from a hitherto safe anchorage without knowing where we may drift."[11]

Perhaps this fear of being morally adrift helped the conference participants forge an agreement. Their most acute concern was to ensure that the burdensome weight of a decision to discontinue treatment did not immobilize the physician. The nightmare case for them was not the unnecessary death of a defective newborn but the survival of such a newborn because physicians had been unable to make tough but necessary choices. Unless doctors took command, warned Zuelzer, the infant nurseries would stand as "the horror chambers we call intensive care units. . . . The operation is a success, the child will live, and now someone will brief the family with averted eyes that they have a mongoloid on their hands. A triumph of modern medicine—or medicine at its worst?"[12] Indeed, physicians' inertia was already beginning to make "the beep of the oscillograph . . . the voice of the new barbarianism."[13]

In this same spirit, Judson Randolph, a professor of surgery at George Washington University, attempted to spell out the conditions under which doctors could justifiably deny treatment in the "hopeless case." He came down on the side of the Johns Hopkins doctors: he would have recommended to the parents to forego surgery. The bioethicists present concurred with the general sentiment. Fletcher offered an admiring restatement of Robert Louis Stevenson's conclusion about the Polynesians: "Out of love for their children they practice infanticide, and at the same time their practice of infanticide makes them treasure their children all the more." Veatch, most concerned with maximizing parental input, testily criticized the physicians for what he took to be their arrogance: "The framing of the question in terms of 'how much the patient should be told or consulted' has been the standard formulation of this meeting. This grates me the wrong way. The question I would tend to ask is: Under what circumstances, if any, should the parents not have control of the decision?" But he, too, was ready to follow the parents' wishes with little concern for the interests of the newborn.[14]

Veatch's complaints notwithstanding, the Ross Conference demonstrated some readiness among the physicians to include in the decision making process not only parents but even third parties. The willingness to support such an unusual step reflected a widely shared sense that resolving the substantive issues was so far beyond the conventional boundaries of medical ethics that physicians had to adopt new strategies. "Here we are really playing God," declared Zuelzer, "and we need all the help we can get. Apart from giving parents a voice—or at least a hearing—we should enlist the support of clergymen, lawyers, sociologists, psychologists, and plain citizens who are not expert at anything, but can contribute their common sense and wisdom." Or, as Judson argued, there should be "an opinion body in every pediatric center to deal with ethical problems in the clinical setting. Such a board might be composed of physicians, administrators, lawyers, chaplains and other representative lay persons."[15]

No one was quite ready to define what such a body was to do, and many of those present feared it might set down rules that would interfere with the doctor–patient relationship. "We have to have some type of guidelines," Zuelzer noted. "I don't know what they are, but the danger lies not so much in our day-to-day decision-making process as in the prospect of some body some day pressing the bureaucratic button and saying: 'This is no longer an acceptable category of human beings and shall be eliminated.' "[16] But in the end, the shared sense of a desperate need for new policies led the conference attendees to two major conclusions:

> The absolute obligation to prolong life under circumstances which impair its quality and dignity needs to be reexamined with a view to arrive at a humane philosophy and guidelines for medical practice.

> One condition for reaching an acceptable ethic is the education of the public and the enlistment of the help of other professional and lay groups.

In short, the physicians were ready to strike a bargain: in order to be able to terminate treatment, they were ready to give nonphysicians a role in decision making. Presumably "a free flow of information from the profession to the laymen" would produce an ethic that would not require treating all patients at all times with all possible resources.[17]

· · ·

The position adopted at the Ross Conference received a far more dramatic and attention-riveting formulation in Raymond Duff and Alexander Campbell's 1973 *New England Journal of Medicine* article on the "Moral and Ethical Dilemmas in the Special-Care Nursery." It was an almost exact analogue to Henry Beecher's 1966 article on human experimentation. Just as Beecher had demonstrated that ethical problems in human experimentation went well beyond the practices of an individual researcher, so Duff and Campbell revealed that the ethical dilemmas in neonatal nurseries extended far beyond the death of a single baby. Like Beecher, too, they were whistle-blowers exposing a secret shared by pediatricians—namely, that the cause of death for a considerable number of newborns was the physician's determination to withhold life-sustaining treatment. "That decisions are made not to treat severely defective infants may be no surprise to those familiar with special-care facilities," wrote Duff and Campbell.[18] The Johns Hopkins baby was merely one in a series.

Unlike Beecher, Duff and Campbell named names—indeed, named themselves. Rather than make a general argument about the ethical dilemmas in a neonatal unit, they were at once precise and specific: at the Yale–New Haven Hospital, 43 of 299 consecutive deaths in the special-care nursery between 1 January 1970 and 30 June 1972 (14 percent) occurred when physicians halted treatment. "The awesome finality of these decisions," they conceded, "combined with a potential for error in prognosis, made the choice agonizing. . . . Nevertheless, the issue has to be faced, for not to decide is an arbitrary and potentially devastating decision of default."[19]

In their exposé Duff and Campbell did not seek to denounce the withdrawal of treatment as unethical—the forty-three deaths were not the counterparts of Beecher's twenty-two cases on the roll of dishonor. Nor were they prepared to invite into the neonatal unit a hospitalwide committee staffed with ethicists and lawyers. Their goal was far more circumscribed: to have parents share in the determinations that once had been the doctors' exclusive preserve. They, like the Ross conferees, strongly supported the propriety of terminating treatment, provided that the decision was reached jointly by physicians and the parents: "We believe the burdens of decision making must be borne by families and their professional advisers because they are most familiar with the respective situations. Since families primarily must live with and are most affected by the decisions, it therefore appears that society and the health professions should provide only general guidelines for decision making." The parents, after all, would be the ones to bear the burden of care should the newborn survive in a compromised state (that is, physically or mentally handicapped, or both). Finally, like Beecher before them, they were convinced that parents, no less than human subjects, were intellectually and emotionally capable of giving informed consent to these decisions. Although some physicians believed that the mysteries of medicine were too esoteric for laypeople to grasp, or that the trauma of giving birth to a disabled infant was too disorienting, Duff and Campbell insisted that "parents are able to understand the implications of such things as chronic dyspnea, oxygen dependency, incontinence, paralysis, contracture, sexual handicaps and mental retardation."[20]

To buttress the case for parental involvement, Duff and Campbell contended that excluding parents would leave physicians to their own devices, which could well mean that the decisions would serve the doctors' purposes, but not necessarily the parents'. Physicians, they pointed out, often face conflicts of interest that "may result in decisions against the individual preferences"; they might, for example, decide to treat a newborn in order to learn more about experimental therapies that might save the life of the next low-weight baby or manage the information so as to aggrandize their own authority.[21] To read Duff and Campbell was to learn that the mind-set of the neonatologist was not significantly different from the mind-set of the researcher, for both might sacrifice the well-being of the particular patient in order to further the progress of medicine.

A companion piece to the Duff and Campbell article appeared in the same *NEJM* issue and adopted an almost identical approach. Anthony Shaw's "Dilemmas of 'Informed Consent' in Children" was more of an opinion piece, without hard data from a specific hospital unit, so it did not capture the same notoriety. But Shaw also centered his arguments on the Johns Hopkins case and rejected a "rigid right-to-life philosophy." Like the others, his fear was not discrimination against the handicapped but the survival of an infant with an unacceptably low quality of life. "My ethic," he wrote, "considers quality of life as a value that must be balanced against a belief in the sanctity of life." Because every year medicine gains the ability to "remove yet another type of malformation from the 'unsalvageable' category . . . we can wind up with 'viable' children . . . propped up on a pillow, marginally tolerating an oral diet of sugar and amino acids and looking forward to another operation." The only escape from the morass, Shaw also recognized, was to reach beyond the medical profession. "Who should make these decisions? The doctors? The parents? Clergymen? A committee? . . . I think that the parents must participate in any decision about treatment and they must be fully informed of the consequences of consenting and withholding consent." As to the standards to be followed: "It may be impossible for any general agreement or guidelines . . . but I believe we should bring these problems into the public forum because whatever the answers may be, they should not be the result of decisions made solely by the attending physicians. Or should they?"[22]

Despite Shaw's tacked-on last question, the message of the two articles—really, the consensus among the pediatric specialists who first tackled the issue—was unmistakable: the critical issue was to know when to terminate treatment, and in reaching this decision, it was valid to consider the quality of life and the consequences of treatment not only for the newborn but for the family. Substantive guidelines were probably too difficult to draw up and were potentially mischievous, but the process of decision making about termination of treatment should involve parents, and probably others as well. To adopt policies that were beyond the scope of traditional medical ethics, to terminate treatment despite injunctions to do no harm, required a new kind of legitimacy, namely, the sanction of the lay as well as the medical world.

This preliminary consensus was short-lived and, as it turned out, deeply controversial. The first critics came from within the profession: the idea that outsiders should participate in medical decision making sparked opposition, and so did the proposition that termination of treatment for handicapped newborns was sometimes ethically appropriate. The debates quickly spilled over from medicine to the laity, to become among the most divisive issues Americans faced in the post–Vietnam War era.

The first complaints about Duff and Campbell's and Shaw's articles came from conservative physicians who feared that these authors conceded too much authority to outsiders. Franz Ingelfinger, the outspoken, traditionalistic editor of the *NEJM*, wrote that what he liked best about the contributions was their case-by-case approach, their preference for "the principles of individualism" over "fairly rigid rules of ethical professional behavior."[23] (Ingelfinger's confusion of "individualism" with Duff and Campbell's commitment to an individual, case-by-case decision making may help explain his tenacity on the subject.) What he liked least about the articles was the suggestion that physicians invite in outsiders—a practice, he was convinced, that would produce "God squad" committees.

Although it was only 1973 and the bioethics movement's most impressive successes were yet to come, Ingelfinger was already bemoaning the fact that "this is the day of the ethicist in medicine. He delineates the rights of patients, of experimental subjects, of fetuses, of mothers, of animals, and even of doctors." And in a well-conceived comparison between the attitudes of the 1950s and those of the 1970s, he observed, "What a far cry from the days when medical 'ethics' consisted of condemning economic improprieties such as fee splitting and advertising." Ingelfinger had little patience with the ethicists whose work he considered to be "the products of armchair exercise," untested in the "laboratory of experience," and he advised his colleagues: "When Duff and Campbell ask, 'Who decides for the child?' the answer is 'you.' " He conceded that "society, ethics, institutional attitudes and committees can provide the broad guidelines, but the onus of decision-making ultimately falls on the doctor in whose care the child has been put."[24] To abdicate this responsibility was to subvert the ethics and standing of the profession itself. "Some will not agree with this thesis," Ingelfinger concluded, "but for those who do . . . a necessary corollary is that current attempts to de-mysticize and debase the status of the physician are compromising his ability to provide leadership (not exercise dictatorship!) when health and life are at stake." The issue came down to who would rule at the bedside—doctors or others.

Equally unhappy were a number of physicians who believed that the emerging consensus in favor of termination violated medicine's ethical norms. These critics condemned the Johns Hopkins Hospital for its handling of the case and denounced Duff and the others for their readiness to halt treatment. One of the first protests came from the Yale–New Haven nursery itself. Two of Duff and Campbell's associates, Doctors Joan Venes and Peter Huttenlocher, with a hostility not ordinarily found in letters to medical journals, disassociated themselves from the Duff–Campbell position. Accusing them of "hyperbole . . . throughout the article," Venes and Huttenlocher, like Ingelfinger, believed it "an abrogation of the physician's role . . . to argue conflicting opinions in the presence of already distraught parents or to leave with them the very difficult decision." But they went even further, rejecting the idea that physicians could use "active means to produce 'an early death' of the child," or should include in their calculus "the financial and psychologic stresses imposed upon a family with the birth of a handicapped child."[25]

This was only the start, though. Any notion of a consensus among physicians soon evaporated in the heat of antagonisms so bitter as to exceed anything heard in human experimentation or transplantation. Two of the physicians involved in the Johns Hopkins incident, Doctors Cooke and Fost, were soon condemning their own earlier behavior and colleagues who would follow that example. In a complete turnabout, Cooke now insisted that whatever the parental sentiments, "the physician must opt for [the] life of his patient. . . . The physician must recognize that the patient is neither his property nor that of the parents, to be disposed of at will." But if parents were too biased against the handicapped and too confused about the implications of a handicap to be trusted, and if Ingelfinger's advice seemed antediluvian, then how was one to proceed in the tough case where treatment might, or might not be, futile? Cooke opted for a "group decision," with input not only from ethicists and other professionals, but from "families who have been through such decisions themselves." In this way, "the handicapped or the potentially handicapped will be accorded treatment equivalent to that of his normal brother."[26]

Fost, also chastened by the Johns Hopkins experience, was even more insistent on treatment, whatever the parental wishes. At an academic conference that both he and Duff attended, he unleashed an impassioned attack on Duff's position: "Dr. Duff has been asked, 'What is to prevent families from deciding *arbitrarily* that a child shouldn't be kept alive?' He says, 'The doctors won't allow it.' I see institutions where children with Down's Syndrome . . . or myelomeningocele [spina bifida] with an excellent prognosis are allowed to starve, without specific criteria as to who is in this class and without a defined process for decision making. What is the definition of arbitrary if not the absence of criteria or a defined process?" He also rejected the simple definition of a "hopeless" case: "I do not understand what is hopeless about Down's Syndrome," [at which point another physician interrupted to say: "Have a child with it of your own—you will soon see."]. "Life, even impaired life, is very important. . . . We should not kill people or allow people to die just because they are going to wind up in wheelchairs or because they have only a 20 percent chance of a normal IQ."

Fost insisted on the need to open up and formalize the decision making process, not to facilitate decisions to terminate treatment, as some of his colleagues urged, but to protect the handicapped. "Dr. Duff rejects committees because members tend to be 'elite . . . quite powerful, and often seek more power. This tends to corrupt.' " But the power of a committee was minimal compared to the authority of physicians to disenfranchise the handicapped, "where an elite of the bright declares mental retardation to be equal to suffering, and an elite of the walking declares wheelchair existence to be 'massive disability.' " Not that Fost himself would treat every case maximally, but in the controversial cases and when long life was possible, he followed "a *process*—where facts, feelings, and interests not always perceived by parents and physicians, [are] brought to bear. . . . I assemble as diverse a group as we can—nurses, lawyers, students, secretaries, philosophers, to talk about it."[27] In sum, physicians were obliged to consult with outsiders to the case, even with outsiders to medicine.

Duff neither retreated from his readiness to terminate treatment at least in some cases, nor did he lack allies of his own. Perhaps the most controversial among them was John Lorber, the English surgeon who in the 1960s had been famous for his aggressiveness in treating spina bifida. In 1971, however, Lorber reversed his position, and as he explained to his American colleagues (at the same conference where Fost was taking on Duff): "The pendulum had swung too far, from one extreme of treating none to the other of treating all. The balance had to be restored. The case for selective treatment was overwhelming." To this end, Lorber formulated clinical criteria—the size of the lesion, degree of paralysis, and extent of hydrocephalus—and used them to guide (really, he conceded, to dictate) parental decisions. When a surgeon examined a newborn with extensive lesions, concluded Lorber, he "should think of the life that lies ahead for the baby. If he would not like such a child of his own to survive, then he should take the logical long-term strategic view and resist the temptation to operate."[28]

Anthony Shaw also continued to support the termination position, even going so far as to devise a mathematical formula that would ostensibly factor in all the relevant social and economic considerations: (N.E.) times (H. plus S.) equals M.L. That is, on a scale of 1 to 10, the child's natural endowments (N.E.) were multiplied by the home (H.) advantages (emotional, financial) plus the society (S.) resources (special education programs, foster homes) to determine a meaningful-life (M.L.) score. Shaw concluded that there could be no definition of a meaningful life, "except to point out that in this formula, a value of 200 would indicate the maximal meaningful life for an infant," and to imply that a score of 25 or 50 or 75 (a very handicapped child born to poor parents in a state unwilling to fund social services) would suggest a meaningless life, and thus permit (encourage?) a decision not to treat.[29]

With proponents like Lorber and formulas composed by Shaw, the termination position grew even more controversial; and for both obvious and less obvious reasons, those outside of medicine soon were drawn into the debate. For one thing, weighing of the issues here, as in human experimentation and transplantation, did not require a mastery of esoteric techniques or complex treatments. The clinical data about retardation, spina bifida, and low birth weights were accessible to laypeople; and the inevitable uncertainty about the neurological and social outcomes for the newborns in these categories heightened a sense that moral values, not medical facts, were fundamental to treatment decisions.

For another, it was ever so easy—and unsettling—to plot a slippery slope: Let the profession abandon a commitment to the preservation of life, and then the Lorbers and Shaws would devise value-laden formulas to decide who lived. Soon enough only the perfect child would be allowed to survive—and at the other end of life, only the perfect adult. This was not medicine but selective eugenics and the worst kind of social engineering, which raised the specter of Nazilike programs and brought greater acrimony to an already bitter dispute.

Still other considerations propelled outsiders to join in this debate. One cannot imagine an issue more likely to galvanize lay opinion and action than the treatment of the handicapped newborn, or imagine a time more auspicious for riveting attention on it than the early 1970s, or more precisely, 1973. Besides being the year of Duff and Campbell's *NEJM* article, 1973 was also the year of the Supreme Court's *Roe v. Wade* decision legalizing abortion. In 1973 Congress also enacted the Vocational Rehabilitation Act, and its Section 504 provided that no one "solely by reason of his handicap, be excluded from the participation in, be denied the benefits of, or be subjected to discrimination under any program or activity receiving Federal financial assistance."[30] The principles underlying both the court finding in *Roe v. Wade* and the congressional legislation in Section 504 were directly relevant to decision making in neonatal units. The difficulty was that the principles of the Court and the Congress were at conflict, pointing policy in opposite directions.

The thrust of *Roe v. Wade* was to maximize parental autonomy in that a mother who wanted a fetus aborted had the right to do so. To be sure, she had to act in cooperation with her physician, and her prerogatives, relative to the rule-making power of the state, declined as the viability of the fetus increased over time. But through most of the first two trimesters it was essentially the mother's choice—and not the doctor's or the legislature's—as to whether the fetus survived. In this way, *Roe v. Wade* expanded the domain of private decision making against both professional and state authority, and thus was most consistent, in the context of newborns and termination of treatment, with the recommendations that Duff and others were proposing. Under *Roe v. Wade* the parent determined whether the fetus would survive—and it was not much of an extension to add, whether a defective newborn would survive. Not that the Court spoke specifically to the fate of the handicapped newborn or that it sanctioned infanticide; rather, in the name of privacy, it championed parental decision making, which was precisely what Duff and others were advocating.

The very fact that *Roe v. Wade* did have this consistency with Duff, however, clarified for the public all the stakes in neonatal decision making and made it seem not only fitting but necessary for outsiders to enter the neonatal intensive care unit. The issue was not only how to respond to gravely ill newborns, which might be defined, in keeping with Franz Ingelfinger and John Lorber, as a medical question in which the doctor essentially calculated the odds and proceeded accordingly. It was also a question of defining life, and the Duff position seemed to exemplify the fears of not only the opponents of legalized abortion, who saw it as the first step on the road to destroying the sanctity of all life, but those essentially sympathetic with *Roe v. Wade* but apprehensive about an unbounded protection of family privacy. Did one begin by discounting the life of the fetus and then move, inexorably, to discounting the life of the newborn, and, eventually the elderly? Was the newborn nursery an inevitable extension of the abortion clinic? As a result of *Roe v. Wade*, the neonatal intensive care unit became a crystal ball in which one might see the future.[31]

Then, at the very moment the Supreme Court was expanding the scope of family privacy, Congress was expanding the rights of the disabled. Although the two developments might appear part of an enlargement of individual liberties, they were in fact on a collision course, destined to meet head-on in the newborn nursery.

According to the 1970 U.S. Census, almost 10 percent of Americans identified themselves as disabled. Despite their numbers, however, they had not yet been a visible or politically active group. Those handicapped by blindness had little to do with the deaf or with the wheelchair-bound, and almost no one among the physically disabled identified with the mentally disabled. Within a few years, however, not only was there a distinct disabilities community, but it was shaping public policy. Advances in medical technology, from prosthetic devices to surgical techniques, enabled the handicapped to live longer and do more. Consequently, the handicapped found their own disabilities less limiting than the social barriers they encountered, from too little access to public space to too much prejudice from potential employers and landlords. The diverse groups came together through a shared experience of exclusion and took as their model for political action the minority rights campaigns. The most notable success for the disabilities movement came in 1973. Just as Title VI in the Civil Rights Act of 1964 banned discrimination in federally financed programs on the basis of race, color, or national origin, and Title IX in the Education Amendments of 1972 banned discrimination on the basis of sex, so Section 504 of the Vocational Rehabilitation Act banned discrimination on the basis of handicap.[32]

The immediate impact of Section 504 on federal policy was negligible. The provision, one small paragraph in a lengthy vocational education bill, had not been debated in Congress; and none of its sponsors anticipated that by the end of the decade Section 504 would be the basis for the expenditure of well over a billion dollars to give the handicapped greater access to mass transportation, public housing, and employment and educational opportunities. But in 1973 Section 504 already reflected and reinforced a new attitude about disabilities diametrically opposed to the negative biases that many of the nonhandicapped, including physicians, shared. As one advocate (from the National Federation of the Blind) testified: "This civil rights for the handicapped provision . . . brings the disabled within the law. . . . It establishes that because a man is blind or deaf or without legs, he is not less a citizen, that his rights of citizenship are not revoked or diminished because he is disabled." Or as Senator Hubert Humphrey explained, "Every child—gifted, normal, and handicapped—has a fundamental right to educational opportunity and the right to health."[33]

It was still too early to foresee all the social consequences of this reorientation. No one, no matter how prescient, could have predicted that ten years later Section 504 would be tacked up on the walls of neonatal units or that medical care might come under its umbrella. But clearly, attitudes toward the handicapped were being transformed, and the impact was bound to be felt not only in modifications to make public buildings wheelchair accessible but in assessments of which conditions should or should not be treated in newborns, and who should be making the decision.

• • •

One more incentive for the public to focus on neonatal ethics arose in 1973: Mondale's long campaign to create a national commission finally succeeded, helped along by Kennedy's ability to use the newest scandals in human experimentation to press for both minority rights and patient rights. Kennedy himself tied all these strands together, convening a one-day hearing on "Medical Ethics: The Right to Survival." The very title made his own orientation toward neonatal decision making apparent; the key consideration for him was how to protect the rights of the newborn, not the prerogatives of doctors or parents. He opened the hearing by observing that just the previous week, Congress had formally established the National Commission for the Protection of Human Subjects, and the new body might well want to add to its agenda the treatment of the newborn, for the plight of handicapped neonates resembled the plight of many human subjects—both were vulnerable to discrimination, deprived of the right to consent, and in need of protection. "In our committee sessions," Kennedy reported, "we heard of prisoners being used in human experimentation . . . we learned of experimental drugs plus medical devices being used," and these experiments often were conducted without the consent of the subjects. "Now," he continued, "we are moving into a different area, but the question of consent still arises. Who has the right to give consent for infants? Is it only the parents? . . . Is it possible that some physicians and families may join in a conspiracy to deny the right of a defective child to live or to die?" The voice of the doctor and the parent were being heard, but not the infant's, and hence his fate might well depend on "which of you doctors the parents take him to."[34] Thus, physicians, even acting in concert with parents, should have an institutional review board–type committee looking over their shoulder.

Just how provocative these points were emerged in the testimony of the hearing's four witnesses. Two took their priorities from a sense of family privacy (staying with the *Roe v. Wade* model); two, closer to Kennedy, made their priority protecting the newborn (drawing on Section 504 and the lessons learned in human experimentation). Raymond Duff and Lewis Sheiner, a physician from the University of California–San Francisco (UCSF) medical school, advocated case-by-case decisions that ultimately reflected the choice of parents with their physicians. "It is disquieting," conceded Duff, "to discover that infants apparently have an identical condition and may be treated differently, and some may survive and some not . . . but that is the way it is." On the opposing side were Robert Cooke and Warren Reich, a bioethicist from the Kennedy Institute at Georgetown, who argued that parents might be so "very biased" that it was unconscionable to allow their preferences to condemn an infant to death. Nor were they persuaded that individual physicians had the insight or the moral authority to prevent such abuses. "Public awareness of the fallibility of its various priesthoods is increasing," noted Reich, "and medicine is no exception. The Tuskegee syphilis study debacle, or the Willowbrook hepatitis study make sensational news and arouse public distrust."[35]

The one point of agreement, although not very firm, was on the need for collective decision making. Far apart in substantive terms, all the witnesses still favored more open and formal decision-making mechanisms—notably, ethics committees with representatives drawn from medicine, the professions, and the lay public. Duff and Sheiner, for their part, emphasized the consultative character of the committee: "A dialogue must be begun." Reich stressed the need to equip such a group with explicit guidelines; otherwise, it, too, might discriminate against the handicapped. "Both Dr. Sheiner and Dr. Duff . . . lay great weight on procedures, as though procedures for decision-making are going to be our only salvation, since it is not possible to establish any kind of norms that can govern our conduct. I would like to say that procedures are indeed important, but they do not carry with them any assurance of truth. . . . Principles should be prior to procedures."[36] But everyone agreed that these committees were to educate both parents and doctors about handicaps, and rebut stereotypes about the effects of disabilities. Collective decision making in which physicians would share authority with a variety of outsiders seemed to be the only way out of the impasse.

The tensions between *Roe v. Wade* and Section 504, between the prerogatives of families, the authority of physicians, and the protections against discrimination due to handicap, also enlarged the cohort of philosophers interested in bioethics. In particular, Daniel Callahan, co-founder of the Hastings Institute, and Albert Jonsen of the UCSF Medical School followed a route into the field that began with abortion, continued through *Roe v. Wade*, and eventually entered the neonatal unit.

Although Callahan had earned a doctorate in philosophy from Harvard in 1961, he chose not to pursue a traditional academic career. He served on the editorial staff for the Catholic-oriented weekly, *Commonweal*, and held a variety of visiting teaching positions. Then, in the late 1960s, he became fascinated with the issue of abortion. With foundation support, he pursued his analysis, not attempting to resolve the controversies but "asking the question, as a philosopher, how one would go about thinking through an issue like that." In the process, Callahan discovered "the whole world of medical ethics, of which abortion was simply one part." In particular, he was drawn to the problems posed by heart transplantation, the definition of death, and the "possibilities and hazards in genetic engineering." He also discovered the critical need for an interdisciplinary approach: "One could see in any issue a philosophical problem, but then there was almost always a legal problem, a political problem, a socio-cultural problem as well."

From this starting point, Callahan joined with his Hastings, New York, neighbor, Willard Gaylin, a psychiatrist who was then writing a book on Vietnam war resisters, to found the Hastings Institute of Society, Ethics and the Life Sciences. The first items on its agenda, as might be expected, were population issues, behavior modification, death and dying, and genetic engineering. Its strategy was to bring together representatives of a variety of disciplines, both theoretical and policy oriented, to define the relevant issues, and, even more notably, to offer rules and guidelines for resolving them. Callahan both then and later insisted on the need for limiting physicians' "absolute autonomy," for devising "accepted ground rules." As he told an interviewer in 1977: "Doctors want . . . to make all the choices. Well, we're saying to them, no. There are some public interests at stake here and some general principles you have to abide by. . . . You're playing in a public ballpark now . . . and you've got to live by certain standards . . . like it or not."[37]

To be sure, not every philosopher who crossed over into medicine was quite so confrontational. Joseph Fletcher, for example, in his exceptionally popular 1966 book, *Situational Ethics* (which sold over

150,000 copies), emphasized the importance of doing right in a particular circumstance over rigidly following universal rules. "The situationist," he wrote, "enters into every decision-making situation fully armed with the ethical maxims of his community and its heritage, and he treats them with respect as illuminators of the problem. Just the same he is prepared in any situation to compromise them or set them aside *in the situation* if love seems better served by doing so." The idea of ethics tied to the particulars of a situation fit well with medicine's case-by-case orientation, and so amorphous a concept as "love" suited the exercise of a very traditional kind of paternalism. But if such a reading was popular among some physicians, Fletcher had other intentions. "Situation ethics" was hostile to what it labeled mindless legalism, but it was also determined to elevate the lay voice, in the first instance in religious controversies, and by implication, in medical controversies as well. Fletcher's aims were essentially democratic. In the process of empowering the congregation against the bishop, he was altogether comfortable in empowering the patient against the doctor.[38]

Albert Jonsen's approach was closer to Callahan than to Fletcher. In May 1974, Jonsen, who had left the Jesuit order and was teaching in the UCSF Health Policy Program, brought together colleagues from the Department of Pediatrics with an interdisciplinary group of outsiders to medicine to explore "Critical Issues in Newborn Intensive Care."[39] At this meeting (and at many others thereafter), laypeople outnumbered physicians, and the recommendations reflected the altered balance of power.

The conference participants proposed "A Moral Policy for Neonatal Intensive Care" (the prominence of "moral" in the title testifying to the leading role of bioethicists). The lead proposition was that parents, not doctors, had responsibility for the "ultimate decisions" affecting the newborn. "Those who engender and willingly bring an infant to birth are morally accountable for its well being. They are closest to the infant and must bear the burdens of its nurture, especially if it is ill or defective." Only as a last resort, when parents abdicated their rightful responsibility, should physicians assume "the heavy burden of rendering final decisions." Here again, as in human experimentation and transplantation, the presumption was that physicians had a conflict of interest. Echoing what had been said at the Ross Conference as well as by Duff and Campbell, the participants explained in the report, "Physicians may feel that their duty extends not only to a particular infant under care but also to all children. For such a reason, some physicians may be devoted to scientific research aimed at improving the quality and effectiveness of neonatal care for all. While this dedication is necessary and praiseworthy, it may, on occasion . . . push a clinician, even unconsciously, to extend a course of care beyond reasonable limits of benefit to the patient."[40] The neonatal nursery was too close to the laboratory to trust to physicians.

The conference's second major recommendation was to urge the creation of guidelines for neonatal decision making. Establishing in advance a series of principles would rein in the discretionary authority of individual physicians and protect the interests of the newborn as well. The neonatologists should devise and circulate "clinical criteria which render more specific the general conditions of prolonged life without pain and the potential for human communication. Resuscitation criteria should be established. . . . Delivery room policy, based on certain criteria, should state conditions for which resuscitation is not indicated."[41]

To these same ends, the final recommendation was to open up neonatal decision making to outsiders: each unit should "establish an advisory board consisting of health professionals and other involved and interested persons." (Imagine how a once autonomous professional would respond to the idea of inviting in "interested persons.") The board would "discuss the problems of the unit and make a periodic retrospective review of the difficult decisions." Its purpose was not to supercede parental authority but to "provide, by bringing a variety of experience, belief, and attitude, a wider human environment for decision-making than would otherwise be available." Thus, the board would supplement—in effect, supplant—the narrow viewpoint of technicians.[42]

Although the recommendations were presented as the conference findings and published in a leading medical journal, *Pediatrics*, the consensus was less complete than it appeared. In quite self-conscious fashion, the bioethicists were laying down a challenge to the medical profession. They conceded that "this moral policy may seem unreal. This is the inevitable result of considering moral decisions apart from the agony of living through the decisions." But, they said, their intellectual distance from the bedside strengthened their position: "The air of unreality is, we believe, the necessary cool moment which philosophers say should precede any reasonable judgment. That judgment will have to be made amid the hard realities, but it may be better made in light of reflection on these propositions."[43] Armchair ethics was more cool, reasonable, and reflective than bedside ethics.

Although the physicians at the conference did not directly confront the philosophers, the split of opinion, particularly about the proper division of authority between doctor and parent, did peek through in the report. Dr. Clement Smith, of the Harvard Medical School, let it be known (albeit in a footnote) that "nonmedical members of the conference insisted . . . with unanimity . . . that life-and-death decisions must be made by the parents, while doctors of medicine with almost equal unanimity saw that as an avoidance of the physician's own responsibility." Dr. Smith preferred—and so did most physicians, he believed—"that the doctor, through intimate participation and full discussion with the parents, interpret their beliefs or wishes clearly enough to act according to those indications rather than confront parents directly with the act of decision."[44] His minority statement makes clear just how novel and controversial it still was to elevate the parent over the doctor.

Although many physicians shared Dr. Smith's frustration and discontent, they were unable to make their case persuasively. Inside the neonatal unit, they might convince parents to accept their advice; but in public forums devoted to exploring normative standards and the principles that should govern neonatal decision making, they were very much on the defensive, and their weakness affected the eventual design of public policy. To counter claims for expanding parental authority, Harvard's Dr. Smith and his peers invoked an almost discredited ideal of paternalism. Moreover, for them to claim that many parents did not want to carry the burden of the decision, and to live for the rest of their lives with the guilt of having "killed" their newborn—even though such instances were real enough—was an inadequate argument, for it conceded that if parents were strong enough and not guilt ridden, they should be making these decisions.

An alternative and potentially more powerful claim on behalf of the exercise of physician authority was to present the doctor as protector of the newborn against the potentially biased and self-interested parents, those who wanted a perfect child and were repelled at the prospect of raising a Down's syndrome baby. But this claim had problems of its own. The medical record was anything but spotless—as evidenced by the events at Johns Hopkins, the writings of Duff and Campbell, the formulas of Shaw, and the guidelines of Lorber. And to pit the doctor against the family even in the guise of the protector of the handicapped inevitably raised well-worn images of a heavy-handed medical paternalism. Indeed, it was against the prospect of continued medical paternalism that the parents of one low-birth-weight newborn wrote, first in an article and then in a book, one of the most widely read and emotionally moving attacks on physician hegemony. In *The Long Dying of Baby Andrew*, Robert and Peggy Stinson described their son's death with a bitterness matched only by ex–mental patients in denouncing psychiatric tyranny.[45] To read their account is to understand all the better why the public agenda gave so much prominence to neonatal decision making, why a variety of outsiders joined physicians in the nursery, and why physicians were not going to be recognized as defenders of handicapped newborns.

The Stinson story began in December 1976, when Peggy, five months pregnant with her second child, suddenly started to bleed heavily. Her physician diagnosed the problem as a low-lying placenta that was liable to hemorrhage, and he counseled her to remain in bed. Peggy and her husband, Robert, a historian teaching at Moravian College in Pennsylvania, considered, but decided against, an abortion. Although Peggy followed her doctor's advice, she entered spontaneous labor, rushed to her local hospital, and after many hours of difficult labor gave birth to an 800-gram baby boy, or what the Stinsons call a "fetal infant."[46] Almost immediately, they informed the physician that they did not want extraordinary measures used to keep the baby alive.

Even without heroics, the baby, Andrew, stabilized and survived his first several days of life. But then he experienced a fluid imbalance, a problem that the physician assured the Stinsons was readily correctable; with their agreement, Andrew was transferred to a tertiary care medical center in Philadelphia, with the expectation that he would remain there for a matter of days and return to the community hospital. However,

Andrew developed problems breathing and was placed on a respirator. When the Stinsons opposed this measure, the Philadelphia physicians summarily informed them that in their opinion Andrew should be treated, and should the Stinsons continue to object, the hospital would obtain a court order. "Mrs. Stinson," Peggy reports one doctor saying, "I wouldn't presume to tell my auto mechanic how to fix my car."[47]

The Stinsons each kept a journal of the events that followed Andrew's birth, and the entries make up *The Long Dying of Baby Andrew*. Their reason for publishing their record of the "tragic failures" and "perils" of the ICU, was, they explain, to help recapture medical decision making from the experts and return it to the family. "The general public—and that includes the parents and potential parents of the babies whose care the specialists are debating—has little exposure to the issues and no voice at all in the debate. While specialists argue abstractions and hospitals impose different 'policies,' suffering babies and their family can get, quite literally, trapped."[48]

One of the Stinsons's most bitter and telling complaints is the sense of exclusion and isolation they experienced throughout the ordeal. "Have they ever saved a baby like Andrew in this I[nfant] ICU?" they wondered. "Does Andrew have a real chance? . . . If only we had someone to trust."[49] Why this acute sense of an absence of trust? In part, because medicine deals with uncertainties. At every critical juncture, physicians (in retrospect, overly optimistic) assured the Stinsons that the interventions would be quick and effective. Place the infant into the tertiary care center to correct a fluid imbalance, or put the infant onto the respirator, and he will be back and stable in a matter of weeks. But Andrew never did leave the tertiary care center or get off the respirator. Indeed, from the start nothing happened as expected. The Stinsons had believed that her spontaneous labor was part of a miscarriage, only to learn to their astonishment that the fetus was breathing. Undoubtedly, other physicians might have been more effective at explaining to them the underlying uncertainties; but even so, the case of Andrew was like a roller coaster, and the parents felt helpless as they watched the ride.

Second, the Stinsons were strangers to the tertiary care hospital. The baby's transfer from the local hospital to the Philadelphia medical center took them, in every sense, away from home. Not only were they forced to travel several hours to visit Andrew, but the hospital itself, as Robert observed, was strange, "an entirely different world from the one I normally inhabit." The internal organization of the infant ICU only exaggerated the distance. Since this was a teaching hospital, a new group of residents rotated through the unit every month, with the result that over six months, the Stinsons met a bewildering number of doctors; no sooner did one face become familiar than the rotation was over and a new face was at the nursery door. "It's hard to find out how Andrew is," Peggy complained. "We never get the same person twice when we call the hospital." Her journal entry a month later noted: "Another stranger to explain ourselves to. . . . The bureaucracy controls Andrew. . . . It rolls inexorably onward. . . . Doctors come and doctors go—there's a schedule in the office somewhere." Ultimately, "The doctor-rotation thing is impossible from the point of view of the parent."[50]

Rotations meant not only adjusting to different styles of communication but to different information. It took weeks for the Stinsons to puzzle out whether or not Andrew had suffered a cerebral bleed, and some of the confusion had to do with a lack of continuity among the caretakers. So too, because the Stinsons continued to object to treatment, the medical teams labeled them difficult and uncooperative, and the label was passed on team to team, the way teachers tell each other about a troublesome student. Under these circumstances, it was virtually impossible for the Stinsons to form a relationship with any of the doctors.

Perhaps most important in understanding their feelings of distrust was the fact that the Stinsons were convinced (and, as we have seen, they were anything but alone in this) that the physicians did not share an identity of interest with them or, they thought, with Andrew. The physicians' primary commitment, they believed, was not to the particular newborn but to the accumulation of knowledge: the ICU was a laboratory, the physicians medical researchers, and Andrew the human subject. "It's not the technology per se that inspires fears—it's the mentality of the people employing it. Fallible people lost sight of their fallibility in the scramble to push back the frontiers of knowledge, to redesign nature and to outwit death." When they confronted one of the physicians directly with the question, "Isn't Andrew's life a kind of experiment, then?" he bridled at the idea, insisting that "our concern here is for the health of each patient." But the Stinsons were not persuaded. "Andrew is interesting to them in some detached way—their own private research project, conveniently underage so that they need no consent for whatever it is that they do. . . . Of course, they don't see it that way; they're saving the life of an unfortunate child. . . . And if it looks like Andrew can't be saved? Why stop there? They're still learning something." Health care in a tertiary center "could be a mask—a partial truth—which covers, however unintended, the research which is just as much a reason for [its] being."[51]

For the Stinsons the entire episode amounted to an unprecedented loss of control. "[Dr.] Farrell controls Andrew's life," Robert noted angrily. And Peggy repeatedly lamented that "everything is out of control. I am out of control. Even the disaster itself is out of control. . . . Andrew is not our baby any more—he's been taken over by a medical bureaucracy." This loss of control was all the more difficult for them to accept in light of *Roe v. Wade*. "A woman can terminate a perfectly healthy pregnancy by abortion at 24½ weeks and that is legal," observed Peggy. "Nature can terminate a problem pregnancy by miscarriage at 24½ weeks and the baby must be saved at all cost; anything less is illegal and immoral." It seemed hopeless to try to explain these points to the hospital staff. "We're irrelevant, just an annoyance, people for them all to patronize and categorize, and then shake their heads about."[52]

In their effort to cope, the Stinsons sought psychological counseling, and their therapist, as they report it, helped promote a sense of control: "You have been powerless. You have to get back in power." Apparently, the therapy helped, and toward the end of Andrew's six-month life, Peggy became pregnant again. The Stinsons interpreted the event as a symbolic victory: "The new baby is an act of will; we take control again."[53]

The Stinsons' account, as would be expected, struck a sympathetic cord in many of its readers (and eventually in many of the viewers of an adapted television program). The book jacket had a blurb from Raymond Duff that people should "apply the lessons from this classic story of irony and tragedy in modern medicine" and another from

Daniel Callahan that this was the story of "extraordinarily sensitive parents coping with a grievous moral problem." The doctors had apparently allowed "technological enthusiasm" to triumph over "human care." Two well-known ethicists, Peter Singer and Helga Kuhse, reviewed the book very favorably, applauding the Stinsons for sharing their ordeal with the readers.[54] Without doubt, many of the Stinsons' criticisms were on target and devastating: the alien character of the hospital setting, the frustrations of following house-staff rotations, and the arrogance of the senior physicians. Their story helps us understand the impulse to elevate the rights of parents against doctors, and by extension, the rights of patients against doctors. It also clarifies why, despite the very strong case that can be made in support of Andrew's doctors, physicians were destined to cede authority to a variety of third parties.

Like the film version of the John Hopkins case, *The Long Dying of Baby Andrew* is designed to impart a particular lesson and empower the Stinsons (and patients) against their doctors. But again, like the film, it is less than clear what this book actually represents. Ostensibly it is the diaries that the Stinsons kept; however, they themselves concede that it is not the complete and actual record, but an edited version, containing only what they have chosen to tell the reader. How many of the book's entries are tailored to make the case, to get revenge at the doctors, we cannot know (and the Stinsons are unwilling to allow an independent examination of the original entries). The opening sections of the journal, for example, do not have a ring of authenticity; it is doubtful that a woman who had never before kept a diary would start one when she began to hemorrhage in her fifth month of pregnancy and anticipated an immediate miscarriage. Nor is it likely that a parent given favorable news about her baby's prospects would on the spot react as skeptically as Peggy did. Rather, one suspects that much of the journal was written with the benefit of hindsight, reviewing the events when the outcome was known, when Andrew turned out to be a losing case.

It is important to keep these doubts in mind, for if we are to reverse the angle of vision and analyze these same events from the perspective of Andrew's physicians, a very different message emerges. After the fact, it is easy to fault physicians for making decisions to treat over parental objections. But go back to the start, bracket the ending, and simple judgments become complicated.

An 800-gram baby born in December 1976 was a newborn with a slim but real chance of survival. Hospitals with infant ICUs on a par with Philadelphia's, like University Hospital in Cleveland, had survival rates of 47 percent in infants between 501 and 1,000 grams.[55] Andrew, it is true, was born very early in the pregnancy, which reduced the odds, but not to the point of hopelessness. A range of neonatal units reported 10 percent success even here, and the Philadelphia hospital may well have been better equipped to treat such cases. What then were the physicians to do? The parents clearly did not want treatment; expecting an aborted fetus, they were having trouble coping with the fact of a breathing infant. But the first crisis of a fluid imbalance seemed to the doctors manageable, and the initial use of the respirator, reasonable; and the doctors were comfortable in not allowing the parents' displeasure to seal the fate of the infant. Over the next several months, when the prognosis for Andrew became more guarded and then dismal, the doctors had great difficulty in backing off—perhaps because the law on terminating treatment was still primitive; because neonatal units have a fierce protreatment ideology; or because the doctors did not want these parents, who had stopped visiting Andrew and were looking for ways to terminate their parental obligations, to be proven right. But being wrong in March or May was not the same as being wrong in December.

After all, what was at the root of the parents' case to terminate treatment? What arguments did they make to the doctors? Most of them had less to do with Andrew and more to do with their own concerns, such as their family, careers, and financial situation. From their perspective, the demands that Andrew would place on the family would deprive his older sister (and future siblings) of a fair share of parental attention. As Andrew's treatment persisted, the Stinsons faced the prospect that his hospitalization would outrun their medical coverage. Robert raised this possibility with one of the physicians, asking him whether, in the event of bankruptcy, he would lose his house. "I wanted to shock him into seeing how extensive and unrealized the consequences of his pursuit were, but he shocked me instead. 'I guess they will,' was all he said. . . . The social or financial consequences of his work, being literally beyond the glass walls of the IICU, are just not real to him. The unit is sterile and intensive in more ways than one thinks." Concluded Robert: "These doctors go on righteously about their business while our lives fall apart."[56]

Clearly, the physicians were not inclined to worry about the Stinson house or Andrew's impact on the Stinson family, however dismaying the predicament. Andrew was the patient, not the parents or the sister, and treatment decisions were not made with one eye on a bank account or the psychological state of siblings. Of course, the doctors should have been better at communicating uncertainties and much less arrogant. But these shortcomings notwithstanding, the crux of the problem was whether conditions external to the neonatal nursery should affect physicians' behavior in the neonatal nursery. The Stinsons insisted that the answer is yes—and Duff and others agreed. But then think of the objections of Cooke and Fost, and we are back to the deadlock of parental rights as against protection from harm.

However compelling the Stinsons' narrative, one has only to imagine a different set of circumstances to see its limits. What would have happened if Andrew had survived; if, despite his parents' reluctance to treat, the physicians had gone ahead and Andrew had made it through? The Stinsons would then have had no story. In other words, they got to publish their account precisely because this was one time (out of how many?) that the parents' reluctance to treat seemed justified by the end result. Had Andrew won, however, it would have been the physicians' turn to write about parents who quit too easily to be trusted with making treatment decisions, but even that would not have resolved the issues. In the end, the Stinsons found no one to trust, but neither does the reader. That Andrew lost does not support the case for parents' rights, any more than does the fact that other infants have won buttress the case for doctors.

Although the contest for control over neonatal decision making in the early 1970s did not yield definitive answers, it did exert a critical influence over how the larger issue of ruling medicine would be resolved. First, the era of the physician as unilateral decision maker in the neonatal nursery (and elsewhere) was clearly over. It was still not apparent what combination of lawyers, legislators, administrators, bioethicists, patients, and parents would affect and control medical decision making. But whatever the mix, it was obvious that the ICU was no longer physicians' exclusive preserve. At the least, some kind of collective mechanism, along the line of the IRBs, was likely to come into place.

At the same time, the prospect was very real that politics would intrude. Whether spurred by reactions to *Roe v. Wade* or Section 504, the neonatal issues resonated with so many others that elected officials and candidates were likely to stake out a position that would win votes. Moreover, no organizations were at hand to reduce the controversies. In human experimentation, the NIH had been able to impose corrective action on the research community, and although the IRBs did not resolve all the social and ethical dilemmas and required a second round of redesign and reinvigoration (following on the exposés that Kennedy highlighted), still this mechanism defused, indeed depoliticized, the problem. Medicine, however, with no counterpart to the NIH, could not reach closure, and gave every opportunity for politicians to grandstand about medical cases.

Second, once the life-and-death decisions in the infant ICU were rendered visible, they could not again be buried. Some commentators tried to make the case for obfuscation, finding a virtue in maintaining unambiguous laws (such as ones condemning euthanasia) and ambiguous practices (such as letting some newborns die). But the curtain had lifted, the spotlight was trained, and there was very little room to maneuver.

Third, any policies adopted were likely to generate invective and hostility. There was no satisfying the views of all parties. Once the battleground for determining the limits of privacy against the state's protective power was the infant nursery, dissension was predictable. How unfortunate for physicians that the extraordinary tension between abortion, on the one hand, and protection for the handicapped, on the other, was fought out on their turf.

Finally, this encounter between physicians and outsiders helped frame what questions would be asked—or not asked—about medical decision making and neonatal care, and whose voice would be most prominent in answering them. Focusing on the Johns Hopkins case as prototypical meant that case-specific assessments of the morality of individual actions would dominate the intellectual and policy agenda, as though the only relevant considerations had to do with what happened in the neonatal nursery itself. The microissue—What should a doctor do about this baby?—not the macroissue—Are expenditures on the neonatal nursery the best use of social resources, or, why are most babies in the neonatal nursery from underprivileged families?—would be the focus of attention. Put another way, the Johns Hopkins case helped ensure that philosophy, not the social sciences, would become the preeminent discipline among academics coming into the field of medicine. This, in turn, meant that principles of individual ethics, not broader assessments of the exercise of power in society, would dominate the intellectual discourse around medicine. The meaning and implication of this fact will become more apparent as we examine the most celebrated of all the medical cases, the case of Karen Ann Quinlan.

CHAPTER 11

New Rules for the Bedside

THE culmination of the decade-long process of bringing strangers to the bedside came in the case of Karen Ann Quinlan. Its impact on opinion and policy outweighed even that of the scandals in human experimentation and the death of a newborn at Johns Hopkins. After Quinlan there was no disputing the fact that medical decision making was in the public domain and that a profession that had once ruled was now being ruled.

The bare facts of the case are well known and easily summarized. On the night of 15 April 1975, Karen Ann Quinlan, age twenty-two, was brought into a New Jersey hospital emergency room in a coma whose etiology was never fully explained and from which she never emerged. After several months of hoping against hope, her parents recognized that she would not recover, and they asked her doctors and the hospital, St. Clair's, to remove her from the respirator that had been assisting her breathing. Joseph and Julia Quinlan, practicing Catholics, had sought church guidance on the issue and had been told that respirator care was "extraordinary" and that returning Karen to her "natural state" (that is, taking her off the machine, even if she would then die) was a morally correct action. Although the Quinlans believed that their decision was in accord with the sentiments of Karen's doctors, the hospital denied their request. St. Clair's staff would not even consider removing Karen from the respirator unless a court formally appointed them Karen's legal guardians. Even then, the hospital reserved judgment, because by any criteria, including the Harvard brain-death standards, Karen was alive; and disconnecting her from the respirator—or "pulling the plug," as it came to be known in the popular jargon—might well violate the medical ethic to "do no harm" and open the doctors and the hospital to criminal prosecution for homicide.

The Quinlans went before the Superior Court of New Jersey to ask that Joseph be appointed Karen's guardian for the express purpose of requesting her removal from the respirator. In November 1975 the lower court rejected the petition, but the Quinlans appealed to the state's supreme court, which accepted the case. (Although the Quinlans did not initially know it, this court was especially active, having already ordered private hospitals to perform abortions and prohibited communities from using zoning statutes to exclude low- and moderate-income housing.)[1] The court heard arguments in January 1976, and on 31 March 1976 returned its verdict in support of the Quinlans. After another two months of wrangling with the hospital and the doctors, Karen was weaned from the respirator and transferred to a long-term-care facility. Despite predictions of imminent death, she survived, off the respirator, for another nine years.

Although the *Quinlan* case had many layers and contexts, legal, medical, theological, ethical, and popular, the heart of the decision involved not so much a patient's "right to die" but something more specific and elemental: Who ruled at the bedside? Strip away the rhetoric and the symbols, and the *Quinlan* case was a contest between physicians, on the one hand, and patients and their legal advocates, on the other. Once doctors had presumed to represent the patient's interest. With *Quinlan*, the role went, amazingly enough, to lawyers and judges.

Certainly, Joseph and Julia Quinlan experienced the shift to the legal arena. According to their account of the events, St. Clair's staff initially responded to their request to discontinue treatment matter-of-factly; the hospital had them sign a paper declaring: "We hereby authorize and direct Dr. Morse to discontinue all extraordinary measures, including the use of a respirator, for our daughter Karen Quinlan." The document noted that the physicians had explained all the consequences of the removal and were thereby released "from any and all liability." "When we left the hospital that night," Julia Quinlan recalled, "all I could think was Karen's ordeal is almost over. And so is ours." But the next day, Dr. Morse called Joseph Quinlan to tell him that he had a "moral problem" with the agreement, and he intended to consult a colleague; the day after, he called again to say he would not remove Karen from the respirator. When the Quinlans persevered and began to consider bringing the case to court, Paul Armstrong, about to become their lawyer, warned them not only of the extensive publicity that was likely to follow, but of the fact that "the medical profession is powerful, and they're not going to like an issue like this being taken to the courts."[2] The Quinlans, however, did not back off and so learned just how right he was.

In making the case for the Quinlans, Armstrong's briefs and oral presentation centered on Karen's (and her surrogate's) constitutional right to determine her own medical care. Relying on the expanded definition of privacy that the U.S. Supreme Court had established in 1965 in *Griswold v. Connecticut* (which guaranteed right of access to contraception) as well as *Roe v. Wade*, Armstrong argued that it is "the role and function of the physician to advise an individual of what his diagnosis is . . . that the physician should advise as to the nature of treatments that are available, what the options are. . . . Then that decision should be made either by the individual or his family."[3] The patient, not the doctor, was entitled to decide whether to pursue treatment.

The hospital and the physicians (as well as the state attorney general) took a different tack, not confronting the *Quinlan* argument directly but insisting that the court had no business interfering with physicians' medical judgments. "Removal of the respirator was not supported by accepted medical practice,"[4] and patients could not invoke the authority of the court to compel physicians to violate the Hippocratic oath. "No court . . . should require a physician to act in derogation of this sacred and time-honored oath."[5] In the past, judges had always "limited their review of the type of treatment prescribed by the physician to whether it was in accordance with ordinary medical practice and not to what the Court, in an exercise of its own judgment, determined to be the proper medical treatment." Thus, "plaintiff seeks relief which would inject the Court into the patient–physician relationship and override the medical treatment decided on by the treating physician."[6]

Leaving unclear whether the doctor or the patient had the last word in the examining room, the defendants insisted that the court did not belong there. "It's the decision of my client," argued the physicians' attorney, "that, from a philosophical point of view, they are opposed to the Court injecting itself into the relationship of the patient and the doctor; and the Court making a decision, so to speak, as to who shall live and who shall die." The attorney general agreed: "I think the difficulty that we have seen here today, and throughout the trial period of the case, demonstrates why, in my judgment, these problems should be left . . . to the medical profession."[7] In essence, the lower court had found that this was "a medical decision, not a judicial one," and the higher court ought to respect the ruling.

On 31 March 1976 the court handed down its opinion in a case it rightly labeled of "transcendent importance." First, it authorized the Quinlan family to have Karen taken off the respirator. Second, and no less remarkable and precedent setting, it installed judges at the bedside, allowing them to instruct doctors in what might or might not be done in the realm of treatment.

The court accepted Armstrong's argument, built on *Roe v. Wade*, that a constitutionally protected right to privacy overlay the doctor–patient relationship. "Presumably," declared the court, "this right is broad enough to encompass a patient's decision to decline medical treatment under certain circumstances, in much the same way that it is broad enough to encompass a woman's decision to terminate pregnancy under certain conditions." Nevertheless, the patient's right to privacy was not absolute; in the case of abortion, for example, the right carried little weight in the third trimester of a pregnancy. Thus, the court had to decide the degree to which the Quinlans' privacy rights were to be balanced or compromised by other considerations—namely, the interest of the state in preserving life and in allowing physicians to exercise their best professional judgment.[8]

Given the facts of the *Quinlan* case, the court disposed quickly of the state-interest question: "We think that the State's interest *contra* [withdrawal from the respirator] weakens and the individual's right to privacy grows as the degree of bodily invasion increases and the prognosis dims. Ultimately there comes a point at which the individual's rights overcome the State interest." And Karen Quinlan in a persistent vegetative state and on a respirator seemed to have reached the point.[9]

What of society's stake in the autonomy of the medical profession, and the charge that the court's "premise [in favor of withdrawal] unwarrantly offends prevailing medical standards?" The truly difficult issue was whether the court could dare to tell physicians how to treat, or not to treat, their patients. The court confronted the challenge of the *Quinlan* case head-on, insisting that the questions raised transcended medical authority. Whatever the physicians' prerogatives, judges should not be prevented from "deciding matters clearly justiciable nor preclude a re-examination by the Court as to underlying human values and rights." The court went even further, declaring that social values and medical values might well diverge, and then, medical practice "must, in the ultimate, be responsive not only to the concepts of medicine but also to the common moral judgment of the community at large." Who was to decide when such a conflict existed and how it should be resolved? The court, for it, and not physicians, was best situated to define and implement community standards.[10]

Such declarations notwithstanding, the court conceded that it still might seem daring or foolhardy for judges "having no inherent expertise . . . to overrule a professional decision made according to prevailing medical practice and standards." How could a court, then, have the temerity to contravene medical practice and medical ethics and order treatment to be discontinued? How could it substitute legal rulings for bedside ethics? The answer was by impeaching medicine; that is, by insisting that what doctors testified to in court and what they did at the bedside were two different things, and that physicians' efforts to smooth over the contradictions were lame. "The question," as the court framed it, "is whether there is such internal consistency and rationality in the application of such standards as should warrant their constituting an ineluctable bar to the effectuation of substantive relief for plaintiff at the hands of the court. We have concluded not."[11]

The court reasoned that while the principles of medical ethics required that physicians not remove life-preserving technologies from patients, the realities of medical practice revealed a "widening ambiguity," as evidenced by the fact that physicians refrained from putting hopelessly ill patients on advanced support systems or resuscitating them when they breathed what should have been their last breath. Doctors, in other words, did "distinguish between curing the ill and comforting and easing the dying," and to this latter end they were ready to use "judicious neglect" by writing in pencil on a patient's chart "the foreboding initials DNR [Do Not Resuscitate]."[12]

Admittedly, physicians saw no conflict between their standards and their practices. Dr. Morse, and the other physicians who testified on his behalf, scrupulously differentiated between withholding treatment in the hopeless case, which was allowable, and withdrawing treatment from the hopeless case, which ostensibly was not. They accepted sins of omission and condemned sins of commission. But the court was unimpressed with the reasoning: "The thread of logic in such distinctions may be elusive to the non-medical lay mind," for the end result was the same—whether by an act of commission or of omission, the patient died.

Why, then, were physicians in general so determined to maintain this distinction, and why, in the *Quinlan* case in particular, were they so unwilling to do for Karen Ann Quinlan what they did as a matter of course for other patients? The reason, concluded the court, had to do with physicians' fears of malpractice suits or, worse yet, of criminal prosecution. Put another way, self-interest and the fear of sanctions, not medical principle or an ethical commitment, explained their refusal to accede to the Quinlans' request. The court, therefore, took as its self-imposed duty to find "a way to free physicians, in the pursuit of their healing vocation, from possible contamination by self-interest or self-protection."[13]

The effort turned out to be more than a little confused and less than appreciated. Just as neonatologists had settled for agreement on process when agreement on substance was impossible, so did the *Quinlan* court. It called for the establishment of hospital ethics committees, expecting this mechanism to resolve the dilemma. The inspiration for its proposal was a 1975 *Baylor Law Review* article by Karen Teel, a pediatrician. Teel contended that physicians assumed unwarranted responsibility and risk in making difficult ethical decisions, for they were "ill-equipped" on intellectual grounds and, "knowingly or not, assumed civil and criminal liability." Along with a growing number of physicians, she recommended that they share responsibility with a formally constituted body, "an Ethics Committee composed of physicians, social workers, attorneys, and theologians." This committee would not only bring a new and valuable dialogue to medical decision making but appropriately, from a legal point of view, share and divide responsibility.[14]

The court took up Teel's suggestion, but with less interest in ensuring the interdisciplinary character of the committee than in promoting "the diffusion of professional responsibility for [termination] decisions, comparable in a way to the value of multi-judge courts in finally resolving on appeal difficult questions of law."[15] Without acknowledging it, however, the court transformed Teel's committee into a prognosis committee, charging it to decide not the ethical issues of a case but the narrower technical question of whether the patient was in a chronic vegetative state. If the committee found she was, the physicians could then remove her from the respirator "without any civil or criminal liability." Through this innovation, the court expected to rescue medicine from its internal contradictions. Once the committees were functioning, physicians would not have to worry about liability, and judges would not have to review decisions to terminate treatment.

The *Quinlan* case, in the tradition of Beecher and Duff and Campbell, exposed a well-hidden secret. Despite a rhetorical commitment to the maxims of "do no harm" and "preserve life," doctors had been in the business of managing death and, until now at least, doing so very much on their own. Writing on the op-ed page of the *New York Times* in 1975, Michael Halberstam, a practicing physician in Washington, D.C., expressed surprise that the case "is in court at all. Each day, hundreds, perhaps thousands, of similar dilemmas present themselves. . . . The decisions are difficult, often agonizing, but they are reached in hospital corridors and in waiting rooms, not courts." The *Quinlan* case, in other words, "represents a failure of the usual—often unspoken deliberately ambiguous—steps in caring for such a patient."[16] Halberstam expected that physicians would not change their pattern of "tacit cooperation with reality"; but, in fact, *Quinlan* changed the reality to make tacit cooperation suspect. Decisions to terminate or withdraw treatment that individual physicians had once made covertly now would take place before an audience. The stage was likely to be a courtroom, and lawyers and judges, the leading actors.

Not surprisingly, many physicians reacted hostilely to the decision, finding *Quinlan* an egregious example of the subversion of their professional discretion. A 1975 editorial in *JAMA*, actually written by a bioethicist, Richard McCormick, distorted the case to make this point. McCormick argued that "decision-making within health care, if it is to remain truly human . . . must be controlled primarily within the patient–doctor–family relationship, and these decisions must be tailormade to individual cases and circumstances. If technology and law were largely to usurp these prerogatives—as they threaten to do as a result of the *Quinlan* case—we would all be the worse off."[17] (One could not know from his comments that the physicians had acted against the family, and that lawmakers were attempting to limit technology.) Physicians interviewed by the news weeklies generally voiced their opposition. A neurologist from the Massachusetts General Hospital (MGH) complained that to allow courts to make such decisions "is taking the judgment of a doctor and putting it in the hands of those not competent to make a decision."[18] A colleague from the University of Chicago insisted that "a court cannot decide in total detail what a physician is to do."[19] Even Dr. Teel, whose article the *Quinlan* court had cited, distanced herself from the opinion. Ethics committees were still a very novel and untested idea: "There are a lot of problems and I'd like to see them ironed out before everyone feels they must jump on ethics committees as the way to handle tough medical cases."[20]

With public scrutiny heightened, a few hospitals took steps to bring greater formality to the decision-making process. The *Quinlan* decision became the occasion for setting up committees to advise and review termination decisions and to formulate guidelines for individual physicians. But these measures represented more of an effort at damage control than an enthusiastic embracing of a new style of practice. Thus, the Massachusetts General Hospital administrators appointed an ad hoc committee to study "how best to manage the hopelessly ill patient," appointing to it a psychiatrist, two physicians, a nursing administrator, a layperson (who had recovered from cancer), and, in a wonderfully distancing phrase, "legal counsel." The committee recommended, and the MGH established, a four-point patient-classification system, ranging from A ("Maximal therapeutic effort without reservation") to D ("all therapy can be discontinued"), which would be "generally reserved for patients with brain death or when there is no reasonable possibility that the patient will return to a cognitive and sapient life." The MGH also organized an Optimum Care Committee to advise "in situations where difficulties arise in deciding the appropriateness of continuing intensive therapy for critically ill patients." The committee, however, met only at the request of the attending physician, and its recommendation went back to this physician, who was free to accept or reject its advice. In a six-month pilot trial of the system in 1976, the committee members reported that "requests for . . . consultation have been rare." They had reviewed the cases of fifteen patients, clarifying misunderstandings, reopening lines of communication, and, by their own estimate, "above all, maximizing support for the responsible physician who makes the medical decision to intensify, maintain or limit effort at reversing the illness."[21]

Boston's Beth Israel Hospital, also citing *Quinlan,* drew up guidelines for ordering a DNR code for a patient. When a physician believed a patient to be "irreversibly and irreparably ill," with death "imminent" (that is, likely to occur within two weeks), the physician could elect to discuss with an ad hoc committee, composed exclusively of doctors, whether death was so certain that resuscitation would serve no purpose. If the committee members unanimously agreed, and the competent patient made it his or her "informed choice," then a DNR order would be entered in the patient's chart; should the patient be incompetent, the physician was to obtain the approval of the family and then enter the order.[22]

Even these innovative measures were implemented with great caution and were not readily adopted in other settings. Both the MGH and Beth Israel committees were dominated by physicians and deferred to the "responsible physician." The MGH code did not emphasize the need to obtain the consent of the competent patient, and Beth Israel did not address the more general issue of termination or withdrawal of treatment. Nevertheless, even these modest innovations remained the exception and drew vigorous attacks. Most hospitals did not adopt guidelines or establish committees, and traditionalistic physicians disdained the new measures. "I am at a loss," observed one doctor, "to understand the need for the various [MGH] committees . . . if the final decision rests with the 'responsible physician.' " As for the Beth Israel

DNR guidelines, "I shudder to think of the innumerable unsalvageable poor souls who would undergo the assault of modern medical technology while awaiting the assemblance of an ad hoc committee . . . who could allow them the dignity of a peaceful departure from this world."[23] Another physician criticized the Beth Israel stipulation that physicians obtain the permission of the competent patient before writing a code: "The consultant-committee requirements are regrettable, but the requirement for the informed consent of the patient is intolerable. It is no longer enough that we let the terminal patient know that his prognosis is grave; he must know that it is utterly hopeless, and he must completely agree with us. If we allow him a slim thread of hope, if he persists in his natural denial of death, he must spend his last moments with someone pounding on his chest 60 times a minute."[24]

In effect, physicians and their institutions did not react any more forcefully to the *Quinlan* case and its aftermath than they had to the Johns Hopkins case and its aftermath. A handful of academic medical centers moved haltingly to meet the challenge, but they did not become the models for emulation. More typically, the professional response amounted to a repetition of now familiar refrains: Trust to the doctor and do not intrude on the doctor–patient relationship. Keep courts and formally constituted committees out of the ICU. But these wishes were destined not to be respected by attorneys, judges, or the patients themselves.

Soon after the *Quinlan* decision came down, the *NEJM* ran an editorial entitled "Terminating Life Support: Out of the Closet," written by a professor at Harvard Law School, Charles Fried. The fact that a lawyer authored a column normally reserved for doctors reinforced its very argument. "That [life-prolonging] measures are in fact regularly withheld or withdrawn is an open secret," observed Fried, "but the course of decision and the testimony in the *Quinlan* case show how wary the medical profession can be when the spotlight of publicity illuminates its practices." However uneasy the physicians were, Fried was certain that lawyers would have "the last word." Conceding that lawyers had typically been involved in medicine through malpractice litigation, and that they had not "been a constructive force in the shaping of the relation of the public to the health professions," Fried contended that "for better or for worse we still shall have to fall back on the lawyers' skills, for they are not only an unavoidable nuisance but the professional adjuvants of the ordinary citizen's autonomy, particularly when this autonomy is threatened by complexity or adversity."[25] Fried spotted what the physicians had missed: that lawyers and judges had not pursued some imperialistic imperative and invaded medicine's domain but, rather, were in alliance with patients in an effort to right an imbalance of power and establish the principles of patient autonomy. This process, shrewdly concluded Fried, would continue. *Quinlan* was a portent of things to come.

His prediction was quickly borne out, for *Quinlan* sparked a new and more sustained involvement of lawyers and judges in medical decision making. It had little in common with compensation-minded malpractice litigation, which only looked back on events to see whether harms had occurred. It was closer to the type of law inspired by human experimentation, especially the substantial case law and legal analyses devoted to informed consent. To be sure, decisions around transplantation had found their way into the courts, with judges ruling that parents could have one child donate a kidney to another. On occasion, so too had withdrawal of treatment issues; for example, in the aftermath of the Johns Hopkins case, a judge in Maine had ordered treatment for a handicapped newborn. But all of these interventions were completely overshadowed by the fallout from the *Quinlan* decision. What had been exceptional now became the rule.

After *Quinlan* a self-perpetuating dynamic took hold. Hospitals that attempted to alter practice in accordance with the ruling required the services of a lawyer to insure that it was on the right track. Thus, both the MGH and Beth Israel, as Fried noted, had used lawyers to help them design their new procedures. Moreover, the *Quinlan* decision provoked questions, analyses, and then in short order, more decisions. Here was a far-reaching case replete with ambiguities and covered with maximum intensity in the press—the only cases more prominent were the Supreme Court decisions in *Brown v. Board of Education* and *Roe v. Wade*. If physicians took comfort in the gaps that the *Quinlan* case left open, the lawyers rushed in to fill them. Just as nature abhors a vacuum, legal minds abhor contradictory standards or confusing stipulations, and *Quinlan* had more than its fair share of them.

Hence, it served as the bridge for lawyers and judges to cross over into medicine.

Take the matter of ethics committees. The *Quinlan* court had responded by the seat of its pants—apparently unaware, to judge by an absence of references, that ethics committees had first been discussed in the context of treatment decisions for newborns. The decision cited Dr. Teel, but her *Baylor Law Journal* article was not so much an article as a short and highly general comment inspired by the Johns Hopkins baby case. Teel did not set out a model for the committees, and she was astonished that the court had picked her suggestion. She got the idea, she later remarked, from a program on educational television (probably the film about the Johns Hopkins baby) and had even expressed some reservations about it in the piece itself. Thus, the court left open even more questions than it answered. "The ethics committee aspect of the *Quinlan* decision is the subject of much confusion, disagreement, and concern," noted a *Rutgers Law Review* article. "For example, would the role of such a body be solely advisory or would its determinations be mandatory? What should be its composition—totally professional or representative of various disciplines? Who should select the members? . . . And of particular importance, is the requirement of committee concurrence in a termination decision reached by a physician and family or guardian constitutional?"[26] The court not only failed to define the role and duties of such a committee, but actually compounded the confusion by mixing ethics with prognosis. Were the committees to address moral values or neurological outcomes? Was this a committee to evaluate the wishes of the patient or the accuracy of medical predictions? The *Quinlan* decision obfuscated the issues, inviting others to clarify them.

Not only the substance but the fact of *Quinlan* set off a reaction that brought more such cases to court, expanding the direct involvement of law in medical decision making. Although the ruling of a New Jersey court was not binding in any other jurisdiction, cautious and prudent physicians and hospital directors elsewhere were soon preparing to go to court rather than unilaterally terminate treatment. Less than a month after *Quinlan*, a Massachusetts court (in the case of *Superintendent of Belchertown State School v. Saikewicz*) was asked by the superintendent of a state school for the retarded to decide whether chemotherapy could be withheld from a mentally retarded adult suffering from leukemia, particularly when similarly situated nonretarded adults would almost certainly take the treatment. The Massachusetts court not only found the issue justiciable and ruled that such withholding of treatment was permissible, but went on to say, even more vigorously than *Quinlan*, that these questions had to come before a court. As against the *Quinlan* court's expectation that ethics committees would obviate judicial involvement, the Massachusetts court insisted:

> We take a dim view of any attempt to shift the ultimate decision-making responsibility away from the duly established courts of proper jurisdiction to any committee, panel or group, ad hoc or permanent. . . . We do not view the judicial resolution of this most difficult and awesome question—whether potentially life-prolonging treatment should be withheld from a person incapable of making his own decision—as constituting a "gratuitous encroachment" on the domain of medical expertise. Rather, such questions of life and death seem to us to require the process of detached but passionate investigation and decision that forms the ideal on which the judicial branch of government was created. Achieving this ideal is our responsibility and that of the lower court, and is not to be entrusted to any other group purporting to represent the "morality and conscience of our society" no matter how highly motivated or impressively constituted.[27]

Once the secret was out, a number of judges defined themselves as the properly constituted authority to render such decisions, unwilling to rely on ad hoc groups with ad hoc procedures.

Not surprisingly, the *Saikewicz* decision infuriated and frightened physicians. Arnold Relman, who succeeded Ingelfinger as the editor of the *NEJM*, could reconcile *Quinlan* with traditional medical ethics, for the court assumed that doctors and patients (if not the doctor alone) should reach life-and-death decisions. But *Saikewicz* represented an all-out war on physicians' authority. The decision, declared Relman, left "no possible doubt of its total distrust of physicians' judgment in such matters. . . . Physicians must not be allowed to use their own professional judgment, but should be guided instead by government regulation." Unhappily, but very accurately, he concluded: "This astonishing opinion can only be viewed as a resounding vote of 'no confidence' in the abilities of physicians and families to act in the best interest of the incapable patient suffering from terminal illness. . . . The court thus asserts in effect that its duty is not simply to remedy abuses and settle disagreements that arise in the practice of medicine but also to take routine responsibility for certain types of medical decisions frequently needed for terminally or hopelessly ill patients."[28]

To be sure, a number of legal scholars and judges shared Relman's conviction that the court was the wrong forum for resolving these issues. They objected to the interventionist position of *Quinlan* and, even more so, of *Saikewicz*, and they were not at all content with so ill-defined a creature as an ethics committee. But the outlook of even these critics was much closer to that of their legal colleagues than that of physicians, for they, too, were unwilling to trust to the discretion of the physician without formulating coherent procedures and a body of agreed-upon principles. They preferred that the legislature, not the court, set policy, but from medicine's perspective that was a minor distinction. For whatever the disagreements among lawyers and judges about the specifics of *Quinlan* and *Saikewicz*, they all wished to narrow the discretion of physicians and enhance predictability through formal rules and regulations.

An example that aptly illustrates both the dynamic set off by the *Quinlan* case and what it means to bring a legal mind-set into medicine, is the grand jury investigation and report of the DNR procedures in effect at New York's La Guardia Hospital as of 1983.[29] The facts of the case were not as unique as one might expect. (An almost exact replay took place several years later at New York Hospital.) Mrs. M., a seventy-eight-year-old woman, was on a respirator in the hospital's ICU, suffering from breathing difficulties of uncertain cause, with no diagnosis of a terminal illness. Although she may have on a few occasions tried to disconnect her respirator, neither she nor her family had asked that treatment be discontinued or given any indication that she wished to die. One night Mrs. M. was found off the respirator (the tube neatly wrapped under her pillow and the monitor alarm turned off) and in the midst of a cardiac arrest. The medical student on duty in the ICU, according to the grand jury finding, "began administering closed chest massage while the nurse reconnected the tubing. Another nurse arrived and asked the student whether she should call a 'Code 33' emergency, the hospital's signal for all available personnel to respond and administer cardiopulmonary resuscitation. . . . As the nurse started to do so, the student indicated that Mrs. M. was not to be coded. According to the testimony of both nurses, the medical student said: 'What am I doing? She's a no-code,' and then ceased the cardiac massage." Mrs. M. died a few minutes later. The next morning the hospital told the patient's relatives that everything possible had been done for her, but an anonymous phone call to the family from someone who identified herself as a nurse at the hospital reported that the patient "had died 'unnecessarily' because 'a no-code' was sent out."

The grand jury investigation did not resolve precisely what happened that night—the medical student denied the nurses' version, and there was no finding on who disconnected the respirator. But the grand jury did evaluate the procedures around the DNR code and found "shocking procedural abuses." The system was arbitrary, capricious, and without accountability. The hospital officials, reported the grand jury, prohibited "any written mention of [DNR] orders on the patients' charts. Instead they instituted a process of designating 'no code' patients by affixing so-called 'purple dots' to file cards which were kept solely by the nurses and only until the particular patient died or was discharged. . . . As a result, the 'no-code' order could never be attributed to any physician and the only record of it would disappear after it was carried out." There was also "no officially formulated policy which required physicians to obtain consent from, or even inform, the patient or his family before the 'no-code' order was given."

The grand jury response, with a good deal of guidance from the state's attorneys, exemplified both the strength of the patient–lawyer alliance around autonomy and the differences between a legal and medical orientation. The grand jury recommended, first, that DNR decisions "be reached jointly" by the physician and the patient; so significant a measure could not be entrusted to the physician alone. Recognizing that many doctors believed that this consultative requirement was a cruel burden to put on a dying patient, the grand jury still insisted that it was an essential aspect of patients' rights and that doctors must not have the authority to decide unilaterally who should be resuscitated and who should be left to die. Second, although the grand jury did not want to impose rigid rules on hospitals—recognizing that all patients were not alike—and did not want to define precisely all the circumstances under which it was proper not to resuscitate a patient, it did insist on "explicit procedural safeguards to prevent the decision from being made carelessly, unilaterally or anonymously." DNR decisions were to be "accurately and permanently documented," entered on the patient's chart, and signed by the responsible physician.

The La Guardia report did not immediately accomplish its aims. Not long afterward, a New York daily newspaper published a photograph surreptitiously taken of Memorial Hospital's "confidential" chalkboard entries of which patients should be treated with maximum therapy and which should not; and New York Hospital faced a well-publicized suit when its staff not only refused to resuscitate a woman patient but prevented her nephew, a doctor who by coincidence was at her bedside when she arrested, from doing so. But the grand jury report, by publicizing how haphazard DNR standards were and recommending more rigorous procedures, helped reduce the tolerance for the individual exercise of discretion without accountability—what physicians considered the exercise of professional discretion. Within a few years New York became one of many states that required extensive consultation with patients, properly executed forms, and properly annotated charts before a patient could be coded DNR.

The *Quinlan* case also helped make medical decision making the stuff of everyday, popular discourse, which had the effect of strengthening the alliance of lawyer and patient against the doctor and the hospital and bringing still more forms, and more formality, to medicine. The case of Brother Fox demonstrates the process at work. A member of a Catholic religious order, Brother Fox, in 1979, at the age of eighty-three, underwent a hernia operation. In the course of the procedure, he suffered a cardiac arrest, and the loss of oxygen to the brain left him in a persistent vegetative state. The brothers in his order asked the hospital officials to disconnect his respirator, which they refused to do without court permission. At the subsequent hearing, the brothers explained that right after the *Quinlan* case, their community, including

Brother Fox, held lengthy discussions about the ethics of withdrawal of treatment, and Brother Fox had firmly stated that were he ever to fall into such a state, he would want the respirator disconnected.[30]

The discussions that Brother Fox and his religious community conducted formally, many other Americans conducted informally, for *Quinlan* took the issue of termination of treatment not only into law review journals but magazines on supermarket racks. The case had almost every necessary ingredient for capturing public and media attention. It had elements of a good-girl-gone-bad story—a twenty-two-year-old from a devout Catholic family who may have used drugs. It also had a grade-B horror-movie quality: Why had Karen Ann Quinlan fallen into a coma, and was there any chance she would awake from it? But perhaps most important, Quinlan's case personalized an issue that had previously seemed abstract. It was one thing for Senator Mondale to inveigh against the future implications of medical technology, but quite another to think about Karen—and to a remarkable degree this became the story of Karen, to the point that even the court decision referred to her by her first name. There she lay, tethered to a machine that kept her alive for no purpose.

Although the media tended to frame the story as a case of the "right to die," as though the villain in the story was the respirator technology itself, many people understood that the real issue at stake was who ruled at the bedside. The cautionary lesson that emerged from *Quinlan* was the need for individuals to find a way to have their wishes respected. Almost no one argued against the Quinlan family's request; the overwhelming majority of the public agreed that families "ought to be able to tell doctors to remove all life-support services and let the patient die." (In 1977, 66 percent of respondents to a poll by Lou Harris approved the proposition and 15 percent were undecided; four years later, 73 percent approved and only 4 percent were undecided.)[31] Rather, the pressing issue was how to avoid the Quinlans' predicament.

The answers were not long in coming. In casual ways, people expressed their preferences to family and friends, more or less as Brother Fox had done. (Numbers here are imprecise, but when termination-of-treatment cases entered the courtroom, judges certainly assumed that once-competent patients would have expressed a preference, and relatives and friends often reported that they had.) There was also mounting interest in more formal documents, such as "living wills." The idea of an advance directive by which individuals could instruct physicians not to use heroic treatment in the event of terminal illness grew apace with respirators and intensive care units. In the early 1970s, the Euthanasia Educational Council drew up a model living will, and when the "Dear Abby" column described it, 50,000 people wrote in for a copy. In April 1974, Dr. Walter Modell published in the *NEJM* a one-page directive "On Medical Intervention." "Because medical advances have outdistanced our expected forms of ethical behavior," the form read, "I believe it is therefore wise to establish an order of preference which can be used to guide those physicians who care for me." Two months later, the *New York Times* Sunday magazine devoted an article to the living will, under the banner: "Thousands have signed a document that says, in effect: If I'm terminally ill, pull the plug." But in these first appearances, the living will was highly controversial. A number of leaders in gerontology and thanatology, concerned that people in good health would be making wrong-headed decisions about what they might want done when they were in poor health, condemned it as a "cop-out."[32]

The *Quinlan* case brought a more favorable consensus and new popularity to the living will. Sissela Bok, a philosopher interested in health policy, explored the "Personal Directions for Care at the End of Life" in the *New England Journal of Medicine*, openly seeking to empower the patient (through a legal document) against the physician and the hospital. "The plight of Karen Quinlan and her family," declared Bok, "touched many readers. More than the fear of death itself, it is the fear of lingering before death and of creating heavy burdens for families that troubles many. . . . Accordingly, a growing number of persons are now signing statements, often known as Living Wills, requesting that their lives not be unduly prolonged under certain conditions." Although the legal status of such documents was uncertain, Bok believed that they should guide physicians' decisions, and she offered a model form:

I,_____, want to participate in my own medical care as long as I am able. But I recognize that an accident or illness may someday make me unable to do so. . . . If my death is near and cannot be avoided . . . I do not want to have my life prolonged. I would then ask not to be subjected to surgery or resuscitation. Nor would I then wish to have life support from mechanical ventilators, intensive care services, or other life prolonging procedures.[33]

Bok insisted that the general tenor of the document was as important as the specific stipulations. As befit the contentious quality of so many of the cases, her first point was that a living will "should use a tone of requesting what is one's due rather than a tone of pleading or begging for consideration." The living will was an expression of a patient's rights—the right to die was part of a right to "participate" in medical care, not only while competent, but even when incompetent.

Neither the real nor the symbolic quality of the living will was lost on doctors. One oncologist suggested an alternative model:

I . . . having been under the care of my physician for a reasonable enough time to realize that he is compassionate, skilled and has my best interests at heart, in the event my conditions become critical and death appears imminent, trust him to continue to act in this manner. . . . I believe he is my best advocate in matters relating to my care. . . . He is a friend and understands my feelings. I do not wish to place potential and real barriers between myself and him by authorizing a third party to act on my behalf.[34]

That the document has the aura of a parody, if not fantasy, demonstrates both the degree to which doctors had actually become strangers (the phrases about friendship and feelings ring hollow) and the extent to which medical paternalism had lost legitimacy.[35] Thus, the reactions to the *Quinlan* case drew on and reinforced the ideology of patients' rights. The living will took its place alongside the AHA Patient Bill of Rights in asserting the new stand against doctors.

These attitudes also increased the pressure on legislatures to regulate medical decision making at the end of life. By the mid-1970s, some dozen states had enacted brain-death statutes, but the fallout from *Quinlan* and similar cases brought to the fore issues that bore even more intimately on the doctor–patient relationship. For one thing, the courts kept asking for legislative guidance in this area. Although a number of judges were ready to pronounce on termination of treatment, they consistently urged the state to enact legislation clarifying the duties and responsibilities of physicians and eliminating the fears of civil or criminal liability. Even the *Saikewicz* court, for example, refrained from formulating comprehensive guidelines to govern the treatment of incompetent patients, insisting that this effort should be left to the legislative branch. For another, the popular interest in living wills prompted calls for legislation that would make the documents binding on doctors and hospitals.

A few months after the *Quinlan* decision, California enacted a living will statute, and although its many qualifications made the document very difficult to use—the patient had to be suffering from a terminal disease, the living will could not be over five years old, and it must have been reexecuted no sooner than fourteen days after the patient learned about a terminal disease—it was still perceived as moving in the right direction. The living will now had legal standing as "the final expression of [the patient's] legal right to refuse medical or surgical treatment and accept the consequences from such refusal," and it absolved physicians who followed the will's instructions from charges of homicide. (It also protected next of kin from losing insurance benefits cancelable in the event of suicide.)[36] To be sure, there were good reasons for legislators to avoid acting on termination of treatment, for the potential to antagonize one or another religious group or state medical association was considerable. Nevertheless, after *Quinlan* it was not only the courts but the legislatures that entered medicine, typically to the end of expanding patient choices and narrowing physician authority.

Finally, the *Quinlan* case not only brought new players into the realm of medical decision making but solidified the position of one group of outsiders already there, namely, the bioethicists. After *Quinlan*, the bioethics movement in the United States had a vitality and a standing that were in every way remarkable. Every national commission addressing medical issues would have among its members a bioethicist, and no media account of a medical breakthrough would be complete without a bioethicist commenting on its implications. Within the decade, most medical schools would have a philosopher teaching a course on bioethics, and many tertiary care centers would have bioethicists serving on one or another of its critical care, IRB, transplant, or human reproduction committees. Once it was assumed that anyone on ward rounds who was not wearing a white coat was a chaplain; after *Quinlan*, he or she was assumed to be a bioethicist.

Renee Fox, one of the leading contemporary medical sociologists, was among the first to analyze this change and to decry both the methods and intellectual assumptions of bioethics. The very year of the *Quinlan* decision, 1976, she wrote an article exploring "the emergence of a new area of inquiry and action that has come to be known as bioethics." Quoting Daniel Callahan, of the Hastings Institute, to the effect that bioethics was "not yet a full discipline," that most of its practitioners "had wandered into the field from somewhere else, more or less inventing it as they go," Fox documented its growing influence. Not only were several academic centers studying and teaching bioethics, but an "impressive array of private foundations, scholarly bodies and government agencies" were supporting such efforts; and an equally impressive interdisciplinary group, composed predominantly of philosophers and concerned physicians, were pursuing them.[37]

Fox was disturbed, however, that bioethics had made such quick and thorough inroads, for she was convinced that it was bringing the wrong set of values to medicine. Some of her dissatisfaction reflected a struggle over turf, for as the bioethicists had moved into medicine, sociologists had moved out; she noted "a remarkable paucity of work by sociologists or other social scientists in this area."[38] But the point of Fox's attack was to criticize bioethicists not so much for excluding sociologists but for excluding the sociological approach. In a formulation that she later repeated and elaborated, Fox charged that bioethicists had no sense of time or place—that is, no awareness of why the movement had succeeded when it did or where it did, nor of why over the past ten years bioethics had become more important in the United States than in any other industrialized nation. Lacking this broader perspective, bioethicists could not recognize their own particular biases and predilections. In particular, they did not understand that they were elevating to a universal status beliefs that reflected nothing more than their own views. Indeed, in their eagerness to extend their reach, they transformed religious questions into ethical questions, giving a narrowly secular quality to discussions that had once been more wide-ranging.

The net result of this failure, Fox contended, was to entrench within bioethics an unyielding and unqualified commitment to individual rights, thereby minimizing all other communal or societal considerations. Insisted Fox:

> In the prevailing ethos of bioethics, the value of individualism is defined in such a way, and emphasized to such a degree, that it is virtually severed from social and religious values concerning relationships between individuals; their responsibilities, commitments, and emotional bonds to one another. . . . To this narrowly gauged conception of individualism bioethics attaches an inflated and inflationary value. Claims to individual rights phrased in terms of moral entitlements tend to expand and to beget additional claims to still other individual rights. In these respects, the individualism of bioethics constitutes an evolution away from older, less secularized and communal forms of American individualism.

Her conclusion was partly judgmental, partly wishful thinking: "It is unclear whether bioethics truly reflects the state of American medical ethics today and whether it can—or ought to—serve as the common framework for American medical morality."[39]

In her determination to fault bioethics for adopting so individualistic an approach, Fox was herself guilty of some of the very charges she leveled at bioethics. She, too, failed to set the movement in a societal framework, leaving the impression that bioethicists were a self-seeking and self-promoting group of academic entrepreneurs, which would hardly suffice to explain their broad appeal. What Fox missed, or was unwilling to consider, was that the movement's strong commitment to individual rights was at the core of its success. This orientation may well have alienated doctors, but it allied bioethicists with other outsiders to medicine—namely, lawyers, public officials, the media, and, even more, patients and their families who, like the Quinlans, had confronted unyielding medical authority.

Just how close the fit was emerges from one telling incident. When the Quinlans' lawyer, Paul Armstrong, was preparing for oral argument before the New Jersey Supreme Court, he first flew to Washington to consult with the bioethicists at Georgetown's Kennedy Institute and then went to the Hastings Institute to review his arguments with Robert Veatch. They peppered him with questions—"Mr. Armstrong, can you draw a distinction between allowing someone to die and actively advancing death? How do we know what Karen's wishes are since she is incompetent?"—and helped him frame answers.[40] In this way, the *Quinlan* case represented both the emergence of a new authority over medicine and a new alliance among outsiders to medicine. The Quinlans first took counsel with the clergy, but to effect their wishes, they had to turn to a lawyer, who, in turn, consulted with bioethicists so as to sharpen his argument before a court.

The great majority of bioethicists, as this incident suggests, came down on the side of the Quinlans, elevating individual rights over medical authority. If Fox was likely to give greater weight to medical traditions, the bioethicists were adamant in championing the patient's claims. *Quinlan* became the occasion for one after another of them to speak out for patient autonomy. Edmund Pellegrino, then a professor of medicine at Yale University and later the head of the Georgetown program in medical ethics, warned against "putting excessive powers into the hands of professionals of any kind. . . . Give the physician too much power, and it can be abused."[41] The proper task for the doctor was to provide patients and their families with the information necessary for them to reach a decision. Tristram Engelhardt, then on the faculty at Georgetown, put the *Quinlan* decision into the framework of the Patient Bill of Rights for strengthening the voice of the patient.[42] And Robert Veatch, having counseled Armstrong, celebrated the court decision, hopeful that it would become the guiding precedent.[43]

Was anything lost by the almost exclusive dedication of bioethics to the principle of patient autonomy? Perhaps the thoroughgoing commitment to autonomy did encourage a polarization of issues, pitting tweed coat against white coat, but it is doubtful whether any modifications in this stance would have made the medical profession more comfortable about losing discretionary authority. More important, as witnessed in the cases of both Karen Ann Quinlan and the Johns Hopkins baby, the individualistic approach of the bioethicists focused their attention more on the one-to-one encounter of patient and doctor than on the societal context of American medicine. A commitment to patient autonomy presumed that the most critical problem in American medicine was the nature of this doctor–patient relationship and that, by implication, such issues as access to health care or the balance between disease prevention and treatment were of lesser import. In this sense Fox was right to observe that bioethics lacked a sociological imagination. Nevertheless, protecting the rights of the individual patient often had a relevance that transcended class lines—emphasizing concepts like consent meant protecting both the poor and the well-to-do from the unscrupulous researcher, and insisting on patient dignity had implications at least as vital for the ward service as for the private pavilion.

In the end, the initial commitment of bioethics to patient rights helps account for its extraordinary accomplishments in the decade from 1966 to 1976. The fit between the movement and the times was perfect. Just when courts were defining an expanded right to privacy, the bioethicists were emphasizing the principle of autonomy, and the two meshed neatly; judges supplied a legal basis and bioethicists, a philosophical basis for empowering the patient. Indeed, just when movements on behalf of a variety of minorities were advancing their claims, the bioethicists were defending another group that appeared powerless— patients. All these advocates were siding with the individual against the constituted authority; in their powerlessness, patients seemed at one with women, inmates, homosexuals, tenants in public housing, welfare recipients, and students, who were all attempting to limit the discretionary authority of professionals. In fact, the bioethicists had far more in common with the new roster of rights agitators than many of its leaders recognized or would have admitted. Ph.D.s, often trained in philosophy, many with a Catholic background, who typically followed conventional life-styles, may not have been personally comfortable with still more left-leaning, agnostic, and aggressive advocates committed to alternative life-styles. But however glaring these differences, the conceptual similarities were critical. All these movements looked at the world from the vantage point of the objects of authority, not the wielders of authority.

Of course, bioethics had one critical advantage that gave it more staying power than these other groups, assuring its successes not only in the late 1960s and early 1970s, but through the 1980s. Bioethics crossed class lines. It was at least as responsive, and perhaps even more so, to the concerns of the haves than the have-nots. Not everyone is poor or a member of a minority group or disadvantaged socially and economically; but everyone potentially, if not already, is a patient. This fact gives a special character and appeal to a movement that approaches the exercise of medical authority from the patient's point of view.

EPILOGUE

IN the fifteen years since the Quinlan decision, the trends that first emerged in the 1966–76 decade have become all the more prominent and powerful. Outsiders to medicine, more conspicuously and successfully than physicians, now define the social and ethical questions facing the profession and set forth the norms that should govern it. The most impressive and thorough undertaking in this area, the President's Commission for the Study of Ethical Problems in Medicine and Biomedical and Behavioral Research, was dominated by lawyers and philosophers (from academic departments rather than schools of theology). Created by Congress in 1978 as the successor organization to the 1973 National Commission on the Protection of Human Subjects, it, too, owed its existence to the energetic intervention of Edward Kennedy. Invoking, once again, the great scandals in human experimentation—Willowbrook, Tuskegee, Brooklyn Jewish Chronic Disease Hospital—Kennedy successfully moved for the establishment of "an interdisciplinary committee of professionals . . . to work together to try to give the society guidance on some of the most difficult, complex, ethical and moral problems of our time."[1] In 1978 substantial political mileage could still be gained from these scandals, bringing more rules and players to the bedside.

The appointment of Morris Abram to the commission chairmanship is inexplicable without an appreciation of the events of 1966–76. In no other way can one fathom the selection of a former civil rights lawyer to head a study of medical ethics. In fact, Abram exemplified not only the influence of lawyers on medicine, but the formidable new authority of the patient as well. Stricken a few years earlier with leukemia, Abram had been as active in directing his own treatment as any patient could be. He arranged for the importation from abroad of an experimental drug (no mean feat in the 1970s), and ordered every doctor who touched him (in his immuno-compromised state) to scrub in his presence; when, after multiple blood drawings, his veins started to close down, Abram compelled the physicians to devise a routine that would satisfy all their daily requirements with one needle stick.[2] Not surprisingly, Abram selected another lawyer, Alexander Capron, to serve as executive director for the commission. Capron, one of the first professors of law to cross over into medicine and an active member of the Hastings Institute, had written extensively and perceptively on many of the issues that composed the bioethics agenda.

Outsiders to medicine dominated the commission's membership. Five of the first eleven commissioners came from bioethics, law, and the social sciences, and three from behavioral research. The group designated to pronounce on ethical problems in medicine had only five M.D.s, of whom three were practicing physicians. The professional staff was even further removed from medicine. Only one was an M.D., while four had law degrees, and five, Ph.D.s. In short, this group was not likely to give great deference to the traditions of bedside ethics.

Structure and personnel did shape substance. Between 1980 and 1983, the commission published over a dozen reports devoted to such concerns as establishing a uniform definition of death, obtaining informed consent, compensating for injuries to research subjects, securing access to health care, and, of course, terminating life-sustaining treatment.[3] In addressing this exceptionally broad range of subjects, the commission was guided by a series of now well-established principles. First, the relationship between patient and doctor should be marked by "mutual participation and respect and by shared decisionmaking."[4] The patient was to be active and involved, the physician, responsive and sharing. Second, the commission insisted that medical decision making conform to explicit principles that would be consistently applied, eschewing case-by-case resolutions. Finally, when confronting almost insoluble ethical problems, the commission opted for collective as opposed to individual judgments; when the issues became intricate, it frequently invoked procedures modeled on IRB deliberations. The commission strove to make medical decision making visible, formal, and predictable, and altogether responsive to the patient's preferences.

Consistent with these ends, the commission made informed consent the cornerstone of its design. "Ethically valid consent is a process of shared decisionmaking based upon mutual respect and participation, not a ritual to be equated with reciting the contents of a form. . . . Patients should have access to the information they need to help them understand their conditions and make treatment decisions. . . . Health care providers should not ordinarily withhold unpleasant information simply because it is unpleasant."[5] Thus, in framing policy for terminating treatment, arguably its most important contribution, the commission gave precedence to "the voluntary choice of a competent and informed patient." It recognized that in some instances the conscience of physicians or the mission of a hospital might conflict with the patient's wishes, and it did not wish to ride roughshod over these differences. It hoped that some of the disputes would be worked out between doctor and patient and that hospitals would develop review mechanisms and policies "to ensure the means necessary to preserve both health and the value of self determination." But when conflict was unavoidable, "the primacy of a patient's interests in self-determination and in honoring the patient's own view of well-being warrant leaving with the patient the final authority to decide."[6]

The commission was equally adamant about protecting the rights of the incompetent patient. It strongly advocated the development of legal mechanisms that would allow patients to make their wishes known in advance, either by living wills or through the appointment of a surrogate decision maker. In the event that the patient had been silent, or had never achieved competence (as in the case of newborns or persons with severe mental disability), the commission again looked to hospital review committees, not individual physicians, to advise on the decisions. Hospitals should formulate "explicit, and publicly available policies regarding how and by whom decisions are to be made."[7]

The initial reception accorded the commission's publications demonstrates the persistence of the distinction between medical insiders and outsiders. Most medical journals ignored the enterprise, not reporting on the commission's birth or passage, or on its substantive findings; well into the 1980s, it was the unusual physician who had read any of its reports. (The one exception was the commission's draft of a Uniform Determination of Death Act, which was endorsed by both the American Medical Association and the American Bar Association, and enacted by many states; but this was primarily a technical matter that did not divide the profession.) Outsiders, on the other hand, were, and still are, far more attentive to the commission's findings. Let a termination-of-treatment case make headlines, and the courts, the media, and the legislature, as well as an enlarged community of concerned academics, will consult and cite the commission's recommendations.

The commission's work, however, has not escaped substantive criticism, and one particular charge casts a harsh light not only on the commission itself but on the degree to which medical decision making has actually changed over the past twenty-five years. Jay Katz, who was among the first to explore in depth the ethics of human experimentation (Capron was his student at Yale Law School), has argued that the commission was far too complacent about the prospect of doctors entering a partnership with patients. Convinced that the hallowed tradition in medicine is for physicians to be silent with patients so as to exercise their own discretion, Katz remains unpersuaded that a fundamental redressing of the balance of authority has come to mark the doctor-patient relationship. Committed to empowering the patient, he is dismayed by the difficulty, if not impossibility, of the task. "I have nothing but admiration," he declared, "for the Commission's remarkable vision, which is so contrary to the medical profession's view of how physicians and patients should converse with one another." But no one should be misled into thinking that such rhetoric has engendered a new reality. The commission, for example, cited an opinion poll which found most physicians ready to share information about a fatal diagnosis with patients; Katz countered that sociologists who observe interactions in psychiatric wards report that physicians manipulate the consent process to render it meaningless. The old attitudes and practices persist, for medicine lacks a tradition of communicating uncertainties to patients and sharing decision making.[8]

Katz is not alone in minimizing the import of the changes that have come to medicine. A number of sociologists contend that medicine's privileged status has not eroded over the past twenty-five years. In the words of one student of the debate, medicine has not lost "its *relative* position of prestige and respect, or expertise, or monopoly over that expertise." Eliot Freidson, one of the most prominent sociologists of medicine, insists also that "the professions . . . continue to possess a monopoly over at least some important segment of formal knowledge that does not shrink over time." Conceding that doctors have lost some individual autonomy over decision making, he believes that this authority has simply been transferred to other doctors, not to outsiders. The internal organization of the profession has been altered, but not the external position of the profession in society.[9]

How accurate are these judgments on the events of 1966–76 and their aftermath? Have physicians merely adopted a different stance toward the pollster but not toward the patient? Have the new rules and players truly made a difference?

The record since 1966, I believe, makes a convincing case for a fundamental transformation in the substance as well as the style of medical decision making. Certainly this is true for the conduct of human experimentation. Although the regulatory performance of the Institutional Review Boards is not without flaws, the experiments that Henry Beecher described could not now occur; even the most ambitious or confident investigator would not today put forward such protocols. Indeed, the transformation in research practices is most dramatic in the area that was once most problematic: research on incompetent and institutionalized subjects. The young, the elderly, the mentally disabled, and the incarcerated are not fair game for the investigator. Researchers no longer get to choose the martyrs for mankind.

To be sure, gaps and deficiencies remain. IRBs in different institutions work with different standards, and just the way that liberal incorporation laws in one state (like New Jersey in the 1900s) undercut regulation elsewhere, so a researcher unhappy with IRB supervision at his home institution can pick up and move his shop—which apparently is what heart surgeon William DeVries did. More, the structure of the IRBs remains flawed. Although mandated to include "community representatives" among their members, the IRBs are at liberty to define the category, to select almost anyone they wish to fill it, and to dismiss out of hand anyone whose performance displeases them. More telling, the IRBs almost never investigate or scrutinize the actual encounter of researcher and subject. They examine the language of the consent form, but do not monitor the consent process or the interaction between investigator and subject.[10]

On the balance, however, the procedures to protect human experimentation are so firmly entrenched that the central issue now, in view of the AIDS crisis, is not how to protect the human subject from the investigator but how to ensure that all those who wish to be human subjects have a fair opportunity to enter a protocol. The nightmare image has shifted from an unscrupulous researcher taking advantage of a helpless inmate to a dying patient desperate to join a drug trial and have a chance at life. The backlash against the IRB is spurred not by researchers impatient with bureaucratic delays but by patients who want to make their own calculations of risks and benefits and to decide for themselves, without the veto power of an IRB, whether a protocol is worth entering. Although this reorientation in large measure reflects the grim fate confronting persons with AIDS, it also testifies to how effectively the IRBs have trained, really tamed, the researcher.[11]

To turn to the examining room, it is evident that the changes that have occurred there since the mid-1960s resemble the changes that followed in the aftermath of *Brown v. Board of Education.* Just as in civil rights one witnessed a powerful legal and societal endorsement of the idea of integration which practice never quite managed to realize, so in medicine one also witnessed a powerful endorsement of patient sovereignty with practice, again, falling short of the model. This has been a period of transition, marked by an exceptional variety of styles characterizing medical decision making. One finds, particularly among older physicians and older patients, a reluctance to adapt to a new set of expectations. Some physicians are unwilling to relinquish the discretionary authority that they exercised for so long, and some patients are unable to exercise the authority that they have won.

Nevertheless, the examining room, like the laboratory, gives ample evidence of the impact of new rules and new players. An unprecedented degree of formality now accompanies a resolution to forego life-sustaining treatment. Some states, and an even larger number of hospitals, require physicians to complete detailed forms and obtain the competent patient's signed consent before entering a Do Not Resuscitate code. Predictably, physicians have complained that, in compelling patients to confront their impending death, these discussions are cruel. For to justify a DNR code, the physician will have to explain that the disease is terminal and death imminent, that resuscitation is medically futile, and that the pounding on the chest, the likely breaking of ribs, and going on a ventilator are more painful than useful. But these protests notwithstanding, public policy and opinion demand that this explicit dialogue occur, preferring such conversations to pencilled notations on nursing charts or chalk entries on blackboards.

To be sure, subterfuge is possible and undoubtedly happens. Hospital resuscitation teams may follow a "slow code," walking, not rushing, to the bedside, and when a patient is incompetent, the physician may manipulate the family into following orders, if not on the first day then on the third. There is also evidence that some physicians find the obligation so distasteful or difficult that they postpone the discussions to the last minute, and then, with the patient in a coma, talk to the family. (This tactic helps explain why one retrospective study of DNR orders found that the family was far more likely than the patient—86 percent compared to 22 percent—to have authorized a DNR code, and another study reported that most DNR orders were written within three days of death.)[12] Still, it is apparent that new procedures have taken hold. Medical decisions now leave a well marked paper trail, and the stacked DNR forms are becoming as prominent on the nursing station desk as any other order sheets.

What is true for DNR orders holds as well for decisions to refuse or withdraw life-sustaining treatment. Ask a medical school class whether physicians should respect the wishes of a competent adult who is a Jehovah's Witness to be allowed to die rather than accept a blood transfusion, and the immediate and unanimous response is yes. That the competent, terminally ill patient can refuse not only high-technology interventions but food and water is now a well established principle, not only in bioethics tracts but in case law, and many physicians have come to respect, and even be comfortable with, this exercise of patient autonomy. (One surgeon recounted to me how much easier it is to function in an atmosphere where openness about prognosis is the norm. In the old days, he would have to pause outside the room to try and recall precisely which deceit he had perpetrated on the patient; now he only had to consult the chart, read the entries, and begin the conversation.) Again, physicians have retained some degree of discretion. They may well consult with patient and family about the use of a respirator or the administration of antibiotics, but reserve for themselves more technical (and covert) decisions about raising or lowering drug dosages that alter cardiac output or blood pressure. Taken as a whole, however, the cloak that covered medical decision making when the end of life approached has been lifted, and determinations on whether to continue or halt treatment are the focus of open deliberation.

These decisions are the substance of hospital committee deliberations as well. The idea of an ethics committee, as we have seen, first captured national attention in the Quinlan decision and commentators were soon suggesting that these committees should address not only the purely medical question (is the illness terminal?), but the truly ethical ones (for example, by what standard should decisions be made on behalf of the incompetent patient?). The catalyst for the spread of ethics committees, however, was not only academic analysis but several well-publicized incidents between 1982 and 1984 in which treatment was withdrawn from handicapped newborns. In these so-called "Baby Doe" cases, replays of the earlier Johns Hopkins case, parents refused to give permission for life-saving surgery because the newborn seemed too severely disabled. Media coverage of these incidents was extensive (confirming the extent to which consciousness had been raised about bioethical questions), and the Reagan administration tried to gain political capital with right-to-life groups by insisting upon life-sustaining treatment under almost all circumstances. The Department of Health and Human Services (HHS) opened an 800 telephone number to receive tips about possible discriminatory treatment of a disabled newborn and organized a Baby Doe squad that would rush to investigate cases and compel treatment. Individual right-to-life proponents joined the campaign. One of them, upon learning that a New York hospital was about to accede to the joint decision of family and physicians to withhold surgery from a severely impaired newborn, asked the state court to order treatment.

Both federal and state courts have rejected these efforts. They found no statutory basis for the federal government to reach into the neonatal nursery, and preferred to empower families and physicians rather than third-party advocates to make the decisions. The Reagan administration persisted, and HHS issued regulations to expand the oversight role of state child protection agencies. At the same time, it urged, but did not require, that hospitals establish neonatal ethics committees.

These same incidents also encouraged other, very different groups to endorse ethics committees. The President's commission urged hospitals with high-tech neonatal units to formulate "explicit policies on decision-making . . . for these infants," and it hoped that an ethics committee would conduct reviews whenever the family and the physician differed about life-sustaining interventions or whenever a dispute occurred on the futility or benefit of such an intervention.[13] In addition, a variety of medical associations, including the American Academy of Pediatrics, the American Medical Association, and the American Hospital Association, went on record favoring ethics committees. Surveys of hospitals between 1983 and 1985 reported that the percentage of hospitals with these committees doubled, with teaching hospitals and large tertiary care centers taking the lead.[14] At the least, ethics committees may obviate the need to go to court (or forestall another effort to bring 800 numbers into the nursery). At best, they may provide a forum for resolving conflicts in which both sides could invoke strong ethical principles.

Although hospital ethics committees come in an almost bewildering variety of shapes and forms, even more so than the IRBs, they do share a number of essential characteristics. Membership is heavily weighted to clinical personnel, with a bioethicist and community representative (again undefined) included. The committees often design and implement teaching programs for staff or assist in drawing up guidelines and procedures for their hospitals, and these activities are generally well accepted. Controversy begins when ethics committees address individual cases, when their members take a place around the bedside. Critics of ethics committees, like critics of IRBs, come both from those who believe they go too far and from those who believe they do not go far enough. One side feels that they violate the privacy of the doctor-patient relationship and promote consensus at the cost of principle; the other complains that the committees mainly serve the needs of the clinician (patients do not always have the right to convene them) and lack real authority (most are only advisory in character). Thus one prefers to trust to the doctor and the family, the other, to a full-fledged court hearing.

Ethics committees are still too new and the data too thin to resolve these differences. Lacking a clear federal mandate, they do not have the authority of the IRB, and their advisory role can be impeded by state legislation. A number of states, for example, have mandated the treatment of all surviving newborns. (Louisiana law, for example, declares that "no infant born alive shall be denied or deprived of food or nutrients, water, or oxygen by any person whatsoever with the intent to cause or allow the death of the child.")[15] A neonatal ethics committee responsive to such laws might find nothing to do. Moreover, the committees may not consistently or meaningfully enhance the voice of the patient. To the degree that they are doctor-convened, they may be doctor-dominated. Nevertheless, their potential benefits are likely to promote their spread and use. Ethics committees, more than courts, may provide a relaxed atmosphere in which to clarify implicit but unexamined assumptions, by the family or the physician, about what it means to have disability and how to cope with it. The committees may also operate without paying scrupulous attention to the letter of the law or by finding a loophole that will sanction their recommendation. For example, even under restrictive state legislation that mandates treatment, an exception may be made when the intervention would be "futile," a term that does not lend itself to strict definition. Thus ethics committees may be able to recommend withholding or foregoing "futile" treatment in a particular situation, whatever the statute's general thrust.[16]

No estimate of the recent impact and future direction of the changes we have been analyzing can be complete without reckoning with the extraordinary growth of economic regulation of medicine over the past twenty-five years. As we noted at the outset, the movement to bring law and bioethics to the bedside was not driven by cost considerations. There was hardly a mention of fiscal matters in the Mondale or Kennedy hearings, in the reports of the national commissions addressing human experimentation or bioethics, in the debates over defining death and facilitating transplantation, or in the controversies that enveloped the Johns Hopkins baby or Karen Ann Quinlan.

This dynamic is not, however, altogether separable from the one that brought federal, state, and corporation administrators to the bedside. In fact, it is difficult to sort out the relationship between these two trends, or to plot which way the arrow of influence points. Both worked to reduce discretion in medical decision making, empowering not only courts, legislatures, and committees but government and business regulatory bodies—who now require (before allowing reimbursement) unambiguous evidence that the patient was sick enough to warrant hospital admission, a stay of however many days, and the particular procedures used. After all, 1966 was not only the year that Beecher published his exposé, but the year that the federal government, through the enactment of Medicare and Medicaid, became the single largest purchaser of services.

Without being dogmatic, it may be that the concerns about trust, deference, and discretion helped to promote the change in regulatory policy. The new and enormous stake of the federal government in medical costs may have been in itself sufficient to explain the origins of cost containment. But it is also worth noting that this effort gathered momentum from the dynamics we have been exploring here. Because the doctor had become a stranger, because the levels of trust had diminished, because technology placed the doctor's hands more often on dials than on patients, it became more legitimate to treat the physician as one more seller of services and medical care as a commodity that should be regulated like any other.

Whatever the causal relationship, it is indisputable that the two trends have been mutually reinforcing. Each of them separately and then both together have brought more outsiders to medicine, and more formality and collective judgment as well. Whatever gaps one has left open, the other filled in. One cannot always be certain which of the two is ultimately responsible for a development, but since they both drive policy in the same direction, the route of change is marked in bold.

There is every reason to expect that for the foreseeable future medical decision making will be a shared enterprise and physicians will not regain the discretionary authority they once enjoyed. The outsiders who have entered medicine will probably remain there, bringing in like-minded successors. Medicine is and will continue to be in the public domain. Programs in bioethics are now entrenched in the medical schools, delineating a relatively fixed career line. The body of law around medical decision making and, concomitantly, the number of jobs in law and health care are great enough to ensure that a new cadre of lawyers will be engaged with these issues. Moreover, the media have their health reporters with refined sensibilities about the legal and ethical dimensions of a story. It is not simply that ethical and legal issues in medicine now abound, but that a cadre of journalists are trained to perceive and pursue them. Let an announcement of a medical advance be made, whether in mapping a gene, prescribing a growth hormone, or transplanting fetal tissue, and the reflex response is to analyze the ethical dimension of the innovation. All the while, of course, the vigorous attempt to contain medical costs will keep a small army of budget-minded officials involved as well.

Patients are also likely to be sparing with the deference and trust they accord to physicians or hospitals, reserving for themselves critical decisions about treatment. Attitude and practice will vary by class, gender, and generation—younger middle-class women are likely to be more assertive than elderly lower-class men. But in crisis situations, particularly around life-sustaining treatments, patients and their families will forcefully advance their own preferences. The structural considerations that originally helped to secure this change have only assumed greater prominence. Doctors are all the more strangers and hospitals the more strange places as the number of physicians in group practice (whether a health maintenance organization or health center) mounts, along with the degree of subspecialization. Simultaneously, the number of community and sectarian hospitals is shrinking and the rural hospital is becoming a relic of the past.

Judicial decisions, directly and indirectly, will encourage patient prerogatives and reinforce proceduralism. State and federal courts have become deeply immersed in medical decision making—by one recent count, between 1976 and 1988 there have been fifty-four reported decisions involving the right to refuse life-sustaining treatment, and the Supreme Court, in the 1990 *Cruzan* decision, has now addressed the issue. The clear consensus, joined by the Supreme Court, is that competent patients have the right to make their own decisions about life-sustaining treatment, and such treatment is to be broadly defined, including the provision of food and water. The principal area of disagreement is on the standards that should be applied in decision making for the incompetent patient. Must the once-competent patient have left clear and convincing evidence of his or her wishes? Can a lower standard suffice, especially when parents are requesting that treatment be terminated?

The case of Nancy Cruzan exemplifies the controversies. As a result of an automobile accident, Cruzan suffered brain damage and loss of oxygen. She remained in a coma for several weeks, then entered a persistent vegetative state. To keep her nourished, the hospital inserted a feeding and hydration tube. When it became apparent to her parents that their daughter would never regain mental functioning, they asked the hospital to remove the tube. The hospital refused, and, as in the case of Karen Ann Quinlan, the dispute entered the courts.

A lower Missouri court sided with the parents, crediting their report of a "somewhat serious conversation" in which Nancy stated that she did not wish to be kept alive unless she could live a halfway normal life. The Missouri Supreme Court adjudged this testimony "unreliable," and ruled that a state may insist, as Missouri does, on "clear and convincing" evidence before terminating treatment for an incompetent patient. The majority opinion from the U.S. Supreme Court agreed, finding this higher standard reasonable and not in contravention of a right to privacy. Although proponents of patients' rights interpreted the *Cruzan* case as a defeat, the initial effect of the Supreme Court ruling has been to publicize the need for competent adults to record their wishes through a living will or the formal appointment of a surrogate decision maker. So too, *Cruzan* is prompting state legislatures to make these stipulations binding on health care personnel and facilities. The fallout from *Cruzan* may thus help to persuade even more Americans to declare their preferences in advance and to secure the legality of such directives. It may soon become standard practice for hospital admission offices to ask patients not only for their insurance card but for their living wills.

Indeed, let a family for one reason or another be frustrated in fulfilling its wishes, and it may even take vigilante action. In one recent case a father, brandishing a revolver to keep the hospital staff from intervening, disconnected the respirator that was keeping his infant daughter alive in a persistent vegetative state. In another incident, a family disconnected the respirator that was keeping their brain-injured father alive, and physically barred hospital personnel from reconnecting the machine. Although one would have thought that vigilante actions had no place in an ICU, neither case led to an indictment. Still more startling, both stories became the occasion for commentators to disparage the tyranny of medicine and the machine over the patient.[17]

By almost every account, these changes have disturbed many physicians and may adversely affect recruitment to the profession. Physicians lament the loss of status and authority, which they link directly to a loss of professional autonomy and discretion. Writing in the *NEJM* in January 1990, Dr. Saul Radovsky asked "why the morale of today's doctor is low," and found much of his answer in the extent to which their professional lives "are more hemmed in and complicated" by rules. "Doctors ethics, morality, and commitment to public service have largely been legislated or are regulated." Physicians now see themselves "cast as wrongdoers and incompetents who yearly require new laws, regulations, admonitions, court decisions, and exposés to make them more honest, ethical, competent, corrigible, and contrite. Perhaps it is no wonder if many of them now look for a change or exit."[18] Reporting in the *New York Times* a month later, Lawrence Altman and Elisabeth Rosenthal found that "the degree of dissatisfaction among doctors is astonishingly high," and they cited a 1989 Gallup Poll that almost 40 percent of physicians questioned said that if they knew then what they know now, they would not have entered medical school.[19] These complaints are in large measure responsible for a notable decline in applications to medical school—among white males, the pool has decreased by half—and one is left to ponder whether this decrease presages a more general demoralization of the profession.

Which brings us to our final consideration. Reviewing these events, and speculating about the future, suggests that the transformations in medical decision making, as vital as they are, have come with a price. To alter the balances between doctor and patient and medicine and society encouraged, unavoidably, the intervention of a greater number of third parties. Ironically, to cope with the doctor as stranger and the hospital as strange, to respond to perceived conflicts of interest and to the power of new technologies, it appeared necessary to bring still more strangers to the bedside. Constraining one authority figure required creating other authority figures. To make certain that the patient's voice would be heard and respected demanded the support of a chorus, and as sometimes happens, the chorus can overwhelm the soloist.

The crowding of so many people around the bedside may be a transitional phenomenon in the history of medical decision making. Successor generations may find it less necessary to draw on outsiders to enhance the prerogatives of the patient; they may be more ready to trust to the patient alone, or the patient together with the doctor. Indeed, one glimpses signs of new alignments, such as doctors and patients uniting against government and corporate officials who attempt to curtail medical expenditures. By the same token, court cases on termination of treatment at times pit patient against hospital, with the doctor siding with the patient. And in the case of handicapped newborns, doctors, families, and courts have closed ranks to keep out third-party, right-to-life advocates and government bureaucrats. Thus, with new configurations emerging, the crowd now gathered around the bedside may disperse.

The process of change may be accelerated because if patients today are more sovereign than ever before, medicine itself is more bureaucratic, enmeshed in forms, committees, and procedures. This bureaucratization can adversely affect patients as well as practitioners. Signing a DNR code sheet is a proper exercise of patient autonomy, but one may still wish for a less formal and cumbersome mechanism. That dying has become a legal process is not an unqualified sign of progress.

In effect, one more aspect of modern life has become contractual, prescribed, and uniform. One more encounter of a primary sort now tends to be disinterested, neutral, and remote. To be sure, medical schools, medical societies, institutes, foundations, and government agencies are attempting to ameliorate the situation. Perhaps bringing the humanities into medical education will humanize the doctor; perhaps there are new ways to teach students not only how to take a case history from a patient but how to give information to a patient. Perhaps the incentives to train family doctors will alter recruitment patterns and strengthen the doctor-patient relationship. And perhaps all the energies devoted to these programs and the discussions that accompany them will help us as a society to resolve the daunting questions of what values we wish to preserve, or abandon, in the effort to prolong human life.

The prospect of accomplishing such an agenda does not breed an easy confidence or optimism. In the end, patients may well continue to experience medicine as modern: powerful and impersonal, a more or less efficient interaction between strangers.

APPENDIX A

Citations to Henry Beecher's 1966 Article

1. Captain Robert Chamovitz, MC, USAF, Captain Francis J. Catanzaro, MC, AUS, Captain Chandler A. Stetson, MC, AUS, and Charles H. Rammelkamp, Jr., M.D., "Prevention of Rheumatic Fever by Treatment of Previous Streptococcal Infections: I. Evaluation of Benzathine Penicillin G," *New England Journal of Medicine* 251 (1954): 466–71.

2. Captain Alton J. Morris, Captain Robert Chamovitz, MC, USAF, Captain Frank J. Catanzaro, MC, Army of the United States, and Charles H. Rammelkamp, Jr., M.D., Cleveland, "Prevention of Rheumatic Fever by Treatment of Previous Streptococcic Infections: Effect of Sulfadiazine," *Journal of the American Medical Association* 160 (1956): 114–16.

3. Pedro T. Lantin, Sr., M.D., Alberto Geronimo, M.D., and Victorino Calilong, M.D., Manila, Philippines, "The Problem of Typhoid Relapse," *American Journal of the Medical Sciences* 245 (1963): 293–98.

4. Howard E. Ticktin, M.D., and Hyman J. Zimmerman, M.D., "Hepatic Dysfunction and Jaundice in Patients Receiving Triacetyloleandomycin," *New England Journal of Medicine* 267 (1962): 964–68.

5. James L. Scott, M.D., Sydney M. Finegold, M.D., Gerald A. Belkin, M.D., and John S. Lawrence, M.D., "A Controlled Double-Blind Study of the Hematologic Toxicity of Chloramphenicol," *New England Journal of Medicine* 272 (1965): 1137–42.

6. Robert M. Zollinger, Jr., M.D., Martin C. Lindem, Jr., M.D., Robert M. Filler,

M.D., Joseph M. Corson, M.D., and Richard E. Wilson, M.D., "Effect of Thymectomy on Skin-Homograft Survival in Children," *New England Journal of Medicine* 270 (1964): 707–9.

7. A. A. Lurie, M.D., R. E. Jones, M.D., H. W. Linde, Ph.D., M. L. Price, A.B., R. D. Dripps, M.D., and H. L. Price, M.D., "Cyclopropane Anesthesia. 1. Cardiac Rate and Rhythm during Steady Levels of Cyclopropane Anesthesia at Normal and Elevated End-Expiratory Carbon Dioxide Tensions," *Anesthesiology* 19 (1958): 457–72.

8. Frank A. Finnerty, Jr., Lloyd Witkin, and Joseph F. Fazekas, with the technical assistance of Marie Langbart and William K. Young, "Cerebral Hemodynamics during Cerebral Ischemia Induced by Acute Hypotension," *Journal of Clinical Investigation* 33 (1954): 1227–32.

9. Angelo G. Rocco, M.D., and Leroy D. Vandam, M.D., Boston, "Changes in Circulation Consequent to Manipulation during Abdominal Surgery," *Journal of the American Medical Association* 164 (1957): 14–18.

10. Eugene Braunwald, Robert L. Frye, Maurice M. Aygen, and Joseph W. Gilbert, Jr., "Studies on Starling's Law of the Heart. III. Observations in Patients with Mitral Stenosis and Atrial Fibrillation on the Relationships between Left Ventricular End-Diastolic Segment Length Filling Pressure, and the Characteristics of Ventricular Contraction," *Journal of Clinical Investigation* 39 (1960): 1874–84.

11. Eugene Braunwald, M.D., and Andrew G. Morrow, M.D., "Sequence of Ventricular Contraction in Human Bundle Branch Block: A Study Based on Simultaneous Catheterization of Both Ventricles," *American Journal of Medicine* 23 (1957): 205–11.

12. Douglas R. Morton, M.D., Karl P. Klassen, M.D., F.A.C.S., Jacob J. Jacoby, M.D., Ph.D., and George M. Curtis, M.D., Ph.D., F.A.C.S., "The Effect of Intrathoracic Vagal Stimulation on the Electrocardiographic Tracing in Man," *Surgery, Gynecology and Obstetrics* 96 (1953): 724–32.

13. Stanley Reichman, William D. Davis, John Storaasli, and Richard Gorlin, "Measurement of Hepatic Blood Flow by Indicator Dilution Techniques," *Journal of Clinical Investigation* 37 (1958): 1848–56.

14. Gerald B. Phillips, M.D., Robert Schwartz, M.D., George J. Gabuzda, Jr., M.D., and Charles S. Davidson, M.D., "The Syndrome of Impending Hepatic Coma in Patients with Cirrhosis of the Liver Given Certain Nitrogenous Substances," *New England Journal of Medicine* 247 (1952): 239–46.

15. Laurens P. White, Elizabeth A. Phear, W. H. J. Summerskill, and Sheila Sherlock, with the technical assistance of Marjorie Cole, "Ammonium Tolerance in Liver Disease: Observations Based on Catheterization of the Hepatic Veins," *Journal of Clinical Investigation* 34 (1955): 158–68.

16. S. Krugman, M.D., Robert Ward, M.D., Joan P. Giles, M.D., Oscar Bodansky, M.D., and A. Milton Jacobs, M.D., "Infectious Hepatitis: Detection of Virus during the Incubation Period and in Clinically Inapparent Infection," *New England Journal of Medicine* 261 (1959): 729–34.

17. Elinor Langer, "Human Experimentation: Cancer Studies at Sloan-Kettering Stir Public Debate on Medical Ethics," *Science* 143 (1964): 551–53.

18. Edward F. Scanlon, M.D., Roger A. Hawkins, M.D., Wayne W. Fox, M.D., and W. Scott Smith, M.D., "Fatal Homotransplanted Melanoma: A Case Report," *Cancer* 18 (1965): 782–89.

19. P. R. Allison, F.R.C.S., and R. J. Linden, M.B., Ch.B., "The Bronchoscopic Measurement of Left Auricular Pressure," *Circulation* 7 (1953): 669–73.
20. Andrew G. Morrow, M.D., F.A.C.S., Eugene Braunwald, M.D., J. Alex Haller, Jr., M.D., and Edward H. Sharp, M.D., "Left Heart Catheterization by the Transbronchial Route: Technic and Applications in Physiologic and Diagnostic Investigations," *Circulation* 16 (1957): 1033–39.

21. John B. Hickam and Walter H. Cargill, "Effect of Exercise on Cardiac Output and Pulmonary Arterial Pressure in Normal Persons and in Patients with Cardiovascular Disease and Pulmonary Emphysema," *Journal of Clinical Investigation* 27 (1948): 10–23.

22. Robert Lich, Jr., Lonnie W. Howerton, Jr., Lydon S. Goode, and Lawrence A. Davis, "The Ureterovesical Junction of the Newborn," *Journal of Urology* 92 (1964): 436–38.

NOTES

Introduction

1. Hans Jonas, "Philosophical Reflections on Experimenting with Human Subjects," *Daedalus* 98 (1969): 219.
2. Marie R. Haug and Bebe Lavin, "Practitioner or Patient—Who's in Charge?" *Journal of Health and Social Behavior* 22 (1981): 215; Boston Women's Health Book Collective, *Our Bodies, Ourselves* (New York: 1973), xx.
3. Letter from Dr. William Bartholome of the University of Kansas Medical School to Mrs. Samuel Mayer, 9 December 1971.
4. See, for example, the discussion in Jeanne Harley Guillemin and Lynda Lytle Holmstrom, *Mixed Blessings: Intensive Care for Newborns* (New York: 1986), chap. 5.

Chapter 1

1. Henry K. Beecher, "Ethics and Clinical Research," *New England Journal of Medicine* 74 (1966): 1354–60 (hereafter cited as *NEJM*). All quotations from Beecher are to this article unless otherwise cited. A synopsis of the argument that follows appeared in my *NEJM* article, "Ethics and Human Experimentation: Henry Beecher Revisited," 317 (1987): 1195–99.
2. C. L. Kaufman, "Informed Consent and Patient Decision Making: Two Decades of Research," *Social Science and Medicine* 17 (1983): 1657–64.
3. Beecher to Richard Field, 3 August 1965, Henry Beecher Manuscripts, Francis A. Countway Library of Medicine, Harvard University (hereafter cited as Beecher MSS).
4. Beecher to Arnold Relman, 21 June 1966, Beecher MSS.

5. See the letters of Beecher to these publications, May–June 1966, Beecher MSS.

6. See Beecher to George Burch, 27 June 1966, Beecher MSS.

7. For two useful surveys see Norman Howard-Jones, "Human Experimentation in Historical and Ethical Perspective," *Social Science Medicine* 16 (1982): 1429–48; J. C. Fletcher, "The Evolution of the Ethics of Informed Consent," in *Research Ethics*, ed. K. Berg and K. E. Tanoy (New York: 1983), pp. 187–228. See also Lawrence K. Altman, *Who Goes First: The Story of Self-Experimentation in Medicine* (New York: 1987).

8. J. P. Bull, "The Historical Development of Clinical Therapeutic Trials," *Journal of Chronic Diseases* 10 (1959): 218–48.

9. Bull, "Clinical Therapeutic Trials," p. 222.

10. D. Baxby, *Jenner's Smallpox Vaccine* (London: 1981), esp. pp. 22–23, 58–63; Lewis H. Roddis, "Edward Jenner and the Discovery of Smallpox Vaccination," *Military Surgeon* 65 (1929): 853–61.

11. Edward Jenner, "Vaccination against Smallpox" (1798; reprint, Harvard Classics, *Scientific Papers* vol. 38, 1910), pp. 164–65.

12. Roddis, "Edward Jenner," pp. 861–64.

13. Howard-Jones, "Human Experimentation," p. 1429.

14. Ibid., pp. 1429–31.

15. William Beaumont, "Experiments and Observations on the Gastric Juice and Physiology of Digestion" (1833; reprint, New York: Peter Smith, 1941), pp. xii–xiii.

16. R. Vallery-Radot, *The Life of Pasteur* (New York: 1926), pp. 404–5. See also Gerald Geison, "Pasteur's Early Work on Rabies: Reexamining the Ethical Issues," *Hastings Center Report* 8 (1978): 26–33; Stephen Paget, *Pasteur and after Pasteur* (London: 1914), p. 79. The recent work of Bruno Latour on Pasteur does not address the ethics of human experimentation: *The Pasteurization of France* (Cambridge, Mass.: 1988).

17. Vallery-Radot, *Pasteur*, pp. 414–17.

18. Pasteur recommended that convicted criminals be the subjects of human experimentation. As he wrote to the emperor of Brazil: "If I were a King, an Emperor, or even the President of a Republic . . . I should invite the counsel of a condemned man, on the eve of the day fixed for his execution, to choose between certain death and an experiment which would consist in several preventive inoculations of rabic virus. . . . If he survived this experiment—and I am convinced that he would—his life would be saved" (Vallery-Radot 1926, p. 405).

19. Claude Bernard, *An Introduction to the Study of Experimental Medicine*, trans. H. C. Greene (New York: 1927), pp. 101–2.

20. J. H. Salisbury, "On the Causes of Intermittent and Remittent Fevers," *American Journal of Medical Science* 26 (1866): 51–68.

21. Cited in Howard-Jones, "Human Experimentation," p. 1430.
22. J. P. Bull, "The Historical Development of Clinical Therapeutic Trials," *Journal of Chronic Disease* 10 (1959): 235.
23. Michael Bliss, *The Discovery of Insulin* (Chicago: 1982).
24. Bull, "Clinical Therapeutic Trials," p. 237.
25. Cited in Walter B. Bean, *Walter Reed; A Biography* (Charlottesville, Va.: 1982), p. 128.
26. Cited in Bean, *Reed*, pp. 131, 147.
27. Ibid.
28. Ibid., pp. 146–47, 165.
29. V. Veeressayev, *The Memoirs of a Physician*, trans. Simeon Linder (New York: 1916), app. B.
30. George M. Sternberg and Walter Reed, "Report on Immunity against Vaccination Conferred upon the Monkey by the Use of the Serum of the Vaccinated Calf and Monkey," *Transactions of the Association of American Physicians* 10 (1895): 57–69.
31. Joseph Stokes, Jr., et al., "Results of Immunization by Means of Active Virus of Human Influenza," *Journal of Clinical Investigation* 16 (1937): 237–43. This was one in a series of his investigations that used institutionalized populations. See, for example, Stokes et al., "Vaccination against Epidemic Influenza," *American Journal of the Medical Sciences* 194 (1937): 757–68.
32. My account here follows the excellent analysis of Susan Lederer, "Hideyop Noguchi's Luetin Experiment and the Antivivisectionists," *Isis* 76 (1985): 31–48.
33. All quotations cited in Lederer, "Noguchi's Luetin Experiment," pp. 321–48.

Chapter 2

1. Chester S. Keefer, "Dr. Richards as Chairman of the Committee on Medical Research," *Annals of Internal Medicine* 71, supp. 8 (1969): 62.
2. E. C. Andrus et al., eds., *Advances in Military Medicine*, 2 vols. (Boston: 1948). For a summary of the work of the CMR, see the foreword to volume 1.
3. Andrus et. al., *Advances*, vol. 1, p. 7.
4. Records of the Office of Scientific Research and Development, Committee on Medical Research, Contractor Records (Contract 120, Final Report), Principal Investigator Stuart Mudd (University of Pennsylvania), 3 March 1943, Record Group 227, National Archives, Washington, D.C., (hereafter cited as Records of the OSRD, CMR; C = Contract, R = Report, PI = Principal Investigator).
5. Records of the OSRD, CMR, Summary Report, Division of Medicine, Status Report, PI E.C. Anderson, 14 December 1944.

NOTES

6. Records of OSRD, CMR, Contractor Records (Children's Hospital), June 1946, 293, L27, pp. 24–45.

7. Ibid.

8. Ibid.

9. Records of the OSRD, CMR, Contractor Records, 120, Monthly Progress Report 18, PI Stuart Mudd, 3 October 1944.

10. A. V. Hardy and S. D. Cummins, "Preliminary Note on the Clinical Response to Sulfadiazine Therapy," *Public Health Reports* 58 (1943): 693–96.

11. J. Watt and S. D. Cummins, "Further Studies on the Relative Efficacy of Sulfonamides in Shigellosis," *Public Health Reports* 60 (1945): 355–61.

12. Andrus et al., *Advances*, vol. 1, p. xlix.

13. Records of the OSRD, CMR, Contractor Records, C 450, R L2, Bimonthly Progress Report, PI Alf S. Alving (University of Chicago), 1 August 1944.

14. Records of the OSRD, CMR, Contractor Records, C 450, R L36, 21 December 1945; Reports L50, L49.

15. *New York Times*, 5 March 1945, pp. 1–3.

16. Andrus et al., *Advances*, vol 1, p. 17.

17. Records of the OSRD, CMR, Contractor Records, C 360, R L 14, Bimonthly Progress Report 8, PI Werner Henle (Children's Hospital of Philadelphia), 1 December 1944.

18. Werner Henle et al., "Experiments on Vaccination of Human Beings against Epidemic Influenza," *Journal of Immunology* 53 (1946): 75–93.

19. For similar research at Ypsilanti State Hospital, see Jonas E. Salk et al., "Immunization against Influenza with Observations during an Epidemic of Influenza A One Year after Vaccination," *American Journal of Hygiene* 42 (1945): 307–21.

20. Thomas Francis, Jr., Jonas E. Salk et al., "Protective Effect of Vaccination against Induced Influenza A," *Proceedings of the Society for Experimental Biology and Medicine* 55 (1944): 104. For details on the research reports, see Jonas E. Salk et al., "Protective Effects of Vaccination against Induced Influenza B," *Journal of Clinical Investigation* 24 (1945): 547–53; see also Francis, Salk, et al., 536–46.

21. Commission on Influenza, "A Clinical Evaluation of Vaccination against Influenza," *Journal of the American Medical Association* 124 (1944): 982–84; see also Monroe D. Eaton and Gordon Meiklejohn, "Vaccination against Influenza: A Study in California during the Epidemic of 1943–44," *American Journal of Hygiene* 42 (1945): 28–44.

22. The account here is based on the material in Records of the OSRD, CMR, General Correspondence, A–F, box 59. See especially the policy memorandums of 16 July 1943; 22 September 1943 (Summary, Penicillin Procedures, Industry Advisory Committee); 13 January 1944; 15 January 1944; 20 January 1944. See also A. N. Richards, "Production of Penicillin in the United States (1941–1946)," *Nature* 201 (1964): 441–45.

23. On the COs' experience, see Records of the OSRD, CMR, box 18. Contracts 206 and 483 provide typical examples, as does the correspondence of E. F. Adolph (University of Rochester) with E. C. Andrus, 14 December 1943 and 6 April 1944. See also Administrative Document 18, Camp Operations Division, 1 October 1943. The seawater experiments are reported in Contract 180, PI Allan Butler, 14 September 1942. Records of the OSRD, CMR, "Human Experiments," box 36.

24. Records of the OSRD, CMR, General Correspondence, "Human Experiments—Venereal Disease" (hereafter cited as Records of the OSRD, CMR, "Human Experiments"), box 39, Moore to Richards, 1 February 1943. Parran to Richards, 9 February 1943.

25. J. E. Moore to A. N. Richards, 6 October 1942. Richards to Moore, 9 October 1942.

26. Richards to Moore, Ibid., 31 October 1942, box 39.

27. R. E. Dyer to Richards, 18 January 1943.

28. Records of the OSRD, CMR, General Correspondence, "Statement of Explanation of the Experiment and Its Risks to Tentative Volunteers," Minutes of a Conference on Human Experimentation in Gonorrhea, filed with Subcommittee of Venereal Disease of the Committee of Medicine, box 39, 29 December 1942. The document may have exaggerated the efficacy of sulfanilamide treatment; there was much dispute about the actual cure rate, and recurrence was noted to be a problem, as was the existence of resistant strains. Indeed, this uncertainty was one of the reasons for the CMR research.

29. Records of the OSRD, CMR, "Human Experiments," box 39, Moore to Richards, 1 February 1943.

30. Ibid., Frank Jewett and Ross Harrison to Vannevar Bush, 5 March 1943.

31. Ibid., Thomas Parran to A. N. Richards, 9 February 1943.

32. James Bennet to J. E. Moore, 26 February 1943; Contractor Records, M3169, Report L7, 7 September 1945–50, pp. 45–50.

Chapter 3

1. For an overview of this history, see Donald C. Swain, "The Rise of a Research Empire: NIH, 1930 to 1950," *Science* 138 (1962): 1233–37; V. A. Harden, *Inventing the NIH: Federal Biomedical Research Policy, 1887–1937* (Baltimore, Md.: 1986), esp. pp. 179–91; Stephen P. Strickland, *Politics, Science, and Dread Disease* (Cambridge: 1972).

2. For a detailed analysis of the transfer of authority from the CMR to the NIH, see Daniel M. Fox, "The Politics of the NIH Extramural Program, 1937–1950," *Journal of the History of Medicine and Allied Sciences* 42 (1987): 447–66. As he makes clear, the transfer was easiest at the ideological level and far more complicated at the contract-grant level.

3. George Rosen, "Patterns of Health Research in the United States, 1900–1960," *Bulletin of the History of Medicine* 39 (1965): 220.

4. Vannevar Bush, "Science, the Endless Frontier: Report to the President on a Program for Scientific Research," (1945): esp. pp. 46–47, 53. In addition to Fox, "The Politics of the NIH," see also *New York Times*, 21 July 1945, 13 August 1945.

5. *New York Times*, 4 July 1945, p. 13.

6. "The National Institutes of Health: A Concerted Effort to Investigate and Study the Many Unconquered Diseases which Afflict Mankind," distributed by the Chemical Foundation, New York (n.d.), pp. 18–19, quoting from the *Congressional Record*.

7. *New York Times*, 6 February 1945, p. 18.

8. Ibid., 12 September 1944, p. 12.

9. Ibid., 21 November 1944, p. 24; see also 29 October 1945, sec. 4, 9.

10. J. E. Rall, epilogue, in *NIH: An Account of Research in Its Laboratories and Clinics*, ed. Dewitt Stetten, Jr., and W. T. Carrigan (New York: 1984), p. 527.

11. "Handbook for Patients at the Clinical Center," Public Health Service (PHS) Publication 315 (1953), esp. p. 2; "Clinical Center: National Institutes of Health," PHS Publication 316 (1956), esp. p. 13; "The Patient's Part in Research at the Clinical Center," PHS Publication (n.d.), pp. 2–3.

12. Minutes, Ad Hoc Committee on Clinical Research Procedures, 28 May 1965, NIH Files, Bethesda, MD., p. 1 (hereafter cited as Minutes, NIH Ad Hoc Committee). "In only a small percentage of instances do patients sign a specific consent."

13. Minutes, NIH Ad Hoc Committee, 19 March 1965, pp. 1–5. The committee was brought together to revise the 1950 publication entitled "Group Consideration of Clinical Research Procedures Deviating from Acceptable Medical Practice or Involving Unusual Hazards." Under the chairmanship of Nathaniel Berlin, the committee members reviewed past procedures in order to make recommendations, which were approved in 1966.

14. Minutes, NIH Ad Hoc Committee, 16 February 1965, p.2.

15. Ibid., 28 May 1965, pp.1–3.

16. Ibid., 22 January 1965, p. 2.

17. Ibid., 19 March 1965, p. 4.

18. Ibid., p.3; 23 April 1965, p.4

19. Ibid., 2 June 1965, pp. 1–2.

20. Ibid., 2 June 1965, pp. 1–3.

21. Mark S. Frankel, *The Public Health Guidelines Governing Research Involving Human Subjects,* George Washington University Program of Policy Studies in Science and Technology Monograph no. 10 (Washington, D.C.: 1972), pp. 6–12.

22. L. G. Welt, "Reflections on the Problems of Human Experimentation," *Connecticut Medicine* 25 (1961): 75–78.

23. Law–Medicine Research Institute of Boston University, Report to the U.S. Public Health Service; Frankel, *Guidelines Governing Research*, p.18

24. Welt, "Human Experimentation," pp. 78; Law–Medicine Institute, "Report." See also chapter 5, note 10.

25. The most useful and accessible compendium of relevant articles and codes is Irving Ladimer and Roger Newman, *Clinical Investigation in Medicine: Legal, Ethical, and Moral Aspects* (Boston: Law–Medicine Institute of Boston University, 1963). Ladimer and Newman were both on the staff of the Boston University Law–Medicine Institute. There was sufficient commentary on the history, ethics, and practice of human experimentation to enable the editors to assemble a 500-page book and a bibliography of 500 references. But several points must be made, quite aside from the tone of the articles and the limits of public action. First, the institute was altogether accurate in describing itself as "a program unique in the United States," and the importance of its own work should not be exaggerated. Second, the great majority of articles reprinted were from physicians—lawyers were second, Ph.D.s in other disciplines a distant third (the most notable were Renee Fox and Margaret Mead). Medical ethics and the ethics of human experimentation were still the province of physicians (see chapter 6), with lawyers making forays into this particular area.

26. *U.S. v. Karl Brandt*, Nuremberg Tribunal, Trials of War Criminals, vol. 2, pp. 71–73.

27. *New York Times*, 4 November 1945, p. 29.

28. Francis D. Moore as quoted in *Clinical Investigation in Medicine*, ed. Ladimer and Newman, p. 433.

29. On the realities of the matter, see the outstanding study by Robert N. Proctor, *Racial Hygiene: Medicine under the Nazis* (Cambridge: 1988). See also Robert Jay Lifton, *The Nazi Doctors* (New York: 1986). Note how recent these two studies are, reflective of how late the turn of attention to these issues has been.

30. See, for example, Cortez Enlow, "The German Medical War Crimes: Their Nature and Significance," *JAMA* 139 (1947): 801–5.

31. "Drug Industry Act of 1962," *Congressional Record*, 23 August 1962, p. 17391.

32. Ibid., pp. 17395, 17397.

33. Ibid., pp. 17398–99, 17401, 17404.

34. Ibid., p. 17400.

35. See National Society for Medical Research, *Report on the National Conference on the Legal Environment of Medical Science*, Chicago, 27–28 May 1959, pp. 5–90; Welt, "Human Experimentation," pp. 75–78; Stuart Sessions, "Guiding Principles in Medical Research Involving Humans, National Institutes of Health," *Hospitals* 32 (1958): 44–64. Even to read A. C. Ivy, who was so intimately involved with the prosecution at Nuremberg, is to feel this tone;

see, for example, "The History and Ethics of the Use of Human Subjects in Medical Experiments," *Science* 108 (1948): 1–5.

36. National Society for Medical Research, *Report on the Conference*, pp. 81–89. Otto Guttentag, a physician writing in *Science*, did describe the ultimate dilemma posed by human experimentation as "tragic in the classical sense," and he suggested a division of authority between the "physician-friend" and the "physician-experimenter." But his recommendation captured little attention in the literature and had no influence on practice. See Guttentag's commentary on Michael Shimkin, "The Problem of Experimentation on Human Beings: The Physician's Point of View," *Science* 117 (1953): 205–10.

37. Ladimer and Newman, in their *Clinical Investigation in Medicine*, list only four American codes: those of the American Medical Association (AMA), the NIH Clinical Center, the American Psychological Association, and the Catholic Hospital Association.

38. "Requirements for Experiments on Human Beings," Report of the Judicial Council, adopted by the House of Delegates of the AMA, December 1946, *JAMA* 132 (1946): 1090.

39. AMA, *Digest of Official Actions* (Adopted December 1952) (Chicago: Author, 1959), pp. 617–18.

Chapter 4

1. In the absence of any biography or scholarly articles about Beecher, one must turn to obituaries and the like. See, for example, the *New England Journal of Medicine* 295 (1976): 730.

2. Henry K. Beecher and Donald P. Todd, "A Study of the Deaths . . . ," *Annals of Surgery* 140 (1954): 2, 5, 17.

3. For Beecher's wartime experience, see his letters to Edward Mallinkrot, 22 December 1943 and 19 June 1945, Henry Beecher manuscripts, Francis A. Countway Library of Medicine, Harvard University (hereafter cited as Beecher MSS). See also his notes to a lecture delivered in Sanders Theater, 16 October 1946, "The Emergence of Anesthesia's Second Power." In his papers there is also an undated memorandum describing the research he wished to carry out: "We have been asked by the Army to study the compounds that have . . . in common: they give access to the subconscious. The Army has a further interest as well: It can be indicated in the question: Can one individual obtain from another, with the aid of these drugs, willfully suppressed information? If we undertake the study this latter question will not be mentioned in the contract application. We request that it not be referred to outside this room." Beecher's rationalization for carrying out the study fit perfectly with the researchers' orientation discussed in chapter 2: "In time of war, at least, the importance of the other [army] purpose hardly appears

debatable." Henry K. Beecher, *Measurement of Subjective Responses* (New York: 1959), esp. pp. viii, 65–72.

4. The link for Beecher between placebo trials and the ethics of experimentation is most clearly made in his editorial, "Ethics and Experimental Therapy," *Journal of the American Medical Association* 186 (1963): 858–59 (hereafter cited as *JAMA*).

5. *New York Times*, 24 March 1965; *Wall Street Journal*, 10 June 1965.

6. Beecher to George Burch, 27 June 1966, Beecher MSS.

7. Beecher to John Talbott, 20 August 1965, 30 August 1965, and Talbott to Beecher, 25 August 1965, Beecher MSS.

8. Talbott to Beecher, 25 October 1965, Beecher MSS.

9. Joseph Garland to Beecher, 30 March 1966, 7 April 1966, and Beecher to Garland, 1 April 1966, Beecher MSS.

10. Beecher to John Knowles, 10 June 1966, Beecher MSS.

11. Henry K. Beecher, "Ethics and Clinical Research," *NEJM* 274 (1966): 1354–60.

12. Beecher to Joseph Sadusk, 7 June 1965, Beecher MSS. Sadusk was the medical director of the FDA. See also Beecher to Geoffrey Edsall, 3 August 1966, Beecher MSS.

13. An excellent compilation of materials in the Southam case can be found in *Experimentation with Human Beings*, ed. Jay Katz (New York: 1972), pp. 9–65.

14. Beecher, "Ethics of Clinical Research," pp. 1354–55.

15. In a personal interview (April 19, 1988), Dr. Braunwald said that he did seek the permission of the patients but did not then or later supply evidence for the assertion. Note the comments of Donald Fredrickson in chapter 3 on these experiments as well. When I asked Dr. Braunwald why he never entered a protest against Beecher's statements about him, he declared (in a point that strengthens my general arguments about the state of research ethics in the period) that no one ever queried him about it. Despite the absence of footnotes in the Beecher article, there could be little doubt about who was doing such research.

16. David J. Rothman and Sheila M. Rothman, *The Willowbrook Wars* (New York: 1984), chap. 11.

17. Henry K. Beecher, "Experimentation in Man," *JAMA* 169 (1959): 461–78.

18. Ibid.

19. Beecher, "Ethics of Clinical Research," p. 1360. This was also the position of his contemporary, Louis Welt; see "Reflections on the Problem of Human Experimentation," *Connecticut Magazine* 25 (1961): 78.

Chapter 5

1. Mark S. Frankel, *The Public Health Service Guidelines Governing Research Involving Human Subjects*, George Washington University Program of Policy Studies

in Science and Technology Monograph no. 10 (Washington, D.C.: 1972), pp. 20–21.

2. Ibid., pp. 23–24.

3. John Sherman to Roman Pucinski, 1 July 1966, National Institutes of Health Files, Bethesda, Md.

4. Frankel, *Guidelines Governing Research*, pp. 23, 31.

5. Ibid., p. 30.

6. Committee on Government Operations report to the Senate Subcommittee on Government Research, *Hearings on the National Commission on Health Science and Society*, 90th Cong., 2d sess., 1968, pp. 211, 212 (hereafter cited as Hearings on Health).

7. Henrik Bendixen to Henry Beecher, March 1966, Henry Beecher Manuscripts, Francis A. Countway Library of Medicine, Harvard University (hereafter cited as Beecher MSS).

8. *Handbook on the Normal Volunteer Patient Program of the Clinical Center*, March 1967, NIH Files, Bethesda, Md., p. 15.

9. In May 1969, PHS-NIH officials did provide a more specific definition of consent; see Frankel, *Guidelines Governing Research*, pp. 38–39. See also Ruth R. Faden and Tom L. Beauchamp, *A History and Theory of Informed Consent* (New York: 1986), pp. 205–15, for a more positive view of the 1966 document as well as the 1969 revisions.

10. The most acute analysis of the FDA regulations in human experimentation remains William J. Curran's "Governmental Regulation of the Use of Human Subjects in Medical Research: The Approach of Two Federal Agencies," *Daedalus* 98 (1969): 542–94; I have relied on it in the paragraphs that follow.

11. Curran, "Governmental Regulation," pp. 558–69.

12. Hearings on Health, pp. 211–12.

13. Paul Ramsey, *The Patient as Person* (New Haven, Conn.: 1970), p. 1.

14. Ibid., p. xiv.

15. Ibid., p. xv.

16. Ibid., pp. xvi, 5–7, xvii.

17. The resulting publication, *Ethical Aspects of Experimentation with Human Subjects*, appeared as vol. 98, Spring 1969.

18. Hans Jonas, "Philosophical Reflections on Experimenting with Human Subjects," *Daedalus* 98 (1969): 219.

19. Jonas, "Philosophical Reflections," p. 245.

20. David J. Rothman, "The State as Parent," in *Doing Good*, ed. Willard Gaylin, Steven Marcus, David J. Rothman, and Ira Glasser (New York: 1978), pp. 84–85.

Chapter 6

1. Hans Jonas, "Philosophical Reflections on Experimenting with Human Beings," *Ethical Aspects of Experimentation with Human Subjects* 98 (1969): 1.
2. Joseph Fletcher, *Morals and Medicine* (Princeton, N.J.: 1954), pp. x–xi, xx.
3. The Rush essay is in his *Sixteen Introductory Lectures* (Philadelphia: 1811), pp. 125–32; see esp. p. 127.
4. Richard Cabot, *Adventures on the Borderlands of Ethics* (New York: 1926), p. 23. See also his "The Use of Truth and Falsehood in Medicine," *American Medicine* 5 (1903): 344–49.
5. American Medical Association, Bureau of Medical Economics, "Economics and the Ethics of Medicine," *Bulletin of the American Medical Association* (May 1936): 58, 59, 61.
6. "Ectopic Gestation," *Linacre Quarterly* 10 (1942): 6–23.
7. Paul Blanshard, *American Freedom and Catholic Power* (Boston: 1950), ch. 6.
8. Joseph Fletcher, *Morals and Medicine*, pp. 18, 35.
9. Ibid., pp. 97, 142, 191.
10. John Burnham, "American Medicine's Golden Age: What Happened to It?" *Science* 215 (1982): 1474–79.
11. Compare the analysis that follows with Edward Shorter, *Bedside Manners* (New York: 1985).
12. Jay Katz, *The Silent World of Doctor and Patient* (New York: 1984). See, too, the perceptive discussion of his approach, as against that of Martin Pernick ("The Patient's Role in Medical Decision-Making," in the President's Commission for the Study of Ethical Problems in Medicine . . . , *Making Health Care Decisions* [Washington, D.C.: 1982], vol. 3), in Faden and Beauchamp, *Informed Consent*, pp. 76–101. I join with them in finding the Pernick case more persuasive, although the argument I make here is a different one.
13. On the history of the medical profession, see John S. Haller, Jr., *American Medicine in Transition* (Urbana, Ill.: 1981), chap. 7.
14. Oliver Wendell Holmes, "The Young Practitioner," *Medical Essays*, vol. 9 of the *Writings of Oliver Wendell Holmes* (Boston: 1891).
15. Quoted in Richard Shryock, *Medicine in America* (Baltimore: 1966), p. 163. See also Joseph McFarland, "How to Choose a Doctor," *Hygea* (August 1931): 743–45, for counsel that patients would not go wrong if they "choose a doctor of whom doctors think highly."
16. Carlo M. Cippola, *Public Health and the Profession of Medicine in the Renaissance* (Cambridge: 1976), p. 115.
17. See, for example, Jacob A. Goldberg, "Jews in Medicine," *Medical Economics*, March 1940, pp. 54–56. Many rural areas did their best to found some sort of medical institution, not only to have a facility nearby but to have as staff familiar, like-minded people. Even when good roads and connections made travel to nearby urban centers practical, the incentive remained to organize

community hospitals to ensure such ties. See, for example, Arthur E. Hertzler, *The Horse and Buggy Doctor* (New York, 1938), pp. 254–56.

18. Selwyn D. Collins, "Frequency and Volume of Doctors' Calls . . . ," *Public Health Reports* 55 (1940): 1977–2012.

19. Commission on Medical Education, *Final Report* (1932), p. 73; 55 percent of doctor–patient contacts were in the office, and 10 percent in the hospital.

20. Francis Weld Peabody, *Doctor and Patient* (New York: 1930), pp. 32–33. Peabody worried that hospital visits were liable to confound matters: "The difficulty is that in the hospital one gets into the habit of using the oil immersion lens instead of the low power, and focuses too intently on the center of the field." Using technology as a metaphor for hospital conditions was clever and suggestive of still larger problems.

21. Lane Gerber, *Married to Their Careers*, p. xiv. Since Gerber was more than a little unhappy about the neglect he believes his family suffered from his father, his account may have less romance about it; this is not a son celebrating his father.

22. Lewis Thomas, *The Youngest Science* (New York: 1983), p. 9.

23. S. J. McNeill, "Where Is the Family Doctor and What Is the Matter with the Public?" *Illinois Medical Journal* (February 1928): 145–146. "The doctor would enter the home, revered and respected, his every wish and judgment acquiesced, for his advice and dictation was paramount and the family . . . had all confidence in his ability as a doctor."

24. Rosemary Stevens, as quoted in Irvine Loudon, "The Concept of the Family Doctor," *Bulletin of the History of Medicine* 58 (1984): 347. Loudon, incidentally, finds both the concept and reality of the family doctor very much alive in pre–World War II England, and uses Stevens's remark as a point of departure. See also Selwyn Collins, "Frequency and Volume of Doctor's Calls," p. 1998.

25. Peabody, *Doctor and Patient*, p. 25. He also feared that doctors were becoming too scientific in their approach to patients; but here, too, he was anticipating a problem, not giving persuasive evidence that it already existed. In addition to the citations below, see also J. Lue Sutherland, "The Passing of the Family Physician," *The Nebraska State Medical Journal* 6 (1921): 305–6.

26. *Final Report of the Commission on Medical Education* (New York: 1932), pp. 65, 115, 173. By now, however, over one-third of the medical school classes were beginning to specialize, which is what made medical educators so sensitive to the change; and the better schools did have higher rates: the percentage of Harvard Medical School graduates entering specialty training and practice was 64 percent; at Johns Hopkins, 75 percent; at Stanford, 55 percent.

27. Daniel Funkenstein, *Medical Students, Medical Schools and Society during Five Eras* (Cambridge: 1968), p. 12.

28. Robert S. Veeder, "Trend of Pediatric Education and Practice," *American Journal of Diseases of Children* 50 (1935): 1–10.

29. J. D. Brook, "The Passing of the Family Doctor and Practice of the Future," *Journal of the Michigan State Medical Society* 29 (1930): 694.

30. Earl L. Koos, *The Health of Regionville* (New York: 1954), pp. 53–59. See also the study by Harold Frum, probably based on Columbus, Ohio ("Choice and Change of Medical Service," Master's thesis, Ohio State University, 1939). He reports that 72.5 percent of the families in his survey saw only one or two physicians in the course of a year; fully 67 percent saw only one or two physicians over five years (p. 49). Frum does add that few families—perhaps 60 of 200—had "family doctors," as very narrowly defined. Even so, he concluded that having a family doctor was the pattern for 40 percent of the population, and certainly more for the middle class than the lower class.

31. Gladys V. Swackhamer, *Choice and Change of Doctors*, Committee on Research in Medical Economics (New York: 1939), esp. pp. 6–23, 27–28, 31.

32. *New York Times*, 14 May 1934, sec. 4, p. 8.

33. Holmes, *Medical Essays*, p. 377. We will return later to the end of the phrase: "and whether they had better live at all or remain unrealized possibilities, as belonging to a stock not worth being perpetuated."

34. Quoted in Robert K. Merton et al., *The Student-Physician* (Cambridge: 1957), p. 26, footnote 12. See also the remark of D. N. Cathell: "You are supposed to know the family's constitution. You will find that 'knowing people's constitutions' is a powerful acquisition" (*The Physician Himself and What He Should Add to His Scientific Acquirements* [Baltimore, Md., 1882], p. 66).

35. Walter L. Bierring, "The Family Doctor and the Changing Order," *Journal of the American Medical Association* 102 (1934): 1996.

36. John Stoeckle and J. Andrew Billings, "A History of History-Taking: The Medical Interview" (Unpublished manuscript, Department of Medicine, Harvard Medical School, 1989).

37. The study of literature and medicine has burgeoned over the past five years, another manifestation of the changes that this book is analyzing. A useful introduction to the nineteenth-century literature is Richard R. Malmsheimer, "From Rappaccini to Marcus Welby: The Evolution of an Image" (Ph.D. diss., University of Minnesota, 1978).

38. George Eliot, *Middlemarch* (New York: Penguin, [1871–72] 1965), esp. pp. 178–80, 193–95.

39. Anton Chekhov, *Uncle Vanya: Scenes from Country Life* (New York: Signet, [1899] 1964), esp. pp. 174, 194, 197, 201, 209, 225.

40. Sidney Kingsley, *Men in White* (New York: 1933).

41. Charles E. Rosenberg, "Martin Arrowsmith: The Scientist as Hero," *American Quarterly* 15 (1963): 447–58.

42. Joseph Jerger, *Here's Your Hat! The Autobiography of a Family Doctor* (New York: 1939), esp. pp. 51, 223; William Allen Pusey, *A Doctor of the 1870s and 80s* (Baltimore: 1932), esp. pp. xi, 85; Robert T. Morris, *Fifty Years a Surgeon* (New York: 1935), esp. p. 7; James B. Herrick, *Memories of Eighty*

Years (Chicago: 1949), esp. pp. 86, 155. The New York Academy of Medicine has an excellent guide to these autobiographies, and an excellent collection of them.

43. Frederic Loomis, *Consultation Room* (New York: 1939), pp. 74–76.

44. D. W. Cathell, *The Physician Himself and What He Should Add to His Scientific Acquirements* (Baltimore: 1882), p. 12. Cathell was professor of pathology at the College of Physicians and Surgeons in Baltimore and the president of its Medical and Surgical Society. Over the course of these decades, it was also common to find physicians in the leadership ranks of the boosters and promoters of new towns and cities. Such political involvement was not without its critics. Holmes, for example, advised that physicians "do not dabble in the muddy sewer of politics." But the general practitioners commonly ignored such advice.

45. Holmes, *Medical Essays*, p. 388.

46. Ibid., p. 377.

47. Alphonso Schwitalla and M. R. Kneift, "The Catholic Hospital of the United States, Canada, and Newfoundland at the Beginning of 1934," *Hospital Progress* 15 (1934): 69–71, 74–75.

48. Ibid., 81–93; Mary Hicks, *Hospitals of Cincinnati, A Survey* (n.p., 1925), chap. 2, pp. 51–53. See also *Story of the First Fifty Years of the Mt. Sinai Hospital, 1852–1902* (New York: 1944).

49. Peter Joseph Barone, "Practical Advice by a Catholic Doctor," *Hospital Progress* 4 (1923): 177; John P. Boland, "Religious Aspects of Sisters' Hospitals," *Hospital Progress* 2 (1921): 285. See also Haven Emerson, *The Hospital Survey for New York*, vol. 1 (New York: 1937), p. 36; E. H. Lewinski-Corwin, *The Hospital Situation in Greater New York* (New York: 1924).

50. Tina Leviton, *Islands of Compassion: A History of the Jewish Hospitals of New York* (New York: 1964), esp. pp. 89–91, 113.

51. Emerson, *Hospital Survey*, vol. 1, pp. 19–31.

52. Ibid., p. 29. See also Haven Emerson et al., *Philadelphia Hospital and Health Survey—1929* (Philadelphia: 1929), pp. 574–79; Michael M. Davis, "Are There Enough Beds? Or Too Many?" *The Modern Hospital* 48 (1937): 149–52; C. Rufus Rorem, "The Percentage of Occupancy in American Hospitals," *JAMA* 98 (1932): 2060–61.

53. Emerson, *Hospital Survey*, vol. 1, p. 27. Length of stay ranged from 12.2 days in voluntary hospitals to 17.8 in municipal hospitals.

Chapter 7

1. Meg Greenfield, "The Land of the Hospital," *Newsweek*, 30 June 1986, p. 74.

2. Eliot Freidson, *Patients' Views of Medical Practice* (New York: 1961), pp. 58–59, 66–67.

3. Charles Rosenberg, *The Care of Strangers: The Rise of America's Hospital System* (New York: 1987), pp. 173–75, 253–57.

4. For an elaboration of this point see David J. Rothman, "The Hospital as Caretaker," *Transactions and Studies of the College of Physicians of Philadelphia* 12 (1990): 151–74.

5. United Hospital Fund, "Hospital Closures in New York City," *Proceedings of the Health Policy Forum* (New York: 1978), pp. 28–31.

6. *New York Times*, 6 June 1987, pp. 1, 11.

7. Elisabeth Kübler-Ross, *On Death and Dying* (New York: 1969), pp. 5, 7, 8, 146–47. See also Terry Mizrachi, *Getting Rid of Patients: Contradictions in the Socialization of Physicians* (New Brunswick, N.J.:1986).

8. Natalie Rogoff, "The Decision to Study Medicine," in *The Student-Physician*, ed. Robert K. Merton et al. (Cambridge: 1957), pp. 110–11.

9. Reported by Alan Gregg, *Challenges to Contemporary Medicine* (New York: 1956), p. 103. Gregg, himself a vice-president of the Rockefeller Foundation, would ask physicians how old they were when they decided on their profession; he reported, "The majority has confirmed the impression that the decision is often made early."

10. Wagner Thielens, Jr., "Some Comparisons of Entrants to Medical and Law School," in *The Student-Physician*, ed. Merton et al., pp. 132–33.

11. Ibid., p. 143.

12. Gregg, *Challenges to Contemporary Medicine*, p. 105.

13. Melvin Konner, *Becoming a Doctor: A Journey of Initiation in Medical School* (New York: 1987), pp. 1–5.

14. Daniel Funkenstein, *Medical Students, Medical Schools, and Society during Five Eras* (Cambridge: 1968), p. 17. He reports much higher percentages for the class of 1971 (68 percent), but then the start of a drop-off by the class of 1976 (down to 59 percent). See also John Colombotos and Corinne Kirchner, *Physicians and Social Change* (New York: 1986).

15. Louis Harris and associates, "Medical Practice," pp. 30–39.

16. Lane A. Gerber, *Married to Their Careers* (New York: 1983), pp. 51, 58, 63, 67, 70.

17. Alice Adams, *Superior Women* (New York: 1984), pp. 234–35.

18. Philip Roth, *The Anatomy Lesson* (New York: Ballantine, 1983), esp. pp. 163, 170, 217, 225, 230–31.

19. C. E. Poverman, *Solomon's Daughter* (New York: Penguin, 1981), p. 256.

20. John Irving, *The Cider House Rules* (New York: 1985).

21. John Burnham, "American Medicine's Golden Age: What Happened to It?" *Science* 215 (1982): 1474–79.

22. Richard Carter, *The Doctor Business* (New York: 1958), pp. 11–17.

23. Selig Greenberg, *The Troubled Calling* (New York: 1965), pp. xi, 1–3.
24. Daniel M. Fox, "Who We Are: The Political Origins of the Medical Humanities," *Theoretical Medicine* 6 (1985): 329, 334, 338.
25. Boston Women's Health Book Collective, *Our Bodies, Ourselves* (New York: 1971), pp. 252–53.
26. Sylvia Law and Steven Polan, *Pain and Profit: The Politics of Malpractice* (New York: 1978). The quotation is from R. Crawford Morris, "Law and Medicine: Problems of Malpractice Insurance," *Journal of the American Medical Association* 215 (1971): 843. See also *Medical Malpractice*, Report of the Secretary's Commission on Medical Malpractice, Department of Health, Education and Welfare (Washington, D.C.: 1973), esp. pp. 3, 69, 71–72, 667–68.
27. Joint Commission on Accreditation of Hospitals, *Accreditation Manual for Hospitals*, Preamble 1–2 (1970).
28. George J. Annas and Joseph M. Healey, Jr., "The Patient Rights Advocate: Redefining the Doctor–Patient Relationship in the Hospital Context," *Vanderbilt Law Review* 27 (1974): 254–57.
29. Willard Gaylin, "The Patient's Bill of Rights," *Saturday Review of Science* 1 (1973): 22.
30. William J. Curran, "The Patient Bill of Rights Becomes Law," *New England Journal of Medicine* 290 (1974): 32–33.
31. D. Oken, "What to Tell Cancer Patients: A Study of Medical Attitudes," *JAMA* 175 (1961): 1120–28; Howard Waitzkin and John D. Stoeckle, "The Communication of Information about Illness," *Advances in Psychosomatic Medicine* 8 (1972): 185–89.

Chapter 8

1. Shana Alexander, "They Decide Who Lives, Who Dies," *Life*, 9 November 1962, p. 103.
2. Delford L. Stickel, "Ethical and Moral Aspects of Transplantation," *Monographs in the Surgical Sciences* 3 (1966): 267–72. As would be expected in 1966, Stickel was a surgeon interested in medical ethics, not a lay ethicist. Moreover, he framed the transplantation issues in the context of human experimentation. See also "Moral Problems in the Use of Borrowed Organs, Artificial and Transplanted," *Annals of Internal Medicine* 60 (1964): 310–13.
3. Thomas E. Starzl, "Ethical Problems in Organ Transplantation," *Annals of Internal Medicine* 67, supplement 7 (1967): 35–36.
4. G. E. W. Wolstenholme and Maeve O'Connor, eds., *Ethics in Medical Progress: With Special Reference to Transplantation* (Proceedings of the CIBA Foundation Symposium, Boston, 1966), p. 6.
5. Ibid., p. 19.

6. Ibid., p. 59. The recognition of this point was widespread; see, for example, the *Annals of Internal Medicine* editorial cited in note 2 ("Borrowed Organs," p. 312), noting that the problem of risk to the donor raised an ethical problem that was "frighteningly real."

7. Wolstenholme and O'Connor, *Ethics in Medical Progress*, pp. 66, 81. William J. Curran, "A Problem of Consent: Kidney Transplantation in Minors," *New York University Law Review* 34 (1959): 891–98.

8. Wolstenholme and O'Connor, *Ethics in Medical Progress*, p. 71.

9. Francis D. Moore, *Give and Take: The Development of Tissue Transplantation* (Philadelphia: 1964).

10. Francis D. Moore, "Medical Responsibility for the Prolongation of Life," *Journal of the American Medical Association* 206 (1968): 384 (hereafter cited as *JAMA*).

11. Howard P. Lewis, "Machine Medicine and Its Relation to the Fatally Ill," *JAMA* 206 (1968): 387.

12. John Shillito, "The Organ Donor's Doctor: A New Role for the Neurosurgeon," *New England Journal of Medicine* 281 (1969): 1071–72 (hereafter cited as *NEJM*).

13. *Newsweek*, 18 December 1967, p. 86. Just how persistent this idea was, is evident in the United Nations Report from the Secretary General that concluded that "human rights need to be protected in the field of surgical transplants," because the rights of the donor might be too easily violated (*New York Times*, 19 April 1970, p. 36).

14. Rene Menguy, "Surgical Drama," *NEJM* 278 (1968): 394–95.

15. John D. Arnold, Thomas F. Zimmerman, and Daniel C. Martin, "Public Attitudes and the Diagnosis of Death," *JAMA* 206 (1968): 1949–54, esp. pp. 1950–51.

16. Ad Hoc Committee of the American Electroencephalographic Society, "Cerebral Death and the Electroencephalogram," *JAMA* 209 (1969): 1505–9, esp. p. 1508.

17. Clarence C. Crafoord, "Cerebral Death and the Transplantation Era," *Diseases of the Chest* 55 (1969): 141–45, esp. p. 142. (Crafoord was a professor of thoracic surgery in Stockholm and the recipient of a 1968 gold medal from the American College of Chest Physicians.) See also "When Is a Patient Dead?" *JAMA* 204 (1968): 142.

18. Henry Beecher to Robert H. Ebert, 30 October 1967, Henry Beecher Manuscripts, Francis A. Countway Library of Medicine, Harvard University (hereafter cited as Beecher MSS).

19. Ebert to Joseph Murray, 4 January 1968, Beecher MSS.

20. Ad Hoc Committee to Examine the Definition of Death, Harvard Medical School, "A Definition of Irreversible Coma," *JAMA* 205 (1968): 337–40.

21. George H. Williams to Henry K. Beecher, 23 January 1968, Beecher MSS.

22. Draft of 11 April 1968; for this and other materials on the Harvard Brain Death Committee, see the file in the Beecher MSS.
23. Ad Hoc Committee, "Definition of Irreversible Coma," pp. 338–39.
24. Henry Beecher, "After the 'Definition of Irreversible Coma,' " *NEJM* 281 (1969): 1070–71. It was accepted, for example, by the Committee on Ethics of the American Heart Association. In this article, Beecher quoted Peter Medawar's brilliant definition of death: A man is legally dead "when he has undergone irreversible changes of a type that make it impossible for him to seek to litigate."
25. "What and When Is Death?" *JAMA* 204 (1968): 219–20.
26. Ebert to Beecher, 1 July 1968, Beecher MSS.
27. Ad Hoc Committee, "Definition of Irreversible Coma," p. 339.
28. Leonard A. Stevens, "When Is Death?" *Reader's Digest* 94 (1969): 225–32; *Time*, 16 August 1968 and also 27 May 1966.
29. *Annals of Internal Medicine* 68 (1968): 695–99.
30 Kenneth Vaux, "A Year of Heart Transplants: An Ethical Valuation," *Postgraduate Medicine* (1969): 201–5.
31. J. Ernest Breed, "New Questions in Medical Morality," *Illinois Medical Journal* 135 (1969): 504–26, esp. p. 506, on a meeting at Perry Hospital. See also "Symposium on Death," *North Carolina Medical Journal* 28 (1967): 457–68; "Clergy–Physician Dialogues," *Maryland State Medical Journal* 18 (1969): 77–84. Religious spokespeople were alert to the issue the moment that the first transplant occurred; see *Newsweek*, 18 December 1967.
32. Irvine H. Page, "The Ethics of Heart Transplantation," *JAMA* 207 (1969): 109–13.
33. Jordan D. Haller and Marcial M. Cerruti, "Progress Report: Heart Transplantation in Man," *American Journal of Cardiology* 124 (1969): 554–63.
34. Quoted in Renee C. Fox and Judith P. Swazey, *The Courage to Fail* (Chicago: 1974), p. 110.
35. "Cardiac Transplantation in Man," *JAMA* 204 (1968): 147–48; "A Plea for a Transplant Moratorium," *Science News* 93 (1968): 256.
36. "Too Many Too Soon," 29 June 1968, pp. 1413–14.
37. Fox and Swazey, *The Courage to Fail*, p. 132.
38. See, for example, *Time*, 15 March 1968, p. 66; 6 December 1968, pp. 59–60; *Newsweek*, 21 April 1969, pp. 76–78; *The Nation*, 30 December 1968, pp. 719–20.
39. Page, "Heart Transplantation," p. 113.
40. Lyman A. Brewer, "Cardiac Transplantation, An Appraisal," *JAMA* 205 (1968): 101–2.
41. Michael E. DeBakey, Editorial, *Journal of Thoracic and Cardiovascular Surgery* 55 (1968): 449.

Chapter 9

1. The resolution prompted hearings and testimony: Committee on Government Operations report to the Senate Subcommittee on Government Research, *Hearings on the National Commission on Health Science and Society*, 90th Cong., 2d sess., 1968 (hereafter cited as Hearings on Health), pp. 315–19.
2. Ibid., p. 24.
3. Ibid., p. 149.
4. Ibid., p. 121.
5. Ibid., p. 200. David Bazelon, the federal judge who had pioneered in creating mental health law, made this same distinction: in his terms, experts decided the degree of a patient's dangerousness, and society decided whether that degree of dangerousness was sufficient to warrant confining the individual (Hearings on Health, p. 280).
6. Hearings on Health, p. 138.
7. Ibid., Beecher, p. 104; Braver, p. 121; Vaux, p. 138; Mendelsohn, pp. 200–201; Bazelon, p. 276.
8. Hearings on Health, p. 70.
9. Ibid., p. 80.
10. Ibid., pp. 81–82.
11. Ibid., p. 77.
12. Ibid., p. 98.
13. Ibid., pp. 100–101.
14. Ibid., pp. 310–17.
15. Ibid., p. 9.
16. Ibid., pp. 41–43.
17. Ibid., pp. 45–52.
18. Ibid., p. 333.
19. Ibid., pp. 292, 333, 338.
20. Report of the National Advisory Commission on Civil Disorder, March 1968, Bantam ed., 269–72.
21. National Advisory Commission on Health Science and Society, Joint Hearing before the Senate Subcommittee on Health . . . of the Committee on Labor and Public Welfare, 92d Cong., 1st sess., 9 November 1971, pp. 49, 112.
22. Hearings on Health, pp. 5–6.
23. Ibid., p. 315.
24. Ibid., pp. 315, 317, 319.
25. Ibid., pp. 46, 53, 55.
26. Ibid., p. 29.
27. Ibid., p. 45.
28. Mark S. Frankel, "Public Policy Making for Biomedical Research: The Case of Human Experimentation" (Ph.D. diss., George Washington University, 1976) p. 293, footnote 85.

29. James Jones, *Bad Blood* (New York, 1981); David J. Rothman, "Were Tuskegee and Willowbrook 'Studies in Nature'?" *Hastings Center Report* (April 1982), pp. 5–7.

30. Jerone Stephens, "Political, Social, and Scientific Aspects of Medical Research on Humans," *Politics and Society* 3 (1973): 409–27; Richard N. Little, Jr., "Experimentation with Human Subjects: Legal and Moral Considerations Regarding Radiation Treatment of Cancer at the University of Cincinnati College of Medicine," *Atomic Energy Law Journal* 13 (1972): 305–30. See also Frankel, "Public Policy Making," pp. 178–83.

31. *Congressional Record*, 24 March 1971 (92nd Cong., 1st sess.), pp. 7670–7678.

32. "Quality of Health Care—Human Experimentation, 1973," pts. 1–4, Hearings before the Senate Subcommittee on Health of the Committee on Labor and Public Welfare, 93d Cong., 1st sess., 1973 (hereafter cited as Hearings on Human Experimentation).

33. Ibid., p. 1055.

34. Ibid., pt. 1, 21 February 1973, p. 2.

35. The alternative policy, to have the FDA monitor actual physician usage, has never been implemented on the grounds that it would restrict physicians' prerogatives too much.

36. Hearings on Human Experimentation, pt. 1, 22 February 1973, pp. 65–66.

37. Ibid., pt. 2, 23 February 1973, p. 354.

38. Ibid., pt. 3, 7 March 1973, p. 841.

39. Ibid., p. 795.

40. Ibid., 8 March 1973, pp. 1045, 1049.

41. Ibid., pt. 2, 23 February 1973, pp. 378–79.

42. Ibid., pt. 3, 7 March 1973, p. 843.

43. Ibid., pt. 4, pp. 1264–65. For evidence of how persistent a theme this was for Kennedy, see also National Advisory Commission on Health Science and Society, Joint Hearings, 9 November 1971, 92d Cong., 1st sess., p. 2.

Chapter 10

1. One of the first analyses of ethics of the case was James Gustafson, "Mongolism, Parental Desires, and the Right to Life," *Perspectives in Biology and Medicine* 16 (1972–73): 529–57.

2. The press reports on the film either missed the fact that this was a re-creation or took the baby to be the actual baby. See, for example, *New Haven Register*, 20 October 1971: "The film opened with the baby's birth."

3. The lead for the story of the conference in the *New York Times*, for example, was "Film Ponders the Right to Life of a Mentally Retarded Infant," 15 October 1971, p. 31.

4. *Annapolis Evening Capital*, 16 October 1971, p. 1; letters to the *Washington Post*, 23 October 1971.

5. D. M. to William Bartholome, 28 October 1971; Mrs. R. H. to Robert Cooke, 18 October 1971. These were part of the letters saved by Bartholome and kindly shared with me.

6. Seemingly, the first use of the term *bioethics* was in an article by Van Rensselaer Potter, "Bioethics, the Science of Survival," *Perspectives in Biology and Medicine* 14 (1970): 127–53. But his use of the term was not what it came to be: "We are in great need of a land ethic, a wildlife ethic, a population ethic, a consumption ethic, an urban ethic, an international ethic, a geriatric ethic, and so on. . . . All of them involve *bioethics*, and survival of the total ecosystem is the test of the value system" (p. 127).

7. *Washington Post*, 2 October 1971, p. 1; and 13 October 1971, "Can Science and Ethics Meet?"

8. William Bartholome to Mrs. S. M., 9 December 1971.

9. *Baltimore Sun*, 21 October 1971.

10. "Ethical Dilemmas in Current Obstetric and Newborn Care," Report of the Sixty-Fifth *Ross Conference on Pediatric Research* (Columbus, Ohio, 1973) (hereafter cited as Ross Conference, "Ethical Dilemmas").

11. Ibid., pp. 12, 16–17.

12. Ibid., p. 18.

13. The "new barbarianism" phrase was Raymond Duff's. "Medical Ethics: The Right to Survival, 1974," Hearings before the Senate Subcommittee on Health of the Committee on Labor and Public Welfare, 93d Cong., 2d sess., 11 June 1974 (hereafter cited as Medical Ethics: The Right to Survival), p. 4.

14. Ross Conference, "Ethical Dilemmas," pp. 58–59, 63, 70–71, 73–74.

15. Ibid., pp. 20, 91.

16. Ibid., p. 77.

17. Ibid., pp. 89–91.

18. Raymond Duff and Alexander Campbell, "Moral and Ethical Dilemmas in the Special-Care Nursery," *New England Journal of Medicine* 289 (1973): 890–94.

19. Ibid., p. 893.

20. Ibid., pp. 893–94.

21. Ibid., p. 894.

22. Anthony Shaw, "Dilemmas of 'Informed Consent' in Children," *NEJM* 289 (1973): 885–90. Shaw later observed that he actually received very few letters in response to the article.

23. Franz Ingelfinger's editorial remarks appeared in the same *NEJM* issue: "Bedside Ethics for the Hopeless Case," 289 (1973): 914–15.

24. In reviewing these lines, one wonders whether it was Ingelfinger who suggested that Shaw add to his article the awkward closing line, "Or should they?"

25. "Correspondence," *NEJM* 290 (1974): 518.
26. Hearings on "Medical Ethics: The Right to Survival," pp. 16–19.
27. Fost's remarks are quoted in Chester Swinyard, ed., *Decision Making and the Defective Newborn* (Proceedings of a [1975] Conference on Spina Bifida and Ethics, Springfield, Illinois, 1978), pp. 228, 247, 562.
28. Ibid., pp. 59–67, esp. pp. 63, 66–67.
29. Ibid., pp. 592–93.
30. The coincidental developments in 1973 first came to my attention in Nelson Lund, "Infanticide, Physicians, and the Law," *American Journal of Law and Medicine* 11 (1985): 1–29.
31. See the discussion in John Fletcher, "Abortion, Euthanasia, and Care of Defective Newborns," *NEJM* 292 (1975): 75–77.
32. Material in this and the next paragraph is drawn from Richard K. Scotch, *From Good Will to Civil Rights: Transforming Federal Disability Policy* (Philadelphia: 1984).
33. Scotch, *From Good Will to Civil Rights*, pp. 43, 55.
34. "Medical Ethics: The Right to Survival," pp. 1–2, 11, 22.
35. Ibid., pp. 17, 19.
36. Ibid., p. 25.
37. Interview with Daniel Callahan, 17 March 1977, conducted by Allan Brandt (who shared the transcript with me); quotations are from pp. 2–6, 49.
38. Joseph Fletcher, *Situation Ethics: The New Morality* (Philadelphia: 1966), p. 261. See also Harvey Cox, *The Situation Ethics Debate* (Philadelphia: 1968), pp. 12–13.
39. A. R. Jonsen et al., "Critical Issues in Newborn Intensive Care: A Conference Report and Policy Proposal," *Pediatrics* 55 (1975): 756–68.
40. Ibid., p. 761.
41. Ibid., p. 763.
42. Ibid., p. 764.
43. Ibid., p. 760.
44. Ibid., p. 764.
45. Robert and Peggy Stinson, *The Long Dying of Baby Andrew* (Boston: 1983). The book is an expansion of an article that originally appeared in *Atlantic Monthly* (July 1978) entitled "On the Death of a Baby."
46. Robert and Peggy Stinson, *Baby Andrew*, p. xi.
47. Ibid., p. 71.
48. Ibid., pp. xii–xiv.
49. Ibid., p. 62.
50. Ibid., pp. 145, 62, 115, 142.
51. Ibid., pp. 57, 145.
52. Ibid., pp. 93, 115, 46–47.
53. Ibid., pp. 301, 358.
54. "The Future of Baby Doe," *New York Review of Books*, 1 March 1984, p. 17.

55. Alistair G. Philip et al., "Neonatal Mortality Risk for the Eighties: The Importance of Birth Weight/Gestational Age Groups," *Pediatrics* 68 (1981): 128; Maureen Hack et al., "The Low-Birth-Weight Infant—Evolution of a Changing Outlook," *NEJM* 301 (1979): 1163.
56. Robert and Peggy Stinson, *Baby Andrew*, pp. 147, 187.

Chapter 11

1. Daniel R. Coburn, *"In Re Quinlan*: A Practical Overview," *Arkansas Law Review* 31 (1977): 63.
2. Joseph and Julia Quinlan with Phyllis Battelle, *Karen Ann* (New York: 1977), pp. 117–18, 127.
3. The briefs, the court argument, and the decision are conveniently collected in *In the Matter of Karen Quinlan*, vol. 2 (Arlington, Va.: University Publications of America, 1976). For appellant brief, see pp. 1–40. See also Transcript of Proceedings, 26 January 1976, p. 237 (hereafter, all references to documents from the case refer to this source).
4. Brief and Appendix on Behalf of the Attorney General of New Jersey, p. 51. Defendants brought in Dr. Sidney Diamond, professor of neurology at Mt. Sinai, to testify: "No physician to my knowledge will ever interrupt a device which is performing a life-saving measure at any time at all" (p. 117).
5. Brief on Behalf of Defendants-Respondents, p. 145.
6. Supplemental Brief on Behalf of . . . St. Clare's Hospital, pp. 187–88.
7. Transcript of Proceedings, pp. 284, 258–59.
8. Docket no. A-116, Supreme Court, State of New Jersey, 31 March 1976.
9. *In the Matter*, p. 305.
10. Ibid., pp. 306–8.
11. Ibid., p. 309.
12. Ibid., p. 310.
13. Ibid., pp. 278–79, 311.
14. Karen Teel, "The Physician's Dilemma: A Doctor's View: What the Law Should Be," *Baylor Law Review* 27 (1975): 6–9.
15. *In the Matter*, p. 312.
16. Michael Halberstam, "Other Karen Quinlan Cases Never Reach Court," Op-Ed, *New York Times*, 2 November 1975.
17. *Journal of the American Medical Association* 234 (1975): 1057.
18. *Time*, 27 October 1975, p. 41.
19. *Time*, 3 November 1975, p. 58. See also Transcript of Proceedings, p. 257, where

counsel for the guardian observed: "If one thing has occurred as a result of this case, I think at least the doctors involved, and probably other doctors, are now going to be much more concerned about judicial approval than might have occurred before this."

20. Quoted in Stephan Bennett, "In the Shadow of Karen Quinlan," *Trial* 12 (1976): 40.

21. "Optimal Care for Hopelessly Ill Patients," Report of the Critical Care Committee of the Massachusetts General Hospital, *New England Journal of Medicine* 295 (1976): 362–64 (hereafter cited as *NEJM*).

22. M. T. Rapkin et al., "Orders Not to Resuscitate," *NEJM* 295 (1976): 364–66.

23. Letter of Jean Pierre Raufmann (Montefiore Medical Center, New York), *NEJM* 295 (1976): 1140.

24. Letter of Allan Parham (Medical University of South Carolina), *NEJM* 295 (1976): 1139.

25. Charles Fried, "Terminating Life Support: Out of the Closet!" *NEJM* 295 (1976): 390–91. And not only patients but medical institutions needed lawyers' help, for both the MGH and Beth Israel drew on lawyers to design their new procedures.

26. Harold L. Hirsch and Richard E. Donovan, "The Right to Die: Medico-Legal Implications of *In Re Quinlan*," *Rutgers Law Review* 30 (1977): 267–303, esp. p. 274.

27. *Superintendent of Belchertown State School v. Saikewicz*, 373 Mass. 728; 370 N.E. 2d 417 (1977).

28. Arnold Relman, "The *Saikewicz* Decision: Judges as Physicians," *NEJM* 298 (1978): 508–9.

29. Supreme Court of the State of New York, "Report of the Special January 3rd, Additional 1983 Grand Jury Concerning 'Do Not Resuscitate' Procedures at a Certain Hospital in Queens County," esp. pp. 4, 14, 23–24.

30. For the Brother Fox case, see *In Re Storer*, 52 N.Y., 2d 363; 420 N.E. 2d 64 (1981).

31. The Harris Survey, 4 March 1985, no. 18, "Support Increases for Euthanasia." In a Gallup poll of 1985, over 80 percent favored the court position in *Quinlan*: Gallup Report, no. 235, April 1985, p. 29. See also John M. Ostheimer, "The Polls: Changing Attitudes toward Euthanasia," *Public Opinion Quarterly* 44 (1980): 123–28.

32. David Dempsey, "The Living Will," *New York Times*, Magazine, 23 June 1974, pp. 12–13; Walter Modell, "A 'Will' to Live," *NEJM* 290 (1974): 907–8; "Death with Dignity," *Hearings before the Special Committee on Aging*, U.S. Senate, 92nd Cong., 2d sess., 7 August 1972, pp. 23–24, 33.

33. Sissela Bok, "Personal Directions for Care at the End of Life," *NEJM* 295 (1976): 367–69.

34. Donald J. Higby, "Letter to the Editor," *NEJM* 295 (1976): 1140.
35. Marquis Childs, "Ethics and Illness," *Washington Post*, 18 November 1985.
36. "The Right to Die a Natural Death," *University of Cincinnati Law Review* 46 (1977): 192–98; "Note: The Legal Aspects of the Right to Die: Before and after the Quinlan Decision," *Kentucky Law Journal* 65 (1976–77): 831–33; Donald Collester, "Death, Dying and the Law: A Prosecutorial View of the Quinlan Case," *Rutgers Law Review* 30 (1977): 328.
37. Renee C. Fox, "Advanced Medical Technology—Social and Ethical Implications," *Annual Review of Sociology* 2 (1976): 231–68.
38. Ibid., p. 414.
39. Renee C. Fox and Judith P. Swazey, "Medical Morality Is Not Bioethics: Medical Ethics in China and the United States," in *Essays in Medical Sociology*, ed. Renee C. Fox (New Brunswick, N.J.: 1988), pp. 645–70, esp. pp. 668–70.
40. Joseph and Julia Quinlan, *Karen Ann*, pp. 252–53.
41. Edmund Pellegrino, Interview, *U.S. News and World Report*, 3 November 1975, p. 53.
42. Tristram Engelhardt, Jr., "But Are They People?" *Hospital Physician* (February 1976): 7. In this same spirit, Sisela Bok promoted living wills so that the patient could "retain some control over what happens at the end of one's life."
43. Robert Veatch, *Death, Dying, and the Biological Revolution* (New Haven, Conn.: 1976), p. 140.

Epilogue

1. United States Senate, 1978. Congressional Hearings.
2. Morris Abram, *The Day is Short* (New York: 1982), ch. 12.
3. There has been little scholarly attention to how the Commission worked, its strengths and weaknesses, and its overall impact. This point is aptly made by Alan Weisbard and John Arras in their introduction to the "Symposium: Commissioning Morality: A Critique of the President's Commission for the Study of Ethical Problems in Medicine and Biomedical and Behavioral Research," *Cardozo Law Review* 6 (1984): 223–355 (hereafter cited as "Commissioning Morality").
4. Alexander M. Capron, "Looking Back at the President's Commission," *Hastings Center Report* (October 1983), pp. 7–10.
5. President's Commission for the Study of Ethical Problems in Medicine and Biomedical and Behavioral Research (hereafter cited as "President's Commission"), *Summing Up: The Ethical and Legal Problems in Medicine and Biomedical and Behavioral Research* (Washington, D.C.: 1983), pp. 20–21.

NOTES

6. President's Commission, *Deciding to Forego Life-Sustaining Treatment* (Washington, D.C.: 1983), p. 44.
7. Ibid., pp. 2–5.
8. Jay Katz, "Limping Is No Sin: Reflections on *Making Health Care Decisions*," in "Commissioning Morality," pp. 243–265. See also his book, *The Silent World of Doctor and Patient* (New York: 1984), and my comments above in chapter 6.
9. See the review article by Fredric Wolinsky, "The Professional Dominance Perspective, Revisited," in the *Milbank Quarterly* 66, Supplement 2 (1988): 33–47, esp. 40–41.
10. See, for example, Bradford H. Gray et al., "Research Involving Human Subjects," *Science* 201 (1978): 1094–1101; Jerry Goldman and Martin Katz, "Inconsistency and Institutional Review Boards," *JAMA* 248 (1982): 197–202.
11. For an elaboration of this point see Harold Edgar and David J. Rothman, "New Rules for New Drugs: The Challenge of AIDS to the Regulatory Process," *The Milbank Quarterly* 68, Supplement 1 (1990): pp. 111–42.
12. Susanna E. Bedell et al., "Do-Not-Resuscitate Orders for Critically Ill Patients in the Hospital," *JAMA* 256 (1986): 233–38; Palmi V. Jonsson et al., "The 'Do not Resuscitate' Order: A Profile of Its Changing Use," *Archives of Internal Medicine* 148 (1988): 2373–75.
13. President's Comission, *Deciding to Forego Life-Sustaining Treatment*, pp. 169–70, 227. To buttress the case for ethics committees, the commission cited the positive contributions of the IRB. However, it also noted how little was known about the actual operation of IRBs, and hoped that as ethics committees proliferated, their functioning would be evaluated more systematically.
14. See the report "Ethics Committees Double Since '83: Survey," *Hospitals* 59 (1985): 60. The literature on the advantages and disadvantages of ethics committees is huge—testimony to the prominence of the "Baby Doe" cases and the number of commentators interested in bioethical questions. A useful guide to the material is "Ethics Committee: Core Resources," available through the Hastings Center. Among the books and articles I found most useful are: Ronald E. Cranford and A. Edward Doudera, *Institutional Ethics Committees and Health Care Decisions* (Ann Arbor: 1984); Bernard Lo, "Behind Closed Doors: Promises and Pitfalls of Ethics Committees," *NEJM* 317 (1987): 46–50; and Alan R. Fleischman, "Bioethical Review Committees in Perinatology," *Clinics in Perinatology* 14 (1987): 379–93.
15. Robert F. Weir, "Pediatric Ethics Committees: Ethical Advisors or Legal Watchdogs?" *Law, Medicine and Health Care* 15 (1987): 105.
16. Mark Siegler, "Ethics Committees: Decisions by Bureaucracy," *Hastings Center Report* (June 1986), pp. 22–24. Weir, "Pediatric Ethics Committees,"

291

p. 109, for the comment by Angela Holder, counsel for medicolegal affairs, Yale University School of Medicine and Yale-New Haven Hospital.

17. "Life Support Forcibly Cut, A Father Dies," *New York Times*, 11 January 1990, p. B1. The medical examiner later ruled that he believed that the man was dead before the incident occurred, and on these weak grounds, dismissed the case.

18. Saul S. Radovsky, "U.S. Medical Practice Before Medicare and Now—Differences and Consequences," *NEJM* 322 (1990): 263–67.

19. Lawrence Altman and Elisabeth Rosenthal, "Changes in Medicine Bring Pain to Healing Profession," *New York Times*, 18 February 1990, p. 1.

INDEX

INDEX

INDEX

160; media attention, 158, 165–67, 171; public opinion, 174; triage, 155–56
Triage: dialysis, 150; and kidney transplants, 155–56, 159
The Troubled Calling (Greenberg), 141
Trust: physician and patient relationship, 109, 190–91, 215
Tuberculosis, research on, 79
Tuskegee research, U.S. Public Health Service, 183, 187, 208, 247
Typhoid, research on, 52

Uncle Tom's Cabin (Stowe), 15
Uncle Vanya (Chekhov), 119–20, 138
Uniform Determination of Death Act, 250
U.S. Public Health Service, 35, 51, 89. *See also* Tuskegee research, U.S. Public Health Service

Vaccines, research for. *See specific diseases*
Vaux, Kenneth, 171
Veatch, Robert, 194, 195, 244
Vietnam War, 209
Vocational Rehabilitation Act, 204, 206
Volunteers for human experimentation: "normal" volunteers, 83, 92
Von Pirquet, Clemens, 28

Wangensteen, Owen, 173
War and the Christian Conscience: How Shall Modern War Be Conducted Justly? (Ramsey), 95
Washkansky, Louis, 157
Waterhouse, Benjamin, 21

Watson, James, 192
Watt, James, 35
Welt, Louis, 60, 67
Wiesel, Elie, 192
Williams, George, 161
Willowbrook State School for the Retarded, 77, 81, 208, 247
Willson, Robert, 194
Women's rights movement, 141–44
Woodruff, Michael, 154–56
World Medical Association, 74
World War II, human experimentation during, 30–50; children as research subjects, 33–34, 38; Committee on Medical Research, 31–48; conscientious objectors as research subjects, 41; dysentery, research on, 32–36, 47–48; 79; gonorrhea, research on, 40, 42–47; influenza, research on, 37–39, 47–48, 79; malaria, research on, 36–37, 47–48, 79; mentally handicapped as research subjects, 34–35, 47, 49; mentally ill as research subjects, 36; Nazi atrocities, 31, 41, 61–63, 68, 83; penicillin, discovery of, 39–40; prisoners as research subjects, 36–38, 44–47; public reaction, impact of, 48–49; soldiers as research subjects, 39

Yale–New Haven Hospital, 197
Yale University, 110, 111, 244; Divinity School, 95
Yellow fever research, 25–27, 47, 52
Ypsilanti State Hospital (Michigan), 38–39

Zuelzer, William, 194–96

ABOUT THE AUTHOR

David J. Rothman is Bernard Schoenberg Professor of Social Medicine, Director of the Center for the Study of Society and Medicine, and Professor of History at Columbia University. His books have explored the consequences of past and present social policies toward the poor, the criminal, and the mentally disabled. In 1971, his book *The Discovery of the Asylum* was co-winner of the Albert J. Beveridge Prize, and in 1987, he received a honorary Doctor of Law degree from the John Jay School of Criminal Justice.

His current research and writing analyzes the social and ethical issues in medical practice and hospital care. He chaired a New York City task force that has explored the advantages and disadvantages of single-disease hospitals and has examined the impact of AIDS on the regulation of new drugs. He is presently completing a study of American attitudes and policies toward the allocation of scarce medical resources.

David Rothman has served as Samuel Paley Lecturer at Hebrew University, as Distinguished Lecturer at the Kyoto American Studies Seminar, as Fulbright Professor to India, and most recently, as a fellow at the Rockefeller Foundation study center at Bellagio.

Making America

Fifth Edition

Making America

A HISTORY OF THE UNITED STATES

VOLUME 1: TO 1877

Carol Berkin
Baruch College, City University of New York

Christopher L. Miller
The University of Texas—Pan American

Robert W. Cherny
San Francisco State University

James L. Gormly
Washington and Jefferson College

WADSWORTH
CENGAGE Learning

Australia • Brazil • Japan • Korea • Mexico • Singapore • Spain • United Kingdom • United States

Making America: A History of the United States volume 1: to 1877, Fifth Edition

Carol Berkin, Christopher L. Miller, Robert W. Cherny, and James L. Gormly

Publisher: Suzanne Jeans

Senior Sponsoring Editor: Ann West

Senior Marketing Manager: Katherine Bates

Senior Development Editor: Lisa Kalner Williams

Senior Project Editor: Bob Greiner

Art and Design Manager: Jill Haber

Cover Design Director: Anthony L. Saizon

Senior Photo Editor: Jennifer Meyer Dare

Senior Composition Buyer: Chuck Dutton

New Title Project Manager: James Lonergan

Editorial Assistant: Evangeline Bermas

Marketing Associate: Lauren Bussard

Editorial Assistant: Laura Collins

Cover Art: *Tontine Coffee House,* c. 1797 (oil on linen) by Francis Guy (1760–1820) © Collection of the New York Historical Society, USA/The Bridgeman Art Library.

Text Credits: p. 354: Map 12.3 from Norton, *A People and A Nation,* Fifth Edition, copyright © 1998 by Houghton Mifflin Company. Reprinted by permission; p. 378: Map 13.2 from Norton, *A People and A Nation,* Fifth Edition, copyright © 1998 by Houghton Mifflin Company. Reprinted by permission; p. 408: Map 14.2 from Norton, *A People and A Nation,* Fifth Edition, copyright © 1998 by Houghton Mifflin Company. Reprinted by permission; p. 426: Map 14.5 from Norton, *A People and A Nation,* Fifth Edition, copyright © 1998 by Houghton Mifflin Company. Reprinted by permission.

For product information and technology assistance, contact us at **Cengage Learning Customer & Sales Support, 1-800-354-9706**

For permission to use material from this text or product, submit all requests online at **www.cengage.com/permissions** Further permissions questions can be emailed to **permissionrequest@cengage.com**

Library of Congress Control Number: 2007933591

ISBN-13: 978-0-618-99485-4

ISBN-10: 0-618-99485-8

Wadsworth
25 Thomson Place
Boston, MA 02210
USA

Cengage Learning is a leading provider of customized learning solutions with office locations around the globe, including Singapore, the United Kingdom, Australia, Mexico, Brazil, and Japan. Locate your local office at **international.cengage.com/region**

Cengage Learning products are represented in Canada by Nelson Education, Ltd.

To learn more about Wadsworth, visit **www.cengage.com/wadsworth**

Purchase any of our products at your local college store or at our preferred online store **www.ichapters.com**

Printed in the United States of America
3 4 5 6 7 11 10 09 08

✔ Brief Contents

✔ Contents

✔ Maps

✔ Features

✔ Preface

Authors of textbooks may dream of cheering audiences and mountains of fan mail, but this is rarely their reality. Yet there are occasional moments of glory. A colleague drops by our office to tell us she has been using our text and the students seem more prepared and more interested in class. A former student, now teaching, sends an e-mail, saying he has used our book as a basis for his first set of class lectures and discussions. Or a freshman in a survey class adds a note at the end of her exam, saying, "thanks for writing a text that isn't boring." Maybe none of this adds up to an Academy Award or a photo on the cover of *People* magazine, but comments like these do assure us that the book we originally envisioned is, if not perfect, at least on the right track. And the improvements we have made in this fifth edition of *Making America* make us even more confident.

From the beginning, our goal has been to create a different kind of textbook, one that meets the real needs of the modern college student. Nearly every history classroom reflects the rich cultural diversity of today's student body, with its mixture of students born in the United States and recent immigrants, both of whom come from many different cultural backgrounds, and its significant number of serious-minded men and women whose formal skills lag behind their interest and enthusiasm for learning. As professors in large public universities located on three of the nation's borders—the Pacific Ocean, the Atlantic, and the Rio Grande—we know the basic elements both the professor and the students need in the survey text for that classroom. These elements include a historical narrative that does not demand a lot of prior knowledge about the American past; information organized sequentially, or chronologically, so that students are not confused by too many topical digressions; and a full array of integrated and supportive learning aids to help students at every level of preparedness comprehend and retain what they read.

Making America has always provided an account of the American past firmly anchored by a political chronology. In it, people and places are brought to life not only through words but also through maps, paintings, photos, and other visual elements. Students see a genuine effort to communicate with them rather than impress them. And *Making America* presents history as a dynamic process shaped by human expectations, difficult choices, and often surprising consequences.

With this focus on history as a process, *Making America* encourages students to think historically and to develop into citizens who value the past.

Yet, as veteran teachers, the authors of *Making America* know that any history project, no matter how good, can be improved. Having scrawled "Revise" across the top of student papers for several decades, we impose the same demands on ourselves. For every edition, we subjected our text to the same critical reappraisal. We eliminated features that professors and students told us did not work as well as we had hoped; we added features that we believed would be more effective; and we tested our skills as storytellers and biographers more rigorously each time around. This fifth edition reflects the same willingness to revise and improve the textbook we offer to you.

The Approach

Professors and students who have used the previous editions of *Making America* will recognize immediately that we have preserved many of its central features. We have again set the nation's complex story within an explicitly political chronology, relying on a basic and familiar structure that is nevertheless broad enough to accommodate generous attention to social, economic, and diplomatic aspects of our national history. We remain confident that this political framework allows us to integrate the experiences of all Americans into a meaningful and effective narrative of our nation's development. Because our own scholarly research often focuses on the experiences of women, immigrants, African Americans, and Native Americans, we would not have been content with a framework that excluded or marginalized their history. *Making America* continues to be built on the premise that all Americans are historically active figures, playing significant roles in creating the history that we and other authors narrate. We have also continued what is now a tradition in *Making America*, that is, providing pedagogical tools for students that allow them to master complex material and enable them to develop analytical skills.

Themes

This edition continues to thread the five central themes through the narrative of *Making America* that professors and students who used earlier editions will recognize. The first of these themes, the political development of the nation, is evident in the text's coverage of the creation and revision of the federal and local governments, the contests waged over domestic and diplomatic policies, the internal and external crises faced by the United States and its political institutions, and the history of political parties and elections.

The second theme is the diversity of a national citizenry created by both Native Americans and immigrants. To do justice to this theme, *Making America* explores not only English and European immigration but immigrant communities from Paleolithic times to the present. The text attends to the tensions and conflicts that arise in a diverse population, but it also examines the shared values and aspirations that define middle-class American lives.

Making America's third theme is the significance of regional subcultures and economies. This regional theme is developed for society before European colonization and for the colonial settlements of the seventeenth and eighteenth centuries. It is evident in our attention to the striking social and cultural divergences that existed between the American Southwest and the Atlantic coastal regions and between the antebellum South and North, as well as significant differences in social and economic patterns in the West.

A fourth theme is the rise and impact of large social movements, from the Great Awakening in the 1740s to the rise of youth cultures in the post–World War II generations, movements prompted by changing material conditions or by new ideas challenging the status quo.

The fifth theme is the relationship of the United States to other nations. In *Making America* we explore in depth the causes and consequences of this nation's role in world conflict and diplomacy, whether in the era of colonization of the Americas, the eighteenth-century independence movement, the removal of Indian nations from their traditional lands, the impact of the rhetoric of manifest destiny, American policies of isolationism and interventionism, or in the modern role of the United States as a dominant player in world affairs.

In this edition, we have continued a sixth theme: American history in a global context. This new focus allows us to set our national development within the broadest context, to point out the parallels and the contrasts between our society and those of other na-

tions. It also allows us to integrate the exciting new scholarship in this emerging field of world or global history.

Learning Features

The chapters in *Making America* follow a format that provides students essential study aids for mastering the historical material. The first page of each chapter begins with "A Note from the Author," a message from the author that sets the tone for each chapter. This feature is new to this edition (read more on "A Note from the Author" in the next section). The page after "Note" provides a topical outline of the material students will encounter in the chapter. The outline sits on the same page as "Individual Choices," a brief biography of a woman or man whose life reflects the central themes of the chapter and whose choices demonstrate the importance of individual agency, or ability to make choices and act on them. Then, to help students focus on the broad questions and themes, we provide critical thinking, or focus, questions at the beginning of each major chapter section. At the end of the chapter narrative, "Individual Voices" provides a primary source and a series of thought-provoking questions about that source. These primary sources allow historical figures to speak for themselves and encourage students to engage directly in historical analysis. Finally, each chapter concludes with a summary that reinforces the most important themes and information the student has read. The "In the Wider World" timeline puts the narrative's most significant events and developments in international context. The "In the United States" chronology provides a more detailed list of key domestic events of the chapter.

To ensure that students have full access to the material in each chapter, we provide an on-page glossary, defining terms and explaining their historically specific usage the first time they appear in the narrative. The glossary also provides brief identifications of the major historical events, people, or documents discussed on the page. This on-page glossary will help students build their vocabularies and review for tests. The glossary reflects our concern about communicating fully with student readers without sacrificing the complexity of the history we are relating.

The illustrations in each chapter provide a visual connection to the past, and their captions analyze the subject of the painting, photograph, or artifact—and relate it to the narrative. For this edition we have selected many new illustrations to reinforce or illustrate the themes of the narrative.

New to the Fifth Edition

In this new edition we have preserved what our colleagues and their students considered the best and most useful aspects of *Making America*. We also have replaced what was less successful, revised what could be improved, and added new elements to strengthen the book.

You will find many features that you told us worked well in the past: Individual Choices, Individual Voices, focus questions, timelines, and maps. You will also find new features that you told us you would like to see. "A Note from the Author" is a personal message from the chapter's author to the reader. Like the book itself, the "Note" bridges the gap between reader and author and between student and historian. In direct terms, the author writes why the events that will unfold in the chapter continue to capture his or her interest. Many of the "Notes" also unveil linkages between the current and previous chapters.

The fifth edition has enhanced "It Matters Today," a feature in each chapter that points out connections between current events and past ones. This feature now includes discussion and reflection questions that challenge students to see the links between past and present. We encourage faculty and students to ask each other additional "It Matters Today" questions and even to create their own "It Matters Today" for other aspects of the textbook's chapters.

Naming in *Making America*

We have thought carefully about the names by which we have identified ethnic groups. As a general rule, we have tried to use terms that were in use among members of that group at the time under consideration. At times, however, this would have distracted readers from the topic to the terminology, and we wanted to avoid that. In such instances, we have tried to use the terms in general use today among members of that group.

Thus, we have used *African American* and *black* relatively interchangeably. The same applies to the terms *American Indian* and *Native American*. If we are writing about a particular Indian group, we have tried to use the most familiar names by which those groups prefer to be identified, for example, *Lakota* rather than *Sioux*.

Sometimes the names by which groups are identified are controversial within the group itself. Thus, in identifying people from Latin America, some prefer *Latino* and others *Hispanic*. Our usage in this regard often reflects our own regional perspective—Bob Cherny has tended to use *Latino* as that term is more widely used in California, and Chris Miller has often used *Hispanic* because that term is more widely used in Texas. In other places, we have used more specific terms; for example, we have used *Mexican* or *Mexican American* to identify groups that migrated to the United States from Mexico and because that is the usage most common among scholars who have studied those migrants in recent years.

Finally, in a few instances when we have discussed nondominant groups, we have indicated the names that such groups used for dominant groups. In some discussions of the Southwest, for example, you will encounter the term *Anglo* to indicate those people who spoke English rather than Spanish, although we are well aware that many who were (and are) called *Anglo* are not of English (or Anglo-Saxon) descent. *Anglo* has to do with language usage, from the perspective of those who spoke Spanish, rather than having to do with those English-speakers' own sense of ethnicity. Similarly, we sometimes use the term *haole* in our discussions of Hawai'i, to indicate those people whom the indigenous Hawaiians considered to be outsiders.

We the authors of *Making America* believe that this new edition will be effective in the history classroom. Please let us know what you think by sending us your views through Cengage Learning's website, located at www.cengage.com.

Learning and Teaching Ancillaries

The program for this edition of *Making America* includes a number of useful learning and teaching aids. These ancillaries ar designed to help students get the most from the course and to provide instructors with useful course management and presentation tools.

Kelly Woestman has been involved with *Making America* through previous editions and has taken an even more substantive role in the fifth edition. We suspect that no other technology author has been so well integrated into the author team as Kelly has been with our team, and we are certain that this will add significantly to the value of these resources.

Website tools

The **Instructor Website** features the **Instructor's Resource Manual** written by Kelly Woestman of Pittsburg State University, primary sources with instructor notes in addition to hundreds of maps, images, audio and video clips, and PowerPoint slides for classroom presentation. The **Diploma Testing**™ CD-ROM provides flexible test-editing capabilities of the Test Items written by Matthew McCoy of the University of Arkansas at Fort Smith.

Cengage Learning's **Eduspace** for *Making America* provides a customizable course management system powered by Blackboard along with interactive homework assignments that engage students and encourage in-class discussion. Assignments include gradable homework exercises, writing assignments, primary sources with questions, and Associated Press Interactives. Eduspace also provides a gradebook and communication capabilities, such as live chats, threaded discussion boards, and announcement postings. Eduspace is also the home of the *Making America* **e-book**, an interactive version of the textbook that provides direct links to quizzing, relevant primary sources, and more.

HistoryFinder, a new Cengage Learning technology initiative, helps instructors create rich and exciting classroom presentations. This online tool offers thousands of online resources, including art, photographs, maps, primary sources, multimedia content, Associated Press interactive modules, and readymade PowerPoint slides. HistoryFinder's assets can easily be searched by keyword, or browsed from pulldown menus of topic, media type, or by textbook. Instructors can then browse, preview, and download resources straight from the website.

The **Student Website** contains a variety of tutorial resources including the **Study Guide** written by Kelly Woestman, ACE quizzes with feedback, interactive maps, primary sources, chronology exercises, flashcards, and other interactivities. The website for this edition of *Making America* will feature two different audio tools for students. These audio files are downloadable as MP3 files. **Audio Notes** provide an auditory counterpart to the textbook's "A Note from the Author," whereby the authors will provide personal insight into each chapter. **Audio Summaries** help students review each chapter's key points.

Please contact your local Cengage Learning sales representative for more information about these learning and teaching tools in addition to the **Rand McNally Atlas of American History**, WebCT and Blackboard cartridges, and transparencies for United States History.

Acknowledgments

The authors of *Making America* have benefited greatly from the critical reading of this edition of the book by instructors from across the country. We would like to thank these scholars and teachers: James Bradford, Texas A&M University; Susan Burch, Gallaudet College; Kathleen Carter, High Point University; Norman Caulfield, Fort Hays State University; Craig Coenen, Mercer County Community College; Lawrence Culver, Utah State University; Rick Elder, Bay Mills Community College; Theresa Kaminsky, University of Wisconsin, Stevens Point; Gene Kirkpatrick, Tyler Junior College; Janilyn Kocher, Richland Community College; Lorraine Lees, Old Dominion University; Greg Miller, Hillsborough Community College; Bryant Morrison, South Texas College; Michael Nichols, Tarrant County College; Elsa Nystrom, Kennesaw State University; William Paquette, Tidewater Community College; Mark Pellatt, Northeastern Technical College; Charles Robinson, South Texas College; David Voelker, University of Wisconsin, Green Bay; David Wolcott, Miami University; and Manuel Yang, Lourdes College.

Carol Berkin, who is responsible for Chapters 3 through 7, thanks the librarians at Baruch College and The Graduate Center of CUNY and the Gilder Lehrman Institute of American History for providing help in locating interesting primary sources, and colleagues and students in the Baruch history department for their ongoing, stimulating discussion of history and historical methods. She thanks her children, Hannah and Matthew, for their patience and support while she revised this book.

Christopher L. Miller, who is responsible for Chapters 1 and 2 and 8 through 14, is indebted to the community at the University of Texas—Pan American for providing the constant inspiration to innovate. Thanks, too, are due to Chris's students and colleagues at Lomonosov Moscow State University during his tenure there as the Nikolay V. Sivachev Distinguished Chair in U.S. History and American Studies. Colleagues on various H-NET discussion lists as always were generous with advice, guidance, and often abstruse points of information.

Robert W. Cherny, who is responsible for Chapters 15 through 22, wishes to thank his students who, over the years, have provided the testing ground for much that is included in these chapters, and especially to thank his colleagues and research assistants who have helped with the previous editions and Rebecca Hodges, his research assistant for this fifth edition. The staff of the Leonard Library at San Francisco State has always been most helpful. Rebecca Marshall Cherny, Sarah Cherny, and Lena Hobbs Kracht Cherny have been unfailing in their encouragement, inspiration, and support.

James L. Gormly, who is responsible for Chapters 23 through 30, would like to acknowledge the support and encouragement he received from Washington and Jefferson College. He wants to gives a special thanks to Sharon Gormly, whose support, ideas, advice, and critical eye have helped to shape and refine his chapters.

As always, this book is a collaborative effort between authors and the editorial staff of Cengage Learning. We would like to thank Ann West, senior sponsoring editor; Lisa Kalner Williams, senior development editor; Bob Greiner, senior project editor; Emily Meyer, editorial assistant; and Amy Pastan, who helped us fill this edition with remarkable illustrations, portraits, and photographs. These talented, committed members of the publishing world encouraged us and generously assisted us every step of the way.

✔ A Note for the Students

Dear Student:

History is about people—brilliant and insane, brave and treacherous, loveable and hateful, murderers and princesses, daredevils and visionaries, rule breakers and rule makers. It has exciting events, major crises, turning points, battles, and scientific breakthroughs. We, the authors of Making America, believe that knowing about the past is critical for anyone who hopes to understand the present and chart the future. In this book, we want to tell you the story of America from its earliest settlement to the present and to tell it in a language and format that helps you enjoy learning that history.

This book is organized and designed to help you master your American History course. The narrative is chronological, telling the story as it happened, decade by decade or era by era. We have developed special tools to help you learn. In the next few pages, we'll introduce you to the unique features of this book that will help you to understand the complex and fascinating story of American history.

At the back of the book, you will find some additional resources. In the Appendix, you will find an annotated, chapter-by-chapter list of suggested readings. You will also find reprinted several of the most important documents in American history: the Declaration of Independence, the Articles of Confederation, and the Constitution. Here, too, are tables that give you quick access to important data on the presidents and their cabinets. In addition, you will find a complete list of glossary terms used in the book. Finally, you will see the index, which will help you locate a subject quickly if you want to read about it.

In addition, you will find a number of useful study tools on the Making America student website. These include "History Connects" activities, map and chronology exercises, chapter quizzes, and primary sources—all geared to help you study, do research, and take tests effectively.

We hope that our textbook conveys to you our own fascination with the American past and sparks your curiosity about the nation's history. We invite you to share your feedback on the book: you can reach us through Cengage Learning's American History website, which is located at http://college.cengage.com/history.

Carol Berkin, Chris Miller, Bob Cherny, and Jim Gormly

CHAPTER

4

The English Colonies in the Eighteenth Century, 1689–1763

A NOTE FROM THE AUTHOR

A Maine farm wife churning butter, a ship captain unloading his cargo in Boston, an African American slave toiling in a rice paddy in South Carolina, a Philadelphia matron shopping for cloth in a local shop—these eighteenth-century figures may have thought they had little in common. In some ways, they were correct. They lived in communities with different economic activities and different labor systems. Some lived in rural areas, others in bustling cities. They were rich and poor; free and unfree; black and white. Whose life was typical? Whose story should a chapter on eighteenth-century colonial life tell?

No historian, no matter how talented, can tell every person's individual story. For me, telling a coherent story of life in eighteenth-century America is a delicate balancing act in which factors that unify historical subjects and factors that divide them must be considered. Common experiences and unique ones both play a part in recreating the past.

What did I find that the colonists had in common? First, they lived on the margins rather than the center of the British Empire. The seat of wealth, power, and prestige was London, not New York or Philadelphia. Second, England, not the colonists, determined the flow of trade across the Atlantic. Third, by mid-century, colonists expected their local elected assemblies rather than the distant British Parliament to govern them. Finally, the competition between England and its rivals, France and Spain, linked the colonists to one another and drew them into bloody imperial wars.

While you'll find trade, politics, and war the three cords that link eighteenth-century colonists in this chapter, you'll also encounter race, region, social class, and gender as factors that divide them. As you read along, consider another issue that will soon divide the colonists: was the British government becoming tyrann...

or the ...

or that ...

Each chapter opens with **A Note from the Author**. Here, the author of the chapter explains what he or she finds most interesting about the events of this period in American history.

Susie King Taylor

Born a slave in rural Georgia, Susie King Taylor attended an illegal school for slaves in antebellum Savannah. After the outbreak of the Civil War, she fled to safety among the Union forces and founded a school for other "contrabands." When her husband, Edward King, joined an all-Black regiment fighting for their freedom, Susie accompanied him, serving as a nurse, aide, and continuing as a teacher. Following the war she became a leading voice in advocating racial equality and educational opportunity for all people. *Library of Congress.*

The "Note" is immediately followed by **Individual Choices**. These biographies show how historical events are the results of real people making real choices. Some of the featured individuals are famous historical figures. Others are ordinary people who played an important role in shaping the events of their era.

✔ Individual Choices

Born a slave in 1848, young Susie Baker attended an illegal school for slave children in Savannah, Georgia, where, by the age of 14, she had learned everything her teachers could offer. Then war came. Early in 1862 Union forces attacked the Georgia coast. Powerless and fearful of what the future might hold, many slaves left the city. Eventually a Union gunboat picked up Susie and a number of **"contrabands"** and ferried them to a Yankee encampment on St. Simon's Island. Before long the community of displaced former slaves exceeded six hundred. Discovering that Susie could read and write, Union officials asked her to open a school, the first legally sanctioned school for African Americans in Georgia.

At St. Simon's Susie met and then married another contraband named Edward King. Like many in the camp, King wanted to fight for his freedom. Finally, Union Captain C. T. Trowbridge arrived on the island with a request for volunteers. Though they were offered no pay, no uniforms, and no official recognition, King and his friends eagerly joined up. Trowbridge drilled them during the day while Susie tutored them at night. Finally, in ... and official recognition (thou...

But such good fortune was not to last. Seeking to break France's dependence on America as a source for food and other supplies, Napoleon sought an alliance with Russia, and in the spring of 1807 his diplomatic mission succeeded. Having acquired an alternative source for grain and other foodstuffs, Napoleon immediately began enforcing the Berlin Decree, hoping to starve England into submission. The British countered by stepping up enforcement of their European blockade and aggressively pursuing impressment to strengthen the Royal Navy.

The escalation in both France's and Britain's economic war efforts quickly led to confrontation with Americans and a diplomatic crisis. A pivotal event occurred in June 1807. The British **frigate** *Leopard*, patrolling the American shoreline, confronted the American warship *Chesapeake*. Even though both ships were inside American territorial waters, the *Leopard* ordered the American ship to halt and hand over any British sailors on board. When the *Chesapeake*'s captain refused, the *Leopard* fired several **broadsides**, crippling the American vessel, killing three sailors, and injuring eighteen. The British then boarded the *Chesapeake* and dragged off four men, three of whom were naturalized citizens of the United States. Americans were outraged.

Americans were not the only ones galvanized by British aggression. Shortly after the *Chesapeake* affair, word arrived in the United States that Napoleon had responded to Britain's belligerence by declaring a virtual economic war against neutrals. In the **Milan Decree,** he vowed to seize any neutral ship that so much as carried licenses to trade with England. What was worse, the Milan Decree stated that ships that had been boarded by British

were on European money and manufactures, Jefferson chose to violate one of his cardinal principles: the U.S. government would interfere in the economy to force Europeans to recognize American neutral rights. In December 1807, the president announced the **Embargo Act,** which would, in effect, close all American foreign trade as of January 1 unless the Europeans agreed to recognize America's neutral rights to trade with anyone it pleased.

Crises in the Nation

→ *How did Jefferson's economic and Indian policies influence national developments after 1808?*

→ *How did problems in Europe contribute to changing conditions in the American West?*

→ *What did the actions of frontier politicians such as William Henry Harrison do to bring the nation into war in 1812?*

Jefferson's reaction to European aggression immediately began strangling American trade and with it America's domestic economic development. In addition, European countries still had legitimate claims on much of North America, and the Indians who continued to occupy most of the continent had enough military power to pose a serious threat to the United States if properly motivated (see Map 9.1). While impressment, blockade, and embargo paralyzed America's Atlantic frontier, a combination of European and Indian hostility along the western frontier added to the air of national emergency. The resulting series of domestic crises played havoc with Jefferson's vision of

> You'll find **Focus Questions** at the beginning of the chapter's major sections. These questions guide you to the most important themes in each section. The questions also connect moments in United States history to relevant events in global history.

their tax money, although each town was required to make one church the established church. New England did not separate church and state entirely until the nineteenth century.

Protection of Property Rights

Members of the revolutionary generation who had a political voice were especially vocal about the importance of private property and protection of a citizen's right to own property. In the decade before the Revolution, much of the protest against British policy had focused on this issue. For free, white, property-holding men—and for those white male servants, tenant farmers, or apprentices who hoped to join their ranks someday—life, liberty, and happiness were interwoven with the right of landownership.

The property rights of some infringed on the freedoms of others, however. Claims made on western lands by white Americans often meant the denial of Indian rights to that land. Masters' rights included a claim to the time and labor of their servants or apprentices. In the white community, a man's property rights usually included the restriction of his wife's right to own or sell land, slaves, and even her own personal possessions. Even the independent-minded Deborah Sampson lost her right to own property when she became Mrs. Gannett. And the institution of slavery transformed human beings into the private property of others.

The right to property was a principle, not a guarantee. Many white men were unable to acquire land during the revolutionary era or in the decades that followed. When the Revolution began, one-fifth of free American people lived in poverty or depended on public charity. The uneven distribution of wealth

several legal reforms were spurred by a commitment to the republican belief in social equality. Chief targets of this legal reform included the laws of **primogeniture** and **entail**. In Britain, these inheritance laws had led to the creation of a landed aristocracy. The actual threat they posed in America was small, for few planters ever adopted them. But the principle they represented remained important to republican spokesmen such as Thomas Jefferson, who pressed successfully for their abolition in Virginia and North Carolina.

The passion for social equality—in appearance if not in fact—affected customs as well as laws. To downplay their elite status as landowners, revolutionaries stopped the practice of adding "**Esquire**" (abbreviated "Esq.") after their names. (George Washington, Esq., became plain George Washington.)

Even unintentional elitist behavior could have embarrassing consequences. When General George Washington and the officers who served with him in the Revolutionary War organized the Society of the Cincinnati in 1783, they were motivated by the desire to sustain wartime friendships. The society's rules, however, brought protest from many Americans, for membership was hereditary, passing from officer fathers to their eldest sons. Grumblings that the club

> The **On-Page Glossary** defines key terms, concepts, and vocabulary in the lower right-hand corner of the page where the term first appears. Use the glossary as a review tool. If English is not your first language, use the glossary to help with difficult words you find in this chapter. Glossary terms are also bolded in the index for your reference.

almshouse A public shelter for the poor.

primogeniture The legal right of the eldest son to inherit the entire estate of his father.

entail A legal limitation that prevents property from being divided, sold, or given away.

Esquire A term used to indicate that a man was a gentleman.

because it held the headquarters of many leading western corporations and partly because it was the western center for finance capitalism—the Pacific Coast counterpart of Wall Street.

By 1900, a few other western cities—Denver, Salt Lake City, Seattle, Portland, and especially Los Angeles—were beginning to challenge the economic dominance of San Francisco. (For Los Angeles, see pages 689–690.)

Water Wars

From the first efforts at western economic development, water was a central concern. Prospectors in the California gold rush needed water to separate worthless gravel from gold. On the Great Plains, a cattle rancher claimed grazing land by controlling a stream. Throughout much of the West, water was scarce, and competition for water sometimes produced conflict—usually in the form of courtroom battles.

Lack of water potentially posed stringent limits on western urban growth. Beginning in 1901, San Francisco sought federal permission to put a dam across the Hetch Hetchy Valley, on federal land adjacent to Yosemite National Park in the Sierra Nevada, in order to create a reservoir. Opposition came from the **Sierra Club,** formed in 1892 and dedicated to preserving Sierra Nevada wilderness. Congress finally approved the project in 1913, and the enormous construction project took more than twenty years to complete. Los Angeles resolved its water problems in a similar way, by diverting the water of the Owens River to its use—even though Owens Valley residents tried to dynamite the **aqueduct** in resistance.

Throughout much of the West, irrigation was vital to the success of farming. As early as 1899, irrigated land in the eleven westernmost states produced $84 million in crops. Although individual entrepreneurs and companies undertook significant irrigation projects, the magnitude of the task led many westerners to look for federal assistance, just as they had sought federal assistance for railroad development. "When Uncle Sam puts his hand to a t-----

▲▲▲▲▲▲▲
IT MATTERS TODAY

WESTERN WATER AND GLOBAL WARMING

Westerners have always struggled with the problem of insufficient water. These days, many western cities draw their water from dams and reservoirs in the mountains, where winter snow gradually melts during the spring and early summer, replacing water that the cities draw from the reservoirs. In California, where precipitation falls mostly in the winter and early spring, both cities and agriculture look to the Sierra Nevada snowpack for water in the summer and fall.

Global warming is likely to force a reconsideration of this century-old solution to the problem of inadequate water. As the climate warms, most scientists project that more of the precipitation that falls in the mountains will be rain. Unlike snow, rain will come into the reservoirs all at once and may overwhelm the capacity of the reservoirs. Downstream areas will likely experience winter and spring flooding. Water that runs off as floods will not be available for use in the summer and autumn. If these scientists' projections are accurate, western cities will need to devise new methods of conserving water.

- Go online and do research in western newspapers (the *Los Angeles Times* or *San Francisco Chronicle*) on the effect of global warming on urban water supplies. Are western city governments planning for future water shortages?

- What effect is global warming likely to have on the urban infrastructure of your city, especially those parts of the urban infrastructure created in the late nineteenth and early twentieth centuries?

It Matters Today shows how a person, event, or idea in every chapter is meaningful today. The questions at the end of each essay prompt you to consider specific connections between the past, the present—and the future.

Maps provide visual representations of how historical events and trends have impacted different regions of the United States. The captions below the maps supply information on ways to interpret what you see.

Mean annual rainfall (inches)
- Over 80
- 60–80
- 40–60
- 20–40
- 10–20
- Under 10
- 28 inch rainfall line

MAP 18.3 Rainfall and Agriculture, ca. 1890 The agricultural produce of any given area depended on the type of soil, the terrain, and the rainfall. Most of the western half of the nation received relatively little rainfall compared with the eastern half, and crops such as corn and cotton could not be raised in the West without irrigation. The line of aridity, beyond which many crops required irrigation, lies between twenty-eight inches and twenty inches of rain annually.

Russian-German immigrants), and began to practice irrigation did agriculture become viable. Even so, farming practices in some western areas failed to protect soil that had formerly-----

steps did those entrepreneurs take to develop their industries?

- How did economic development in the West during

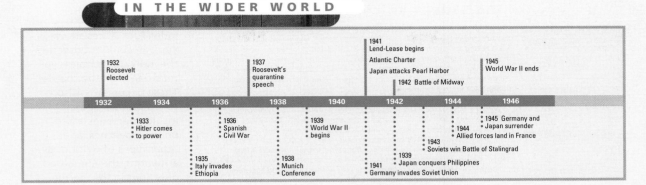

IN THE WIDER WORLD

1932
Roosevelt
elected

1937
Roosevelt's
quarantine
speech

1941
Lend-Lease begins
Atlantic Charter
Japan attacks Pearl Harbor
1942 Battle of Midway

1945
World War II ends

| 1932 | 1934 | 1936 | 1938 | 1940 | 1942 | 1944 | 1946 |

1933
Hitler comes
to power

1936
Spanish
Civil War

1939
World War II
begins

1945 Germany and
Japan surrender
1944
Allied forces land in France

1943
Soviets win Battle of Stalingrad

1935
Italy invades
Ethiopia

1938
Munich
Conference

1939
Japan conquers Philippines
1941
Germany invades Soviet Union

The **"In the Wider World" timeline** provides a quick review of the major events in the chapter so you can see what was happening in both the United States and around the world.

In the United States

The **"In the United States" chronology** provides a fuller listing of the important events covered in the chapter.

New Frontiers

1960 Sit-ins begin

SNCC formed

Students for a Democratic Society formed

Boynton v. Virginia

John F. Kennedy elected president

1961 Peace Corps formed

Alliance for Progress

Yuri Gagarin orbits the Earth

Bay of Pigs invasion

Freedom rides begin

Vienna summit

Berlin Wall erected

1962 Michael Harrington's *The Other America*

SDS's *Port Huron Statement*

James Meredith enrolls at the University of Mississippi

Cuban missile crisis

Rachel Carson's *Silent Spring*

1963 Report on the status of women

Betty Friedan's *The Feminine Mystique*

Equal Pay Act

Martin Luther King's "Letter from a Birmingham Jail"

Limited Test Ban Treaty

March on Washington

16,000 advisers in Vietnam

Diem assassinated

Kennedy assassinated; Lyndon Baines Johnson becomes president

1964 War on Poverty begins

Freedom Summer in Mississippi

Civil Rights Act

Office of Economic Opportunity created

Johnson elected president

1965 Malcolm X assassinated

Selma freedom march

Elementary and Secondary Education Act

Medicaid and Medicare

Voting Rights Act

Watts riot

Immigration Act

1966 Black Panther Party formed

National Organization for Women founded

Stokely Carmichael announces Black Power

Model Cities Act

1967 Urban riots in over 75 cities

1968 Kerner Commission Report

Martin Luther King Jr. assassinated

1969 Woodstock

Stonewall Riot

Neil Armstrong lands on moon

> **Examining a Primary Source**

✔ Individual Voices

Susie King Taylor

① *In Taylor's mind, what conditions did the end of the Spanish-American War leave unresolved? What does this say about her perceptions concerning her role in the Civil War?*

② *In 1886, Taylor was one of the co-founders of the Women's Relief Corp, an organization devoted to aiding Civil War veterans and furthering recognition for American soldiers. She was the president of the Massachusetts auxiliary in 1898, leading the organization to send aid to soldiers in the Spanish-American War.*

③ *What is Taylor suggesting here about the way in which the contributions of African American Civil War veterans were regarded? What does this suggest about her motivations for writing about her experiences in that war?*

Like all African Americans, Susie King Taylor had a deep personal investment in the outcome of the American Civil War. A slave herself, she ran away to the Union lines seeking asylum and, like many other "contrabands," joined the Union cause. Unlike most others, however, Taylor recorded her experiences during the war, giving her contemporaries and modern historians a unique insight into the accomplishments and disillusionments that came with fighting for the freedom and equality that the war seemed to promise.

With the close of the Spanish war, and on the entrance of the Americans into Cuba, the same conditions confront us as the war of 1861 left. The Cubans are free, but it is a limited freedom, for prejudice, deep-rooted, has been brought to them and a separation made between the white and black Cubans, a thing that had never existed between them before; but to-day there is the same intense hatred toward the negro in Cuba that there is in some parts of this country. ①
I helped to furnish and pack boxes to be sent to the soldiers and hospitals during the first part of the Spanish war; ② *there were black soldiers there too. At the battle of San Juan Hill, they were in the front, just as brave, loyal, and true as those other black men who fought for freedom and the right; and yet their bravery and faithfulness were reluctantly acknowledged, and praise grudgingly given.* ③ *All we ask for is "equal justice," the same that is accorded to all other races who come to this country, of their free will (not forced to, as we were), and are allowed to enjoy every privilege, unrestricted, while we are denied what is rightfully our own in a country which the labor of our forefathers helped to make what it is.*

Individual Voices shows you a document related to the Individual Choices you read earlier in the chapter. These documents (also called primary sources) include personal letters, poems, speeches, and other types of writing. By answering the numbered questions in the margin, you'll analyze the primary sources the way a historian would.

SUMMARY

Each chapter concludes with a **Summary** that reinforces the most important themes and information in the chapter.

After Jefferson's triumphal first four years in office, factional disputes at home and diplomatic deadlocks with European powers began to plague the Republicans. Although the Federalists were in full retreat, many within Jefferson's own party rebelled against some of his policies. When Jefferson decided not to run for office in 1808, tapping James Madison as his successor, Republicans in both the Northeast and the South bucked the president, supporting George Clinton and James Monroe, respectively.

To a large extent, the Republicans' problems were the outcome of external stresses. On the Atlantic frontier, the United States tried to remain neutral in the wars that engulfed Europe. On the western frontier, the Prophet and Tecumseh were successfully unifying dispossessed Indians into an alliance devoted to stopping U.S. expansion. Things went from bad to worse when Jefferson's use of economic sanctions gave rise to the worst economic depression since the beginnings of English colonization. The embargo strangled the economy in port cities, and the downward spiral in agricultural prices threatened to bankrupt many in the West and South.

The combination...

justifying the conquest of the rest of North America. Despite Madison's continuing peace efforts, southern and western interests finally pushed the nation into war with England in 1812.

Although some glimmering moments of glory heartened the Americans, the war was mostly disastrous. But after generations of fighting one enemy or another, the English people demanded peace. When their final offensive in America failed to bring immediate victory in 1814, the British chose to negotiate. Finally, on Christmas Eve, the two nations signed the Treaty of Ghent, ending the war. From a diplomatic point of view, it was as though the war had never happened: everything was simply restored to pre-1812 status.

Nevertheless, in the United States the war created strong feelings of national pride and confidence, and Americans looked forward to even better things to come. In the Northeast, the constraints of war provoked entrepreneurs to explore new industries, creating the first stage of an industrial revolution in the country. In the West, the defeat of Indian resistance combined with bright economic opportunities to trigger a wave of westward migration. In the South, the ...revolutionized both...

The **Student Website** contains a variety of review materials and resources, including ACE quizzes with feedback, interactive map and chronology exercises, "History Connects" activities, flashcards, and other study tools. Here's the place to download MP3 **Audio Notes** and chapter **Audio Summaries** to help you prepare for class. If your instructor uses Eduspace®, Cengage Learning's course management system, you will have access to a multimedia e-book version of *Making America* that directly links the text to quizzes, audio files, Associated Press interactive activities, and more. Start by going to http://www.college.cengage.com/history.

✔ About the Authors

Carol Berkin

Born in Mobile, Alabama, Carol Berkin received her undergraduate degree from Barnard College and her Ph.D. from Columbia University. Her dissertation won the Bancroft Award. She is now Presidential Professor of history at Baruch College and the Graduate Center of City University of New York. She has written *Jonathan Sewall: Odyssey of an American Loyalist* (1974); *First Generations: Women in Colonial America* (1996); *A Brilliant Solution: Inventing the American Constitution* (2002); and *Revolutionary Mothers: Women in the Struggle for America's Independence* (2005). She has edited *Women of America: A History* (with Mary Beth Norton, 1979); *Women, War and Revolution* (with Clara M. Lovett, 1980); *Women's Voices, Women's Lives: Documents in Early American History* (with Leslie Horowitz, 1998) and *Looking Forward/Looking Back: A Women's Studies Reader* (with Judith Pinch and Carole Appel, 2005). She was contributing editor on southern women for *The Encyclopedia of Southern Culture* and has appeared in the PBS series *Liberty! The American Revolution; Ben Franklin;* and *Alexander Hamilton* and The History Channel's *Founding Fathers*. Professor Berkin chaired the Dunning Beveridge Prize Committee for the American Historical Association, the Columbia University Seminar in Early American History, and the Taylor Prize Committee of the Southern Association of Women Historians, and she served on the program committees for both the Society for the History of the Early American Republic and the Organization of American Historians. She has served on the Planning Committee for the U.S. Department of Education's National Assessment of Educational Progress, and chaired the CLEP Committee for Educational Testing Service. She serves on the Board of Trustees of The Gilder Lehrman Institute of American History and The National Council for History Education.

Christopher L. Miller

Born and raised in Portland, Oregon, Christopher L. Miller received his Bachelor of Science degree from Lewis and Clark College and his Ph.D. from the University of California, Santa Barbara. He is currently associate professor of history at the University of Texas—Pan American. He is the author of *Prophetic Worlds: Indians and Whites on the Columbia Plateau* (1985), which was recently (2003) republished as part of the Columbia Northwest Classics Series by the University of Washington Press. His articles and reviews have appeared in numerous scholarly journals and anthologies as well as standard reference works. Dr. Miller is also active in contemporary Indian affairs, having served, for example, as a participant in the American Indian Civics Project funded by the Kellogg Foundation. He has been a research fellow at the Charles Warren Center for Studies in American History at Harvard University and was the Nikolay V. Sivachev Distinguished Chair in American History at Lemonosov Moscow State University (Russia). Professor Miller has also been active in projects designed to improve history teaching, including programs funded by the Meadows Foundation, the U.S. Department of Education, and other agencies.

Robert W. Cherny

Born in Marysville, Kansas, and raised in Beatrice, Nebraska, Robert W. Cherny received his B.A. from the University of Nebraska and his M.A. and Ph.D. from Columbia University. He is professor of history at San Francisco State University. His books include *Competing Visions: A History of California* (with Richard Griswold del Castillo, 2005); *American Politics in the Gilded Age, 1868-1900* (1997); *San Francisco, 1865–1932: Politics, Power, and Urban Development* (with William Issel, 1986); *A Righteous Cause: The Life of William Jennings Bryan* (1985, 1994); and *Populism, Progressivism, and the Transformation of Nebraska Politics, 1885–1915* (1981). He is co-editor of *American Labor and the Cold War: Unions, Politics, and Postwar Political Culture* (with William Issel and Keiran Taylor, 2004). His articles on politics and labor in the late nineteenth and early twentieth centuries have appeared in journals, anthologies, and historical dictionaries and encyclopedias. In 2000, he and Ellen Du Bois co-edited a special issue of the *Pacific Historical Review* that surveyed woman suffrage movements in nine locations around the Pacific Rim. He has been an NEH Fellow, Distinguished Fulbright Lecturer at Lomonosov Moscow State University (Russia), and Visiting Research Scholar at the University of Melbourne (Australia). He has served as president of H-Net (an association of more than one hundred electronic networks for scholars in the humanities and social sciences), the Society for Historians of the Gilded Age and Progressive Era and of the Southwest Labor Studies Association; as treasurer of the Organization of American Historians; and as and a member of the council of the American Historical Association, Pacific Coast Branch.

James L. Gormly

Born in Riverside, California, James L. Gormly received a B.A. from the University of Arizona and his M.A. and Ph.D. from the University of Connecticut. He is now professor of history and chair of the history department at Washington and Jefferson College. He has written *The Collapse of the Grand Alliance* (1970) and *From Potsdam to the Cold War* (1979). His articles and reviews have appeared in *Diplomatic History, The Journal of American History, The American Historical Review, The Historian, The History Teacher,* and *The Journal of Interdisciplinary History.*

Making America

Making a "New" World, to 1588

A NOTE FROM THE AUTHOR

Where should we begin the story of Making America? We started this project without a clear answer to that question. Traditionally this story begins with the voyages of a confused but daring Genoese sailor, Christopher Columbus, who accidentally stumbled upon a chain of continents that some suspected lay between Europe and Asia. This makes a convenient starting point, but it is terribly misleading. As you will learn in the pages to come, Columbus discovered a world populated by ancient and sophisticated societies whose presence would prove essential to the process of European conquest and colonization of this "New World." We decided that the history of those societies before Columbus's arrival had to be included in our story.

Our story of Making America would thus go deeper in time than more traditional accounts. But we also realized that it would have to range farther in space. Making America was a truly global process. For generations exotic items from China, Persia, and other mysterious places wound their way westward along the Silk Road and northward across the Sahara Desert bringing novel luxuries into an evolving cosmopolitan marketplace. Atlantic nations like Portugal and Spain sought to make these transactions more efficient by substituting sailing ships for camels, hoping to enhance their own importance in that marketplace. This explosion in commerce helps explain why Columbus and other adventurers of his day risked the open seas of the Atlantic. And this is why Asia and Africa, as much as Europe, were essential to the process of making America.

Yet America was equally essential in the making of the Europe, Africa, and Asia that we know today. The influx of wealth from America and the demand for labor to harness that wealth changed the face of the globe. Old ideas, unchallenged certainties fell away, or were shattered by rising new intellectual traditions. In the process new states, new churches, new generations of leaders sprang up—all of which would drive American and global history onward.

This was a story that we found compelling and explains why we begin our discussion of Making America as we do. And this thread of how the world influenced America and America has influenced the world will be woven throughout our narrative as our story unfolds.

Hienwatha

New conditions in North America led to increasing conflicts among the five northeastern Iroquois tribes during the fifteenth and sixteenth centuries. Hienwatha overcame resistance—even the murder of his family—to convince Iroquois leaders to form the Iroquois League, a political, military, and religious alliance that helped them survive massive changes and made them a major force in world diplomacy. *The Newberry Library, Chicago.*

✔ Individual Choices

Things were bad, and getting worse, for the people who lived in North America's northeastern woodlands (see Map 1.3). For generations they had lived peacefully in their largely self-sufficient villages on the corn that the women grew and the game that the men hunted. Warfare was infrequent, and famine all but unknown. But around 600 years ago a long-lasting change in the weather made corn production less dependable, and the people were forced to hunt and gather more wild foods to supplement their diets. As hunters from individual villages roamed deeper and deeper into the forests looking for food, they encountered others who, like themselves, were desperate to harvest the diminishing resources. Conflicts became common. "Everywhere there was peril and everywhere mourning," says one version of the story. "Feuds with outer nations and feuds with brother nations, feuds of sister towns and feuds of families and clans made every warrior a stealthy man who liked to kill."

In the midst of the crisis, a child who would be called Hienwatha (or Hiawatha, Maker of Rivers) was born among the woodland people. Oral accounts among the various Indian groups disagree about Hienwatha's early life. According to some sources, he was born among the Onondaga Nation sometime shortly after 1400 but came to live with the neighboring Mohawks. If so, he may well have been a war captive, taken to replace a Mohawk killed in the ever-accelerating violence that raged through the woodlands.

Having grown to adulthood among the Mohawks, the still young and unmarried outsider left his village to seek survival on his own in the woods. Food was scarce, and Hienwatha became a cannibal, killing lone travelers to eat their flesh. One day, as Hienwatha was butchering a victim, he discovered that he had a visitor. The man, a Huron Indian called Dekanahwideh (Two River Currents Flowing Together), shamed Hienwatha for his sad and dishonorable state. The stranger then told him of a spirit being called Peacemaker, who had given Dekanahwideh a vision and a mission: he was to unify all the Iroquois into a great and peaceful nation. Inspired by the stranger's words, Hienwatha vowed never to eat human flesh again and to spend his life making Dekanahwideh's vision a reality.

3

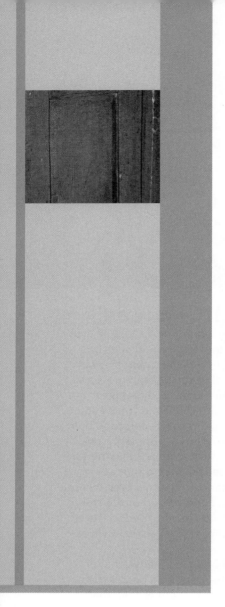

Hienwatha moved back among the Mohawks, married, and began telling the people about Dekanahwideh's vision and Peacemaker's message. Although many found his words inspiring, some, including Onondaga leader Tadadaho, opposed him. Tadadaho and his supporters finally attacked Hienwatha, killing his family and forcing him to flee once again into the woods.

Undaunted, Hienwatha tried to think of some way to convince his enemies among the Iroquois to accept the idea of cooperation. His solution was to weave a belt of wampum-shell strings that showed a great chain connecting the five northern Iroquois nations—Mohawk, Oneida, Onondaga, Cayuga, and Seneca. Carrying his belt, Hienwatha traveled among the five nations, telling them that they could survive only if they ceased fighting among themselves and began cooperating. He finally won over even Tadadaho, whose Onondaga Nation became the keeper of the council fires. Together Hienwatha, Dekanahwideh, Tadadaho, and the other leaders of the Five Nations created a confederation government that Europeans later would call the League of the Iroquois. Under its provisions each member nation maintained complete sovereignty in its own affairs, but all agreed fully to defend the others, share resources, and promote the confederation's overall welfare. They also vowed to carry forward Peacemaker's design by offering peace to all who would agree to live with them under the Great Tree of Peace that symbolized the new covenant. Many agreed, but many also resisted what they saw as Iroquois aggression. That included Dekanahwideh's own Huron people, who formed their own alliance system to oppose the Iroquois League.

As remarkable as Hienwatha's story is, his experience was not entirely unique. Faced with changing conditions, natural ones at first and then those brought by invading Europeans, Indians throughout the Americas struggled valiantly and creatively to restructure their societies and their lives. Sometimes the effort brought success, as it did for the Iroquois, but the new political, diplomatic, and spiritual alignments just as often triggered more struggle and war, as it did between the Iroquois and the Hurons. But whatever else might be said for the achievements of Hienwatha and his contemporary visionaries, they succeeded in reshaping America, crafting what Europeans naively—but in this one sense quite correctly—called the New World. And in the process, they helped shape the entire Atlantic world, where the making of America would soon take center stage.

INTRODUCTION

For nearly a thousand years before the Iroquois formed their league, a combination of natural and human forces truly global in scope was having a profound impact throughout the Atlantic world. For example, in 632, a vibrant new religion swept out of the Arabian Peninsula to conquer much of the Mediterranean world. Eventually Europeans, who had themselves adopted a new and dynamic religion, Christianity, only a few centuries earlier, struck back in a protracted series of Crusades designed to break Islamic power. At the same time, climatic changes encouraged expansion by Viking warlords out of Scandinavia southward into the European mainland and westward all the way into North America. Together these expansive societies introduced new technologies and knowledge of distant and mysterious worlds that would engender an air of restlessness throughout Europe.

One of those mysterious worlds lay to the south of the forbidding Sahara Desert in Africa. There, as in both America and Europe, people had been dealing with changing conditions by crafting societies and economies that made the most of varying environments. When Islamic trading caravans began penetrating this region in the eighth century, they found highly developed cities that could draw on massive populations and natural resources to produce goods that were in great demand throughout the evolving Atlantic world. Like Native Americans, Africans too would be drawn into the restlessness that characterized this dynamic age.

Within decades after the Five Nations united, Christopher Columbus, a Genoese navigator in Spain's employ, rediscovered the **Western Hemisphere** while trying to find the hidden and distant worlds known to Islamic traders. Columbus's accident brought two historical streams together, and from that point onward, the history of each helped to form the future of both. On a global scale, this event launched a new era in human history. On a more local scale, it began a process we call *Making America.*

A World of Change

→ *How did environmental changes influence the development of various societies in North America during the millennia before the emergence of the Atlantic world?*

→ *What forces came into play in the centuries before 1500 that would launch Europeans on a program of outward exploration?*

→ *What factors in sub-Saharan African history helped lead to the development of the slave trade?*

Christopher Columbus's accidental encounter with the Western Hemisphere came after nearly a thousand years of increasing restlessness and dramatic change that affected all of the areas surrounding the Atlantic Ocean. After **millennia** of relative isolation, the natural and human environments in America were opened to the flow of people, animals, and goods from the rest of the Atlantic world. During the centuries before 1492, Christian monarchs and church leaders conducted a series of **Crusades** to wrest control of the **Holy Land** from the **Muslims.** As armies of Crusaders pushed their way into the region, they came into contact with many desirable commodities—fine silks, exotic spices, and precious stones and metals. As word spread of the finery Muslims obtained through trade with Africa and Asia, enterprising individuals began looking for ways to profit by supplying such luxuries to European consumers. At the same time, northern European **Vikings** were extending their holdings throughout many parts of Europe and westward all the way to North America. Both Crusaders and Vikings came into contact with

equally restless and vibrant societies in Africa and the Western Hemisphere, lending greater impetus to continuing exploration.

American Origins

American history, both before and after Columbus's intrusion, was shaped by the peculiar landscape that had developed over millennia in the Western Hemisphere. Floating plates of the earth's crust meet along the continent's western flank, rubbing and sometimes crashing together. Like a car fender after a collision, the earth has crumpled from the impact, forming rugged mountain ranges all the way from the Arctic to the extreme tip of South America. These collisions also left gaps and weak points in the earth's crust that gave rise to volcanoes and other geological activity. The resulting upheavals constantly changed the region's face: whole mountains were created and then destroyed, rich veins of minerals formed and then were buried, and varied local habitats emerged that would house an incredible array of plant and animal species.

While upheaval was shaping the western portion of the hemisphere, erosion was the sculptor in the east. Old granite rock formations were carved by winter frosts and running water. Thousands of rivers and streams crisscrossed the flattening land, carrying the

---

Western Hemisphere   When discussing the world longitudinally (lengthwise), geographers often divide the globe into two halves (hemispheres). The **Western Hemisphere** includes North America, Mexico, Central America, and South America; the **Eastern Hemisphere** includes Europe, Asia, and Africa.

millennia   The plural of *millennium*, a period of one thousand years.

Crusades   Military expeditions undertaken by European Christians in the eleventh through the thirteenth centuries to recover the Holy Land from the Muslims.

Holy Land   Palestine, which now is divided between Israel, Jordan, and Syria; called the Holy Land because it is the region in which the events described in the Old and New Testaments of the Bible took place; it is sacred to Christians, Jews, and Muslims.

Muslims   People who practice the religion of Islam, a monotheistic faith that accepts Mohammed as the chief and last prophet of God.

Vikings   Medieval Danish, Swedish, and Norwegian groups who responded to land shortages and climatic conditions in Scandinavia by taking to the sea and establishing communities in various parts of western Europe, Iceland, Greenland, and North America.

minerals eroding from higher ground to form rich and deep soil downstream. Upstream, often all that remained was bedrock with only a shallow cover of topsoil. Throughout these regions, too, different habitats supported varied life forms.

About 2.5 million years ago, a new force came to dominate the landscape with the onset of the Great Ice Age. During the height of the Ice Age, great sheets of ice advanced and withdrew across the world's continents. Glaciers moved southward, grinding away at the central part of North America, carving a flat corridor all the way from the Arctic Circle to the Gulf of Mexico. During the last ice advance, the Wisconsin glaciation, a sheet of ice more than 8,000 feet thick covered the northern half of both Europe and North America.

Not only did this massive ice sheet affect the underlying geology, but so much water was frozen into the glaciers that sea levels dropped as much as 450 feet. Migratory animals found vast regions closed to them by the imposing ice fields and ventured into areas exposed by the receding sea. One such region, Beringia, lay between present-day Siberia on the Asian continent and Alaska in North America (see Map 1.1). Now covered by the waters of the Bering Sea and Arctic Ocean, Beringia during the Ice Age was a dry, frigid grassland—a perfect grazing ground for animals such as giant bison and huge-tusked woolly mammoths. Hosts of predators, including large wolves and saber-toothed cats, followed them.

Sea levels were low enough to expose Beringia about 70,000 years ago, and the area remained above sea level more or less continually until about 10,000 years ago. Although movement southward into North America would have been difficult because of the rugged terrain and mountainous glaciers, determined migrating species may have begun populating the continent at any time between these dates.

What was true for other species may also have been true for humans. Each of the indigenous peoples who continue to occupy this hemisphere has its own account of its origins, some of which involve migration while others do not. Biological evidence suggests that the majority of Native Americans did migrate here; three distinct groups arrived seemingly at different times. The first of these groups, called the Paleo-Indians, probably entered the continent between 30,000 and 40,000 years ago, and their descendants eventually occupied the entire area of the Western Hemisphere. The second group, collectively called the Na-Dene people, appears to have arrived very near the end of the Wisconsin era, between 10,000 and 11,000 years ago, and their descendants are concentrated in

Although some archaeologists and many Native Americans dispute the accuracy of this forensic reconstruction, many experts consider this bust of the Kenniwick Man based on a skull discovered on the banks of the Columbia River in 1996 to be the best indication of both the deep antiquity and diversity of Native American peoples. *James Chatters and Thomas McClelland.*

the subarctic regions of Canada and the southwestern United States. The final group, the Arctic-dwelling Inuits, or Eskimos, arrived sometime later, perhaps after Beringia had flooded again (see Map 1.1). Though science paints a clear picture of this process, a great many anomalies exist. Recent archaeological finds and isolated discoveries such as that of the **Kenniwick Man** suggest that many different groups of migrating or truly indigenous people may have coexisted or succeeded each other over this 60,000-year period.

Until about 9,000 years ago the presence of Ice Age animals supplied human hunters with their primary source of meat and set the tempo for Paleo-Indian life. However as temperatures warmed, these species began to die out. The hunters faced the unpleasant prospect of following the large animals into extinction if they kept trying to survive by hunting big game.

People everywhere in North America abandoned big-game hunting and began to explore the newly emerging local environments for new sources of food, clothing, shelter, and tools. In the forests that grew

Kenniwick Man The name given to a human skeleton discovered next to the Columbia River near Kenniwick, Washington, in 1996. The skeleton is believed to be over 9,000 years old and appears to have facial features unlike those of other ancient Indian relics.

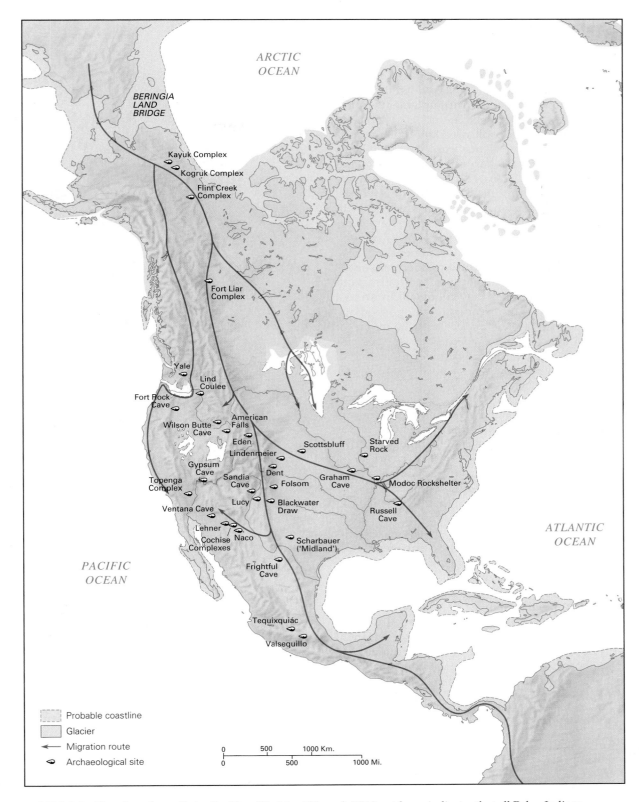

MAP 1.1 **First Americans Enter the New World** Although DNA evidence indicates that all Paleo-Indians were genetically related, at least two cultural groups moved into different parts of North America between 70,000 and 40,000 years ago. The Old Cordilleran group, to the west of the Rocky Mountains, and the Clovis group, to the east, left records of their passing at numerous sites, the most prominent of which are labeled here.

up to cover the eastern half of the continent, they developed finely polished stone tools, which they used to make functional and beautiful implements out of wood, bone, shell, and other materials. There and along the Pacific shore, people used large, heavy stone tools to hollow out massive tree trunks, making boats from which they could harvest food from inland waterways and from the sea. During this time domesticated dogs were introduced into North America, probably by newly arriving migrants from Asia. With boats for river transportation and dogs to help carry loads on land, Native American people were able to make the best use of their local environments by moving around to different spots during different seasons of the year. Thus they did not establish permanent towns or villages. Rather, they followed an annual round of movement from camp to camp—perhaps collecting shellfish for several weeks at the mouth of a river, then moving on to where wild strawberries were ripening, and later in the summer relocating to fields in which maturing wild onions or sunflower seeds could be harvested.

Although these ancestors of modern Native Americans believed in and celebrated the animating spirits of the plants and animals that they depended on for survival, they nonetheless engaged in large-scale environmental engineering. They used fire to clear forests of unwanted scrub and to encourage the growth of berries and other plants they found valuable. In this way they produced vegetables for themselves and also provided food for browsing animals such as deer, which increased in number while other species, less useful to people, declined. They also engaged in genetic engineering. A highly significant example comes from north-central Mexico, where, beginning perhaps 7,000 years ago, human intervention helped a wild strain of grass develop bigger seedpods with more nutritious seeds. Such intervention eventually transformed a fairly unproductive plant into an enormously nourishing and prolific food crop: **maize.**

Maize (corn), along with other engineered plants like beans, squash, and chilies, formed the basis for an agricultural revolution in North America, allowing many people to settle in larger villages for longer periods. Successful adaptation—including plant cultivation and eventually agriculture—along with population growth and the constructive use of spare time allowed some Indians in North America to build large, ornate cities. The map of ancient America is dotted with such centers. Beginning about 3,000 years ago, the Ohio and Mississippi Valleys became the home for a number of **mound builder** societies whose cities became trading and ceremonial centers

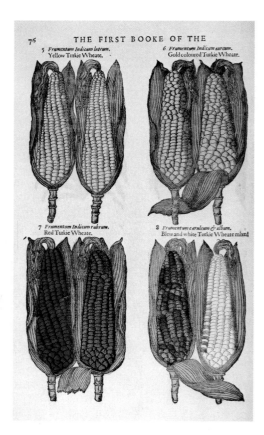

Maize (corn), which was genetically engineered by Native Americans in what is now Mexico some 7,000 years ago, became one of the staple food sources for many Indian groups in North America. As it passed through trade from one group to another, further genetic engineering produced the wide variety of corn types illustrated here. *The Granger Collection, New York.*

that had enormous economic and social outreach. Large quantities of both practical and purely decorative artifacts from all over North America have been found at these sites. Then, about 800 years ago, midwestern mound builder sites fell into decline, and the people who once had congregated there withdrew to separated villages or bands. No single satisfactory explanation accounts for why this happened, but it is

maize   Corn; the word *maize* comes from an Indian word for this plant.
mound builder   Name applied to a number of Native American societies, including the Adena, Hopewell, and Mississippian cultures, that constructed massive earthen mounds as monuments and building foundations.

IT MATTERS TODAY

NATIVE AMERICANS SHAPE A NEW WORLD

It may be hard to imagine why understanding the original peopling of North America and how Native cultures evolved during the millennia before Columbus could possibly matter to the history of the United States or, more specifically, to how we live our lives today. Without this chapter in our history, there would likely have been no United States history at all. Europeans in the fifteenth century lacked the tools, the organization, the discipline, and the economic resources to conquer a true wilderness—such a feat would have been the equivalent of our establishing a successful colony on the moon today. But the environmental and genetic engineering conducted through the millennia of North American history created a hospitable environment into which European crops, animals, and people could easily insinuate themselves. And while the descendants of those Europeans may fool themselves into thinking that they constructed an entirely new world in North America, the fact is that they simply grafted new growth onto ancient rootstock, creating the unique hybrid that is today's America.

- Describe what you think it would take technologically, economically, and politically for the United States to establish a successful permanent colony on the Moon. How would the presence of a biologically identical indigenous population change those requirements?
- In what ways are the Indian heritages of America still visible in our society today?

interesting to note that other changes were taking place at around this time elsewhere in the Atlantic world that would have profound effects on the American story.

Change and Restlessness in the Atlantic World

During the few centuries following the death of the prophet **Mohammed** in 632, Muslim Arabs, Turks, and **Moors** made major inroads into western Asia and northern Africa, eventually encroaching on Europe's southern and eastern frontiers (see Map 1.2). During these same years, Scandinavian Vikings, who controlled the northern frontiers of Europe, began expanding southward and westward. Accomplished and fearless seamen, the Vikings swept down Europe's western shore and through Russia by river to the Mediterranean. They also began colonizing Iceland and Greenland. Then, according to Viking sagas, a captain named Bjarni Herjólfsson sighted North America in 986. Fourteen years later, Viking chieftain Leif Eriksson led an expedition to the new land, and over the decades that followed, Vikings established several American colonies.

By about the year 1000, then, the heartland of Europe was surrounded by dynamic societies that served as conduits to a much broader world. Although Europeans resented and resisted both Viking and Islamic invasion, the newcomers brought with them tempting new technologies, food items, and expansive knowledge. These contributions not only enriched European culture but also improved the quality of life. For example, new farming methods increased food production so much that Europe began to experience a population explosion. Soon Europeans would begin turning this new knowledge and these new tools against the people who brought them.

Iberians launched a **Reconquista**, an effort to break Islamic rule on the peninsula, and in 1096, European Christians launched the first in a series of Crusades to sweep the Muslims from the Holy Land. With the aid of English Crusaders, Portugal attained independence in 1147. Meanwhile in the Holy Land, hordes of Crusaders captured key points only to be expelled by Muslim counterattacks. The effort to dislodge Islamic forces from Jerusalem and other sacred sites came largely to an end in 1291, but the struggle continued

Mohammed Born ca. 570 into an influential family in Mecca, on the Arabian Peninsula, around 610 Mohammed began having religious visions in which he was revealed as "the Messenger of God." The content of his various visions was recorded as the Qur'an, the sacred text that is the foundation for the Islamic religion.

Moors Natives of northern Africa who converted to Islam in the eighth century, becoming the major carriers of the Islamic religion and culture both to southern Africa and to the Iberian Peninsula (Spain and Portugal), which they conquered and occupied from the eighth century until their ouster in the late fifteenth century.

Reconquista The campaign undertaken by European Christians to recapture the Iberian Peninsula from the Moors.

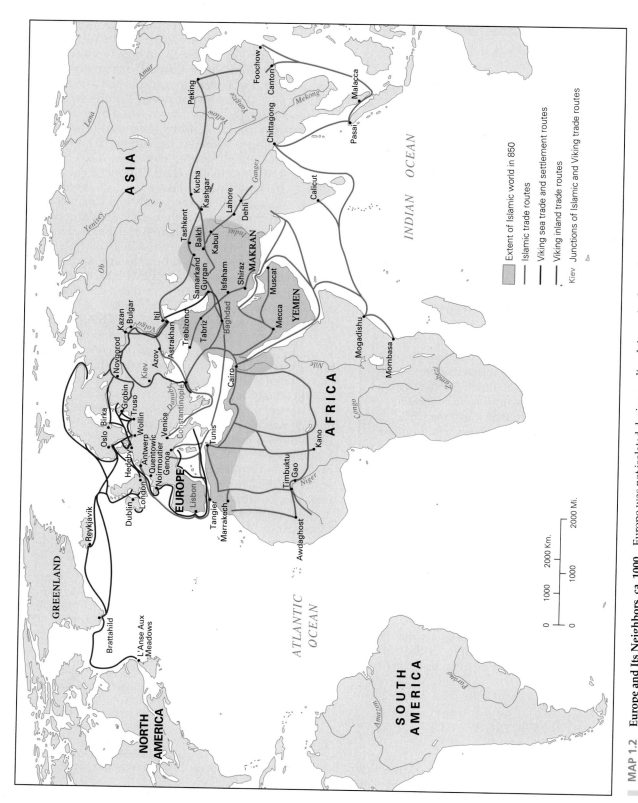

MAP 1.2   Europe and Its Neighbors, ca. 1000   Europe was not isolated during medieval times. As shown here, Viking and Islamic empires surrounded western Europe, and their trade routes crisscrossed the region, bringing faraway goods and ideas from many lands, including North America, long before Columbus "discovered" the New World.

Beginning in about the year 1000, two dynamic seafaring societies controlled the European continent's perimeters: various allied Islamic societies to the south and Vikings on all other sides. Both groups used innovative technologies and advanced geographical knowledge to continually expand their holdings, including holdings in North America. Their ships carried many new commodities as well as new knowledge into Europe, helping to create a restless, exploring spirit among Europeans. *Left: The Pierpont Morgan Library/Art Resource, NY; right: Bibliothèque Nationale, France.*

in the Iberian Peninsula. By 1380 Portugal's King John I had united that country's various principalities under his rule. In Spain, unification took much longer, but in 1469 **Ferdinand and Isabella**, heirs to the rival thrones of Aragon and Castile, married and created a united state in Spain. Twenty-three years later, in 1492, the Spanish subdued the last Moorish stronghold on the peninsula, completing the Reconquista.

Dealings with the Vikings in the north took a somewhat different turn. Although they maintained trading contacts with North America for several hundred years, the Vikings began to retreat in the middle of the 1300s. By 1450 or so, they had withdrawn entirely from their transatlantic colonies. The most likely cause of their departure was a shift in climate. Although experts disagree about the exact timing, it appears that at some time between 1350 and 1450 a significant climatic shift called the Little Ice Age began to affect the entire world. In the Arctic and subarctic, temperatures fell, snowfall increased, and sea ice became a major hazard to navigation. This shift made it impossible for the Vikings to practice the herding, farming, and trading that supported their economy in Greenland and elsewhere. Finding themselves cut off from a vibrant North Atlantic empire, Viking settlements in the British Isles, Russia, France, and elsewhere merged with local populations.

These Viking refugees often joined with their neighbors in recognizing the value of large-scale political organization. Consolidation began in France in around 1480, when Louis XI took control of five rival provinces to create a unified kingdom. Five years later in England, Henry Tudor and the House of Lancaster defeated the rival House of York in the Wars of the Roses, ending nearly a hundred years of civil war. Tudor, now styling himself King Henry VII, cemented this victory by marrying into the rival house, wedding Elizabeth of York to finally unify the English throne. As in Spain and Portugal, the formation of unified states in France and England opened the way to new expansive activity that would accelerate the creation of an Atlantic world.

The Complex World of Indian America

The world into which Vikings first sailed at the beginning of the second millennium and into which other

> **Ferdinand and Isabella**   Joint rulers of Spain (r. 1469–1504); their marriage in 1469 created a united Spain from the rival kingdoms of Aragon and Castile.

MAP 1.3 **Indian Culture Areas in North America** Social scientists who study Native American societies have divided them into a complex of "culture areas": regions in which cultural similarities outnumber differences between resident groups. While there is some disagreement among scholars about the exact number and extent of specific areas, this map provides a representative view of the various culture areas in North America.

Europeans would intrude half a millennium later was not some static realm stuck in the Stone Age. Native American societies were every bit as progressive, adaptable, and historically dynamic as those that would invade their homes. In fact, adaptive flexibility characterized Indian life throughout North America, and so the vast variety in environmental conditions that characterize the continent led to the emergence of enormous differences between various Indian groups. **Anthropologists** have tried to make the extremely complicated cultural map of North America understandable by dividing the continent into a series of culture areas—regions where the similarities among native societies were greater than the differences. Map 1.3 shows eleven such areas: Arctic, Subarctic, Northwest Coast, Plateau, California, Great Basin, Southwest, Great Plains, Eastern Woodlands, Southeast, and Mexico Middle-America.

In the southeastern region of North America, peoples speaking Siouan, Caddoan, and Muskogean languages formed vibrant agricultural and urban societies that had ties with exchange centers farther north as well as with adventurous traders from Mexico. At places like Natchez, fortified cities housed gigantic pyramids, and farmland radiating outward provided food for large residential populations. These were true cities and, like their counterparts in Europe and Asia, were magnets attracting ideas, technologies, and religious notions from the entire hemisphere.

Farther north, in the region called the Eastern Woodlands, people lived in smaller villages and combined agriculture with hunting and gathering. The Iroquois, for example, lived in towns numbering three thousand or more people, changing locations only as soil fertility, firewood, and game became exhausted. Before Hienwatha and the formation of the Iroquois League, each village was largely self-governed by clan mothers and their chosen male civil servants. Each town was made up of a group of **longhouses**, structures often 60 feet or more in length.

A tradition that may go back to the time when the Iroquois lived as nomadic hunters and gatherers dictated that men and women occupy different spheres of existence. The women's world was the world of plants, healing, nurturing, and order. The men's was the world of animals, hunting, and war. By late **pre-Columbian** times, the Iroquois had become strongly agricultural, and because plants were in the women's sphere, women occupied places of high social and economic status in Iroquois society. Families were matrilineal, meaning that they traced their descent through the mother's line, and matrilocal, meaning that a man left his home to move in with his wife's family upon

Iroquois towns consisted of rows of longhouses, often surrounded by defensive walls. This partial reconstruction of a sixteenth-century Iroquois town that stood near what is now London, Ontario, illustrates how such sites looked. The staked areas to the right of the rebuilt longhouses show where neighboring longhouses used to stand. *Richard Alexander Cooke III.*

marriage. Women distributed the rights to cultivate specific fields and controlled the harvest.

Variations on this pattern were typical throughout the Eastern Woodlands and in the neighboring Great Plains and Southwest. Having strong ties with agriculturalists in the east, Plains groups such as the Mandans

anthropologists Scholars who study human behavior and culture in the past or the present.

longhouses Communal dwellings, usually built of poles and bark and having a central hallway with family apartments on either side (see illustration).

pre-Columbian Existing in the Americas before the arrival of Columbus.

began settling on bluffs overlooking the many streams that eventually drain into the Missouri River. Living in substantial houses insulated against the cold winters, these people divided their time among hunting, crop raising, and trade. Over a five-hundred-year period, populations increased, and agricultural settlements expanded. By 1300, such villages could be found along every stream ranging southward from North Dakota into present-day Kansas.

In the Southwest, groups with strong ties to Mexico began growing corn as early as 3,200 years ago, but they continued to follow a migratory life until about 400 when they began building larger and more substantial houses and limiting their migrations. The greatest change, however, came during the eighth century, when a shift in climate made the region drier and a pattern of late-summer thunderstorms triggered dangerous and erosive flash floods.

There seem to have been two quite different responses to this change in climate. A group called the Anasazi expanded their agricultural ways, cooperating to build flood-control dams and irrigation canals. The need for cooperative labor meant forming larger communities, and between about 900 and 1300 the Anasazi built whole cities of multistory apartment houses along the high cliffs, safe from flooding but near their irrigated fields. In these densely populated towns Anasazi craft specialists such as potters, weavers, basket makers, and tool smiths manufactured goods for the community while farmers tended fields and priests attended to the spiritual needs of the society.

Another contingent of southwestern Indians abandoned the region, moving southward into Mexico. Here they came upon the remnants of classical city-states like Teotihuacán. One of several highly developed societies of central Mexico, Teotihuacán was the largest city-state in the Western Hemisphere, with a population of nearly 200,000. However, by around the year 600, Teotihuacán and other such societies were in decline. Over the next several hundred years, migrants from southwestern North America—so-called Chichimecs or "wild tribes"—borrowed architectural and agricultural skills from the fallen societies and built new monumental cities. The first of these, Tula, entered its heyday in about the year 1000, but a civil war two centuries later brought that civilization to an end. Shortly thereafter, another Chichimec tribe rose to prominence in central Mexico. The **Aztecs** arrived in the Valley of Mexico soon after 1200, settling on a small island in the middle of a brackish lake. From this unappealing center, a series of strong leaders used a combination of diplomacy and brutal warfare to establish a **tributary empire** that eventually ruled as many as 6 million people.

Other major changes occurred in the Southwest after 1300. During the last quarter of the thirteenth century, a long string of summer droughts and bitterly cold winters forced the Anasazi to abandon their cities. They disappeared as a people, splitting into smaller communities that eventually became the various Pueblo groups. At the same time, an entirely new population entered the region. These hunter-gatherers brought new technologies, including the bow and arrow, into the Southwest. About half of them continued to be hunter-gatherers, while the rest borrowed cultivating and home-building techniques from the Pueblos. Europeans who later entered the area called the hunter-gatherers Apaches and the settled agriculturalists Navajos.

In other regions agriculture was practiced only marginally, if at all. In areas like the Great Basin, desert conditions made agriculture too risky, and in California, the Northwest Coast, and the intermountain Plateau (see Map 1.3), the bounty of available wild foods made it unnecessary. In these regions, hunting and gathering remained the chief occupations. For example, the Nez Percés and their neighbors living in the Plateau region occupied permanent village sites in the winter but did not stay together in a single group all year. Rather, they formed task groups—temporary villages that came together to share the labor required to harvest a particular resource—and then went their separate ways when the task was done. These task groups brought together not only people who lived in different winter villages but often people from different tribes and even different language groups. In such groups, political authority passed among those who were best qualified to supervise particular activities. If the task group was hunting, the best and most senior hunters—almost always men—exercised political authority. If the task group was gathering roots, then the best and most senior diggers—almost always women—ruled. Thus among such hunting-gathering people, political organization changed from season to season, and social status depended on what activities were most important to the group at a particular time.

Aztecs   An Indian group living in central Mexico; the Aztecs used military force to dominate nearby tribes; their civilization was at its peak at the time of the Spanish conquest.

tributary empire   An empire in which subjects rule themselves but make payments, called tribute, to an imperial government in return for protection and services.

After being separated from the rest of Africa by the formation of the Sahara Desert, the Bantu people—aided perhaps by their mastery of iron-smelting technology—expanded throughout the sub-Saharan portion of the continent. This painting rendered by non-Bantu Bushmen, records a battle between themselves and Bantus. Note the relatively huge size and menacing quality of the Bantus compared with the retreating Bushmen, an indication of how the newly dominant group was perceived by its neighbors. *Private Collection.*

As these examples illustrate, variations in daily life and social arrangements in pre-Columbian North America reflected variations in climate, soil conditions, food supplies, and cultural heritages from place to place across the vast continent. But despite the enormous size of the continent and the amazing variety of cultures spread across it, economic and social connections within and between ecological regions tied the people together in complex ways. For example, varieties of shell found only along the Northwest Pacific Coast passed in trade to settlements as far away as Florida, having been passed from hand to hand over thousands of miles of social and physical space.

A World of Change in Africa

Like North America, Africa was home to an array of societies that developed in response to varying natural and historical conditions. But unlike contemporary Indian groups, Africans maintained continual if perhaps only sporadic contacts with societies in Europe and Asia, societies to which they had at one time been intimately linked.

Tendrils of trade between the Mediterranean and **sub-Saharan Africa** can be traced back to ancient Egypt and before, but the creation of the Sahara Desert, the product of a 1,500-year-long drought that began about 4,500 years ago, cut most of Africa off from the fertile areas of the Mediterranean coast. The people living south of the new desert were forced largely

to reinvent civilization in response to changing conditions. They abandoned the wheat and other grain crops that had predominated in earlier economies, domesticating new staples such as **millet** and native strains of rice. They also abandoned the cattle and horses that had been common in earlier times, adopting sheep and goats, which were better suited to arid environments. Depending on immediate conditions, groups could establish large villages and live on a balance of vegetables, meat, and milk or, if necessary, shift over to a purely nomadic lifestyle following their herds.

Social organization tended to follow a similar adaptive strategy. The entire region was dominated by a single group of people, speakers of closely related dialects of the common Bantu language (see Map 1.4). Among these Bantu descendants and their neighbors, the social structure was based on the belief that large subgroups were descended from a common **fictive ancestor.** These

sub-Saharan Africa   The region of Africa south of the Sahara Desert.

millet   A large family of grain grasses that produce nutritious, carbohydrate-rich seeds used for both human and animal feed.

fictive ancestor   A mythical figure believed by a social group to be its founder and from whom all members are believed to be biologically descended.

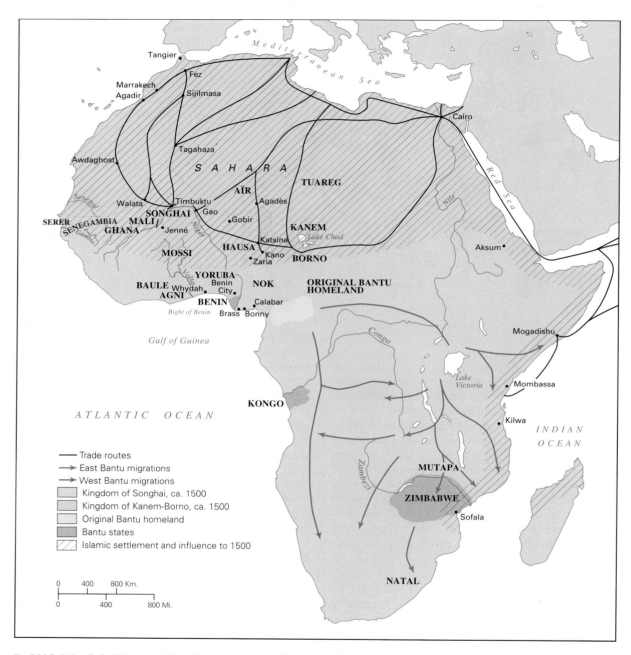

MAP 1.4 Sub-Saharan Africa Before Sustained European Contact During the many centuries that followed the formation of the Sahara Desert, Bantu people expanded throughout the southern half of Africa. They and other groups established a number of powerful kingdoms, the capitals of which served as major trading centers among these kingdoms and for Islamic traders, who finally penetrated the desert after the year 750.

larger organizations were then subdivided into smaller and smaller groups, each independent—as a modern nuclear family might be—but tied through an elaborate family tree to hundreds or even thousands of other similar groups.

The status of each group was determined by seniority in the line of descent—those descended from the oldest offspring of the common ancestor were socially and politically superior to those descended from younger branches. This fundamental hierarchy created

Introducing camels as draft animals made it possible for Arab and other traders to penetrate the forbidding Sahara Desert to open up a highly profitable trade with sub-Saharan states that were rich with gold, ivory, and other valuable commodities. This gold and diamond miniature (the sculpture is only about two-and-a-half inches tall) celebrates the riches that these animals carried out of Africa. *The Metropolitan Museum of Art, Gift of The Shaw Foundation, Inc., 1959. (59.44.1) Photograph (c) 1966 The Metropolitan Museum of Art.*

an organizational structure that permitted large-group cooperation and management when appropriate but also permitted each small band to function independently when conditions required. Within each group, seniority also determined political and social status: the eldest descendant of the common ancestor within each group held superior power, whereas those on the lowest branch of the family tree were treated more or less as slaves.

Much of the technology in place in sub-Saharan Africa can be traced to common roots that preceded the formation of the desert. Evidence suggests that pottery and simple metallurgy were part of an ancient pan-African technological tradition. However, sometime between two and three thousand years ago, sub-Saharan groups appear to have discovered iron smelting. Inventing a furnace shaped like a long tube that permitted both the high heat and air draft necessary for melting iron ore, craftsmen were able to make use of abundant raw iron deposits common in southern Africa to produce tools, vessels, and weapons. This discovery may, in fact, have aided the Bantu-speakers in their extensive expansion throughout most of the continent. It certainly gave African groups an edge in

carving settlements out of the jungles and grasslands. Often, large cities with elaborate social hierarchies grew in neighborhoods where iron and other ores were particularly abundant. These would then become centers for trade as well as political hubs, the seeds from which later kingdoms and empires would sprout.

These trading centers became particularly important when Islamic expansion brought new, outside sources for trade into the sub-Saharan world. The first mention of trade between Islamic adventurers and African communities stems from the eighth century, and it seems to have developed slowly over the next several hundred years. One catalyst to the trade growth was the introduction of the camel as a draft animal. Native to Asia and the Arabian Peninsula, camels were ideally suited for crossing the inhospitable desert, making it possible to establish regular caravan routes that linked sub-Saharan trading centers with the outside world. Increasingly after 1100, metal goods—iron, gold, and precious gems—and slaves were carried across the desert by Arab, Berber, and other Muslim traders, who gave African middlemen silks, spices, and other foreign goods in exchange. This trade tended to enhance the power of African elites, leading to ever larger and more elaborate states.

Exploiting Atlantic Opportunities

→ *How did various groups of Europeans seek to exploit opportunities that arose from new discoveries leading up to and following 1492?*

→ *Why did Columbus's entry into the Western Hemisphere prove to be a major turning point in the development of the Atlantic world?*

→ *How did Native Americans and Africans respond initially to European expansion?*

Dynamic forces in America, Europe, Africa, and beyond seemed unavoidably to be drawing the disparate societies that occupied the Atlantic shore into a complex world of mutual experience. But this process was not automatic. Enterprising people throughout the globe seized opportunities created by the spirit of restlessness and the merging of historical streams, advancing the process and giving it peculiar shape. Generally seeking profits for themselves and advancement for their own nations, tribes, or classes, those who sought to exploit the emerging new world nonetheless had enormous impact on the lives of all who occupied it. The process of outreach and historical evolution that helped to launch the American experience grew directly from these efforts at exploitation.

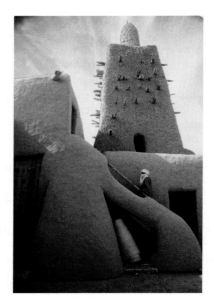
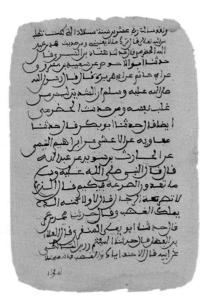

During the years before European penetration into the region, western Africa became a center for Islamic culture. Islamic scholars congregated at holy sites like the Sankoré Mosque in Timbuktu (left). Here they discussed Islamic law and wrote scholarly treatises like Sayyid al-Mukhtur ibn Ahmed ibn Abi Bakr al-Kunti al-Kabir's "An Argument for Peace," which emphasized the Qur'an's message of peace and harmony (right). Writings like these not only helped win more Africans over to Islam but also influenced Qur'anic scholarship throughout the expanding Muslim world. *Left: Photo © www.danheller.com; right: Mamma Haidara Commemorative Library, Timbuktu, Mali.*

The Portuguese, Africa, and Plantation Slavery

The first of the European states to pull itself together was also the first to challenge Islamic dominance in both the Asian and African trade. Portugal's John I encouraged exploration by establishing a school of navigation on his kingdom's southwestern shore. Under the directorship of John's son **Henry the Navigator**, the school sent numerous expeditions in search of new sources of wealth. By the 1430s, the Portuguese had discovered and taken control of islands off the western shore of Africa, and within thirty years Prince Henry's protégés had pushed their way to Africa itself, opening relations with the Songhai Empire.

The **Songhai Empire** was typical of the sub-Saharan trading states that emerged through Muslim contacts (see Map 1.4). As was common in the region, the Songhai state consisted of numerous smaller societies, all related through a common ancestor and organized along hierarchical lines. Society remained largely village based, with slaves at the bottom, skilled craftsmen in the middle, and a small noble class at the top. These nobles assembled in Timbuktu, a trading hub and the Songhai capital, which became a cosmopolitan center

where African and Islamic influences met. Its art, architecture, and the accomplishments of its scholars impressed all who ventured there. From Timbuktu, Songhai traders shipped valuable trade goods across the Sahara by means of caravans. The Portuguese, however, offered speedier shipment and higher profits by carrying trade goods directly to Europe by sea.

By the end of the fifteenth century, Portuguese navigators had gained control over the flow of prized items such as gold, ivory, and spices out of West Africa, and Portuguese colonizers were growing sugar and other crops on the newly conquered Azores and Canary Islands. From the beginning of the sixteenth century onward, the Portuguese also became increasingly involved in slave trafficking, at first to their own plantations and then to Europe itself. By 1550, Por-

Henry the Navigator   Prince who founded an observatory and school of navigation and directed voyages that helped build Portugal's colonial empire.

Songhai Empire   A large empire in West Africa whose capital was Timbuktu; its rulers accepted Islam around the year 1000.

tuguese ships were carrying African slaves throughout the world.

The Continued Quest for Asian Trade

Meanwhile, the Portuguese continued to venture outward. In 1487 Bartolomeu Dias became the first European to reach the **Cape of Good Hope** at the southern tip of Africa. Ten years later Vasco da Gama sailed around the cape and launched the Portuguese exploration of eastern Africa and the Indian Ocean.

By the end of the fifteenth century, England, Spain, and France were vying with Portugal to find the shortest, cheapest, and safest sea route between Europe and Asia. Because of its early head start, Portugal remained fairly cautious in its explorations, hugging the coast around Africa before crossing the ocean to India. As latecomers, Spain and England could not afford to take such a conservative approach to exploration. Voyagers from those countries took advantage of technologies borrowed from China and the Arab world to expand their horizons. From China, Europeans acquired the magnetic compass, which allowed mariners to know roughly in what direction they were sailing, even when out of sight of land. An Arab invention, the **astrolabe**, which allowed seafarers to calculate the positions of heavenly bodies, also reduced the uncertainty of navigation. These inventions— together with improvements in steering mechanisms and hull design that improved a captain's control over his ship's direction, speed, and stability—made voyages much less risky.

Eager to capitalize on the new technology and knowledge, an ambitious sailor from the Italian port city of Genoa, **Christopher Columbus**, approached John II of Portugal in 1484 and asked him to support a voyage westward from Portugal, across the Atlantic, to the East Indies. The king refused when his geographers warned that Columbus had underestimated the distance. Undeterred, Columbus peddled his idea to various European governments over the next several years but found no one willing to take the risk. Finally, in 1492, Ferdinand and Isabella's defeat of the Moors provided Columbus with an opportunity.

The Spanish monarchs had just thrown off Islamic rule in the coastal province of Granada and were eager to break into overseas trading, dominated in the east by the Arabs and in the south and west by the Portuguese. Ferdinand and Isabella agreed to equip three ships in exchange for a short, safe route to the Orient. On August 3, 1492, Columbus and some ninety

sailors departed on the *Niña, Pinta,* and *Santa Maria* for the uncharted waters of the Atlantic. More than three months later, they finally made landfall. Columbus thought he had arrived at the East Indies, but in fact he had reached the islands we now call the **Bahamas**.

Over the next ten weeks, Columbus explored the mysteries of the Caribbean, making landfalls on the islands now known as Cuba and Hispaniola. He collected spices, coconuts, bits of gold, and some native captives. He described the natives as "a loving people" who, he thought, would make excellent servants. Columbus then returned to Spain, where he was welcomed with great celebration and rewarded with backing for three more voyages. Over the next several years, the Spanish gained a permanent foothold in the region that Columbus had discovered and became aware that the area was a world entirely new to them.

England, like Spain, was jealous of Portugal's trade monopoly, and in 1497 Henry VII commissioned another Italian mariner, Giovanni Caboto, to search for a sea route to India. **John Cabot**, as the English called him, succeeded in crossing the North Atlantic, arriving in the area that Leif Eriksson had colonized nearly five hundred years earlier. Shortly thereafter, another Italian, **Amerigo Vespucci**, sailing under the Spanish flag, sighted the northeastern shore of South America and sailed northward into the Caribbean in search of a passage to the East. Finally, in 1524, Giovanni da Verrazano, sailing for France, explored the Atlantic coast of North America, charting the coastline of what later became the thirteen English mainland colonies.

Cape of Good Hope   A point of land projecting into the Atlantic Ocean at the southern tip of Africa; to trade with Asia, European mariners had to sail around the cape to pass from the South Atlantic into the Indian Ocean.

astrolabe   An instrument for measuring the position of the sun and stars; using these readings, navigators could calculate their latitude—their distance north or south of the equator.

Christopher Columbus   (Cristoforo Colombo) Italian explorer in the service of Spain who attempted to reach Asia by sailing west from Europe, thereby arriving in America in 1492.

Bahamas   A group of islands in the Atlantic Ocean east of Florida and Cuba.

John Cabot   (Giovanni Caboto) Italian explorer who led the English expedition that sailed along the North American mainland in 1497.

Amerigo Vespucci   Italian explorer of the South American coast; Europeans named America after him.

A New Transatlantic World

At first, European monarchs greeted the discovery of a new world as bad news: they wanted access to the riches of Asia, not contact with some undiscovered place. As knowledge of the **New World** spread, the primary goal of exploration became finding a route around or through it—the fabled **Northwest Passage**. But gradually Europeans learned that the new land had attractions of its own.

Ambitious adventurers from Britain, France, and Iberia began exploring the fertile fishing grounds off the northern shores of North America. By 1506, such voyages became so commonplace and so profitable that the king of Portugal placed a 10 percent tax on fish imported from North America in an effort to harness this new source of wealth. But these voyages did more than feed the European imagination and the continent's appetite for seafood. It appears that these fishermen established temporary camps along the shores of North America to provide land support for their enterprises. Gradually, as the Native Americans and the fishermen came to know each other, they began to exchange goods. Europeans, even relatively poor fishermen, had many things that the Indians lacked: copper pots, knives, jewelry, woolen blankets, and hundreds of other novelties. For their part, the Indians provided firewood, food, ivory, and furs. Apparently the trade grew quickly. By 1534, when **Jacques Cartier** made the first official exploration of the Canadian coast for the French government, he was approached by party after party of Indians offering to trade furs for the goods he carried. He could only conclude that many other Europeans had come before him.

The presence of explorers such as Verrazano and Cartier and of unknown numbers of anonymous fishermen and part-time traders had several effects on the native population. The Micmacs, Hurons, and other northeastern Indian groups approached the invading Europeans in friendship, eager to trade and to learn more about the strangers. In part this response was a sign of natural curiosity, but it also reflected some serious changes taking place in the native world of North America.

As we have noted, the onset of the Little Ice Age had far-reaching effects. As the climate grew colder, hunter-gatherers in the subarctic responded by withdrawing farther south, where they began to encroach on Algonquin and Iroquoian Indians. Meanwhile, the deteriorating climate made it more difficult for groups like the Iroquois to depend on their corn crops for food. Forced to rely more on hunting and gathering, the Iroquois had to expand their territory, and in doing so they came into conflict with their neighbors. As warfare became more common, groups increasingly formed alliances for mutual defense—systems like the Iroquois League. And Indians found it beneficial to welcome European newcomers into their midst—as trading partners bearing new tools, as allies in the evolving conflicts with neighboring Indian groups, and as powerful magicians whose **shamans** might provide explanations and remedies for the hard times that had befallen them.

The Challenges of Mutual Discovery

→ *How did Native Americans respond to increasing contact with European explorers and settlers?*

→ *In what ways did Europeans seek to incorporate Africans and Native Americans into their world of understanding?*

→ *In what ways was the world made different through the process called the Columbian Exchange?*

Europeans approached the New World with certain ideas in mind and defined what they found there in terms that reflected what they already believed. American Indians approached Europeans in the same way. Both of these groups—as well as Africans—were thrown into a new world of understanding that challenged many of their fundamental assumptions. They also exchanged material goods that affected their physical well-being profoundly.

New World   A term that Europeans used during the period of early contact and colonization to refer to the Americas, especially in the context of their discovery and colonization.

Northwest Passage   The rumored and much-hoped-for water route from Europe to Asia by way of North America was sought by early explorers.

Jacques Cartier   French explorer who, by navigating the St. Lawrence River in 1534, gave France its primary claim to territories in the New World.

shamans   People who act as a link between the visible material world and an invisible spirit world; a shaman's duties include healing, conducting religious ceremonies, and foretelling the future.

 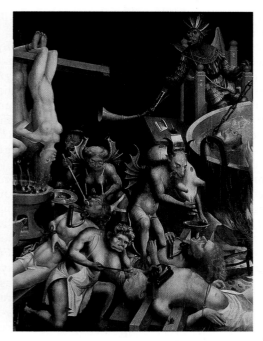

Europeans had trouble fitting American Indians into their preconceived ideas about the world. Native Americans were sometimes cast as noble savages and other times as devils. The Brazilian Indian shown in these two works illustrates the conflicting views. In one, the feather-clad Indian is shown as a wise magus paying homage to the Christ-child; in the other, an Indian devil wears the same costume while presiding over the tortures of Hell. *Left: "Adoration of the Magi" by Master of Viseu. Museu de Grao Vasco; right: "Inferno" anonymous, Portuguese. Giraudon/ Art Resource, NY.*

A Meeting of Minds in America

Most Europeans had a firm sense of how the world was arranged, who occupied it, and how they had come to be where they were. The existence of America—and even more the presence there of American Indians—challenged that secure knowledge. In the first stages of mutual discovery in America, most Europeans were content mentally to reshape what they found in the New World to fit with what they expected to find. Columbus expected to find India and Indians, and he believed that was precisely what he had found. Other Europeans understood that America was a new land and that the Indians were a new people, but they attempted to fit both into the cosmic map outlined in the Bible.

Columbus's initial comments about the American Indians set the tone for many future encounters. "Of anything that they possess, if it be asked of them, they never say no," Columbus wrote; "on the contrary, they invite you to share it and show as much love as if their hearts went with it." Such writings were widely circulated in Europe and led to a perception of the Indians as noble savages, men and women free from the temptations and vanities of modern civilization.

Not all Europeans held this view of American Indians. Amerigo Vespucci, for one, found them less than noble. "They marry as many wives as they please," he explained. "The son cohabits with mother, brother with sister, male cousin with female, and any man with the first woman he meets. . . . Beyond the fact that they have no church, no religion and are not **idolaters**, what more can I say?" Much more, actually. Vespucci reported that the Indians practiced cannibalism and prostitution and decorated themselves in gaudy and "monstrous" ways.

idolaters   A person who practices *idolatry*, idol worship, a practice forbidden in the Judeo-Christian and Muslim traditions.

In some ways, the arrival of Europeans may have been easier for American Indians to understand and explain than the existence of American Indians was for the Europeans. To Indians, the world was alive, animated by a spiritual force that was both universal and intelligent. This force took on many forms. Some of these forms were visible in the everyday world of experience, some were visible only at special times, and some were never visible. Social ties based on fictive kinship and **reciprocal trade** linked all creatures—human and nonhuman—together into a common cosmos. These connections were chronicled in myth and were maintained through ritual, which often involved the exchange of ceremonial items believed to have spiritual value. Such objects included quartz and volcanic-glass crystals, copper, mica, shells, and other rare and light-reflecting objects. In the pre-Columbian trading world, such prized goods passed from society to society, establishing a spiritual bond between the initial givers and the eventual receivers, even though the two groups might never meet.

Europeans and European goods slipped easily into this ceremonial trading system. The trade items that the Europeans generally offered to American Indians on first contact—glass beads, mirrors, brass bells—resembled closely the items that the Indians traditionally used to establish friendly spiritual and economic relations with strangers. The perceived similarity of the trade goods offered by the Europeans led Indians to accept the newcomers as simply another new group in the complex social cosmos uniting the spiritual and material worlds.

On the other hand, Europeans perceived such items as worthless trinkets, valuing instead Indian furs and Indian land. This difference in perception became a major source of misunderstanding and conflict. To the Indians, neither the furs nor the land was of much value because by their understanding they did not "own" either. According to their beliefs, all things had innate spirits and belonged to themselves. Thus passing animal pelts along to Europeans was simply extending the social connection that had brought the furs into Indian hands in the first place. Similarly, according to Indian belief, people could not own land: the land was seen as a living being—a mother—who feeds, clothes, and houses people as long as she receives proper respect. The idea of buying or selling land was unthinkable to Indians. When Europeans offered spiritually significant objects in exchange for land on which to build, farm, or hunt, Indians perceived the offer as an effort to join an already existing relationship, and not as a contract transferring ownership.

The Columbian Exchange

Even though Europeans and American Indians saw some similarities in each other, their worlds differed greatly, sometimes in ways hidden to both groups. The natural environments of these worlds were different, and the passage of people, plants, and animals among Europe, Africa, and North America wrought profound changes in all three continents. Historians call this process the **Columbian Exchange**.

Perhaps the most tragic trade among the three continents came about as the direct and unavoidable consequence of human contact. During the period leading up to the age of exploration, many Europeans lost their lives to epidemic diseases. The Black Death of the fourteenth century, for example, wiped out over a third of Europe's population. Exposure to smallpox, measles, typhus, and other serious diseases had often had devastating results, but Europeans gradually developed resistance to infection. In contrast, the Indian peoples whom Columbus and other European explorers encountered lived in an environment in which contagious diseases were never a serious threat until the Europeans arrived. They had no **acquired immunity** to the various bacteria and viruses that Europeans carried. As a result, the new diseases spread very rapidly and were much more deadly among the native peoples than they were among Europeans.

Controversy rages over the number of Indians killed by imported European diseases. Estimates of how many people lived in America north of Mexico in 1492 run from a high of 25 million to a low of 1 million. At the moment, most scholars accept a range of from 3 to 10 million. Even if the most conservative estimate is correct, the raw numbers of people who died of smallpox, typhus, measles, and other imported diseases were enormous. In areas of early and continuing association between Europeans and Indians, between 90 and 95 percent of the native population appear to

---

reciprocal trade   A system of trading in which the objective is equal exchange of commodities rather than profit.

Columbian Exchange   The exchange of people, plants, and animals between Europe, Africa, and North America that occurred after Columbus's arrival in the New World.

acquired immunity   Resistance or partial resistance to a disease; acquired immunity develops in a population over time as a result of exposure to harmful bacteria or viruses.

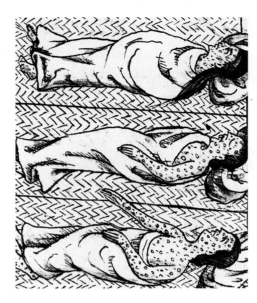

European diseases killed many millions of Indians during the initial stages of contact because they had no immunity to such epidemic illnesses as influenza, measles, and plague. Smallpox was one of the deadliest of these imported diseases. This Aztec drawing illustrates smallpox's impact, from the initial appearance of skin lesions through death. Not only were traditional Indian medical practices unable to cure such diseases, but physical contact between shamans and patients actually helped to spread them. *Biblioteca Medicea Laurenziana.*

have died of disease during the first century of contact. Although the percentage was probably lower in areas where contact was infrequent and where native populations were sparse, disease took a terrible toll as it followed the lines of kinship and trade that held native North America together.

Disease, however, did not flow in only one direction. Some diseases that originated in Africa found their way to both North America and Europe and at least one, **syphilis**, may have originated in the Western Hemisphere and migrated eastward. American Indians appear to have been less debilitated physically by syphilis, to which they may have possessed partial immunity. Africans were largely unaffected by various **malarial** fevers that ravaged both European and native populations. Europeans found measles to be a mildly unpleasant childhood disease, but for both Africans and Indians it was a mass killer. The march of exchanged diseases across the North American landscape and their effects on various populations provided a constant backdrop for the continent's and for global history.

Less immediate but perhaps equally extreme ecological effects arose from the passage of plants among Europe, North America, and Africa. The introduction of plants into the New World extended a process that had been taking place for centuries in the Old World. Trade with Asia had carried exotic plants such as bananas, sugar cane, and rice into Africa as early as 2,300 years ago. From Africa, these plants were imported to Iberian-claimed islands such as the Canaries and eventually to America, where, along with cotton, indigo, coffee, and other imports, they would become **cash crops** on European-controlled plantations. Grains such as wheat, barley, and millet were readily transplanted to some areas in North America, as were grazing grasses and various vegetables, including turnips, spinach, and cabbage.

North American plants also traveled from west to east in the Columbian Exchange. Leading the way in economic importance was tobacco, a stimulant used widely in North America for ceremonial purposes and broadly adopted by Europeans and Africans as a recreational drug. Another stimulant, cocoa, also enjoyed significant popularity among Old World consumers. In addition, New World vegetables helped to revolutionize world food supplies. Remarkably easy to grow, maize thrived virtually everywhere. In addition, the white potato, tomato, **manioc**, squash, and beans native to the Western Hemisphere were soon cultivated throughout the world. Animals also moved in the Columbian Exchange. Europeans brought horses, pigs, cattle, oxen, sheep, goats, and domesticated fowl to America, where their numbers soared.

The transplanting of European grain crops and domesticated animals reshaped the American landscape. Changing the contours of the land by clearing trees and undergrowth, and by plowing and fencing altered the flow of water, the distribution of seeds, the nesting of birds, and the movement of native animals.

syphilis An infectious disease usually transmitted through sexual contact; if untreated, it can lead to paralysis and death.

malarial Related to malaria, an infectious disease characterized by chills, fever, and sweating; malaria is often transmitted through mosquito bites.

cash crops A crop raised in large quantities for sale rather than for local or home consumption.

manioc Also called cassava, a root vegetable native to South America that became a staple food source throughout the tropical world after 1500.

Gradually, imported livestock pushed aside native species, and imported plants choked out indigenous ones.

Probably the most important and far-reaching environmental impact of the Columbian Exchange was its overall influence on human populations. Although exchanged diseases killed many millions of Indians and lesser numbers of Africans and Europeans, the transplantation of North American plants significantly expanded food production in what had been marginal areas of Europe and Africa. At the same time, the environmental changes that Europeans wrought along the Atlantic shore of North America permitted the region to support many more people than it had sustained under Indian cultivation. The overall result in Europe and Africa was a population explosion that eventually spilled over to repopulate a devastated North America.

New Worlds in Africa and America

As the Columbian Exchange redistributed plants, animals, and populations among Europe, Africa, and North America, it permanently altered the history of both hemispheres. In North America, for example, the combination of disease, environmental transformation, and immigrant population pressure changed American Indian life and culture in profound ways.

Clearly, imported disease had the most ruinous influence on the lives of Indians. Cooperative labor was required for hunting and gathering, and native groups that continued to depend on those activities faced extinction if disease caused a shortage of labor. Also, most societies in North America were **nonliterate**: elders and storytellers passed on their collective knowledge from one generation to another. Wholesale death by disease wiped out these bearers of practical, religious, and cultural knowledge. The result of this loss was confusion and disorientation among survivors. In an effort to avert extinction, remnant groups banded together to share labor and lore. Members of formerly self-sustaining kinship groups joined together in composite villages or, in some cases, intertribal leagues or confederacies. And the devastation that European diseases wrought eased the way for the deeper penetration of Europeans into North America as Indians sought alliances with the newcomers in order to gain new tools, new sources of information, and new military partners, pushing Indians into increasingly tangled relationships with Europeans.

The Columbian Exchange also severely disrupted life in Africa. Africa had long been a key supplier of labor in the Old World. The ancient Egyptians had imported slaves from Ethiopia and other regions south

Parties of captured villagers from Africa's interior were bound together and marched to trading centers on the coast, where they were sold to European or Arab traders. The slave drivers were heavily influenced by outside contact. One of those shown here is wearing an Arab-influenced turban, while the clothing of the other is more European. Note, too, that the latter carries both a gun and a traditional African spear. *The Granger Collection, New York.*

of the Sahara Desert, a practice that continued through Roman times. But it was Islamic traders who turned the enslavement of Africans into a thriving enterprise. When North African Muslims established regular caravan routes across the desert into sub-Saharan Africa, slaves quickly became a dominant trade item, second only to gold in overall value. Perhaps as many as 4 million slaves were carried across the desert between 800 and the time the Portuguese redirected the trade in the sixteenth century.

Portuguese entry revolutionized this economy. European technology, wealth, and ideas fostered the development of aggressive centralized states along the

nonliterate   Lacking a system of reading and writing, relying instead on storytelling and mnemonic (memory-assisting) devices such as pictures.

Slave Coast on the western shore of Africa's Gulf of Guinea (see Map 1.5). Armed with European firearms, aggressive tribes such as the Ashanti engaged in large-scale raiding deep into the Niger and Congo river regions. These raiders captured millions of prisoners, whom they herded back to the coast and sold to Portuguese, Spanish, Dutch, and other European traders to supply labor for mines and plantations in the New World.

It is difficult to determine the number of people sold in the West African slave trade between 1500 and 1800. The most recent estimates suggest that more than 9.5 million enslaved Africans arrived in the New World during this three-hundred-year period. And they were only a small portion of the total number of Africans victimized by the system. On average, between 10 and 20 percent of the slaves shipped to the Americas died in transit. Adding in the numbers who were shipped to other locations in the Eastern Hemisphere, who were kept in slavery within Africa, and who died during the raids and on the marches to the coast yields a staggering total.

A New World in Europe

The discovery of America and the Columbian Exchange also had staggering repercussions on life in Europe. New economic opportunities and new ideas demanded new kinds of political and economic organization. The discovery of the New World clearly forced a new and more modern society onto Europeans.

Europe's population was already rising when potatoes, maize, and other New World crops began to revolutionize food production. Populations then began to soar despite nearly continuous wars and a flood of migration to the New World. With populations on the rise and overseas empires to run, European rulers and their advisers saw that centralized states appeared to offer the most promising device for harnessing the riches of the New World while controlling ever-increasing numbers of people at home. The sons and daughters of Europe's first generation of **absolute monarchs** chose to continue the consolidation of authority begun by their parents.

As Europeans responded to social, political, and economic changes, traditional patterns of authority broke down, especially in the realm of religion. A particularly devastating blow to religious authority came from the pen of Martin Luther, a German monk. Luther preached that salvation was God's gift to the faithful. In 1517 he presented a set of arguments, the **Ninety-five Theses**, maintaining that only individual repentance and the grace of God could save sinners. The implications of this simple formula were profound: if Luther was right, then Christians could achieve salvation without the intercession of the Roman Catholic or any other church, undermining the keystone of both religious and political authority upon which order in Europe was based.

Luther's ideas took root among a generation of theologians who were dissatisfied with the corruption and superstition they found in the medieval Catholic Church, launching the period known as the **Reformation**. A Frenchman, John Calvin, further undermined the church's authority by suggesting that God had preselected only some people for salvation. Calvin called these individuals **the Elect**. For all others, no earthly effort—no good works, no prayers, no church intervention—could save them. Thus neither popes nor kings had any claim to authority, and no one held the keys to salvation except God, but happiness on earth might be attained by wresting worldly authority from the hands of kings and putting it into the hands of the Elect.

Known as **Protestantism**, the doctrines of Luther, Calvin, and others who wanted to reform the Catholic Church formed an ideology that appealed to a broad audience in the rapidly changing European world of the sixteenth century. Ever critical of entrenched

---

Slave Coast   A region of coastal West Africa adjacent to the Gold Coast; it was the principal source of the slaves taken out of West Africa from the sixteenth to the early nineteenth century (see Map 1.5).

absolute monarchs   The ruler of a kingdom in which every aspect of national life—including politics, religion, the economy, and social affairs—comes under royal authority.

Ninety-five Theses   A document prepared by Martin Luther in 1517 protesting certain Roman Catholic practices that he believed were contrary to the will of God as revealed in Scripture.

Reformation   The sixteenth-century rise of Protestantism, with the establishment of state-sponsored Protestant churches in England, the Netherlands, parts of Germany and Switzerland, and elsewhere.

the Elect   According to Calvinism, the people chosen by God for salvation.

Protestantism   From the root word *protest*, the beliefs and practices of Christians who broke with the Roman Catholic Church; rejecting church authority, the doctrine of "good works," and the necessity of the priesthood, Protestants accepted the Bible as the only source of revelation, salvation as God's gift to the faithful, and a direct, personal relationship with God as available to every believer.

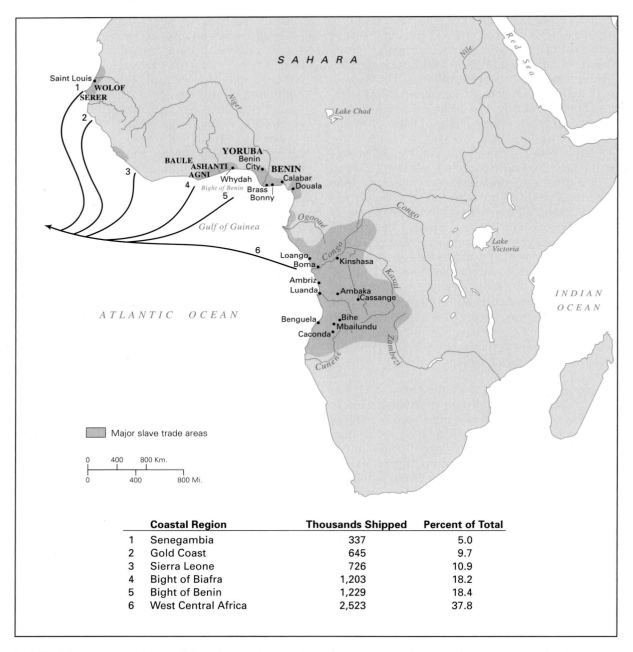

| | Major slave trade areas |

	Coastal Region	Thousands Shipped	Percent of Total
1	Senegambia	337	5.0
2	Gold Coast	645	9.7
3	Sierra Leone	726	10.9
4	Bight of Biafra	1,203	18.2
5	Bight of Benin	1,229	18.4
6	West Central Africa	2,523	37.8

MAP 1.5 **Western Africa and the Atlantic Slave Trade**   Africa's western shore was the major source for slaves that were transported to European colonies on the Atlantic islands, the Caribbean islands, and mainland North and South America. Powerful coastal kingdoms mounted organized raids into many inland areas to capture people who were then marched to the coast for shipment to the New World. This map shows the several regions from which slaves were extracted, and the accompanying table gives approximate numbers of people who were exported from each.

authority, the new doctrines attracted lawyers, bureaucrats, merchants, and manufacturers, whose economic and political status was on the rise thanks to increased prosperity generated by the Columbian Exchange. But many in the ruling classes also found aspects of the new theology attractive. In Germany, Luther's challenge to the priesthood, and by extension to the Catholic Church itself, led many local princes to question the **divine right** to authority claimed by the ruler of the **Holy Roman Empire**. Similarly, **Henry VIII** of England, at one time a critic of Luther's ideas, found Protestantism convenient when he wanted to resist the authority of the pope and expand English national power.

Henry VIII, the son of Henry VII and Elizabeth of York, was the first undisputed heir to the English throne in several generations, and he was consumed with the desire to avoid renewed civil war by having a son who could inherit the Crown. When his wife Catherine of Aragon, daughter of Spain's Ferdinand and Isabella, failed to bear a boy, Henry demanded in 1527 that Pope Clement VII grant him a divorce and permission to marry someone else. Fearful of Spanish reprisals on Catherine's behalf, Clement refused. In desperation, Henry launched an English Reformation by seizing the Catholic Church in England, gaining complete control of it by 1535.

Henry was not a staunch believer in the views aired by Luther and others, but the idea of unifying religious and civil authority under his personal control did appeal to him. In addition, the Catholic Church owned extensive and valuable lands in England, estates that Henry could use to enhance his wealth and power. He needed Protestant support in his war against the pope's authority, so he reluctantly opened the door to Protestant practices in his newly created Church of England.

After Henry's death, his very young son—finally born to his third wife, Jane Seymour—ascended the throne as Edward VI. In the absence of a strong king, Protestants had virtual free rein, and the pace of reform quickened. Young King Edward, however, was a frail child and died after ruling for only six years. Mary, his oldest sister, succeeded him. The daughter of Henry's first wife, Mary had married Philip II of Spain and was a devout Roman Catholic. She attempted to reverse the reforming trend, cruelly suppressing Protestantism by executing several hundred leading reformers. But her brutality only drove the movement underground and made it more militant. By the time her half-sister Elizabeth, who was born and raised a Protestant, inherited the crown in 1558, the Protestant underground had become powerful and highly motivated. In fact, **Elizabeth I** spent her entire half-century reign trying to reach a workable settlement with Protestant **dissenters** that would permit them free worship without endangering her control over church and state.

---

divine right   The idea that monarchs derive their authority to rule directly from God and are accountable only to God.

Holy Roman Empire   A political entity, authorized by the Catholic Church in 1356, unifying central Europe under an emperor elected by four princes and three Catholic archbishops.

Henry VIII   King of England (r. 1509–1547); his desire to divorce his first wife led him to break with Catholicism and establish the Church of England.

Elizabeth I   Queen of England (r. 1558–1603); she succeeded the Catholic Mary I and reestablished Protestantism in England; her reign was a time of domestic prosperity and cultural achievement.

dissenters   People who do not accept the doctrines of an established or national church.

Examining a Primary Source

✔ Individual Voices

The Five Nations Adopt the Great Law

Pressed on all sides by radically changing conditions, five Indian nations among the Iroquoian-speaking people in the Eastern Woodlands listened to Hienwatha (Hiawatha) and joined him in embracing the message of Dekanahwideh. The Peacegiver presented a plan for government, often referred to as "The Great Law," which would become the constitution for the Iroquois League. But Dekanahwideh's

① *Clearly Dekanahwideh chose the image of the "great tree" for a reason. What do you see as the meaning behind this image? What do you think the four "great, long, white roots" symbolize?*

② *What is Dekanahwideh advocating in this passage? How do you suppose this advice steered Five Nations policy during the three centuries after the adoption of the Great Law?*

③ *What does the Great Law suggest about the responsibility of each of the Five Nations to the confederacy as a whole? How would the scheme advocated here help the Iroquois deal with changing historical conditions?*

vision included much more than just peace among the Five Nations. Like similar strategies for cooperation that were being crafted by Indian groups throughout North America during this critical time, in the mid-1400s, the Great Law was a creative device that would carry the Iroquois into a new era of history.

Then Dekanahwideh said: "We have now completed arranging the system of our local councils and we shall hold our annual Confederate Council at the settlement of Thadodahho, the capitol or seat of government of the Five Nations Confederacy."

Dekanahwideh said: "Now I and you lords of the Confederate Nations shall plant a tree Ska-renj-heh-se-go-wah (meaning a tall and mighty tree) and we shall call it Jo-ne-rak-deh-ke-wah (the tree of the great long leaves)."

"Now this tree which we have planted shall shoot forth Jo-doh-ra-ken-rah-ko-wah (four great, long, white roots). These great, long, white roots shall shoot forth one to the north and one to the south and one to the east and one to the west, and we shall place on the top of it Oh-don-yonh (an eagle) which has great power of long vision, and we shall transact all our business beneath the shade of this great tree. **①** The meaning of planting this great tree, Skareh-hehsegowah, is to symbolize Ka-yah-ne-renh-ko-wa, which means Great Peace, and Jo-deh-ra-ken-rah-ke-wah, meaning Good Tidings of Peace and Power. The nations of the earth shall see it and shall accept and follow the roots and shall follow them to the tree and when they arrive here you shall receive them and shall seat them in the midst of your confederacy. **②** The object of placing an eagle on the top of the great, tall tree is that it may watch the roots which extend to the north and to the south and to the east and to the west, and whose duty shall be to discover if any evil is approaching your confederacy, and he shall scream loudly and give the alarm and all the nations of the confederacy at once shall heed the alarm and come to the rescue." **③**

SUMMARY

Making America began many thousands of years ago. Over millennia the continent's residents continually crafted economic strategies, social arrangements, and political systems to preserve and enhance their lives. The result was a rich and flourishing world of different cultures, linked by common religious and economic bonds.

At first, the arrival of Europeans only added another society to an already cosmopolitan sphere. The Vikings came and went, as perhaps did other non-Indians. But ultimately, the dynamic European society that arose after the Crusades and plagues of the Middle Ages became more intrusive. As a result, Native Americans faced challenges that they had never imagined: economic crises, disease, war, and the unfolding environmental changes wrought by the Europeans who followed Columbus.

In addition, influences from the New World reached out to accelerate processes that were already

affecting the Old. The flow of wealth and food out of the West was increasing populations, and this growth, with the accompanying rise of powerful kings and unified nations, led to continuing conflict over newfound resources. In Africa, strong coastal states raided weaker neighboring groups, more than doubling the flow of slaves out of Africa. This, in turn, influenced further developments in America. As disease destroyed millions of Indians, newcomers from the entire Atlantic rim poured in to replace them. These newcomers came from very different physical environments and had distinctly foreign ideas about nature. Their novel practices and ideas helped to create a new America on top of the old, rendering drastic changes to the landscape. Continuing interactions among these various newcomers, and between them and the survivors of America's original people, would launch the process of Making America.

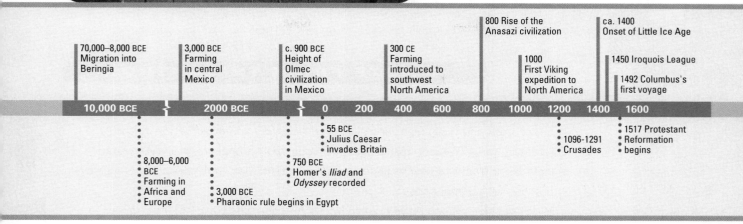

IN THE WIDER WORLD

800 Rise of the
Anasazi civilization

ca. 1400
Onset of Little Ice Age

70,000–8,000 BCE
Migration into
Beringia

3,000 BCE
Farming
in central
Mexico

c. 900 BCE
Height of
Olmec
civilization
in Mexico

300 CE
Farming
introduced to
southwest
North America

1000
First Viking
expedition to
North America

1450 Iroquois League

1492 Columbus's
first voyage

| 10,000 BCE | 2000 BCE | 0 | 200 | 400 | 600 | 800 | 1000 | 1200 | 1400 | 1600 |

8,000–6,000
BCE
Farming in
Africa and
Europe

3,000 BCE
Pharaonic rule begins in Egypt

750 BCE
Homer's *Iliad* and
Odyssey recorded

55 BCE
Julius Caesar
invades Britain

1096-1291
Crusades

1517 Protestant
Reformation
begins

In the United States

The New World

ca. 70,000–8,000 BCE	Human migration from Asia into Beringia
ca. 7000 BCE	Plant cultivation begins in North America
ca. 1400 BCE	Sub-Saharan Africans perfect iron smelting
ca. 34 CE	Death of Jesus of Nazareth and beginning of Christianity
632	Death of Mohammed and beginning of Islamic expansion
ca. 750	Islamic caravans travel to West Africa; African slave trade begins
ca. 500–1000	Rise of Hopewell culture
ca. 800–1700	Rise of Mississippian culture
ca. 1000–1400	Vikings in North America
1096–1291	The Crusades

ca. 1200	Aztecs arrive in the Valley of Mexico
ca. 1400	Beginning of Little Ice Age
ca. 1450	Hienwatha and Dekanahwideh found Iroquois League
1492	Reconquista completed; Columbus's first voyage
1500	Portuguese begin to transport and trade African slaves
1517	Martin Luther presents Ninety-five Theses
1527–1535	Henry VIII initiates English Reformation
1558	Elizabeth I becomes queen of England

Note: BCE means "before the common era."

A Continent on the Move, 1400–1725

A NOTE FROM THE AUTHOR

In Chapter 1 we put to rest the notion that before 1492 the Americas were an unoccupied and virgin frontier waiting for discovery and exploitation by the "civilized world." We also highlighted the cosmopolitan nature of the American experience from the very beginning of colonization. Making America was a global process with global consequences.

How this process played out in North America, the topic of this chapter, is then, by necessity, a complicated story. But it is a story we confront every day. Last night for dinner I ate roasted meat with tortillas and piquante sauce. You will find this same meal in various forms being served throughout the Mexican American Borderlands. In some places the meat is goat, in others it is beef. In some places, the tortillas are made from corn, in others from flour. In some places the sauce has green chilies, in others they are red. In all cases, this simple meal gives dramatic testimony to how native and colonizing forces blended into each other in a wide variety of ways.

Each colonizing nation confronted different circumstances at each point of entry to the continent. The French, for example, found that the climate, natural environment, and human populations in Louisiana were radically different from anything they had known at home and perhaps even more radically different from what they had encountered in Canada. For their part, the Dutch thought they would incorporate the Indians of the Hudson Valley into a profitable fur monopoly but found themselves clients in a monopoly controlled by the Iroquois. Successful settlement meant adaptability, and actual settlers often found themselves at odds with colonial officials back home who knew nothing about conditions in the field.

By the beginning of the eighteenth century, the entire North American continent was dotted with a wide variety of sophisticated and cosmopolitan communities that continued to evolve as they interacted with each other and with the administrative authorities in their own and other homelands. Much of what Americans are today—even down to what we eat for dinner—can be traced to these early confrontations and their peculiar outcomes.

Bartolomé de las Casas

Himself a former conquistador, Bartolomé de Las Casas was ordained as a Catholic priest in 1512 and became one of the most vocal opponents of Spain's brutal exploitation of Native American people. He was responsible for major reforms in the way Spaniards were supposed to treat Indians and in 1550 debated Juan Ginés de Sepúlveda, a well-respected court scholar, who insisted that Native Americans were not human and deserved no protections under law. Las Casas brought his biblical learning and his New World experience to bear, winning the debate and Catholic support for continued reforms in Spanish colonial policy. *Archivo de Indias, Seville, Spain/Bridgeman Art Library Ltd.*

✔ Individual Choices

In 1550 Spanish church officials ordered a council of learned theologians to assemble in the city of Valladolid to hear a debate over an issue so important that it challenged the entire underpinning of Spain's New World empire. At issue was the question of whether Native American Indians were human beings. Arguing that they were not was the well-respected scholar Juan Ginés de Sepúlveda. Arguing on the Indians' behalf was a former conquistador and **encomandero** named Bartolomé de Las Casas.

Born in 1474, Las Casas was the son of a small merchant in Seville. His family was privileged enough that young Bartolomé had both access and the leisure time to study at Seville's cathedral school. Like many of his contemporaries, Las Casas decided to pursue a military career, going to Granada as a soldier in 1497. Then in 1502 he embarked to the West Indies to seek his fortune in the conquest of the Americas.

Apparently Las Casas was successful as a **conquistador**: within a few years he had earned an imperial land grant with a full complement of Indian laborers. Meeting the demands of both church and king, he taught the Indians Catholicism while he exploited their labor. Unlike many of his neighbors, Las Casas came to believe that Indians were every bit as much the children of God as the Spanish, and he took his religious duty to them seriously. Finally, after a decade as a soldier and land baron Las Casas took the vows to become a priest and devoted himself to the spiritual protection of the Indians. He devised a plan that would organize Indians into farming communities under church protection, allowing them to become self-sufficient contributors to the Spanish Empire. His plan won support from

encomandero A land owner/proprietor in the encomienda system, Spain's system of bonded labor in which Indians were assigned to Spanish plantation and mine owners in exchange for a tax payment and an agreement to "civilize" and convert them to Catholicism.

conquistadors Spanish soldiers who conquered Indian civilizations in the New World.

the archbishop of Toledo and the Spanish Parliament. In 1519 he was given permission to start an experimental community in what is now Venezuela. But Indians in the region understandably were suspicious, and Spanish landlords were hostile; the experiment failed. Despite this setback, Las Casas remained convinced that Indians deserved full Christian recognition. He joined the Dominican order in 1523 and began writing a history of the Spanish Empire in America. As an outgrowth, he sent a series of long letters to the Council of the Indies in Madrid exposing the harsh exploitation of the natives throughout Spanish America. Las Casas then took his case personally to Spain. In 1540 he petitioned for an audience with King Charles V. As he waited for Charles to respond, he wrote a report, *Brevísima relación de la destrucción de las Indias* ("A Brief Report on the Destruction of the Indians") summarizing his experiences and views.

By the time he finally met with Charles V, Las Casas was well prepared to argue for wholesale reform of Spanish Indian policy in America. And Charles was convinced. He signed a series of new laws in 1542—the *Leyes Nuevas*—reforming the *encomienda* system and placing Indian relations under church authority. To ensure that these reforms would be carried out, Las Casas was appointed bishop of Chiapas and sent back to the New World with forty fellow Dominicans to oversee the enforcement of the laws.

Las Casas served as bishop until 1547, when hostility from landowners in America and growing opposition to humane colonization at home prompted him to return to Spain. The chief spokesman for that growing opposition was Juan Ginés de Sepúlveda, a well-respected scholar whose star was rising in court circles. Las Casas's return prompted demands for a face-off between the two, leading to the Council of Valladolid.

The debate went on for a year, extending through 1550 into 1551. Speaking for Spanish investors and court-based politicians who, like himself, had never been to the Western Hemisphere, Sepúlveda based his argument solely on logic and Scripture. According to his view, it was impossible for Indians in the Americas to be descendants of Adam and Eve; hence they were, in his words, "as apes are to men." As such, Indians did not deserve protection from the church. Las Casas countered with firsthand evidence, drawing on his varied experiences as priest, historian, conquistador, and *encomendero* in an attempt to prove that Indians truly were human beings.

Despite Sepúlveda's great learning and his influence at court, he lost the debate: his writings were denied official recognition by the church, whereas Las Casas's were accepted. But this official victory for Las Casas made little immediate difference. Though Sepúlveda's views were rejected by the church, they were embraced by conquistadors as justification for the continuing conquest and enslavement of the native population. In arguing effectively for the recognition of Indians as human beings, however, Las Casas established an undercurrent of official disapproval that served as a braking mechanism against the extreme abuse of the Native population. The resulting three-way tension—between those who would exploit the Indians, those who sought to protect them, and the Indians themselves—would shape the colonial process and would punctuate life in the Americas for generations to come.

INTRODUCTION

The debate in the Council of Valladolid in 1550 focused early attention on a situation that all European colonizers would have to face. Despite Sepúlveda's claims, the population native to the Americas *was* human. Of course, changing natural conditions and the influx of new forces such as epidemic disease had weakened them, but for centuries successful European settlement continued to require Indian cooperation. Court-based scholars like Sepúlveda might fool themselves into thinking that the Indians did not matter, but experienced veterans like Las Casas knew better. Conflicts with the Indians could spell disaster for vulnerable overseas colonies.

Conflicts with other imperial powers could lead to disaster as well. It was virtually inevitable that other nations would join Spain in seeking a share of the wealth promised by the New World. Forced into a defensive posture and unable to fend off the ambitions of numerous European rivals, Spain had to watch as the Dutch and the French carved out substantial inroads into North America.

The presence of so many, and such varied, Europeans presented both challenges and exceptional opportunities for Indians. In areas where a single European power was asserting dominance, Indians could often do little but bear up under relentless economic and religious pressures. Sometimes the encounter facilitated friendship, intermarriage, and the formation of complex composite societies; sometimes it led to open hostilities and even war. But in areas where two or more European powers were contesting for control, Indians could take advantage of their pivotal position and play one side off against the other in seeking their own ends.

The constant interplay among different European traditions, a novel physical environment, and a dynamic Indian presence forged a series of new societies across the North American continent. Throughout the colonial era and beyond, these hybrid societies continued to influence historical development and to color the life of the people and the nation.

The New Europe and the Atlantic World

→ *Why did European rulers promote exploration and colonization in North America?*

→ *How did religious and political rivalries influence the ways in which each European power approached New World colonization?*

Expansion into the New World and the subsequent economic and political pressures of colonization aggravated the crisis of authority in Europe. Eager to enlist political allies against Protestants, popes during this era used land grants in the New World as rewards to faithful monarchs. At the same time, Henry VIII and Elizabeth I, constantly fearful of being outflanked by Catholic adversaries, promoted the development of a powerful English navy and geographical exploration as defensive measures.

Spanish Expansion in America

Spain's entry into Atlantic exploration first sparked a diplomatic crisis between the Spanish and Portuguese. Portugal feared that Spain's intrusion might endanger

The differences between European and Native American styles and conceptions of warfare were often striking. This scene, from the Codex Durán, illustrates a Spanish force besieged by Aztec warriors. Note the contrast in clothing, for example. For most Indian groups, warfare was a highly spiritual affair surrounded by ceremony, often involving colorful and fanciful costumes. The European battle dress, however, bespeaks a very different conception of warfare: practical and deadly. *Archivo fotografico.*

its hard-won trading enterprises in Africa and the Atlantic islands. Spain, however, claimed the right to explore freely. In 1493 the pope settled the dispute by drawing a line approximately three hundred miles west of Portugal's westernmost holdings. Spanish exploration, he declared, was to be confined to areas west of the line (that is, to the New World) and Portuguese activity to areas east of it (to Africa and India). A year later, Spain and Portugal updated the agreement in the **Treaty of Tordesillas**, which moved the line an additional 1,000 miles westward. Most of the Western Hemisphere fell exclusively to Spain, at least in the eyes of Roman Catholics.

Over the next several decades the Spanish monarchs recruited hardened veterans of the Reconquista (see page 9) to lead its New World colonization efforts. **Hernando Cortés** was one such figure. In 1519 Cortés landed on the mainland of Mexico with an army of six hundred soldiers. Within three years he and his small force had conquered the mighty Aztec Empire. Although it is tempting to suppose that Cortés's victory was the product of technological superiority, his weapons made less difference in the outcome than did several other factors. More important than guns and swords were the warhorses and attack dogs that Cortés used to instill anxiety. More important than even these, however, was the Spanish philosophy of war, which emphasized hard strikes against both armed and civilian targets. This type of campaign stood in stark contrast to the Aztec art of war, which was much more ceremonial in nature and limited in scope. Cortés was also adept at cultivating diplomatic advantages. An Indian woman whom he called Doña Marina served as his translator and cultural adviser, and with her help the conquistadors gained military support from numerous tribes of Mexican Indians who resented the Aztecs' power and their continuous demands for tribute. And finally, crucially, smallpox and other European germs weakened the Aztecs during the two years in which Cortés maintained strained but peaceful relations with them.

The Spanish Crown supported many other exploratory ventures designed to bring new regions under Spain's control. In 1513 and again in 1521, Juan Ponce de León led expeditions to Florida. Following up on these voyages, Pánfilo de Narváez embarked on a colonizing mission to Florida in 1527. When his party became stranded, local Indians killed most of its members but took a few captives. One of these captives, Álvar Núñez Cabeza de Vaca, escaped with three others in 1534. The stories they told upon returning to Mexico led the Spanish to send Hernando de Soto to claim the Mississippi River, and he penetrated into the heart of the mound builders' territory in present-day Louisiana and Mississippi. One year later, **Francisco Vásquez de Coronado** left Mexico to look for seven cities that Cabeza de Vaca had heard glittered with gold. Coronado eventually crossed what are now the states of New Mexico, Arizona, Colorado, Oklahoma, and Kansas. These explorations were but a few of the ambitious adventures undertaken by Spanish conquistadors.

Coronado never found Cabeza de Vaca's "cities of gold," but other Spaniards did locate enormous sources of wealth. In Bolivia, Colombia, and north-central Mexico, rich silver deposits rewarded the conquistadors. To the south, in present-day Peru, Francisco Pizarro in 1532 conquered the Inca Empire, an advanced civilization that glittered with gold. Enslaving local Indians for labor, Spanish officials everywhere in the New World quickly moved to rip precious metals out of the ground and from what they characterized as "heathen temples." Between 1545 and 1660, Indian and later African slaves extracted over 7 million pounds of silver from Spanish-controlled areas, twice the volume of silver held by all of Europe before 1492. In the process, Spain became the richest nation in Europe, perhaps in the world.

Dreams of an English Eden

Given the stormy political and religious climate that prevailed during the sixteenth century, it is not surprising that Spain's early successes in the New World stirred up conflict with the other emerging states in Europe. To England, France, and other European countries, the massive flow of wealth made Spanish power a growing threat that had to be checked. The continuing religious controversies that accompanied the Reformation (see page 25) worsened the situation. Economic, religious, and political warfare was the rule

Treaty of Tordesillas   The agreement, signed by Spain and Portugal in 1494, that moved the line separating Spanish and Portuguese claims to territory in the non-Christian world, giving Spain most of the Western Hemisphere

Hernando Cortés   Spanish soldier and explorer who conquered the Aztecs and claimed Mexico for Spain.

Francisco Vásquez de Coronado   Spanish soldier and explorer who led an expedition northward from Mexico in search of fabled cities of gold, passing through present-day New Mexico, Arizona, Colorado, Oklahoma, and Kansas, giving Spain a claim to most of the American Southwest.

Acting on information collected from Indians on Mexico's frontiers, in 1540 Francisco Vásquez de Coronado set out with an armed party to find seven cities of gold rumored to exist in the northern wilderness. Though the party crisscrossed much of the American Southwest, venturing as far as modern-day Kansas, they found no golden cities. Such parties, however, increased the Spaniards' knowledge of America and, through numerous encounters, increased Americans' knowledge of the new invaders in their land. *The Granger Collection, New York.*

throughout the century. One of the most celebrated of these early conflicts involved Spain and England.

Tension between Spain and England had been running high ever since Henry VIII had divorced his Spanish wife, Catherine of Aragon. That he quit the Catholic Church to do so and began permitting Protestant reforms in England added to the affront. Firmly wedded to the Catholic Church politically and religiously, Spain was aggressive in denouncing England. For his part, Henry was concerned primarily with domestic issues and steered away from direct confrontations with Spain or any of the other outraged Catholic countries.

The main exception to Henry's isolationism was an effort to bring Ireland and other outlying parts of his realm more firmly under his control. In 1541 Henry assumed the title "King of Ireland" and used his new status to institute both religious and political reforms. He confiscated lands controlled by Irish Catholic monasteries and the estates of local lords who opposed him, channeling the money into building a stronger administrative structure. During the years to come, both Henry's heirs and the **Stuart kings** who would follow them continued a systematic policy of colonization in Ireland. In the process, British authorities instituted a new set of colonial offices and encouraged generations of military adventurers, both of which would shape and advance later ventures in North America.

During the reign of Henry's younger daughter, Elizabeth, the continuing flow of New World wealth into Spain and that nation's anti-Protestant aggression led to an upturn in hostile activity. When Philip II of Spain, Elizabeth's brother-in-law and most vehement

critic, sent an army of twenty thousand soldiers to root out Protestantism in **the Netherlands**, only a few miles across the English Channel from Elizabeth's kingdom, the English queen began providing covert aid to the Protestants rebels. Elizabeth also struck at Philip's most valuable and vulnerable possession: his New World empire. In 1577 Elizabeth secretly authorized English **privateer** and explorer Francis Drake to attack Spanish ships in the area reserved for Spain under the Treaty of Tordesillas. Drake carried out his task with enthusiasm, raiding Spanish ships and seizing tons of gold and silver during a three-year cruise around the world.

Elizabeth was open to virtually any venture that might vex her troublesome brother-in-law. New World colonizing efforts promised to do that and had the potential for enriching the kingdom as well. Although Elizabeth's father had confiscated and redistributed large tracts of church-owned land during his reign, farmland was becoming extremely scarce, and

---

Stuart kings The dynasty of English kings who claimed the throne after the death of Elizabeth I, who left no heirs.

the Netherlands/Holland/Dutch Often used interchangeably, the first two terms refer to the low-lying area in western Europe north of France and Belgium and across the English Channel from Great Britain; the Dutch are the inhabitants of the Netherlands.

privateer A ship captain who owned his own boat, hired his own crew, and was authorized by his government to attack and capture enemy ships.

Queen Elizabeth I used her charm and intelligence to turn England into a major world power and restored order to a kingdom shaken by religious and political turmoil following the death of her father, Henry VIII. This pendant from the 1570s not only captures the queen's elegance and austere grace, but was also a powerful political statement. Note the intertwining of white and red roses—emblems of the Houses of York and Lancaster, respectively—symbolizing the unified monarchy forged by her grandfather. On the reverse is an image of a phoenix rising from the flames of its nest, symbolizing the renewal of the true monarchy. Already in her 40s by the time the "Phoenix Jewel" was crafted, it may have been the last portrait to capture Elizabeth's true age; future images of the queen always depict her as being much younger than she really was. While this may have been the product of vanity, it seems more likely that the queen wanted to diminish concerns among her subjects that aging might undermine her resolve and bring back an era of disorder. © *Trustees of The British Museum.*

members of both the traditional nobility and the **gentry**—a class that was becoming increasingly important because of its investments in manufacturing and trading ventures—wanted more space for expansion. A relatively small island, England could acquire more territory only by carving it out of the New World.

Thus in 1578, when Sir Humphrey Gilbert claimed that John Cabot's voyages gave England rightful ownership of the North American coast, Elizabeth granted him permission to settle two hundred colonists between the St. Lawrence River and the mythical land of Norumbega in what is now Newfoundland. Though he succeeded in reaching the site, one disaster after another plagued the effort, and Gilbert himself died at sea while trying to return to England. Thereafter, Gilbert's half-brother, **Sir Walter Raleigh**, took over the

colonizing effort. This time, Elizabeth commanded Raleigh to locate farther south on the border of Spanish Florida, where an English base would facilitate raids on Philip's treasure fleets. Raleigh chose an island off the coast of present-day North Carolina. He advertised **Roanoke Island** as an "American Eden," where "the earth bringeth forth all things in abundance, as in the first Creation, without toile or labour." To honor his benefactor, he decided to call this paradise Virginia, tribute to the unwed, and thus officially virgin, queen.

In 1585 Elizabeth further angered the Spanish king by openly sending an army of six thousand troops across the Channel to aid Dutch rebels. In the meantime, Philip was supporting various Catholic plots within England to subvert Elizabeth's authority and bring down the Protestant state. As tensions increased, so did English piracy. In 1586 Drake intensified his campaign, not only raiding Spanish ships at sea but attacking settlements in the Caribbean. Thus by 1586, British troops were fighting the Spanish alongside Dutch rebels in Holland; Spanish spies were encouraging rebellion in England, Scotland, and Ireland; and British ships were raiding Spanish settlements in the New World. War loomed on the horizon.

The Decline of Spanish Power

The enormous inflow of wealth from the New World brought Spain power that no European country since the Roman Empire had enjoyed, but such rapid enrichment was a mixed blessing. Starting in Spain and radiating outward, prices began to climb as the growth of the money supply outpaced the growth of European economies. Too much money was chasing too few goods. Between 1550 and 1600, prices doubled in much of Europe, and **inflation** continued to soar for another half-century.

In addition, the social impact of the new wealth was forcing European monarchs to expand geographically

gentry   The class of English landowners ranking just below the nobility.

Sir Walter Raleigh   English courtier, soldier, and adventurer who attempted to establish the Virginia Colony.

Roanoke Island   Island off North Carolina that Raleigh sought to colonize beginning in 1585.

inflation   Rising prices that occur when the supply of currency or credit grows faster than the available supply of goods and services.

and crack down domestically. As prices rose, the traditional landholding classes earned enormous profits from the sale of food and other necessities. Other groups fared less well. Artisans, laborers, and landless peasants—by far the largest class of people in Europe—found the value of their labor constantly shrinking. Throughout Europe, social unrest increased as formerly productive and respected citizens were reduced to poverty and begging. Overseas expansion seemed an inviting solution to the problem of an impoverished population. It was a safety valve that relieved a potentially dangerous source of domestic pressure while opening opportunities for enhancing national wealth through the development of colonies.

Sitting at the center of the new economy, Philip's Spain had the most to lose from rapid inflation and popular unrest. It also had the most to lose from New World expansion by any other European nation. Each New World claim asserted by England, France, or some other country represented the loss of a piece of treasure that Spain claimed as its own. Philip finally chose to confront building tensions by taking a desperate gamble: he would destroy England. This ploy, he thought, would effectively remove the Protestant threat, rid him of Elizabeth's ongoing harassment, and demonstrate to the rest of Europe that Spain intended to exercise absolute authority over the Atlantic world. In the spring of 1585, when tensions were at their peak, Philip began massing what was to be the largest marine force Europe had ever witnessed.

In 1588 Philip launched an **armada** of 132 warships carrying more than three thousand cannon and an invasion force of thirty thousand men. Arriving off the shores of England in July, the so-called Invincible Armada ran up against small, maneuverable British defense ships commanded by Elizabeth's skilled pirate captains. Drake and his fleet harassed the Spanish ships, preventing them from launching a successful attack. Then a storm blowing down from the North Sea scattered the Spanish fleet, ruining Philip's expected conquest of England. Though Spanish power remained great for some time to come, the Armada disaster effectively ended Spain's near-monopoly over New World colonization.

European Empires in America

→ *What similarities and differences characterized Spanish, French, and Dutch patterns of empire building in North America?*

→ *What role did natural environments play in shaping the colonial enterprises engineered by the Spanish, the French, and the Dutch?*

→ *How did the colonists' experiences challenge and help to reshape imperial policies?*

In the seventeenth and eighteenth centuries, Spain, France, England, and a number of other European nations vied for control of the Americas and for domination of the transatlantic trade (see Map 2.1). For reasons that are explained in Chapter 3, England was somewhat delayed in its colonizing efforts, and by the time it became deeply involved in New World ventures, Spain, France, and Holland had already made major progress toward establishing empires in America. These European settlements not only affected England's colonization process profoundly, but through their interactions among themselves and with the Native Americans, they also created unique societies in North America whose presence influenced the entire course of the continent's history.

The Troubled Spanish Colonial Empire

Although the destruction of the Armada in 1588 struck a terrible blow at Spain's military power and its New World monopoly, the Spanish Empire continued to grow. By the end of the seventeenth century, it stretched from New Mexico southward through Central America and much of South America into the Caribbean islands and northward again into Florida. Governing such a vast empire was difficult, and periodic efforts to reform the system usually failed. Two agencies in Spain, the House of Trade and the Council of the Indies, set Spanish colonial policy. In the colonies, Crown-appointed viceroys wielded military and political power in each of the four divisions of the empire. The Spanish colonies set up local governments as well; each town had a **cabildo secular**, a municipal council, as well as judges and other minor officials. The colonial administrators were appointed rather than elected, and most were envoys from Spain rather than native-born individuals.

---

armada   A fleet of warships.

cabildo secular   Secular municipal council that provided local government in Spain's New World empire.

MAP 2.1 European and Indian Settlements in the Americas   Although Europeans were at first unsure about the implications of stumbling over a portion of the world that was new to them, they quickly came to understand the economic, political, and military potential involved in American colonization. As this map shows, exploration continued into the seventeenth century as Europeans scrambled to claim individual pieces of New World real estate.

Over the centuries, as the layers of bureaucracy developed, corruption and inefficiency developed as well. The Spanish government made efforts to regulate colonial affairs, sending *visitadores* to inspect local government operations and creating new watchdog agencies. Despite these safeguards, colonial officials ignored their written instructions and failed to enforce laws.

One major source of corruption and unrest stemmed from a persistent New World problem: the shortage of labor. The Spanish had adapted traditional institutions to address the demand for workers in mines and on plantations. In Spain, work was directed by **feudal** landlords, *encomenderos*, whose military service to the king entitled them to harness the labor of Spanish peasants. In New Spain, Indians took the place of the peasants in what was called the *encomienda* system. Under a law passed in 1512, when an Indian group was first encountered by the Spanish, the conquistador was required to explain to them that they were subject to the Spanish king and to the Catholic Church, offering to absorb them peacefully. Having satisfied this *requiremento*, the *encomenderos* gained the right to use the Indians' labor for nine months each year. For his part, the *encomendero* paid a tax to the Crown for each Indian he received and agreed to teach his workers the Catholic faith, Spanish language and culture, and a "civilized" vocation.

Despite some commitment to uplifting local Indians, the system in reality was brutally exploitative. As Bartolomé de Las Casas reported both to the Council of the Indies and to the king himself, landlords frequently overworked their Indian **serfs** and failed in their "civilizing" responsibilities. As the result of Las Casas's appeal, the Leyes Nuevas turned Indian relations in New Spain over to the church, and priests were assigned to enforce the laws. Among the new regulations was a stipulation that a priest accompany all expeditions to certify the proper execution of the *requiremento* and serve as witnesses that Indians were treated lawfully. As Las Casas discovered, however, colonists often ignored even these slim protections. Some simply forged a priest's signature, anticipating that by the time the document reached administrators in faraway Madrid, no one would know the difference. Others disregarded the law altogether.

Bureaucratic and church interference in the labor system was one source of tension. Taxes were another. Spanish colonists were taxed to support the huge and largely corrupt, unrepresentative, and self-serving imperial bureaucracy. But for many decades the wealth produced within this empire overshadowed all governing problems. The gold, silver, and copper mined by Indian and later African slaves so dazzled Spanish officials that imperial authorities took few serious steps toward practical reform until the end of the seventeenth century.

The Dutch Enterprise

Interestingly, it was a former colony, the Netherlands, that presented one of the most serious threats to Spain's New World monopoly. The Armada disaster in 1588 had tipped the scales in favor of Dutch Protestant rebels, and the newly independent nation quickly developed a thriving commercial economy. Holland's first serious claim to American territory came in 1609, when Dutch sea captain **Henry Hudson** explored the East Coast in search of the elusive Northwest Passage (see page 20). He sailed up a large river that he hoped would lead him west to the Pacific. After realizing that he had not found the hoped-for route to the Far East, he returned to Holland and reported to his sponsor, the Dutch East India Company, that the territory surrounding this river—which he named after himself—was "pleasant with Grasse & Flowers and Goodly Trees" and that the Indians were friendly. Surely, he added, profits could be made there. Hudson's employers did not share his enthusiasm for settlement; however, a fashion trend that seized Europe late in the sixteenth century provided a powerful incentive for some investment in the region. The immense popularity of the broad-brimmed beaver felt hat created a nearly insatiable demand for fur, and the experiences of early explorers and fishermen along America's North Atlantic shore indicated that a near endless supply was ripe for the trapping (see page 20). Seeking to tap in on this "brown gold," the Dutch built a trading post on the Hudson River at Albany and an export station on Manhattan Island in 1614. Real Dutch efforts at New World colonization, however, did not begin until investors formed the **Dutch West India Company** in 1621. The new company financed Dutch privateers who successfully raided Spanish and Portuguese treasure ships and, in 1634, overcame weak Spanish and Portuguese resistance to conquer a number of islands in the Caribbean.

feudal Relating to a system in which landowners held broad powers over peasants or tenant farmers, providing protection in exchange for loyalty and labor.

requiremento A provision in Spanish colonial law that required conquistadors to inform Indians that they were subject to Spanish authority and to absorb them peacefully.

serfs Peasants who were bound to a particular estate but, unlike slaves, were not the personal property of the estate owner and received traditional feudal protections.

Henry Hudson Dutch ship captain and explorer who sailed up the Hudson River in 1609, giving the Netherlands a claim to the area now occupied by New York.

Dutch West India Company Dutch investment company formed in 1621 to develop colonies for the Netherlands in North America.

Its location at the mouth of the Hudson River made the Dutch settlement of New Amsterdam a particularly important colonial trading center. Furs flowed down the river from Fort Orange (near modern Albany, New York), while guns, tools, and other trade goods traveled the other way. This etching (detail), based on a watercolor illustration painted around 1653, captures the city's colorful vibrancy after Peter Stuyvesant and the Dutch burghers merged their power to bring order and prosperity. The weighing beam in the foreground illustrates both the prosperity and quest for order: it was used not only to weigh the loads of goods flowing through the town, but was also used as a whipping post and gallows when necessary. *Museum of the City of New York. Gift of Dr. N. Sulzberger.*

The Dutch also pushed the Portuguese aside to take control of the transatlantic slave trade.

Farther north, the Company instructed official Peter Minuit to negotiate a lease for the entire island of Manhattan from the Manhates Indians in 1626. This acquisition gave it control over the mouth of the river that Hudson had discovered and the land of "Grasses & Flowers" that it drained. The Dutch focus remained upriver, however; the company did nothing to attract settlers, and by 1629 only three hundred colonists had spread themselves in a thin ribbon from the capital, New Amsterdam, on Manhattan Island, upriver to Albany. But in that year, the Dutch West India Company drew up a comprehensive business plan to maximize profits and minimize dependence on local Indians for food and other support. To encourage the agricultural development necessary to support the fur industry, the company offered huge estates called **patroonships** to any company stockholder willing to bring fifty colonists to **New Netherland** at his own expense. In exchange, the patroons would enjoy near-feudal powers over their tenants. But few prosperous Dutchmen were interested in becoming New World barons. Rensselaerswyck, the estate of Kilian van Rensselaer, was the only patroonship to develop in accordance with the company's plan. The colony's development came to rely instead on many poorer migrants who were drawn by unofficial promises of land ownership and economic betterment.

Settlers from just about anywhere were welcome in New Netherland—the colony attracted an extremely

patroonships Huge grants of land given to any Dutch West India Company stockholder who, at his own expense, brought fifty colonists to New Netherland; the colonists became the tenants of the estate owner, or patroon.

New Netherland The colony founded by the Dutch West India Company in present-day New York; its capital was New Amsterdam on Manhattan Island.

THE FELT HAT FAD

Changes in fashion come and go, and we seldom give much thought to them as being historically significant. But the sudden popularity of felt hats in the late sixteenth century had a profound impact on not just America's history, but the history of the entire world. The flood of new wealth flowing into Europe from America permitted people of means—not just the nobility, but the landed gentry and even urban craftsmen and small business owners—to keep up with the latest fashion trends. Being in style became increasingly important to status-conscious merchants, manufacturers, and other beneficiaries of the New World boom. Demand for the beaver fur to make the felt became so steep that virtually the entire population of Old World beavers was wiped out, and entire industries arose in France, the Netherlands, Great Britain, and Russia to import this "brown gold" from the Americas. Fur drew Europeans up virtually every waterway in North America, leading to the founding of many of the most prominent cities in America today. It is safe to say that without this seemingly silly fashion trend that little in the United States would be as we know it today.

- Another important trade item during this era was deerskins. Research the demand for deerskins and then discuss what this tells us about socioeconomic changes during this era.

- Identify a current fashion trend and discuss its impact on global society. What differences do you think this trend will make on the future?

diverse population, including German and French Protestants, free and enslaved Africans, Catholics, Jews, and Muslims. In 1638 the Dutch even encouraged Swedish fur traders to create their own colony, New Sweden, within its boundaries. Local government in such a disparate community was a persistent problem. Although the Dutch West India Company was officially in charge, the actual conduct of day-to-day affairs was run by an elite group of **burghers**, men in New Amsterdam whose economic and political successes gave them significant influence. In an effort to reassert its power, the company reorganized its New World operations in 1645, appointing Peter Stuyvesant

to manage all of its affairs in the Western Hemisphere. Stuyvesant immediately came into conflict with the local burghers in New Amsterdam, and in 1647 he was forced to create a compromise government that gave the burghers an official voice through a council of nine appointed representatives. Six years later, Stuyvesant and the council created a municipal government modeled on those back home in Holland. Despite this nod to democratic government, Stuyvesant ran company affairs with an iron hand, significantly tightening operations throughout the colony. In 1655 he even invaded and rooted out the Swedes, eliminating that source of dissension and competition.

The French Presence in America

Although France made a number of efforts to compete with Spain's New World projects during the sixteenth century, Spanish power was sufficient to prevent any major successes. For example, when a force of French Protestants established a colony in Florida in 1564, Spanish authorities sent an army to root them out. This led to increased Spanish vigilance, prompting Pedro Menéndez de Aviles to build the city of **Saint Augustine** the following year.

Unable to penetrate Spain's defenses in the south, the French concentrated their efforts farther north. Early in the seventeenth century, **Samuel de Champlain**, the "father of **New France**," established trading posts in Nova Scotia and elsewhere, founded the city of Quebec, and in 1608 formed an enduring alliance with the Huron Indians. But despite these efforts and the potential profitability of the fur trade, French colonial authorities at first took little interest in overseas enterprises.

burghers   Town dwellers who were free from feudal obligations and were responsible for civic government during the medieval period in Europe; in New Amsterdam these were men who were not Dutch West India Company officials, but who governed civic affairs through their political influence.

Saint Augustine   First colonial city in the present-day United States; located in Florida and founded by Pedro Menéndez de Aviles for Spain in 1565.

Samuel de Champlain   French explorer who traced the St. Lawrence River inland to the Great Lakes, founded the city of Quebec, and formed the French alliance with the Huron Indians.

New France   The colony established by France in what is now Canada and the Great Lakes region of the United States.

In 1627 French minister Cardinal Richelieu chartered the **Company of New France**, awarding a group of the king's favorites a license to establish plantations in Canada, but the venture failed to attract much interest. French Protestants, who might have emigrated to avoid religious persecution, were forbidden to move to the colony, and few French Catholics wanted to migrate to America. Thus the colonizing effort did not attract enough rent-paying tenants to make the envisioned estates profitable. Equally important was the fact that the few French peasants and small farmers who did venture to the New World found life in the woods and the company of Indians preferable to life as tenant farmers. So-called *coureurs de bois*, or "runners of the woods," married Indian women and lived among the tribes, returning to the French settlements only when they had enough furs to sell to make the trip worthwhile.

Frustrated by the lack of profits, Richelieu reorganized the Company of New France in 1633, dispatching Champlain, now bearing the title Lieutenant of New France, with three ships of supplies, workmen, and soldiers who, it was hoped, would breathe new life into the colony. In its new form, the company ignored the government's demands that it establish agricultural settlements and focused instead on the fur trade. Setting up posts in Quebec, Montreal, and a few more remote locations, the company became the primary outfitter of and buyer from the *coureurs de bois* and amassed huge profits by reselling the furs in Europe. After Richelieu's death in 1642, queen mother and French regent Anne of Austria acted on complaints filed by both fur trade investors and Jesuit missionaries that the Company of New France was not governing effectively. She chose to empower a new company, the **Community of Habitants of New France**, with a monopoly on the fur trade and the privilege of granting land claims. Then, in 1647, Anne approved the formation of a council that consisted of the governor, the local director of the Jesuits, the colony's military commandant, and three elected officials. Meanwhile, the Company of New France continued technically to own the land and retained the power to appoint the governor and court officials in the colony.

Local authorities managed most of the colony's affairs until 1663, when the Crown began to intervene seriously in Canada. Having taken the functions of state into his own hands, young Louis XIV gave his finance minister, Jean-Baptiste Colbert, considerable authority over all monetary matters, including colonial enterprises. Seeking to make New France more efficient and to increase its contribution to the empire at large, Colbert founded the **Company of the West**,

Although this scene in Quebec was not painted until 1820, back streets in the old part of the city still looked very much as they had during the heyday of the French *coureurs de bois*. So did the people. Shops, like the one on the left, sold provisions and tools—often on credit—to the outward-bound runners of the woods, binding them to bring their next load of furs back to satisfy their debt. Thus, while the French Crown did little to encourage the fur business, it formed the core for Canada's woodland and urban economies. *With permission of the Royal Ontario Museum © ROM.*

Company of New France   Company established by Cardinal Richelieu to bring order to the running of France's North American enterprises.

coureurs de bois   Literally, "runners of the woods"; independent French fur traders who lived among the Indians and sold furs to the French.

Community of Habitants of New France   Company chartered by Anne of Austria to make operations in New France more efficient and profitable; it gave significant political power to local officials in Canada.

Company of the West   Company chartered by Colbert after New France became a royal colony; modeled on the Dutch West India Company, it was designed to maximize profits to the Crown.

modeled on the highly successful Dutch West India Company. He also revoked the land titles held by the Company of New France, putting them directly into the king's hands, and overturned the political power of the Community of Habitants, making New France a royal colony.

Although the king reaped enormous profits from the fur trade, his colonial interests ranged beyond this single source of income. In 1673 a French expedition led by Louis Joliet and Jacques Marquette set out on a systematic exploration of New France's many waterways. They discovered what appeared to be a major river, but it fell to **Robert Cavelier, Sieur de La Salle**, to prove the strategic and economic value of that discovery. In 1683 he and a party of French *coureurs de bois* and Indians retraced the earlier expedition and then followed the Mississippi River all the way to the Gulf of Mexico. La Salle immediately claimed the new territory for Louis XIV of France, naming it **Louisiana** in his honor. In 1698 the king sent settlers to the lower Mississippi Valley under the leadership of Pierre LeMoyne d'Iberville, who in 1699 raised Louisiana's first French fort, near present-day Biloxi, Mississippi. In 1718 French authorities built the city of New Orleans to serve as the capital of the new territory.

The acquisition of Louisiana was a major accomplishment for La Salle and for France. The newly discovered river way gave the French a rich, untapped source of furs as well as an alternative shipping route, allowing them to avoid the cold, stormy North Atlantic. Also, if an agricultural venture could be started in the new territory, it might serve as an inexpensive source of supplies to support both the fur trade in Canada and France's sugar plantations in the Caribbean. But perhaps of greatest importance was Louisiana's strategic location between Spain's claims in the Southwest and the Dutch and other colonies along the eastern seaboard. Controlling this piece of real estate gave Louis considerable leverage in international diplomacy.

Indians and the European Challenge

→ *How did changes in the natural environment affect Indian societies during the early colonial period?*

→ *How did the arrival of Europeans influence continuing adaptations by Native American groups?*

Native Americans did not sit idly by while the European powers carved out empires in North America. Some joined the newcomers, serving as advisers and companions. Others sought to use the Europeans as allies to accomplish their own economic, diplomatic, or military goals (see Map 2.2). Still others, overwhelmed by the onset of European diseases and shifting population pressures, withdrew into the interior. The changes in native America created both obstacles and opportunities, giving shape to the patterns of expansion and conflict that characterized the colonial world.

The Indian Frontier in New Spain

Indian assistance had been critical in Spain's successful campaigns against the Aztecs and Incas. In Mexico, for example, groups who had been forced to pay tribute to the Aztec Empire gladly allied themselves with the Spanish in what the natives perceived as an opportunity to win their independence. Their hopes were soon dashed when the Spanish simply replaced the Aztecs as the new lords of a tributary empire.

Once their New World empire was firmly rooted, Spanish expansion met little native resistance until 1598, when a particularly brutal conquistador named **Don Juan de Oñate** led a large expedition to the Rio Grande region of New Mexico. When some Pueblos resisted Oñate's efforts to impose Spanish culture and religion, the conquistador chose to make an example of **Ácoma pueblo**. It took Oñate's troops three days to subdue the settlement, but Spanish steel finally overcame Ácoma clubs and stone knives. When the battle was over, Oñate ordered eight hundred Indians executed and made slaves of the nearly seven hundred survivors, mostly women and children. In addition, each male survivor over the age of 25 had one foot chopped off to prevent his escape from slavery. Two **Hopi Indians** who had been visiting Ácoma at the time

Robert Cavelier, Sieur de La Salle French explorer who followed the Mississippi River from present-day Illinois to the Gulf of Mexico in 1683, giving France a claim to the entire river way and adjoining territory.

Louisiana French colony south of New France; it included the entire area drained by the Mississippi River and all its tributary rivers.

Don Juan de Oñate Spaniard who conquered New Mexico and claimed it for Spain in the 1590s.

Ácoma pueblo Pueblo Indian community that resisted Spanish authority in 1598 and was subdued by the Spanish.

Hopi Indians Indians who were related to the Comanches and Shoshones and took up residence among the Pueblo Indians as agricultural town-dwellers; their name means "peaceful ones."

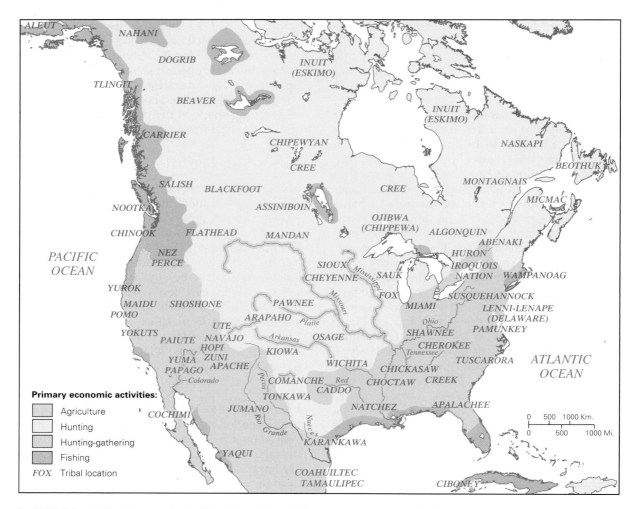

MAP 2.2 **Indian Economies in North America** Indian economic activities helped to shape patterns of European settlement and investment in the New World. Regions that were primarily agricultural, like the Atlantic shoreline, lent themselves to European farming activities. Farther north and west, however, where hunting played a more prominent role in native life, the fur trade was a more attractive investment for European settlers.

of the battle had their right hands cut off and then were sent home as examples of the price of resistance.

This blatant cruelty disgusted even the most cynical authorities in New Spain, and both the church and state stepped in. Oñate was removed, and the surviving Indians were placed under joint military and religious protection. Some members of Oñate's company remained, however, founding the town of **Santa Fe** in 1609. Others scattered to set up ranches throughout the region.

Thanks in part to Las Casas's efforts, the church played a key role in developing the colonies, especially in the stark regions along Mexico's northern frontier

where there were no gold mines or profitable plantations. The Franciscan order led church efforts in New Mexico and put a peculiar stamp on the pattern of Indian relations. A highly **ascetic** and disciplined order, the Franciscans were particularly offended by Pueblo

Santa Fe Spanish colonial town established in 1609; eventually the capital of the province of New Mexico.

ascetic Practicing severe abstinence or self-denial, generally in pursuit of spiritual awareness.

For thousands of years, Indians in the arid Southwest had carved out a rich existence by maintaining careful balance in using the region's natural resources. Katsinas (sometimes spelled Kachinas) represented the various forces in nature that demanded attention and respect. Icons like this one were a physical reminder of the spiritual dynamics alive in the world of the various Pueblo peoples. Seeing these figures as "pagan idols," Roman Catholic missionaries destroyed them whenever they could. In 1680 the Indians struck back: the wanton destruction of the Indians' religious traditions was a key cause of the Pueblo Revolt, which drove the Spanish out of New Mexico for nearly a decade. *The Museum of Fine Arts, Houston. The Bridgeman Art Library.*

Before the arrival of European explorers like Hernando de Soto in the early 1540s, Indians in the American Southeast had lived in huge cities characterized by monumental architecture and a stratified class system with priest kings at the top, skilled craftsmen and traders in the middle, and common farmers and laborers at the bottom. This painting by archaeological reconstruction artist Tom Hall captures the bustling marketplace at Moundville, a large pre-Columbian city in present-day Alabama. Moundville appears to have begun to decline in around 1350—perhaps a consequence of climate change—and collapsed altogether following the introduction of European diseases. Scholars are unsure about what became of Moundville's survivors, but it is likely that they formed smaller villages that were easier to support in the new environment. All of the Southeastern Indian societies—the Cherokees, Choctaws, Creeks, Natchez, and many others—went through a similar transition during this period. *Tom Hall/National Geographic Society Image Collection.*

religion and the Pueblo lifestyle. Indian ceremonies that involved various types of traditional religious objects smacked of idolatry to the Franciscans. Seeking to root out what they viewed as evil, the priests embarked on a wholesale effort to destroy every vestige of the Indians' religion. One priest, Fray Alonso de Benavides, bragged in the 1620s that in one day he confiscated "more than a thousand idols of wood," which he then burned. The priests also interfered in the most intimate social aspects of Pueblo life, imposing foreign ideas about sexual relations and family structure, punishing most of the Pueblos' traditional practices as sinful.

After nearly a century of enduring these assaults on their most fundamental values, the Pueblos struck back. In 1680 a traditional leader named Popé led an uprising that united virtually all of the Indians in New Mexico against Spanish rule. The **Pueblo Revolt** left four hundred Spaniards dead as the rebels captured Santa Fe and drove the invaders from their land. It took almost a decade for the Spanish to regroup sufficiently to reinvade New Mexico. In 1689 troops moved back into the region and over the next several years waged a brutal war to recapture the territory. The fighting continued off and on until the end of the century, but Spanish settlers began returning to New Mexico after the recapture of Santa Fe in 1693.

Elsewhere along the northern frontier of New Spain, the unsettled nature of Indian life and the arid and uninviting character of the land made settlement unappealing to the Spaniards. Efforts at mining, raising livestock, and missionizing in Arizona and Texas were largely unsuccessful until after 1700.

The Indian World in the Southeast

Members of Spanish exploring expeditions under would-be conquistadors such as Ponce de León and de Soto were the first Europeans to contact the mound builder societies and other Indian groups in the Southeast. Although their residential and ceremonial centers often impressed the Spaniards, these Mississippian agricultural groups had no gold and could not easily be enslaved. The conquistadors moved on without attempting to force Spanish rule or the Catholic religion on them.

Given sufficient incentive, however, the Spanish were quick to strike at Indian independence and culture. In Florida, for example, the need to protect Spanish ships from French settlers led Spain to establish garrisons such as Saint Augustine. With this and other similar military posts in place, Jesuit and Franciscan missionaries ranged outward to bring Catholicism to Indians in the region. By 1600 they had established missions from the gulf coast of Florida all the way to Georgia.

Although the Spanish presence in the region was small, its impact was enormous. The Spanish introduced European diseases into the densely populated towns in the Mississippi River region. Epidemics wiped out entire Native American civilizations and forced survivors to abandon their towns and entirely modify their ways of life. Certain groups, among them the Cherokees and Creeks, formed village-based economies that combined agriculture, hunting, and gathering. As had happened earlier in the Northeast among the Iroquois and others, this change in economy led to increasing intergroup warfare. And like the Iroquois,

many southeastern groups created formal confederacies as a way of coping. One example is the **Creek Confederacy**, a union of many groups who had survived the Spanish epidemics. Internally, members created an economic and social system in which each population contributed to the welfare of all and differences were settled through athletic competition—a ballgame not unlike modern lacrosse—rather than warfare. And when new Europeans arrived in the seventeenth and eighteenth centuries, the Creeks and other confederacies found it beneficial to welcome them as trading partners and allies, balancing the competing demands of the Spanish and French, and later the English. To some degree, they took advantage of the European rivalries to advance their own interests against those of neighboring confederacies.

The Indian World in the Northeast

By the time Europeans had begun serious exploration and settlement of the Northeast, the economic and cultural changes among Eastern Woodlands Indians that had begun between 1350 and 1450 had resulted in the creation of two massive—and opposing—alliance systems. On one side were the Hurons, Algonquins, Abenakis, Micmacs, Ottawas, and several smaller tribes. On the other was the Iroquois League.

The costs and benefits of sustained European contact first fell to the Hurons and their allies. The Abenakis, Micmacs, and others who lived along the northern shore of the Atlantic were the first groups drawn into trade with the French, and it was among them that the *coureurs de bois* settled and intermarried. These family ties became firm economic bonds when formal French exploration brought these groups into more direct contact with the European trading world. Seeking advantage against the Iroquois, the Hurons and their neighbors created a great wheel of alliance with the fur trade at its hub and France as its axle.

The strong partnership between these Indians and the French posed a serious threat to the Iroquois. Much of the territory being harvested for furs by the

Pueblo Revolt   Indian rebellion against Spanish authority in 1680 led by Popé; succeeded in driving the Spanish out of New Mexico for nearly a decade.

Creek Confederacy   Alliance of Indians living in the Southeast; formed after the lethal spread of European diseases to permit a cooperative economic and military system among survivors.

Alfred Jacob Miller based this 1837 painting of eighteenth-century mounted buffalo hunters on interviews with Shoshone Indians he met on a trip through the American West. It illustrates clearly the enormous impact the arrival of horses had on Plains Indian life. Note how few mounted men it took to drive vast numbers of animals over a cliff to their deaths. At the bottom of the cliff, women would butcher the dead animals and the meat, bones, and hides would provide food, clothing, tools, tents, and trade goods sufficient to support an entire band of Indians for some time. The arrival of the horse on the Great Plains in the late 1600s marked the beginning of 150 years of unprecedented wealth and power for the Indians in the region. *The Walters Art Museum, Baltimore.*

Hurons had once belonged to the Iroquois, and the Confederacy wanted it back. The presence of the French and the fur trade made this objective all the more desirable. If they could push the Hurons and their allies out and take control of the St. Lawrence River, the French would then have to trade exclusively with them. But the French presence also complicated the situation in that the Hurons had a ready source for guns, iron arrowheads, and other tools that gave them a military edge.

The arrival of the Dutch in Albany, however, offered the Iroquois an attractive diplomatic alternative. In 1623 the Dutch West India Company invited representatives from the Iroquois League to a meeting at **Fort Orange**, offering them friendship and trade. The Iroquois responded enthusiastically, but in a way that the Dutch had not anticipated. Instead of entering peacefully into the trade, the Iroquois imposed their authority over all of the Indian groups already trading with the Dutch. They began a bloody war with the **Mohicans**, who had been the Dutch traders' main

source for furs in the Hudson Valley. By 1627 the Iroquois had driven the Mohicans out of the Hudson Valley and had taken control over the flow of furs.

Trade was so vigorous that the Iroquois soon wiped out fur supplies in their own territory and began a serious push to acquire new sources. Beginning in the late 1630s, the Iroquois Confederacy entered into a long-term aggressive war against the Hurons and their allies in New France; against the Munsees, Delawares, and other groups in the Susquehanna and Delaware River valleys to the south; and even against the Iroquois-speaking Eries to the west. Citing Hienwatha's

Fort Orange   Dutch trading post established near present-day Albany, New York, in 1614.

Mohicans   Algonquin-speaking Indians who lived along the Hudson River, were dispossessed in a war with the Iroquois confederacy, and eventually were all but exterminated.

legacy, the Iroquois justified their aggression by claiming that their conquests were simply bringing more people into the shelter of the Great Tree of Peace, expanding the confederacy to include all the northeastern Indians.

The New Indian World of the Plains

Though largely unexplored and untouched by Europeans, the vast area of the Great Plains also underwent profound transformation during the period of initial contacts. Climate change, the pressure of shifting populations, and the introduction of novel European goods through lines of kinship and trade created an altogether new culture and economy among the Indians in this region.

Before about 1400, Indians living on the plains rarely strayed far from the river ways that form the Missouri River drainage, where they lived in villages sustained by agriculture, hunting, and gathering (see pages 13-14). The climate cooldown that affected their neighbors to the east had a similar effect on the Plains Indians: growing seasons became shorter, and the need to hunt became greater. But at the same time, this shift in climate produced an increase in one food source: **buffalo**.

A survivor of the great ice ages, the American bison is particularly well adapted to cold climates. Unlike European cattle, which often starve when snow buries the grasses on which they graze, buffalo use their hooves to dig out the grass they need, and their efficient metabolism extracts nutrients from even poor-quality pasturage. Although buffalo had long been a presence on the plains, the cold weather during the Little Ice Age spurred a massive increase in their numbers. Between 1300 and 1800, herds numbering in the millions emerged in the new environment created by the climate change.

Some groups—such as the **Caddoan**-speaking Wichitas, Pawnees, and Arikaras—virtually abandoned their agricultural villages and became hunters. Others, such as the Hidatsas, split in two: a splinter group calling themselves Crows went off permanently to the grasslands to hunt while the remainder stayed in their villages growing corn and tobacco. These and others who chose to continue their agricultural ways, the Mandans, for example, established a thriving trade with the hunters, exchanging vegetables and tobacco for fresh meat and other buffalo products.

The increase in buffalo not only provided a welcome resource for the Indians already on the Great Plains but also drew new populations to the area. As the climate farther north became unbearably severe, the Blackfeet and other Indians swept down from the subarctic Northeast to hunt on the plains. Other Algonquin-speaking Indians, including the Gros Ventres, Cheyennes, and Arapahos, soon followed. These were then joined by other northeastern groups fleeing the violence and disease that were becoming endemic in the Eastern Woodlands. Some groups, even war-weary Hurons and Iroquois, came as small parties and sought adoption among Great Plains societies. Others came en masse. The **Lakotas**, for example, once the westernmost family of Siouan agriculturalists, were pushed onto the plains by continuing pressure from the east, but they maintained close relations with their **Dakota** neighbors in Minnesota, who continued to farm and harvest wild rice and other crops. This continued tie, like that between the Crows and Hidatsas, increased both the hunters' and the farmers' chances for survival in an ever more hostile world by expanding available resources. Intergroup trade became the key to the welfare of all.

The buffalo also began to play an important role on the southern plains. There, groups such as the Apaches, Comanches, and Kiowas specialized in hunting the ever-increasing herds and then exchanging part of their kill for village-based products from their neighbors and kinsmen, the Navajos, Hopis, and Pueblos. And it was in these intergroup trades that the Plains Indians would acquire a new advantage in their efforts to expand their hunting economy: the horse.

One unintentional outcome of the Pueblo Revolt was the liberation of thousands of Spanish horses. The Pueblos had little use for these animals, but their trading partners, the Kiowas and Comanches, quickly adopted them. Horses could carry much larger loads than dogs and could survive on a diet of grass rather

---

buffalo   The American bison, a large member of the ox family, native to North America and the staple of the Plains Indian economy between the fifteenth and mid-nineteenth centuries.

Caddoan   A family of languages spoken by the Wichitas, Pawnees, Arikaras, and other Plains Indians.

Lakotas/Dakotas   Subgroups of the Sioux Nation of Indians; Lakotas make up the western branch, living mostly on the Great Plains; Dakotas, the eastern branch, live mostly in the prairie and lakes region of the Upper Midwest.

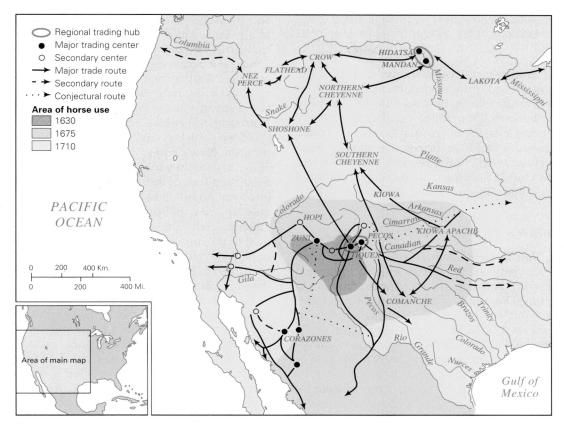

MAP 2.3   **Intergroup Trading on the Plains**   Although movies portray Plains Indians as unsophisticated hunters and warriors, Native American societies in America's midsection maintained extremely complex and cosmopolitan trading networks. As this map shows, trade routes that had existed before Europeans entered the region acquired added importance in distributing the novel technologies and ideas that the newcomers brought with them. The most important of these was horses, which were passed very quickly from group to group along these trade routes.

than taking a share of the meat. In less than a generation, horses became a mainstay of the buffalo-hunting cultures on the southern plains. And from there, horses spread quickly to other hunting people.

Northern plains dwellers such as the Shoshones quickly began acquiring horses from their southwestern kinsmen. Following a northward path along the eastern flank of the Rocky Mountains, horses were passed from one group to another in the complex trading system that had come into existence in the plains region. Well adapted to grasslands, virtually free from natural predators or diseases, and highly prized and thus well protected by their new human owners, horses greatly increased in number. By 1730, virtually all of the plains hunting peoples had some horses and were clamoring for more.

The steady demand for horses and hunting grounds created a new dynamic on the Great Plains and set a new economy into motion (see Map 2.3). After the Spanish reconquest of New Mexico, Indians could obtain horses only through warfare and trade, and both increased significantly. Surprise raids to steal horses from neighboring Indian groups and European settlements brought both honor and wealth to those who were successful.

Conquest and Accommodation in a Shared New World

→ *What forces shaped the day-to-day lives of settlers in New Mexico, Louisiana, and New Netherland?*

→ *How did settlers and American Indians adapt to changing conditions in the different regions of colonial occupation?*

Old World cultures, Native American historical dynamics, and New World environmental conditions combined to create vibrant new societies in European pioneer settlements. Despite the regulatory efforts of Spanish bureaucrats, French royal officials, and Dutch company executives, life in the colonies developed in its own peculiar ways. Entire regions in what would become the United States assumed cultural contours that would shape all future developments in each.

New Spain's Northern Frontiers

Life along New Spain's northern fringe was punctuated by friction between the empire's highly organized official structure and the disorderliness common to frontier settings. For the Spanish, notions of civil order were rooted in the local community—city, town, or village—and its ruling elite. Responsibility for maintaining order belonged to the *cabildo secular*, the municipal town council composed of members of the elite or their appointees. Spain established towns in all of its New World colonies and immediately turned over local authority to a ruling *cabildo*. In Mexico, Peru, and elsewhere this practice was appropriate and usually successful, but in the high desert of New Mexico the *cabildo* system was at odds with environmental and cultural conditions.

After suppressing the Pueblo Revolt during the 1690s, Spaniards began drifting back into New Mexico. Unlike areas to the south, New Mexico offered no rich deposits of gold or silver, and the climate was unsuitable for large-scale agriculture. With neither mines nor plantations to support the *encomienda* system, the basic underpinnings of the traditional ruling order never emerged. Even so, the Spanish colonial bureaucracy followed conventional imperial procedures and made Santa Fe the official municipal center for the region after its recapture from the Indians in 1693. But there were no *encomenderos* to provide wealth. The church, which was channeling money to missions, and the Spanish government, which allocated both military and civic support funds, were the only major employers in the region. Those in neither church's nor state's employ had to scramble for a living.

As in the days before the Pueblo Revolt, the most rewarding economic enterprise in the region was ranching. Under Pueblo control following the revolt, the small flocks of sheep abandoned by the fleeing Spanish grew dramatically. By the time the Spanish returned,

sheep ranching had become a reliable way to make a living. Thus, rather than concentrating near the municipal center in Santa Fe, the population in New Mexico spread out across the land, forming two sorts of communities. South of Santa Fe, people settled on scattered ranches. Elsewhere, they gathered in small villages along streams and pooled their labor to make a living from irrigated **subsistence farming**.

Like colonists elsewhere in Spain's New World empire, the New Mexico colonists were almost entirely male. Isolated on sheep ranches or in small villages, these men sought Indian companionship and married into local populations. These marriages gave birth not only to a new hybrid population but also to lines of kinship, trade, and authority that were in sharp contrast to the imperial ideal. For example, when Navajo or Apache raiding parties struck, ranchers and villagers turned to their Indian relatives for protection rather than to Spanish officials in Santa Fe.

Far away from the imperial economy centered in Mexico City, New Mexicans looked northward for trading opportunities. Southern Plains Indians—Apaches, Comanches, Kiowas, and their kin—needed a continuous supply of horses. They could obtain them by raiding Spanish ranches, but doing so brought reprisals by ranchers and their Indian relatives. Trade was a safer option. Facing labor shortages and too poor to take advantage of traditional Spanish labor systems, New Mexicans accepted Indian slaves—especially children—in exchange for horses. Soon, these young captives became another important commodity in the already complex trading and raiding system that prevailed among the southwestern Indians and Spanish New Mexicans.

In this frontier world, unlike the rest of Spanish America, a man's social status came to depend less on his Spanish connections than on his ability to work effectively in the complicated world of kinship that prevailed in the Indian community. The people who eventually emerged as the elite class in New Mexico were those who best perfected these skills. Under their influence, Santa Fe was transformed from a traditional mission and imperial town into a cosmopolitan frontier trading center. During the next two centuries, this multiethnic elite absorbed first French and then Anglo-American newcomers while maintaining its own social, political, and economic style.

---

subsistence farming   Farming that produces enough food for survival but no surplus that can be sold.

San Esteban Rey, a Catholic church built at Pueblo de Ácoma in about 1642, stands as a monument to the mixing of cultures in colonial New Mexico. The building's adobe construction, rising towers, and curving corners reflect traditional Pueblo architecture, while the crosses on the top identify its European purpose. Churches like this provided an anchor for the multicultural society that emerged in the region. *Lee Marmon.*

The Dutch Settlements

The existence of Rensselaerswyck and other great landed estates made it seem as though the New Netherland colony was prosperous and secure, but it actually was neither. Few of the wealthy stockholders in the Dutch West India Company wanted to trade their lives as successful gentleman investors for a pioneering existence on a barely tamed frontier. The economy in Holland was booming, and only the most desperate or adventurous wanted to leave. But having no one to pay their way, even the few who were willing were hard-pressed to migrate to the colony.

Desperate to draw settlers, the Dutch West India Company created an alternative to patroonship, agreeing to grant a tract of land to any free man who would agree to farm it. This offer appealed to many groups in Europe who were experiencing hardship in their own countries but who, for one reason or another, were unwelcome in the colonies of their homelands. French Protestants, for example, were experiencing terrible persecution in France but were forbidden from going to Canada or Louisiana. Roman Catholics, Quakers, Jews, Muslims, and a wide variety of others also chose to migrate to New Netherland. Most of the colonists settled on small farms, called *bouweries* in Dutch, and engaged in the same agricultural pursuits they had practiced in Europe. Thus New Netherland was dotted with little settlements, each having its own language, culture, and internal economy.

Farming was the dominant activity among the emigrants, but some followed the example of the French *coureurs de bois* and went alone or in small groups into the woods to live and trade with the Indians. Called *bosch loopers*, these independent traders traveled through the forests, trading cheap brandy and rum for the Indians' furs, which they then sold for enormous profits. Although both tribal leaders and legitimate traders complained about the *bosch loopers'* illegal activities, company officials could not control them.

In fact, the Dutch West India Company was unable to control much of anything in New Netherland. The incredible diversity of the settlers no doubt contributed to this administrative impotence. For example, Dutch law and company policy dictated that the **Dutch Reform Church** was to be the colony's official and only religion. But instead of drawing everyone into one congregation, the policy had the opposite effect. As late as 1642 not a single church of any denomination had been planted. Poor leadership and unimaginative policies also contributed to the general air of disorder. Following Peter Minuit's dismissal by the company in 1631, a long line of incompetent governors ruled the colony. In the absence of any legislative assembly or other local body to help keep matters on track, for years one bad decision followed another. It took a major reorganization by the West India Company and its appointment of Peter Stuyvesant in 1645 to turn the colony around.

Life in French Louisiana

France's colony in Louisiana had many of the same qualities and faced many of the same problems as Holland's and Spain's North American possessions. Like most European settlements, Louisiana suffered from a critical shortage of labor, leading first to dependence on the Indians and eventually to the wholesale adoption of African slavery. And like all Europeans who settled in North America, Louisianans found themselves embroiled in a complicated Native American world that usually defied European understanding.

Despite the territory's strategic location, fertile soils, and fur-bearing animals, few Frenchmen showed any interest in settling there. In the first years of the colony's

bosch loopers   Dutch term meaning "woods runners"; independent Dutch fur traders.
Dutch Reform Church   Calvinistic Protestant denomination; the established church in the Dutch Republic and the official church in New Netherland.

The French had difficulty persuading settlers to come to their New World province in Louisiana. As a result, the region's development depended on a mixture of various European refugees, native Indians, and imported Africans for labor. Alexander de Batz's 1735 painting gives us a good idea of what the population around New Orleans looked like at that time. As in neighboring New Mexico, a multiracial and multicultural society emerged in Louisiana that left a permanent legacy in the region. *Peabody Museum, Harvard University 41-72-10/20 T2377.*

existence, the population consisted primarily of three groups: military men, who were generally members of the lower nobility; *coureurs de bois* from Canada looking for new and better sources of furs; and French craftsmen seeking economic independence in the New World. The men in each group had little in common with those in the other groups, and, more important, none had knowledge of or interest in food production. In the absence of an agricultural establishment, the small number of settlers in Louisiana had to depend on imported food. At first, ships from France carried provisions to the colonies, but war in Europe frequently interrupted this source. In desperation, the colonists turned to the Indians.

The **Natchez**, **Chickasaws**, and **Choctaws** were all close by and well provisioned. The Chickasaws refused to deal with the French, and the Natchez, divided into quarreling factions, were sometimes helpful and sometimes hostile. But the Choctaws, locked into a war with the Chickasaws and a tense relationship with the Natchez, found the prospect of an alliance with the French quite attractive. In the realignment process, the Choctaws helped shape France's Indian policies

and expansion plans. For example, they were able to convince the French to expand onto Natchez land rather than in Choctaw territory. When the Natchez resisted French incursion, the Choctaws helped their European allies destroy the tribe. The Choctaws also assisted the French in a thirty-year-long conflict with the Chickasaws, though with less success.

Natchez An urban, mound-building Indian people who lived on the lower Mississippi River until they were destroyed in a war with the French in the 1720s; survivors joined the Creek Confederacy.

Chickasaws An urban, mound-building Indian people who lived on the lower Mississippi River and became a society of hunters after the change in climate and introduction of disease after 1400; they were successful in resisting French aggression throughout the colonial era.

Choctaws Like the Chickasaws, a mound-building people who became a society of hunters after 1400; they were steadfast allies of the French in wars against the Natchez and Chickasaws.

Despite the Choctaw alliance, which guaranteed ample food supplies and facilitated territorial acquisitions, Louisiana remained unappealing to Frenchmen. Although local officials advised against it, the French government finally resorted to recruiting paupers, criminals, and religious or political refugees from central Europe and elsewhere to people the new land. But even with these newcomers, labor was inadequate to ensure survival, much less prosperity. Increasingly, settlers in Louisiana followed their Spanish neighbors' example by importing African slaves to do necessary work. By 1732, slaves made up two-thirds of the population.

As unappealing as the colony was to Frenchmen, it was even more so to French women. As a result, French men, like their Spanish neighbors, married Indians and, later, African slaves, creating a hybrid **creole** population that would come to dominate the region and set its cultural tone.

> **creole**   In colonial times, a term referring to anyone of European or African heritage who was born in the colonies; in Louisiana, refers to the ethnic group resulting from intermarriage by people of mixed languages, races, and cultures.

Examining a Primary Source

✔ Individual Voices

Bartolomé de Las Casas Argues for the American Indians

In his debate with Juan Ginés de Sepúlveda before the Council of Valladolid in 1550 and 1551, Bartolomé de Las Casas repeatedly stressed the many remarkable accomplishments made by Indians, both in creating advanced civilizations of their own and in adapting to Spanish civilization. Many witnesses (most of whom had never been to America) disputed these claims, but more damaging was the argument that such accomplishments were irrelevant. Though perhaps clever, Sepúlveda argued, Indians lacked souls and therefore could never become truly civilized Christians. Like animals, then, they could be exploited but never embraced. Las Casas thought otherwise, and drew on Church doctrine to refute this claim. In the end, Las Casas's argument won the day and became the official position for the Catholic Church and the Spanish Crown.

① *What, exactly, is Las Casas asserting in this sentence? How does this proposition set up the rest of his argument?*

Who, therefore, except one who is irreverent toward God and contemptuous of nature, has dared to write that countless numbers of natives across the ocean are barbarous, savage, uncivilized, and slow witted when, if they are evaluated by an accurate judgment, they completely outnumber all other men? **①** *This is consistent with what Saint Thomas writes: "The good which is proportionate to the common state of nature is to be found in most men and is lacking only in a few. . . . Thus it is clear that the majority of men have sufficient knowledge to guide their lives, and the few who do not have this knowledge are said to be half-witted or fools." Therefore, since barbarians of that kind, as Saint Thomas says, lack that good of the intellect which is knowledge of the truth, a good proportionate to the common condition of rational nature, it is evident that in each part of the world, or anywhere among the nations, barbarians of this sort or freaks of rational nature can only be quite rare. For since God's love of mankind is so great and it is his will to save all men, it is in accord with his wisdom that in the whole universe, which is perfect in all its parts, his supreme wisdom should shine more and more in the most perfect thing: rational nature. Therefore, the barbarians of the kind we have placed in the third category are most rare, because with such natural endowments*

② *What does the reference to writings by Saint Thomas tell us about Las Casas's view of human nature? How does it refute Sepúlveda's claims concerning Indians?*

③ *Judging from this brief excerpt from Las Casas's argument, why do you suppose he won the debate? Why would the Catholic Church have chosen to endorse and publicize his views and not Sepúlveda's*

they cannot seek God, know him, call upon him, or love him. They do not have a capacity for doctrine or for performing the acts of faith or love. **②**

Again, if we believe that such a huge part of mankind is barbaric, it would follow that God's design has for the most part been ineffective, with so many thousands of men deprived of the natural light that is common to all peoples. And so there would be a great reduction in the perfection of the entire universe—something that is unacceptable and unthinkable for any Christian. **③**

Source: Bartolomé de las Casas, *In Defense of the Indians: The Defense of the Most Reverend Lord, Don Fray Bartolomé de las Casas, of the Order of Preachers, Late Bishop of Chiapa, Against the Persecutors and Slanderers of the Peoples of the New World Discovered Across the Seas.* Translated, edited and annotated by Stafford Poole (Dekalb, Northern Illinois University Press, © 1974). Used by permission of Northern Illinois University Press.

SUMMARY

Spain's opening ventures in the Americas had been wildly successful, making the Iberian kingdom the envy of the world. Hoping to cash in on the bounty, other European nations challenged Spain's monopoly on American colonization, creating an outward explosion. Although slow to consolidate an imperial presence in North America, England was the first to confront the Spanish in force, wounding them severely. France and the Netherlands took advantage of the situation to begin building their own American empires.

For Native Americans, the entry of Europeans into their realms combined with other forces to create an air of crisis. Presented with a series of new challenges, Indians sought new ways to solve their problems and created altogether new societies. This often involved difficult choices: perhaps allying with the newcomers, resisting them, or fleeing. As different groups exercised different options, the outcome was a historically dynamic world of interaction involving all of the societies that were coming together in North America.

This dynamic interaction yielded interesting fruit. In New Spain, New France, Louisiana, New Netherland, and throughout the Great Plains, truly cosmopolitan societies emerged. Bearing cultural traits and material goods from throughout the world, these new transatlantic societies set the tone for future development in North America. As we will see in Chapter 3, societies on the Atlantic coast, too, were evolving as English colonists interacted with the land and its many occupants. The outcome of such interchange, over the centuries, was the emergence of a multicultural, multiethnic, and extraordinarily rich culture—an essential element in Making America.

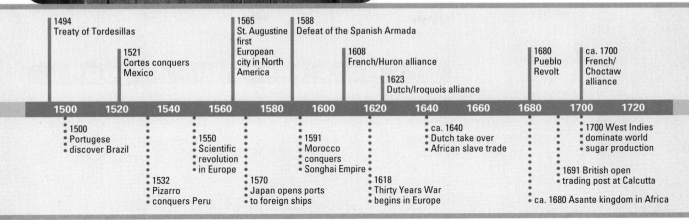

IN THE WIDER WORLD

1494
Treaty of Tordesillas

1521
Cortes conquers Mexico

1565
St. Augustine first European city in North America

1588
Defeat of the Spanish Armada

1608
French/Huron alliance

1623
Dutch/Iroquois alliance

1680
Pueblo Revolt

ca. 1700
French/ Choctaw alliance

| 1500 | 1520 | 1540 | 1560 | 1580 | 1600 | 1620 | 1640 | 1660 | 1680 | 1700 | 1720 |

1500
Portugese discover Brazil

1532
Pizarro conquers Peru

1550
Scientific revolution in Europe

1570
Japan opens ports to foreign ships

1591
Morocco conquers Songhai Empire

1618
Thirty Years War begins in Europe

ca. 1640
Dutch take over African slave trade

1691 British open trading post at Calcutta

1700 West Indies dominate world sugar production

ca. 1680 Asante kingdom in Africa

In the United States

New World Colonies and Native Americans

1494 Treaty of Tordesillas

1512 Creation of the *encomienda* system

1519–1521 Hernando Cortés invades Mexico

1542 Las Casas convinces Spain to implement the Leyes Nuevas

1551 Council of Valladolid rules that American Indians are human beings with souls

1558 Elizabeth I becomes queen of England

1565 Spanish found St. Augustine in present-day Florida

1588 English defeat Spanish Armada

1598 Don Juan de Oñate destroys Ácoma pueblo

1608 French-Huron alliance

1609 Henry Hudson sails up Hudson River; Spanish found Santa Fe in present-day New Mexico

1623 Beginning of Dutch-Iroquois alliance

1627 Creation of Company of New France

1645 Dutch West India Company reorganized under Peter Stuyvesant

1680 Pueblo Revolt

1683 La Salle expedition down the Mississippi River to the Gulf of Mexico

ca. 1700 Beginning of French-Choctaw alliance

Founding the English Mainland Colonies, 1585–1732

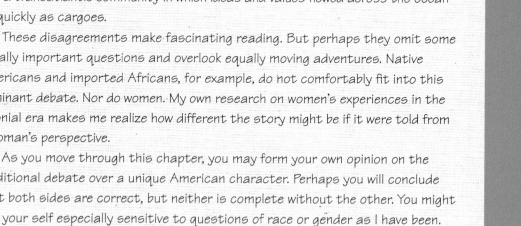

A NOTE FROM THE AUTHOR

Strange vegetation. Exotic animals. Dangerous aliens. Deadly diseases. This may sound like a science fiction movie, but it is actually a description of the colony of Virginia in 1607. The first English settlers at Jamestown were probably as nervous and frightened as a spaceship crew landing on Mars. Yet during the seventeenth century, thousands of English colonists chose to follow these adventurers. Like modern immigrants, these colonists were pushed out of their homelands by poverty, religious persecution, and political conflicts and pulled toward colonial North America by the promise of land, religious freedom, and the expectation of a better life.

Many historians have pored over the diaries, letters, and ship's logs from these days of early settlement. The stories they tell are exciting, but somehow they remain incomplete. Most scholars seem to focus on one overriding question: Was the new American society unique? Some argue that the new environment and the isolation created by a vast ocean forged a unique American character—more practical, more ambitious, more egalitarian than the character of those who remained behind. But other historians remind us that the colonists crisscrossed the Atlantic frequently to visit relatives and conduct business, and they emphasize a transatlantic community in which ideas and values flowed across the ocean as quickly as cargoes.

These disagreements make fascinating reading. But perhaps they omit some equally important questions and overlook equally moving adventures. Native Americans and imported Africans, for example, do not comfortably fit into this dominant debate. Nor do women. My own research on women's experiences in the colonial era makes me realize how different the story might be if it were told from a woman's perspective.

As you move through this chapter, you may form your own opinion on the traditional debate over a unique American character. Perhaps you will conclude that both sides are correct, but neither is complete without the other. You might find your self especially sensitive to questions of race or gender as I have been. Or, you might raise new questions of your own, because the past is always being debated, rewritten, and rediscovered. History, like housework, is "never done." And this is what ensures that the old and often-told story of American colonization will always be, in some respect, new.

Nathaniel Bacon

Nathaniel Bacon came to Virginia as a gentleman in the 1670s, but his resentment of the economic and political domination of the colony by a small group of planters transformed him into a backwoods rebel. In 1676, Bacon led an army of discontented farmers, servants, and slaves against the powerful coastal planters—and almost won. In this stained glass window, discovered and restored in the twentieth century, Bacon's social class and his commanding presence are both evident. *Courtesy of The Association for the Preservation of Virginia Antiquities.*

✔Individual Choices

In 1674 a charismatic young Englishman named Nathaniel Bacon arrived in Virginia. He was wealthy enough to buy a large plantation near Jamestown and a large tract of land on the frontier, and he was quickly appointed to Governor William Berkeley's elite advisory council. Yet, within two years, Bacon had become the leader of a rebellion of poor farmers that almost toppled the colonial government.

Bacon could have lived out his days comfortably among the planter elite. Why, then, did he become a rebel? He had arrived in Virginia at a tense moment when the colony's backcountry farmers' dream of prosperity was threatened by drought, Indian raids, a drop in the price of tobacco, and unfair taxing policies by Berkeley's administration. When Indians attacked, Bacon sympathized with these farmers. When Indians attacked his own frontier farm, he threw in his lot with his neighbors.

Bacon demanded that the Governor raise a militia to rid the area of all Indians. The Governor refused—and Bacon took matters into his own hands. He raised a vigilante army and began a war against all nearby Indians, even the peaceful tribes. The amazed, and enraged, governor branded Bacon a traitor. Bacon quickly struck back. Over five hundred men flocked to join "General" Bacon, and together they seized control of the colony's capital. By mid-October Bacon's rebels controlled over two-thirds of Virginia. Then tragedy struck. On October 26, 1676, Nathaniel Bacon suddenly died of dysentery. Without his leadership, the revolution faltered and by spring of 1677, it had been crushed.

For the next hundred years, the royal governors and the wealthy coastal planters dominated Virginia political life. To these elite colonists, Nathaniel Bacon symbolized a dangerous breakdown of law and order. To backcountry families, Bacon remained a frontier hero. But villain or hero, Nathaniel Bacon would not be the last colonist to fight against unfair treatment.

INTRODUCTION

Bacon's Rebellion reflects many of the contradictory themes and patterns of the early colonial period: the determination to create new communities and the willingness to uproot Native American communities in the process; the sense of new opportunities for success and the continuing influence of wealth and social prestige in a frontier world; and the challenge of creating a unified society in the face of the conflicting economic interests of coastal planters and backcountry farmers.

The seventeenth century saw thousands of English men and women risk the dangers of the Atlantic crossing, the hardships of frontier life, the threat of violence from other settlers and local Indian groups, and the often overwhelming sense of isolation that were all part of the colonizing experience. What motivated them? Many left England to escape religious persecution or, at the least, discrimination and harassment because of their dissenting religious views. Puritans, Catholics, and Quakers all felt compelled to resist demands for allegiance to the Church of England. Given a choice between silence and exile, many chose to journey to what Europeans called the "New World." These English religious radicals were not alone in seeking freedom of worship. Jews, French Protestants, and German Pietists also came to America to escape persecution.

Still other colonists faced the difficult choice of poverty or flight. The economic transformation of England from a feudal society to a market society disrupted the lives of the country's rural population of tenant farmers. Thrown off their land as wealthy landlords turned to sheep raising, thousands of these victims of an emerging capitalism became nomads and vagabonds, traveling from country towns to seaport cities in search of work. Desperation drove them to sign away several years of their lives to a ship captain or plantation owner in Virginia or Maryland in exchange for passage to America.

But if desperation prompted them to leave England, dreams and expectations often motivated them too. These young men and woman agreed to years of servitude and backbreaking labor in the tobacco fields of the **Chesapeake,** without wages and with the most meager rations, because they hoped to acquire land when they were released from bondage. The promise of land was perhaps the most powerful appeal to more fortunate colonists as well. Families of modest means sold off their belongings and said their goodbyes to familiar faces and a familiar landscape, determined

to build new and more independent lives for themselves in the colonies.

This expectation of opportunity was not the monopoly of English men and women. Dutch colonists, Swedes, Finns, and Germans also risked life and limb to reach America in order to improve their economic circumstances. Only one group of colonists, enslaved Africans, arrived on the mainland against their wills. Although their numbers were small in the seventeenth century, thousands of enslaved men, women, and chil-

---

IT MATTERS TODAY

GRASSROOTS MOVEMENTS, THEN AND NOW

Bacon's Rebellion is one of the first instances of a grassroots movement in American history. These movements often give voice to people who feel they are not being heard by the government on important issues. Many things we take for granted today began as demands by grassroots movements, including the end to slavery, the direct election of senators, and women's suffrage. The antiwar movement of the 1960s, the environmental movements of the 1990s, and the antismoking movement of today are recent examples of grassroots movements. Often grassroots movements provide insights into changing values in American society, and, equally often, they arise as part of a cluster of reform movements.

- Research a modern grassroots movement. What tactics has it employed to win support? How successful do you think these tactics have been?

- Do you think grassroots protest is a valuable part of the American political process today, or do we have institutions and political processes that make such protests unnecessary?

Chesapeake   The Chesapeake was the common term for the two colonies of Maryland and Virginia, both of which border on Chesapeake Bay.

dren would become unwilling colonists in the decades that followed.

Colonists recorded their experiences in diaries, letters, journals, and reports to government, church, or trading company officials. These accounts dramatize the hardships and risks that settlers confronted and testify that many did not survive. Ships carrying colonists sank in ocean storms or fell victim to pirates or enemy vessels. Diseases unknown in England decimated settlements. Poor planning and simple ignorance of survival techniques destroyed others. Conflicts with local Indian populations produced violence, bloodshed, and atrocities on both sides. And though colonists lived far from the seats of power in Europe, the rivalries between English, French, Dutch, and Spanish governments spilled across the ocean, erupting in border raids and full-scale wars throughout the century.

Yet the records left by these colonists were not always tales of tragedy. New Englanders recorded the wonders of new vegetation and towering forests. New Yorkers described rolling farmlands, wide rivers, deep harbors. Virginians marveled at rich black soil, exotic flowers, and blooming plants. And throughout the colonies that emerged during the seventeenth and eighteenth centuries, settlers observed, with equal measures of amazement and contempt, the customs and appearances of a race of people entirely new to them: Native Americans.

England and Colonization

→ *What was the impact of the failure of the Roanoke Colony on England's colonizing effort?*

→ *What circumstances or conditions in England prompted people to migrate to America?*

By the end of the century, twelve distinct colonies hugged the Atlantic coastline of English America. The thirteenth, Georgia, was founded in 1732. Although each colony had its own unique history, climate and geography produced four distinct regions: New England, the Middle Colonies, the Chesapeake, and the Lower South. The colonies within each region shared a common economy and labor system, or a similar religious heritage, or a special character that defined the population, such as ethnic diversity. And by the end of the century, as frontier outposts developed into well-established communities, certain institutions emerged in every colony. Thus, whether its founders had been religious refugees or wealthy businessmen, each colony developed a representative assembly, established

courts, built houses of worship—and constructed jails. Carolinians may have thought they shared little in common with the people of Connecticut, but both sets of colonists were subject to English law, English trade policies, and English conflicts with rival nations. Separate, yet linked to one another and to what they affectionately called the "Mother Country" in crucial ways, between 1607 and 1700 the colonies transformed themselves from struggling settlements to complex societies.

England's First Attempts at Colonization

In July 1584, two small ships entered the calm waters between the barrier islands and the mainland of North Carolina. On board were a group of Englishmen, sent by the wealthy nobleman Sir Walter Raleigh with orders to reconnoiter the area and locate a likely spot for settlement. The men were impressed by the peaceful, inviting scene before them: a forest of cypress, sweet gums, pines, and flowering dogwood rising up from the sandy shores; the scent of flowers; and the gentle rustling of treetops filled with birds. The exhausted travelers could not fail to see the contrast between this exotic, lush environment, seemingly untamed by human efforts, and the carefully cultivated farmlands and pastures of their native land. But if they were awed, they were not naive. To protect themselves from unseen dangers, each man wore a suit of armor and carried weapons. Sometime that afternoon, the Englishmen got their first glimpse of the local population as three Indians approached in a canoe. It would be difficult to say which group was more amazed by what they saw. Despite all that they had read, and the many sketches they had seen, the Englishmen surely found these native people strange to behold, dressed as they were in loincloths, their bodies decorated with tattoos and adorned with necklaces and bracelets of shells. The Indians were perhaps equally astonished by the sight of strangers, encased in heavy metal on a humid summer's day.

The encounter passed without incident. Within a month, the Englishmen were gone, returning to make their report to the eagerly awaiting Raleigh. But the following year, a new group of Englishmen sank anchor off the North Carolina shore. These men, many of them soldiers recruited by Raleigh, settled on Roanoke Island. Among them was a 25-year-old historian, surveyor, and cartographer, Thomas Harriot, who published his remarkable account of his nation's first colonizing attempt, *A Briefe and True Report of the New*

Found Land of Virginia, in 1588. In his *Briefe and True Report,* Harriot described the Indians the colonists encountered but failed to report the almost immediate clashes between natives and invaders. The Englishmen's unshakable sense of superiority, despite their dependence on the Indians for food, destroyed the possibility of cooperation. Before the year was over, Harriot and his shipmates returned to England.

Raleigh tried a second time in 1587, spending most of his remaining fortune to send over a hundred colonists to the area. Unfortunately, war with Spain made it impossible for Raleigh to send supplies to his colony for over three years. When a ship finally did reach the colony, the men on board could find no trace of the colonists. Instead they found abandoned ruins, and a single word carved into the bark of a nearby tree: "Croatan." Whether the Roanoke colonists had fled from attack by the Croatan Indians, or been rescued by them in the face of starvation, epidemic, or some other natural disaster, such as a severe drought, no one knows. News of the Roanoke mystery spread rapidly. So too did news that Sir Walter Raleigh had lost his entire fortune in his attempts at colonization. Thus, although Harriot's account stressed the possibilities for wealth and profit in America, the chilling outcome discouraged others from following Raleigh's lead.

Turmoil and Tensions in England

Although no one was willing to risk personal fortune on colonizing America, many English aristocrats believed the country needed to get rid of its numerous poor and, in their minds, dangerous men and women. Pamphlets suggested that the solution to crime and riots was to find a dumping ground for the thousands who had been displaced by the changing economy—desperate people without money or shelter, removed from their lands without any means of livelihood. As farmlands were turned into pastures for sheep that supplied the new woolens industries, the resentful evicted farmers carried signs reading "Sheep Eat Men."

The kings and their advisers also worried about the unrest stirred by growing demands for religious reform within the **Church of England.** The movement to "purify" the church had grown steadily, led by men and women who believed it had kept too many Catholic rituals and customs despite its claim to be Protestant. For the seventeenth-century monarchs, the Stuart kings, this Puritan criticism smacked of treason since the king was not only head of the nation but also head of the Anglican Church. Mistrust between Puritan re-

formers and the Crown grew under King James I and his son Charles I, for both men were rumored to be secretly practicing Catholicism.

There were other tensions in English society in the early decades of the century. A political struggle between the Crown and the legislative branch of the English government, the **Parliament,** was building to a crisis. In 1642 a civil war erupted, bringing together many of the threads of discontent and conflict. A Puritan army led by Oliver Cromwell overthrew the monarchy and in 1649 took the radical step of executing King Charles I. Cromwell's success established the supremacy of the Parliament. For almost a dozen years, the nation was a **Commonwealth,** a republic dominated by Puritans, merchants, and gentry rather than noblemen. Cromwell headed the government until his death in 1658, but to many English citizens his rule was as dictatorial as an absolute monarch's. In 1660 the Stuart family was invited to take the throne once again. For twenty-five years, a period called the **Restoration,** Charles II ruled the nation. But when the Crown passed to his brother James II, an avowed Catholic, a second revolution occurred. This time, no blood was shed in England. James fled to the safety of France, and his Protestant daughter Mary and her Dutch husband, William, came to the English throne. This **Glorious Revolution** of 1688 ended almost a century of political, ideological, and economic instability. By then, twelve American colonies were already perched on the mainland shores.

Church of England   The Protestant church established in the sixteenth century by King Henry VIII as England's official church; also known as the Anglican Church.

Parliament   The lawmaking branch of the English government, composed of the House of Lords, representing England's nobility, and the House of Commons, an elected body of untitled English citizens.

Commonwealth   The republic established after the victory of Oliver Cromwell in the English civil war; the Commonwealth lasted from 1649 until the monarchy was restored in 1660.

Restoration   The era following the return of monarchy to England, beginning in 1660 with King Charles II and ending in 1688 with the exile of King James II.

Glorious Revolution   A term used to describe the removal of James II from the English throne and the crowning of the Protestant monarchs, William and Mary.

Settling the Chesapeake

→ *What were the goals of the Virginia Company and of the Calvert family in creating their Chesapeake colonies? Did the colonies achieve these goals?*

→ *What events illustrate the racial, class, and religious tensions in the Chesapeake?*

→ *How did the Chesapeake colonists resolve conflicts within their communities?*

Fears of financial ruin had prevented any Englishman from following in Sir Walter Raleigh's footsteps. But English **entrepreneurs** had developed a new method of financing high-risk ventures, the **joint-stock company,** and it was soon applied to planting colonies. In a joint-stock company, investors joined together and purchased shares in a venture. Any profits had to be shared by all, but likewise any losses would be absorbed by all. In 1603 both the Plymouth Company and the London Company asked King James I for a charter to settle Virginia. The king agreed to both requests.

Although in theory these two joint-stock companies were rivals, neither worried much about its settlements intruding on the other's. Virginia was, after all, a huge and vaguely defined region, covering much of the Atlantic coast of North America and extending from one ocean to the other. The Plymouth Company chose a poor site for its colony, however. The rocky coast of Maine proved uninviting to the settlers, and sickness and Indian attacks soon sent the survivors hurrying home to England. With its sole rival out of the way, the London Company (now calling itself simply the Virginia Company) launched its enterprise. The first colonists did not set out until December 1606, heading far to the south of the ill-fated Maine colony. Here, near the Chesapeake Bay, they would create the first successful English colony in America.

The Jamestown Colony

The 101 men and four boys sent by the Virginia Company aboard the *Susan Constant,* the *Godspeed,* and the *Discovery* had been tossed on the Atlantic waters for over five months when at last they entered the calm, broad waters of the Chesapeake Bay and made their way up a river they would name the James in honor of their king. Happy at last to feel dry land under their feet, the men disembarked on a small peninsula that jutted out into the river. They named their settlement **Jamestown.** If they had known what lay in store for them in the next decade, they might have sailed home at once.

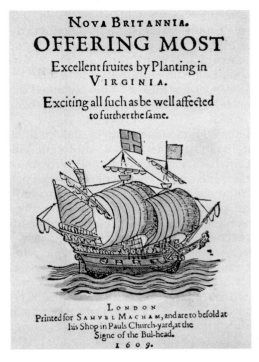

Advertisements like this one were designed to promote settlement of England's first permanent mainland colony. Recruiters hoped that the promise of economic opportunity would offset the fears of settling in a dangerous, strange and distant land. *The Granger Collection, New York*

The early years of this Jamestown colony were a seemingly endless series of survival challenges. The colonists discovered, too late, that they had encamped in an unhealthy spot. Summer brought intense heat, and the men were attacked by swarms of insects, bred in the wetlands that surrounded them. The water of the James was polluted by ocean salt water, making it dangerous to drink. One by one, the settlers fell ill, suffering typhus, malaria, or dysentery. Few of the men

---

entrepreneur   A person who organizes and manages a business enterprise that involves risk and requires initiative.

joint-stock company   A business financed through the sale of shares of stock to investors; the investors share in both the profits and losses from a risky venture.

Jamestown   First permanent English settlement in mainland America, established in 1607 by the Virginia Company and named in honor of King James I.

had any experience in wilderness survival. Indeed, most were gentlemen adventurers, hoping to discover gold and other precious metals just as the Spanish had in Central and South America. These adventurers, as one Englishman bluntly put it, "never knew what a day's labour meant." They assumed that they could enslave the local Indians and force them to do all the work.

Had they known more about the local Indians, they might not have relied on this solution. The Powhatan Confederacy, made up of some thirty Algonquin-speaking tribes on the coastal plains, was a powerful force in the Indian world of the east coast of North America. The chief of the Powhatans had forged this confederacy in the 1570s, in response to Spanish attempts at colonization. When the English arrived, the confederacy was led by Wahunsonacock, who effectively controlled tidewater Virginia and the eastern shore of Chesapeake Bay. Although Wahunsonacock's Powhatan tribe had only about forty warriors, he could count on the assistance of some three thousand others, drawn from member tribes such as the Pamunkeys, Mattoponis, and Arrohatecks. While the English adventurers expended their energies on a futile search for gold rather than on building shelters or stockpiling food for the winter, the Indians harvested their corn—and waited to see what this group of Europeans would do.

What the English did was not impressive. Lacking any farming skills, disorganized, and unaccustomed to following orders or working hard, the colonists soon faced disease, starvation, and exposure to the elements. Temporary relief came when John Smith took command. Smith was hardly a well-liked man: he was over-confident and self-centered, full of exaggerated tales of his heroic deeds as a mercenary in exotic lands. He had narrowly escaped execution on the voyage from England for his role in organizing a mutiny. Smith did have some survival knowledge, however, and he did know how to discipline men. He established a "no work, no food" policy, and he negotiated with the Powhatans for corn and other supplies. When Smith left in 1609, the discipline and order he had established quickly collapsed. The original colonists and those who joined them the following spring remembered that winter as "the starving time." The desperate colonists burned their housing to keep warm and ate dogs, cats, mice, snakes, even shoe leather in their struggle to survive. Only sixty settlers were alive at winter's end.

The Powhatans had little sympathy for the desperate colonists. Even before Smith had departed, cooperation between the two groups had begun to disintegrate, for despite all their problems, the English exhibited

The relationship between the Powhatan Indians and the Virginia colonists deteriorated quickly, despite early signs of cooperation. In this engraving, the adventurer and mercenary John Smith, who claimed to have once been saved by the Indian princess Pocahontas, is shown capturing a Powhatan warrior. Note the difference in weaponry used by the two opponents. *The Granger Collection, New York*

a sense of superiority and entitlement that alienated Wahunsonacock and his confederacy. By 1609 tension and resentment had turned to bloodshed, and raids and counterattacks defined Anglo-Indian relationships for over a decade. Wahunsonacock made several efforts to establish peace, but English encroachments on Indian lands made any lasting truce impossible. Wahunsonacock and his successor, Opechancanough, the chief of the Pamunkeys, recognized that dealing with the English colonists would require warfare, not words.

If the settlers were learning hard lessons in survival, the Virginia Company was learning hard lessons, too. The colony was hanging on by a thread, but the stockholders saw no profits. Their yearly expenses—passage for new colonists, supplies for old ones—gave them a new, more realistic understanding of the slow and costly nature of colonization. The Virginia Company seemed caught in an investor's nightmare, pumping good money after bad in hopes of delaying a total collapse. Prospects seemed bleak: the only gold the colonists had found was "fool's gold," and the investors could see nothing else of economic value in the Chesapeake.

Fortunately the investors were wrong. Tobacco, a weed native to the Americas, proved to be the colony's salvation. Pipe smoking had been a steady habit in England since the mid-sixteenth century, and Englishmen were a steady market for this "brown gold." The local strain of tobacco in Virginia was too harsh for English tastes, but one of the colonists, an enterprising young planter named John Rolfe, managed to transplant a milder strain of West Indian tobacco to the colony. This success changed Rolfe's life, earning him both wealth and the admiration of his neighbors. Rolfe made a second contribution to the colony soon afterward, easing the strained Indian-white relationships by his marriage to an Indian princess, Pocahontas, who John Smith insisted had saved his life.

By 1612, the Virginia Colony was caught up in a tobacco craze as its settlers engaged in a mad race to plant and harvest as many acres of tobacco as possible. Yet the Virginia Company was unable to take full advantage of this unexpected windfall, for it had changed its policies in an effort to ease its financial burdens. In the beginning the company owned all the land but also bore all the costs of colonization. But by 1618, the company's new policy allowed individual colonists to own land if they paid their own immigration expenses. This **head right system** granted each male colonist a deed for 50 acres of land for himself and for every man, woman, or child whose voyage he financed. In this way the Virginia Company shifted the cost of populating and developing the colony to others. But the head rights also ended the company's monopoly on the suddenly valuable farmland.

Other important concessions to the colonists soon followed. The military-style discipline instituted by John Smith and continued by later leaders was abandoned. At the same time, a measure of self-government was allowed. In 1618 the company created an elected, representative lawmaking body called the **House of Burgesses,** which gave the landholders—tobacco planters—of Virginia some control over local political matters. In effect, a business enterprise had finally become a colonial society.

The Virginia Company did retain one of the colony's earliest traditions: a bad relationship with the Powhatan Indians. By 1622, the English seemed to have the upper hand, for the population had grown and tobacco had brought a measure of prosperity. As Virginia planters pressed farther inland, seizing Indian land along local rivers, the new Powhatan chief, Opechancanough, decided to strike back. On what the Christian settlers called Good Friday, he mounted

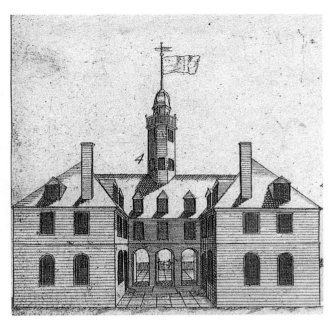

The Virginia House of Burgesses was the first representative assembly to be established in the British colonies. The legislators held their first session in a small Jamestown church, but by 1669, the tobacco planters who served in this assembly had moved into elegant quarters in the colonial capital of Williamsburg. The imposing building sent a clear message to all Virginians that government was the proper domain of gentlemen of wealth and social standing. *Library of Congress.*

a deadly attack on Jamestown, killing a quarter of the colonists in a single day. The company responded as quickly as it could, sending weapons to the Virginians. For two years, war raged between Indians and the English. Although the bloodshed became less frequent by 1625, a final peace was not reached for a decade. By that time, disease and violence had taken its toll on the Powhatans. Once over forty thousand strong, they had dwindled to fewer than five hundred people.

The Good Friday Massacre, as the English called it, brought important changes for the colony. King James I had already begun an investigation of the Virginia Company's management record—and the

---

head right system The grant of 50 acres of land for each settler brought over to Virginia by a colonist.

House of Burgesses The elected lawmaking body of Virginia, established by the Virginia Company in 1618; the assembly first met in 1619.

Baltimore was founded in 1629 and served as a shipping center for Maryland tobacco growers. By 1752, when this view was drawn, it had begun to show signs of developing into a prosperous port city. After the American Revolution, Baltimore expanded and by the 1790s boasted a population of over twenty thousand. *"Baltimore 1752," from a sketch by John Moale, Esq. The Maryland Historical Society, Baltimore.*

colony's growing profit potential. When he learned of the renewed conflict between Indians and colonists, he decided to take action. The king took away the company's charter and declared Virginia to be a royal possession.

If the king's advisers had tallied the cost in human life for the planting of this first English colony in the same manner that the company tallied expenses in pence and pounds, they would have found the outcome sobering. By 1624, only 1,275 of the 8,500 settlers who had arrived since 1607 remained alive. Fortunately, no other English colony would pay such a price for its creation.

Maryland: A Catholic Refuge

As Virginians spread out along the riverways of their colony, searching for good tobacco land, plans for a second Chesapeake colony were brewing in England. The man behind this project was not a merchant or entrepreneur, and profit was not his motive. George Calvert, a wealthy Catholic who King Charles I had just made Lord Baltimore, was motivated by a strong concern for the fate of England's dwindling number of Catholics. He envisioned a religious refuge in America, a safe haven in the face of growing harassment and discrimination against members of his faith. Calvert acquired a charter from the king that granted him a generous tract of land east and north of Chesapeake Bay. Here, he planned to establish a highly traditional society, dominated by powerful noblemen and populated by obedient tenant farmers. Thus, in the 1630s,

George Calvert was a reactionary thinker with a radical vision.

Calvert never realized his dream. He died before a single colonist could be recruited for his Maryland. His oldest son, Cecilius Calvert, the second Lord Baltimore, took on the task of establishing the colony. To Calvert's surprise, few English Catholics showed any enthusiasm for the project. When the first boatload of colonists sailed up the Chesapeake Bay in 1634, most of these two hundred volunteers were young Protestants seeking a better life. Calvert wisely adopted the head right system developed by the Virginia Company to attract additional settlers. The lure of land ownership, he realized, was the key to populating Maryland.

Calvert's colony quickly developed along the same lines as neighboring Virginia. Marylanders immediately turned to planting the profitable **staple crop,** tobacco, and joined the scramble for good riverfront land. Like the Virginians, these colonists used trickery, threats, and violence to pry acres of potential farmland from resisting Indians. By midcentury, the Chesapeake colonies could claim a modest prosperity, even though their populations grew slowly. But they could not claim a peaceful existence. The political crises that shook England during the mid-seventeenth century sent shock waves across the Atlantic Ocean to

---

staple crop   A basic or necessary agricultural item, produced for sale or export.

the American shores. These crises intertwined with local tensions among colonists or between colonists and Indians to produce rebellions, raids, and civil wars.

Troubles on the Chesapeake

In Maryland, tensions ran high between the Catholic minority, who had political influence beyond their numbers because of Lord Baltimore's support, and the Protestant majority in the colony. But with the rise to power of the Puritan leader Oliver Cromwell and his Commonwealth government in England, Calvert realized that his power to protect Maryland's Catholics was in jeopardy. Hoping to avoid persecution of the Catholic colonists, Calvert offered religious toleration to all Marylanders. In 1649 he issued the innovative Toleration Act, protecting all Christians from being "troubled [or] molested . . . in respect of his or her religion." Calvert's liberal policy offended the staunchly Puritan Cromwell, who promptly repealed the act. In 1654 the Puritan-dominated Parliament went further, seizing Maryland from the Calvert family and establishing a Protestant assembly in the colony. The outcome was exactly as Calvert had feared: a wave of anti-Catholic persecution swept over Maryland.

Within a year, a bloody civil war was raging in Maryland. Protestant forces won the fiercely fought Battle of the Severn, but their victory proved futile when Oliver Cromwell died and the monarchy was restored. Charles II returned Maryland to the Calvert family, who had always been loyal supporters of the Stuart dynasty. Despite this reversal of fortunes, Protestants in Maryland continued their struggle, organizing unsuccessful rebellions in 1659, 1676, and again in 1681. Then, in 1689, William and Mary ascended to the throne of England in the Glorious Revolution, and Maryland's Protestants rallied once again. Led by an unlikely looking hero, the stooped and nearly crippled minister **John Coode**, colonists formed an army they called the Protestant Association. By 1691, Coode had persuaded the Crown to make Maryland a royal colony. The story did not end here, however. In 1715 the fourth Lord Baltimore gave up the Catholic faith and joined the Church of England. Maryland was once again returned to the Calverts.

Virginia was less affected by religious controversy than its neighbor. There, colonists were primarily Anglicans although small communities of Quakers, Puritans, and even members of the radical Dutch Labadist sect were scattered throughout Virginia. Religious differences, however, did not spark hostilities. Instead, the fault lines in Virginia society developed between the wealthy planters of the tidewater region and the ambitious newcomers seeking to make their fortunes in the backcountry.

The antagonism between the western, or backcountry, colonists and their more prosperous tidewater rivals was coming to a head as tobacco prices fell in the 1660s. It was in this highly volatile atmosphere that the brash young Nathaniel Bacon rose to challenge the established order of the Virginia Colony. While Bacon's rebellion ultimately failed after the death of its leader, many of the ideas behind the rebellion would resurface one hundred years later during the events leading up to the Revolutionary War.

Colonial Chesapeake Life

Every aspect of life in the Chesapeake colonies, observers noted, seemed to be shaped by tobacco. Its cultivation set rhythms of work and play in both Maryland and Virginia that were dramatically different from those in England. Planting, tending, harvesting, and drying tobacco leaves took almost ten months of the year, beginning in late winter and ending just before Christmas. In the short period between the holiday and the start of a new planting cycle, Chesapeake planters, their families, and their servants worked frantically to catch up on other, neglected farm chores. They did repairs, sewed and mended, built new cabins and sheds, cut timber and firewood. They also compressed what meager social life they had into these winter weeks, engaging—whenever possible—in hasty courtships followed by marriage.

Because tobacco quickly exhausted the soil in which it grew, planters moved frequently to new acres on their estates or to newly acquired lands farther west. Because they rarely stayed in one place very long, planters placed little value on permanent homes or on creating permanent social institutions such as schools. Throughout the century, Chesapeake colonists sacrificed many of the familiar forms of community life to the demands of their profitable crop.

Planters needed a labor force large enough and cheap enough to ensure their profits. As long as poverty and social unrest plagued England, they found the workers they needed from their homeland. Over 175,000 young, single, and impoverished immigrants flooded the Chesapeake during the seventeenth century, their passages paid by the ship captain or the

John Coode   Leader of a rebel army, the Protestant Association, that won control of Maryland in 1691.

THIRTY DOLLARS REWARD.

RAN away, on the 22d of August laſt, *a handſome Negro Lad,* named

A R C H,

Notices of runaway slaves like this one appear frequently in newspapers or as posters. Historians learn a good deal from the descriptions provided of the runaway, often including the monetary value, age, appearance, and special skills of the enslaved man or woman. *The Granger Collection, New York*

planter. In exchange for their transatlantic voyage, these **indentured servants** worked for several years in the tobacco fields without pay. Planters preferred a male work force, for they shared the general European assumption that farming was a masculine activity. As a result, these colonies had an unusual population profile: men outnumbered women in most areas of Virginia and Maryland by 3 to 1. In some areas, the ratio was a remarkable 6 to 1 until the end of the century.

For these indentured servants, and often for their masters as well, life was short and brutal. They spent long, backbreaking days in the fields. Their food rations were meager, their clothing and bedding inadequate, and their shoulders frequently scarred by the master's whip. Servants wrote letters home describing their miserable existence. "People cry out day, and night," wrote one young man, who told his father that most servants would give up "any limb to be in England again."

Most servants also expressed doubts that they would survive to win their freedom. In many cases, they were correct. Disease and malnutrition took the lives of perhaps a quarter of these bound laborers. Free colonists fared little better than servants. Typhus, dysentery, and malaria killed thousands. Over one-quarter of the infants born in the Chesapeake did not live to see their first birthdays; another quarter of the population died before reaching the age of 20. Early death, the skewed ratio of men to women, and high infant mortality combined to create a **demographic disaster** that continued until the last decades of the century.

By the end of the 1600s, the labor force had become increasingly biracial. The steady supply of English workers dried up as economic conditions in England improved. At the same time, the cost of purchasing an African slave declined. During the next century, the shift from English servants to African slaves would be completed.

New England: Colonies of Dissenters

→ *Why did English religious dissenters settle in New England?*

→ *What type of society did the Puritans create in Massachusetts?*

→ *How did the Puritan authorities deal with dissent?*

While Captain John Smith was barking orders at the settlers in Jamestown, some religious dissenters in a small English village were preparing to escape King James's wrath. These residents of Scrooby Village were people of modest means, without powerful political allies or a popular cause. But they had gone one step further than the majority of Puritans, who continued to be members of the Anglican Church despite their criticisms of it. The Scrooby villagers had left the church altogether, forming a separate sect of their own. James I despised these **separatists** and declared his intention to drive them out of England—or worse.

The Scrooby separatists took James's threats seriously. In 1611 they fled to the city of Leyden in the Netherlands. They saw themselves as **Pilgrims** on a spiritual journey to religious freedom. The Dutch welcomed them warmly, but several Pilgrims feared that the comfortable life they had found in Holland was diminish-

indentured servants People working out their compulsory service for a fixed period of time, usually from four to seven years; the terms were most often agreed to in exchange for passage to the colonies; a labor contract called an indenture spelled out the agreement.

demographic disaster The outcome of a high death rate and an unbalanced ratio of men to women in the Chesapeake colonies.

separatists English Protestants who chose to leave the Church of England because they believed it was corrupt.

Pilgrims A small group of separatists who left England in search of religious freedom and sailed to America on the *Mayflower* in 1620.

The Bible was the most cherished book, and often the only book, in a colonist's home. To safeguard this treasure, many Pilgrims stored their Bibles in hand-carved boxes like this one belonging to William Bradford. This box, once decorated with the lion and unicorn symbol of England, was politicized during the American Revolution, when the British lion was scraped off. *Courtesy of the Pilgrim Hall Museum, Plymouth, Massachusetts.*

MAP 3.1 **New England Settlement in the Seventeenth and Early Eighteenth Centuries** This map shows the major towns and cities of New England and their settlement dates. By the end of the seventeenth century, the region had four colonies. Colonists seeking land moved west and south toward the New York border and north toward French Canada. Those involved in trade, shipping, and crafts migrated to the seaport cities.

ing their devotion to God. By 1620, **William Bradford** was leading a small group of these transplanted English men and women on a second pilgrimage—to America.

The Plymouth Colony

The Leyden Pilgrims were joined by other separatists in England. Together, they set sail on an old, creaky ship called the *Mayflower*. On board, too, were a band of "strangers," outsiders to the religious sect who simply wanted passage to America. Crammed together in close and uncomfortable quarters, Pilgrims and strangers weathered a nightmare voyage of violent storms and choppy waters. After nine weeks at sea, the captain anchored the *Mayflower* at Cape Cod, almost 1,000 miles north of the original Virginia destination (see Map 3.1). The exhausted passengers did not complain; they fell to the ground to give thanks. Once the thrill of standing on dry land had passed,

however, many of them sank into depression. The early winter landscape of New England was dreary, alien, and disturbingly empty. William Bradford's own wife, Dorothy, may have committed suicide in the face of this bleak landscape.

Talk of setting sail for Virginia spread through the ranks of the ship's crew and the passengers. Mutiny was in the air. To calm the situation, Bradford negotiated an unusual contract with every man aboard the ship—Pilgrim, crew, servant, and stranger.

This document, known as the **Mayflower Compact,** granted political rights to any man willing to remain and to abide by whatever laws the new colony enacted. Here was an unheard-of opportunity for poor men to participate in governing themselves. All agreed, and the new colony of Plymouth Plantations began to prepare for the long winter ahead.

In Plymouth Plantations, as in Virginia, the first winter brought sickness, hunger, and death. Half of the colonists did not survive. When a Patuxet Indian,

---

William Bradford   The separatist who led the Pilgrims to America; he became the first governor of Plymouth Plantations.

Mayflower Compact   An agreement drafted in 1620 when the Pilgrims reached America that granted political rights to all male colonists who would abide by the colony's laws.

Squanto, came upon the remaining men and women in the spring of 1621, he found them huddled in flimsy shelters, trapped between a menacing forest and a dangerous ocean. Squanto sympathized with their confusion and their longings for home, for he had crossed the Atlantic in 1605 aboard an English trading ship and spent several years in an alien environment. He also understood what it meant to be a survivor, for the Pilgrims had settled where his own village had once stood. His entire family and tribe had been wiped out by diseases carried by English traders and fishermen.

Squanto helped the colonists, teaching them how to plant corn, squash, and pumpkins. Perhaps his greatest service, however, was in helping William Bradford negotiate a peace treaty with Massasoit, leader of the local Wampanoag Indians. The Wampanoags also agreed to spread the word to neighboring Indian communities that the Pilgrims were allies rather than enemies. The combined efforts of Squanto and Massasoit saved the Plymouth Colony, and in the fall of 1621, English settlers and Indian guests sat down together in a traditional harvest celebration of thanksgiving.

Plymouth grew slowly, its colonists earning their livings by farming, fishing, and lumbering. A few Pilgrims grew wealthy by developing a fur trade with the Indians. Unlike the Jamestown settlers, the Plymouth community purchased land rather than seizing it, and they proved to be strong allies when warfare broke out between Massasoit's people and their enemies. In fact, the colonists proved to be such ferocious fighters that they were known as Wotoroguenarge, or "Cutthroats."

Massachusetts Bay and Its Settlers

A second colony soon appeared beside Plymouth Plantations. In 1629 a group of prosperous Puritans, led by the 41-year-old lawyer and landowner **John Winthrop,** secured a charter for their Massachusetts Bay Company from King Charles I. These Puritans had grown increasingly worried about the government's attitude toward dissenters. This harassment, coupled with a deepening economic depression in England, spurred them to set sail for New England. Advertising their colony as "a refuge for many who [God] means to save out of the general calamity," Winthrop and his colleagues had no trouble recruiting like-minded Puritans to migrate.

From the beginning, the Massachusetts Bay Colony had several advantages over Jamestown and Plymouth Plantations. The colonists were well equipped and well prepared for their venture. The company had

even sent an advance crew over to clear fields and build shelters for them. As religious tensions and economic distress increased in England, Massachusetts attracted thousands of settlers. This **Great Migration** continued until Oliver Cromwell's Puritan army took control of England.

While profit motivated the Virginia colonists and a desire to worship in peace prompted the Pilgrims to sail to America, the Puritans of Massachusetts were people with a mission. They hoped to create a model Christian community, a "city upon a hill" that would persuade all English men and women that the reforms they proposed in the Anglican Church were correct. John Winthrop set out their mission in a speech to the passengers aboard the *Arabella*. "The eyes of all peoples are upon us," Winthrop warned, and, more importantly, God was watching them as well. If they abandoned or forgot their mission, the consequences would surely include divine punishment.

This sense of mission influenced the physical as well as spiritual shape of the colony. Massachusetts colonists created tight-knit farming villages and small seaport towns in which citizens could monitor one another's behavior as well as come together in prayer. This settlement pattern fit well with the realities of New England's climate and terrain, since the short growing season and the rocky soil made large, isolated plantations based on staple crops impossible. The colonists, homesick for English villages in regions such as East Anglia, did their best to reproduce familiar architecture and placement of public buildings. The result was often a hub-and-spoke design, with houses tightly clustered around a village green or common pasture, a church beside this green, and most of the fields and farms within walking distance of the village center. This design set natural limits on the size of any village because beyond a certain point—usually measured in a winter's walk to church—a farm family was considered outside the community circle. As a town's population grew and the available farmland was farther from the village green, settlers on the outer rim of the town usually chose to create a new community for

---

Squanto   A Patuxet Indian who taught the Pilgrims survival techniques in America and acted as translator for the colonists.

John Winthrop   One of the founders of Massachusetts Bay Colony and the colony's first governor.

Great Migration   The movement of Puritans from England to America in the 1630s, caused by political and religious unrest in England.

This statue of Anne Hutchinson conveys her as a courageous and determined woman. Massachusetts Bay's Puritan officials would not have approved. They considered her a dangerous heretic who overstepped her proper place as a woman by challenging the established religious and political authorities. Like Roger Williams, Anne Hutchinson was exiled from the colony for her unorthodox views. *Picture Research Consultants & Archives.*

themselves. The Puritans called this process of establishing a new village "hiving off."

Massachusetts and other New England settlements that followed were societies of families. Many, although not all, of the colonists arriving during the Great Migration came as members of a family. Of course, each ship carried unmarried male and female servants too, but unlike in the Chesapeake, the gender ratio in the northern colonies was never dramatically skewed. Imbalances between the sexes did occur in border towns decimated by war with the Indians or in older communities where land was scarce and the young men ventured farther west. On the whole, however, the number of men and women was roughly equal. And, unlike their Chesapeake counterparts, New Englanders never endured a demographic disaster. The cool temperatures and clean drinking water made the region a healthy place for Europeans, healthier than England itself. Infant mortality was low, and most children lived to marry and produce families of their own. A couple could expect to live a long life together and raise a family of five to seven children. One outcome of this longevity was a rare phenomenon in the seventeenth-century English world: grandparents.

Both Puritans and neighboring Pilgrims spoke of the family as "a little commonwealth," the building block on which the larger society was constructed. They set a high priority on obedience in child rearing, in part because they believed that sinfulness and disobedience were the twin results of **original sin.** Breaking a child's will was thus a necessary step toward ensuring the child's salvation. The larger society actively supported a parent's right to demand respect and a child's duty to obey. In fact, Massachusetts law made criticizing a parent a crime punishable by death. The penalty was rarely administered, but the existence of such a harsh law shows the importance of obedience within the family.

A wife was also expected to obey her husband. Puritan ministers reinforced this ideal of a **hierarchy,** or well-defined chain of command, within a family. "Wives," they preached, "are part of the House and Family, and ought to be under a Husband's Government: they should Obey their own Husbands." A husband, however, was bound by sacred obligations to care for and be respectful toward his wife. He must rule his household, he was instructed, without "rigour, haughtiness, harshness, severity; but with the greatest love, gentleness, kindness, tenderness." Marriage involved many practical duties as well. Wives were expected to strive to be "notable housewives"— industrious, economical managers of resources and skilled at several crafts. They were to spin yarn, sew, cook, bake, pickle, butcher farm animals, cure meat, churn butter, and set cheeses. In close-knit New England communities, women were able to help one

original sin In Christian doctrine, the condition of sinfulness that all humans share because of Adam and Eve's disobedience to God in the Garden of Eden.

hierarchy A system in which people or things are ranked above one another.

another by exchanging butter for eggs, assisting with a neighbor's childbirth, or nursing the sick back to health. Husbands were expected to labor in the fields, or in the shop, in order to provide for their families.

Although obligated to be tender and loving, the husband controlled the resources of the family. This was true in all English colonies, although in the Chesapeake, a husband's early death often left the wife in charge of the family farm or shop and its profits until sons came of age. Under English law, a married woman, as a *femme couverte*, lost many of her legal rights because, in law, she came under the protection and governance of her husband. Married women could not acquire, sell, or bequeath property to another person. They could not sue or be sued or claim the use of any wages they earned. They could gain such basic legal rights only through special contracts made with their husbands. Puritan communities, however, frowned on any such arrangements. In the "little commonwealth" of the family, a man was the undisputed head of the household and thus had authority over all its economic resources and all its members. He also represented the family's interests in the realm of politics. No matter how wise or wealthy a woman might become, she was denied a political voice.

Government in Puritan Massachusetts

In order to create the "city upon a hill" the directors of the Massachusetts Bay Company needed, and expected, the full cooperation of all colonists. This did not mean that all colonists had an equal voice or an equal role in fulfilling this vision of a perfect community. During his speech aboard the *Arabella*, John Winthrop made it clear that the "wilderness Zion" was not intended to be an egalitarian society. Like most of his audience, Winthrop believed that it was natural and correct for some people to be rich and some to be poor—"some high and eminent in power and dignity, others mean and in subjugation." Women, children, servants, young men, and adult men without property owed obedience to others in most English communities. But in Massachusetts, there were further limitations on participation. Not even all free males with property were granted a voice in governing the colony. The first government, in fact, consisted solely of Winthrop and the eleven other stockholders of the company who had emigrated to New England. Later, the company relaxed its control and allowed a representative assembly to be elected, but the qualifications for political participation were dramatically different from those set by Mary-

land or Virginia. No man in Massachusetts had a full political voice unless he was an acknowledged church member, not just a churchgoer. Church membership, or **sainthood,** was granted only after a person testified to an experience of "saving grace," a moment of intense awareness of God's power and a reassuring conviction of personal salvation. Thus Massachusetts made religious qualifications as important as gender or economic status in the colony's political life.

Massachusetts differed from the Chesapeake colonies in other significant ways. The colony's government enforced biblical law as well as English civil and criminal law. This meant that the government regulated a colonist's religious beliefs and practices, style of dress, sexual conduct, and personal behavior. For example, every colonist was required to attend church and to observe the Sabbath as Puritan custom dictated. The church played a role in supervising business dealings, parent-child relationships, and marital life.

In the early decades of the colony, the Puritan sense of mission left little room for religious toleration. Colonial leaders saw no reason to welcome anyone who disagreed with their religious views. English America was large, they argued, and people of other faiths could settle elsewhere. Winthrop's government was particularly aggressive against members of a new sect called the **Quakers,** who came to Massachusetts on a mission of their own—to convert Puritans to their faith. Quakers entering the colony were beaten, imprisoned, or branded with hot irons. If they returned, they were hanged. Puritan leaders showed just as little tolerance toward members of their own communities who criticized or challenged the rules of the Bay Colony or the beliefs of its church. They drove out men and women who they perceived to be **heretics,** or religious traitors, including Roger Williams and Anne Hutchinson.

Almost anyone could be labeled a heretic—even a popular Puritan minister. Only a year after the colony

---

femme couverte From the French for "covered woman"; a legal term for a married woman; this legal status limited women's rights, denying them the right to sue or be sued, own or sell property, or earn wages.

sainthood Full membership in a Puritan church.

Quakers Members of the Society of Friends, a radical Protestant sect that believed in the equality of men and women, pacifism, and the presence of a divine "inner light" in every individual.

heretic A person who does not behave in accordance with an established attitude, doctrine, or principle, usually in religious matters.

was established, the church at Salem made **Roger Williams** its assistant minister. His electrifying sermons and his impressive knowledge of Scripture attracted a devoted following. But he soon attracted the attention of local authorities as well, for his sermons were highly critical of the colonial government. From his pulpit, Williams condemned political leaders for seizing Indian land, calling their tactics of intimidation and violence a "National Sinne." He also denounced laws requiring church attendance. True religious faith, he said, was a matter of personal commitment. It could not and should not be compelled. "Forced religion," he told his congregation, "stinks in God's nostrils."

In 1635 John Winthrop's government banished Roger Williams from the colony. With snow thick on the ground, Williams left Salem and sought refuge with the Narragansett Indians. When spring came, many of his Salem congregation joined him in exile. Together, in 1635, they created a community called Providence that welcomed dissenters of all kinds, including Quakers, Jews, and Baptists.

Providence also attracted other Massachusetts colonists tired of the tight controls imposed on their lives by Winthrop and his colleagues. In 1644 the English government granted Williams a charter for his colony, which he eventually called Rhode Island. Within their borders, Rhode Islanders firmly established the principle of separation of church and state.

Soon after the Massachusetts authorities rid the colony of Roger Williams, a new challenge arose. In 1634 Puritan **Anne Hutchinson,** her husband, William, and their several children emigrated to Massachusetts. The Hutchinsons made an impressive addition to the colonial community. He was a successful merchant. She had received an exceptionally fine education from her father and was eloquent, witty, and well versed in Scripture. In addition, she was clearly knowledgeable about the religious debates of the day. Like Williams, Hutchinson put little stock in the power of a minister or in any rules of behavior to assist an individual in the search for salvation. She believed that only God's grace could save a person's soul. And she declared that God made a "covenant of grace," or a promise of salvation, that did not depend on any church, minister, or worship service.

Hutchinson's opinions, aired in popular meetings at her home, disturbed the Puritan authorities. That she was a woman made her outspoken defiance even more shocking. Men like John Winthrop believed that women ought to be silent in the church and had no business criticizing male authorities, particularly ministers and **magistrates,** or government officials. A surprising number of Puritans, however, were untroubled by Hutchinson's sex. Male merchants and craftsmen who lacked political rights because they were not members of the saintly elect welcomed her attacks on these authorities. Hutchinson also attracted Puritan saints who resented the tight grip of the colonial government on their business, personal, and social lives.

In the end, none of Hutchinson's supporters could protect her against the determined opposition of the Puritan leadership. In 1637 she was arrested and brought to trial. Although she was in the last months of a troubled pregnancy, her judges forced her to stand throughout their long, exhausting, repetitive examination. Hutchinson seemed to be winning the battle of words despite her physical discomfort, but eventually she blundered. In one of her answers, she seemed to claim that she had direct communication with God. Such a claim went far beyond the acceptable bounds of Puritan belief. Triumphantly, John Winthrop and his colleagues declared her a heretic, "unfit to our society." They banished her from Massachusetts. Even after her departure, the government seemed to worry about her influence. They encouraged rumors that she was a witch and claimed that the miscarriage she suffered shortly after the trial indicated a demonic fetus.

Many Puritans who left Massachusetts did so by choice, not because they were banished. For example, in 1636 the Reverend Thomas Hooker and his entire Newton congregation abandoned Massachusetts and resettled in the Connecticut River valley. They sought freedom from Winthrop's domination, and the richer soils of the river valley attracted them. Other Puritan congregations followed these Newton families. By 1639 the Connecticut Valley towns of Hartford, Wethersfield, and Windsor had drafted their own governments, and in 1644 they united with the Saybrook settlement at the mouth of the Connecticut River to create the colony of Connecticut. In 1660 the independent New Haven community joined them. Other Bay colonists, searching for new or better lands, made their way north to

Roger Williams   Puritan minister banished from Massachusetts for criticizing its religious rules and government policies; in 1635, he founded Providence, a community based on religious freedom and the separation of church and state.

Anne Hutchinson   A religious leader banished from Massachusetts in 1636 because of her criticism of the colonial government and what were judged to be heretical beliefs.

magistrates   Civil officers charged with administering the law.

what later became Maine and New Hampshire. New Hampshire settlers won a charter for their own colony in 1679, but Maine remained part of Massachusetts until it became a state in 1820.

Indian Suppression

Although the Puritan colonists hoped to create a godly community, they were often motivated by greed and jealousy. Between 1636 and the 1670s, New Englanders came into conflict with one another over desirable land. They also waged particularly violent warfare against the Indians of the region.

When the Connecticut Valley towns sprang up, for example, Winthrop tried to assert Bay Colony authority over them. His motives were personal: he and his friends had expected to develop the valley area lands themselves someday. The Connecticut settlers ignored Winthrop's claims and blocked his attempts to prevent their independence from Massachusetts. But they could not ignore the Indians of the area, who understood clearly the threat that English settlers posed to their territories and their way of life. Sassacus, leader of the Pequots, hoped that an armed struggle would break out between Winthrop and the new Connecticut towns, destroying them both. Instead, however, the two English rivals concentrated on destroying the Pequots.

By 1636, the **Pequot War** had begun, with the Indians under attack from both Massachusetts and Connecticut armies and their Indian allies, the Narragansetts and the Mohicans. Mounting a joint effort, the colonists targeted the Pequot town of Mystic Village. Although the village was defenseless and contained only civilians, Captain John Mason gave the orders for the attack. Captain John Underhill of the Massachusetts army recorded the slaughter with obvious satisfaction: "Many [Pequots] were burnt in the fort, both men, women, and children." When the survivors tried to surrender to the Narragansetts, Puritan soldiers killed them. The brutal war did not end until all the Pequot men had been killed and the women and children sold into slavery. Connecticut claimed credit for this victory and, despite the massacre at Mystic, Massachusetts grudgingly conceded. If the Narragansett Indians believed their alliance with Winthrop would protect them, they were mistaken. Within five years the Puritans had assassinated the Narragansett chief, an act of insurance against problems with these Indian allies.

For almost three decades, an uneasy peace existed between New England colonists and Indians. But the struggle over the land continued. When war broke out again, it was two longtime allies—the Plymouth colo-

No portrait of Metacomet, or King Philip, was painted during his lifetime. In this nineteenth-century painting, Metacomet wears traditional New England Indian clothing, yet he is armed with a European musket. This provides a stark reminder that even the bitterest enemies borrowed from one another's culture. *Library of Congress.*

nists and the Wampanoags—who took up arms against each other. By 1675, the friendship between these two groups had been eroded by Pilgrim demands for new Indian lands. Chief **Metacomet,** known to the English as King Philip, made the difficult decision to resist. When Metacomet used **guerrilla tactics** effectively, staging raids on white settlements, the colonists retaliated by burning Indian crops and villages and sell-

Pequot War Conflict in 1636 between the Pequot Indians inhabiting eastern Connecticut and the colonists of Massachusetts Bay and Connecticut: the Indians were destroyed and driven from the area.

Metacomet A Wampanoag chief, known to the English as King Philip, who led the Indian resistance to colonial expansion in New England in 1675.

guerrilla tactics A method of warfare in which small bands of fighters in occupied territory harass and attack their enemies, often in surprise raids; the Indians used these tactics during King Philip's War.

ing Indian captives into slavery. By the end of the year, Metacomet had forged an alliance with the Narragansetts and several small regional tribes. Metacomet's early, devastating raids on white settlements terrified the colonists, but soon the casualties grew on both sides. Atrocities were committed by everyone involved in this struggle, which the English called King Philip's War. With the help of Iroquois troops sent by the governor of New York, the colonists finally defeated the Wampanoags. Metacomet was murdered, and his head was impaled on a stick.

Indian objections to colonial expansion in New England had been silenced. Indeed, few native peoples remained to offer resistance of any sort. Several tribes had been wiped out entirely in the war, or their few survivors sold into slavery in the Caribbean. Those who escaped enslavement or death scattered to the north and the west. The victory had cost the English dearly also. More than two thousand New England colonists lost their lives as the war spread from Plymouth to nearby settlements. And the war left a legacy of hate that prompted Indian tribes west of Massachusetts to block Puritan expansion whenever possible. The costs of New England's Indian policy prompted colonial leaders in other regions to try less aggressive tactics in dealing with local Indians. For the Wampanoags, the Narragansetts, and the Pequots, however, this decision came too late.

Change and Reaction in England and New England

Both Pilgrim and Puritan leaders had expected the broad expanse of the Atlantic Ocean to protect their colonies from the political and religious tensions that wracked seventeenth-century England. Like their Chesapeake counterparts, they were wrong. From the beginning, of course, Puritan migration to New England had been prompted by Charles I's hostility to dissenters. When Puritan armies challenged the Stuart king in 1642, Bay Colony settlers rejoiced. Many chose to return home to fight in this Puritan Revolution. Throughout the decade, the Massachusetts population shrank.

Massachusetts faced a crisis in the post–civil war years. The sense of mission and the religious commitment that had accompanied its founding seemed to be declining. Few native-born colonists petitioned for full membership, or sainthood, in their local churches, perhaps because of their growing involvement with commerce or because their mission seemed to have been fulfilled by Cromwell and his followers. Few new saints migrated to the Bay Colony after Cromwell's

victory or during the Restoration era. In fact, most of the newcomers in the 1660s were not Puritans at all but Anglicans or members of other Protestant groups seeking economic opportunities. The Bay Colony leaders could not prevent them from settling, as John Winthrop had once done, for King Charles II would not allow it.

The decline in religious zeal troubled ministers and government officials alike, for it marked a sharp decline in eligible voters and officeholders. It troubled the saints, who feared their own children would never join the church and thus never become full citizens in the colony. The problem was made worse by the growing demands of prosperous non-Puritan men for an active role in the government. Some towns began to compromise, allowing men of property and good standing in the community to participate in local decision making. But the saints were not willing to set aside the church membership requirement. In 1662 they decided to introduce the **Half-Way Covenant,** an agreement that allowed the children of church members to join the church even if they did not make a convincing declaration of their own salvation. This compromise kept political power in the hands of Puritans—for the moment.

Pressures from England could not be dealt with so easily, however. Charles II cast a doubtful eye on a colony that sometimes ignored English civil law if it conflicted with biblical demands. In 1683 Charles insisted that the Bay Colony revise its charter to weaken the influence of biblical teachings and eliminate the stringent voting requirements. The Massachusetts government said no. With that, Charles revoked the charter. Massachusetts remained in political limbo until 1685, when James II came to the throne. Then conditions worsened.

In an effort to centralize administration of his growing American empire, King James II combined several of the northern colonies into one large unit under direct royal control. This megacolony, the **Dominion of New England,** included Massachusetts, Rhode Island, Connecticut, Plymouth Plantations, and the newly acquired

---

Half-Way Covenant   An agreement (1662) that gave partial membership in Puritan churches to the children of church members even if they had not had a "saving faith" experience.

Dominion of New England   A megacolony created in 1686 by James II that brought Massachusetts, Plymouth Plantations, Connecticut, Rhode Island, New Jersey, and New York under the control of one royal governor; William and Mary dissolved the Dominion when they came to the throne in 1689.

colonies of New Jersey and New York. James expected the Dominion to increase the **patronage,** or political favors, he could provide to his loyal supporters—favors such as generous land grants or colonial administrative appointments. He also expected to increase revenues by imposing duties and taxes on colonial goods in the vast region he now controlled.

What King James did not expect was how strongly colonists resented his Dominion and the man he chose to govern it. That man was the arrogant and greedy Sir Edmund Andros. Andros immediately offended New England Puritans by establishing the Church of England as the official religion of the new colony. Then he added insult to injury by commandeering a Puritan church in Boston for Anglican worship. Andros also alienated many non-Puritans in Massachusetts by abolishing the representative assembly there. These men had been struggling to be included in the assembly, not to have the assembly destroyed. Andros's high-handed tactics united Massachusetts colonists who had been at odds with each other. One sign of this cooperation surfaced when the Dominion governor imposed new taxes: saints and nonsaints alike refused to pay them.

When Boston citizens received news of the Glorious Revolution, they imprisoned Edmund Andros and shipped him back to England to stand trial as a traitor to the nation's new Protestant government. Massachusetts Puritans hoped to be rewarded for their patriotism, but they were quickly disappointed. Although William and Mary abolished the Dominion, they chose not to restore the Bay Colony charter. In 1691 Massachusetts became a royal colony, its governor appointed by the Crown. **Suffrage,** or voting rights, was granted to all free males who met an English **property requirement.** Church membership would never again be a criterion for citizenship in the colony.

Over the course of its sixty-year history, Massachusetts had undergone many significant changes. The Puritan ideal of small, tightly knit farming communities whose members worshiped together and shared common values and goals had been replaced for many colonists by an emerging "Yankee" ideal of trade and commerce, bustling seaport cities, diverse beliefs, and a more secular, or nonreligious, orientation to daily life. This transition increased tensions in every community, especially during the difficult years of the 1680s. Those tensions contributed to one of the most dramatic events in the region's history: the Salem witch trials.

In 1692 a group of young women and girls in Salem Village began to show signs of what seventeenth-century society diagnosed as bewitchment. They fell into violent fits, contorting their bodies and showing great emotional distress. Under questioning, they named several local women, including a West Indian slave named Tituba, as their tormentors. The conviction that the devil had come to Massachusetts spread quickly, and the number of people accused of witchcraft mushroomed. By summer, more than a hundred women, men, and children were crowded into local jails, awaiting trial. Accusations, trials, and even executions—nineteen in all—continued until the new royal governor, Sir William Phips, arrived in the colony and forbade any further arrests. Phips dismissed the court that had passed judgment based on "spectral evidence"—that is, testimony by the alleged victims that they had seen the spirits of those tormenting them. In January 1693, Phips assembled a new court that acquitted the remaining prisoners.

What had prompted this terrible episode in colonial history? In part, the witch trials reflected a struggle between Puritan farmers of Salem Village and the town's more worldly merchants, for the accusers were often members of the farming community while the accused were often associated with commercial activities. In part, they revealed the fact that, despite the busy port towns and the prosperity of the older farming communities, danger continued to lurk nearby. French and Indian attacks on the border settlements were frequent and brutal, and refuges from this violence could be seen in many older towns. In the despair that followed these attacks, colonists looked for someone to blame for their losses. Finally, the witch-hunts reflected the belief among people—whether farmers or merchants—that the devil and his disciples could work great harm in a community.

The Pluralism of the Middle Colonies

→ *Why did the Dutch and the English encourage a multicultural population in New York?*

→ *What cultural and economic tensions came to a head in Leisler's Rebellion?*

---

patronage   Jobs or favors distributed on a political basis, usually as rewards for loyalty or service.

suffrage   The right to vote.

property requirement   The limitation of voting rights to citizens who own certain kinds or amounts of property.

→ *What made William Penn's vision for Pennsylvania so distinctive?*

Between the Chesapeake and New England lay the vast stretch of forest and farmland called New Netherland, a Dutch colony that was home to settlers from Holland, Sweden, Germany, and France. In the 1660s, Charles II seized the area and drove the Dutch from the Atlantic coast of North America. The English divided the conquered territory into three colonies: New York, New Jersey, and Pennsylvania. Although the region changed hands, it did not change its character: the Middle Colonies remained a multicultural, commercially oriented, and competitive society no matter whose flag flew over them.

From New Netherland to New York

Before 1650, Europe's two major Protestant powers, England and Holland, had maintained a degree of cooperation, and their American colonies remained on friendly terms, assisting each other, for example, in conflicts with Indians. But a growing rivalry over the transatlantic trade and conflicting land claims in the Connecticut Valley soon eroded this neighborliness. Beginning in 1652, these rivals fought three naval wars as both nations tried to control the transatlantic trade in raw materials and manufactured goods. After each, the Dutch lost ground, and their decline made it likely that the New Netherland settlement would be abandoned.

King Charles II of England wanted New Netherland very much, and James, Duke of York (later King James II), was eager to satisfy his brother's desires. In 1664 Charles agreed to give James control of the region lying between the Connecticut and Delaware Rivers—if James could wrest it from the Dutch (see Map 3.2). The promise and the prize amounted to a declaration of war on New Netherland.

When the duke's four armed ships arrived in New Amsterdam harbor and aimed their cannon at the town, Governor Peter Stuyvesant tried to rally the local residents to resist. They refused. Life under the English, they reasoned, would probably be no worse than life under the Dutch. Perhaps it might be better. The humiliated governor surrendered the colony, and in 1664 New Netherland became New York without a shot being fired.

In many ways, James proved to be a very liberal ruler, allowing the Dutch and other European colo-

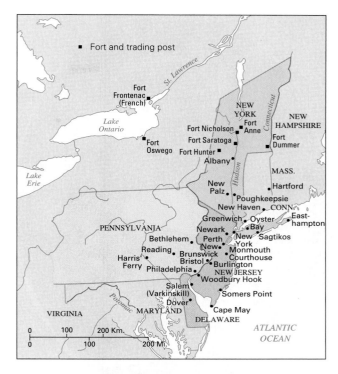

MAP 3.2 **The Middle Colonies** This map shows the major towns, cities, and forts in the colonies of New York, Pennsylvania (including Delaware), and New Jersey. The prosperity of the region was based on the thriving commerce of its largest cities, Philadelphia and New York, and on the commercial production of wheat.

nists to keep their lands, practice their religions, and conduct their business in their native languages. But the duke's generosity and tolerance did not extend to taxation matters. James saw his colonists much as his brother the king saw every colonist: as a source of personal revenue. James taxed New Yorkers heavily and allowed no representative assembly that might interfere with his use of the treasury. All political offices in the new colony, high or low, went to the duke's friends, creating a patronage system that impressed even King Charles.

James's colony did not develop as he had hoped, however. Settlement did not expand to the north and east as he wished. He could not enlist the aid of influential New Yorkers in his expansion plans, even though he offered them the incentive of a representative assembly in 1682. By 1685, James—now king of England—had lost interest in the colony, abandoning his schemes for its growth and abolishing the representative assembly as well.

This portrait of Peter Stuyvesant, the governor of the Dutch colony of New Netherland, was painted by Henrick Courturier when the feisty Stuyvesant was fifty years old. Stuyvesant governed with a heavy hand, flying into a rage if colonists challenged his decisions. He was not popular, but he did bring much-needed order to the colony. *Collection of the New York Historical Society.*

Leisler's Rebellion

Although James viewed New York as a failure, the colony actually grew rapidly during his rule. The population doubled between 1665 and 1685, reaching fifteen thousand the year the duke ascended to the English throne. These new settlers added to the cultural diversity that had always characterized the region. The colony became a religious refuge for French Protestants, English Quakers, and Scottish **Presbyterians.** New York's diverse community, however, did not always live in harmony. English, Dutch, and German merchants competed fiercely for control of New York City's trade and for dominance in the city's cultural life. An equally intense rivalry existed between Manhattan's merchants and Albany's fur traders. Only one thing united these competitors: a burning resentment of James's political control and the men he chose to en-

force his will. Their anger increased when James created the Dominion of New England, merging New York with the Puritan colonies.

In 1689 news of the Glorious Revolution prompted a revolt in New York City similar to the one that shook Boston. **Jacob Leisler,** a German merchant, emerged as its leader. Although Leisler lacked the charisma and commanding presence that had allowed Nathaniel Bacon to rise to power in 1667, he was able to take control of the entire colony. Acting in the name of the new English monarchs, William and Mary, he not only removed Dominion officials but imprisoned several of his local opponents, declaring them enemies of Protestantism. He then called for city elections to oust James's remaining appointees. Leisler expected an era of home rule to follow his rebellion, but England's new monarchs had no intention of leaving a local merchant in charge of a royal colony. When William and Mary sent a new governor to New York, Leisler refused to surrender the reins of government. This time, the abrasive, headstrong merchant found few supporters, and eventually he was forced to step down. To Leisler's surprise, he was then arrested and charged with treason. Both he and his son-in-law were tried, found guilty, and executed. As befit traitors in the seventeenth century, the two rebels were hanged, disemboweled while still alive, and then beheaded. Afterward, their mutilated bodies were quartered. In death, Leisler became a hero and a martyr. Popular anger was so great that to quiet the discontent, the new governor had to permit formation of a representative assembly. Several of the men elected to this new legislature were ardent Leislerians, and for many years New York politics remained a battleground between home rule advocates and supporters of the royal governor and the king.

William Penn's Holy Experiment

More than most dissenting sects, Quakers had paid a high price for their strongly held convictions. Members of the Society of Friends had been jailed in England and

> **Presbyterians** Members of a Protestant sect that eventually became the established church of Scotland but which in the seventeenth century was sometimes persecuted by Scotland's rulers.
>
> **Jacob Leisler** German merchant who led a revolt in New York in 1689 against royal officials representing the Dominion of New England; he was executed as a traitor when he refused to surrender control of the colony to a governor appointed by William and Mary.

William Penn was about 50 years old when this chalk drawing was done. Although Pennsylvania was famous for its religious tolerance and welcoming of non-English immigrants, Penn held many views in common with New England's Puritan leaders. He believed that government should impose and enforce a moral code, because drunkenness, luxury, gambling, and cursing were not only "sins against Nature" but "sins against Government." *"William Penn" by Francis Place. The Historical Society of Pennsylvania.*

Scotland and harassed by their neighbors throughout the empire. Quaker leaders had strong motives to create a refuge for members of their beleaguered church. In the 1670s, a group of wealthy Friends purchased New Jersey from its original proprietors and offered religious freedom and generous political rights to its current and future colonists, many of whom were Puritans. The best known of these Quaker proprietors was **William Penn,** who had given up a life of privilege, luxury, and self-indulgence in Restoration society and embraced the morally demanding life of the Friends.

Penn's father, Admiral Sir William Penn, was one of England's naval heroes and a political adviser to King Charles II. The senior Penn and his son had little in common except their loyalty to the king and their willingness to provide liberal loans to support their monarch's extravagant lifestyle. Eventually, Charles rewarded the Penns' devotion. In 1681, he granted the younger Penn a charter to a huge area west of the Delaware River. This gave Penn the opportunity to create for Quakers a refuge that fully embodied their religious principles.

Penn called his new colony Pennsylvania, meaning "Penn's Woods," in memory of his father. (The southernmost section of Penn's grant, added later by Charles II, developed independent of Penn's control and in 1776 became the state of Delaware.) Like most colonial proprietors, Penn expected to profit from his charter, and he set a quitrent, or small fee, on all land purchased within his colony. But his religious devoutness ensured that he would not govern by whim. Instead, Quaker values and principles were the basis for his "holy experiment." At the heart of the Quaker faith was the conviction that the divine spirit, or "inner light," resided in every human being. Quakers thus were expected to respect all individuals. By their plain dress and their refusal to remove their hats in the presence of their social "betters," Quakers demonstrated their belief that all men and women were equal. In keeping with their egalitarian principles, Quakers also recognized no distinctions of wealth or social status in their places of worship. At the strikingly simple Quaker meeting, or worship service, any member who felt moved to speak was welcome to participate, no matter how poor or uneducated and no matter what sex or age. Although they actively sought converts, Quakers were always tolerant of other religions.

Pennsylvania's political structure reflected this **egalitarianism.** All free male residents had the right to vote during Penn's lifetime, and the legislature they elected had full governing powers. Unlike his patron, Charles II, William Penn had no intention of interfering in his colony's lawmaking process. He honored the legislature's decisions even when they disturbed or amazed him. The political quarrels that developed in Pennsylvania's assembly actually shocked Penn, but his only action was to urge political leaders not to be "so noisy, and open, in your dissatisfactions."

Penn's land policy also reflected Quaker principles. Unlike many proprietors, he wanted no politically powerful landlords and no economically dependent tenant farmers. Instead, he actively promoted a society of independent, landowning farm families. Penn also insisted that all land be purchased fairly from the Indians, and he pursued a policy of peaceful coexistence between the two cultures. William Penn took an active role in making Pennsylvania a multicultural society, recruiting non-English settlers through pamphlets that stressed the religious and political freedoms and economic opportunities his colony offered. More than eight thousand immigrants poured into the colony in the first four years. Many did come from England, but Irish, Scottish, Welsh, French, Scandinavian, and

William Penn   English Quaker who founded the colony of Pennsylvania in 1681.

egalitarianism   A belief in human equality.

This sketch of a Quaker meeting highlights one of the most radical of Quaker practices: allowing women to speak in church. Most Protestant denominations, because of their reading of Saint Paul, enforced the rule of silence on women. But Quakers struck a blow at seventeenth-century gender notions by granting women an active ministerial role, a voice in church policy, and decision-making responsibilities on issues relating to the church and the family. *"The Quaker Meeting" (detail) by Egbert Van Heemskerk. The Quaker Collection, Haverford College Library.*

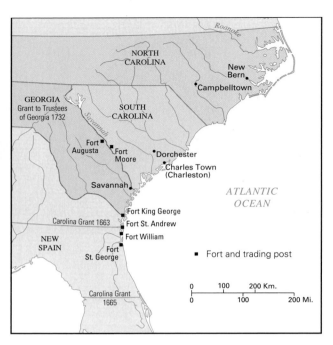

MAP 3.3   The Settlements of the Lower South   This map shows the towns and fortifications of North Carolina, South Carolina, and Georgia, as well as the overlapping claims by the Spanish and the English to the territory south and west of Fort King George. The many Georgia forts reflect that colony's role as a buffer state between rice-rich South Carolina and the Spanish troops stationed in Florida.

German settlers came as well. To their English neighbors who did not speak German, newcomers from Germany such as the Mennonites and Amish were known as the "Pennsylvania Dutch" (*Deutsch*, meaning "German," would have been correct).

When William Penn died in 1717, he left behind a successful, dynamic colony. Philadelphia was already emerging as a great shipping and commercial center, rivaling the older seaports of Boston and New York City. But this success came at some cost to Penn's original vision and to his Quaker principles. The commercial orientation here, as in Puritan Massachusetts, attracted colonists who were more secular in their interests and objectives than the colony's founders. These colonists had no strong commitment to egalitarianism. Many newcomers saw Penn's Indian policy as a check on their ambitions and preferred to seize land from the Indians rather than purchase it. The demand for military protection from Indians by these land-hungry farmers in the western part of the colony became a major political issue and a matter of conscience for Quakers, whose religious principles included **pacifism.** Eventually many Quakers chose to resign from the colonial government rather than struggle to uphold a holy experiment their neighbors did not support.

The Colonies of the Lower South

→ *What type of society did the founders of Carolina hope to create? How did the colony differ from their expectations?*

→ *Why did philanthropists create Georgia? Why did the king support this project?*

William Penn was not the only Englishman to benefit from the often extravagant generosity of King Charles II. In 1663 the king surprised eight of his favorite supporters by granting them several million acres lying south of Virginia and stretching from the Atlantic to the Pacific Ocean. This gesture by Charles was both grand and calculated. France, Spain, Holland, and the Indian tribes that inhabited this area all laid claim to it, and Charles thought it would be wise to secure Eng-

pacifism   Opposition to war or violence of any kind.

The Lynch family, wealthy rice planters of South Carolina, built this elegant home on the banks of the North Santee River in the 1730s. Hopsewee Plantation is a striking example of the luxury enjoyed by the small number of elite white planters whose fortunes depended on the labor of enslaved African field workers. *Courtesy of the Hopsewee Plantation.*

land's control of the region by colonizing it. The eight new colonial proprietors named their colony Carolina to honor the king's late father, who had lost his head to the Puritan Commonwealth (and whose name in Latin was Carolus; see Map 3.3).

The Carolina Colony

The proprietors' plan for Carolina was similar to Lord Baltimore's medieval dream. The philosopher John Locke helped draw up the Fundamental Constitution of Carolina, an elaborate blueprint for a society of great landowners, **yeomen** (small, independent farmers), and serfs (agricultural laborers) bound to work for their landlords. Locke later became famous for his essays on freedom and human rights (see Chapter 4)—a far cry from the social hierarchy proposed in the Carolina constitution. Like the Calverts, however, the Carolina proprietors discovered that few English people were willing to travel 3,000 miles across the ocean to become serfs. Bowing to reality, the proprietors offered the incentive of the head right system used in Virginia and Maryland decades earlier.

The early settlers in Carolina, many of them relocating from the Caribbean island of Barbados, made their way to the southeastern portion of the colony, drawn there by the fine natural harbor of the port city, Charles Town (later Charleston), and its fertile surroundings. Despite the dangers of the Spanish to the south in Florida and the Yamasee Indians to the southwest, Charles Town grew rapidly, becoming the most important city in the southern colonies. The early Carolinians experimented with several moneymaking activities. Some

established trade with the Indians of the region, exchanging English goods for deerskins and for captive victims of tribal warfare. The deerskins were shipped to England. The Indians were shipped as slaves to the Caribbean. Other colonists tapped the region's pine forests to produce naval stores—the timber, tar, resin, pitch, and turpentine that were used in building and maintaining wooden ships.

Carolinians experimented with several cash crops, including sugarcane, tobacco, silk, cotton, ginger, and olives. But none of these crops was particularly profitable. The first real success turned out to be cattle raising, a skill the settlers learned from African slaves brought into the colony by the settlers from Barbados. In the 1680s, Carolina cattlemen turned to a new and very profitable enterprise: rice cultivation. In 1719, Carolina's elite rice planters took control of the southern section of the colony from the original proprietors and named it South Carolina. These planters quickly became the richest English colonists on the mainland.

The northern region of Carolina did not fare as well. Bordered by the Great Dismal Swamp to the north and by smaller swamps to the south, this isolated area attracted few colonists. The land around Albemarle Sound was fertile enough, but the remaining coastline was cut off from the Atlantic by a chain of barrier islands that blocked access to oceangoing vessels. Despite all these constraints, some poor farm

yeoman Independent landowner entitled to suffrage.

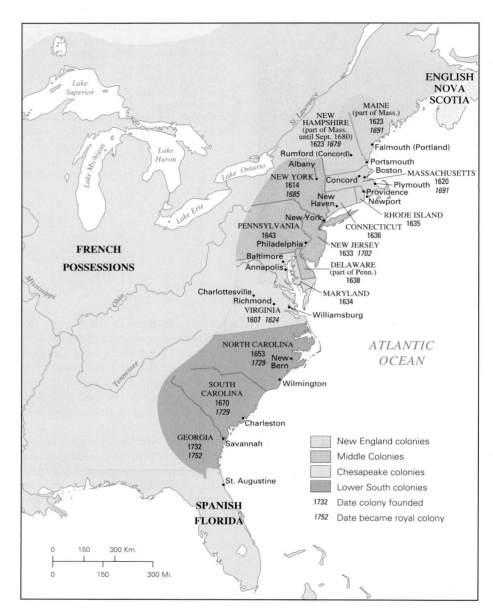

MAP 3.4 **The Colonies and Their Major Cities** The creation of the English mainland colonies spanned almost 125 years, from the first settlement at Jamestown, Virginia, in 1607 to the founding of the last colony of Georgia in 1732. This map indicates the year each colony was founded, the type of charter governing it, and the date in which eight of these colonies came directly under royal control. The map also locates the major colonial cities in each region.

Georgia, the Last Colony

More than one hundred years after the first Jamestown colonists struggled against starvation and disease in Virginia, the last of the original thirteen colonies was established in the Lower South. In 1732 **James Oglethorpe**, a wealthy English social reformer, and several of his friends requested a charter for a colony on the Florida border. Oglethorpe and his colleagues were not seeking to make a profit from this colony; instead they hoped to provide a new, moral life for English men and women imprisoned for minor debts. King George II had other motives for granting the charter, however. He was anxious to create a protective buffer between the valuable rice-producing colony of South Carolina and the Spanish in Florida. The king inserted a clause in the Georgia charter requiring military service from every male settler. Thus he guaranteed that the poor men of Georgia would protect the rich men of South Carolina (see Map 3.4).

families and freed white indentured servants had drifted in from Virginia, searching for unclaimed land and a fresh start. They had modest success in growing tobacco and producing naval stores.

In 1729 the Albemarle colonists followed the lead of their elite neighbors around Charleston and rid themselves of proprietary rule. Then these North Carolinians went one step further: they officially separated from the rice-rich southern section of the colony. The Crown thus recovered what Charles II had given away, for both South Carolina and North Carolina had become royal colonies.

> **James Oglethorpe**   English philanthropist who established the colony of Georgia in 1732 as a refuge for debtors.

Oglethorpe and his associates added their own special restrictions on the lives of the Georgia colonists. Because they believed that poverty was the result of a weak character or, worse, of an addiction to vice, they did not think debtors could govern themselves. They forbade a representative assembly and denied the settlers a voice in selecting political leaders and military officers. In an effort to reform the character of their colonists, the trustees set other rules, including a ban on all alcoholic beverages. To ensure that these settlers worked hard, they kept individual land grants small, and they banned slavery.

Oglethorpe interviewed many imprisoned debtors, searching for members of the "deserving poor" who would benefit from Georgia. But few of these debtors met his standards. In the end, most of the colony's settlers turned out to be middle-class English immigrants and South Carolinians looking for new land. These colonists did not welcome the trustees' paternalistic attitudes, and they soon challenged all the restrictive rules and regulations in the charter. They won the right to accumulate and sell land. They introduced slave labor in defiance of the trustees. By the 1740s, illegal slave auctions were a common sight in Georgia's largest town, Savannah. By 1752, Oglethorpe and his fellow trustees had lost enthusiasm for their reform project and, with relief, returned Georgia to the king.

✔ Individual Voices

Nathaniel Bacon: Manifesto Concerning the Troubles in Virginia, 1676

Nathaniel Bacon began his defiance of the colonial government with one specific objective: to remove the threat of Indian aggression in the backcountry of Virginia. Yet Bacon soon found himself the leader of a civil war between backcountry farmers, apprentices, and servants on the one hand and the wealthy coastal planters and the royal governor on the other. Labeled a traitor by Governor Berkeley, Bacon defended himself and his actions in "The Declaration of the People." In it, he also listed his followers' many grievances against the governor.

① Here Bacon declares that a just God would condone his attacks on the Indian population since they had slaughtered innocent colonists. Yet Bacon attacked peaceful Indians as well as those who had threatened white settlements. Do Bacon's attacks on these peaceful Indian communities suggest a larger issue of racism in the colonies?

② In this section Bacon reminds his readers that the haughty tidewater planters came to Virginia as poor men, not as gentlemen, and are thus no better than his followers. Today, they would be accused of "putting on airs" or of being social climbers.

If virtue be a sin, if piety be guilt, all the principles of morality, goodness and justice be perverted, we must confess that those who are now called rebels may be in danger of those high imputations. Those loud and several bulls would affright innocents and render the defense of our brethren and the inquiry into our sad and heavy oppressions, treason. **①** *But if there be, as sure there is, a just God to appeal to; if religion and justice be a sanctuary here; if to plead the cause of the oppressed; if sincerely to aim at his Majesty's honour and die public good without any reservation or by interest; if to stand in the gap after so much blood of our dear brethren bought and sold; if after the loss of a great part of his Majesty's colony deserted and dispeopled, freely with our lives and estates to endeavour to save the remainders be treason; God Almighty judge and let guilty die. But since we cannot in our hearts find one single spot of rebellion or treason, or that we have in any manner aimed at the subverting of the settled government or attempting of the person of any either magistrate or private man, notwithstanding the several reproaches and threats of some who for sinister ends were disaffected to us and censured our innocent and honest designs, and since all people in all places where we have yet been can attest our civil, quiet, peaceable behaviour far different from that of rebellion and tumultuous persons, let truth be bold and all the world know the real foundations of pretended guilt. We appeal to the country itself what and of what nature their oppressions have been, or by what cabal and mystery the designs of many of those whom we call great men have been transacted and carried on; but let us trace these men in authority and favour to whose hands the dispensation of the country's wealth has been committed.* **②** *Let us observe the sudden rise of their estates composed with the quality in which they first*

(3) Bacon argues that the governor and his friends have done nothing to earn the public's trust or admiration, and have failed to provide basic protection for the citizens of the colony. One hundred years later, American revolutionaries will make the same claim against the king and Parliament of Great Britain. Do you think Bacon's claims are accurate?

entered this country, or the reputation, they have held here amongst wise and discerning men. And let us see whether their extractions and education have not been vile, and by what pretence of learning and virtue they could so soon [come] into employments of so great trust and consequence. (3) Let us consider their sudden advancement and let us also consider whether any public work for our safety and defence or for the advancement and propagation of trade, liberal arts, or sciences is here extant in any way adequate to our vast charge. Now let us compare these things together and see what sponges have sucked up the public treasure, and whether it has not been privately contrived away by unworthy favourites and juggling parasites whose tottering fortunes have been repaired and supported at the public charge. Now if it be so, judge what greater guilt can be than to offer to pry into these and to unriddle the mysterious wiles of a powerful cabal; let all people judge what can be of more dangerous import than to suspect the so long safe proceedings of some of our grandees, and whether people may with safety open their eyes in so nice a concern.

SUMMARY

In 1607, the English created their first permanent colony at Jamestown. By 1732, thirteen English colonies hugged the coast of the Atlantic Ocean. Some, like Maryland, Pennsylvania, and Massachusetts, were founded as religious refuges; others were founded for profit. Four distinct regions soon emerged, based primarily on how the settlers made their livings: the Chesapeake, where tobacco was the staple crop; New England, with its small farms, shipping, and lumbering industries; the Middle Colonies, which grew and exported wheat through the major port cities of New York and Philadelphia; and the Lower South, where rice plantations, worked by African slaves, dominated.

Virginia and Maryland made up the Chesapeake region. Here tobacco shaped every aspect of life. Thousands of poor young Englishmen were brought over to work in the tobacco fields. They came as indentured servants, working without pay in exchange for passage to America. Few women were recruited, and the combination of an unbalanced sex ratio and frequent deaths caused by an unhealthy climate, grueling labor, and poor diet produced what historians call a "demographic disaster" in the seventeenth-century Chesapeake.

The colonies of the Lower South, the Carolinas and Georgia, were established many decades after the Chesapeake by two groups of wealthy Englishmen. Carolina's proprietors tried to create a feudal society, and Georgia's founders wanted to build a haven for debtors. In the end, however, neither goal was achieved. After experiments in cattle-raising and other enterprises, the settlers of what became South Carolina focused on rice production, using African slave labor, and these planters became the richest group in the colonies. North Carolinians were poorer, growing tobacco and farming.

Plymouth Plantations, Massachusetts, Rhode Island, Connecticut and later New Hampshire made up the New England colonies. Here, the earliest settlers were dissenters who sought religious freedom. In 1620, separatists known as the Pilgrims founded the first New England colony, Plymouth Plantations. Their leaders drafted a radical document known as the Mayflower Compact, which assured broad political rights to all the men on board their ship, including the crew and servants. In 1630, Massachusetts Bay was founded by the Puritans who intended it to be a model Protestant community. They demanded conformity to their religious views and drove out those who challenged them, especially Quakers. When Puritans like Roger Williams and Anne Hutchinson challenged the colony's leadership and its religious practices, they too were exiled. Williams went on to found Rhode Island on the principle of separation of church and state. Other colonists left Massachusetts voluntarily and founded Connecticut. In 1691, Massachusetts was taken over by the King, and the Puritans' religious experiment ended. The anxiety produced by this political change coupled with economic tensions and dangers on the frontier contributed to the Salem witch-hunts of 1691.

The Middle Colonies region was originally settled by the Dutch and the Swedes, but the English seized the area in 1664. New Sweden and New Netherland became New Jersey and New York. In 1681 William Penn created the colony of Pennsylvania, west of New Jersey, as a home for Quakers. Unlike the Puritans, however, he welcomed people of all faiths into his "holy experiment." The Middle Colonies were noted for their diverse populations and policies of religious toleration.

Religious, economic, and political conflicts were common back in England, and it was often no more peaceful in the colonies. English settlers brought with them all the old prejudices and rivalries. In Maryland, Protestants and Catholics warred with each other and in Virginia, poor backcountry farmers, led by Nathaniel Bacon, rose up against the wealthier coastal planters in 1676. The desire for land also led to bloodshed. Land hungry colonists in Virginia made war against the Indians and New Englanders fought two brutal wars with local tribes in 1636 and 1675. Finally, English policies prompted rebellions, as colonists in Boston and New York rose up to overthrow the hated Dominion of New England in 1689.

As you will see in Chapter 4, colonists continued to think of England as "home" even as they developed their own societies and their own institutions. Some developments, like widespread African slavery, would seem to widen the differences among the colonial regions; some, like the rise of local representative government would seem to bring them together. Slowly, however, they developed interests and goals that conflicted with the policies of the Mother Country. One thing was certain: great changes would take place in the eighteenth century.

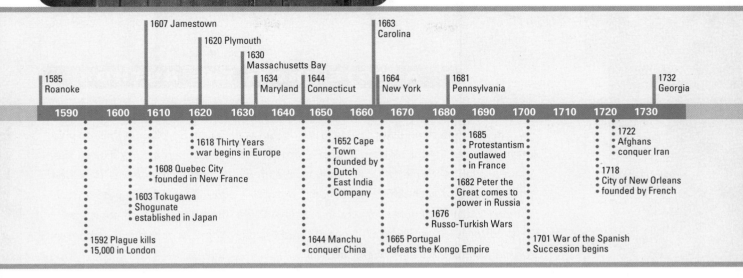

IN THE WIDER WORLD

1607 Jamestown
1620 Plymouth
1630 Massachusetts Bay
1585 Roanoke
1634 Maryland
1644 Connecticut
1663 Carolina
1664 New York
1681 Pennsylvania
1732 Georgia

1590 1600 1610 1620 1630 1640 1650 1660 1670 1680 1690 1700 1710 1720 1730

1618 Thirty Years war begins in Europe
1652 Cape Town founded by Dutch East India Company
1685 Protestantism outlawed in France
1722 Afghans conquer Iran
1608 Quebec City founded in New France
1682 Peter the Great comes to power in Russia
1718 City of New Orleans founded by French
1603 Tokugawa Shogunate established in Japan
1676 Russo-Turkish Wars
1592 Plague kills 15,000 in London
1644 Manchu conquer China
1665 Portugal defeats the Kongo Empire
1701 War of the Spanish Succession begins

In the United States

Settling the Mainland Colonies

1585	English colonize Roanoke Island
1607	Virginia Company founds Jamestown
1619	Virginia House of Burgesses meets
1620	Pilgrims found Plymouth Plantations
1625	Charles I becomes king of England
1630	Puritans found Massachusetts Bay Colony
1634	Lord Baltimore establishes Maryland
1635	Roger Williams founds Providence
1636	Anne Hutchinson banished from Massachusetts
	Pequot War in New England
	Connecticut settled
1642–1648	English civil war
1649	Charles I executed; Cromwell and Puritans come to power in England

1655	Civil war in Maryland
1660	Restoration of English monarchy
1663	Carolina chartered
1664	New Netherland becomes New York
1675	King Philip's War in New England
1676	Bacon's Rebellion in Virginia
1681	Pennsylvania chartered
1685	James II becomes king of England
1686	Dominion of New England established
1688	Glorious Revolution in England
1689	Leisler's Rebellion in New York
1691	Massachusetts becomes royal colony
1692	Salem witch trials
1732	Georgia chartered

CHAPTER 4

The English Colonies in the Eighteenth Century, 1689–1763

A NOTE FROM THE AUTHOR

A Maine farm wife churning butter, a ship captain unloading his cargo in Boston, an African American slave toiling in a rice paddy in South Carolina, a Philadelphia matron shopping for cloth in a local shop—these eighteenth-century figures may have thought they had little in common. In some ways, they were correct. They lived in communities with different economic activities and different labor systems. Some lived in rural areas, others in bustling cities. They were rich and poor; free and unfree; black and white. Whose life was typical? Whose story should a chapter on eighteenth-century colonial life tell?

No historian, no matter how talented, can tell every person's individual story. For me, telling a coherent story of life in eighteenth-century America is a delicate balancing act in which factors that unify historical subjects and factors that divide them must be considered. Common experiences and unique ones both play a part in recreating the past.

What did I find that the colonists had in common? First, they lived on the margins rather than the center of the British Empire. The seat of wealth, power, and prestige was London, not New York or Philadelphia. Second, England, not the colonists, determined the flow of trade across the Atlantic. Third, by mid-century, colonists expected their local elected assemblies rather than the distant British Parliament to govern them. Finally, the competition between England and its rivals, France and Spain, linked the colonists to one another and drew them into bloody imperial wars.

While you'll find trade, politics, and war the three cords that link eighteenth-century colonists in this chapter, you'll also encounter race, region, social class, and gender as factors that divide them. As you read along, consider another issue that will soon divide the colonists: was the British government becoming tyrannical? In 1763, neither the Maine housewife, the ship captain, the slave, or the Philadelphia matron knew how important this question would become— or that it would lead many colonists to choose independence.

Eliza Lucas Pinckney's Gown

As the daughter of one prosperous South Carolina planter and the wife of another, Eliza Lucas Pinckney could afford luxury goods most colonists could not hope to enjoy. But the gown shown above was made of silk produced on her own plantation and sent to England to be woven and dyed. Eliza Lucas Pinckney, who became the manager of her father's three plantations when she was only a teenager, took great pride in experimenting with new crops, including silk from silkworms and the blue dye indigo. *National Museum of American History, Smithsonian Institution, Behring Center.*

✔ Individual Choices

Eliza Lucas of South Carolina was only sixteen when her father was called away to war and left her in charge of his three plantations. The decision would have surprised most eighteenth-century colonists, but George Lucas believed Eliza was no ordinary young woman. Eliza quickly proved her father right for, under her management, the family plantations prospered. She even introduced a new crop, **indigo,** from which a valuable blue dye was made. While other wealthy young women thought about marriage and children, Eliza busied herself with planting, paying bills, directing overseers, and selling crops. But she also made time for traditional female tasks like attending teas, visiting the sick, and learning how to dance and play the piano. To do all this, she set herself a grueling daily schedule, beginning each day at 5:00 A.M.

Eliza's father had encouraged many nontraditional skills in his daughter. For example, he opened his legal library to her and educated her fully on her legal rights as a single woman, or *femme sole.* She put her legal expertise to good use, helping her neighbors write their wills and sue for their debts.

Eliza stubbornly protected her independence. When she finally married it was to an old and respected friend, Charles Pinckney, a widower twice her age who was a leading lawyer and political figure in the colony. As a wife, Eliza turned her full attention to domestic concerns and to the education of her five children. She rejected the traditional notion that children were burdened by original sin and raised her family according to John Locke's theories of the power of nurture and encouragement. Locke's advice served her well: Eliza and Charles's two surviving sons grew up to be political leaders during the revolutionary struggle and her only daughter followed in Eliza's footsteps, eventually running her own plantation.

> **indigo** Shrublike plant with clusters of red or purple flowers, grown on plantations in the South; it was a primary source of blue dye in the eighteenth century.
>
> *femme sole* From the French for "woman alone"; a legal term for an unmarried, widowed, or divorced woman with the legal right to own or sell property, sue or be sued, or earn wages.

INTRODUCTION

Even the most casual observer of colonial society could not fail to note major regional changes and developments during the eighteenth-century. A new system of slave labor was defining the Southern colonies; cities were growing dramatically in the Middle Colonies; and in New England, a Puritan world was transforming into a world of enterprising Yankees.

These differences among the regions were offset by many shared experiences. The colonists were all part of a common imperial structure. They were also part of a sprawling transatlantic community, in which goods, people, and ideas steadily flowed between England, Europe, the Americas, and Africa. Although some three thousand miles of ocean separated New Yorkers from Londoners, colonists journeyed between the two worlds, bringing news of developments in politics, changes in fashion, and popular books. Events in Europe, in England, and in the Caribbean had an impact on everything in colonial life from the religious background of new immigrants to debates over slavery in Virginia to the safety of life on the Maine frontier.

Although Americans eagerly awaited news from an England they still called "home," few members of the English elite followed American developments closely—or at all. Most continued to think of the colonies as a dumping ground for misfits and hayseeds who would struggle to survive, or die, on a violent frontier. Members of the English Parliament viewed the colonists as a collective source of endless problems. They expected insubordinate colonial legislatures, defiant merchants who violated trade regulations, and a dangerously unstable political atmosphere in a society that gave common men an **unprecedented** voice in government. Yet it was the colonists who often suffered from decisions made by Parliament and King. England's fierce rivalries with European nations produced a long series of imperial wars that disrupted colonial life and cast a long shadow over communities from the Maine border to Georgia. In the end, England would triumph over every rival for a North American empire. The outcome of this victory would prove surprising to everyone.

The English Transatlantic Communities of Trade

→ *What were the main regional differences in colonial commerce?*

→ *In which region, and for what reasons, did new immigrants seem to have the best economic choices?*

→ *How were the Carolina plantation owners' profits affected by rising tensions between England and Spain and Portugal?*

Although the English spoke of "the colonial trade," British America did not have a single, unified economy. Instead, four distinctive regional economies had developed on the mainland, concentrated along the Atlantic coastline and bordered on the west by the primarily **subsistence society** that was commonly found on the edge of white settlement. To the south, the sugar islands of the Caribbean made up a fifth unique regional economy. Each of these economies was shaped by environmental conditions, natural resources, English commercial policy, the available labor force, and the available technological know-how.

Regions of Commerce

The sugar-producing islands of the West Indies were the brightest jewels in the English imperial crown. Spain had first laid claim to most of these islands, but England had gobbled up many of them when the Spanish chose to concentrate instead on the gold- and silver-mining colonies of Peru and Mexico. By the eighteenth century, the English flag flew over St. Kitts, Barbados, Nevis, Montserrat, and Jamaica. On each island, English plantation owners built fabulous fortunes on the sugar that African slaves produced. While the **absentee planters** lived in luxury in England, black slaves lived—and died in staggering numbers—on the islands, working the cane fields and tending the fires that burned day and night under the sugar vats of the "great Boiling houses."

Few mainland colonists enjoyed the wealth of this "Sugar Interest." Still, in the Lower South, planters of South Carolina and Georgia, like Eliza Lucas Pinckney,

unprecedented   Unheard of or novel.

subsistence society   A society that produces the food and supplies necessary for its survival but that does not produce a surplus that can be marketed.

absentee planters   An estate owner who collects profits from farming or rent but does not live on the land or help cultivate it.

The sugar-producing islands of the Caribbean were the jewels in the British empire of trade. Ship captains and ship owners made their fortunes out of the sugar, or as it was often called in the eighteenth century, molasses they carried from the West Indies to the mainland colonies, as well as to England and to Africa. The sugar planters lived in luxury in England, among the wealthiest men in the empire. Meanwhile, slaves labored in the cane fields in order to produce the profits these men enjoyed. *British Library; London, UK/Bridgeman Art Library Ltd.*

amassed considerable fortunes by growing rice in the lowlands along the Atlantic coast. By the 1730s, this American rice was feeding the people of the Mediterranean, Portugal, and Spain. By midcentury, planters were making additional profits from indigo, which Eliza Lucas Pinckney had recently introduced to the region. Other Carolinians found cattle raising a profitable enterprise. Like the sugar planters, Carolina and Georgia rice growers based their production on slave labor, but unlike the island moguls, these plantation masters never became permanent absentee landowners.

Tobacco continued to dominate the economy of the Chesapeake, although by the eighteenth century, "brown gold" was no longer the only crop Virginians and Marylanders were willing to plant. In fact, at the turn of the century, when the price of tobacco was driven down by high taxes and competition from Mediterranean sources, many **tidewater** planters chose to diversify. They began producing wheat and other grains for export. As a result, tobacco production shifted west to the area along the Potomac, the James River valley, and the **piedmont** foothills. The second major shift came in the labor force used in tobacco cultivation. By the eighteenth century, African slaves had replaced indentured servants in the fields. Planters who could afford to purchase a number of slaves enjoyed a competitive advantage over their neighbors in both the old and the new tobacco areas because they had enough workers to plant and harvest bigger crops. This large-scale production kept tobacco the number one export of the mainland colonies.

Together, these two southern regions provided the bulk of the mainland's agricultural exports to Great Britain. By contrast, the New England regional economy depended far less on Britain as a market. Except in the Connecticut River valley, where tobacco was grown, the rocky soil of their region made large-scale farming unfeasible for New Englanders. Instead, they developed both a lumbering and a fishing industry, and shipped the timber and dried fish to the West Indies. But it was shipbuilding and the ambitious **carrying trade** connected to it that dominated New England's economy. Colonists made great profits from an extensive shipping network that carried colonial exports across the Atlantic and distributed foreign goods and English manufactured products to the colonies. Some merchant-shippers—the slave traders of Newport, Rhode Island, for example—specialized in a certain commodity, but most were willing to carry any cargo that promised a profit. By the eighteenth century, New England shipping made these colonists rivals of English merchants rather than useful sources of profit for the Mother Country.

Sandwiched between the South and New England, the colonies of New York, New Jersey, Pennsylvania, and later Delaware developed their own regional economy. The Middle Colonies combined the successes of

---

tidewater Low coastal land drained by tidal streams in Maryland and Virginia.

piedmont Land lying at the foot of a mountain range.

carrying trade The business of transporting goods across the Atlantic or to and from the Caribbean.

IT MATTERS TODAY

WOMEN'S OPPORTUNITIES, THEN AND NOW

In her character and her life choices, Eliza Lucas Pinckney seems remarkably modern. Yet she lived in an era when women were assumed to be best suited for the domestic duties known as "house-wifery." Of course, Pinckney had advantages many other eighteenth-century women did not enjoy: wealth, social standing, and a father and a husband who had confidence in her abilities. Without these advantages, Pinckney might never have been able to venture outside the domestic realm. Today, Pinckney would find herself in the company of many women who are able to succeed in careers in business, medicine, scientific research—and in an area completely closed out to Pinckney, politics. The contrast between a life that was extraordinary in the eighteenth century but ordinary in the twenty-first century prompts us to examine what changes have occurred in women's lives between the colonial era and today.

- Choose a profession such as law, medicine, or the military. Research the entrance of women into that profession. What arguments have been offered for and against allowing women into this profession? What factors do you feel have been most significant in opening up opportunities for women in this field? What obstacles still remain?

their neighbors, creating profits from both staple-crop farming and trade. The forests of the Pocono Mountains and upper New York were a source of wood and wood products for the shipbuilding industry, and locally harvested flaxseed was exported to Ireland for its linen industry. The central crop, however, was wheat. Fortunately for the colonists of this area, the price of wheat rose steadily during the eighteenth century. The carrying trade was equally important in this region's mixed economy. Ships carrying cargoes of grain and flour milled in New York City across the Atlantic and into the Caribbean crossed paths with other colonial ships bringing manufactured goods and luxury items from Europe through the region's two major port cities,

New York and Philadelphia. By 1775, Philadelphia had become the second-largest city in the British Empire.

Not everyone in Maryland grew tobacco for the market, of course, and not everyone in Massachusetts was a sailor, lumberjack, ship captain, or urban shop-keeper. The market-oriented activity was largely confined to the older coastal settlements of each region, where harbors and river ways provided the necessary transportation routes for the shipment of crops, goods, and supplies. Inland from these farms, towns, and cities, most colonies had a backcountry that was sparsely populated and farmed by European immigrants, ex-servants, or the families of younger sons from older communities. There, on what white settlers thought of as the frontier and Indians despised as the invasion line, colonists struggled to produce enough for survival. They lacked the labor force to clear the land or work sufficient acreage for a marketable crop, or they lacked the means to get that crop to market. And with no financial or political resources, they had little hope of solving either the manpower or the transport problem. As a result, this belt of subsistence economy extended like a border from Maine to western Pennsylvania, to inland Carolina, along every region of the mainland colonies. But even these backcountry farms had a fragile link to the world of international trade, for settlers brought with them the farm tools and the basic house-hold supplies that had been manufactured in England or imported through colonial ports.

The Cords of Commercial Empire

England's mainland colonists traded, both directly and indirectly, with many European nations and their colonies. Salt, wine, and spices reached colonial tables from southern Europe, and sugar, rum, molasses, and cotton came to their households from the West Indies. But the deepest and broadest channels in the transatlantic trade were those that connected the Mother Country and the colonies. The British purchased over half of all the crops, furs, and mined resources that colonists produced for market and supplied 90 percent of all colonial imports. Strong cords of exchange thus bound America to England, even if many colonists were second-, third-, or even fourth-generation Americans and others traced their roots to different nations and even different continents. The English mainland colonies were also bound to one another, despite a deserved reputation for dispute, disagreement, and endless rivalries. New Englanders might exchange insults with Pennsylvanians, but in the shops and on the wharfs, Pennsylvania flour, Massachusetts mackerel,

Carolina rice, and scores of domestic products and produce changed hands in a lively and cheerful commerce. Domestic trade was greater in volume, although lower in value, than all foreign trade in this eighteenth-century world.

Community and Work in Colonial Society

→ *How did Yankee society differ from Puritan society in early eighteenth-century New England?*

→ *Why did non-English settlers migrate to the British North American colonies?*

→ *Why did colonists in the Chesapeake and Lower South shift from indentured servants to slaves as their primary labor force? What problems faced Africans in slavery?*

→ *What was distinctive about life in the Middle Colonies?*

→ *What motivated colonists to migrate to the backcountry?*

Despite the belief of many observers that there was an "American character," visitors could not fail to note striking physical and social differences as they traveled from New England to the Lower South. Moving from the carefully laid-out towns of New England, through the crowded seaport cities of the Middle Colonies, and into the isolated rural worlds of the plantation South, they could see that the Yankee culture of Connecticut was strikingly different from the elegant lifestyle and social attitudes of Charles Town planter elite.

The Emergence of the "Yankee"

In the early eighteenth century, New England's seaport towns and cities grew steadily in size and economic importance. With the rise of a profitable international commerce, the Puritan culture of the village gave way to a more secular "Yankee" culture. In this milieu, a wealthy man could rise to political prominence without any need to demonstrate his piety. Economic competition and the pursuit of profit eclipsed older notions that the well-being of the community was more important than the gains of the individual. Not merely sentiments, these changes were substantive: seventeenth-century laws regulating prices and interest rates, for example, were repealed or simply ignored. Still, some sense of obligation to the community remained in New Englanders' willingness to create and maintain public institutions such as schools and colleges. In 1701, for example, Yale College opened its doors in New Haven, Connecticut, giving the sons of elite New Englanders an alternative to Massachusetts's Harvard College, founded in 1636. And New Englanders supported newspapers and printing presses that kept their communities informed about local, regional, and even international events.

Even in more traditional New England villages, changes were evident. By the eighteenth century, many fathers no longer had enough farmland to provide adequately for all their sons. Thus many younger sons left their families and friends behind and sought their fortunes elsewhere. Some chose to go west, pushing the frontier of settlement as they searched for fertile land. Others went north, to less developed areas such as Maine. In the process, they created new towns and villages, causing the number of backcountry New England towns to grow steadily until the end of the colonial period. Still other young men abandoned farming entirely and relocated to the commercial cities of the region. Whatever their expectations, urban life often disappointed them, for inequality of wealth and opportunity went hand in hand with the overall prosperity. In Boston a growing number of poor widows and landless young men scrambled for employment and often wound up dependent on public charity. As news spread about the scarcity of farmland in the countryside and the poverty and competition for work in the cities, European immigrants to America tended to bypass New England and settle in the Middle Colonies or along the southern frontier.

Planter Society and Slavery

Southern society was changing as dramatically as New England's. By the end of the seventeenth century, the steady supply of cheap labor from England had begun to disappear. The English economy was improving, and young men who might once have signed on as indentured servants in Virginia or Maryland now chose to remain at home. Those who did immigrate preferred to indenture themselves to farmers and merchants of the Middle Colonies, where work conditions were bearable and economic opportunities were brighter. While this supply of indentured servants was declining, however, a different labor supply was beginning to increase: enslaved Africans.

Although a small number of Africans had been brought to Virginia as early as 1619, the legal differences between black workers and white workers

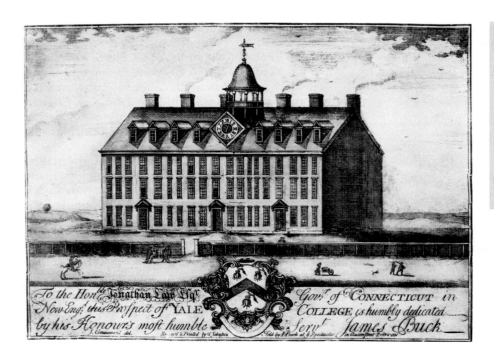

Yale College was founded in 1701, making it the third oldest college in the United States. Its benefactor, Elihu Yale, was born in Boston but spent most of his life in England. By 1749, when this illustration appeared, there were five colleges in the colonies: Harvard, Yale, King's College, the College of New Jersey, and the College of William and Mary. Only the wealthiest young men were likely to attend these schools. *The Granger Collection, New York.*

remained vague until the 1660s. By that time, the slowly increasing numbers of African Americans elicited the different, and harsher, treatment that defined slavery in the Caribbean and South America. By midcentury, it became the custom in the Chesapeake to hold black servants for life terms, although their children were still considered free. By the 1660s, colonists turned these customs of **discrimination** into law. In 1662 Virginia took a major step toward making slavery an inherited condition by declaring that "all children born in this country shall be held bond or free according to the condition of the mother."

Slaves did not become the dominant labor force in southern agriculture until the end of the century, although southern planters were probably well aware of the advantages of slave labor over indentured servitude. First, a slave, bound for life, would never compete with his former master the way freed white servants did. Second, most white colonists did not believe that the English customs regulating a master's treatment of servants had to be applied to African workers. For example, Christian holidays need not be honored for African laborers, and the workday itself could be lengthened without any outcry from white neighbors. Why, then, were the early Chesapeake planters reluctant to import slaves as colonists in the Caribbean and South America had done? Two factors made them hesitate. Dutch control of the African slave trade

kept purchasing prices high, and the disease environment of the Chesapeake cut human life short. Until the end of the seventeenth century, therefore, planters considered the financial investment in African laborers both too costly and too risky.

In the 1680s, however, the drawbacks to African slavery began to vanish. Mortality rates fell in the Chesapeake, and the English broke the Dutch monopoly on the slave trade. Fierce competition among English slavers drove prices down and at the same time ensured a steady supply of slaves. Under these conditions, the demand for slaves grew in the Chesapeake. Although only 5 percent of the roughly 9.5 million Africans brought to the Americas came to the North American mainland colonies, their numbers in Virginia and Maryland rose dramatically in the eighteenth century. By 1700, 13 percent of the Chesapeake population was African or of African descent. In Virginia, where only 950 Africans lived in 1660, the black population grew to 120,000 by 1756. At the end of the colonial period, blacks made up 40 percent of Virginia's population.

discrimination Treatment based on class, gender, or racial category rather than on merit; prejudice.

Colonists who could not afford to purchase African slaves now found themselves at an economic disadvantage. These poorer white Virginians and Marylanders moved west, and new immigrants to the colonies avoided the coastal and piedmont plantation society altogether. Colonial merchants and skilled craftspeople also avoided the Chesapeake, for the planters purchased goods directly from England or used slave labor to manufacture barrels, bricks, and other products. As a result, this region saw the development of few towns or cities that could provide a dense community life. The Chesapeake remained a rural society, dominated by a slaveowning class made prosperous by the labor of African Americans who lived in bondage all their lives.

If tobacco provided a comfortable life for an eighteenth-century planter, rice provided a luxurious one. The Lower South, too, was a plantation society, headed by the wealthiest mainland colonists, the rice growers of the coastal regions of Carolina and Georgia. Members of this planter elite concentrated their social life in elegant Charles Town, where they moved each summer to avoid the heat, humidity, and unhealthy environment of their lowland plantations. With its beautiful townhouses, theaters, and parks, Charles Town was the single truly cosmopolitan city of the South and perhaps the most sophisticated of all mainland cities in North America.

The prosperity that these Lower South planters enjoyed, like the prosperity of the tidewater planters, was based on the forced labor of their slaves. Indeed, the families from Barbados who settled South Carolina had never relied on indentured servants because they arrived with slaves from their Caribbean plantations. By 1708, one-half of the colonial population in Carolina was black, and by 1720, Africans and African Americans outnumbered their white masters. Farther south, in Georgia, the colonists openly defied the trustees' ban on slavery until that ban was finally lifted.

Slave Experience and Slave Culture

Most slaves brought to the mainland colonies did not come directly from Africa. Instead, these men and women were reexported to the Chesapeake or the Lower South after a short period of **seasoning** in the tropical climate of the West Indies. But all imported slaves, whether seasoned or new to the Americas, began their bondage when African slavers, often armed with European weapons, captured men, women, and children and delivered them in chains to European

ships anchored along the coast of West Africa (see Map 4.1). While many of those enslaved were considered war captives, others were simply kidnap victims. The slave trader John Barbot recounted the theft of "little Blacks" who had been sent by their parents to "scare away the devouring small birds" in the family cornfield. Even before these captives reached the coast and the European slave ships waiting there, they were introduced to the horrors of slavery. Their captors treated them "severely and barbarously," beating them and inflicting wounds on their bodies. The many who died on the long march from the interior to the coast were left unburied, their bodies to be "devoured by . . . beasts of prey." As the surviving captives were branded and then put into canoes to be rowed to the waiting ships, some committed suicide, leaping overboard into the ocean waters. Slave traders tried to prevent these suicides—every death meant a smaller profit—but were not surprised by them. The slaves, they commented, dreaded life in America more than their captors dreaded hell.

The transatlantic voyage, or **middle passage,** was a nightmare of death, disease, suicide, and sometimes mutiny. The casualties included the white officers and crews of the slave ships, who died of diseases in such great numbers that the waters near Benin in West Africa were known as the "white man's grave." But the loss of black lives was far greater. Slave ships were breeding grounds for scurvy, yellow fever, malaria, dysentery, smallpox, measles, and typhus—each bringing painful death. When smallpox struck his slave ship, one European recorded that "we hauled up eight or ten slaves dead of a morning. The flesh and skin peeled off their wrists when taken hold of." Perhaps 18 percent of all the Africans who began the middle passage died on the ocean.

Until the 1720s, most Chesapeake slaves worked alone on a tobacco farm with the owner and his family or in small groups of two or three, in a system known as "gang labor." This isolation made both marriage and the emergence of a slave community almost impossible. Even on larger plantations, community formation was discouraged by the use of "gangs" made up entirely of women and children or of men only. The

---

seasoning A period during which slaves from Africa were held in the West Indies so they could adjust to the climate and disease environment of the American tropics.

middle passage The transatlantic voyage of indentured servants or African slaves to the Americas.

Both Africans and Europeans played critical roles in the African slave trade. In this illustration, African slave drivers march their captives, wearing chains and neck-clamps, from their village. Their likely destination: European ships waiting along the west coast of Africa. *Journey of the Discovery of the Source of the Nile, New York, 1869.*

steady influx of newly imported slaves, or "outlanders," during the first decades of the eighteenth century also made it difficult for African Americans to work together to create a culture in response to their disorienting circumstances. The new arrivals had to be taught to speak English and to adapt to the demands of slavery. Slowly, however, these involuntary immigrants from different African societies, speaking different languages, practicing different religions, and surviving under the oppressive conditions of slavery, did create a sense of community, weaving together African and European traditions. The result was an African American culture that gave meaning to, and a sense of identity within, the slave's oppressive world.

In the Lower South, where Eliza Lucas Pinckney ran her plantation, slaves were concentrated on large plantations where they had limited or no contact with white society. This isolation from the dominant society allowed them an earlier opportunity to develop a creole, or native, culture. In contrast to gang labor, here a "task labor" system prevailed, in which slaves were assigned certain chores to be completed within a certain time period. This alternative gave rice plantation slaves some control over their pace of work and some opportunities to manage their free time. Local languages evolved that mixed a basic English vocabulary with words from a variety of African tongues. One of these languages, Gullah, spoken on the Sea Islands off the coast of Georgia and South Carolina, remained the local dialect until the end of the nineteenth century.

For many slaves, the bonds of community that were fostered and forged within this culture became a form of resistance to the enslavement they were forced to endure. But African Americans also developed other ways to show their hatred of slavery. The diary of Virginia planter William Byrd is filled with accounts of daily resistance: slaves who challenged orders, field hands who broke tools and staged work slowdowns, men who pretended sickness and women who claimed pregnancies, household servants who stole supplies and damaged property, and slaves of all ages who ran away to the woods for a day or two or to the slave quarters of a neighboring plantation. African Americans with families, and those who understood the odds against escape, preferred to take disruptive actions like these rather than risk almost certain death in open rebellion.

The Urban Culture of the Middle Colonies

The small family farms of Pennsylvania, with their profitable wheat crops, earned the colony its reputation as the "best poor man's country." Tenant farmers, hired laborers, and even African slaves were not unknown in eastern Pennsylvania, but the colony boasted more comfortable or middling-class farm families than neighboring New York or New Jersey. In New York great estates along the Hudson River controlled much of the colony's good land, and in New Jersey wealthy

This depiction of the African slave trade focuses on the despair and grief produced by the traffic in human beings during the colonial and early national period. Those taken aboard the slave ship would endure the horrors of the "middle passage," the long voyage across the Atlantic Ocean to the Americas. *The Granger Collection, New York.*

owners dominated the choicest acreage, a situation that often resulted in tensions between the landlords and their tenants.

What made the Middle Colonies distinctive was not the expansive Hudson River estates or the comfortable farmhouses in seas of wheat. The region's distinguishing feature was the dynamic urban life of its two major cities, New York and Philadelphia. Although only 3 percent of the colonial population lived in the eighteenth-century cities, they were a magnet for young men and women, widows, free African Americans and slaves, and some of the immigrant population pouring into the colonies from Europe. By 1770, Philadelphia's 40,000 residents made it the second-largest city in the British Empire. In the same year, 25,000 people crowded onto the tip of New York's Manhattan Island.

New York residents shared their cramped living spaces with chickens and livestock and their streets with roving packs of dogs and pigs. On the narrow cobblestone or gravel streets, pedestrians jostled one another and struggled to avoid being run down by carts, carriages, men on horseback, or cattle being driven to slaughter. Although colonial cities were usually thought to be cleaner than European cities, with better sewerage and drainage systems, garbage and excrement left to rot on the streets provided a feast for flies and scavenging animals, including free-roaming pigs.

City residents faced more serious problems than runaway carts and snarling dogs. Sailors on the ships docked at Philadelphia or New York often carried venereal diseases. These and other communicable diseases spread rapidly in overcrowded areas. Fires also raced through these cities of wooden houses, wharfs, and shops. And crime—especially robbery and assault—was no stranger in the urban environment, where taverns, brothels, and gambling houses were common.

These eighteenth-century cities offered a wide range of occupations and experiences that attracted many a farmer's daughter or son but sometimes overwhelmed a new arrival from the countryside. One farm boy wrote to his father of the "Noise and confusion and Disturbance. I must confess, the jolts of Waggons, the Ratlings of Coaches, the crying of meat for the Market, the [hollering] of negroes and the ten thousand junggles and Noises, that continually Surround us in every Part almost of the Town, confuse my Thinking."

Young men who could endure the noise and confusion sought work as **apprentices** in scores of artisan trades ranging from the luxury crafts of silver- and goldsmithing or cabinet making to the profitable trades of shipbuilding, blacksmithing, or butchering, to the more modest occupations of ropemaking, baking, barbering, or shoemaking. The poorest might find work on the docks or as servants, or they might go to sea.

apprentice   A person bound by legal agreement to work for an employer for a specific length of time in exchange for instruction in a trade, craft, or business.

Young women had fewer choices because few trades were open to them. Some might become dressmakers or **milliners,** but domestic service or prostitution were more likely choices. In the Middle Colony cities, as in Boston, widowed farm wives came seeking jobs as nurses, laundresses, teachers, or seamstresses. A widow or an unmarried woman who had a little money could open a shop or set up a tavern or a boarding house.

New York City had the highest concentration of African Americans in the northern colonies. The city attracted many free African American men and women. Only perhaps 5 percent of all mainland colony African Americans were free, and those **manumitted** by their plantation masters frequently chose to remain in the South, although they faced legal and social harassment, including special taxes and severe punishments—for example, striking a white person in self-defense could cost a black man his life. Others, though, made their way to the cities of New England and the Middle Colonies, making a living as laborers and servants or sailors. In addition, although slave labor was not common in New England or on the family farms of the Middle Colonies, slaves were used on New York's docks and wharfs as manual laborers.

Life in the Backcountry

Thomas Malthus, a well-known English economist and diligent student of **demographics,** believed the eighteenth-century population explosion in the English mainland colonies was "without parallel in history." The colonial white population climbed from 225,000 in 1688 to over 2 million in 1775, and the number of African Americans reached 500,000 in the same year. Natural increase accounted for much of this growth, and over half of the colonists were under age 16 in 1775. But hundreds of thousands of white immigrants arrived during the eighteenth century, risking hunger, thirst, discomfort, fear, and death on the transatlantic voyage to start life over in America. The majority of these immigrants ended up in the backcountry of the colonies.

The migration west, whether by native-born or immigrant white colonists, gradually shifted the population center of mainland society. Newcomers from Europe and Britain, as well as descendants of original New England settlers and the younger sons of the tidewater Chesapeake, all saw their best opportunities in the sparsely settled regions of western New York, northern New England, western Pennsylvania, Virginia's Shenandoah Valley, or the Carolina backcountry. Many of these settlers were squatters who cleared a few acres

Few women worked in the skilled trades or crafts, although widows and daughters might manage a shop after a husband or father died. The mantua maker shown here was considered an artisan and could command a good price for her skills, which were making fancy gowns and other elaborately sewn clothing. *Courtesy of the American Antiquarian Society.*

and laid claim by their presence to a promising piece of land.

The westward flow of settlers was part of the American landscape throughout the century, but it became a flood after 1760. A seemingly endless train of carts, sledges, and wagons moved along Indian paths to the west, and the rivers were crowded with rafts and canoes carrying families, farm tools, and livestock. Many of these new immigrants traveled south from Pennsylvania along a wagon road that ran 800 miles from Philadelphia to Virginia, North Carolina, and Augusta, Georgia. Others chose to remain in the Middle Colo-

milliner   A maker or designer of hats.
manumit   To free from slavery or bondage.
demographics   Statistical data on population.

nies. New York's population rose 39 percent between 1760 and 1776, and in 1769, on the day the land office opened at Fort Pitt (Pittsburgh), over twenty-seven hundred applicants showed up to register for land.

By 1760, perhaps 700,000 new colonists had made their homes in the mainland colonies. In the early part of the century, the largest immigrant group was the **Scots-Irish.** Later, German settlers dominated. But an occasional traveler on the wagon roads might be Italian, Swiss, Irish, Welsh, or a European Jew. Most striking, the number of British immigrants swelled after 1760, causing anger and alarm within the British government. The steady stream of young English men and women out of the country prompted government officials to consider passing laws curbing emigration. What prompted this transatlantic population shift? It was not always desperation or oppression. Many arrived with enough resources to finance their new life in the colonies. Some became indentured servants or redemptioners only to preserve those savings. While unemployment, poverty, the oppression of landlords, and crop failures pushed men and women out of Europe or Britain, it is also true that the availability of cheap land, a greater likelihood of religious freedom, and the chance to pursue a craft successfully pulled others toward the colonies.

Conflicts Among the Colonists

→ *What events illustrated the tensions between races in colonial society?*

→ *What conflicts arose between elites and poorer colonists?*

The strains of economic inequality being felt in every region of mainland British America frequently erupted into violent confrontations. At the same time, tensions between Indians and colonists continued, and tensions between black and white colonists increased as both slave and free black populations grew during the eighteenth century. In almost every decade, blood was shed as colonist battled colonist over economic opportunity, personal freedom, western lands, or political representation.

Slave Revolts, North and South

White slave masters in both the Chesapeake and the Lower South knew that a slave revolt was always a possibility, for enslaved Africans and African Americans shared with other colonists what one observer called a "fondness for freedom." Planters thus took elaborate precautions to prevent rebellions, assembling armed patrols that policed the roads and woods near their plantations. These patrols were usually efficient, and the punishment they inflicted was deadly. Even if rebels escaped immediate capture, few safe havens were available to them. Individual runaways had a hard time sustaining their freedom, but dozens of rebels from one plantation were usually doomed once whites on neighboring plantations were alerted. Despite these odds, slaves continued to seek their liberty, often timing their revolts to coincide with epidemics or imperial wars that distracted the white community.

The most famous slave revolt of the eighteenth century, the **Stono Rebellion,** took place in the midst of a yellow fever epidemic in Charles Town just as news of war between England and Spain reached the colony of South Carolina. Early on a Sunday morning in September 1739, about twenty slaves gathered at the Stono River, south of Charles Town. Their leader, Jemmy, had been born in Africa, possibly in the Congo but more likely Angola, for twenty or more of those who eventually joined the revolt were Angolan. The rebels seized guns and gunpowder, killed several planter families and storekeepers, and then headed south. Rather than traveling quietly through the woods, the rebels marched boldly in open view, beating drums to invite slaves on nearby plantations to join them in their flight to Spanish Florida. Other slaves answered the call, and the Stono rebels' ranks grew to almost one hundred. But in Charleston, planters were gathering to put an end to the uprising. By late Sunday afternoon white militias had overtaken and surrounded the escaping slaves. The Stono rebels stood and fought, but the militiamen killed almost thirty of them. Those who were captured were executed. Those who escaped into the countryside were hunted down.

The Stono Rebellion terrified white South Carolinians, who hurried to make the colony's already harsh slave codes even more brutal. The government increased the slave patrols in both size and frequency. It also raised the bounties, or rewards offered for the

---

Scots-Irish Protestant Scottish settlers in British-occupied northern Ireland, many of whom migrated to the colonies in the eighteenth century.

Stono Rebellion Slave revolt in South Carolina in 1739; it prompted the colony to pass harsher laws governing the movement of slaves and the capture of runaways.

capture of runaways, to make sure that fleeing slaves taken alive and unharmed, or brought in dead and scalped, were worth hunting down.

Hostilities between black colonists and white colonists were not confined to the South. In the crowded environment of New York City, white residents showed the same fear of slave rebellions as Carolina or Virginia planters. Their fears became reality at midnight on April 6, 1712, when two dozen blacks, armed with guns, hatchets, and swords, set fire to a downtown building. Startled New Yorkers who rushed to keep the flames from spreading were attacked by the rebels, leaving nine people shot, stabbed, or beaten to death. Six more were wounded. Militia units from as far away as Westchester were called out to quell the riot and to cut off any hope of escape for the slaves. Realizing the hopelessness of their situation, six committed suicide. Those who were taken alive suffered horrible punishment. According to the colonial governor, Robert Hunter, "some were burnt, others were hanged, one broke on the wheel, and one hung alive in chains in the town." Twenty-nine years later, the mere rumor of a conspiracy by African Americans to commit arson was enough to move white residents to violent reprisals. Despite the lack of any evidence to support the charge, 101 of the city's black residents were arrested—18 of them were hanged and 18 burned alive.

Clashes Between the Rich and the Poor

Most often, class tensions erupted into violence as tenant farmers battled landlords or their agents and backcountry farmers took up arms against the elite planters who dominated their colonial governments. New York tenant farmers had long resented the legal and economic power that manor lords wielded over their lives, and protests, labeled "land riots" by the wealthy landlords, were common throughout the century. Likewise, New Jersey landlords who tried to squeeze higher rents out of their tenants provoked bitterness—and frequent bloodshed. In January 1745, for example, tenants in Essex County, New Jersey, rioted after three of their number were arrested by local authorities. When the sheriff tried to bring one of the alleged troublemakers to the county courthouse, he was "assaulted by a great number of persons, with clubbs and other weapons," who rescued the prisoner. Later, a "multitude" armed with axes stormed the jail and rescued the remaining prisoners. Such tenant uprisings in both colonies continued during the 1750s and 1760s, as landless men

expressed their resentment and frustration at their inability to acquire land of their own.

In the backcountry, settlers were likely to face two enemies: Indians and the established political powers of their own colonies. Often the clashes with the colonial government were about Indian policy. Eighteenth-century colonial legislatures and governors preferred diplomacy to military action, but western settlers wanted a more aggressive program to push Indians out of the way. Even when frontier hostilities led to bloodshed, the colonists of the coastal communities were reluctant to spend tax money to provide protection along the settlement line. In the end, bitter western settlers frequently took matters into their own hands. Bacon's Rebellion was the best example of this kind of vigilante action in the seventeenth century.

The revolt by Pennsylvania's Paxton Boys was the most dramatic eighteenth-century episode. More than most colonies, Pennsylvania's Quaker-dominated government encouraged settlers to find peaceful ways to coexist with local tribes. But the eighteenth-century Scots-Irish settlers did not share the Quaker commitment to pacifism. They demanded protection against Indian raids on isolated homesteads and small frontier towns. In 1763 frustrated settlers from Paxton, Pennsylvania, attacked a village of peaceful Conestoga Indians. Although the murder of these Indians solved nothing and could not be justified, hundreds of western colonists supported this vigilante group known as the Paxton Boys. The group marched on Philadelphia, the capital city of Pennsylvania, to press their demands for an aggressive Indian policy. With Philadelphia residents fearing their city would be attacked and looted, the popular printer and political leader Benjamin Franklin met the **Paxton Boys** on the outskirts of the city and negotiated a truce. The outcome was a dramatic shift in Pennsylvania Indian policy, illustrated by an official bounty for Indian scalps.

Vigilante action, however, was not always connected to Indian conflicts. In South Carolina, trouble arose because coastal planters refused to provide basic government services to the backcountry. Settlers in western South Carolina paid their taxes, but because their counties had no courts, they had to travel long distances to register land transactions or file lawsuits.

Paxton Boys   Settlers in Paxton, Pennsylvania, who massacred Conestoga Indians in 1763 and then marched on Philadelphia to demand that the colonial government provide better defense against the Indians.

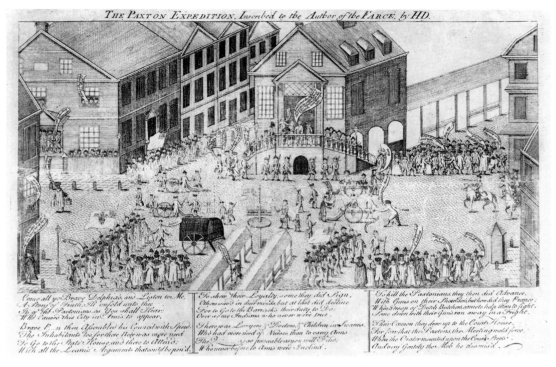

The vigilantes known as the Paxton Boys were backcountry farmers, angry that
Pennsylvania's government would not protect them from the threat of Indian attack.
In 1763, they turned their anger on the scattered communities of Conestoga Indians who
were living peacefully nearby, killing many. The following year, 500 of these vigilantes
marched on Philadelphia. As this engraving illustrates, British troops were called on to
suppress this rebellion in the colonial capital. *The Granger Collection, New York.*

The government provided no sheriffs either, and out-laws preyed on these communities. With the coastal planters refusing to admit any backcountry representatives to the colonial legislature, settlers could do little but complain, petition, and demand relief. In the 1760s, the farmers took matters into their own hands, choosing to "regulate" backcountry affairs themselves through vigilante action. These **Regulators** pursued and punished backcountry outlaws, dispensing justice without the aid of courts or udges.

In North Carolina, a similar power struggle led to a brief civil war. Here, a Regulator movement was organized against legal outlaws, a collection of corrupt local officials in the backcountry appointed because of their political connections to the colony's slave-holding elite. These officials awarded contracts to friends for building roads and bridges. They charged exorbitant fees to register deeds, surveys, or even the sale of cattle. And they set high poll taxes on their backcountry neighbors. The North Carolina Regulators wanted these men removed, and when their demands were ignored, they mounted a taxpayers' rebellion. When tax collection dried up, the governor acted, raising a militia of twelve hundred men to march on the rebels. The showdown took place in 1771 near the Alamance River, where the governor's army easily defeated the two thousand poorly armed Regulators. Six of the movement's leaders were then hanged. The brief east-west war ended in North Carolina, but the bitterness remained. During the Revolutionary War, when most of North Carolina's coastal

> **Regulators** Frontier settlers in the Carolinas who protested the lack or abuse of government services in their area; the North Carolina Regulators were suppressed by government troops in 1771.

elite cast their lot for independence, many of the farmers of the backcountry—disgusted with colonial government—sided with England.

Reason and Religion in Colonial Society

→ *What political and personal expectations arose from Enlightenment philosophy?*

→ *What was the impact of the Great Awakening on colonial attitudes toward authority?*

Trade routes tied the eighteenth-century colonial world to parent societies across the Atlantic. The bonds of language and custom tied the immigrant communities in America to their homelands too. In addition to these economic and cultural ties, the flow of ideas and religious beliefs helped sustain a transatlantic community.

The Impact of the Enlightenment

At the end of the seventeenth century, a new intellectual movement arose in Europe: the **Enlightenment.** Enlightenment thinkers argued that reason, or rational thinking, rather than divine revelation, tradition, intuition, or established authority, was the true path to reliable knowledge and to human progress. A group of brilliant French thinkers called **philosophes,** including Voltaire, Rousseau, Diderot, Buffon, and Montesquieu, were among the central figures of the Enlightenment, along with English philosophers such as John Locke and Isaac Newton and Scotland's David Hume. These philosophers, political theorists, and scientists disagreed about many issues, but all embraced the belief that nature could provide for all human wants and that human nature was basically good rather than flawed by original sin. Humans, they insisted, were rational and capable of making progress toward a perfect society if they studied nature, unlocked its secrets, and carefully nurtured the best human qualities in themselves and their children. This belief in progress and perfectibility became a central Enlightenment theme.

The Enlightenment was the handiwork of a small, intensely intellectual elite in Europe, and only the colonial elite had access to the books and essays that these philosophers produced. Elite colonists were drawn to two aspects of Enlightenment thought: its new religious philosophy of **deism** and the political theory of the "social contract." Deism appealed to colonists such as the Philadelphia scientist, writer, and political leader Benjamin Franklin and Virginia planters George Washington and Thomas Jefferson, men who were intensely interested in science and the scientific method. Deists believed that the universe operated according to logical, natural laws, without divine intervention. They thus denied the existence of any miracles after the Creation and rejected the value of prayer in this rational universe.

The most widely accepted Enlightenment ideas in the colonies were those of the English political theorist John Locke, who published his *Essay Concerning Human Understanding* in 1690 and *Two Treatises of Government* in 1691. In his political essays Locke argued that human beings have certain natural rights that they cannot give away—or alienate—and that no one can take from them. Those rights include the right to own themselves and their own labor and the right to own that part of nature on which they have labored productively—that is, their property. However, in exchange for the government's protection of their natural rights to life, liberty, and property, people make a social contract to give up absolute freedom and to live under a rule of law. According to Locke, the government created by the **social contract** receives its political power from the consent of those it governs, and it cannot claim a divine right to rule. In Locke's scheme, the people express their will, or their demands and interests, through a representative assembly, and the government is obligated to protect and respect the natural rights of its citizens and serve their interests. If the government fails to do this, Locke said, the people have a right, even a duty, to rebel. Locke's theory was especially convincing because it meshed with political developments in England from the civil war to the Glorious Revolution that were familiar to the colonists.

Enlightenment   An eighteenth-century intellectual movement that stressed the pursuit of knowledge through reason and challenged the value of religious belief, emotion, and tradition.

philosophe   Any of the popular French intellectuals or social philosophers of the Enlightenment, such as Voltaire, Diderot, or Rousseau.

deism   The belief that God created the universe in such a way that it could operate without any further divine intervention such as miracles.

social contract   A theoretical agreement between the governed and the government that defines and limits the rights and obligations of each.

Religion and Religious Institutions

Deism attracted little attention among ordinary colonists, but many eighteenth-century Americans were impressed by the growing religious diversity of their society. The waves of immigration had greatly increased the number of Protestant sects in the colonies, and colonists began to see religious toleration as a practical matter. The commitment to religious toleration did not come at an even pace, of course, nor did it extend to everyone. No colony allowed Catholics to vote or hold elective office after Rhode Island disfranchised Catholics in 1729, and even Maryland did not permit Catholics to celebrate Mass openly until Catholics in the city of Baltimore broke the law and founded a church in 1763. Connecticut granted freedom of worship to "sober dissenters" such as Anglicans, Quakers, and Baptists as early as 1708, but in 1750 its legislature declared it a felony to deny the **Trinity.** When colonists spoke of religious toleration, they did not mean the separation of church and state. On the contrary, the tradition of an **established church,** supported by taxes from all members of a community regardless of where they worshiped, went unchallenged in the southern colonies, where Anglicanism was established, and in Massachusetts and Connecticut, where **Congregationalism** was established.

As the diversity in churches was growing, the number of colonists who did not regularly attend any church at all was growing too. Some colonists were more preoccupied with secular concerns, such as their place in the economic community, than with spiritual ones. Others were losing their devotion to churches where the sermons were more intellectual than impassioned and the worship service was more formal than inspiring.

Into this moment stepped that group of **charismatic** preachers who, like Jonathan Edwards, denounced the obsession with profit and wealth they saw around them, condemned the sinfulness and depravity of all people, warned of the terrible punishments of eternal hellfires, and praised the saving grace of Jesus Christ. In a society divided by regional disputes, racial conflicts, and economic competition, these preachers held out a promise of social harmony based on the surrender of individual pride and a renewed love and fear of God. In voices filled with "Thunder and Lightning," they called for a revival of basic Protestant belief.

The Great Awakening

The religious revival of the eighteenth century was based as much on a new approach to preaching as on the message itself. This new-style preaching first appeared in New Jersey and Pennsylvania in the 1720s, when two **itinerant** preachers—Theodore Frelinghuysen and William Tennent Jr.—began calling the local churches to task for lack of devotion to God and for "cold" preaching. Tennent established what he called a "log college" to train fiery preachers who could spread a Christian revival throughout the colonies. Soon afterward, Jonathan Edwards spread the revival to Massachusetts. Like Frelinghuysen and Tennent, Edwards berated the lukewarm preaching of local ministers and then turned to the task of saving lost souls. The revival, or **Great Awakening,** sparked by men like Edwards and Tennent, spread rapidly throughout the colonies, carried from town to town by the wandering ministers called "Awakeners." These preachers stirred entire communities to renewed religious devotion.

The Great Awakening's success was ensured in 1740, when **George Whitefield** toured the colonies from Charles Town to Maine. Everywhere this young preacher went, crowds gathered to hear him. Often the audiences grew so large that church sanctuaries could not hold them and Whitefield would finish his service in a nearby field or village green. His impact was electric. "Hearing him preach gave me a heart wound," wrote one colonist, and even America's most committed deist, Benjamin Franklin, confessed that Whitefield's sermons moved him. Whitefield himself recorded his effect on a crowd: "A wonderful power

Trinity In Christian doctrine, the belief that God has three divine aspects—Father, Son, and Holy Spirit.

established church The official church of a nation or colony, usually supported by taxes collected from all citizens, no matter what their religious beliefs or place of worship.

Congregationalism A form of Protestant church government in which the local congregation is independent and self-governing; in the colonies, the Puritans were Congregationalists.

charismatic Having a spiritual power or personal quality that stirs enthusiasm and devotion in large numbers of people.

itinerant Traveling from place to place.

Great Awakening A series of religious revivals based on fiery preaching and emotionalism that swept across the colonies during the second quarter of the eighteenth century.

George Whitefield English evangelical preacher of the Great Awakening whose charismatic style attracted huge crowds during his preaching tours of the colonies.

The English evangelical minister, George Whitefield, inspired awe and prompted renewed commitment to Christianity everywhere he preached. Crowds overflowed into the fields outside of colonial country churches, and men and women in his audiences often fainted or cried out in ecstasy. As the leading figure of the Great Awakening, Whitefield was loved by thousands and criticized by ministers who opposed the religious enthusiasm he represented. *Bridgeman Art Library Ltd.*

was in the room and with one accord they began to cry out and weep most bitterly for the space of half an hour." As the sermon progressed, the audience response became more intense: "Some of the people were as pale as death; others were wringing their hands; others lying on the ground; others sinking into the arms of their friends; and most lifting their eyes to heaven, and crying to God for mercy."

The Great Awakening did not go unchallenged. Some ministers had gladly turned over their pulpits to Awakeners. But others, angered by the criticisms of their preaching and suggestions that they themselves were unsaved, launched a counterattack against the revivalists and their "beastly brayings." Members of the colonial elite were roused to political action against a movement that constantly condemned the worldly amusements they enjoyed, such as dancing, gambling, drinking, theater, and elegant clothing. In Connecticut, for example, the assembly passed a law banning itinerant ministers from preaching outside their own parishes.

Bitter fights within congregations and denominations also developed. "Old Light" Congregationalists upheld the established service but "New Lights" chose revivalism, and "Old Side" Presbyterians battled "New Sides" over preaching styles and the content of the worship service. Congregations split, and the minority groups hurriedly formed new churches. Many awakened believers left their own **denominations** entirely, joining the Baptists or the Methodists. Antirevivalists also left their strife-ridden churches and became Anglicans. These religious conflicts frequently became intertwined with secular disputes. Colonists who had long-standing disagreements over Indian policy or economic issues lined up on opposite sides of the Awakening. Class tensions influenced religious loyalties, as poor colonists pronounced judgment on their rich neighbors using religious vocabulary that equated luxury, dancing, and gambling with sin.

Thus, rather than fulfilling its promise of social harmony, the Great Awakening increased strife and tension among colonists. Yet it had positive effects as well. For example, the Awakening spurred the growth of higher education. During the complicated theological arguments between Old Lights and Awakeners, the revivalists came to see the value of theological training. They founded new colleges, including Rutgers, Brown, Princeton, and Dartmouth, to prepare their clergy just as the Old Lights relied on Harvard and Yale to train theirs. One of the most important effects of the Great Awakening was also one of the least expected. The resistance to authority, the activism involved in creating new institutions, the participation in debate and argument—these experiences reinforced a sense that protest and resistance were acceptable, not just in religious matters but in the realm of politics as well.

Government and Politics in the Mainland Colonies

→ *What circumstances limited a colonial governor's exercise of royal power?*

→ *What was the result of the struggle for power between the colonial assemblies and the colonial governors?*

denomination A group of religious congregations that accept the same doctrines and are united under a single name.

The English mainland colonies were part of a large and complex empire, and the English government had created many agencies to set and enforce imperial policy. Parliament passed laws regulating colonial affairs, the royal navy and army determined colonial defense, and English diplomats decided which foreign nations were friends and which were foes. But from the beginning, most **proprietors,** joint-stock companies, and kings had also found it convenient to create local governments within their colonies to handle day-to-day affairs. Virginia's House of Burgesses was the first locally elected legislative body in the colonies, but by 1700 every mainland colony boasted a representative assembly generally made up of its wealthiest men.

In the first half of the eighteenth century, the British government decided to restructure its colonial administration, hoping to make it more efficient. Despite this reorganization, the government was notably lax in enforcing colonial regulations. Even so, colonists often objected to the constraints of imperial law and challenged the role of the king or the proprietors in shaping local political decisions. This **insubordination** led to a long and steady struggle for power between colonial governors and colonial assemblies. Over the first half of the century, the colonists did wrest important powers from the governors. But the British government remained adamant that ultimate power, or **sovereignty,** rested in the hands of king and Parliament.

Imperial Institutions and Policies

By the eighteenth century, the British government had divided responsibility for colonial regulation and management among several departments, commissions, and agencies. Even though the Lords Commissioners of Trade and Plantations had been created in 1696 to coordinate the Empire's rules and regulations for the colonies, authority remained fragmented. The treasury board, for example, continued to supervise all colonial financial affairs, and its customs office collected all trade revenues. The admiralty board, however, had the authority to enforce trade regulations. The potential for conflict among all these departments, commissions, and agencies was great. But British indifference to colonial affairs helped to preserve harmony.

Parliament set the tone for colonial administration in the eighteenth century with a **policy** that came to be known unofficially as **salutary neglect.** Salutary, or healthy, neglect meant the government was satisfied with relaxed enforcement of most regulations as long as the colonies remained dutifully loyal in military and economic matters. As long as specific, or **enumerated,** colonial raw materials continued to flow into British hands and the colonists continued to rely on British manufactured goods, salutary neglect suited the expectations of the king, Parliament, and most government officials.

Salutary neglect did not mean that the colonists were free to do exactly as they pleased. Even in purely domestic matters the colonial governments could not operate as freely as many of them desired. The most intense political conflicts before the 1760s centered on the colonial assemblies' power to govern local affairs as they chose.

Local Colonial Government

The eighteenth-century mainland colonies remained a mixture of royal, proprietary, and corporate colonies, although the majority were held directly by the king. Whatever the form of ownership, however, the colonies were strikingly similar in the structure and operation of their governments. Each colony had a governor appointed by the king or the proprietor or, in Connecticut and Rhode Island (the two **corporate colonies**), elected to executive office. Each had a council, usually appointed by the governor, though sometimes elected by the assembly, which served as an advisory body to the governor. And each had an elected representative assembly with lawmaking and taxing powers.

The governor was the linchpin of local government because he represented royal authority and imperial interests in the local setting. In theory, his powers were impressive. He alone could call the assembly into session, and he had the power to dismiss it. He also could veto any act passed by the assembly. He had the sole power to appoint and dismiss judges, justices of the

---

proprietor   In colonial America, a proprietor was a wealthy Englishman who received a large grant of land in America from the king or queen in order to create a new colony.

insubordination   Resistance to authority; disobedience.

sovereignty   The ultimate power in a nation or a state.

policy   A course of action taken by a government or a ruler.

salutary neglect   The British policy of relaxed enforcement of most colonial trade regulations as long as the mainland colonies remained loyal to the government and profitable within the British economy.

enumerated   Added to the list of regulated goods or crops.

corporate colony   A self-governing colony, not directly under the control of proprietors or the Crown.

Historians are sometimes simply wrong. For over a century, experts in New York history were certain that this was a portrait of Lord Cornbury, royal governor of New York from 1702 to 1708. Cornbury, it was said, bore a striking resemblance to his cousin Queen Anne and had dressed in women's clothing in order to emphasize his connection to her authority and power. But recently a scholar has proven that this is not Lord Cornbury. Now the task is to discover who the person in the portrait really is. *Collection of the New York Historical Society.*

peace, and all government officials. He could grant pardons and reprieves. The governor made all land grants, oversaw all aspects of colonial trade, and conducted all diplomatic negotiations with the Indians. Because he was commander in chief of the military and naval forces of the colony, he decided what action, if any, to take in conflicts between colonists and Indians. Armed with such extensive powers, the man who sat in the English colonial governor's seat ought to have been respected—or at least obeyed.

A closer look, however, reveals that the governor was not so powerful after all. First, in many cases he was not free to exercise his own judgment because he was bound by a set of instructions written by the board of trade. Though highly detailed and specific, these instructions often bore little relation to the realities the governor encountered in his colony. Instead, by limiting his ability to improvise and compromise, they proved more burdensome than helpful to many a frustrated governor.

Second, the governor's own skills and experience were often limited. Few men in the prime of their ca-

reers sought posts 3,000 miles from England, in the provinces. Thus governorships went to **bureaucrats** nearing the end of sometimes unimpressive careers or to younger men who were new to the rough-and-tumble games of politics. Many colonial governors were honorable and competent, but enough of them were fools, scoundrels, or eccentrics to give the office a poor reputation.

Finally, most governors served brief terms, sometimes too brief for them to learn which local issues were critical or to discern friend from foe in the colonial government. For many, the goal was simply to survive the ordeal. They were willing to surrender much of their authority to the local assemblies in exchange for a calm, uneventful, and, they hoped, profitable term in office.

Even the most ignorant or incompetent governor might have managed to dominate colonial politics had he been able to apply the grease that oiled eighteenth-century political wheels: patronage. The kings of England had learned that political loyalty could be bought on the floor of Parliament with royal favors. By midcentury, over half of the members of Parliament held Crown offices or had received government contracts. Unfortunately for the colonial governor, he had few favors to hand out. The king could also bribe voters or intimidate them to ensure the election of his supporters to Parliament, but the governor lacked this option as well. The number of eligible voters in most colonies was far too great for a governor's resources.

The most significant restraint on the governor's authority was not his rigid instructions, his inexperience, or his lack of patronage, but the fact that the assembly paid his salary. England expected the colonists to foot the bill for local government, including compensation for the governor. Governors who challenged the assembly too strongly or too often usually found a sudden, unaccountable budget crisis delaying or diminishing their allowances. Those who bent to assembly wishes could expect bonuses in the form of cash or grants of land.

While the governors learned that their great powers were not so great after all, the assemblies in every colony were making an opposite discovery: they learned they could broaden their powers far beyond the king's intent. They fought for and won more freedom from the governor's supervision and influence, gaining the

> **bureaucrat** A government official, usually appointed, who is deeply devoted to the details of administrative procedures.

right to elect their own speaker of the assembly, make their own procedural rules, and settle contested elections. They also increased their power over taxation and the use of revenues, or, in eighteenth-century parlance, their **power of the purse.**

In their pursuit of power, these local political leaders had several advantages besides the governor's weakness. They came from a small social and economic elite who were regularly elected to office for both practical and social reasons. First, they could satisfy the high property qualifications set for most officeholding. Second, they could afford to accept an office that cost more to win and to hold than its modest salary could cover. Third, a habit of **deference**—respect for the opinions and decisions of the more educated and wealthy families in a community—won them office. Although as many as 50 to 80 percent of adult free white males in a colony could vote, few were considered suitable to hold office. Generations of fathers and sons from elite families thus dominated political offices. These men knew one another well, and although they fought among themselves for positions and power, they could effectively unite against outsiders such as an arrogant governor. Finally, through long careers in the legislature they honed the political, administrative, and even **oratorical** skills that would enable them to contend successfully with the royal appointees.

Conflicting Views of the Assemblies

The king and Parliament gave local assemblies the authority to raise taxes, pay government salaries, direct the care of the poor, and maintain bridges and roads. To the colonists, this division of authority indicated an acceptance of a two-tiered system of government: (1) a central government that created and executed imperial policy and (2) a set of local governments that managed colonial domestic affairs. If these levels of government were not equal in their power and scope, at least—in the minds of the colonists—they were equally legitimate. On both points, however, the British disagreed. They did not acknowledge a multilevel system. They saw a single vast empire ruled by one government consisting of king and Parliament. The colonial governments may have acquired the power to establish temporary operating procedures and to pass minor laws, but British leaders did not believe they had acquired a share of the British government's sovereign power. As the governor of Pennsylvania put it in 1726, the assembly's actions and decisions should in "no ways interfere . . . with the Legal Prerogative of the Crown or the true Legislative Power of the Mother State." "True Legislative Power" belonged with Parliament, and most British political leaders considered the assemblies to be little more than **ad hoc** bodies, specially created to meet immediate needs and serve as surrogates, or deputies, for those with real authority.

North America and the Struggle for Empire

→ *What were the diplomatic and military goals of Europeans and American Indians in North America?*

→ *What were the major effects of the imperial wars on the American colonists?*

→ *How did the English victory in 1763 affect people in North America?*

During the seventeenth century, most of the violence and warfare in colonial America arose from struggles either between Indians and colonists over land or among colonists over political power and the use of revenues and resources. These struggles continued to be important during the eighteenth century. By 1690, however, the most persistent dangers to colonial peace and safety came from the fierce rivalries between the French, Spanish, and the English (see Map 4.1). Between 1688 and 1763, these European powers waged five bloody and costly wars. Most of these conflicts were motivated by politics at home, although colonial ambitions spurred the last and most decisive of them. No matter where these worldwide wars began, or what their immediate cause, colonists were usually drawn into them.

When imperial wars included fighting in America, English colonists were expected to fight without the assistance of British troops. Often the enemy the colonists faced was neither French nor Spanish but Indian, a result of the alliances Indians had formed with Europeans to advance their own interests. For

---

power of the purse   The political power that is enjoyed by the branch of government that controls taxation and the use of tax monies.

deference   Yielding to the judgment or wishes of a social or intellectual superior.

oratorical   Related to the art of persuasive and eloquent public speaking.

ad hoc   Created for, or concerned with, one specific purpose; Latin for "to this [end]."

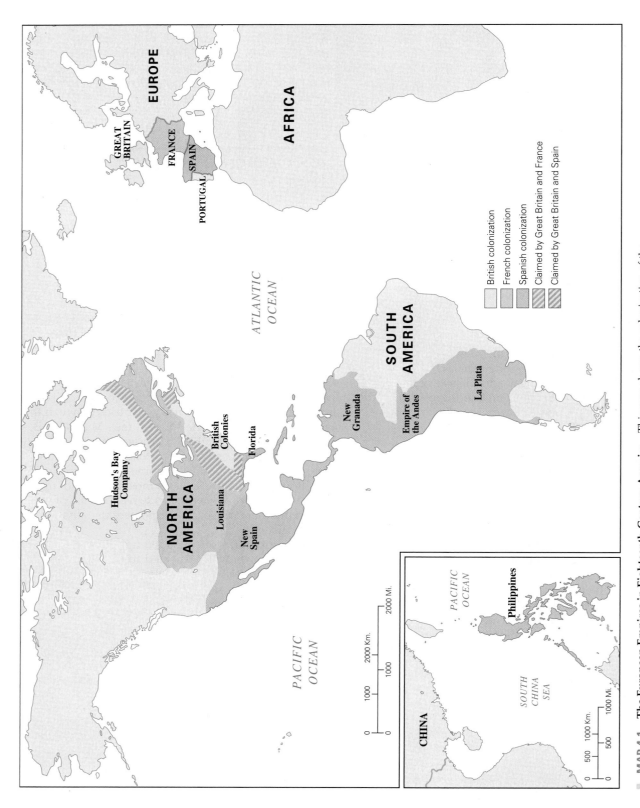

MAP 4.1 **The European Empires in Eighteenth-Century America** This map shows the colonization of the Americas and the Philippines by three rival powers. It is clear from the map why British colonists felt vulnerable to attack by England's archenemies, France and Spain, until English victory in the Great War for Empire in 1763.

Legend:
- British colonization
- French colonization
- Spanish colonization
- Claimed by Great Britain and France
- Claimed by Great Britain and Spain

example, until the mid-seventeenth century, the Huron-dominated confederacy to the north supported the French (see Map 4.2). These two allies had a strong economic bond: the French profited from the fur trade while the Hurons enjoyed the benefits of European manufactured goods. The English colonists were not without their Indian allies, however. Although the older, seventeenth-century alliances between the Wampanoags and the Plymouth settlers had ended in violence, other alliances held. Ties with the Iroquois League were carefully nurtured by the English, who appreciated the advantages of friendship with Indians living south of the Great Lakes, along crucial fur trading routes. For their part, the Iroquois were willing to cooperate with a European power who was the enemy of their perpetual rival, the Hurons. The southern English colonists turned to the **Creek Confederacy** when wars with Spain erupted. Yet the colonists' own land hunger always worked to undermine—if not unravel—these Indian alliances. Thus the southern tribes' support was unreliable, and the Iroquois, wary of the English westward expansion, often chose to pursue an independent strategy of neutrality.

The wars that raged from 1689 until 1763 were part of a grand effort by rival European nations to control the balance of power at home and abroad. The colonists often felt like pawns in the hands of the more powerful players, and resentment sometimes overshadowed their patriotic pride when England was victorious. Whatever their views on imperial diplomacy, few colonists escaped the impact of this nearly century-long struggle for power between England, France, and Spain, for periods of peace were short and the long shadow of war hung over them until Britain's major triumph in 1763.

An Age of Imperial Warfare

William and Mary's ascent to the throne in 1689 ushered in an era of political stability and religious tolerance in Britain. But it also ushered in an age of imperial warfare. Almost immediately, France took up arms against England, Holland, Sweden, and Spain in what the Europeans called the War of the League of Augsburg but which colonists called simply King William's War. With France as the enemy, New England and northern New York bore the brunt of the fighting. Because the English sent no troops to defend the border communities there, colonial armies, composed largely of untrained militia companies, and their Iroquois allies defended British interests—and their own families—in this long and vicious war. As reports of atrocities mounted, the governments of Massachusetts,

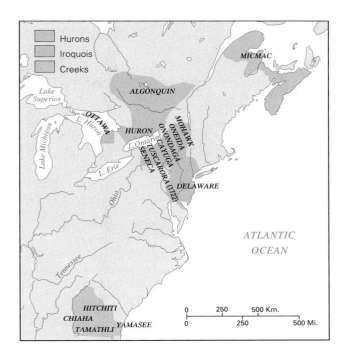

MAP 4.2   The Indian Confederacies   This map shows the three major Indian military and political coalitions—the Huron, Iroquois, and Creek Confederacies. Unlike the squabbling English mainland colonies, these Indian tribes understood the value of military unity in the face of threats to their land and their safety and the importance of diplomatic unity in negotiating with their European allies.

Plymouth, Connecticut, and New York made a rare attempt at cooperation. They pledged to combine their resources in order to invade Canada. In the end, however, few made good on their promises of men or money, and colonial attacks on Montreal and Quebec both failed. When the war finally ended with the Treaty of Ryswick in 1697, 659 New Englanders had died in battle, in raids, or in captivity. The death toll for the Iroquois nations was higher—between 600 and 1,300. The lessons of the war were equally apparent. First, colonists paid a high price for their disunity and lack of cooperation. Second, no New Englander could ever feel secure until the French had been driven out of Canada. Third, the colonists needed the aid of the English army and navy to effectively drive the French away.

The colonists had little time to enjoy peace. Five years later, in 1702, the conflict colonists called Queen

Creek Confederacy   Alliance of the Creeks and smaller Indian tribes living in the Southeast.

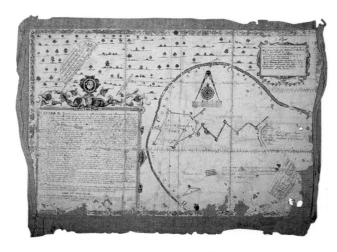

Imperial wars between England and her rivals often drew the colonists and neighboring Indian tribes into conflict. Between 1711 and 1713, land-hungry North Carolinians, joined by South Carolina and Virginia militias and by Creek and Yamasee troops, turned Queen Anne's War into a brutal and successful war on the nearby Tuscarora Indians. *From the collections of the South Carolina Historical Society.*

Anne's War began, once again pitting France and its now dependent ally, Spain, against England, Holland, and Austria. In this eleven-year struggle, colonists faced enemies on both their southern and northern borders. Once again, those enemies included Indians. Between 1711 and 1713, southern colonists were caught up in fierce warfare with the Tuscaroras, who were angered by North Carolina land seizures. The casualties were staggering. Some 150 settlers were killed in the opening hours of the war, and in the following months both sides outdid one another in cruelty. Stakes were run through the bodies of women, children were murdered, and Indian captives were roasted alive. South Carolina and Virginia sent arms and supplies to aid the North Carolina colonists, and the Creek and Yamasee Indians fought beside the white settlers against the Tuscaroras. When this war-within-a-war ended in 1713, more than a thousand Tuscaroras were dead and nearly four hundred had been sold into slavery. The survivors took refuge in the land of the Iroquois.

The war in the north was just as deadly. Indian and French raids, such as the one on Deerfield, Massachusetts, cost the lives of many New Englanders. Despite repeated calls for help, the British did not send troops to defend their northern colonies. Disappointed New Englanders raised an army of nearly thirty-five hundred men and, in 1710, triumphantly took control of the military post at Port Royal and with it all of Acadia, or as the English called it, Nova Scotia.

The war, which ended in 1713, cost New Englanders dearly. The high death toll of King William's War and Queen Anne's War was staggering: nearly one of every four soldiers in uniform had died. The financial cost was equally devastating. Four-fifths of Massachusetts revenues in 1704–1705 went for military expenses. Homeowners in Boston saw their taxes rise 42 percent between 1700 and 1713. The city's streets were filled with beggars and its homes with widows. In Connecticut and Massachusetts, colonists spoke bitterly of the Mother Country's failure to protect them. Yet this time New Englanders could see tangible gains from the imperial struggle. The English flag now flew over Nova Scotia, Newfoundland, and Hudson Bay, which meant that Maine settlers no longer had to fear enemy raids. New England fleets could fish the cod-rich waters of Newfoundland more safely. And colonial fur traders could profit from Hudson Bay's resources.

For a generation, Europeans kept the peace. In America, however, violence continued along the line of settlement, with New Englanders battling Indian allies of the French and southern colonists making war on their own former allies, the Yamasees. The short but ferociously fought Yamasee War of 1715 left four hundred of South Carolina's five thousand colonists dead in the first twelve months of fighting, a higher death rate than white Massachusetts had sustained in King Philip's War.

At the end of the 1730s, the calm in Europe was fractured. By 1740, France, Spain, and Prussia were at war with England and its ally, Austria. This war, known in the colonies as King George's War, again meant enemy attacks on both the northern and southern colonies. New Englanders, swept up in the Great Awakening, viewed the war as a Protestant crusade against Catholicism, a holy war designed to rid the continent of religious enemies. Yet when the war ended in 1748, France still retained its Canadian territories.

The Great War for Empire

Despite three major wars and countless border conflicts, the map of North America had changed very little. Colonial efforts to capture Canada or to rid the southwest of Indian enemies had not succeeded. Yet veterans of the wars, and their civilian colonial supporters, spoke with pride of the colonial armies as excellent military forces. Without assistance from British regulars or the British navy, militiamen and volunteer armies had defended their communities, defeated Indian enemies, and captured important French forts.

Many colonists remained angry and bewildered, however, by the Mother Country's military neglect.

George Washington was a young man when the British General Edward Braddock was sent to the colonies to drive the French out of the Ohio Valley. Washington volunteered to join this disastrous campaign. When Braddock's troops were caught by surprise and routed by an Indian and French force near the Monongahela River, Washington was one of the officers who carried the mortally wounded Braddock off the field of battle. Washington escaped unharmed. *The Granger Collection, New York.*

From their perspective, they were being dragged into European wars that did not concern them. Then, in 1756, the tables seemed to turn: this time, Europe was dragged into a colonial war. Westward expansion deeper into North America triggered a great war for empire, referred to in Europe as the Seven Years' War and in the colonies as the French and Indian War.

The problem began in the 1740s, as the neutral zone between the French colonial empire and the British mainland settlements began to shrink. As thousands of new immigrants poured into the English colonies, the colonists pressed farther westward, toward the Ohio Valley. Virginia land speculators began to woo the Indians of the region with trading agreements. The English colonial interest in the valley alarmed the French, who had plans to unite their mainland empire, connecting Canada and Louisiana with a chain of forts, trading posts, and missions across the Ohio Valley.

Virginia's governor, Robert Dinwiddie, was troubled by French military buildup in the Ohio Valley. He warned the British that a potential crisis was developing thousands of miles from London. In 1754 Britain responded; the government agreed to send an expedition to assess French strength and warn the French to abandon a new fort on French Creek. Dinwiddie chose an inexperienced Virginia planter and colonial militia officer, Major George Washington, to lead the expedition. When Washington conveyed the warning, the French commander responded with insulting sarcasm. Tensions escalated rapidly. Dinwiddie later sent Major Washington to challenge the French at Fort Duquesne, near present-day Pittsburgh, but the French forced him to surrender.

Fearing another war, colonial political leaders knew it was time to act decisively—and to attempt cooperation. In June 1754, seven colonies sent representatives to Albany, New York, to organize a united defense. Unfortunately this effort at cooperation failed. When the Albany Plan of Union was presented to the colonial assemblies, none was willing to approve it. Instead, American colonists looked to Britain to act. This time, Britain did. Parliament sent Major General Edward Braddock, a battle-hardened veteran, to drive the French out of Fort Duquesne. Braddock's humiliating failure was only the first of many for the English in America.

English and French forces engaged each other in battle four times before war was officially declared in 1756. Soon, every major European power was involved, and the fighting spread rapidly across Europe, the Philippines, Africa, India, the Caribbean, and North America.

For most Americans, the English victory in the Battle of Quebec was the most dramatic event of the Seven Years' War. When Benjamin West painted "The Death of General Wolfe," he acknowledged the role Indian allies had played on both sides of this imperial struggle by adding an Indian observer to the scene. *National Gallery of Canada, Ottawa.*

In America, France's Indian allies joined the war more readily than England's. Iroquois tribes opted for neutrality, waiting until 1759 to throw in their lot with the English. Although Mohawks fought as mercenaries in New York and Iroquois in western Pennsylvania suppressed Delaware attacks on English colonists there, Iroquois support was erratic. In fact, some members of the League, including the Senecas, fought with the French in 1757 and 1758. Given these circumstances, a British defeat seemed likely.

In the south, the Cherokees played the French and English against each other. About 250 Cherokee warriors did sign up to fight with the Virginia militia in 1757, but as mercenaries rather than allies. By 1760, a full-scale war between colonists and Cherokees had erupted in the southern colonies. Although this Cherokee Rebellion of 1759–1761 ended in Indian defeat, the war drained off many of the southern colonial resources that might have been used against the French.

In 1756 the worried British government turned over the direction of the war to the ardent imperialist William Pitt. More than willing to take drastic steps, Pitt committed the British treasury to the largest war expenditures the nation had ever known and then put together the largest military force that North America had ever seen, combining 25,000 colonial troops with 24,000 British regulars. The fortunes of war soon reversed. By the end of 1759, the upper Ohio Valley had been taken from the French. And in August of that year, General James Wolfe took the war to the heart of French Canada: the fortress city of Quebec.

With his piercing eyes and his long red hair, the 31-year-old Wolfe looked the part of the military hero he was. Despite his eighteen years of military service, even Wolfe admitted he was daunted by the difficult task ahead of him. Quebec, heavily manned and well armed, sat on top of steep cliffs rising high above the St. Lawrence River. Inside, the formidable French general Louis-Joseph Montcalm was in command. The only possible approach was from the west of the city, across the Plains of Abraham. The problem was how to get to that battlefield.

Wolfe was uncharacteristically hesitant until he discovered a blockaded roadway running to the top of the 175-foot cliff. On the evening of September 12, forty-five hundred British soldiers climbed this diagonal path to the top. When the thoroughly surprised Montcalm saw a double line of scarlet uniforms forming on the plain at dawn, he gathered a force of more than four thousand and marched out to meet the British. The French fired several rounds, but Wolfe ordered his men to hold their fire until the enemy was within 60 yards. Then the redcoats fired, and the French turned and ran. Among the British wounded was General James Wolfe, shot through the chest. Hearing that the French were in retreat, the dying general murmured, "Now, God be praised, I will die in peace." Among the French casualties was Louis-Joseph, Marquis de Montcalm, who died the following day from internal injuries caused by a musket ball to his midsection.

Five days after the Battle of the Plains of Abraham, Quebec formally surrendered. In 1760 the city of Montreal also fell to the British. With that, the French governor surrendered the whole of New France to his enemies, and the war in North America was over. The fighting in this most global of eighteenth-century wars continued elsewhere until 1763. Spain entered the struggle as a French ally in 1761, but English victories in India, the Caribbean, and the Pacific squelched

TABLE 4.1 — **Imperial and Colonial Wars**

Name	Date	Participants	Treaty
In colonies: King William's War *In Europe:* War of the League of Augsburg	1688–1697	*In Europe:* France vs. England, Holland, Sweden, and Spain *In North America:* Colonists and their Iroquois allies vs. French and their Indian allies *Area:* New England and Northern New York	Treaty of Ryswick (1697) *Results* Port Royal in Acadia (Nova Scotia) is returned to France France is still a presence in North America
In colonies: Queen Anne's War *In Europe:* War of the Spanish Succession	1702–1713	*In Europe:* England, Holland, and Austria vs. France and Spain *In North America:* English colonists vs. French and Spanish powers in North and South and their Indian allies	Treaty of Utrecht (1713) *Results* France renounces plans to unite with Spain under one crown England gains Caribbean islands, St. Kitts, Gibraltar, and Minorca English flag flies over Nova Scotia, New Foundland, and Hudson Bay War takes a financial toll on the colonies
War of Jenkins's Ear	1739–1740	*In Europe:* England vs. Spain *In North America:* English colonists clash with Spanish in interior regions (Georgia, South Carolina, Virginia	None—Conflict expands into King George's War
In colonies: King George's War *In Europe:* War of the Austrian Succession	1740–1748	*In Europe:* Austria and England vs. Prussia, France, and Spain *In North America:* English colonists in New England vs. French and their Indian allies	Treaty of Aix-la-Chapelle (1748) *Results* England returns Louisbourg to French in exchange for Madras (in India)
In colonies: French and Indian War *In Europe:* Seven Years' War	1756–1763	*In Europe:* England and Prussia vs. France and Austria *In North America:* English colonists vs. French and their Indian allies *Area:* Global war; in colonies, all regions	Treaty of Paris (1763) *Results* French Empire shrinks France's presence in North America is greatly reduced France loses trading posts in Africa and exits India Britain takes Florida from Spain and Canada from France France gives up Louisiana to Spain for compensation for Florida British government is deeply in debt The borders of Britain's North American colonies are secured

any hopes the French had. The **Treaty of Paris** established the supremacy of the British Empire.

The Outcomes of the Great War for Empire

The war had redrawn the map of the world (see Table 4.1). The French Empire had shriveled, with nothing remaining of New France but two tiny islands between Nova Scotia and Newfoundland. Ten thousand Acadians—French colonists of Nova Scotia—were

Treaty of Paris The treaty ending the French and Indian War in 1763; it gave all of French Canada and Spanish Florida to Britain.

refugees of the war, deported from their homes by the English because their loyalty was suspect. These Acadians, who either relocated to France, settled in New England, or made the exhausting trek to French-speaking Louisiana, were living reminders of the French Empire's eclipse. The only other remnants of the French Empire in the Western Hemisphere were the sugar islands of Guadeloupe, Martinique, and St. Domingue, left to France because England's so-called Sugar Interest wanted no further competition in the British market. Across the ocean, France lost trading posts in Africa, and on the other side of the world, the French presence in India vanished.

The 1763 peace treaty dismantled the French Empire but did not destroy France itself. Although the nation's treasury was empty, its borders were intact. France's alliance with Spain held firm, cemented by the experience of defeat. Britain was victorious, but victory did not mean Britain had escaped unharmed.

The British government was deeply in debt and faced new problems associated with managing and protecting its greatly enlarged empire.

In the mainland colonies, people lit bonfires and staged parades to celebrate Britain's victory and the safety of their own borders. But the tension of being both members of a colonial society and citizens of a great empire could not be easily dismissed. The war left scars, including memories of the British military's arrogance toward provincial soldiers and lingering resentment over the quartering of British soldiers at colonial expense. The colonists were aware that the British had grounds for resentment also, particularly the profitable trade some Americans had carried on with the enemy even in the midst of the war. Suspicion and resentment, a growing sense of difference, a tug of loyalties between the local community and the larger empire—these were the unexpected outcomes of a glorious victory.

Examining a Primary Source

✔ Individual Voices

Eliza Lucas Challenges Traditional Plantation Life

The eighteenth-century plantation world of South Carolina was a patriarchal society dedicated to the production of a single staple crop, rice. When Eliza Lucas began experimenting with indigo, figs, and hemp at Wappoo, her family plantation, it was the beginning of a new era of prosperity and diversification in the South Carolina plantation economy. As one of the few women to manage a large plantation at the time, Lucas was unique in her desire to experiment with new crops and stretch old gender roles. In her letters, Eliza Lucas provides insight into the experiences of a woman succeeding in a male-dominated society. In this letter to her young niece, Lucas describes the demanding schedule she maintained in order to balance her roles as a society woman and a plantation master.

① In this section Eliza Lucas shows us some of the ways in which she juggles her feminine and masculine roles. Do you think the men of the period spent the same amount of time devoted to learning?

② Eliza Lucas hoped that the two African American slave girls she was educating would educate other slaves on the plantation. What arguments could be raised against this program to educate slaves? What benefits might come from the education of slaves?

Dr. Miss B.

. . . Why, my dear Miss B, will you so often repeat your desire to know how I triffle away my time in our retirement in my fathers absence. Could it afford you advantage or pleasure I should not have hesitated, but as you can expect neither from it I would have been excused; however, to show you my readiness in obeying your commands, here it is.

① *In general then I rise at five o'Clock in the morning, read till Seven, then take a walk in the garden or field, see that the Servants are at their respective business, then to breakfast. The first hour after breakfast is spent at my musick, the next is constantly employed in recolecting something I have learned least for want of practise it should be quite lost, such as French and short hand.* **②** *After that I devote the rest of the time till I dress for dinner to our little Polly and two* black girls who I teach to read, and if I have my papa's approbation (my Mamas I have got) I intend [them] for school mistres's for the rest of the negro children—another scheme you see. But to proceed, the first hour after dinner as the first after breakfast at musick, the rest of the afternoon in Needle work till candle light, and from that time to bed time read or write. 'Tis the fashion here to carry our work abroad so that having company, without they are great strangers, is no interruption to that affair; but I have particular matters for particular days, which is an interruption of mine. Monday my musick Master is here. Tuesdays my friend Mrs. Chardon (about 3 mile distant) and I are constantly engaged to each other, she at our house one Tuesday—I at hers the next and this is one of the happiest days I spend at Woppoe. Thursday the whole day except what necessary affairs of the family take up is spent in writing, either on the business of the plantations, or letters to my friends. Every other Fryday, if no company, we go a vizeting so that I go abroad once a week and no oftener.

O! I had like to forgot the last thing I have done a great while. I have planted a large figg orchard with design to dry and export them. ③ I have reconed [reckoned] my experience and the propfets [profits] to arise from these figgs, but was I to tell you how great an Estate I am to make this way, and how 'tis to be laid out you would think me far gone in romance. Your good Uncle I know has long thought I have a fertile brain at schemeing. I only confirm him in his opinion; but I own I love the vegitable world extremly. I think it an innocent and useful amusement. Pray tell him, if he laughs much at my project, I never intend to have my hand in a silver mine and he will understand as well as you what I mean . . .

③ Lucas is clearly proud of her latest moneymaking project, yet she doesn't want to go into too much detail about her plans to her friend. What reason does she give for this hesitancy?

SUMMARY

Important changes emerged in the British mainland colonies during the eighteenth century. In New England, increased commercial activity and a royal government produced a shift from a "Puritan" culture to a more secular "Yankee" culture. In the South, the planter elite shifted from a labor force of indentured servants to one of African slaves. By midcentury, these enslaved workers had begun to develop their own community life and their own African American culture. The Middle Colonies developed a lively urban culture that contrasted with the backcountry or culture of newly arrived immigrants.

Intellectual life in the eighteenth century also changed. The colonial elite embraced the Enlightenment notion that progress would come through the application of reason rather than faith. They developed a skepticism about religious dogmas and accepted John Locke's theory of natural right. At the same time, the Great Awakening unleashed a second, and opposing, intellectual current. Revivalists such as Jonathan Edwards and George Whitefield spurred a renewed pursuit of religious salvation among ordinary colonists. Their message had radical implications, for these "Awakeners" challenged all authority except the individual spirit.

A similar challenge to authority emerged in politics and imperial relations. Despite England's policy of salutary neglect in governing the colonies, colonial assemblies resented royal officials and asserted their own claims to power as the legitimate representatives of the local interests.

England, France, and Spain fought five major wars between 1688 and 1763. Colonists were expected to defend their own borders in most of the wars. In the French and Indian War, however, the British played an active role in driving the French out of mainland America. Their victory in 1763 altered the colonial map of North America and changed power relations throughout the European world.

Dramatic events like the British victory often have unexpected consequences. As you will see in the next chapter, that victory carried with it a long trail of problems for the British government. The war had been costly, but peace proved to be costlier. Where would the government find the money to operate their vastly increased empire? What policies should they pursue toward the French colonists in Canada and the Indians of the Ohio Valley? Perhaps most surprising, tensions between the English colonists and the Mother Country intensified as the colonial celebration and appreciation quickly turned into resentment, protest, and resistance. How this happened is the focus of Chapter 5.

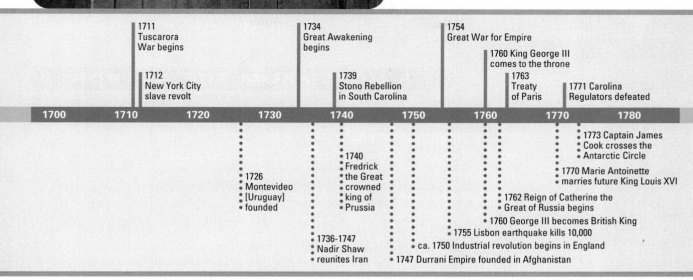

IN THE WIDER WORLD

1711
Tuscarora
War begins

1712
New York City
slave revolt

1734
Great Awakening
begins

1739
Stono Rebellion
in South Carolina

1754
Great War for Empire

1760 King George III
comes to the throne

1763
Treaty
of Paris

1771 Carolina
Regulators defeated

1700	1710	1720	1730	1740	1750	1760	1770	1780

1726
Montevideo
[Uruguay]
founded

1740
Fredrick
the Great
crowned
king of
Prussia

1736-1747
Nadir Shaw
reunites Iran

1773 Captain James
Cook crosses the
Antarctic Circle

1770 Marie Antoinette
marries future King Louis XVI

1762 Reign of Catherine the
Great of Russia begins

1760 George III becomes British King

1755 Lisbon earthquake kills 10,000

ca. 1750 Industrial revolution begins in England

1747 Durrani Empire founded in Afghanistan

In the United States

From Settlements to Societies

1690–1691 John Locke's essays *Concerning Human Under-standing* and *Two Treatises of Government*

1701 Yale College founded

1702 Queen Anne's War begins

1704 Pro-French Indians attack Deerfield, Massachusetts

Tuscarora War begins in North Carolina

1712 New York City slave revolt

1715 Colonists defeat Creek and Yamasee Indians of Georgia

1734 Great Awakening spreads to New England

1739 Stono Rebellion in South Carolina

1740 King George's War begins

George Whitefield begins his preaching tour

1756 Great War for Empire begins

1759 British capture Quebec

1771 North Carolina Regulator movement defeated

Deciding Where Loyalties Lie, 1763–1776

A NOTE FROM THE AUTHOR

In 1763, English colonists toasted King George III and hailed the British government as the greatest protector of liberties the world had ever known. Yet you will see in this chapter that by 1776 many of these same colonists considered the king a tyrant and a "royal brute" and many believed the British government was conspiring to enslave them. Clearly, something had gone terribly wrong. You will see that, after the war, Britain changed its approach to the colonies. Parliament tried to tighten its control over trade and raise money from the colonists. When they met with resistance, British leaders attempted to weaken the powers of the colonial assemblies and impose their own will on the colonists. Americans responded by evading the laws, committing acts of violence against royal officials, and using mass protests and boycotts of English goods in order to get new laws repealed. By 1776, no compromise seemed possible—and war seemed the only answer.

But can the movement for independence be explained simply by looking at events after 1763? Most historians look for long-term as well as immediate or short-term causes to explain a choice as important as this one. And, good historians recognize that there are at least two sides to every question.

If you were writing a history of the path to independence, where would you begin? Are there long-term political or economic trends and developments that set the stage for the conflict after 1763? Can you detect significant shifts in the understanding of the British Empire's goals, its benefits and rewards, and the obligations of its citizens? Or were the disagreements and the violence after 1763 so dramatic that they explain the revolution?

You can probably see how difficult it is to choose the critical causes of the Revolution. Deciding what to emphasize, what to give priority to, and how to weave together all the complex strands into a coherent account—these are the major challenges facing any historian of the American Revolution. Like each of you, each scholar will make different choices when writing that story. This explains why there are so many books on the independence movement—and why there will be so many more in the future.

Charles Inglis

This portrait of the Anglican minister and later bishop Charles Inglis reveals a proud, intelligent, self-confident gentleman. Yet Inglis, like many loyalists, was spurned by his fellow colonists after he wrote a pamphlet urging all Americans to remain loyal to the king. He risked his neighbors' ridicule, he said, because he was a true patriot and a friend to America's best interests. *National Portrait Gallery, London.*

✓ Individual Choices

Charles Inglis was born in Ireland in 1734. He became an Anglican minister and served six years as a missionary among the Mohawk Indians. In 1765 he became the assistant rector of New York City's prestigious Trinity Church. His delight at the appointment soon turned to dismay, however. The Stamp Act was passed that same year, and many of the colony's leading political figures and ordinary citizens linked the Church of England with the king's plans to oppress the colonists. Despite the open hostility Inglis soon faced, he chose to speak out in defense of both his church and his king.

By the 1770s, Inglis was dangerously at odds with his neighbors. Yet he would not be silent. He wrote pamphlets and published letters in the local newspapers in support of Parliament's right to tax the colonies and the colonists' duty to submit. When Thomas Paine published his radical *Common Sense* in 1776, Charles Inglis was one of the few conservatives who dared to challenge this open call for revolution. He condemned Paine and warned of the "evils which inevitably must attend our separating" from the Mother Country. He carefully listed the advantages of a reconciliation with Great Britain and then listed the horrors that would befall the colonies if they continued on the reckless path to rebellion. He painted a portrait of "the greatest confusion, and most violent convulsions" that would be the inevitable outcome of American protest and resistance to the king's sovereignty. Pointing out the hopelessness of waging a war against the most powerful navy and army in the world, he reminded Americans that they were still "properly Britons . . . [with] . . . the manners, habits, and ideas of Britons. . . ." Those ideas, he added emphatically, did not include a republican form of government.

In 1777 Charles Inglis was named rector of Trinity Church. From his pulpit, he continued boldly to pray for the king's well-being, despite the Declaration of Independence. He would not allow the revolutionaries to constrain him; he would not let their threats silence him. He remained an outspoken loyalist even when his church was burned and his personal property was confiscated by the new state government.

When the British evacuated New York in 1783, Inglis joined thousand of other loyalists in exile in Nova Scotia. Despite all that he had suffered at the hands of the revolutionaries, he refused to speak bitterly of his American enemies. Instead he wrote: "I do not leave behind me an individual against whom I have the smallest degree of resentment or ill-will."

117

INTRODUCTION

Many colonists believed that Britain's victory in 1763 would usher in a new era of economic growth, westward expansion, and improved cooperation between Mother Country and colonies. But the colonists' hopes for harmony and good will were quickly dashed. Less than two years after the Treaty of Paris ended the war, colonists were protesting Britain's Indian policy and its new trade regulations. In the next thirteen strife-filled years, the colonists and the British government discovered the fundamental political differences that existed between them. They found that they did not agree over the meaning of representative government or the proper division of power between Parliament and the local elected assemblies. And they found themselves in conflict over major imperial policies. English officials, for example, thought it made good sense to curtail westward settlement in order to prevent costly Indian wars. But American colonists believed loyal citizens deserved the economic opportunity that westward settlement would provide. The British government and the colonists also disagreed on the obligations the colonists owed to the empire. The British insisted that the Americans ought to help pay the costs of maintaining that empire, but the colonists believed that this was the duty of those who remained in the Mother Country. By the 1770s, Americans who had once toasted the king and his government now drank instead to liberty and resistance to tyrants. By 1775, a new choice faced the colonists: loyalty or rebellion. And men such as Charles Inglis seemed caught in the midst of a struggle they had never anticipated and could not avoid.

The colonists who chose to protest taxation by the British government in 1765 and 1767, or to oppose the creation of juryless courts, or to complain of the presence of troops in their towns in peacetime did not know they were laying the groundwork for a revolution. Indeed, most of them would have been shocked at the suggestion that they were no longer loyal British patriots. Yet events between 1763 and 1776 forced these colonists to choose between two versions of patriotism—loyalty to the king or loyalty to colonial independence—and between two visions of the future—as members of a great and powerful empire or as citizens of a struggling new nation. These events also forced Indians and African American slaves to choose an alliance with the king or with the rebels, just as it forced churchmen and royal officials such as Inglis to decide if the solemn oath of allegiance they had taken to the king was binding under all circumstances.

IT MATTERS TODAY

THE RIGHT TO DISSENT

Charles Inglis was a man of integrity who considered himself as much an American patriot as his opponent in the pamphlet wars, Alexander Hamilton. But unlike Hamilton, Inglis believed that the protests against Parliament and the king were dangerous and unjustified and would lead to an unjust and tragic war. Throughout American history, men and women have opposed political and social choices made by the nation, including the entrance of the United States into World War I, woman suffrage, Prohibition, and the wars in Vietnam and Iraq. The right to dissent, guaranteed by the Constitution, has been a critical part of the American political tradition since the nation began. Examining how dissent has been offered and how it has been received is part of the story of all major controversial events.

- Consider your position on dissent in times of national crisis. Do you believe the government has the right to suppress dissent during times of war or major disasters? Why or why not?

- Examine the key provisions of the Alien and Sedition Acts of 1789 and the Patriot Act of 2001. Discuss the impact modern technology has had on the ability to enforce such laws and on the ability of citizens to oppose or resist them.

The war for independence set neighbor against neighbor, father against son, wife against husband, and slave against master. For thousands, the outcome of this crisis of loyalty was exile from home and family. For others, it meant death or injury on the battlefield, widowhood, or life as an orphan. In 1776, however, its outcome was unclear.

Victory's New Problems

→ *Why did Prime Minister Grenville expect the colonists to accept part of the burden of financing the British Empire in 1764?*

→ *How did mercantile theory affect the colonies' trade with other nations?*

→ *Why were the colonists alarmed by Grenville's 1765 stamp tax?*

→ *How did the colonists protest Parliament's taxation policies?*

In the midst of the French and Indian War, King George II died in his bed. Loyal subjects mourned the old king and in 1760 crowned his young grandson **George III.** At 22, the new monarch was hardworking but highly self-critical, and he was already showing the symptoms of an illness that produced **delusions** and severe depression. Although he was inexperienced in matters of state, George III meant to rule—even if he had to deal with politicians, whom he distrusted, and engage in politics, which he disliked. He chose **George Grenville,** a no-nonsense, practical man to assist him. It fell to Grenville to handle the two most pressing post-war tasks: negotiating England's victory treaty with France and its allies, and designing Britain's peacetime policies.

Grenville's diplomats met with little resistance at the negotiating table. France was defeated, and it was up to the British government to decide what the spoils of war would be. England could take possession of a French Caribbean sugar island or the French mainland territory of Canada, a vast region stretching north and northwest of the English colonies. English sugar planters raised loud objections to the first option, for another sugar island would mean new competitors in the profitable English sugar markets. There was strong support, however, for adding Canada (see Map 5.1). Doing so would ensure the safety of the mainland colonies, whose people were increasingly important as consumers of English-made goods. With Canada, too, would come the rich fishing grounds off the Newfoundland coast and the fertile lands of the Ohio Valley. Such arguments in favor of Canada carried the day. By the end of 1763, George III could look with pride on an empire that had grown in physical size, on a nation that dominated the markets of Europe, and on a navy that ruled the seas.

Unfortunately, victory also brought new problems. First, the new English glory did not come cheaply. To win the war, William Pitt had spent vast sums of money, leaving the new king with an enormous war debt. English taxpayers, who had groaned under the wartime burden, now demanded tax relief, not tax increases. Second, the new Canadian territory posed serious governance problems because the Indians were unwilling to pledge their allegiance to the English king and, despite the change in flag, the French Cana-dians were unwilling to abandon their traditions, laws, or the Catholic Church.

Dealing with Indian and French Canadian Resistance

Both the Canadian tribes and Spain's former Indian allies along the southeastern borders of the English colonies felt threatened by Britain's victory. For dec-ades, Indian diplomats had protected their lands by playing European rivals against one another, but with the elimination of France and the weakening of Spain in mainland America, this strategy was impossible. The Creeks and Cherokees of the Southeast expected the worst—and it soon came. English settlers from the southern colonies poured into their lands, and although the Cherokees mounted full-scale resistance along the Virginia and Carolina western settlement line, the Brit-ish crushed their resistance. Cherokee leaders were forced to sign treaties that opened their lands to both English settlement and military bases.

A similar invasion of Delaware and Mingo territory began in the Ohio Valley and the Great Lakes region in 1763. The British added insult to injury by raising the price of the weapons, tools, clothing, and liquor that, by now, the tribes depended on. The crisis united the Indians, who acted quickly to create an intertribal al-liance known as the **Covenant Chain.** The Covenant Chain brought together Senecas, Ojibwas, Potowa-tomis, Hurons, Ottawas, Delawares, Shawnees, and Mingoes, all of whom stood ready to resist colonial settlers, British trading policy, and the terms of military occupation of frontier forts. Led by the Ottawa chief **Pontiac,** the Indians mounted their attack on British forts and colonial settlements in the spring of 1763. By

---

George III   King of England (r. 1760–1820); his govern-ment's policies produced colonial discontent that led to the American Revolution in 1776.

delusions   A false belief strongly held in spite of evidence to the contrary.

George Grenville   British prime minister who sought to tighten controls over the colonies and to impose taxes to raise revenues.

Covenant Chain   An alliance of Indian tribes estab-lished to resist colonial settlement in the Ohio Valley and Great Lakes region and to oppose British trading policies.

Pontiac   Ottawa chief who led the unsuccessful resistance against British policy in 1763.

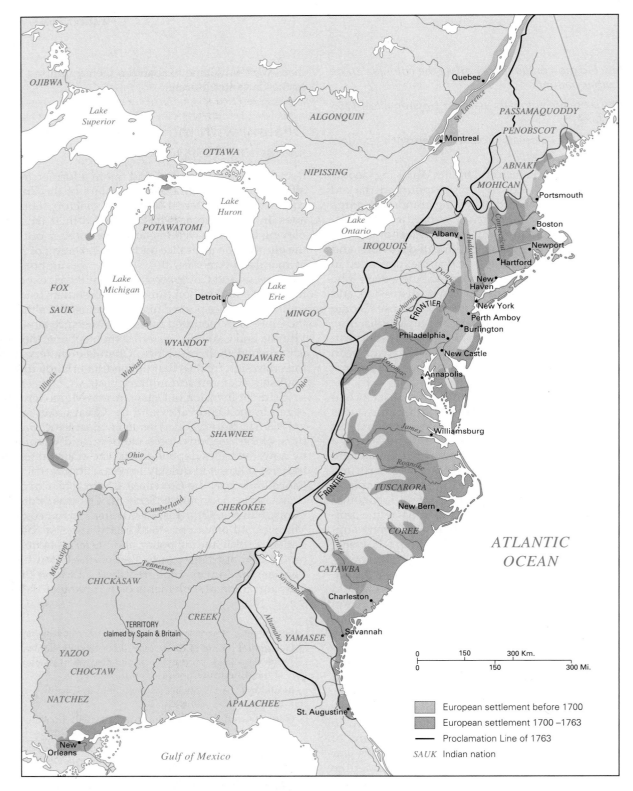

MAP 5.1 The Proclamation Line of 1763 This map shows European settlement east of the Appalachian Mountains and the numerous Indian tribes with territorial claims to the lands between the Appalachians and the Mississippi River. The Proclamation Line, which roughly follows the mountain range, was the British government's effort to temporarily halt colonial westward expansion and thus to prevent bloodshed between settlers and Indians. This British policy was deeply resented by land-hungry colonists.

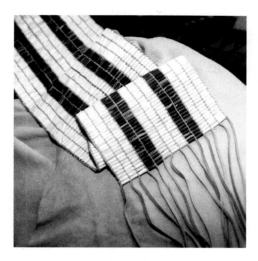

Among the Iroquois nations, wampum belts were the equivalent of the written documents familiar to English and European officials. The belt above was a treaty, stating the terms and conditions under which white people were welcomed to Indian lands. The two strands of yellow signified the equality of colonist and Iroquois, or as the Oneida explained, "We will not be like Father and Son, but like Brothers." *Oneida Indian Nation.*

fall, their resistance had evaporated, and the Covenant Chain tribes were forced to acknowledge British control of the Ohio Valley.

The British realized that such costly victories would not ensure permanent peace in the West. As long as the "middle ground" between Indian and colonial populations continued to shrink, Indians would mount resistance. And as long as Indians resisted what Creeks bluntly called "people greedily grasping after the lands of red people," settlers would demand expensive military protection as they pushed westward. If the army did not respond, settlers were ready to take action on their own. When the Paxton Boys of western Pennsylvania avenged an Indian raid by murdering a village of innocent Conestogas (see page 98), the dangers of this type of vigilante action became painfully clear. Violence would lead to violence—unless Grenville could keep Indians and settlers at arm's length. Grenville's solution was a proclamation, issued in 1763, temporarily banning all colonial settlement west of the Appalachian Mountains.

Grenville's **Proclamation Line of 1763** outraged colonists hoping to move west and wealthy land speculators hoping to reap a profit from their western investments. With the Indian enemy reeling from defeat, settlers insisted that this was the perfect moment to cross the mountains and stake claims to the land. Most colonists simply ignored Grenville's Proclamation Line.

Over the next decade, areas such as Kentucky began to fill with eager homesteaders, creating a wedge that divided northern from southern Indian tribes and increasing Indian anxiety about their own futures.

Because of their long tradition of anti-Catholic sentiment, American colonists also objected to Grenville's policy toward French-speaking Catholic Canadians. George III's advisers preferred to win over these new subjects rather than strong-arm them. Thus, to balance the French Canadians' loss of their fishing and fur-trading industries, Grenville promised them the right to preserve their religious and cultural way of life. Britain's colonists were scandalized by this concession to the losers in the war.

Demanding More from the Colonists

Colonists were not the only ones growing discontent. In London, the king, his ministers, and many members of Parliament were impatient with colonial behavior and attitudes. Hadn't the colonists benefited more than anyone from the French defeat? asked George Grenville. And hadn't they contributed less than anyone to securing that victory? Such questions revealed the subtle but important rewriting of the motives and goals of the French and Indian War. Although Britain had waged the war to win dominance in European affairs, not to benefit the colonies, Grenville now declared that the war had been fought to protect the colonists and to expand their opportunities for settlement.

This new interpretation fit well with the government's increasing doubts about colonial commitments to the empire's trade interests. It seemed clear to Grenville that something had gone wrong in the economic relationship between England and the colonies. Colonial cities such as Boston, Philadelphia, and New York had grown considerably, yet their growth did not make England as rich as **mercantile theory** said it should. One reason was that in every colony locally produced

---

Proclamation Line of 1763   Boundary that Britain established in the Appalachian Mountains, west of which white settlement was banned; it was intended to reduce conflict between Indians and colonists.

mercantile theory   The economic notion that a nation should amass wealth by exporting more than it imports; colonies are valuable in a mercantile system as a source of raw materials and as a market for manufactured goods.

goods competed with English-made goods. A more important reason, however, was illegal trade. Colonists seized economic opportunity wherever they found it—even in trade with England's rivals. In fact, to English amazement, colonials had continued to trade with the French Caribbean islands throughout the French and Indian War. In peacetime, colonists avoided paying **import duties** on foreign goods by bribing customs officials or landing cargoes where no customs officers were stationed.

George Grenville was often mocked for having a bookkeeper's mentality, but few laughed at what the prime minister discovered when he examined the imperial trade books. By the 1760s, the Crown had collected less than £2,000 in revenue from colonial trade with other nations while the cost of collecting these duties was over £7,000 a year. Such discoveries fueled British suspicions that the colonies were underregulated and undergoverned, as well as ungrateful and uncooperative. When the strong doubts about colonial loyalty met the reality of the British government debts and soaring expenses, something drastic could be expected to follow. And it did. In 1764 Parliament approved the reforms of colonial policy proposed by Grenville. Colonists greeted those reforms with shock and alarm.

Separately, each of Grenville's measures addressed a loophole in the proper relationship between Mother Country and colonies. For example, a **Currency Act** outlawed the use of paper money as legal tender in the colonies. In part, this was done to ensure the colonial market for English manufacturers. Although the colonists had to pay for imported English products with hard currency (gold and silver), they could use paper money to pay for locally produced goods. With paper money now banned, local manufacturers would be driven out of business.

Grenville believed the major problem was smuggling. Lawbreakers were so common, and customs officers so easily bribed, that smuggling had become an acceptable, even respectable, form of commerce. To halt this illicit traffic, Grenville set about to reform the **customs service.** In his 1764 American Revenue Act, he increased the powers of the customs officers, allowing them to use blanket warrants, called writs of assistance, to search ships and warehouses for smuggled goods. He also changed the regulations regarding key foreign imports, including sugar, wine, and coffee. This startling shift in policy, known popularly as the **Sugar Act,** revealed Grenville's practical bent. He knew that any attempt to stop the flow of French sugar into the colonies was a waste of time and resources. So he decided to make a profit for the Crown from this trade.

He would lower the tax on imported sugar—but he would make sure it was collected. Until 1764, a colonist accused of smuggling was tried before a jury of his neighbors in a **civil court.** He expected, and usually got, a favorable verdict from his peers. Grenville now declared that anyone caught smuggling would be tried in a juryless **vice-admiralty court,** where a conviction was likely. Once smuggling became too costly and too risky, Grenville reasoned, American shippers would declare their cargoes of French sugar and pay the Crown for the privilege of importing them.

The Colonial Response

Grenville's reforms were spectacularly ill timed as far as Americans were concerned. The colonial economy was suffering from a postwar **depression,** brought on in part by the loss of the British army as a steady market for American supplies and of British soldiers as steady customers who paid in hard currency rather than paper money. In 1764 unemployment was high among urban artisans, dockworkers, and sailors. Colonial merchants were caught in a credit squeeze—unable to pay their debts to British merchants because their colonial customers had no cash to pay for their purchases. These colonists were not likely to cheer a currency act that shut off a source of money or a Sugar Act that established a new get-tough policy on foreign trade. In the eyes of many colonists, the English government was turning into a greater menace than the French army had ever been.

Some colonists, however, saw these hard times and the need to tighten their belts as a welcome brake on their society's **materialism.** These Americans believed

---

import duties   Taxes on imported goods.

Currency Act   British law of 1764 banning the printing of paper money in the American colonies.

customs service   A government agency authorized to collect taxes on foreign goods entering a country.

Sugar Act   British law of 1764 that taxed sugar and other colonial imports to pay for some of Britain's expenses in protecting the colonies.

civil court   Any court that hears cases regarding the rights of private citizens.

vice-admiralty court   Nonjury British court in which a judge heard cases involving shipping.

depression   A period of drastic economic decline, marked by decreased business activity, falling prices, and high unemployment.

materialism   Excessive interest in worldly matters, especially in acquiring goods.

that a love of luxuries weakened people's spirit, sapped their independence, and would soon lead to the same moral decay they saw in England, where they believed extravagance and corruption infected society and tainted the nation's political leaders. After 1763, these colonists appealed to their neighbors to embrace simplicity and sacrifice. They urged prosperous women, for example, to abandon fashion, with its "gaudy, butterfly, vain, fantastick and expensive Dresses bought from Europe," and put on the "decent plain Dresses made in their own Country." Convinced that the eighteenth-century **consumer revolution** in the colonies had eroded virtue, these colonists called for a **boycott** of all goods manufactured in England.

Other views and other proposals for action soon filled the pages of colonial newspapers. This concern suggested that Grenville's reforms had raised profound issues of liberty and the rights of citizens and of the relationship between Parliament and the colonial governments—issues that needed to be resolved. The degree to which Parliament had, or ought to have, power over colonial economic and political life required serious, public pondering. Years later, with the benefit of hindsight, Massachusetts lawyer and revolutionary John Adams stressed the importance of the Sugar Act in starting America down the road to independence. "I know not why we should blush to confess," wrote Adams, "that molasses [liquid sugar] was an essential ingredient in American independence. Many great events have proceeded from much smaller causes." But in 1764 colonists were far from agreement over the issue of parliamentary and local political powers. They were not even certain how to respond to the Sugar Act.

The Stamp Act

Did Grenville stop to consider the possibility of "great events" arising from his postwar policies? Probably not. He was hardly a stranger to protest and anger, for he had often heard British citizens grumble about taxes and assert their rights against the government. As he saw it, his duty was to fill the treasury, reduce the nation's staggering debt, arm its troops, and keep the royal navy afloat. The duty of loyal British citizens, he believed, was to obey the laws of their sovereign government. Grenville had no doubt that the measures he and Parliament were taking to regulate the colonies and their revenue-producing trade were constitutional. Some colonists, however, had doubts. Thus the next piece of colonial legislation Grenville proposed was designed not only to raise revenue but to settle the principle of parliamentary sovereignty.

The **Stamp Act** of 1765 was to be the first **direct tax** ever laid on the colonies by Parliament, and its purpose was to raise revenue by taxing certain goods and services. There was nothing startling or novel about the revenue-collecting method Grenville proposed to use. A stamp tax raised money by requiring the use of government "stamped paper" on certain goods or as part of the cost for certain services. It was simple and efficient, and several colonial legislatures had adopted this method themselves. What was startling, however, was that Parliament would consider imposing a tax on the colonists that was not aimed at regulation of foreign trade. Up until 1765, Parliament had passed many acts regulating colonial trade. Sometimes these regulations on imports generated revenue for the Crown, and the colonists accepted them as a form of **external taxation.** But colonists expected direct taxation only from their local assemblies. If Grenville's Stamp Act became law, it would mark a radical change in the distribution of political power between assemblies and Parliament. It would be the powerful assertion of Parliament's sovereignty that Grenville intended.

Most members of Parliament saw the Stamp Act as an efficient and modest redistribution of the burdens of the empire—and a constitutional one. Colonists were certainly not being asked to shoulder the entire burden, since the estimated £160,000 in revenue from the stamped paper would cover only one-fifth of the cost of maintaining a British army in North America. Under these circumstances, Parliament saw no reason to deny Grenville's proposed tax. Thus the Stamp Act passed in February 1765 and was set to go into effect in November. The nine-month delay gave Grenville time to print the stamped paper, arrange for its shipment across the Atlantic, and appoint agents to receive and distribute the stamps in each colony. News of the tax, however, crossed the ocean rapidly and was

---

consumer revolution   The rising market for manufactured goods, particularly luxury items, that occurred in the early eighteenth century in the colonies.

boycott   An organized political protest in which people refuse to buy goods from a nation or group of people whose actions they oppose.

Stamp Act   British law of 1765 that directly taxed a variety of items, including newspapers, playing cards, and legal documents.

direct tax   A tax imposed to raise revenue rather than to regulate trade.

external taxation   Revenue raised in the course of regulating trade with other nations.

greeted with outrage and anger. Opposition was widespread among the colonists because virtually every free man and woman was affected by a tax that required stamps on all legal documents, on newspapers and pamphlets, and even on playing cards and dice. Grenville was reaching into the pockets of the rich, who would need stamped paper to draw up wills and property deeds and to bring suit in court. And he was emptying the pockets of the poor, who would feel the pinch when dealing a hand of cards in a tavern or buying a printed **broadside** filled with advertising. Other segments of the colonial society would also feel the sting of the new tax. Unless colonial merchants and ship captains used stamped clearances for all shipments, the royal navy could seize their cargoes. Lawyers feared the loss of clients if they had to add the cost of the stamps to their fees. With the stamp tax Grenville united northern merchants and southern planters, rural women and urban workingmen, and he riled the most articulate and argumentative of all Americans: lawyers and newspaper publishers.

The Popular Response

Many colonists were ready to resist the new legislation. Massachusetts, whose smugglers were already choking on the new customs regulations, and whose assembly had a long history of struggle with local Crown officers, led the way. During the summer of 1765, a group of Bostonians formed a secret resistance organization called the **Sons of Liberty.** Spearheading the Sons was the irrepressible **Samuel Adams,** a Harvard-educated member of a prominent Massachusetts family who preferred the company of local working men and women to the conversation of the elite. More at home in the dockside taverns than in the comfortable parlors of his relatives, Adams was a quick-witted, dynamic champion of working-class causes. He had a genius for writing propaganda and for mobilizing popular sentiment on political and community issues. Most members of the Sons of Liberty were artisans and shopkeepers, and the group's main support came from men of the city's laboring classes who had been hard hit by the postwar depression and would suffer from the stamp tax. These colonists had little influence in the legislature or with Crown officials, but they compensated by staging public demonstrations and protests to make their opinions known.

The Sons of Liberty had been created to oppose British policies, but with class divisions widening in Boston, they sometimes added protests against local issues and local elites. Prosperous Bostonians saw a potential danger in the mobilization of lower-class crowds. For these elites, crowd protest was a double-edged sword, a useful weapon that could be deadly in the wrong hands. By January 1765, New York City also had a Sons of Liberty organization, and by August, the Sons could be found in other cities and towns across the colonies.

Demonstrations and protests escalated, and once again Boston led the way. On August 14, shoemaker **Ebenezer McIntosh** led a crowd to protest the appointment of the colony's stamp agent, wealthy merchant Andrew Oliver. Until recently, McIntosh had headed one of two major workers' organizations in town, a **fraternal** group of artisans, apprentices, and day laborers known to the city's disapproving elite as the South End "gang." But on this August day, city gentlemen disguised themselves as workingmen and joined McIntosh's gang members as they paraded through the city streets, carrying an effigy of Oliver. The crowd destroyed the stamp agent's dockside warehouse and later broke all the windows in his home. The message was clear—and Oliver understood it well. The following day Andrew Oliver resigned as stamp agent. Boston Sons of Liberty celebrated by declaring the tree on which they hanged Oliver's effigy the "liberty tree."

Oliver's resignation did not end the protest. Customs officers and other Crown officials living in Boston were threatened with words and worse. The chief target of abuse, however, was the haughty merchant **Thomas Hutchinson,** hated by many of the ambitious younger political leaders because he monopolized appointive offices in the colony's government and by the workingmen because of his obvious disdain for ordinary people. Late one August evening, a large crowd surrounded Hutchinson's elegant brick man-

broadside An advertisement, public notice, or other publication printed on one side of a large sheet of paper.

Sons of Liberty A secret organization first formed in Boston to oppose the Stamp Act.

Samuel Adams Massachusetts revolutionary leader and propagandist who organized opposition to British policies after 1764.

Ebenezer McIntosh Boston shoemaker whose workingman's organization, the South End "gang," became the core of the city's Sons of Liberty in 1765.

fraternal Describes a group of people with common purposes or interests.

Thomas Hutchinson Boston merchant and judge who served as lieutenant governor and later governor of Massachusetts; Stamp Act protesters destroyed his home in 1765.

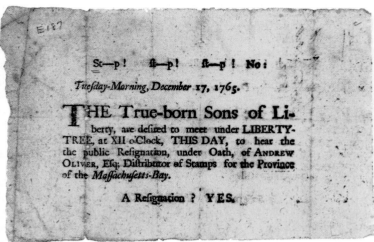

The Sons of Liberty first appeared in Boston, but this organization that united elite and working-class protesters spread quickly to other American cities. In 1765, the Boston Sons demanded the resignation of local stamp agent, Andrew Oliver. Ten years later, New York's pro-British editor, James Rivington, used the illustration above while reporting that a New Brunswick mob had hanged him in effigy. The New York Sons promptly attacked his office, destroyed his press, and forced his paper to close. *Mr. Rivington: Library of Congress; Sons of Liberty Broadside: Massachusetts Historical Society.*

sion. Warned of the impending attack, Hutchinson and his family had wisely fled, escaping just before rocks began to shatter the parlor windows. By dawn, the house was in ruins, and Hutchinson's furniture, clothing, and personal library had been trashed.

Thomas Hutchinson was a political target of those who opposed the Stamp Act. But because he represented the privilege and power of the few and the well placed, he was also a social target of the working people in the crowd. The savage destruction of his home led many of Boston's elite to withdraw their support from popular protests of any kind. Perhaps, they reasoned, the tensions between rich and poor were more dangerous than any parliamentary reform. Like the challenge to authority of the Great Awakening, these political protests carried the seeds of social revolution.

The campaign against the stamp agents spread like a brushfire across the colonies. Agents in Connecticut, Rhode Island, Maryland, and New York were mercilessly harassed. Most stamp agents resigned. When the stamps reached colonial ports in November, only the young and conservative colony of Georgia could produce anyone willing to distribute them. Colonial governors retaliated by refusing to allow any colonial ships to leave port. They hoped this disruption of trade would persuade local merchants to help end the resistance. Their strategy backfired. Violence increased as hundreds of unemployed sailors took to the streets, terrorizing customs officers and any colonists suspected of supporting the king's taxation policy.

Political Debate

While the Sons of Liberty and their supporters demonstrated in the streets, most colonial political leaders were proceeding with caution. Virginia lawyer and planter **Patrick Henry** briefly stirred the passions of his colleagues in the House of Burgesses when he suggested that the Stamp Act was evidence of the king's tyranny. Not everyone agreed with him that the measure was so serious. Many did agree, however, that the heart of the matter was not stamped paper but parliamentary sovereignty versus the rights of colonial citizens. "No taxation without representation"—the principle that citizens cannot be taxed by a government unless they are represented in it—was a fundamental assumption of free white Englishmen on both sides of the Atlantic. The crucial question was, Did the House of Commons represent the colonists even though no

Patrick Henry Member of the Virginia House of Burgesses and American revolutionary leader noted for his oratorical skills.

When Parliament enacted the Stamp Tax of 1765, the government designed this special embossed tax stamp to be used on the items that came under the new law. These items included newspapers, most legal documents, playing cards, and dice. The Stamp Tax provoked the first major protest and boycott by colonists against the Mother Country. *The Granger Collection, New York.*

colonist sat in the House and none voted for its members? If the answer was no, then the Stamp Act violated the colonists' most basic "rights of Englishmen."

Stating the issue in this way led to other concerns. Could colonial political leaders oppose a single law such as the Stamp Act without completely denying the authority of the government that was responsible for its passage? Massachusetts lawyer James Otis pondered this question when he sat down to write his *Rights of the British Colonists Asserted and Proved.* Any opposition to the Stamp Act, he decided, was ultimately a challenge to parliamentary authority over the colonies, and it would surely lead to colonial rebellion and a declaration of colonial independence. He, for one, was not prepared to become a rebel.

The logic of his own argument disturbed Otis and prompted him to propose a compromise: the colonists should be given representation in the House of Commons. Few political leaders took this suggestion seriously. Even if Parliament agreed, a small contingent of colonists could be easily ignored in its decision making. Most colonial leaders thought it best to de-

clare that American rights and liberties were under attack and to issue warnings that the assemblies would oppose any further threats to colonial rights. They carefully avoided, however, any treasonous statements or threats of rebellion. In the most popular pamphlet of 1765, Pennsylvania lawyer Daniel Dulaney captured this combination of criticism and caution. His *Considerations on the Propriety of Imposing Taxes on the British Colonies* reaffirmed the dependence of the colonies on Great Britain. But it also reminded Parliament that Americans knew the difference between dependence and slavery.

Colonial assemblymen knew that a final question hung in the air. If Parliament asserted its right to govern the colonies directly, what powers would remain to them as members of the colonial legislatures? These men had much to lose—status, prestige, and the many benefits that came from deciding how tax monies would be allocated. In the end, the majority agreed that a firm stand had to be taken. After much debate, most assemblies followed the lead of the Virginia House of Burgesses and issued statements condemning the Stamp Act and demanding its repeal. Massachusetts reinforced this unusual show of unity among the colonies when its assembly put out a call for an intercolonial meeting of delegates to discuss the Stamp Act crisis. The call to meet was greeted with enthusiasm.

Grenville's policies appeared to be bringing about what had once seemed impossible: united political action by the colonies. Until the Stamp Act, competition among the colonial governments was far more common than cooperation. Yet in the fall of 1765 delegates from nine colonies met in New York "to consider a general and unified, dutiful, loyal and humble Representation [petition]" to the king and Parliament. The petitions this historic Stamp Act Congress ultimately produced were far bolder than the delegates first intended. They were powerful, tightly argued statements that conceded parliamentary authority over the colonies but denied Parliament's right to impose any direct taxes on them. "No taxes," the Congress said, "ever have been, or can be Constitutionally imposed" on the colonies "but by their respective Legislatures." Clearly Americans expected this tradition to be honored.

Repeal of the Stamp Act

Neither the protest in the streets nor the arguments of the Stamp Act Congress moved the king or Parliament to repeal the stamp tax. But economic pressure did. English manufacturers relied heavily on their colonial markets and were certain to be hurt by any in-

Virginia planter and lawyer Patrick Henry may have acquired his oratorical brilliance from his uncle, a fiery Virginia preacher. Henry chose politics rather than the pulpit, and throughout the 1760s and 1770s, he stirred the House of Burgesses to resist British policy and the British king. *The Colonial Williamsburg Foundation.*

terruption in the flow and sale of goods to America. Thus the most powerful weapon in the colonial arsenal was a refusal to purchase English goods. On Halloween night, just one day before the stamp tax officially went into effect, two hundred New York merchants announced that they would not import any new British goods. Local artisans and laborers rallied to support this boycott. A mixture of patriotism and self-interest motivated both these groups. The merchants saw the possibility of emptying warehouses bulging with unsold goods because of the postwar depression. Unemployed and underemployed artisans and laborers saw the chance to sell their own products if the supply of cheaper English-made goods dried up. The same combination of interests existed in other colonial cities, and thus the nonimportation movement spread quickly. By the end of November, several colonial assemblies had publicly endorsed the nonimportation agreements signed by local merchants. Popular support widened as well. In many cities and towns, women publicly announced their commitment to nonimportation and vowed to spend long hours spinning and weaving their own cloth rather than purchase it ready-made from England. Their participation was crucial to the success of the boycott.

English exporters complained bitterly of the damage done to their businesses and pressured Parliament to take colonial protest seriously. Talk of repeal grew bolder and louder in the halls of Parliament. The Grenville government reluctantly conceded that enforcement of the Stamp Act had failed miserably. Even in colonies where royal officials dared to distribute the stamped paper, Americans refused to purchase it. Colonists simply ignored the hated law and continued to sue their neighbors, sell their land, publish their newspapers, and buy their playing cards as if the stamped paper and the Stamp Act did not exist.

By winter's end, Grenville was no longer prime minister. For the king's new head of state, Lord Rockingham, the critical issue was not whether to repeal the Stamp Act but how to do so without appearing to cave in to colonial pressure. After much debate and political maneuvering, the government came up with a satisfactory solution. In 1766, Great Britain repealed the Stamp Act but at the same time passed a Declaratory Act, which asserted that the colonies "have been, are, and of right ought to be subordinate unto, and dependent upon the imperial Crown and parliament of Great Britain," and thus Parliament's right to pass legislation for and raise taxes from the North American colonies was reaffirmed as absolute.

Colonists celebrated the repeal with public outpourings of loyalty to England that were as impressive as their public protests had been. There were cannon salutes, bonfires, parades, speeches, and public toasts to the king and Rockingham. In Boston, Sons of Liberty built a pyramid and covered its three sides with patriotic poetry. In Anne Arundel County, Maryland, colonists erected a "liberty pillar" and buried "Discord" beneath it. And in a spectacular but poorly executed gesture, the Liberty Boys of Plymouth, Massachusetts, tried to move Plymouth Rock to the center of town. When the famous rock on which the Pilgrims were said to have landed split in two, half of it was carried to Liberty Pole Square, where it remained until 1834.

Asserting American Rights

→ *Why did Charles Townshend expect his revenue-raising measures to be successful?*

→ *What forms of resistance did the colonists use to force the repeal of Townshend's measures?*

→ *How did the Townshend Acts affect the northern colonies' trade with the West Indies?*

→ *What were the results of colonial resistance?*

The Declaratory Act firmly asserted that Parliament had "the sole and exclusive right" to tax the colonists.

This was a clear rejection of the colonial assemblies' claim to power, yet the colonists responded with indifference. Those who commented on it at all dismissed it as a face-saving device. To a degree, they were correct. But the Declaratory Act expressed the views of powerful men in Parliament, and within a year they put it to the test.

By the summer of 1766, William Pitt had returned to power within George III's government. But Pitt was old and preoccupied with his failing health. He lacked the energy to exercise the control over the government he had demonstrated during the French and Indian War. A young playboy named Charles Townshend, serving as chancellor of the exchequer, rushed in to fill the leadership void. This brash young politician wasted little time foisting a new package of taxes on the colonies.

The Townshend Acts and Colonial Protest

During the Stamp Act crisis, Benjamin Franklin had assured Parliament that American colonists accepted indirect taxation even if they violently protested a direct tax such as the Stamp Act. In other words, Americans conceded the British government's right to any revenue arising from the regulation of colonial trade. In 1767 Townshend decided to test this distinction by proposing new regulations on a variety of imported necessities and luxuries. But the Townshend Acts were import taxes unlike any other the colonies had ever seen: they were tariffs on products made in Britain.

The Townshend Acts taxed glass, paper, paint, and lead products made in England, all part of the luxury trade. The acts also placed a three-penny tax on tea, the most popular drink among colonists everywhere and considered a necessity by virtually everyone. Townshend wanted to be certain these taxes were collected, so he ordered new customs boards established in the colonies and created new vice-admiralty courts in the major port cities of Boston, Charleston, and Philadelphia to try any cases of smuggling or tax evasion that might occur. In case Americans tried to harass customs officials, as they had so effectively done during the stamp tax protests, Townshend ordered British troops transferred from the western regions to the major colonial port cities. He knew this troop relocation would anger the colonists, but he was relying on the presence of uniformed soldiers—known as "redcoats" because of their scarlet jackets—to keep the peace. To help finance this military occupation of key cities, Townshend invoked the 1766 Quartering Act, a law requiring colonists to provide room and board, "candles, firing, bedding, cooking utensils, salt and vinegar" and a ration of beer, cider, or rum to troops stationed in their midst.

Clearly, Townshend was taking every precaution to avoid the embarrassment Grenville had suffered in the Stamp Act disaster. But he made a serious error in believing that colonists would meekly agree to pay import duties on British-made goods. When news of the new regulations reached the colonies, the response was immediate, determined, and well-organized resistance.

If the newspapers reflected popular sentiment accurately, the colonists were united in their opposition to the Townshend Acts and to the Mother Country's repressive enforcement policies. Some were incensed that the government was once again trampling on the principle of "no taxation without representation." In Boston, Samuel Adams voiced his outrage: "Is it possible to form an idea of Slavery, more compleat, more miserable, more disgraceful than that of a people, where justice is administer'd, government exercis'd, and a standing army maintain'd at the expense of the people, and yet without the least dependence upon them?" Others worried more about the economic burden of the new taxes and the quartering of the troops than about political rights. Boston lawyer Josiah Quincy Jr. asked readers of the *Boston Gazette*: "Is not the bread taken out of the children's mouths and given unto the Dogs?"

John Dickinson, a well-respected Pennsylvania landowner and lawyer, laid out the basic American position on imperial relations in his pamphlet *Letters from a Farmer in Pennsylvania* (1767). Direct taxation without representation violated the colonists' rights as English citizens, Dickinson declared. But by imposing any tax that did not regulate foreign trade, Parliament also violated those rights. Dickinson also considered, and rejected, the British claim that Americans were represented in the House of Commons. According to the British argument, colonists enjoyed "virtual representation" because the House of Commons represented the interests of all citizens in the empire who were not members of the nobility, whether those citizens participated directly in elections to the House or not. Like most Americans, Dickinson discounted virtual representation. What Englishmen were entitled to, he wrote, was *actual* representation by men they had elected to government to protect their interests. For qualified voters in the colonies, who enjoyed actual representation in their local assemblies, virtual representation was nothing more than a weak excuse for exclusion and exploitation. As one American quipped: "Our privileges are all virtual, our sufferings are real."

While political theorists set out the American position in newspaper essays and pamphlets, protest leaders organized popular resistance against acts that were clearly designed to raise revenue as well as make daily life more expensive in the colonies. Samuel Adams set in motion a massive boycott of British goods to begin on January 1, 1768. Just as before, some welcomed the chance a boycott provided to "mow down luxury and high living." But simple economics also contributed forcefully to support for the boycott. Boston artisans remained enthusiastic about any action that stopped the flow of inexpensive English-made goods to America. Small-scale merchants were also eager to see nonimportation enforced. They had little access to British credit or goods under normal circumstances, and the boycott would eliminate the advantages enjoyed by the merchant elite who did. Merchants and shippers who made their living smuggling goods from the West Indies supported the boycott because it cut out the competing English-made products. The large-scale merchants who had led the 1765 boycott were not enthusiastic, however. By 1767, their warehouses were no longer overflowing with unsold English stock, and the boycott might cut off their livelihoods. Many of these elite merchants delayed signing the agreements. Others did not sign at all.

The strongest voices raised against the boycott, and against resistance to the Townshend Acts in general, were the voices of colonists holding Crown-appointed government offices. These fortunate few—including judges and customs men—shared their neighbors' sensitivity to abuse or exploitation by the Crown. But they had sworn to uphold and carry out the programs and policies of the British government. And many of their salaries came from England. Because their careers and their identities were closely tied to the power and authority of the Crown, they were inclined to see British policymakers as well intentioned and acceptance of British policy as a patriotic duty. Jonathan Sewall, the king's attorney general in Massachusetts, was perhaps typical of these royal officeholders. Sewall had deep roots in his colonial community, for his family went back many generations and included lawyers, judges, merchants, and assemblymen. His closest friend was John Adams, cousin of Samuel Adams, and the wealthy Boston merchant and smuggler John Hancock would soon become his brother-in-law. Yet Sewall became a staunch public defender of Crown policy. In his newspaper articles he urged his neighbors to ignore the call to resistance, and he questioned the motives of the leading activists, suggesting that greed, thwarted ambition, and envy rather than high-minded principles motivated the rabble-rousers. But despite their pres-

Samuel Adams, whose family owned a Boston brewery, was the undisputed leader of the popular protest movement in Massachusetts during the 1760s and 1770s. Adams was one of the organizers of the Sons of Liberty, a group responsible for many of the demonstrations against British policies as well as some of the violence against British officials. After the Revolution, he served as Governor of Massachusetts. *The Granger Collection, New York.*

tige and their positions of authority, Crown officers like Sewall were no more able to prevent the boycott or slow the spread of resistance than Anglican ministers like Charles Inglis.

Just as the Sons of Liberty and the Stamp Act demonstrations brought common men into the political arena, the 1768 boycott brought politics into the lives of women. When in 1765 the inexpensive, factory-made cloth produced in England had been placed high on the list of boycotted goods, an old, neglected, and tedious domestic skill became both a real and a symbolic element in the American protest strategy. In 1768 many women responded to the challenge. Taking a bold political stance, women, including wealthy mothers and daughters, formed groups called the Daughters of Liberty and staged large public spinning bees to show support for the boycott. Wearing clothing made of "homespun" became a mark of honor and a political statement. As one male observer noted, "The ladies . . . while they vie with each other in skill and industry in their profitable employment, may vie with the men in contributing to the preservation and prosperity of their country and equally share in the honor of it." Through the boycott, politics had entered the domestic circle.

The British Humiliated

Townshend and his new taxation policy faced sustained defiance in almost every colony, but Massachusetts provided the greatest embarrassment for Parliament and the king. Massachusetts governor Francis Bernard had lost his control over local politics ever since he tried to punish the assembly for issuing a call in 1768 for collective protest, called a Circular Letter, against the Townshend Acts to other colonies. Although Bernard forced the assembly to rescind, or call back, the letter, the men chosen for the legislature in the next election simply reissued it. The helpless governor could do nothing to save face except dismiss the assembly, leaving the colony without any representative government. Bernard's ability to ensure law and order eroded rapidly after this. Throughout 1768, enforcers of the boycott roamed the streets of Boston, intimidating pro-British merchants and harassing anyone wearing British-made clothing. Boston mobs of men and women openly threatened customs officials, and the Sons of Liberty protected smuggling operations. Despite the increased number of customs officers policing the docks and wharves, the colony was doing a thriving business in smuggling foreign goods and the items listed in the hated Townshend Acts. One of the town's most notorious smugglers, the flamboyant John Hancock, grew more popular with his neighbors each time he broke the customs laws and unloaded his illegal cargoes of French and Spanish wines or West Indian sugar. When customs officers seized Hancock's vessel, aptly named the *Liberty*, in June 1768, protesters beat up senior customs men, and mobs visited the homes of other royal officials. The now-desperate Governor Bernard sent an urgent plea for help to the British government.

In October 1768, four thousand troops arrived in Boston. The Crown clearly believed that the presence of one soldier for every four citizens would be enough to restore order quickly. John Adams marveled at what he considered British thickheadedness. The presence of so many young soldiers, far from home and surrounded by a hostile community, was certain to worsen the situation. Military occupation of Boston, Adams warned, made more violence inevitable. Adams was right. With time on their hands, the soldiers passed the hours courting any local women who would speak to them and pestering those who would not. They angered local dockworkers by moonlighting in the ship-

yards when off duty and taking jobs away from colonists by accepting lower pay. For their part, civilians taunted the sentries, insulted the soldiers, and refused the military any sign of hospitality. News of street-corner fights and tavern brawls inflamed feelings on both sides. Samuel Adams and his friends did their best to fan the flames of hatred, publishing daily accounts of both real and imaginary confrontations in which soldiers threatened the honor or endangered the safety of innocent townspeople.

The military occupation dragged on through 1769 and early 1770. On March 5, the major confrontation most people expected occurred. An angry crowd began throwing snowballs—undoubtedly laced with bricks and rocks—at British sentries guarding the customs house. The redcoats, under strict orders not to fire on civilians, issued a frantic call for help in withdrawing to safety. When Captain Thomas Preston and his men arrived to rescue the sentries, the growing crowd immediately enveloped them. How, and under whose orders, Preston's soldiers began to fire is unknown, but they killed five men and wounded eight other colonists. Four of the five victims were white laborers. The fifth, Crispus Attucks, was a free black sailor.

Massachusetts protest leaders' account of what they called the Boston Massacre appeared in colonial newspapers everywhere and included a dramatic anti-British illustration engraved by silversmith Paul Revere. A jury of colonists later cleared Preston and all but two of his men of the charges against them. But nothing that was said at their trial—no sworn testimony, no lawyer's arguments—could erase the image of British brutality against British subjects.

Even before the bloodshed of March 5, Edmund Burke, a member of Parliament known for his sympathy to the colonial cause, had warned the House of Commons that the relationship between Mother Country and colonies was both desperate and tragic. "The Americans," Burke said, "have made a discovery, or think they have made one, that we mean to oppress them; we have made a discovery, or think we have made one, that they intend to rise in rebellion. We do not know how to advance; they do not know how to retreat." Burke captured well the growing American conviction of a conspiracy or plot by Parliament to deprive the colonists of their rights and liberties. He also captured the British government's growing sense that a rebellion was being hatched. But Parliament was ready to act to ease the crisis and make a truce possible. A new minister, Frederick Lord North, was given the reins of government, and on the very day Captain Preston's men fired on the crowd at Boston, Lord North repealed the Townshend Acts and allowed the hated

Paul Revere's engraving of the Boston Massacre appeared in newspapers the day after the confrontation between redcoats and Boston citizens. Despite the fact that Captain Preston and most of his soldiers were acquitted of wrongdoing, Revere's striking image of innocent civilians and murderous soldiers remained fixed in the popular mind. It reinforced suspicion that the British were plotting to deprive Americans of their rights and liberties. *"Boston Massacre" by Paul Revere. Library of Congress.*

Quartering Act to expire. Yet Lord North wanted to give no ground on the question of parliamentary control of the colonies. For this reason, North kept the tax on tea—to preserve a principle rather than fill the king's treasury.

Success Weakens Colonial Unity

Repeal of the Townshend Acts allowed the colonists to return to the ordinary routine of their lives. But it was not true that all tensions had vanished. Troubling ones remained—and they were largely among the colonists themselves.

The economic boycott begun in 1768 exposed and deepened the growing divisions between the merchant elite and the coalition of smaller merchants, artisans, and laborers in the urban centers of the North. During the years of nonimportation, many of the wealthy merchants had secretly imported and sold British goods whenever possible. When repeal came in 1770, the demand for locally manufactured goods was still low, and artisans and laborers still faced poor economic prospects. These groups were reluctant to

abandon the boycott even after repeal. But few merchants, large or small, would agree to continue it.

Many elite colonists gladly abandoned the radical activism they had shown in the 1760s in favor of social conservatism. Their fear of British tyranny dimmed, but their fear of the lower classes' clamor for political power grew. Artisans and laborers did indeed continue to press for broader participation in local politics and for more representative political machinery. The tyranny that some of them opposed was close to home. "Many of the poorer People," observed one supporter of expanded political participation, "deeply felt the Aristocratic Power, or rather the intolerable Tyranny of the great and opulent." The new political language in which these common men justified their demands made their social superiors uneasy. Their own impassioned appeals for rights and liberties were returning to haunt some of the colonial elite.

The Crisis Renewed

→ *What British policies led Americans to imagine a plot against their rights and liberties?*

→ *How did the king hope to crush resistance in Massachusetts?*

→ *How did the Continental Congress respond to the Intolerable Acts?*

Lord North's government took care not to disturb the calm created by the repeal of the Townshend Acts. Between 1770 and 1773, North proposed no new taxes on the colonists and made no major changes in colonial policy. American political leaders took equal care not to make any open challenges to British authority. Both sides recognized that their political truce had its limits. It did not extend to smugglers and customs men, who continued to lock horns; it did not end the bitterness of southern colonists who wished to settle beyond the Proclamation Line; nor did it erase the distrust colonial political leaders and the British government felt for each other.

Disturbing the Peace of the Early 1770s

Despite the repeal of the Townshend duties, the British effort to crack down on American smuggling continued. New England merchants whose fortunes were built on trade with the Caribbean resented the sight of customs officers at the docks and customs ships patrolling the coastline (see Map 5.2). Rhode Island

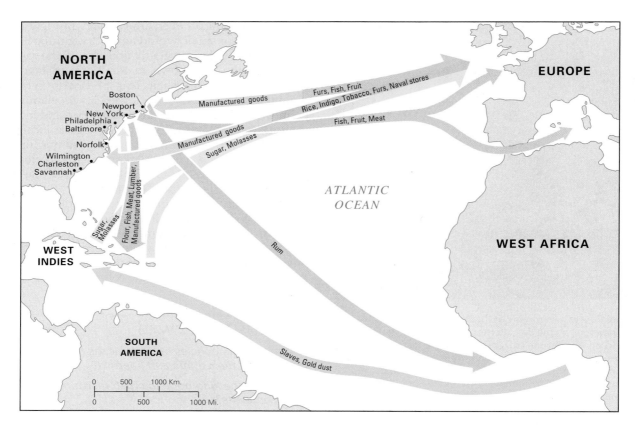

MAP 5.2 **Colonial Transatlantic Trade in the 1770s** This map shows the major trade routes between the British mainland colonies, West Africa, the Caribbean, and Europe and the most important export and import cargoes carried along these routes. The central role northern seaport cities played in carrying colonial agricultural products across the Atlantic and bringing British manufactured goods into the colonies is clear. Note also the role the northern colonies played in the slave trade.

merchants were especially angry and frustrated by the determined—and highly effective—customs operation in their colony. They took their revenge one June day in 1772 when the customs patrol boat, the *Gaspée,* ran aground as it chased an American vessel. That evening a band of colonists boarded the *Gaspée,* taunted the stranded customs men, and then set fire to their boat.

Rhode Islanders called the burning of the *Gaspée* an act of political resistance. The English called it an act of vandalism and appointed a royal commission to investigate. To their amazement, no witnesses came forward, and no evidence could be gathered to support any arrests. The British found the conspiracy of silence among the Rhode Islanders appalling.

Many American political leaders found the royal commission equally appalling. They were convinced that the British government had intended to bring its suspects to England for trial and thus deprive them of a jury of their peers. They read this as further evidence of the plot to destroy American liberty, and they decided to keep in close contact in order to monitor British moves. Following the Virginia assembly's lead, five colonies organized a communications network called the committees of correspondence, instructing each committee to circulate detailed accounts of any questionable royal activities in its colony. These committees of correspondence were also a good mechanism for coordinating protest or resistance should the need arise. Thus the colonists put in place their first permanent machinery of protest.

The Tea Act and the Tea Party

During the early 1770s, colonial activists worked to keep the political consciousness of the 1760s alive. They commemorated American victories over British policy and observed the anniversary of the Boston Massacre with solemn speeches and sermons. The New York Sons of Liberty celebrated their founding day with dinners, endless toasts, and rituals that linked the Sons with a tradition of English radicalism. Without major British provocation, however, a revival of mass action was unlikely.

In 1773 Parliament provided that provocation. This time the government was not setting new colonial policy. It was trying to save a major commercial enterprise, the East India Tea Company. Mismanagement, coupled with the American boycott and the tendency of colonists to buy smuggled Dutch tea, had left the company in serious financial trouble. With its warehouses bursting with unsold tea, the company appealed to Parliament to rescue them.

The company directors had a plan: if Parliament allowed them to ship their tea directly to the colonial market, eliminating the English merchants who served as middlemen, they could lower their prices and compete effectively against the smuggled Dutch tea. Even with the three-penny tax on tea that remained from the Townshend era, smart consumers would see this as a bargain. Lord North liked the plan and saw in it the opportunity for vindication: Americans who purchased the cheaper English tea would be confirming Parliament's right to tax the colonies. With little debate, Parliament made the company's arrangement legal through passage of the Tea Act. No one expected the colonists to object.

Once again, British politicians had seriously misjudged the impact of their decisions. Colonists read the Tea Act as an insult, a challenge, another chilling sign of a conspiracy against their well-being and their liberty. They distrusted the arrangement, believing that the East India Tea Company would raise its prices dramatically once all foreign teas were driven off the market. And they were concerned that if other British companies marketing products in the colonies followed the East India Tea Company's example, prices for scores of products would soar. These objections, however, paled beside the colonists' immediate grasp of Lord North's strategy: purchasing cheaper English tea would confirm Parliament's right to tax the colonies. The tea that Americans drank might be cheap, but the price of conceding the legitimacy of the tea tax was too high.

Colonists mobilized their resistance in 1773 with the skill acquired from a decade of experience. In several cities, crowds met the ships carrying the East India tea and prevented the unloading of their cargoes. They used the threat of violence to persuade ship cap-

The famous "Boston Tea Party" of December 1773 was neither secretive nor quiet. As this illustration shows, a noisy crowd gathered on the docks to cheer the men who boarded British ships to toss thousands of pounds' worth of tea into the harbor. Although the radicals donned Indian disguises, most of them were no doubt easily recognized by their supporters. Although this artist painted an all-male crowd, written accounts tell us that women were present at the Tea Party too. *Library of Congress.*

tains to return to England with the tea still on board. As long as both the captains and the local royal officials gave in to these pressures, no serious confrontation occurred. But in Massachusetts, the most famous victim of mob violence, now Governor Thomas Hutchinson, was not willing to give in. A stalemate resulted: colonists refused to allow crews to unload the tea, but Hutchinson refused to allow the tea ships to depart without unloading. Boston activists broke the stalemate on December 16, 1773, when some sixty men, thinly disguised as Mohawk Indians, boarded the tea ships. Working calmly and methodically, they dumped 342 chests of tea, worth almost £10,000, into the waters of Boston Harbor.

The Intolerable Acts

The Boston Tea Party delighted colonists everywhere. The Crown, however, failed to see the humor in this deliberate destruction of valuable private property. The tea chests had barely settled into the harbor mud before Parliament retaliated. The king and his minister meant to make an example of everyone in Boston, the source of so much trouble and embarrassment over the past decade. Americans on the scene in England warned friends and family back home of the growing rage against the colonies. Arthur Lee, serving in London as Massachusetts's colonial agent, drew a gloomy picture of the dangers ahead in a letter to his brother. "The storm, you see, runs high," he wrote, "and it will require great prudence, wisdom and resolution, to save our liberties from shipwreck."

The four acts that Parliament passed in 1774 to discipline Massachusetts were as harsh and uncompromising as Arthur Lee predicted. The colonists called them the Intolerable Acts. The Port Act declared the port of Boston closed to all trade until the citizens compensated the East India Tea Company fully for its losses. This was a devastating blow to the colony's economy. The Massachusetts Government Act transferred much of the power of the colony's assembly to the royal governor, including the right to appoint judges, sheriffs, and members of the colonial legislature's upper house. The colony's town meetings, which had served as forums for anti-British sentiment and protests, also came under the governor's direct control. A third measure, the Justice Act, allowed royal officials charged with capital crimes to stand trial in London rather than before local juries. And a new Quartering Act gave military commanders the authority to house troops in private homes. To see that these laws were enforced, the king named General Thomas Gage, commander of the British troops in North America, as the acting governor of Massachusetts.

At the same time that Parliament passed these punitive measures, the British government issued a comprehensive plan for the government of Canada. The timing of the Quebec Act may have been a coincidence, but its provisions infuriated Americans. The Quebec Act granted the French in Canada the right to worship as Catholics, retain their language, and keep many of their legal practices—all marks of a tolerance that the Crown had refused to show its English colonists. The Quebec Act also expanded the borders of Canada into the Ohio Valley at the expense of the English-speaking colonies' claim to western land. This dealt a harsh blow to Virginia planters who hoped to profit from land speculation in the region. The endorsement of Catholicism and the stifling of western expansion seemed to connect the Quebec Act to the attack on American liberty that Parliament had launched with the Intolerable Acts.

The king expected the severe punishment of Massachusetts to isolate that colony from its neighbors. But the Americans resisted this divide-and-conquer strategy. In every colony, newspaper essays and editorials urged readers to see Boston's plight as their own. "This horrid attack upon the town of Boston," said the *South Carolina Gazette*, "we consider not as an attempt upon that town singly, but upon the whole Continent." George Washington, by now an influential Virginia planter and militia officer—and a major land speculator—declared that "the cause of Boston now is and ever will be the cause of America." Indeed, the Intolerable Acts produced a wave of sympathy for the beleaguered Bostonians, and relief efforts sprang up across the colonies. The residents of Surry County, Virginia, declared they had gathered "upwards of 150 barrels of Indian corn and wheat . . . for the benefit of those firm and intrepid sons of Liberty." Throughout the year, much-needed supplies found their way to Boston despite British efforts to isolate the city.

Colonists did not stop at sympathy for the victims of the Intolerable Acts. In pamphlets and political essays, they placed these acts into the larger context of systematic oppression by the Mother Country. Political writers referred to the British government as the "enemy," conspiring to deprive Americans of their liberty, and urged colonists to defend themselves against the "power and cunning of our adversaries." This unity of sentiments, however, was more fragile than it appeared. In the cities, bitter divisions quickly developed, and artisans struggled with merchants to control the mass meetings that would make strategy choices. Samuel Adams and the radical artisans and workers of Boston suggested what might be at stake in this struggle between elites and ordinary citizens when they formed a "solemn league and covenant" to lead a third intercolonial boycott of British goods. As most Bostonians knew, the words *solemn league* referred to a pact between the Scottish Presbyterians and English Puritans who had overthrown royal government in the 1640s and beheaded a king. Adams and his allies had made their choice: armed rebellion. Yet even in crisis-torn Boston, not everyone wanted matters to go that far. And in the southern colonies, planters fearful of the social instability that resistance might bring worried that slave revolts and class antagonisms between the elite and the poorer farmers might be the ultimate outcome of escalating protest.

Creating a National Forum: The First Continental Congress

On September 5, 1774, delegates from every colony but Georgia gathered in Philadelphia for a continental congress. Few of the delegates or the people they represented thought of themselves as revolutionaries. "We want no revolution," a North Carolina delegate bluntly stated. Yet in the eyes of their British rulers, he and other colonists were treading dangerously close to treason. After all, neither the king nor Parliament had authorized the congress to which colonial assemblies and self-appointed committees had sent representatives. And that congress was intent on resisting acts of Parliament and defying the king. English men and women had been hanged as traitors for far less serious betrayals of the English government.

Some of the most articulate political leaders in the colonies attended this First Continental Congress. Conservative delegates such as Joseph Galloway of Pennsylvania hoped to slow the pace of colonial resistance by substituting petitions to Parliament for the total boycott proposed by Samuel Adams. Their radical opponents—including Samuel Adams and his cousin John, Patrick Henry, and delegates from the artisan community of Philadelphia—demanded the boycott and more. Most of the delegates were desperately searching for a third choice: a way to express their grievances and demand that injustices be corrected without further eroding their relationship with England.

The mounting crisis in Massachusetts diminished the chances of a moderate solution. Rumors spread that the royal navy was planning to bombard Boston and that General Gage was preparing to invade the countryside. Thousands of Massachusetts militiamen had begun mustering in Cambridge. The growing conflict drove many delegates into the radical camp. In this atmosphere of dread and anxiety, the Continental Congress approved the Continental Association, a boycott of all English goods to begin on December 1, 1774. The Congress also passed strong resolutions demanding the repeal of the Intolerable Acts.

The First Continental Congress had chosen radical tactics, but many delegates were torn between loyalties to two governments and their conflicting claims to power. Parliament insisted on an unconditional right to make laws for and regulate the colonies. The colonial assemblies claimed that they alone had the right to tax the colonists. Thomas Jefferson, a young Virginia planter and intellectual, tried to find a way out of this dilemma by separating loyalty to the king from resistance to Parliament. He argued that the colonists owed allegiance to the nation's king, not to Parliament, and that each colony did indeed have the right to legislate for itself. Not everyone agreed.

If no compromise could be reached, the delegates—and Americans everywhere—would have to choose where their strongest loyalties lay. Joseph Galloway believed that he had worked out the necessary compromise. In his Plan of Union, Galloway proposed a drastic restructuring of imperial relations. The plan called for a Grand Council, elected by each colonial leg-islature, that would share with Parliament the right to originate laws for the colonies. The Grand Council and Parliament would have the power to veto or disallow each other's decisions if necessary. A governor-general, appointed by the Crown, would oversee council operations and preserve imperial interests.

After much discussion and debate, Congress rejected Galloway's compromise by the narrowest of margins. Then it was John Adams's turn to propose a solution. Under his skillful urging and direction, the Congress adopted the Declaration of Rights and Grievances. The declaration politely but firmly established the colonial standard for acceptable legislation by Parliament. Colonists, said the declaration, would consent to acts meant to regulate "our external commerce." But they absolutely denied the legitimacy, or lawfulness, of an "idea of taxation, internal or external, for raising a revenue on the subjects of America, without their consent."

George III, or George William Frederick, was only 22 when he became the King of Great Britain and Ireland in 1760. During his reign, Britain won a major war against France in 1763, but lost most of its mainland colonies in 1783, when American independence was recognized. Thomas Paine called him "the royal brute;" American revolutionaries called him a tyrant; but supporters viewed him as a statesman. In this portrait George III shows no signs of the illness that would lead to blindness and senility, as well as bouts of insanity, later in his life. *Library of Congress.*

The delegates knew that the force behind the declaration came neither from the logic of its argument nor from the genius of its political reasoning. Whatever force it carried came from the unspoken but nevertheless real threat that rebellion would occur if the colonists' demands were not met. To make this threat clearer, Congress endorsed a set of resolutions rushed to Philadelphia from Suffolk County, Massachusetts. These Suffolk Resolves called on the residents of that county to arm themselves and prepare to resist British military action. Congressional support for these resolves sent an unmistakable message that American leaders were willing to choose rebellion if politics failed.

The delegates adjourned and headed home, bringing news of the Congress's decisions with them to their families and their communities. There was nothing to do now but wait for the Crown's response. When it came, it was electric. "Blows must decide," declared King George III, "whether they are to be subject to this country or independent."

The Decision for Independence

→ *Could the Revolutionary War have been avoided?*

→ *What alternatives might have kept compromise alive?*

→ *What motivated some colonists to become loyalists and others to become patriots?*

Americans were anxious while they waited for the king and Parliament to respond to the Declaration of Rights and Grievances, but they were not idle. In most colonies, a transfer of political power was occurring as the majority of Americans withdrew their support for and obedience to royal governments and recognized the authority of anti-British, patriot governments. The king might expect blows to decide the issue of colonial autonomy, but independent local governments were becoming a reality before any shots were fired.

Taking Charge and Enforcing Policies

Imperial control broke down as communities in each colony refused to obey royal laws or acknowledge the authority of royal officers. For example, when General Thomas Gage, the acting governor of Massachusetts, refused to convene the Massachusetts assembly, its members met anyway. Their first order of business was to prepare for military resistance to Gage and his

army. While the redcoats occupied Boston, the rebellious assembly openly ordered the colonists to stockpile military supplies near the town of Concord (see Map 5.3).

The transition from royal to patriot political control was peaceful in communities where anti-British sentiment was strong. Where it was weak, or where the community was divided, radicals used persuasion, pressure, and open intimidation to advance the patriot cause. These radicals became increasingly impatient with dissent, disagreement, or even indecision among their neighbors. They insisted that people choose sides and declare loyalties.

In most colonial cities and towns, patriot committees arose to enforce compliance with the boycott of British goods. These committees publicly exposed those who did not obey the Continental Association, publishing violators' names in local newspapers and calling on the community to shun them. These tactics were effective against merchants who wanted to break the boycott and consumers willing to purchase English goods if they could find them. When public shaming did not work, most committees were ready to use threats of physical violence and to make good on them.

Colonists suspected of sympathizing with the British were brought before committees and made to swear oaths of support for the patriot cause. Such political pressure often gave way to violence. In Connecticut a group of patriots hauled a 70-year-old Anglican man from his bed, dragged him naked into the winter night, and beat him brutally because his loyalty to the Church of England made him suspect. In New England, many pro-British citizens, or **loyalists,** came to fear for their lives. In the wake of the Intolerable Acts, hundreds of them fled to the city of Boston, hoping General Gage could protect them from their neighbors.

The Shot Heard 'Round the World

The American situation was frustrating, but King George continued to believe that resistance in most colonies would fade if the Massachusetts radicals were crushed. In January 1775, he ordered General Gage to arrest the most notorious leaders of rebellion in that colony, Samuel Adams and John Hancock. Although storms on the Atlantic prevented the king's orders from

---

loyalist An American colonist who remained loyal to the king during the Revolution.

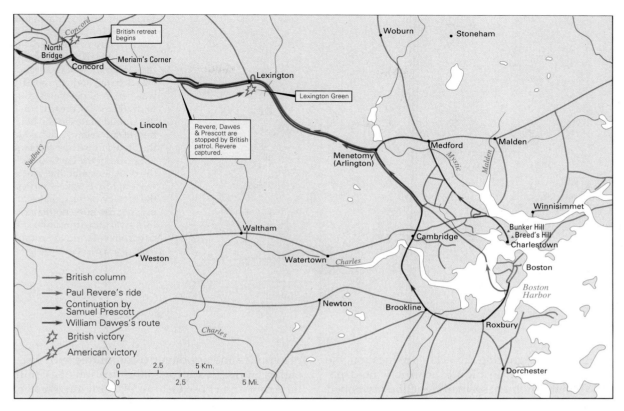

MAP 5.3   The First Battles in the War for Independence, 1775   This map shows the British march to Concord and the routes taken by the three Americans who alerted the countryside of the enemy's approach. Although Paul Revere was captured by the British and did not complete his ride, he is the best remembered and most celebrated of the nightriders who spread the alarm.

reaching Gage until April, the general had independently decided it was time to take action. Gage planned to dispatch a force of redcoats to Concord with orders to seize the rapidly growing stockpile of weapons and arrest the two radical leaders along the way.

The patriots, of course, had their spies in Boston. Reports of the arrest orders and of suspicious troop preparations reached the militias gathered outside the occupied city. The only question was when and where Gage would attack. The Americans devised a warning system: as soon as Gage's troops began to move out of Boston, spies would signal the route with lanterns hung in the bell tower of the North Church. On April 18, 1775, riders waiting outside Boston saw one lantern, then another, flash from the bell tower. Within moments, silversmith Paul Revere and his fellow messengers rode off to give news of the British army's approach to the militia and the people living in the countryside.

Around sunrise on April 19, an advance guard of a few hundred redcoats reached the town of Lexington, where they expected to apprehend Adams and Hancock. In the pale light, they saw about seventy colonial militiamen waiting on the village green. As the badly outnumbered colonists began to disperse, eager and nervous redcoats broke ranks and rushed forward, sending up a triumphant cheer. No order came to fire, but in the confusion shots rang out. Eight Americans were killed, most of them shot in the back as they ran for safety. Nine more were wounded. Later Americans who told the story of the skirmish at Lexington would insist that the first musket fired there sounded a "shot heard 'round the world."

The British troops marched from Lexington to Concord. Surprised to find the town nearly deserted, they began a methodical search for weapons. All they uncovered were five hundred musket balls, which they dumped into a nearby pond. They then burned the

The Pennsylvania State House in Philadelphia is best known to modern-day Americans as Independence Hall. It was here that the Declaration of Independence was debated and approved, and it was here that delegates gathered to draft a new Constitution for the United States in the hot and humid summer of 1787. Although the State House boasted large windows in the East Room where the delegates met, the shutters were tightly closed—to preserve the secrecy of the debates and to prevent the huge bottlenecked flies swarming throughout the city from entering the room. *Independence National Historic Park.*

town's liberty tree. Ignoring this act of provocation, the Concord **Minutemen,** in hiding nearby, waited patiently. When the moment seemed right, they swooped down on the unsuspecting British troops guarding the town's North Bridge.

The sudden attack by the Americans shocked the redcoats, who fled in a panic back toward Boston. The Minutemen followed, gathering more men along the path of pursuit. Together, these American farmers, artisans, servants, and shopkeepers terrorized the young British soldiers, firing on them at will from behind barns, stone walls, and trees. When the shaken troops reached the British encampment across the Charles River from Boston, 73 of their comrades were dead, 174 were wounded, and 26 were missing. The day after the **Battles of Lexington and Concord,** thousands of New England militiamen poured in from the surrounding countryside, dug trenches, and laid siege to Boston. As far as they and thousands of other Americans were concerned—including the loyalist refugees crowded into the city—war had begun.

The Second Continental Congress

When the Continental Congress reconvened in May 1775, it began at once to ready the colonies for war. This Second Continental Congress authorized the printing of American paper money for the purchase of supplies and appointed a committee to oversee foreign relations. It approved the creation of a Continental Army and chose George Washington, the Virginia veteran of the French and Indian War, to serve as its commander.

The Congress was clearly ready to defend Americans' rights and protect their liberties. But was it ready to declare a complete break with England? Some delegates still hoped to find a peaceful solution to the crisis, despite the bloodshed at Lexington and Concord. This sentiment led the Congress to draft the **Olive Branch Petition,** which offered the king a choice: the colonists would end their armed resistance if the king would withdraw the British military and revoke the

Minutemen Nickname first given to the Concord militia because of their speed in assembling and later applied generally to colonial militia during the Revolution.

Battles of Lexington and Concord Two confrontations in April 1775 between British soldiers and patriot Minutemen; the first recognized battles of the Revolution.

Olive Branch Petition Resolution, adopted by the Second Continental Congress in 1775 after the Battles of Lexington and Concord, that offered to end armed resistance if the king would withdraw his troops and repeal the Intolerable Acts.

Intolerable Acts. Many delegates must have doubted the king's willingness to make such concessions, for the very next day the Congress issued a public statement in defense of the war preparations. This "Declaration of the Causes and Necessity of Taking Up Arms" boldly accused the British government of tyranny. It stopped short, however, of declaring colonial independence.

Across the Atlantic, British leaders struggled to find some negotiating points despite the king's refusal to bend. Almost two months before the battles at Lexington and Concord, Lord North had drafted a set of Conciliatory Propositions for Parliament and the American Continental Congress to consider. North's proposals gave no ground on Parliament's right to tax the colonies, but they did offer to suspend taxation if Americans would raise funds for their own military defense. Members of Parliament who were sympathetic toward the Americans also pressed for compromise. They insisted that it made better sense to keep the colonies as a market for English goods than to lose them in a battle over raising revenue.

Cooler heads, however, did not prevail. Americans rejected Lord North's proposals in July 1775. The king, loathe to compromise, rejected the Olive Branch Petition. George III then persuaded Parliament to pass an **American Prohibitory Act** instructing the royal navy to seize American ships engaged in any form of trade, "as if the same were the ships . . . of open enemies." For all intents and purposes, King George III declared war on his colonies before the colonies declared war on their king.

The Impact of "Common Sense"

War was a fact, yet few American voices were calling for a complete political and emotional break with Britain. Even the most ardent patriots continued to justify their actions as upholding the British constitution. They were rebelling, they said, to preserve the rights guaranteed English citizens, not to establish an independent nation. Their drastic actions were necessary because a corrupt Parliament and corrupt ministers were trampling on those rights.

Although in 1764 Patrick Henry had dramatically warned the king to remember that tyrants were often deposed, few colonists had yet traced the source of their oppression to George III himself. If any American political leaders believed the king was as corrupt as his advisers and his Parliament, they did not make this view public. Then, in January 1776, Thomas Paine, an Englishman who had emigrated to America a few years earlier, published a pamphlet he called *Common*

Sense. Paine's pamphlet broke the silence about King George III.

Tom Paine was a corsetmaker by trade but a political radical by temperament. As soon as he settled in Philadelphia, he became a wholehearted and vocal supporter of the colonial protest to defend colonial rights, but he preferred American political independence. In *Common Sense,* Paine spoke directly to ordinary citizens, not to their political leaders. Like the preachers of the Great Awakening, he rejected the formal language of the elite, adopting instead a plain, urgent, and emotional vocabulary and writing style designed to reach a mass audience.

Common Sense was unique in its content as well as its style. Paine made no excuses for his revolutionary zeal. He expressed no admiration for the British constitution or reverence for the British political system. Instead, he attacked the **sanctity** of the monarchy head-on. He challenged the idea of a hereditary ruler, questioned the value of monarchy as an institution, and criticized the personal character of the men who ruled as kings. The common man, Paine insisted, had the ability to be his own king and was surely more deserving of that position than most of the men who had worn crowns. Paine put it bluntly and sarcastically: "Of more worth is one honest man to society, and in the sight of God, than all the crowned ruffians that ever lived." He dismissed George III as nothing more than a "Royal Brute," and he urged Americans to establish their own republic. No wonder Charles Inglis felt compelled to respond to such radical and treasonous arguments!

Common Sense sold 120,000 copies in its first three months in print. Paine's defiance of traditional authority and open criticism of the men who wielded it helped many of his readers, both male and female, discard the last shreds of loyalty to the king and to the empire. The impact of Paine's words resounded in the taverns and coffeehouses, where ordinary farmers, artisans, shopkeepers, and laborers took up his call for independence and the creation of a republic. Political leaders acknowledged Paine's importance,

---

American Prohibitory Act British law of 1775 that authorized the royal navy to seize all American ships engaged in trade; it amounted to a declaration of war.

Common Sense Revolutionary pamphlet written by Thomas Paine in 1776; it attacked George III, argued against monarchy, and advanced the patriot cause.

sanctity Saintliness or holiness; the quality of being sacred or beyond criticism.

although some begrudged the popular admiration lavished on this poorly educated artisan. The Harvard-trained John Adams reluctantly admitted that *Common Sense* was a "tolerable summary of the arguments I have been repeating again and again in Congress for nine months." But Adams's social snobbery led him to criticize Paine's language and his flamboyant writing style, suitable, Adams insisted, only "for an emigrant from new Gate [an English prison] or one chiefly associated with such company." Unshaken by such criticism, Tom Paine was content to see his message move so many into the revolutionary camp.

Declaring Independence

The Second Continental Congress, lagging far behind popular sentiment, inched its way toward a formal declaration of independence. But even John Adams, who had fumed at its snail's pace, took heart when the Congress opened American trade to all nations except Great Britain in early April 1776 and instructed the colonies to create official state governments. Then, on June 7, Adams's close ally in the struggle to announce independence, Virginia lawyer Richard Henry Lee, rose on the floor of the Congress and offered this straightforward motion: "That these United Colonies are, and of right ought to be, free and independent States, that they are absolved from all allegiance to the British Crown, and that all political connection between them and the State of Great Britain is, and ought to be, totally dissolved."

Lee's resolution was no more than a statement of reality, yet the Congress chose to postpone its final vote until July. The delay would give members time to win over the few fainthearted delegates from the Middle Colonies. It also would allow the committee appointed to draft a formal declaration of independence time to complete its work.

Congress had chosen an all-star group to draft the declaration, including John Adams, Connecticut's Roger Sherman, Benjamin Franklin, and New York landowner Robert Livingston. But these men delegated the task of writing the document to the fifth and youngest member of the committee, Thomas Jefferson. They chose well. The 33-year-old Virginian was not a social radical like Samuel Adams and Tom Paine. He was not an experienced politician like John Adams and Benjamin Franklin. And he lacked the reputation of fellow Virginians George Washington and Richard Henry Lee. But he had his strengths, and the committee members recognized them. Jefferson could draw on a deep and broad knowledge of political theory and phil-

In 1776, patriots everywhere celebrated independence by destroying local symbols of royal authority. New Yorkers, however, combined the practical with the symbolic, tearing down an imposing statue of King George III that had stood near the tip of Manhattan since 1770 and recycling its lead to make ammunition for the Revolutionary army. *"Pulling Down the Statue of George III" by William Walcott. Private Collection.*

osophy. He had read the works of Enlightenment philosophers, classical theorists, and seventeenth-century English revolutionaries. And though shy and somewhat halting in his speech, Thomas Jefferson was a master of written prose. Jefferson began the **Declaration of Independence** with a defense of revolution based on "self-evident" truths about humanity's "inalienable rights"—rights that included life, liberty, and the pursuit of property. (In a later draft, the rights became "unalienable" and "property" became "happiness.") Jefferson argued that these rights were natural rather than historical. In other words, they came from the "Creator" rather than developing out of human law, government, or tradition. Thus they were broader and more sacred than the specific "rights of Englishmen." With this philosophical groundwork in place, Jefferson moved on to list the grievances that demanded that America end its relationship with Britain. He focused on the king's abuse of power rather than on the oppressive legislation passed by Parliament. All gov-

Declaration of Independence   A formal statement, adopted by the Second Continental Congress in 1776, that listed justifications for rebellion and declared the American mainland colonies to be independent of Britain.

ernment rested on the consent of the governed, Jefferson asserted, and the people had the right to overthrow any government that tyrannized rather than protected them, that threatened rather than respected their unalienable rights.

The genius of Jefferson's Declaration was not that it contained novel ideas but that it contained ideas that were commonly accepted by America's political leaders and by most ordinary citizens as well. Jefferson gave voice to these beliefs, clearly and firmly. He also gave voice to the sense of abuse and injustice that had been growing in colonial society for several decades.

Declaring Loyalties

Delegates to the Second Continental Congress approved the Declaration of Independence on July 2, 1776, and made their approval public on July 4 (the text of the Declaration is reprinted in the Documents section at the end of this book). As John Adams was fond of saying, "The die had been cast," and Americans had to weigh loyalty to king against loyalty to a new nation. For Americans of every region, religion, social class, and race, this decision weighed heavily. In the face of such a critical choice, many wavered. Throughout the war that followed the Declaration, a surprising number of colonists clung to neutrality, hoping that the breach could be resolved without their having to participate or choose sides.

Those who did commit themselves based their decisions on deeply held beliefs and personal considerations, as well as fears. Many loyalists believed that tradition, commitment, and common sense argued for acknowledging parliamentary supremacy and the king's right to rule. These colonists had an abiding respect for the structure of the British government, with its balance between royalty, aristocracy, and the common people, and its ability to preserve the rights of each group. In their judgment, the advantages of remaining within the protective circle of the most powerful nation in Europe seemed too obvious to debate. And the likelihood of swift and bloody defeat at the hands of the British army and navy seemed too obvious to risk. Many of the men who articulated the loyalist position were members of the colonial elite. They frankly admitted their fears that a revolution would unleash the "madness of the multitude." The tyranny of the mob, they argued, was far more damaging than the tyranny of which the king stood accused.

Not all colonists who chose loyalism feared the mob or revered the principles on which the British political system was based. For many, the deciding issues were economic. Holders of royal offices and

Peter Salem (1750–1816) was an African American soldier who fought in the battle of Concord on April 19, 1775 and later in the Battle of Bunker Hill. He reinlisted in 1776 and fought once again in the battles of Saratoga and Stony Point. After the war, he returned to his home state of Massachusetts where he died in a poor house at the age of 66. *Schomburg Center/Art Resource, NY.*

merchants who depended on trade with British manufacturers found loyalty the compelling option. The loyalist ranks were also filled with colonists from the "multitude." Many small farmers and tenant farmers gave their support to the Crown when their political and economic foes—the great planters of the South or the New York manor lords—became patriots. The choice of which side to back often hinged, therefore, on local struggles and economic conflicts rather than on imperial issues.

For some of the perhaps 150,000 active loyalists, loyalism was a matter of personal character as much as conscious self-interest. Reluctance to break a solemn oath of allegiance to the king, anxiety over cutting ties with the past, fear of the chaos and violence that were a real part of revolution—any and all of these feelings could motivate a colonist to remain loyal rather than rebel.

For African Americans, the rallying call of liberty was familiar long before the Revolution began. Decades of slave resistance and rebellion demonstrated that black colonists did not need the impassioned language of a Patrick Henry or a Samuel Adams to remind them of the value of freedom. Instead, many slaves viewed the Revolution as they viewed epidemics and imperial warfare: as a potential opportunity to gain their own liberty. In the same way, free blacks saw the Revolution as a possible opportunity to win civil rights they had been denied before 1776.

African Americans had pointed out the inconsistencies of the radical position even before the Declaration of Independence. In 1773, a group of enslaved blacks in Boston petitioned the governor and the assembly for their freedom, "in behalf of all those, who . . . are held in a state of SLAVERY, within the bowels of a FREE country." There were white colonists who appreciated the injustice of a white slaveholding community in crisis over threats to its liberty. In 1774, while John Adams debated the threat of political slavery for colonial Englishmen in the First Continental Congress, his wife Abigail observed: "It always appeared a most iniquitous [sinful] scheme to me—to fight ourselves for what we are daily robbing and plundering from those who have as good a right to freedom as we have." Tom Paine agreed. Writing as "Humanus" in a Philadelphia newspaper, Paine urged white patriots to abolish slavery and give freed blacks western land grants.

Other patriots worried that slaves would seek their freedom by supporting the British in the war. The royal governor of Virginia was ready to make an offer of freedom to the colony's slaves. In 1775 Governor Dunmore expressed his intention to "arm all my own Negroes and receive all others that will come to me whom I shall declare free." Rumors of this plan horrified neighboring Maryland planters, who demanded that their governor issue arms and ammunition to protect against slave **insurrection.** Throughout the South, white communities braced themselves for a black struggle for freedom that would emerge in the midst of the colonial struggle for independence.

When Dunmore did offer freedom to "all indentured Servants, negroes or others . . . able and willing to bear Arms who escaped their masters," he was more interested in disrupting the slave-based plantation economy of his American enemies than in African American rights. Yet slaves responded, crossing into British lines in great enough numbers to create an "Ethiopian Regiment" of soldiers. These black loyalists wore a banner across their uniforms that read "Liberty to Slaves." Only six hundred to two thousand slaves managed to escape their masters in 1775–1776, but in the southern campaigns of the long war that followed, thousands of black men, women, and children made their way to the British lines. Once in uniform, black soldiers were usually assigned to work in road construction and other manual labor tasks rather than participate in combat. Perhaps as many as fifty thousand slaves gained their freedom during the war, as a result of either British policy or the disruptions that made escape possible.

Indians' responses to news of the war were far from uniform. At first, many considered the Revolution a family quarrel that should be avoided. The revolutionaries would have been satisfied to see Indians adopt this policy of neutrality. They knew they were unlikely to win Indian support given the legacy of border warfare and the actions of land-hungry settlers. As early as 1775, the Second Continental Congress issued a proclamation warning Indians to remain neutral. But the British, recognizing their advantage, made strong efforts to win Indian support. Indian leaders proceeded cautiously, however. When a British negotiator boasted to Flying Crow that British victory was inevitable, the Seneca chief was unimpressed. "If you are so strong, Brother, and they but as a weak Boy, why ask our assistance?" The chief was unwilling to commit his tribe based on issues that divided Crown and colonists but meant little to the welfare of his own people. "You say they are all mad, foolish, wicked, and deceitful— I say you are so and they are wise for you want us to destroy ourselves in your War and they advise us to live in Peace."

The British continued to press for Indian participation in the war, and many Indian tribes and confederations eventually decided that the Crown would better serve their interests and respect their rights than would the colonists. First, the British were much more likely than the colonists to be able to provide a steady supply of the manufactured goods and weapons the Indians relied on in the eighteenth century. Second, colonial territorial ambitions threatened the Indians along the southern and northwestern frontiers. Third, an alliance with the British offered some possibility of recouping land and trading benefits lost in the past. No uniformity emerged, however. Among the Iroquois, for example, conflicting choices of loyalties led pro-British Senecas to burn the crops and houses of Oneidas who had joined forces with the patriots. Among the Potowatomis, similar divisions occurred. Intertribal rivalries and Indians' concerns about the safety of their own villages often determined alignments. In the southern backcountry, fierce fighting between Indians and revolutionaries seemed a continuation of the century's many border wars. But even there, alignments could shift. Although the Cherokees began the war as British allies, a split developed, producing an internal civil war similar to the one among the Iroquois tribes.

insurrection   An uprising against a legitimate authority or government.

Fewer than half of the colonists threw in their lot with the revolutionaries. Among those who did were people whose economic interests made independence seem worth the risk, including artisans and urban laborers, merchants who traded outside the British Empire, large and small farmers, and many members of the southern planter elite. For these Americans, it was not simply a matter of escaping unfair taxation. A release from Britain's mercantile policies, which restricted colonial trade with other nations, held out the promise of expanded trade and an end to the risks of smuggling. Sometimes the pressure for independence came from below rather than from a colony's political leadership. For example, although Virginia's elite produced many radical spokesmen for independence such as Patrick Henry, many southern planters only reluctantly endorsed independence in order to retain their authority over the more radical ordinary farmers. Colonists affected by the Great Awakening and by its message of egalitarianism often chose the patriot side.

Americans with a conscious, articulated radical vision of society—the Tom Paines and Samuel Adamses—supported the Revolution and its promise of a republic. Many who became revolutionaries shared the hope for a better life under a government that encouraged its citizens to be virtuous and to live in simplicity.

As Americans—English, European, Indian, and African American—armed themselves or fled from the violence and bloodshed they saw coming, they realized that the conflict wore two faces: this was a war for independence, but it was also a civil war. In the South, it pitted slave against master, Cherokee against Cherokee, and frontier farmer against tidewater planter. In New England, it set neighbor against neighbor, forcing scores of loyalist families to flee. In some instances, children were set against parents, and wives refused to support the cause their husbands had chosen. Whatever the outcome of the struggle ahead, Americans knew that it would come at great cost.

✔ Individual Voices

Charles Inglis Calls for Reconciliation

Charles Inglis, Anglican minister and rector of New York City's Trinity Church, was one of the few loyalists who dared take issue with Thomas Paine's dramatic and powerful call to revolution, *Common Sense.* His response came in the form of a 1776 pamphlet called *The True Interest of America Impartially Stated.* In the portion of his pamphlet reprinted below, Inglis expresses horror at the prospect of breaking a sacred oath of allegiance to the Church of England and the Crown. Most loyalists who held appointed office and most Anglican ministers shared his feelings on this issue. In *The True Interest,* Inglis also predicts that the British army and navy would crush the rebellion at the cost of many American lives. His vision of the chaos, devastation, and humiliation the rebellious colonists would suffer was echoed in the private letters of loyalists everywhere. Finally, he points to the loss of property and the resulting poverty that would befall the colonies if they rose up against the Crown. Although fighting had already begun at Lexington and Concord, and the Continental Congress had started to muster an army, Inglis pleaded for the colonists to seek a reconciliation with Britain. But as John Adams was so fond of saying, "The die had been cast"; the Declaration of Independence was issued on July 4, 1776.

In many ways, Inglis proved correct. Much American blood was spilled during the Revolution, and the long home-front war saw much devastation. Many of the ministers and officeholders who remained loyal saw the new state governments confiscate and sell their land and their homes. Once-wealthy loyalists such as Jonathan Sewall of Massachusetts and Joseph Galloway of Pennsylvania ended their lives in exile and in poverty. Inglis was wrong, however, about the outcome of the war: in one of the greatest military upsets of Western history, the Americans defeated the proud British empire.

(1) *Inglis is referring to the battles in Massachusetts at Lexington, Concord, and Bunker Hill, in April and June 1775.*

(2) *Although revolutionaries suffered the loss of crops, homes, and livestock, it was the loyalists who, in the end, saw their estates seized by the state governments and sold to patriotic neighbors. Do you think that confiscating their lands and possessions was justified?*

The blood of the slain, the weeping voice of nature cries—it is time to be reconciled, it is time to lay aside those animosities which have pushed on Britons to shed the blood of Britons; **(1)** *it is high time that those who are connected by the endearing ties of religion, kindred and country, should resume their former friendship, and be united in the bond of mutual affection, as their interests are inseparably united. . . . By a Reconciliation with Great-Britain, Peace—that fairest offspring and gift of Heaven—will be restored. . . . What uneasiness and anxiety, what evils, has this short interruption of peace with the parent-state, brought on the whole British empire!*

Suppose we were to revolt from Great-Britain, declare ourselves Independent, and set up a Republic of our own—what would be the consequence? I stand aghast at the prospect—my blood runs chill when I think of the calamities, the complicated evils that must ensue. . . . All our property throughout the continent would be unhinged; the greatest confusion, and most violent convulsions would take place. . . . What a horrid situation would thousands be reduced to who have taken the oath of allegiance to the King; yet contrary to their oath, as well as inclination, must be compelled to renounce that allegiance, or abandon all their property in America! **(2)** *How many thousands more would be reduced to a similar situation; who, although they took not that oath, yet would think it inconsistent with their duty and a good conscience to renounce their Sovereign. . . .*

(3) Modern nations have also established colonies and fought wars to keep them. What economic advantages do colonies provide? Can you think of noneconomic reasons why colonies might be valuable?

(4) If you were writing a response to Inglis's dire scenario, how would you refute his predictions of American defeat? What American advantages would you cite? What British disadvantages? What do you think were the most important factors in the American victory?

By a Declaration of Independency, every avenue to an accommodation with Great-Britain would be closed; the sword only could then decide the quarrel; and the sword would not be sheathed till one had conquered the other.

The importance of these colonies to Britain need not be enlarged on, it is a thing so universally known. **(3)** *The greater their importance is to her, so much the more obstinate will her struggle be not to lose them. . . . Great-Britain therefore must, for her own preservation, risk everything, and exert her whole strength, to prevent such an event from taking place. This being the case—Devastation and ruin must mark the progress of this war along the sea coast of America. Hitherto, Britain has not exerted her power. . . . But as soon as we declare for independency . . . ruthless war, with all its aggravated horrors, will ravage our once happy land. . . . Torrents of blood will be spilt, and thousands reduced to beggary and wretchedness. . . .* **(4)**

SUMMARY

The British victory in the Great War for Empire produced many new problems. The British had to govern the French population in Canada and maintain security against Indians on a greatly expanded colonial frontier. They had to pay an enormous war debt but continue to finance strong and well-equipped armed forces to keep the empire they had won. To deal with these new circumstances, the English government chose to impose revenue-raising measures on the colonies.

The Sugar Act of 1764 tightened customs collections, the Stamp Act of 1765 placed a direct tax on legal documents, and the Townshend Acts of 1767 set import taxes on English products such as paint and tea. Colonists protested this sharp shift in policy for they saw Parliament's revenue-raising actions as an abuse of power. Political debate in the colonies began to focus on endangered rights and on the possibility that the British government meant to curtail American liberties.

Crowds directed by the Sons of Liberty attacked royal officials, and in Boston five civilians died in a clash with British troops known as the Boston Massacre. Colony-wide boycotts of British goods were the most effective form of protest. They led to the repeal of all three taxes.

Political activists prepared for a quick and united response to any new crises by creating organizations such as the committees of correspondence. In 1773 the British passed the Tea Act. They expected little American opposition, but they were wrong. In Boston a group of activists dumped thousands of pounds' worth of tea into the harbor.

The "Boston Tea Party" enraged British officials. As a punishment, the English closed the port of Boston to all trade. This and other Intolerable Acts infuriated colonists, who took united action in support of Massachusetts. A new colonial forum, the First Continental Congress, met in 1774 to debate the colonies' relationship to England and to issue a united protest. A Declaration of Rights and Grievances was sent to the king, but he rejected the colonists' appeal for compromise. Instead he declared that "blows must decide."

After British troops and militiamen fought at Lexington and Concord, the Second Continental Congress prepared for war. Tom Paine's pamphlet *Common Sense* pushed many reluctant colonists into the revolutionary camp. Not even a reasoned rebuttal of this call to revolution, such as the one written by Charles Inglis, could halt the progress toward independence after this. In July 1776, Congress issued the Declaration of Independence, drafted by Thomas Jefferson. It defended the colonists' right to resist a tyrannical king. In 1776 Americans faced the difficult task of choosing sides: loyalty to the Crown or revolution. African Americans and Indians had to decide whether to offer support to one side or the other or try to remain neutral in the midst of revolution. The outcome was both a war for colonial independence and a civil war that divided families and communities across America. In Chapter 6, you will see how independence was won.

IN THE WIDER WORLD

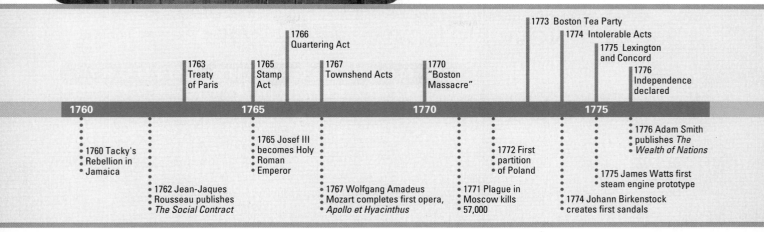

1760   1765   1770   1775

1763 Treaty of Paris

1765 Stamp Act

1766 Quartering Act

1767 Townshend Acts

1770 "Boston Massacre"

1773 Boston Tea Party

1774 Intolerable Acts

1775 Lexington and Concord

1776 Independence declared

1760 Tacky's Rebellion in Jamaica

1762 Jean-Jaques Rousseau publishes *The Social Contract*

1765 Josef III becomes Holy Roman Emperor

1767 Wolfgang Amadeus Mozart completes first opera, *Apollo et Hyacinthus*

1771 Plague in Moscow kills 57,000

1772 First partition of Poland

1774 Johann Birkenstock creates first sandals

1775 James Watts first steam engine prototype

1776 Adam Smith publishes *The Wealth of Nations*

In the United States

Loyalty or Rebellion?

1763 Treaty of Paris ends French and Indian War

Pontiac's Rebellion

Proclamation Line

1764 Sugar Act

1765 Stamp Act

Sons of Liberty organized

Stamp Act Congress

Nonimportation of British goods

1766 Stamp Act repealed

Declaratory Act

1767 Townshend Acts

John Dickinson's *Letters from a Farmer in Pennsylvania*

1768 Nonimportation of British goods

Massachusetts Circular Letter

1770 Boston Massacre

Townshend Acts repealed

1772 Burning of the *Gaspée*

1773 Tea Act

Boston Tea Party

1774 Intolerable Acts

First Continental Congress

Continental Association

Declaration of Rights and Grievances

Suffolk Resolves

1775 Battles of Lexington and Concord

Second Continental Congress

Olive Branch Petition

Declaration of the Causes and Necessity of Taking Up Arms

1776 Tom Paine's *Common Sense*

Declaration of Independence

Recreating America: Independence and a New Nation, 1775–1783

A NOTE FROM THE AUTHOR

Americans are drawn to the stories of bravery, daring, and betrayal in the American Revolution. In part, the appeal lies in the unlikely victory of a ragtag army over the greatest military and naval force in the eighteenth-century world. In part, it is because the war marks the birth of our nation. In part, it is because the cast of characters—from the elegant young Marquis de Lafayette to the luxury-loving British general "Gentleman Johnny" Burgoyne to the fearless George Washington to the treacherous General Arnold—seem so much larger than life.

A chapter on the American Revolution must focus on the war itself. Yet, the complete story does not take place on the battlefield. It also takes place in Congress and Parliament where the money was raised to arm and equip these men. It takes place in the homes of civilians who had to be mobilized to support or oppose this home-front war. It takes place in Paris where diplomats gathered to draft the peace treaty, for their negotiating skills determined which military gains and losses would be permanent. And, it takes place in the intellectual and social spheres—or as John Adams put it, in the hearts and minds of the participants—for the war produced revolutions in the way people thought about themselves and about others, in the way they behaved within their families and communities, and in the way they defined their rights and duties to their government

In the end, the lines that separate military, political, diplomatic, social, and intellectual history vanish as soon as an historian begins to reconstruct past events. Instead of isolating these categories, the historian must weave the strands together to create a picture with breadth and depth. Thus, although I have placed the war itself at the center of Chapter 6, ideas and events off the battlefield surround it.

Deborah Sampson

Whether attracted by adventure, the promise of a pension, or the bounty soldiers received upon enlistment, Deborah Sampson decided to disguise herself as a man and enlist in the Continental Army in 1781. She served for over two years before officers discovered she was a woman and discharged her. This portrait, drawn by Joseph Stone Framingham in 1797, depicts Sampson in female dress but surrounds her with the military emblems befitting a veteran of the Revolutionary War. *Courtesy the Rhode Island Historical Society.*

✔ Individual Choices

Deborah Sampson was born into a poor Massachusetts family in 1760 and was hired out as a servant when she was a young child. By the time the revolutionary war began, her future held few choices. With no dowry or inheritance, she was unlikely to marry; with no special training, she was likely to remain a servant. But Sampson discovered another option—and she took it. Disguising herself as a man, she enlisted as a soldier in the Continental Army. Just as the colonies changed themselves into an independent nation, Deborah Sampson changed herself into Private Robert Shurtleff.

As a woman, Sampson might have played a role in the war by serving as a **courier** or a spy. Or she might have joined thousands of other women in the army camps, performing valuable services such as cooking, laundering, or nursing. She might have remained safely at home, knitting socks or making uniforms for the poorly clad soldiers serving under General Washington. But none of these alternatives would have given her what military service offered: the chance to see new places and have new experiences, an enlistment bonus, a pension if she survived, and a promise of land when the war ended. Thousands of poor young men risked the dangers of the battlefield for these rewards. Why not Deborah Sampson?

Perhaps patriotism also prompted her to abandon her petticoats for a uniform. But whatever her motives, Deborah Sampson proved herself a fine soldier and a clever one for she managed to hide her identity for several years, even when she was wounded in the leg by a musket ball. The truth of her sex was finally discovered when she was hospitalized for a fever.

On October 25, 1783, Deborah Sampson was granted an honorable discharge—and Robert Shurtleff disappeared. The next Spring, she married Benjamin Gannett and began a family. As a wife and mother, she was expected to give up any role in the public sphere. But once again she proved herself a rebel: in 1802 she traveled throughout New England giving public lectures on her military career. The tales she told the crowds who flocked to see her were undoubtedly full of exaggerated claims of battlefield heroics. Yet dressed in her uniform once again, performing a precision drill on stage, Deborah Sampson demonstrated the unexpected impact of the Revolution on an ordinary American's life.

courier   A messenger carrying official information, sometimes secretly.

INTRODUCTION

The war that changed Deborah Sampson's life, and the lives of most colonists, began in April 1775 as a skirmish at Concord's North Bridge. Great Britain expected an easy victory over the colonial rebels, and, on paper, at least, the odds against an American victory were staggering. To crush the colonial rebellion, Great Britain could commit vast human and material resources. The well-trained and harshly disciplined British ground troops were assisted and supplied by the most powerful navy in the world, and they carried the flag of Europe's richest imperial power. Many Indian tribes, including most of the Iroquois, allied with the British, and the Crown could expect thousands of white and black loyalists to fight beside them as well.

The American resources were far less impressive. The Continental Congress had a nearly empty treasury, and the country had none of the foundries or factories needed to produce arms, ammunition, or other military supplies. The army administration was inefficient, the population was wary of professional soldiers, and the new state governments were unwilling to raise tax monies to contribute to Congress's war chest. Through most of the war, therefore, American officers and enlisted men could expect to be underpaid or not paid at all. They were likely to go into battle poorly equipped, often half-starved, and frequently dressed in rags. Unlike the British redcoats, these Americans had little military skill or formal military training. Most were as new to military life as Deborah Sampson.

Britain's advantage was not absolute, however. The British had to transport arms, provisions, and men across thousands of miles of ocean. They risked delays, disasters, and destruction of supplies on the open seas. The Americans, on the other hand, were fighting on familiar terrain, and geography gave them an additional advantage: their vast, rural society could not be easily conquered even if major colonial cities were taken or an entire region were occupied. Long-standing European rivalries gave the Americans valuable allies. Holland, France, and Spain all stood to gain from England's distress, and they willingly lent money and provided much-needed supplies to the

American artist John Trumbull painted *The Battle of Bunker Hill* in 1786, over a decade after the bloody encounter between redcoats and American militiamen. Trumbull was a student of the famous American painter Benjamin West, who had won his reputation celebrating the English victories of the French and Indian War. Trumbull and other American students of West built their reputations by celebrating American victories in the artistic style that West taught them. *"The Death of General Warren at Bunker Hill" by John Trumbull, Yale University Art Gallery/ Art Resource, NY.*

rebellion. In 1778, when France and Spain decided to formally recognize American independence, the war suddenly expanded into a global struggle. The support of the French navy transformed General Washington's military strategy and led eventually to the defeat of the British army at Yorktown.

No matter what eighteenth-century Americans felt about the war, no matter which side they supported or what role they played, they shared the experience of extraordinary events and the need to make extraordinary choices when the war disrupted their ordinary lives. In this most personal and immediate sense, the war was as revolutionary for them as it was for a young woman who became, for a brief but critical moment, a soldier in the name of liberty.

The First Two Years of War

→ *What were the British and American strategies in the early years of the war?*

→ *What decisions and constraints kept the British from achieving the quick victory many expected?*

In 1775 **Thomas Gage**, the British general serving as military governor of Massachusetts and commander of the British army of occupation there, surely wished he were anywhere but Boston. The town was unsophisticated by British standards, many of its inhabitants were unfriendly, and its taverns and lodging houses bulged at the seams with complaining loyalist refugees from the countryside. Gage's army was restless, and his officers were bored. The American encampments outside the city were growing daily, filling with local farmers and artisans after the bloodshed of Lexington and Concord. These thousands of colonial **militiamen** gathering on the hills surrounding Boston were clearly the military enemy. Yet in 1775 they were still citizens of the British Empire, not foreign invaders or foes. Gage, like his American opponents, was caught up in the dilemmas of an undeclared war.

The Battle for Boston

With proper artillery, well placed on the hills surrounding the city, the Americans could have done serious damage to Gage's army of occupation. The problem was that the rebels had no cannon. A New Haven druggist named **Benedict Arnold** joined forces with a Vermont farmer named Ethan Allen to solve the problem. In May 1775 their troops captured Fort Ticonderoga in New York and began the difficult task of transporting the fort's cannon across hundreds of miles of mountains and forests to Boston. By the time the artillery reached the city, however, a bloody battle between Gage and the American militia had already taken place.

In early June, Gage had issued a proclamation declaring all armed colonists traitors, but he offered **amnesty** to any rebel who surrendered to British authorities. When the militiamen ignored the general's offer, Gage decided a show of force was necessary. On June 17, 1775, under cover of cannon fire from a British warship in Boston harbor, Gage's fellow officer **William Howe** led a force of twenty-four hundred soldiers against rebel-held Breed's Hill. Despite the oppressive heat and humidity of the day, General Howe ordered his men to advance in full dress uniform, weighed down with wool jackets and heavy knapsacks. Howe also insisted on making a "proper" frontal attack on the Americans. From the top of the hill, Captain William Prescott's militiamen immediately opened fire on the unprotected redcoats. The result was a near massacre. The tables turned, however, when the Americans ran out of ammunition. Most of Prescott's men fled in confusion, and the British soldiers bayoneted the few who remained to defend their position.

Even battle-worn veterans were shocked at the carnage of the day. The British suffered more casualties that June afternoon than they would in any other battle of the war. The Americans, who retreated to the safety of Cambridge, learned a costly lesson on the importance of an effective supply line of arms and ammunition to their fighting men. Little was gained by either side. That the battle was misnamed the

Thomas Gage   British general who was military governor of Massachusetts and commander of the army occupying Boston in 1775.

militiamen   Soldiers who were not members of a regular army but ordinary citizens called out in case of an emergency.

Benedict Arnold   Pharmacist-turned-military-leader whose bravery and daring made him an American hero and a favorite of George Washington until he committed treason in 1780.

amnesty   A general pardon granted by a government, especially for political offenses.

William Howe   British general in command at the Battle of Bunker Hill; three years later he became commander in chief of British forces in America.

Battle of Bunker Hill captured perfectly the confusion and the absurdity of the encounter.

Congress Creates an Army

While militiamen and redcoats turned the Boston area into a war zone, the Continental Congress took its first steps toward recruiting and supplying an army. The "regular" army that took shape was not really a national force. It was a collection of small state armies whose recruits preserved their local or regional identities. While this army was expected to follow the war wherever it led, the Continental Congress still relied on each state's militia to join in any battles that took place within its borders.

Congress chose French and Indian War veteran **George Washington** to command the Continental forces. Washington wrote gloomily of the enormity of the task before him. Nothing he saw when he reached Massachusetts on July 3, 1775, made him more optimistic. A carnival atmosphere seemed to prevail inside the militiamen's camps. Farm-boys-turned-soldiers fired their muskets at random, often using their weapons to start fires or to shoot at geese flying overhead. In the confusion, they sometimes accidentally wounded or killed themselves and others. "Seldom a day passes but some persons are shot by their friends," Washington noted in amazement.

The camps resembled pigsties. The stench from open latrines was terrible, and rotting animal carcasses, strewn everywhere, added to the aroma. The men were dirty and infected with lice, and most soldiers were constantly scratching, trying to relieve an itch that left them covered with scabs and raw, peeling skin. General Washington was disturbed but not surprised by what he saw. He knew that the men in these camps were country boys, away from home for the first time in their lives. The chaos they created resulted from a combination of fear, excitement, boredom, inexperience, and plain homesickness, all brewing freely under poor leadership. Despite his sympathy for these young men, Washington acted quickly to reorganize the militia units, replace incompetent officers, and tighten discipline within the camps.

The British meanwhile laid plans for the evacuation of Boston, spurred in part by the knowledge that Arnold's wagon train of cannon was nearing Massachusetts. In March 1776 a fleet arrived to carry Thomas Gage, his officers, the British army, and almost a thousand loyalist refugees north to the safety of Halifax, Nova Scotia. By this time, command of

His Majesty's war was in the hands of the Howe brothers—General William Howe, commander of the Breed's Hill attack, and **Richard Howe**, an admiral in the royal navy. With the help of military strategists and the vast resources of the Crown, the Howes were expected to bring the rebellion to a speedy end and restore order to the colonies.

The British Strategy in 1776

General Howe was less concerned with suppressing the radicalism of New England than the king had been. He thought the most effective strategy would be to locate areas with high concentrations of loyalists and mobilize them to secure the allegiance of their undecided and even rebellious neighbors. Howe and his advisers targeted two reputed centers of loyalist strength. The first—New York, New Jersey, Pennsylvania—had a legacy of social and economic conflicts, such as the revolt of the Paxton Boys, that had caused many of the region's elite families to fear that independence threatened their prosperity. But loyalism was not confined to the conservative and wealthy. Its second stronghold was among the poor settlers of the Carolina backcountry. There, decades of bitter struggle between the coastal planters and the backcountry farmers had led to the Regulator movement (see page 99) and to intense loyalist sentiment among many of the embattled westerners.

General Howe's strategy had its flaws, however. First, although many people in these two regions were loyal, their numbers were never as great as the British assumed. Second, everywhere they went, British and **Hessian troops** left behind a trail of destruction and memories of abuse that alienated many Americans who might have considered remaining loyal. Howe was not likely to win over families who saw their

---

Battle of Bunker Hill   British assault on American troops on Breed's Hill near Boston in June 1775; the British won the battle but suffered heavy losses.

George Washington   Commander in chief of the Continental Army; he led Americans to victory in the Revolution and later became the first president of the United States.

Richard Howe   British admiral who commanded British naval forces in America; he was General William Howe's brother.

Hessian troops   German soldiers from the state of Hesse who were hired by Britain to fight in the American Revolution.

"cattle killed and lying about the fields and pastures . . . household furniture hacked and broken into pieces . . . wells filled up and . . . tools destroyed."

Nevertheless, in 1776 Howe launched his first major military assaults in the South and the mid-Atlantic region. The campaign in the South, directed by General Henry Clinton, went badly. In North Carolina, loyalists did turn out to fight for the Crown, but the British failed to provide them the military support they needed. Poorly armed and badly outnumbered, Carolina loyalists were decisively defeated by the rebel militia on February 27 in the Battle of Moore's Creek. Rather than rush to their defense, the British abandoned their loyalist allies in favor of taking revenge on South Carolina. Clinton and an impressive fleet of fifty ships and three thousand men sailed into Charleston harbor. But the British had unexpected bad luck. As the troops started to wade ashore, they found themselves stranded on small islands surrounded by a sudden rush of tidal waters. The Americans, on the other hand, had unexpected good luck. Working frantically to defend the harbor, they constructed a flimsy fort out of local palmetto wood. To the surprise of both sides, the cannon balls fired by British ships sank harmlessly into the absorbent, pulpy palmetto stockade. The fort—and the city of Charleston—remained standing.

Embarrassed and frustrated, the British command abruptly ended its southern campaign. General Clinton, a gloomy man under the best of circumstances, sailed north, eager to escape the scene of his humiliation. The South Carolina loyalists, however, could not escape British failures. They had been denounced, mobbed, imprisoned, and sometimes tortured since 1775. Their situation grew even worse after the British withdrew.

Escape from New York

While Clinton was failing in the Carolinas, the Howe brothers were preparing a massive invasion of the mid-Atlantic region. In July 1776, Admiral Howe and General Howe sailed into New York harbor with the largest expeditionary force of the eighteenth century. With thirty thousand men, one-third of them Hessian mercenaries, this British army was larger than the peacetime population of New York City.

The Howes were not eager to demolish New York, however. Unlike most British officers, the brothers were genuinely fond of Americans, and they preferred to be agents of compromise and negotiation rather than of destruction. They hoped that a spectacular show of force and a thorough humiliation of rebel commander George Washington would be enough to bring the Americans to their senses and end the rebellion.

General Washington rushed his army south from Massachusetts to defend the city, but he had few illusions that his twenty-three thousand men, many of them sick and most of them inexperienced at war, could repel the invading British forces. In the middle of his defense preparations, Washington received a copy of the newly approved Declaration of Independence. He immediately ordered his brigades to line up on the parade grounds so that he could read Thomas Jefferson's stirring words aloud to them. He was gratified to hear the men cheer the Declaration. But privately, Washington wondered if these men would fight when they faced the enemy in battle.

For a month, the Howes made no move on the city. Finally, in the early morning of August 22, 1776, the British began their advance, landing unopposed, and moving toward the Brooklyn neck of Long Island (see Map 6.1). Just as Washington had feared, his raw and inexperienced troops quickly broke when fighting began five days later. Cut off from one another, confused by the sound and sight of the attack, almost all the American troops surrendered or ran. A single Maryland regiment made a heroic stand against the landing forces but was destroyed by the oncoming British. Washington, at the scene himself, might have been captured had the Howes pressed their advantage. But they withdrew, content that they had made the American commander look foolish.

Washington took advantage of the Howes' delay to bring his troops to the safety of Manhattan Island. The safety proved temporary, for on September 15, a British attack again sent his farm-boys-turned-soldiers into flight. Angry and frustrated, Washington threw his hat to the ground and shouted, "Are these the men with whom I am to defend America!"

Washington's army fled north, with the British in hot pursuit. In a skirmish at Harlem Heights, the American commander was relieved to see his men stand their ground and win their first combat victory. He was even more relieved by the strange failure of the British to press their advantage. The British had only to follow his army into Westchester County and deliver a crushing blow, but they did not. When the redcoats finally engaged the Continentals again at White Plains, the Americans managed to retreat safely. Soon afterward, Washington took his army across the Hudson River to New Jersey and marched them farther west, across the Delaware River into Pennsylvania.

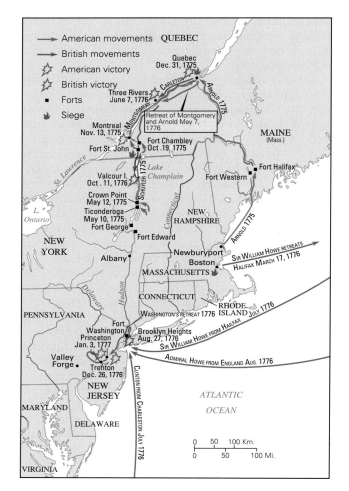

MAP 6.1 **The War of the North, 1775–1777** The American attempt to capture Canada and General George Washington's effort to save New York from British occupation were failures, but Washington did manage to stage successful raids in New Jersey before retreating to safety in the winter of 1777. This map details the movements of both British and American troops during the Northern Campaign, and it indicates the victories and defeats for both armies.

Winter Quarters and Winter Victories

Following European customs, General Howe established winter quarters for his troops before the cold set in. Redcoats and Hessians made their camps in the New York area and in Rhode Island that December, expecting Washington to make camp somewhere as well. But Washington, safe for the moment in Pennsylvania, was too restless to settle in just yet. Enlistment terms in his army would soon be up, and

without some encouraging military success he feared few of his soldiers would reenlist. Thus Washington looked eagerly for a good target to attack—and found one. Across the Delaware, on the Jersey side, two or three thousand Hessian troops held a garrison near the town of Trenton.

On Christmas night, amid a howling storm, General Washington led twenty-four hundred of his men back across the river. Marching 9 miles through a raging blizzard, the Americans arrived to find the Hessians asleep. The surprised enemy surrendered immediately. Without losing a single man, Washington had captured nine hundred prisoners and many badly needed military supplies. Taking full advantage of the moment, Washington made a rousing appeal to his men to reenlist. About half of the soldiers agreed to remain.

The **Battle of Trenton** was a crucial victory, but Washington enjoyed his next success even more. In early January he again crossed into New Jersey from the safety of Pennsylvania and made his way toward the British garrison at Princeton. On the way, his advance guard ran into two British regiments. As both sides lined up for battle, Washington rode back and forth in front of his men, shouting encouragement and urging them to stand firm. His behavior was reckless, for it put him squarely in the line of fire, but it was also effective. When the British turned in retreat, Washington rashly rode after them, clearly delighted to be in pursuit for once in the war.

The Trenton and Princeton victories raised the morale of the Continental Army as it settled at last into its winter quarters near Morristown, New Jersey. They stirred popular support also. Americans everywhere referred to the two winter raids as a "nine-day wonder." Of course, Howe's army was still poised to march on Philadelphia when warm weather revived the war again. And Congress still had few resources to spare for Washington and his men. When Washington pleaded for supplies, Congress urged him to commandeer what he needed from civilians nearby. The general wisely refused. English high-handedness and cruelty had turned many people of the area into staunch supporters of the Revolution, and Washington had no intention of alienating them by seizing their livestock, food, or weapons.

Battle of Trenton Battle on December 26, 1776, when Washington led his troops by night across the Delaware River and captured a Hessian garrison wintering in New Jersey.

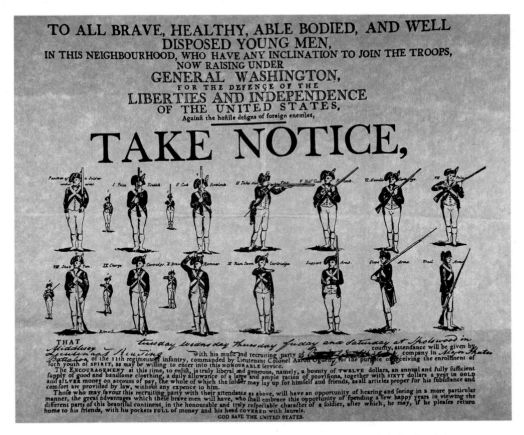

This recruiting poster for the Continental Army invites young men to join in the defense of American liberty and independence. As an incentive, a bounty of $12 is offered, as well as "good and handsome clothing," a daily allowance of provisions and $60 a year, paid in gold. *The Granger Collection, New York.*

Burgoyne's New York Campaign

In July 1777 General William Howe sailed with fifteen thousand men up the Chesapeake Bay toward Philadelphia. The Continental Congress had already fled the city, knowing that Washington could not prevent the enemy occupation. Although the Americans made two efforts to block Howe, first at Brandywine Creek and then at Germantown, the British had little difficulty capturing Philadelphia. The problems they did face in 1777 came not from Washington but from the poor judgment of one of their own, a flamboyant young general named **John Burgoyne**.

Burgoyne had won approval for an elaborate plan to sever New England from the rest of the American colonies. He would move his army south from Montreal, while a second army of redcoats and Iroquois, commanded by Colonel Barry St. Leger, would veer east across the Mohawk Valley from Fort Oswego. At the same time, William Howe would send a third force north from New York City. The three armies would rendezvous at Albany, effectively isolating New England and, it was assumed, giving the British a perfect opportunity to crush the rebellion.

The plan was daring and—on paper—seemed to have every chance of success. In reality, however, it had serious flaws. First, neither Burgoyne nor the British officials in England had any knowledge of the American terrain that had to be covered. Second, they badly misjudged the Indian support St. Leger would

John Burgoyne British general forced to surrender his entire army at Saratoga, New York, in October 1777.

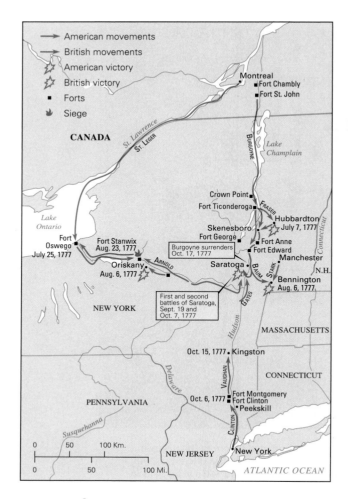

MAP 6.2 The Burgoyne Campaign, 1777 The defeat of General John Burgoyne and his army at Saratoga was a major turning point in the war. It led to the recognition of American independence by France and later by Spain and to a military alliance with both these European powers. This map shows American and British troop movement and the locations and dates of the Saratoga battles leading to the British surrender.

In true eighteenth-century British style, "Gentleman Johnny" Burgoyne chose to travel well rather than lightly. The thirty wagons moving slowly behind the general contained over fifty pieces of artillery for the campaign. They also contained Burgoyne's mistress, her personal wardrobe and his, and a generous supply of champagne. When the caravan encountered New York's swamps and gullies, movement slowed to a snail's pace. The Americans took full advantage of Burgoyne's folly. Ethan Allen and his Green Mountain Boys harassed the British as they entered Allen's home region of Vermont. A bloody, head-on battle near Bennington further slowed Burgoyne's progress. When the general's army finally reached Albany in mid-September, neither St. Leger nor Howe were in sight.

The full support St. Leger had counted on from the Iroquois had not materialized, and he met fierce resistance as he made his way to the rendezvous point. When news reached him that Benedict Arnold and an army of a thousand Americans were approaching, St. Leger simply turned around and took his exhausted men to safety at Fort Niagara. Howe, of course, had no idea that he was expected in Albany. This left John Burgoyne stranded in the heart of New York. By mid-September 1777, his supplies dwindling, he realized his only option was to break northward through the American lines and take refuge in Canada—or surrender. On September 19, Burgoyne attacked, hoping to clear a path of retreat for his army. The elderly American general, **Horatio "Granny" Gates**, was neither bold nor particularly clever, but it took little daring or genius to defeat Burgoyne's weary, dispirited British soldiers. When Burgoyne tried once again to break through on October 7, Gates and his men held their ground. On October 17, 1777, General John Burgoyne surrendered.

News that a major British army had been defeated spread quickly on both sides of the Atlantic. It was a powerful boost to American confidence and an equally powerful blow to British self-esteem. The report also reversed the fortunes of American diplomatic efforts. Until Saratoga, American appeals to the governments of Spain, France, and Holland for supplies, loans, and military support had met with only moderate success. Now, hopes ran high that France would recognize independence and join the war effort.

Horatio "Granny" Gates Elderly Virginia general who led the American troops to victory in the Battle of Saratoga.

---

receive. Third, General Howe, no longer in New York City, knew absolutely nothing of his own critical role in the plan. Blissfully unaware of these problems, Burgoyne led his army from Montreal in high spirits in June 1777 (see Map 6.2). The troops floated down Lake Champlain in canoes and flatbottom boats and easily retook Fort Ticonderoga. From Ticonderoga, the invading army continued to march toward Albany. From this point on, however, things began to go badly for Burgoyne.

Friedrich Wilhelm Augustus von Steuben, or Baron Von Steuben, served in the Prussian army. He came to America in 1777, to join General George Washington's troops at Valley Forge. He took on the task of turning the amateur soldiers into a well trained army. Because he spoke little or no English, he swore and yelled at the troops in German and French. When this proved ineffective, he instructed his French speaking aide to deliver the curses for him in English! *The Granger Collection, New York.*

Winter Quarters in 1777

John Adams, who never wore a uniform, had once toasted a "short and Violent war." After Burgoyne's defeat, many Americans believed that Adams's wish was coming true. General Washington, however, did not share their optimism. French help might be coming, he pointed out, but who knew when? In the meantime, he reminded Congress the Continental Army still needed funds and supplies. Congress ignored all his urgent requests. The result was the long and dreadful winter at Valley Forge. **Valley Forge** was 20 miles from Philadelphia, where General Howe and his army were comfortably housed for the winter. Throughout December 1777, Washington's men labored to build the huts and cabins they needed. While two officers were assigned to share quarters, a dozen enlisted men were expected to crowd into a 14-by-16-foot hut. Rations were a problem from the start. Technically, each man was entitled to raw or cured meat, yet most soldiers at Valley Forge lived entirely on a diet of fire cakes, made of flour and water baked in the coals or over the fire on a stick. Blankets were scarce, coats were rare, and firewood was precious. An army doctor summed up conditions when he wrote: "Poor food—hard lodgings—cold weather—fatigue—nasty clothes—nasty cookery—vomit half my time—smoked out of my senses—the devil's in it—I can't endure it."

The doctor, however, did endure it. So did the soldiers he tended to daily, men such as the barefoot, half-naked, dirty young man who cried out in despair, "I am sick, my feet lame, my legs are sore, my body covered with this tormenting itch." While civilians mastered the steps of the latest dance craze, "the Burgoyne surrender," soldiers at Valley Forge traded the remains of their uniforms and sometimes their muskets for the momentary warmth and sense of well-being provided by liquor.

The enlisted men who survived the winter at Valley Forge were strangers to luxury even in peacetime. Like Deborah Sampson, most were from the humblest social classes: farm laborers, servants, apprentices, even former slaves. They were exactly the sort of person most Americans believed ought to fight the war. But if poverty had driven them into the army, a commitment to see the war through kept them there. The contrast between their own patriotism and the apparent indifference of the civilian population made many of these soldiers bitter. Private Joseph Plumb Martin expressed

> **Valley Forge** Winter encampment of Washington's army in Pennsylvania in 1777–1778; because the soldiers suffered greatly from cold and hunger, the term *Valley Forge* has become synonymous with "dire conditions."

the feelings of most when he said "a kind and holy Providence" had done more to help the army while it was at Valley Forge "than did the country in whose service we were wearing away our lives by piecemeal."

What these soldiers desperately needed, in addition to new clothes, good food, and hot baths, was professional military training. And that is the one thing they did get, beginning in the spring of 1778, when an unlikely Prussian volunteer arrived at Valley Forge. **Baron Friedrich von Steuben** was almost 50 years old, dignified, elegantly dressed, with a dazzling gold and diamond medal always displayed on his chest. Like most foreign volunteers, many of whom plagued Washington more than they helped him, the baron claimed to be an aristocrat, to have vast military experience, and to have held high rank in a European army. In truth, he had purchased his title only a short time before fleeing his homeland in bankruptcy and he had only been a captain in the Prussian army. A penniless refugee, von Steuben hoped to receive a military pension for his service in the American army. He had not, however, exaggerated his talent as a military drillmaster. All spring, the baron could be seen drilling Washington's troops, alternately shouting in rage and applauding with delight. Washington had little patience with most of the foreign volunteers who joined the American cause, but he considered von Steuben a most unexpected and invaluable surprise.

In the spring of 1778, Washington received the heartening news that France had formally recognized the independence of the United States. He immediately declared a day of thanks, ordering cannon to be fired in honor of the new alliance. That day, the officers feasted with their commander, and Washington issued brandy to each enlisted man at Valley Forge. American diplomacy had triumphed; Washington hoped the combined forces of France and America would soon bring victory as well.

Diplomacy Abroad and Profiteering at Home

→ *Why did the French assist the Americans secretly in the early years of the war?*

→ *Why did France enter the war after Saratoga?*

→ *Besides the French, what other European power supported the American colonists' struggle against the British?*

→ *How did the French alliance affect the war effort and wartime spending?*

Like most wars, the Revolutionary War was not confined to the battlefields. Diplomacy was essential, and popular morale and support had to be sustained for any war to be won. American diplomats hoped to secure supplies, safe harbors for American ships, and if at all possible, formal recognition of independence and the open military assistance that would allow. British diplomats, on the other hand, worked to prevent any formal alliances between European powers and the American rebels. Both sides issued propaganda to ensure continued popular support for the war. General Burgoyne's defeat, and the widening of the war into an international struggle, affected popular morale in both America and Britain.

The Long Road to Formal Recognition

In 1776 England had many enemies and rivals in Europe who were only too happy to see George III expend his resources and military personnel in an effort to quell a colonial rebellion. Although these nations expected the American Revolution to fail, they were more than eager to keep the conflict going as long as possible. Before Saratoga, they preferred to keep their support for the Revolution unofficial. Thus, with the help of King Louis XVI's chief minister, the comte de Vergennes, an American entrepreneur named Arthur Lee set up a private commercial firm, supposedly for trading with France. In reality, the firm siphoned weapons and funds from France to the revolutionaries. France also agreed to open ports to American privateers and to provide French ships and seamen for raids on British commercial shipping.

The Americans hoped for more, however. In December 1776, Congress sent the printer-politician-scientist **Benjamin Franklin** to Paris in hopes of winning formal recognition of American independence. The charming and witty Franklin was the toast of Paris, adored by aristocrats and common people alike, but even he could not persuade the king to support the Revolution openly. Burgoyne's surrender changed everything. After Saratoga, the British government began scram-

Baron Friedrich von Steuben Prussian military officer who served as Washington's drillmaster at Valley Forge

Benjamin Franklin American writer, inventor, scientist, and diplomat instrumental in bringing about a French alliance with the United States in 1778 and who later helped negotiate the treaty ending the war.

bling to end a war that had turned embarrassing, and the French government began scrambling to reassess its diplomatic position. Vergennes suspected that the English would quickly send a peace commission to America after Burgoyne's defeat. If the American Congress agreed to a compromise ending the rebellion, France could gain nothing more. But if the French kept the war alive by giving Americans reason to hope for total victory, perhaps they could recoup some of the territory and prestige lost to England in the Seven Years' War. This meant, of course, recognizing the United States and entering a war with Britain. Vergennes knew a choice had to be made—but he was not yet certain what to do.

Meanwhile, the English government was indeed preparing a new peace offer for Congress. At the heart of the British offer were two promises that George III considered to be great concessions. First, Parliament would renounce all intentions of ever taxing the colonies again. Second, the Intolerable Acts, the Tea Act, and any other objectionable legislation passed since 1763 would be repealed. Many members of Parliament thought these overtures were long overdue. They had been vocal critics of their government's policies in the 1760s and 1770s and had refused to support the war. After Burgoyne's defeat, popular support for compromise also increased in England. The Americans, however, were unimpressed by the offers. For Congress, a return to colonial status was now unthinkable.

Benjamin Franklin knew that Congress would reject the king's offer. But he was too shrewd to relieve the comte de Vergennes's fear that a compromise was in the works. Franklin warned that France must act quickly and decisively or accept the consequences. His gamble worked, and in 1778 France and the United States signed a treaty. The pact linked French and American fates tightly together, for under its provisions neither country could make a separate peace with Great Britain. By 1779, Spain had also formally acknowledged the United States, and in 1780 the Netherlands did so too. George III had little choice but to declare war against these European nations.

The Revolution had grown into an international struggle that taxed British resources further and made it impossible for Britain to concentrate all its military might and naval power in America. With ships diverted to the Caribbean and to the European coast, Britain could no longer blockade American ports as effectively as before or transport troops to the American mainland as quickly. Above all, the entry of the French into the war opened new strategic possibilities for General Washington and his army. If the Americans could count on the cooperation of the French fleet, a British army could be trapped on American soil, cut off by French ships from supplies, reinforcements, and any chance of escape.

War and the American Public

News of the alliance with France helped release an orgy of spending and purchasing by American civilians. The conditions were ripe for such a spree in 1778. With the value of government-issued paper money dropping steadily, spending made more sense than saving. And with profits soaring from the sale of supplies to the army, many Americans had more money to spend than ever before. Also, not all of the credit that diplomats had negotiated with European allies went toward military supplies. Some of it was available for the purchase of manufactured goods. This combination of optimism, **cheap money**, and plentiful foreign goods led to a wartime spending bonanza.

Many of the goods that were imported into America in the next few years were actually British-made. American consumers apparently saw no contradiction between their strong patriotism and the purchase of enemy products. A **black market**—a network for the sale of illegally imported English goods—grew rapidly, and profits from it skyrocketed. Abandoning the commitment to "virtuous simplicity" that had led them to dress in homespun, Americans stampeded to purchase tea and other imported luxuries.

Both the government and the military succumbed to this spirit of self-indulgence. Corruption and **graft** grew common, as both high- and low-ranking officials sold government supplies for their own profit or charged the army excessive rates for goods and services. Cheating the government and the army was a game civilians could play, too. Wagoners carting pickled meat to military encampments drained the brine from the barrels to lighten their load so they could carry more. The results were spoiled meat, soldiers suffering from food poisoning—and a greater profit for the cartmen. Soldiers became accustomed to defective weapons, defective shoes, and defective ammunition, but many of them joined the profit game by selling off their army-issued supplies to any available buyers. Recruiters pocketed the bounties given to them

---

cheap money   Paper money that is readily available but has declined in value.

black market   The illegal business of buying and selling goods that are banned or restricted.

graft   Misuse of one's position for profit or advantage.

The state governments, like the Continental Congress, printed paper money in order to finance the war effort. These certificates were used to pay soldiers and civilians who supplied the army with food, horses, or lodgings. Unfortunately, there was little in many of the state treasuries to back these paper certificates, and this, combined with inflation, soon made some paper money worthless. The Continental Congress's paper money declined in value faster than most. "Not worth a continental" became popular slang for anything that was worthless. *Picture Research Consultants & Archives.*

to attract enlistees. Officers accepted bribes from enlisted men seeking discharges.

Popular optimism and the spending frenzy unleashed by the French treaty contrasted sharply with the financial realities facing Congress. Bluntly put, the government was broke. By 1778, both Congress and the states had exhausted their meager sources of hard currency. The government met the crisis by printing more paper money. The result was rampant inflation. The value of the "continental," as the congressional paper money was called, dropped steadily with each passing day. The government's inability to pay soldiers became widely known—and enlistments plummeted. Both the state militias and the Continental Army resorted to impressment, or forced military service, to fill their ranks. Men forced to serve, however, were men more likely to mutiny or to desert. Officers did not know whether to sympathize with their unpaid and involuntary soldiers or to enforce stricter discipline upon them. Some officers executed deserters or

mutineers; some ordered the men whipped. And some pardoned their men, despite the severity of their crimes. Congress acknowledged the justice of the soldiers' complaints by giving them pay raises in the form of certificates that they could redeem—after the war.

From Stalemate to Victory

→ *What did France hope to achieve by coming to the aid of the struggling American army?*

→ *What led to General Cornwallis's surrender at Yorktown?*

→ *What were the most important results of the peace treaty negotiations?*

The French presence in the war did not immediately alter the strategies of British or American military leaders. English generals in the North displayed caution after Burgoyne's surrender, and Washington waited impatiently for signs that the French fleet would come to his aid. The result was a stalemate. The active war shifted to the South once again in late 1778 as the British mounted a second major campaign in the Carolinas.

The War Stalls in the North

Sir Henry Clinton, now the commander of the British army in North America, knew that the French fleet could easily blockade the Delaware River and thus cut off supplies to occupied Philadelphia. So, by the time warm weather had set in, his army was on the march, heading east through New Jersey en route to New York. Clinton's slow-moving caravan, burdened by a long train of bulky supply wagons, made an irresistible target—and Washington decided to strike.

Unfortunately, Washington entrusted the unreliable **General Charles Lee** with the initial attack. Lee marched his men to Monmouth, New Jersey, and as the British approached, the Americans opened fire. Yet as soon as the British army began to return fire, Lee ordered his men to retreat. When Washington arrived

Sir Henry Clinton General who replaced William Howe as commander of the British forces in America in 1778 after the British surrender at Saratoga.

General Charles Lee Revolutionary general who tried to undermine Washington's authority on several occasions; he was eventually dismissed from the military.

on the scene, the Americans were fleeing and the British troops were closing in.

Washington rallied the retreating Americans, calling on them to re-form their lines and stand their ground. Trained by von Steuben, the men responded well. They moved forward with precision and speed, driving the redcoats back. The **Battle of Monmouth** was not the decisive victory Washington had dreamed of, but it was a fine recovery from what first appeared to be certain defeat. As for Lee, Washington saw to it that he was discharged from the army.

Monmouth was only the first of several missed opportunities that summer of 1778. In August the French and Americans launched their first joint effort, sending a combined land and naval attack against the British base at Newport, Rhode Island. At the last minute, however, French admiral D'Estaing decided that the casualty rate would be too high. He abruptly gathered up his own men and sailed to safety on the open seas. The American troops were left to retreat as best they could.

Throughout the fall and winter of 1778 Washington waited in vain for French naval support for a major campaign. Early news coming from the western front did little to improve Washington's bleak mood. In Kentucky and western Virginia, deadly Indian attacks had decimated many American settlements. The driving force behind these attacks was a remarkable British official named Harry Hamilton, who won the nickname "Hair Buyer" because of the bounties he paid for American scalps. In October Hamilton led Indian troops from the Great Lakes tribes into the Illinois-Indiana region and captured the fort at Vincennes. The American counterattack was organized by a stocky young frontiersman, **George Rogers Clark**, whose own enthusiasm for scalping earned him the nickname "Long-Knife." To Washington's relief, Clark and his volunteer forces managed to drive the British from Vincennes.

Border conflict with Britain's Indian allies remained a major problem, and when loyalist troops joined these Indians, the danger increased. So did the atrocities. When patriot General John Sullivan's regular army was badly defeated by Mohawk chief **Thayendanegea**, known to the Americans as Joseph Brant, and local loyalists, Sullivan took revenge by burning forty Indian villages. It was an act of violence and cruelty that deeply shocked and shamed General Washington.

Spring and summer of 1779 passed and still Washington waited for the French navy's cooperation. Fall brought the general the worst possible news: Admiral D'Estaing and his fleet had sailed for the West

Mohawk chief Thayendanegea (Joseph Brant) believed that Iroquois lands would be lost if the Americans were victorious. He urged an Iroquois alliance with the British, fought for the British, and directed a series of deadly raids against settlements in New York. After the war—as Brant had feared—his people were forced to relocate to Canada. *"Joseph Brant" by Wilhelm von Moll Berczy, ca. 1800. National Gallery of Canada, Ottawa.*

Indies under orders to protect valuable French possessions in the Caribbean and, if possible, to seize English possessions there. News of D'Estaing's departure spurred a new wave of discipline problems among Washington's idle troops. Mutinies and desertions increased. From his winter headquarters in Morristown Heights, New Jersey, Washington wrote to von Steuben: "The prospect, my dear Baron, is gloomy, and the storm thickens." The real storm, however, was raging not in New Jersey but in the Carolinas.

Battle of Monmouth   New Jersey battle in June 1778 in which Charles Lee wasted a decisive American advantage.

George Rogers Clark   Virginian who led his troops to successes against the British and Indians in the Ohio Territory in 1778.

Thayendanegea   Mohawk chief known to the Americans as Joseph Brant; his combined forces of loyalists and Indians defeated John Sullivan's expedition to upstate New York in 1779.

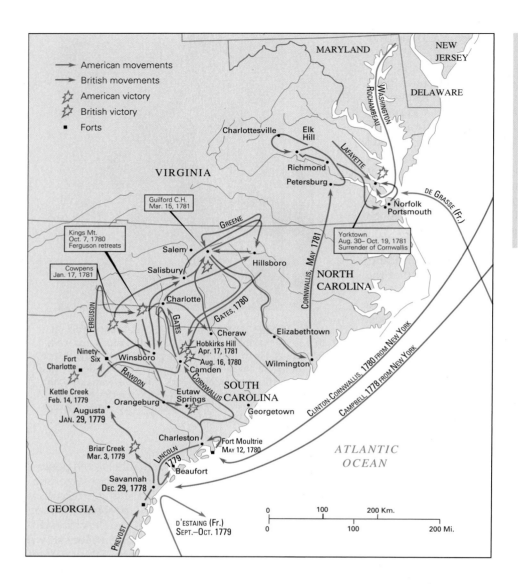

MAP 6.3 **The Second Southern Campaign, 1778–1781** This map of the second attempt by Britain to crush the rebellion in the South shows the many battles waged in the Lower South before Cornwallis's encampment at Yorktown and his surrender there. This decisive southern campaign involved all the military resources of the combatants, including British, loyalist, French, and American ground forces and British and French naval fleets.

The Second Carolinas Campaign

Since the fall of 1778, the British had been siphoning off New York-based troops for a new invasion of the South. The campaign began in earnest with the capture of Savannah, Georgia (see Map 6.3). Then, in the winter of 1779, General Henry Clinton sailed for Charleston, South Carolina, eager to avenge his embarrassing retreat in the 1776 campaign. Five thousand Continental soldiers hurried to join the South Carolina militia in defense of the city. From the Citadel, a fortification spanning the northern neck of the city's peninsula, these American forces bombarded the British with all they could find, firing projectiles made of glass, broken shovels, hatchets, and pickaxes. From aboard their ships, the British answered with a steady stream of mortar shells. On May 12, 1780, after months of deadly bombardment and high casualties on both sides, the Citadel fell. The American commander, General Benjamin Lincoln, surrendered his entire army to the British, and a satisfied General Clinton returned to New York.

Clinton left the southern campaign in the hands of **Charles Cornwallis**, an ambitious and able general

> **Charles Cornwallis** British general who was second in command to Henry Clinton; his surrender at Yorktown in 1781 brought the Revolution to a close.

Patrick Ferguson, who served in the Royal North British Dragoons during the Seven Years War, was a fine marksman and the inventor of the Ferguson rifle. By 1777, he was in America, serving under General Howe. Seriously wounded at Monmouth, he taught himself to fight with a sword and fire a rifle with his left hand. On October 7, 1780, at the battle of King's Mountain, he was shot from his horse and killed. Legend has it that one of his two girlfriends pointed him out to the American soldiers. Legend also has it that his other girlfriend, Virginia Sal, is buried with him in his grave. *The Granger Collection, New York.*

who set out with more than eight thousand men to conquer the rest of South Carolina. Cornwallis and his regular army were joined by loyalist troops who were as eager to take their revenge on their enemies as Clinton had been. Since the British had abandoned the South in 1776, small, roving bands of loyalist guerrillas had kept resistance to the Revolution alive. After the British victory at Charleston, the guerrillas increased their attacks, and a bloody civil war of ambush, arson, and brutality on both sides resulted. By the summer of 1780, fortunes had reversed: the revolutionaries were now the resistance, and the loyalists were in control.

The revolutionary resistance produced legendary guerrilla leaders, including **Francis Marion**, known as the "Swamp Fox." Marion organized black and white recruits into raiding bands that steadily ha-

rassed Cornwallis's army and effectively cut British lines of communication between Charleston and the interior. While Marion did his best to trouble the British, Thomas Sumter's guerrillas and other resistance forces focused their energies on the loyalists. When these guerrillas and loyalists met head-on in battle, they honored few of the rules of war. In October 1780, for example, in the **Battle of King's Mountain**,

Francis Marion South Carolina leader of guerrilla forces during the war; known as the "Swamp Fox," he harassed British forces during the second southern campaign.

Battle of King's Mountain Battle fought in October 1780 on the border between the Carolinas in which revolutionary troops defeated loyalists.

revolutionaries surrounded loyalist troops and picked them off one by one. As this bitter civil war continued, marauding bands terrorized civilians and plundered their farms. Often the worst damage was done by outlaws posing as soldiers.

The regular American army, under the command of the Saratoga hero, "Granny" Gates, had little success against Cornwallis. In August 1780, Gates and his men suffered a crushing defeat at Camden, South Carolina. That fall, Washington wisely replaced Gates with a younger, more energetic officer from Rhode Island, **Nathanael Greene**. The fourteen hundred Continental soldiers Greene found when he arrived in South Carolina were tired, hungry, and clothed in rags. They were also, Greene discovered, "without discipline and so addicted to plundering that the utmost exertions of the officers cannot restrain them." Greene's first steps were to ease the strains caused by civil war, raids, and plundering by offering pardons to loyalists and proposing alliances with local Indian tribes. In the end, Greene managed to win all but the Creeks away from the British.

Greene's military strategy was attrition: wear the British out by making them chase his small army across the South. He sent Virginian Daniel Morgan and six hundred riflemen to western South Carolina to tempt troops under the command of Banastre Tarleton into pursuit. Tarleton finally caught up with Morgan on an open meadow called the Cowpens in January 1781. When the outnumbered Americans stood their ground, ready to fight, the tired and frustrated British soldiers panicked and fled. Annoyed by this turn of events, Cornwallis decided to take the offensive. Now it was Greene's turn to lead the British on a long, exhausting chase. In March 1781, the two armies finally met at Guilford Courthouse, North Carolina. Although the Americans lost the battle and withdrew, British losses were so great that Cornwallis had to rethink the southern campaign. He decided that the price of conquering the Lower South was more than he was willing to pay. Disgusted, Cornwallis ordered his army northward to Virginia. Perhaps, he mused, he would have better luck there.

Treason and Triumph

In the fall of 1780, the popular general Benedict Arnold, one of Washington's protégés, defected to the British. Although Arnold's bold plot to turn over control of the Hudson River by surrendering the fort at **West Point**, New York, to the British was foiled, Arnold's treason saddened Washington and damaged American morale. Washington's unhappiness

over Arnold's betrayal was eased the following spring, however, when news came that French help was at last on its way. The general sat down at a strategy session with his French counterpart, General Rochambeau, in May 1781. The results were not exactly what Washington had hoped for: he had pressed for an attack on British-occupied New York, whereas Rochambeau insisted on a move against Cornwallis in Virginia. Since the French general had already ordered Admiral de Grasse and his fleet to the Chesapeake, Washington had little choice but to concur.

Thus, on July 6, 1781, a French army joined Washington's Continental forces just north of Manhattan for the long march to Virginia. The French soldiers, elegant in their sparkling uniforms, were openly amazed and impressed by their bedraggled allies. "It is incredible," wrote one French officer, "that soldiers composed of whites and blacks, almost naked, unpaid, and rather poorly fed, can march so well and stand fire so steadfastly."

Within a few months, General Cornwallis too would be forced to admire the American army's stamina. In July, however, the British commander was unaware that a combined army was marching toward him. His first clue that trouble lay ahead came when a force of regular soldiers, led by Baron von Steuben and the marquis de Lafayette, appeared in Virginia. Soon afterward, Cornwallis moved his army to the peninsula port of Yorktown to prepare for more serious battles ahead. The choice of **Yorktown** was one he would heartily regret.

By September 1781, the French and American troops coming from New York had joined forces with von Steuben and Lafayette's men. Admiral de Grasse's fleet of twenty-seven ships, seventy-four cannon, and an additional three thousand French soldiers were in place in Chesapeake Bay. General Clinton, still in New York, had been devastatingly slow to realize what the enemy intended. In desperation, he now sent a naval squadron from New York to rescue the trapped Cornwallis. He could do little more, since most of the British fleet was in the Caribbean.

Nathanael Greene American general who took command of the Carolinas campaign in 1780.

West Point Site of a fort overlooking the Hudson River, north of New York City.

Yorktown Site of the last major battle of the Revolution; American and French troops trapped Cornwallis's army here, on a peninsula on the York River near the Chesapeake Bay, and forced him to surrender.

John Trumbull celebrates the surrender of Cornwallis at Yorktown in this painting. However, neither Cornwallis nor Washington actually participated in the surrender ceremonies. The British commander claimed illness and sent his general of the guards as his deputy. Washington, always sensitive to status as well as to protocol, promptly appointed an officer of equal rank, General Benjamin Lincoln, to serve as his deputy. *"Surrender of Lord Cornwallis" by John Trumbull. Yale University Art Gallery/ Art Resource, NY.*

Admiral de Grasse had no trouble fending off Clinton's rescue squadron. Then he turned his naval guns on the redcoats at Yorktown. From his siege positions on land, Washington also directed a steady barrage of artillery fire against the British, producing a deafening roar both day and night. The noise dazed the redcoats and prevented them from sleeping. On October 19, 1781, Lord Cornwallis admitted the hopelessness of his situation and surrendered. Despite the stunning turn of events at Yorktown, fighting continued in some areas. Loyalists and patriots continued to make war on each other in the South for another year. Bloody warfare against the Indians also meant more deaths along the frontier. The British occupation of Charleston, Savannah, and New York continued. But after Yorktown the British gave up all hope of military victory against their former colonies. On March 4, 1782, Parliament voted to cease "the further prosecution of offensive war on the Continent of North America, for the purpose of reducing the Colonies to obedience by force." The war for independence had been won.

Winning Diplomatic Independence

What Washington and his French and Spanish allies had won, American diplomats had to preserve. Three men represented the United States at the peace talks in Paris: Benjamin Franklin, John Adams, and John Jay. At first glance, this was an odd trio. The elderly Franklin, witty and sophisticated, had spent most of the war years in Paris, where he earned a deserved reputation as an admirer of French women and French wines. Adams, competitive, self-absorbed, and socially inept, did not hide his distaste for Franklin's flamboyance. Neither man found much comfort in the presence of the prudish, aristocratic John Jay of New York. Yet they proved to be a highly effective combination. Franklin brought a crafty skill and a love of strategy to the team as well as a useful knowledge of French politics. Adams provided the backbone, for in the face of any odds he was stubborn, determined, fiercely patriotic, and a watchdog of American interests. Jay was calm, deliberate, and though not as aggressive as his New England colleague, he matched Adams in patriotism and integrity.

European political leaders expected the Americans to fare badly against the more experienced British and French diplomats. But Franklin, Jay, and Adams were far from naive. They were all veterans of wartime negotiations with European governments, having pursued loans, supplies, and military support. And they understood what was at stake at the peace table. They knew that their chief ally, France, had its own agenda and that England still wavered on the degree of independence America had actually won at Yorktown. Thus, despite firm orders from Congress to rely on France at every phase of the negotiations, the American diplomats quickly put their own agenda on the table. They issued a direct challenge to Britain: you must formally recognize American independence as a precondition to any negotiations at all. The British commissioner reluctantly agreed. Negotiations continued for more than a year, with all sides debating, arguing, and compromising until the terms of a treaty were finally set.

In the **Treaty of Paris of 1783** the Americans emerged with two clear victories. First, although the British did not give up Canada as the Americans had hoped, the boundaries of the new nation were extensive. Second, the treaty granted the United States unlimited access to the fisheries off Newfoundland, a particular concern of New Englander John Adams. It was difficult to measure the degree of success on other issues, however, since the terms for carrying out the agreements were so vague. For example, Britain ceded the Northwest to the United States. But the treaty said nothing about approval of this transfer of power by the Indians of the region, and it failed to set a timetable for British evacuation of the forts in the territory. This lack of clarity would cause problems for the Americans. In other cases, however, the treaty's vague language worked to American advantage. The treaty contained only the most general promise that the American government would not interfere with collection of the large prewar debts southern planters owed to British merchants. The promise to urge the states to return confiscated property to loyalists was equally inexact.

The peacemakers were aware of the treaty's shortcomings and its lack of clarity on key issues. But this was the price for avoiding stalemate and dangerous confrontation on controversial issues. Franklin, Adams, and Jay knew the consequences might be serious, but for the moment they preferred to celebrate rather than to worry.

Republican Expectations in a New Nation

→ *How did the Revolution affect Americans' expectations regarding individual rights, social equality, and the role of women in American society?*

→ *What opportunities were open to African Americans during and after the Revolution?*

→ *What was the fate of the loyalists?*

As an old man, John Adams reminisced about the American Revolution with his family and friends. Although he spoke of the war as a remarkable military event, Adams insisted that the Revolution was more than battlefield victories and defeats. The Revolution took place, Adams said, "in the hearts and the minds of the people." What he meant was that changes in American social values and political ideas were as critical as artillery, swords, and battlefield strategies in creating the new nation. "The people" were, of course, far more diverse than Adams was ever willing to admit. And they often differed in their "hearts and minds." Race, region, social class, gender, religion, even the national origin of immigrants—all played a part in creating diverse interests and diverse interpretations of the Revolution. Adams was correct, however, that significant changes took place in American thought and behavior during the war and the years immediately after. Many of these changes reflected a growing identification of the new American nation as a **republic** that ensured not only representative government but also the protection of individual rights, an educated citizenry, and an expanded suffrage.

The Protection of Fundamental Rights

The Declaration of Independence expressed the commonly held American view that government must protect the fundamental rights of life, liberty, property, and, as Jefferson put it, "the pursuit of happiness." The belief that Britain was usurping these rights was a major justification for the Revolution. Thus, whatever form Americans chose for their new, independent government, they were certain to demand the protection of these fundamental rights. This emphasis had many social consequences.

The protection of many individual rights—freedom of speech, assembly, and the press, and the right to a trial by jury—were written into the new constitutions of several states. But some rights were more difficult to define than others. While many Americans supported "freedom of conscience," not all of them supported separation of church and state. In the seventeenth century, individual dissenters such as Roger Williams and Anne Hutchinson had fought for the separation of church and state. After the Great Awakening, the same demands were made by organized dissenter communities such as the Baptists, who protested the privileges that established churches enjoyed in most colonies. When Virginia took up the question in 1776, political leaders were not in agree-

---

Treaty of Paris of 1783 Treaty that ended the Revolutionary War in 1783 and secured American independence.

republic A nation in which supreme power resides in the citizens, who elect representatives to govern them.

ment. The House of Burgesses approved George Mason's Declaration of Rights, which guaranteed its citizens "the free exercise of religion," yet Virginia continued to use tax monies to support the Anglican Church. Even with the strong support of Thomas Jefferson, dissenters' demands were not fully met until 1786, when the Statute of Religious Freedom ended tax-supported churches and guaranteed complete freedom of conscience, even for atheists. Other southern states followed Virginia's lead, ending tax support for their Anglican churches.

The battle was more heated in New England. Many descendants of the Puritans wished to continue government support of the Congregational Church. Others simply wished to keep the principle of an established church alive. As a compromise, communities were sometimes allowed to decide which local church received their tax money, although each town was required to make one church the established church. New England did not separate church and state entirely until the nineteenth century.

Protection of Property Rights

Members of the revolutionary generation who had a political voice were especially vocal about the importance of private property and protection of a citizen's right to own property. In the decade before the Revolution, much of the protest against British policy had focused on this issue. For free, white, property-holding men—and for those white male servants, tenant farmers, or apprentices who hoped to join their ranks someday—life, liberty, and happiness were interwoven with the right of landownership.

The property rights of some infringed on the freedoms of others, however. Claims made on western lands by white Americans often meant the denial of Indian rights to that land. Masters' rights included a claim to the time and labor of their servants or apprentices. In the white community, a man's property rights usually included the restriction of his wife's right to own or sell land, slaves, and even her own personal possessions. Even the independent-minded Deborah Sampson lost her right to own property when she became Mrs. Gannett. And the institution of slavery transformed human beings into the private property of others.

The right to property was a principle, not a guarantee. Many white men were unable to acquire land during the revolutionary era or in the decades that followed. When the Revolution began, one-fifth of free American people lived in poverty or depended on public charity. The uneven distribution of wealth among white colonists was obvious on the streets of colonial Boston, in the rise in **almshouses** in Philadelphia, and in the growth of voluntary relief organizations that aided the homeless and the hungry in other cities and towns. For some, taking advantage of opportunities to acquire property was difficult even when those opportunities arose. Washington's Continental soldiers, for example, were promised western lands as delayed payment for their military service. But when they left the army in 1783, most were penniless, jobless, and sometimes homeless. They had little choice but to sell their precious land warrant certificates, trading their future as property owners for bread today.

Legal Reforms

Although economic inequality actually grew in the decades after the Revolution, several legal reforms were spurred by a commitment to the republican belief in social equality. Chief targets of this legal reform included the laws of **primogeniture** and **entail**. In Britain, these inheritance laws had led to the creation of a landed aristocracy. The actual threat they posed in America was small, for few planters ever adopted them. But the principle they represented remained important to republican spokesmen such as Thomas Jefferson, who pressed successfully for their abolition in Virginia and North Carolina.

The passion for social equality—in appearance if not in fact—affected customs as well as laws. To downplay their elite status as landowners, revolutionaries stopped the practice of adding "**Esquire**" (abbreviated "Esq.") after their names. (George Washington, Esq., became plain George Washington.)

Even unintentional elitist behavior could have embarrassing consequences. When General George Washington and the officers who served with him in the Revolutionary War organized the Society of the Cincinnati in 1783, they were motivated by the desire to sustain wartime friendships. The society's rules, however, brought protest from many Americans, for membership was hereditary, passing from officer fathers to their eldest sons. Grumblings that the club

---

almshouse   A public shelter for the poor.

primogeniture   The legal right of the eldest son to inherit the entire estate of his father.

entail   A legal limitation that prevents property from being divided, sold, or given away.

Esquire   A term used to indicate that a man was a gentleman.

In this portrait of Mary Harvey Champneys and her step-daughter, Sarah Champneys, the two women pose in the respectable attire of a matron and an unmarried girl. The artist, Edward Savage, began his career making copies of paintings by more notable artists such as John Singleton Copley, but later managed to earn his living as a portraitist. In an era without photography, family portraits served as memorials as well as a display of wealth. *The Gibbes Museum of Art/Carolina Art Association.*

would spawn a military aristocracy—incompatible with republican government—drove Washington and his comrades to revise the offending society bylaws.

In some states, the principle of social equality had concrete political consequences. Pennsylvania and Georgia eliminated all property qualifications for voting among free white males. Other states lowered their property requirements for voters but refused to go as far as universal white manhood suffrage. They feared that the outcome of such a sweeping reform was unpredictable. Even women might demand a political voice.

Women in the New Republic

The war did not erase differences of class, race, region, or age for either men or women. Thus its impact was not uniform for all American women. Yet some experiences, and the memories of them, were probably shared by the majority of white and even many black women. They would remember the war years as a time of constant shortages, anxiety, harassment, and unfamiliar and difficult responsibilities. Men going off to war left women to manage farms or shops in addition to caring for large families and household duties. Women had to cope with the critical shortages of food and supplies and to survive on meager budgets in inflationary times. Many, like the woman who pleaded with her soldier husband to "pray come home," may have feared they would fail in these new circumstances. After the war, however, many remembered with satisfaction how well they had adapted to new roles. They expressed their sense of accomplishment in letters to husbands that no longer spoke of "your farm" and "your crop" but of "our farm" and even "my crop."

Many women found they enjoyed the sudden independence from men and from the domestic hierarchy that men ruled in peacetime. Even women in difficult circumstances experienced this new sense of freedom. Grace Galloway, wife of loyalist exile Joseph Galloway of Pennsylvania, remained in America during the war in an effort to preserve her husband's property. Shunned by her patriot neighbors, reduced from wealth to painful poverty, Grace Galloway nevertheless confided to her diary that "Ye liberty of doing as I please Makes even Poverty more agreable than any time I ever spent since I married." If Galloway experienced new self-confidence and liberty during wartime, not all women were so fortunate. For the victims of rape and physical attack by soldiers on either side, the war meant more traditional experiences of vulnerability. American soldiers sang songs of flirtation and of their hopes for kisses from admiring young women, but occupying armies, guerrilla bands, and outlaws posing as soldiers left trails of abuse, particularly in New Jersey, along the frontier, and in the Carolinas.

For women, just as for men, the war meant adapting traditional behavior and skills to new circumstances. Women who followed the eighteenth-century custom of joining husbands or fathers in army camps took up the familiar domestic chores of cooking, cleaning, laundering, and providing nursing care. Outside the army camps, loyalist and patriot women served as spies or saboteurs and risked their lives by shelter-

Sheet music such as "The Ladies Patriotic Song" found its way into the parlors of many revolutionary and early republic homes. This song, which celebrates the heroes of independence, George Washington and John Adams, also celebrates what postwar society considered to be feminine virtues: beauty, innocence, and patriotic devotion. *Chicago Historical Society.*

ing soldiers or hiding weapons in their cellars. Sometimes they opted to burn their crops or destroy their homes to prevent the enemy from using them. These were conscious acts of patriotism rather than wifely duties. On some occasions, women crossed gender boundaries dramatically. Although few behaved like Deborah Sampson and disguised themselves as men, women such as **Mary Ludwig** and Margaret Corbin did engage in military combat. These "Molly Pitchers" carried water to cool down the cannon in American forts across the country; but if men fell wounded, nearby women frequently took their place in line. After the war, female veterans of combat, including Corbin, applied to the government for pensions, citing as evidence the wounds they had received in battle.

In the postwar years, members of America's political and social elite engaged in a public discussion of women's role in the family and in a republican society. Spurred by Enlightenment assertions that all humans were capable of rational thought and action and by the empirical evidence of women's patriotic commitments and behavior, these Americans set aside older colonial notions that women lacked the ability to reason and to make moral choices. They urged a new role for women within the family: the moral training of their children. This training would include the inculcating of patriotism and republican principles. Thus the republic would rely on wives and mothers to sustain its values and to raise a new generation of concerned citizens.

This new ideal, "**republican womanhood,**" reflected Enlightenment ideals, but it also had roots in economic and social changes that began before the Revolution, including the growth of a prosperous urban class able to purchase many household necessities. No longer needing to make cloth or candles or butter, prosperous urban wives and mothers had time to devote to raising children. Republican womanhood probably had little immediate impact in the lives of ordinary free women, who remained unable to purchase essential goods or to pay others to do household chores, or in the lives of African American or Indian women.

Although women's active role in the education of the next generation was often applauded as a public, political contribution, not simply a private, family duty, it did not lead to direct political participation for female Americans. The Constitution left suffrage qualifications to the state governments, and no state chose to extend voting rights to women. Only one state, New Jersey, failed to stipulate "male" as a condition

Mary Ludwig Wife of a soldier at Fort Monmouth; one of many women known popularly as "Molly Pitchers" because they carried water to cool down the cannon their husbands fired in battle.

republican womanhood A role for mothers that became popularized following the Revolution; it stressed women's importance in instructing children in republican virtues such as patriotism and honor.

Margaret Cochran Corbin was the wife of an American soldier serving at Fort Washington. On November 16, 1776, her husband was killed and she took over his place, firing a cannon against the British enemy. She was severely wounded, and lost the use of her left arm. In 1779 the Continental Congress granted Margaret Corbin a military pension, a rare acknowledgement of women's service in battle. In 1926, a monument was erected to honor her. *Private Collection.*

IT MATTERS TODAY

TRACKING CHANGES IN GENDER ROLES

Eighteenth-century women like Deborah Sampson and Esther DeBerdt Reed tested the limits of traditional gender roles, demonstrating bravery on the battlefield and political organizing skills during the American Revolution. But it would be over 140 years before their descendants could vote in a national election and decades more before they could serve in the military. The impact of this social change can be seen today in the accomplishments of women such as Lt. General Claudia J. Kennedy, the United States Army's first female three-star general; Sandra Day O'Connor, the first woman to become a Supreme Court justice; Madeleine Albright, the first woman secretary of state; and Geraldine Ferraro, the first woman to be the vice-presidential nominee of a national party. Tracking major changes in gender roles and examining why those changes occurred is a critical part of the historian's task.

- Do you think a woman president is likely to be elected in your lifetime? Explain the factors on which you base your opinion.

for suffrage in its first constitution, and this oversight was soon revised.

Although American republicanism expected mothers to instill patriotism in their children, it also expected communities to provide formal education for future citizens. Arguing that a citizen could not be both "ignorant and free," several states allotted tax money for public elementary schools. Some went even further. By 1789, for example, Massachusetts required every town to provide free public education to its children. After the Revolution, *children* meant girls as well as boys.

This new emphasis on female education was a radical departure for women. Before the Revolution, the education of daughters was haphazard at best. Colleges and the preparatory schools that trained young men for college were closed to female students. A woman got what formal knowledge she could by reading her father's or her brother's books. Some women, most notably Anne Hutchinson and the Massachusetts revolutionary propagandist Mercy Otis Warren, were lucky enough to receive fine educations from the men in their family. But most women had to be content to learn domestic skills rather than geography, philosophy, or history. After the Revolution, however, educational reformers reasoned that mothers must be well versed in history and even political theory if they were to teach their children the essential principles of citizenship. By the 1780s, private academies had opened to educate the daughters of wealthy American families. These privileged young women enjoyed the rare opportunity to study mathematics, history, and geography. Although their curriculum was often as rigorous as that in a boys' preparatory school, the addition of courses in fancy needlework reminded the girls that their futures lay in marriage and motherhood.

The War's Impact on Slaves and Slavery

The protection of liberty and the fear of enslavement were major themes of the Revolution. Yet the denial

The blessings of liberty and equality at the heart of the Revolution did not extend to all Americans. In New England, slavery was abolished after the war, but free blacks were not welcomed into white society. The illustration above of a celebration sponsored in 1793 by Massachusetts governor John Hancock for free African Americans was accompanied by a satiric poem that mocked blacks and what the poet saw as their crude attempts to mimic polite society. *Library Company of Philadelphia.*

of liberty was a central reality in the lives of most African Americans. As the movement for independence developed, slaves' political and military loyalties reflected their best guess as to which side offered them the greatest chance of freedom. Ironically, the desire for freedom set many of them against the Revolution. Of the fifty thousand or so slaves who won their freedom in the war, half did so by escaping to the British army. Only about five thousand African American men joined the Continental Army once Congress opened enlistment to them in 1776. Black soldiers were generally better treated by the British than by the revolutionaries. In both armies, however, African American troops received lower pay than white soldiers and were often assigned to the most dangerous or menial duties.

With American victory in 1781, African American loyalist soldiers faced a difficult decision: to remain in America and risk re-enslavement or to evacuate along with the British army. Many stayed, prompting a group of angry owners to complain that there was "reason to believe that a great number of slaves which were taken by the British army are now passing in this country as free men." The British transported those who chose to leave to Canada, to England, to British Florida, to the Caribbean, or to Africa. Three thousand former slaves settled initially in Nova Scotia, but the racism of their white loyalist neighbors led more than a thousand of these veterans to emigrate a second time. Led by an African-born former slave named Thomas Peters, they sailed to Sierra Leone, in West Africa, where they established a free black colony. Slaves found other routes to freedom besides

military service during the war. Some escaped from farms and plantations to the cities, where they passed as free people. Others fled to the frontier, where they joined sympathetic Indian tribes. Women and children, in particular, took advantage of wartime disruptions to flee their masters' control.

The long war affected the lives of those who remained in slavery. Control and discipline broke down when the southern campaigns dragged on, distracting slave owners and disrupting work routines. Slave masters complained loudly and bitterly that their slaves "all do now what they please every where" and "pay no attention to the orders of the overseer." These exaggerated complaints point to real but temporary opportunities for slaves to alter the conditions under which they worked and lived.

In the northern states, the revolutionaries' demand for liberty undermined black slavery. Loyalists taunted patriots, asking, "How is it that we hear the loudest yelps for liberty among the drivers of negroes?" The question made the contradiction between revolutionary ideals and American reality painfully clear. Not all slave owners, however, needed to be shamed by others into grappling with the hypocrisy of their position. In the 1760s and 1770s, influential political leaders such as James Otis, Thomas Paine, and Benjamin Rush campaigned against the continuation of slavery. In Boston, Phillis Wheatley, a young African-born slave whose master recognized and encouraged her literary talents, called on the revolutionaries to acknowledge the universality of the wish for freedom. "In every human breast," Wheatley wrote, "God had implanted a Principle, which we call love

As a child, Phillis Wheatley was brought from Africa and sold to a Boston couple who came to recognize and encourage her literary talent. Wheatley's patriotic poetry won approval from George Washington and praise from many revolutionary leaders. She died free but in poverty in the 1780s. *Library of Congress.*

of freedom; it is impatient of Oppression, and pants for Deliverance. . . . I will assert, that the same Principles live in us." George Washington was among those who admired Wheatley's talents and respected her demands for black freedom, and he publicly acknowledged her as an American poet.

Free black Americans joined with white reformers to mobilize antislavery campaigns in Pennsylvania, Massachusetts, Rhode Island, and Connecticut. In Boston and Philadelphia, slaves petitioned on their own behalf to be "liberated from a state of Bondage, and made Freemen of this Community." Of course, these states were home to few slaves, and the regional economy did not depend on unfree labor. Thus it was easier there to acknowledge the truth in the slave's cry: "We have no property! . . . we have no children! . . . we have no city! . . . we have no country!"

Manumission increased during the 1770s, especially in the North. In 1780, Pennsylvania became the first state to pass an emancipation statute, making manumission a public policy rather than a private matter of conscience. Pennsylvania lawmakers, however, compromised on a gradual rather than an immediate end to slavery. Only slaves born after the law was enacted were eligible, and they could not expect

to receive their freedom until they had served a twenty-eight-year term of indenture. By 1804, all northern states except Delaware had committed themselves to a slow end to slavery.

Slavery was far more deeply embedded in the South, as a labor system and as a system that regulated race relations. In the Lower South, white Americans ignored the debate over slavery and took immediate steps to replace missing slaves and to restore tight control over work and life on their plantations. Manumission did occur in the Upper South. Free black communities grew in both Maryland and Virginia after the Revolutionary War, and planters openly debated the morality of slavery in a republic and the practical benefits of slave labor. They did not all reach the same conclusions. George Washington freed all his slaves on the death of his wife, but Patrick Henry, who had often stirred his fellow Virginia legislators with his spirited defense of American liberty, justified his decision to continue slavery with blunt honesty. Freeing his slaves, he said, would be inconvenient (see Figure 6.1).

The Fate of the Loyalists

Before independence was declared, white Americans loyal to the Crown experienced the isolation and disapproval of their communities. Some faced the physical danger of tarring and feathering, imprisonment, or beatings. Still others saw their property destroyed. After 1775, loyalists flocked to the safety of British-occupied cities, crowding first into Boston and later into New York City and Philadelphia. When the British left an area, the loyalists evacuated with them. More than a thousand Massachusetts loyalists boarded British ships when Boston was abandoned in 1776, and fifteen thousand more sailed out of New York harbor when the war ended in 1781. Altogether, as many as a hundred thousand men, women, and children left their American homes to take up new lives in England, Canada, and the West Indies.

Wealth often determined a loyalist's destination. Rich and influential men such as Thomas Hutchinson of Massachusetts took refuge in England during the war. But life in England was so expensive that it quickly ate up their resources and drove them into debt. Accustomed to comfort, many of these exiles passed their days in seedy boarding houses in the small cities outside London. They lost more than servants and fine clothes, however. In a society dominated by

manumission   Freedom from slavery or bondage.

aristocrats and royalty, loyalist men who had enjoyed status and prestige in America suddenly found themselves socially insignificant, with no work and little money. Loyalists in England grew more desperately homesick each day.

When the war ended, most of the loyalists in England departed for Nova Scotia, New Brunswick, or the Caribbean. Many of these exiles were specifically forbidden to return to the United States by the new state governments. Others refused to go back to America because they equated the new republican society with mob rule. Those who were willing to adjust to the new American nation returned slowly.

Less prosperous loyalists, especially those who served in the loyalist battalions during the war, went to Canada after 1781. The separation from family and friends, as much as the bleak climate of Canada, at first caused depression and despair in some exiles. One woman who had bravely endured the war and its deprivations broke down and cried when she landed at Nova Scotia. Like the revolutionaries, these men and women had chosen their political loyalty based on a mixture of principle and self-interest. Unlike the revolutionaries, they had chosen the losing side. They lived with the consequences for the rest of their lives.

Canada became the refuge of another group of loyalists: members of the Indian tribes that had supported the Crown. The British ceded much of the Iroquois land to the United States in the Treaty of Paris, and American hostility toward "enemy savages" made peaceful postwar coexistence unlikely. Thus, in the 1780s, Mohawks, Onondagas, Tuscaroras, Senecas, Oneidas, and Cayugas along with Delawares, Tutelos, and Nanticokes created new, often multiethnic settlements on the

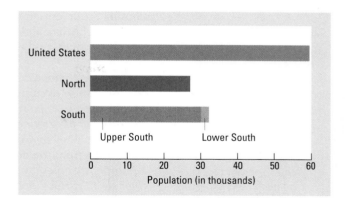

FIGURE 6.1   Free Black Population, 1790   This graph shows the number of free African Americans in the United States in 1790, as well as their regional distribution. These almost 60,000 free people were less than 10 percent of the African American population of the nation. Although 40 percent of northern blacks were members of this free community, only about 5.5 percent of the Upper South African Americans and less than 2 percent of those in the Lower South lived outside the bounds of slavery.

banks of the Grand River in Ontario. These communities marked an end to the dislocation and suffering many of these refugees had experienced during the Revolution, when steady warfare depleted Indian resources and made thousands dependent on the British for food, clothing, and military supplies. A majority of the Indians who settled in Canada had already spent years in makeshift encampments near Fort Niagara after American armies destroyed their farms, homes, and villages.

Examining a Primary Source

✔ Individual Voices

Esther DeBerdt Reed Glories in the Usefulness of Women

Deborah Sampson took the most daring path to participation in the Revolution. But other women also pushed the boundaries of women's traditional sphere by organizing to play a public role in the war effort. Wealthy Philadelphia matron Esther DeBerdt Reed, for example, helped organize women's voluntary associations to raise funds and supplies for the American army. Openly political activities by women were not always greeted favorably by the community, however. Women who expressed their patriotism through public actions were accused of overstepping the boundaries of their gender—that is, of unfeminine behavior. Reed defended her activism in "The Sentiments of an American Woman," printed in 1780. In this

① *Here, Constitution does not mean a written plan of government but the natural characteristics and appropriate behaviors of women—and of men. Do you think Reed is challenging the notion that women are constitutionally, or naturally, weak and incapable of making decisions and acting on them? Or is she saying that women are decisive and competent only in times of great crisis?*

② *Male revolutionary leaders often drew analogies between their choices and actions and those of biblical heroes and leaders of the Roman republic. Why do you think Reed referred to the women of the Bible and Ancient Rome?*

③ *If you were opposed to the activities Reed was engaged in what arguments would you make against this type of female activism?*

unusual document, she connects the patriotic women of the Revolution with heroic women of history, and she discusses female patriotism in terms that Deborah Sampson would surely have applauded.

> *On the commencement of actual war, the Women of America manifested a firm resolution to contribute as much as could depend on them, to the deliverance of this country. Animated by the purest patriotism they are sensible of sorrow at this day, in not offering more than barren wishes for the success of so glorious a Revolution. They aspire to render themselves more really useful; and this sentiment is universal from the north to the south of the Thirteen United States.* **①** *Our ambition is kindled by the fame of those heroines of antiquity, who have rendered their sex illustrious, and have proved to the universe, that, if the weakness of our Constitution, if opinion and manners did not forbid us to march to glory by the same paths as the Men, we should at least equal and sometimes surpass them in our love for the public good. I glory in all that which my sex has done great and commendable.* **②** *I call to mind with enthusiasm and with admiration, all those acts of courage, of constancy and patriotism, which history has transmitted to us: The people favoured by Heaven, preserved from destruction by the virtues, the zeal and the resolution of Deborah, of Judith, of Esther! . . . Rome saved from the fury of a victorious enemy by the efforts of Volunia, and other Roman ladies: So many famous sieges where the Women have been seen forgetting the weakness of their sex, building new walls, digging trenches with their feeble hands; furnishing arms to their defenders, they themselves darting the missile weapons on the enemy, resigning the adornments of their apparel, and their fortunes to fill the public treasury, and to hasten the deliverance of their country. . . . [We are] Born for liberty, disdaining to bear the irons of a tyrannic Government. . . .* **③** *Who knows if persons disposed to censure, and sometimes too severely with regard to us, may not disapprove our appearing acquainted even with the actions of which our sex boasts? We are at least certain, that he cannot be a good citizen who will not applaud our efforts for the relief of the armies which defend our lives, our possessions, our liberty.*

SUMMARY

When the colonies declared their independence, many people on both sides doubted they could win the war. The British outnumbered and outgunned the Americans, and their troops were better trained and better equipped. The Americans' major advantage was logistic: they were fighting a war on familiar terrain.

The early British strategy was to invade New York and the southern colonies, where they expected to rally strong loyalist support. This strategy failed, not only because they were waging war on unfamiliar territory but also because they had overestimated loyalist strength and alienated would-be sympathizers. Washington's hit-and-run tactics made it impossible for the British to deliver a crushing blow.

The turning point in the war came in 1777 when British general John Burgoyne's plan to isolate New England from the other rebel colonies failed. Burgoyne was forced to surrender at Saratoga, New York. The surprising American victory led to an alliance between France and the United States and the expansion of the war into an international conflict. The British invaded the South again in 1778, but despite early victories, their campaign ended in disaster. American victory was assured when French and American forces defeated General Cornwallis at Yorktown, Virginia, in October 1781. Fighting continued for a time, but in March 1782, the British Parliament ended the conflict. The Treaty of Paris was negotiated in 1783, and to the surprise of many European diplomats, the Americans gained important concessions.

Victory led to significant transformations in American society. Individual rights were strengthened for free white men. A republican spirit changed the outlook, if not the condition, of many Americans, as customs that fit a hierarchical society gave way to more egalitarian behavior. The wartime experiences of women such as Deborah Sampson led American intellectuals to reconsider women's "nature" and their abilities. Although full citizenship was not granted, white women's capacity for rational thought was acknowledged, and their new role as the educators of their children led to expanded formal education for women. Black Americans also made some gains. Fifty thousand slaves won their freedom during the war, thousands by serving in the Continental Army. Northern states moved to outlaw slavery, but southern slaveholders decided to preserve the institution despite intense debate. For most Loyalists, the end of the war meant permanent exile from their homeland.

Independence had been won. But could it be preserved? In Chapter 7, you will read about the struggles to create governments that could protect the young nation and preserve the liberties its citizens had fought to insure.

IN THE WIDER WORLD

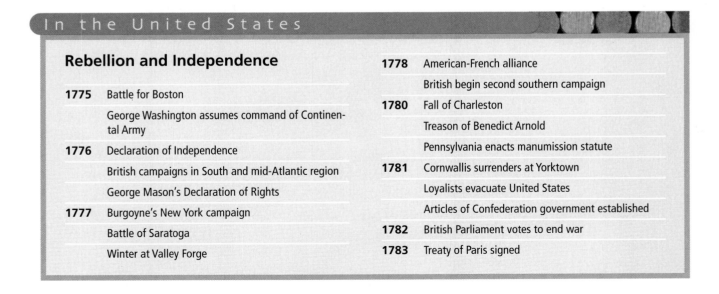

1775
Battle for Boston

Washington takes command

1776 Declaration of Independence

1777
Battle of Saratoga

Winter at Valley Forge

1778
United States alliance with France

1780
Fall of Charleston

Pennsylvania's manumission statute

1781
Cornwallis surrenders at Yorktown

1783
Treaty of Paris

1774	1775	1776	1777	1778	1779	1780	1781	1782	1783	1784

1774
George Louis Lesage invents the electric telegraph

1777
King Chôngjo builds Kyujanggak library, Seoul

1780
Peruvian Indian revolt against Spain

1783
Catherine the Great of Russia annexes the Crimea

1784
John Wesley Charters Methodist Church

In the United States

Rebellion and Independence

1775 Battle for Boston

George Washington assumes command of Continental Army

1776 Declaration of Independence

British campaigns in South and mid-Atlantic region

George Mason's Declaration of Rights

1777 Burgoyne's New York campaign

Battle of Saratoga

Winter at Valley Forge

1778 American-French alliance

British begin second southern campaign

1780 Fall of Charleston

Treason of Benedict Arnold

Pennsylvania enacts manumission statute

1781 Cornwallis surrenders at Yorktown

Loyalists evacuate United States

Articles of Confederation government established

1782 British Parliament votes to end war

1783 Treaty of Paris signed

CHAPTER 7

Competing Visions of the Virtuous Republic, 1770–1796

A NOTE FROM THE AUTHOR

America was now an independent nation—but could it last? Unlike you, anxious Americans of the time could not read ahead in the textbook. For the revolutionary generation, the future held many uncertainties. Would the economy recover from a postwar depression? Could the nation pay off its huge debts to France, Holland, and its own citizens? Would the states return to their old habits of rivalry and competition with one another? Most importantly, were the limited powers of the Articles of Confederation government enough to ensure the survival of the United States?

In 1787, delegates from twelve of the thirteen states gathered in Philadelphia to debate what should be done to save the country. Most of them believed a stronger central government was necessary and that the states would have to give up or share some powers with that national government. After four months of deliberation, these "framers" produced a new Constitution that divided power between the states and the national government, and incorporated the checks and balances that they hoped would prevent abuses of power. That Constitution has lasted, with amendments, until today.

But was such a drastic change necessary? Historians do not agree on this question. Some argue there was no real economic or political crisis in 1787 and that the Confederation was a workable, and more democratic, government than the new Constitution created. Others argue that the framers were correct and that the Constitution paved the way to prosperity and to the rise of the United States as a respected nation. Their debates echo the debates of the pro- and anti-Constitution forces in 1787 that you'll see in this chapter.

The issues raised by this debate are not just academic ones, however. Every day, you can find Americans questioning whether local control or central control of schools, social services, and tax monies serves the community best. And, throughout American history the proper division of powers between state governments and the central government in our federal system has been hotly contested. In fact, the tension between states' rights and the authority of the national government was, and is, one of the most controversial issues in our nation's history.

Mercy Otis Warren

Massachusetts playwright, poet, and historian Mercy Otis Warren penned some of the most popular and effective propaganda for the American cause. In her plays, she portrayed pro-British officeholders as greedy, power-hungry traitors, while she praised Boston radicals as noble heroes. *"Mercy Otis Warren" by John Singleton Copley. Courtesy of the Museum of Fine Arts, Boston, bequest of Winslow Warren; © 2008 Museum of Fine Arts, Boston.*

Individual Choices

Mercy Otis Warren was the sister of one Massachusetts revolutionary and the wife of another. But she was a revolutionary in her own right. She never held elective office, gave a public speech, or donned a uniform to fight for independence for these were male roles in the eighteenth century. Instead she waged her revolution with pen and paper. During the 1770s, she wrote biting satirical plays that mocked royal officials and their supporters. In *The Adulateur* and *The Group* she drew the imperial struggle in stark moral terms as a battle between tyranny and representative government, greed and self-sacrifice, and ambitions and virtue. Patriots like John Adams praised her as an effective propagandist for the revolutionary cause.

After the Revolution, however, Warren and Adams became political enemies. He believed the country needed a powerful central government, but Warren continued to believe in local self-rule. When the Constitution was proposed, Warren, like its other opponents, argued that a central government with taxing powers was the first step toward re-creating the tyranny of the British king.

Warren never changed her mind. In 1805 she published the first history of the Revolution. In it, she argued that "no taxation without representation" applied to any central government, not simply to the government of King George III. Adams never changed his mind either. He believed the Constitution saved the American experiment in representative government. Their disagreement would live on long after these two were gone.

On other issues, however, Warren found an ally in John's wife, Abigail Adams. Both women urged the nation's leaders to "remember the ladies" when they spoke of equality and liberty. Warren stressed the need for formal educational opportunities for women. She lived to see young ladies academies established in many states, but the first women's college, Mt. Holyoke, was not founded until 1837, 23 years after her death.

INTRODUCTION

Between 1776 and 1783, Americans fought to create an independent nation. But what kind of nation would that be? Most free white Americans rejected the notion of an American monarchy and embraced the idea of a republic. Yet a republic could take many forms, and Americans who enjoyed a political voice disagreed on what form was best for the new nation. As a consequence, the transition from independence to nationhood generated heated debate.

How should power be divided between state and national governments? How should laws be made, and by whom? Who should administer those laws? What programs and policies should the national government pursue? How could the government be designed to protect the unalienable individual rights that free white Americans believed they possessed? These questions had to be answered, and soon.

The Articles of Confederation, which joined the states in a "league of friendship," was the nation's first effort at republican government. It guided Americans through the last years of the war and the peace negotiations. It also organized the northwest territories and established the steps toward statehood for a territory. These were major achievements. But many political leaders believed this government was too weak to solve America's economic and social problems or set its course for the future.

In 1787 delegates to a Constitutional Convention produced a new plan of government, the Constitution. It was the result of compromises between the interests of small states and large ones, between southern and northern regional interests, and between those who sought to preserve the sovereignty of the states and those who wished to increase the power of the national government. The Constitution created a stronger national government with the right to regulate interstate and foreign trade, and the power to tax.

Antifederalists, who opposed the new government, argued that it threatened the basic ideals of the Revolution, especially the commitment to local representative government. Revolutionaries such as Mercy Otis Warren and Patrick Henry insisted that state governments were the best guarantee that republican values would survive. Others feared the new government would be dominated by the wealthiest citizens. Federalists, who supported the constitution, argued that the new government would save America from economic disaster, international scorn, and domestic unrest. Leading patriots of the 1760s and 1770s could

The men who drafted the New Jersey constitution took care to include a property qualification for voting but forgot to specify the sex of an eligible voter. Thus women who owned property had the right to vote from 1776 to 1807, when the "error" was corrected. New Jersey did not choose to grant women the vote again for over a century. © *Bettmann/ CORBIS.*

be found on both sides of this debate, but the Federalists carried the day.

The adoption of the Constitution did not magically solve all America's problems. Tensions between northern and southern states were growing more serious. The nation was deeply divided over foreign policy and the lineup of allies and enemies in Europe. And even after the Constitution was ratified, many Americans continued to believe that strong local governments protected their liberties best. Nevertheless, when President George Washington said his farewells to public life in 1796, most Americans were confident that their young nation would survive.

America's First Constitutions

→ *What types of legislatures did the states create?*

→ *What were the major elements of the Articles of Confederation?*

→ *What problems arose in ratifying the Articles?*

The writers of state constitutions were the first to grapple with troubling but fundamental issues—in particular, the definition of citizenship and the extent of political participation. Should women be allowed to vote? Could landless men, servants, free blacks, or apprentices enjoy a political voice? These were exactly the kinds of questions John Adams feared might arise in any discussion of voting rights, or suffrage. They raised the specter of democracy, which he considered a dangerous system. Once the question was posed, he predicted, "There will be no end of it . . . women will demand a vote, lads from twelve to twenty-one will think their rights are not enough attended to, and every man who has not a **farthing** will demand an equal voice with any other in all acts of state."

English political tradition supported Adams's view that political rights were not universal. Under English law, "rights" were, in fact, particular *privileges* that a group enjoyed because of special social circumstances—including age, sex, wealth, or family ties. In their first constitutions, several states extended these privileges to all free white men, a democratic reform but one that still set special conditions of race and sex.

The state constitutions reflected the variety of opinion on this matter of democracy within a republic. At one end of the spectrum was Pennsylvania, whose constitution abolished all property qualifications and granted the vote to all white males in the state. At the other end were states such as Maryland, whose constitution continued to link the ownership of property to voting. To hold office, a Marylander had to meet even higher standards of wealth than the voters.

While constitution writers in every state believed that the legislature was the primary branch of government, they were divided over other issues. Should there be a separate executive branch? Should the legislature have one house or two? What qualifications should be set for officeholders? Again, Pennsylvania produced the most democratic answer to this question. Pennsylvania's constitution concentrated all power to make and to administer law in a one-house, or **unicameral,** elected assembly. The farmers and artisans who helped draft this state constitution eliminated both the executive office and the upper house of the legislature, remembering that these had been strongholds for the wealthy in colonial times. Pennsylvania also required annual elections of all legislators to ensure that the assembly remained responsive to the people's will. In contrast, Maryland and the other states divided powers among a governor, or executive branch, and a **bicameral** legislature, although the legislature enjoyed the broader powers. Members of the upper house in Maryland's legislature had to meet higher property qualifications than those in the lower

house, or assembly. In this manner, political leaders in this state ensured their elite citizens a secure voice in lawmaking.

Pennsylvania and Maryland represented the two ends of the democratic spectrum. The remaining states fell between these poles. The constitutions of New Hampshire, North Carolina, and Georgia followed the democratic tendencies of Pennsylvania. New York, South Carolina, and Virginia chose Maryland's more conservative or traditional approach. New Jersey and Delaware took the middle ground, with at least one surprising result. New Jersey's first constitution, written in 1776, gave the vote to "all free inhabitants" who met certain property qualifications. This requirement denied the ballot to propertyless men but granted voting rights to property-holding women. A writer in the *New York Spectator* in 1797 snidely remarked that New Jersey women "intermeddl[ing] in political affairs" made that state's politics as strange as those of the "emperor of Java [who] never employs any but women in his embassies." Nevertheless, for thirty-one years, at least a few New Jersey women regularly exercised their right to elect the men who governed them. Then, in 1807, state lawmakers took away that right, arguing that "the weaker sex" was too easily manipulated by political candidates to be allowed to vote.

A state's particular history often determined the type of constitution it produced. For example, coastal elites and lowland gentry had dominated the colonial governments of New Hampshire, South Carolina, Virginia, and North Carolina. These states sought to correct this injustice by ensuring representation to small farming districts in interior and frontier regions. The memory of high-handed colonial governors and elitist upper houses in the legislature led Massachusetts lawmakers to severely limit the powers of their first state government. The constitutions in all of these states reflected the strong political voice that ordinary citizens had acquired during the Revolution.

Beginning in the 1780s, however, many states revised their constitutions, increasing the power of the government. At the same time, they added safeguards they believed would prevent abuse. The 1780 Massachusetts constitution was the model for many of these revisions. Massachusetts political leaders built in a

---

farthing   A British coin worth one-fourth of a penny and thus a term used to indicate something of very little value.

unicameral   Having a single legislative house.

bicameral   Having a legislature with two houses.

system of so-called checks and balances among the legislative, judicial, and executive branches to ensure that no branch of the government could grow too powerful or overstep its assigned duties. Over the opposition of many farmers and townspeople, these newer state constitutions also curbed the democratic extension of voting and officeholding privileges. Thus wealth returned as a qualification to govern, although the revised constitutions did not allow the wealthy to tamper with the basic individual rights of citizens. In seven states, these individual rights were safeguarded by a **bill of rights** guaranteeing freedom of speech, religion, and the press as well as the right to assemble and to petition the government.

The Articles of Confederation

There was little popular support for a powerful central government in the early years of the Revolution. Instead, as John Adams later recalled, Americans wanted "a Confederacy of States, each of which must have a separate government." When Pennsylvania's **John Dickinson** submitted a blueprint for a strong national government to the Continental Congress in July of 1776, he watched in wonder and dismay as his colleagues transformed his plan, called **Articles of Confederation,** into a government that preserved the rights and privileges of the states.

Members of the one-house Continental Congress agreed that the new government should also be a unicameral legislature, without an executive branch or a separate judiciary. Democrats like Tom Paine and Samuel Adams praised the Articles' concentration of lawmaking, administrative, and judicial powers in the hands of an elected assembly, whereas conservatives like John Adams condemned the new government as "too democratical," lacking "any equilibrium" among the social classes.

Both Paine and Adams were eager to see a government that could protect the nation from tyranny. Paine, however, feared tyranny from above, from a power-grasping executive or an aristocratic upper house. Adams feared tyranny from below, from a majority of ordinary citizens who might exercise their will recklessly. Tyranny of any sort seemed unlikely from the proposed Confederation government since its powers were so limited. It had no authority to tax or to regulate trade or commerce. These powers remained with the state governments, reflecting the view of many Americans that the behavior of their local governments could be closely monitored. Because it had no taxing power, the Confederation had to depend on the states to finance its operations.

IT MATTERS TODAY

HAVING A VISION FOR THE FUTURE
In 1791, Alexander Hamilton outlined his vision for the economic future of the United States. When Hamilton predicted that manufacturing would, and should, overtake agriculture as the basis for the American economy, he knew he would be setting himself against some of the most important people in the nation. Hamilton's *Report on Manufactures* was not adopted by Congress, but the ideas set forth in it would eventually become central to the economy of the United States. Hamilton's belief that a strong central government with broad economic powers could encourage the fledgling manufacturing industries of the new country set the stage for this country to become the economic superpower it is today.

- Presidential candidates often outline their vision for the nation's future in their inaugural addresses. Select one such inaugural address and analyze the vision it offers.

- In the nineteenth century, reformers established utopian communities. In modern times, minorities and women have put forward their plans for a more egalitarian society. Select one example of these social visions and analyze its contents and the historical circumstances in which it developed.

Dickinson's colleagues agreed that the state legislatures, not the voters themselves, should choose the members of the Confederation Congress. But they did not agree on how many members each state should be allotted. The question boiled down to this: should the states have equal representation or **proportional representation** based on population? Dickinson ar-

---

bill of rights   A formal statement of essential rights and liberties under law.

John Dickinson   Philadelphia lawyer and revolutionary pamphleteer who drafted the Articles of Confederation.

Articles of Confederation   The first constitution of the United States; it created a central government with limited powers, and it was replaced by the Constitution in 1788.

proportional representation   Representation in the legislature based on the population of each state.

MAP 7.1   Western Land Claims After American Independence   This map indicates the claims made by several of the thirteen original states to land west of the Appalachian Mountains and in the New England region. The states based their claims on the colonial charters that governed them before independence. Until this land was ceded to the federal government, new states could not be created here as they were in the Northwest Territory.

gued for a one-state, one-vote rule, but fellow Pennsylvanian Benjamin Franklin insisted that large states such as his own deserved more influence in the new government. This time, Dickinson's argument carried the day, and the Articles established that each state, large or small, was entitled to a single vote when the Confederation roll was called. The same jealous protection of state power also shaped the Confederation's amendment process. Any amendment required the unanimous consent of the states.

Arguments over financial issues were as fierce as those over representation and sovereignty. How was each state's share of the federal operating budget to be determined? Dickinson reasoned that a state's contribution should be based on its population, including inhabitants of every age, sex, and legal condition (free or unfree). This proposal brought southern political leaders to their feet in protest. Because their states had large, dependent slave populations, the burden of tax assessment would fall heavily on slave masters and other free white men. In the end, state as-

sessments for the support of the new federal government were based on the value of land, buildings, and improvements rather than on population. The Continental Congress thus shrewdly avoided any final decision on the larger question of whether slaves were property or people.

When Congress finally submitted the Articles to the states for their approval in November of 1777, the fate of the western territories proved to be the major stumbling block to **ratification.** In his draft of the Articles, Dickinson had designated the Northwest Territory as a national domain. The states with colonial charters granting them land from the Atlantic to the Pacific Oceans protested, each claiming the exclusive right to portions of this vast region bounded by the Ohio River, the Great Lakes, and the Mississippi River (see Map 7.1). New Jersey, Maryland, and other

---

ratification   The act of approving or confirming a proposal.

states whose colonial charters gave them no claim to western territory disagreed. While New Jersey and others eventually gave in, Maryland delegates dug in their heels, insisting that citizens of any state ought to have the right to pioneer the northwestern territories. Maryland's ultimatum—no national domain, no ratification—produced a stalemate. To resolve the problem, Virginia, which claimed the lion's share of the Northwest, agreed to cede all claims to Congress. The other states with claims followed suit, and the crisis was over. In 1781 Maryland became the thirteenth and final state to ratify the Confederation government. Establishing this first national government had taken three and a half years. (The text of the Articles of Confederation is reprinted in the Documents appendix at the back of this book.)

Challenges to the Confederation

→ *What problems undermined the Confederation, and what changes did they produce?*

→ *What was the impact of Shays's Rebellion on national politics?*

→ *What gains did nationalists expect from a stronger central government?*

→ *How did the Confederation establish relations with other nations of the world?*

The members of the first Confederation Congress had barely taken their seats in 1781 when Cornwallis surrendered at Yorktown and peace negotiations began in Paris. Even the most optimistic of the Confederation leaders could see that the postwar problems of the new nation were more daunting than negotiations with French or British diplomats. The physical, psychological, and economic damage caused by the long and brutal home-front war was extensive. In New Jersey and Pennsylvania, communities bore the scars of rape and looting by the British occupying armies. In the South, where civil war had raged, a steady stream of refugees filled the cities. In Charleston, "women and children . . . in the open air round a fire without blanket or any Cloathing but what they had on" were a common sight. In many communities, livestock had vanished, and crops had been seized or ruined. In New England, a natural disaster magnified problems created by the war: insects wiped out wheat crops, worsening food shortages and the local economic depression.

After the war, economic depression spread rapidly throughout the states. Four years after the American victory, Thomas Jefferson wrote enthusiastically from France that a visit to Europe would make Americans "adore [their] country, its climate, its equality, liberty, laws, people and manners." America's unemployed sailors, debt-ridden farmers, and destitute widows and orphans would have found it difficult to share his enthusiasm.

Depression and Financial Crisis

Financial problems plagued wealthy Americans as well as poor farmers and unpaid Revolutionary War veterans. Many merchants had overextended their credit importing foreign goods after the war. Land **speculators** had also borrowed too heavily in order to grab up confiscated loyalist lands or portions of the Northwest Territory. Merchants whose fortunes depended on English markets paid a high price for an American victory that cut ties with England. Planters were hard hit when the demand for staple crops such as rice dropped dramatically after the war, and by 1786 the New England fisheries were operating at only about 80 percent of their prewar level. Not surprisingly, the English did nothing to ease the plight of their former colonists. In fact, Britain banned the sale of American farm products in the West Indies and limited the rights of American vessels to carry goods to and from Caribbean ports. These restrictions hit New England shipbuilding so hard that whole communities were impoverished.

The Confederation government did not create these economic problems, but it had little success in dealing with them. In fact, it was helpless to solve its own most pressing problem—debt. To finance the war, the Continental Congress had printed more than $240 million in paper money backed by "good faith" rather than by the hard currency of gold and silver. As doubts grew that the government could ever **redeem** these continentals for hard currency, their value fell rapidly. The scornful phrase "not worth a continental" indicated popular attitudes about the government as

---

speculators A person who buys and sells land or some other commodity in the hope of making a profit.

redeem To pay a specified sum in return for something; in this case, to make good on paper money issued by the government by exchanging it for hard currency, silver or gold.

well as its finances. Congress was also embarrassed by the substantial debts to foreign nations it was unable to repay.

In 1781 the government turned to Philadelphia shipper and merchant **Robert Morris** for advice on how to raise funds. Morris, known as a financial wizard, came up with a solution: ask the states to approve federal **tariffs,** or import taxes, on certain foreign goods. The tariffs would provide desperately needed income for the Confederation and relieve the states from having to contribute funding many could scarcely afford. For three years, beginning in 1782, Congress sought the necessary unanimous approval for a duty of 5 percent on imported goods, payable in hard currency rather than paper money. But the plan failed because both Virginia and Rhode Island said no. To add insult to injury, some states promptly passed their own tariffs on imported goods. The failure of the tariff strategy prompted one critic of the Confederation government to comment: "Thirteen wheels require a steady and powerful regulation to keep them in good order." Until Congress could act without the unanimous consent of all states, nothing could "prevent the machine from becoming useless."

The Northwest Ordinances

Still in financial crisis, the Confederation pinned its hopes for solvency on the sale of western lands in the Northwest Territory. Here at least Congress had the authority to act, for it could set policy for the settlement and governance of all national territories. In 1784, 1785, and 1787, a national land policy took shape in three **Northwest Ordinances.** These regulations had political significance beyond their role in raising money for the government: they guaranteed that the men and women who moved west would not be colonial dependents of the original states.

The 1784 ordinance established that five new states would be carved out of the region, each to stand on an equal footing with the older, original states. In the earliest stages of settlement, each territory would have an appointed governor. As soon as the number of eligible voters in the territory increased sufficiently, however, they could elect a representative assembly, and the territory could begin to govern itself. Once a state constitution was drafted and approved by the territory's voters, the new state could send elected representatives to the Confederation Congress. Ohio, Indiana, Illinois, Michigan, and Wisconsin each followed this path to full statehood (see Map 7.2).

Author of many of *The Federalist Papers* essays and first secretary of the treasury, Alexander Hamilton was admired for his intellectual brilliance and his political vision, even by bitter political opponents. Hamilton was a true American success story: an illegitimate son of a Scottish merchant, he immigrated to the mainland during his teenage years, where he enjoyed a spectacular career. Hamilton served as Washington's aide-de-camp, became a leader of the New York bar, and entered New York's social elite by his marriage into the Schuyler family. In 1804, a political enemy, Aaron Burr, killed Hamilton in a duel. *"Alexander Hamilton" by Charles Wilson Peale. Courtesy of the Independence National Historical Park Collection.*

The ordinance of 1785 spelled out the terms for sale of the land. Mapmakers divided the region into five districts and subdivided each district into townships. Each township, covering 36 square miles, was broken down in a gridlike pattern of thirty-six 640-acre plots. Congress intended to auction these plots off to individual settlers rather than to land speculators, but when the original selling price of $1 per acre in hard

Robert Morris Pennsylvania merchant and financial expert who advised the Continental Congress during the Revolution and served as a fundraiser for the Confederation government.

tariffs A tax on imported or exported goods.

Northwest Ordinances Three laws (1784, 1785, 1787) that dealt with the sale of public lands in the Northwest Territory and established a plan for the admission of new states to the Union.

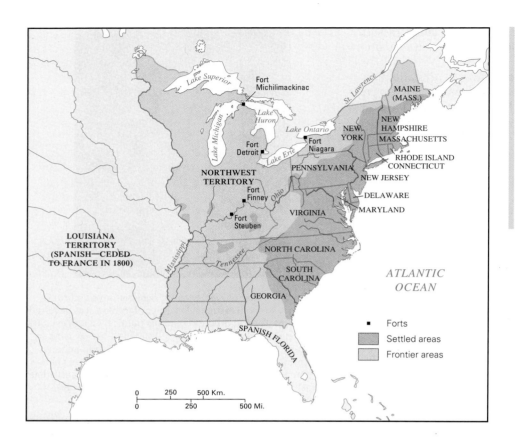

MAP 7.2 The United States in 1787 This map shows the extent of American westward settlement in 1787 and the limits placed on that settlement by French and Spanish claims west of the Mississippi and in Florida. Plans for the creation of five states in the Northwest Territory were approved by Congress in 1787, ensuring that the settlers in this region would enjoy the same political rights as the citizens of the original thirteen states.

currency proved too high for the average farm family, Congress lowered the price and lifted the ban on sales to speculators.

The ordinance of 1787 established that sixty thousand white males were needed for a territory to apply for admission as a state. Thomas Jefferson, who drafted this ordinance, took care to protect the liberties of the settlers with a bill of rights and to ban slavery north of the Ohio River. Jefferson's provisions trampled on the rights of American Indians, however, for their claims to the land were ignored in favor of white settlement.

Diplomatic Problems

The Confederation's diplomatic record was as discouraging as its financial plight. Problems with the British and the Indians arose in the West as settlers began to pour into the Northwest Territory. Although the British had agreed in the Treaty of Paris (1783) to evacuate their western forts, they refused to take any steps until the Americans honored their treaty obligations to repay their war debts and return loyalists' confiscated property. From their strongholds in the

territories, the British encouraged Indian resistance by selling arms and supplies to the Shawnees, Miamis, and Delawares. These tribes, and others, denied the legitimacy of the two treaties that turned over the northwest territories to the Americans.

American claims to western lands rested on the 1784 **Treaty of Fort Stanwix** and the 1785 **Hopewell Treaties.** The former, negotiated with the remnants of the Iroquois confederacy, opened all Iroquois lands to white settlement; the second, signed by Choctaw, Chickasaw, and Cherokee chiefs, granted Americans settlement rights in what was then the Southwest. The Shawnees and their allies challenged both treaties. By what right, they asked, did those tribes speak for them?

Treaty of Fort Stanwix Treaty signed in 1784 that opened all Iroquois lands to white settlement.
Hopewell Treaties Treaties signed by 1785 in which the Choctaws, Chickasaws, and Cherokees granted American settlement rights in the Southwest.

Throughout the 1780s, the Confederation and the Indians resorted to warfare rather than negotiation.

The Confederation preferred diplomacy to armed conflict when dealing with European powers. Congress sent John Adams to Great Britain, but not even this persistent and dedicated New Englander could wring any concessions from the British. The American bargaining position was weak. Commercial ties with France and Holland had not developed as rapidly after independence as some patriots had predicted, and thus American merchants remained economically dependent on England as a source of manufactured goods, and on British possessions in the Caribbean for trade. Britain had no desire to end America's economic dependency.

The Confederation had problems with allies as well as with enemies. Spain, for example, was alarmed by American settlers pouring into the land east of the Mississippi. Almost fifty thousand Americans had already moved into what would become Kentucky and Tennessee, and thousands more were eager to farm the rich, river-fed lands of the region. The Spanish government, which controlled access to the Mississippi River and the port of New Orleans, responded by banning all American traffic on the river. The Confederation appointed **John Jay,** fresh from his success as a Paris peace commissioner, to negotiate with Spain on this and other issues, but Jay could make no headway.

The Confederation had no better luck in dealing with the **Barbary pirates.** For many years, the rulers of Algiers, Tunisia, Tripoli, and Morocco had taken advantage of their location along the Barbary Coast of North Africa to attack European vessels engaged in Mediterranean trade. Most European nations kept this piracy under control by paying blackmail or by providing armed escorts for their merchant ships. The Barbary pirates showed no mercy to American ships, which were no longer protected by the British bribes or the royal navy. In 1785 a New England ship was captured, its cargo seized, and the crew stripped and sold into slavery. Though appalled and outraged, the Confederation Congress, with no navy and no authority to create one, could do little to ensure safe passage for American ships on the Mediterranean.

A Farmers' Revolt

From the "Wild Yankees" of Pennsylvania's Susquehanna Valley to the "Liberty-Men" of Maine, eighteenth-century backcountry settlers organized to resist speculators' claims on the land and to demand that political power remain with local communities rather than state governments. After the Revolution,

these rebels used the language of republicanism to defend their protests and to justify the occasional violence that erupted in their areas. "We fought for land & liberty, & it is hard if we can't enjoy either," wrote one **squatter** in response to a land speculator's claim to his farm. "Who can have a better right to the land than we who have fought for it, subdued it & made it valuable?" Farmers suffering from the postwar economic depression had a long list of complaints, including high rents and land prices, heavy taxes, debts, burdensome legal fees, and the failure of central governments to provide protection from Indian attacks and frontier bandits. These backcountry settlers often made members of the political and economic elite uneasy just as their colonial counterparts—the Regulators and the Paxton Boys—had done. When farmers in western Massachusetts began an organized protest in 1786, this uneasiness reached crisis proportions.

The farmers of western Massachusetts were among the hardest hit by the postwar depression and the rising inflation that accompanied it. Many were deeply in debt to creditors who held mortgages on their farms and lands. In the 1780s, these farmers looked to the state government for temporary relief, hoping that it would pass **stay laws** that would temporarily suspend creditors' rights to foreclose on, or seize, lands and farm equipment. The Massachusetts assembly responded sympathetically and thus aroused the anger of merchants and other creditors who were themselves deeply in debt to foreign manufacturers. The upper house of the state legislature, with its more elite members, sided with the creditors and blocked the passage of stay laws. The Massachusetts government then shocked the farmers by raising taxes.

In 1786 hundreds of farmers revolted. They believed they were protecting their rights and their communities as true republicans must do, but their creditors

John Jay New York lawyer and diplomat who negotiated with Great Britain and Spain on behalf of the Confederation; he later became the first chief justice of the Supreme Court and negotiated the Jay Treaty with England.

Barbary pirates Pirates along the Barbary Coast of North Africa who attacked European and American vessels engaged in Mediterranean trade.

squatter A person who settles on unoccupied land to which he or she has no legal claim.

stay laws Laws suspending the right of creditors to foreclose on debtors; they were designed to protect indebted farmers from losing their land.

In 1786, western Massachusetts farmers began an agrarian revolt against high taxes and mortgage foreclosures that soon spread to other New England states. Most of the leaders of the uprising, known as Shays's Rebellion, were veteran officers of the American Revolution; many had participated in the protest and resistance that preceded the war. The government of Massachusetts crushed the rebellion, jailing some leaders and driving Daniel Shays to seek asylum in Vermont. News of the uprising prompted elite political leaders like George Washington and Alexander Hamilton to press for a more powerful central government, able to ensure "law and order" throughout the nation. *National Portrait Gallery, Smithsonian Institution/Art Resource, NY.*

viewed their actions quite differently. To them, the farmers appeared to be dangerous rebels threatening the state with "anarchy, confusion, and total ruin." They accused **Daniel Shays,** a 39-year-old veteran of Bunker Hill, of leading the revolt.

In 1786, farmers known as Shays's rebels closed several courts and freed a number of their fellow farmers from debtors' prison. Their actions struck a chord among desperate farmers in other New England states, and the rebellion began to spread. Fear of a widespread uprising spurred the Massachusetts government to action. It sent a military force of six hundred to Springfield, where more than a thousand farmers, most armed with pitchforks rather than guns, had gathered to close the local courthouse. When the farmers were within range, the troops let loose a cannon barrage that killed four and set the remaining men to flight. Then, on February 4, 1787, four thousand troops surprised the remaining "rebels" in the village of Petersham. Although Daniel Shays managed to escape, the farmers' revolt was over.

Shays's Rebellion revealed the temper of the times. When the government did not respond to their needs, the farmers acted as they had been encouraged to act in the prerevolutionary years. They organized, and they protested—and when government still did not respond, they took up arms against what they considered to be injustice. Across the country, many Americans sympathized with these farmers. But just as many did not. Abigail Adams, whose husband, John, had been labeled an irresponsible troublemaker by loyalist opponents only a decade earlier, turned this language against the leaders of the farmers' revolt. She condemned them as "ignorant, restless, desperadoes,

without conscience or principles," who were persuading a "deluded multitude to follow their standards."

The revolt stirred up fears of slave rebellions and pitched battles between debtors and creditors, haves and have-nots. Above all, it raised doubts among influential political figures about the ability of either state governments or the Confederation to preserve the rule of law. To men such as George Washington, now a planter and private citizen, Shays's Rebellion was a national tragedy, not for its participants but for the reputation of the United States. When the farmers' protest began, Washington wrote to authorities in Massachusetts urging them to act fairly but decisively. "If they have real grievances," he said, the government should acknowledge them. But if not, authorities should "employ the force of government against them at once. . . . To be more exposed to the eyes of the world, and more contemptible than we already are, is hardly possible."

The Revolt of the "Better Sort"

In important ways, the Articles of Confederation embodied the desires of the revolutionary generation for a limited central government that directed diplomacy and coordinated military defense but left the major tasks of governing to local representative governments. Yet such a government was proving to have troubling

Daniel Shays Revolutionary War veteran considered the leader of the farmers' uprising in western Massachusetts called Shays's Rebellion.

In 1876, Thomas Pritchard Rossiter painted his *Signing of the Constitution of the United States* honoring a group of statesmen that included James Madison, Alexander Hamilton, and George Washington, who presided over the Constitutional Convention. Thomas Jefferson, absent because of his duties as ambassador to France, referred to the fifty-five delegates who crafted the Constitution as a gathering of "demigods." *Signing of the Constitution of the United States by Thomas Pritchard Rossiter, 1867. Fraunces Tavern Museum.*

costs and trying consequences. By 1786, members of the nation's elite, or the "better sort," believed the survival of the nation was in question. Washington predicted "the worst consequences from a half-starved, limping government, always moving upon crutches and tottering at every step." For him, for Hamilton, and for others like them who thought of themselves as **nationalists,** the solution was clear. "I do not conceive we can long exist as a nation," Washington remarked, "without having lodged somewhere a power which will pervade the whole Union in as energetic a manner as the authority of the State government extends over the several states." Here was a different form of republican government to consider.

Support for a stronger national government grew in the key states of Virginia, Massachusetts, and New York. Men of wealth and political experience urged a reform agenda that included giving the central government taxing powers, devising an easier amendment process, and providing some legal means to enforce national government policies that a state might oppose. They wanted a government that could establish stable diplomatic and trade relations with foreign countries. They also wanted a national government able to preserve their property and their peace of mind. One of the driving forces behind this appeal for reform was Alexander Hamilton.

In 1786 a group of influential Virginians called for a meeting on interstate trade restrictions that placed import taxes on goods carried from state to state. The Confederation Congress approved a meeting of state delegates at Annapolis, Maryland, to discuss this issue. But the meeting organizers had a second agenda: to test the waters on revising the nation's constitution. Although only a third of the states participated in the Annapolis conference, nationalists were convinced that their position had substantial support. They asked Congress to call a convention in Philadelphia so that political leaders could continue to discuss interstate commerce problems—and other aspects of government reform. Some members of Congress were reluctant, but news of Shays's Rebellion tipped the balance in favor of the convention.

Creating a New Constitution

→ *What major compromises did the framers make in writing the new constitution?*

→ *What safeguards did James Madison see in his "checks and balances" system?*

Late in May 1787, George Washington called the convention to order in Philadelphia. Before him sat

nationalists Americans who preferred a strong central government rather than the limited government prescribed in the Articles of Confederation.

delegates from eleven of the thirteen states (New Hampshire's delegates did not arrive until late July), closeted behind curtained windows and locked doors in the heat and humidity of a Philadelphia summer. These secrecy precautions stemmed, they said, from their wish to speak frankly about the nation's political and economic problems without fear that foreign governments would use that information to their advantage. They were also looking out for their own reputations in their home states for they quickly realized they might have to make compromises that would be unpopular with their state governments. Only Rhode Island refused to participate, accusing the convention of masquerading as a discussion of interstate trade in order to drastically revise the national government. The accusation by "Rogue's Island," as critics called the smallest state, was correct. The fifty-five prominent and prosperous men did expect to make significant changes in the structure of the government. Here was another reason to keep the deliberations secret.

Most of the men gathered in that room were lawyers, merchants, or planters—Americans of social standing though not necessarily intellectual achievement. When the absent Thomas Jefferson later referred to the convention members as "demigods," he was probably thinking of the likes of 81-year-old Benjamin Franklin, whose sparkling wit and crafty political style set him apart from his colleagues despite his advanced age; or of the articulate, brilliant Alexander Hamilton of New York, whose reputation as a financial mastermind equal to the Confederation's adviser Robert Morris was well established; or of Pennsylvania's Gouverneur Morris, who was widely admired for his intelligence as well as for his literary skills, and his fellow delegate, the logical and learned James Wilson; and finally of **James Madison,** the prim Virginia planter who turned out to be the chief architect of a new constitution. Several notable men were absent. Jefferson, author of the Declaration of Independence, was abroad serving as ambassador to France. John Adams, driving force behind the influential Massachusetts constitution of 1780, was representing the United States in the same capacity in London. And the two great propagandists of the Revolution, Samuel Adams and Thomas Paine, were also absent, for both opposed any revision of the Articles of Confederation.

Revise or Replace?

Most of the delegates were nationalists, but they did not necessarily agree on how best to proceed. Should they revise the Articles or abandon them? Eventually,

Edmund Randolph of Virginia, Charles Pinckney of South Carolina, William Paterson of New Jersey, and Alexander Hamilton himself would present blueprints for the new government. But it was the Virginia planter and lawyer Edmund Randolph who first captured the convention's attention with his delegation's proposal, which effectively amended the Articles of Confederation out of existence.

Although Randolph introduced the **Virginia Plan** on the convention floor, James Madison was its guiding spirit. The 36-year-old Madison was no dashing figure. He was small, frail, charmless, and a hypochondriac. But he was highly respected as a scholar of philosophy and history and as an astute political theorist, and his long service as a member of the Virginia legislature and in the Confederation Congress gave him a practical understanding of politics and government. At the convention, Madison brought all his knowledge to bear on this question: what was the best form of government for a strong republic? He concluded, as John Adams had done early in the 1780s, that the fear of tyranny should not rule out a powerful national government. Any dangerous abuse of power could be avoided if internal checks and balances were built into the republican structure.

Madison's Virginia Plan embodied this conviction. It called for a government with three distinct branches—legislative, executive, and judicial—to replace the Confederation's Congress, which was performing all three functions. By dividing power in this way, Madison intended to ensure that no individual or group of men could wield too much authority, especially for self-interested reasons. Madison's plan also gave Congress the power to **veto** laws passed by the state legislatures and the right to intervene directly if a state acted to interrupt "the harmony of the United States."

The notion of a strong government able, as Madison put it, "to control the governed" but also "obliged to control itself" was endorsed by the delegates. But they were in sharp disagreement over

James Madison   Virginia planter and political theorist known as the "father of the Constitution"; he became the fourth president of the United States.

Virginia Plan   Fourteen proposals by the Virginia delegation to the Constitutional Convention for creating a more powerful central government and giving states proportional representation in a bicameral legislature.

veto   The power or right of one branch of government to reject the decisions of another branch.

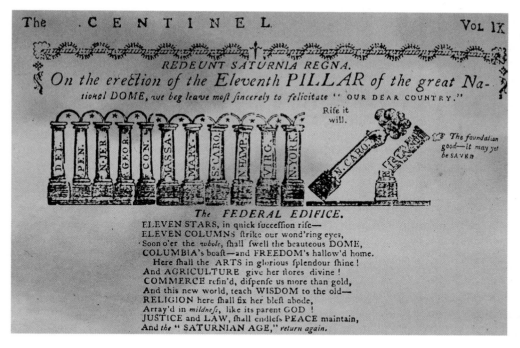

The battles over ratification of the Constitution began in Fall of 1787. It took only 9 states to ensure the constitution would go into effect. As this newspaper drawing illustrates, Delaware was the first to approve the new government and New Hampshire the ninth. But it was ratification by the critical states of Virginia and New York that ensured the establishment of that government. By 1788, only North Carolina and the state others called "Rogues Island" remained. *The Granger Collection, New York.*

many specific issues in the Virginia Plan. The greatest controversy swirled around representation in the legislative branch—Congress—a controversy familiar to those who had helped draft the Articles of Confederation. Madison proposed a bicameral legislature with membership in each house based on proportional representation. Large states supported the plan, for representation based on population worked to their advantage. Small states objected heatedly, calling for equal representation for each state. Small states argued that proportional representation would leave them helpless against a federal government dominated by the large ones. Small-state delegates threw their support behind a second proposal, the **New Jersey Plan,** which also called for three branches of government and gave Congress the power to tax and to control national commerce. This plan, however, preserved an equal voice and vote for every state within a unicameral legislature.

Debate over the two plans dragged on through the steamy days of a June heat wave. Tempers flared, and at times the deadlock seemed hopeless. Threats to walk out of the convention came from both sides. A compromise was needed to prevent distrust and hostility from destroying the convention. That compromise, hammered out by a special committee, was presented by Roger Sherman of Connecticut. Their **Great Compromise** used the idea of a two-house legislature in order to satisfy both sides. It proposed proportional representation in the lower house (the House of Representatives) and equal representation in the upper house (the Senate).

The Great Compromise resolved the first major controversy at the convention but opened the door to the

New Jersey Plan A proposal submitted by the New Jersey delegation at the Constitutional Convention for creating a government in which the states would have equal representation in a unicameral legislature.

Great Compromise A proposal calling for a bicameral legislature with equal representation for the states in one house and proportional representation in the other.

next one. The delegates had to decide how the representatives to each house were to be elected. A compromise also settled this issue. State legislatures would select senators, and the eligible voters of each state would directly elect their state's representatives to the lower house. This formula allowed the delegates to acknowledge the sovereignty of the state governments but also to accommodate the republican commitment to popular elections in a representative government.

The delegates faced one last stumbling block over representation: which Americans were to be counted to determine a state's population? This issue remained as divisive as it had been when the Articles of Confederation were drafted. Southern delegates took care to argue that slaves, who composed as much as one-third and sometimes more of each plantation state's residents, should not be included in the population count on which a state's tax assessments were based. On the other hand, they insisted that these slaves should be included in the population count that determined a state's seats in the House of Representatives. Northern delegates protested, declaring that slaves should be considered property in both instances. These delegates were motivated by self-interest rather than a desire for consistency, for if slaves were considered property, not people, the North would dominate the lower house.

A compromise that defied reason but made brilliant political sense settled this question. The **Three-Fifths Compromise** established that three-fifths of the slave population would be included in a state's critical headcount. A clause was then added guaranteeing that the slave trade would continue for a twenty-year period. Some southern leaders, especially in South Carolina, wanted this extension badly because they had lost many slaves during the Revolution. But not all slave owners concurred. Virginia's George Mason, a slave owner himself, spoke passionately of the harm slavery did to his region. It not only prevented white immigration to the South, Mason said, but infected the moral character of the slave master. "Every master of slaves," Mason argued, "is born a petty tyrant." Slave owners "bring the judgment of heaven upon a country," particularly one intended as a republic.

Drafting an Acceptable Document

The Three-Fifths Compromise ended weeks of debate over representation. No other issue arose to provoke such controversy, and the delegates proceeded calmly to implement the principle of checks and balances.

For example, the president, or executive, was named commander in chief of the armed forces and given primary responsibility for foreign affairs. To balance these **executive powers,** Congress was given the right to declare war and to raise an army. Congress received the critical "power of the purse," but this power to tax and to spend the revenues raised by taxation was checked in part by the president's power to veto congressional legislation. As yet another balance, Congress could override a presidential veto by the vote of a two-thirds majority. Following the same logic of distributing power, the delegates gave authority to the president to name federal court judges, but the Senate had to approve all such appointments.

Occasionally, as in the system for electing the president, the convention chose awkward or cumbersome procedures. For example, many delegates opposed direct popular election of the president. Some agreed with the elitist sentiments of George Mason, who said this "would be as unnatural . . . as it would [be] to refer a trial of colours to a blind man." Others simply doubted that the citizens of one state would be familiar enough with a candidate from a distant state to make a valid judgment. In an age of slow communication, few men besides George Washington had a truly national reputation. Should the president be chosen by state legislators who had perhaps worked in government with political leaders from outside their states? Delegates rose to object that this solution threatened too great a concentration of power in the legislators' hands. As a somewhat clumsy compromise, the delegates created the **Electoral College,** a group of special electors to be chosen by the states to vote for presidential candidates. Each state would be entitled to a number of electors equal to the number of its senators and representatives sitting in Congress, but no one serving in Congress at the time of a presidential election would be eligible to be an elector. If two presidential candidates received the same number of Electoral

Three-Fifths Compromise   An agreement to count three-fifths of a state's slave population for purposes of determining a state's representation in the House of Representatives.

executive powers   Powers given to the president by the Constitution.

Electoral College   A body of electors chosen by the states to elect the president and vice president; each state may select a number of electors equal to the number of its senators and representatives in Congress.

College votes, or if no candidate received a majority of the Electoral College votes, then the House of Representatives would choose the new president. This complex procedure honored the **discretion** of the state governments in appointing the electors but limited the power of individuals already holding office.

The long summer of conflict and compromise ended with a new plan for a national government. Would the delegates be willing to put their names to the document they had created in secrecy and by overreaching their authority? Benjamin Franklin fervently hoped so. Though sick and bedridden, Franklin was carried by friends to the convention floor, where he pleaded for unanimous support for the new government. When a weary George Washington at last declared the meetings adjourned on September 17, 1787, only a handful of delegates left without signing what the convention hoped would be the new American constitution.

Resolving the Conflict of Vision

→ *What were the Antifederalists' arguments against the Constitution? What were the Federalists' arguments in its favor?*

→ *What was the outcome of the ratification process?*

The framers of the Constitution called for special state **ratifying conventions** to discuss and then vote on the proposed change of government. They believed that these conventions would give citizens a more direct role in this important political decision. But the ratifying procedure also gave the framers two advantages. First, it allowed them to bypass the state legislatures, which stood to lose power under the new government and were thus likely to oppose it. Second, it allowed them to nominate their supporters and campaign for their election to the ratifying conventions. The framers added to their advantage by declaring that the approval of only nine states was necessary to establish the Constitution. Reluctantly, the Confederation Congress agreed to all these terms and procedures. By the end of September 1787, Congress had passed the proposed Constitution on to the states, triggering the next round of debates over America's political future.

The Ratification Controversy

As Alexander Hamilton boasted, "The new Constitution has in favor of its success . . . [the] very great weight of influence of the persons who framed it." Hamilton was correct. Men of wealth, political experience, and frequently great persuasive powers put

their skills to the task of achieving ratification. But what Hamilton did not mention was that many revolutionary heroes and political leaders opposed the Constitution with equal intensity—most notably Patrick Henry, Samuel Adams, and George Clinton, the popular governor of New York. Boston's most effective revolutionary propagandist, Mercy Otis Warren, immediately took up her pen to attack the Constitution and even **canvassed** her neighbors to stand firm against what she called an assault on republican values. Thus the leadership on both sides of the issue was drawn from the political elite of the revolutionary generation.

The pro-Constitution forces won an early and important victory by clouding the language of the debate. They abandoned the label "nationalists," which drew attention to their belief in a strong central government, and chose to call themselves **Federalists,** a name originally associated with a system of strong state governments and limited national government. This shrewd tactic cheated opponents of the Constitution out of their rightful name. The pro-Constitution forces then dubbed their opponents **Antifederalists.** This label implied that their adversaries were negative thinkers, pessimists, and a group lacking a program of its own.

Although the philosophical debate over the best form of government for a republic was an important one, voters considered other, practical factors in choosing a Federalist or Antifederalist position. Voters in states with a stable or recovering economy were likely to oppose the Constitution because the Confederation system gave their states greater independent powers. Those in small, geographically or economically disadvantaged states were likely to favor a strong central government that could protect them from their competitive neighbors. Thus the small states of Delaware and Connecticut ratified the Constitution quickly, but in New York and Virginia ratification was hotly contested.

To some degree, Federalist and Antifederalist camps matched the divisions between the relatively urban,

---

discretion The power or right to act according to one's own judgment.

ratifying conventions A meeting of delegates in each state to determine whether that state would ratify the Constitution.

canvass A survey that is taken.

Federalists Supporters of the Constitution; they desired a strong central government.

Antifederalists Opponents of the Constitution; they believed a strong central government was a threat to American liberties and rights.

market-oriented communities of the Atlantic coast and the frontier or rural communities of the inland areas (see Map 7.3). For example, the backcountry of North and South Carolina and the less economically developed areas of Virginia saw little benefit in a stronger central government, especially one that might tax them. But coastal centers of trade and overseas commerce such as Boston, New York City, and Charleston were eager to see an aggressive and effective national policy regarding foreign and interstate trade. In these urban centers, artisans, shopkeepers, and even laborers joined forces with wealthy merchants and shippers to support the Constitution as they had once joined them to make the Revolution. No generalization can explain every political choice, of course. No economic or social group was unified under the Federalist or the Antifederalist banner. On the whole, however, it can be said that the Federalists were better organized, had more resources at their disposal, and campaigned more effectively than the Antifederalists.

In the public debates, the political differences between the Federalists and Antifederalists were sharply defined. Antifederalists rejected the claim that the nation was in a "critical period," facing economic and political collapse. As one New Yorker put it: "I deny that we are in immediate danger of anarchy and commotions. Nothing but the passions of wicked and ambitious men will put us in the least danger. . . . The country is in profound peace . . . and the lives, the liberty and property of individuals is protected." Nevertheless, the Federalists were successful in portraying the moment as a crisis or turning point for the young republic—and in insisting that their plan for recovery was better than no plan at all.

The Antifederalists struck hard against the dangerous elitism they believed they saw in the Constitution. They portrayed the Federalists as a privileged, sophisticated minority, ready and able to tyrannize the people if their powerful national government were ratified. Be careful, one Massachusetts man warned, because "these lawyers, and men of learning, and moneyed men, that talk so finely and gloss over matters so smoothly, to make us poor illiterate people swallow down the pill, expect to get into Congress themselves." And New York Antifederalist Melancton Smith predicted that the proposed new government would lead inevitably to rule by a wealthy, unrepresentative minority. Smith argued with simple eloquence that members of a House of Representatives who had so much power ought to "resemble those they represent . . . and be disposed to seek their true interests." But this was impossible, Smith reasoned, when the representative body was so small

and the political ambitions and financial resources of the elite were so great. The Virginia revolutionary leader Richard Henry Lee was flabbergasted that his generation would even consider ratification of the Constitution. "'Tis really astonishing," he wrote to a New York opponent in the summer of 1788, "that the same people, who have just emerged from a long and cruel war in defense of liberty, should agree to fix an elective **despotism** upon themselves and posterity."

The Antifederalists' most convincing evidence of elitism and its potential for tyranny was that the Constitution lacked a bill of rights. The proposed new national Constitution contained no written guarantees of the people's right to assemble or to worship as they saw fit, and it gave no assurances of a trial by jury in civil cases or the right to bear arms. The framers believed these rights were secure because most state constitutions contained strong guarantees of these rights. But Antifederalists put the question to both voters and delegates: what did this glaring omission tell Americans about the framers' respect for republican ideals? The only conclusion, Antifederalists argued, was that the Constitution was a threat to republican principles of representative government, a vehicle for elite rule, and a document unconcerned with the protection of the people's individual liberties. Its supporters, Antifederalists warned, were "crying 'wolf'" over economic and social problems in order to seize power.

The Federalist strategy was indeed to portray America in crisis. They pointed to the stagnation of the American economy, to the potential for revolt and social anarchy, and to the contempt that other nations showed toward the young republic. They also argued that the Constitution fulfilled and could preserve the republican ideals of the Revolution far better than the Articles of Confederation. Their cause was put forward most convincingly by Alexander Hamilton, James Madison, and John Jay, who entered the newspaper wars over ratification in the key state of New York. Together, they produced a series of essays known today as the *Federalist Papers*. Although these 85 essays were all signed "Publius," Hamilton wrote 51 of them, Madison 29, and Jay 5. Their common theme was the link between American prosperity and a strong central government.

despotism   Rule by a tyrant.
Federalist Papers   Essays written by Alexander Hamilton, John Jay, and James Madison in support of the Constitution.

MAP 7.3 **The Federalist and Antifederalist Struggle over the Constitution** The battle over ratification of the Constitution was fiercely fought throughout 1787 and 1788. This map shows the areas of strong antifederalism, the areas of Federalist strength, and the scattered pockets where opinion was evenly divided.

The Federalist Victory

Practical politics rather than political theory seemed to influence the outcome of many of the ratifying conventions. Delaware, New Jersey, Georgia, and Connecticut—all small states—quickly approved the Constitution. In Pennsylvania, Antifederalists in the rural western regions lost control of the convention to the Federalists and thus that state also endorsed the Constitution. In the remaining states, including

Massachusetts, Virginia, and New York, the two sides were more evenly matched.

Antifederalists were in the majority in the Massachusetts convention, where most of the delegates were small farmers from the western counties and more than twenty of them had participated in Shays's Rebellion. The Federalists' strategy was to make political deals with key delegates, winning over Antifederalists such as Samuel Adams and John Hancock, for example, with promises to demand the addition of a bill of rights to the Constitution. Class divisions, however, turned out to be critical during the convention balloting. Men of high social and economic status voted 107 to 34 for ratification. The less wealthy delegates were more divided, voting against the Constitution by a ratio of 2 to 1. At the final count, a 19-vote margin gave the Federalists a narrow victory in Massachusetts.

After Massachusetts ratified, the fight shifted to New Hampshire. Here, too, Federalists won by a small majority. Rhode Island, true to its history of opposition to strong central authority, rejected the Constitution decisively. But Maryland and South Carolina ratified it, and the tide in favor of the new government influenced the next critical vote: that of Virginia. There, Antifederalist leaders Lee, Henry, and James Monroe focused on the absence of a bill of rights in the proposed Constitution. James Madison and George Washington directed the Federalist counterattack. In the end, the presence of Washington proved irresistible because Virginians knew that this war hero and admired colleague was certain to be the first president of the United States if the Constitution went into effect. When the vote was taken on June 25, 1788, Virginia became the tenth state to ratify the new government.

New York's battle was equally intense. Acknowledging that the absence of a bill of rights was a major political error, Federalist leaders Jay and Hamilton made a public pledge to support its inclusion. By then, however, ten states had already ratified the Constitution, and so the new government was a **fait accompli.** Realizing this, on July 26, 1788, a majority of New York delegates voted yes on ratification.

President George Washington

The election of senators and Congress members was almost complete by February 4, 1789, when presidential electors met in each state to choose the nation's first president. Although George Washington did not seek the position, he knew the nation expected him to

The unknown artist of *The Federal Procession in New York, 1788* captured the jubilant mood of Americans as they celebrated their new Constitution with parades, bonfires, and banquets. As the "Ship of State" float indicates, New Yorkers were particularly eager to acknowledge the role of their own Alexander Hamilton in launching the new government. *Library of Congress.*

serve. The general was among the very few in the revolutionary generation to have a national reputation. He was hailed as the hero of the Revolution, and he looked and acted the part of the dignified, virtuous patriot. Washington became president by a unanimous vote of the Electoral College. For regional balance, New Englander John Adams was chosen vice president.

In April 1789, as Washington made his way from Virginia to his inauguration in New York City, the temporary national capital, Americans thronged to greet him with parades, sharply dressed military escorts, and choruses of church bells and cannon fire. Near Trenton, New Jersey, the scene of his first victory in the Revolutionary War, he passed through a triumphal arch 20 feet high, supported by thirteen pillars, and inscribed in gold with the date of the Battle of Trenton. As his barge took him across the Hudson River, private boats sailed alongside, their passengers singing songs composed in his honor. Thousands of supporters gathered to see him take the oath of office. Yet amid the celebration, Washington and his closest

---

fait accompli   An accomplished deed or fact that cannot be reversed or undone.

TABLE 7.1   Ratification of the U.S. Constitution

State	Date of Ratification	Vote
Delaware	December 7, 1787	30-0
Pennsylvania	December 12, 1787	46-23
New Jersey	December 18, 1787	38-0
Georgia	January 2, 1788	26-0
Connecticut	January 9, 1788	128-40
Massachusetts	February 6, 1788	187-168
Maryland	April 28, 1788	63-11
South Carolina	May 23, 1788	149-73
New Hampshire	June 21, 1788	57-47
Virginia	June 25, 1788	89-79
New York	July 26, 1788	30-27
North Carolina	November 21, 1789	194-77
Rhode Island	May 29, 1790	34-32

advisers knew the future was uncharted and uncertain. "We are in a wilderness," Madison observed, "without a single footstep to guide us."

Washington agreed. The new president understood that he symbolized a national experiment in government and that friends and critics of the United States would be closely watching his behavior in office. Since he was the first to hold the presidency, his every action had the potential to become a ritual and to set a precedent for those who followed. "Few . . . can realize," he wrote, "the difficult and delicate part which a man in my situation has to act. . . . I walk on untrodden ground."

Washington proceeded with caution and deliberation. He labored carefully over each of his selections to the almost one thousand federal offices waiting to be filled. He took particular care in choosing the men to head four executive departments created with approval from Congress. Naming his **protégé** Alexander Hamilton to the Treasury Department was probably Washington's easiest decision. He asked the Massachusetts military strategist Henry Knox to head the War Department and fellow Virginian Edmund Randolph to serve as attorney general. Washington chose another Virginian, Thomas Jefferson, to be secretary of state. Over time, the president established a pattern of meeting with this **cabinet** of advisers on a regular basis to discuss policy matters. Together, they made major decisions and, as Washington expected, expressed serious disagreements that exposed him to differing viewpoints on policy.

protégé   An individual whose welfare or career is promoted by an influential person.

cabinet   A body of officials appointed by the president to run the executive departments of the government and to act as the president's advisers.

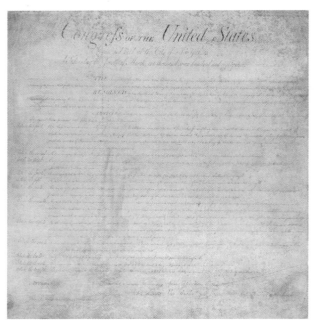

The strongest case the AntiFederalist made against the Constitution was that it did not explicitly state the rights of the people. Although the framers had assumed that these rights were ensured by the states, Federalists quickly realized they had made a serious mistake in failing to include them in the Constitution. Pro-Constitution leaders promised to amend the constitution as soon as it was approved—and they did. Our first ten amendments, guaranteeing such rights as freedom of speech, religion and the press and the right of habeus corpus, are commonly known as the Bill of Rights. *National Archives.*

Competing Visions Re-emerge

→ *How did Alexander Hamilton's expectations for the new nation differ from those of Thomas Jefferson? What were the consequences of this conflict of vision?*

→ *How did the French Revolution affect Washington's diplomatic policy?*

A remarkable but, as it turned out, short-lived spirit of unity marked the early days of Washington's administration. Federalists had won the overwhelming majority of seats in the new Congress, and this success enabled them to work quickly and efficiently on matters they felt had priority. But the unity was fragile. By 1792, sectional divisions were deepening, and as the government debated foreign policy and domestic affairs, two distinct groups, voicing serious differences of opinion, began to form. Alexander Hamilton's

vision for America guided one group. At the heart of the other was the vision of Thomas Jefferson.

Unity's Achievements

In addition to creating the four executive departments that became the cabinet, the First Congress passed the **Judiciary Act of 1789.** This act established a Supreme Court, thirteen district courts, and three circuit courts. It also empowered the Supreme Court to review the decisions of state courts and to nullify any state laws that violated either the Constitution or any treaty made by the federal government. President Washington chose John Jay to serve as first chief justice of the Supreme Court.

The First Congress also managed to break the stalemate on the tariff issue. Southern leaders had opposed a tariff because a tax on imports added to the cost of the consumer goods that southern agriculturalists had to purchase. Northeastern leaders had favored tariff legislation because such a tax, by making foreign goods more expensive, would benefit their region's merchants and manufacturers. During Washington's first term, southerner James Madison took the lead in conducting the delicate negotiations over tariffs. The result was an import tax on certain items such as rum, cocoa, and coffee.

Madison also prodded Congress to draft the promised **Bill of Rights.** Although more than two hundred suggestions were submitted to Congress, Madison honed them down to twelve. On December 15, 1791, ten of these were added to the Constitution as the Bill of Rights, and soon after, both Rhode Island and North Carolina ratified the Constitution and joined the union. Eight of these original constitutional amendments spelled out the government's commitment to protect individual **civil liberties.** They guaranteed that the new national government could not limit free speech, interfere with religious worship, deny U.S. cit-

Judiciary Act of 1789   Law establishing the Supreme Court and the lower federal courts; it gave the Supreme Court the right to review state laws and state court decisions to determine their constitutionality.

Bill of Rights   The first ten amendments to the U.S. Constitution, added in 1791 to protect certain basic rights of American citizens.

civil liberties   Fundamental individual rights such as freedom of speech and religion, protected by law against interference from the government.

For several years, New York City served as the capital of the new United States. But plans were soon laid for a new capital city to be created on the banks of the Potomac River, on land donated by Virginia and Maryland. This new city was to be named Washington, in honor of the hero of the Revolution and the first president of the new nation. Although elaborate plans for elegant, tree-lined streets such as this one were drawn up, for many years visitors and residents alike described Washington, D.C., as a dismal town of muddy streets and dreadful climate. *Library of Congress.*

izens the right to keep or bear arms, force the quartering of troops in private homes, or allow homes to be searched without proper search warrants. The amendments prohibited the government from requiring persons accused of crimes to testify against themselves, nor could it deny citizens the right to a trial by jury. The government also could not deprive a citizen of life, liberty, or property without "due process of law," or impose excessive bail, or administer "cruel and unusual punishments." The Ninth Amendment made clear that the inclusion of these protections and rights did not mean that others were excluded. The Tenth Amendment stated that any powers not given to the federal government or denied to the states belonged solely to the states or the people.

Condensed into these ten amendments was a rich history of struggle for individual rights in the face of abusive power. It was a history that recalled the experiences of colonists protesting the illegal search and seizure of cargoes in Boston harbor, the British government's insistence on quartering troops in New York homes, and the religious persecution of men and women who dissented from established churches both in England and in the colonies.

Hamilton and Jefferson's Differences

Alexander Hamilton was consumed by a bold dream: to transform agricultural America into a manufacturing society that rivaled Great Britain. His blueprint for achieving this goal called for tariffs designed to protect developing American industry rather than simply raise revenue. It also called for **subsidies,** or government financial support, for new enterprises and incentives to support new industries. And it relied on strong economic and diplomatic ties with the mercantile interests of England. Hamilton's vision had great appeal in the Northeast but few advocates in the southern states. Indeed, his ambitious development program seemed to confirm Patrick Henry's worst fears: that the new government would produce "a system which I have ever dreaded—subserviency of Southern to Northern Interests."

Virginia planters Thomas Jefferson and James Madison offered a different vision of the new nation: a prosperous, agrarian society. Instead of government tariffs designed to encourage American manufacturing, they advocated a national policy of **free trade** to keep consumer prices low. The agrarian view did not entirely rule out commerce and industry in the United States. As long as commercial society remained "a handmaiden to agriculture," Jefferson saw no danger that citizens would be exploited or lured into the love of luxury that destroyed republics. In the same fashion, Hamilton was content to see agriculture thrive as long as it did not drain away the scarce resources of the national government or stand in the way of commercial or industrial growth. Hamilton and men of similar vision around him spoke of themselves as true **Federalists.**

subsidies   Financial assistance that a government grants to an enterprise considered to be in the public interest.

free trade   Trade between nations without any protective tariffs.

Federalists   Political group formed during Washington's first administration; led by Alexander Hamilton, they favored an active role for government in encouraging commercial and manufacturing growth.

Those who agreed with Jefferson and Madison identified themselves as **Republicans.**

The emergence of two political camps was certain to trouble even the men who played a role in creating them. The revolutionary generation believed that **factions,** or special-interest parties, were responsible for the corruption of English politics. John Adams seemed to speak for all these political leaders when he declared: "A division of the republic into two great parties . . . is to be dreaded as the greatest political evil." Yet as President Washington was quick to see, **sectionalism** fueled the growth of just such a division.

Hamilton's Economic Plan

As secretary of the treasury, Alexander Hamilton was expected to seek solutions to the nation's **fiscal** problems, particularly the foreign and domestic debts hanging over America's head. His proposals were the source of much of the conflict that divided Congress in the early 1790s.

In January 1790 Hamilton submitted a *Report on Public Credit* to the Congress. In it, he argued that the public debt fell into three categories, each requiring attention: (1) foreign debt, owed primarily to France; (2) state debts, incurred by the individual states to finance their war efforts; and (3) a national debt in the form of government securities (the notorious paper continentals) that had been issued to help finance the war. To establish credit, and thus to be able to borrow money and attract investors in American enterprises, Hamilton declared that the nation had to make good on all it owed.

Hamilton proposed that the federal government assume responsibility for the repayment of all three categories of debt. He insisted the continentals be redeemed for the amount shown on the certificate, regardless of what their current value might be. And he proposed that *current* holders of continentals should receive that payment regardless of how or when they had acquired them. These recommendations, and the political agenda for economic growth they revealed, raised furious debate within Congress.

Before Hamilton's *Report on Public Credit,* James Madison had been the voice of unity in Congress. Now, Madison leapt to his feet to protest the treasury secretary's plan. The government's debt, both financial and moral, Madison argued, was not to the current creditors holding the continentals but to the *original* holders. Many of the original holders were ordinary citizens and Continental soldiers who had sold these certificates to speculators at a tremendous loss during the postwar depression. The state treasuries of New York, Pennsylvania, and Maryland were three of the largest speculators, buying up great quantities of these bonds when they were disgracefully cheap. If Hamilton's plan were adopted, Madison protested, these speculators, rather than the nation's true patriots, would reap enormous unfair profits.

Madison's emotional opposition to Hamilton's debt program came from a deep distrust of certain ways of attaining wealth. Although enslaved men and women performed the work done on Madison's plantation, the Virginia planter believed that wealth acquired by productive labor was moral whereas wealth gained by the manipulation of money was corrupt. Hamilton simply sidestepped the moral issue by explaining the difficulty of identifying and locating the original holders of the continentals. Whatever the ethical merits of Madison's argument, Hamilton said, his solution was impractical. Congress supported Hamilton, but the vote reflected the growing rift between regions.

Madison was far from silenced, however. Next, he led the opposition to Hamilton's proposal that the federal government assume, or take over, the states' debts. Here, Hamilton's motives were quite transparent: as a fierce nationalist, he wished to concentrate both political and economic power in the federal government at the expense of the states. He knew that creditors, who included America's wealthiest citizens, would take a particular interest in the welfare and success of any government that owed them money. By concentrating the debt in the federal government, Hamilton intended to give America's elite a clear stake in America's success. Hamilton also knew that a sizable debt provided a compelling reason for raising revenue. By assuming the state debts, the federal government could undercut state governments' need for new taxes—and justify its own.

Republicans   Political group formed during Washington's first administration; led by Thomas Jefferson and James Madison, they favored limited government involvement in encouraging manufacturing and the continued dominance of agriculture in the national economy.

factions   A political group with shared opinions or interests.

sectionalism   Excessive concern for local or regional interests.

fiscal   Relating to finances.

Congress saw the obvious **inequities** of the plan. Members from states such as Maryland and Virginia quickly reminded Congress that their governments had paid all their war debts during the 1780s. If the national government assumed state debts and raised taxes to repay them, responsible citizens of Maryland and Virginia would be taxed for the failure of Massachusetts or New York to honor their obligations. Although the Senate approved the assumption of state debts, members of the House strongly objected and deferred a decision. Hamilton, realizing he faced defeat, moved to break the deadlock by a behind-the-scenes compromise with Madison and his ally Jefferson. Hamilton was confident he held a valuable bargaining chip: the location of the national capital.

In 1789 the new government had made New York its temporary home until Congress could settle on a permanent site. The choice turned out to be politically delicate because of regional jealousy and competition. Hamilton was willing to put the capital right in Jefferson's backyard in exchange for the Virginian's support on assumption of state debts. The deal clearly appealed to southern regional pride, but Madison and Jefferson had deeper motives for agreeing to it. Like many good Republicans, they believed it was important to monitor the deliberations of a powerful government. But in an age of slow land travel and slower communication, it was difficult to keep watch from a distance. New Englanders also knew that "watching" meant the chance to influence the government. "The climate of the Potomac," one New Englander quipped, would prove unhealthy, if not deadly, to "northern constitutions." Nevertheless, by trading away the capital location, Hamilton ensured the success of his assumption plan.

The year 1791 began with another controversial proposal from the secretary of the treasury. This time, Hamilton outlined a plan for chartering a national bank. The bank, modeled on the Bank of England, would serve as fiscal agent for the federal government, although it would not be an exclusively public institution. Instead, the bank would be funded by both the government and private sources in a partnership that fit nicely with Hamilton's plan to tie national prosperity to the interests of private wealth.

Once again, James Madison led the opposition. He argued that the government had neither the express right nor the **implied power** to create a national institution such as the bank. The majority of Congress did not agree, but Madison's argument that the bank was unconstitutional did cause President Washington to hesitate over signing the congressional bill into law. As usual, Washington decided to consult advisers on the matter. He asked both Secretary of State Jefferson and the treasury head Hamilton to set down their views.

Like Madison, Jefferson was at that time a **strict constructionist** in his interpretation of the Constitution. On February 15, 1791, he wrote of the dangers of interpreting the government's powers broadly. "To take a single step beyond the boundaries . . . specifically drawn around the powers of Congress," he warned, "is to take possession of a boundless field of power." A **broad constructionist,** Hamilton saw no such danger in the bank. He based his argument on Article 1, Section 8, of the Constitution, which granted Congress the right to "make all Laws which shall be necessary and proper" to exercise its legitimate powers. As he put it on February 23: "The powers contained in a constitution . . . ought to be construed liberally in advancement of the public good." And because it seemed obvious that "a bank has a natural relation to the power of collecting taxes," Hamilton believed there could be no reasonable constitutional argument against it. Hamilton's argument persuaded the president, and the bank was chartered on February 25, 1791. By July 4, 1791, stock in the newly established Bank of the United States was offered for sale.

Hamilton's assumption strategy and the creation of a bank were just preliminaries to the ambitious economic development program that he put forward in 1792 in his *Report on Manufactures*. But this time his package of policies for aggressively industrializing the nation—including protective tariffs and government incentives and subsidies—was too extreme to win support in Congress. Still, the Bank of the United States, which provided much-needed working **capital** for new commercial and manufacturing enterprises, and the establishment of sound national credit, which

---

inequities   Unfair circumstances or proceedings.

implied power   Power that is not specifically granted to the government by the Constitution but can be viewed as necessary to carry out the governing duties listed in the Constitution.

strict constructionist   A person who believes the government has only the powers specifically named in the Constitution.

broad constructionist   A person who believes the government can exercise any implied powers that are in keeping with the spirit of the Constitution.

capital   Money needed to start or sustain a commercial enterprise.

attracted foreign capital to the new nation, had gone far toward moving the economy in the direction of Hamilton's vision.

Foreign Affairs and Deepening Divisions

In 1789, just as George Washington became the first president of the United States, the **French Revolution** began. And in the years in which Hamilton was advancing his economic programs, that revolution stirred new controversy within American politics.

The first signs of serious resistance to the French monarchy came when **Louis XVI,** king of France, asked for new taxes. Reformers within the French parliament, or Estates General, refused, choosing instead to reduce the king's power and create a constitutional monarchy. Outside the halls of government, crowds took to the streets in the name of broad social reform. On July 14, 1789, Parisian radicals stormed the Bastille prison, a symbol of royal oppression, tearing down its walls and liberating its political prisoners. The crowds filling the Paris streets owed some of their political rhetoric and ideals to the American Revolution. The marquis de Lafayette acknowledged this debt when he sent his old friend President Washington the key to the Bastille. Like most Americans in these early days of the French Revolution, Washington was pleased to be identified with this new struggle for the "rights of man." Briefly, enthusiasm for the French Revolution united Hamilton's Federalists and Jefferson's Republicans.

By 1793, however, American public opinion began to divide sharply on the French Revolution. Popular support faded when the revolution's most radical party, the Jacobins, imprisoned and then executed the king and his wife. Many shocked Americans denounced the revolution completely when the Jacobins, in their **Reign of Terror** against any who opposed their policies, began marching moderate French reformers as well as members of the nobility to the guillotine to be beheaded.

Soon after eliminating their revolutionary opponents, the Jacobin government vowed to bring "liberty, equality, and brotherhood" to the peoples of Europe, by force if necessary. This campaign to spread the revolution led France into war with England, Spain, Austria, and **Prussia.** At the very least, France expected the Americans to honor the terms of the treaty of 1778, which bound the United States to protect French possessions in the West Indies from enemy attack. The enemy most likely to strike was England,

a fact that suddenly made a second war between England and the United States a possibility.

American opinion on a second war with England was contradictory and complex. George Blake, a Boston lawyer and political figure, reminded his fellow citizens, "The [French] cause is half our own, and does not our policy and our honor urge us to most forcibly cherish it?" But others who continued to support the French Revolution, including Thomas Jefferson, did not want the United States to become embroiled in a European war. Many who condemned the French Revolution nevertheless were eager to use any excuse to attack the British, who still were occupying forts in the Northwest and restricting American trade in the Caribbean. Political leaders such as Hamilton who were working toward better relations with England were appalled not only by the French assault on other nations but also by the prospect of American involvement in it. While Americans struggled with these contradictory views, the French plotted to mobilize American support directly.

In 1793 the new French republic sent a diplomatic minister to the United States. When Citizen **Edmond Genêt** arrived in Charleston, he wasted no time on formal matters such as presenting his credentials as an official representative from France to either the president or the secretary of state. Instead, he immediately launched a campaign to recruit Americans to the war effort. By all accounts, Genêt was charming, affable, and in the words of one observer, so humorous that he could "laugh us into the war." President Washington, however, was not amused. Genêt's total disregard for formal procedures infuriated Washington, who was undecided about whether to officially recognize the French minister. Genêt's bold attempts to

---

French Revolution   Political rebellion against the French monarchy and aristocratic privileges; it began in 1789 and ended in 1799.

Louis XVI   The king of France (r. 1774–1792) when the French Revolution began; he and his wife, Marie Antoinette, were executed in 1793 by the revolutionary government.

Reign of Terror   The period from 1793 to 1794 in the French Revolution when thousands of people were executed as enemies of the state.

Prussia   A northern European state that became the basis for the German Empire in the late nineteenth century.

Edmond Genêt   Diplomat sent by the French government to bring the United States into France's war with Britain and Spain.

On July 14, 1789, Parisian citizens stormed the Bastille prison, in search of the ammunition said to be found within the prison walls. To these men and women, the Bastille was a symbol of the brutality of France's absolute monarchy. Americans celebrated this event, which marked the beginning of a Revolution that promised to establish "liberty, equality, and fraternity" in France. Yet, as the revolution continued, and spread to a war between England and France, Americans would become deeply divided over who to support. *Reúnion des Musées Nationaux/Art Resource, NY.*

provoke incidents between the United States and Spain stunned Hamilton. Even Thomas Jefferson grew uncomfortable when the Frenchman used the port of Philadelphia to transform a captured British ship into a French privateer!

On April 22, 1793, Washington decided to act. Publicly, the president issued a proclamation that declared American **neutrality** without actually using the term. While allowing Washington to avoid a formal **repudiation** of America's treaty with France, the proclamation made clear that the United States would give no military support to the French. Privately, Washington asked the French government to recall Genêt.

The Genêt affair had domestic as well as diplomatic repercussions. For the first time, George Washington came under public attack. A Republican newspaper whose editor was employed by Jefferson in the state department questioned the president's integrity in refusing to honor the Franco-American treaty. Washington was furious with this assault on his character. Federalist newspapers struck back, insisting that Jefferson and his followers had actively encouraged the outrageous behavior of Genêt, and Federalists issued resolutions condemning Genêt. By the end of 1793, Jefferson had resigned from Washington's government, more convinced than ever that Hamilton and his supporters posed a serious threat to the survival of the American republic.

More Domestic Disturbances

Hamilton's Federalists agreed that the republic was in danger—from Jefferson's Republicans. By Washington's second term (he was reelected in 1792), both political groups were trying to rouse popular sentiment for their programs and policies and against those of their opponents. Just as in the prerevolutionary years, these appeals to popular opinion broadened participation in the debate over the future of the nation. Ordinary citizens did not always wait until their political leaders solicited their views, however. In the wake of the French Revolution and British interference in the West and on the seas, organizations rose up to make demands on the government. The most troubling of these to President Washington were the **Democratic-Republican societies.**

neutrality The policy of treating both sides in a conflict the same way and thus favoring neither.
repudiation The act of rejecting the validity or the authority of something.
Democratic-Republican societies Political organizations formed in 1793 and 1794 to demand greater responsiveness by the state and federal governments to the needs of the citizens.

Between 1793 and 1794, thirty-five Democratic-Republican societies were created. Made up primarily of craftsmen and men of the "lower orders," these pro-French political groups also had their share of professional men, merchants, and planters. In Philadelphia, for example, noted scientist and inventor David Rittenhouse and Alexander Dallas, secretary to the governor of Pennsylvania, were society members. In Kentucky, which had split from Virginia in 1792, local elites organized their own society, separate from the one made up of western farmers. No matter what the background of the membership, these societies shared a common agenda: to serve as a platform for expressing the public's will. They insisted that political officeholders were "the agents of the people," not their leaders, and thus should act as the people wished.

In 1794 many western farmers were dismayed over what they considered the government's indifference toward the people. Kentucky settlers fretted about the navigation of the Mississippi, while Pennsylvania and Carolina farmers resented a new federal **excise** tax on whiskey. Although the Democratic-Republican societies denied an active role in spurring a new farmers' revolt against the government, a belief that the government ought to respond to its citizens' demands did seem to motivate Pennsylvania, Carolina, and Kentucky farmers to tar and feather **excise men,** burn the barns of tax supporters, and intimidate county officials. The most determined and organized resistance came from Pennsylvania, where, in July 1794, a crowd ransacked and burned the home of the federal excise inspector and then threatened to march on Pittsburgh if the tax on whiskey were not repealed.

President Washington, haunted by the memory of Shays's Rebellion and worried that the radical spirit of the French Revolution was spreading throughout America, determined to crush this **Whiskey Rebellion** firmly. Calling up thirteen thousand militiamen, the president marched into the countryside to do battle with a few hundred citizens armed with rifles and pitchforks. In the face of such an overwhelming military force, the whiskey rebels abruptly dispersed.

Washington publicly laid the blame for the western insurrection on the Democratic-Republican societies. Federalists in Congress rushed to propose a resolution condemning those groups. Fisher Ames, an ardent Massachusetts Federalist, delivered an impassioned condemnation of the societies, accusing them of spreading "jealousies, suspicions, and accusations" against the government. They had, Ames declared, "arrogantly pretended sometimes to be the people and sometimes the [people's] guardians, the champi-

ons of the people." Instead, he said, they represented no one but themselves.

The Jeffersonians, generally believed to be sympathetic to the societies, knew it would be politically damaging to defend them in the aftermath of the Whiskey Rebellion. Instead, they worked to see a more moderate expression of disapproval emerge from Congress.

By 1796, the Democratic-Republican organizations had vanished from the American political scene. The president's public condemnation and Congress's censure undoubtedly damaged them. But improvements on the western borders also diminished the farmers' interest in protest organizations. In October 1795, Carolina planter Thomas Pinckney won the concession from Spain that Jay had been unable to obtain in earlier negotiations: free navigation of the Mississippi River. Pinckney's **Treaty of San Lorenzo** not only gave western farmers an outlet to ocean trade through the port of New Orleans but also ensured that Indian attacks would not be launched from Spanish-held territories.

Jay's Treaty

During Washington's second administration, the diplomatic crisis continued to worsen. England resented America's claim to neutrality, believing it helped France. The British, therefore, ignored American claims that "free ships made free goods" and began to seize American vessels trading with the French Caribbean islands. These seizures prompted new calls for war with Great Britain.

Anti-British emotion ran even higher when the governor of Canada actively encouraged Indian resistance to American settlement in the Northwest. Washington and the general public considered Indian relations dismal enough without such meddling, es-

---

excise   A tax on the production, sale, or consumption of a commodity or on the use of a service within a country.

excise men   Men who collected taxes on an article of trade or sale.

Whiskey Rebellion   A protest by grain farmers against the 1794 federal tax on whiskey; militia forces led by President Washington put down this Pennsylvania uprising.

Treaty of San Lorenzo   Treaty between the United States and Spain, negotiated in 1795 by Thomas Pinckney; Spain granted the United States the right to navigate the Mississippi River and use the port of New Orleans as an outlet to the sea.

In 1794, the new federal government passed an excise tax on whiskey made from surplus American grains. Farmers in western Pennsylvania rose up in protest against what they considered an unfair assault on their livelihood. Using tactics straight out of the pre-Revolutionary War era, including tarring and feathering the "revenooer" assigned to collect the taxes, the "Whiskey Rebels" challenged the federal government's authority. President Washington met this challenge by assembling an army of almost thirteen thousand men to put down the Whiskey Rebellion. Critics declared the president's response excessive. Do you agree? *Library of Congress.*

pecially since efforts to crush the Miamis of Ohio had recently ended in two embarrassing American defeats. In February 1794, as General Anthony Wayne headed west for a third attempt against the Miamis, the Canadian governor's fiery remarks were particularly disturbing.

Jefferson's departure left little anti-British sentiment in the cabinet. But it remained strong in the Congress, where the House of Representatives considered restricting trade with England. Outside the government, war hysteria showed itself as mobs attacked English seamen and tarred and feathered Americans expressing pro-British views. What would Washington do?

Early in 1794, the president sent Chief Justice John Jay to England as his special **envoy.** Jay's mission was to produce a compromise that would prevent war between the two nations. Jay, however, was pessimistic. Britain wanted to avoid war with the United States, but what would British diplomats concede to his weak nation?

Jay's negotiations did resolve some old nagging issues. In the treaty that emerged, Britain agreed to evacuate the western forts although it did not promise to end support for Indian resistance to American western settlement. Britain also granted some small trade favors to America in the West Indies. For its part,

the United States agreed to see that all prewar debts owed to British merchants were at last paid. Jay, a committed abolitionist, did not press for any provision compensating slaveholders for slaves lost during the Revolution. In the end, Jay knew he had given up more than he gained: he had abandoned America's demand for freedom of the seas and acknowledged the British navy's right to remove French property from any neutral ship.

Jay's Treaty did little to enhance John Jay's reputation or popularity. After reading it, fellow New Yorker Robert R. Livingston said bluntly: "Mr. Jay has sacrificed the essential interests of this country." In Congress, judgments on the treaty were openly **partisan.** Federalists credited Jay's Treaty with preserving the

> **envoy** A government representative charged with a special diplomatic mission.
>
> **Jay's Treaty** Controversial 1794 treaty negotiated between the United States and Great Britain by John Jay to ensure American neutrality in the French and English war.
>
> **partisan** Taking a strong position on an issue out of loyalty to a political group or leader.

On August 3, 1795, after an American victory in the Battle of Fallen Timbers, representatives from a number of tribes, including Wyandots, Delawares, Shawnee, Ottawa, Miami, and Potawatomi, signed a treaty with the United States. In exchange for goods such as blankets, utensils, and domestic animals the Indians turned over a large territory that would include much of modern-day Ohio and modern Chicago. The treaty established the "Greenville Treaty Line," marking the boundary between Indian and white territories for several years, which white settlers often ignored. *Ohio Historical Society.*

peace, but Republicans condemned it as an embarrassment and a betrayal of France. Worried that the angry debate over ratification would fan popular outrage, the president banned public discussion of the treaty. Republican congressmen, however, leaked accounts to the press. Once again, the president came under attack, and Kentucky settlers threatened rebellion, warning Washington that if he signed Jay's Treaty, "western America is gone forever—lost to the Union." The treaty finally squeaked through the Senate in the spring of 1795 with only two southern senators supporting ratification. The House debate on appropriations for the treaty was equally bitter and prolonged. In the end, however, Congress endorsed Jay's handiwork. Despite the criticism, Jay knew he had accomplished his mission, for American neutrality in the European war continued.

Jay's negotiations with England damaged the prestige and authority of Washington's administration. The president did far better, however, in military and dip-

lomatic affairs in the West. In August 1794, Anthony Wayne's army defeated the northwestern Indians at the **Battle of Fallen Timbers.** Wayne then lived up to his reputation as "Mad Anthony" by rampaging through enemy villages, destroying all that he could. These terror tactics helped produce the **Treaty of Greenville** in August 1795. By this treaty, the Indians ceded most of the land that later became the state of Ohio. These victories, combined with the auspicious terms of Pinckney's Treaty of San Lorenzo, won praise for the troubled president.

Battle of Fallen Timbers   1794 battle in which Kentucky riflemen defeated Indians of several tribes, helping to end Indian resistance in the Northwest.

Treaty of Greenville   1795 treaty in which the United States agreed to pay northwestern Indians about $10,000 for the land that later became the state of Ohio.

Washington's Farewell

The bitter political fight over Jay's Treaty, combined with the steady and nagging criticism of his policies in the press and the hardening of party lines between Federalists and Republicans, helped George Washington make an important decision: he would not seek a third term as president. Instead, in 1796 he would return to his beloved Virginia home, Mount Vernon, and resume the life of a gentleman planter.

When Washington retired, he left behind a nation very different from the one whose independence he had helped win and whose survival he had helped secure. The postwar economic depression was over, and the war raging in Europe had produced a steadily rising demand for American foodstuffs. More fundamentally, in the fifteen years since the Revolution, the U.S. economy had moved decisively in the direction that Alexander Hamilton had envisioned. The values and expectations of a **market economy**—with its stress on maximizing profit and the pursuit of individual economic interests—had captured the imagination and shaped the actions of many white Americans. Hamilton's policies as secretary of the treasury had both reflected and advanced a growing interest in the expansion of trade, the growth of markets, and the development of American manufacturing and industry. In its political life, the republic had been reorganized and the relationships between the states and the central government redefined. The new Constitution granted greater diplomatic and commercial powers to the federal government but protected individual citizens through the Bill of Rights. America's political leaders, though convinced that factions were dangerous to the survival of the republic, had nevertheless created and begun to work within an evolving party system.

In his Farewell Address to the public, Washington expressed his thoughts on many of these changes. Although Jefferson had believed the president was a Federalist partisan, Washington spoke with feeling against parties in a republic, urging the nation to return to nonpartisan cooperation. Washington also warned America and its new leaders not to "interweave our destiny with any part of Europe" or "entangle our peace and prosperity in the toils of European ambition." An honorable country must "observe good faith and justice toward all nations," said the aging Virginian, but Americans must not let any alliance develop that draws the nation into a foreign war. The final ingredient in Washington's formula for America's success and its "permanent felicity" was the continuing virtue of its people.

> **market economy**   An economy in which production of goods is geared to sale or profit.

✔ Individual Voices

Mercy Otis Warren Criticizes Boston Citizens

① *The terms "whigs" and "tories" come from seventeenth-century English politics. Whigs opposed the religious policies of, and abuse of power by, King Charles II. Tories, on the other hand, supported both the king's power and his church. Why do you think American loyalists would resent being labeled as Tories?*

Mercy Otis Warren believed that a republic would survive only as long as its citizens remained patriots. For her, as for her fellow Massachusetts radical Samuel Adams, a patriot was a citizen who worked hard, lived simply, and was willing to sacrifice life and fortune for the sake of his or her country. Even before the war ended, she began to worry that such virtuous men and women were no longer in the majority. Her own Massachusetts society, she feared, had turned its back on virtue in the pursuit of luxury and frivolous enjoyments. In 1779, she satirized these selfish characteristics in her play, *The Motley Assembly, a Farce, published for the entertainment of the curious.* She ends her play with this condemnation of her neighbors and former friends:

> *Blush Boston! Blush! Thy honest sons bewail,*
> *That dance and song over patriol zeal prevail,*
> *That Whigs and Tories (joined by wayward chance* ①

(2) An apostate is a person who betrays a trust or an allegiance. What events in 1779 might have led the people of Boston to believe that the worst of the war was over and that they did not need to make as many sacrifices to the cause of independence as they had in 1775 or 1776?

Should hand in hand lead on the sprightly dance,
Or sword to sword as harmlessly oppose
As all such heroes would their country's foes,
Here lured by fashion, opposite interests join,
And lull their cares and rage, in cards and wine.
Here friends to freedom, vile apostate meet, (2)
And here unblushing can each other greet.
In mixed assembly, see they crowd the place.
Stain to their country, to their sires disgrace.
Hell in some hearts, but pleasure in each face,
All, all are qualified to join this tribe,
Who have a hundred dollars to subscribe. (3)

(3) Why does Warren point out the cost of joining this social assembly?

SUMMARY

After independence was declared, Americans faced the challenge of creating a new nation out of thirteen distinct states. Faced with enormous debt and still surrounded by real and potential enemies, the new nation's ability to survive seemed doubtful to many. As colonies became states, they drafted their own constitutions. Some put in place democratic forms of government while others built in more restrictive features such as high property qualifications for office-holding. The first national government, created by the Articles of Confederation, reflected the states' desire to preserve their individual sovereignty. It also embodied the revolutionary generation's opposition to a strong centralized government. The Confederation government thus lacked basic powers: it could not raise taxes or regulate commerce.

The Confederation could point to several achievements, however: it negotiated the peace treaty of 1783, and it established, through three Northwest Ordinances, the process by which territories became states on an equal footing with the original states. But with limited powers, the Confederation could not resolve the nation's financial problems, deal effectively with foreign nations, or ensure social order within its borders. Efforts to raise funds through the sale of western land led to new conflict with both the British and the Indians. Settlement on the southern frontier provoked retaliation by the Spanish. Barbary pirates seized American trading ships in the Mediterranean. Domestic violence erupted when Massachusetts farmers,

hard hit by the postwar depression, rose up in revolt in Shays's Rebellion in 1786. By that time, many of the nation's elite political figures were calling for a stronger national government.

In the summer of 1787, these nationalists met in Philadelphia to consider a new constitution. The Constitution they produced, after long months of debate, steered a middle ground between a central government that was too powerful and one that was too weak. It established executive, legislative, and judicial branches, which could "check and balance" one another and thus, hopefully, safeguard the nation from tyranny. The new government could both raise taxes and regulate commerce. The new Constitution was ratified by the states in 1788 after intense battles between pro-Constitution forces, known as Federalists, and their Antifederalist opponents. Despite strong arguments on both sides, the Federalist leaders won their victory.

Soon after George Washington took office as the first president, serious differences in political opinion again emerged. Alexander Hamilton's vision of a vigorous commercial and industrial nation conflicted with Thomas Jefferson's desire for an agrarian nation. These two factions disagreed over economic and foreign policy. The French Revolution intensified the divisions: while Hamilton argued against American support for the French in their war with England, Jefferson pressed the administration to support their fellow revolutionaries. Washington managed to steer a neutral course in this European conflict. By the end of Washington's second term, the United States had expanded its borders, negotiated with Spain for access to the Mississippi River, and under Hamilton's guidance, it had established a national bank at the center of an economic system that promoted market-oriented growth. The country had survived domestic unrest and the development of political parties. The departing Washington urged Americans to continue to cooperate and cautioned them not to allow competing visions of America's future to harm the new nation.

As you will read in the next chapter, the political battles between Hamilton's Federalist party and Jefferson's Republican party continued to shape national politics and diplomacy. Could one party turn over the reins of government to the other peacefully—or would civil war destroy the young republic?

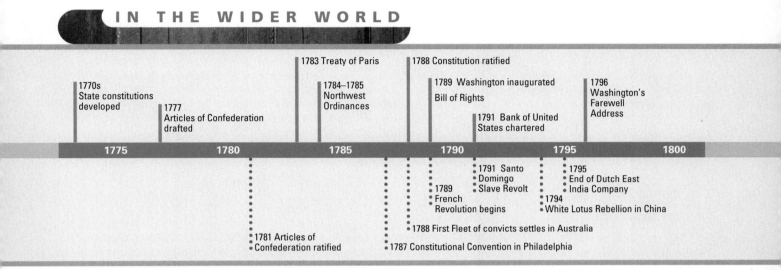

IN THE WIDER WORLD

1770s State constitutions developed

1777 Articles of Confederation drafted

1781 Articles of Confederation ratified

1783 Treaty of Paris

1784–1785 Northwest Ordinances

1787 Constitutional Convention in Philadelphia

1788 Constitution ratified

1788 First Fleet of convicts settles in Australia

1789 Washington inaugurated
Bill of Rights

1789 French Revolution begins

1791 Bank of United States chartered

1791 Santo Domingo Slave Revolt

1794 White Lotus Rebellion in China

1795 End of Dutch East India Company

1796 Washington's Farewell Address

1775　1780　1785　1790　1795　1800

In the United States

From Revolution to Nationhood

1770s State constitutions developed	George Washington inaugurated as first president
1776 Oversight in New Jersey constitution gives property-holding women right to vote	Judiciary Act of 1789
1777 Congress adopts Articles of Confederation	**1791** First Bank of the United States chartered
1781 States ratify Articles of Confederation	Bill of Rights added to Constitution
Cornwallis surrenders at Yorktown	Alexander Hamilton's *Report on Manufactures*
1784–1785 First two Northwest Ordinances	**1792** Washington reelected
1786 Annapolis Convention	**1793** Genêt affair
Shays's Rebellion	Jefferson resigns as secretary of state
1787 Constitutional Convention	**1794** Whiskey Rebellion in Pennsylvania
Third Northwest Ordinance	Battle of Fallen Timbers
1787–1788 States ratify U.S. Constitution	**1795** Congress approves Jay's Treaty
1789 First congressional elections	Treaty of San Lorenzo
	1796 Washington's Farewell Address

The Early Republic, 1796–1804

A NOTE FROM THE AUTHOR

It is hard for us to remember that the Founders, people we are used to seeing immortalized in marble statues, were just people. Like our political leaders today they had faults, uncertainties, biases, and lack of foresight. At the same time, they understood that they occupied a peculiar place in history and were conscious of their legacy. For example, historians have learned that in retirement Thomas Jefferson edited file copies of letters he had sent earlier in his life in order to enhance his reputation. This willful manipulation of the historical record aggravates the already difficult task of sorting out the complexities of our past, yet it makes the people who set the nation on its initial course all the more fascinating and the history they made all the more worthy of reexamination.

Too often we treat this era in our history as something, like the likenesses of the Founders themselves, carved in stone. Realizing that they themselves were uncertain about where the nation was to go and struggled over which course to follow makes clear that we can never accept uncritical assertions about the intentions of the Founders. We must wade through intentional deceptions, naïve misrepresentations, expressions of confusion and uncertainty, and try to piece together how it all happened. We should always be willing to reexamine what we thought we knew in order to better understand not only where we came from, but where we are now.

Much that you will read in the chapter to come is very different from what was written in this chapter in previous editions of this book. This is not a measure of an earlier lack of judgment on our part nor of a desire to make changes for their own sake. It is, instead, a result of the fact that the ultimate version of any historical era can never be written; our story must change as we learn new things about what happened in the past. As you apply your critical thinking skills to the material to come, you might catch a glimpse of something surprising hiding in the shadows of the marble men who launched this nation.

George Logan

The United States was caught up in a wave of patriotism when the French slighted President Adams's ambassadors in the XYZ affair. Federalists promoted a war against France, but George Logan chose to resist emotionalism and Federalist pressure by going to France to iron out the two nations' difficulties, thus ending the threat of war. *"George Logan" by Gilbert Stuart. Courtesy of the Historical Society of Pennsylvania Collection, Atwater Kent Museum of Philadelphia.*

✔ Individual Choices

Even the suggestion of the United States fighting a war presented a serious problem for George Logan. Like many descendants of Pennsylvania's first families, Logan was a Quaker and was morally opposed to war. His father, a conscientious objector during the Revolutionary War, had sent him to study medicine in Scotland and Paris while the war continued. Returning to the United States in 1780, George learned that his family was dead and that much of the considerable Logan estate had been destroyed.

Logan turned to farming to support himself and then, in 1785, to politics, winning a seat in the Pennsylvania assembly. Ever a critic of Federalist economic and diplomatic strategies, he followed his friend Thomas Jefferson when the Republican faction became an opposition party.

By 1798, Logan seemed well on his way to recovering the fortune and prominence that the war had taken. But then a diplomatic crisis with France made war again seem inevitable. Recalling his father's frustration as the colonies were drawn into war in 1776, Logan made a fateful choice: he risked his property, his reputation, even his life, to prevent another war.

Quietly Logan began selling off property to raise cash to support a private peace effort. He then went to his friend Jefferson, who gave him letters of introduction to important people in France. Government agents learned of Logan's aims and put him under surveillance, but he slipped their noose and sailed for Germany during the summer of 1798. There he met with the marquis de Lafayette (see page 164), who used his influence to get Logan into France and arrange an audience with French foreign minister Talleyrand.

Facing a formidable coalition of absolutist antirevolutionary European powers, the last thing Talleyrand wanted was to further alienate the only other democratic nation in the world. Meeting with Talleyrand and other French officials in early August, Logan capitalized on this fact. He told them that most Americans supported democracy in France but warned that French seizure of American ships and other hostile actions were undermining that support. He assured them that if the French released the American sailors they were holding and ended the embargo placed on American ships, American popular support would turn back to France

and force the American government to end the Quasi-War. Talleyrand was convinced, assuring Logan that France would be happy to meet with a peace delegation if Adams would send one.

Logan's news was warmly received by his fellow Republicans and, surprisingly, by President Adams, who ignored his party's advice and immediately sought peace with France. Within a year, American ambassador William Vans Murray and Napoleon finalized the peace Logan had initiated. Logan had succeeded. Choosing to risk all for peace, he overcame official constraints and averted a war.

INTRODUCTION

When George Washington stepped down as president, the stability that his leadership lent to a new and uncertain government retired with him. And Washington's replacement, John Adams, seemed incapable of calming national anxieties. Under his watch, the United States became involved in an undeclared war with France and saw its international reputation consistently decline. And domestic unrest prevailed as well. Led by Alexander Hamilton, hardcore Federalists had tried to undermine the electoral process in 1796 and then used the war crisis to wage an internal war against their political enemies. Far from succeeding in the destruction of their critics, these Federalist efforts actually helped to crystallize opposition, giving Hamilton's key rival, Thomas Jefferson, a forum from which to assault the party in power. In 1800 these efforts backfired on the Federalists: despite trying to rig the national election again, Federalists were soundly defeated and turned out of office.

Assuming the presidency in 1801, Jefferson ushered in a new era in American politics. Jefferson instituted a series of reforms that would launch the country on a heady, freewheeling adventure of continental expansion and global trade. His secretary of the treasury, Albert Gallatin, implemented radical tax cuts and equally radical cuts in government spending. At the same time, Jefferson waged an aggressive foreign policy designed to restore American international trading and win new territory from along the nation's borders. His successes could be measured by a mounting federal treasury surplus, increased national income, and expanding borders.

Under Jefferson's leadership most Americans saw significant improvement in their everyday lives, and the nation became increasingly optimistic. But the Jeffersonian promise was not made to everyone. For women, Native Americans, and African Americans,

life improved, and opportunities certainly expanded, but underlying prejudices and rigid codes of public behavior prevented their full realization. Contradictions shot through the whole of Jeffersonian America, counterbalancing the enthusiastic optimism and giving peculiar shape to national life.

Conflict in the Adams Administration

→ *How did diplomatic affairs in Europe affect Americans in the closing years of the eighteenth century?*

→ *How did Federalists manipulate the crisis with France in 1798 for their own political advantage?*

→ *What steps did Republicans take to counter Federalist manipulations?*

Retiring president George Washington spoke for many in 1796 when he warned in his Farewell Address of "the baneful effects of the spirit of party." Both Hamilton and Jefferson and their followers were thoroughgoing republicans, but their conceptions of republicanism were essentially different. Hamiltonians tended to be "classical republicans," and espoused the belief that states are fragile and must be led by men of substance and property who stood above private interest; in short, by an aristocracy that could protect the people from themselves. Jeffersonians, on the other hand, tended to be "liberal republicans," asserting that the people could care for themselves and that the state existed solely to guarantee free and equal participation for citizens pursuing private interests in the political and economic realm. For Federalists, aristocratically led republicanism in England provided the appropriate model; for Republicans, popularly led republicanism in revolutionary France came closer to the ideal. These views were fundamentally incompatible and led each side to conviction that the other sought to destroy "real" republicanism. These differences led to serious political conflict during the years following Washington's retirement.

The Split Election of 1796

As the broadly accepted leader of the opposition to Hamilton's policies, Thomas Jefferson was the Republicans' logical choice to represent them in the presidential election in 1796. Most people at the time were not surprised that Republicans chose **Aaron Burr,** a brilliant young New York attorney and member of the Senate, to balance the ticket. Though many years apart in age and from vastly different backgrounds, both Jefferson and Burr were veterans of the revolutionary struggles in 1776 and outspoken champions of liberal republicanism.

Although he styled himself a spokesman for the common man, Burr definitely was not one—his grandfather was the famous evangelical minister Jonathan Edwards (see page 101), and his family continued to have enormous influence. During the Revolutionary War, Burr accepted a commission in the Continental Army, where he found common cause with the radical democrats who had formed the Sons of Liberty (see pages 124–125). By 1784, he had used his political connections and backing from the Sons of Liberty to win a place in the New York state assembly. In 1791 the New York Sons of Liberty, now calling themselves the Society of St. Tammany, maneuvered Burr's election to the U.S. Senate.

Meanwhile, Jefferson had returned from Paris in 1789 to join Washington's cabinet as secretary of state. He was deeply disturbed to find that the once-unified revolutionary forces he knew from 1776 had divided into what he called a "republican side" and a "kingly one," and he complained that "a preference of kingly over republican government was evidently the favorite sentiment." His own preferences put him in league with, and eventually on the same ticket as, Burr and his associates in the Society of St. Tammany, who were equally dismayed.

The apparent unity among Republicans contrasted sharply with divisions in the Federalist faction. Most Federalists assumed that Vice President Adams would succeed Washington as president, but Hamilton and some other hardcore party members doubted the New Englander's loyalty to the party. They favored **Thomas Pinckney** of South Carolina. The younger son of a prestigious South Carolina planter, Pinckney emerged as a major political force when he successfully negotiated the treaty with Spain that opened the Mississippi River to American commerce. This coup won Pinckney the unreserved admiration of both southerners and westerners (see page 202). Hamilton supported him, though, both because Pinckney was less associated with radical causes than was Adams and because Hamilton felt he could exercise more influence over the mild-mannered South Carolinian than he could over the stiff-necked Yankee.

Most Federalists, however, aligned behind the old warhorse from Massachusetts. A descendant of New England Calvinists (see page 101), Adams was a man of strong principles, fighting for what he believed was right despite anyone's contrary opinion. Though a thorough Federalist, he remained Thomas Jefferson's close friend: both he and his wife, Abigail, maintained a spirited correspondence with the red-haired Virginian during his stay in Paris. Like Washington, Adams was seen by many old revolutionaries as above politics, as a **statesman** whose conscience and integrity would help the new nation avoid the pitfalls of **factionalism.**

It was precisely Adams's statesmanship that led Hamilton to oppose him; he sought to use a loophole in the Constitution to rig the election against Adams. According to the Constitution, each member of the Electoral College could cast votes for any two candidates; the highest vote getter became president, and the runner-up became vice president. Hamilton urged Pinckney supporters to cast only one vote—for Pinckney—so that Adams could not get enough votes to win the presidency. But Hamilton underestimated Pinckney's unpopularity in the North, Adams's unacceptability to some southerners, and Jefferson's growing popularity among northerners. Nor did the treasury secretary expect Adams supporters to learn of the plot; when they did, they withheld votes from Pinckney to make up for the votes being withheld from Adams.

Aaron Burr   New York lawyer and vice-presidential candidate in 1796; he became Thomas Jefferson's vice president in 1801 after the House of Representatives broke a deadlock in the Electoral College.

Thomas Pinckney   South Carolina politician and diplomat who was an unsuccessful Federalist candidate for president in 1796.

statesman   A political leader who acts out of concern for the public good and not out of self-interest.

factionalism   In politics, the emergence of various self-interested parties (factions) that compete to impose their own views onto either a larger political party or the nation at large.

Because of the squabbling within the Federalist faction, Jefferson received the votes of disgruntled Federalist electors as well as electors within Republican ranks. He thus ended up with more votes than Pinckney—and only three fewer than Adams. So the nation emerged from the first truly contested presidential election with a split administration: the president and vice president belonged to different factions and held opposing political philosophies.

Adams was ill suited to lead a deeply divided nation. Although he disavowed any aristocratic sentiments in his inaugural address, the new president's aloofness did little to put liberal Republicans' fears to rest. In fact, Adams retained Oliver Wolcott, James McHenry, and Timothy Pickering from Washington's cabinet, all of whom were Hamilton men through and through. This move thoroughly angered Republicans, who had hoped Hamilton's influence would wane now that he had retired from government service to practice law. Clearly the divisions between classical and liberal republicans were still alive and the two views remained locked in conflict. This disunity enticed interested parties both at home and abroad to try to undermine Adams's authority and influence.

XYZ: The Power of Patriotism

One group seeking to take advantage of the divisions in the United States was the revolutionary government in France. America's minister in Paris, James Monroe, sympathized with the French cause, but the pro-British impact of Jay's Treaty (see pages 202–203) and the antirevolutionary rhetoric adopted by Federalists led the French to suspect American sincerity. During the election of 1796, France sought to influence American voting by actively favoring the Republican candidates, threatening to terminate diplomatic relations if the vocally pro-British Federalists won. True to its word, the revolutionary government of France broke off relations with the United States as soon as Adams was elected.

Angry at the French, Adams retaliated in 1796 by calling home the sympathetic Monroe and replacing him with devout Federalist **Charles Cotesworth Pinckney,** the older brother of Hamilton's favored candidate for the presidency. The French refused to acknowledge Pinckney as ambassador and began seizing American ships. Faced with what was fast becoming a diplomatic crisis, and possibly a military one as well, Adams wisely chose to pursue two courses simultaneously. Asserting that the United States would not be "humiliated under a colonial spirit of fear and a sense

One of the fathers of the American Revolution, John Adams seemed the perfect choice to step into the presidency when George Washington chose to step down at the end of his second term. Though many were comforted by Adams's conservative statesmanship, the rigid New Englander was poorly qualified to deal with the partisan politics that came to haunt his administration. *Library of Congress.*

of inferiority," he pressed Congress in 1797 to build up America's military defenses. At the same time, he dispatched John Marshall and Elbridge Gerry to join Pinckney in Paris, where they were to arrange a peaceful settlement of the two nations' differences.

Playing a complicated diplomatic game, French foreign minister **Charles Maurice de Talleyrand-Périgord** declined to receive Pinckney and the peace delegation. As weeks passed, three businessmen residing in Paris, whose international trading profits stood at risk, offered themselves as go-betweens in solving the stalemate. According to Pinckney's report, these men sug-

---

Charles Cotesworth Pinckney   Federalist politician and brother of Thomas Pinckney; he was sent on a diplomatic mission to Paris in 1796 during a period of unfriendly relations between France and the United States.

Charles Maurice de Talleyrand-Périgord   French foreign minister appointed by the revolutionary government in 1797; he later aided Napoleon Bonaparte's overthrow of that government and served as his foreign minister.

Americans saw the XYZ affair as proof of European corruption standing in sharp contrast to American virtue. In this 1798 engraving by Charles Williams, a maidenly America is flattered to distraction by courtly Europeans while members of the French Directory prepare to plunder her wealth. *Courtesy Lilly Library, Indiana University, Bloomington, IN.*

gested that if the Americans were willing to pay a bribe to key French officials and guarantee an American loan of several million dollars to France, the three businessmen would be able to get them a hearing. Offended at such treatment, Pinckney broke off diplomatic relations. Reporting the affair to President Adams, Pinckney refused to name the would-be go-betweens, calling them only "X," "Y," and "Z."

Americans' response to the **XYZ affair** was overwhelming. France's diplomatic slight seemed a slap in the face to a new nation seeking international respect. In Philadelphia, people paraded in the streets to protest French arrogance. The crowds chanted Pinckney's reported response: "No, no, not a sixpence!" This wave of patriotism overcame the spirit of division that had plagued the Adams administration, giving the president a virtually unified Congress and country. In the heat of the moment, Adams pressed for increased military forces, and in short order Congress created the Department of the Navy and appropriated money to start building a fleet of warships. Then, on July 7, 1798, Congress rescinded all treaties with France and authorized privateering against French ships. Congress also created a standing army of twenty thousand troops and ordered that the militia be expanded to thirty thousand men. Washington added his prestige to the effort by coming out of retirement to lead the new army, with Hamilton as his second-in-command. Although running sea battles between French and American ships resulted in the sinking or capture of

many vessels on both sides, Congress shied away from actually declaring war, which led to the conflict being labeled the **Quasi-War.**

The Home Front in the Quasi-War

Still disappointed over their failure to steal the presidential election, Federalists immediately seized upon the war as a means to crush their political enemies. In Congress, they began referring to Jefferson and his supporters as the "French Party" and accused the vice president and his faction of treason whenever they advised a moderate course. Arguing that the presence of this "French Party" constituted a danger to national security, congressional Federalists proposed a series of new laws to destroy all opposition to their conception of true republicanism.

One source of opposition was **naturalized** American citizens. The revolutionary promises of "life, liberty, and the pursuit of happiness" had drawn many immigrants to the United States. Disappointed by Hamilton's approach to government and economics, they were drawn to Jefferson's political rhetoric—especially his stress on equal opportunity and his attacks on aristocracy. In 1798 Federalists in Congress passed three acts designed to counter political activities by immigrants. The Naturalization Act extended the residency requirement for citizenship from five to fourteen years. The Alien Act authorized the president to deport any foreigner he judged "dangerous to the peace and safety of the United States." The Alien Enemies Act permitted the president to imprison or banish any foreigner he considered dangerous during a national emergency. The Naturalization Act was designed to prevent recent immigrants from supporting the Republican cause by barring them from the political process. The other two acts served as a constant

XYZ affair   A diplomatic incident in which American envoys to France were told that the United States would have to loan France money and bribe government officials as a precondition for negotiation.

Quasi-War   Diplomatic crisis triggered by the XYZ affair; fighting occurred between the United States and France between the early summer of 1798 and the official end of the conflict in September 1800, but neither side issued a formal declaration of war.

naturalized   Granted full citizenship (after having been born in a foreign country).

reminder that the president or his agents could arbitrarily imprison or deport any resident alien who stepped out of line.

The other source of support for Jefferson was a partisan Republican press, which attempted to balance the biased news and criticism spewing forth from Federalist news sources with biased accounts of its own. To counter this, congressional Federalists passed the Sedition Act. In addition to outlawing conspiracies to block the enforcement of federal laws, the Sedition Act prohibited the publication or utterance of any criticism of the government or its officials that would bring either "into contempt or disrepute." In the words of one Federalist newspaper, "It is patriotism to write in favour of our government, it is **sedition** to write against it." Federalists brandished the law against all kinds of criticism directed toward either the government or the president, including perfectly innocent political editorials. Not surprisingly, most of the defendants in the fifteen cases brought by federal authorities under the Sedition Act were prominent Republican newspaper editors.

Republicans complained that the **Alien and Sedition Acts** violated the Bill of Rights, but Congress and the federal judiciary, controlled as they were by Hamilton loyalists, paid no attention. Dissidents had little choice but to take their political case to the state governments, which they did in the fall of 1798. One statement, drafted by Madison, came before the Virginia legislature, and another, by Jefferson, was considered in Kentucky.

Madison and Jefferson based their **Virginia and Kentucky Resolutions** on the Tenth Amendment, contending that powers not specifically granted to the federal government under the Constitution or reserved to the people in the Bill of Rights fell to the states. By passing laws such as the Alien and Sedition Acts that were not explicitly permitted in the text of the Constitution, Congress had violated the states' rights. The two authors differed, however, in the responses they prescribed for states to take. For his part, Madison asserted that when the majority of states agreed that a federal law had violated their Tenth Amendment rights, they could collectively overrule federal authority. But Jefferson went further, arguing that each individual state had the "natural right" to **interpose** its own authority to protect its own rights and the rights of its citizens.

The Virginia and Kentucky Resolutions passed in their respective state legislatures, but no other states followed suit. Even within Kentucky and Virginia, great disagreement arose over how far state authority should extend. Nevertheless, this response to the Fed-

eralists' use of federal power brought the disputed relationship between federal law and **states' rights** into national prominence.

Another bone of contention was the methods used to finance the Quasi-War with France and the impact these methods had on various groups of Americans. Consistent with Hamilton's views on finance, tariffs and excises were to be the primary source of revenue, and they had the greatest impact on people who needed manufactured or imported items but had little hard cash. In addition, Federalists imposed a tax on land, hitting cash-poor farmers especially hard. In 1799 farmers in Northampton County, Pennsylvania, refused to pay the tax and began harassing tax collectors. Several tax resisters were arrested, but an auctioneer named John Fries, himself a Federalist, raised an armed force to break them out of jail. Later, federal troops sent by Adams to suppress what Federalists characterized as **Fries's Rebellion** arrested Fries and two of his associates. Charged with treason, the three were tried in federal court, found guilty, and condemned to death.

Settlement with France

The Federalists' seeming overreaction to French provocation and domestic protest alienated increasing numbers of Americans. Adams himself was eager to

---

sedition   Conduct or language inciting rebellion against the authority of a state.

Alien and Sedition Acts   Collectively, the four acts—Alien Act, Alien Enemies Act, Naturalization Act, and Sedition Act—passed by Congress in 1798 designed to prevent immigrants from participating in politics and to silence the anti-Federalist press.

Virginia and Kentucky Resolutions   Statements that the Virginia and Kentucky legislatures issued in 1798 in response to the Alien and Sedition Acts; they asserted the right of states to overrule the federal government.

interpose   To place a barrier between two objects or forces; to Jefferson, the principle of interposition meant that states had the right to use their sovereign power as a barrier between the federal government and the states' citizens when the natural rights of those citizens were at risk.

states' rights   The political position in favor of limiting federal power to allow the greatest possible self-government by the individual states.

Fries's Rebellion   A tax revolt by Pennsylvania citizens in 1799 that was suppressed by federal forces; leader John Fries was condemned to death for treason but received a presidential pardon from John Adams.

end the conflict, and when George Logan sent news from France that Foreign Minister Talleyrand was asking that a new American delegation be sent, Adams seized the opportunity to end the Quasi-War. Telling the Federalist-dominated Congress that he would give them the details later, Adams instructed the American minister to the Netherlands, William Vans Murray, to go immediately to Paris. As rumors of negotiations began to circulate, Hamilton and his supporters became furious, all but accusing Adams of treason. This gave the president the ammunition he needed: he fired Pickering, Wolcott, and McHenry, Hamilton's primary supporters in his cabinet, and then embarrassed the Federalist judiciary by granting a presidential pardon to John Fries and his fellow Pennsylvania rebels.

Adams's diplomatic appeal to France was well timed. When Murray and his delegation arrived in Paris in November 1799, they found that whatever ill feeling might have existed toward the United States had been swept away. On November 9, 1799, **Napoleon Bonaparte** had overthrown the government that was responsible for the XYZ affair. Napoleon was more interested in establishing an empire in Europe than in continuing an indecisive conflict with the United States. After some negotiation, Murray and Napoleon drew up and signed the Convention of Mortefontaine, ending the Quasi-War on September 30, 1800.

The "Revolution of 1800"

→ *What did Thomas Jefferson mean by the statement "Every difference of opinion is not a difference of principles"?*

→ *How did Federalists respond to losing the election of 1800? What does this response reveal about their political attitudes?*

→ *How did Jefferson's vision for America differ from that of Hamilton, Adams, and other Federalists?*

According to the partisan press, the political situation in 1800 was as simple as the contrast between the personalities of the major presidential candidates. The Republican press characterized Adams as an aristocrat and a **spendthrift,** charging that Adams's efforts to expand the powers of the federal government were really attempts to rob citizens of freedom and turn the United States back into a colony of England. In contrast, the Republican press characterized Jefferson as a man of the people, sensitive to the appeals of southern and western agricultural groups who felt perpetually ignored or abused by northeastern Federalists

and their constituents. According to Federalist newspapers, however, Vice President Jefferson was a dangerous radical and an atheist, a man who shared French tastes for radical politics, **dandyism,** and immorality. In the eyes of the Federalists, Adams was a man whose policies and steady-handed administration would bring stability and prosperity, qualities that appealed to manufacturers and merchants in New England, as well as to Calvinists and other supporters of classical republicanism. The rhetoric became so hateful that even Adams and Jefferson got caught up in it—the old friends stopped speaking to each other; nearly twenty years passed before they renewed their friendship.

The Lesser of Republican Evils

As the election of 1800 approached, the split between Adams and Hamilton widened. Both agreed on the necessity of dumping Jefferson as vice president, putting forward Charles Cotesworth Pinckney, hero of the XYZ affair, to replace him. But Adams's behavior in the wake of George Logan's mission to France had angered the Hamiltonians; they now wanted Adams to be gone as well. Having gotten Pinckney into the Electoral College balloting, Hamilton again tried to steal the 1800 election. As before, he advised delegates to withhold votes, but this time he engaged in direct lobbying, even writing a pamphlet in which he questioned Adams's suitability for the presidency.

Hamilton's methods backfired again: Federalists cast one more vote for Adams than for Pinckney. But more important, Hamilton's scheming and his faction's consistent promanufacturing stance had so alienated southern Federalists that many chose to support Jefferson. With Jefferson pulling in the southern vote and his running mate—Burr again—pulling in the craftsmen and small-farm vote in New York and Pennsylvania, the Republicans outscored the Federalists by 16 votes in the Electoral College. But that still did not settle the election. Burr and Jefferson won the same number of electoral votes (see Map 8.1). The tie threw

Napoleon Bonaparte   General who took control of the French government in November 1799, at the end of France's revolutionary period; he eventually proclaimed himself emperor of France and conquered much of the continent of Europe.

spendthrift   A person who spends money recklessly or wastefully.

dandyism   Dressing and behaving in an overly ornate and flamboyant fashion.

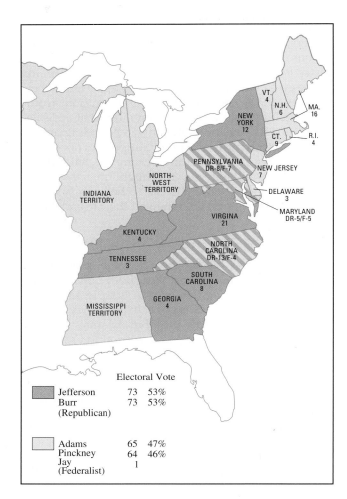

Electoral Vote

Jefferson	73	53%
Burr	73	53%
(Republican)		

Adams	65	47%
Pinckney	64	46%
Jay	1	
(Federalist)		

MAP 8.1   Election of 1800   The political partnership between Thomas Jefferson and Aaron Burr allowed the Republicans to unseat Federalist John Adams in the election of 1800. As this map shows, only New England voted as a bloc for the Federalist, while Burr's political home, New York, went entirely to Jefferson.

the election into the House of Representatives, which was still stocked with hard-line Federalists elected during the Quasi-War hysteria in 1798.

Undoubtedly many Federalists in the House wished they could overturn the election of 1800 altogether, but the Constitution specifically barred them from doing so. Instead, they faced the task of choosing between two men whom most of them viewed as being dangerous radicals bent on destroying the Federalists' hard work. Indecision was plain: in ballot after ballot over six grueling days early in 1801, neither Jefferson nor Burr could win the necessary majority.

In addition to exhaustion and frustration, two things finally combined to break the deadlock. First, Hamil-

ton convinced several Federalists that even though Jefferson's rhetoric was dangerous, the Virginian was a gentleman of property and integrity—a suitable guardian under classical republican theory—whereas Burr was "the most dangerous man of the community." Second, Virginia and Pennsylvania mobilized their militias, intent on preventing a "legislative usurpation" of the popular will. As Delaware senator James Bayard described the situation, "we must risk the Constitution and a Civil War or take Mr. Jefferson." Finally, on the thirty-sixth ballot, on February 17, 1801, Jefferson emerged as the winner.

Federalists and Republicans agreed about very little, but the threat of civil war frightened both factions equally. Not long after Jefferson's election, both parties aligned briefly to pass the **Twelfth Amendment** to the Constitution, which requires separate balloting in the Electoral College for president and vice president, thereby preventing deadlocks like the one that nearly wrecked the nation in 1800. The new electoral procedure led to new sorts of political intrigues, but the manipulation that Hamilton attempted was no longer possible after the Twelfth Amendment was ratified in 1804.

Federalist Defenses and a Loyal Opposition

The Federalists had outmaneuvered themselves in the election of 1800, but they were not about to leave office without erecting some defenses for the political and economic machinery they had constructed. The Federalist-controlled judiciary, which had proved its clout during the controversy over the Alien and Sedition Acts, appeared to offer the strongest bulwark to prevent Republicans from tampering with the Constitution. Thus, during their last days in office, the Federalist **lame ducks** in Congress passed the **Judiciary Act of 1801,** which created sixteen new federal judge-

Twelfth Amendment   Constitutional amendment, ratified in 1804, that provides for separate balloting in the Electoral College for president and vice president.

lame duck   An officeholder who has failed to win, or is ineligible for, reelection but whose term in office has not yet ended.

Judiciary Act of 1801   Law that the Federalist Congress passed to increase the number of federal courts and judicial positions; President Adams rushed to fill these positions with Federalists before his term ended.

Painted while he was at the height of his power and influence, this portrait of Chief Justice John Marshall captures the jurist's imposing presence—he dominated the Supreme Court and American constitutional law for over thirty years after his appointment in 1801, setting many precedents that remain in force today. *Boston Athenaeum.*

ferson's inaugural address was oddly **conciliatory**. "We are all Republicans; we are all Federalists," Jefferson said, seeming to abandon partisan politics and align himself with those who had recently labeled him a "brandy-soaked defamer of churches" and a "contemptible hypocrite." In his mind, all Americans shared the same fundamental principles—the principles of 1776. But even Jefferson considered the election of 1800 a revolution—"as real a revolution in the principles of our government as that of 1776 was in its form."

Jefferson was right in many respects about the revolutionary nature of the election of 1800. Although his inaugural address preached kinship between Federalists and Republicans, the new president repeatedly criticized his opponents for their lack of faith in democracy and the American people. Unlike the Federalists, Jefferson was unalterably opposed to using the power of government against those who opposed his political position. "If there be any among us who would wish to dissolve this Union or to change its republican form," he said, "let them stand undisturbed as monuments of the safety with which error of opinion may be tolerated, where reason is left free to combat it."

As a result of Jefferson's reassuring address, the nation began to share the president's view that "every difference of opinion is not a difference of principles." Even extreme Federalists such as Fisher Ames came to understand that a "party is an association of honest men for honest purposes, and when the State falls into bad hands, is the only efficient defense; a champion who never flinches, a watchman who never sleeps." Ames went on to describe how a loyal **opposition party** should behave. "We are not to revile or abuse

ships, six additional **circuit courts,** and a massive structure of **federal marshals** and clerks. President Adams then rushed to fill all these positions with loyal Federalists, signing appointments right up to midnight on his last day in office. The appointments came in such large numbers and so late in the day that **John Marshall,** Adams's secretary of state, was unable to deliver all the appointment letters before his own term ran out. But Marshall did deliver one letter promptly: the one addressed to himself, making him chief justice of the Supreme Court.

Considering the ill will evident in the Alien and Sedition Acts and the presidential electioneering, Jef-

circuit courts   A court of appeals that has the power to review and either uphold or overturn decisions made by lower courts; in terms of authority, these stand between federal district courts and the Supreme Court.

federal marshal   A law enforcement officer who works directly for the federal district court; each district court has one marshal, who in turn employs a staff of deputies to carry out orders from the court.

John Marshall   Virginia lawyer and politician whom President Adams made chief justice of the Supreme Court; his legal decisions helped shape the role of the Supreme Court in American government.

conciliatory   Striving to overcome distrust or to regain good will.

opposition party   A political party opposed to the party or government in power.

CLASSICAL VERSUS LIBERAL REPUBLICANISM

Political disputes that took place in this country over a century ago remain at the core of national discussion today. One of these has to do with the proper role of a republican government. "Classical" republicans like Alexander Hamilton saw the power of the state as the sole defense against dangerous forces from abroad and lawlessness at home. "Liberal" republicans like Thomas Jefferson claimed that the state itself was the most serious threat to freedom. Classical republicans accused their liberal counterparts of promoting anarchy: John Rutledge, for example, asserted in the House of Representatives in 1798 that liberals "believe it to be their duty to do all in their power to overturn the whole system . . . , they may think a French army and a French invasion necessary." John Nicholas countered, saying "More evil is to be apprehended in this country from the **votaries** of despotism, than from the votaries of France." These charges and countercharges will sound familiar to generations of Americans who have continued to debate which form of republicanism, Classical or Liberal, is the true basis of our American political tradition.

- Reflect upon Jefferson's inaugural assertion that "every difference of opinion is not a difference of principles" by applying it to the debate between classical and liberal republicans in the years directly following the "Revolution of 1800."

- Identify a moment in United States history since 1800 when this debate again became a serious issue in national politics. How were the conflicts resolved in that later situation?

magistrates, or lie even for good cause," he said. "We must act as good citizens, using only truth, and argument, and zeal to impress them." With parties such as these, a system of loyal opposition could become a permanent part of a republican government without risk to security or freedom. And in keeping with the two-party spirit and Jefferson's philosophical commitment to free speech, Congress let the Sedition Act and the Alien Acts expire in 1801 and 1802, and did

not seek to replace them. It also repealed the Naturalization Act, replacing its fourteen-year probationary interval with a five-year naturalization period.

Confident in Americans' ability to reason, Jefferson outlined a plan for a "wise and frugal government" that would seek "equal and exact justice to all men of whatever state or persuasion, religious or political." He would, he said, support state governments "in all their rights" but would not tear down the federal structure or fail to pay its debts.

Jefferson's Vision for America

Jefferson had a strong, positive vision for the nation, and the party made every effort to put his policies into effect. He embraced a specific notion of proper political, economic, and social behavior. The greatest dangers to a republic, he believed, were (1) high population density and the social evils it generated and (2) the concentration of money and power in the hands of a few. Accordingly, Jefferson wanted to steer America away from the large-scale, publicly supported industry so dear to Hamilton and toward an economy founded on yeoman farmers—men who owned their own land, produced their own food, and were beholden to no one. Such men, Jefferson believed, could make political decisions based solely on pure reason and good sense.

But Jefferson was not naive. He knew Americans would continue to demand the comforts and luxuries found in industrial societies. His solution was simple. In America's vast lands, he said, a nation of farmers could produce so much food that "its surplus [could] go to nourish the now perishing births of Europe, who in return would manufacture and send us in exchange our clothes and other comforts." Overpopulation and **urbanization**—the twin causes of corruption in Europe—would not occur in America, for here, Jefferson said, "the immense extent of uncultivated and fertile lands enables every one who will labor, to marry young, and to raise a family of any size."

Making such a system work, however, would require a radical change in economic policy. The government would have to let businesses make their own decisions and succeed or fail in a marketplace free of

votaries   Strict loyalists to a particular ideology.
urbanization   The growth of cities in a nation or region and the shifting of the population from rural to urban areas.

government interference. In an economy with absolutely free trade and an open marketplace, the iron law of **supply and demand** would determine the cost of goods and services. This view of the economy was a direct assault on mercantilist notions of governments controlling prices and restricting trade to benefit the nation-state.

Jefferson believed that, given the shortage of raw materials and foodstuffs in war-torn and overcrowded Europe and its oversupply of manufactured items, free trade in a truly open international economy would benefit the United States. If the European nations could be convinced to drop trade restrictions and let the marketplace decide the value of goods, the principles of supply and demand would ensure profits for American producers and shippers.

Republicanism in Action

→ *How did Republicans deal with the defenses that Federalists put in place in 1801? What successes did they have?*

→ *What policies did Jefferson pursue to carry out his vision for the country? What obstacles did he encounter?*

When Jefferson assumed office, he ushered a new spirit into national politics and the presidency. A combination of circumstances moved him to lead a much simpler life than had his predecessors. For one thing, he was the first president to be inaugurated in the new national capital, the still largely uncompleted Washington City, which afforded quite different and much more limited **amenities.** Washington lacked the taverns, **salons,** and entertaining social circles that both previous capitals, New York and Philadelphia, had offered. Personal preferences also moved him in a simpler direction. He refused, for example, to ride in a carriage, choosing to go by horseback through Washington's muddy and rutted streets. He continued to give parties as he had done in Paris, but he sat his guests at a round table so that no one might be seen as more important than the others. He abandoned the fashion of wearing a wig, letting his red hair stand out, and he sometimes entertained with startling informality, wearing frayed slippers and work clothes.

But this show of simplicity and his conciliatory inaugural address were somewhat misleading. Jefferson was a hardworking partisan politician and administrator whose main objective was to turn the nation around to his vision of republican virtue with all pos-

Suffering a lifelong sensitivity to cold as well as a dislike for formality, Thomas Jefferson usually chose to dress practically, in fairly plain clothes that kept him warm. This 1822 portrait by Thomas Sully captures the former president in his customary greatcoat, unadorned suit, and well-worn boots. *"Thomas Jefferson" by Thomas Sully. West Point Museum, United States Military Academy, West Point, N.Y.*

sible speed. He quickly launched a program to revamp the American economy and give the United States a place in the international community. Along the way, he captured many Americans' affection and their political loyalty but also alienated those who did not share his vision or who lacked his zeal.

supply and demand   The two factors that determine price in an economy based on private property: (1) how much of a commodity is available (supply) and (2) how many people want it (demand).
amenities   Conveniences, comforts, and services.
salon   A gathering place, generally in a private home, where people came together to discuss their common interests; in the eighteenth and early nineteenth centuries, these were often the places where politicians gathered to discuss philosophy and policy issues.

Assault on Federalist Defenses

Aware of the partisan purpose behind the Judiciary Act of 1801 and Adams's midnight appointments, Republicans chose to wage an equally aggressive partisan war to reverse Federalist control of the justice system. In January 1802, Republicans in Congress proposed the repeal of the 1801 Judiciary Act, arguing that the new circuit courts were outrageously expensive and unnecessary. Federalists countered that if Congress repealed the act, it would in effect be terminating judges for reasons other than the "high crimes and misdemeanors" mentioned in the Constitution, thereby violating the separation of powers. Congress proceeded anyway, replacing the Judiciary Act of 1801 with the Judiciary Act of 1802, and awaited the response of the Federalist courts.

The **constitutionality** of the new Judiciary Act was never tested, but the power of the judicial branch to interpret and enforce federal law did become a major issue the following year. On taking office, Jefferson's secretary of state, James Madison, held back the appointment letters that John Marshall had been unable to deliver before the expiration of his term. One jilted appointee was William Marbury, who was to have been **justice of the peace** for the newly created District of Columbia (see pages 197; 199). Marbury, with the support of his party, filed suit in the Supreme Court. According to Marbury, the Judiciary Act of 1789 gave the federal courts the power to order the executive branch to deliver his appointment.

Marbury v. Madison was Chief Justice Marshall's first major case, and in it he proved his political as well as his judicial ingenuity. Marshall was keenly aware that in a direct confrontation between the executive and judicial branches, the judiciary was sure to lose. Rather than risking a serious blow to the dignity of the Supreme Court, Marshall ruled in 1803 that the Constitution contained no provision for the Supreme Court to issue such orders as the Judiciary Act of 1789 required and that therefore the law was unconstitutional.

This decision put Jefferson and Madison in a difficult political position. On one hand, the authors of the Virginia and Kentucky Resolutions were on record for arguing that the states and not the courts should determine the constitutionality of federal laws. But political realities forced them to accept Marshall's decision in this case if they wanted to block Adams's handpicked men from assuming lifetime appointments in powerful judicial positions. Although this **precedent** for **judicial review** did not immediately invalidate the principles set forth in Jefferson's and Madison's earlier **manifestos,** it established the standard that federal courts, rather than states, could decide the constitutionality of acts of Congress.

Marshall's decision in *Marbury v. Madison* gave the Republicans the power to withhold undelivered letters of appointment from the Adams administration, but it gave them no power to control the behavior of judges whose appointments were already official. Thus, in the aftermath of the Marbury decision, Republican radicals in Congress decided to take aim at particularly partisan Federalist judges.

John Pickering of New Hampshire was an easy first target. A mentally ill alcoholic, he was known to rave incoherently both on and off the bench, usually about the evils of Jefferson and liberal republicanism. No one, not even staunch Federalists, doubted that the besotted man was incompetent, but it was far from certain that he had committed the "high crimes and misdemeanors" for which he was **impeached** in 1803. Whether he had or not, the Senate found him guilty and removed him from office.

Emboldened by that easy victory and armed with a powerful precedent, radical Republicans took on Supreme Court justice Samuel Chase. Chase was notorious for making partisan decisions—such as condemning John Fries to death—and for using the federal bench as an anti-Republican soapbox. Unlike Pickering, Chase defended himself very competently, making the political motivations behind the impeachment effort obvious to all observers. In the end, both

---

constitutionality Accordance with the principles or provisions of the Constitution.

justice of the peace The lowest level of judge in some state court systems, usually responsible for hearing small claims and minor criminal cases; because Washington, the District of Columbia, is a federal territory rather than a state, the justice of the peace for that district is a federal appointee.

Marbury v. Madison Supreme Court decision (1803) declaring part of the Judiciary Act of 1789 unconstitutional, thereby establishing an important precedent in favor of judicial review.

precedent An event or decision that may be used as an example in similar cases later on.

judicial review The power of the Supreme Court to review the constitutionality of laws passed by Congress and by the states.

manifesto A written statement publicly declaring the views of its author.

impeach To formally charge a public official with criminal conduct in office; once the House of Representatives has impeached a federal official, the official is then tried in the Senate on the stated charges.

Although Jefferson's efforts to stop Barbary pirate looting against American shipping in the Mediterranean were largely a failure, the struggle provided a wonderful training ground for future military leaders. Young naval commander Stephen Decatur was one such figure. In the course of the fighting, Decatur boarded a pirate ship and engaged in hand-to-hand fighting against the crew, eventually winning the fight even though he had already been wounded by a bullet through his arm. *Naval Historical Center.*

Federalists and many Republicans voted to dismiss the charges, returning Chase to his position on the Supreme Court. The failure to impeach Chase demonstrated that the political structure was not going to tip decisively to either side and made Jefferson's inaugural statement of principle a guideline for political reality: both sides would have to compromise in charting the course for the nation.

Implementing a New Economy

Still, Republicans were determined on one partisan agenda item: tearing down Hamilton's economic structure and replacing it with a new one more consistent with Jefferson's vision. Responsibility for planning and implementing this economic policy fell to Treasury Secretary **Albert Gallatin.** Gallatin's first effort as secretary of the treasury was to try to settle the nation's debts. His ambitious goal was to make the United States entirely debt free by 1817. With Jefferson's approval, Gallatin implemented a radical course of budget cutting, going so far as to close several American embassies overseas to save money. At home, Gallatin and Jefferson pared administrative costs by reducing staff and putting an end to the fancy receptions and other social events that President Adams had so enjoyed. The administration cut the military by half, reducing the army from four thousand to twenty-five hundred men and the navy from twenty-five ships to a mere seven.

But Gallatin's cost cutting did much more than just reduce the national budget. First, Gallatin was able to mask the firing of loyal Federalists still employed in civil service in a seemingly nonpartisan appeal to fiscal responsibility. He accomplished another ideological goal by reducing the overall federal presence, putting more responsibilities onto the states, where his and Jefferson's philosophy said they belonged. In addition, Gallatin's plan called for a significant change in how the government raised money. In 1802 the Republican Congress repealed all **internal taxes,** leaving customs duties and the sale of western lands as the sole sources of federal revenue. With this one sweeping gesture, Gallatin struck a major blow for Jefferson's economic vision by tying the nation's financial future to westward expansion and foreign trade. But this vision would soon face serious challenges.

Threats to Jefferson's Vision

One threat to Jefferson's commitment to foreign trade came from pirates who patrolled the northern coast of Africa from Tangier to Tripoli, controlling access to the Mediterranean Sea. Ever since gaining independence,

Albert Gallatin   Treasury secretary in Jefferson's administration; he favored limited government and reduced the federal debt by cutting spending.

internal taxes   Taxes collected directly from citizens, like Alexander Hamilton's various excise taxes (see page 202), as opposed to tariffs or other taxes collected in connection with foreign trade.

the United States had in effect been bribing the Barbary pirates not to attack American ships (see page 185). By 1800, fully a fifth of the federal budget was earmarked for this purpose, a cost Gallatin wished to see eliminated as he tried to balance the nation's books. To Jefferson, principle was as important as financial considerations. Jefferson decided on war. Asserting presidential privilege as commander in chief, he dispatched navy ships to the Mediterranean in 1801.

The war that followed was a fiasco from anyone's point of view. After some indecisive engagements between the American fleet and the pirates, Jefferson's navy suffered a major defeat with the capture of a prize warship, the *Philadelphia*, and its entire crew. A bold but unsuccessful attempt to invade Tripoli by land across the Libyan Desert led only to a threat to kill the crew of the *Philadelphia* and other hostages. The war dragged along until 1805, when the United States finally negotiated peace terms, agreeing to pay $60,000 for the release of the hostages and accepting the pirates' promise to stop raiding American shipping.

In the meantime, France and Spain posed a serious threat to Jefferson's dream of rapid westward expansion. As settlers continued to pour into the region between the Appalachian Mountains and the Mississippi River, the commercial importance of that inland waterway increased. Whoever controlled the mouth of the Mississippi—the place where it flows past New Orleans and into the Gulf of Mexico and the open seas—would have the power to make or break the interior economy.

In accordance with the Treaty of San Lorenzo (1795) (see page 202), Spain had granted American farmers the right to ship cargoes down the Mississippi without paying tolls, and had given American merchants permission to **transship** goods from New Orleans to Atlantic ports without paying export duties. In 1800, however, Napoleon had traded some of France's holdings in southern Europe to Spain in exchange for Spain's land in North America. The United States had no agreement with France concerning navigation on the Mississippi, so the deal between Spain and France threatened to scuttle American commerce on the river. Anxiety over this issue turned to outright panic when, preparatory to the transfer of the land to France, Spanish officials suspended free trade in New Orleans.

Jefferson responded on two fronts. Backing away from his usual anti-British position, he announced, "The day France takes possession of New Orleans we must marry ourselves to the British fleet and nation," and he dispatched James Monroe to talk with the British about a military alliance. He also had Monroe

With French backing, François Dominique Toussaint L'Ouverture (center) led his fellow slaves in a revolt against their French and Spanish masters, driving the Europeans from the West Indian island of Santo Domingo in 1791. Emperor Napoleon Bonaparte double-crossed Toussaint in 1802, sending a French army to seize the island. Although Toussaint was captured, his army defeated the French, creating the republic of Haiti in 1804. *"Toussaint L'Ouverture" by William Edouard Scott. Amistad Research Center, Tulane University, New Orleans, AFAC Collection.*

instruct the American minister to France, Robert Livingston, that he could spend as much as $2 million to try to purchase New Orleans and as much adjacent real estate as possible.

Napoleon may have been considering the creation of a Caribbean empire when he acquired Louisiana from Spain. Rich with sugar, the island of **Santo Domingo**

---

transship   The practice of shipping cargo to a secondary port and then transferring it to other ships for transport to a final destination; cargos from up the Mississippi River were shipped by barge to New Orleans and then loaded onto ocean-going vessels to be carried to American ports along the Atlantic coast.

Santo Domingo   Caribbean island (originally named Hispaniola by Christopher Columbus and also known as Saint Domingue) shared by the modern nations of Haiti and the Dominican Republic.

was strategically well placed to serve as a hub for French exploitation of the North American interior. France and Spain had shared ownership of the island until an army under the leadership of a former slave named **François Dominique Toussaint L'Ouverture** liberated the French half in 1791 and the Spanish half ten years later. With backing from the French, Toussaint made himself president of the unified nation, but in 1802 Napoleon betrayed him by sending an invasion force to reclaim Santo Domingo. Americans feared that the French army's next destination would be New Orleans.

The French army was able to defeat and capture Toussaint, but no more. The rebels' military skills and yellow fever, malaria, and other tropical diseases destroyed the French force. Stymied in the Caribbean, Napoleon turned his full attention back to extending his holdings in Europe and was seeking funds to finance a continental war. Thus, by the time Monroe and Livingston entered into negotiations with the French in 1803, Napoleon had instructed Foreign Minister Talleyrand to offer the whole of Louisiana to the Americans for $15 million.

Pushing Westward

Although Livingston and Monroe had been authorized to spend only $2 million for the purchase of Louisiana, they jumped at the deal offered by Talleyrand, hoping that President Jefferson would approve. The president not only approved but was overjoyed. The deal contained three important benefits for Jefferson and the nation. It removed one European power—France—from the continent and saved Jefferson from having to ally the United States with Britain. It secured the Mississippi River for shipments of American agricultural products to industrial Europe. And it doubled the size of the United States, opening uncharted new expanses for settlement by yeoman farmers.

The **Louisiana Purchase** was immensely popular among most Americans, but it raised significant ideological and constitutional questions. Some Federalists *and* Republicans questioned whether the United States could acquire this territory and its many residents without becoming an empire; something entirely at war with the rhetoric of our Revolution against the British. To this Jefferson responded by spinning the term "empire" into the phrase "empire of liberty," emphasizing that the new territory would aid Americans in securing and extending the benefits of our revolutionary tradition. Members of both parties also pointed out that the framers of the Constitution had made no provision for the acquisition of new territories by the United States, saying that the nation was prohibited from extending

westward beyond its then-current boundaries without specific constitutional authorization. Again, Jefferson parried with rhetoric, saying: "Strict observance to the written laws is doubtless one of the high duties of a good citizen, but it is not the highest. The laws of necessity, of self-preservation, of saving our country when in danger, are of a higher obligation." In the end, Jefferson got his way: Congress voted overwhelmingly for ratification of the treaty in November 1803.

Even before the Louisiana Purchase, "laws of necessity" had led Jefferson to exert presidential power in an unusual way. Although Spanish, French, and American fur traders, outlaws, and soldiers of fortune had crisscrossed Louisiana over the years, little systematic exploration had been done. When rumors of the land transfer between France and Spain began circulating, Jefferson started preparations to send a covert spy mission. In a series of confidential letters, Jefferson informed his private secretary, **Meriwether Lewis,** that he was to form a party that would pretend to be on a scientific mission, and the president issued false papers to that effect. Their primary mission, however, was to note the numbers of French, Spanish, and other agents in the area, along with the numbers and condition of the Indians, and to chart major waterways and other important strategic sites (see Map 8.2). They were also to open the way for direct dealings between the Indians and the United States, undermining the Indians' relations with the Spanish and French whenever possible. Early in 1803, months before Congress authorized the Louisiana Purchase, the president sought and received a secret congressional **appropriation** granting the funds necessary to finance the mission.

Lewis, his co-commander **William Clark,** and the rest of the Corps of Discovery set out by boat in the

François Dominique Toussaint L'Ouverture   Black revolutionary who liberated the island of Santo Domingo, only to see it reinvaded by the French in 1802.

Louisiana Purchase   The U.S. purchase of Louisiana from France for $15 million in 1803; the Louisiana Territory extended from the Mississippi River to the Rocky Mountains.

Meriwether Lewis   Jefferson aide who was sent to explore the Louisiana Territory in 1803; he later served as its governor.

appropriation   Public funds authorized for a specific purpose.

William Clark   Soldier and explorer who joined Meriwether Lewis as co-leader on the expedition to explore the Louisiana Territory; he was responsible for mapmaking.

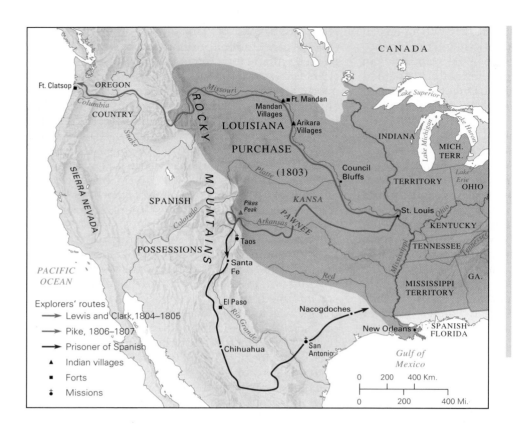

MAP 8.2   Louisiana Purchase and American Exploration As this map shows, President Jefferson added an enormous tract of land to the United States when he purchased Louisiana from France in 1803. The president was eager to learn about the new territory and sent two exploration teams into the West. In addition to collecting information, Lewis and Clark's and Pike's expeditions sought to commit Indian groups along their paths to alliances with the United States and to undermine French, Spanish, and British relations with the Indians, even in those areas that were not officially part of the United States. In Pike's case, this covert intelligence assignment led to his arrest by Spanish authorities and eventual expulsion from their territory.

spring of 1804. Pushing its way up the Missouri River, the party arrived among the Mandan Indians (see pages 13–14) in present-day North Dakota in the late fall. They chose to winter among the Mandans, a decision that may have ensured the expedition's success. The Mandans were a settled agricultural group who had been farming along the upper Missouri for over a thousand years. Unlike many of their neighbors, they had resisted the temptation to abandon their villages for mounted buffalo hunting when horses had arrived on the northern plains after 1700. Their villages, which offered food and shelter for the wandering hunting tribes, soon became hubs in the evolving Plains trading and raiding system (see pages 48–49). By wintering with the Mandans, the expedition came into contact with many of the Indian and European groups that participated in the complex economy of the West. Lewis and Clark acted on Jefferson's secret instructions by learning all they could from the Mandans and their visitors about the fur trade, the nature of military alliances, and the tribes that lived farther west.

One particularly important contact Lewis and Clark made during the Mandan winter was with a French trapper named Charbonneau and his Shoshone wife, **Sacajawea.** Between the two of them, Sacajawea and Charbonneau spoke several of the languages understood by the Indians in the Far West and possessed knowledge about the geography and the various peoples in the area. With their help, Lewis and Clark were able to make contact with the Shoshones, who aided them in crossing the Rocky Mountains. From there, the expedition passed from Indian group to Indian group along a chain of friendship. The Nez Perce Indians, for example, were allied to the Shoshones and accepted the party hospitably. The Nez Perces then sent word down the Columbia River that these men were allies, ensuring their safe and speedy passage. Following this chain of Indian hospitality, the expedition finally reached the Pacific Ocean in November 1805.

While many Native American groups genuinely welcomed Lewis and Clark, others remained dubious about the newcomers. On the return trip, part of the

Sacajawea   Shoshone woman who served as guide and interpreter on the Lewis and Clark expedition.

Daring though they were, Lewis and Clark and the men who accompanied them on their transcontinental exploring (and spy) mission would not have succeeded, or possibly even have survived, had it not been for the assistance of the Indian people who helped them at every stage of their voyage. One in particular, the Shoshone woman Sacajawea, shown here with the expedition's leaders, was instrumental in guiding them across the Rocky Mountains and on to the Pacific. *The Granger Collection, New York.*

expedition ventured off its original outward course to explore new territory and encountered a party of **Piegan Indians.** Allied closely with trading interests in Canada and involved in sporadic war with the Shoshones, the Piegans afforded the party no special diplomatic status, attempting to steal a gun from them while they slept. The Americans thwarted the theft and, in the melee that followed, were able to fight the Piegans off long enough to make a strategic retreat. Years later, Piegan Indians and their allies in the northern Rockies cited this encounter as justification for continuing hostilities toward Americans and their Indian trading partners.

Europeans in the interior were also skeptical of American "scientific" parties. In 1806 Lieutenant Zebulon M. Pike set out on a venture to explore the territory between the Missouri and Red Rivers south of Lewis and Clark's route. The Pawnee and Kansa Indians in the region received Pike with great reserve,

pointing out that the Spanish had recently sent an army through their territory demanding Indian allegiance. Undaunted, Pike continued his journey by following the trail left by the Spanish force, eventually arriving in what is now Colorado (see Map 8.2). From there, he pushed southward, venturing into New Mexico. Though he claimed that this trespass was an innocent navigational error, his party nonetheless was captured by a Spanish army detachment and held for three months. Pike and his men were finally escorted back to the United States and set free with a warning to stay out of Spanish lands and Spanish affairs.

Challenge and Uncertainty in Jefferson's America

→ *How did the life of the average American change during Jefferson's presidency?*

→ *What place did Native Americans and African Americans have in the America Jefferson envisioned? How did each of these groups respond to these roles?*

Jefferson's policies not only put the nation on a new road politically and economically but also brought a new spirit into the land. The Virginian's commitment to opportunity and progress, to openness and frugality, offered a stark contrast in approach and style to the policies of his predecessors. The congressional elections of 1802 and the presidential election in 1804 proved Jefferson's popularity and the Republican Party's strong appeal. Nevertheless, some disturbing social and intellectual undercurrents began to surface during his second term. National expansion strained conventional social institutions as white farmers, entrepreneurs, and adventurers seized the opportunities that Republican economic and expansion policies offered. Adding to the strain was the fact that the Jeffersonian spirit was more of a promise than a commitment and that Jefferson's vision for the republic excluded many.

The Heritage of Partisan Politics

The popularity of Jefferson's party was abundantly clear in 1804. Jefferson had won an extremely narrow

Piegan Indians The branch of the Blackfoot Indians who resided in areas of what is now Montana during the late eighteenth and early nineteenth centuries.

victory in 1800, and his Republican Party had won significant but hardly overwhelming majorities in Congress. The congressional elections of 1802, however, had virtually eclipsed Federalist power, and Federalists faced the presidential election of 1804 with dread. Former president John Adams commented, "The power of the Administration rests upon the support of a much stronger majority of the people throughout the Union than the former administrations ever possessed since the first establishment of the Constitution."

Despite an abiding faith in the emerging two-party system, staunch Federalist congressman Fisher Ames withdrew from public life, followed by John Jay and other prominent leaders. Some traditional Federalists, however, continued to fight. The party tapped former vice-presidential candidate Charles Cotesworth Pinckney to head the 1804 presidential ticket. For the vice presidency, the Federalists chose Rufus King, a defender of the notion of loyal opposition and the two-party system.

Federalists had trouble identifying issues on which to build a viable platform. Hoping to capitalize on **anti-expansionist** fears in New England and sentiments favoring states' rights in the South, the Federalists focused their campaign on Jefferson's acquisition of Louisiana. In a direct appeal to Yankee **frugality**, Federalists charged that Jefferson had paid too much for the new territory and was attempting to use the region to build a unified agrarian political faction. Pinckney accused Jefferson of violating his own political principles by exerting a federal power not explicitly granted in the Constitution. As noted above, some Republicans shared these views, but no one could question Jefferson's overall success in accomplishing the party's goals. During his first administration, Jefferson had eliminated internal taxes, stimulated westward migration, eliminated the hated Alien and Sedition Acts, and rekindled hope in the hearts of many disaffected Americans.

At the same time, he had proved that he was no threat to national commerce or to individual affluence. Despite Federalist fears, the economy continued to grow at the same rate during Jefferson's tenure in office as it had under the Federalists. In the process, those who engaged in international trade amassed enormous fortunes. Such economic growth permitted Jefferson to maintain a favorable **balance of payments** throughout his first administration, a feat the Federalists had never achieved. And with Gallatin's help, Jefferson had proved his fiscal responsibility by building up a multimillion-dollar Treasury surplus.

The enormous scope of Jefferson's successes and the limited scope of his opponent's platform helped swing the election of 1804 firmly over to the Republicans. Jefferson won 162 electoral votes to Pinckney's 14, carrying every state except Connecticut and Delaware.

Westward Expansion and Social Stress

Eastern Federalists and other critics of Jefferson's vision had some justification for their concerns about the rapid growth of the West. A baby boom had followed the Revolution, and as new territories opened in the West, young people streamed into the region at a rate that alarmed many. This had an unsettling effect on communities in the East. During the eighteenth century, older people maintained authority by controlling the distribution of land to their children. With only so much worthwhile land to go around, sons and daughters lived with and worked for their parents until their elders saw fit to deed property over to them. As a result, children living in the East generally did not become independent—that is, they did not become church members, marry, or operate their own farms or businesses—until they were in their thirties. Economic opportunities available in the west, however, lessened young people's need to rely on their parents for support and lowered the age at which they began to break away. During the early part of the nineteenth century, the age at which children attained independence fell steadily. By the 1820s, children were joining churches in their teens and marrying in their early to mid-twenties. Breathing the new air of independence, intrepid young people not only migrated west but also challenged their parents' authority at home. Obviously social and political traditionalists were upset. Business interests in the East were also upset as they witnessed westward expansion drawing off population, which in time would drive up the price of labor and reduce profits.

Conditions out west were even less stable as rapid growth put enormous stress on conventional institutions. The population of Ohio, for example, grew from

---

anti-expansionist   One opposed to the policy of expanding a country by acquiring new territory.

frugality   An unwillingness to spend money for unnecessary things; by stereotype, New Englanders (Yankees) supposedly have an ingrained tendency to frugality.

balance of payments   The difference between a nation's total payments to foreign countries and its total receipts from abroad.

The Mississippi River drainage system was the only reliable transportation route for Americans moving into the West during the early 1800s. Farmers moved produce to market on keelboats like the one depicted here. Above decks, cargo and livestock endured weather and exposure to mosquitoes and other river menaces. Below decks, however, there was a cabin-like environment where people could eat, drink, and sleep in comfort during the trip downriver. One problem with this mode of transport was that the current on the giant river made upstream travel impossible during much of the year, so boats like this one were often sold for lumber after they reached New Orleans. *The New York Public Library/Art Resource, NY; (inset)* **interior of a Flatboat by Charles-Alexander Lesueur, 1826,** *Muséum d'histoire naturelle, Le Havre, France.*

45,000 in 1800 to 231,000 in 1810, and similar rates of growth occurred in the new states of Tennessee and Kentucky and in territories from Louisiana north to Michigan and west to Missouri. Authorities in the West found these increases challenging as they tried to deal with the practical matters of maintaining governments, economies, and peaceful relations among the new settlers and between the settlers and neighboring Indians.

Most of the people who moved west looked forward to achieving the agrarian self-sufficiency that Jefferson advocated, but life in the West was far more complicated. Inexpensive, reliable transportation was impossible in the vast, rugged interior, and Jefferson's notion of breadbasket America trading with industrial Europe was doomed without it. No navigable streams ran eastward from America's interior across the Appalachians to the Atlantic, and the ridges of those mountains made road building extremely difficult.

Only two reliable routes existed for transporting produce from the interior to shipping centers in the East. The Ohio-Mississippi-Missouri drainage system provided a reliable watercourse, and huge cargoes flowed along its stream. Shipping goods on the Mississippi, however, was a dangerous and expensive operation. Because of the river's strong current, loads could be shipped only one way—downstream. Rafts were built for the purpose and then were broken up and sold for lumber in New Orleans. Shippers had to return home by foot on the **Natchez Trace.** On both

> **Natchez Trace**   A road connecting Natchez, Mississippi, with Nashville, Tennessee; it was commercially and strategically important in the late eighteenth and early nineteenth centuries.

legs of the journey, travelers risked attack by river pirates, Indians, and sickness. Moreover, it was virtually impossible for shippers to take manufactured goods back with them because of the condition of the roads and the distances involved. The other river route—the St. Lawrence River, flowing east from the Great Lakes to the northern Atlantic—presented similar problems. In addition, that river passed through British Canada and therefore was closed to American commercial traffic.

As a result of geographical isolation and the rapid pace of settlement, the economy in the West became highly localized. Settlers arriving with neither food nor seed bought surplus crops produced by established farmers. The little capital that was generated in this way supported the development of local industries in hundreds of farming villages. Enterprising craftsmen ranging from **coopers** to **wheelwrights** produced hand-manufactured items on demand. As long as people kept moving into an area, local economies boomed. But when new arrivals slowed and then stopped, the market for surplus crops and local manufactures collapsed, and the economy went bust. Swinging from boom to bust and back again became a way of life in newly settled areas.

Along with economic instability, social instability was also common. The odd mixture of ethnic, religious, and national groups found in western villages did little to bring cohesiveness to community life.

The Religious Response to Social Change

The changes taking place in the young republic stirred conflicting religious currents. One was liberalism in religious thought. The other was a new **evangelicalism.**

Born of the Enlightenment (see page 100) in France, Scotland, and England, liberal religious thought emphasized the connection between **rationalism** and faith. To rationalists like both Jefferson and Adams, the possibility that a being as perfect as God might behave irrationally was unthinkable. In fact, for such men, the more plain, reasonable, and verifiable religious claims were, the more likely it was that they emanated from God. Less perfect than God, it was man who had cluttered the plain revealed truth with irrational claims and insolvable mysteries. For his part, Jefferson was so convinced of this logic that he edited his own version of the Bible, keeping only the moral principles and the solid historical facts and discarding anything supernatural.

This liberal creed led many, including Jefferson, to abandon organized religion altogether. Not all liberals were so quick to bolt organized worship however. John Adams, for example, continued to adhere to New England Congregationalism, but he and others used their influence to promote a young and more liberal clergy who sought to insert a heavy dose of rationalism into the old Puritan structure. Rejecting such traditional mysteries as the **Trinity** and the literal divinity of Christ, a so-called **Unitarian** movement emerged and expanded inside Congregational churches during the years just before and following the American Revolution. Liberal influence within Congregationalism became so prominent in New England that Unitarians were able to engineer the election of their own **Henry Ware** as the senior professor of theology at Harvard College, formerly the educational heart of orthodox Calvinist America. Though outraged, more traditional Congregationalists did little immediately to oust liberals from their churches. In the decades to come, however, doctrinal disagreements between the parties led to virtual religious warfare.

While deism and Unitarianism were gaining strong footholds in eastern cities, disorder, insecurity, and missionizing activities were helping to foster a very different kind of religious response in the West. Although Methodists, Baptists, Presbyterians, and evangelical Congregationalists disagreed on many specific

cooper   A person who makes or repairs wooden barrels.

wheelwright   A person who makes or repairs wheels for carts, wagons, or other vehicles.

evangelicalism   A Protestant religious persuasion that emphasizes the literal truth of the Gospels and salvation through faith alone; in the early nineteenth century, it became infused with increasing amounts of romantic emotionalism and an emphasis on converting others.

rationalism   The theory that the exercise of reason, rather than the acceptance of authority or spiritual revelation, is the only valid basis for belief and the best source of spiritual truth.

Trinity   The Christian belief that God consists of three divine persons: Father, Son, and Holy Spirit.

Unitarian   A religion that denies the Trinity, teaching that God exists only in one person; it also stresses individual freedom of belief and the free use of reason in religion.

Henry Ware   Liberal Congregationalist who was elected senior theologian at Harvard College in 1805, making Unitarianism the dominant religious view at the previously Calvinist stronghold.

Evangelical denominations gained ever wider followings during the early nineteenth century as the uncertainties accompanying rapid expansion took their toll on national self-confidence. Mass baptisms like this one painted by Russian tourist Pavel Svinin celebrated the emotional moment of conversion and the individual's rebirth as a Christian. *"A Philadelphia Anabaptist Immersion During a Storm" by Pavel Svinin. The Metropolitan Museum of Art, Rogers Fund, 1942. (42.95.20). Photograph © 1979 The Metropolitan Museum of Art.*

principles, they all emphasized the spirited preaching that could bring about the emotional moment of conversion—the moment of realization that without the saving grace of God, every soul is lost. Each of these denominations concentrated on training a new, young ministry and sending it to preach in every corner of the nation. In this way, another religious awakening swept across America, beginning in Cane Ridge, Kentucky, in 1801 and spreading throughout the South and West.

The new evangelicalism stressed the individual nature of salvation but at the same time emphasized the importance of Christian community. Looking back to the first generation of Puritans in America, the new evangelicals breathed new life into the old Puritan notion of God's plan for the universe and the leading role that Americans were to play in its unfolding. As early nineteenth-century Presbyterian divine Lyman Beecher put it, "It was the opinion of [Jonathan] Edwards that the millennium would commence in America . . . all providential signs of the times lend corroboration to it."

Early nineteenth-century evangelicals formed official **synods,** councils, and conventions as well as hundreds of voluntary associations designed to carry out what they characterized as God's plan for America. These organizations helped counterbalance the forces of extreme individualism and social disorder by providing ideological underpinnings for the expansive behavior of westerners and a sense of mission to ease the insecurities produced by venturing into the unknown. They also provided an institutional framework that brought some stability to communities in which traditional controls were lacking.

synod   An official governing council of a religious denomination that makes decisions on theological matters and matters of church law.

These attractive features helped evangelicalism to sweep across the West. During the early nineteenth century, it became the dominant religious persuasion in that region.

The Problem of Race in Jefferson's Republic

Jefferson's policies enabled many Americans to benefit from the nation's development, but they certainly did not help everyone. Neither Native Americans nor African Americans had much of a role in Jefferson's republic, and each group was subject to different forms of unequal treatment during the Jeffersonian era.

A slaveholder himself, Jefferson expressed strong views about African Americans. In his *Notes on the State of Virginia* (1781), Jefferson asserted that blacks were "inferior to whites in the endowments both of body and mind." Even when presented with direct evidence of superior black intellectual accomplishments, Jefferson remained unmoved. When the well-respected African American mathematician, astronomer, and engineer Benjamin Banneker sent a copy of an almanac he had prepared to Jefferson, the then secretary of state replied, "No body wishes more than I do to see such proofs as you exhibit, that nature has given to our black brethren, talents equal to those of the other colors of men." However, he refused to acknowledge that Banneker's work provided such proofs. "I have a long letter from Banneker," Jefferson later told his friend Joel Barlow, "which shows him to have had a mind of very common stature indeed." He went on to suggest that the almanac had actually been written by a white engineer who was intent on "puffing" Banneker's reputation.

Jefferson was convinced, and stated publicly on many occasions, that the white and black races could not live together without inevitably polluting both. This was the key reason for what little opposition he voiced to slavery and for his continued involvement in various projects to remove African Americans by colonizing them in Africa. And yet despite this attitude, many of his contemporaries believed that he kept a slave mistress, Sally Hemings, by whom he fathered several children, a contention that modern DNA evidence has demonstrated as credible. Even so, almost no documentary evidence about the relationship exists despite the fact that hundreds of the nation's most prolific writers (and gossips) passed through Jefferson's home regularly. Circumstantial evidence, however, suggests that their relationship was an exclusive one and lasted for a long period of time. And traditions passed down through generations of Sally Hemings's descendants claim that theirs was a sentimental, even romantic bond.

Given his belief in racial inequality, it seems contradictory that Jefferson could have had a long-term affectionate relationship with an African American woman. If so, it reflects equally deep-seated contradictions that shot through American society at the time. Truly a man of his century and his social class, Jefferson was convinced that women, like slaves, existed to serve and entertain men. Thus his entanglement with Hemings, who probably was the half-sister of Jefferson's deceased wife, seemed no more unequal or unnatural than his marriage. But while the relationship may have seemed perfectly natural behind closed doors, the race code to which Jefferson gave voice in his various publications and official utterances defined it as entirely unacceptable in public. This rigid separation between public and private behavior led Jefferson to keep the relationship secret, and his friends and family—even most of his political enemies—joined him in a conspiracy of silence. This, too, was reflective of broader social ambiguities, contradictions that defined the sex lives of masters and slaves in Jefferson's South.

Throughout the Jeffersonian era, the great majority of African Americans lived in that South, and most of them were slaves. But from the 1790s onward, the number of free blacks increased steadily. Emancipation did not bring equality, however, even in northern states. Many states did not permit free blacks to testify in court, vote, or exercise other fundamental freedoms accorded to whites. Public schools often refused admission to black children. Even churches were often closed to blacks who wished to worship.

Some African Americans began to respond to systematic exclusion and to express their cultural and social identity by forming their own institutions. In Philadelphia, tension between white and free black Methodists led former slave Richard Allen to form the Bethel Church for Negro Methodists in 1793. Two years later, Allen became the first black deacon ordained in America. Ongoing tension with the white Methodist hierarchy, however, eventually led Allen to secede from the church and form his own **African Methodist Episcopal Church** (Bethel) in 1816. Similar controversies in New York led black divine James Varick to

> **African Methodist Episcopal Church**   African American branch of Methodism established in Philadelphia in 1816 and in New York in 1821.

found an African Methodist Episcopal Church (Zion) in that city in 1821.

African American leadership was not confined to religious and intellectual realms. **James Forten,** for example, a free-born African American, followed up on his experience as a sailor in the Revolutionary navy with a career as a sail maker in Philadelphia. Despite both overt and subtle racial discrimination, he acquired his own company in 1798, eventually becoming a major employer of both African American and white workers. Though himself a Quaker, Forten often cooperated with Richard Allen but did not subscribe to projects designed to separate the races, working consistently—even to the point of petitioning Congress and the Pennsylvania assembly—to pass laws ensuring desegregation and equal treatment. In cooperation with other African American entrepreneurs, such as Boston's Paul Cuffe, Forten invested expertise, capital, and personal influence in an effort to create jobs for black city-dwellers and opportunities for budding black businessmen. Despite these efforts, the overall racial atmosphere in Jefferson's America significantly limited the number of African American leaders who attained positions of wealth or influence.

Jefferson thought differently of Native Americans than he did of African Americans. He considered Indians to be "savages" but was not convinced that they were biologically inferior to Europeans: "They are formed in mind as well as in body, on the same module with the 'Homo Sapiens Europaeus,'" he said. Jefferson attributed the differences between Indians and Europeans to what he termed the Indians' cultural retardation. He was confident that if whites lifted Indians out of their uncivilized state and put them on an equal footing with Europeans, Indian populations would grow, their physical condition would improve, and they would be able to participate in the yeoman republic on an equal footing with whites.

Jefferson's Indian policy reflected this attitude. Jefferson created a series of government-owned trading posts at which Indians were offered goods at cheap prices. He believed that Indians who were exposed to white manufactures would come to agree that white culture was superior and would make the rational decision to adopt that culture wholesale. At the same time, both the government and right-minded philanthropists should engage in instructing Native Americans in European methods of farming, ensuring that these former "savages" would emerge as good, Republican-voting frontier farmers. Until this process of **acculturation** was complete, however, Jefferson believed the Indians, like children, should be protected from those who might take advantage of them or lead them astray.

Unlike many of his contemporaries, Thomas Jefferson was convinced that the American Indians could eventually become full participants in the American republic. Members of the "Five Civilized Tribes" (Cherokee, Choctaw, Chickasaw, Creek, and Seminole) often owned large plantations and practiced lifestyles not unlike those of their white neighbors. Unfortunately, Jefferson's hopes fell before the racism and greed of white settlers. Even sophisticated leaders like Cherokee chief Tah Chee, pictured here, were driven from their land; he and his band eventually took up residence in Texas to escape persecution in their native Arkansas. *Library of Congress.*

Also like children, the Indians were not to be trusted to exercise the rights and responsibilities of citizenship. Thus Indian rights were left to the whims of the Senate—which drafted and ratified Indian treaties—and of the army—which enforced those treaties.

James Forten   African American entrepreneur with a successful sail making business in Philadelphia who provided leadership for black business enterprises and advocated both racial integration and equal rights during the Jeffersonian era.

acculturation   Changes in the culture of a group or an individual as a result of contact with a different culture.

The chief problem for Jeffersonian Indian policy was not the Indians' supposed cultural retardation but their rapid modernization. Among groups such as the Cherokees and Creeks, members of a rising new elite led their people toward greater prosperity and diplomatic independence. Alexander McGillivray of the Creeks, for example, deftly manipulated American, French, and Spanish interests to Creek advantage while building a strong economic base founded on both communally and privately owned plantations. In similar fashion, the rising Cherokee elite in 1794 established a centralized government that began pushing the Cherokees into a new era of wealth and power.

Although Jefferson might have greeted such acculturation with enthusiasm, the Indians' white neighbors generally did not. Envisioning all-out war between the states and the Indians—war that his reduced government and shrunken military was helpless to prevent—Jefferson advanced an alternative. Having acquired Louisiana, Jefferson suggested the creation of large reserves to which Indians currently residing within states could relocate, taking themselves out of state jurisdictions and removing themselves from the corrupting influence of the "baser elements" of white society. Although he did not advocate the use of force to move Indians west of the Mississippi, he made every effort to convince them to migrate. This idea of segregating Native Americans from other Americans formed the basis for Indian policy for the rest of the century.

✔ Individual Voices

Congress Debates George Logan's Mission to France

① *What is Otis saying here? What does he perceive as the motive behind the Republican criticism of a bill to outlaw acts like Logan's?*

② *This speech is quoted from The Debates and Proceedings in the Congress of the United States, the official record of Congress from 1789 through 1824. In this source, speeches were generally reported in the third person; hence Otis is referred to as "he."*

③ *What is Otis saying was the actual motivation for proposing this bill? What conclusions can you draw from this statement about the nature of partisan politics in 1798? To what extent is such political practice in play today?*

Even before any official news had reached Washington, rumors were flying about George Logan's trip to France to negotiate an end to the diplomatic crisis that was plaguing the nation. Less than a month after Logan had set off for Europe, Federalists in Congress proposed a new law that would make any such efforts at unofficial peacemaking a federal crime. Republican representative Albert Gallatin urged patience: wait for the president to present the facts to Congress as he had promised to do. But the Federalists persisted, leading Gallatin to ask why they were so eager to criminalize Logan's actions. In a moment of heated candor, Massachusetts Federalist Harrison G. Otis blurted out the answer, revealing what was really at work inside the radical circle.

Again: it is insisted that the secret of the resolution on the table, was to perpetuate the division of party, and that, although but few real causes of dissension remain, yet we are determined to throw down the gauntlet and excite the greatest possible irritation. **①** *This accusation he denied.* **②** *He did not believe that the resolution was introduced with any such design; but if such had been the object of the mover, the blame would not attach to him or to his friends. They might even then have justified themselves upon principles of self-defence. He appealed to the whole House that, within a few days after the commencement of this session, they were threatened with a notice that motions might be expected in favor of repealing the Alien and Sedition acts; which could owe their origin to no other intention but that of inflaming the public mind, and of persevering in the endeavor to expose the Administration and its friends to odious imputations. Therefore we should stand acquitted, if, instead of giving time to our adversaries to furnish their weapons, and carry war into our borders, we had seized this occasion to strike the first blow.* **③**

SUMMARY

Americans faced a difficult choice in 1796: to continue in a Federalist direction with John Adams or to move into new and uncharted regions of republicanism with Thomas Jefferson. Factionalism and voter indecision led to Adams's election as president and Jefferson's as vice president. The split outcome frightened Federalists, and they used every excuse to make war on their political opponents. Diplomatically, they let relations with France sour to the point that the two nations were at war in all but name. At home, they used repressive measures such as the Alien and Sedition Acts to try to silence opponents, and they imposed tariffs and taxes that were hateful to many. Reminded of what they had rebelled against in the Revolution, in 1800 the American people decided to give Jefferson and the Republican faction a chance.

Although Jefferson called the election "the revolution of 1800," even hard-line Federalists such as Hamilton were sure that the general direction in government would not change. Just to be safe, however, Federalists stacked the court system so that Republicans would face insurmountable constraints if they tried to change government too much. At the same time, they organized themselves into a true political party, an ever-present watchdog on the activities of their rivals.

Jefferson's inaugural address in 1801 seemed to announce an end to partisan warfare, but both Madison and hard-line Republicans in Congress attempted to restrict Federalist power in the court system. The Republican program, however, was not entirely negative. Jefferson looked toward a future in which most Americans could own enough land to produce life's necessities for themselves and were beholden to no one and thus free to vote as their consciences and rationality dictated. To attain this end, Jefferson ordered massive reductions in the size of government, the elimination of internal federal taxes, and rapid westward expansion, including the purchase of the vast territory called Louisiana. For some the outcome was a spirit of excitement and optimism, but not everyone was so hopeful. Many were unsure and fearful of the new order's novelty and of the stresses that rapid expansion engendered; social change disrupted lives and communities.

Jefferson clearly wanted most Americans to share in the bounty of an expanded nation, but not all were free to share equally. For American Indians, the very success of Jefferson's expansion policy meant a contraction in their freedom of action. African Americans also found that the equality Jefferson promised to others was not intended for them, though many like Benjamin Banneker and Paul Cuffe grasped for it anyway. As to women, Jefferson himself observed, "The appointment of a woman to office is an innovation for which the public is not prepared, nor am I"; they were encouraged to play an active role in the new nation but were expected to do so only through their roles as wives and mothers.

IN THE WIDER WORLD

1796
Adams
elected

Washington's
farewell
address

1798
Quasi-War

Alien and
Sedition Acts

Kentucky and
Virginia Resolutions

1801
Jefferson
elected

1803 *Marbury v. Madison*

Louisiana Purchase

1804
Jefferson reelected

Lewis and Clark expedition

| 1770 | 1792 | 1794 | 1796 | 1798 | 1800 | 1802 | 1804 | 1806 |

1802 France invades
Santo Domingo

1800 Spain cedes Louisiana to France

1799 Napoleon seizes power

1791
Slave revolt in Santo Domingo

1798 France invades Egypt

Second Coalition against France

1769–1795
British Empire expands into
Australia, Africa, Ceylon

In the United States

Partisan Tension and Jeffersonian Optimism

1796 George Washington's Farewell Address

First contested presidential election: John Adams elected president, Thomas Jefferson vice president

1797 XYZ affair

1798 Quasi-War with France begins

Alien and Sedition Acts

Kentucky and Virginia Resolutions

George Logan's mission to France

1799 Fries's Rebellion

Napoleon seizes control in France

1800 Convention of Mortefontaine ends Quasi-War

Jefferson and Aaron Burr tie in Electoral College

Spain gives Louisiana back to France

1801 Jefferson elected president in House of Representatives; Burr vice president

Judiciary Act of 1801

John Marshall becomes chief justice

War begins between American navy ships and Barbary pirates

Outdoor revival meeting at Cane Ridge, Kentucky

1802 Congress repeals all internal taxes

Congress repeals Judiciary Act of 1801

French invade Santo Domingo

1803 *Marbury v. Madison*

Impeachment of Justices John Pickering and Samuel Chase

Louisiana Purchase

1804 Twelfth Amendment ratified

Jefferson reelected

1804–1806 Lewis and Clark expedition

1806–1807 Zebulon Pike's expedition

1816 African Methodist Episcopal Church formed in Philadelphia

Increasing Conflict and War, 1805–1815

A NOTE FROM THE AUTHOR

Less than twenty years ago, historians spent little time discussing the War of 1812, leading one young scholar to dub it "A Forgotten Conflict." Given the traditional emphasis in American historiography on politics and diplomacy, this is not surprising. Politically the war seems to have made little difference: Jeffersonians controlled national politics both before and after the conflict. Diplomatically the war appeared to make even less difference: the Treaty of Ghent ended the conflict by simply ignoring that it had ever occurred.

New developments in historical scholarship have changed all that. Close examination of the political scene, for example, shows that while Republicans continued to dominate national politics, leadership within the party underwent radical change. A new generation of Republicans, men born after the Revolution and steeped in continental nationalism, came to dominate Congress and pushed the nation in aggressive new directions. In the realm of diplomacy, while the war won nothing for the United States directly, the nation emerged with a new confidence that made it a major player in global affairs in the near future.

Perhaps the most important impacts of the war happened almost accidentally. The first of these was the product of an interruption in the global economy. No longer able to depend on cheap imports from Europe, Americans increasingly turned to manufacturing their own consumer goods. In the years between 1808 and 1815, the United States experienced a budding industrial revolution that changed the course of the nation's economy. At the same time, the cultivation of cotton made the American South one of the key economic players in the global marketplace. Another incidental outcome of the war was the destruction of Indian resistance along the nation's western frontier. With Indian power largely broken, there was nothing to prevent aggressive Americans from expanding in overwhelming numbers into the west, forever changing the map of the continent.

Taken together, these changes that came out of the War of 1812 pushed the United States in radical new directions. It is safe to say that this was the onset of American modernization, the beginning of an America that we recognize today as forming the foundation for our everyday lives.

Tecumseh

Tecumseh followed in his father's footsteps by becoming an influential war leader among the Shawnee people. And following his mother's influence, a Creek Indian who had married across tribal lines, he emphasized the unity between all Native American people. Both influences would lead him to undertake heroic efforts to preserve what remained of the Indians' territory in the years following the American Revolution. According to many experts, this particular portrait, a composite of several sketches, comes closest to capturing what this Indian leader looked like at the peak of his career. *Benson J. Lossing,* The Pictorial Field Book of the War of 1812.

✔ Individual Choices

In the opening days of the nineteenth century, most Americans believed the Native Americans were doomed to extinction. History mandated that the Indians would vanish and that European Americans would inherit their land. The Indians disagreed, and one of their most prominent leaders, Tecumseh, did as much as possible to stop the loss of Indian land that whites deemed inevitable.

Tecumseh stood in stark contrast to dominant white theories about Indian life. Whites thought of Indians living in isolated and constantly warring tribes, yet Tecumseh's parents came from different tribes: his father was a Shawnee from Ohio and his mother was a Creek from Alabama. In the sophisticated Indian world of the American interior, peaceful visitations between tribes were common, as were intergroup marriages.

A combination of his family connections and a distinguished military career led to Tecumseh's emergence as war chief in the late 1780s, and he played a key role in the continuing defense against American incursions. But defeat at the Battle of Fallen Timbers in 1794 temporarily broke the Indian defenses. Taking advantage of Indian vulnerability, American agents used a combination of bribery, coercion, and outright violence to convince **civil chiefs** to cede more land. Seeking to stop these new invasions, Tecumseh approached war chiefs from a variety of tribes suggesting a vast alliance system in which the warriors would stop civil chiefs from selling land and form a military force to turn back the Americans.

Bent on continuing expansion, white leaders like Indiana territorial governor William Henry Harrison found Tecumseh's actions frightening. Finally in November 1811 Harrison resorted to direct action, leading an army to invade the Tecumseh's headquarters at Prophetstown on Tippecanoe Creek. Tecumseh was absent, seeking new allies, and Harrison's forces

---

civil chiefs   In many Native American societies, leadership was shared among different classes of chiefs, each of which was responsible for specific political tasks; civil chiefs generally were responsible for overseeing domestic affairs, while war chiefs were responsible for diplomacy.

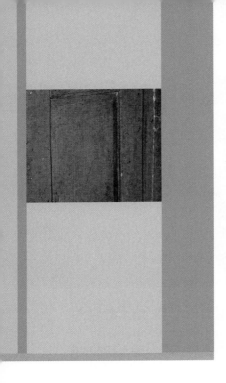

were able to overcome a spirited defense and burn the town, destroying its winter food supply. By the time Tecumseh reached Tippecanoe in January, few of his followers remained. Thinking first of the survivors' welfare, Tecumseh traveled to Canada seeking emergency supplies.

While he was in Canada, war again broke out, this time between the United States and Great Britain. He decided that the only hope for the Shawnees' future lay in a British victory, and he committed what was left of his alliance to the British. His army enjoyed great success against the Americans, but at the Battle of the Thames, on October 5, 1813, Tecumseh's forces were overrun, and Tecumseh was shot. After the battle, triumphant American troops mutilated his body and left it lying on the field.

Hopes for a unified Indian resistance died with Tecumseh, and his mutilated body foreshadowed the future for the Indian land base. Stinging from military defeats and with no more strong voices urging common cause, the once-cosmopolitan world of the Indian interior became what whites imagined it to be: isolated tribes constantly warring among themselves. Expansionists like Harrison used this desperation to play one group off against another, carving piece after piece out of the Indian domain until, by 1850, virtually no Indians remained in the territory Tecumseh had tried to preserve.

INTRODUCTION

Tecumseh's situation in Indiana reflected many of the more troubling problems that beset the nation during the opening decades of the nineteenth century. Sitting at the juncture of three worlds—the dynamic republican world of Jeffersonian America, the European imperial world in Canada, and his own Native American world—Tecumseh perceived that unless something happened soon, all three worlds were heading for a crisis.

Jefferson had set an ambitious agenda for the country that was extremely popular with many Americans, but it created serious stresses within the nation and across the world. Along the Atlantic frontier, imperial powers such as Great Britain and France challenged Jefferson's commitment to open trade and freedom of the seas. A war of words, blustering threats, and some open confrontations pushed the United States increasingly toward crisis and triggered economic disaster. Along the western frontier, a variety of Indian groups opposed Jefferson's vision of rapid westward expansion. Here too, verbal and some armed conflicts engendered an air of crisis. And to many, including Harrison, these seemed not to be isolated phenomena. Convinced that a conspiracy was afoot between Indian dissidents like Tecumseh and imperial agents from Great Britain

and France, an increasing number of Jeffersonians demanded aggressive action.

Try as they might to ease the growing tensions, neither Jefferson and his successor, James Madison, nor Federalist and Republican dissidents could stem the tide of crisis. Harrison finally took matters over the edge: his attack on Prophetstown precipitated a general call for a war that set the nation on a new course altogether.

Troubling Currents in Jefferson's America

→ How did varying interests between regions of the country complicate Jefferson's political situation during his second term as president?

→ What impact did European politics have on the American economy between 1804 and 1808?

Jefferson's successes, culminating in his victory in the 1804 election, seemed to prove that Republicans had absolute control over the nation's political reins. But factions challenging Jefferson's control were forming. A small but vocal coalition of disgruntled Federalists threatened to **secede** from the Union. Even within his own party, Jefferson's supremacy eroded, and dissidents emerged. Diplomatic problems also joined domestic ones to trouble Jefferson's second administration.

Emerging Factions in American Politics

The Federalists' failure in the election of 1804 nearly spelled the troubled party's demise. With the West and the South firmly in Jefferson's camp, disgruntled New England Federalists found their once-dominant voice being drowned out by those who shared Jefferson's rather than Hamilton's view of America's future (see pages 197–198). Proclaiming that "the people of the East cannot reconcile their habits, views, and interests with those of the South and West," Federalist leader Timothy Pickering advocated radical changes in the Constitution that he thought might restore balance. Among other things, northeasterners demanded much stricter standards for admitting new states in the West and the elimination of the Three-Fifths Compromise. Pickering brought together a tight political coalition called the **Essex Junto** to press for these changes.

Regional fissures began to open inside Jefferson's party as well. Throughout Jefferson's first administration, some within his party, especially those from the South, criticized the president for turning his back on republican principles by expanding federal power and interfering with states' rights. One of Jefferson's most vocal critics was his cousin **John Randolph.**

The two Virginia Republicans clashed on the eve of the 1804 election over the **Yazoo affair.** This complicated legal tangle had begun back in 1794 when a group of politically well-connected land speculators used bribes and other questionable methods to secure over 40 million acres of land from the State of Georgia for a mere five hundred thousand dollars. Georgia voters were outraged and in the next election threw the corrupt state congressmen out of office. When the new state legislature convened in 1796, it overturned the previous sale, but in the meantime, much of the land had already been sold to individual farmers, who had already taken possession. Georgia ordered these individuals to move off the disputed land, offering them financial compensation, but many refused, taking the matter to court. The political and legal infighting continued until 1802, when Georgia finally joined the other original states in ceding its western lands to the United States as part of the compromise necessary to

gain ratification for the Constitution (see pages 181–182). With Jefferson's approval, Georgia included the disputed Yazoo lands with other claims, turning the state conflict into a federal one and involving the national government in a matter that Randolph and others believed should have been worked out by the state.

In 1806 Jefferson again irritated Randolph by approaching Congress for a $2 million appropriation to be used to win French influence in convincing Spain to sell Florida to the United States. Citing these and other perceived violations of Republican principles, Randolph announced, "I found I might co-operate or be an honest man." Randolph chose honesty, splitting with Jefferson to form a third party, the **Tertium Quid,** fracturing the Republican united political front.

A second fissure in the party opened over controversial vice president Aaron Burr's political scheming. Upset that Burr had not conceded the presidency immediately after the tied Electoral College vote in 1800, Jefferson snubbed him throughout his first four years in office and then dropped him as his vice-presidential nominee in 1804. But Burr's political failures constituted an opportunity for the Essex Junto: Pickering offered to help Burr become governor of New York if Burr delivered the state to the northern confederacy. Burr agreed, but mainstream New York Federalists

---

secede   To withdraw formally from membership in a political union; threats of secession were used frequently during the early nineteenth century to bring attention to political issues.

Essex Junto   A group of political conspirators who sought power outside of the regular political process—composed of radical Federalists in Essex County, Massachusetts, who at first advocated constitutional changes that would favor New England politically and later called for New England and New York to secede from the United States

John Randolph   Virginia Republican politician who was a cousin of Thomas Jefferson; he believed in limited government and objected to several of Jefferson's policies.

Yazoo affair   Corrupt deal in which the Georgia legislature sold a huge tract of public land to speculators for a low price but later overturned the sale; the basis for the Supreme Court case of *Fletcher v. Peck,* discussed in more detail in Chapter 10, which in 1810 established the sanctity of civil contracts over state legislation.

Tertium Quid   Republican faction formed by John Randolph in protest against Jefferson's plan for acquiring Florida from Spain; the name is Latin and means a "third thing," indicating Randolph's rejection of both the Federalist and Republican Parties.

were furious, especially Alexander Hamilton. During the New York state election in the spring of 1804, Hamilton was quoted by the press as saying that Burr was "a dangerous man, and one who ought not to be trusted with the reins of government." Burr lost the election in a landslide, wrecking the junto's scheme and pushing himself into an even greater personal and political crisis. Never willing to accept defeat gracefully, Burr demanded that Hamilton retract his statements. When Hamilton refused, Burr challenged him to a duel. Though personally opposed to dueling, in the honor-driven culture that permeated early-nineteenth-century politics, Hamilton could not refuse. An excellent shot, the vice president put a bullet directly through Hamilton's liver and into his spine, killing him.

Killing Hamilton did not solve Burr's problems. Though an indictment for murder was eventually dropped, Burr was forced into hiding and in the process fell in with a former Revolutionary War commander, James Wilkinson, who was employed simultaneously by Spain and the United States. Wilkinson's real loyalties and intentions remain mysterious, but one point seems clear: with Burr's help he intended to carve out a personal domain in the borderland between American and Spanish territories in the Mississippi region. When Congress reconvened in the fall of 1804 and Burr resumed his seat as president of the Senate, he used his political connections to gain an appointment for Wilkinson to be governor of the Louisiana Territory, providing an institutional foundation for whatever plot they had hatched. Then, when his vice-presidential term expired in 1805, Burr ventured west, sailing down the Mississippi to recruit associates. Rumors of intrigue soon surfaced, and investigations began when federal authorities received a letter from Wilkinson late in 1806 implicating Burr in a "deep, dark, wicked, and widespread conspiracy" against the United States. Learning that Wilkinson had turned him in, Burr tried to reach Spanish Florida but was captured early in 1807 and put on trial for treason.

Burr's trial provided an open arena for Jefferson and his critics to air their views on such touchy subjects as presidential power, westward expansion, and national loyalty. Presiding over the case, Chief Justice John Marshall made it clear that he believed Burr was a victim, not the perpetrator, of a conspiracy. Jefferson, however, was determined to have Burr prosecuted to the full extent of the law. Using the powers of his office, Jefferson offered pardons to conspirators who would testify against Burr, and he leaked information that made his former vice president look guilty. He also refused to honor a subpoena issued by Marshall requiring Jefferson to appear in court and to produce official documents that might have a bearing on the case. In this instance, Jefferson embarrassed the chief justice by recalling that Marshall had supported George Washington's assertion of presidential privilege during investigations into Jay's Treaty (see page 204). Marshall backed down, and neither Jefferson nor his executive papers appeared in court.

But Marshall struck back in his own way: he turned Jefferson's insistence upon strict constitutional constructionism against the president. In his instructions to the jury, Marshall noted that the Constitution defined treason as "levying war against the United States or adhering to their enemies" and that a guilty verdict required direct evidence from two witnesses. Because Burr had not waged war, and because neither Spain nor Britain was at the moment an enemy of the United States, the jury acquitted the former vice president, to the glee of Jefferson's critics.

The Problem of American Neutrality

Internal tensions in American politics were matched by growing stress in the nation's diplomatic and economic relations. Jefferson's economic successes had been the product of continuing warfare in Europe. With their fleets engaged in naval battles, their people locked in combat, and their lands crisscrossed by opposing armies, Europeans needed American ships and the fruits of American labor, especially food. American neutrality ensured continued prosperity as long as the contending parties in Europe agreed to the diplomatic principle of neutrality.

Americans immediately grasped at this opportunity. An upsurge in European campaigning in 1803 helped raise the total value of American exports by over 65 percent. A significant proportion of the increase came from the shipment of foreign goods to foreign markets by way of neutral American ports: sugar from the Caribbean, for example, frequently passed through the United States on its way to Europe. These so-called re-exports rose in value from $14 million in 1803 to $60 million in 1807, prompting a rapid growth in earnings for American shipping. In 1790, net income from shipping amounted to a mere $5.9 million; by 1807 the volume had surged to $42.1 million.

Prospects seemed bright for America's economic and diplomatic future and for Jefferson's dream of agricultural America feeding overcrowded, war-torn Europe. But politicians in both England and France cared about their own military victories, not about American prosperity. Their decisions, especially those

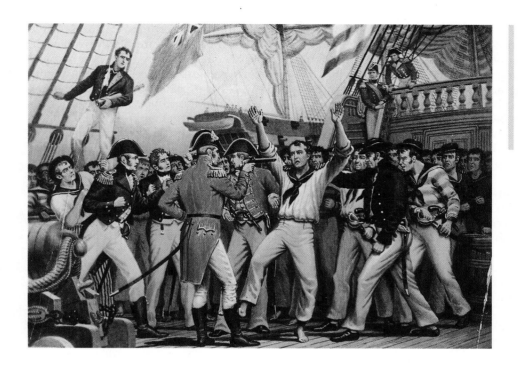

The impressment of sailors into the British navy from American ships was one of the more prominent causes of the War of 1812. This 1790 engraving shows an American sailor being seized at gunpoint while those who might try to assist him are elbowed aside. *Library of Congress.*

relating to neutral shipping, disrupted American trade and created an atmosphere of hostility.

Another source of tension was a British law that empowered the king's warships to engage in **impressment.** For decades, British sailors had protested the exceedingly cruel conditions and low pay in His Majesty's navy by jumping ship in American ports and enlisting as merchant sailors on American vessels. Strapped for mariners by renewed warfare, England pursued a vigorous policy of reclaiming British sailors after 1803, even if they were on neutral American ships and, more provocatively, even if they had become citizens of the United States. It is estimated that the British abducted as many as eight thousand sailors from American ships between 1803 and 1812. The loss of so many seamen hurt American shippers economically, but it wounded American pride even more. Like the XYZ affair, impressment seemed to be a direct denial of the United States' status as a legitimate nation.

Economic Warfare

Pressure on American neutrality increased after 1805, when a military deadlock emerged in the European war: Britain was supreme at sea, while France was in control on the continent of Europe. Stuck in a stalemate, both sides used whatever nonmilitary advantages were available in an effort to tip the balance in their favor. Thus the war changed from one of military campaigning to one of diplomatic and economic maneuvering. Seeking to close off foreign supplies to England, in November 1806 Napoleon issued the **Berlin Decree,** barring ships that had anchored at British harbors from entering ports controlled by France. The British Parliament responded by issuing a series of directives that permitted neutral ships to sail to European ports only if they first called at a British port to pay a transit tax. It was thus impossible for a neutral ship to follow the laws of either nation without violating the laws of the other. All this European blustering, however, had little immediate effect on the American economy. From the issuance of the Berlin Decree to the end of 1807, American exports and shipping rose more than they had risen during any similar period.

impressment   Procedure permitted under British maritime law that authorized commanders of warships to force English civilian sailors into military service.

Berlin Decree   Napoleon's order declaring the British Isles under blockade and authorizing the confiscation of British goods from any ship found carrying them.

But such good fortune was not to last. Seeking to break France's dependence on America as a source for food and other supplies, Napoleon sought an alliance with Russia, and in the spring of 1807 his diplomatic mission succeeded. Having acquired an alternative source for grain and other foodstuffs, Napoleon immediately began enforcing the Berlin Decree, hoping to starve England into submission. The British countered by stepping up enforcement of their European blockade and aggressively pursuing impressment to strengthen the Royal Navy.

The escalation in both France's and Britain's economic war efforts quickly led to confrontation with Americans and a diplomatic crisis. A pivotal event occurred in June 1807. The British **frigate** *Leopard,* patrolling the American shoreline, confronted the American warship *Chesapeake.* Even though both ships were inside American territorial waters, the *Leopard* ordered the American ship to halt and hand over any British sailors on board. When the *Chesapeake*'s captain refused, the *Leopard* fired several **broadsides,** crippling the American vessel, killing three sailors, and injuring eighteen. The British then boarded the *Chesapeake* and dragged off four men, three of whom were naturalized citizens of the United States. Americans were outraged.

Americans were not the only ones galvanized by British aggression. Shortly after the *Chesapeake* affair, word arrived in the United States that Napoleon had responded to Britain's belligerence by declaring a virtual economic war against neutrals. In the **Milan Decree,** he vowed to seize any neutral ship that so much as carried licenses to trade with England. What was worse, the Milan Decree stated that ships that had been boarded by British authorities—even against their crew's will—were subject to immediate French capture.

Many Americans viewed the escalating French and English sanctions as insulting treachery that cried out for an American response. The *Washington Federalist* newspaper observed, "We have never, on any occasion, witnessed . . . such a thirst for revenge." If Congress had been in session, the legislature surely would have called for war, but Jefferson stayed calm. War with England or France or, worse still, with both would bring Jefferson's whole political program to a crashing halt. He had insisted on inexpensive government, lobbied for American neutrality, and hoped for renewed prosperity through continuing trade with Europe. War would destroy his entire agenda. But clearly Jefferson had to do something.

Believing that Europeans were far more dependent on American goods and ships than Americans were on European money and manufactures, Jefferson chose to violate one of his cardinal principles: the U.S. government would interfere in the economy to force Europeans to recognize American neutral rights. In December 1807, the president announced the **Embargo Act,** which would, in effect, close all American foreign trade as of January 1 unless the Europeans agreed to recognize America's neutral rights to trade with anyone it pleased.

Crises in the Nation

→ *How did Jefferson's economic and Indian policies influence national developments after 1808?*

→ *How did problems in Europe contribute to changing conditions in the American West?*

→ *What did the actions of frontier politicians such as William Henry Harrison do to bring the nation into war in 1812?*

Jefferson's reaction to European aggression immediately began strangling American trade and with it America's domestic economic development. In addition, European countries still had legitimate claims on much of North America, and the Indians who continued to occupy most of the continent had enough military power to pose a serious threat to the United States if properly motivated (see Map 9.1). While impressment, blockade, and embargo paralyzed America's Atlantic frontier, a combination of European and Indian hostility along the western frontier added to the air of national emergency. The resulting series of domestic crises played havoc with Jefferson's vision of a peaceful, prosperous nation.

frigate   A very fast warship, rigged with square sails and carrying from thirty to fifty cannon on two gun decks.

broadside   The simultaneous discharge of all the guns on one side of a warship.

Milan Decree   Napoleon's order authorizing the capture of any neutral vessels sailing from British ports or submitting to British searches.

Embargo Act   Embargo (a government-ordered trade ban) announced by Jefferson in 1807 in order to pressure Britain and France to accept neutral trading rights; it went into effect in 1808 and closed down all U.S. foreign trade.

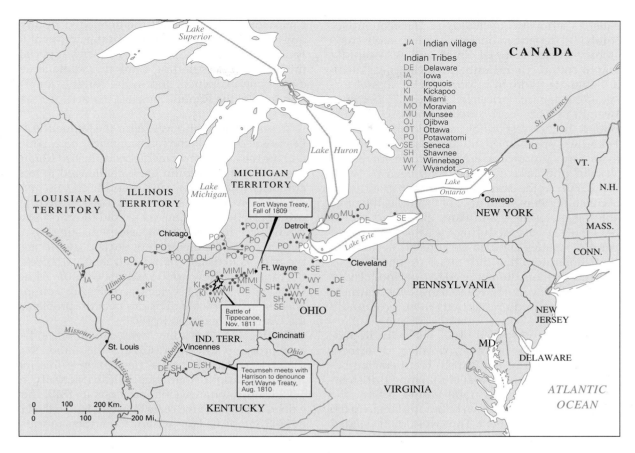

MAP 9.1 **Indian Territory, ca. 1812** Frontier leaders like William Henry Harrison were worried about unified Indian resistance in the years leading up to the War of 1812. This map shows why. Strong Indian groups, some of which were allied with Tecumseh, formed a nearly solid frontier line on the nation's western borders. Harrison's efforts and the War of 1812 virtually destroyed this constraint on American expansion.

Economic Depression

Although Jefferson felt justified in suspending free trade to protect neutral rights, the result was the worst economic depression since the founding of the British colonies in North America. Critics such as John Randolph pronounced Jefferson's solution worse than the problem—like trying "to cure corns by cutting off the toes." And while Jefferson's "damn-bargo," as critics called it, was only halfheartedly enforced, the economy slumped disastrously. Taken together, all American exports fell from $109 million to $22 million, and net earnings from shipping fell by almost 50 percent. During 1808, earnings from legitimate business enterprise in America declined to less than a quarter of their value in 1807.

The depression shattered economic and social life in many eastern towns. It has been estimated that thirty thousand sailors were thrown out of work and that as many as a hundred thousand people employed in support industries were laid off. During 1808 in New York City alone, 120 businesses went bankrupt, and the combination of unemployment and business failure led to the imprisonment of twelve hundred New Yorkers for debt. New England, where the economy was almost entirely dependent on foreign trade, was hit harder still. In light of Jefferson's policies and the collapsing economy, the extremism expressed by the Essex Junto three years earlier began to sound reasonable.

New Englanders screamed loudest about the impact of the embargo, but southerners and westerners were just as seriously affected by it. The economy of the South had depended on the export of staple crops like tobacco since colonial times and was rapidly turning to cotton. There, embargo meant near-death to all legitimate trade. In response to the loss of foreign markets, tobacco prices fell from $6.75 per hundredweight to $3.25, and cotton from 21 to 13 cents per pound. In the West, wholesale prices for agricultural products spiraled downward also. Overall, the prices of farm products were 16 percent lower between 1807 and 1811 than they had been between 1791 and 1801. At the same time, the price of virtually every consumer item went up. For example, the price of building materials—hardware, glass, and milled lumber—rose 11 percent during the same period, and the price of textiles climbed 20 percent. In fact, the only consumer item that did not go up in price was the one item farmers did not need to buy: food. Faced with dropping incomes and soaring costs, farmers probably felt the trade restrictions more profoundly than others.

Rather than blaming their problems on the Republican administration, however, disaffected farmers directed their anger at the British. Frontiersmen believed, rightly or wrongly, that eliminating British interference with American trade would restore the boom economy that had drawn so many of them to the edge of American settlement. Thus westerners banded together to raise their voices in favor of American patriotism and war against Britain.

Political Upheaval

Despite the escalating crisis in the country, Jefferson remained popular and powerful, but like Washington, he chose to step down from the presidency after serving two terms, making it clear to party officials that he favored James Madison to replace him in the upcoming presidential election of 1808. Although Madison and Jefferson had much in common and were longtime friends, they seemed very different from each other. Few could say they knew Madison well, but those who did found him captivating: a man of few words but of piercing intellect and unflinching conviction. Those less well acquainted with him thought the quiet Virginian indecisive: where Jefferson tended to act on impulse, Madison approached matters of state as he approached matters of political philosophy—with caution, patience, and reason.

Riding his reputation as a brilliant political thinker and his status as Jefferson's chosen successor, Madison easily defeated his Federalist opponent, Charles Cotesworth Pinckney. But the one-sided results disguised deep political divisions in the nation at large. Federalist criticism of Jefferson's policies, especially of the embargo, was finding a growing audience as the depression deepened, and in the congressional election in 1808 the Republicans lost twenty-four seats to Federalists.

Internal dissent also weakened the Republican Party. Dissatisfied with Jefferson's policies, both southern and northeastern party members contested Madison's succession. The Tertium Quid challenged Jefferson's authority in the **party caucus** and tried to secure the nomination for the stately and conservative **James Monroe.** Jefferson managed to hold the party's southern wing in line, but northeasterners, stinging under the pressure of the embargo, bucked the decision of the party caucus and nominated their own presidential candidate: New Yorker George Clinton. Although Clinton polled only six electoral votes, his nomination was a sign of growing divisions over the problems that the United States faced in 1808.

During Madison's first two years in office, lack of any progress toward resolving the nation's woes seemed to confirm critics' perception of his indecisiveness. Despite that, Republicans actually made gains in the congressional elections in 1810: they regained fourteen of the seats they had lost in the House in 1808 and picked up two additional Senate seats. But this was no vote of confidence in Madison. Though the new congressmen were Republicans, sixty-three of them did not support Madison or his commitment to a conciliatory policy toward the British. These new members of Congress were mostly very young, extremely patriotic, and represented frontier constituents who were being ravaged by the agricultural depression. In the months to come, their increasingly strident demands for aggressive action against England earned them the nickname **War Hawks.**

---

party caucus A meeting of members of a political party to decide on questions of policy or leadership or to register preferences for candidates running for office.

James Monroe Republican politician from Virginia who served in diplomatic posts under George Washington, John Adams, and Thomas Jefferson; he later became the fifth president of the United States.

War Hawks Members of Congress elected in 1810 from the West and South who campaigned for war with Britain in the hopes of stimulating the economy and annexing new territory.

The Rise of the Shawnee Prophet

A key reason for War Hawk militancy was the unsettled conditions along the western frontier. Relations with Indians in the West had been peaceful since the Battle of Fallen Timbers in 1794. The Shawnees and other groups had been thrown off their traditional homelands in Ohio by the Treaty of Greenville (see page 204) and forced to move to new lands in Indiana. There, food shortages, disease, and continuing encroachment by settlers caused many young Indians to lose faith in their traditional beliefs and in themselves as human beings.

In the midst of the crisis, one disheartened, diseased alcoholic rose above his afflictions to lead the Indians into a brief new era of hope. Tecumseh's younger brother Lalawethika had bragged that he would play an influential role in his people's affairs (his name meant "Noisemaker"). But his prospects had declined along with those of his people. Lacking his brother's training as a warrior, Lalawethika felt increasingly hopeless, turned to alcohol, and finally in 1805 became critically ill. He claimed that he remembered dying and meeting the Master of Life, who showed him the way to lead his people out of degradation and commanded him to return to the world of the living so he could tell the Indians what they must do to recover their dignity. He then awoke, cured of his illness. Launching a full-fledged religious and cultural revival designed to teach the ways revealed to him by the Master of Life, he adopted the name Tenskwatawa ("the Way"). Whites called him **"The Prophet."**

Blaming the decline of his people on their adoption of white ways, the Prophet taught them to go back to their traditional lifestyle—to discard whites' clothing, religion, and especially alcohol—and live as their ancestors had lived. He also urged his followers to unify against the temptations and threats of white exploiters and to hold on to what remained of their lands. If they followed his teachings, the Prophet insisted, the Indians would regain control of their lives and their lands, and the whites would vanish from their world. In 1807 the Prophet established a religious settlement, Prophetstown, on the banks of Tippecanoe Creek in Indiana Territory. This community was to serve as a center for the Prophet's activities and as a living model for revitalized Indian life. The residents of Prophetstown worked together using traditional forms of agriculture, hunting, and gathering.

Although the Prophet preached a message of ethnic pride, nonviolence, and passive resistance, as white settlers continued to pressure his people, he began to advocate more forceful solutions to the Indians' problems. In a speech to an intertribal council in April 1807, he suggested for the first time that warriors unite to resist white expansion. Although he did not urge his followers to attack the whites, he made it clear that the Master of Life would defend him and his followers if war were pressed on them.

Prophecy and Politics in the West

While Tenskwatawa continued to stress spiritual means for stopping white aggression, his brother **Tecumseh** pushed for a more political course of action. Seven years older than the Prophet, Tecumseh had always inclined more toward politics and warfare. Known as a brave fighter and a persuasive political orator, Tecumseh traveled throughout the western frontier, working out political and military alliances designed to put a stop to white expansion once and for all. Although he did not want to start a war against white settlers, Tecumseh exhorted Indians to defend every inch of land that remained to them. In 1807 he warned Ohio governor Thomas Kirker that they would do so with their lives.

Tecumseh's plan might have brought about his brother's goals. Faced by a unified defensive line of Indians stretching along the American frontier from Canada to the Gulf of Mexico, the United States probably would have found it virtually impossible to expand any farther, and the Indian confederacy would have become a significant force in America's future. The very brilliance of Tecumseh's reasoning and his success at organizing Indian groups caused a great deal of confusion among whites. Various white officials were convinced that the Shawnee leader was a spy either for the French or for the British and that his activities were an extension of some hidden plot by one European power or another. Though wrong, such theories helped to escalate the air of crisis in the West and in the nation at large.

Indiana governor William Henry Harrison had good reason to advance the impression of a conspiracy

> **The Prophet (Tenskwatawa)** Shawnee religious visionary who called for a return to Indian traditions and founded the community of Prophetstown on Tippecanoe Creek in Indiana.
>
> **Tecumseh** Shawnee leader and brother of the Prophet; he established an Indian confederacy along the frontier that he hoped would be a barrier to white expansion.

Although they had enormous respect for each other, Indiana territorial governor William Henry Harrison and Tecumseh were both ferocious when it came to defending their political and diplomatic positions. This painting of their confrontation at the 1810 peace conference held at Vincennes makes this point clearly. The two never actually came to blows at this meeting or at another held one year later, but they never were able to find common ground. Tecumseh's refusal to compromise his people's rights to their land eventually led to renewed warfare and his own death. *Cincinnati Museum Center—Cincinnati Historical Society Library.*

between Tecumseh and the British. Harrison and men like him believed the United States had the right to control all of North America and, accordingly, to brush aside anything standing in the way by any means available (see Map 9.1). Britain and the Indians were thus linked in their thinking. Both were seen as obstacles to national destiny—and many War Hawks prayed for the outbreak of war between the United States and the British with the Indians in between. Such a war would provide an excuse for attacking the Indians along the frontier to break up their emerging confederation and dispossess them of their land. In addition, a war would justify invading and seizing Canada, fulfilling what many considered a logical but frustrated objective of the American Revolution. At the same time, taking Canada from the British would open rich timber, fur, and agricultural lands for American settlement. More important, it would secure American control of the Great Lakes and St. Lawrence River—potentially a very valuable shipping route for agricultural produce from upper New York, northern Ohio, and the newly opening areas of the **Old Northwest.**

Choosing War

With the nation reeling from the economic squeeze of the embargo, Congress replaced it with the **Non-Intercourse Act** early in 1809. The new law forbade trade only with England and France and gave the president the power to reopen trade if either of the

combatants lifted its restrictions against American shipping. Even though this act was much less restrictive than the embargo, American merchants were relieved when it expired in the spring of 1810. At that point, Congress passed an even more permissive boycott, **Macon's Bill No. 2.** According to this new law, merchants could trade with the combatants if they wanted to take the risk, but if either France or England lifted its blockade, the United States would stop trading with the other.

Hoping to cut England off from needed outside supplies, Napoleon responded to Macon's Bill in August by sending a letter to the American government promising to suspend French restrictions on American shipping. In secret, however, the French emperor issued an order to continue seizing American ships. Despite Napoleon's devious intentions, Madison

Old Northwest   The area of the United States referred to at the time as the Northwest Territory, it would eventually be broken into the states of Indiana, Illinois, Michigan, and Wisconsin.

Non-Intercourse   Law passed by Congress in 1809 reopening trade with all nations except France and Britain and authorizing the president to reopen trade with them if they lifted restrictions on American shipping.

Macon's Bill No. 2   Law passed by Congress in 1810 that offered exclusive trading rights to France or Britain, whichever recognized American neutral rights first.

sought to use the French peace overture as a lever: he instructed the American mission in London to tell the British that he would close down trade with them unless they joined France in dropping trade restrictions. Sure that Napoleon was lying, the British refused, backing the president into a diplomatic corner. In February 1811, the provisions of Macon's Bill forced Madison to close trading with Britain for its failure to remove economic sanctions, stepping up tensions all around.

Later in the year, events in the West finally triggered a crisis. The underlying origin of the problem was an agreement, the Fort Wayne Treaty, signed in the fall of 1809 between the United States and representatives of the Miami, Potawatomi, and Delaware Indians. In return for an outright bribe of $5,200 and individual **annuities** ranging from $250 to $500, civil chiefs among these three tribes sold over 3 million acres of Indian land in Indiana and Illinois—land already occupied by many other Indian groups.

In August 1810, Tecumseh met with Governor Harrison in Vincennes, Indiana, to denounce the Fort Wayne Treaty. Harrison insisted that the agreement was legitimate. Speaking for those whose lands had been sold out from under them, Tecumseh said, "They want to save that piece of land, we do not wish you to take it. . . . I want the present boundary line to continue. Should you cross it, I assure you it will be productive of bad consequences." But Harrison refused to budge.

The Vincennes meeting convinced the Indians that they must prepare for a white attack. The Prophet increasingly preached the Master of Life's commitment to support the faithful in a battle against the whites. Tecumseh traveled up and down the American frontier, enlisting additional allies into his growing Indian confederacy. Meanwhile, Harrison grew more and more eager to attack the Indians before they could unite fully. He got his chance when a second peace conference, also held at Vincennes in the summer of 1811, also failed. Citing the failed peace effort and sporadic skirmishes between frontier settlers and renegade bands of Indians, none of whom were directly connected to Tecumseh, Harrison ordered an attack. On November 7, in the so-called **Battle of Tippecanoe**, an army of enraged frontiersmen burned Prophetstown. Then, having succeeded in setting the Indian frontier ablaze, Harrison called for a declaration of war against the Indians and the British.

Headlining Harrison's call for war, a Kentucky newspaper proclaimed, "The war on the Wabash is purely BRITISH, the SCALPING KNIFE and TOMAHAWK of British savages, is now, again devastating

IT MATTERS TODAY

THE BATTLE OF TIPPECANOE

Americans today generally think that Indians never really mattered in the nation's history. This modern dismissal of Indian significance is entirely incorrect. For years before the Battle of Tippecanoe, William Henry Harrison warned officials in Washington that if Tecumseh was successful he really could stop American westward expansion. This was not baseless exaggeration. As Harrison himself said of Tecumseh, "He is one of those uncommon geniuses, which spring up occasionally to produce revolutions and overturn the established order of things." We will never know how close Tecumseh came to overturning the established order. We do know that he experienced considerable success in raising a unified defense. Historians disagree about whether he could have succeeded in stopping American expansion, but there is no question that such a unified force along the American frontier would have compelled politicians like Jefferson to reconsider their policies. In either case, America today would be a profoundly different place had Harrison not destroyed Prophetstown and undermined the growing Indian confederacy.

- How might the Jefferson administration have dealt differently with the demands made by Tecumseh and his allies? In what ways would the United States be different today had this alternative course been followed?

- Since the early nineteenth century, the United States has encountered resistance to national expansion on a number of fronts. Choose another situation from later in the nation's history in which such resistance was dealt with. What similarities and/or differences do you see between this event and the handling of Tecumseh's resistance movement?

annuity   An allowance or income paid annually.
Battle of Tippecanoe   Battle near Prophetstown in 1811, where American forces led by William Henry Harrison defeated the followers of the Shawnee Prophet and destroyed the town.

our frontiers." Coming as it did while Congress was already embroiled in debate over economic sanctions and British impressment, the outbreak of violence on the frontier was finally enough to push Madison into action. Still hoping for some sort of peaceful resolution, the president chose his words carefully when he told Congress, "We behold . . . on the side of Great Britain, a state of war against the United States; and on the side of the United States, a state of peace toward Britain." As chairman of the House Foreign Relations Committee, however, **John C. Calhoun** was less circumspect: "The mad ambition, the lust of power, and the commercial avarice of Great Britain have left to neutral nations an alternative only between the base surrender of their rights, and a manly vindication of them." He then introduced a war bill in Congress.

When the vote was finally cast in 1812, the war bill passed by a vote of 79 to 49 in the House and 19 to 13 in the Senate. Although they seemed to have the most to lose from continued indecisive policies, representatives from the heavily Federalist regions that depended the most on overseas trade—Massachusetts, Connecticut, and New York, for example—voted against war, whereas strongly Republican western and southern representatives voted in favor.

The Nation At War

→ *What geographic and economic factors impeded American war efforts against Great Britain and Britain's Indian allies?*

→ *How did events in Europe influence the war in America?*

→ *To what extent were Americans' objectives in going to war accomplished?*

The nation was dreadfully unprepared when the breach with England finally came. With virtually no army or navy, the United States was taking a terrible risk in engaging what was fast becoming the most awesome military power in the world. Not surprisingly, defeat and humiliation were the main fruits of American efforts as the two nations faced off.

The Fighting Begins

Despite years of agitation, the war's actual arrival in 1812 caught the United States terribly unprepared. Republican cost cutting had virtually disbanded the military during Jefferson's first term in office. Renewed fighting with pirates in the Mediterranean and build-

ing tensions in the Atlantic had forced Republicans to increase military spending, but the navy still had fewer than twenty vessels, and the army could field fewer than seven thousand men. And for all its war fever, Congress balked at appropriating new funds even after war had been declared. Thus the first ventures in the war went forward with only grudging financial support.

In line with what the War Hawks wanted, the first military campaign was a three-pronged drive toward Canada and against the Indians (see Map 9.2). One force, commanded by Harrison, was successful in raiding undefended Indian villages but was unable to make any gains against British troops. Farther east, a force led by Major General Stephen Van Rensselaer was defeated by a small British and Indian army. Meanwhile, the third force, commanded by Henry Dearborn, lunged at Montreal but nervously withdrew back into U.S. territory after an inconclusive battle against the British.

American sailors fared much better during the war's opening days. Leading the war effort at sea were three frigates: the *Constitution* (popularly known as **Old Ironsides**), the *President,* and the *United States.* In mid-August, the *Constitution* outmaneuvered and eventually sank what the British described as "one of our stoutest frigates," the H.M.S. *Guerrière.* The *United States,* under the command of Stephen Decatur, enjoyed a victory against the British frigate the H.M.S. *Macedonian.* Enduring thirty broadsides fired by the *Macedonian,* Decatur's gunners splintered the British ship with seventy broadsides of their own. Though no stranger to the horrors of war, Decatur was shocked by what he found when he boarded the crippled vessel: "fragments of the dead scattered in every direction, the decks slippery with blood, and one continuous agonizing yell of the unhappy wounded." American privateers also enjoyed success, capturing 450 British merchant ships valued in the millions during the first six months of the war.

American naval victories were all that kept the nation's morale alive in 1812. Former Treasury secretary Albert Gallatin summarized the nation's humiliating

John C. Calhoun   Congressman from South Carolina who was a leader of the War Hawks and the author of the official declaration of war in 1812.

Old Ironsides   Nickname of the U.S.S. *Constitution,* the forty-four-gun American frigate whose victory over the *Guerrière* bolstered sagging national morale during the War of 1812.

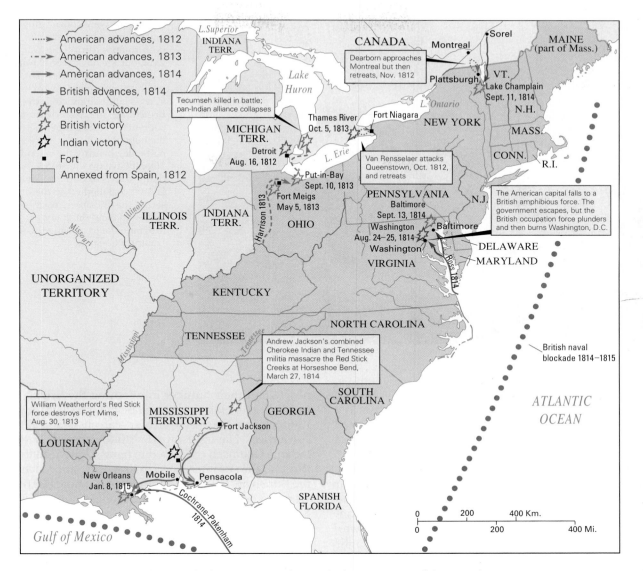

MAP 9.2 **The War of 1812** The heaviest action during the first two years of the War of 1812 lay along the U.S./Canadian border. In 1814 the British sought to knock the United States out of the war by staging three offensives: one along the northern frontier at Plattsburgh, New York; one into the Chesapeake; and a third directed at the Mississippi River at New Orleans. All three offensives failed.

military efforts: "The series of misfortunes," he wrote to Jefferson, "exceeds all anticipations made even by those who had least confidence in our inexperienced officers and undisciplined men." The land war had been, as another politician recalled, a "miscarriage, without even the heroism of disaster." Vowing to reverse the situation, Congress increased the size of the army to fifty-seven thousand men and offered a $16 bonus to encourage enlistments.

Thus in 1812 Madison stood for reelection at a time when the nation's military fate appeared uncertain and his own leadership seemed shaky. Although the majority of his party's congressional caucus supported him for reelection, nearly a third of the Republican congressmen—mostly those from New York and New England—rallied around New Yorker DeWitt Clinton, nephew and political ally of Madison's former challenger George Clinton. Like his uncle, DeWitt Clinton

Americans were consistently disappointed by the army's performance during the War of 1812, but the navy scored numerous significant victories. This painting celebrates Oliver Hazard Perry's landmark victory over the British fleet in Lake Erie during September 1813. Draped across the bow of his boat is Perry's battle flag bearing the legend "Don't Give up the Ship," the dying words of Captain James Lawrence, killed when the British seized the *Chesapeake* back in 1807—an incident that was instrumental in causing the war. *Library of Congress.*

was a Republican who favored Federalist economic policies and agreed with New England Federalists that the war was unnecessary. Most Federalists supported Clinton, and the party did not field a candidate of its own.

When the campaign was over, the outcome was nearly the same as the congressional vote on the war bill earlier in the year. New York and New England rallied behind Clinton. The South and West continued to support Madison, the Republicans, and war. Madison won but was in no position to gloat. His share of electoral votes had fallen from 72 percent in 1808 to 58.9 percent. At the same time, Republican Party strength in the House dropped by over 13 percent, in the Senate by about 8 percent.

The War Continues

When military campaigning resumed in the spring of 1813, it appeared that the U.S. Army would fare as badly as it had the previous fall. Fighting resumed when British colonel Henry Proctor and Tecumseh, with a joint force of nine hundred British soldiers and twelve hundred Indians, laid siege to Harrison's command camped at Fort Meigs on the Maumee Rapids in Ohio. An army of twelve hundred Kentucky militiamen finally arrived and drove the enemy off, but they were so disorganized that they lost

nearly half their number in pursuing the British and Indian force. Harrison was shocked, proclaiming the Kentuckians' "excessive ardour scarcely less fatal than cowardice." Having escaped virtually unscathed, Proctor and Tecumseh continued to harass American forces through the summer. Then, with winter approaching, the British and Indians withdrew to Canada. Harrison, who had been busy raising additional troops, decided to pursue.

No doubt Harrison's new effort would have proved as fruitless as his earlier ones, but an unexpected event turned the odds in his favor. One key problem plaguing Harrison and other commanders in the field was that the British controlled the Great Lakes and so could depend on an uninterrupted supply line. In contrast, American forces and their supplies moved along undeveloped roads and were easy targets for Indian and British attackers. **Oliver Hazard Perry,** a young naval tactician, had been given command of a small fleet assigned to clear the lakes of British ships. After months of playing hide-and-seek among the shore islands, British and American ships met in battle at Put-in-Bay in

Oliver Hazard Perry   American naval officer who led the fleet that defeated the British in the Battle of Put-in-Bay during the War of 1812.

Choosing to side with the British against the United States in the War of 1812, Tecumseh joined British commander Henry Proctor in leading a joint force of Indians and British regulars. On October 5, 1813, their force was attacked by an army led by Tecumseh's old rival William Henry Harrison. As shown in this painting of the battle, a penetrating cavalry charge (upper left) broke the British line while the Indian forces continued fighting. In the clash, Tecumseh was shot and died on the field. In this romanticized view, we see him, gun down and tomahawk raised as a bullet from a mounted officer's pistol moves unerringly toward him. *Library of Congress.*

September 1813. Two hours of cannon fire left Perry's **flagship,** the *Lawrence,* nearly destroyed, and 80 percent of the crew lay dead or wounded. Perry refused to surrender. He slipped off his damaged vessel and took command of another ship standing nearby. What remained of his command then sailed back into the heart of the British force and after three hours of close combat subdued and captured six British ships. Perry immediately sent a note to Harrison stating, "We have met the enemy and they are ours."

Buoyed by this news, Harrison's army closed in on Proctor and Tecumseh at the Thames River, about 50 miles northeast of Detroit, on October 5. The British force faced a piercing cavalry charge and lacking naval support was soon forced to surrender. The Indians held out longer, but when word spread that Tecumseh had been killed, they melted into the woods, leaving the body of their fallen leader to be torn apart by the victorious Americans.

Another war front had also opened farther south during 1813. Although the Creek Confederacy as a whole wished to remain neutral, one faction calling themselves the Red Sticks had allied with Tecumseh

in 1812. In the summer of 1813, Red Stick leader William Weatherford led a force against Fort Mims, killing all but about thirty of the more than three hundred occupants. The so-called Fort Mims massacre enraged whites in the Southeast. In Tennessee, twenty-five hundred militiamen rallied around **Andrew Jackson,** a young brawler and Indian fighter. Already called "Old Hickory" because of his toughness, Jackson made a bold promise: "The blood of our women & children shall not call for vengeance in vain." In the course of that summer and fall, Jackson's frontier ruffians fought multiple engagements against the Red Stick Creeks, driving them into hiding.

---

flagship   The ship that carries the fleet commander and bears the commander's flag.

Andrew Jackson   General who defeated the Creeks at Horseshoe Bend in 1814 and the British at New Orleans in 1815; he later became the seventh president of the United States.

While these battles raged on land, the British shut down American forces at sea. Embarrassed by the success of Old Ironsides and the other American frigates, the British admiralty ordered that "the naval force of the enemy should be quickly and completely disposed of" and sent sufficient ships to do the job. The American naval fleet and **merchant marine** found themselves bottled up in port by the world's strongest navy.

The Politics of War

The war had wound down for the winter by the time Congress reconvened in December 1813, but the outlook was not good. Disappointed that American forces had not knocked the British out of the war, Republican representative William Murfree spoke for many when he said, "The result of the last campaign disappointed the expectations of every one." President Madison tried to be optimistic. Recalling the victories during the year, he said, "The war, with its **vicissitudes,** is illustrating the capacity and destiny of the United States to be a great, a flourishing, and a powerful nation."

Madison's optimism seemed justified later in December when the British offered to open direct peace negotiations with the Americans. The president quickly formed a peace commission, but until its work was done, Madison and Congress still had to worry about the practical issues of troops and money, both of which were in critically short supply.

Despite increases in army pay and bonuses for new recruits, enlistments were falling off in 1813. Congressional Republicans responded by adding further enticements for new recruits, including grants of 160 acres of land in the western territories. Congress also authorized the president to extend the term of enlistment for men already in service. By 1814, Congress had increased the size of the army to more than sixty-two thousand men but had not figured out how to pay for all the changes.

Presenting the federal budget for 1814, Treasury Secretary William Jones announced that the government's income would be approximately $16 million, but its expenses would amount to over $45 million. Traditional enemies of internal taxes, the Republicans faced a dilemma. Shortly after convening, members of Congress had passed a set of new taxes and could not imagine explaining another increase to their constituents. So congressional Republicans decided to borrow instead, authorizing a $35 million deficit.

Adding to the money problem was the fact that, to this point in the war, the United States had permitted neutral nations to trade freely in American ports, carrying American exports to England and Canada and

English goods into eastern ports. As a result of this flourishing trade, American currency was flooding out of the United States at an alarming rate, weakening the nation's economy. At the same time, American food was rolling directly into British military commissaries, strengthening the enemy's ability and will to fight.

In a secret message to Congress, the president proposed an absolute embargo on all American ships and goods—neither were to leave port—and a complete ban on imports that were customarily produced in Great Britain. Federalists, especially those from New England, screamed in protest. They called the proposal "an engine of tyranny, an engine of oppression," no different, they said, from the Intolerable Acts imposed on American colonies by Britain in 1774 (see pages 133–134). But congressional Republicans passed the embargo a mere eight days after Madison submitted it.

The **Embargo of 1813** was the most far-reaching trade restriction bill ever passed by Congress. It confined all trading ships to port, and even fishing vessels could put to sea only if their masters posted sizable **bonds.** Government officials charged with enforcing the new law had unprecedented **discretionary powers.** The impact was devastating: the embargo virtually shut down the New England and New York economies, and it severely crippled the economy of nearly every other state.

New British Offensives

While Congress debated matters of finance and trade restrictions, events in Europe were changing the entire character of the war. On March 31, 1814, the British and their allies took Paris, forcing Napoleon to abdicate his throne. Few in America mourned the French emperor's fall. Jefferson wrote, "I rejoice . . . in the downfall of Bonaparte. This scourge of the world has occasioned the deaths of at least ten millions of human beings." Napoleon's defeat, however, left the

---

merchant marine   A nation's commercial ships.

vicissitudes   Sudden or unexpected changes encountered during the course of life.

Embargo of 1813   An absolute embargo on all American trade and British imports.

bond   A sum of money paid as bail or security.

discretionary powers   Powers to be used at one's own judgment; in government, powers given to an administrative official to be used without outside consultation or oversight.

Although the British were successful in capturing the United States capital in August 1814, defenders stalled the invasion long enough for the government to escape. In frustration, the British pillaged the city and then burned the public buildings. This painting captures the disordered scene as city dwellers try to quench the flames while the capitol building blazes in the background. © *Bettmann/CORBIS.*

United States as Great Britain's sole military target. Republican Joseph Nicholson expressed a common lament when he observed, "We should have to fight hereafter not for 'free Trade and sailors rights,' not for the Conquest of the Canadas, but for our national Existence."

As Nicholson feared, a flood of combat-hardened British veterans began arriving in North America, and the survival of the United States as an independent nation was indeed at issue. By the late summer of 1814, British troop strength in Canada had risen to thirty thousand men. From this position of power, the British prepared a chain of three offensives to bring the war to a quick end.

In August 1814, twenty British warships and several troop transports sailed up Chesapeake Bay toward Washington, D.C. The British arrived outside Washington at midday on August 24. The troops defending the city could not withstand the force of hardened British veterans, but they delayed the invasion long enough for the government to escape. Angered at being foiled, the British sacked the city, torching most of the buildings. They then moved on toward the key port city of Baltimore.

At Baltimore, the British navy had to knock out Fort McHenry and take the harbor before the army could take the city. On September 13, British ships armed with heavy **mortars** and rockets attacked the fort. Despite the pounding, when the sun rose on September 14, the American flag continued to wave over Fort McHenry. The sight moved a young Georgetown volunteer named **Francis Scott Key,** who had watched the shelling as a prisoner aboard one of the British ships, to record the event in a poem that was later set to music and became the national anthem of the United States. Having failed to reduce the fort, the British were forced to withdraw, leaving Baltimore undisturbed.

mortar   A portable, muzzle-loading cannon that fires large projectiles at high trajectories over a short range; traditionally used by mobile troops against fixed fortifications.

Francis Scott Key   Author of "The Star-Spangled Banner," which chronicles the British bombardment of Fort McHenry in 1814; Key's poem, set to music, became the official U.S. national anthem in 1931.

While this strike at the nation's midsection was raging, Sir George Prevost, governor-general of Canada, massed ten thousand troops for an invasion in the north. The British force arrived just north of Plattsburgh, New York, on September 6, where it was to join the British naval fleet that controlled Lake Champlain. However, a small American flotilla under the command of Lieutenant Thomas Macdonough outmaneuvered the imposing British armada and forced a surrender on September 11. Prevost had already begun his attack against the defenders at Plattsburgh, but when he learned that the British lake fleet was defeated and in flames, he lost his nerve and ordered his men to retreat.

On yet another front, the British pressed an offensive against the Gulf Coast designed to take pressure off Canada and close transportation on the Mississippi River. The defense of the Gulf Coast fell to Andrew Jackson and his Tennesseans. Having spent the winter raising troops and collecting supplies, in March 1814 Jackson and his army of four thousand militiamen and Cherokee volunteers resumed their mission to punish the Red Stick Creeks. Learning that the Red Sticks had established a camp on the peninsula formed by a bend in the Tallapoosa River, Jackson led his men on a forced march to attack. On March 27 in what was misleadingly called the **Battle of Horseshoe Bend,** Jackson's force trapped the Creeks and slaughtered nearly eight hundred people, destroying Red Stick opposition and severely crippling Indian resistance in the South.

After the massacre at Horseshoe Bend, Jackson moved his army toward the Gulf of Mexico, where a British offensive was in the making. Arriving in New Orleans on December 1, he found the city ill prepared to defend itself. The local militia, consisting mostly of French and Spanish residents, would not obey American officers. "Those who are not for us are against us, and will be dealt with accordingly," Jackson proclaimed. He turned increasingly to unconventional sources of support. Free blacks in the city formed a regular army corps, and Jackson created a special unit of black refugees from Santo Domingo under the command of Colonel Jean Baptiste Savary. White citizens protested Jackson's arming of runaway slaves, but he ignored their objections. "Legitimate citizens" protested too when Jackson accepted a company of river pirates under the command of **Jean Lafitte,** awarding them a blanket pardon for all past crimes. "Hellish Banditti," Jackson himself called them, but the pirate commander and the general hit it off so well that Lafitte became Jackson's constant companion during the campaign.

Having pulled his ragtag force together, Jackson settled in to wait for the British attack. On the morning of January 8, 1815, it came. The British force, commanded by General Edward Pakenham, emerged from the fog at dawn, directly in front of Jackson's defenses. Waiting patiently behind hastily constructed barricades, Jackson's men began firing cannon, rifles, and muskets as the British moved within range. According to one British veteran, it was "the most murderous fire I have ever beheld before or since."

When it was all over, more than two thousand British troops had been killed or wounded in the **Battle of New Orleans,** while a mere seventy-one Americans fell. This was by far the most successful battle fought by American forces during the War of 1812. But ironically, it was fought after the war was over.

The War's Strange Conclusion

While the British were closing in on Washington in the summer of 1814, treaty negotiations designed to end the war were beginning in Ghent, Belgium. Confident that their three-pronged attack against the United States would soon knock the Americans out of the war, the British delegates were in no hurry to end it by diplomacy. They refused to discuss substantive issues, insisting that all of the matters raised by Madison's peace commission were nonnegotiable.

At that point, however, domestic politics in England began to play a deciding role. After nearly a generation of armed conflict, the English people were war-weary, especially the taxpayers. As one British official put it, "Economy & relief from taxation are not merely the War Cry of Opposition, but they are the real objects to which public attention is turned." The failures at Plattsburgh and Baltimore made it appear that at best the war would drag on at least another year, at an estimated cost to Britain of an additional $44 million. Moreover, continuation of the

Battle of Horseshoe Bend   Battle in 1814 in which Tennessee militia massacred Creek Indians in Alabama, ending Red Stick resistance to white westward expansion.

Jean Lafitte   Leader of a band of pirates in southeast Louisiana; he offered to fight for the Americans at New Orleans in return for the pardon of his men.

Battle of New Orleans   Battle in the War of 1812 in which American troops commanded by Andrew Jackson destroyed the British force attempting to seize New Orleans.

The nearly miraculous American victory in the Battle of New Orleans—fought two weeks after the Americans and British had signed a peace treaty—helped launch a new era in American nationalism. And, as this illustration from a popular magazine shows, it made Andrew Jackson, shown waving his hat to encourage his troops, a national hero of greater-than-human proportions. *Library of Congress.*

American war was interfering with Britain's European diplomacy. Trying to arrive at a peace settlement for Europe at the **Congress of Vienna,** a British official commented, "We do not think the Continental Powers will continue in good humour with our Blockade of the whole Coast of America." Speaking for the military, the **Duke of Wellington** reviewed British military successes and failures in the American war and advised his countrymen, "You have no right . . . to demand any **concession** . . . from America."

In the end, the **Treaty of Ghent,** completed on December 24, 1814, simply restored diplomatic relations between England and the United States to what they had been prior to the outbreak of war. The treaty said nothing about impressment, blockades, or neutral trading rights. Neither military action nor diplomatic finagling netted Canada for the War Hawks. And the treaty did nothing about the alleged conspiracies between Indians and British agents. Although Americans called the War of 1812 a victory, they actually won none of the prizes that Madison's war statement had declared the nation was fighting for.

Peace and the Rise of New Expectations

→ *How did events during the War of 1812 help to move the American economy in new directions after peace was restored?*

→ *What impact did changes in the economy have on the institution of slavery and on the lives of slaves?*

Despite repeated military disasters, loss of life, and diplomatic failure, the war had a number of positive effects on the United States. Just to have survived a war against the British was enough to build national confidence, but to have scored major victories such as those at Plattsburgh, Baltimore, and especially New Orleans was truly worth boasting about. Americans emerged from the conflict with a new sense of national pride and purpose. And many side effects from the fighting itself gave Americans new hopes and plans.

Congress of Vienna   Conference between ambassadors from the major powers in Europe to redraw the continent's political map after the defeat of Napoleon; it also sought to uproot revolutionary movements and restore traditional monarchies.

Duke of Wellington   The most respected military leader in Great Britain at this time; Wellington was responsible for the defeat of Napoleon.

concession   In diplomacy, something given up during negotiations.

Treaty of Ghent   Treaty ending the War of 1812, signed in Belgium in 1814; it restored peace but was silent on the issues over which the United States and Britain had gone to war.

New Expectations in the Northeastern Economy

Although trading interests in the Northeast suffered following Jefferson's embargo and were nearly ruined by the war and Madison's embargo, a new avenue of economic expansion opened in New England. Cut off from European manufactured goods, Americans started to make more textiles and other items for themselves.

Samuel Slater, an English immigrant who had been trained in manufacturing in Britain, introduced the use of machines for spinning cotton yarn to the United States in 1790. His mill was financially successful, but few others tried to copy his enterprise. Even with shipping expenses, tariffs, and other added costs, buying machine-made British cloth was still more practical than investing large sums at high risk to build competing factories in the United States. And after 1800, Jefferson's economic policies discouraged such investment. But his embargo changed all that. After it went into effect in 1808, British fabrics became increasingly unavailable, and prices soared. Slater and his partners moved quickly to expand their spinning operations to fill the void. And now his inventiveness was widely copied.

Another entrepreneur, Francis Cabot Lowell, went even further than Slater. Left in the lurch economically by the embargo, Lowell ventured to England in 1810. While there, he engaged in wholesale industrial espionage, observing British textile-manufacturing practices and machinery and making detailed notes and sketches of what he saw. Returning to the United States just before war broke out in 1812, Lowell formed the Boston Manufacturing Company. In 1813 the company used the plans Lowell had smuggled back to the United States to build a factory in Waltham, Massachusetts. The new facility included spinning machines, power looms, and all the equipment necessary to **mechanize** every stage in the production of finished cloth, bringing the entire process under one roof. Like Slater's innovations, Lowell's too were soon duplicated by economically desperate New Englanders.

The spread of textile manufacturing was astonishing. Prior to 1808, only fifteen cotton mills of the sort Slater had introduced had been built in the entire country. But between the passage of the embargo and the end of 1809, eighty-seven additional mills had sprung up, mostly in New England. And when war came, the pace increased, especially when Lowell's idea of a mechanized textile factory proved to be highly efficient and profitable. The number of people employed in manufacturing increased from four thousand in 1809 to perhaps as many as a hundred thousand in 1816. In the years to come, factories in New England and elsewhere supplied more and more of the country's consumer goods.

New Opportunities in the West

But business growth was not confined to the Northeast. Following the war, pioneers poured into the West in astounding numbers. The population of Ohio had already soared from 45,000 in 1800 to 231,000 in 1810, but it more than doubled again by 1820, reaching 581,000. Indiana, Illinois, Missouri, and Michigan experienced similar growth. Most of those who flooded into the newly opened West were small farmers, but subsistence agriculture was not the only economic opportunity that drew expectant Americans into the region. Big business, too, had great expectations for finding new wealth in the West.

One of the designs behind the Lewis and Clark and the Zebulon Pike expeditions had been to gain entry for the United States into the burgeoning economy in North America's interior (see pages 223–225). That economy was complex, with many commodities being traded, and few entirely understood all of its intricacies. There was one facet, though, that was well known and very desirable to entrepreneurs: the brown gold of beaver, mink, and other animal furs.

Even before the War of 1812, individual fur traders had tried to break the monopoly wielded by the English and Canadians over the trade along the northern frontier and by the Spanish and French farther south. One particularly visionary businessman had already put a plan in motion before the war to create a continent-wide trading network. John Jacob Astor, a German immigrant who had arrived in the United States in 1783, announced that he intended to establish "a range of Posts or Trading houses" along the route that Lewis and Clark had followed from St. Louis to the Pacific (see Map 8.2).

Another visionary entrepreneur sought a similar fortune in the Southwest. Auguste Chouteau was French by birth, but like many frontiersmen, he changed nationalities as frequently as the borderlands changed owners. Chouteau had helped to found the town of St. Louis and had been instrumental in establishing that city as the capital for a fur-trading empire. He, his brother Pierre, and an extended family of business partners used intermarriage to create a massive kin-

---

mechanize   To substitute machinery for human labor.

Generally, when we think of the Far West in the early nineteenth century, especially the fur trade, we think of wild adventures experienced by colorful men who had little thought for responsibilities or wealth. The fact is that the early American fur trade was big business and the entrepreneurs who succeeded at it became true captains of industry. Here we see the home that fur profits built for the Chouteau family in St. Louis, a considerable mansion by any standards. *"St. Louis the Fourth City, 1764–1909" by Walter B. Stevens. S. J. Clarke Publishing Co., 1909.*

ship network that included important French, Spanish, and Indian connections. With kinship ensuring cooperative trading partners, the Chouteau brothers were able to extend their reach deep into the Missouri region and establish trade between St. Louis and the Spanish far western trading capital at Santa Fe (see Map 2.3 and pages 49-50). As Americans began to penetrate the area, the Chouteau brothers took the change in stride, inviting William Clark of the Corps of Discovery and fur entrepreneur Andrew Henry to join forces with them in founding the Missouri Fur Company in 1809.

The war disrupted both Astor's and the Missouri Fur Company's operations, but when the war was over, the fur business resumed with increasing vigor. Pierre Chouteau and his various American partners pushed continually farther into the West, using their strategy of forming traditional Indian trading partnerships, often rooted in intermarriage, to expand business. Chouteau also used his kin partnerships and capital from the fur trade to branch into other businesses. He was a cofounder of the Bank of Missouri and served as its president for a number of years. He also operated flour mills and distilleries and speculated in real estate. Members of his extended family later helped to found Kansas City, pioneered mining in Colorado, and financed railroad building in the Dakotas.

The joint efforts of individual farmers and business tycoons such as Astor and the Chouteaus opened the West and proved to the satisfaction of many that great fortunes and good lives could be had on the frontier. Though the promise was nearly always greater than the reality, the allure of the West was unmistakable. And after the War of 1812, the nation's aspirations became more and more firmly tied to that region's growth and development.

But American westward expansion posed a terrible threat to Native Americans. When Harrison's soldiers burned Prophetstown and later killed Tecumseh, they wiped out all hopes for a pan-Indian confederacy. In addition, the civil war among the Creeks, followed by Jackson's victories against the Red Stick faction, removed all meaningful resistance to westward expansion in the South. Many Indian groups continued to wield great power, but accommodationist leaders such as those who formed the Cherokee government suggested that cooperation with federal authorities was the best course.

Collaboration between the United States and Native Americans helped to prevent renewed warfare, but at enormous cost to the Indians. Within a year of the Battle of Horseshoe Bend, Jackson forced the Creeks to sign the Treaty of Fort Jackson, which confiscated over 20 million acres of land from the Creek Confederacy. A similar but more gradual assault on Indian landholding began in the Northwest in 1815. In a council meeting at Portage des Sioux in Illinois Territory, the United States signed peace accords with the various tribes that had joined the British during the war. Both sides pledged that their earlier hostilities

Following the War of 1812 and the death of Tecumseh, aggressive American expansionists put great pressure on Indians living on the eastern side of the Mississippi River to move farther west. In location after location, American Indian agents and their military escorts set up treaty negotiations designed to acquire ever-increasing amounts of land that would accommodate ambitious would-be farmers. This painting captures one of the largest of these, the Prairie du Chien conference of 1825, at which the Sauk, Fox, Chippewa, and other Indians in Illinois, Wisconsin, and Michigan ceded huge portions of land in hopes of winning peace. *Wisconsin Historical Society.*

would be "forgiven and forgotten" and that all the agreeing parties would live in "perpetual peace and friendship." The northwestern Indians, however, possessed some 2 million acres of prime real estate between the Illinois and Mississippi Rivers—land that the United States government had already given away as enlistment bonuses to white war volunteers. Moving the Indians off that land as quickly as possible thus became a matter of national priority.

Over the next several years, **federal Indian agents** used every tactic they could think of to coerce groups like the Kickapoo Indians into ceding their lands. Finally, in 1819, the Kickapoo Nation signed the Treaty of Edwardsville, turning over most of the land the United States had demanded. Having secured this massive tract, government agents then turned their attention to the vast holdings of more distant tribes—the Sauk, Fox, Chippewa, and Dakota Indians in western Illinois, Wisconsin, and Michigan. As they had done

with the Kickapoos, American negotiators used bribery, threat, and manipulation of local tensions to pursue their goal, eventually winning an enormous cession of land in the Prairie du Chien treaties of 1825.

A Revolution in the Southern Economy

Indian dispossession and westward expansion also promised great economic growth for the South. In the years before the War of 1812, the southern economy

---

federal Indian agents Government officials who were responsible for negotiating treaties with Native American groups; at this time they were employed by the War Department.

had been sluggish, and the future of the region's single-crop agricultural system was doubtful. Tobacco, the mainstay of the South's economy, was no longer the glorious profit maker it had been during the colonial period. Sea Island cotton, rice, sugar, and other products continued to find markets, but they grew only in limited areas. However, the technological and economic changes that came in the war's wake pumped new energy into the South. In only a few decades, an entirely new South emerged.

The mechanization of the British textile industry in the late eighteenth century created an enormous new demand for cotton. Southern planters had been growing the fibrous plant since colonial times, but soil and climatic conditions limited the growing area for the sort of **long-staple cotton** that could be harvested and sold economically. Large areas of the South and Southwest had proved suitable for growing **short-staple cotton,** but the time and labor required to pick the sticky seeds from the compact **cotton bolls** made the crop unprofitable. In 1793 a young Yale College graduate, **Eli Whitney,** was a guest at a plantation in Georgia, where he learned about the difficulty of removing the seeds from short-staple cotton. In a matter of weeks, Whitney helped to perfect a machine that allowed a small and unskilled work force to quickly comb out the seeds without damaging the fibers. He obtained a **patent** for the cotton gin (short for "cotton engine") in 1794 and set up a factory in New Haven, Connecticut, to manufacture the machine. Whitney's engine, though revolutionary in its impact, was a relatively simple mechanism, and despite his patent, other manufacturers and individual planters stole the design and built their own cotton gins.

The outcome of Whitney's inventiveness was the rapid spread of short-staple cotton throughout inland South Carolina and Georgia. Then, just as it seemed that the southern economy was about to bloom, embargo and war closed down exports to England. Although some cotton growers were able to shift sales from England to the rising new factories in New England, a true explosion of growth in cotton cultivation had to await war's end.

With the arrival of peace and the departure of the British naval blockade, cotton growing began to spread at an astounding rate. The massacre of the Red Stick Creeks removed the final major threat of Indian resistance in the South, and southerners rushed into frontier areas, spreading cotton agriculture into Alabama and Mississippi and then into Arkansas and northern Louisiana. Even the Mississippi River seemed to present no serious barrier to this runaway expansion. In 1821 Spanish authorities gave long-time western land speculator Moses Austin permission to settle three hundred American families within a 200,000-acre tract in Texas between the Brazos and Colorado Rivers. When the elder Austin died, his son, **Stephen F. Austin,** took over the enterprise and in the aftermath of the Panic of 1819 was able to offer families large plots of land for a filing fee of only 12½ cents an acre. "I am convinced," he exclaimed, "that I could take on fifteen hundred families as easily as three hundred if permitted to do so." Throughout the 1820s and 1830s, Austin and other *empresarios* helped thousands of hopeful cotton capitalists to expand into Mexican territory. As a result of this expansion, the South's annual cotton crop grew by leaps and bounds. By 1840, annual exports reached nearly a million and a half bales, and increasing volumes were consumed within the United States by the mushrooming textile factories in the Northeast.

Reviving and Reinventing Slavery

Before the emergence of cotton, when the South's agricultural system was foundering, many southerners began to question the use of slaves. In 1782 Virginia made it legal for individual masters to free their slaves, and many did so. In 1784 Thomas Jefferson proposed (but saw defeated) a land ordinance that would have prohibited slavery in all of the nation's territories after 1800. Some southern leaders advocated abolishing slavery and transporting freed blacks to Africa. But

long-staple cotton   A variety of cotton with long and loosely packed pods of fiber that is easy to comb out and process.

short-staple cotton   A variety of cotton with short and tightly packed pods of fiber in which the plant's seeds are tangled.

cotton boll   The pod of the cotton plant; it contains the plant's seeds surrounded by the fluffy fiber that is spun into yarn.

Eli Whitney   American inventor and manufacturer; his perfecting of the cotton gin revolutionized the cotton industry.

patent   A government grant that gives the creator of an invention the sole right to produce, use, or sell that invention for a set period of time.

Stephen F. Austin   American colonizer in Texas and leading voice in the Texas Revolution.

empresario   In the Spanish colonies, a person who organized and led a group of settlers in exchange for land grants and the right to assess fees.

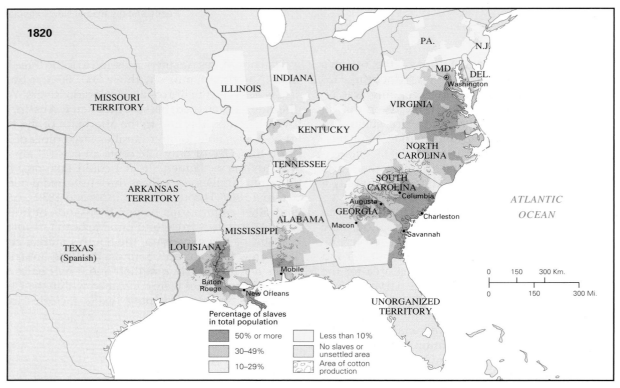

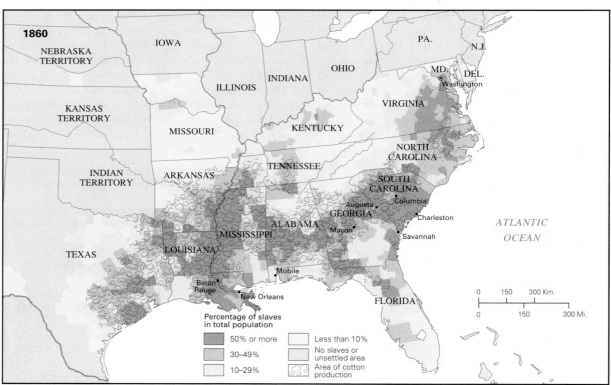

MAP 9.3 **Cotton Agriculture and Slave Population** Between 1820 and 1860, the expansion of cotton agriculture and the extension of slavery went hand in hand. As these maps show, cotton production was an isolated activity in 1820, and slavery remained isolated as well. By 1860, both had extended westward.

The invention of the cotton gin and the spread of cotton agriculture throughout the American South created an enormous new demand for slave workers and changed the nature of their work. A handful of slaves (only two in this illustration of the process) could comb through large amounts of fiber, but it took armies of field workers to produce the raw cotton that kept the machinery (and the plantation system) working. *The Granger Collection, New York.*

the booming southern economy after the War of 1812 required more labor than ever. As a result, African American slavery expanded as never before.

Viewed side by side, a map showing cotton agriculture and one showing slave population appear nearly identical (see Map 9.3). In the 1820s, when cotton production was most heavily concentrated in South Carolina and Georgia, the greatest density of slaves occurred in the same area. During the 1840s, as cotton growing spread to the West, slavery followed. By 1860, both cotton growing and slavery appear on the map as a continuous belt stretching from the Carolinas through Georgia and Alabama and on to the Mississippi River.

The virtually universal shift to cotton growing throughout the South brought about not only the expansion and extension of slavery but also substantial modifications to the institution itself. The wide variety of economic pursuits in which slave labor had been employed from the colonial period onward led to varied patterns in slave employment. In many parts of the South, slaves traditionally exercised a great deal of control over their work schedules as they completed assigned tasks (see page 94). But the cotton business called for large gangs of predominantly unskilled workers, and increasingly slaves found themselves regimented like machines in tempo with the demands of cotton production.

At the same time, as northeastern factories were able to provide clothing, shoes, and other manufactured goods at ever more attractive prices and western farmers shipped cheap pork and grain into southern markets, plantation managers found it more practical to purchase such goods rather than to produce them. Thus slaves who formerly had performed various skilled tasks such as milling and weaving found themselves pressed into much less rewarding service as brute labor in the cotton fields. To a large extent, then, specialized manufacturing in the North and large-scale commercial food production in the West permitted an intensified cotton industry in the South and helped foster the increasing dehumanization of the peculiar labor system that drove it.

Examining a Primary Source

✔ Individual Voices

Tecumseh Describes American Indian Policy Under William Henry Harrison

Between 1808 and 1811, Shawnee political spokesman Tecumseh and Indiana Territory governor William Henry Harrison engaged in a running war of words. In the course of these discussions, Tecumseh became increasingly frustrated at Harrison's apparent ignorance of political and social organization among the various groups of Indians in the American interior. He repeatedly explained that though relations among the various Indians were complex, they nevertheless constituted a single people and not a patchwork of separate nations. Finally, at a conference in Vincennes on August 20, 1810, Tecumseh lost his temper and accused Harrison of intentionally misunderstanding the nature of Native American inter-group relations as part of a larger effort to defraud the Indians of their land. The original handwritten transcript of this speech contains many abbreviations as well as some unusual spelling and punctuation. The excerpt that follows has been modernized for easier reading.

① What exactly is Tecumseh charging Harrison and his agents of doing? What does this suggest about Tecumseh's understanding of the nature of Indian organization and Harrison's misunderstandings about it?

② Why would Tecumseh insist that warriors rather than village chiefs decide policy toward the United States?

You try to force the red people to do some injury. It is you that is pushing them on to do mischief. You endeavor to make distinctions. You wish to prevent the Indians to do as we wish them to: unite and let them consider their land as the common property of the whole. You take tribes aside and advise them not to come into this measure. . . .

The reason I tell you this is [that] you want by your distinctions of Indian tribes in allotting to each a particular tract of land to make them to war with each other. You never see an Indian come and endeavor to make the white people do so. You are continually driving the red people when at last you will drive them into the great Lake where they can't either stand or work. **①**

You ought to know what you are doing with the Indians. Perhaps it is by direction of the President to make those distinctions. It is a very bad thing and we do not like it. Since my residence at Tippecanoe, we have endeavored to level all distinctions to destroy village chiefs by whom all mischief is done; it is they who sell our land to the Americans [so] our object is to let all our affairs be transacted by Warriors. **②**

This land that was sold and the goods that were given for it was only done by a few. The treaty was afterwards brought here and the Weas were induced to give their consent because of their small numbers. The treaty at Fort Wayne was made through the threats [by] Winamac, ③ but in future we are prepared to punish those chiefs who may come forward to propose to sell their land. If you continue to purchase [land from] them, it will produce war among the different tribes, and at last I do not know what will be the consequences to the white people. . . .

I now wish you to listen to me. If you do not it will appear as if you wished me to kill all the chiefs that sold you the land. I tell you so because I am authorized by all the tribes to do so. I am at the head of them all. I am a Warrior and all the Warriors will meet together in two or three moons from this. Then I will call for those chiefs that sold you the land and shall know what to do with them. If you do not restore the land, you will have a hand in killing them. ④

③ The Wea Indians, a small Miami Indian group, did not sign the Fort Wayne Treaty but later were pressured by Harrison and his accomplice, Winamac, to give their approval. A political headman among the Potawatomi Indians, Winamac worked closely with Harrison, using threats and bribes to convince many of his peers to sign away their lands.

④ What did Tecumseh propose to do if Harrison persisted in conducting Indian policy and land acquisition as he had done at Fort Wayne? Why do you think Tecumseh chose this particular approach?

SUMMARY

After Jefferson's triumphal first four years in office, factional disputes at home and diplomatic deadlocks with European powers began to plague the Republicans. Although the Federalists were in full retreat, many within Jefferson's own party rebelled against some of his policies. When Jefferson decided not to run for office in 1808, tapping James Madison as his successor, Republicans in both the Northeast and the South bucked the president, supporting George Clinton and James Monroe, respectively.

To a large extent, the Republicans' problems were the outcome of external stresses. On the Atlantic frontier, the United States tried to remain neutral in the wars that engulfed Europe. On the western frontier, the Prophet and Tecumseh were successfully unifying dispossessed Indians into an alliance devoted to stopping U.S. expansion. Things went from bad to worse when Jefferson's use of economic sanctions gave rise to the worst economic depression since the beginnings of English colonization. The embargo strangled the economy in port cities, and the downward spiral in agricultural prices threatened to bankrupt many in the West and South.

The combination of economic and diplomatic constraints brought aggressive politicians to power in 1808 and 1810. Men such as William Henry Harrison expected that war with England would permit the United States finally to realize independence—forcing freedom of the seas, eliminating Indian resistance, and justifying the conquest of the rest of North America. Despite Madison's continuing peace efforts, southern and western interests finally pushed the nation into war with England in 1812.

Although some glimmering moments of glory heartened the Americans, the war was mostly disastrous. But after generations of fighting one enemy or another, the English people demanded peace. When their final offensive in America failed to bring immediate victory in 1814, the British chose to negotiate. Finally, on Christmas Eve, the two nations signed the Treaty of Ghent, ending the war. From a diplomatic point of view, it was as though the war had never happened: everything was simply restored to pre-1812 status.

Nevertheless, in the United States the war created strong feelings of national pride and confidence, and Americans looked forward to even better things to come. In the Northeast, the constraints of war provoked entrepreneurs to explore new industries, creating the first stage of an industrial revolution in the country. In the West, the defeat of Indian resistance combined with bright economic opportunities to trigger a wave of westward migration. In the South, the economy was revolutionized by the cotton gin and the growing demand for fiber among English and then American manufacturers. Throughout the country, economic progress promised to improve life for most Americans, but as before, both African Americans and Native Americans bore much of the cost.

IN THE WIDER WORLD

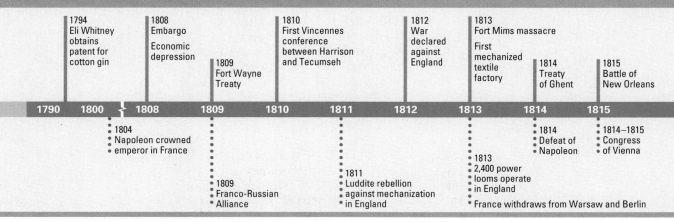

1790	1800	1808	1809	1810	1811	1812	1813	1814	1815

1794 Eli Whitney obtains patent for cotton gin

1808 Embargo Economic depression

1809 Fort Wayne Treaty

1810 First Vincennes conference between Harrison and Tecumseh

1812 War declared against England

1813 Fort Mims massacre
First mechanized textile factory

1814 Treaty of Ghent

1815 Battle of New Orleans

1804 Napoleon crowned emperor in France

1809 Franco-Russian Alliance

1811 Luddite rebellion against mechanization in England

1813 2,400 power looms operate in England
France withdraws from Warsaw and Berlin

1814 Defeat of Napoleon

1814–1815 Congress of Vienna

Domestic Expansion and International Crisis

1794	Eli Whitney patents cotton gin
1803	Britain steps up impressments
1804	Duel between Alexander Hamilton and Aaron Burr
	Jefferson reelected
1805	Beginning of Shawnee religious revival
1807	Burr conspiracy trial
	Founding of Prophetstown
	Chesapeake affair
1808	Embargo of 1808 goes into effect
	Economic depression begins
	James Madison elected president
1809	Non-Intercourse Act
	Fort Wayne Treaty
	Chouteau brothers form Missouri Fur Company
1810	Macon's Bill No. 2
	Vincennes Conference between Harrison and Tecumseh
	Formation of War Hawk faction
1811	United States breaks trade relations with Britain

	Second Vincennes Conference between Harrison and Tecumseh
	Battle of Tippecanoe and destruction of Prophetstown
1812	United States declares war against England
	United States invades Canada
	James Madison reelected
1813	Fort Mims massacre
	Battle of Put-in-Bay
	Embargo of 1813
	First mechanized textile factory, Waltham, Massachusetts
	Battle of the Thames
1814	Battle of Horseshoe Bend
	British capture and burn Washington, D.C.
	Battle of Plattsburgh
	Treaty of Ghent
1815	Battle of New Orleans
	Treaty of Fort Jackson
	Portage des Sioux treaties
1819	Treaty of Edwardsville
1825	Prairie du Chien treaties

10

The Rise of a New Nation, 1815–1836

A NOTE FROM THE AUTHOR

Here in the opening decades of the twenty-first century we watch the beginning of what many experts believe is a new era in human existence; a post-modern era. We are presented day after day with uncertainty after uncertainty as long-standing traditions fall away. We are increasingly confronted by events in faraway places that refuse to stay faraway: satellite television brings a high definition world into our living rooms, and the Internet invites us to interact with it at every level of our existence. It is frightening, exciting, challenging; it gives free play to both our best and our worst characteristics as individuals and as societies.

Two centuries ago Americans sat in a similar place and faced similar dilemmas. During the opening decades of the nineteenth century, the modern era was crashing in on equally frightened and excited Americans. Like us, they saw traditions falling away and confronted new realities and challenges in an atmosphere of uncertainty. In the process, they created many of the institutions and habits that we long took for granted; precisely those same traditions that are now giving way to new, post-modern behaviors.

As I deal on a day-to-day basis with the changes that seem to be happening at an ever-accelerating rate, I reflect on the experiences of Americans two hundred years ago and try to imagine how foreign and frightening the emerging modern world—the world I have always clung to for a sense of tradition and stability—must have seemed to them. It gives me a much greater respect for those earlier Americans who weathered this transformation and a much greater optimism for our future, knowing that out of the insecurities of the past grew the anchors that until recently provided our own sense of security. I have no doubt that new anchors will develop as we enter this new post-modern world, and we can learn a lot from our nineteenth-century ancestors about how to weather change gracefully, if not always gratefully.

John C. Calhoun

As a young congressman in the years bracketing the War of 1812, John C. Calhoun was celebrated as a leading American nationalist. But in the years following the economic panic of 1819 and the sectional crisis in Missouri, Calhoun chose to abandon nationalism in favor of states' rights and southern sectionalism. As vehement in his new sentiments as he had been in his earlier ones, Calhoun became an icon among states' rights advocates for generations to come. *National Portrait Gallery, Smithsonian Institution/Art Resource, NY.*

Individual Choices

Little in John C. Calhoun's background would have suggested that he would emerge as a controversial and divisive figure. A political prodigy, he had been elected to the U.S. House of Representatives at age 29, where he joined forces with other up-and-coming legislators as part of the hyper-patriotic War Hawk faction. After the War of 1812 he continued to act as a dedicated nationalist, working closely with Henry Clay to build the American System—Clay's plan for a national **market economy.** Calhoun drafted specific bills necessary to the program; won House support for chartering a new national bank, spending federal funds for transportation development, and creating the nation's first protective tariff package; and convinced President Madison of the program's constitutionality. Calhoun quickly established a reputation as a solid nationalist; his admiring colleague John Quincy Adams found him to be "above all sectional and factious prejudices more than any other statesman of this Union with whom I have ever acted."

But in the wake of the economic Panic of 1819, Calhoun began entertaining serious "sectional and factious prejudices." To a large extent this was because of proposals on the part of his northeastern colleagues to use tight credit and higher tariffs as a way of fighting off the effects of the depression. While these solutions made sense to manufacturers and some other beneficiaries of the postwar boom, they threatened to strangle the growing cotton industry that was fast becoming the centerpiece in the economy of the South. But population growth in the Northeast and increasing economic specialization in parts of the West gave protariff forces all the votes they needed to promote their political agenda in Congress. Soon, Calhoun came to believe, the Northeast would emerge as a tyrannical mother country, and the rest of the nation would become its oppressed and dependent colonies.

---

market economy   An economic system based on the buying and selling of goods and services, in which prices are determined by the forces of supply and demand.

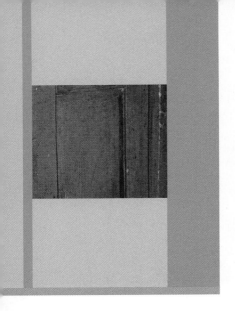

Fearful that incoming president Andrew Jackson was even more nationalistic than his predecessors, in 1828 Calhoun drafted a pamphlet called *The South Carolina Exposition and Protest*. Drawing on ideas enunciated years before by James Madison and Thomas Jefferson in their Virginia and Kentucky Resolutions, Calhoun argued that the federal union was nothing more than a convenient mechanism for carrying out the collective will of the states. As such, its sovereignty was not superior to that of the states. More importantly, if a state determined that a federal law violated the basic rights of its citizens, a popular assembly could declare that law null—having no legal force—within its borders. This doctrine became known as nullification.

By the time of his death in 1850, Calhoun's role as a leading nationalist had been all but forgotten, replaced by his new legacy as the virtual patron saint for southern independence. The transformations that unsettled the nation turned Calhoun completely around, and his new legacy would affect the nation every bit as profoundly as had his earlier one.

INTRODUCTION

Though certainly more talented than many Americans and more powerful than most, John C. Calhoun nonetheless was typical of his generation in many ways. Like most of his contemporaries he was angered by British invasions of American sovereignty and lobbied for war in 1812. Following the war he embraced the spirit of national unity and good feelings to promote economic consolidation, leading Congress to revolutionize public finance laws in order to encourage expansive growth. And these policies succeeded: the United States experienced an exciting growth spurt after 1815. But when the speculative bubble burst in 1819, the optimism and unity that had characterized the country faltered.

Calhoun was also typical of a growing number of Americans in his views on politics. Like his fellow prodigies Henry Clay and William Henry Harrison, Calhoun had made politics a career from very early in life. Of course, Calhoun, Clay, and Harrison were property owners, and their families had always exercised political rights, but during the 1820s more and more Americans gained those same rights and took politics every bit as seriously as Calhoun and his privileged colleagues. In this highly charged atmosphere, matters of state became for the first time in the nation's history a topic for debate among people from all regions and from a broad cross-section of occupations and communities. As for Calhoun, politics for these newly enfranchised voters was not some gentleman's game but a form of personal combat designed to make their own lives better and to test their wills and their loyalties. To such highly motivated men, even the risk of civil war was an acceptable price for claiming their personal and sectional rights.

An "Era of Good Feelings"

→ *What were the sources for Americans' optimism as they emerged from the War of 1812?*

→ *What steps did the American government take to capitalize on this optimism?*

→ *How did new developments in the nation influence foreign affairs?*

→ *How did events in North Africa and Europe influence developments in the United States?*

James Madison had been the butt of jokes and the cause of dissension within his own party during the War of 1812, but he emerged from the war a national hero with considerable political clout. Although his fellow Republicans may have considered his wartime policies indecisive, after the war Madison immediately seized the political initiative to inaugurate vigorous new diplomatic and domestic programs. His successor, James Monroe, then picked up the beat, pressing on with a new nationalistic Republican agenda. The nationalism that arose after the war seemed to bring political dissension to a close. Commenting on the decline of partisan politics, a Federalist newspaper in Boston proclaimed the dawn of an **"Era of Good Feelings."**

The "American System" and New Economic Direction

The nation was much more unified politically in 1815 than it had been for years. The war's outcome and the growth that began to take place immediately following the peace settlement had largely silenced Madison's critics within the Republican Party. And during the waning days of the war, extreme Federalists had so embarrassed their party that they were at a severe political disadvantage.

The Essex Junto was primarily responsible for the Federalists' embarrassment. The junto had capitalized on the many military blunders and growing national debt to cast Republicans in a bad light and was drawing increasing support in the Northeast. In mid-December 1814 the Essex Junto staged the Hartford Convention, voting to secede from the union unless Congress repealed the Embargo of 1813 and passed the slate of constitutional reforms the junto had been pushing since its formation (see page 239). However, news of the Treaty of Ghent, which ended the War of 1812, and of the American victory in the Battle of New Orleans caused many to view the Federalists' efforts as either foolish or treasonous, and party popularity underwent a steep decline.

Facing no meaningful opposition, Madison chose in December 1815 to launch an aggressive new domestic policy. He challenged Congress to correct the economic ills that had caused the depression and helped to propel the nation into war. He also encouraged the states to invest in the nation's future by financing transportation systems and other internal improvements. Former critics such as DeWitt Clinton, Henry Clay, and John C. Calhoun quickly rallied behind the president and his nationalistic economic and political agenda.

Clay took the lead. He had come to Congress as one of the War Hawks in 1810 and had quickly become the dominant voice among the younger representatives. Born in Virginia in 1777, Clay had moved at the age of 20 to the wilds of Kentucky to practice law and carve out a career in politics. He was fantastically successful, becoming Speaker of the Kentucky state assembly when he was only 30 years old and winning a seat in the House of Representatives four years later. He became Speaker of the House during the prewar crisis. Now aligning himself firmly with the new economic agenda, Clay became its champion, calling it the **American System.**

What congressional Republicans had in mind was to create a national market economy. In the colonial period and increasingly thereafter, local market economies grew up around the trading and manufacturing centers of the Northeast. Individuals in these areas produced single items for cash sale and used the cash they earned to purchase goods produced by others. Specialization was the natural outcome. Farmers, for example, chose to grow only one or two crops and to sell the whole harvest for cash, which they used to buy various items they had once raised or made for themselves. Calhoun and others wanted to see such interdependence on a much larger scale. They envisioned a time when whole regions would specialize in producing commodities for which geography, climate, and the temperament of the people made each locale most suitable. Agricultural regions in the West, for example, would produce food for the industrializing Northeast and the fiber-producing South. The North would depend on the South for efficiently produced cotton, and both South and West would depend on the Northeast for manufactured goods. Improved transportation systems would make this flow of goods possible, and a strong national currency would ensure orderly trade between states. Advocates of the American System were confident that the balance eventually established among regions would free the nation as a whole from economic dependence on manufacturing centers in Europe.

Clay and his cohorts recognized that one of the first steps in bringing all this about would have to be a national banking authority. True, Republicans had persistently opposed Alexander Hamilton's Bank of the United States (see page 199) and had killed it in 1811. During the war, however, bankers, merchants, and foreign shippers had chosen not to accept the paper currency issued by local and state banks. The postwar call for a unified national economy prompted Republicans to press again for a national currency and for a national bank to regulate its circulation. In 1816 Calhoun introduced legislation chartering a Second Bank

Era of Good Feelings   The period from 1816 to 1823, when the decline of the Federalist Party and the end of the War of 1812 gave rise to a time of political cooperation.

American System   An economic plan sponsored by nationalists in Congress; it was intended to capitalize on regional differences to spur U.S. economic growth and the domestic production of goods previously bought from foreign manufacturers.

of the United States, which Congress approved overwhelmingly. The Second Bank had many of the same powers and responsibilities as Hamilton's bank. Congress provided $7 million of its $35 million in opening capital and appointed one-fifth of its board of directors. The Second Bank opened for business in Philadelphia on January 1, 1817.

Proponents also saw improvements in transportation and communications as essential. Access to reliable transportation by means of the Great Lakes and the Ohio and Mississippi Rivers had been one of the principal planks in the War Hawk platform in 1812, and poor lines of supply and communication had spelled disaster for American military efforts during the war itself. Announcing that they would "bind the republic together with a perfect system of roads and canals," Republicans in Congress put forward a series of proposals designed to improve transportation and communications.

Finally, Calhoun took the lead in advocating **protective tariffs** to help the fledgling industries that had hatched during the war. Helped by the embargoes, American cotton-spinning plants had increased rapidly between 1808 and 1815. But with the return of open trade at war's end, British merchants dumped accumulated inventories of cotton and woolen cloth onto the U.S. market below cost in an effort to hamper further American development. Although some New England voices protested tariffs as unfair government interference, most northeasterners supported protection. Most southerners and westerners, however, remained leery of its impact on consumer prices. Still, shouting with nationalistic fervor about American economic independence, westerners such as Clay and southerners such as Calhoun were able to raise enough support to pass Madison's proposed **Tariff of 1816,** opening the way for continued tariff legislation in the years to come.

The popularity of these measures was apparent in the outcome of the 1816 elections. Madison's handpicked successor, fellow Virginian James Monroe, won by a decisive electoral majority: 184 votes to Federalist Rufus King's 34. Congressional Republicans enjoyed a similar sweep, winning more than three-fourths of the seats in the House of Representatives and the Senate. Presented with such a powerful mandate and the political clout necessary to carry it out, Republicans immediately set about expanding on the new nationalistic agenda.

The Transportation Problem

In the years before the War of 1812, travel on the nation's roads was a wearying experience. People who could afford transportation by stagecoach were crammed into an open wagon bouncing behind four horses on muddy, rutted, winding roads. Stagecoaches crept along at 4 miles per hour—when weather, equipment, and local **blue laws** permitted them to move at all. And the enjoyment of such dubious luxury did not come cheaply: tolls for each mile of travel equaled the cost of a pint of good whiskey.

Recognizing the need for more and better roads, entrepreneurs sought to profit by building private **turnpikes** between heavily traveled points. In 1791, for example, a private company opened a 66-mile-long road between Philadelphia and Lancaster, Pennsylvania, hoping to make money on tolls. Between that time and the outbreak of war in 1812, private companies invested millions of dollars to construct several thousand miles of turnpikes.

Despite such private efforts, it was clear to many after the war that only the large-scale resources available to state and federal governments could make a practical difference in the transportation picture. Immediately after the war, Calhoun introduced legislation in Congress to finance a national transportation program. Congress approved, but Madison vetoed the bill, stating that the Constitution did not authorize federal spending on projects designed to benefit the states. But Calhoun finally won Madison's support by convincing the president that a government-funded national road between Cumberland, Maryland, and Wheeling, Virginia, was a military and postal necessity and therefore the initial federal expenditure of $30,000 for the **Cumberland Road** was permissible under the

protective tariff Tax on imported goods intended to make them more expensive than similar domestic goods, thus protecting the market for goods produced at home.

Tariff of 1816 First protective tariff in U.S. history; its purpose was to protect America's fledgling textile industry.

blue laws Local legislation designed to enforce Christian morality by forbidding certain activities, including traveling, on Sunday.

turnpike A road on which tolls are collected at gates set up along the way; private companies hoping to make a profit from the tolls built the first turnpikes.

Cumberland Road The initial section of what would be called the "National Road," a highway built with federal funds; this section stretched from Cumberland, Maryland, to Wheeling, Virginia. Later the road would be extended to Vandalia, Illinois, and beyond.

Before the transportation revolution, traveling was highly risky and uncomfortable. This painting shows a rather stylish stagecoach, but its well-dressed passengers are clearly being jostled. Note how the man in the front seat is bracing himself, while the man behind him loses his hat under the wheels. *"Travel by Stagecoach Near Trenton, New Jersey" by John Lewis Krimmel. The Metropolitan Museum of Art, Rogers Fund, 1942 (42.95.11). Photograph © 1984 The Metropolitan Museum of Art.*

Constitution. That constitutional hurdle cleared, actual construction began in 1815.

Although people and light cargoes might move efficiently along the proposed national road, water transportation remained the most economical way to ship bulky freight. Unfortunately, with few exceptions, navigable rivers and lakes did not link up conveniently to form usable transportation networks. Holland and other European countries had solved this problem by digging canals to expand the areas served by waterways. Before the War of 1812, some Americans had considered this solution, but enormous costs and engineering problems had limited canal construction to less than 100 miles. After the war, however, the entry of the state and federal governments into transportation development opened the way to an era of canal building.

New York State was most successful at canal development. In 1817 the state started work on a canal that would run more than 350 miles from Lake Erie at Buffalo to the Hudson River at Albany. Aided by Governor DeWitt Clinton's unswerving support and the gentle terrain in western New York, engineers planned the **Erie Canal.** Three thousand workers dug the huge ditch and built the **locks,** dams, and **aqueducts** that would transport barges carrying freight and passengers across the state. This vision became reality when the last section of the canal was completed and the

first barge made its way from Buffalo to Albany and then on to New York City in 1825.

Canals were really little more than extensions of natural river courses, and fighting the currents of the great rivers that they connected remained a problem. Pushed along by current and manpower, a barge could make the trip south from Pittsburgh to New Orleans in about a month. Returning north, against the current, took more than four months, if a boat could make the trip at all. As a result, most shippers barged their freight downriver, sold the barges for lumber in New Orleans, and walked back home along the Natchez Trace, a well-used path that eventually became another national road (see page 227).

In 1807 Robert Fulton wedded steam technology borrowed from England with his own boat design to prove that steam-powered shipping was possible. Steam-driven water wheels pushed his 160-ton ship,

Erie Canal   A 350-mile canal stretching from Buffalo to Albany; it revolutionized shipping in New York State.

lock   A section of canal with gates at each end, used to raise or lower boats from one level to another by admitting or releasing water; locks allow canals to compensate for changes in terrain.

aqueduct   An elevated structure raising a canal to bridge rivers, canyons, or other obstructions.

the *Clermont,* upstream from New York City to Albany in an incredibly quick thirty-two hours. Unfortunately, the design of the *Clermont* required deep water and large amounts of fuel to carry a limited **payload,** demands that rendered what many called "Fulton's Folly" impractical for most of America's rivers. After the war, however, Henry M. Shreve, a career boat pilot and captain, began experimenting with new designs and technologies. Borrowing the hull design of the shallow-draft, broad-beamed keelboats that had been sailing up and down inland streams for generations, Shreve added two lightweight high-compression steam engines, each one driving an independent side wheel. He also added an upper deck for passengers, creating the now-familiar multistoried steamboats of southern lore. Funded by merchants in Wheeling, Virginia—soon to be the western terminus for the Cumberland Road—Shreve successfully piloted one of his newly designed boats upriver, from Wheeling to Pittsburgh. Then, in 1816, he made the first successful run south, all the way to New Orleans.

Legal Anchors for New Business Enterprise

President Madison had raised serious constitutional concerns when Henry Clay and his congressional clique proposed spending federal money on road development. Though Calhoun was able to ease the president's mind on this specific matter, many constitutional issues needed clarification if the government was going to play the economic role that nationalists envisioned.

In 1819 the Supreme Court took an important step in clarifying the federal government's role in national economic life. The case arose over an effort by the state of Maryland to raise money by placing **revenue stamps** on federal currency. When a clerk at the Bank of the United States' Baltimore branch, James McCulloch, refused to apply the stamps, he was indicted by the state. In the resulting Supreme Court case, *McCulloch v. Maryland* (1819), the majority ruled that the states could not impose taxes on federal institutions and that McCulloch was right in refusing to comply with Maryland's revenue law. But more important, in rejecting Maryland's argument that the federal government was simply a creation of the several states and was therefore subject to state taxation, Chief Justice John Marshall wrote, "The Constitution and the laws made in pursuance thereof are supreme: that they control the constitution and laws of the respective states, and cannot be controlled by them." With this, Mar-

shall declared his binding opinion that federal law was superior to state law in all matters.

Marshall demonstrated this principle again and reinforced it five years later in the landmark case of *Gibbons v. Ogden* (1824). In 1808 the state of New York had recognized Robert Fulton's accomplishments in steamboating by granting him an exclusive contract to run steamboats on rivers in that state. Fulton then used this monopoly power to sell licenses to various operators, including Aaron Ogden, who ran a ferry service between New York and New Jersey. Another individual, Thomas Gibbons, was also running a steamboat service in the same area, but he was operating under license from the federal government. When Ogden accused Gibbons of violating his contractual monopoly in a New York court, Gibbons took refuge in federal court. It finally fell to Marshall's Supreme Court to resolve the conflict. Consistent with its earlier decision, the Court ruled in favor of Gibbons, arguing that the New York monopoly conflicted with federal authority and was therefore invalid. In cases of interstate commerce, it ruled, Congress's authority "is complete in itself" and the states could not challenge it.

But it was going to take more than federal authority and investment to revolutionize the economy. Private money would be needed as well, and that too required some constitutional clarification. At issue were contracts, the basis for all business transactions, and their security from interference by either private or public challengers.

One case from before the war was important in clarifying how federal authorities would deal with matters of contract. The issue was the Yazoo affair, in which the Georgia state legislature had contracted to sell vast tracts of land to private investors (see page 239). The decision by the legislature to overturn that

---

payload   The part of a cargo that generates revenue, as opposed to the part needed to fire the boiler or supply the crew.

revenue stamps   Stickers affixed to taxed items by government officials indicating that the tax has been paid.

McCulloch v. Maryland   Supreme Court case (1819) in which the majority ruled that federal authority is superior to that of individual states and that states cannot control or tax federal operations within their borders.

Gibbons v. Ogden   Supreme Court case (1824) in which the majority ruled that the authority of Congress is absolute in matters of interstate commerce.

THE FEDERAL ROLE IN INTERSTATE COMMERCE

Gibbons v. Ogden (1824) established a strong precedent that had far-reaching consequences. At the time of the ruling, interstate commerce was fairly inconsequential; most people in the United States depended on themselves and their immediate neighbors for their needs. But with this ruling in place, as interstate commerce expanded, the power of the federal government expanded, too. It is now virtually impossible to engage in any sort of activity that does not involve interstate commerce. Even in the most private and intimate moments of our lives, objects we use often were manufactured, in whole or in part, in another state; if not, they likely were carried to our local community on interstate highways; and in all cases they were paid for using federal reserve notes. Marshall's decision granting absolute federal authority over interstate commerce thus justified central government jurisdiction over a wide variety of our everyday activities. For example, many civil rights cases during the 1960s and after landed in federal court because interstate commerce was involved. This is a reality that forms one of the most fundamental aspects of our lives in the United States today.

- Reflecting upon the development of canal and road systems during the early nineteenth century, how did the Supreme Court's decisions concerning interstate commerce and federal supremacy influence the way the nation developed?
- Choose an activity in which you engage on a regular basis—an athletic event, cultural activity, religious act, or something entirely personal and private; virtually anything—and examine what role interstate commerce plays in it. In what ways might the involvement of interstate commerce give the federal government the right to influence or even control that activity? Do you think that degree of influence is justified?

contract was fraudulently obtained, it still was binding and that the state legislature had no right to overturn it. Nor, it ruled in a later case, could a state modify a standing contract. That case, *Dartmouth College v. Woodward* (1819), involved Dartmouth College's founding charter, which specified that new members of the board of trustees were to be appointed by the current board. In 1816 the New Hampshire state legislature tried to take over the college by passing a bill that would allow the state's governor to appoint board members. The college brought suit, claiming that its charter was a legal contract and that the legislature had no right to abridge it. Announcing the Court's decision, Marshall noted that the Constitution protected the sanctity of contracts and that state legislatures could not interfere with them.

These and other cases helped ease the way for the development of new business ventures. With private contracts and federal financial bureaus safe from state and local meddling and the superiority of Congress in interstate commerce established, businesses had the security they needed to expand into new areas and attempt to turn Clay's dream of a national market economy into a reality. And private investors knew that their involvement in often risky ventures was protected, at least from the whims of politicians.

James Monroe and the Nationalist Agenda

While Congress and the courts were firmly in the hands of forward-looking leaders, the presidency passed in 1816 to the seemingly old-fashioned James Monroe. Personally conservative, Monroe nonetheless was a strong nationalist as well as a graceful statesman. He had served primarily as a diplomat during the contentious period that preceded the War of 1812, and as president he turned his diplomatic skills to the task of calming political disputes. He was the first president since Washington to take a national goodwill tour, during which he persistently urged various political

Fletcher v. Peck Supreme Court case (1810) growing out of the Yazoo affair in which the majority ruled that the original land sale contract rescinded by the Georgia legislature was binding, establishing the superiority of contracts over legislation.

Dartmouth College v. Woodward Supreme Court case (1819) in which the majority ruled that private contracts are sacred and cannot be modified by state legislatures.

contract led to a great deal of political fuss, but it created a legal problem also: could a state legislature dissolve an executed contract? This came before Marshall's Court in 1810 with the case of *Fletcher v. Peck* (1810). In this case, the Court ruled that even if the original

With a long and distinguished career as a diplomat behind him, the handsome and elegant James Monroe brought a statesmanlike demeanor into the White House. He managed to soothe long-standing disputes between various political factions, ushering in what would be called "The Era of Good Feelings." *The Granger Collection, New York.*

factions to merge their interests for the benefit of the nation at large.

Monroe's cabinet was well chosen to carry out the task of smoothing political rivalries while flexing nationalistic muscles. He selected John Quincy Adams, son and heir of Yankee Federalist John Adams, as secretary of state because of his diplomatic skill and to win political support in New England. Monroe tapped southern nationalist John C. Calhoun for secretary of war and balanced his appointment with that of southern states' rights advocate William C. Crawford as secretary of the treasury. With his team assembled, Monroe launched the nation on a course designed to increase its control over the North American continent and improve its position in world affairs.

Madison had already taken steps toward initiating a more aggressive diplomatic policy, setting the tone for the years to come. Taking advantage of U.S. involvement in the War of 1812, Barbary pirates (see page 222) had resumed their raiding activity against American shipping. In June 1815, Madison ordered a military force back to the Mediterranean to put an end to those raids. Naval hero Stephen Decatur returned to the region with a fleet of ten warships. Training his guns on the port of Algiers itself, Decatur threatened to level the city if the pirates did not stop raiding American shipping. The Algerians and the rest of the Barbary pirates signed treaties ending the practice of exacting **tribute.** They also released all American hostages and agreed to pay compensation for past seizures of American ships. Celebrating the victory, Decatur gave voice to a militant new American nationalism, proclaiming, "Our Country! In her intercourse with foreign nations may she always be in the right; but our country, right or wrong."

As though in direct response to Decatur's pronouncement, Monroe maintained Madison's firm stand as he attempted to resolve important issues not settled by earlier administrations. Secretary of State Adams began negotiating for strict and straightforward treaties outlining America's economic and territorial rights.

The first matter Adams addressed was the Treaty of Ghent (1814)—specifically, the loose ends it had left dangling. One problem had been the **demilitarization** of the Great Lakes boundary between the United States and British Canada. In the 1817 Rush-Bagot Agreement, both nations agreed to cut back their Great Lakes fleets to only a few vessels. A year later, the two nations drew up the Convention of 1818: the British agreed to honor American fishing rights in the Atlantic, to recognize a boundary between the Louisiana Territory and Canada at the 49th parallel, and to occupy the Oregon Territory jointly with the United States.

With these northern border issues settled, Adams set his sights on defining the nation's southern and southwestern frontiers. Conditions in Spanish Florida were extremely unsettled. Pirates and other renegades used Florida as a base for launching raids against American settlements and shipping, and runaway slaves found it a safe haven in their flight from southern plantations. By December 1817, matters in the Florida border region seemed critical. Reflecting on the situation there, General Andrew Jackson wrote the president advocating the invasion of Spanish Florida. "Let it be signified to me through any channel . . . that the posses-

tribute   A payment of money or other valuables that one group makes to another as the price of security.

demilitarization   The removal of military forces from a region and the restoration of civilian control.

sion of the Floridas would be desirable to the United States, and in sixty days it will be accomplished."

A short time later, Secretary of War Calhoun ordered Jackson to lead a military expedition into southern Georgia. Jackson's orders read that he was to patrol the border to keep raiders from crossing into the United States and runaway slaves from going out, but he later claimed that Monroe secretly authorized him to invade Florida. Whatever the case, Jackson crossed the border, forcing the Spanish government to flee to Cuba. Spain vigorously protested, and Secretary of War Calhoun and others recommended that the general be severely disciplined. Adams, however, saw an opportunity to settle the Florida border issue. He announced that Jackson's raid was an act of self-defense that would be repeated unless Spain could police the area adequately. Fully aware that Spain could not guarantee American security, Adams knew that the Spanish would either have to give up Florida or stand by and watch the United States take it by force. Understanding his country's precarious position, Spanish minister Don Luis de Onís chose to cede Florida in the **Adams-Onís Treaty** of 1819. The United States got all of Florida in exchange for releasing Spain from $5 million in damage claims resulting from border raids. Spain also relinquished all previous claims to the Oregon Country in exchange for acknowledgment of its claims in the American Southwest.

Spain's inability to police its New World territories also led to a more general diplomatic problem. As the result of Spain's weakness, many of its colonies in Latin America had rebelled and established themselves as independent republics. Fearful of the anticolonial example being set in the Western Hemisphere, most members of the Congress of Vienna (see page 255) seemed poised to help Spain reclaim its overseas empire. Neither England, which had developed a thriving trade with the new Latin American republics, nor the United States felt that Europe should be allowed to intervene in the affairs of the Western Hemisphere. In 1823 British foreign minister George Canning proposed that the United States and England form an alliance to end European meddling in Latin America. Most members of Monroe's cabinet supported allied action, but Adams protested that America would be reduced to a "cock-boat in the wake of the British man-of-war." Instead, he suggested a **unilateral** statement to the effect that "the American continents by the free and independent condition which they have assumed, and maintain, are henceforth not to be considered as subject for future colonization by any European power."

Monroe remained undecided. He trusted Adams's judgment but did not share the secretary of state's confidence in the nation's ability to fight off European colonization without British help. Monroe nevertheless conceded the nationalistic necessity for the United States to "take a bolder attitude . . . in favor of liberty." The president's indecision finally vanished in November 1823 when he learned that the alliance designed to restore Spain's colonies was faltering. With the immediate threat removed, Monroe rejected Canning's offer and in his annual message in December announced that the United States would regard any effort by European countries "to extend their system to any portion of this hemisphere as dangerous to our peace and safety." He went on to define any attempt at European intervention in the affairs of the Western Hemisphere as a virtual act of war against the United States and at the same time promised that the United States would steer clear of affairs in Europe.

The **Monroe Doctrine,** as this statement was later called, was exactly the proud assertion of principle "in favor of liberty" that Monroe had hoped for. It immediately won the support of the American people. The Monroe Doctrine, like Decatur's "Our country, right or wrong" speech, seemed to announce the arrival of the United States on the international scene. Both Europeans and Latin Americans, however, thought it was a meaningless statement. Rhetoric aside, the policy depended on the British navy and on Britain's informal commitment to New World autonomy.

Dynamic Growth and Political Consequences

→ *How did the global economic situation contribute to American economics between 1815 and 1820?*

→ *How did postwar economic optimism help lead to economic panic in 1819?*

→ *How did economic growth and panic contribute to sectional conflict and political contention?*

Adams-Onís Treaty   Treaty between the United States and Spain in 1819 that ceded Florida to the United States, ended any Spanish claims in Oregon, and recognized Spanish rights in the American Southwest.

unilateral   Undertaken or issued by only one side and thus not involving an agreement made with others.

Monroe Doctrine   President Monroe's 1823 statement declaring the Americas closed to further European colonization and discouraging European interference in the affairs of the Western Hemisphere.

During the **Napoleonic wars,** massive armies had drained Europe's manpower, laid waste to crops, and tied up ships, making European nations dependent on America. After those wars ended in 1815, Europeans continued to need American food and manufactures as they rebuilt a peacetime economy. Encouraged by a ready European market and expanding credit offered by the Second Bank of the United States and by various state banks, budding southern planters, northern manufacturers, and western and southwestern farmers embarked on a frenzy of speculation. They rushed to borrow against what they were sure was a golden future to buy equipment, land, and slaves.

Although all shared the same sense of optimism, entrepreneurs in the North, West, and South had different ideas about the best course for the American economy. As the American System drew the regions together into increasing mutual dependency, the tensions among them increased as well. As long as economic conditions remained good, there was little reason for conflict, but when the speculative boom collapsed, sectional tensions increased dramatically.

The Panic of 1819

Earlier changes in federal land policy had contributed to the rise of speculation. In 1800 and again in 1804, Congress had passed bills lowering the minimum number of acres of federal land an individual could purchase and the minimum price per acre. After 1804 the minimum purchase became 160 acres and the minimum price, $1.64 per acre. The bill also permitted farmers to pay the government in **installments.** For most Americans, the minimum investment of $262.40 was still out of reach, but the installment option encouraged many to take the risk and buy farms they could barely afford.

Land speculators complicated matters considerably. Taking advantage of the new land prices, they too jumped into the game, buying land on credit. Unlike farmers, however, speculators never intended to put the land into production. They hoped to subdivide and sell it to people who could not afford to buy 160-acre lots directly from the government. Speculators also offered installment loans, pyramiding the already huge tower of debt.

Banks—both relatively unsupervised state banks and the Second Bank of the United States—then added to the problem. Farmers who bought land on credit seldom had enough cash to purchase farm equipment, seed, materials for housing, and the other supplies necessary to put the land to productive use. So the banks extended liberal credit on top of the credit al-

THE REMEMBRANCER,
OR
DEBTORS PRISON RECORDER.

" HE WHO'S ENTOMB'D WITHIN A PRISON'S WALLS
ENDURES THE ANGUISH OF A LIVING DEATH "

VOL. I.   NEW-YORK, SATURDAY APRIL 8, 1820.   No. I.

THE
DEBTORS PRISON RECORDER
IS ISSUED FROM THE PRESS OF
CHARLES N. BALDWIN,
AND PUBLISHED BY
JOHN B. JANSEN,
No. 15 Chatham-street,
NEW-YORK,
At two dollars per annum, payable quarterly in advance.
Persons at a distance may have the paper regularly forwarded to them by mail, provided they forward the requisite advance, *post paid.*

TO THE PUBLIC.
THE chief object of this publication will be to spread before an enlightened public the deplorable effects resulting from the barbarous practice of imprisonment for debt—to exhibit the misery of its wretched victims, and the unfeeling conduct of unpitying creditors. By these means, " with truth as its guide, and justice for its object," it will, it is hoped, gradually prepare the minds of the community for the entire abolition of a law which exists a dishonor to the precepts of Christianity, and as a blot on the statute book.
It will be published weekly, in an octavo form, each number to consist of eight pages, comprising a succinct and correct history of the interesting incidents which daily occur in the debtors prison—a correct Journal of prisoners received and discharged from

time to time, with such remarks as may grow out of peculiar persecution or other causes; nor will it neglect to announce the number of those who are supplied with food from that inestimable body, the Humane Society, to whom the profits of this publication will be faithfully applied, as a small testimonial of the gratitude felt by the unfortunate inmates of the prison, for their distinguished beneficence. It will contain interesting extracts from the latest European and American publications. In its columns will be found a variety of communications on various interesting subjects, from gentlemen without the prison walls, who have kindly volunteered their services to furnish us with essays on the ARTS and SCIENCES, criticisms on the DRAMA, POETRY, &c.
This work will be edited, and its matter carefully revised by several prisoners, who, if they cannot themselves enjoy the benefits of their labor, may at least feel a pleasure in the reflection that after ages will bestow a pitying tear on their sufferings, and bless them for the exertions made to rescue their country from the only vestage of feudal tyranny remaining in a land that boasts of freedom.
The small pittance paid for its perusal, will, it is believed, procure for it the patronage of a generous public, who will be amply remunerated in performing a duty subserving the great and benign ends of Charity, while in return they are furnished with a species of reading not to be met with in any other publication

Before the adoption of modern bankruptcy laws, it was common for people to be put in prison when they could not pay their debts. One impact of the Panic of 1819 was a huge upturn in such imprisonments. Newspapers like *The Remembrancer, or Debtors Prison Recorder,* which began publication with this issue on April 8, 1820, called for reform in debtor laws and also reported gruesome stories about the sufferings of previously respectable people who found themselves in debtors' prison through no fault of their own. Debtors Prison Recorder, *Vol. 1., No. 1, New York, Saturday, April 8, 1820.*

ready extended by the government and by land developers. Farmers thus had acreage and tools, but they also had an enormous debt.

Two developments in the international economy combined to undermine the nation's tower of debt. The economic optimism that fed the speculative frenzy

Napoleonic wars Wars in Europe waged by or against Napoleon Bonaparte between 1803 and 1815.

installments Partial payments of a debt to be made at regular intervals until the entire debt is repaid.

rested on profitable markets. But as the 1810s drew to a close and recovery began in Europe, the profit bandwagon began to slow, and optimism to slip. Not only was Europe able to supply more of its own needs, but Europeans were also importing from other regions of the globe. Led by Great Britain, European nations were establishing colonies in Asia, Africa, and the Pacific. In addition, the recent independence of many of Europe's Latin American colonies deprived the Europeans of the gold and silver that had driven international economics since the discovery of America. Europe became less and less dependent on American goods and, at the same time, less and less able to afford them. Thus the bottom began to fall out of the international market that had fueled speculation within the United States.

Congress noted the beginning of the collapse late in 1817 and tried to head off disaster by tightening credit. The government stopped installment payments on new land purchases and demanded that they be transacted in hard currency. The Second Bank of the United States followed suit in 1818, demanding immediate repayment of loans in either gold or silver. State banks then followed and were joined by land speculators. Instead of curing the problem, however, tightening credit and recalling loans drove the economy over the edge. The speculative balloon burst, leaving nothing but a mass of debt behind. This economic catastrophe became known as the **Panic of 1819.**

Six years of economic depression followed the panic. As prices declined, individual farmers and manufacturers, unable to repay loans for land and equipment, faced **repossession** and imprisonment for debt. In Cincinnati and other agricultural cities, bankruptcy sales were a daily occurrence. In New England and the West, factories closed, throwing both employees and owners out of work. In New York and other manufacturing and trading cities, the ranks of the unemployed grew steadily. The number of **paupers** in New York City nearly doubled between 1819 and 1820, and in Boston thirty-five hundred people were imprisoned for debt. Shaken by the enormity of the problem, John C. Calhoun observed in 1820: "There has been within these two years an immense revolution of fortunes in every part of the Union; enormous numbers of persons utterly ruined; multitudes in deep distress."

Economic Woes and Political Sectionalism

Despite Monroe's efforts to merge southern, northern, and nationalist interests during the Era of Good Feel-

ings, the Panic of 1819 drove a wedge between the nation's geographical sections. The depression touched each of the major regions differently, calling for conflicting solutions. For the next several years, the halls of Congress rang with debates rooted in each section's particular economic needs.

Tariffs were one proven method for handling economic emergencies, and as the Panic of 1819 spread economic devastation throughout the country, legislators from Pennsylvania and the Middle Atlantic states, southern New England, and then Ohio and Kentucky began clamoring for protection. Others disagreed, turning tariffs into the issue that would pit region against region more violently than any other during these years.

Farmers were split on the tariff issue. Irrespective of where they lived, so-called yeoman farmers favored a free market that would keep the price of the manufactures they had to buy as low as possible. In contrast, the increasing number of commercial farmers—those who had chosen to follow Henry Clay's ideas and were specializing to produce cash crops of raw wool, hemp, and wheat—joined mill owners, factory managers, and industrial workers in supporting protection against the foreign dumping of such products. So did those westerners who were producing raw minerals such as iron and tin that were in high demand in the industrializing economy.

Southern commercial farmers, however, did not join with their western counterparts in favoring protection. After supporting the protective Tariff of 1816, Calhoun and other southerners became firm opponents of tariffs. Their dislike of protection reflected a complex economic reality. Britain, not the United States, was the South's primary market for raw cotton and its main supplier of manufactured goods. Protective tariffs raised the price of such goods as well as the possibility that Britain might enact a **retaliatory tariff**

Panic of 1819 A financial panic that began when the Second Bank of the United States tightened credit and recalled government loans.

repossession The reclaiming of land or goods by the seller or lender after the purchaser fails to pay installments due.

paupers A term popular in the eighteenth and nineteenth centuries to describe poor people; cities like New York and Boston often registered paupers so as to provide local relief.

retaliatory tariff A tariff on imported goods imposed neither to raise revenue nor control commerce but to retaliate against tariffs charged by another nation.

on cotton imports from the South. If that happened, southerners would pay more for manufactures but receive less profit from cotton.

When, in 1820, northern congressmen proposed a major increase in tariff rates, small farmers in the West and cotton growers in the South combined to defeat the measure. Northerners then wooed congressmen from the West, where small farmers were begging for a relief from high land prices and debt. The northerners supported one bill that lowered the minimum price of public land to $1.25 per acre and another that allowed farmers who had bought land before 1820 to pay off their debts at the reduced price. The bill also extended the time over which those who were on the installment plan could make payments. Then, in 1822, northerners backed a bill authorizing increased federal spending on the Cumberland Road, an interest vital to westerners. Such **blandishments** finally had the desired outcome. In 1824 western congressmen joined with northern manufacturing interests to pass a greatly increased tariff.

This victory demonstrated an important new political reality. Of the six western states admitted to the Union after 1800, three—Ohio, Indiana, and Illinois—were predominantly farming states, split between commercial and nonspecialized farming. The other three—Louisiana, Mississippi, and Alabama—were increasingly dominated by cotton growing. As long as northern commercial interests could pull support from Ohio, Indiana, and Illinois, the balance of power in Congress remained relatively even. But new expansion in either the North or South had the potential to tip the political scale. As all three regions fought to implement specific solutions to the nation's economic woes, the regional balance of power in Congress became a matter of crucial importance.

The Missouri Compromise

The delicate balance in Congress began to wobble immediately in 1819 when the Missouri Territory applied for statehood. New York congressman James Tallmadge Jr. realized that if Missouri was admitted as a free state, its economy would resemble the economies of states in the Old Northwest, and its congressmen would be susceptible to northern political deal making. This realization led Tallmadge to propose that no new slaves be taken into Missouri and that those already in the territory be emancipated gradually. Southerners likewise understood that if Missouri was admitted as a slave state, its economy would resemble the economies of the southern states and its congres-

sional **bloc** would undoubtedly support the southern position on tariffs and other key issues. They unified to oppose the **Tallmadge Amendment.**

Both sides in the debate were deeply entrenched, but in 1820 Henry Clay suggested a compromise. Late in 1819, Maine had separated from Massachusetts and applied for admission to the United States as a separate state. The compromise proposed by Clay was to admit Missouri as a slave state and Maine as a free state. Clay also proposed that after the admission of Missouri, slavery be banned forever in the rest of the Louisiana Territory above 36°30' north latitude, the line that formed Missouri's southern border (see Map 10.1). With this provision, Congress approved the **Missouri Compromise,** and the issue of slavery in the territories faded for a while.

The Missouri crisis was more than a simple debate over economic interests and congressional balances. Although economic issues had caused the conflict, slavery—its expansion and, for a few, its very existence—had become part of a struggle between sections over national power. For former Federalists such as Rufus King, the crisis offered an opportunity to use the slavery issue to woo northerners and westerners away from the traditionally southern-centered Republican coalition. Thus DeWitt Clinton and other northeastern dissidents joined with former Federalists to criticize their party's southern leadership and challenge Monroe's dominance. Wise to this political "party trick," Jefferson observed that "King is ready to risk the union for any chance of restoring his party to power and wriggling himself to the head of it." Still, the "trick" was an effective one: from 1820 onward, opportunistic politicians would attempt to use slavery to their own advantage.

---

blandishment   The use of flattery or manipulation to convince others to support a particular project or point of view.

bloc   A group of people united for common action.

Tallmadge Amendment   An amendment to a statehood bill for Missouri proposed by New York congressman James Tallmadge Jr. that would have banned slavery from the new state; it created a deadlock in Congress that necessitated the Missouri Compromise.

Missouri Compromise   Law proposed by Henry Clay in 1820 admitting Missouri to the Union as a slave state and Maine as a free state and banning slavery in the Louisiana Territory north of latitude 36°30'.

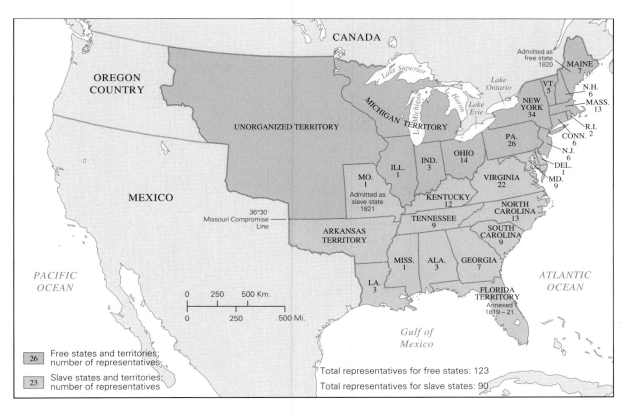

MAP 10.1 **Missouri Compromise and Representative Strength** The Missouri Compromise fixed the boundary between free and slave territories at 36°30' north latitude. This map shows the result both in geographical and political terms. While each section emerged from the compromise with the same number of senators (24), the balance in the House of Representatives and Electoral College tilted toward the North.

New Politics and the End of Good Feelings

Conducted in the midst of the Missouri crisis, the presidential election of 1820 went as smoothly as could be: Monroe was reelected with the greatest majority ever enjoyed by any president except George Washington. Despite economic depression and sectional strife, the people's faith in Jefferson's party and his handpicked successors remained firm. As the election of 1824 approached, however, it became clear that the nation's continuing problems had broken Republican unity and destroyed the public's confidence in the party's ability to solve domestic problems.

Approaching the end of his second term, Monroe could identify no more gentleman Republicans from Virginia to carry the presidential torch. Although he probably favored John Quincy Adams as his succes-

sor, the president carefully avoided naming him as the party's **standard bearer,** leaving that task to the Republican congressional caucus. If Monroe was hoping that the party would nominate Adams, he was disappointed when the southern-dominated party caucus tapped Georgia states' rights advocate William Crawford as its candidate. Certainly Clay and Adams were disappointed: each immediately defied party discipline by deciding to run against Crawford without the approval of the caucus. Encouraged by the apparent death of the caucus system for nominating presidential candidates, the Tennessee state legislature chose to put forward its own candidate, Andrew Jackson.

---

standard-bearer The recognized leader of a movement, organization, or political party.

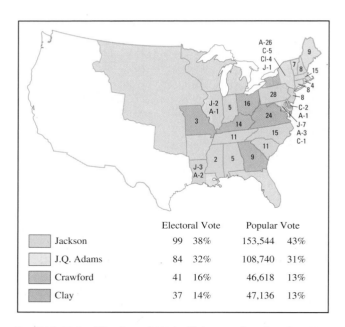

	Electoral Vote		Popular Vote	
Jackson	99	38%	153,544	43%
J.Q. Adams	84	32%	108,740	31%
Crawford	41	16%	46,618	13%
Clay	37	14%	47,136	13%

MAP 10.2 **Election of 1824** This map showing the 1824 presidential election illustrates how divided the nation had become politically. William Crawford, the official Republican Party nominee, placed third in the Electoral College. The two most successful candidates, Andrew Jackson and John Quincy Adams, represented no political party. Speaker of the House Henry Clay, who finished fourth, played a key role in the outcome. Under his leadership, the House elected Adams.

The election that followed was a painful demonstration of how deeply divided the nation had become. Northern regional political leaders rallied behind Adams, southern sectionalists supported Crawford, and northwestern commercial farmers and other backers of the American System lined up behind Clay. But a good portion of the American people—many of them independent yeoman farmers, traditional craftsmen, and immigrants—defied their political leaders by supporting the hero of New Orleans: Jackson.

The source of Jackson's political popularity is something of a mystery because the Tennessean remained almost entirely silent during the campaign. But his posture as a man of action—a doer rather than a talker—and the fact that he was a political outsider certainly played key roles. For whatever combination of reasons, once the ballots were cast, it became apparent that this groundswell of popular enthusiasm was a potent political force. Though a political **dark horse,** Jackson won the popular election, but the Electoral College vote was another matter (see Map 10.2). Jackson had 99 electoral votes to Adams's 84, Crawford's 41, and Clay's 37, but that was not enough to win the election. Jack-

son's opponents had a combined total of 162 of the 261 electoral votes cast. Thus Jackson won a **plurality** of electors but did not have the "majority of the whole number of electors" required by the Constitution. The Constitution specifies that in such cases, a list of the top three vote getters be passed to the House of Representatives for a final decision.

By the time the House had convened to settle the election, Crawford, the third-highest vote getter, had suffered a disabling stroke, so the list of candidates had only two names: John Quincy Adams and Andrew Jackson. Because Clay had finished fourth, he was not in contention in the **runoff election.** As Speaker of the House, however, he was in a particularly strategic position to influence the outcome, and friends of both hopefuls sought his support. Adams's and Clay's views on tariffs, manufacturing, foreign affairs, and other key issues were quite compatible. Clay therefore endorsed Adams, who won the House election and in 1825 became the nation's sixth president.

Jackson and his supporters were outraged. They considered Clay a betrayer of western and southern interests, calling him the "Judas of the West." Then when Adams named Clay as his secretary of state—the position that had been the springboard to the presidency for every past Republican who held it—Jacksonians exploded. Proclaiming Adams's election a "corrupt bargain," Jackson supporters withdrew from the party of Jefferson, bringing an end to the one-party system that had emerged under the so-called **Virginia Dynasty** and dealing the knockout blow to the Era of Good Feelings.

The "New Man" in Politics

→ *What factors helped change Americans' political options during the mid-1820s?*

dark horse A political candidate who has little organized support and is not expected to win.

plurality In an election with three or more candidates, the number of votes received by the leading candidate but which amount to less than half of the total number of votes cast.

runoff election A final election held to determine a winner after an earlier election has eliminated the weakest candidates.

Virginia Dynasty Term applied to the U.S. presidents from Virginia in the period between 1801 and 1825: Jefferson, Madison, and Monroe.

→ *How did the election of Andrew Jackson in 1828 reflect those new options?*

Since Washington's day the presidency had been considered an office for gentlemen and statesmen. The first several presidents had tried to maintain an air of polite dignity while in office, and voters were generally pleased with that orderly approach. But with the massive social changes taking place after the War of 1812, the conduct of national politics changed drastically. New voters from new occupations with radically varying political and economic views began making demands. Many felt isolated from a political system that permitted the presidency to pass from one propertied gentleman to another. Clearly, changing times called for political change, and the American people began to press for it in no uncertain terms.

Adams's Troubled Administration

John Quincy Adams may have been the best-prepared man ever to assume the office of president. The son of revolutionary giant and former president John Adams, John Quincy had been born and raised in the midst of America's most powerful political circles. By the time of his controversial election in 1825, Adams had been a foreign diplomat, a U.S. senator, a Harvard professor, and an exceptionally effective secretary of state. Adams conducted himself in office as his father had, holding himself above partisan politics and refusing to use political favors to curry support. As a result, Adams had no effective means of rallying those who might have supported him or of pressuring his opponents. Thus, despite his impressive résumé, Adams's administration was a deeply troubled one.

Adams's policy commitments did nothing to boost his popularity. The new president promised to increase tariffs to protect American manufacturing and to raise funds necessary to pay for "the improvement of agriculture, commerce, and manufactures." He also wanted the Second Bank of the United States to stabilize the economy while providing ample loans to finance new manufacturing ventures. And he advocated federal spending to improve "the elegant arts" and advance "literature and the progress of the sciences, ornamental and profound." High sounding though Adams's objectives were, Thomas Jefferson spoke for many when he observed that such policies would establish "a single and splendid government of an aristocracy . . . riding and ruling over the plundered ploughman and beggared yeomanry." Jefferson's criticism seemed particularly apt in the economic turmoil that followed the Panic of 1819. Moreover, the increase in federal power implied by Adams's policies frightened southerners, and this fear, combined with their traditional distaste for tariffs, virtually unified opposition to Adams in the South.

Led by John C. Calhoun, Adams's opponents tried to manipulate tariff legislation to undercut the president's support. Calhoun proposed that Congress should propose an unprecedented increase in tariff rates. Northeastern Jacksonians should then voice support for the increase while Jackson supporters in the West and South opposed them. Calhoun and his colleagues envisioned a win-win situation: northeastern Jacksonians would win increasing support from manufacturing interests in their region by appearing to support tariffs; southern and western Jackson supporters could take credit for sinking tariff increases, cementing support in their districts; and Adams, who had promised increases as part of his political agenda, would appear ineffectual and his support undermined. But Calhoun and his fellow conspirators had miscalculated: when the tariff package came to the floor in May 1828, key northeastern congressmen engineered its passage. The resulting **Tariff of Abominations** was not what Calhoun had expected, but it served his ends by establishing tariff rates that were unpopular with almost every segment of the population, and the unpopular president would bear the blame.

Democratic Styles and Political Structure

Adams's demeanor and outlook compounded his problems. He seemed more a man of his father's generation than of his own. The enormous economic and demographic changes that occurred during the first decades of the nineteenth century created a new political climate, one in which Adams's archrival Andrew Jackson felt much more at ease than did the stiff Yankee who occupied the White House.

One of the most profound changes in the American political scene was an explosion in the number of voters. Throughout the early years of the republic's history, voting rights were limited to white men who held real estate. In a nation primarily of farmers, most men owned land, so the fact of limited suffrage raised

Tariff of Abominations Tariff package designed to win support for anti-Adams forces in Congress; its passage in 1828 discredited Adams but set off sectional tension over tariff issues.

little controversy. But as economic conditions changed, a smaller proportion of the population owned farms, and while bankers, lawyers, manufacturers, and other such men often were highly educated, economically stable, and politically concerned, their lack of real estate barred them from political participation. Not surprisingly, such elite and middle-class men urged suffrage reform. In 1800 only three of the sixteen states—Kentucky, Vermont, and New Hampshire—had no property qualifications for voting, and Georgia, North Carolina, and Pennsylvania permitted taxpayers to vote even if they did not own real property. By 1830, only five of the twenty-four states retained property qualifications, nine required tax payment only, and ten made no property demands at all. Of course, all of the states continued to bar women from voting, no matter how much property they may have owned, and most refused the ballot to African Americans, whether free or slave. Still, the raw number of voters grew enormously and rapidly. In the 1824 election, 356,038 men cast ballots for the presidency. Four years later, more than three times that number of men voted.

Complementing the impact of the expanding **electorate** were significant changes in the structure of politics itself. Key among them was the method for selecting members of the Electoral College (see page 190). Gradually, state after state adopted the popular election of electors until, by 1828, state legislatures in only two states continued to appoint them. At the same time, more and more government jobs that had traditionally been appointive became elective. Thus more voters would vote to fill more offices and could affect the political process in new, profound ways. In addition, states increasingly dropped property qualifications for officeholding as well as voting, opening new opportunities for breaking the gentlemanly monopoly on political power.

Political opportunists were not slow to take advantage of the new situation. Men such as New Yorker **Martin Van Buren** quickly came to the fore, organizing political factions into tightly disciplined local and statewide units. A longtime opponent of Governor DeWitt Clinton's faction in New York, Van Buren molded disaffected Republicans into the so-called Bucktail faction. In 1820 the Bucktails used a combination of political patronage—the ability of the party in power to distribute government jobs—**influence peddling,** and fiery speeches to draw newly qualified voters into the political process and swept Clinton out of office.

Many new voters were gratified at finally being allowed to participate in politics but sensed that

their participation was not having the impact it should. They resented the "corrupt bargain" that had denied the presidency to the people's choice—Andrew Jackson—in the election of 1824. Voters in upstate New York and elsewhere pointed at organizations such as the **Masons,** claiming that they used secret signs and rituals to ensure the election of their own members, thus maintaining the supremacy of political parties and thwarting the popular will. In the fall of 1826, William Morgan, a bricklayer and Mason from Canandaigua, New York, decided to publish some of the organization's lesser secrets. Morgan was promptly arrested—charged with owing a debt of $2.69—and jailed. What happened after that remains a mystery. Some unknown person paid Morgan's debt, and he was released. But as he emerged from jail, he was seized, bound and gagged, and dragged into a carriage that whisked him out of town. He was never seen again.

Morgan's disappearance caused a popular outcry, and political outsiders demanded a complete investigation. When no clues turned up, many assumed that a Masonic conspiracy was afoot. Within a year, opportunistic young politicians, including New Yorkers Thurlow Weed and William Seward and Pennsylvanian **Thaddeus Stevens,** had harnessed this political anxiety by forming the **Antimasonic Party.** Based exclusively on the alienation felt by small craftsmen, farmers, and other marginalized groups, the Anti-

electorate The portion of the population that possesses the right to vote.

Martin Van Buren New York politician known for his skillful handling of party politics; he helped found the Democratic Party and later became the eighth president of the United States.

influence peddling Using one's influence with people in authority to obtain favors or preferential treatment for someone else, usually in return for payment.

Masons An international fraternal organization with many socially and politically prominent members, including a number of U.S. presidents.

Thaddeus Stevens Opportunistic politician who was one of the founders of the Antimasonic Party; he later became a leader of the "Conscience Whigs" and later still became one of the key organizers of the Republican Party. During and after the Civil War, he was the leader of the Radical Republican faction in Congress.

Antimasonic Party Political party formed in 1827 to capitalize on popular anxiety about the influence of the Masons; it opposed politics-as-usual without offering any particular substitute.

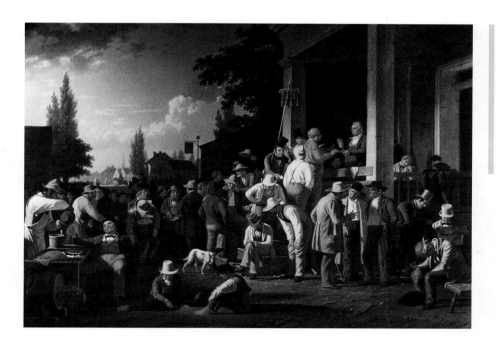

As suffrage requirements loosened, politics went from being a sedate parlor game among gentlemen to a rough-and-tumble contest that often spilled out into streets of the nation's cities and villages. This painting by George Caleb Bingham captures the colorful spirit of the new politics in depicting a county election in early nineteenth-century Missouri. *Francis G. Mayer/CORBIS.*

masons had no platform beyond their shared faith in conspiracies and opposition to them. The Antimasonic Party was, in effect, a political party whose sole cause was to oppose political parties.

What was happening in New York was typical of party and antiparty developments throughout the country. As the party of Jefferson dissolved, a tangle of political factions broke out across the nation. This was precisely the sort of petty politics that Adams disdained, but the chaos suited a man like Jackson perfectly. So, while the Antimasons were busy pursuing often highly fanciful conspiracy theories, Van Buren was busy forging with the hero of New Orleans an alliance that would fundamentally alter American politics.

The Rise of "King Andrew"

Within two years of Adams's election, Van Buren had brought together northern outsiders like himself, dissident southern Republicans like John C. Calhoun, and western spokesmen like **Thomas Hart Benton** of Missouri and John H. Eaton of Tennessee into a new political party. Calling themselves Democratic-Republicans—**Democrats** for short—this party railed against the neofederalism of Clay's and Adams's National Republican platform. The Democrats called for a return to Jeffersonian simplicity, states' rights, and democratic principles. Behind the scenes, however, they employed the tight organizational discipline and

manipulative techniques that Van Buren had used to such good effect against the Clintonians in New York. Lining up behind the recently defeated popular hero Andrew Jackson, the new party appealed to both opportunistic political outsiders and democratically inclined new voters. In the congressional elections of 1826, Van Buren's coalition drew the unqualified support of both groups, unseating enough National Republicans to gain a twenty-five-seat majority in the House of Representatives and an eight-seat advantage in the Senate.

Having Andrew Jackson as a candidate was probably as important to the Democrats' success as their ideological appeal and tight political organization. In many ways, Jackson was a perfect reflection of the new voters. Like many of them, he was born in a log cabin under rustic circumstances. His family had faced more than its share of hardships: his father had died two weeks before Andrew's birth, and he had lost his

Thomas Hart Benton   U.S. senator from Missouri and legislative leader of the Democrats; he was a champion of President Jackson and a supporter of westward expansion.

Democrats   Political party that brought Andrew Jackson into office; it recalled Jeffersonian principles of limited government and drew its support from farmers, craftsmen, and small businessmen.

The presidential election of 1828 pitted two totally opposite kinds of men against each other. The elderly-looking John Quincy Adams (right), who had been involved in national politics for over a quarter of a century, represented old style gentlemanly politics. The flamboyant military hero Andrew Jackson (left), on the other hand, was a political outsider and seemed to have much more in common with the new generation of American voters. *Library of Congress.*

two brothers and his mother during the Revolutionary War. In the waning days of the Revolution, at the age of 13, Jackson joined a mounted militia company and was captured by the British. His captors beat their young prisoner and then let him go, a humiliation he would never forgive.

At the end of the war, Jackson set out to make his own way in the world. Like many of his contemporaries, he chose the legal profession as the route to rapid social and economic advancement. In 1788 he was appointed **public prosecutor** for the North Carolina district that later split off to become Tennessee. Driven by an indomitable will and a wealth of native talent, Jackson became the first U.S. congressman from the state of Tennessee and eventually was elected to the Senate. He also was a judge on the Tennessee Supreme Court. Along the way, Jackson's exploits established his solid reputation as a heroic and natural leader. Even before the War of 1812, his toughness had earned him the nickname "Old Hickory" (see page 251). Also, in the popular view, it was Jackson's brashness, not Adams's diplomacy, that had finally won Spanish Florida for the United States.

Jackson's popular image as a rough-hewn man of the people was somehow untarnished by his political alliance with business interests, his activities as a land speculator, and his large and growing personal fortune and stock of slaves. In the eyes of frontiersmen, small farmers, and to some extent urban workingmen, he remained a common man like them. Having started with nothing, Jackson seemed to have drawn from a combination of will, natural ability, and divine favor to become a man of substance without becoming a snob.

Caricature and image making rather than substantive issues dominated the election campaign of 1828. Jackson supporters accused Adams of being cold, aristocratic, and corrupt in bowing to speculators and

---

public prosecutor   A lawyer appointed by the government to prosecute criminal actions on behalf of the state.

caricature   An exaggerated image of a person, usually enhancing their most uncomplimentary features.

special interests when defining his tariff and land policies. Adams supporters charged Jackson with being a dueler, an insubordinate military adventurer, and an uncouth backwoodsman whose disregard for propriety had led him to live with a woman before she divorced her first husband.

The characterization of Adams as cold was accurate, but charges of corruption were entirely untrue, though Adams's refusal to respond led many to believe them. The charges against Jackson were all too true, but voters saw them as irrelevant. Rather than damaging Jackson's image, such talk made him appear romantic and daring. When all was said and done, the Tennessean polled over a hundred thousand more popular votes than did the New Englander and won the vast majority of states, taking every one in the South and West (see Map 10.3).

As if in response to his supporters' desires and his opponents' fears, Jackson swept into the White House on a groundswell of unruly popular enthusiasm. Ten thousand visitors crammed into the capital to witness Jackson's inauguration on March 4, 1829. Showing his usual disdain for tradition, Jackson took the oath of office and then pushed through the crowd and mounted his horse, galloping off toward the White House followed by a throng of excited onlookers. When they arrived, the mob flowed behind him into the presidential mansion, where they climbed over furniture, broke glassware, and generally frolicked. The new president was finally forced to flee the near-riot by climbing out a back window. Clearly a boisterous new spirit was alive in the nation's politics.

Launching Jacksonian Politics

That he was a political outsider was a major factor in Jackson's popularity. Antimasons and others were convinced that politics consisted primarily of conspiracies among political insiders, and Jackson curried their support by promising **retrenchment** and reform in the federal system. In the process he initiated a personal style in government unlike that of any of his predecessors in office and alienated many both inside and outside Washington.

Retrenchment was first on the new president's agenda. Jackson challenged the notion that government work could be carried out best by an elite core of professional civil servants. Such duties, Jackson declared, were "so plain and simple that men of intelligence may readily qualify themselves for their performance." And in order to keep such men from becoming entrenched, Jackson promised to institute regular rotation in office for federal bureaucrats: ap-

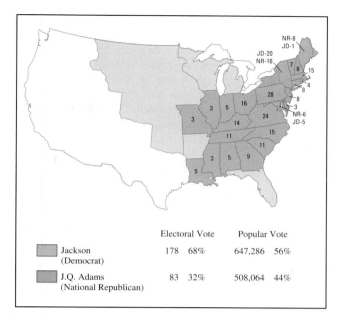

MAP 10.3   Election of 1828   This map shows how the political coalition between Andrew Jackson and Martin Van Buren turned the tables in the election of 1828. Jackson's Democratic Party won every region except Adams's native New England.

pointments in his administration would last only four years, after which civil servants would have to return to "making a living as other people do."

Like many of Jackson's policies, this rotation system was designed to accomplish more than a single goal. Because no new party had come to power since Jefferson's election in 1800, Jackson inherited some ten thousand civil servants who owed their jobs to Republican patronage. Rotation in office gave the president the excuse to fire people whom he associated with the "corrupt bargain" and felt he could not fully trust. It also opened up an unprecedented opportunity for Jackson to reward his loyal supporters by placing them in the newly vacated civil service jobs. The Jacksonian adage became "To the victor belong the **spoils**," and the Democrats made every effort to advance their

special interest   A person or organization that seeks to benefit by influencing legislators to support particular policies.

retrenchment   In government, the elimination of unnecessary jobs or functions for reform or cost-cutting purposes.

spoils   Jobs and other rewards for political support.

party's hold on power by distributing government jobs to loyal party members.

Patronage appointments extended to the highest levels in government. Jackson selected cabinet members not for their experience or ability but for their political loyalty and value in satisfying the various factions that formed his coalition. The potential negative impact of these appointments was minimized by Jackson's decision to abandon his predecessors' practice of regularly seeking his cabinet members' advice on major issues: the president called virtually no cabinet meetings and seldom asked for his cabinet's opinion. Instead, he surrounded himself with an informal network of friends and advisers. This so-called **Kitchen Cabinet** worked closely with the president on matters of both national policy and party management.

Jackson's relationship with everyone in government was equally unconventional. He was known to rage, pout, and storm at suspected disloyalty. Earlier presidents had at least pretended to believe in the equal distribution of power among the three branches of government, but Jackson avowed that the executive should be supreme because the president was the only member of the government elected by all the people. He made it clear that he would stand in opposition to both private and congressional opponents and was not above threatening military action to get his way. Reflecting his generally testy relationship with the legislative branch, he vetoed twelve bills in the course of his administration, three more than all his predecessors combined. Nor did he feel any qualms about standing up to the judiciary. Such arrogant assertions of executive power led Jackson's opponents to call the new president "King Andrew."

The Reign of "King Andrew"

→ *What was President's Jackson role in shaping U.S. Indian policy? How does his background account for his policy choices?*

→ *How did conditions in each region of the country influence the national divisions reflected in the nullification crisis and the Bank War?*

Jackson had promised the voters "retrenchment and reform." He delivered retrenchment, but reform was more difficult to arrange. Jackson tried to implement reform in four broad areas: (1) the nation's banking and financial system, (2) internal improvements and public land policy, (3) Indian affairs, and (4) the collection of revenue and enforcement of federal law. The

steps that Jackson took appealed to some of his supporters but strongly alienated others. Thus, as Jackson tried to follow through on his promise to reform the nation, he nearly tore the nation apart.

Jackson and the Bank

The Second Bank of the United States, chartered in 1816, was an essential part of Clay and Calhoun's American System. In addition to serving as the depository for federal funds, the Second Bank issued national currency, which could be exchanged directly for gold, and it served as a national clearing-house for notes issued by state and local banks. In that capacity, the Second Bank could regulate currency values and credit rates and help to control the activities of state banks by refusing to honor their notes if the banks lacked sufficient gold to back them. The Second Bank could also police state and local banks by calling in loans and refusing credit—actions that had helped bring on the Panic of 1819 and had made the Second Bank very unpopular.

In 1823 **Nicholas Biddle** became president of the Second Bank. An able administrator and talented economist, Biddle enforced firm and consistent policies that restored some confidence in the bank and its functions. But many Americans still were not ready to accept the notion of an all-powerful central banking authority. The vast majority of opponents were Americans who did not understand the function of the Second Bank, viewing it as just another instrument for helping the rich get richer. These critics tended instinctively to support the use of hard currency, called **specie**. Other critics, including many state bankers, opposed the Second Bank because they felt that Biddle's controls were too strict and that they were not receiving their fair share of federal revenues. Speculators and debtors also opposed the bank: when they gambled correctly, they could benefit from the sort of economic instability the bank was designed to prevent.

Hoping to fan political turmoil in the upcoming presidential election, Jackson's opponents in Congress proposed to renew the bank's twenty-year char-

---

Kitchen Cabinet President Jackson's informal advisers, who helped him shape both national and Democratic Party policy.

Nicholas Biddle President of the Second Bank of the United States; he struggled to keep the bank functioning when President Jackson tried to destroy it.

specie Coins minted from precious metals.

Published in 1833, this political cartoon entitled "The Diplomatic Hercules [Andrew Jackson] Attacking the Political Hydra [The Second Bank of the United States]" illustrates why the Bank War enhanced rather than hurt Jackson at the polls. Many voters saw the bank as a monster that used its tentacles of complicated financial policy to choke common people while enriching the speculators and merchants who supported it. *Collection of The New-York Historical Society.*

ter four years early, in 1832. They hoped that Biddle's leadership had established the bank as a necessary part of the nation's economy, even in critics' minds, and that Democratic Party discipline would break down if the president tried to prevent the early renewal of the charter. They were partially right—Congress passed the renewal bill, and Jackson vetoed it—but the anticipated rift between Jackson and congressional Democrats did not open. The president stole the day by delivering a powerful veto message geared to appeal to the mass of Americans on whose support his party's congressmen depended. Jackson denounced the Second Bank as an example of vested privilege and monopoly power that served the interests of "the few at the expense of the many" and injured "humbler members of society—the farmers, the mechanics, and laborers—who have neither the time nor the means of securing like favors to themselves." And Jackson went even further, asserting that foreign interests, many of which were seen as enemies to American rights, had used the bank to accumulate large blocks of American securities.

Although the charter was not renewed, the Second Bank could operate for four more years on the basis of its unexpired charter. Jackson, however, wanted to kill the Second Bank immediately, to "deprive the conspirators of the aid which they expect from its money and power." The strategy Jackson chose was to withdraw federal funds and redeposit the money in state banks. Although this move was illegal, Jackson nonetheless ordered Treasury Secretary Louis McLane to withdraw the federal funds. When he refused, the president fired and replaced him with William J. Duane,

who also refused to carry out Jackson's order. Jackson quickly fired him too and appointed Kitchen Cabinet member Roger B. Taney to head the Treasury Department. Stepping around the law rather than breaking it, Taney chose not to transfer federal funds directly from the Second Bank to state banks, but instead simply kept paying the government's bills from existing accounts in the Second Bank while placing all new deposits in so-called **pet banks.**

Bank president Biddle was not going to give up without a fight. Powerless to stop Taney's diversion of federal funds, Biddle sought to replace dwindling assets by raising interest rates and by calling in loans owed by state banks. In this way, the banker believed, he would not only head off the Second Bank's collapse but also trigger a business panic that might force the government to reverse its course. "Nothing but the evidence of suffering . . . will produce any effect," Biddle said as he pushed the nation toward economic instability. Biddle was correct that there would be "evidence of suffering," but the full effect of the **Bank War** would not be felt until after the reign of "King Andrew" had ended.

---

pet banks   State banks into which Andrew Jackson ordered federal deposits to be placed to help deplete the funds of the Second Bank of the United States.

Bank War   The political conflict that occurred when Andrew Jackson tried to destroy the Second Bank of the United States, which he thought represented special interests at the expense of the common man.

Jackson and the West

Although Jackson was a westerner, his views on federal spending for roads, canals, and other internal improvements seemed based more on politics than on ideology or regional interest. For example, when Congress passed a bill calling for federal money to build a road in Kentucky—from Maysville, on the Ohio border, to Lexington—Jackson vetoed it, claiming that it would benefit only one state and was therefore unconstitutional. But three practical political issues influenced his decision. First, party loyalists in places such as Pennsylvania and New York, where Jackson hoped to gain support, opposed federal aid to western states. Second, Lexington was the hub of Henry Clay's political district, and by denying aid that would benefit that city, Jackson was putting his western competitor in political hot water. Finally, Jackson's former congressional district centered on Nashville—already the terminus of a national road and therefore a legitimate recipient of federal funds. Thus Jackson could lavish money on his hometown while seeming to stand by strict constitutional limitations on federal power.

Disposing of the **public domain** was the other persistent problem Jackson faced. By the time he came to power, land policy had become a major factor in sectional politics. Although the price of $1.25 per acre for public land established in the wake of the Panic of 1819 was a significant improvement over the previous price, it was still too high for many hopeful farmers. Abandoning his predecessors' notion that public land sales should profit the government, Jackson took the position that small farmers should be able to buy federal land for no more than it cost the government to **survey** the plot and process the sale.

Jackson thus directed Congress that "public lands shall cease as soon as practicable to be a source of revenue," and western Jacksonians responded immediately. One of them, Senator Thomas Hart Benton of Missouri, proposed in 1830 that the price of government land be dropped gradually from $1.25 to just 25 cents an acre and that any lands not sold at that price simply be given away. He also suggested that squatters—anyone who was currently settled illegally on public land—be given the first chance to buy the tract where they were squatting when the government offered it for sale.

Such measures pleased Jackson's western supporters but frightened easterners and southerners. His supporters in the East and South feared that migration would give the West an even bigger say in the

Throughout the West, people without money simply camped on publicly owned land. This painting by George Caleb Bingham captures one such family as they pause outside their log cabin. Western politicians like Thomas Hart Benton argued that such "squatters" had a legitimate right to claim the land they settled and fought for legislation protecting squatters' rights. *"The Squatters" by George Caleb Bingham, 1850. Photograph © 2008 Museum of Fine Arts, Boston.*

nation's economic and political future. In addition, southerners were concerned that Congress would replace revenues lost from the sale of public land by raising tariffs, threatening the South's economic relationship with Europe. Northerners were afraid that as people moved west, the drain on population would drive up the price of labor, increasing the cost of production and lowering profits. The result was nearly three years of debate in Congress. A frustrated Henry Clay, desperate to save any scrap of his economic plans for the nation, suggested that the distribution of public land be turned over to the states. Congress, relieved to have the matter taken out of its hands, passed Clay's bill in 1833, but Jackson vetoed it, taking another slap at Clay and affirming that the distribution of the public domain was a federal matter.

public domain   Land owned and controlled by the federal government.
survey   To determine the area and boundaries of land through measurement and mathematical calculation.

Jackson and the Indians

At the end of the War of 1812, the powerful Cherokees, Choctaws, Seminoles, Creeks, and Chickasaws—the so-called **Five Civilized Tribes**—numbered nearly seventy-five thousand people and occupied large holdings within the states of Georgia, North and South Carolina, Alabama, Mississippi, and Tennessee. These Indians had embraced Jefferson's vision of acculturation but were seen as an obstruction to westward migration, especially by grasping planters on the make who coveted Indian land for cotton fields. A similar situation prevailed in the Northwest. Though neither as numerous nor as Europeanized as the Civilized Tribes, groups such as the Peorias, Kaskaskias, Kickapoos, Sauks, Foxes, and Winnebagos were living settled and stable lives along the northern frontier.

Throughout the 1820s, the federal government tried to convince tribes along the frontier to move farther west. Promised money, new land, and relief from white harassment, many Indian leaders agreed. Others, however, resisted, insisting that they stay where they were. The outcome was terrible factionalism within Indian societies as some lobbied to sell out and move west while others fought to keep their lands. Playing on this factionalism, federal Indian agents were able to extract land cessions that consolidated the eastern tribes onto smaller and smaller holdings. One such transaction, the 1825 Treaty of Indian Springs, involved fraud and manipulation so obnoxious that President Adams overturned the ratified treaty and insisted on a new one.

Adams's protective attitude did not extend to all Indians, however. The Prairie du Chien treaties (see page 258) called for the gradual removal of the northwestern tribes to the west side of the Mississippi. Drawn by the presence of gold and rich soil, impatient white miners and farmers moved onto the treaty lands even before the Indians left. In 1827 the Winnebagos, under Red Bird, resisted this invasion by raiding mining settlements in what was still legally Indian territory. White miners called for federal troops to assist their militia companies in suppressing Winnebago resistance. Despite the illegality of the miners' actions, the Adams administration complied, driving Red Bird and his people out of the disputed region.

Adams at least paid lip service to honest dealings with the Indians and the sanctity of treaties. Jackson scoffed at both. In 1817 he had told President Monroe, "I have long viewed treaties with the Indians an absurdity not to be reconciled to the principles of our government." As president, Jackson advocated removing all the eastern Indians to the west side of the Mississippi, by force if necessary (see Map 10.4). Following Jackson's direction, Congress passed the **Indian Removal Act** in 1830, appropriating the funds necessary to purchase all of the lands held by Indian tribes east of the Mississippi River and to pay for their resettlement in the West.

It did not take Jackson long to begin implementing his new authority. Like the Winnebagos, the Sauk and Fox Indians also resisted violations of the Prairie du Chien treaties. When white farmers penetrated Sauk Indian territory during the summer of 1831, the Jackson administration authorized federal troops to forcibly move the entire band of more than a thousand Indian men, women, and children across the Mississippi. During the following spring, however, one Sauk leader, **Black Hawk,** led a party back "home." Harassed by Illinois militia units, Black Hawk's resistance force clung to their territory until federal troops marched in from Illinois and Missouri, killing more than three hundred Indians and capturing Black Hawk.

At the same time, whites were exerting similar pressure on the southern tribes. The case of the Cherokees provides an excellent illustration of the new, more aggressive attitude toward Indian policy. Having allied with Jackson against the Creeks in 1813, the Cherokees emerged from the War of 1812 with their lands pretty well intact, and a rising generation of progressive leaders pushed strongly for the tribe to embrace white culture. In the early 1820s the Cherokees created a formal government with a bicameral legislature, a court system, and a professional, salaried civil service. In 1827 the tribe drafted and ratified a written constitution modeled on the Constitution of the United States. In the following year the tribe began publication of its own newspaper, the *Cherokee Phoenix*, printed in both English and Cherokee, using the alphabet devised

Five Civilized Tribes Term used by whites to describe the Cherokee, Choctaw, Seminole, Creek, and Chickasaw Indians, many of whom were planters and merchants.

Indian Removal Act Law passed by Congress in 1830 providing for the removal of all Indian tribes east of the Mississippi and the purchase of western lands for their resettlement.

Black Hawk Sauk leader who brought his people back to their homeland in Illinois; he was captured in 1832 when U.S. troops massacred his followers.

earlier in the decade by tribal member **George Guess (Sequoyah).**

Rather than winning the acceptance of their white neighbors, however, those innovations led to even greater friction. From the frontiersmen's point of view, Indians were supposed to be dying out, disappearing into history, not founding new governments and competing successfully for economic power. Thus in 1828 the Georgia legislature **annulled** the Cherokee constitution. In the following year, gold was found on Cherokee land. As more than three thousand greedy prospectors violated tribal territory, the state of Georgia extended its authority over the Cherokees and ordered all communal tribal lands seized.

That was the first in a series of laws that the Georgia legislature passed to make life as difficult as possible for the Cherokees in hopes of driving them out of the state. When Christian missionaries living with the tribe protested the state's actions and encouraged the Cherokees to seek federal assistance, Georgia passed a law that required teachers among the Indians to obtain licenses from the state—a law expressly designed to eliminate the missionaries' influence. When two missionaries, Samuel Austin Worcester and Elizur Butler, refused to comply, a company of Georgia militia invaded their mission in the heart of Cherokee country, arrested the teachers, and marched them off to jail.

Two notable lawsuits came out of the combined efforts of the missionaries and Cherokees to get justice. In the first case, *Cherokee Nation v. Georgia* (1831), the Cherokees claimed that Georgia's action in extending authority over them and enforcing state law within Cherokee territory was illegal because they were a sovereign nation in a treaty relationship with the United States. The U.S. Supreme Court refused to hear this case. Speaking for the Court, Chief Justice John Marshall stated that the Cherokee Nation was neither a foreign nor a domestic state but was a "domestic dependent nation" and as such had no standing in federal court.

As American citizens, however, Worcester and Butler did have legitimate standing under federal law, and in 1832 Marshall was able to render a decision in the case of *Worcester v. Georgia.* In this case, the Court ruled that the Cherokee Nation was a distinct political community recognized by federal authority and that Georgia did not have legitimate power to pass laws regulating Indian behavior or to invade Indian land. He thus declared all the laws Georgia had passed to harass the Cherokees null and void and ordered the state to release Worcester and Butler from jail.

Although the Cherokees had grounds for celebration, their joy was short-lived. Jackson refused to use any federal authority to carry out the Court's order.

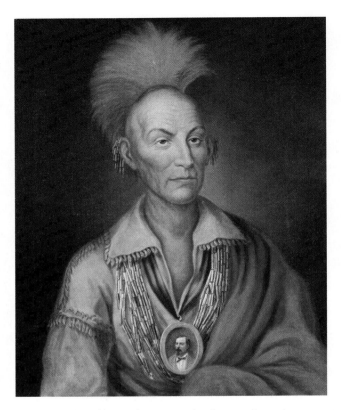

When white farmers began moving into territory that legally belonged to the Sauk and Fox Indians during the summer of 1831, Andrew Jackson's Department of War removed the Indians by force. Black Hawk resisted by moving his band back to their homeland to plant crops in the spring of 1832. Harassed by Illinois militia, the Sauk band attempted to flee back across the Mississippi River but were headed off by federal troops and massacred at the Battle of Bad Axe: the official report noted that 150 Indians were killed—though it acknowledged that number was too low "as a large proportion were slain in endeavoring to swim to the islands" and their bodies lost—while 40, including Black Hawk, were captured. *Chicago Historical Society.*

George Guess (Sequoyah) Cherokee silversmith and trader who created an alphabet that made it possible to transcribe the Cherokee language according to the sounds of its syllables.

annul To declare a law or contract invalid.

Cherokee Nation v. Georgia Supreme Court case (1831) concerning Georgia's annulment of all Cherokee laws; the Supreme Court ruled that Indian tribes did not have the right to appeal to the federal court system.

Worcester v. Georgia Supreme Court case (1832) concerning the arrest of two missionaries to the Cherokees in Georgia; the Court found that Georgia had no right to rule in Cherokee territory.

It is easy to gloss over the brutality that was part of removing the Cherokees and other Indians from the Southeast during the 1830s, but this blockhouse at the former site of Fort Marr in Tennessee provides gruesome testimony to the actualities of the "Trail of Tears." It was one of four corner guard towers that were connected by high walls that contained Indians waiting to be transported to Indian Territory. Confinement often lasted for months, during which time food, fresh water, adequate shelter, and sanitary facilities were either minimal or not supplied at all. Armed sentinels in the blockhouses could shoot through specially drilled gun ports if the Indian detainees protested their inhumane treatment.
© Copyright 1994–2003 by Golden Ink. All Rights Reserved. Used with permission.

When the Cherokees and their sympathizers pressed Jackson on the matter, he claimed that he was powerless to help and that the only way the Indians could get protection from the Georgians was to relocate west of the Mississippi.

Under this sort of pressure, tribal unity broke down. The majority of Cherokees stood fast with their stalwart leader John Ross, fighting Georgia through the court system. But another faction emerged advocating relocation. Preying on the division, federal Indian agents named the dissenters as the true representatives of the tribe and convinced them to sign the **Treaty of New Echota** (1835), in which the minority faction sold the last 8 million acres of Cherokee land in the East to the U.S. government for $5 million.

A similar combination of pressure, manipulation, and outright fraud led to the dispossession of all the other Civilized Tribes. During the winter of 1831–1832, the Choctaws in Mississippi and Alabama became the first tribe to be forcibly removed from their lands to a designated Indian Territory between the Red and Arkansas Rivers in what is now Oklahoma. They were joined by the Creeks in 1836 and by the Chickasaws in 1837. John Ross and the other antitreaty Cherokee leaders continued to fight in court and to lobby in Congress, but in 1838 federal troops rounded up the entire Cherokee tribe and force-marched them to

Treaty of New Echota Treaty in 1835 by which a minority faction gave all Cherokee lands east of the Mississippi to the U.S. government in return for $5 million and land in Indian Territory.

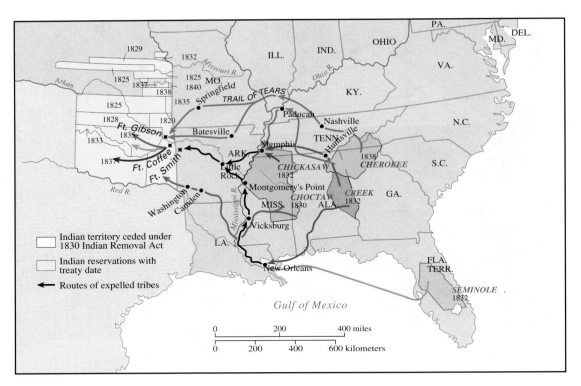

MAP 10.4   **Indian Removal**   The outcome of Andrew Jackson's Indian policy appears clearly on this map. Between 1830 and 1835, all of the Civilized Tribes except Osceola's faction of Seminoles were forced to relocate west of the Mississippi River. Thousands died in the process. © *Martin Gilbert,* The Routledge Atlas of American History, *Fourth Edition, ISBN: 0415281512 HB & 0415281520 PB.*

Indian Territory. Like all of the Indian groups who were forcibly removed from their native lands, the Cherokees suffered terribly. In the course of the long trek, which is known as the **Trail of Tears** (see Map 10.4), nearly a fourth of the twenty thousand Cherokees who started the march died of disease, exhaustion, or heartbreak.

The only one of the Civilized Tribes to abandon legal defenses and adopt a policy of military resistance was the Seminoles. Like the other tribes, the Seminoles were deeply divided. Some chose peaceful relocation; others advocated rebellion. After the conciliatory faction signed the Treaty of Payne's Landing in 1832, a group led by **Osceola** broke with the tribe, declaring war on the protreaty group and on the United States. After years of guerrilla swamp fighting, Osceola was finally captured in 1837, but the antitreaty warriors fought on. The struggle continued until 1842, when the United States withdrew its troops, having lost fifteen hundred men during the ten-year conflict. Eventually, even the majority of Osceola's followers

agreed to move west, though a small faction of the Seminoles remained in Florida's swamps, justly proud that they were neither conquered nor dispossessed by the United States.

The Nullification Crisis

Southern concerns about rising tariffs during the debate over western lands reflected the South's abiding political and economic posture during the Jackson administration. For years, southerners had complained

Trail of Tears   Forced march of the Cherokee people from Georgia to Indian Territory in the winter of 1838, during which thousands of Cherokees died.

Osceola   Seminole leader in Florida who opposed removal of his people to the West and led resistance to U.S. troops; he was captured by treachery while bearing a flag of truce.

that tariffs discriminated against them. From their point of view, they were paying at least as much in tariffs as the North and West but were not getting nearly the same economic benefits.

This matter had come to a head in 1829 when the impact of the ill-considered Tariff of Abominations (1828) began to be felt throughout the nation. The new tariffs roused loud protest from states such as South Carolina, where soil exhaustion and declining prices for agricultural produce were putting strong economic pressure on men who were deeply invested in land and slaves. Calhoun, who took office as Jackson's vice president in 1829, spearheaded the protest.

Though it guarded the author's identity, the South Carolina legislature published Calhoun's *South Carolina Exposition and Protest* in 1828, fanning the flames of sectionalism. Calhoun's **nullification** sentiments reflected notions being expressed throughout the nation. And as Calhoun's pamphlet circulated to wider and wider audiences, nationalists such as Clay and Jackson grew more and more anxious about the potential threat to federal power. The test came in 1830, when Senator Robert Y. Hayne of South Carolina and Senator **Daniel Webster** of Massachusetts entered into a debate over Calhoun's ideas. Hayne zealously supported Calhoun; Webster appealed to nationalism. Many have maintained that Hayne's speech was better argued than Webster's, but what mattered was how the president and the nation viewed the debate. Jackson soon made his position clear. At a political banquet, he offered the toast, "Our Federal Union—It must be preserved," indicating that he would brook no nullification arguments. Calhoun, who was sitting near the president, then rose and countered Jackson's toast with one of his own: "The Union—next to our liberty most dear." For Jackson, who valued loyalty above all else, his vice president's insubordination was inexcusable. Still, two years passed before the crisis finally came.

In 1832 nullification advocates in South Carolina called for a special session of the state legislature to consider the matter of state versus federal power. The convention met in November and voted overwhelmingly to nullify the despised tariff. The legislature also elected Hayne, nullification's most prominent spokesman, as governor and named Calhoun as his replacement in the Senate. The vice president, who realized that he would not be Jackson's running mate in the coming election, finally admitted writing the *Exposition and Protest* and resigned from the vice presidency to lead the pro-nullification forces from the Senate floor.

Jackson quickly proved true to his toast of two years before. Bristling that nullification violated the Constitution and was "destructive of the great object for which it was formed," Jackson immediately reinforced federal forts in South Carolina and sent warships to guarantee the tariff's collection. He also asked Congress to pass a "force bill" giving him the power to invade the rebellious state if doing so proved necessary to carry out federal law. In hopes of placating southerners and winning popular support in the upcoming election, Congress passed a lowered tariff, but it also voted to give Jackson the power he requested.

South Carolina nullifiers immediately called a new convention, which withdrew its nullification of the previous tariff but passed a resolution nullifying the force bill. Because Jackson no longer needed the force bill to apply federal law and collect the new tariff, he chose to ignore this action. Thus there was no real resolution to the problem, and the gash over federal versus states' rights remained unhealed. The wound continued to fester until it was finally cauterized thirty years later by civil war.

nullification Refusal by a state to recognize or enforce a federal law within its boundaries.

Daniel Webster Massachusetts senator and lawyer who was known for his forceful speeches and considered nullification a threat to the Union.

✔ Individual Voices

John C. Calhoun Justifies the Principle and Practice of Nullification

After resigning from the vice presidency in 1832 over the nullification crisis, John C. Calhoun was appointed by the South Carolina legislature to fill a vacancy in its U.S. Senate delegation. One year later, in February 1833, Calhoun stood before the Senate defending South Carolina's actions and the principle of nullification. In a brief statement, Calhoun summarized his views and attempted to justify his home state's act of disobedience in refusing to comply with federal tariff laws.

① *What is the significance of Calhoun's assertion that the federal union is a "union of States" and "not of individuals"?*

② *How does Calhoun's description of the process by which the Constitution was ratified justify his claims concerning the rights of a statewide convention to declare federal laws null and void?*

③ *The expression "meum and tuum" is Latin for "mine and thine." Here Calhoun is saying that a citizen's claim that the government has wrongly taken his or her property—a conflict between "mine and thine"—would be an appropriate matter to take to court. In cases, however, where all citizens believe themselves deprived by the government, it falls to the state and not to the courts to act on their behalf.*

The people of Carolina believe that the Union is a union of States, and not of individuals; that it was formed by the States, and that the citizens of the several States were bound to it through the acts of their several States; that each State ratified the Constitution for itself, and that it was only by such ratification of a State that any obligation was imposed upon its citizens. **①** *Thus believing, it is the opinion of the people of Carolina that it belongs to the State which has imposed the obligation to declare, in the last resort, the extent of this obligation, as far as her citizens are concerned; and this upon the plain principles which exist in all analogous cases of compact between sovereign bodies. On this principle the people of the State, acting in their sovereign capacity in convention, precisely as they did in the adoption of their own and the Federal Constitution, have declared, by the ordinance, that the acts of Congress which imposed duties under the authority to lay imposts, were acts not for revenue, as intended by the Constitution, but for protection, and therefore null and void.* **②** *. . . It ought to be borne in mind that, according to the opinion which prevails in Carolina, the right of resistance to the unconstitutional acts of Congress belongs to the State, and not to her individual citizens; and that, though the latter may, in a mere question of* meum *and* tuum, **③** *resist through the courts an unconstitutional encroachment upon their rights, yet the final stand against usurpation rests not with them, but with the State of which they are members; and such act of resistance by a State binds the conscience and allegiance of the citizen . . . .*

④ On what basis does Calhoun justify the expulsion of federal authorities from a state? What assumptions is he making about federal rights versus states' rights?

The Constitution has admitted the jurisdiction of the United States within the limits of the several States only so far as the delegated powers authorize; beyond that they are intruders, and may rightfully be expelled; and that they have been efficiently expelled by the legislation of the State through her civil process, as has been acknowledged on all sides in the debate, is only a confirmation of the truth of the doctrine for which the majority in Carolina have contended. ④

SUMMARY

With the end of the War of 1812, President Madison and the Republicans promoted a strong agenda for the nation. Joining with former critics such as Henry Clay and John C. Calhoun, Madison pushed for a national market economy by sponsoring federal legislation for a national bank, controlled currency, and tariff protection for American industry. In addition, Madison gave free rein to nationalists such as Stephen Decatur, John Quincy Adams, and Andrew Jackson, who succeeded in enhancing the nation's military reputation and expanding its sphere of influence.

While the nation moved forward in accomplishing its diplomatic goals, the Republicans' economic agenda suffered from a lack of viable transportation and communication systems. Expecting quick and enormous profits, New York built the Erie Canal, the first successful link between the increasingly urban and manufacturing East and the rural, agricultural West. Convinced finally that transportation improvements were necessary for national defense and for carrying out the work of the government, Madison and his successors joined with state officials to begin the process of building a truly national system of roads and canals.

But what had begun as an age of optimism closed in a tangle of conflict and ill will. A much-hoped-for prosperity dissolved in the face of shrinking markets, resulting in economic panic in 1819 and a collapse in the speculative economy. Economic hard times, in turn, triggered increased competition between the nation's geographical sections, as leaders wrestled for control over federal power in an effort to rid particular areas of economic despair. Supporters of the American System tried to craft a solution, but their compromise did not entirely satisfy anyone. And in the sea of contention that swelled around the Missouri Compromise, the Era of Good Feelings collapsed.

Meanwhile, distressed by what seemed an elite conspiracy to run American affairs, newly politicized voters swept the gentlemanly John Quincy Adams out of office and replaced him with the more exciting and presumably more democratic Andrew Jackson. Backed by a political machine composed of northern, western, and southern interests, Jackson had to juggle each region's financial, tariff, and Indian policy demands while trying to hold his political alliance and the nation together. The outcome was a series of regional crises—the Bank War, nullification, and Indian removal—that alienated each region and together constituted a crisis of national proportions.

IN THE WIDER WORLD

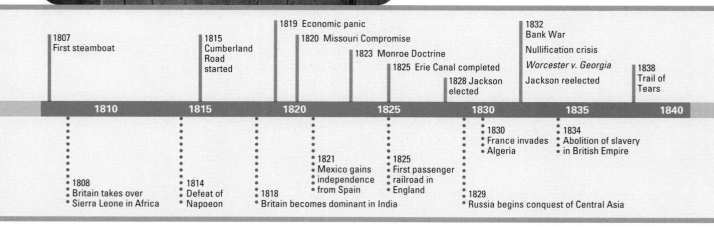

New Optimism and a New Democracy

1807   Robert Fulton tests steam-powered *Clermont*

1810   *Fletcher v. Peck*

1814   Treaty of Ghent ends War of 1812

1814–1815   Hartford Convention

1815   Government funds Cumberland Road

Stephen Decatur defeats Barbary pirates

1816   Tariff of 1816

First successful steamboat run, Pittsburgh to New Orleans

James Monroe elected president

1817   Second Bank of the United States opens for business

Rush-Bagot Agreement

Construction of Erie Canal begins

Congress suspends installment payments on public land purchases

1818   Convention of 1818

Andrew Jackson invades Spanish Florida

1819   *Dartmouth College v. Woodward*

McCulloch v. Maryland

Adams-Onís Treaty

Missouri Territory applies for statehood

Panic of 1819

1820   Monroe reelected

Missouri Compromise

Northeastern congressmen propose protective tariffs and reduction of public land prices

1823   Monroe Doctrine

1824–1828   Suffrage reform triples voter population

1824   *Gibbons v. Ogden*

Western congressmen join northeastern congressmen to pass increased protective tariffs

Jackson wins electoral plurality and popular majority in presidential election

1825   House of Representatives elects John Quincy Adams president

Prairie du Chien treaties

Completion of Erie Canal

1826   Disappearance of William Morgan and beginning of Antimasons

1827   Ratification of Cherokee constitution

Federal removal of Winnebagos

1828   Tariff of Abominations

Jackson elected president

Publication of *The South Carolina Exposition and Protest*

First issue of the *Cherokee Phoenix*

1830   Webster-Hayne debate

Indian Removal Act

1831   Federal removal of Sauks and Choctaws

Cherokee Nation v. Georgia

1832   *Worcester v. Georgia*

Bank War

Nullification crisis

Black Hawk War

Seminole War begins

1836–1838   Federal removal of Creeks, Chickasaws, and Cherokees

The Great Transformation: Growth and Expansion, 1828–1848

A NOTE FROM THE AUTHOR

You may have noticed as you have been reading this book that the time span covered by each chapter has become shorter and shorter. This trend will continue throughout the rest of the text. Why does Chapter 1 cover almost 70,000 years of history, and the two you are about to read collectively span only twenty? Part of the explanation is that quite honestly most people are more interested in what took place closer to our own lifetime—that which can be seen to have a more immediate influence on our lives—than on things that seem more distant. And we know more about the recent past than we do about what happened a very long time ago. But another reason is that the pace of history itself has accelerated. Generations might pass before people in colonial Massachusetts or Virginia noticed a momentous change. But by the beginning of the nineteenth century people were seeing the entire foundation of their society change before their eyes. And today, things that were cutting edge last week will be obsolete by the end of the month. This phenomenon has fascinated generations of historians and caused them to wonder what the future could possibly hold—should it continue. That is another reason why studying history can be rewarding; to help us orient ourselves to the increasing rate of change we experience daily by seeing how past generations have done the same.

Helen Jewett

With natural beauty and a quick mind, Helen Jewett became a very successful prostitute in New York City. Although she had no valid claim to genteel status, she passed herself off as the dishonored daughter of an elite family. Pretenders like Jewett used the anonymity possible in newly emerging American cities in the 1830s to insinuate themselves into polite social circles. The press coverage of Helen Jewett's grisly murder brought attention to these unsavory types, and her death was used as a moral lesson illustrating the costs that might accompany sneaking through social barriers. *Courtesy of the American Antiquarian Society.*

✔ Individual Choices

The story of Helen Jewett's fateful choice begins with a little girl named Dorcas Doyen, the daughter of a poor Maine shoemaker. Her mother died when she was 10 years old, and her father decided to put her out as a domestic servant. Dorcas eventually became a maid in the household of a prominent judge. She was encouraged to better herself and succeeded so well that visitors often mistook her for one of the judge's own daughters.

But she was not one of the judge's daughters. Rapidly approaching womanhood, Dorcas faced the unpleasant reality that as long as she remained in the relatively closed, face-to-face village world of rural Maine, she could never be anything more than the serving girl that everyone knew her to be. At age 17 she chose to assume a new name and move to Portland, where her beauty, charm, and wit soon made her a much-sought-after companion by the upwardly mobile young men in the city. Though no one in polite society at the time would have used such an expression, she had become a high-class call girl, and a successful one; so successful that she decided to break into the big time by moving to New York City.

Adopting the name Helen Jewett she took up residence in one of the most fashionable brothels in America's most fashionable city. There she entertained a following of educated, economically comfortable young clerks and junior managers who were putting off marriage while launching their careers. Whenever asked about her background, Jewett told her clients that she had once been a genteel and proper girl but had fallen in with the reckless son of a wealthy merchant, who seduced and then abandoned her. Homeless and friendless, deserted on the cruel streets of New York, she turned to the only profession open to a dishonored woman.

"Soiled" and yet still genteel, she slipped through the cracks of social convention, living out a polite existence despite her fallen condition. And she probably would have continued this successful life if horror had not intervened. Late on the night of April 10, 1836, the fallen but fashionable woman was hacked to death with an ax and then set on fire. The sparkling quality of Jewett's life and the gruesome nature of her death made her murder an overnight media sensation—newspapers scrambled for the latest tidbits about the death, and life, of this conventionally contradictory young woman.

299

In the terminology of the time, Dorcas Doyen had become a "painted woman," a pretender to social status that the new anonymous urban space in New York City made possible. Of course moralistic journalists were quick to point out that her deception caused her grisly death, but her story revealed not only the risks but also the expanding range of choices that were coming into being. Free to invent new identities for themselves, a new generation of Americans slipped loose from the traditional constraints of village life to choose where and how they wanted to live in a new, modern, and urbanizing America.

INTRODUCTION

Helen Jewett might be considered an exceptional woman in any era, but all the more so in the early nineteenth century. At a time when expectations for women increasingly constrained their public roles—confining them, at least ideally, to positions as mothers, teachers, and churchgoers at the high end of the social spectrum or factory workers or domestic servants at the lower end—her decision to become a prostitute certainly stands out. But in a way, her experience typifies much broader patterns in American life during this period. Like many in her generation, she followed the economic opportunities that were fleeing the countryside and concentrating in the newly arising cities. She also made a conscious choice to forgo marriage and childbearing in exchange for a career. And like so many of her contemporaries, her success in that career was itself a product of changing times: the anonymity that came with the rise of cities permitted prostitution to thrive, just as the deferral of marriage for the sake of personal development may have encouraged upwardly mobile young men to seek out women like her. At the same time, the worsening of conditions for working people certainly provided an incentive for young Dorcas Doyen to create a false identity for herself that would allow her to transcend her lowly origins. She came to the city to make something new and better of herself—transforming herself in line with the great transformation happening around her.

But the urbanization that was taking place in the northeastern section of the country was only one manifestation of the upheaval that was affecting the nation at large. As cotton production continued to offer staggering profits for efficient and lucky southern planters, that industry and its various features—especially slavery—underwent significant growth and change. That in turn affected the everyday lives of everyone, of every race, in the ever-expanding Cotton Belt. Another alternative was to move west. This era saw an explosion in westward expansion as hopeful cotton capitalists and independent farmers sought new opportunities in both the northwest and southwest.

The New Cotton Empire in the South

→ *Why did living conditions for southerners—black and white—change after 1820?*

→ *How did elite white southerners respond to the change? What were the impacts of their response on slaves, free blacks, and poor whites?*

The South exploded outward, seeking new lands on which to grow the glamour crop of the century: cotton. In 1820 cotton was being grown heavily in parts of Virginia, South Carolina, and Georgia. Within a matter of decades, the cotton empire had expanded to include most of Alabama, Mississippi, and Louisiana, and extensive portions of eastern Texas, Kentucky, Tennessee, Arkansas, and southern Missouri (see Map 9.3). The new dependence on a single crop changed the outlook and experiences not just of large planters but also of the slaves, free blacks, and poor whites whose labor made cotton king.

A New Birth for the Plantation System

Few images have persisted in American history longer than that of the "typical" courtly southern planters in the years before the Civil War. Often characterized as the direct heirs of the colonial era patriarchs and the conservators of an older, stately way of life, the cotton barons of the **antebellum** South were really a new sort of men who carved out a new sort of existence. These new aristocrats were generally not related to the old colonial plantation gentry, but had begun their careers as land speculators, financiers, and rough-and-tumble yeoman farmers who had capitalized on both ruthlessness and lucky speculations in the burgeoning cotton market to amass large landholdings and armies of slaves.

And these were far from typical. First off, the total number of slaveholders constituted less than one-third of all white southerners. Of the minority who actually owned slaves, nearly three-quarters owned only 80 to 160 acres of land and fewer than ten slaves; another 15 percent owned up to 800 acres and between ten and twenty slaves, leaving only about 12 percent who possessed more than 800 acres and twenty or more slaves. Though few in number, slaveholders in general, and the planter class in particular, controlled the biggest share of productive land and labor. As a result, their economic, political, and social importance was far out of proportion to their numbers.

This is not to say that the image of grand plantations and lavish aristocratic living is entirely false. The owners of cotton plantations made an excellent living from the labor of their slaves. Although they often complained of debt and poor markets, it appears that large-scale planters could expect an annual return on capital that was the equivalent of what the most successful northern industrialists were making. Agricultural profits in non-cotton-producing areas were significantly lower, but even there slavery netted white landowners major profits. The enormous demand for workers in the heart of the **Cotton Belt** created a profitable interstate trade in slaves, especially after Congress outlawed the importation of slaves from abroad in 1808. Although an unknown number of slaves continued to be smuggled in, mostly from the nearby Caribbean islands, most came to the Cotton Belt from the plantations of former tobacco, rice, and sugar growers who now went into the business of breeding and selling slaves. Thus even planters who did not grow cotton came to have a significant investment in its cultivation and in the labor system that was its cornerstone.

The increasing demand for slaves had a terribly unsettling effect on social stability in the plantation world. Whereas generations of slaves had coexisted with generations of slave owners on the traditional plantations in the colonial South, now the appeal of quick profits led planters in places like Virginia and Maryland to sell off their slaves, often breaking up families and deeply rooted social connections in the process. This fragmentation of slave society helped to further dehumanize an already dehumanizing institution and drove a deeper wedge between the races.

The enormous profits earned from cotton in the 1840s and 1850s permitted some planters—or, more often, the children of successful cotton capitalists—to build elegant mansions and to affect the lifestyle that they associated with a noble past. Voracious readers of romantic literature, planters assumed what they imagined were the ways of medieval knights, adopting courtly manners and the nobleman's **paternalistic** obligation to look out for the welfare of social inferiors, both black and white. Women decked out in the latest gowns flocked to formal balls and weekend parties. Young men were sent to academies where they could learn the twin aristocratic virtues of militarism and honor. Young women attended private "seminaries" where they were taught, in the words of one southern seminary mistress, "principles calculated to render them useful and rational companions." Courtship became highly ritualized, an imitation of imagined medieval court manners.

Practical concerns, however, always threatened to crack this romantic veneer. Although huge profits might be made in cotton planting, successful ventures required major capital investment. If land suitable for cotton could be purchased directly from the federal government, it might be had for as little as 25 cents an acre, but efficient planting called for huge blocks of land, and planters often had to pay a premium to get them. Contrary to popular perception, slave labor was not cheap. At the height of the slave trade, a healthy male field hand in his mid-twenties sold for an average of $1,800. Younger and older men or those in less than perfect health sold for less, but even a male child too young to work in the fields might cost anywhere from $250 to $500.

Often planters purchased slaves and fields on credit and genuinely feared that their carefully constructed empires and lifestyles might collapse in an instant. Aristocratic parents sought to use marriage as a means of adding to family and economic security. "As to my

antebellum   The decades before the Civil War, the period from 1815 to 1860; Latin for "before the war."

Cotton Belt   The region in the southeastern United States in which cotton is grown.

paternalistic   Treating social dependents as a father treats his children, providing for their needs but denying them rights or responsibilities.

Despite the popular image that antebellum planters lived lives of idle luxury in great mansions, most actually lived in modest homes and worked alongside their employees and slaves, as this 1838 painting by an anonymous artist shows. *"Ye Southern Planter" 1838. Private collection.*

having any sweethearts that is not thought of," one young southern woman complained. "Money is too much preferred, for us poor Girls to be much caressed."

Even those girls whose fortunes earned caresses faced a strange and often difficult life. Planters' wives bore little resemblance to their counterparts in popular fiction. Far from being frail, helpless creatures, southern plantation mistresses carried a heavy burden of responsibility. A planter's wife was responsible for all domestic matters. She supervised large staffs of slaves, organized and ran schools for the children on the plantation, looked out for the health of everyone, and managed all plantation operations in the absence of her husband. All those duties were complicated by a sex code that relegated southern women to a peculiar position in the plantation hierarchy—between white men and black slaves. On the one hand, southern white women were expected to exercise absolute authority over their slaves. On the other, they were to be absolutely obedient to white men. "He is master of the house," said plantation mistress Mary Boykin Chesnut about her husband. "To hear [him] is to obey." This contradiction put great pressure on southern women, adding severe anxiety to their other burdens. "All the comfort of my life depends upon his being in a good humor," Chesnut remarked. And while in some respects planters treated their slaves like machines, slaves were nonetheless human—and sexual—beings, a fact that produced even more stress for plantation mistresses. Like Thomas Jefferson before them (see page 230), antebellum planters found that their power over slave women afforded them sexual

as well as financial benefits. One southerner rationalized this situation, saying, "The intercourse which takes place with enslaved females is less depraving in its effects [on white men] than when it is carried on with females of their own caste." As a result, a particularly beautiful young slave woman, who like Sally Hemings might herself have been the daughter of such a relationship, could bring as much as $5,000 at auction. Constrained as they were by the region's strict rules of conduct, the wives of these men generally were powerless to intercede. Though some may not have minded release from sexual pressures, they had to be mindful of slave concubines and their children, both of whom occupied an odd place in the domestic power structure. It is little wonder, then, that Chesnut concluded her observations about southern womanhood with the statement, "There is no slave . . . like a wife."

Life Among Common Southern Whites

As noted above, fully two-thirds of free southern families owned no slaves. A small number of these families owned stores, craft shops, and other urban businesses in Charleston, New Orleans, Atlanta, and other southern cities. Some were attorneys, teachers, doctors, and other professionals. The great majority, however, were proud small farmers who owned, leased, or simply squatted on the land they farmed.

Often tarred with the label "poor white trash" by their planter neighbors, these people were often pro-

Slave life in the antebellum South presented an array of complex and often contradictory sides, as these two images illustrate. On the left, a parlor scene shows two young house slaves in absolute subjugation— one even serves as a footstool for his mistress. The nicely framed daguerreotype on the right, however, depicts slaves in a very different light; this couple either had the means to bear the cost of the expensive photograph or their owner thought highly enough of them to do so. These are but two striking images of a complex evolving world that emerged in the cotton South, the legacy of which we continue to live with today. *(Left) Rare Books & Manuscripts, The Ohio State University Libraries; (right) The Maryland Historical Society, Baltimore.*

ductive stock raisers and farmers. They concentrated on growing and manufacturing by hand what they needed to live, but all aspired to end up with small surpluses of grains, meat products, and other commodities that they could sell either to neighboring plantations or to merchants for export. Many of these small farmers tried to grow cotton in an effort to raise cash, though they generally could not do so on a large scale. Whatever cash they raised they usually spent on necessary manufactures, as well as on land and slaves.

These small farmers had a shaky relationship with white planters. On the one hand, many wanted to join the ranks of the great planters, hoping they could transform their small holdings into cotton empires. On the other hand, they resented the aristocracy and envied the planters' exalted status and power. They also feared the expansion of large plantations, which often forced small holders to abandon their hard-won farms and slaves.

Although they seldom rebelled openly against their social superiors, common white people often used the power of the ballot box to make their dissatisfactions known. For despite the enormous power of the plantation elite, they were greatly outnumbered by the lesser class of whites, who had the power to wreck the entire social and economic structure if they became sufficiently disgruntled. Thus the *noblesse oblige* practiced by aristocrats toward poorer whites

was as much a practical necessity as it was a romantic affectation.

Large-scale planters also used racial tensions as a device for controlling their contentious neighbors. Although they were not above taking slave concubines or trusting African Americans with positions of authority on plantations, the white elite nonetheless emphasized white supremacy when conversing with their poorer neighbors. They acknowledged that poor farmers felt underprivileged when compared with planters, but slavery spared them from the most demeaning work. What freedoms and privileges poor whites enjoyed, planters asserted, existed only because of the existence of slavery; should slavery ever end, planters avowed, whether because of poor white political maneuverings or outside pressures, it would be the farmers who would have the most to lose.

Free Blacks in the South

Caught in the middle between southern planters, slaves, and poor white farmers, African Americans in the South who were not slaves often faced extreme

noblesse oblige The belief that members of the elite are duty-bound to treat others charitably, especially those of lower status than themselves.

discrimination. Some communities of free blacks could trace their origins back to earliest colonial times, when Africans, like Europeans, served limited terms of indenture. The majority, however, had been freed recently because of diminishing plantation profits during the late 1700s. Most of these people lived not much differently from slaves, working for white employers as day laborers.

Mounting restrictions on free blacks during the first half of the nineteenth century limited their freedom of movement, economic options, and the protection they could expect to receive by law. In the town of Petersburg, Virginia, for example, when a free black woman named Esther Fells irritated her white neighbor, he took it upon himself to whip her for disturbing his peace. The sheriff did not arrest the assailant but instead took Mrs. Fells into custody, and the court ordered that she be given fifteen more lashes for "being insolent to a white person." Skin color left free African Americans open to abuses and forced them to be extremely careful in their dealings with their white neighbors.

Still, some opportunities were available for a handful of free blacks who had desirable skills. In the Upper South—Delaware, Maryland, and Virginia—master craftsmen hired young African American boys as apprentices, and those who could stick out their apprenticeship might eventually make an independent living. The situation was different for African American girls. They had few opportunities as skilled laborers. Some became seamstresses and washers, others became cooks, and a few grew up to run small groceries, taverns, and restaurants. Folk healing, **midwifery,** and prostitution also led to economic independence for some black women.

It is worth noting that perhaps as many as 10 percent of free southern African American heads of household were slaveowners, but by itself this statistic is somewhat misleading. Many free black men were forced to buy their wives and children in order to reunite families and often were prevented by restrictive slave codes from legally freeing them. Still, a good many people of African descent owned plantations and gangs of slave laborers, though these possessions seldom earned them entry into local elite circles.

Living Conditions for Southern Slaves

A delicate balance between power and profit shaped planters' policies toward slaves and set the tone for slave life. Maintaining profitability prompted slave-

Although slaves increasingly were being used in the growing cotton industry during the antebellum years, some continued to practice skilled trades throughout the South. Horace King, for example, was a civil engineer who designed and built bridges and public buildings, including sections of the Alabama state capitol building. *Collection of the Columbus Museum, Columbus, Georgia; Museum purchase.*

owners to enforce severe discipline and exercise careful supervision over slaves, leading southern states to write increasingly harsh **slave codes** during the early nineteenth century, giving slaveowners virtual life-and-death control over their human chattels. But slaves were expensive: damaging or, worse, killing a healthy slave meant taking a significant financial loss. Still, given the need to keep up productivity, slaveowners were not shy about using measured force. "I always punish according to the crime," one plantation owner declared. "If it is a Large one I give him a genteel flogging with a strop, about 75 Lashes I think

---

midwifery   The practice of assisting women in childbirth.

slave codes   Laws that established the status of slaves, denying them basic rights and classifying them as the property of slaveowners.

This early photograph, taken on a South Carolina plantation before the Civil War, freezes slave life in time, giving us a view of what slave cabins looked like, how they were arranged, how the largest majority of slaves dressed, and how they spent what little leisure time they had. *Collection of William Gladstone.*

is a good whipping." Noting the practical limitations even to this "genteel" form of discipline, he continued, "When picking cotton I never put on more than 20 stripes and very frequently not more than 10 or 15." But not all plantation owners were gentle or even practical when it came to discipline. The historical record is filled with accounts of slaveowners who were willing to take a financial loss by beating slaves until they became useless or even died.

In keeping with demands for profitability, housing for slaves was seldom more than adequate. Generally, slaves lived in one-room log cabins with dirt floors and a fireplace or stove. Mindful of the need to maintain control and keep slaves productive, slaveowners tried to avoid crowding people into slave quarters. As one slaveowner explained, "The crowding [of] a number into one house is unhealthy. It breeds contention; is destructive of delicacy of feeling, and it promotes immorality between the sexes." Though not all planters shared this view, census figures suggest that the average slave cabin housed five or six people.

Though not crammed fifty to a house, as were workers in some New York slums, slave quarters were not particularly comfortable. The cabins had windows, but generally only wooden shutters and no glass. The windows let in flies in summer and cold in winter, but closing the shutters shut out the light. When the shutters were closed against flies and cold, the most reliable

source of light was an open fireplace or stove, which was also used for heat and cooking. Ever-present fires increased the danger of cabins burning down, especially because chimneys were generally made of sticks held together with dried mud. As one slave commented, "Many the time we have to get up at midnight and push the chimney away from the house to keep the house from burning up."

As in the cabin homes of common southern whites, furnishings in slave houses were usually fairly crude and often were crafted by the residents themselves. Bedding generally consisted of straw pallets stacked on the floor or occasionally mounted on rough bedsteads. Other furnishings were equally simple—rough-hewn wooden chairs or benches and plank tables.

Clothing was very basic. One Georgia planter outlined the usual yearly clothing allowance for slaves: "The proper and usual quantity of clothes for plantation hands is two suits of cotton for spring and summer, and two suits of woolen for winter; four pair of shoes and three hats." Women generally wore simple dresses or skirts and blouses, while children often went naked in the summer and were fitted with long, loose-hanging shirts during the colder months.

It appears that the slave diet, like slave clothing and housing, was sufficient to maintain life but not particularly pleasing. One slave noted that there was "plenty to eat sich as it was," but in summer flies swarmed all over the food. Her master, she said, would laugh about that, saying the added nutrition provided by the flies "made us fat." Despite justified complaints, the fact is that the average slave diet was rich by comparison with the diet of many other Americans. Slaves in the American South ate significantly more meat than workers in the urban North. In addition to meat, slaves consumed milk and corn, potatoes, peas and beans, molasses, and fish. Generally the planter provided this variety of food, but owners also occasionally permitted slaves to hunt and fish and to collect wild roots, berries, and vegetables. Theft also added to the quantity and variety of foods available in the slave quarters.

Although the diet provided to slaves kept them alive and functioning, the southern diet in general lacked important nutrients, and diet-related diseases plagued southern communities. Slaves were also subject to hernia, pneumonia, and **lockjaw,** of which each, in its way, was the product of slaves' working and living conditions. Because of the lack of proper sanitation, slaves also suffered from dysentery and **cholera.**

One major public health risk that was **endemic** among slaves was in the realm of circulatory disease. Recent research reveals that slave children were generally undernourished because slaveowners would not allocate ample resources to feed people who did not work. Once children were old enough to work, however, they had access to a very high-calorie diet. Such early malnutrition followed by an instant transition to a high-calorie and often high-fat diet may well have led to the high incidence of heart attacks, strokes, and similar ailments among slaves found in the historical record. And given the balance-sheet mentality among plantation owners, this phenomenon may not have been unwelcome. Old people who could not work hard were, like children, a liability; thus having slaves die from circulatory disease in middle age saved planters from unnecessary expenditures later on.

As to the work itself, cotton planting led to increasing concentration in the tasks performed by slaves. A survey of large and medium-size plantations during the height of the cotton boom shows that the majority of slaves (58 percent of the men and 69 percent of the women) were employed primarily as **field hands.** Of the rest, only 2 percent of slave men and 17 percent of slave women were employed as **house slaves.** The remaining 14 percent of slave women were employed in nonfield occupations such as sewing, weaving, and food processing. Seventeen percent of slave men were employed in nonfield activities such as driving wag-ons, piloting riverboats, and herding cattle. Another 23 percent were managers and craftsmen.

The percentage of slave craftsmen was much higher in cities, where slave **artisans** were often allowed to hire themselves out on the open job market in return for handing part of their earnings over to their owners. In Charleston, Norfolk, Richmond, and Savannah, slave artisans formed guilds. Feeling threatened by their solidarity, white craftsmen appealed to state legislatures and city councils for restrictions on slave employment in skilled crafts. Such appeals, and the need for more and more field hands, led to a decline in the number of slave artisans during the 1840s and 1850s.

Whether on large plantations or small farms, the burden of slavery was a source of constant stress for both slaves and masters in the newly evolving South. The precarious nature of family life, the ever-present threat of violence, and the overwhelming sense of powerlessness weighed heavily on slaves. And among masters, the awareness that they often were outnumbered and thus vulnerable to organized slave rebellion was a source of anxiety. Locked into this fear- and hate-laden atmosphere, everyone in the cotton South was drawn into what would become a long-lasting legacy of racial tension and distrust.

The Manufacturing Empire in the Northeast

→ *How did the process of manufacturing change in the United States after 1820? How did this change affect the nature of work?*

→ *In what ways did the American system of manufacturing change the traditional patterns of trade between the United States and the rest of the world?*

lockjaw   A popular name for tetanus, an often fatal disease resulting primarily from deep wounds.

cholera   An infectious disease of the small intestines whose bacteria is often found in untreated water.

endemic   Present among a particular group or groups of people or geographical area.

field hands   People who do agricultural work such as planting, weeding, and harvesting.

house slaves   People who did domestic work such as cleaning and cooking.

artisan   A person whose primary employment is the specialized production of hand-manufactured items; a craftsperson.

→ *How did the developing factory system affect the lives of artisans, factory owners, and middle-class Americans?*

Although the South changed radically during the opening years of the nineteenth century, one thing persisted: the economy remained rooted in people's homes. Before the 1820s, households in the North also produced most of the things they used. For example, more than 60 percent of the clothing that Americans wore was spun from raw fibers and sewn by women in their own homes. Some householders even crafted sophisticated items—furniture, clocks, and tools—but skilled artisans usually made such products. These craftsmen, too, usually worked in their homes, assisted by family members and an extended family of artisan employees: **apprentices** and **journeymen.**

Beginning with the cotton-spinning plants that sprang up during the War of 1812, textile manufacturing led the way in pushing production in a radical new direction (see page 256). From 1820 onward, manufacturing increasingly moved out of the home and into factories, and cities began to grow up around the factories. The intimate ties between manufacturers and workers were severed, and both found themselves surrounded by strangers in the new urban environments. "In most large cities there may be said to be two nations, understanding as little of one another, having as little intercourse, as if they lived in different lands," said Unitarian minister William Ellery Channing in 1841. "This estrangement of men from men, of class from class, is one of the saddest features of a great city."

The "American System of Manufacturing"

The transition from home manufacturing to factory production did not take place overnight, and the two processes often overlapped. Pioneer manufacturers such as Samuel Slater relied on home workers to carry out major steps in the production of textiles. Using what was called the **putting-out system,** cotton spinners supplied machine-produced yarn to individual households, where families then wove fabric on their own looms during their spare time. Such activities provided much-needed cash to farm families, enabled less productive family members (like the elderly or children) to contribute, and gave entire families worthwhile pastimes during lulls in the farming calendar.

But innovations in manufacturing soon began displacing such home crafting. The factory designs pioneered by Francis Cabot Lowell and his various partners were widely copied during the 1820s and 1830s. Spinning and weaving on machines located in one building significantly cut both the time and the cost of manufacturing. Quality control became easier because the tools of the trade, owned by the manufacturer rather than by the worker, were standardized and employees were under constant supervision. As a result, the putting-out system for turning yarn into cloth went into serious decline, falling off by as much as 90 percent in some areas of New England. Even home production of clothes for family use slid into decline. Women discovered that spending their time producing cheese or eggs or other marketable items could bring in enough cash to purchase clothing and still have money left over. Throughout the 1830s and 1840s, ready-made clothing—often cut, machine-sewn, and finished by semiskilled workers in factory settings—became standard wearing apparel.

A major technological revolution helped to push factory production into other areas of manufacturing as well during these years. In traditional manufacturing, individual artisans crafted each item one at a time, from the smallest part to the final product. A clockmaker, for example, either cast or carved individually by hand all of the clock's internal parts. As a result, the mechanisms of a clock worked together only in the clock for which they had been made. If that clock ever needed repair, new parts had to be custom-made for it. The lack of **interchangeable parts** made manufacturing extremely slow and repairs difficult, and it limited employment in the manufacturing trades to highly skilled professionals.

While serving as ambassador to France, Thomas Jefferson had encountered the idea of standardizing parts, so that a wheel from any given clock could be used in any other similar clock. Eli Whitney, perfecter of the cotton gin (see page 259), was the first American to propose the large-scale use of interchangeable parts—for a gun-manufacturing scheme in 1798. Whitney's efforts failed because he lacked money and

apprentice   A person who is bound by contract to a craftsman, providing labor in exchange for learning the skills associated with the craft.

journeyman   A person who has finished an apprenticeship in a trade or craft and is a qualified worker in the employ of another.

putting-out system   Manufacturing system through which machine-made components were distributed to individual families who used them to craft finished goods.

interchangeable parts   Parts that are identical and which can be substituted for one another.

As American industry became increasingly mechanized in the decades after 1820, suitable mill sites—places with solid foundations for factory buildings and reliable water flow for powering machinery—became highly prized. Often long stretches of riverbanks would sprout factory after factory. This was the case in Brandywine Village near the present site of Wilmington, Delaware, which became the leading mechanized, flour-producing center in the United States during the early nineteenth century. *From the permanent collection of the Historical Society of Delaware.*

precision machine tools. But a quarter-century later, in 1822, one of Whitney's partners in this pioneering venture, John H. Hall, brought together the necessary skill, financing, and tools to prove that manufacturing guns from interchangeable parts was practical. Within twenty years this "American system of manufacturing," as it was called, was being used to produce a wide range of products—farm implements, padlocks, sewing machines, and clocks. Formerly, clocks had been a status symbol setting apart people of means from common folks; however, using standardized parts, pioneer manufacturers like Seth Thomas and Chauncey Jerome revolutionized clock making to the point where virtually all Americans could afford them. Not only that, Thomas's and Jerome's breakthroughs produced clocks so inexpensive and reliable that even the British and Europeans began importing them. This reversed the long-standing pattern of manufactures moving exclusively from Europe to America, a trend that would grow in the years to come.

New Workplaces and New Workers

With machines now producing standardized parts for complex mechanisms such as clocks, the worker's job was reduced to simply assembling premade components. The centuries-old **guild** organization for artisans—preserved in the hierarchical system of apprentices, journeymen, and master craftsmen—rapidly fell away as extensive training in the manufacturing arts became irrelevant.

At first, owners found they had to use creative means to attract workers into the new factories. Some entrepreneurs developed **company towns.** In New England these towns resembled traditional New England villages. Families recruited from the economically depressed countryside were installed in neat row houses, each with its own small vegetable garden. The company employed each family member. Women worked on the production line. Men ran heavy machinery and worked as **millwrights,** carpenters, haulers, or as day laborers dredging out the **millraces.**

guild   An association of craftspeople with the same skills who join together to protect their common interests.

company town   A town built and owned by a single company; its residents depend on the company for jobs, stores, schools, and housing.

millwright   A person who designs, builds, or repairs mills or mill machinery.

millrace   The channel for the fast-moving stream of water that drives a mill wheel.

IT MATTERS TODAY

MANUFACTURING AND THE REVOLUTION IN TIME

In 1838, Chauncey Jerome introduced the first mass-produced brass clock at a price that virtually any American could afford. The distribution of clocks and the means by which Jerome produced them reinforced each other. Factory production required that workers, clerks, managers, shippers, and others essential to industry be coordinated if factories were going to function effectively. All of these employees, from the highest to the lowest in status, needed to have a reliable way of telling time. Jerome's clocks provided that reliability, contributing to a revolution in the way Americans began thinking about time itself. Increasingly people looked to mechanical devices to punctuate their lives. Time management, a concept that would have been foreign to a previous generation of Americans, had now become a reality. We now are almost entirely dependent on day planners or electronic personal information managers to keep track of time, a heritage of the revolution in time-keeping that was born in 1838 with the introduction of cheap brass clocks.

- How were the lives of Americans in the early nineteenth century changed by the increased regimentation that accompanied the manu-facturing revolution? In what ways does your life reflect these changes that took place so long ago?

- Try to imagine experiencing one day without referring to any sort of mechanical or electronic time management device. Describe what your day would be like.

Children did light work in the factories and tended gardens at home.

Lowell's company developed another system at its factories. Hard-pressed to find enough families to leave traditional employment and come to work in the factories, Lowell recruited unmarried farm girls. The company built dormitories to house these young working women, offering cash wages and reasonable prices for room and board, as well as cultural events and educational opportunities. Because most of the girls saw factory work as a transitional stage between girlhood and marriage, Lowell assured them and their families that the company would strictly control the moral atmosphere so that the girls' reputations would remain spotless.

In New York, Philadelphia, and other cities, immigrant slums offered opportunistic manufacturers an alternative source of labor. In the shoe industry, for example, one family would make soles, while a neighboring family made heels, and so forth. This type of operation was not as efficient as large shoe factories, but the money that urban manufacturers saved by not building factories and by paying rock-bottom wages to desperate slum-dwellers made it possible for the companies to compete successfully in the open market.

The combination of machine production and a growing pool of labor proved economically devastating to workers. No longer was the employer a master craftsman or a paternalistic entrepreneur who felt some responsibility to look out for his workers' domestic needs. Factory owners were obligated to investors and bankers and had to squeeze the greatest possible profit out of the manufacturing process. They kept wages low, regardless of the workers' cost of living. As the swelling supply of labor allowed employers to offer lower and lower wages, increasing numbers of working people faced poverty and squalor.

Immigration supplied much of this labor. Between 1820 and 1830 slightly more than 151,000 people immigrated to the United States. In the decade that followed, that number increased to nearly 600,000; between 1840 and 1850, well over a million and a half people moved to the United States from abroad (see Map 11.1). This enormous increase in immigration changed not only the **demographic** but also the cultural and economic face of the nation. The flood of immigrants collected in the port and manufacturing cities of the Northeast, where they joined Americans fleeing financial depression in the countryside after the economic panics of 1819 (see pages 276–278) and 1837 (discussed in Chapter 12). Adding to the resulting brew were former master craftsmen, journeymen, and apprentices who no longer had a secure place in the changing economy. Together, though seldom cooperatively, these groups helped to form a new social class in America.

Nearly half of all the immigrants who flooded into the United States between 1820 and 1860 came from

demographic The statistical distribution of subpopulations (ethnic groups, for example) among the larger population of a community or nation.

Water powered textile factories were complex, noisy, and dangerous places to work. As shown here, many machines were powered by a common drive shaft and so remained in motion all the time. Working around the constantly whirring equipment often led to injury or death for what one nineteenth-century magazine described as "the human portion of the machine." *The Granger Collection, New York.*

Ireland—a nation beset with poverty, political strife, and starvation. Because of land tenancy laws imposed by the British government in Ireland, by the early 1840s poverty was so wide-spread that one third of all Irish farmers could not support their families. Then in the mid-1840s a new crisis in the form of a blight that killed the one staple food source for Irish peasants—the potato—led millions to flee the island. Most Irish immigrants had few marketable skills or more money than the voyage to America cost; they arrived penniless and with little or no chance of finding employment.

Similar conditions beset many members of the second most numerous immigrant group: the Germans. Economic change and political upheaval in Germany were putting both peasants and skilled craftsmen to flight. Like Irish peasants, German farmers arrived in America destitute and devoid of opportunities. Trained German craftsmen had a better chance of finding employment, but the changeover from handicraft to industrial production—the very change that in many cases had driven them from Germany—was also taking place in America. And like the Irish, few spoke English well.

Not only were the new immigrants poor and often unskilled, but also most were culturally different from native-born Americans. Religion was their most notable cultural distinction: the majority was Roman Catholic. Their Catholicism separated them from most Americans, who claimed to be Protestant whether they

worshiped actively or not. It also made them suspect in the minds of people steeped in anti-Catholic sentiments handed down from earlier generations of Protestant immigrants who had fled Catholic persecution. In religion, then, as well as in language, dress, and eating and drinking habits, the new immigrants were very different from the sorts of people whose culture had come to dominate American society.

Poverty, cultural distinctiveness, and a desire to live among people who understood their ways and spoke their language brought new immigrants to neighborhoods where their countrymen had already found places to live. In New York, Philadelphia, and other cities, people with the same culture and religion built churches, stores, pubs or beer halls, and other familiar institutions that helped them cope with the shock of transplantation from Europe and gave them a chance to adapt gradually to life in the United States. They also started fraternal organizations and clubs to overcome the loneliness, isolation, and powerlessness they were experiencing.

Because the new immigrants were poor, housing in their neighborhoods was often substandard, and living conditions were crowded, uncomfortable, and unsanitary. Desperate for work and eager to make their own way in their new country, these fresh immigrants were willing to do nearly anything to earn money. Lacking the resources to buy farms and lacking the skills to enter professional trades, they were the perfect work force for the newly evolving

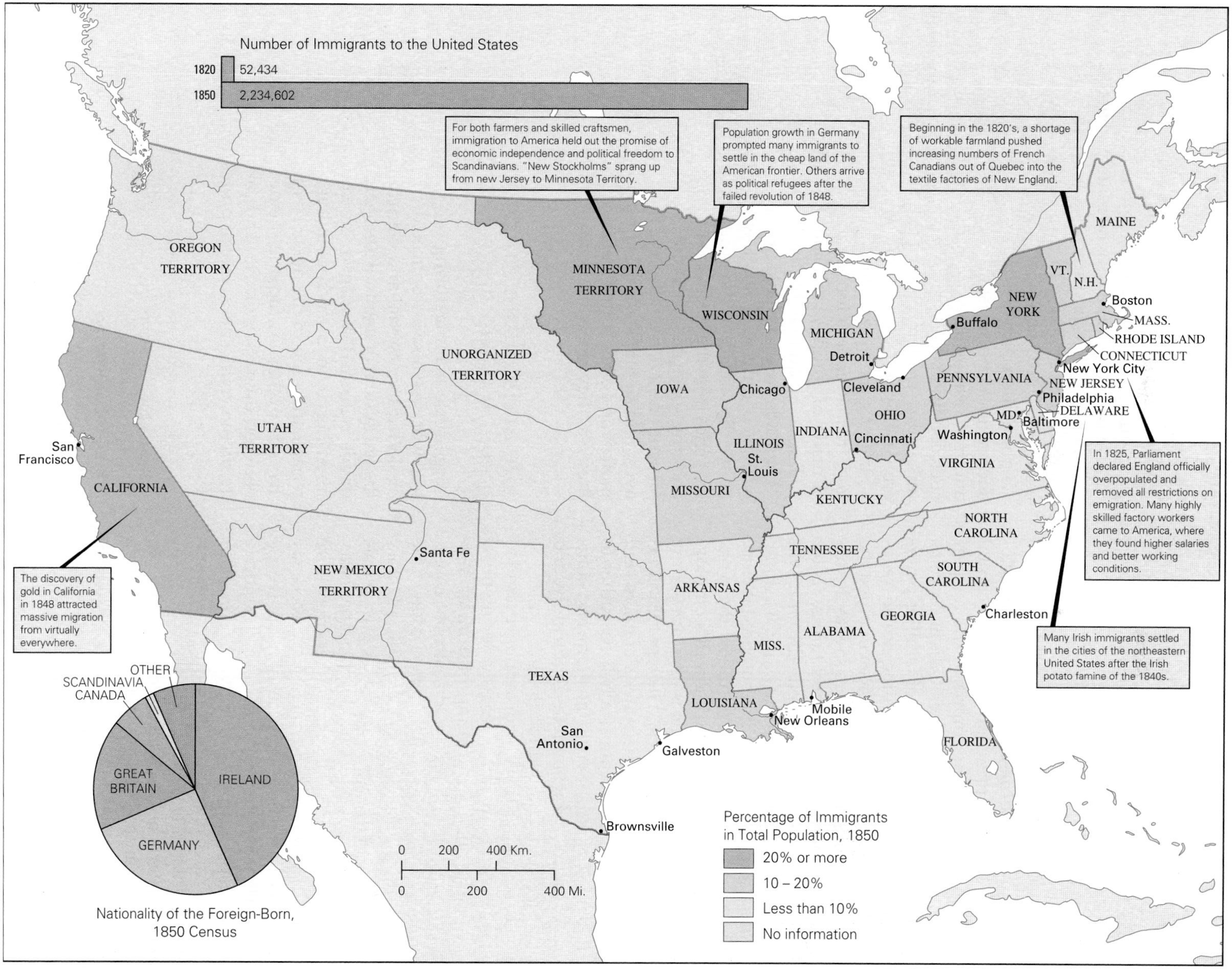
Number of Immigrants to the United States
1820 52,434
1850 2,234,602
For both farmers and skilled craftsmen, immigration to America held out the promise of economic independence and political freedom to Scandinavians. "New Stockholms" sprang up from new Jersey to Minnesota Territory.
Population growth in Germany prompted many immigrants to settle in the cheap land of the American frontier. Others arrive as political refugees after the failed revolution of 1848.
Beginning in the 1820's, a shortage of workable farmland pushed increasing numbers of French Canadians out of Quebec into the textile factories of New England.
In 1825, Parliament declared England officially overpopulated and removed all restrictions on emigration. Many highly skilled factory workers came to America, where they found higher salaries and better working conditions.
Many Irish immigrants settled in the cities of the northeastern United States after the Irish potato famine of the 1840s.
The discovery of gold in California in 1848 attracted massive migration from virtually everywhere.
OREGON TERRITORY
MINNESOTA TERRITORY
WISCONSIN
MICHIGAN
MAINE
VT.
N.H.
NEW YORK
Boston
MASS.
RHODE ISLAND
CONNECTICUT
New York City
NEW JERSEY
Philadelphia
DELAWARE
MD.
Baltimore
Washington
Buffalo
Detroit
Cleveland
Chicago
PENNSYLVANIA
OHIO
INDIANA
Cincinnati
ILLINOIS
St. Louis
IOWA
MISSOURI
KENTUCKY
VIRGINIA
NORTH CAROLINA
SOUTH CAROLINA
Charleston
TENNESSEE
GEORGIA
ALABAMA
MISS.
ARKANSAS
LOUISIANA
Mobile
New Orleans
FLORIDA
TEXAS
San Antonio
Galveston
Brownsville
UNORGANIZED TERRITORY
UTAH TERRITORY
NEW MEXICO TERRITORY
Santa Fe
CALIFORNIA
San Francisco
OTHER
SCANDINAVIA
CANADA
GREAT BRITAIN
IRELAND
GERMANY
Nationality of the Foreign-Born, 1850 Census
0 200 400 Km.
0 200 400 Mi.
Percentage of Immigrants in Total Population, 1850
20% or more
10 – 20%
Less than 10%
No information

MAP 11.1 Origin and Settlement of Immigrants, 1820–1850 Immigration was one of the most important economic, political, and social factors in American life during the antebellum period. As this map shows, with the exception of Louisiana, immigration was confined almost exclusively to areas where slavery was not permitted. This gave the North, Northwest, and California a different cultural flavor from the rest of the country and also affected the political balance between those areas and the South.

industrial economy. As the flow of immigrants increased, the traditional labor shortage in America was replaced by a **labor glut,** and the social and economic status of all workers declined accordingly.

Living Conditions in Blue-Collar America

Working conditions for **blue-collar workers** in factories reflected the labor supply, the amount of capital available to the manufacturing company, and the personal philosophy of the factory owner. Girls at Lowell's factories described an environment of familiar paternalism. Factory managers and boarding-house keepers supervised every aspect of their lives in much the same manner that authoritarian fathers saw to the details of life on traditional New England farms. As for the work itself, one mill girl commented that it was "not half so hard as . . . attending the dairy, washing, cleaning house, and cooking." What bothered factory workers most was the repetitive nature of the work and the resulting boredom. One of Lowell's employees described the tedium. "The time is often apt to drag heavily till the dinner hour arrives," she reported. "Perhaps some part of the work becomes deranged and stops; the constant friction causes a belt of leather to burst into a flame; a stranger visits the room, and scans the features and dress of its inmates inquiringly; and there is little else to break the monotony."

She went on to note that daydreaming provided relief from the boredom and the ear-shattering noise of the machinery. But daydreaming in front of fast-moving equipment could have disastrous consequences for what a New Jersey magazine called "the human portion of the machine." Inattentive factory workers were likely to lose fingers, hands, or whole arms to whirring, pounding, slashing mechanisms. Not a few lost their lives. Though managers may have wanted to make factories safer, investors vetoed any additional costs that safety devices might have incurred. Samuel Slater, for example, complained bitterly to his investors after a child was chewed up in a factory machine. "You call for yarn but think little about the means by which it is to be made."

Gradually Slater's and Lowell's well-meaning paternalism became rare as factory owners withdrew from overseeing day-to-day operations. The influx of laborers from the depressed countryside and of foreign immigrants wiped out both decent wages and the sorts of incentives the early manufacturing pioneers had employed. Not only did wages fall but laborers were also expected to find their own housing, food, and entertainment. Soon hulking **tenements** sprang up, replacing the open fields and clusters of small homes that once had dominated the urban landscape. Large houses formerly occupied by domestic manufacturers and their apprentices were broken up into tiny apartments by profit-hungry speculators who rented them to desperate laborers. Cellars and attics became living spaces like the rest of the building. In cities like New York, laborers lived 50 to a house in some working-class areas. As population densities reached 150 people an acre in such neighborhoods, sewage disposal, drinking water, and trash removal became difficult to provide. Life in such conditions was grossly unpleasant and extremely unhealthy: epidemics of typhus, cholera, and other crowd diseases swept through the slums periodically.

Investigating living and working conditions, a *New York Tribune* reporter found them deplorable. "The floor is made of rough plank laid loosely down, and the ceiling is not quite so high as a tall man," he reported. "The walls are dark and damp and the miserable room is lighted only by a shallow sash partly projecting above the surface of the ground and by the light that struggles from the steep and rotting stairs." In this dark and tiny space, he observed, "often lives the man and his work bench, the wife, and five or six children of all ages; and perhaps a palsied grandfather and grandmother and often both. Here they work, here they cook, they eat, they sleep, they pray."

Life and Culture Among a New Middle Class

Large-scale manufacturing not only changed industrial work but also introduced demands for a new class of skilled managerial and clerical employees. Under the old system of manufacturing, the master craftsman or his wife had managed the company's accounts, hired journeymen and apprentices, purchased raw materials, and seen to the delivery of finished products. The size of the new factories made such direct contact between owners, workers, and products impossible. To fill the void, a new class of professionals came into

---

labor glut   Oversupply of labor in relation to the number of jobs available.

blue-collar workers   Workers who wear work clothes, such as coveralls and jeans, on the job; their work is likely to involve manual labor.

tenement   An urban apartment house, usually with minimal facilities for sanitation, safety, and comfort.

Living conditions for working people in America's new industrializing cities were often terrible, as this illustration of a working class tenement apartment makes clear. "The walls are dark and damp and the miserable room is lighted only by a shallow sash," a *New York Tribune* reporter observed. "Here they work, here they cook, they eat, they sleep, they pray." *The Granger Collection, New York.*

being. In these days before the invention of the typewriter, firms such as Lowell's Boston Manufacturing Company employed teams of young men as clerks. These clerks kept accounts, wrote orders, and drafted correspondence, all in longhand. As elite owners such as Lowell and his partners became wrapped up in building new factories, pursuing investors, and entering new markets, both clerical and manufacturing employees were increasingly supervised by professional managers.

One distinguishing characteristic of the new **white-collar workers** was their relative youth. These young people, many of them the sons and daughters of rural farmers, had flocked to newly emerging cities in pursuit of formal education. They stayed to seek employment away from the economic instability and **provincialism** of the farm. The experience of Elizabeth Yale Hancock, a country girl from upstate New York, was fairly typical. After attending public school in Champlain, Elizabeth transferred to the Plattsburgh Academy. She studied there full-time for two terms before taking a job teaching at a public school while continuing classes at the academy part-time. She then went to the Female Seminary in Buffalo, where she enrolled in college-level classes. While pursuing her studies there, she worked as a nanny and resident tutor. Finally graduating from the seminary, Elizabeth took a job as a teacher at a select school.

Men too attended school when and where they could get financial assistance and then settled down where they could find employment and the company of others like themselves. And, as Elizabeth Hancock's experience indicates, women joined men in moving into new professions. While middle-class men found employment as clerks, bookkeepers, and managers, middle-class women parlayed their formal education and their gender's perceived gift for nurturing children into work as teachers. It became acceptable for women to work as teachers for several years before marriage, and many avoided marriage altogether to pursue their hard-won careers.

Middle-class men and women tended to put off marriage as long as possible while they established themselves socially and economically. They also tended to have fewer children than their parents. In the new urban middle-class setting, parents felt compelled to send their children to school so that they could take their place on the career ladder chosen by their parents. Adding nothing to family income, children thus became economic liabilities rather than assets, and middle-class adults used a combination of late marriage and various forms of birth control to keep families small.

A lack of traditional ties affected the lives of both married and unmarried middle-class people. Many unmarried men and women seeking their fortunes in town boarded in private homes or rooming houses. After marriage, middle-class men and women often

white-collar workers Workers able to wear white shirts on the job because they do no grubby manual labor.

provincialism The limited and narrow perspective thought to be characteristic of people in rural areas.

moved into private town homes, isolating themselves and their children from perceived dangers in the faceless city but also cutting them off from the comforting sociability of traditional country life. Accordingly, these young people crafted new urban structures that might provide the missing companionship and guidance.

Obviously some sought the company of women like Helen Jewett. Most, however, found companionship in **voluntary associations.** Students in colleges and universities formed a variety of discussion groups, preprofessional clubs, and benevolent societies. After graduation, groups such as the Odd Fellows and the Masons brought people together for companionship. Such organizations helped enforce traditional values through rigid membership standards stressing moral character, upright behavior, and, above all, order.

The *Odd Fellows' Manual* summarized the philosophy of these organizations well. "In the transaction of our business we pursue strict parliamentary rules, that our members may be qualified for any public stations to which they may be called by their fellow-citizens," the manual asserts. "And when business has been performed, we indulge in social intercourse, and even in cheerful and innocent hilarity and amusement. But all in strict order and decorum, good fellowship and prudence are constantly to be kept in view." In such clubs, people could discuss the latest books or world affairs with others of similar education and lifestyle in an affable setting. As the *Odd Fellows' Manual* went on to say, "Exercise yourself in the discussions of your Lodge not for the purpose of mere debate, contention, or 'love of opposition,' but to improve yourself in suitably expressing your sentiments." Young people also created and joined professional and trade groups. These associations served a social function, but they also became forums for training novices and for setting standards for professional methods and modes of conduct.

Members of the new middle class also used their organizing skills to press for reforms. While the elite class of factory owners and financiers generally formed the leadership for such organizations as the American Tract Society, the American Bible Society, and the American Board of Commissioners for Foreign Missions—each a multimillion-dollar reforming enterprise—young middle-class men and women provided the rank and file of charity workers.

In addition to their youth, another characteristic that prevailed among this newly forming class was deep anxiety. Although their education and skills earned them jobs with greater prestige than those of the average worker, these clerks and supervisors could be laid off or demoted to working-class status at any time.

Also, because of the anonymity in the new cities, it was virtually impossible to know if a stranger was truly a member of one's own class or an imposter who might use the trappings of gentility to take advantage of the new urban scene. Such suspicions led to a very strict set of rules for making social connections, and the wary atmosphere also helps to explain the fascination with a woman like Helen Jewett, whose life, and especially whose death, illustrated the dangers posed by and to pretenders to middle-class gentility.

Social Life for a Genteel Class

The changes in lifestyle that affected working-class and middle-class Americans were in large part an outcome of changes in the daily lives of those who owned and operated manufacturing businesses. In earlier years, when journeymen and apprentices had lived with master craftsmen, they were in effect members of a craftsman's extended family. The master craftsman/owner exercised great authority over his workers but felt obligated to care for them almost as a parent would have done. Such working arrangements blurred the distinction between employee and employer. Crammed together in the same household, owner and workers shared the same general lifestyle, kept the same hours, ate the same food, and enjoyed the same leisure activities. The factory system ended this relationship. The movement of workers out of the owners' homes permitted members of the emerging elite class to develop a **genteel** lifestyle that set them off from the army of factory workers and lesser number of clerks. Genteel families aimed at the complete separation of their private and public lives. Men in the manufacturing elite class spent their leisure time in new activities. Instead of drinking, eating, and playing with their employees, business owners began to socialize with one another in private clubs and in church and civic organizations. Instead of attending the popular theater, elite patrons began endowing opera companies and other highbrow forms of entertainment.

The lives of the factory owners' wives also changed. The mistress of a traditional manufacturing household had been responsible for important tasks in the oper-

---

voluntary association An organization or club through which individuals engage in voluntary service, usually associated with charity or reform.

genteel The manner and style associated with elite classes, usually characterized by elegance, grace, and politeness.

ation of the business. Genteel women, in contrast, were expected to leave business dealings to men. Ensconced in private houses set apart from the new centers of production and marketing, genteel women found themselves with time on their hands. To give themselves something to do, they sought areas of activity that would provide focus and a sense of accomplishment without imperiling their elite status by involving them in what was now perceived as the crass, masculine world of commerce. Many found outlets for their creative energies in fancy needlework, reading, and art appreciation societies. But some wished for more challenging activities. Sarah Huntington Smith, for example, a member of Connecticut's elite, spoke for many when she complained in 1833, "To make and receive visits, exchange friendly salutations, attend to one's wardrobe, cultivate a garden, read good and entertaining books, and even attend religious meetings for one's own enjoyment; all this does not satisfy me."

One activity that consumed genteel women was motherhood. Magazines and advice manuals, which began appearing during the 1820s and 1830s, rejected the traditional adage of "spare the rod, spoil the child," replacing it with an insistence on gentle nurturing. One leader in this movement was author and teacher Bronson Alcott. Alcott denied the concept of **infant depravity** that had so affected Puritan parents during the colonial era and led them to break their children's will, often through harsh measures (see page 69). Instead, he stated emphatically that "the child must be treated as a free, self-guiding, self-controlling being."

Alcott was equally emphatic that child rearing was the mother's responsibility. As his wife, Abigail, wrote of family management in Alcott's household, "Mr. A aids me in general principles, though nobody can aid me in the detail." And, according to Alcott, women should feel especially blessed for having such an opportunity.

Books like Alcott's *Conversations with Children on the Gospels* (1836–1837) flooded forth during these years and appealed greatly to isolated and underemployed women. Many adopted the advertised **cult of domesticity** completely. Turning inward, these women centered their lives on their homes and children. In doing so, they believed they were performing an important duty for God and country and fulfilling their most important, perhaps their only, natural calling.

Other genteel women agreed with the general tone of the domestic message but widened the woman's supposedly natural sphere outward, beyond the nursery, to encompass the whole world. They banded together with like-minded women to get out into the

Voluntary associations and fraternal organizations sprang up by the hundreds in the new urban America that was emerging in the 1830s and 1840s. These organizations provided companionship and, more importantly, a sense of order for the newly emerging middle class. The Odd Fellows was one prominent example. This sheet music cover, from a piece entitled "The Oddfellows March," is but one piece of evidence of the enormous cultural contributions that these organizations made to emerging modern American life. *The Maryland Historical Society, Baltimore.*

world in order to reform it. "I want to be where every arrangement will have unreserved and constant reference to eternity," Sarah Huntington Smith explained. Smith herself chose to become a missionary. Others during the 1830s and 1840s involved themselves in

---

infant depravity The idea that children are naturally sinful because they share in the original sin of the human race but have not learned the discipline to control their evil instincts.

cult of domesticity The belief that women's proper role lies in domestic pursuits.

a variety of reform movements, such as founding Sunday schools or opposing alcohol abuse. These causes let them use their nurturing and purifying talents to improve what appeared to be an increasingly chaotic and immoral society, the world represented by Helen Jewett.

A New Empire in the West

→ *How did most Americans imagine "the West"? To what extent were their imaginings accurate?*

→ *Who generally were the first pioneers to move into the West? How did they and those who followed actually move westward and establish communities there?*

While life in the cotton South and manufacturing Northeast underwent radical change in their way, the American West too was experiencing wholesale transformation. Enterprising capitalists often led the way in systematic exploration, looking for furs, gold, and other sources of quick profit. But it did not take long before a wide variety of others followed. Whether they expected a wasteland, a paradise, or something in between, what all of these newcomers to the West did find was a natural and cultural world that was much more complex than anything they had imagined.

Moving Westward

The image of the solitary trapper braving a hostile environment and even more hostile Indians is the stuff of American adventure novels and movies. Although characters such as Christopher "Kit" Carson and Jeremiah "Crow Killer" Johnson really did exist, these men were merely advance agents for an **extractive industry** geared to the efficient removal of animal pelts.

What drew men like Carson and Johnson into the Far West in the 1830s and 1840s was an innovation in the fur business instigated by long-time entrepreneur, William Henry Ashley. Taking advantage of the presence of large numbers of underemployed young men seeking fortune and adventure in the West, Ashley broke the long tradition of depending exclusively on Indian labor for collecting furs. In 1825 he set up the highly successful rendezvous system. Under this arrangement, individual trappers—white adventurers like Carson and Johnson, African Americans such as James Beckwourth, and a large number of Indians— combed the upper Missouri, trapping, curing, and packing furs. Once each year Ashley conducted a fur rendezvous in the mountains, where the trappers

The mountain fur trade is a colorful part of the nation's history and folklore. While millionaire fur entrepreneurs like John Jacob Astor lived in luxury in Eastern cities, trappers like Joe Meek (pictured here) occupied the wild and lawless territory of the upper Missouri River. Like many of his contemporaries, Meek survived his wilderness experiences to become an economic and political leader in the Far West when the fur business finally wound down in the 1840s. *Yale Collection of Western Americana. Beinecke Rare Book and Manuscript Library.*

brought their furs and exchanged them for goods. Pioneer missionary Pierre Jean de Smet called these gatherings "one of the most picturesque features of early frontier life in the Far West."

Various large-scale strategies for extracting wealth from the Far West were successful and made their owners very rich and important. But the success of their complex business inadvertently led to its decline. The expansion in international commerce flowing out of the fur trade helped open the way for importing vast amounts of silk from Asia. Soon silk hats became a fashion rage among luxury-loving consumers in both America and Europe, displacing the beaver hats that had consumed most American furs. In addition, the

> **extractive industry** An industry, such as fur trapping, logging, or mining, that removes natural resources from the environment.

This painting by Alfred Jacob Miller captures the color and spirit of the annual fur rendezvous and shows the wide variety of colorful people the event brought together—not only Indians and mountain men, but sightseeing English lords like William Drummond Steward (shown here on his white horse). *"Encampment on Green River" by Alfred Miller. Joslyn Art Museum, Omaha, Nebraska. Gift of the Enron Foundation.*

efficiency with which these gigantic organizations extracted fur from the western wilderness virtually wiped out beaver populations in the Rocky Mountains. Through the 1830s and 1840s, the beaver business slowed to a near standstill.

Many beaver hunters stayed in the West, however, becoming founding members of new communities. As early as 1840, fur trapper Robert "Doc" Newell reportedly told his companion Joe Meek, "Come, we are all done with this life in the mountains. . . . The fur trade is dead in the Rocky Mountains, and it is no place for us now, if ever it was." The two men then headed to the Willamette Valley in Oregon to become settlers. The great captains in the fur industry came to similar conclusions, pulling their capital out of trapping and diverting it to more attractive ventures: banks, mills, real estate, and the burgeoning canal and rail systems.

Often the first people to join the former fur trappers in settling the West were not rugged yeoman farmers but highly organized and well-financed land speculators and developers. From the earliest days of the republic, federal public land policy favored those who could afford large purchases and pay in cash. Liberalization of the land laws during the first half of the nineteenth century put smaller tracts—for less money and on credit terms—within reach of more citizens, but speculators continued to play a role in land distribution by offering often even smaller tracts and more liberal credit (see page 276). This was particularly true as states granted rights-of-way, first to canal companies and then, increasingly, to railroad developers as a way of financing internal improvements. Land

along transportation routes was especially valuable, and developers could often turn an outright grant into enormous profits.

A third group of expectant fortune hunters was lured into the Far West by the same magnet that had drawn the Spanish to the American Southwest: gold. Since colonial times, Americans had persistently hunted precious metals, usually without much success. The promise of gold continued to draw people westward, however, onto Winnebago lands in 1827 and into Cherokee territory in 1829 (see pages 289; 290). But the most impressive case of gold fever would not strike until 1848, when a group of laborers digging a millrace in northern California found flakes and then chunks of gold. Despite efforts to suppress the news, word leaked out, and by mid-May 1848 men were rushing from all over California and Oregon into the Sierra foothills northeast of Sacramento to prospect for gold. By September, news reached the East that the light work of panning for gold in California could yield $50 a day, two months' wages for an average northern workingman. In 1849 more than a hundred thousand **forty-niners** took up residence in California.

As in earlier gold rushes, most of these fortune hunters did not discover gold, but many of them

forty-niners   Prospectors who streamed into California in 1849, after the discovery of gold northeast of New Helvetia in 1848.

stayed to establish trading businesses, banks, and farms. Others moved on, still seeking their fortunes. But eventually they too, for the most part, settled down to become shopkeepers, farmers, and entrepreneurs.

Distinct waves of Americans pushed westward into the areas opened by gold seekers, fur trappers, and land speculators. All of these migrants were responding to promises of abundant land in America's interior. But different groups were reacting to very different conditions in the East, and those differences gave shape to their migrations and to the settlements they eventually created.

"To make money was their chief object," one young pioneer woman in Texas commented; "all things else were subsidiary to it." Like her family, many settlers went west to improve their fortunes. Many, too, were pushed by economic forces to seek new lives in the West, especially after the panics of 1819 and 1837. Throughout New England, for example, people faced a choice between moving into cities or migrating westward. Others, however, saw the unsettled nature of the West as a refuge for establishing or expanding particular religious or social practices. Many Protestant sects sent battalions of settlers and missionaries to carve out new "Plymouth Colonies" in the West. The most notable of these religious pioneer groups was the Mormons, who came to dominate the Great Basin Region.

This movement was founded in upstate New York in 1830 by **Joseph Smith Jr.** Announcing that he had experienced a revelation that called for him to establish a community in the wilderness, Smith led his congregation as a unit out of New York in 1831 to settle in the northeastern Ohio village of Kirtland. There the Mormons thrived for a while, stressing notions of community, faith, and hard work. But religious persecution eventually convinced Smith to lead his followers farther west into Missouri. Again the Mormons faced serious resentment from frontiersmen. Smith then decided to relocate his congregation to the Illinois frontier, founding the city of Nauvoo in 1839. Continuing conversions to the new faith brought a flood of Mormons to Smith's Zion in Illinois. In 1844 Nauvoo, with a population of fifteen thousand Mormons, dwarfed every other Illinois city.

Despite their growth in numbers and prosperity, Smith's community in Nauvoo continued to be victims of religious and economic persecution. On June 27, 1844, Smith was murdered by a mob in neighboring Carthage, Illinois. The remaining church leaders concluded that the Mormons would never be safe until they moved far from mainstream American civilization. **Brigham Young,** Smith's successor, decided to search for a safe refuge beyond the Rocky Mountains

and led sixteen hundred Mormons to the valley of the **Great Salt Lake.** Young immediately assigned some followers to begin an irrigation project and sent others on to California to buy livestock. The rest of the congregation soon arrived, and within a matter of weeks the Mormon community had become a thriving settlement of nearly two thousand.

Whether they were hopeful cotton planters from the South, Yankee farmers from New England, or religious refugees in the **Great Basin,** most people went west not as the stalwart individualists immortalized by western movies, but as part of a larger community. Beginning with early parties going to Ohio or Texas in the 1820s, most traveled in small-to-medium-size groups. Even those few who arrived alone seldom stayed that way. "Those of us who have no families of our own, reside with some of the families in the settlement," one young migrant observed. "We remain here notwithstanding the scarcity of provisions, to assist in protecting the settlement."

During the 1830s and 1840s, migrating parties became larger and more organized. Describing an Oregon-bound wagon train in the 1840s, one young woman reported that "Probably there were sixty-five or seventy, or possibly more than that, wagons in our train, and hundreds of loose cattle and horses." "We were not allowed to travel across the plains in any haphazard manner," she continued. "No family or individual was permitted to go off alone from the company." Among such groups on the **Oregon Trail,** life remained much as it had been at home. "Everybody was supposed to rise at daylight, and while the women were preparing breakfast, the men rounded

Joseph Smith Jr. Founder of the Church of Jesus Christ of Latter-day Saints, also known as the Mormon Church, who transcribed the Book of Mormon and led his congregation westward from New York to Illinois; he was later murdered by an anti-Mormon mob.

Brigham Young Mormon leader who took over in 1844 after Joseph Smith's death and guided the Mormons from Illinois to Utah, where they established a permanent home for the church

Great Salt Lake A shallow, salty lake in the Great Basin near which the Mormons established a permanent settlement in 1847.

Great Basin A desert region of the western United States including most of Nevada and parts of Utah, California, Idaho, Wyoming, and Oregon.

Oregon Trail The overland route from St. Louis to the Pacific Northwest followed by thousands of settlers in the 1840s.

Although modern movies and traditional folklore portray early Texas as a barely settled cowboy frontier, the region actually was attractive because vast areas in its eastern and central regions could support large-scale cotton, sugar, and other lucrative plantation businesses. This painting from 1845 captures the more genteel side of Texas life during the pioneer era. *Texas Memorial Museum, The University of Texas, Austin.*

up the cattle, took down the tents, yoked the oxen to the wagons and made everything ready for an immediate start after the morning meal was finished." Even social customs remained the same. "Life on the plains was a primitive edition of life in town or village," the same pioneer woman remarked. "We were expected to visit our neighbors when we paused for rest. If we did not, we were designated as 'high-toned' or 'stuck-up.' . . . Human nature is the same the world over. Bickerings and jealousies arose just as they would have done in a settlement of the same size." And so life went on during the six months it took to cross the more than 2,000 miles separating the settled part of the nation from the **Oregon Country.**

One other thing most pioneers had in common was that hard cash was always in short supply. Frontier farmers in every region of the West lived on a shoestring, barely making ends meet when conditions were good and falling into debt when weather or other hazards interrupted farming. Still, those who were lucky and exercised careful management were able to carve out excellent livings. Strongly centralized authority and a deeply felt sense of community helped the Mormons, for example, to overcome even bad luck and deficient skills. Many in other communities, however, had to sell out to satisfy creditors or saw their land repossessed for debts. Pulling up stakes again, they often moved to new lands exhausted of furs and opened to settlement by merchant-adventurers and Indian agents.

Many pioneers had no legal claim to their lands. People bankrupted by unscrupulous speculators or by their own misfortune or mismanagement often settled wherever they could find a spread that seemed unoccupied. Thousands of squatters living on unsold federal lands were a problem for the national government when the time came to sell off the public domain. Always with an eye to winning votes, western politicians frequently advocated "squatter rights," as Thomas Hart Benton had done in 1830 (see page 288). Western congressmen finally maneuvered the passage of a **preemption bill** in 1841, allowing squatters to settle on unsurveyed federal land. Of course, this right did not guarantee that they would have the money to buy the land once it came on the market, or that they would make profitable use of it in the meantime. Thus shoestring farming, perpetual debt, and an uncertain future continued to challenge frontier farmers.

Pioneer Life in the New Cotton Country

Migrants to cotton country in the Mississippi Valley and beyond brought a particular lifestyle with them.

Oregon Country The region to the north of Spanish California extending from the crest of the Rocky Mountains to the Pacific Coast.

preemption bill A temporary law that gave squatters the right to buy land they had settled on before it was offered for sale at public auction.

Though highly idealized, this painting of an emigrant wagon train settling down for the night on the Oregon Trail does capture many accurate details. Notice, for example, the division of labor: women are washing, cooking, and tending to small children while men are drawing water, herding animals, and preparing to hunt for food. Diaries kept by actual emigrants confirm this was the way life was on the trail. *The Corcoran Gallery of Art, Washington, D.C. Gift of Mr. & Mrs. Lansdell K. Christie.*

Often starting out as landless herders, migrating families carved out claims beyond the **frontier line** and survived on a mixture of raised and gathered food until they could put the land into agricultural production. The Indians who preceded them in the Mississippi Valley unintentionally simplified life for these families; the Indians had already cleared large expanses of land for agriculture. Removal of the Indians to the Far West and the continuing devastation of Indian populations by disease meant that southern frontiersmen could plant corn and cotton quickly and reap early profits with minimal labor.

Although some areas were cleared and extremely fertile, others were swampy, rocky, and unproductive. In these less desirable locales, settlers were allowed to survey their own claims. The result was odd-shaped farms, differences in the quality of land owned by neighboring farmers, and the re-creation of the southern class system in the new lands. Those fortunate enough to get profitable lands might become great planters; those not so fortunate had to settle for lesser prosperity and lower status.

During the pioneer phase of southern frontier life, all the members of migrating families devoted most of their time to the various tasks necessary to keep the family alive. Even their social and recreational lives tended to center on practical tasks. House building, planting, and harvesting were often done in cooperation with neighbors. Such occasions saw plenty of food and homemade whiskey consumed, and at day's end, music and dancing often lasted long into the night.

Women gathered together separately for large-scale projects such as group quilting. Another community event for southwestern settlers was the periodic religious revival, which brought people from miles around to revival meetings that might last for days (see pages 229–230). Here they could make new acquaintances, court sweethearts, and discuss the common failings in their souls and on their farms.

Life among Westering Yankees

For migrants to areas such as Michigan and Oregon, the overall frontier experience differed in many respects from that in the Mississippi Valley. In the Old Northwest, Indians had also cleared the land for planting; pioneers snatched up the Indians' deserted farms. Here however professional surveyors had already carved the land into neat rectangular lots. These surveys generally included provision for a township, where settlers quickly established villages similar to those left behind in New England, in which they re-created the social institutions they already knew and respected—first and foremost, law courts, churches, and schools.

Conditions in the Oregon Country resembled those farther east in most respects, but some significant dif-

frontier line　The outer limit of agricultural settlement bordering on areas still under Indian control or unoccupied.

Using Indian labor, Franciscan missionaries transformed the dry California coastal hill country into a blooming garden and built a long string of missions in which to celebrate their religion. This painting of Mission San Gabriel conveys the beauty and the awesome size of these mission establishments. *Courtesy of the Santa Barbara Mission Archive-Library.*

ferences did exist. Most important, the Indians in the Oregon Country had never practiced agriculture—their environment was so rich in fish, meat, and wild vegetables that farming was unnecessary—and they still occupied their traditional homelands and outnumbered whites significantly. Although both of these facts might have had a profound impact on life in Oregon, early pioneers were bothered by neither. Large open prairies flanking the Columbia, Willamette, and other rivers provided abundant fertile farmland. And the Indians helped rather than hindered the pioneers.

Like their southwestern counterparts, pioneers in both the Old and the Pacific Northwest cooperated in house building, annual planting and harvesting, and other big jobs, but a more sober air prevailed at these gatherings among the descendants of New England Puritans. Religious life was also more solemn. Religious revivals swept through Yankee settlements during the 1830s and 1840s, but the revival meetings tended to be held in churches at the center of communities rather than in outlying campgrounds. As a result, they were usually briefer and less emotional than their counterparts on the cotton frontier and strongly reinforced the Yankee notion of village solidarity.

The Hispanic Southwest

The physical and cultural environment in the Southwest differed greatly from that in the Pacific Northwest. One major reason for the difference was that Spain and then Mexico had controlled the region and had left a lasting cultural imprint.

Although they could assert a claim extending back to the mid-1500s, systematic Spanish exploration into most of the American Southwest did not begin until the eighteenth century (see page 34). In California, for example, Russian expansion into the Oregon region prompted the Spanish to begin moving northward; garrisons were established at San Diego and Monterey in 1769 and 1770. **Junípero Serra,** a Franciscan friar, accompanied this expedition and established a mission, San Diego de Alcalá, near the present city of San Diego. Eventually Serra and his successors established twenty-one missions extending from San Diego to the town of Sonoma, north of San Francisco.

The mission system provided a framework for Spanish settlement in California. Established in terrain that resembled the hills of Spain, the missions were soon surrounded by groves, vineyards, and lush farms. California Indians were harnessed for the labor needed to create this new landscape, but not willingly: the missionaries often forced them into the missions, where they became virtual slaves. The death rate from disease

Junípero Serra Spanish missionary who went to California in 1769; he and his successors established near the California coast a chain of missions that depended on Indian labor.

and harsh treatment among the mission Indians was terrible, but their labor turned California's coastal plain into a vast and productive garden.

The Franciscans continued to control the most fertile and valuable lands in California until after Mexico won independence from Spain. Between 1834 and 1840, however, the Mexican government seized the mission lands in California and sold them off to private citizens living in the region. An elite class of Spanish-speaking **Californios** snatched up the rich lands.

At first, the Californios welcomed outsiders as neighbors and trading partners. Ships from the United States called at California ports regularly, picking up cargoes of beef **tallow,** cow hides, and other commodities to be shipped around the world, and settlers who promised to open new lands and business opportunities were given generous grants and assistance. **John Sutter,** for example, received an outright grant of land extending from the Sierra foothills southwest to the Sacramento Valley, where in 1839 he established a colony called New Helvetia. A tribute to the cosmopolitanism in Northern California, people of many races and classes could be found strolling the lanes in New Helvetia and other settlements.

A similar pattern of interracial cooperation existed in other Spanish North American provinces. In 1821 trader William Becknell began selling and trading goods along the Santa Fe Trail from St. Louis to New Mexico. By 1824, the business had become so profitable that people from all over the frontier moved in to create a permanent Santa Fe trade. As had taken place in St. Louis, an elite class emerged in Santa Fe from the intermingled fortunes and intermarriages among Indian, European, and American populations, and a strong kinship system developed. Thus, based on kinship, the Hispanic leaders of New Mexico consistently worked across cultural lines, whether to fight off Texan aggression or eventually to lobby for **annexation** to the United States.

Intercultural cooperation also characterized the early history of Texas settlement. Spanish and then Mexican officials aided the empresarios, hoping that the aggressive Americans would form a frontier line between southern Plains Indians and prosperous silver-mining communities south of the **Rio Bravo.** Tensions rose, however, as population increased. Despite the best efforts of the Mexican government to encourage Hispanics to settle in Texas, fully four-fifths of the thirty-five hundred land titles perfected by the empresarios went to non-Hispanics.

In Texas, economic desperation combined with cultural insensitivity and misunderstanding to create the

sort of tensions that were rare in New Mexico. As a result of the relative lack of harmony and the enormous stretches of land that separated ethnic groups in Texas, both **Texians** and **Tejanos** tended to cling to their own ways.

The Mormon Community

Physical and cultural conditions in the Great Basin led to a completely different social and cultural order in that area. Utah is a high-desert plateau where water is scarce and survival depends on careful management. The tightly knit community of Mormons was perfectly suited to such an inhospitable place, and their social order responded well to the hostile environment.

Mormons followed a simple principle: "Land belongs to the Lord, and his Saints are to use so much as they can work profitably." The church measured off plots of various sizes, up to 40 acres, and assigned them to settlers on the basis of need. Thus a man with several wives, a large number of children, and enough wealth to hire help might receive a grant of 40 acres, but a man with one wife, few children, and little capital might receive only 10. The size of a land grant determined the extent to which the recipient was obligated to support community efforts. When the church ordered the construction of irrigation systems or other public works, a man who had been granted 40 acres had to provide four times the amount of labor as one who had been granted 10 acres. Like settlers elsewhere, the Mormons in Utah joined in community work parties, but cooperation among them was more rigidly controlled and formal. As on other frontiers, when the

Californios Spanish colonists in California in the eighteenth and nineteenth centuries.

tallow Hard fat obtained from the bodies of cattle and other animals and used to make candles and soap.

John Sutter Swiss immigrant who founded a colony in California; the discovery of gold on his property in the Coloma Valley, northeast of New Helvetia (Sacramento) in 1848 attracted hordes of miners who seized his land, leaving him financially ruined.

annexation The incorporation of a territory into an existing political unit such as a neighboring country.

Rio Bravo The Spanish and then Mexican name for the river that now forms the border between Texas and Mexico; the Rio Grande.

Texians Non-Hispanic settlers in Texas in the nineteenth century.

Tejanos Mexican settlers in Texas in the nineteenth century.

With two wives and several children to help share the burden of work, this Mormon settler was in a good position to do well, even in the harsh conditions that prevailed in the near-desert environment of Utah. Sensitive to disapproval from more traditional Christians, families like this tended to associate exclusively with other Mormons and pressured outsiders to leave as quickly as possible. *Denver Public Library, Western History Division.*

system worked it was because it was well suited to natural conditions.

Mormons had their own peculiar religious and social culture, and because of their bad experiences in Missouri and Illinois, they were unaccepting of strangers. The General Authorities of the church made every effort to keep Utah an exclusively Mormon society, welcoming all who would embrace the new religion and its practices but making it difficult for non-Mormons to stay in the region. The one exception was the American Indian population. Because Indians occupied a central place in Mormon sacred literature, the Mormons practiced an accepting and gentle Indian policy. Like other missionaries, Mormons insisted that Indians convert to their religion and lifestyle, but the Mormon hierarchy used its enormous power in Utah to prevent private violence against Indians whenever possible.

Tying the West to the Nation

Rapid expansion created an increased demand for reliable transportation and communications between the new regions in the West and the rest of the nation. An early first step in meeting this demand was building the so-called National Road, which between 1815 and 1820 snaked its way across the Cumberland Gap in the Appalachian Mountains and wound from the Atlantic shore to the Ohio River at Wheeling, Virginia. Then, in 1822, a political deal between northeastern congressmen and their western colleagues extended funding and further extended the road (see page 270).

By 1838 this state-of-the-art highway—with its evenly graded surface, gravel pavement, and stone bridges—had been pushed all the way to Vandalia, Illinois. Within a few more years, it reached St. Louis, the great jumping-off point for the Far West.

At the same time, a series of other roads were beginning to merge into a transportation network. The Natchez Trace (see page 271) also enjoyed federal patronage, as did the so-called Military Road connecting Nashville even more directly to New Orleans. The Nashville Road, in turn, connected Nashville to Knoxville, where a traveler could pick up the Great Valley Road to Lynchburg, Virginia, and from there the Valley Turnpike, which connected with the Cumberland Road. Eventually towns from Portland, Maine, to Saint Augustine, Florida, and from Natchez, Mississippi, to New Haven, Connecticut, were linked by intersecting highways (Map 11.2). Increasing numbers of people used these new roads to head west looking for new opportunities. Farmers, craftsmen, fur hunters, and others already settled in the West used them too, moving small loads of goods to the nearby towns and small cities that always sprang up along the unfolding transportation routes. But the new roads did little to advance large-scale commerce. Heavy and bulky products were too expensive to move: at a minimum, hauling a ton of freight along the nation's roads cost 15 cents a mile. At that rate, the cost of shipping a ton of oats from Buffalo to New York City amounted to twelve times the value of the cargo.

But the new roads also linked rural America to an ever-expanding network of waterways that made

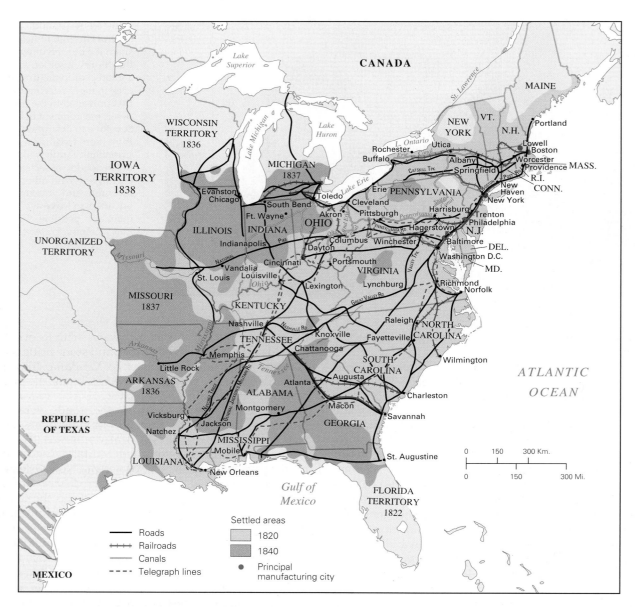

MAP 11.2 **Roads, Canals, Railways, and Telegraph Lines in 1850** A transportation and communications revolution took place between 1820 and 1850 as roads, canals, rails, and telegraph lines reached out to bind together the nation. The connections made by the lines of communications shown here ensured economic growth, but brought to light the vast differences between regional cultures.

relatively inexpensive long-distance hauling possible. Completed in 1825, the Erie Canal revolutionized shipping (see page 271): transporting a ton of oats from Buffalo to Albany fell from $100 to $15, and the transit time dropped from twenty days to just eight. All of New York State celebrated. Businessmen in New York City were particularly happy. During the early nineteenth century, the flood of goods from

America's interior made New York City the most important commercial center in the nation.

The spectacular success of the Erie Canal prompted businessmen, farmers, and politicians throughout the country to promote canal building. State governments offered exclusive charters to canal-building companies, giving them direct financial grants, guaranteeing their credit, and easing their way in every possible

Surprisingly enough, the first steam locomotive manufactured in the United States did not go into service in the rapidly modernizing Northeast but rather in the equally, though differently, modernizing South. The *Best Friend of Charleston* was commissioned by the Charleston and Hamburg Railroad to haul cotton and other bulky freight as well as passengers in South Carolina. *Courtesy of Norfolk Southern Corp.*

manner. The result was an explosion in canal building that lasted through the 1830s (see Map 11.2).

But this new mobility did not come cheaply. Canals cost as much as $20,000 to $30,000 a mile to build, and financing was always a problem. Hoping for large profits, entrepreneurs such as John Jacob Astor invested heavily in canal building. Before 1836, careful investors could make a 15 to 20 percent **return on capital** in canal building, but after that, most canal companies faced bankruptcy, as did the states that had helped finance them.

Steam power took canal building's impact on inland transportation a revolutionary step further. After Shreve's pioneer voyage in 1816, the cost of shipping a ton of goods down American rivers fell annually (see page 272). By 1840, the price had declined from an average of 1¼ cents a mile to less than half a cent, and the cost of upstream transport from over 10 cents a mile to less than a cent. In addition, steamboats could carry bulky and heavy objects that could not be hauled upstream for any price by any other means. The impact of steam technology on the economies of the South and West was staggering. The presence of dependable transportation on the Mississippi drew cotton cultivation farther into the nation's interior, western farmers flooded into the Ohio Valley, and fur trappers and traders pressed up the Missouri River.

Steam technology also had applications in areas without navigable rivers. Towns lacking water routes to the interior began losing revenue from inland trade to canal towns such as Albany and Philadelphia. Predictably, entrepreneurs in places like Baltimore looked for other ways to move cargo. In fact, demands from Baltimore merchants spurred Maryland to take the lead

in developing a new transportation technology: the steam railroad. In 1828 the state chartered the **Baltimore and Ohio Railroad** (B&O). The B&O soon demonstrated its potential when inventor Peter Cooper's steam locomotive *Tom Thumb* sped 13 miles along B&O track. Steam railroading, however, did not seem destined to succeed. In 1829, England's Liverpool and Manchester Railway drew attention and investment by pitting horse-drawn and steam-drawn trains against each other. The steam engines won easily. When Cooper tried the same stunt in the following year, however, the horse won. The B&O abandoned steam power, replacing it with coaches pulled along the rails by horses.

Despite the B&O failure, South Carolina chose to invest in steam technology and chartered a 136-mile rail line from Charleston to Hamburg. Here, the first full-size American-built locomotive, the *Best Friend of Charleston,* successfully pulled cars until the engine exploded, taking much of the train and many of its passengers with it. Rather than giving up on the idea of steam power, however, the Charleston and Hamburg Railroad had the engine rebuilt and began putting "buffer" cars filled with cotton bales between the engine and the other cars to protect passengers and cargoes from boiler explosions. Massachusetts followed

return on capital   The yield on money that has been invested in an enterprise or product.

Baltimore and Ohio Railroad   First steam railroad commissioned in the United States; it resorted to using horse-drawn cars after a stagecoach horse beat its pioneer locomotive in a race.

this practice as well, as it tried to compete with New York by building a railroad from Boston to Albany.

Although rail transport enjoyed some success during this early period, it could not rival water-based transportation systems. By 1850 individual companies had laid approximately 9,000 miles of track, but not in any coherent network. Rails were laid with little or no standardization of track size, and the distance between tracks varied from company to company. As a result, railcars with their loads could not be transferred from one company's line to another's. Other problems also plagued the fledgling industry. Boiler explosions, fires, and derailments were common because pressure regulators, spark arresters, and brakes were inadequate. And in state capitals, investors who hoped to profit from canals, roads, and steam shipping lobbied to prevent legislatures from supporting rail expansion.

Distance impaired not only American commerce but also the conduct of the republic itself. Since the nation's founding, American leaders had expressed the fear that the continent's sheer size would make true federal democracy impractical. Voting returns, economic data, and other information crucial to running a republic seemed to take an impossibly long time to circulate, and the problem promised to get worse as the nation grew. During the 1790s, for example, it took a week for news to travel from Virginia to New York City and three weeks for a letter to get from Cincinnati to the Atlantic coast. This difficulty led Thomas Jefferson and others to speculate that the continent would become a series of allied republics, each small enough to operate efficiently given the slow speed of communication. The transportation revolution, however, made quite a difference in how quickly news got around. After the Erie Canal opened, letters posted in Buffalo could reach New York City within six days and might get to New Orleans within two weeks.

As the nation expanded, and as economics and social life became more complicated, Americans felt growing pressure to keep up with news at home and in the nation's new territories. The revolution in transportation helped them do so by making the transport of printed matter faster and cheaper. At the same time, revolutions in printing technology and paper production significantly lowered the cost of printing and speeded up production. Organizations such as the American Bible Society and the American Tract Society joined newspaper and magazine publishers in producing a literal flood of printed material. In 1790 the 92 newspapers being published in America had a total **circulation** of around 4 million. By 1835 the number of periodicals had risen to 1,258, and circulation had surpassed 90 million.

The explosion in the volume and velocity of communications was enhanced by a true revolution in information technology that was in its starting phases. In the mid-1830s, both Samuel F. B. Morse in the United States and Charles Wheatstone and William Cooke in Great Britain began experimenting with the world's first form of electronic communication: the **electric telegraph.** Morse won the contest, perfecting his version in 1836. Simple in design, Morse's transmitter consisted of a key that closed an electrical circuit, thereby sending a pulse along a connected wire. Morse developed a code consisting of dots (short pulses) and dashes (longer pulses) that represented letters of the alphabet. With this device a skilled operator could quickly key out long messages and send them at nearly the speed of light. Over the next several years, Morse worked on improvements to extend the distance that the impulses would travel along the wires. Finally, in 1843, Congress agreed to finance an experimental telegraph line from Washington, D.C., to Baltimore. Morse sent his first message on the experimental line on May 24, 1844. His message, "What hath God wrought!" was a fitting opening line for the telecommunications revolution.

---

circulation The number of copies of a publication sold or distributed.

electric telegraph Device invented by Samuel F. B. Morse in 1836 that transmits coded messages along a wire over long distances; the first electronic communications device.

✔ **Individual Voices**

The Press "Remembers" Helen Jewett

① *Although it was generally known that young Dorcas was actually hired as a serving girl in Judge Weston's household, this story suggests that she was a guest or companion in the justice's home. Why would a news writer choose to "revise" the facts?*

② *How does the account of the seduction of the teenage Dorcas add to the story? Why might this version have had more appeal than the truth for popular audiences?*

③ *Aspasia was the mistress of Pericles, the foremost Athenian statesman of classical Greece. Despite a disreputable background, Aspasia used her intelligence and wit to charm the political elite of Athens in the fifth century BCE. Though charming, she frequently was the target of public attacks that painted her as a common harlot.*

④ *Whom does the writer want the audience to blame for Dorcas Doyen's descent into prostitution? Why?*

The United States in 1836 was rapidly becoming more modern. One measure of its emerging modernity, a feature with which we are all too familiar today, was the rise of a sensationalist press. The murder of Helen Jewett (really Dorcas Doyen) presented an irresistible opportunity for this new medium. Although a few responsible newspapers printed factually based stories about the victim's early life, sensationalist newspapers seeking larger sales and plumped-up reputations for being investigative published ever more exaggerated accounts of Jewett's life and death. The *New York Herald,* for example, continued to print romanticized stories about Jewett even after it became generally known that her early life was rather unremarkable and that the charming Miss Jewett was a fictional creation by an intelligent and inventive woman who was intent on shaping her life on her own terms. The following is taken from a story printed in the *Herald* on April 12, 1836.

> *Her private history is most remarkable—her character equally so. . . . In Augusta, Maine, lived a highly respectable gentleman, Judge Western [sic], by name. Some of the female members of his family pitying the bereaved condition of young Dorcas invited her to live at the Judge's house. At that time Dorcas was young, beautiful, innocent, modest, and ingenuous. Her good qualities and sprightly temper won the good feelings of the Judge's family. She became a chere-amie of his daughters— a companion and a playmate. . . .* **①**
>
> *After having continued at the Academy for some time, Dorcas, during the summer of 1829, went to spend the vacation at a distant relative's at Norridgewock, a town on the Kennebeck river, about 28 miles above Augusta. Dorcas was then sixteen years of age—and one of the most lovely, interesting, black eyed girls, that ever appeared in that place.*
>
> *In this town, in the course of visiting, she became acquainted with a young man, by the name of H—— Sp——y, a fine youth, elegant and educated, since said to be a Cashier in one of the banks of Augusta. After a short acquaintance with him, all was gone that constitutes the honor and ornament of the female character. . . .* **②**
>
> *She returned after a short season to Augusta. Her situation soon became known in the Judge's family. A quarrel ensued. She left her protector, after having in a moment of passion lost all the rules of virtue and morality.*
>
> *After having recovered from her first lapse from the path of virtue, she retreated to Portland, took the name of Maria B. Benson, and became a regular Aspasia* **③** *among the young men, lawyers, and merchants.* **④**

SUMMARY

Although seemingly the most old-fashioned region of the country, the South that emerged during the years leading up to 1840 was a profoundly different place from what it had been before the War of 1812. As an industrial revolution overturned the economies in Great Britain and the American Northeast, economic options for southerners also changed radically. Although they clothed their new society in romanticized medieval garb, they were creating an altogether new kind of economy and society. The efficient production of cotton by the newly reorganized South was an essential aspect of the emerging national market economy and a powerful force in the Great Transformation.

Change in the North was more obvious. As factories replaced craft shops and cities replaced towns, the entire fabric of northern society seemed to come unraveled. The new economy and new technology created wonderful new opportunities but also imposed serious constraints. A revamped social structure replaced the traditional order as unskilled and semiskilled workers, a new class of clerks, and the genteel elite carved out new lives. The new cities also developed a dark underside where the tawdry glamour that characterized Helen Jewett's life often led to grotesque death. As in the South, the outcome was a remarkable transformation in the lives of everyone in the region.

Meanwhile, the westward movement of Americans steadily gained momentum. Some successful entrepreneurs such as William Henry Ashley made enormous profits from their fur-trading empires. Land speculators and gold seekers, too, helped open areas to settlement. Such pioneers were usually followed by distinct waves of migrants who went west in search of land and opportunity. In Texas, Oregon, California, Utah, and elsewhere in the West, communities sprang up like weeds. Here they interacted—and often clashed—with one another, with those who had prior claims to the land, and with the land itself. As a result, a variety of cultures and economies developed in the expansive section of the country.

Tying the regions together was a new network of roads, waterways, and communications systems that accelerated the process of change. After 1840, it was possible to ship goods from any one section of the country to any other, and people in all sections were learning more about conditions in far distant parts of the growing country. Often this new information promised prosperity, but it also made more and more people aware of the enormity of the transformation taking place and the glaring differences between the nation's various regions. The twin outcomes would be greater integration in the national economy and increasing tension between mutually dependent participants in the new marketplace.

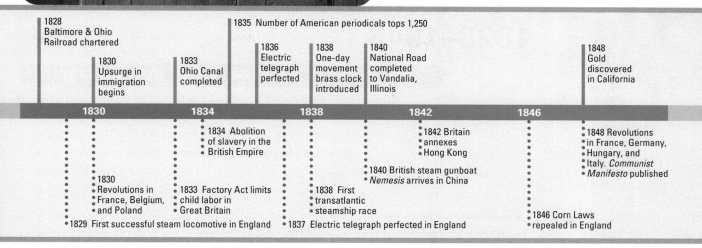

IN THE WIDER WORLD

1828
Baltimore & Ohio
Railroad chartered

1830
Upsurge in
immigration
begins

1833
Ohio Canal
completed

1835 Number of American periodicals tops 1,250

1836
Electric
telegraph
perfected

1838
One-day
movement
brass clock
introduced

1840
National Road
completed
to Vandalia,
Illinois

1848
Gold
discovered
in California

| 1830 | 1834 | 1838 | 1842 | 1846 | |

1834 Abolition
of slavery in the
British Empire

1842 Britain
annexes
Hong Kong

1848 Revolutions
in France, Germany,
Hungary, and
Italy. *Communist
Manifesto* published

1840 British steam gunboat
Nemesis arrives in China

1830
Revolutions in
France, Belgium,
and Poland

1833 Factory Act limits
child labor in
Great Britain

1838 First
transatlantic
steamship race

1829 First successful steam locomotive in England

1837 Electric telegraph perfected in England

1846 Corn Laws
repealed in England

In the United States

The Dawn of Modernization

1821   William Becknell opens Santa Fe Trail to American traders

1822   John H. Hall perfects interchangeable parts for gun manufacturing

1828   Baltimore and Ohio Railroad commissioned

1830   Steam locomotive *Tom Thumb* beaten in race by stagecoach horse

       Church of Latter Day Saints (Mormons) founded in New York

1830–1840   Ten-year immigration figure for United States exceeds 500,000

1833   Ohio Canal completed

1834   Mexican government begins seizing California missions

1835   Number of U.S. periodicals exceeds 1,250, with combined circulation of 90 million

1836   Samuel F. B. Morse invents electric telegraph

       Bronson Alcott's *Conversations with Children on the Gospels*

       Murder of Helen Jewett

1838   National Road completed to Vandalia, Illinois

       First mass-produced brass clock

1839   John Sutter founds New Helvetia

       Mormons build Nauvoo, Illinois

1841   Congress passes preemption bill

1844   Murder of Joseph Smith

1847   Mormons arrive in Utah

1848   Gold discovered in California

Responses to the Great Transformation, 1828–1848

A NOTE FROM THE AUTHOR

Generations of popular writers and motivational speakers have claimed that the Chinese word for "crisis" consists of the conjoined symbols for "danger" and "opportunity." Despite complaints by linguists that this is too simple an analogy, the conjunction of danger and opportunity in any crisis seems apparent. A generation ago, historian Theodore K. Rabb noted the onset of modern Western civilization in what he termed a crisis in Early-Modern Europe. In the same way, the rise of modern America can be traced to a crisis—or a sequence of crises—that took place during the first half of the nineteenth century. Traditionally historians have been torn as to whether this was primarily an era of great progress or one of disastrous conflict. Actually it was both; like the simplified representation of a Chinese "crisis," this was an era fraught with both danger and opportunity. Americans reacted strongly to both potentials. And like the previous generation—the founders of the nation—these Americans were fully conscious of the fact that they were living at a momentous moment. Their actions tell us a lot about how they perceived their crisis-ridden world and how those actions helped to shape ours.

Lydia Sigourney

Giving voice to the Romantic sentimentalism that was setting the tone for middle-class culture in early nineteenth-century America, women writers like Lydia Sigourney became virtual overnight celebrities, selling thousands of books to newly emerging urban consumers. *Watkinson Library, Trinity College, Hartford, Connecticut.*

✔ Individual Choices

Nothing in her family background or upbringing would have marked Lydia Howard Huntley's potential as a leading literary light. Her father, a revolutionary war veteran, was just a gardener and handyman on the estate of a Connecticut matron. But his employer recognized a budding talent in the young girl and encouraged her. Under the older woman's patronage, Lydia began writing poetry and essays at a young age, and when the time came, her sponsor's patrician family saw to it that the girl received the solid education thought fitting for young ladies in New England. Like many young women of modest means in her generation, Lydia followed up her education by becoming a teacher and then, with the help of her benefactors, started an academy for young women in Hartford. Her educational career culminated with the publication in 1815 of collected teaching materials under the title *Moral Pieces, in Prose and Verse.*

Shortly after reaching this pinnacle, she met and married a Hartford area widower, Charles Sigourney. Now a married woman, Lydia gave up her career in teaching and writing to devote herself to service as a wife. However, her desire to write continued. For years she published poems and short prose pieces anonymously, much to the chagrin of her conservative husband. However, his declining fortunes and the failing health of her parents led Lydia to rebel against conventions and begin selling her work and trading on her name. Between 1833 and 1835, she sold nine books under her own name and a number of articles and other pieces to well-known periodicals. In the process, she became the first American woman to earn an entirely independent living as a commercial writer.

Though many contemporary and modern critics have dismissed Sigourney's writing—Edgar Allan Poe called her work shallow and **mawkish**—and certainly would not classify her with Longfellow and other of her male contemporaries, her work may have had a greater influence in her own time than theirs. Focusing on themes that were popular among

mawkish Mushy, exaggerated, and insincere sentimentality.

women of the elite and emerging middling classes, her words and sentiments helped to form a literary basis for female culture during the middle decades of the nineteenth century. Awareness of a literature designed especially for them also encouraged many young women to pursue and attain literacy. In part because of writers like Lydia Sigourney, women's literacy grew at a revolutionary pace, from about 50 percent of that of white males in 1780 to over 90 percent by 1850. As Lydia Sigourney chose to write and take credit for her writing, a generation of American women chose to read, and American society and culture was forever changed in the process.

INTRODUCTION

Lydia Sigourney reflected many of the forces that were shaping America in the years before midcentury. These were years of both growing anxiety and growing hopefulness. Anxiety was rising over industrialization and urbanization that was sweeping across the American North and by the expansion of cotton capitalism in the American South. She shared with born again Christians, transcendentalists, socialists, and other communitarians a belief in human perfectibility that drove them all into a frenzy of work and experimentation. In northern cities, on southern plantations, and at western revival meetings, members of all social classes were crafting cultural expressions designed to give meaning to their lives and lend shape to a society that seemed to be losing all direction. At the same time, ambitious politicians were re-creating the art of politics in line with new economic and cultural imperatives. A new, modern, and much more complicated America clearly was in the making.

And looming over it all was the promise and the challenge of the American West. For many, the West offered a destination for those who sought wealth or free expression. For others, the region provided an arena in which to contest economic and political issues facing the nation at large. Most agreed that the nation's destiny lay in the largely unexplored region, but exactly how this destiny was to unfold remained murky and divided loyalties at every level of society.

Reactions to Changing Conditions

→ *How did developments in American arts and letters reflect the spirit of change during the Jacksonian era?*

→ *What were the cultural consequences of their actions?*

→ *To what extent were American cultural expressions influenced by international forces?*

As industrialization and urbanization mushroomed in the Northeast, cotton cultivation and its peculiar cultural and labor systems expanded across the South, and hundreds of communities grew up in the West, diversity in American life expanded as well. At the same time, however, increasing economic interdependence between regions and revolutionary transportation and communications systems pulled the geographically expansive nation closer together. These opposing forces not only helped to define the social and political tendencies throughout the country, but also the trends that would shape a peculiar American culture.

Romanticism and Genteel Culture

Underlying the new mood in American culture was an artistic and philosophical attitude that swept across the Atlantic and found a fertile new home in North America. **Romanticism,** the European rebellion against Enlightenment reason (see page 100), stressed the heart over the mind, the wild over the controlled, the mystical over the rational. The United States, with its millions of acres of wilderness, teeming populations of wild animals, and colorful frontier myths, was the perfect setting for romanticism to flower. Many of the era's leading intellectuals emphasized the positive aspects of life in the United States, celebrating it in

> **romanticism** Artistic and intellectual movement characterized by interest in nature, emphasis on emotion and imagination over rationality, and rebellion against social conventions.

forms of religious, literary, and artistic expression. In the process, they launched new forms of thought and presentation that won broad recognition among the genteel and middle classes.

This new influence had its earliest impact in the religious realm. Reeling under the shock of social change that was affecting every aspect of life, many young people sought a religious anchor to bring themselves some stability. Many, especially in the rising cities in the Northeast, found a voice in New Englander **Ralph Waldo Emerson.**

Emerson was pastor of the prestigious Second Unitarian Church in Boston when tragedy struck: his young wife, Ellen Louisa, died in 1831. Emerson experienced a religious crisis and, looking for new inspiration, traveled to Europe. There he met the famous Romantic writers William Wordsworth and Thomas Carlyle, who influenced him to seek truth in nature and spirit rather than in rationality and order. Emerson combined this Romantic influence with his already strong Unitarian leaning, creating a new philosophical creed called **transcendentalism.** Recovered from his grief, he returned to the United States to begin a new career as an essayist and lecturer, spreading the transcendentalist message.

"Historical Christianity has fallen into the error that corrupts all attempts to communicate religion," Emerson told the students at the Harvard Divinity School in 1838. "Men have come to speak of revelation as somewhat long ago given and done, as if God were dead." But for Emerson, God was "everywhere active, in each ray of the star, in each wavelet of the pool." Only through direct contact with the **transcendent** power in the universe could men and women know the truth.

Although Emerson emphasized **nonconformity** and dissent in his writings, his ideas were in tune with the cultural and economic currents of his day. In celebrating the individual, Emerson validated the surging individualism of Jacksonian America. In addition, because each person had to find his or her own path to knowledge, Emerson could extol many of the disturbing aspects of modernizing America as potentially liberating forces. Rather than condemning the grasping for wealth that many said characterized Jacksonian America, Emerson stated that money represented the "prose of life" and was, "in its effects and laws, as beautiful as roses."

Emerson not only set the tone for American philosophical inquiry but also suggested a bold new direction for American literature. In 1837 he issued a declaration of literary independence from European models in an address at Harvard University entitled "The American Scholar." Young American writers responded enthusiastically. During the twenty years following this speech, Henry David Thoreau, Walt Whitman, Henry Wadsworth Longfellow, and other writers and poets elaborated the transcendentalist gospel, emphasizing the uniqueness of the individual and the role of literature as a vehicle for self-discovery. "I celebrate myself, and sing myself," Whitman wrote. They also carried the Romantic message, celebrating the primitive and the common. Longfellow mythologized Hiawatha (Hienwatha; see pages 3–4) and sang the praise of the village blacksmith. In "I Hear America Singing," Whitman conveyed the poetry present in the everyday speech of mechanics, carpenters, and other common folk.

Perhaps the most radical of the transcendentalists was Emerson's good friend and frequent houseguest **Henry David Thoreau.** Emerson and his other followers made the case for self-reliance, but Thoreau embodied it, camping on the shore of Walden Pond near Concord, Massachusetts, where he did his best to live independent of the rapidly modernizing market economy. "I went to the woods because I wished to live deliberately," Thoreau wrote, "and not, when I came to die, discover that I had not lived."

Like Thoreau, a number of women were also seeking meaning through their writing. Sarah Moore Grimké published a well-received essay on women's rights called *Letters on the Equality of the Sexes and the Condition of Women* in 1838. Margaret Fuller picked up on the same theme in her *Woman in the Nineteenth Century* (1845), after demonstrating her own equality by editing the highly influential transcendentalist magazine *The Dial* as well as serving as chief literary critic for the *New York Tribune.*

Ralph Waldo Emerson Philosopher, writer, and poet whose essays and poems made him a central figure in the transcendentalist movement and an important figure in the development of literary expression in the United States.

transcendentalism A philosophical and literary movement asserting the existence of God within human beings and in nature, and the belief that intuition is the highest source of knowledge.

transcendent Lying beyond the normal range of experience.

nonconformity Refusal to accept or conform to the beliefs and practices of the majority.

Henry David Thoreau Writer and naturalist and friend of Ralph Waldo Emerson; his best-known work is *Walden* (1854).

This 1827 painting by Thomas Cole, capturing a scene from James Fenimore Cooper's *Last of the Mohicans*, illustrates the romantic mood current during the early nineteenth century. In line with artistic romanticism, nature dwarfs all else. Even a large Indian camp seems insignificant in size, lost in an exaggerated image of the mountains in the Hudson River region of New York. *"Last of the Mohicans" by Thomas Cole. Fenimore Art Museum, Cooperstown, New York.*

But the most popular women writers of the day were those who were most successful at communicating the sentimentalized role for the new genteel woman. Lydia Sigourney was one of the first American women to carve out an independent living as a writer. Catharine Beecher was another woman writer who enjoyed enormous success for her practical advice guides aimed at making women more effective homemakers. The novels of women writers E. D. E. N. Southworth and Susan Warner were among the most popular books published in the first half of the nineteenth century.

Other authors joined Sigourney, Southworth, and Warner in pushing American literature in Romantic directions. James Fenimore Cooper and Nathaniel Hawthorne each helped to popularize American themes and scenes in their writing. Even before Emerson's "American Scholar," Cooper had launched a new sort of American novel and American hero. In *The Pioneers* (1823), Cooper introduced Natty Bumppo, also called Hawkeye, a frontiersman whose honesty, independent-mindedness, and skill as a marksman represented the rough-hewn virtues so beloved by Romantics and popularly associated with the American frontier. Eventually, Cooper wrote five novels featuring the plucky Bumppo, and they all sold well.

Nathaniel Hawthorne explored a different but equally American literary theme: the tension between good and evil. In *Twice-Told Tales* (1837), Hawthorne presented readers with a collection of moral **allegories** stressing the evils of pride, selfishness, and secret guilt among puritanical New Englanders. He brought these themes to fruition in his novel *The Scarlet Letter* (1850), in which adulteress Hester Prynne overcomes shame to gain redemption while her secret lover, Puritan minister Arthur Dimmesdale, is destroyed by his hidden sins.

George Bancroft did for American history what novelists like Cooper did for American literature. A prominent Jacksonian, Bancroft set out to capture in writing the unique nature of the American experience. His history of the United States from the first settlement of the continent through the American Revolution eventually filled ten volumes, published between 1834 and 1874. From Bancroft's perspective, Jacksonian democracy was the perfect form for human government and was the product of the complex history of the American nation. Focusing on strong leaders who carried out God's design by bringing liberty into the world, Bancroft made clear that the middle-class

allegory   A story in which characters and events stand for abstract ideas and suggest a deep, symbolic meaning.

IT MATTERS TODAY

THE SPREAD OF MASS LITERACY

During the colonial and early national eras, literacy beyond basics like signing your name was reserved to a small number of elite people in American society. Books were expensive, and newspapers were few in number; there was little opportunity for most people to read and little incentive for them to do so. During the early nineteenth century, however, both opportunity and incentive for using, as well as availability for acquiring literacy expanded greatly. During this era the spread of public education, creation of literary and self-improvement societies, and mass publication of books and magazines caused an upsurge in both the availability and demand for literacy. Leaders like Horace Mann saw in universal literacy a device that would ensure continuation of the American democratic republic, and writers like Lydia Sigourney saw in it a burgeoning marketplace for making personal fortunes. For their part, young men and women saw in literacy an opportunity to break away from traditional roles in a traditional political and economic system to forge new lives in a new society. From this era onward, Americans took widespread literacy among all classes for granted as part of our national life.

- What developments arose during the early nineteenth century that helped to produce mass literacy in the United States?

- How would American society today be different if only a wealthy elite minority could read? How would your life be different in such a society?

qualities of individualism, self-sufficiency, and a passionate love of liberty were the essence of the American experience and the American genius. Bancroft's history became the definitive work of its kind, influencing generations of American students and scholars in their interpretations of the nation's past.

The drive to celebrate American scenes and the young nation's uniqueness also influenced the visual arts during this period. **Neoclassicism** had dominated the art scene during the late eighteenth century and first decades of the nineteenth. Influenced by Enlightenment rationalism, neoclassical artists brought to their painting and sculpture the simple, logical lines

found in Greek and Roman art. They often used classical imagery in their portrayals of contemporary figures and events. Horatio Greenough's statue of George Washington, for example, presented the nation's first president wrapped in a toga, looking like a Roman statesman.

After 1825, however, classical scenes were gradually being replaced by American ones. Englishman Thomas Cole came to the United States in 1818 hoping to find a romantic paradise. Disappointed by the neoclassical art scene in Philadelphia, Cole began traveling into the American interior. In the Hudson River valley Cole found the paradise he was seeking, and he began painting romantically exaggerated renderings of these locales. The refreshing naturalness and Americanness of Cole's landscapes attracted a large following, and other artists took up the style. This group of landscapists is known as the **Hudson River school,** after the area where most of its members painted.

Another movement in American art that reflected the temper of the time is exemplified by the paintings of George Caleb Bingham. Bingham was born in Virginia and educated for a time in Pennsylvania before he went west to Missouri. There he painted realistic pictures of common people engaged in everyday activities. The flatboat men, marketplace-dwellers, and electioneering politicians in Bingham's paintings were artistic testimony to the emerging democratic style of America in the Jacksonian period (see illustrations on pages 283 and 288).

Culture Among Workers and Slaves

Most genteel people in the antebellum era would have denied that working people, whether the wage-earning immigrants in northern cities or slaves in the South, had a "culture." But each of these groups crafted viable cultures that suited their living and working conditions and were distinct from the genteel culture of their owners or supervisors.

neoclassicism   A revival in architecture and art in the eighteenth and nineteenth centuries inspired by Greek and Roman models and characterized by order, symmetry, and simplicity of style.

Hudson River school   The first native school of landscape painting in the United States (1825–1875); it attracted artists rebelling against the neoclassical tradition.

Slave artisans often fashioned beautiful and functional items that incorporated both European and African design motifs, creating a unique material culture in the American South. A potter, now known only as Dave, crafted enormous storage jars that he inscribed with original poetry. Slave women often used needlework as a means of self-expression, as exemplified by this Star of Bethlehem quilt, crafted by a slave in Texas known only as Aunt Peggy. *Storage jar: All rights reserved, McKissick Museum, The University of South Carolina; quilt: Cincinnati Art Museum. Gift of Mrs. Cletus T. Palmer.*

Wretched living conditions and dispiriting poverty encouraged working-class people in northern cities to choose social and cultural outlets that were very different from those of upper- and middle-class Americans. Offering temporary relief from unpleasant conditions, drinking was the social distraction of choice among working people. Whiskey and gin were cheap and available during the 1820s and 1830s as western farmers used the new roads and canals to ship distilled spirits to urban markets. In the 1830s, consumers could purchase a gallon of whiskey for 25 cents.

Even activities that did not center on drinking tended to involve it. While genteel and middle-class people remained in their private homes reading Sigourney or Hawthorne, working people attended popular theaters cheering entertainments designed to appeal to their less polished tastes. **Minstrel shows** featured fast-paced music and raucous comedy. Plays, such as Benjamin Baker's *A Glance at New York in 1848*, presented caricatures of working-class "Bowery B'hoys" and "G'hals" and of the well-off Broadway "pumpkins" they poked

fun at. To put the audience in the proper mood, theater owners sold cheap drinks in the lobby or in basement pubs. Alcohol was also sold at sporting events that drew large working-class audiences—bare-knuckle boxing contests, for instance, where the fighting was seldom confined to the boxing ring.

Stinging from their low status in the urbanizing and industrializing society, angry about living in hovels, and freed from inhibitions by hours of drinking, otherwise rational workingmen often pummeled one another to let off steam. And in working-class neighborhoods, where police forces were small, fistfights often turned into brawls and then into riots pitting Protestants against Catholics, immigrants against the native-born, and whites against blacks. Notable

minstrel show A variety show in which white actors made up as blacks presented jokes, songs, dances, and comic skits.

ethnic riots shook New York, Philadelphia, and Boston during the late 1820s and 1830s. In 1834, for example, rumors began circulating in Boston that innocent girls were being held captive and tortured in a Catholic convent in nearby Charlestown. A Protestant mob stormed the building, leaving it a heap of smoldering ashes. A year later, in New York's notoriously overcrowded and lawless Five Points District, roving gangs of native-born Protestant and immigrant Irish Catholic men battled in the streets. The ethnic tension evident in these and other riots was the direct result of declining economic power and terrible living conditions—and worker desperation. Native-born journeymen blamed immigrants for lowered wages and loss of status. Immigrants simmered with hatred at being treated like dirt by their native-born coworkers.

Working-class women experienced the same dull but dangerous working conditions and dismal living circumstances as working-class men, but their lives were even harder. Single women were particularly bad off. They were paid significantly less than men but had to pay as much and sometimes more for living quarters, food, and clothing. Marriage could reduce a woman's personal expenses—but at a cost. While men congregated in the barbershop or candy store drinking and socializing during their leisure hours, married women were stuck in tiny apartments caring for children and doing household chores.

Like their northern counterparts, slaves fashioned for themselves a culture that helped them to survive and to maintain their humanity under dehumanizing conditions. The degree to which African practices endured in America is remarkable, for slaves seldom came to southern plantations directly from Africa. What evolved was a truly unique African American culture.

Traces of African heritage were visible in slaves' clothing, entertainment, and folkways. Often the plain garments that masters provided were upgraded with colorful headscarves and other decorations similar to ornaments worn in Africa. Hairstyles often resembled those characteristic of African tribes. Music, dancing, and other forms of public entertainment and celebration also showed strong African roots. Musical instruments were copies of traditional ones, modified only by the use of New World materials. And stories that were told around the stoves at night were a New World adaptation of African **trickster tales.** Other links to Africa abounded. Healers among the slaves used African ceremonies, Christian rituals, and both imported and native herbs to effect cures. Taken together, these survivals and adaptations of African traditions provided a strong base underlying a solid African American culture.

Anti-Catholic and anti-immigrant feelings often caused rioting in American cities during the 1830s and 1840s. In 1834, street violence escalated into a full-fledged riot in Massachusetts, leading to the burning of a Catholic convent in Charlestown, a Boston suburb. This engraving, which adorned the covers of a number of pamphlets that purported to tell the true lurid story of the events surrounding the fire, shows the convent ablaze as fire companies try in vain to smother the flames. Though the most notorious event of this kind that occurred during this era, this riot was anything but exceptional. *The Nun of St. Ursula: Burning of the Convent by Harry Hazel.*

Abiding family ties helped to make this cultural continuity possible. Slave families endured despite kinship ties made fragile by their highly precarious life. Children could be taken away from their parents, husbands separated from wives at the whim of masters. And anyone might be sold at any time. Families that remained intact, however, remained stable. When families did suffer separation, the **extended family** of grandparents and other relatives offered emotional support and helped maintain some sense of continuity. Another African legacy, the concept of fictive kinship (see page 15) also contributed to family stability by turning the whole community of slaves into a vast network of aunts and uncles.

Within families, the separation of work along age and gender lines followed traditional patterns. Slave women, when not laboring at the assigned tasks of

trickster tales   Stories that feature as a central character a clever figure who uses his wits and instincts to adapt to changing times; a survivor, the trickster is used by traditional societies, including African cultures, to teach important cultural lessons.

extended family   A family group consisting of various close relatives as well as the parents and children.

plantation work, generally performed domestic duties and tended children, while the men hunted, fished, did carpentry, and performed other "manly" tasks. Children were likely to help out by tending family gardens and doing other light work until they were old enough to join their parents in the fields or learn skilled trades.

Slaves' religion, like family structure, was another means for preserving unique African American traits. White churches virtually ignored the religious needs of slaves before the mid-eighteenth century. During the Great Awakening (see pages 101–102), however, many white evangelicals turned their attention to the spiritual life of slaves. "Your Negroes may be ignorant and stupid as to divine Things," evangelical Samuel Davies told slaveowners, "not for Want of Capacity, but for Want of Instruction; not through their Perverseness, but through your Negligence." In the face of slaveowners' negligence, evangelical Presbyterians, Baptists, and Methodists took it upon themselves to carry the Christian message to slaves.

Though the designation Baptist or Methodist would suggest that the Christianity practiced by slaves resembled the religion practiced by southern whites, it differed in significant ways. Slave preachers untrained in white theology often equated Christian and African religious figures, creating unique African American religious symbols. Ceremonies too combined African practices such as group dancing with Christian prayer. The merging of African musical forms with Christian lyrics gave rise to a new form of Christian music: the **spiritual.** Masters often encouraged such worship, thinking that the Christian emphasis on obedience and meekness would make slaves more productive and more peaceful servants. Some, however, discouraged religion among their slaves, fearing that large congregations of slaves might be moved to rebellion. Thus some religious slaves had to meet in secret to practice their own particular form of Christianity.

Radical Attempts to Regain Community

To many of all classes, society seemed to be spinning out of control as modernization rearranged basic lifestyles during the antebellum period. Some religious groups and social thinkers tried to ward off the excesses of Jacksonian individualism by forming **utopian** communities that experimented with various living arrangements and ideological commitments. They hoped to strike a new balance between self-sufficiency and community support.

A wealthy Welsh industrialist, Robert Owen, began one of the earliest experiments along these lines. In 1825 he purchased a tract of land on the Wabash River in Indiana called **New Harmony.** Believing that the solution to poverty in modern society was to collect the unemployed into self-contained and self-supporting villages, Owen opened a textile factory in which ownership was held communally by the workers and decisions were made by group consensus. Even though the community instituted innovations like an eight-hour workday, cultural activities for workers, and the nation's first school offering equal education to boys and girls, New Harmony did not succeed. Owen and his son, Robert Dale Owen, were outspoken critics of organized religion and joined their close associate **Frances (Fanny) Wright** in advocating radical causes. These leanings made the Owenites unpopular with more traditional Americans, and when their mill experienced economic hardship in 1827, New Harmony collapsed.

A more famous experiment, **Brook Farm,** had its origin in the transcendentalist movement but later flirted with **socialistic** ideas like those practiced at New Harmony. The brainchild of George Ripley, Brook Farm was designed to "prepare a society of liberal, intelligent and cultivated persons, whose relations with each other would permit a more wholesome and simple life than can be led amidst the pressure of our

spiritual A religious folk song originated by African Americans, often expressing a longing for deliverance from the constraints and hardships of their lives.

utopian Idealistic reform sentiment based on the belief that a perfect society can be created on Earth and that a particular group or leader has the knowledge to actually create such a society.

New Harmony Utopian community that Robert Owen established in Indiana in 1825; economic problems and discord among members led to its failure two years later.

Frances (Fanny) Wright Infamous nineteenth-century woman who advocated what at the time were considered radical causes, including racial equality, equality for women, birth control, and open sexuality.

Brook Farm An experimental farm based on cooperative living; established in 1841, it first attracted transcendentalists and then serious farmers before fire destroyed it in 1845.

socialist Practicing socialism, the public ownership of manufacturing, farming, and other forms of production so that they benefit society rather than produce individual or corporate profits.

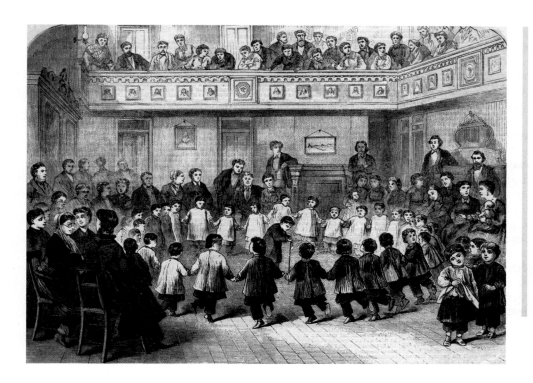

As the nation underwent wrenching economic and social changes, many sought radical solutions for the rising anxieties they were experiencing. Religious, socialist, and a variety of other experimental communities dotted the landscape. In one, the Oneida Community, everything was done collectively, including marriage: all men and women were considered to be married to each other. Children who were born in the commune were raised in common by all of the adults and, as this early nineteenth-century etching shows, were often at the center of community life. © Bettmann/CORBIS.

competitive institutions." To carry out this enterprise Ripley set up a joint-stock company, selling the initial twenty-four shares of stock for $500 each. Most of the stockholders were transcendentalist celebrities such as Nathaniel Hawthorne and Ralph Waldo Emerson. Rather than living and working at the site as Ripley had hoped they would, most just dropped in from time to time. Disappointed, in 1844 Ripley adopted a new constitution based on the socialist ideas of Frenchman Charles Fourier. **Fourierism** emphasized community self-sufficiency, the equal sharing of earnings among members of the community, and the periodic redistribution of tasks and status to prevent boredom and elitism. With this new disciplined ideology in place, Brook Farm began to appeal to serious artisans and farmers, but a disastrous fire in 1845 cut the experiment short. Other Fourierist communities were also founded during this period—nearly a hundred such organizations sprang up from Massachusetts to Michigan and southward into Texas—and although none achieved Brook Farm's notoriety, all shared the same unsuccessful fate.

Some communal experiments were grounded in various religious beliefs. The **Oneida Community,** established in central New York in 1848, for example, reflected the notions of its founder, John Humphrey Noyes. Though educated in theology at Andover and Yale, Noyes could find no church willing to ordain

him because of his strange belief that his followers could escape sin through faith in God, communal living, and group marriage. Unlike Brook Farm and New Harmony, the Oneida Community was very successful financially, establishing thriving logging, farming, and manufacturing businesses. It was finally dissolved as the result of local pressures directed at the "free love" practiced by its members.

Economically successful communes were also operated by the **Shakers,** an offshoot of the Quakers. Free love never disturbed their settlements; Shakers practiced absolute celibacy. Founded in Britain in 1770 and

---

Fourierism   Social system advanced by Frenchman Charles Fourier, who argued that people were capable of living in perfect harmony under the right conditions, which included communal life and republican government.

Oneida Community   A religious community established in central New York in 1848; its members shared property, practiced group marriage, and reared children under communal care.

Shakers   A mid-eighteenth-century offshoot of the Quakers, founded in England by Mother Ann Lee; Shakers engaged in spirited worship, including dancing and rhythmic shaking, hence their name, and practiced communal living and strict celibacy.

then transported to America in 1774, the sect grew slowly at first, but in the excitement of the early nineteenth century, it expanded at a more vigorous rate. By 1826 eighteen Shaker communities had been planted in eight states. Throughout the Jacksonian era and after, the Shakers established communal farms and grew to a population of nearly six thousand. The Shaker communities succeeded by pursuing farming activities and the manufacture and sale of furniture and handcrafts admired for their design and workmanship. But like the Oneida Community, the Shakers' ideas about marriage and family stirred up controversy. In a number of cases, converts deserted husbands or wives in order to join the organization, often bringing their children with them. This led to several highly publicized lawsuits. Controversy also raged over the practice in some areas of turning orphaned children or other public **wards** over to the Shakers. Like most such experiments, the Shaker movement went into decline after 1860, though vestiges of it remain operative today.

A Second Great Awakening

While some were drawn to transcendentalism and a handful chose to follow radical communitarian leaders, others sought solace within existing, mainstream denominations. Beginning in the 1790s both theologians and popular preachers sought to create a new Protestant creed that would maintain the notion of Christian community in an atmosphere of increasing individualism and competition.

Mirroring tendencies in the political and economic realms, Protestant thinking during the opening decades of the nineteenth century emphasized the role of the individual. Preachers such as Jonathan Edwards and George Whitefield had moved in this direction during the Great Awakening of the 1740s, but many Protestant theologians continued to share the conviction that salvation was a gift from God that individuals could do nothing to earn (see page 25). Timothy Dwight, Jonathan Edwards's grandson, took the first step toward liberalizing this position in the 1790s, but it fell to his students at Yale College, especially Nathaniel Taylor, to create a new theology that was entirely consistent with the prevailing secular creed of individualism. According to this new doctrine, God offers salvation to all, but it is the individual's responsibility to seek it. Thus the individual has "free will" to choose or not choose salvation. Taylor's ideas struck a responsive chord in a restless and expanding America. Hundreds of ordained ministers, licensed preachers, and **lay exhorters** carried the message of individual empowerment to an anxious populace.

Unlike Calvinist Puritanism, which characterized women as the weaker sex, the new evangelicalism stressed women's spiritual equality with—and even spiritual superiority to—men. Not surprisingly, young women generally were the first to respond to the new message: during the 1820s and 1830s, women often outnumbered men by two to one in new evangelical congregations. The most highly effective preachers of the day took advantage of this appeal, turning women into agents spreading the word to their husbands, brothers, and children.

Charles Grandison Finney was one of the most effective among the new generation of preachers. A former schoolteacher and lawyer, Finney experienced a soul-shattering religious conversion in 1821. Declaring that "the Lord Jesus Christ" had retained him "to plead his cause," Finney performed on the pulpit as a spirited attorney might argue a case in court. Arguing for souls was like moving a judge to make the right decision in a lawsuit—the result of effective persuasion. Seating those most likely to be converted on a special "anxious bench," Finney focused on them as a lawyer might a jury. The result was likely to be dramatic. Many of the targeted people fainted, experienced bodily spasms, or cried out in hysteria. Such dramatic presentations and results brought Finney enormous publicity, which he and an army of imitators used to gain access to communities all over the West and Northeast. The result was a nearly continuous season of religious revival. The **Second Great Awakening** spread from rural community to rural community like a wildfire until, in the late 1830s, Finney carried the fire into Boston and New York City.

The new revivals led to the breakdown of traditional church organizations and the creation of various Christian denominations. **Evangelical sects** such as the Presbyterians, Baptists, and Methodists split into groups who supported the new theology and those who clung to more traditional notions. Church splits also occurred for reasons that now seem petty.

ward A child who is legally put into the care of someone other than a parent.

lay exhorter A church member who preaches but is not an ordained minister.

Second Great Awakening An upsurge in religious fervor that began around 1800 and was characterized by revival meetings.

evangelical sects Protestant groups that emphasized the sole authority of the Bible and the necessity of actively striving to convert others.

Revival meetings were remarkable affairs. Often lasting several days, they drew huge crowds who might listen to as many as forty preachers in around-the-clock sessions. The impact on the audience frequently was dramatic: one attendee at a New York revival commented that there were "loud ejaculations of prayer . . . some struck with terror . . . others, trembling weeping and crying out . . . fainting and swooning away." *Collection of the New-York Historical Society, USA/The Bridgeman Art Library.*

One Baptist congregation, for example, split over the hypothetical question of whether it would be a sin to lie to marauding Indians in order to protect hidden family members. Those who said lying to protect one's family was no sin formed a separate congregation of so-called Lying Baptists. Those who said lying was sinful under any circumstances gathered as Truth-Telling Baptists.

In the face of such fragmentation, all denominations voiced concern that state support of any one church would give that denomination an artificial advantage in the continuing competition for souls. In fact, those most fervent in their Christian beliefs joined deists and other Enlightenment-influenced thinkers in arguing steadfastly for the continued and even more stringent separation of church and state. This, in turn, added to the spirit of competition as individual congregations vied for voluntary contributions to keep their churches alive.

Even though religious conversion had become an individual matter and competition for tithes a genuine concern, revivalists did not ignore the notion of community. "I know this is all algebra to those who have never felt it," Finney said. "But to those who have experienced the agony of wrestling, prevailing prayer, for the conversion of a soul, you may depend on it, that soul . . . appears as dear as a child is to the mother who brought it forth with pain." This intimate connection forged bonds of mutual responsibility, giving a generation of isolated individuals something to rally around, a common starting point for joint action.

The Middle Class and Moral Reform

The missionary activism that accompanied the Second Great Awakening dovetailed with a reforming inclination among genteel and middle-class Americans; witnessing the squalor and violence in working-class districts and the deteriorating condition for slaves led many to push for reforms. The **Christian benevolence** movement gave rise to hundreds of voluntary societies ranging from maternal associations designed to improve child rearing to political lobby groups aiming at outlawing alcohol, Sunday mail delivery, and other perceived evils. Such activism drew reformers together in common causes and led to deep friendships and a shared sense of commitment—antidotes to the alienation and loneliness common in the competitive world of the early nineteenth century.

The new theology reinforced the reforming impulse by emphasizing that even the most depraved might be saved if proper means were applied. This idea had immediate application in the realm of crime and punishment. Reformers characterized criminals not as evil but as lost and in need of divine guidance. In Auburn, New York, an experimental prison system put prisoners to work during the day, condemned them to absolute silence during mealtimes, and locked them away in solitary confinement at night. Reformers believed that this combination of hard work, discipline, and solitude would put criminals on the path to productive lives and spiritual renewal.

Mental illness underwent a similar change in definition. Rather than viewing the mentally ill as hopeless cases doomed by an innate spiritual flaw, reformers now spoke of them as lost souls in need of help. **Dorothea Dix**, a young, compassionate, and reform-minded teacher, advocated publicly funded asylums for the insane. She told the Massachusetts state legislature in 1843: "I tell what I have seen. . . . Insane persons confined within the Commonwealth, in cages, closets, cellars, stalls, pens! Chained, naked, beaten with rods, and lashed into obedience!" For the balance of the century, Dix toured the country pleading the cause of the mentally ill, succeeding in winning both private and public support for mental health systems.

A hundred other targets for reform joined prisons and asylums on the agenda of middle-class Christian activists. Embracing the Puritan tradition of strict observance of the Sabbath, newly awakened Christians insisted on stopping Sunday mail delivery and demanded that canals be closed on Sundays. Some joined Bible and tract societies that distributed Christian literature; others founded Sunday schools or operated domestic missions devoted to winning either the **irreligious** or the wrongly religious (as Roman Catholics were perceived to be) to the new covenant of the Second Great Awakening.

Many white-collar reformers acted in earnest and were genuinely interested in forging a new social welfare system. A number of their programs, however, seemed more like social control because they tried to force people to conform to a middle-class standard of behavior. For example, reformers believed that immigrants should willingly discard their traditional customs and beliefs and act like Americans. Immigrants who chose to cling to familiar ways were suspected of disloyalty. This aspect of benevolent reform was particularly prominent in two important movements: public education and **temperance.**

Before the War of 1812, most Americans believed that education was the family's or the church's responsibility and did not require children to attend school. But as the complexity of economic, political, and cultural life increased during the opening decades of the nineteenth century, **Horace Mann** and other champions of education pushed states to introduce formal public schooling. Like his contemporary Charles G. Finney, Mann was trained as a lawyer, but unlike Finney, he believed that ignorance, not sin, lay at the heart of the nation's problems. When Massachusetts made Mann the superintendent of a state-wide board of education, he immediately extended the school year to a minimum of six months and gradually replaced classical

Christian benevolence   A tenet in some Christian theology teaching that the essence of God is self-sacrificing love and that the ultimate duty for Christians is to perform acts of kindness with no expectation of reward in return.

Dorothea Dix   Philanthropist, reformer, and educator who was a pioneer in the movement for specialized treatment of the mentally ill.

irreligious   Hostile or indifferent to religion.

temperance   Moderation or abstinence in the consumption of alcoholic drinks.

Horace Mann   Educator who called for publicly funded education for all children and was head of the first public board of education in the United States.

Prison reformers insisted that idleness was symptomatic of the criminal personality and insisted that a combination of exhausting physical exercise, solitary confinement, and silence was necessary to affect rehabilitation. At the experimental prison in Auburn, New York, officials erected a huge step-wheel, chaining prisoners and forcing them to climb for extended periods of time, seeking to instill discipline. © *Collection of the New-York Historical Society.*

learning with such practical courses as arithmetic, practical geography, and physical science.

But Mann and other reformers were interested in more than "knowledge"; they were equally concerned that new immigrants and the children of the urban poor be trained in Protestant values and middle-class habits. Thus the books used in public schools emphasized virtues such as promptness, perseverance, discipline, and obedience to authority. In Philadelphia and other cities where Roman Catholic immigrants concentrated, Catholic parents resisted the cultural pressure applied on their children by Protestant-dominated public school boards. They supported the establishment of **parochial schools**—a development that aggravated the strain between native-born Protestants and immigrant Catholics.

Another source of such tension was a Protestant crusade against alcohol. Drinking alcohol had always been common in America and before the early nineteenth century was not broadly perceived as a significant social problem. But during the 1820s and 1830s, three factors contributed to a new, more ominous perception. One was the increasing visibility of drinking and its consequence, drunkenness, as populations became more concentrated in manufacturing and trading cities. In Rochester, New York, for example, a town that went through the throes of modernization in the late 1820s, the number of drinking establishments multiplied rapidly as the population grew. Anyone with

a few cents could get a glass of whiskey at grocery stores, either of two candy stores, barbershops, or even private homes—all within a few steps of wherever a person might be. By 1829 this proliferation of public drinking led the county grand jury to conclude that strong drink was "the cause of almost all of the crime and almost all of the misery that flesh is heir to."

The second factor was alcohol's economic impact in a new and more complex world of work. Factory owners and managers recognized that workers who drank often and heavily, on or off the job, threatened the quantity and quality of production. Owners and supervisors alike rallied around the temperance movement as a way of policing the undisciplined behavior of their employees, both in and out of the factory. By promoting temperance, these reformers believed they could clean up the worst aspects of city life and turn the raucous lower classes into clean-living, self-controlled, peaceful workers, increasing their productivity and business profits.

The third factor was a social and religious one. Like most of the reform movements, the temperance movement began in churches touched by the Second Great

parochial school A school supported by a church parish; in the United States, the term usually refers to a Catholic school.

Awakening. Drunkenness earned special condemnation from reawakened Protestants, who believed that people were responsible not only for their sins but also for their own salvation. A person whose reason was besotted by alcohol simply could not rise to the demand. Christian reformers, therefore, believed that temperance was necessary not only to preserve the nation but also to win people's souls.

The institution of slavery also became a hot topic among the nation's reborn Christians. Although some people had always had doubts about the morality of slavery, little organized opposition to it appeared before the American Revolution. By the end of the Revolution, only Georgia and South Carolina continued to allow the importation of slaves, while Massachusetts specifically prohibited slavery altogether and Pennsylvania had begun to phase it out gradually. Even the plantation states showed increasing flexibility in dealing with slavery, as some elite southerners began to realize the unprofitability, though generally not the immorality, of the institution. After Virginia authorized owners to free their slaves in 1782, Delaware and Maryland soon did likewise. By the mid-1780s, most states, including those in the South, had active antislavery societies. In 1807, when Congress voted to outlaw permanently the importation of slaves in the following year, little was said in defense of slavery as an institution.

Public feeling about slavery during these years is reflected in the rise of the **American Colonization Society,** founded in 1817. This society was rooted in economic pragmatism, humanitarian concern for slaves' well-being, and a belief that blacks were not equal to whites. Such ideas prompted the organization to propose that if slave owners emancipated their slaves, or if funds could be raised to purchase their freedom, the freed slaves should immediately be shipped to Africa. Others noted that because many slaves had embraced Christianity, they might be agents in the extension of enthusiastic religious conversion. Theologian Samuel Hopkins, who believed slavery to be a sin, pointed out that God had allowed it "so that blacks could embrace the gospel in the New World and then bear the glad tidings back to Africa."

Most preachers active in the Second Great Awakening supported the idea of colonization, but a few individuals pressed for more radical reforms. The most vocal leader among the antislavery forces during the early nineteenth century was **William Lloyd Garrison.** In 1831 he founded the nation's first prominent abolitionist newspaper, *The Liberator.* In it he advocated immediate emancipation for African Americans, with no compensation for slaveholders. In the following year,

Not all African Americans supported the idea of transporting free-born and liberated slaves to Africa, but Paul Cuffe believed that the opportunity should be encouraged. The son of a former slave and an American Indian woman, Cuffe became a sailor. He eventually purchased his own ship and then a fleet of ships, becoming a very successful Boston-area merchant and whaler. He supported many efforts to promote the welfare of African Americans, even supplying money and ships to transport freed slaves who wished to leave the United States to live in the former slave colony of Liberia in Africa. This portrait of a "Black Sailor" is thought to be the mature Paul Cuffe. *Christie's Images, Inc.*

Garrison founded the New England Anti-Slavery Society and then, in 1833, branched out to found the national American Anti-Slavery Society.

At first, Garrison stood alone. Some Christian reformers joined his cause, but the majority held back. In eastern cities, workers fearful for their jobs lived in dread of either enslaved or free blacks flooding in, lowering wages, and destroying job security. In western states such as Indiana and Illinois, farmers feared that competition could arise from a slaveholding aristoc-

American Colonization Society   Organization founded in 1817 to end slavery gradually by assisting individual slave owners to liberate their slaves and then transporting them to Africa.

William Lloyd Garrison   Abolitionist leader who founded and published *The Liberator,* an antislavery newspaper.

racy. In both regions, white supremacists argued that the extension of slavery beyond the Mississippi River and north of the **Mason-Dixon Line** would eventually lead to blacks mixing with the white population, a possibility they found extremely distasteful. Thus most whites detested the notion of immediate emancipation, and radical **abolitionists** at this early date were almost universally ignored or, worse, attacked when they denounced slavery. Throughout the 1830s, riots often accompanied abolitionist rallies, and angry mobs stormed stages and pulpits to silence abolitionist speakers. Still, support for the movement gradually grew. In 1836 petitions flooded into Congress demanding an end to the slave trade in Washington, D.C. Not ready to engage in an action quite so controversial, Congress passed a **gag rule** that automatically **tabled** any petition to Congress that addressed the abolition of slavery. The rule remained in effect for nearly a decade.

Despite this official denial by the national Congress, a neglect shared by many state assemblies, not all governments remained closed to the discussion of slavery. In these state battles, a new group often led the fight against slavery: women.

Having assumed the burden of eliminating sin from the world back in the 1830s (see pages 315–316), many evangelical women became active in the antislavery cause. Moved by their activism, in 1840 Garrison proposed that a woman be elected to the executive committee of the American Anti-Slavery Society. And later that year women were members of Garrison's delegation to the first World Anti-Slavery Convention in London, but British antislavery advocates considered the presence of women inappropriate and refused to seat them.

One prominent female abolitionist, Angelina Grimké, gave voice to her contemporaries' frustration at such treatment: "Are we aliens, because we are women? Are we bereft of citizenship because we are mothers, wives and daughters of a mighty people? Have women no country—no interests staked in public weal—no liabilities in the common peril—no partnership in a nation's guilt and shame?" In that same year, her sister Sarah went further, writing a powerful indictment against the treatment of women in America and a call for equality. In *Letters on the Equality of the Sexes and the Condition of Woman,* Sarah proclaimed, "The page of history teems with woman's wrongs . . . and it is wet with woman's tears." Women must, she said, "arise in all the majesty of moral power . . . and plant themselves, side by side, on the platform of human rights, with man, to whom they were designed to be companions, equals and helpers in every good word and work."

Though they were often in the majority in the various reform movements that arose during the 1830s and 1840s, women were consistently denied leadership roles and forbidden to express their views in public. In 1848, a number of women led by reformers Lucretia Mott and Elizabeth Cady Stanton (pictured here) brought attention to their unequal status by holding a women's rights convention in Seneca Falls, New York. This marked the beginning of a self-conscious movement designed to win full equality for women in the United States; an objective for which women continue to struggle today. © *Bettmann/CORBIS.*

Mason-Dixon Line   The boundary between Pennsylvania and Maryland; it marked the northern division between free and slave states before the Civil War.

abolitionist   An individual who supported national legislation outlawing slavery, either gradually or immediately, with or without compensation to slave owners.

gag rule   A rule that limits or prevents debate on an issue.

table   Action taken by a legislative body (Congress, for example) to postpone debate on an issue until a positive vote to remove the topic from the table is taken.

Like Sarah Grimké, many other women backed away from male-dominated causes and began advancing their own cause. In 1848 two women who had been excluded from the World Anti-Slavery Convention, **Lucretia Mott** and **Elizabeth Cady Stanton,** called concerned women to a convention at Seneca Falls, New York, to discuss their common problems. At Seneca Falls, they presented a Declaration of Sentiments that cited "the history of repeated injuries and usurpations on the part of man toward woman, having in direct object the establishment of an absolute tyranny over her." The convention adopted eleven resolutions relating to equality under the law, rights to control property, and other prominent gender issues. A twelfth resolution, calling for the right to vote, failed to receive unanimous endorsement.

Free and Slave Labor Protests

Like the predominantly white and middle-class women who were founding female protest movements in America, some northern workers and southern slaves began to perceive their miseries not as the product of sin but of their exploitation by others. In view of their grim working and living conditions, it is not surprising that some manufacturing workers and slave laborers protested their situations and embraced increasingly active strategies for dealing with them.

The first organized labor strike in America took place in 1806, when a group of journeyman shoemakers stopped work to protest the hiring of unskilled workers to perform some tasks that higher-paid journeymen and apprentices had been doing. The strike failed when a New York court declared the shoemakers' actions illegal, but in the years to come many other journeymen's groups would try the same tactic. In large part they were reacting to the mechanization that threatened their jobs and their social position. Industrialization robbed them of their status as independent contractors, forcing many to become wage laborers, and they bemoaned their loss of power in having to accept set hours, conditions, and wages for the work they performed.

Instead of attacking or even criticizing industrialization, however, journeymen simply asked for what they believed was their fair piece of the pie: decent wages and working conditions and some role in decision making. Throughout the industrializing cities of the Northeast and the smaller manufacturing centers of the West, journeymen banded together in **trade unions:** assemblies of skilled workers grouped by specific occupation. During the 1830s, trade unions from neighboring towns merged with one another to form the

beginnings of a national trade union movement. In this way, house carpenters, shoemakers, handloom weavers, printers, and comb makers established national unions through which they attempted to enforce uniform wage standards in their industries. In 1834 journeymen's organizations from a number of industries joined to form the **National Trades' Union,** the first labor organization in the nation's history to represent many different crafts.

Not surprisingly, factory owners, bankers, and others who had a vested interest in keeping labor cheap used every device available to prevent unions from gaining the upper hand. Employers countered the national trade unions by forming associations to resist union activity and used the courts to keep organized labor from disrupting business. Despite such efforts, a number of strikes affected American industries during the 1830s. In 1834 and again in 1836, women working in the textile mills in Lowell, Massachusetts, closed down production in the face of wage reductions and rising boarding house rates. Such demonstrations of power by workers frightened manufacturers, and gradually over the next two decades, employers replaced native-born women in the factories with immigrants, who were less liable to organize successfully and, more important, less likely to win approval from sympathetic judges or consumers.

Still, workers won some small victories in the battle to organize. A significant breakthrough finally came in 1842 when the Massachusetts Supreme Court decided in the case of *Commonwealth v. Hunt* that Boston's journeymen boot makers were within their rights to organize "in such manner as best to subserve their own interests" and to call strikes. By that time, however, economic changes had so undermined labor's ability to withstand the rigors of strikes and court cases that legal protection became somewhat meaningless.

Not all labor protests were as peaceful as the shoemakers' strike. In 1828, for example, immigrant weav-

---

Lucretia Mott Quaker minister who founded the Philadelphia Female Anti-Slavery Society (1833) and co-organized the Seneca Falls Women's Rights Convention in 1848.

Elizabeth Cady Stanton Pioneering woman suffrage leader, co-organizer of the first Women's Rights Convention, held in Seneca Falls, New York, in 1848.

trade union A labor organization whose members work in a specific trade or craft.

National Trades' Union The first national association of trade unions in the United States; it was formed in 1834.

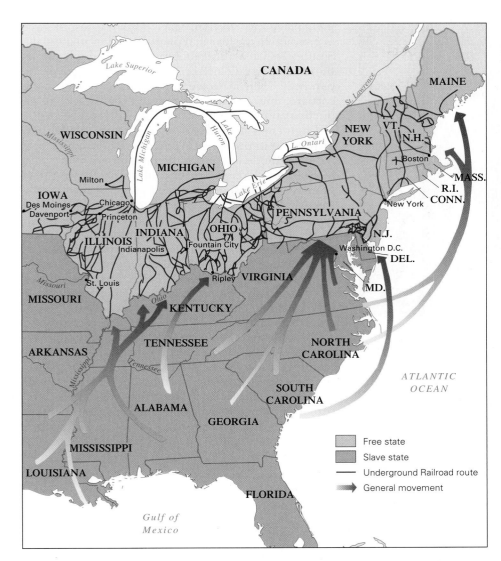

MAP 12.1 **Escaping from Slavery** Running away was one of the most prominent forms of slave resistance during the antebellum period. Success often depended on help from African Americans who had already gained their freedom and from sympathetic whites. Beginning in the 1820s an informal and secret network called the Underground Railroad provided escape routes for slaves who were daring enough to risk all for freedom. The routes shown here are based on documentary evidence, but the network's secrecy makes it impossible to know if they are drawn entirely accurately.

that is, Brother—Rabbit, a classic trickster figure who uses deceit to get what he wants. In one particularly revealing tale, Br'er Rabbit is caught by Br'er Fox, who threatens Rabbit with all sorts of horrible tortures. Rabbit begs Br'er Fox to do anything but throw him into the nearby briar patch. Seizing on Rabbit's apparent fear, Fox unties Br'er Rabbit and pitches him deep into the middle of the briar patch, expecting to see the rabbit struggle and die amid the thorns. Br'er Rabbit, however, scampers away through the briars, calling back over his shoulder that he was born and bred in a briar patch and laughing at Br'er Fox's gullibility. Such stories taught slaves how to deal cleverly with powerful adversaries.

Not all slave resistance was passive. Perhaps the most common form of active resistance was running away (see Map 12.1). The number of slaves who escaped may never be known, though some estimate that an average of about a thousand made their way to freedom each year. But running away was always a

ers protested the pitiful wages paid by Alexander Knox, New York City's leading textile employer. Storming Knox's home to demand higher pay, the weavers invaded and vandalized his house and beat Knox's son and a cordon of police guards. The rioters then marched to the garret and basement homes of weavers who had refused to join the protest and destroyed their looms.

Unlike workers in the North, who at least had some legal protections and civil rights, slaves had nothing but their own wits to protect them against a society that classed them as disposable personal property. Slaves were skilled at the use of **passive resistance**. The importance of passive resistance was evident in the folk tales and songs that circulated among slaves. Perhaps the best-known example is the stories of Br'er—

passive resistance Resistance by nonviolent methods.

No pictures of famed slave revolt leader Nat Turner are known to exist, but this nineteenth-century painting illustrates how one artist imagined the appearance of Turner and his fellow conspirators. White southerners lived in terror of scenes such as this and passed severe laws designed to prevent African Americans from ever having such meetings. *The Granger Collection, New York.*

dangerous gamble. One former slave recalled, "No man who has never been placed in such a situation can comprehend the thousand obstacles thrown in the way of the flying slave. Every white man's hand is raised against him—the patrollers are watching for him—the hounds are ready to follow on his track."

The most frightening form of slave resistance was open and armed revolt. Despite slaveholders' best efforts, slaves planned an unknown number of rebellions during the antebellum period, and many of them were actually carried out. The most serious and violent of these uprisings was the work of a black preacher, Nat Turner. After years of planning and organization, in 1831 Turner led a force of about seventy slaves in a predawn raid against the slaveholding households in Southampton County, Virginia. It took four days for white forces to stop the assault. During that time, the slaves slaughtered and mutilated fifty-five white men, women, and children. Angry, terrified whites finally captured and executed Turner and sixteen of his followers.

In the wake of Nat Turner's Rebellion, fear of slave revolts reached paranoid levels in the South, especially in areas where slaves greatly outnumbered whites. After reading about and seeing a play depict-

ing a slave insurrection, Mary Boykin Chesnut gave expression to the fear that plagued whites in the slave South: "What a thrill of terror ran through me as those yellow and black brutes came jumping over the parapets! Their faces were like so many of the same sort at home. . . . How long would they resist the seductive and irresistible call: 'Rise, kill, and be free!'"

Frightened and often outnumbered, whites felt justified in imposing stringent restrictions and using harsh methods to enforce them. Southern courts and legislatures clapped stricter controls on the freedoms granted to slaves and to free blacks. In most areas, free African Americans were denied the right to own guns, buy liquor, hold public assemblies, testify in court, and vote. Slaves were forbidden to own any private property, to attend unsupervised worship services, and to learn reading and writing. Also, codes that prevented slaves from being unsupervised in towns virtually eliminated slaves as independent urban craftsmen after 1840. In many areas of the South, white citizens formed local **vigilance committees,** bands of armed men who rode through the countryside to overawe slaves and dissuade them from attempting to escape or rebel. Local authorities pressed court clerks, ship captains, and other officials to limit the freedom of blacks. White critics of slavery—who had been numerous, vocal, and well respected before the birth of King Cotton—were harassed, prosecuted, and sometimes beaten into silence.

The Whig Alternative to Jacksonian Democracy

→ *What did Jackson's opponents hope to accomplish when they built their coalition to oppose the Democrats?*

→ *Did the coalition accomplish their purposes? Why or why not?*

The same fundamental structural changes that led to such social and cultural transformations had an enormous impact on politics as well. Although Andrew Jackson was quite possibly the most popular president since George Washington, not all Americans agreed with his philosophy, policies, or political style. As the Bank War illustrates (see pages 286–287), men like Henry Clay and Daniel Webster, who inherited the

vigilance committees Groups of armed private citizens who use the threat of mob violence to enforce their own interpretation of the law.

crumbling structure of Jefferson's Republican Party, continually opposed Jackson in and out of Congress but seemed unable to overcome sectional differences and culture wars enough to challenge Jackson's enormous national power. Gradually, however, anger over Jackson's policies and anxiety about change forged cooperation among the disenchanted, who coalesced into a new national party.

The End of the Old Party Structure

The last full year of Jackson's first term in office, 1832, was a landmark year in the nation's political history. In the course of that single year, the Seminoles declared war on the United States, Jackson declared war on the Second Bank, South Carolina declared war on the binding power of the Constitution, and the Cherokees waged a continuing war in the courts to hold on to their lands. The presidential election that year reflected the air of political crisis.

Henry Clay had started the Bank War for the purpose of creating a political cause to rally Jackson's opponents. The problem was that Jackson's enemies were deeply divided among themselves. Clay opposed Jackson because the president refused to support the American System (see page 286) and used every tool at his disposal to attack Clay's economic policies. Southern politicians like Calhoun, however, feared and hated Clay's nationalistic policies as much as they did Jackson's assertions of federal power. And political outsiders like the Antimasons distrusted all political organizations. These divisions were underscored in the 1832 election.

The Antimasons (see pages 282–283) kicked off the anti-Jackson campaign in September 1831 when they held the nation's first nominating convention in Baltimore. Thurlow Weed's skillful political manipulation had pulled in a wide range of people who were disgusted with what Jefferson had called "political party tricks," and the convention drew a broad constituency. Using all his charm and influence, Weed cajoled the convention into nominating William Wirt, a respected lawyer from Maryland, as its presidential candidate.

Weed and Wirt fully expected that when the Republicans met in convention later in the year, they would rubber-stamp the Antimasonic nomination and present a united front against Jackson. But the Republicans, fearful of the Antimasons' odd combination of **machine politics** and antiparty paranoia, nominated Clay as their standard-bearer. The Republicans then issued the country's first formal **party platform,** a ringing document supporting Clay's economic ideas and attacking Jackson's use of the **spoils system** (see page 285).

Even having two anti-Jackson parties in the running did not satisfy some. Distrustful of the Antimasons and put off by Clay's nationalist philosophy, southerners in both parties refused to support any of the candidates. They finally backed nullification (see pages 292–293) advocate John Floyd of Virginia.

Lack of unity spelled disaster for Jackson's opponents. Wirt and Floyd received votes that might have gone to Clay. But even if Clay had gotten those votes, Jackson's popularity and the political machinery that he and Van Buren controlled would have given the victory to Jackson. The president was reelected with a total of 219 electoral votes to Clay's 49, Wirt's 7, and Floyd's 11. Jackson's party lost five seats in the Senate but gained six in the House of Representatives. Despite unsettling changes in the land and continuing political chaos, the people still wanted the hero of New Orleans as their leader.

The New Political Coalition

If one lesson emerged clearly from the election of 1832, it was that Jackson's opponents needed to pull together if they expected to challenge the growing power of "King Andrew." Imitating political organizations in Great Britain, Clay and his associates began calling Jackson supporters Tories—supporters of the king—and calling themselves Whigs. The antimonarchical label stuck, and the new party formed in 1834 was called the **Whig Party.**

The Whigs eventually absorbed all the major factions that opposed Jackson. At the heart of the party were Clay supporters: advocates of strong government and the American System in economics. The nullifiers in the South, however, quickly came around when Clay and Calhoun found themselves on the same side in defeating Jackson's appointment of Van Buren as

machine politics   The aggressive use of influence, favors, and tradeoffs by a political organization, or "machine," to mobilize support among its followers.

party platform   A formal statement of the principles, policies, and promises on which a political party bases its appeal to the public.

spoils system   System associated with American politics in which a political party, after winning an election, gives government jobs to its voters as a reward for working toward victory.

Whig Party   Political party that came into being in 1834 as an anti-Jackson coalition and that charged "King Andrew" with executive tyranny.

BORN TO COMMAND.

OF VETO MEMORY.

HAD I BEEN CONSULTED.

KING ANDREW THE FIRST.

Calling themselves Whigs after the English political party that opposed royal authority, Henry Clay, John C. Calhoun, and Daniel Webster joined forces to oppose what they characterized as Andrew Jackson's kingly use of power. This lithograph from 1834 depicting Jackson in royal dress stepping on the Constitution expresses their view quite vividly. *New-York Historical Society.*

American minister to England. This successful campaign, combined with Calhoun's growing awareness that Jackson was perhaps more dangerous to his constituents' interests than was Clay, led the southerner and his associates back into Clay's camp. The Antimasons also joined the Whig coalition. Disgusted by Jackson's use of patronage and back-alley politics—not to mention the fact that the president was a Mason—they overcame their distrust of Clay's party philosophy. A final major group to rally to the Whigs was the collection of Christian reformers whose campaigns to eliminate alcohol, violations of the Sabbath, and dozens of other perceived evils had become increasingly political during the opening years of the 1830s. Evangelicals disapproved of Jackson's personal lifestyle, his views on slavery, his Indian policy, and his refusal to involve government in their moral causes. The orderly and sober society that Clay and the Whigs envisioned appealed to such people.

The congressional elections in 1834 provided the first test for the new coalition. In this first electoral contest, the Whigs won nearly 40 percent of the seats in the House of Representatives and more than 48 percent in the Senate. Clearly cooperation was paying off.

Van Buren in the White House

Jackson had seemed to be a tower of strength when he was first elected to the presidency in 1828, but by the end of his second term, he was aging and ill. Nearly 70 years old and plagued by various ailments, Old Hickory decided to follow Washington's example and not run for a third term. Instead, Jackson used all the power and patronage at his command to ensure that Martin Van Buren, his most consistent loyalist, would win the presidential nomination at the Democratic Party convention.

If Jackson personified the popular charisma behind Democratic Party success, Van Buren personified its political machinery. A skilled organizer, his ability at creating unlikely political alliances had earned him the nickname "the Little Magician." Throughout Jackson's first term, Van Buren had headed up the Kitchen Cabinet (see page 286) and increasingly became Jackson's chief political henchman. In 1832 Jackson had repaid his loyalty by making him vice president, with the intention of launching him into the presidency.

Meanwhile, Clay and his Whig associates were hatching a plot to deny the election to the Democrats. Instead of holding a convention and thrashing out a platform, the Whigs let each region's party organization nominate its own candidates. Whig leaders, especially the experienced political manipulator Thurlow Weed, hoped a large number of candidates would confuse voters and throw the election into the House of Representatives, where skillful political management and Van Buren's unpopularity might unseat the Democrats. As a result, four **favorite sons** ran on the Whig ticket. Daniel Webster of Massachusetts represented the Northeast. Hugh Lawson White, a Tennessean and former Jackson supporter, ran for the Southwest. South Carolina nullifier W. P. Mangum represented the South. William Henry Harrison, former governor of Indiana Territory and victor at the Battle of Tippecanoe in 1811, was tapped to represent the Northwest.

Weed underestimated the Democrats' hold on the minds of the voters. Van Buren captured 765,483 pop-

favorite son   A candidate nominated for office by delegates from his or her own region or state.

ular votes—more than Jackson had won in the previous election—but his performance in the Electoral College was significantly weaker than Jackson's had been. Van Buren squeaked by with a winning margin of less than 1 percent, but it was a victory, and the presidential election did not go to the House of Representatives. House Democrats lost thirty-seven seats to Whigs. In the Senate, however, Democrats increased their majority to more than 62 percent. Even with that slight edge, Van Buren could expect trouble getting Democratic policies through Congress. This handicap was worsened by a total collapse in the economy just weeks after he took office.

The **Panic of 1837** was a direct outcome of the Bank War and Jackson's money policies, but it was Van Buren who would take the blame. The crisis had begun with Nicholas Biddle's manipulation of credit and interest rates in an effort to discredit Jackson and have the Second Bank rechartered in spite of the president's veto (see page 287). Jackson had added to the problem by removing paper money and credit from the economy in an effort to win support from hard-money advocates. Arguing that he wanted to end "the monopoly of the public lands in the hands of speculators and capitalists," Jackson had issued the **Specie Circular** on August 15, 1836. From that day forward payment for public land had to be made in specie.

The contraction in credit and currency had the same impact in 1836 as it had in 1819: the national economy collapsed. By May 1837, New York banks were no longer accepting any paper currency, and soon all banks had adopted the policy of accepting specie only. Unable to pay back or collect loans, buy raw materials, or conduct any other sort of commerce, hundreds of businesses, plantations, farms, factories, canals, and other enterprises spiraled into bankruptcy by the end of the year. More than a third of the population was thrown out of work, and people who were fortunate enough to keep their jobs found their pay reduced by as much as 50 percent. Fledgling industries and labor organizations were cast into disarray, and the nation sank into both an economic and an emotional depression.

As credit continued to collapse through 1838 and 1839, President Van Buren tried to address the problems. First, he extended Jackson's hard-money policy, which caused the economy to contract further. Next, in an effort to keep the government solvent, Van Buren cut federal spending to the bone, shrinking the money supply even more. Then, to replace the stabilizing influence lost when the Second Bank was destroyed, he created a national treasury system endowed with many of the powers formerly wielded by the bank. The new regional treasury offices accepted only specie in payment for federal lands and other obligations and used that specie to pay federal expenses and debts. As a result, specie was sucked out of local banks and local economies. While fiscally sound by the wisdom of the day, Van Buren's decisions only made matters worse for the average person and drove the last nail into his political coffin.

The Log-Cabin and Hard-Cider Campaign of 1840

The Whigs had learned their lesson in the election of 1836: only a unified party could possibly destroy the political machine built by Jackson and Van Buren. As the nation sank into depression, the Whigs lined up behind a single candidate for the 1840 election, determined to use whatever means were necessary to break the Democrats' grip on the voters.

Once again, Henry Clay hoped to be the party's nominee, but Thurlow Weed convinced the party that William Henry Harrison would have a better chance in the election. Weed chose Harrison because of his distinguished military record and because the general, who had been a political lion thirty years earlier, had been out of the public eye for a long time and had few enemies left. For Harrison's running mate, the party chose **John Tyler,** a Virginia senator who had bolted from Jackson's Democratic Party during the Bank War. Weed clearly hoped that the Virginian would draw votes from the planter South while Harrison carried the West and North.

Although the economy was in bad shape, the Whig campaign avoided addressing any serious issues. Instead, the Whigs launched a smear campaign against Van Buren. Although he was the son of a lowly tavern keeper, the Whig press portrayed him as an aristocrat whose expensive tastes in clothes, food, and furniture were signs of dangerous excess during an economic

Panic of 1837 An economic collapse that came as the result of Andrew Jackson's fiscal policies and led to an extended national economic depression.

Specie Circular Order issued by President Jackson in 1836 stating that the federal government would accept only specie—gold and silver—as payment for public land; one of the causes of the Panic of 1837.

John Tyler Virginia senator who left the Democratic Party after conflicts with Andrew Jackson; he was elected vice president in 1840 and became president when William Henry Harrison died in office.

Democrats tried to discredit Whig candidate William Henry Harrison by characterizing the one-time Ohio governor as an unsophisticated backwoods hick; funny considering that he was the son of one of the first families of Virginia. Whigs responded by characterizing Martin Van Buren as an urban sophisticate, out of touch with everyday people; also funny, considering that he was the son of a rural tavern keeper. This clever pull card illustrates the Whig view: with the pull lever in one position, Van Buren smiles as he sips "Whitehouse champagne" (left); pull the lever and he grimaces at the taste of simple "log cabin hard cider." *The Granger Collection, New York.*

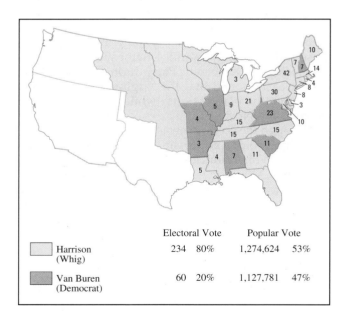

MAP 12.2　Election of 1840　Although the difference in popular votes between William Henry Harrison and Martin Van Buren was small in the election of 1840, Harrison won a landslide victory in the Electoral College. This map shows why. After floundering through several elections, the Whig Party was finally able to organize a national coalition, giving it solid victories in all of the most populous regions of the country. Only the Far West, which was still sparsely settled, voted as a block for Van Buren.

depression. Harrison really was an aristocrat, but the Whigs played on the Romantic themes so popular among their genteel and middle-class constituents by characterizing him as a simple frontiersman—a Natty Bumppo—who had risen to greatness through his own efforts. Whig claims were so extravagant that the Democratic press soon satirized Harrison in political cartoons showing a rustic hick swilling hard cider. The satire backfired. Whig newspapers and speechmakers seized on the image and sold Harrison, the long-time political insider, as a simple man of the people who truly lived in a log cabin.

Van Buren had little with which to retaliate. Harrison had a fairly clean and certainly a distinguished political and military career behind him. Tyler, too, was well respected. And Van Buren had simply not done a good job of addressing the nation's pressing economic needs. Voters, from former Antimasons to Christian reformers, cried out for change, and Van Buren could not offer them one. The combination of political dissatisfaction and campaign hype brought the biggest voter turnout to that time in American history: nearly twice as many voters came to the polls in 1840 as had done so in 1836. And while Harrison won only 53 percent of the popular vote, Weed's successful political manipulations earned the Whigs nearly 80 percent of the electoral votes, sweeping the Democrats out of the White House (see Map 12.2).

The Triumph of Manifest Destiny

→ *What forces in American life contributed to the concept of manifest destiny?*

→ *To what extent did the actions taken by American settlers in Oregon and Texas reflect the ideal of manifest destiny?*

→ *What were the global implications of manifest destiny?*

The key to Harrison's success was the Whig Party's skillful manipulation of the former general's reputation as a frontiersman and popular advocate for westward expansion. Bogged down in debates over tariffs, states' rights, public finance, and dozens of other practical, if boring policy matters, the allure of the west—and the nationalistic appeals of seizing and occupying it—brought an air of excitement to political discussion. It was this allure that helped to draw out the thousands of new voters in 1840 and would provide a new basis for political cooperation and contention in the years to come.

The Rise of Manifest Destiny

The new spirit that came to life in American politics and rhetoric in the years after 1840 found expression in a single phrase: Manifest Destiny. To some extent, manifest destiny can be traced back to the sense of mission that had motivated colonial Puritans (see page 70). Like John Winthrop and his Massachusetts Bay associates, many early nineteenth-century Americans believed they had a duty to go into new lands. During the antebellum period, romantic nationalism, land hunger, and the evangelicalism of the Second Great Awakening shaped this sense of divine mission into a new and powerful commitment to westward expansion. As the American Board of Commissioners for Foreign Missions noted in its annual report for 1827, "The tide of emigration is rolling westward so rapidly, that it must speedily surmount every barrier, till it reaches every habitable part of this continent." The power of this force led many to conclude that the westward movement was not just an economic process but was part of a divine plan for North America and the world.

Not surprisingly, the earliest and most aggressive proponents of expansion were Christian missionary organizations, whose many magazines, newsletters, and reports were the first to give it formal voice. Politicians, however, were not far behind. Democratic warhorse and expansion advocate Thomas Hart Benton of Missouri borrowed both the tone and content of missionary rhetoric in his speeches promoting generous land policies, territorial acquisition, and even overseas expansion. In 1825, for example, Benton argued in favor of American colonization of the Pacific coast and of the world, bringing "great and wonderful benefits" to the western Indians and allowing "science, liberal principles in government, and true religion [to] cast their lights across the intervening sea."

Expansion to the North and West

One major complication standing in the way of the nation's perceived manifest destiny was the fact that Spain, Britain, Russia, and other countries already owned large parts of the continent. The continued presence of the British, for example, proved to be a constant source of irritation. During the War of 1812, the War Hawks had advocated conquering Canada and pushing the British from the continent altogether (see page 246). Although events thwarted this ambition, many continued to push for that objective by either legal or extralegal means.

One confrontation flared in 1838 when Canadian loggers moved into a disputed area on the Maine border and began cutting trees. American lumberjacks resolved to drive them away, and fighting soon broke out. The Canadian province of New Brunswick and the state of Maine then mobilized their militias, the American Congress nervously called up fifty thousand men in case of war, and President Van Buren ordered in General **Winfield Scott.** Once on the scene, Scott was able to calm tempers and arrange a truce, but tension continued to run high.

Another source of dispute between the United States and Great Britain was the **Oregon Question.** The vast Oregon tract had been claimed at one time or another by Spain, Russia, France, England, and the United States (see Map 12.3). By the 1820s, only England and the United States continued to contest for its

---

Winfield Scott Virginia soldier and statesman who led troops in the War of 1812 and the War with Mexico; he was still serving as a general at the start of the Civil War.

Oregon Question The question of the national ownership of the Pacific Northwest; the United States and England renegotiated the boundary in 1846, establishing it at 49° north latitude.

MAP 12.3 **Oregon Territory** This map shows the changing boundaries and shifting possession of the Oregon Country. As a result of Polk's aggressive stance and economic pressures, Britain ceded all land south of the 49th parallel to the United States in 1846.

ownership. At the close of the War of 1812, the two countries had been unable to settle their claims, and in 1818 had agreed to joint occupation of Oregon for ten years (see page 274). They extended this arrangement indefinitely in 1827, with the **proviso** that either country could end it with one year's notice.

Oregon's status as neither British nor American presented its occupants with an unstable situation. One early incident occurred in 1841 when a wealthy pioneer died without leaving a will. Because the Oregon Country had no laws, no guidelines existed on who was entitled to inherit his property. Settlers finally created a **probate court** and instructed it to follow the statutes of the state of New York and appointed a committee to frame a constitution and draft a basic code of laws. Opposition from the British put an end to this early effort at self-rule, but the movement continued. Two years later, Americans in Oregon began agitating again, this time because of wolves preying on their livestock. They held a series of "Wolf Meetings" in 1843 to discuss joint protection and resolved to create a civil government. Although the British tried to prevent it, the assembly passed the **First Organic Laws** of Oregon on July 5, 1843, making Oregon an independent republic

in all but name. Independence, however, was not the settlers' long-term goal. The document's preamble announced that the code of laws would continue in force "until such time as the United States of America extend their jurisdiction over us."

Revolution in Texas

Similar problems faced American settlers who had taken up residence in Spain's, then Mexico's territories in the Southwest. Although the Spanish and then the Mexican government had invited Anglo-Americans to settle in the region, these pioneers generally ignored Mexican customs, including their pledge to practice Roman Catholicism, and often disregarded Mexican law. This was particularly the case after 1829, when Mexico began attaching duties to trade items moving between the region and the neighboring United States. Mexico also abolished importing slaves. Bad feelings grew over the years, but the distant and politically unstable Mexican government could do little to enforce laws, customs, or faith. In addition, despite the friction between cultures in Texas, many Tejanos were disturbed by the corruption and political instability in Mexico City and were as eager as their Texian counterparts to participate in the United States' thriving cotton market.

Assuming responsibility for forging a peaceful settlement to the problems between settlers in Texas and the Mexican government, Stephen F. Austin (see page 259) went to Mexico City in 1833. While Austin was there, **Antonio López de Santa Anna** seized power after a series of revolutions and disputed elections. A former supporter of federalism and a key figure in the adoption of a republican constitution in 1824, Santa Anna had come to the conclusion that

proviso A clause making a qualification, condition, or restriction in a document.

probate court A court that establishes the validity of wills and administers the estates of people who have died.

First Organic Laws A constitution adopted by American settlers in the Oregon Country on July 5, 1843, establishing a government independent from Great Britain and requesting annexation by the United States.

Antonio López de Santa Anna Mexican general who was president of Mexico when he led an attack on the Alamo in 1836; he again led Mexico during its war with the United States in 1846–1848.

Mexico was not ready for democracy. Upon assuming power, he suspended the constitution, dismissed congress, and set himself up as the self-declared "Napoleon of the West."

Throughout Mexico, former revolutionaries and common citizens who had anticipated democracy were outraged by Santa Anna's actions. To the south, in Yucatán and elsewhere, provinces openly rebelled. The same potential existed along the northern frontier as well. Trying to avoid an open break, Austin met with Santa Anna in 1834 and presented several petitions advocating reforms and greater self-government in Texas, but Santa Anna made it clear that he intended to exert his authority over the region. On his arrival back in Texas in 1835, Austin declared, "War is our only recourse." He was immediately made chairman of a committee to call for a convention of delegates from all over Texas. Members of the group that convened referred to themselves as the "Consultation."

Mexican officials, viewing the unrest in Texas as rebellion against their authority, issued arrest warrants for all the Texas troublemakers they could identify and **deployed** troops to San Antonio. Austin's committee immediately sent out word for Texans to arm themselves. The **Texas Revolution** started quickly thereafter when the little town of Gonzales refused to surrender a cannon to Mexican officials on September 29, 1835, and a battle ensued several days later (see Map 12.4).

Angered by the rebellion, Santa Anna personally led the Mexican army into Texas, arriving in San Antonio on February 23, 1836. Knowing that Santa Anna was on his way, Texas commander William Travis moved his troops into the **Alamo.** On March 6 Santa Anna ordered an all-out assault and despite sustaining staggering casualties was able to capture the former mission. Most of the post's defenders were killed in the assault, and Santa Anna executed those who survived the battle, including former American congressman and frontier celebrity Davy Crockett.

Despite the loss at the Alamo, Texans continued to underestimate Santa Anna's strength and his resolve to put down the rebellion. After a series of defeats, however, the Texans scored a stunning victory on April 21 at the San Jacinto River. Disguised in a private's uniform, Santa Anna attempted to escape but was captured and brought to Houston. In exchange for his release, in May 1836 the Mexican president signed the **Treaty of Velasco,** officially recognizing Texas's independence and acknowledging the Rio Grande as the border between Texas and Mexico.

As in Oregon, many leaders in Texas hoped their actions would lead to swift annexation by the United States. In 1838 Houston, by then president of the

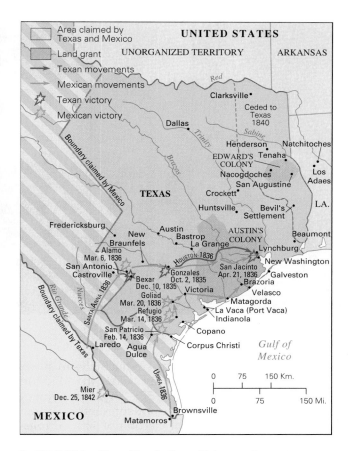

MAP 12.4 Texas Revolution This map shows troop movements and the major battles in the Texas Revolution, as well as the conflicting boundary claims made by Texans and the Mexican government. The Battle of San Jacinto and the Treaty of Velasco ended the war, but the conflicting land claims continued when Mexico repudiated the treaty.

deploy To position military resources (troops, artillery, equipment) in preparation for action.

Texas Revolution A revolt by American colonists in Texas against Mexican rule; it began in 1835 and ended with the establishment of the Republic of Texas in 1836.

Alamo A fortified Franciscan mission at San Antonio; rebellious Texas colonists were besieged and annihilated there by Santa Anna's forces in 1836.

Treaty of Velasco Treaty that Santa Anna signed in May 1836 after his capture at the San Jacinto River; it recognized the Republic of Texas but was later rejected by the Mexican congress.

Following the Battle of San Jacinto, Mexican president Antonio López de Santa Anna was captured while trying to escape disguised as a private. Texas forces brought him to Sam Houston, who had been wounded in the battle, in order to convey his formal surrender. A month later, the captured president signed the Treaty of Valasco, granting Texas its independence in exchange for his own release and return to Mexico. *Texas State Library and Archives Commission.*

Republic of Texas, invited the United States to annex Texas. Because all of Texas lay below the Missouri Compromise line (see pages 278–279), John Quincy Adams, elected to the House of Representatives after his loss in the presidential election of 1828, **filibustered** for three weeks against the acquisition of such a massive block of potential slave territory. Seeking to avoid national controversy, Congress refused to ratify the annexation treaty.

The Politics of Manifest Destiny

Although Adams was typical of one wing of the Whig coalition, he certainly did not speak for the majority of Whigs on the topic of national expansion. The party of manufacturing, revivalism, and social reform inclined naturally toward the blending of political, economic, and religious evangelicalism that was manifest destiny. William Henry Harrison himself, the united party's first national candidate, was a colorful figure in American westward expansion. He had been a prominent War Hawk and Indian fighter in the years leading up to the War of 1812 (see pages 246–248), and his political campaign in 1840 celebrated the simple pleasures and virtues of frontier life, appealing to a westering population. When Harrison died soon after taking office in 1841, his vice president, John Tyler, picked up the torch of American expansionism.

Tyler was a less typical Whig than even Adams. A Virginian and a states' rights advocate, he had been a

staunch Democrat until the nullification crisis, when he bolted the party to protest Jackson's strong assertion of federal power (see page 293). As president, Tyler seemed still to be more Democrat than Whig. Although he had objected to Jackson's use of presidential power, like Old Hickory, Tyler as president was unyielding where political principles were concerned. He vetoed high protective tariffs, internal improvement bills that he perceived as unnecessary, and attempts to revive the Second Bank of the United States. In fact, during Tyler's administration, Whigs accomplished only two moderate goals: they eliminated Van Buren's hated treasury system, and they passed a slightly higher tariff. Tyler's refusal to promote Whig economic policies led to a general crisis in government in 1843, when his entire cabinet resigned over his veto of a bank bill.

Tyler did share his party's desire for expansion, however. He assigned his secretary of state, Daniel Webster, to negotiate a treaty with Britain to settle the Maine matter once and for all. The resulting **Webster-**

---

filibuster To use obstructionist tactics, especially prolonged speechmaking, in order to delay legislative action.

Webster-Ashburton Treaty Treaty that in 1842 established the present border between Canada and northeastern Maine.

This campaign banner celebrating the candidacy of James K. Polk and George M. Dallas on the Democratic ticket carries a subtle message conveying the party's platform. Surrounding Polk's picture are twenty-five stars, one for each state in the Union. Outside the corner box, a twenty-sixth star stands for Texas, which Polk promised to annex. *Collection of David J. and Janet L. Frent.*

Ashburton Treaty (1842) gave more than half of the disputed territory to the United States and finally established the nation's northeastern border with Canada. Tyler also adopted an aggressive stance on the Oregon Question by appointing a federal Indian agent for the region in 1842—an act of doubtful legality in view of the mutual occupation agreement between the United States and Great Britain. His appointee, former missionary Elijah White, was one of the organizers of the Wolf Meetings and had helped draft the First Organic Laws. Historians have speculated that Tyler also encouraged Marcus Whitman to help guide a large party of immigrants into Oregon in 1843 as a way of bolstering the U.S. claim to the region.

Tyler also pushed a forceful policy toward Texas and the Southwest. In 1842 **Sam Houston** repeated his invitation for the United States to annex Texas, only to be rebuffed by Secretary of State Webster, a New Englander who shared Adams's views. When Webster resigned with the other cabinet officers in 1843, however, Tyler replaced him with fellow Virginian Abel P. Upshur, who immediately reopened the matter of Texas annexation.

Negotiations between Houston's representatives and Tyler's secretary of state—Upshur at first, then, after Upshur's death, John C. Calhoun—led to a treaty of annexation on April 11, 1844. In line with the Treaty of Velasco, the annexation document named the Rio Grande as the southern boundary of Texas. Annexation remained a major arguing point between proslavery and antislavery forces, however, and the treaty failed ratification in the Senate. The issue of Texas annexation then joined the Oregon Question as a major campaign issue in the presidential election of 1844.

Expansion and the Election of 1844

As the Whigs and the Democrats geared up for a national election, it became clear that expansion would be the key issue. This put the two leading political figures of the day, Democrat Martin Van Buren and Whig Henry Clay, in an uncomfortable position. Van Buren was on record as opposing the extension of slavery and was therefore against the annexation of Texas. Clay, the architect of the American System (see page 269), was opposed to any form of uncontrolled expansion, especially if it meant fanning sectional tensions, and he too opposed immediate annexation of Texas. Approaching the election, both issued statements to the effect that they would back annexation only with Mexico's consent.

Clay's somewhat ambiguous stance on expansion contrasted sharply with Tyler's efforts to advance the cause of manifest destiny. However, President Tyler's constant refusal to support the larger Whig political agenda led the party to nominate Clay anyway. Van

> **Sam Houston** American general and politician who fought in the struggle for Texas's independence from Mexico and became president of the Republic of Texas.

Buren was not so lucky. The strong southern wing of the Democratic Party was so put off by Van Buren's position on slavery that it blocked him, securing the nomination of Tennessee congressman **James K. Polk.**

The Democrats based their platform on the issues surrounding Oregon and Texas. They implied that the regions rightfully belonged to the United States, stating "that the *re-occupation* of Oregon and the *re-annexation* of Texas at the earliest practicable period are great American measures." Polk vowed to stand up to the British by claiming the entire Oregon Country up to 54°40' north latitude and to defend the territorial claims of Texas. The Democrats played up both regions to appeal to the manifest destiny sentiments of both northerners and southerners. For his part, Clay continued to waffle on expansionism, emphasizing economic policies instead.

The election demonstrated the people's commitment to manifest destiny. Clay was a national figure, well respected and regarded as one of the nation's leading statesmen, whereas Polk was barely known outside Tennessee. Still, Polk polled forty thousand more popular votes than Clay and garnered sixty-five more electoral votes. Seeing the election as a political barometer, outgoing president Tyler prepared a special message to Congress in December 1844 proposing a **joint resolution** annexing Texas. Many congressmen who had opposed annexation could not ignore the clear mandate given to manifest destiny in the presidential election, and the bill to annex Texas passed in February 1845, just as Tyler prepared to turn the White House over to his Democratic successor.

Holding to the position he had taken prior to the election, in his annual message for 1845 Polk asked Congress to end the joint occupation of Oregon. Referring to the largely forgotten Monroe Doctrine (see page 275), the president insisted that no nation other than the United States should be permitted to occupy any part of North America and urged Congress to assert exclusive control over the Oregon Country even if doing so meant war.

Neither the United States nor Britain intended to go to war over Oregon. The only issue—where the border would be—was a matter for the bargaining table, not the battlefield. Recalling the rhetoric that had gotten him elected, Polk insisted on 54°40'. The British lobbied for the Columbia River as the boundary, but their position softened quickly. The fur trade along the Columbia was in rapid decline and had become unprofitable by the early 1840s. As a result, in the spring of 1846, the British foreign secretary offered Polk a compromise boundary at the 49th parallel. The Senate recommended that Polk accept the offer, and a treaty

settling the Oregon Question was ratified on June 15, 1846. Sectional politics, however, delayed the admission of Oregon as a territory for a few years.

The War with Mexico and Sectional Crisis

Though the nation's border issues were now settled from Congress's point of view, the joint resolution annexing Texas and establishing the Rio Grande as its southern border led Mexico's popular press to demand an end to diplomatic relations with the United States. The government did so immediately, threatening war. Polk added to the tension, and seemed to confirm Mexican fears, by declaring that the entire Southwest should be annexed.

Late in 1845, the president dispatched John Slidell to Mexico City to negotiate the boundary dispute. He also authorized Slidell to purchase New Mexico and California if possible. At the same time, Polk dispatched American troops to Louisiana, ready to strike if Mexico resisted Slidell's offers. He also notified Americans in California that if war broke out with Mexico the Pacific fleet would seize California ports and support an insurrection against Mexican authority.

Nervous but bristling over what seemed to be preparations for war, the Mexican government refused to receive Slidell; in January 1846 he sent word to the president that his mission was a failure. Polk then ordered **Zachary Taylor** to lead troops from New Orleans toward the Rio Grande. Shortly thereafter, an American military party led by **John C. Frémont** entered California's Salinas Valley. Reaching an end to its patience, on April 22 Mexico proclaimed that its territory had been violated by the United States and declared war. Two days later, Mexican troops engaged a detachment of Taylor's army at Matamoros on the Rio Grande, killing eleven and capturing the

---

James K. Polk   Tennessee congressman who was a leader of the Democratic Party and the dark-horse winner of the presidential campaign in 1844.

joint resolution   A formal statement adopted by both houses of Congress and subject to approval by the president; if approved, it has the force of law.

Zachary Taylor   American general whose defeat of Santa Anna at Buena Vista in 1847 made him a national hero and the Whig choice for president in 1848.

John C. Frémont   Explorer, soldier, and politician who explored and mapped much of the American West and Northwest; he later ran unsuccessfully for president.

MAP 12.5 **The Southwest and the Mexican War** When the United States acquired Texas, it inherited the Texans' boundary disputes with Mexico. This map shows the outcome: war with Mexico in 1846 and the acquisition of the disputed territories in Texas as well as most of Arizona, New Mexico, and California through the Treaty of Guadalupe Hidalgo.

rest. When news of the battle reached Washington, Polk immediately called for war. Although the nation was far from united on the issue, Congress agreed on May 13, 1846 (see Map 12.5).

The outbreak of war disturbed many Americans. In New England, for example, protest ran high. Transcendentalist Henry David Thoreau chose to be jailed rather than pay taxes that would support the war. It was not expansion as such that troubled Thoreau, but the connection between Texas annexation and slavery. To southerners, the broad stretch of land lying south of 36°30' (the Missouri Compromise line) represented both economic and political power: the adoption of proslavery constitutions in newly acquired territories would ensure the installation of congenial governments strengthening the South's economic and political interests in Congress. Northerners were perturbed by these implications but saw something even more alarming in the southern expansion movement. Since the Missouri Compromise (1820), some northerners had come to believe that a slaveholding **oligarchy** controlled life and politics in the South.

Abolitionists warned that this "Slave Power" sought to expand its reach until it controlled every aspect of American life. Many viewed Congress's adoption of the gag rule in 1836 and the drive to annex Texas as evidence of the Slave Power's influence. Thus debates over Texas pitted two regions of the country against each other in what champions of both sides regarded as mortal combat.

Serious political combat began in August 1846 when David Wilmot, a Democratic representative from Pennsylvania, proposed an amendment to a military appropriations bill specifying that "neither slavery nor involuntary servitude shall ever exist" in any territory gained in the War with Mexico. The **Wilmot Proviso**

oligarchy A small group of people or families who hold power.

Wilmot Proviso Amendment to an appropriations bill in 1846 proposing that any territory acquired from Mexico be closed to slavery; it was defeated in the Senate.

Slaves look on in obvious interest as men gathered at the post office devour the latest news from the front in the war with Mexico. One newspaperman in Baltimore reported, "The news from the army on the Rio Grande has caused more general excitement in this city than has before taken place, perhaps during the present generation." *"War News from Mexico" by Richard Caton Woodville, 1848. The Manogian Foundation © 1996. Board of Trustees, National Gallery of Art, Washington, D.C.*

passed in the House of Representatives but failed in the Senate, where equal state representation gave the South a stronger position. At Polk's request, Wilmot refused to propose his proviso when the House reconsidered the war appropriations bill, but Van Buren Democrats defied Polk by attaching the amendment again, and the House approved it once more. Again the Senate rejected the amended bill. The House finally decided in April to appropriate money for the war without stipulating whether or not slavery would be permitted.

While all this political infighting was going on in Washington, D.C., a real war was going on in the Southwest. In California, American settlers rallied in open rebellion in the Sacramento Valley. The rebels captured the town of Sonoma in June 1846 and declared themselves independent. They crafted a flag depicting a grizzly bear and announced the birth of the Bear Flag Republic. Rushing to Sonoma, Frémont's force joined the Bear Flag rebels, and when the little army

arrived in Monterey on July 19, they found that the Pacific fleet had already acted on Polk's orders and seized the city. The Mexican forces were in full flight southward.

To round out the greater southwestern strategy, Polk ordered Colonel Stephen Kearny to invade New Mexico on May 15. After leading his men across 800 miles of desert to Santa Fe, Kearny found a less-than-hostile enemy force facing him. Members of the interracial upper class of Santa Fe had already expressed interest in joining the United States. Given the opportunity, they surrendered without firing a shot.

Within a short time, all of the New Mexico region and California were securely in the hands of U.S. forces. Zachary Taylor in Texas, however, faced more serious opposition. Marching across the Rio Grande, Taylor headed for the Mexican city of Monterrey, which he attacked in September 1846. He managed to capture the city, but only at the cost of agreeing to let the enemy garrison pass unmolested through his lines. From Monterrey, Taylor planned to turn southward toward Mexico City and lead the main attack against the Mexican capital, but politics intervened.

After Taylor's successful siege at Monterrey, Polk began to perceive the popular general as a political threat. In an attempt to undermine Taylor's political appeal, Polk turned the war effort over to Winfield Scott, ordering Scott to gather an army at the port of Tampico, on the Gulf of Mexico. Drawing men from Taylor's and other forces, Scott was then to sail down to Veracruz, from which the army was to move inland to take Mexico City (see Map 12.4).

Polk complicated the military situation by plotting with deposed Mexican president Santa Anna, who had been exiled to Cuba after his defeat at San Jacinto. In secret correspondence with the president, Santa Anna promised that he would end the war and settle the border dispute in Polk's favor if Polk would help him return to Mexico. The American president agreed to sneak Santa Anna back into Mexico, where he soon resumed the presidency. Going back on his agreement, however, Santa Anna also picked up his sword and vowed to resist American territorial expansion into the disputed territory. Thus, while Scott and Taylor were realigning the American forces, Mexico's most able general resumed command of the army and chose to strike.

Planning to crush Taylor's remaining force and then wheel around to attack Scott, Santa Anna and his numerically superior army encountered Taylor at Buena Vista in February 1847. Tired and dispirited from a forced march across the desert, the Mexican army was in no shape to fight, but Santa Anna ordered an attack

An American private, Samuel E. Chamberlain, made this drawing of the Battle of Buena Vista. Present at the battle, Chamberlain watched as Mexican forces overran an artillery emplacement. The Americans eventually turned the tide, and the battle came out a draw. Even so, troops under Santa Anna were forced to retreat into the Mexican interior, spoiling the general's hope for a quick and easy victory against the invading Americans. *"Battle of Buena Vista" by Samuel Chamberlain, 1847. San Jacinto Museum of History Association.*

anyway. Tactically speaking, the **Battle of Buena Vista** was a draw, but it was a strategic victory for the Americans: Taylor's fresher troops stalled Santa Anna's forces, permitting Scott's forces to capture Veracruz on March 9. His eyes firmly on a quick victory, Scott moved relentlessly toward Mexico City. By May 15, however, Scott found himself out of critical forces and supplies. After three months of waiting, Scott finally received relief and resumed his march on Mexico City. Staging a crushing assault, Scott and his force routed the Mexican defenders and captured the city on September 13, 1847.

With Mexico City, all of Texas, New Mexico, and California in American hands, the direction of treaty talks should have been fairly predictable. Scott's enormous success, however, caused Santa Anna's government to collapse, leaving no one to negotiate with American peace commissioner Nicholas Trist. After a month had passed with no settlement, Polk concluded that Trist was not pressing hard enough and removed him as peace commissioner. But by the time Polk's orders arrived, the Mexican government had elected a new president and on November 11 told Trist that Mexico was ready to begin negotiations. When Trist re-

ceived Polk's removal order, he ignored it and pressed on with negotiations. Finally, on February 2, 1848, Trist and the Mexican delegation signed the **Treaty of Guadalupe Hidalgo,** granting the United States all the territory between the Nueces River and the Rio Grande and between there and the Pacific. In exchange, Trist agreed that the United States would pay Mexico $15 million, and he committed the United States to honoring all claims made by Texans for damages resulting from the war.

Polk was very angry when he heard the terms of the treaty. Although the United States had obtained everything it had gone to war for, Polk felt that Scott's sweeping victory at Mexico City should have netted the

Battle of Buena Vista   Battle in February 1847 during which U.S. troops led by Zachary Taylor forced Santa Anna's forces to withdraw into the interior of Mexico.

Treaty of Guadalupe Hidalgo   Treaty (1848) in which Mexico gave up Texas above the Rio Grande and ceded New Mexico and California to the United States in return for $15 million.

United States more territory for less money. Political realities in Washington, however, prevented Polk from trying to get a more aggressive treaty ratified by the Senate. Although the president had strong support for his own position in favor of annexing all of Mexico, many antislavery voices loudly protested bringing so much land south of the Missouri Compromise line into the Union. Others opposed the annexation of Mexico because they feared that the largely Roman Catholic population might be a threat to Protestant institutions in the United States. Still others, many of whom had opposed the war to begin with, had moral objections to taking any territory by force. Perhaps more convincing than any of these arguments, however, was the fact that the war had cost a lot of money, and congressmen were unwilling to allocate more if peace was within reach. Thus Polk submitted the treaty Trist had negotiated, and the Senate approved it by a vote of 38 to 14.

✔ Individual Voices

**Individual Voices:
The American
Tract Society,
The Moral Threat
from Reading
Fiction**

As mass literacy spread throughout the nation, a culture war began to emerge. Producers of popular magazines and booksellers sought to tap into a burgeoning new market by reprinting both European classic fiction and the newly emerging fiction being produced by such American authors as James Fenimore Cooper and Nathaniel Hawthorne. But Christian reformers like those who founded and financed the American Tract Society, feared that such frivolous literature would undermine the nation's morals and compromise the republic itself. To counter this threat, the Tract Society, American Bible Society, and dozens of other benevolent organizations put out volumes of more uplifting literature, often at very low price or for free, in an effort to drive sinful fictional literature off the market. The plan did not succeed—light and entertaining writing became a mainstay of American literature—and ironically by flooding the marketplace with easy to read inexpensive texts, the Tract Society actually helped to expand literacy and the demand for an ever greater variety of written work.

① *What is it about fiction that the governors of the American Tract Society find objectionable?*

② *Why does the publication of fiction in cheap forms present a particular threat to American morals and stability?*

③ *How does the American Tract Society feel about a free market in literature? What role should publishers have played in American society?*

④ *How did the Tract Society characterize the relationship between fictional literature and alcohol? Why were these particularly dangerous in their view?*

Fiction *also lamentably pervades our own country: deluding our youth with dreams of unreal bliss; pandering to the taste of the licentious; seducing the innocent; profaning all sacred things; prostituting the press, and sacrificing the welfare, temporal and eternal, of thousands, for the sake of pecuniary gain.* ① *Not only is the gilded volume furnished for the wealthy and tasteful, but leaves rudely and roughly printed and thrown together find acceptance with the novel-reader.* ② *Corrupt European writers, with principles as base as their imaginations are vivid, and with pretended sympathy for the depraved masses to whose level their publications tend to debase their readers, have found eager publishers among those from whom we might have hoped better things, and too many readers and admirers in all parts of our country.* ③ *This misnamed "literature" had demoralized thousands of the unsuspecting, and is known to have been the occasion of ruin to many of both sexes by its polluting pages. Its ravages are scarcely less wide spread than those of intemperance: like ardent spirits, producing inattention to present duties; deadening the conscience to the claims of the gospel; undermining or counteracting influences that might result, with the divine blessing, in the salvation of the soul. An immense proportion of the issues of the popular press are of this sort, too vast a proportion for the temporal or spiritual well-being of this reading nation, or for the safety of institutions based on sound intelligence and virtue of the people.* ④

SUMMARY

The acquisition of Texas and the Southwest, even at the cost of war, marked the end of an era of dynamic growth and change. By the end of this era, the United States extended from Atlantic to Pacific, and while vast areas in between remained unexplored and unsettled, the nation's manifest destiny to occupy every inch of North America seemed well on its way to completion.

Americans responded in many different ways to the many unsettling changes that had been taking place as part of this Great Transformation. Different economic classes responded by creating their own cultures and by adopting specific strategies for dealing with anxiety. Some chose violent protest, some passive resistance. Some looked to heaven for solutions and others to earthly utopias. And out of this complex swirl, something entirely new and unexpected emerged: a new America, on its way to being socially, politically, intellectually, and culturally modern.

A new generation emerged that grasped greedily at the new opportunities offered by new economic and cultural arrangements. Literacy grew as never before in the nation's history and with it a thirst for new knowledge. Book publishers, magazine editors, and charitable societies competed to meet this new demand for information and entertainment. And this group of young readers sought to express itself not only in literature, but in politics as well. As expanding media made more people more aware of issues taking place nationwide, they were drawn into politics as never before. In the presidential election of 1840 almost two and a half million men cast ballots, more than a million more than had voted four years earlier.

In that election, Andrew Jackson, a man who had become a national figure by fighting against Indian sovereignty and for westward expansion, swept a new sentiment into national politics. Increasingly Americans came to believe that the West would provide the solutions to the problems ushered in during the Great Transformation. In the short term, this notion led to an exciting race by Americans toward the Pacific. But different visions about how the West would solve the nation's problems soon added to the ever-growing air of crisis. The admission of Texas, California, and other western areas into the United States raised political and economic issues that the mass of readers and voters would need to resolve before the nation could fully realize its perceived destiny.

IN THE WIDER WORLD

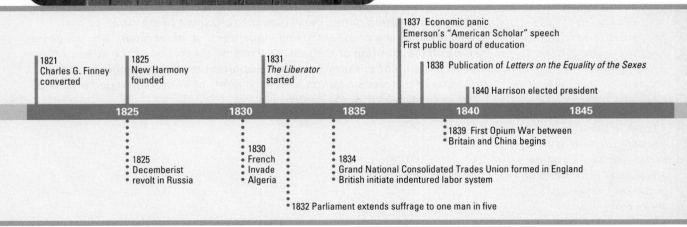

1821 Charles G. Finney converted

1825 New Harmony founded

1831 *The Liberator* started

1837 Economic panic
Emerson's "American Scholar" speech
First public board of education

1838 Publication of *Letters on the Equality of the Sexes*

1840 Harrison elected president

1825 — 1830 — 1835 — 1840 — 1845

1825 Decemberist revolt in Russia

1830 French Invade Algeria

1834 Grand National Consolidated Trades Union formed in England
British initiate indentured labor system

1839 First Opium War between Britain and China begins

1832 Parliament extends suffrage to one man in five

Modernization and Rising Stress

1806   Journeyman shoemakers' strike in New York City

1821   Charles G. Finney experiences a religious conversion

1823   James Fenimore Cooper's *The Pioneers*

1825   Thomas Cole begins Hudson River school of painting

     Robert Owen establishes community at New Harmony, Indiana

1826   Shakers have eighteen communities in the United States

1828   Weavers protest and riot in New York City

1829   Grand jury in Rochester, New York, declares alcohol most prominent cause of crime

1831   Nat Turner's Rebellion

     William Lloyd Garrison begins publishing *The Liberator*

1832   Jackson reelected

1833   Lydia Sigourney publishes bestsellers *Letters to Young Ladies* and *How to Be Happy*

1834   Riot in Charlestown, Massachusetts, leads to destruction of Catholic convent

     George Bancroft publishes volume 1 of his American history

     Formation of National Trades' Union

     Formation of Whig Party

1835   Five Points riot in New York City

     Texas Revolution begins

1836   Congress passes the gag rule

     Martin Van Buren elected president

1837   Horace Mann heads first public board of education

     Panic of 1837

     Ralph Waldo Emerson's "American Scholar" speech

     Senate rejects annexation of Texas

     Armed confrontation between Maine and New Brunswick

1838   Emerson articulates transcendentalism

     Sarah Grimké publishes *Letters on the Equality of the Sexes and the Condition of Women*

1840   Log-cabin campaign

     William Henry Harrison elected president

1841   Brook Farm established

     Death of President Harrison; John Tyler becomes president

1842   *Commonwealth v. Hunt*

     Elijah White named federal Indian Agent for Oregon

1843   Dorothea Dix advocates state-funded insane asylums

     First wagon train into Oregon

     Oregon adopts First Organic Laws

1844   James K. Polk elected president

1845   United States annexes Texas

     Term "manifest destiny" coined

1846   War with Mexico begins

     Oregon boundary established

     California declares itself a republic

1848   Treaty of Guadalupe Hidalgo

Sectional Conflict and Shattered Union, 1848–1860

A Civil War—states divided against other states, families divided among themselves, brothers killing brothers in grisly hand-to-hand combat. Over a four-year period, it would claim more American lives and break more American bodies than any other war in the nation's history. How could this have happened?

American historians have written more about this event than any other in our history, and explanations for it abound. Immediately after the war, writers in the North blamed southerners for their antiquated and immoral practice of slavery. Southerners countered by blaming selfish northern industrial and commercial interests for wanting to colonize the South in order to enhance their own profits. During the early decades of the twentieth century, some historians identified key structural problems in the Constitution that were beyond compromise. Others emphasized that a "bumbling generation" of American politicians was incapable of effecting reasonable compromises. More recently, some pointed to fundamental contradictions between northern and southern versions of capitalism, a structural contest that only a war could resolve. And in the last few years, historians have dusted off a version of the "bumbling generation" argument by claiming that an excess of democracy led to emotional rather than rational approaches to national problems.

As you read this chapter, you will encounter evidence that might be used to support any of these arguments. The progression toward war was a complicated series of events into which millions of individual decisions factored. In this chapter, you'll see these events from many points of view and be able to weigh the various decisions and actions of all the participants. And while we encourage you to analyze this evidence and come to conclusions about why this terrible event happened, we encourage you not to leap to conclusions prematurely.

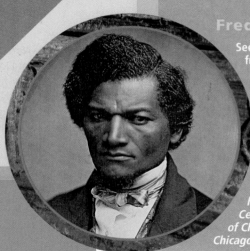

Frederick Douglass

Seeking economic self-sufficiency and personal freedom, Douglass chose to escape from slavery in 1838 to seek employment as a free man in Massachusetts. Facing the constraint of severe racial discrimination, Douglass had difficulty making a living until abolitionist William Lloyd Garrison heard him speak at an antislavery rally. Garrison promoted Douglass as a lecturer and he soon became recognized as one of the most effective abolitionist activists in the country. *Samuel J. Miller, American, 1822–1888, Frederick Douglass, 1847–52, Cased half-plate daguerreotype, Major Acquisitions Centennial Endowment, 1996.433, The Art Institute of Chicago. Photography © The Art Institute of Chicago.*

✓ Individual Choices

In 1838, Frederick Douglass, a slave living in Baltimore, decided that he would try to escape. This was no sudden impulse; Douglass had been thinking about escape and freedom for most of his life. As a young boy he told his white friends, "You will be free as soon as you are twenty-one, *but I am a slave for life!*" And he had tried once before to make his way to freedom, but was captured and returned to his owner. Though his master threatened to sell him to a cotton plantation in Alabama, Douglass's intelligence and skills were worth more in Baltimore: he was made an apprentice at the local shipyard, eventually becoming a master ship caulker. His productivity earned him a lot of freedom: he made his own contracts, set his own work schedule, and collected his own earnings. "I was now of some importance to my master," Douglass recalled. "I was bringing him from six to seven dollars per week." But he also remembered his liberty. "I have observed this in my experience of slavery," Douglass commented, "that whenever my condition was improved, instead of its increasing my contentment, it only increased my desire to be free."

Like most successful runaways, Douglass had the advantage of living in a border region, near free territory, and had an unusual degree of personal freedom and economic independence. Using a wide network of personal connections, he raised money and secured forged documents that entitled him to pass unmolested through slave territory. On September 3, Douglass disguised himself as a merchant sailor and boarded a train heading north out of Baltimore. Switching from train to ferry boat, ferry boat to steamship, steamship back to train, and finally train back to ferry boat, Douglass made his way northward, arriving in New York City early on the morning of September 4. Although he had a couple of close calls, Douglass's escape had succeeded.

Douglass now was free, but the promised land of the non-slave North proved disappointing. Moving to the town of New Bedford, Massachusetts, where he hoped to earn a living in the boatyards, Douglass found that "such was the strength of prejudice against color, among the white caulkers, that they refused to work with me, and of course I could get no employment." For three years he was forced to do odd jobs to keep himself and his wife alive. "There was no work too hard—none too dirty," he recalled. Despite this decline in status and earnings, Douglass never regretted his choice of

freedom, and when he attended an antislavery conference in Nantucket, Douglass stood to speak about his experiences. Famed abolitionist William Lloyd Garrison heard Douglass's speech, declaring that "Patrick Henry, of revolutionary fame, never made a speech more eloquent in the cause of liberty." Garrison was so moved that he offered to support Douglass as a lecturer in the antislavery cause, and Douglass accepted. Having experienced both slavery in the South and racial discrimination in the North, Douglass chose to speak out for the cause of racial equality for the next fifty years.

INTRODUCTION

Though not a politician, Frederick Douglass certainly was not immune to the political wrangling going on around him. Like many Americans, Douglass's life was in a state of constant upheaval as politicians engaged in abstract power games that had all-too-real consequences.

Struggles over tariffs, coinage, internal improvements, public land policy, and dozens of other practical issues intersected in complicated ways with the over-inflated egos of power-hungry politicians to create an air of political contention and national crisis. The discovery of gold in California followed by a massive rush of Americans into the new territory added greed to the equation. Then strong-willed men such as Jefferson Davis and Stephen A. Douglas threw more fuel on the fire as they fought over the best—that is, most profitable and politically advantageous—route for a transcontinental railroad that would tie California's wealth to the rest of the nation. The halls of Congress rang with debate, denunciation, and even physical violence.

Beneath it all lurked an institution that Frederick Douglass knew all too well: slavery. In a changing society rife with the problems of expansion, immigration, industrialization, and urbanization, political leaders tried either to seek compromise or to ignore the slavery question altogether. In reality, they could do neither. As the nation's leaders wrestled with a host of new issues, the confrontation between northern and southern societies peaked. Although many people wanted peace and favored reconciliation, ultimately both sides rejected compromise, leading to the end of the Union and the beginning of America's most destructive and deadly war.

New Political Options

→ *How did the presidential election in 1848 help to foster political dissent?*

→ *How did events in Europe help to push the American economy forward during the 1850s? In what ways did this contribute to growing political tensions?*

→ *What new political options affected the political system during the 1850s? In what ways?*

The presidential election in 1848 had celebrated American expansion and nationalism, but at the same time it revealed a strong undercurrent of dissent. The political system held together during the election, and the existing parties managed to maintain the politics of avoidance, but the successes enjoyed by Free Soil challengers were evidence that significant problems churned under the surface. It was clear to many that the nation's political system was not meeting their economic and ideological needs, and they began looking for new options. Efforts at compromise might save the nation from the immediate consequences of growth, modernization, and sectional tension, but crisis clearly was in the air.

Politicizing Slavery: The Election of 1848

The American victory in the War with Mexico was an enormous shot in the arm for American nationalism and manifest destiny, but it also brought the divisive issue of slavery back into mainstream politics to a degree unknown since the Missouri Compromise. Opposed to slavery expansion for both political and ethical reasons, David Wilmot (see pages 359–360) had broken a gentlemen's agreement among congressmen to skirt around slavery issues, firmly wedding American expansion and slavery in the minds of many. Even a largely apolitical nonconformist like Henry David Thoreau found the connection obvious, and protested the war for that reason.

Of course, being opposed to the expansion of slavery was not the same thing as opposing the institution

Sojourner Truth was a remarkable woman for her time, or for any time. One anecdote claims that a white policeman in New York state demanded that she identify herself. Using her cane to thrust herself upright to her full six feet of height, she boomed out the same words that God used to identify himself to Moses: "I am that I am." The policeman was unnerved and scurried away. Showing such bravery and pride in both her race and sex, it is little wonder that she commanded great respect in both antislavery and women's rights circles throughout her lifetime. *Sophia Smith Collection, Smith College.*

of slavery itself, and antislavery sentiments were still not widespread among the American people during the 1840s. However, as the debates over the Mexican War indicate, abolitionist voices were getting louder and more politically insistent. Despite strong and sometimes violent opposition, the abolition movement had continued to grow, especially among the privileged and educated classes in the Northeast. Throughout the 1830s, evangelicals increasingly stressed the sinful nature of slavery, urging the immediate, uncompensated liberation of slaves.

Garrison, however, consistently alienated his followers. Calling the Constitution "a covenant with death and an agreement with hell," Garrison burned a copy of it, telling his followers, "so perish all compromises with tyranny," and he urged them to have no dealings with a government that permitted so great an evil as slavery. Citing the reluctance of most organ-

ized churches to condemn slavery outright, Garrison urged his followers to break with them as well. He also offended many of his white evangelical supporters by associating with and supporting free black advocates of abolition.

During the 1830s, even moderates within the abolition movement had celebrated Frederick Douglass, **Sojourner Truth,** and other African American abolitionists, welcoming them as members of the American Anti-Slavery Society. But more insistent black voices frightened white abolitionists. African American abolitionist David Walker cried, "The whites want slaves, and want us for their slaves, but some of them will curse the day they ever saw us." Walker advocated that African Americans should "kill or be killed." Another black spokesman, Henry Highland Garnet, proclaimed, "Strike for your lives and liberties. Now is the day and hour. Let every slave in the land do this and the days of slavery are numbered. Rather die freemen than live to be slaves."

Garrison's sentiments mobilized some, but most of his followers were more conservative. In 1840 this and other controversial issues caused many of those moderates to bolt from Garrison's American Anti-Slavery Society to form the more temperate American and Foreign Anti-Slavery Society. This new group forged strong ties with mainstream politicians and church leaders who, while opposed to any extension of slavery and sympathetic to moderate abolitionist proposals, had been relatively silent because of Garrison's reputation for radicalism.

Efforts by moderate antislavery supporters to bring limited abolitionism into the political mainstream meshed with the political aspirations of both those who opposed slavery's expansion primarily for political and economic reasons and those who were motivated by purely ethical concerns. Hoping to cash in on the popular attention created by debates over slavery during the War with Mexico, moderates in 1840 challenged both Whig and Democrat ambivalence by forming a third political party: the **Liberty Party.**

Specifically disavowing Garrison's radical aims, Liberty Party leaders argued that slavery would eventually die on its own if it could be confined geographically. In addition, the Liberty Party called for the

Sojourner Truth Abolitionist and feminist who was freed from slavery in 1827 and became a leading preacher against slavery and for the rights of women.
Liberty Party The first antislavery political party; it was formed in Albany, New York, in 1840.

abolition of slavery in Washington, D.C., and in all the territories where it already existed. Though certainly more popular than Garrison's radical appeals, this moderate message drew little open political support: in 1840 Liberty Party presidential candidate James G. Birney had garnered only about 7,000 out of the nearly 2.5 million votes cast. But in 1844, when he again ran on the Liberty Party ticket, he won 62,000 popular votes. Clearly a moderate antislavery position was becoming more acceptable.

Even in the face of such evidence, both major parties continued to practice the politics of avoidance. Suffering ill health, Polk chose not to run for a second term in 1848, leaving the Democrats scrambling for a candidate. They chose Lewis Cass of Michigan—a longtime moderate on slavery issues—as their presidential candidate and balanced the ticket with General William Butler of Kentucky. The Whigs hoped to ride a wave of nationalism following the War with Mexico by running military hero Zachary Taylor, a Louisianan and a slaveholder, for president and moderate New Yorker Millard Fillmore for vice president.

Disaffected Voices and Political Dissent

It did not take long after the election of 1848 for cracks in the system to become more prominent. In an effort to compete with Democrats in northeastern cities, the Whigs had tried to win Catholic and immigrant voters away from the rival party. The strategy backfired. Not only did the Whigs not attract large numbers of immigrants, but they alienated two core groups among their existing supporters. One such group was artisans, who saw immigrants as the main source of their economic and social woes. The other was Protestant evangelicals, to whom Roman Catholic Irish and German immigrants symbolized all that was wrong in the world and threatening to the American republic. Whig leaders could do little to address these voters' immediate concerns, and increasing numbers left the Whig Party to form state and local coalitions more in tune with their hopes and fears.

One of the most prominent of these locally oriented groups was the anti-Catholic, anti-immigrant **Know-Nothings.** This loosely knit political organization traced its origins back to secret **nativist** societies that had come into existence during the ethnic tension and rioting in Philadelphia, Boston, and New York in the 1830s. These secret fraternal groups at first dabbled in politics by endorsing candidates who shared their **xenophobic** views. Remaining underground, they told their mem-

bers to say "I know nothing" if they were questioned about the organization or its political intrigues, hence the name Know-Nothings.

Increasingly after 1848, these secretive groups became more public and more vocal. To the artisans and others who formed the core of the Know-Nothing movement, the issues of slavery and sectionalism that seemed to dominate the national political debate were nothing but devices being used by political insiders and the established parties to divert ordinary Americans from real issues of concern. The Know-Nothings pointed instead at immigration, loss of job security, urban crowding and violence, and political corruption as the true threats to American liberties. They built a platform charging that immigrants were part of a Catholic plot to overthrow democracy in the United States. Seeking to counter this perceived threat, they contended that "Americans must rule America" and urged a twenty-one-year naturalization period, a ban against naturalized citizens holding public office, and the use of the Protestant Bible in public schools.

Know-Nothings from different regions disagreed about many things, but they all agreed that the Whig and Democratic Parties were corrupt and that the only hope for the nation lay in scrapping traditional politics and starting anew. Like the Antimasonic movement in the 1820s (see pages 282–283), in which many Know-Nothing leaders got their start in politics, the Know-Nothing Party expressed antiparty sentiments, alleging wholesale voter fraud and government corruption by both major parties. As future president Rutherford B. Hayes noted, the people were expressing a "general disgust with the powers that be."

Many Know-Nothings had deep ties with the evangelical Protestant movement and indeed represented one dimension of Christian dissent, but not all Protestant dissenters shared their single-mindedness. Many evangelical reformers believed the nation was beset by a host of evils that imperiled its existence. Progress without Christian principles and individual morality, they thought, posed a great danger for the United States, and they viewed slavery, alcohol, Catholicism, religious heresy, and corrupt government as threats to

Know-Nothings Members of anti-Catholic, anti-immigrant organizations who eventually formed themselves into a national political party.

nativist Favoring native-born inhabitants of a country over immigrants.

xenophobic Fearful of or hateful toward foreigners or those seen as being different.

Convinced that slavery and other sectional issues were blinding Americans to the true dangers stemming from uncontrolled immigration and foreign influence, the Know-Nothing Party ran Millard Fillmore for president in 1856. Banners like this one warned Americans and solicited their votes. Fillmore succeeded in getting 21 percent of the popular vote. *Milwaukee County Historical Society.*

the nation's moral fiber. In their efforts to create moral government and to direct national destiny, these reformers advocated social reform through both religious and political action. Temperance was one of the more prominent topics of their political concern (see page 342). The war on alcohol had made great gains since the 1830s: thirteen states had enacted laws prohibiting the manufacture and sale of liquor. Overall, however, progress seemed slow, and like Know-Nothings and others, temperance advocates became increasingly impatient with the traditional political parties.

While none of these movements alone was capable of overturning the ruling political order, they were symptomatic of serious problems perceived by growing numbers of citizens. Though there were serious differences in the problems that each of these groups emphasized, they shared a number of perceptions in common. All that was missing was a catalyst that could bind them together into a unified dissenting force.

The Politics of Compromise

While dissidents of various types attacked the political parties from outside, problems raised by national expansion were continuing to erode party unity from within. Immediately after Zachary Taylor's election in 1848, California's future became a new divisive issue.

California presented a peculiar political problem. Once word reached the rest of the nation that California was rich with gold, politicians immediately began grasping for control over the newly acquired territory. Although large parts of the area lay below the 36°30' line that the Missouri Compromise had set for slavery expansion, that legislation had applied only to territory acquired in the Louisiana Purchase, and the failure of Congress to pass Wilmot's Proviso left the question of slavery in the new territories wide open.

Having been primarily responsible for crafting the earlier compromise (see pages 278–279), Henry Clay took it upon himself to find a solution to the new situation. Clay was convinced that any successful agreement would have to address all sides of the issue. He thus proposed a complex **omnibus** bill to the Senate on

omnibus Including or covering many matters; an omnibus bill is a piece of legislation with many parts.

CONGRESSIONAL SCALES,
A TRUE BALANCE.

The question of how territory acquired in the war with Mexico might unbalance the nation politically weighed heavily on people's minds as the nation entered the 1850s. In this cartoon, lithographer Nathaniel Currier—who later would found the famous graphic art company Currier and Ives—illustrates the problem. Trying himself to balance the Wilmot Proviso against Southern Rights, the president seeks to keep congressional representatives from the North and the South in balance as well. *Library of Congress.*

January 20, 1850. California would enter the Union as a free state, but the slavery question would be left to popular sovereignty in all other territories acquired through the Treaty of Guadalupe Hidalgo (see page 361). The bill also directed Texas to drop a continuing border dispute with New Mexico in exchange for federal assumption of Texas's public debt. Then, to appease abolitionists, Clay called for an end to the slave trade in Washington, D.C., and balanced that with a clause popular with southerners: a new, more effective **fugitive slave law.**

Though Clay was trying to please all sectional interests, the omnibus bill satisfied no one; Congress debated it without resolution for seven months. Despite appeals to reason by Clay and Daniel Webster, Congress remained hopelessly deadlocked. Finally,

in July 1850, Clay's proposals were defeated. The 73-year-old political veteran left the capital tired and dispirited, but **Stephen A. Douglas** of Illinois set himself to the task of reviving the compromise. Using practical economic arguments and backroom political arm twisting, Douglas proposed each component of Clay's omnibus package as a separate bill, steering each for-

fugitive slave law Law providing for the return of escaped slaves to their owners.

Stephen A. Douglas Illinois senator who tried to reconcile northern and southern differences over slavery through the Compromise of 1850 and the Kansas-Nebraska Act.

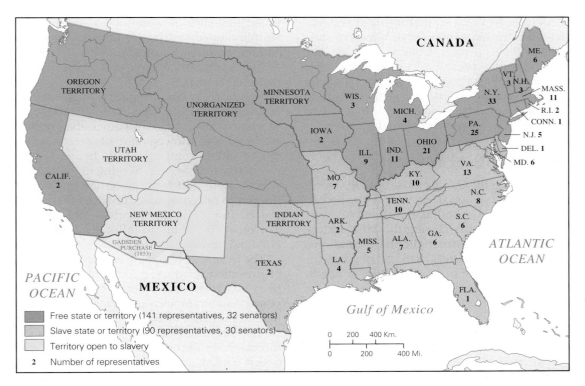

MAP 13.1   The Compromise of 1850   The acquisition of Texas and California brought a showdown between North and South over representation in the national government. As this map shows, the Compromise of 1850 permitted Texas and California to be admitted to the Union without seriously undermining the balance of power in the Senate. In the House of Representatives, however, the balanced favored the North.

ward toward a comprehensive compromise. Finally, in September, Congress passed the **Compromise of 1850** (see Map 13.1).

Silenced by the political machinations of their mainstream colleagues, both antislavery and evangelical Whigs chafed at the provision that allowed slave catchers to follow runaway slaves into the North. Striking back, they increasingly joined forces with African Americans to seek solutions outside the political realm. Throughout the 1850s, both white and African American activists sought to help slaves escape from the South on the **Underground Railroad.** This covert network provided hiding places and aid for runaway slaves along routes designed to carry them from southern plantations through American territory made hostile by the fugitive slave law and on to safety in Canada. Individuals like **Harriet Tubman** made frequent excursions into the South. Along with Frederick Douglass and others, she also delivered lectures on their life in slavery to white audiences across the North, increasing northern awareness of the plight of slaves

and stirring hostility toward the fugitive slave provisions of the Douglas package.

The Compromise of 1850 did little to relieve underlying regional differences and only aggravated political dissent. The fact that slaveowners could pursue runaway slaves into northern states and return them into bondage brought slavery too close to home for

Compromise of 1850   Plan intended to reconcile North and South on the issue of slavery; it recognized the principle of popular sovereignty and included a strong fugitive slave law.

Underground Railroad   The secret network of northerners who helped fugitive slaves escape to Canada or to safe areas in free states.

Harriet Tubman   One of the most famous and most effective of the many African American "conductors" on the Underground Railroad; she is thought to have been personally responsible for leading at least three hundred slaves into freedom.

many northerners. Nor did southerners find any reason to celebrate: admission of another nonslave state further drained their power in Congress and slavery had gained no positive protection, either in the territories or at home. Still, the compromise created a brief respite from the slavery-extension question at a time when the nation's attention increasingly needed to focus on other major changes in national life.

A Changing Political Economy

In the years following the Compromise of 1850, American economic and territorial growth continued to play a destabilizing role in both national and regional development. Most notably, during the 1850s industrial growth accelerated, further altering the nation's economic structure. By 1860 less than half of all northern workers made a living from agriculture as northern industry became more concentrated. Steam began to replace water as the primary power source, and factories were no longer limited to locations along rivers and streams. The use of interchangeable parts became more sophisticated and intricate. In 1851, for example, Isaac Singer devised an assembly line using this technology and began mass-producing sewing machines, fostering a boom in ready-made clothing. As industry expanded, the North became more reliant on the West and South for raw materials and for the food consumed by those working in northeastern factories.

Railroad development stimulated economic and industrial growth. Between 1850 and 1860, the number of miles of railroad track in the United States increased from 9,000 to more than 30,000. The vast majority of these lines linked the Northeast with the Midwest, carrying produce to eastern markets and eastern manufactures to western consumers. In 1852 the Michigan Southern Railroad completed the first line into Chicago from the East, and by 1855 that city had become a key transportation hub linking regions farther west with the eastern seaboard.

Developing this transportation system was difficult. A lack of bridges over major rivers, particularly over the Ohio, impeded rail traffic. Because there still was no standard **rail gauge**—at least twelve different measurements were used—cargo frequently had to be carted from one rail line to another. Despite these problems, railroads quickly became an integral part of the expanding American economy. Western farmers who had previously shipped their products downriver to New Orleans now sent them much more rapidly by rail to eastern industrial centers. The availability of reliable transportation induced farmers to cultivate more land, and enterprising individuals started up related

businesses such as warehouses and **grain elevators,** simplifying storage and loading along railroad lines. Mining boomed, particularly the iron industry; the railroads not only transported ore but also became a prime consumer.

Building a railroad required huge sums of money. In populous areas, where passenger and freight traffic was heavy, the promise of a quick and profitable return on investment allowed railroads to raise sufficient capital by selling company stock. In sparsely settled regions, however, where investment returns were much slower, state and local governments loaned money directly to rail companies, financed them indirectly by purchasing stock, or extended state tax exemptions. The most crucial aid to railroads, however, was federal land grants.

The federal government, which owned vast amounts of unsettled territory, gave land to developers who then leased or sold plots of ground along the proposed route to finance construction. In 1850 one such federal proposal made by Illinois senator Stephen A. Douglas resulted in a 2.6-million-acre land grant to Illinois, Mississippi, and Alabama for a railroad between Chicago and Mobile. Congress also invested heavily in plans for a transcontinental railroad and on March 4, 1853, appropriated $150,000 to survey potential routes across the continent.

While Americans were enjoying the rail boom, events in Europe were creating new markets for American produce. Several years of bad weather spurred crop failures throughout the region. In the face of rising public protest over the high cost of food, in 1846 the British Parliament repealed the Corn Laws, which had outlawed the importation of grain since 1804. Two years later, revolutions spread throughout much of continental Europe, followed by the outbreak of several wars. During the 1850s, the price of grain rose sharply in world markets. Railroads allowed western farmers to ship directly to eastern seaports and on to Europe. Meanwhile, technological advances in farming equipment enabled American farmers to harvest enough grain to meet world demand.

Using the steel plow devised in 1837 by **John Deere,** farmers could cultivate more acres with greater

---

rail gauge The distance between train tracks.

grain elevator A building equipped with mechanical lifting devices and used for storing grain.

John Deere American industrialist who pioneered the manufacture of steel plows especially suited for working hard-packed prairie soil.

The expansion of railroads facilitated transportation in a number of ways. Not only could western farmers get their produce to market and buy bulky manufactured goods delivered by train, but other modes of transportation were made easier. This illustration shows thirty stagecoaches built by a New Hampshire firm being hauled in a single load to the Wells Fargo Company in Omaha, Nebraska, which, in turn, used them to haul passengers and small freight to places where the trains did not go. *New Hampshire Historical Society, Concord.*

ease. The mechanical reaper invented in 1831 by **Cyrus McCormick** allowed a single operator to harvest as much as fourteen field hands could by hand. Railroads distributed these new pieces of heavy equipment at a reasonable cost. The combination of greater production potential and speedy transportation prompted westerners to increase farm size and concentrate on cash crops. The outcome of these developments was a vast increase in the economic and political power of the West.

Western grain markets provided the foodstuffs for American industrialization, and Europe provided much of the labor. Factories employed unskilled workers for the most part, and immigrants made up the majority of that labor pool as food shortages, poverty, and political upheaval drove millions from Europe, especially from Ireland and Germany (see pages 309–310; Map 11.1). Total immigration to the United States exceeded 100,000 for the first time in 1848, and in 1851, 221,000 people migrated to the United States from Ireland alone. In 1852 the number of German immigrants reached 145,000. Many of these newcomers, particularly the Irish, were not trained in skilled crafts and wound up settling in the industrial urban centers of the Northeast, where they could find work in the factories.

This combination of changes set the stage for political crisis. Liberalized suffrage rules transformed naturalized immigrants into voters, and both parties courted them, adding their interests to the political pot. Meanwhile, a mechanized textile industry, hungry for southern fiber, lent vitality to the continued growth of the cotton kingdom and the slave labor system that gave it life. Northern political leaders visualized an industrial nation based on free labor, but that view ran counter to the southern elites' ideals of **agrarian capitalism** based on slavery. In the West, most continued to believe in the Jeffersonian ideal of an agricultural nation of small and medium-size farms and could not accept either industrial or cotton capitalism as positive developments.

Cyrus McCormick   Virginia inventor and manufacturer who developed and mass-produced the McCormick reaper, a machine that harvested grain.

agrarian capitalism   A system of agriculture based on the efficient, specialized production of crops intended to generate profits rather than subsistence.

New technologies responded to but also drove an economic revolution in the United States during the decades just prior to the Civil War. Power looms in the Northeast, cotton gins in the South, and farming machinery in the West increased productivity and launched the emergence of a national capitalist economy. Advertisements like this one often prompted western farmers to borrow the money to buy new machinery that promised to ease their labors while increasing their profits. In the process, they became increasingly enmeshed in a world bounded by high finance, advertising, and economic dependency. *CORBIS.*

Political Instability and the Election of 1852

Dynamic economic progress improved material life throughout the nation, but it also raised serious questions about what course progress should take. As one clear-sighted northern minister pointed out in 1852, the debate was not about whether America should pursue progress but about "different kinds and methods of progress." Contradictory visions of national destiny were about to cause the breakdown of the existing party system.

Slavery seemed to loom behind every debate, but most Americans, even southerners, had no personal investment in the institution. Two-thirds of southerners owned no slaves, tolerating the institution but hav-

ing only fleeting contact with the great plantations and the peculiar labor system operating on them. Northerners, too, were largely indifferent. Men like young Illinois state congressman **Abraham Lincoln** believed the institution was wrong but were not inclined to do anything about it. What mattered to these people was not slavery but autonomy—control over local affairs and over their own lives.

The slavery question challenged notions of autonomy in both the North and the South. In their widely disseminated rhetoric, abolitionists expanded the specter of the Slave Power conspiracy (see page 359), especially in the aftermath of the Compromise of 1850. Growing numbers perceived this conspiracy as intent on imposing southern ways onto all parts of the country and installing southern elites or their sympathizers in seats of power in every section of the nation. Whether they were farmers in western states like Illinois or artisans in Pennsylvania, common people were jealous of their own local institutions and would resist a southern takeover. Nor would common people in the South accept interference from outsiders, and the ever more vigorous antisouthern crusade by northern radicals alarmed them as well.

The Compromise of 1850 momentarily eased regional fears, but sectional tensions still smoldered beneath the surface. These embers flamed anew in 1852 with the publication of *Uncle Tom's Cabin* by **Harriet Beecher Stowe.** Stowe portrayed the darkest inhumanities of southern slavery in the first American novel to include African Americans as central characters. *Uncle Tom's Cabin* sold three hundred thousand copies in its first year. Adapted for the stage, it became one of the most popular plays of the period. The book stirred public opinion and breathed new life into antislavery sentiments, leading Free-Soilers and so-called **conscience Whigs** to renew their efforts to limit or end slavery. When these activists saw that the Whig Party was incapable of addressing the slavery question in any effective way, they began to look for other political options.

Abraham Lincoln Illinois lawyer and politician who argued against popular sovereignty in debates with Stephen Douglas in 1858; he lost the senatorial election to Douglas but was elected president in 1860.

Harriet Beecher Stowe American novelist and abolitionist whose novel *Uncle Tom's Cabin* fanned antislavery sentiment in the North.

conscience Whigs Members of the Whig Party who supported moderate abolitionism, as opposed to cotton Whigs, members who opposed abolitionism.

Not only did Harriet Beecher Stowe's *Uncle Tom's Cabin* fire up northern antislavery sentiments, but it also was the first American novel that featured African American characters in prominent roles. It was issued in various editions with many different covers, but most of them featured the lead character, Uncle Tom—another first in American publishing. This particular cover, from an early "Young Folks' Edition" of the book, depicts the stooped old man with his young, sympathetic white mistress. *Collection of Picture Research Consultants & Archives.*

Superficially, the Whigs seemed well organized and surprisingly unified as a new presidential election approached. They passed over Millard Fillmore, who had advanced into the presidency when Zachary Taylor died in office in July 1850, in favor of General Winfield Scott, Taylor's military rival in the War with Mexico. The Democrats remained divided through forty-nine ballots, unable to decide between Lewis Cass of Michigan, Stephen A. Douglas of Illinois, and **James Buchanan** of Pennsylvania. They finally settled on the virtually unknown **Franklin Pierce** of New Hampshire, who pledged to live by and uphold the Compromise of 1850 and keep slavery out of politics. This promise was enough to bring Martin Van Buren back to the Democrats, and he brought many Free-Soilers back with him. Many others, though, abandoned Van Buren and joined forces with conscience Whigs.

Scott was a national figure and a distinguished military hero, but Pierce gathered 254 electoral votes to Scott's 42. This one-sided victory, however, revealed more about the disarray in the Whig Party than it did about Pierce's popularity or Democratic Party strength. Splits between "cotton" and "conscience" groups splintered Whig unity. Regional tension escalated as Free-Soil rhetoric clashed with calls for extending slavery. Confrontations between Catholics and Protestants and between native-born and immigrant laborers caused bitter animosity. In the North, where immigration, industrialization, and antislavery sentiment were most prevalent and economic friction was most pronounced, massive numbers of voters, believing the Whigs incapable of addressing current problems, deserted the party.

Increasing Tension Under Pierce

The Democratic Party and Franklin Pierce, its representative in the White House, were also not immune to the pressures of a changing electorate. Pierce was part of the **Young America Movement,** which, as a whole, tried to ignore the slavery issue, advocating romantic and aggressive nationalism, manifest destiny, and republican revolutions throughout the Americas. In line with the Young America agenda, Pierce emphasized expansion; choosing a route for a transcontinental railroad became the keystone in his agenda for the nation.

Southerners knew that a railroad based in the South would channel the flow of gold from California through their region and would also open new areas for settlement and allow cotton agriculture to spread beyond the waterways that had proved so necessary to its expansion so far. Eventually the new territories would become states, increasing the South's national political power.

That model of development was totally unacceptable to several groups: to northern evangelicals, who viewed slavery as a moral blight on the nation; to Free-Soil advocates, who believed the spread of slavery would degrade white workers; and to northern manufacturers, who wanted to maintain dominance in Congress to ensure continued economic protection.

James Buchanan   Pennsylvania senator who was elected president in 1856 after gaining the Democratic nomination as a compromise candidate.

Franklin Pierce   New Hampshire lawyer and Democratic politician nominated as a compromise candidate and elected president in 1852.

Young America Movement   A political movement popular among young voters during the 1840s and early 1850s that advocated free-market capitalism, national expansionism, and American patriotism.

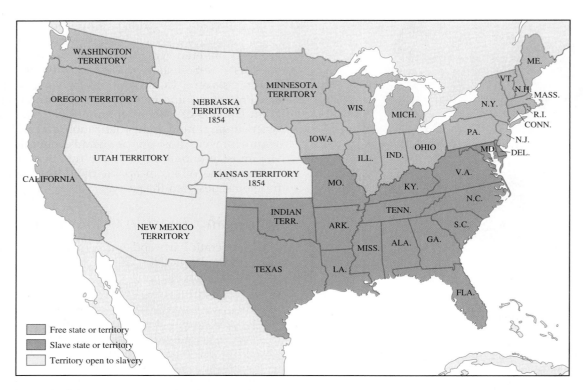

MAP 13.2 **The Kansas-Nebraska Act** This map shows Stephen Douglas's proposed compromise to resolve the dilemma of organizing the vast territory separating the settled part of the United States from California and Oregon. His solution, designed in part to win profitable rail connections for his home district in Illinois, stirred a political crisis by repealing the Missouri Compromise and replacing it with popular sovereignty.

In May 1853, only two months after assuming office, Pierce inflamed all of these groups by sending James Gadsden, a southern railroad developer, to Mexico to purchase a strip of land lying below the southern border of the New Mexico Territory. Any rail line built westward from a southern city would have to cross that land as it proceeded from Texas to California, and Pierce and his southern supporters wanted to make sure that it was part of the United States. The **Gadsden Purchase,** signed on December 30, 1853, added 29,640 square miles of land to the United States for a cost of $10 million. It also finalized the southwestern border of the United States.

Rather than enhancing Pierce's reputation as a nationalist, the Gadsden Purchase fed the perception that he was a southern sympathizer promoting the extension of slavery. It also led to a more serious sectional crisis. The Gadsden Purchase prompted proponents of a southern route for the transcontinental railroad, led by Secretary of War **Jefferson Davis,** to push for gov-

ernment sponsorship of the project. Rooted politically in Chicago and having invested his own money in rail development, Illinois senator Stephen A. Douglas rose to the challenge. He used his position as chairman of the Senate's Committee on Territories to block Davis's effort to build a transcontinental railroad through the South and pushed for a route westward from Chicago. This route passed through territory that had been set aside for a permanent Native American homeland and thus had not been organized into a federal territory. To rectify this problem, Douglas intro-

Gadsden Purchase A strip of land in present-day Arizona and New Mexico that the United States bought from Mexico in 1853 to secure a southern route for a transcontinental railroad.

Jefferson Davis Secretary of war under Franklin Pierce; he later became president of the Confederacy.

duced a bill on January 4, 1854, incorporating the entire northern half of Indian Territory into a new federal entity called Nebraska.

Douglas knew that he would need both northern and southern support to get his bill through Congress, so he tried to structure the legislation so as to alienate neither section. Fearful that the bill would spark yet another debate over slavery, Douglas sought to silence possible opposition by proposing that the matter be left to popular sovereignty within the territory itself—let the voters of Nebraska decide. Noting that the proposed territory was above the Missouri Compromise line, southerners pointed out that Congress might prohibit popular sovereignty from functioning. Douglas responded that the Compromise of 1850 superseded the 1820 Missouri Compromise, but he finally supported an amendment to his original bill dividing the territory in half—Nebraska in the north and Kansas in the south (see Map 13.2). The amended legislation—now called the **Kansas-Nebraska Act**—was based on the assumption that popular sovereignty would lead to slavery in Kansas and a system of free labor in Nebraska; Douglas calculated that both northerners and southerners would be satisfied and support the bill.

Toward a House Divided

→ *How did various political coalitions react to the Kansas-Nebraska Act?*

→ *What was the effect of these various reactions on the national political climate?*

Once again slavery threatened national political stability. In the North, opponents of the bill formed local coalitions to defeat it. On January 24, 1854, a group of Democrats including Salmon P. Chase, Gerrit Smith, Joshua Giddings, and **Charles Sumner** published "The Appeal of the Independent Democrats in Congress, to the People of the United States." They called the bill an "atrocious plot" to make Nebraska a "dreary region of despotism, inhabited by masters and slaves." On February 28, opponents of the Kansas-Nebraska bill met in Ripon, Wisconsin, and recommended the formation of a new political party. Similar meetings took place in several northern states as opposition to the bill grew. In the wake of these meetings, the existing party system would collapse and a new one would arise to replace it.

A Shattered Compromise

Despite this strong opposition, Douglas and Pierce rallied support for the Kansas-Nebraska Act in Con-

gress. On May 26, 1854, after gaining approval in the House of Representatives, the bill passed the Senate, and Pierce soon signed it into law. Passage of the act crystallized northern antislavery sentiment. To protest, many northerners threatened **noncompliance** with the fugitive slave law of 1850. As Senator William Seward of New York vowed, "We will engage in competition for the virgin soil of Kansas, and God give the victory to the side which is stronger in numbers as it is in right."

Antislavery forces, however, remained divided into at least three major groups. The Free-Soil contingent opposed any extension of slavery but did not necessarily favor abolishing the institution. The other two groups—Garrisonians and evangelicals—wanted immediate abolition but disagreed on many particulars. William Lloyd Garrison and his followers believed that slavery was the primary evil facing the nation, and they embraced anyone who held that position. Evangelicals agreed that slavery was evil, but they believed it was one among many vices undermining the virtuous republic. All three groups constantly agitated against slavery and what they perceived as southern control of national politics. They weakened the Democratic Party's strength in the North but could not bring themselves to align behind a single opposition party.

Talk of expansion also threatened Democratic unity in the South. Many southerners believed that extending slavery was necessary to prevent northern domination. Increased northern wealth and continued conflict over the expansion of slavery convinced many southern Democrats that northern manufacturing and commercial power threatened to reduce the South to a "colony" controlled by northern bankers and industrialists.

Some southerners attempted to neutralize this perceived threat by acquiring colonies of their own in the Caribbean and Central America. Although all these efforts were the work of a few power-hungry individuals, many northerners believed them to be part of the Slave Power conspiracy. President Pierce

---

Kansas-Nebraska Act Law passed by Congress in 1854 that allowed residents of Kansas and Nebraska territories to decide whether to allow slavery within their borders.

Charles Sumner Massachusetts senator who was brutally beaten by a southern congressman in 1856 after delivering a speech attacking the South.

noncompliance Failure or refusal to obey a law or request.

unintentionally aggravated this sentiment by pushing to acquire Cuba, which he hoped to purchase from Spain. The Spanish, however, were unwilling to negotiate, and in October 1854 three of Pierce's European ministers met in Ostend, Belgium, and secretly drafted a statement outlining conditions that might justify taking Cuba by force. When the so-called **Ostend Manifesto** became public in 1855, many northerners felt betrayed, fearing that Pierce and the Democratic Party approved of undercover adventurism to expand slavery. These perceptions stirred antislavery anxieties and fueled the growth of the newly formed anti-Democratic coalitions.

Bleeding Kansas

Meanwhile, political friction was about to ignite Kansas. In April 1854, abolitionist Eli Thayer of Worcester, Massachusetts, organized the New England Emigrant Aid Society to encourage antislavery supporters to move to Kansas. They reasoned that flooding a region subject to popular sovereignty with right-minded residents could effectively "save" it from slavery. This group eventually sent two thousand armed settlers to Kansas, founding Lawrence and other communities. With similar designs, proslavery southerners, particularly those in Missouri, also encouraged settlement in the territory. Like their northern counterparts, these southerners came armed and ready to fight for their cause.

President Pierce appointed governors in both Kansas and Nebraska and instructed them to organize elections for territorial legislatures. As proslavery and antislavery settlers vied for control of Kansas, the region became a testing ground for popular sovereignty. When the vote came on March 30, 1855, a large contingent of armed slavery supporters from Missouri—so-called border ruffians—crossed into Kansas and cast ballots for proslavery candidates. According to later Senate investigations, 60 percent of the votes cast were illegal. These unlawful ballots gave proslavery supporters a large majority in the Kansas legislature. They promptly expelled all abolitionist legislators and enacted the Kansas Code—a group of laws meant to drive all antislavery forces out of the territory. Antislavery advocates refused to acknowledge the validity of the election or the laws. They organized their own free-state government and drew up an alternative constitution, which they submitted to the voters.

Bloodshed soon followed. Attempting to bring the conflict to conclusion, proslavery territorial judge Samuel LeCompte called a grand jury of slavery supporters that indicted members of the free-state government for treason and sent a **posse** of about eight hundred men armed with rifles and five cannon to Lawrence. There they "arrested" the antislavery forces and sacked the town, burning buildings and plundering shops and homes. But the violence did not end there. Hearing news of the "Sack of Lawrence," **John Brown,** an antislavery zealot, vowed to "fight fire with fire." Reasoning that at least five antislavery supporters had been killed since the conflict erupted, he and seven others abducted five proslavery men living along the Pottawatomie River south of Lawrence and murdered them. The "Pottawatomie Massacre" triggered a series of episodes in which more than two hundred men were killed. Much of the violence was the work of border ruffians and zealots like Brown, but to many people in both the North and the South, the events symbolized the "righteousness" of their cause.

The Kansas issue also led to violence in Congress. During the debates over the admission of the territory, Charles Sumner, a senator from Massachusetts, delivered an abusive and threatening speech against proslavery advocates. In particular, he made insulting remarks about South Carolina and its 60-year-old senator Andrew Butler. Butler was out of town, but Butler's nephew, Representative Preston Brooks, accosted Sumner and nearly beat him to death with a cane. Though **censured** by the House of Representatives, Brooks was overwhelmingly reelected by his home district and openly praised for his actions—he received canes as gifts from admirers all over the South.

Meanwhile the presidential election of 1856 was approaching. The Pierce administration's actions, southern expansionism, and the Kansas-Nebraska controversy swelled the ranks of dissenters like those who had convened in Ripon. Now formally calling themselves the **Republican Party,** these northern and

---

Ostend Manifesto Declaration by American foreign ministers in 1854 that if Spain refused to sell Cuba, the United States might be justified in taking it by force.

posse A group of citizens deputized by a court or peace officer to assist in law enforcement.

John Brown Abolitionist who fought proslavery settlers in Kansas in 1855; he was hanged for treason after seizing the U.S. arsenal at Harpers Ferry in 1859 as part of an effort to liberate southern slaves.

censure To issue an official rebuke, as by a legislature to one of its members.

Republican Party Political party formed in 1854 that opposed the extension of slavery into the western territories.

Though no one would deny that their cause was noble, many of the men who flocked to Kansas to resist the expansion of slavery were no less violent than their proslavery adversaries. This photograph taken in 1859 shows a gang of armed antislavery men who had just broken an accomplice (John Doy, seated) out of jail in neighboring St. Joseph, Missouri. Like proslavery border ruffians, many of these men also served in guerrilla bands during the Civil War, and some went on to careers as famous outlaws after the war was over. *Kansas State Historical Society.*

western groups began actively seeking support. Immigration also remained a major issue, but the Know-Nothings, despite their success at the local and state levels, split over slavery at their initial national convention in 1855. Disagreement over a **plank** dealing with the Kansas-Nebraska Act caused most northerners to bolt from the convention. Some formed an antislavery group called the Know-Somethings, but many joined Republican coalitions. In 1856 the remaining Know-Nothings reconvened and nominated former president Millard Fillmore as the party's standard-bearer. John C. Frémont, a moderate abolitionist who had achieved fame as the liberator of California (see page 360), got the Republican nomination. The few remaining Whigs endorsed Fillmore at their convention, while some former Know-Nothings met separately and endorsed Frémont. The Democrats rejected both Pierce and Douglas and nominated James Buchanan from Pennsylvania, selecting John C. Breckinridge of Kentucky as Buchanan's running mate to balance the ticket between the North and the South.

The election became a contest for party survival rather than a national referendum on slavery. Buchanan received 45 percent of the popular vote and 163 electoral votes. Frémont finished second with 33 percent of the popular vote and 114 electoral votes. Fillmore received 21 percent of the popular vote but only 8 electoral votes. Frémont's surprisingly narrow margin of defeat demonstrated the appeal of the newly

formed Republican coalition to northern voters. The Know-Nothings, fragmented over slavery, disappeared and never again attempted a national organization.

Bringing Slavery Home to the North

On March 4, 1857, James Buchanan became president of the United States. The 65-year-old Pennsylvanian had begun his political career in Congress in 1821 and owed much of his success to southern support. His election came at a time when the nation needed strong leadership, but Buchanan seemed unable to provide it. During the campaign, he had emphasized national unity, but he proved incapable of achieving a unifying compromise. His attempt to preserve the politics of avoidance only strengthened radicalism in both the North and the South. **Regionalism** colored all political issues, and every debate became a contest between competing social, political, and economic ideologies.

Though Buchanan's shortcomings contributed to the rising crisis, an event occurred within days of his

plank   One of the articles of a political platform.
regionalism   Loyalty to the interests of a particular region of the country.

In attempting to win his freedom, Dred Scott unintentionally set a legal process in motion that would deny Congress's right to control the extension of slavery. This 1858 painting captures Scott's resolution and strength of character. *"Dred Scott" by Louis Schultze, 1881. Missouri State Historical Society, St. Louis.*

inauguration that sent shock waves through the already troubled nation. **Dred Scott,** a slave once owned by John Emerson, resided in Missouri, a slave state. But between 1831 and 1833, Emerson, an army surgeon, had taken Scott with him during various postings, including stints in Illinois and Wisconsin, where the Missouri Compromise banned slavery. Scott's attorney argued that living in Illinois and Wisconsin had made Scott a free man. When, after nearly six years in the Missouri courts, the state supreme court rejected this argument in 1852, Scott, with the help of abolitionist lawyers, appealed to the United States Supreme Court. In a 7-to-2 decision, the Court ruled against Scott. Chief Justice Roger B. Taney, formerly a member of Andrew Jackson's Kitchen Cabinet and a stalwart Democrat (see page 286), argued that in the eyes of the law slaves were not people but property; as such, they could not be citizens of the United States and had no right to petition the Court. Taney then ignited a political powder keg by ruling that Congress had no constitutional authority to limit slavery in a federal territory, thereby declaring the Missouri Compromise unconstitutional.

While southerners generally celebrated the decision, antislavery forces and northern evangelical leaders called the *Dred Scott* decision a mockery of justice and a crime against a "higher law." Some radical abolitionists argued that the North should separate from the Union. Others suggested impeaching the Supreme Court. Already incensed by events in Kansas, antislavery leaders predicted that the next move by the Slave Power conspiracy would be to get the Supreme Court to strike down antislavery laws in northern states.

Meanwhile, the Kansas issue still burned. The fact that very few slaveholders actually moved into the territory did nothing to deter proslavery leaders, who met in Lecompton, Kansas, in June 1857 to draft a state constitution favoring slavery. When the **Lecompton constitution** was submitted for voters' approval, antislavery forces protested by refusing to vote, so it was easily ratified. But when it was revealed that more than two thousand nonresidents had voted illegally, both Republicans and northern Democrats in Congress roundly denounced it. The Buchanan administration joined southerners in support of admitting Kansas to the Union as a slave state and managed to push the statehood bill through the Senate, but the House of Representatives rejected it. Congress then returned the Lecompton constitution to Kansas for another vote. This time Free-Soilers participated in the election and defeated the proposed constitution. Kansas remained a territory.

The Kansas controversy proved a hard pill for Douglas to swallow. He believed in popular sovereignty but could not support the fraudulent election that brought the Lecompton constitution to Congress for approval. And the *Dred Scott* decision had virtually nullified his pet solution by ruling that even popular sovereignty could not exclude slavery from a state or territory. Still entertaining presidential ambitions, Douglas sought a solution that might win him both northern and southern support in a run for the office

Dred Scott   Slave who sued for his liberty in the Missouri courts, arguing that four years on free soil had made him free; the Supreme Court's 1857 ruling against him negated the Missouri Compromise.

Lecompton constitution   State constitution written for Kansas in 1857 at a convention dominated by proslavery forces; it would have allowed slavery, but Kansas voters rejected it.

IT MATTERS TODAY

THE DRED SCOTT CASE

Frederick Douglass was disappointed to discover that freedom for African Americans did not also mean equality. This personal revelation was soon reinforced by one of the most important cases ever to reach the Supreme Court. Denying once and for all that freedom and equality for people of African heritage were identical, the Court's decision in *Dred Scott v. Sanford* declared that because no state at the time that the Constitution was ratified had included African Americans as citizens, then no one of African descent could become a citizen of the United States. Ever! It would take the Thirteenth, Fourteenth, and Fifteenth Amendments to the Constitution to remove the legal justification behind the Court's opinion, but even these did not reverse the racism underlying the decision. The *Dred Scott* case and the amendments designed to correct the constitutional defects that led to it still play a key role in dozens of cases in the nation's courts each year as men and women of many backgrounds seek to make real the tie between freedom and equality that Dred Scott and Frederick Douglass only dreamed of.

- To what extent do you think that the *Dred Scott* case made Civil War in the United States inevitable? Explain.

- Choose a post–Civil War court case dealing with racial equality issues (the American Civil Liberties Union and other organizations as well as the federal government maintain catalogues of important cases). In what ways does the case you have chosen reflect the *Dred Scott* case and the constitutional amendments passed in response? Assess the continuing legacy of this case in American life and justice.

in 1860. His immediate goal, however, was reelection to the Senate.

Illinois Republicans selected Abraham Lincoln to run against Douglas for the Senate in 1858. Born on the Kentucky frontier in 1809, Lincoln had accompanied his family from one failed farm to another, picking up schooling in Indiana and Illinois as opportunities arose. As a young man he worked odd jobs—farm worker, ferryman, flatboatman, surveyor, and store clerk—and

was a member of the Illinois militia during the Black Hawk War in 1832 (see page 289). Two years after the war, Lincoln was elected to the Illinois legislature and began a serious study of law. He was admitted to the Illinois state bar in 1836. A strong Whig, Lincoln followed Henry Clay's economic philosophy and steered a middle course between the "cotton" and "conscience" wings of the Whig Party. Lincoln acknowledged that slavery was evil but contended that it was the unavoidable consequence of black racial inferiority. The only way to get rid of the evil, he believed, was to prevent the expansion of slavery into the territories, forcing it to die out naturally, and then make arrangements to separate the two races forever, either by transporting them to Africa or creating a segregated space for them in the Americas.

Lincoln was decidedly the underdog in the contest with Douglas and sought to improve his chances by challenging the senator to a series of debates about slavery and its expansion. Douglas agreed to seven debates in various parts of the state. During the debate at Freeport, Lincoln asked Douglas to explain how the people of a territory could exclude slavery in light of the *Dred Scott* ruling. Douglas's reply became known as the **Freeport Doctrine.** Slavery, he said, needed the protection of "local police regulations." In any territory, citizens opposed to slavery could elect representatives who would "by unfriendly legislation" prevent the introduction of slavery. Lincoln did not win Douglas's Senate seat, but the debate drew national attention to the Illinois race, and Lincoln won recognition as an up-and-coming Republican force.

Radical Responses to Abolitionism and Slavery

Southerners bristled at claims by Lincoln and others that slavery was immoral. Charles C. Jones and other southern evangelical leaders, for example, offered a religious defense of slavery. Such apologists argued that whites had a moral responsibility to care for blacks and instruct them in the Christian faith. Those who claimed that the Bible condoned slavery pointed out that the Israelites practiced slavery and that when Jesus walked among slaves he never mentioned freedom.

Freeport Doctrine   Stephen Douglas's belief, stated at Freeport, Illinois, that a territory could exclude slavery by writing local laws or regulations that made slavery impossible to enforce.

Hoping to trigger a full-scale revolt against slavery, or perhaps even a civil war, Kansas radical John Brown seized the federal armory at Harpers Ferry, Virginia on October 16, 1859. As shown here, a military force led by then colonel Robert E. Lee finally overcame Brown and his volunteer army. Taken prisoner, Brown was eventually tried for treason and was hanged in the following December. Many proclaimed him martyr, and his name became a rallying cry for those who sought an immediate end to slavery. © *Bettmann/CORBIS.*

The apostle Paul, they argued, even commanded slaves to obey their masters.

Many southerners, like some of their Republican opponents, were less interested in the slave than in how slavery affected white society and white labor. When the Republicans argued that slavery defiled labor, southern apologists countered that slavery was a "mudsill," or foundation, supporting democracy. Southerners contended that whites in the South enjoyed a greater degree of freedom than northern whites because slaves did all the demeaning work, freeing whites for more noble pursuits. Moreover, southern lawyer George Fitzhugh argued, both the North and the South relied equally on a subjugated work force: southerners on **chattel slavery** and northerners on **wage slavery.** Fitzhugh charged that poor northern whites were a "mudsill" as surely as slaves were in the South. The only meaningful difference between wage slaves and southern slaves, Fitzhugh concluded, was that northerners accepted no responsibility for housing and feeding their work force, condemning laborers to suffer at below-subsistence conditions.

These ideas infuriated northerners as much as antislavery arguments angered southerners because they challenged deeply held cultural and social values. Northern radicals increasingly called for the violent overthrow of slavery, and Kansas zealot John Brown moved to oblige them. In 1857 Brown came to the East, where he convinced several prominent antislavery leaders to finance a daring plan to raise an army of

slaves in an all-out insurrection against their masters. Brown and a small party of followers attacked the federal arsenal at **Harpers Ferry,** Virginia, on October 16, 1859, attempting to seize weapons. The arsenal proved an easy target, but no slaves joined the uprising. Local citizens surrounded the arsenal, firing on Brown and his followers until federal troops commanded by Colonel **Robert E. Lee** arrived. On October 18, Lee's forces battered down the barricaded entrance and arrested Brown. He was tried, convicted of treason, and hanged on December 2, 1859.

Brown's raid on Harpers Ferry captured the imagination of radical abolitionists. Republican leaders denounced it, but other northerners proclaimed Brown a martyr. Church bells tolled in many northern cities on

chattel slavery   The bondage of people who are considered to be the movable personal property of their owners.

wage slavery   The bondage of workers who, though legally free, are underpaid, trapped in debt, and living in extreme poverty.

Harpers Ferry   Town in present-day West Virginia and site of the U.S. arsenal that John Brown briefly seized in 1859.

Robert E. Lee   A Virginian with a distinguished career in the U.S. Army who resigned to assume command of the Confederate army in Virginia when the Civil War began.

the day of his execution. In New England, Ralph Waldo Emerson proclaimed Brown "that new saint." Such reactions caused many appalled southerners—even extreme moderates—to seriously consider **secession.** In Alabama, Mississippi, and Florida, state legislatures resolved that a Republican victory in the upcoming presidential election would provide sufficient justification for such action.

The Divided Nation

→ *How did the realignment of the political party system during the 1850s contribute to the conduct and results of the presidential election in 1860?*

→ *Why did the election results have the political effects that they did?*

The Republicans were a new phenomenon on the American political scene: a purely regional political party. Rather than making any attempt to forge a national coalition, the party drew its strength and ideas almost entirely from the North. The Republican platform— "Free Soil, Free Labor, and Free Men"—stressed the defilement of white labor by slavery and contended that the Slave Power conspiracy was eroding the rights of free whites everywhere. By taking up a cry against "Rum, Romanism, and Slavery," the Republicans drew former Know-Nothings and temperance advocates into their ranks. The Democrats hoped to maintain a national coalition, but as the nation approached a new presidential election, their hopes began to fade.

The Dominance of Regionalism

During the Buchanan administration, Democrats found it increasingly difficult to achieve national party unity. Facing Republican pressure in their own states, northern Democrats realized that any concession to southern Democratic demands for extending or protecting slavery would cost them votes at home. In April 1860, as the party convened in Charleston, South Carolina, each side was ready to do battle for its political life.

The fight began when northern supporters of Stephen A. Douglas championed a popular sovereignty position. Southern radicals demanded a plank calling for the legal protection of slavery in the territories. After heated debates, neither side would compromise. When the delegates finally voted, the Douglas forces carried the day. Disgusted delegates from eight southern states walked out of the convention. Shocked, the remaining delegates adjourned the convention;

they would reconvene in Baltimore in June. Most southern delegates boycotted the Baltimore proceedings, and Douglas easily won the Democratic presidential nomination. Moderate southerner Herschel V. Johnson of Georgia was his running mate. Hoping to attract moderate voters from both the North and the South, the party's final platform supported popular sovereignty and emphasized allegiance to the Union.

The southern Democratic contingent met one week later, also in Baltimore, and nominated Vice President John C. Breckinridge of Kentucky as its presidential candidate and Joseph Lane of Oregon as his running mate. The southern Democrats' platform vowed support for the Union but called for federal protection of the right to own slaves in the territories and for the preservation of slavery where it already existed.

In May 1860, a group of former Whigs and Know-Nothings along with some disaffected Democrats convened in Baltimore and formed the **Constitutional Union Party.** They nominated John Bell, a former southern Know-Nothing and wealthy slaveholder from Tennessee, for president and Edward Everett of Massachusetts, a former Whig leader, as his running mate. Hoping to resurrect the politics of compromise, the party resolved to take no stand on the sectional controversy and pledged to uphold the Constitution and the Union and to enforce the laws of the nation.

Having lost most of its moderates to the Constitutional Union coalition and having virtually no southerners in its ranks to start with, the Republican convention faced few ideological divisions, but personality conflicts were rife. The front-runner for the Republican nomination appeared to be William Seward of New York. A former Whig and longtime New York politician, Seward had actively opposed any extension of slavery during the early 1850s but had switched to the popular-sovereignty position during the Kansas controversy. Several other Republican favorites—Salmon P. Chase of Ohio, Simon Cameron of Pennsylvania, and Edward Bates of Missouri— agreed with Seward's position but sought their own nominations. Eventually, however, Illinois favorite son Abraham Lincoln emerged as Seward's major competition. Many delegates considered Seward too radical.

---

secession Withdrawal from the United States.
Constitutional Union Party Political party that organized on the eve of the Civil War with no platform other than preservation of the Constitution, the Union, and the law.

As this cartoon makes clear, the *Dred Scott* case set the agenda for the presidential election of 1860. Here Scott provides the music as each of the four presidential candidates dances with a partner who symbolizes his perceived political orientation. John C. Breckinridge (upper left) dances with fellow southern Democrat James Buchanan, illustrating his alignment with southern proslavery hard-liners. John H. Bell (lower right) dances with a Native American, symbolizing his nativist Know-Nothing affiliations, suggesting avoidance of the slavery issue. Meanwhile, Stephen A. Douglas (lower left) escorts a disheveled Irishman, suggesting his alignment with northeastern urban interests including immigrants and other "undesirables." Finally, Abraham Lincoln (upper right) is seen with an African American woman, an obvious reference to his party's perceived abolitionist leanings. *Courtesy Lilly Library, Indiana University, Bloomington, IN.*

Moreover, he and his campaign manager, Thurlow Weed (see pages 282–283), had earned the distrust of many prominent Republicans for their political wheeling and dealing. Lincoln, in contrast, had a reputation for integrity and had not seriously alienated any of the Republican factions. He won the nomination on the third ballot.

The Election of 1860

The 1860 presidential campaign began as several separate contests. Lincoln and Douglas competed for northern votes; the Republicans were not even on the ballot in the **Deep South**. Douglas proclaimed himself the only national candidate but received most of his support from northerners who feared the consequences of a Republican victory. By the same token, Breckinridge and the southern Democrats expected

no support in the North. Bell and the Constitutional Unionists attempted to campaign in both regions but attracted mostly southern voters anxious to stave off the crisis of disunion.

Slavery and sectionalism were the key issues. Even when a congressional investigation revealed evidence of graft, bribery, and shady dealings in the Buchanan administration, Republicans linked these charges to the supposed Slave Power conspiracy. The slaveholding elite, they contended, not only had attempted to subvert liberty but had used fraudulent means to keep

Deep South   The region of the South farthest from the North, usually said to comprise the states of Alabama, Florida, Georgia, Louisiana, Mississippi, and South Carolina.

the Democratic Party of Buchanan—and Douglas—in power. "Honest Abe Lincoln," the man of the people, would lead the fight against the forces of slavery and corruption. This argument drew in many northern voters, including a lot of former Know-Nothings.

Sensing that Lincoln would win the North, Douglas launched a last-ditch effort to win the election and hold the Union together by pushing his campaign into the South. Douglas and his forces tried unsuccessfully to form a coalition between moderate Democrats and Constitutional Unionists. Already in poor health, Douglas all but exhausted himself trying to prevent disunion.

As the election drew near, the likelihood of a Republican victory deeply alarmed southerners. Even moderate southerners started to believe that the Republicans intended to crush their way of life and to enslave southern whites economically while freeing southern blacks. Northern qualms were aroused as well when the pro-Democrat *New York Herald* contended that the election of Lincoln would bring "hundreds of thousands" of slaves north to compete with whites for jobs, resulting in "African amalgamation with the fair daughters of the Anglo-Saxon, Celtic, and Teutonic races."

Seeking to counter such scare tactics, national Republican leaders forged a platform that advocated limits on slavery's expansion but contained no planks seeking an end to slavery in areas where it already existed. They also called for higher tariffs (to appeal to northern industrialists) and for internal improvements and public lands legislation (to appeal to westerners). Particularly in the Midwest, party leaders worked hard to portray themselves as "the white man's party." In line with the position Lincoln had taken in his 1858 debates with Douglas, Republicans argued that excluding slavery meant excluding blacks from competition with whites. These tactics alienated a few abolitionists but persuaded many northerners and westerners to support the party.

On November 6, 1860, Abraham Lincoln was elected president of the United States with 180 electoral votes— a clear majority—but only 40 percent of the popular vote. Lincoln carried all the northern states, California, and Oregon (see Map 13.3). Douglas finished second with 29 percent of the popular vote but just 12 electoral votes. He won only Missouri. Bell won the 39 electoral votes of Virginia, Kentucky, and Tennessee. Breckinridge, as expected, carried the Deep South but tallied only 72 electoral votes and 18 percent of the popular vote nationwide. For the first time in American history, a purely regional party held the presidency. The Republicans, who had made no effort to win votes

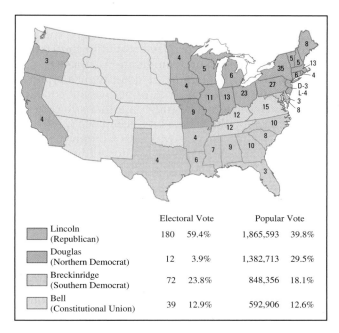

		Electoral Vote		Popular Vote	
Lincoln (Republican)		180	59.4%	1,865,593	39.8%
Douglas (Northern Democrat)		12	3.9%	1,382,713	29.5%
Breckinridge (Southern Democrat)		72	23.8%	848,356	18.1%
Bell (Constitutional Union)		39	12.9%	592,906	12.6%

MAP 13.3 Election of 1860 The election of 1860 confirmed the worst fears expressed by concerned Union supporters during the 1850s: changes in the nation's population made it possible for one section to dominate national politics. As this map shows, the Republican and southern Democratic Parties virtually split the nation, and the Republicans were able to seize the presidency.

in the South, also swept congressional races in the North and secured a large majority in the House of Representatives for the upcoming term.

The First Wave of Secession

After the Republican victory, southern sentiment for secession snowballed, especially in the Deep South. The Republicans were a "party founded on a single sentiment," stated the *Richmond Examiner*: "hatred of African slavery." The *New Orleans Delta* agreed, calling the Republicans "essentially a revolutionary party." But this party now controlled the national government. To a growing number of southerners, the Republican victory was proof that secession was the only alternative to political domination.

Calls for secession had been heard for decades, and most Republicans did not believe that the South would actually leave the Union. Seward had ridiculed threats of secession as an attempt "to terrify or alarm" the northern people. Lincoln himself believed that the "people of the South" had "too much sense" to launch an "attempt to ruin the government." During the campaign, he had promised "no interference by the government, with slaves or slavery within the states," and he continued to urge moderation.

In a last-ditch attempt at compromise, **John J. Crittenden** proposed a block of permanent constitutional amendments—amendments that could never be repealed—to the Senate on December 18, 1860. He suggested extending the Missouri Compromise line westward across the continent, forbidding slavery north of the line, and protecting slavery to the south. Crittenden's plan also upheld the interstate trade in slaves and called for compensation to slaveowners who were unable to recover fugitive slaves from northern states. Although this plan seemed to favor the South, it had some appeal in the North, especially among businessmen who feared that secession would cause a major depression. Thurlow Weed, Seward's political adviser, seemed ready to listen to such a compromise, but Lincoln was "inflexible on the territorial question." The extension of the Missouri Compromise line, Lincoln warned, would "lose us everything we gained by the election." He let senators and congressmen know that he wanted no "compromise in regard to the extension of slavery." The Senate defeated Crittenden's proposals by a vote of 25 to 23. The Kentuckian then proposed putting the measure to a vote of the people, but Congress rejected that idea as well.

Meanwhile, on December 20, 1860, delegates in South Carolina met to consider seceding from the Union. South Carolina had long been a hotbed of resistance to federal authority, and state officials determined to take action to protect slavery before the newly elected Republican administration came to power. Amid general jubilation, South Carolina delegates voted unanimously to dissolve their ties with the United States. Just as the radicals hoped, other southern states followed. During January 1861, delegates convened in Mississippi, Florida, Alabama, Georgia, and Louisiana and voted to secede (see Map 13.4).

On February 4, 1861, delegates from the six seceding states met in Montgomery, Alabama, and formed the provisional government for the **Confederate States of America.** During the several weeks that followed, the provisional congress drafted a constitution, and the six Confederate states ratified it on March 11, 1861.

The Confederate constitution emphasized the "sovereign and independent character" of the states and guaranteed the protection of slavery in any new territories acquired. It allowed tariffs solely for the purpose of raising government revenue and prohibited government funding of internal improvements. It also limited the president and vice president to a single six-year term. A cabinet composed of six executive department heads rounded out the executive branch. In all other respects, the Confederate government was identical to that in the United States. In fact, the U.S. Constitution was acknowledged as the supreme law in the Confederacy except in those particulars where it conflicted with provisions in the Confederate Constitution.

While this process was under way, the Confederate cause got a significant boost when Texas, which had been holding back, declared itself part of the new nation. Despite unionist pleas from Governor Sam Houston, the heavily populated cotton-growing region in the eastern part of the state opted to join neighboring Louisiana in rebellion, and the rest of the state followed suit. The Confederacy now numbered seven states.

Responses to Disunion

Even as late as March 1861, not all southerners favored secession. John Bell and Stephen Douglas together had received more than 50 percent of southern votes in 1860, winning support from southerners who desired compromise and had only limited stakes in upholding slavery. These "plain folk" joined together with some large planters, who stood to suffer economic loss from disunion, in calls for moderation and compromise. And the border states, which were less invested in cotton and had numerous ties with the North, were not strongly inclined toward secession. In February, Virginia had called for a peace conference to meet in Washington in an effort to forestall hostilities, but this attempt, like Crittenden's effort, also failed to hold the Union together.

The division in southern sentiments was a major stumbling block to the election of a Confederate president. Many moderate delegates to the constitutional convention refused to support radical secessionists, believing them to be equally responsible with the Republicans for initiating the crisis. The convention re-

---

John J. Crittenden Kentucky senator who made an unsuccessful attempt to prevent the Civil War by proposing a series of constitutional amendments protecting slavery south of the Missouri Compromise line.

Confederate States of America Political entity formed by the seceding states of South Carolina, Georgia, Florida, Alabama, Mississippi, and Louisiana in February 1861; Texas, Virginia, Arkansas, Tennessee, and North Carolina joined later.

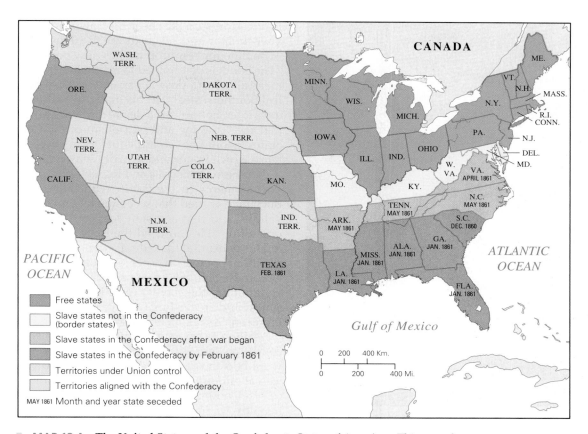

MAP 13.4 **The United States and the Confederate States of America** This map shows the breakup of the Union begun by South Carolina's secession in December 1860. The Cotton Belt followed South Carolina's lead in January, and the rest of the confederate states joined them later in the spring of 1861. Free states then aligned to oppose southern secession, while the border states and inland territories were caught in the middle.

mained deadlocked until two prosecession Virginia legislators nominated Mississippi moderate Jefferson Davis as a compromise candidate.

Davis appeared to be the ideal choice. Austere and dignified, he had not sought the job but seemed extremely capable of handling it. A West Point graduate, he served during the War with Mexico, was elected to the Senate soon afterward, then left the Senate in 1851 to run unsuccessfully for governor in Mississippi. After serving as secretary of war under Franklin Pierce, he returned to the Senate in 1857. Although Davis had long championed southern interests and owned many slaves, he was no romantic, fire-eating secessionist. Before 1860 he had been a strong **Unionist,** arguing only that the South be allowed to maintain its own economy, culture, and institutions, including slavery. He had supported the Compromise of 1850. When he had fought for a southern route for a transcontinental

railroad as secretary of war, he believed that it would benefit the South economically, but he also felt that it would tie the whole nation more firmly together. Like many of his contemporaries, however, Davis had become increasingly alarmed by the prospect of declining southern political power. Immediately after Mississippi's declaration of secession, Davis resigned his Senate seat and threw in with the Confederacy.

To moderates like Davis, the presidential election of 1860 was simply a forceful demonstration of a fact already in evidence: unless the South took a strong stand against outside interference, the region would no longer be able to control its own internal affairs.

Unionist Loyal to the United States of America.

A few months before being nominated by the Republican Party as its presidential candidate, Abraham Lincoln permitted Illinois artist Leonard Volk to cast the future president's face in plaster. Preserved for all these years, this casting and the many reproductions that have been struck from it remain the most accurate picture we have of Lincoln before the secession crisis tore the nation apart. Captured in time, we can see the noble and serious man whose unflinching determination saw the nation through its worst historical crisis. As the many hundreds of photographs and other images of Lincoln during his presidency attest, he would never look this young and confident again. *Picture History.*

The initial northward tilt in the Senate created by California's admission in 1850 had been aggravated in 1858 by the admission of Minnesota and by Oregon's statehood in 1859. Southerners, Davis believed, needed to act in concert to convince northerners to either leave the South alone or face the region's withdrawal from the nation. "To rally the men of the North, who would preserve the government as our fathers found it," Davis proclaimed, "we . . . should offer no doubtful or divided front."

Elected provisional president of the Confederate States of America unanimously on February 9, 1861, Davis addressed the cheering crowds in Montgomery a week later and set forth the Confederate position: "The time for compromise has now passed," he said. "The South is determined to maintain her position, and make all who oppose her smell Southern powder and feel Southern steel." In his inaugural address several days later, he stressed a desire for peace but reiterated that the "courage and patriotism of the Confederate States" would be "found equal to any measure of defense which honor and security may require."

Northern Democrats and Republicans alike watched developments in the South with dismay. President Buchanan argued that secession had no constitutional validity and that any state leaving the Union did so unlawfully. He confused the issue, however, by stating his belief that the federal government had no constitutional power to "coerce a State" to remain in the Union. He blamed the crisis on "incessant and violent agitation on the slavery question," chiding northern states for disregarding fugitive slave laws and calling for a constitutional amendment protecting slavery.

Waiting to assume the office he had just won, Lincoln wrestled with the twin problems of what he would do about secession and slavery. African American abolitionist Frederick Douglass summed up Lincoln's dilemma. "Much as I value the current apparent hostility to Slavery," Douglass stated, "I plainly see that it is less the outgrowth of high and moral conviction against Slavery, as such, than because of the trouble its friends have brought upon the country." The South had divided the nation by seceding, and as Douglass indicated, many northerners were much more concerned about the breakup of the nation and potential hostilities between the North and the South than they ever had been about slavery. Lincoln wrote, "My opinion is that no state can, in any way, lawfully get out of the Union, without the consent of the others." He attempted to clarify his position in a letter to Alexander H. Stephens, who would soon become vice president of the Confederacy. Trying to reassure him that "a republican administration" would not "directly or indirectly, interfere with their slaves, or with them, about their slaves," the president-elect still refused to consider any compromise on disunion or the extension of slavery.

Before he could do anything else, Lincoln first had to unite his party. In an attempt to appease all the Republican factions, he chose his cabinet with great care. His vice president, the moderate Hannibal Hamlin of Maine, had supported Lincoln but was also a friend of William Seward and had been chosen to balance the ticket factionally. Lincoln continued this balancing act by appointing to his cabinet his four main rivals for party control. Seward received the job of secretary of state. Moderate Edward Bates of Missouri became attorney general. Although many Republicans considered Simon Cameron of Pennsylvania to be "destitute of honor and integrity," in the interest of appeasing Cameron's supporters and maintaining party unity, Lincoln reluctantly named him secretary of war. Salmon P. Chase of Ohio, a longtime politician and sometime radical on the slavery question, became secretary of the Treasury. Despite Lincoln's evenhandedness, his political balancing act was not easy to maintain. Chase and Seward, for instance, had a long history of political infighting and hated each other. That Lincoln would appoint Chase to any position so angered Seward that he threatened to resign, and Lincoln had to persuade him to remain.

The Nation Dissolved

→ *What problems confronted Abraham Lincoln and Jefferson Davis in March 1861?*

→ *How did their actions contribute to the escalating national crisis?*

Abraham Lincoln was inaugurated on March 4, 1861. In his inaugural address he repeated themes that he had been stressing since the election: no interference with slavery in states where it existed, no extension of slavery into the territories, and no tolerance of secession. "The Union," he contended, was "perpetual." The Constitution, according to its **Preamble,** had been written to form a "more perfect union," and no state could withdraw. Lincoln believed that the nation remained unbroken, and he pledged to see "that the laws of the Union be faithfully executed in all the States." This policy, he continued, necessitated "no bloodshed or violence, and there shall be none, unless it is forced upon the national authority. The power confided in me will be used to hold, occupy, and possess the property and places belonging to the government, and to collect the duties and imposts." If war came, he argued, it would be over secession, not slavery, for the federal government had a duty to maintain the Union by any means, including force.

Lincoln, Sumter, and War

Lincoln's first presidential address drew mixed reactions. Most Republicans found it firm and reasonable, applauding its tone. Union advocates in both the North and the South thought the speech held promise for the future. Even former rival Stephen Douglas

stated, "I am with him." Moderate southerners commended Lincoln's "temperance and conservatism" and believed the speech was all "any reasonable Southern man" could have expected. Confederates and their sympathizers, however, branded the speech a "Declaration of War." Lincoln had hoped the address would foster a climate of reconciliation, show his commitment to maintaining the Union, and demonstrate his determination to find a peaceful solution, for he desperately needed time to organize the new government and formulate a plan of action. But such luxuries were not forthcoming.

Even before Lincoln assumed office, South Carolina officials had ordered the state militia to seize two federal forts—Fort Moultrie and Castle Pinckney—and the federal arsenal at Charleston. In response, Major Robert Anderson had moved all federal troops from Charleston to **Fort Sumter,** an island stronghold in Charleston Harbor. The Confederate congress determined that "immediate steps be taken to obtain possession" of forts still under U.S. control and demanded that President Buchanan remove all federal troops from the sovereign territory of the Confederacy. Despite his sympathy for the southern cause, Buchanan had announced that Fort Sumter would be defended "against all hostile attacks, from whatever quarter." On January 9, 1861, a Charleston Harbor **battery** fired on a supply ship, the *Star of the West,* as it attempted to reach the fort. Buchanan denounced the action but did nothing.

Immediately after taking office in March, Lincoln received a report from Fort Sumter that supplies were running low. Under great pressure from northern public opinion to do something without starting a war, he responded cleverly. He informed South Carolina governor Francis Pickens of his peaceful intention to send unarmed boats carrying food and supplies to the besieged fort. Lincoln thus placed the Confederacy in a no-win position: if Pickens accepted the resupply of federal forts he would lose face, but firing on an unarmed ship would be sufficiently dishonorable to justify stronger federal action. After studying the situation,

---

preamble   An introductory paragraph in a formal document setting out its underlying justification and purpose.

Fort Sumter   Fort at the mouth of the harbor of Charleston, South Carolina; it was the scene of the opening engagement of the Civil War in April 1861.

battery   An army artillery unit, usually supplied with heavy guns.

In this vivid engraving, South Carolina shore batteries under the command of P. G. T. Beauregard shell Fort Sumter, the last federal stronghold in Charleston Harbor, on the night of April 12, 1861. Curious and excited civilians look on from their rooftops, never suspecting the horrors that would be the outcome of this rash action. *Library of Congress.*

Confederate officials determined to beat Lincoln to the punch. President Davis ordered the Confederate commander at Charleston, General P. G. T. Beauregard, to demand the evacuation of Sumter and, if the federals refused, to "proceed, in such a manner as you may determine, to reduce it." On April 11, while the supply ships were still on their way, Beauregard called on Anderson to surrender. When Anderson rejected the ultimatum on the following day, shore batteries opened fire on the island fortress. After a thirty-four-hour artillery battle, Anderson surrendered. Neither side had inflicted casualties on the other, but civil war had officially begun.

Across the North, newspapers contrasted the president's resolute but restrained policy with the violent aggression of the Confederates, and the public rallied behind the Union cause. In New York City, where southern sympathizers had once vehemently criticized abolitionist actions, a million people attended a Union rally. Even northern Democrats rallied behind the Republican president, hearkening to Stephen Douglas's statement that "there can be no neutrals in this war, only patriots—or traitors." Spurred by the public outcry and confident of support, Lincoln called for seventy-

five thousand militiamen to be mobilized "to maintain the honor, the integrity, and the existence of our National Union, and the perpetuity of popular government." Northern states responded immediately and enthusiastically. Across the Upper South and the border regions, however, the call to arms meant that a decision had to be made: whether to continue in the Union or join the Confederacy.

Choosing Sides in Virginia

The need for southern unity in the face of what he saw as northern aggression pushed Jefferson Davis to employ a combination of political finesse and force to create a solid southern alignment. He selected his cabinet with this in mind, choosing one cabinet member from each state except his own Mississippi and appointing men of varying degrees of radicalism. But unity among the seven seceding states was only one of Davis's worries. A perhaps more pressing concern was alignment among the eight slave states that remained in the Union. These states were critical, for they contained more than half of the entire southern population (two-thirds of its white population), possessed most of the South's industrial capacity, produced most of its food, and raised more than half of its horses. In addition, many experienced and able military leaders lived in these states. If the Confederacy was to have any chance of survival, the human and physical resources of the whole South were essential.

It was not Davis's appeal for solidarity but Lincoln's call to mobilize the militia that won most of the other slave states for the Confederate cause. In Virginia, Governor John Letcher refused to honor Lincoln's demand for troops, and on April 17 a special convention declared for secession. Voters in Virginia overwhelmingly ratified this decision in a popular referendum on May 23. By then Letcher had offered **Richmond** as a site for the new nation's capital. The Confederate congress accepted the offer in order to strengthen ties with Virginia and because facilities in Montgomery were less than adequate.

Not all Virginians were flattered at becoming the seat for the Confederacy. Residents of the western portion of the state had strong Union ties and long-standing political differences with their neighbors east of the Allegheny Mountains. Forty-six counties called

Richmond   Port city on the James River in Virginia; already the state capital, it became the capital of the Confederacy.

mass Unionist meetings to protest the state's secession, and in a June convention at Wheeling, they elected their own governor, Francis H. Pierpoint, and drew up a constitution. The document was ratified in an election open only to voters willing to take an oath of allegiance to the Union. Eastern Virginians considered the entire process illegal, but the West Virginia legislature finally convened in May 1862 and requested admission to the United States.

For many individuals in the Upper South, the decision to support the Confederacy was not an easy one. Virginian Robert E. Lee, for example, was deeply devoted to the Union. A West Point graduate and career officer in the U.S. Army, he had a distinguished record in the war with Mexico and as superintendent of West Point. General Winfield Scott, commander of the Union forces, called Lee "the best soldier I ever saw in the field." Recognizing his military skill, Lincoln offered Lee field command of the Union armies, but the Virginian refused, deciding that he should serve his native state instead. Lee agonized over the decision but told a friend, "I cannot raise my hand against my birthplace, my home, my children." He resigned his U.S. Army commission in April 1861. When he informed Scott, a personal friend and fellow Virginian, of his decision, Scott replied, "You have made the greatest mistake of your life, but I feared it would be so." Scott chose to remain loyal to the Union.

A Second Wave of Secession

Influenced by Virginia and by Lee's decision, three other states joined the Confederacy. Arkansas had voted against secession in March, hoping that bloodshed might be averted, but when Lincoln called for militia units, Governor Henry M. Rector answered, "None will be furnished. The demand is only adding insult to injury." The state then called a second convention and on May 6 seceded from the Union. North Carolinians had also hoped for compromise, but moderates turned secessionist when Secretary of War Simon Cameron **requisitioned** "two regiments of militia for immediate service" against the Confederacy. Governor John W. Ellis replied, "I regard the levy of troops made by this administration for the purpose of subjugating the states of the South [to be] in violation of the Constitution and a gross usurpation of power." North Carolina seceded on May 20.

Tennessee, the eleventh and final state to join the Confederacy, was the home of many moderates, including John Bell, the Constitutional Union candidate in 1860. Eastern residents favored the Union, and those in the west favored the Confederacy. The state's voters at first rejected disunion overwhelmingly, but after the fighting began, Governor Isham C. Harris and the state legislature initiated military ties with the Confederacy, forcing another vote on the issue. Western voters carried the election, approving the agreement and seceding from the Union on June 8. East Tennesseans, who remained loyal Unionists, tried to divide the state much as West Virginians had done, but Davis ordered Confederate troops to occupy the region, thwarting the effort.

Trouble in the Border States

Four slave states remained in the Union, and the start of hostilities brought political and military confrontation in three of the four. Delaware quietly stayed in the Union. Voters there had given Breckinridge a plurality in 1860, but the majority of voters disapproved of secession, and few of the state's citizens owned slaves. Maryland, Missouri, and Kentucky, however, each contained large, vocal secessionist minorities and appeared poised to bolt to the Confederacy.

Maryland was particularly vital to the Union, for it enclosed Washington, D.C., on the three sides not bordered by Virginia. If Maryland were to secede, the Union would be forced to move its capital. Maryland voters had overwhelmingly supported Breckinridge in 1860, and southern sympathizers controlled the legislature. But Governor Thomas Hicks, a Unionist, refused to call a special legislative session to consider secession.

On April 6, a Massachusetts regiment responding to Lincoln's call for troops passed through Baltimore on the way to the capital. A mob confronted the soldiers, and rioters attacked the rear companies with bricks, bottles, and pistols. The soldiers returned fire. When the violence subsided, twelve Baltimore residents and four soldiers lay dead, and dozens more were wounded. Secessionists reacted violently, destroying railroad bridges to keep additional northern troops out of the state. In effect, Washington, D.C., was cut off from the North.

Lincoln and General Scott ordered the military occupation of Baltimore and declared **martial law.** The state legislature finally met and voted to remain

---

requisition   To demand for military use.
martial law   Temporary rule by military authorities, imposed on a civilian population in time of war or when civil authority has broken down.

As momentum built toward civil war in the United States, loyalties were severely tried. In border regions of the South, places like Virginia and Tennessee, many remained loyal to the Union and tried to stop the outbreak of violence. Northern Border States were equally torn. In April, 1861, a mob in Baltimore staged a protest—then a full-scale riot—in response to federal troops marching through the city on their way to the nation's capital. As shown in this illustration, bricks and rocks, then bullets and bayonets, gave voice to the anger and frustration besetting a nation in crisis. *The Granger Collection, New York.*

neutral. Lincoln then instructed the army to arrest suspected southern sympathizers and hold them without formal hearings or charges. When the legislature met again and appeared to be planning secession, Lincoln ordered the army to surround Frederick, the legislative seat—just as Davis had dispatched Confederate troops to occupy eastern Tennessee. With southern sympathizers suppressed, new state elections were held. The new legislature, overwhelmingly Unionist, voted against secession.

Kentucky had important economic ties to the South but was strongly nationalistic. Like Kentuckians Henry Clay and John Crittenden, most in the state favored compromise. The governor refused to honor Lincoln's call for troops, but the state legislature voted to remain neutral. Both the North and the South honored that neutrality. Kentucky's own militia, however, split into two factions, and the state became a bloody battleground where even members of the same family fought against one another.

In Missouri, Governor Claiborne F. Jackson, a former proslavery border ruffian, pushed for secession arguing that Missourians were bound together "in one brotherhood with the States of the South." When Unionists frustrated the secession movement, Jackson's forces seized the federal arsenal at Liberty and wrote to Jefferson Davis requesting artillery to support an assault on the arsenal at St. Louis. Union sympathizers, however, fielded their own forces and fought Jackson at every turn. Rioting broke out in St. Louis as civilians clashed with soldiers, and mob violence marred the nights. Jackson's secessionist movement sent representatives to the Confederate congress in Richmond, but Union forces maintained nominal control of the state and drove prosouthern leaders into exile.

✔ Individual Voices

Frederick Douglass: What to the Slave Is the Fourth of July?

After escaping from slavery and then experiencing continuing denigration in the North, Frederick Douglass eventually became a very effective speaker for the abolition cause. Always very direct, Douglass often said things to white audiences that they *really* did not want to hear. In 1852 the Ladies' Anti-Slavery Society of Rochester invited Douglass to speak at their Fourth of July celebration. They were extremely shocked by what he said.

(1) *To whom is Douglass referring here? Who did he consider his constituency to be?*

> *Fellow-citizens, pardon me, allow me to ask, why am I called upon to speak here to-day? What have I, or those I represent, to do with your national independence?* **(1)** *Are the great principles of political freedom and of natural justice, embodied in that Declaration of Independence, extended to us? and am I, therefore, called upon to bring out humble offering to the national altar, and to confess the benefits and express devout gratitude for the blessings resulting from your independence to us? . . .*

(2) *Ironically, Douglass's statement predicted one of Roger Taney's points in the Dred Scott decision five years later. "In the opinion of the court, the legislation and histories of the times, and the language used in the declaration of independence, show, that neither the class of persons who had been imported as slaves, nor their descendants, whether they had become free or not, were then acknowledged as a part of the people, nor intended to be included in the general words used in that memorable instrument."*

> *But such is not the state of the case. I say it with a sad sense of the disparity between us. I am not included within the pale of this glorious anniversary!* **(2)** *Your high independence only reveals the immeasurable distance between us. The blessings in which you, this day, rejoice, are not enjoyed in common. The rich inheritance of justice, liberty, prosperity and independence, bequeathed by your fathers, is shared by you, not by me. The sunlight that brought life and healing to you, has brought stripes and death to me. This Fourth [of] July is yours, not mine. . . .* **(3)**

> *Fellow-citizens; above your national, tumultuous joy, I hear the mournful wail of millions! whose chains, heavy and grievous yesterday, are, to-day, rendered more intolerable by the jubilee shouts that reach them. If I do forget, if I do not faithfully remember those bleeding children of sorrow this day, "may my right hand forget her cunning, and may my tongue cleave to the roof of my mouth!"* **(4)** *To forget them, to pass lightly over their wrongs, and to chime in with the popular theme, would be treason most scandalous and shocking, and would make me a reproach before God and the world.*

(3) *What is Douglass's point in denying connection to the holiday about which he had been invited to speak?*

(4) *Douglass is quoting here from Psalm 137, which he had recited in full earlier in the speech. This Psalm, which relates to the fall of Israel and the Babylonian Captivity, is cited again when Douglass discusses the fate of nations that defy God. What point was Douglass making in citing this Psalm?*

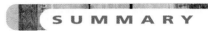

SUMMARY

The presidential election in 1848 raised, and then the Compromise of 1850 failed to alleviate, regional tension and debates. Slavery dominated the political agenda. The Whig Party, strained by fragmentation among its factions, disintegrated, and two completely new groups—the Know-Nothings and the Republicans—competed to replace it. A series of events—including the Kansas-Nebraska Act and the *Dred Scott* decision—intensified regional polarization, and radicals on both sides fanned the flames of sectional rivalry.

The new regional political coalitions of the 1850s more accurately reflected the changed composition of the electorate, but their intense commitment to regional interests left them far less able than their more nationally oriented predecessors to achieve compromise. Even the Democratic Party could not hold together, splitting into northern and southern wings. By 1859, the young Republican Party, committed to restricting slavery's expansion, seemed poised to gain control of the federal government. Fearing that the loss of political power would doom their way of life, southerners recoiled in terror. Neither side felt it could afford to back down.

With the election of Abraham Lincoln in 1860, six southern states withdrew from the Union. Last-minute efforts at compromise, such as the Crittenden proposal, failed, and on April 12, 1861, five weeks after Lincoln's inauguration, Confederate forces fired on federal troops at Fort Sumter in Charleston Harbor. Certain that secession was illegal, Lincoln's constituency expected action, but the president's options were limited by the varied ideologies of his supporters. Similarly, Jefferson Davis and the newly created Confederacy faced problems resulting from disagreement about secession. But Lincoln believed that he had to call the nation to arms, and this move forced wavering states to choose sides. Internal divisions in Virginia, Tennessee, Maryland, Kentucky, and Missouri brought further violence and military action. Before summer, a second wave of secession finally solidified the lineup, and the boundary lines, between the two competing societies. The stakes were set, the division was complete: the nation was poised for the bloodiest war in its history.

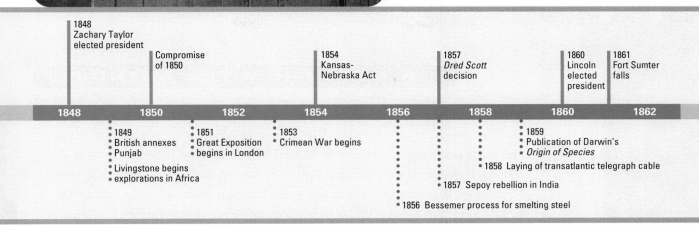

IN THE WIDER WORLD

1848
Zachary Taylor
elected president

Compromise
of 1850

1854
Kansas-
Nebraska Act

1857
Dred Scott
decision

1860
Lincoln
elected
president

1861
Fort Sumter
falls

| 1848 | 1850 | 1852 | 1854 | 1856 | 1858 | 1860 | 1862 |

1849
British annexes
Punjab

Livingstone begins
explorations in Africa

1851
Great Exposition
begins in London

1853
Crimean War begins

1859
Publication of Darwin's
Origin of Species

1858 Laying of transatlantic telegraph cable

1857 Sepoy rebellion in India

1856 Bessemer process for smelting steel

In the United States

Toward a Shattered Union

1848 Zachary Taylor elected president

Immigration to United States exceeds 100,000

1850 Compromise of 1850

1852 First railroad line completed to Chicago

Harriet Beecher Stowe's *Uncle Tom's Cabin*

Franklin Pierce elected president

Whig Party collapses

Know-Nothing Party emerges

1853 Gadsden Purchase

1854 Republican Party formed

Kansas-Nebraska Act

Ostend Manifesto

1855 Proslavery posse sacks Lawrence, Kansas

Pottawatomie Massacre

1856 James Buchanan elected president

Demise of Know-Nothing Party

1857 *Dred Scott* decision

Proslavery Lecompton constitution adopted in Kansas

1858 Lincoln-Douglas debates

Minnesota admitted to Union

1859 Oregon admitted to Union

John Brown's raid on Harpers Ferry

1860 Abraham Lincoln elected president

Crittenden compromise fails

1861 Confederate States of America formed

Fort Sumter shelled

Federal troops occupy Maryland and Missouri

Confederate troops occupy east Tennessee

A Violent Choice: Civil War, 1861–1865

A NOTE FROM THE AUTHOR

It may strike you, as it has some other readers, that this chapter does not focus exhaustively upon military details. In some sense, that is a valid criticism. Like many landmark wars, the American Civil War marked significant changes in the way that war was conducted, even in the way war was envisioned. For generals like Ulysses S. Grant and William Tecumseh Sherman, war was not a glamorous spectacle; it was a practical balance-sheet affair with successes and failures calculated in terms of profits (objectives gained) and losses (lives and other "resources" spent). Certainly there was gallantry, pageantry, and enormous bravery—all worth recording and celebrating. But our objective in this book and in this chapter is to trace the more general history of all the American people: those who fought and those for whom the fighting was little more than a distant echo. Our question is what difference all of these experiences have made to our lives in the United States today.

Obviously we cannot go into detail about every battle, every legislative vote, every family decision, or any number of thousands of events that were important to the everyday experiences of Americans during this terrible and revolutionary time. We hope, however, that the information we can present will guide you to a fuller understanding of the era and inspire you to pursue the aspects you find most compelling, whether those follow horses and battles, the consumer price of sugar, or the aspirations of newly freed slaves.

✔ Individual Choices

Born a slave in 1848, young Susie Baker attended an illegal school for slave children in Savannah, Georgia, where, by the age of 14, she had learned everything her teachers could offer. Then war came. Early in 1862 Union forces attacked the Georgia coast. Powerless and fearful of what the future might hold, many slaves left the city. Eventually a Union gunboat picked up Susie and a number of **"contrabands"** and ferried them to a Yankee encampment on St. Simon's Island. Before long the community of displaced former slaves exceeded six hundred. Discovering that Susie could read and write, Union officials asked her to open a school, the first legally sanctioned school for African Americans in Georgia.

At St. Simon's Susie met and then married another contraband named Edward King. Like many in the camp, King wanted to fight for his freedom. Finally, Union Captain C. T. Trowbridge arrived on the island with a request for volunteers. Though they were offered no pay, no uniforms, and no official recognition, King and his friends eagerly joined up. Trowbridge drilled them during the day while Susie tutored them at night. Finally, in October, the brigade got uniforms and official recognition (though still no pay) and went off to war. Susie went with them.

She spent the rest of the war traveling with the troops, tending to their wounds, their clothes, and their minds; in her words, she "did not fear shell or shot, cared for the sick and dying; camped and fared as the boys did." Then the war ended, and her husband died. She taught school for a while, and though she eventually remarried and settled in the North, she never forgot her wartime experiences.

"These things should be kept in history before the people," she declared, and she made it her business to tell the story. "There has never been a greater war in the United States than the one of 1861, where so many lives were lost—not men alone but noble women as well." Her efforts and

> **contrabands** Term coined by Gen. Benjamin F. Butler
> to describe fugitive slaves who sought refuge among
> Union troops in the South.

those of people like her, people who made hard choices and wrenching sacrifices, had wrought a revolution. "What a wonderful revolution!" she concluded.

"In 1861 the Southern papers were full of advertisements for 'slaves,' but now, despite all the hindrances and 'race problems,' my people are striving to attain the full standard of all other races born free in the sight of God, and in a number of instances have succeeded. Justice we ask—to be citizens of these United States, where so many of our people have shed their blood with their white comrades, that the stars and stripes should never be polluted."

INTRODUCTION

Writing of the Civil War, Susie King Taylor described it as a "revolution." To her mind, the mind of a former slave, it was the liberation of the slaves that marked its revolutionary character. But at the outbreak of war, that revolution was only in the minds of a handful of radicals. When Jefferson Davis and southerner leaders spoke of a revolution, it was against a domineering North that they compared to the England of George III. Lincoln, meanwhile, spoke of a revolution being waged by a rebellious South that would destroy the Union and the Constitution with it.

Many shared the perception that this was a revolutionary moment, but disillusionment seemed to wait behind every event. The South would find it more and more difficult to withstand the superior manpower and resources controlled by the Union. And the North would suffer frustrations of its own as President Lincoln's generals let opportunity after opportunity slip by. In desperation, Lincoln would finally redefine the war by invoking Taylor's revolutionary cause, issuing the Emancipation Proclamation. From that point forward, hopes for a peaceful resolution evaporated: both sides would demand total victory or total destruction.

The war would affect many people in many different ways. For some, like Susie King Taylor, it would afford great opportunities for advancement. For others, it would be a long, torturous ordeal. But one thing was true for everyone and for the nation at large: nothing would be the same after the conflagration was over. Truly it would be a revolution.

The Politics of War

→ *What problems did Abraham Lincoln and Jefferson Davis face as they led their respective nations into war?*

→ *How did each chief executive deal with those problems?*

→ *What role did European nations play during the opening years of the war?*

Running the war posed complex problems for both Abraham Lincoln and Jefferson Davis. At the outset, neither side had the experience, soldiers, or supplies to wage an effective war; and foreign diplomacy and international trade were vital to both. But perhaps the biggest challenge confronting both Davis and Lincoln was internal politics. Lincoln had to contend not only with northern Democrats and southern sympathizers but also with divisions in his own party. Not all Republicans agreed with the president's war aims. Davis also faced internal political problems. The Confederate constitution guaranteed a great deal of autonomy to the Confederate states, and each state had a different opinion about war strategy and national objectives.

Union Policies and Objectives

Abraham Lincoln took the oath of office in March 1861, but Congress did not convene until July. This delay placed Lincoln in an awkward position. The Constitution gives Congress, not the president, the power "to declare war" and "to provide for calling forth the militia to execute the laws of the Union, suppress insurrection, and repel invasions." The secession of the southern states and the imminent threat to federal authority at Fort Sumter, however, required an immediate response.

In effect, Lincoln ruled by executive proclamation for three months, vastly expanding the wartime powers of the presidency. Lincoln called for seventy-five thousand militiamen from the states to put down the rebellion. And ignoring specific constitutional provisions, he suspended the civil rights of citizens in

"It is easy to understand how men catch the contagion of war," civilian relief worker Mary Ashton Rice Livermore asserted. Many on both sides certainly caught it during the opening days of the Civil War. These two Union cavalrymen *(left)* and Confederate infantrymen *(right)*, father and son, volunteered for service and obviously were eager to fight. Such enthusiasm seldom lasted long as days and weeks of boredom, often accompanied by disease, punctuated by brief but heated battles caused enormous anxiety that eroded their fighting spirit. *Left: Richard Carlile; right: Bill Turner.*

Maryland when it appeared likely that the border state would join the Confederacy (see pages 393–394). At various times during the war, Lincoln would resort to similar invasions of civil liberties when he felt that dissent threatened either domestic security or the Union cause.

Having assumed nearly absolute authority, Lincoln faced the need to rebuild an army in disarray. When hostilities broke out, the Union had only sixteen thousand men in uniform, and nearly one-third of the officers resigned to support the Confederacy. What military leadership remained was aged: seven of the eight heads of army bureaus had been in the service since the War of 1812, including General in Chief Winfield Scott, who was 74 years old. Only two Union officers had ever commanded a **brigade,** and both were in their seventies. Weapons were old, and supplies were low. On May 3, Lincoln again exceeded his constitutional authority by calling for regular army recruits to meet

the crisis. "Whether strictly legal or not," he asserted, such actions were based on "a popular demand, and a public necessity," and he expected "that Congress would readily ratify them."

Lincoln had also ordered the U.S. Navy to stop all incoming supplies to the states in rebellion. The naval blockade became an integral part of Union strategy. Though the Union navy had as few resources as the army, leadership in the Navy Department quickly turned that situation around. Navy Secretary Gideon Welles, whom Lincoln called "Father Neptune," purchased ships and built an effective navy that could both blockade the South and support land forces. By the

> **brigade** A military unit consisting of two or more regiments and composed of between 1,500 and 3,500 men.

Though many northerners thought it was too passive, General Winfield Scott's "anaconda plan" was actually very well conceived. As this 1861 lithograph shows, Scott called for a naval blockade of the South and seizure of the Mississippi River, shutting down transportation routes to ruin the Confederate economy. Scott retired at the end of the war's first year, but his plan continued to shape the Union's overall strategy. *Library of Congress.*

end of 1861, the Union navy had 260 warships on the seas and a hundred more under construction.

The aged Winfield Scott drafted the initial Union military strategy. He ordered that the blockade of southern ports be combined with a strong Union thrust down the Mississippi River, the primary artery in the South's transportation system. This strategy would break the southern economy and split the Confederacy into two isolated parts. Like many northerners, Scott believed that economic pressure would bring southern moderates forward to negotiate a settlement and perhaps return to the Union. However, this passive, diplomacy-oriented strategy did not appeal to war-fevered northerners who hungered for complete victory over those "arrogant southerners." The northern press ridiculed what it called the **anaconda plan.**

When Congress finally convened on July 4, 1861, Lincoln explained his actions and reminded congressmen that he had neither the constitutional authority to abolish slavery nor any intention of doing so. Rebellion, not slavery, had caused the crisis, he said, and the seceding states must be brought back into the Union, regardless of the cost. "Our popular government has been called an experiment," he argued, and the point to be settled now was "its successful maintenance against a formidable internal attempt to overthrow it." On July 22 and 25, 1861, both houses of Congress passed resolutions validating Lincoln's actions.

This seemingly unified front lasted only a short time. Viewing vengeance as the correct objective, **Radical Republicans** pressured Congress to create a special committee to oversee the conduct of the war. Radical leader Thaddeus Stevens (see page 282) of Pennsylvania growled, "If their whole country must be laid waste, and made a desert, in order to save this union, so let it be." Stevens and the Radicals pressed for and passed a series of confiscation acts that inflicted severe penalties against individuals in rebellion. Treason was punishable by death, and anyone aiding the Confederacy was to be punished with imprisonment, attachment of property, and confiscation of slaves. All persons living in the eleven seceding states, whether loyal to the Union or not, were declared enemies of the Union and subject to the provisions of the law.

anaconda plan Winfield Scott's plan (named after a snake that smothers prey in its coils) to blockade southern ports and take control of the Mississippi River, thus splitting the Confederacy, cutting off southern trade, and causing an economic collapse.

Radical Republicans Republican faction that tried to limit presidential power and enhance congressional authority during the Civil War; Radicals opposed moderation toward the South or any toleration of slavery.

The Radicals splintered any consensus Lincoln might have achieved in his own party, and northern Democrats railed against his accumulation of power. To keep an unruly Congress from undermining his efforts, Lincoln shaped early Union strategy to appease all factions and used military appointments to smooth political feathers. His attitudes frequently enraged radical abolitionists, but Lincoln maintained his calm in the face of their criticism and merely reinforced his intentions. "What I do about slavery and the colored race," he stated in 1862, "I do because it helps to save the Union; and what I forbear, I forbear because I do not believe it would help to save the Union."

Nevertheless, Lincoln had far greater physical and human resources at his command than did the Confederates (see Table 14.1). The Union was home to more than twice as many people as the Confederacy, had vastly superior manufacturing and transportation systems, and enjoyed almost a monopoly in banking and foreign exchange. Lincoln also had a well-established government structure and formal diplomatic relations with other nations of the world. Still, these advantages could not help the war effort unless properly harnessed.

TABLE 14.1

Comparison of Union and Confederate Resources

	Union (23 States)	Confederacy (11 States)
Total population	20,700,000	9,105,000[a]
Manufacturing establishments	110,000	18,000
Manufacturing workers	1,300,000	110,000
Miles of railroad	21,973	9,283
Troop strength (est.)	2,100,000	850,000

Source: Data from *Battles and Leaders of the Civil War* (1884–1888; reprinted ed., 1956).
[a]Includes 3,654,000 blacks, most of them slaves and not available for military duty.

Confederate Policies and Objectives

At the start of the war, the Confederacy had no army, no navy, no war supplies, no government structure, no foreign alliances, and a political situation as ragged as the Union's. Each Confederate state had its own ideas about the best way to conduct the war. After the attack on Fort Sumter, amassing supplies, troops, ships, and war materials was the main task for Davis and his cabinet. Politics, however, influenced southern choices about where to field armies and who would direct them, how to run a war without offending state leaders, and how to pursue foreign diplomacy.

The Union naval blockade posed an immediate problem. The Confederacy had no navy and no capacity to build naval ships. But it did have the extremely resourceful Stephen Mallory as secretary of the navy. Under Mallory's direction, southern coastal defenders converted river steamboats, tugboats, and **revenue cutters** into harbor patrol gunboats, and they developed and placed explosive mines at the entrances to southern harbors.

Confederates pinned their main hope of winning the war on the army. Fighting for honor was praise-worthy behavior in the South, and southerners strongly believed they could "lick the Yankees" despite their disadvantage in manpower and resources. Southern boys rushed to enlist to fight the northern "popinjays," expecting a quick and glorious victory. Thousands volunteered before the Confederate war department was even organized. By the time Lincoln issued his call for seventy-five thousand militiamen, the Confederates already had sixty thousand men in uniform.

Despite this rush of fighting men, the South faced major handicaps. Even with the addition of the four Upper South states (Virginia, North Carolina, Tennessee, and Arkansas), as of 1860, the South built only 4 percent of all locomotives and only 3 percent of all firearms manufactured in the United States. The North produced almost all of the country's cloth, **pig iron,** boots, and shoes. Early in the war, the South could

revenue cutter   A small, lightly armed boat used by government customs agents to apprehend merchant ships violating customs laws.

pig iron   Crude iron, direct from a blast furnace, that is cast into rectangular molds called pigs in preparation for conversion into steel, cast iron, or wrought iron.

produce enough food but lacked the means to transport it where it was needed. Quartermaster General Abraham Myers drew the mammoth task of producing and delivering tents, shoes, uniforms, blankets, horses, and wagons. All were in short supply.

The miracle worker in charge of supplying southern troops with weapons and ammunition was Josiah Gorgas, who became chief of **ordnance** in April 1861. Gorgas purchased arms from Europe while his ordnance officers bought or stole copper pots and tubing to make **percussion caps,** bronze church bells to make cannon, and lead weights to make bullets. He built factories and foundries to manufacture small arms. But despite his extraordinary skill, he could not supply all of the Confederate troops. When the Confederate congress authorized the enlistment of four hundred thousand additional volunteers in 1861, the war department had to turn away more than half of the enlistees because it lacked equipment for them.

Internal politics also plagued the Davis administration. First, he alienated his high-spirited populace by advocating a defensive war in the belief that counterattacking and yielding territory when necessary would buy time, making war so costly that the Union would give up. As one southern editor put it, the "idea of waiting for blows, instead of inflicting them is altogether unsuited to the genius of our people." But even a defensive posture proved hard to maintain. Despite the shortage of arms, state governors hoarded weapons seized from federal arsenals for their own state militias and demanded that their states' borders be protected, spreading troops dangerously thin. Politics also played a role in determining southern military leadership. Although the South had many more qualified officers at the beginning of the war than did the North, powerful state politicians with little military experience—such as Henry A. Wise of Virginia and Robert A. Toombs of Georgia—received appointments as generals.

The Diplomatic Front

Perhaps the biggest challenge facing the Confederacy was gaining international recognition and foreign aid. The primary focus of Confederate foreign policy was Great Britain. For years, the South had been exporting huge amounts of cotton to Britain, and many southerners felt that formal recognition of Confederate independence would immediately follow secession. Political and economic realities as well as ethical issues doomed them to disappointment. After all, the Union was still an important player in international affairs, and the British were not going to risk offending the emerging industrial power without good cause. Also, many English voters were morally opposed to slavery and would have objected to an open alliance with the slaveholding Confederacy. Thus, while the British allowed southern agents to purchase ships and goods, they crafted a careful policy. On May 13, 1861, Queen Victoria proclaimed official neutrality but granted **belligerent status** to the South. This meant that Britain recognized the Confederates as responsible parties in a legitimate war, but did not recognize the Confederate States of America as yet ready to enter the international community.

The British pronouncement set the tone for other European responses and was much less than southerners had hoped for. It was also a major blow to the North, however, for Britain rejected Lincoln's position that the conflict was rebellion against duly authorized government. Lincoln could do little but accept British neutrality, for to provoke Britain might lead to full recognition of the Confederacy or to calls for arbitration of the conflict. At the same time, he cautiously continued efforts to block all incoming aid to the Confederacy. In November 1861, however, an incident at sea nearly scuttled British-American relations. James Murray Mason, the newly appointed Confederate emissary to London, and John Slidell, the Confederate minister to France, were traveling to their posts aboard the *Trent,* a British merchant ship bound for London. After the *Trent* left Havana, the U.S. warship *San Jacinto,* under the command of Captain Charles Wilkes, stopped the British ship. Wilkes had Mason, Slidell, and their staffs removed from the *Trent* and taken to Boston for confinement at Fort Warren.

Northerners celebrated the action and praised Wilkes, but the British were not pleased. They viewed the *Trent* affair as aggression against a neutral government, a violation of international law, and an affront to their national honor. President Lincoln, Secretary of State William Seward, and U.S. Ambassador to England Charles Francis Adams (son of former president John Quincy Adams) calmed the British by arguing that

---

ordnance Weapons, ammunition, and other military equipment.

percussion cap A thin metal cap containing an explosive compound, needed to fire the guns used in the Civil War.

belligerent status Recognition that a participant in a conflict is a nation engaged in warfare rather than a rebel against a legally constituted government; full diplomatic recognition is one possible outcome.

Wilkes had acted without orders. They ordered the release of the prisoners and apologized to the British, handling the incident so adroitly that the public outcry was largely forgotten when Mason and Slidell arrived in London.

The Union's First Attack

Like most southerners, northerners were confident that military action would bring the war to a quick end. General Irvin McDowell made the first move when his troops crossed into Virginia to engage troops led by General P. G. T. Beauregard (see Map 14.1 and Table 14.2). McDowell's troops, though high-spirited, were poorly trained and undisciplined. They ambled along as if they were on a country outing, allowing Beauregard enough time to position his troops in defense of a vital rail center near Manassas Junction along a creek called **Bull Run.**

McDowell attacked on Sunday, July 21, and maintained the offensive most of the day. He seemed poised to overrun the Confederates until southern reinforcements under **Thomas J. Jackson** stalled the Union advance. Jackson's unflinching stand at Bull Run earned him the nickname "Stonewall," and under intense cannon fire, Union troops panicked and began fleeing into a throng of northern spectators who had brought picnic lunches and settled in to watch the battle. Thoroughly humiliated before a hometown crowd, Union soldiers retreated toward Washington. Jefferson Davis immediately ordered the invasion of the Union capital, but the Confederates were also in disarray and made no attempt to pursue the fleeing Union forces.

This battle profoundly affected both sides. In the South, the victory stirred confidence that the war would be short and victory complete. Northerners, disillusioned and embarrassed, pledged that no similar retreats would occur. Under fire for the loss and hoping to improve both the management of military affairs and the competence of the troops, Lincoln fired McDowell and appointed **George B. McClellan.** McClellan was assigned to create the **Army of the Potomac** to defend the capital from Confederate attack and spearhead any offensives into Virginia. Lincoln also replaced Secretary of War Simon Cameron with Edwin Stanton, a politician and lawyer from Pennsylvania. Scott remained in place as general in chief until his retirement at the end of the year.

General McClellan's strengths were in organization and discipline. Both were sorely needed. Before Bull Run, Union officers had lounged around Washington while largely unsupervised raw recruits in army camps received no military instruction. Under McClellan,

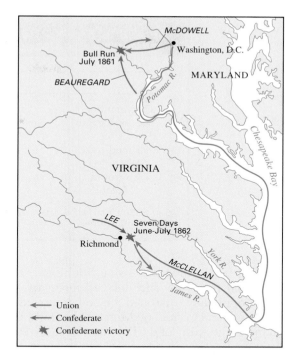

MAP 14.1   Union Offensives into Virginia, 1861–1862
This map shows two failed Union attempts to invade Virginia: the Battle of Bull Run (July 1861) and the Peninsular Campaign (August 1862). Confederate victories embarrassed the richer and more populous Union.

months of training turned the 185,000-man army into a well-drilled and efficient unit. Calls to attack Richmond began anew, but McClellan, seemingly in no hurry for battle, continued to drill the troops and remained in the capital. Finally on January 27, 1862,

Bull Run   A creek in Virginia not far from Washington, D.C., where Confederate soldiers forced federal troops to retreat in the first major battle of the Civil War, fought in July 1861.

Thomas J. Jackson   Confederate general nicknamed "Stonewall"; he commanded troops at both battles of Bull Run and was mortally wounded by his own soldiers at Chancellorsville in 1863.

George B. McClellan   U.S. general tapped by Lincoln to organize the Army of the Potomac; a skillful organizer but slow and indecisive as a field commander. He eventually replaced Winfield Scott as general in chief of Union forces.

Army of the Potomac   Army created to guard the U.S. capital after the Battle of Bull Run in 1861; it became the main Union army in the East.

TABLE 14.2	Battle of Bull Run, July 22, 1861	
	Union Army	**Confederate Army**
Commanders	Irvin McDowell	P. G. T. Beauregard
Troop strength	17,676	18,053
Losses		
Killed	460	387
Wounded	1,124	1,582
Captured	1,312	13
Total Losses	2,896	1,982

Source: Data from *Battles and Leaders of the Civil War* (1884–1888; reprinted ed., 1956).

Lincoln called for a broad offensive, but his general in chief ignored the order and delayed for nearly two months. Completely frustrated, Lincoln removed McClellan as general in chief on March 11 but left him in command of the Army of the Potomac. Even so, Union forces in the East mounted no major offensives.

From Bull Run to Antietam

→ *How did military action during the opening years of the war affect the people's perceptions of the war in the North and South?*

→ *In what ways did international diplomacy play into Lincoln's decision making as the war unfolded?*

→ *Why did Lincoln issue the Emancipation Proclamation when and in the way he did? What sorts of responses did it elicit?*

Reorganizing the military and forming the Army of the Potomac did not accomplish Lincoln's and the nation's goal of toppling the Confederacy quickly and bringing the rebellious South back into the Union. In the second year of the war, frustration followed frustration as Confederate forces continued to outwit and outfight numerically superior and better-equipped federal troops. After Bull Run it was clear that the war would be neither short nor glorious. Military, political, and diplomatic strategies became increasingly entangled as both North and South struggled for the major victories that would end the war.

The War in the West

While the war in the East slid into inactivity, events in the West seemed almost as futile for the Union forces.

In the border state of Missouri, the conflict rapidly degenerated into guerrilla warfare. Confederate William Quantrill's Raiders matched atrocities committed by Unionist guerrilla units called Jayhawkers. Union officials seemed unable to stop the ambushes, arson, theft, and murder, and Missouri remained a lawless battleground throughout the war.

Both the United States and the Confederacy coveted the western territories nearly as much as they did the border states. In 1861 Confederate Henry Hopkins Sibley attempted to gain control of New Mexico and Arizona. Bearing authority directly from Jefferson Davis, Sibley recruited thirty-seven hundred Texans and marched into New Mexico. He defeated a Union force at Valverde, but his losses were high. Needing provisions to continue the operation, he sent units to raid abandoned Union storehouses at Albuquerque and Santa Fe, but withdrawing federal troops had burned whatever supplies they could not carry. The small Confederate force at Santa Fe encountered a much larger federal force and won a miraculous victory, but the effort left the Confederates destitute of supplies. Under constant attack, the starving Confederate detachment evaded Union troops and retreated back into Texas.

As the war intensified, leaders on both sides were forced to concentrate on regional defenses and focus on potential confrontations with enemy armies. Union officers pulled most of their troops back into the areas of concentrated fighting, leaving vast areas of the sparsely settled West with no military protection. In 1862 the Santee Sioux took advantage of the situation by attacking and killing more than eight hundred settlers in the Minnesota River valley. An army of fourteen hundred volunteers finally put down the uprising, but the lack of federal troops in frontier regions created severe anxiety in western communities.

Angered by years of systematic mistreatment at the hands of federal authorities, many Native Americans in Indian Territory were eager to enlist for service with the Confederacy. Confederate president Jefferson Davis chose his Indian agents carefully in order to take advantage of this much-needed source of aid: his ambassador to Indian Territory, General Albert Pike, for example, had represented the Creeks in their battle against removal in the 1830s. As this daguerreotype illustrates, Davis's diplomacy was highly successful; many young Indians flocked to Confederate recruitment rallies to join the army. *Wisconsin Historical Society.*

Confederate leaders sought alliances with several Indian tribes at the onset of war, particularly tribes in the newly settled Indian Territory south of Kansas. Many of the residents there had endured the Trail of Tears (see page 292) and had no particular love for the Union. If these Indian tribes aligned with the Confederacy, they not only could supply troops but might also form a buffer between Union forces in Kansas and the thinly spread Confederate defenses west of the Mississippi River. Davis appointed General Albert Pike, an Arkansas lawyer who had represented the Creeks in court, as special commissioner for the Indian Territory in March 1861. Pike negotiated with several tribes

and on October 7 signed a treaty with John Ross, chief of the Cherokee Nation (see pages 291–292). The treaty, which applied to some members of the Cherokee, Choctaw, Creek, Chickasaw, and Seminole tribes, granted the Indians more nearly equal status—at least on paper—than any previous federal treaty, and it guaranteed that Indians would be asked to fight only to defend their own territory. One Cherokee leader, Stand Watie, became a Confederate general and distinguished himself in battle, leading his Confederate troops in guerrilla warfare against Union forces.

Struggle for the Mississippi

While McClellan stalled in the East, one Union general finally had some success in the western theater of the war. Following the strategy outlined in General Scott's anaconda plan, **Ulysses S. Grant** moved against southern strongholds in the Mississippi Valley in 1862. On February 6, he took Fort Henry along the Tennessee River and ten days later captured Fort Donelson on the Cumberland River near Nashville, Tennessee (see Map 14.2). As Union forces approached Nashville, the Confederates retreated to Corinth, Mississippi. In this one swift stroke, Grant successfully penetrated Confederate western defenses and brought Kentucky and most of Tennessee under federal control.

At Corinth, Confederate general Albert Sidney Johnston finally reorganized the retreating southern troops while Grant was waiting for reinforcements. Early on April 6, to Grant's surprise, Johnston attacked at Pittsburg Landing, Tennessee, near a small country meetinghouse called Shiloh Church (see Table 14.3). Some Union forces under General **William Tecumseh Sherman** were driven back, but the Confederate attack soon lost momentum as Union defenses stiffened. The **Battle of Shiloh** raged until midafternoon. When Johnston was mortally wounded, General Beauregard took command and by day's end believed the enemy defeated. But Union reinforcements arrived during the night,

Ulysses S. Grant U.S. general who became general in chief of the Union army in 1864 after the Vicksburg campaign; he later became president of the United States.

William Tecumseh Sherman U.S. general who captured Atlanta in 1864 and led a destructive march to the Atlantic coast.

Battle of Shiloh Battle in Tennessee in April 1862 that ended with an unpursued Confederate withdrawal; both sides suffered heavy casualties for the first time, but neither side gained ground.

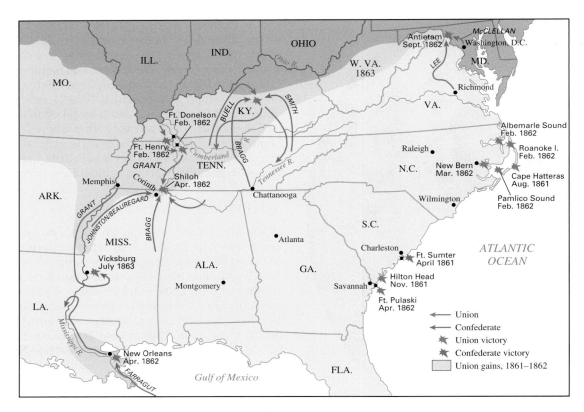

MAP 14.2 **The Anaconda Plan and the Battle of Antietam** This map illustrates the anaconda plan at work. The Union navy closed southern harbors while Grant's troops worked to seal the northern end of the Mississippi River. The map also shows the Battle of Antietam (September 1862), in which Confederate troops under Robert E. Lee were finally defeated by the Union army under General George McClellan.

and the next morning Grant counterattacked, pushing the Confederates back to Corinth.

The losses on both sides were staggering. The Battle of Shiloh made the reality of war apparent to everyone but made a particularly strong impression on the common soldier. After Shiloh, one Confederate wrote: "Death in every awful form, if it really be death, is a pleasant sight in comparison to the fearfully and mortally wounded." Few people foresaw that the horrible carnage at Shiloh was but a taste of what was to come.

Farther south, Admiral David G. Farragut led a fleet of U.S. Navy gunboats against New Orleans, the commercial and banking center of the South, and on April 25 forced the city's surrender. Farragut then sailed up the Mississippi, hoping to take the well-fortified city of **Vicksburg,** Mississippi. He scored several victories until he reached Port Hudson, Louisiana, where the combination of Confederate defenses and shallow water forced him to halt. Meanwhile, on June 6,

Union gunboats destroyed a Confederate fleet at Memphis, Tennessee, and brought the upper Mississippi under Union control. Vicksburg remained the only major obstacle to Union control over the entire river (see Map 14.2).

Realizing the seriousness of the situation in the West, the Confederates regrouped and invaded Kentucky. Union forces under General William S. Rosecrans stopped Confederate general Braxton Bragg's force on December 31 at Stone's River and did not pursue when the Confederates retreated. Back in Mississippi, Grant launched two unsuccessful attacks against Vicksburg in December, but then Union efforts stalled. Never-

> **Vicksburg** Confederate-held city on the Mississippi River that surrendered on July 4, 1863, after a lengthy siege by Grant's forces.

TABLE 14.3 Battle of Shiloh, April 6–7, 1862		
	Union Army	**Confederate Army**
Commanders	William Tecumseh Sherman Ulysses S. Grant	Albert Sidney Johnston (killed) P. G. T. Beauregard
Troop strength	75,000	44,000
Losses		
Killed	1,754	1,723
Wounded	8,408	8,012
Captured, missing	2,885	959
Total Losses	13,047	10,694

Source: Data from *Battles and Leaders of the Civil War* (1884–1888; reprinted ed., 1956).

theless, northern forces had wrenched control of the upper and lower ends of the river away from the Confederacy.

Lee's Aggressive Defense of Virginia

The anaconda plan was well on its way to cutting the Confederacy in two, but the general public in the North thought that the path to real victory led to Richmond, capital of the Confederacy. Thus, to maintain public support for the war, Lincoln needed victories over the Confederates in the East, and campaigns there were given higher priority than campaigns in the West. Confederate leaders, realizing that Richmond would be an important prize for the North, took dramatic steps to keep their capital city out of enemy hands. In fact, defending Richmond was the South's primary goal: more supplies and men were assigned to campaigns in Virginia than to defending Confederate borders elsewhere.

Hoping to clear Virginia's coastline of Union blockaders and protect their capital from amphibious invasion, Confederate naval architects had redesigned a captured Union ship named the *Merrimac.* They encased the entire ship in iron plates and renamed it the *Virginia.* Learning of Confederate attempts to launch an armored ship, the Union navy began building the *Monitor,* a low-decked ironclad vessel with a revolving gun turret. In March the *Virginia* and the *Monitor* shelled each other for five hours. Both were badly damaged but still afloat when the *Virginia* withdrew, making its way back to Norfolk, never to leave harbor again.

With the *Virginia* out of service, McClellan devised precisely the amphibious assault that Virginians had feared. Expecting to surprise the Confederates by attacking Richmond from the south, he transported the entire Army of the Potomac by ship to Fort Monroe, Virginia. Initiating what would be called the **Peninsular Campaign,** the army marched up the peninsula between the York and James Rivers (see Map 14.1). In typical fashion, McClellan proceeded cautiously. The outnumbered Confederate forces took advantage of his indecision and twice slipped away, retreating toward Richmond while McClellan followed. Hoping to overcome the odds by surprising his opponent, General Joseph E. Johnston, commander of the Confederate Army of Northern Virginia, wheeled about and attacked at Seven Pines on May 31. Though the battle was indecisive—both sides claimed victory—it halted McClellan's progress and disabled Johnston, who was seriously wounded.

With McClellan stalled, Confederate stalwart Stonewall Jackson staged a brilliant diversionary thrust down the Shenandoah Valley toward Washington. Jackson, who had grown up in the region, seemed to be everywhere at once. In thirty days, he and his men (who became known as the "foot cavalry") marched 350 miles, defeated three Union armies in five battles, captured and sent back to Richmond a fortune in provisions and

> **Peninsular Campaign**   McClellan's attempt in the spring and summer of 1862 to capture Richmond by advancing up the peninsula between the James and York Rivers; Confederate forces under Robert E. Lee drove his troops back.

Desperate to break the grip of the Union anaconda, the Confederate navy converted the captured Union ship U.S.S. *Merrimac* into the ironclad C.S.S. *Virginia*. Virtually immune to any weapon carried by Union frigates, the *Virginia* dominated the sea-lanes out of Norfolk Harbor. Though the *Virginia* carried cannon, its iron hull was its most effective weapon, as illustrated by this painting of the Confederate ironclad ramming the Union blockade vessel *Cumberland*. The Union navy eventually completed construction of its own ironclad, the U.S.S. *Monitor*, which defeated the *Virginia* in a dramatic sea battle, eliminating that weapon from the Confederate arsenal. *"Ramming of the U.S.S. Cumberland and the U.S.S. Virginia" by Alexander Charles Stuart. Courtesy of the Charleston Renaissance Gallery, Charleston, SC.*

equipment, inflicted twice as many casualties as they received, and confused and immobilized Union forces in the region.

Meanwhile, Union forces were marking time near Richmond while McClellan waited for reinforcements. Determined to remove this threat, Confederate forces launched a series of attacks to drive McClellan away from the Confederate capital. Though his army had already proved itself against the Confederates at Seven Pines, a new factor weighed in against McClellan. With Johnston wounded, Davis had been forced to replace him, choosing Robert E. Lee. Lee was probably the Confederacy's best general. Daring, bold, and tactically aggressive, he enjoyed combat, pushed his troops to the maximum, and was well liked by those serving under him. Lee had an uncanny ability to read the character of his opponents, predict their maneuvers, and exploit their mistakes. In a move that became typical of his generalship, Lee split his forces and attacked from all sides over a seven-day period in August, forcing McClellan into a defensive position. The Peninsular Campaign was over. The self-promoting Union general had been beaten in part by his own indecisiveness.

Fed up with McClellan, Lincoln transferred command of the Army of the Potomac to General John Pope, but Pope's command was brief. Union forces encountered Lee's army again at the Manassas rail line on August 30. The Confederates pretended to retreat, and when Pope followed, Lee soundly defeated Lincoln's new general in the **Second Battle of Bull Run.** Thoroughly disappointed with Pope's performance, but lacking any other viable replacement, Lincoln once again named McClellan commander of the Army of the Potomac.

Lee's Invasion of Maryland

Feeling confident after the second victory at Bull Run, Lee devised a bold offensive against Maryland. His plan had three objectives. First, he wanted to move the fighting out of war-torn Virginia so that farmers could harvest food. Second, he hoped that he might attract volunteers from among the many slave owners and southern sympathizers in Maryland to beef up his undermanned army. Third, he believed that a strong thrust against Union forces might gain diplomatic recognition for the Confederacy from Europe. In the process, he hoped to win enough territory to force the Union to sue for peace. On September 4, Lee crossed the Potomac into Maryland, formulating an intricate offensive by dividing his army into three separate attack wings. But someone was careless—Union soldiers found a copy of Lee's detailed instructions wrapped around some cigars at an abandoned Confederate campsite.

Second Battle of Bull Run Union defeat near Bull Run in August 1862; Union troops led by John Pope were outmaneuvered by Lee.

If McClellan had acted swiftly on this intelligence, he could have crushed Lee's army piece by piece, but he waited sixteen hours before advancing. By then, Lee had learned of the missing orders and quickly withdrew. Lee reunited some of his forces at Sharpsburg, Maryland, around **Antietam Creek** (see Map 14.2). There, on September 17, the Army of the Potomac and the Army of Northern Virginia engaged in the bloodiest single-day battle of the Civil War.

The casualties in this one battle were more than double those suffered in the War of 1812 and the War with Mexico combined. "The air was full of the hiss of bullets and the hurtle of grapeshot," one Union soldier said, and "the whole landscape turned red." The bitter fighting exhausted both armies. After a day of rest, Lee retreated across the Potomac. Stonewall Jackson, covering Lee's retreat, soundly thrashed a force that McClellan sent in pursuit. But for the first time, General Lee experienced defeat.

Although Lee's offensive had been thwarted, Lincoln was in no way pleased with the performance of his army and its leadership. He felt that McClellan could have destroyed Lee's forces if he had attacked earlier or, failing that, had pursued the fleeing Confederate army with all haste. He fired McClellan again, this time for good, and placed Ambrose E. Burnside in command of the Army of the Potomac.

Burnside moved the Army of the Potomac to the east bank of the Rappahannock River overlooking **Fredericksburg,** Virginia (see Map 14.3), where he delayed for almost three weeks. Lee used the time to fortify the heights west of the city with men and artillery. On December 13, in one of the worst mistakes of the war, Burnside ordered a day-long frontal assault. The results were devastating. Federal troops, mowed down from the heights, suffered tremendous casualties, and once again the Army of the Potomac retreated to Washington.

Diplomacy and the Politics of Emancipation

The first full year of the war ended with mixed results for both sides. Union forces in the West had scored major victories, breaking down Confederate defenses and taking Memphis and New Orleans. But the failure of the Army of the Potomac under three different generals and against Lee and Jackson's brilliant maneuvers seemed to outweigh those successes. Lee's victories, however, carried heavy casualties, and the South's ability to supply and deploy troops was rapidly diminishing. A long, drawn-out conflict favored

the Union unless Jefferson Davis could secure help for the Confederacy from abroad.

The Confederacy still expected British aid, but nothing seemed to shake Britain's commitment to neutrality. In addition to the practical and ethical issues discussed earlier, this resistance was due to the efforts of Charles Francis Adams, Lincoln's ambassador in London, who demonstrated his diplomatic skill repeatedly during the war. Also, Britain possessed a surplus of cotton and did not need southern supplies, neutralizing the South's only economic lever and frustrating Davis's diplomatic goals.

Radical Republicans were also frustrated. No aspect of the war was going as they had expected. They had hoped that the Union army would defeat the South in short order. Instead the war effort was dragging on. More important from the Radicals' point of view, nothing was being done about slavery. They pressed Lincoln to take a stand against slavery, and they pushed Congress for legislation to prohibit slavery in federal territories.

Politically astute as always, Lincoln acted to appease the Radical Republicans, foster popular support in the North for the war effort, and increase favorable sentiment for the Union cause abroad. During the summer of 1862, he drafted a proclamation freeing the slaves in the Confederacy and submitted it to his cabinet. Cabinet members advised that he postpone announcing the policy until after the Union had achieved a military victory. In August, **Horace Greeley,** founder of the *New York Tribune,* called for the immediate emancipation of all slaves, but Lincoln reiterated that his objective was "to save the Union," not "to save or destroy slavery." On September 22, however, five days after the Battle of Antietam, Lincoln unveiled the **Emancipation Proclamation,** which abolished slavery in the states "in rebellion" and would go into effect on January 1, 1863.

Antietam Creek   Site of a battle that occurred in September 1862 when Lee's forces invaded Maryland; both sides suffered heavy losses, and Lee retreated into Virginia.

Fredericksburg   Site in Virginia of a Union defeat in December 1862, which demonstrated the incompetence of the new Union commander, Ambrose E. Burnside.

Horace Greeley   Journalist and politician who helped found the Republican Party; his newspaper, the *New York Tribune,* was known for its antislavery stance.

Emancipation Proclamation   Lincoln's order abolishing slavery as of January 1, 1863, in states "in rebellion" but not in border territories still loyal to the Union.

Although the Emancipation Proclamation was a major step toward ending slavery, it actually freed no slaves. The proclamation applied only to slavery in areas controlled by the Confederacy, not in any area controlled by the Union. Some found this exception troubling, labeling the proclamation an empty fraud, but the president's reasoning was sound. He could not afford to alienate the four slave states that had remained in the Union, nor could he commit any manpower to enforce emancipation in the areas that had been captured from the Confederacy. Lincoln made emancipation entirely conditional on a Union military victory, a gambit designed to force critics of the war, whether in the United States or Great Britain, to rally behind his cause.

Whether or not it was successful as a humanitarian action, issuing the Emancipation Proclamation at the time he did and in the form he did was a profoundly successful political step for Lincoln. Although a handful of northern Democrats and a few Union military leaders called it an "absurd proclamation of a political coward," more joined Frederick Douglass in proclaiming, "We shout for joy that we live to record this righteous decree." Meanwhile, some in Britain pointed to the paradox of the proclamation: it declared an end to slavery in areas where Lincoln could not enforce it, while having no effect on slavery in areas where he could. But even there, most applauded the document and rallied against recognition of the Confederacy.

Still, Lincoln's new general in chief, Henry Halleck, was chilled by the document. As he explained to Grant, the "character of the war has very much changed within the last year. There is now no possible hope of reconciliation." The war was now about slavery as well as secession, and the Emancipation Proclamation committed the Union to conquering the enemy. As Lincoln told one member of his cabinet, the war would now be "one of subjugation."

The Human Dimensions of the War

→ *How did the burdens of war affect society in the North and the South during the course of the fighting?*

→ *How did individuals and governments in both regions respond to those burdens?*

The Civil War imposed tremendous stress on American society. As the men marched off to battle, women faced the task of caring for families and property alone. As casualties increased, the number of voluntary enlistments decreased, and both sides searched for ways to find replacements for dead and wounded soldiers. The armies consumed vast amounts of manufactured and agricultural products—constantly demanding not only weapons and ammunition but also food, clothing, and hardware. Government spending was enormous, hard currency was scarce, and inflation soared as both governments printed paper money to pay their debts. Industrial capability, transportation facilities, and agricultural production often dictated when, where, and how well armies fought. Society in both North and South changed to meet an array of hardships as individuals facing unfamiliar conditions attempted to carry on their lives amid the war's devastation.

Instituting the Draft

By the end of 1862, heavy casualties, massive desertion, and declining enlistments had depleted both armies. Although the North had a much larger population pool than the South to draw from, its enlistments sagged with its military fortunes during 1862. More than a hundred thousand Union soldiers were absent without official leave. Most volunteers had enlisted in 1861 for limited terms, which would soon expire. Calling on state militias netted few replacements because the Democrats, who made tremendous political gains at the state level in 1862, openly criticized Republican policies and at times refused to cooperate. In March 1863, Congress passed the **Conscription Act,** trying to bypass state officials and ensure enough manpower to continue the war. The law in effect made all single men between the ages of 20 and 45 and married men between 20 and 35 eligible for service. Government agents collected names in a house-to-house survey, and draftees were selected by lottery.

The conscription law did offer "escape routes." Drafted men could avoid military service by providing—that is, hiring—an "acceptable substitute" or by paying a $300 fee to purchase exemption. The burden of service thus fell on farmers and urban workers—a large proportion of whom were immigrants—who were already suffering from the economic burden of high taxation and inflation caused by the war. Added to that was workers' fear that multitudes of former slaves freed by the Emancipation Proclamation would pour into the already crowded

Conscription Act Law passed by Congress in 1863 that established a draft but allowed wealthy people to escape it by hiring a substitute or paying the government a $300 fee.

Many soldiers entered the Civil War expecting excitement and colorful pageantry, but the realities of war were harsh and ugly. And the new art of photography, introduced to the United States shortly before the war, brought the harsh reality home to Americans on both sides in the fighting. Scenes like this one became so common that veterans reported becoming numb to the shock of death and the meaning of death itself changed in the minds of many Americans. *Library of Congress.*

job market, further lowering the value of their labor. Together, conscription and emancipation created among the urban poor a sense of alienation, which exploded in the summer of 1863.

The trouble started on July 13 in New York City. Armed demonstrators protesting unfair draft laws engaged in a spree of violence, venting their frustration over the troubles plaguing working people. During three nights of rioting, white workingmen beat many African Americans and lynched six. The Colored Orphan Asylum and several homes owned by blacks were burned. Mobs ransacked businesses owned by African Americans and by people who employed them. Irish men and women and members of other groups that seemed to threaten job security also felt the fury as mobs attacked their churches, businesses, and homes. The rioters also expressed their frustration against Republican spokesmen and officials. Republican journalist Horace Greeley was **hanged in effigy,** and the homes of other prominent Republicans and abolitionists were vandalized. Protesting draft exemptions for the rich, rioters also set upon well-dressed strangers on the streets. After four days of chaos, federal troops put down the riot. Fearful of future violence, the city council of New York City voted to pay the $300 exemp-

tion fee for all poor draftees who chose not to serve in the army.

The Confederacy also instituted a draft after the first wave of enlistments dried up. Conscription in the South, as in the North, met with considerable resentment and resistance. Believing that plantations were necessary to the war effort and that slaves would not work unless directly overseen by masters, in 1862 Confederate officials passed the **Twenty Negro Law,** which exempted planters owning twenty or more slaves from military service. Like the exemptions in the North, the southern policy fostered the feeling that the poor were going off to fight while the rich stayed safely at home. The law was modified in 1863, requiring exempted planters to pay $500, and in 1864, the number of slaves

hang in effigy   To hang, as if on a gallows, a crude likeness or dummy—an effigy—representing a hated person.

Twenty Negro Law   Confederate law that exempted planters owning twenty or more slaves from the draft on the grounds that overseeing farm labor done by slaves was necessary to the war effort.

Angered by the fact that rich men were virtually exempt from the draft, frightened by the prospect of job competition from freed southern slaves, and frustrated by the lack of resolution on the battlefield, workingmen took to the streets in New York City during the summer of 1863 to protest against the war. Well-dressed men, African Americans, and leading war advocates were the main targets of mob violence during three nights of uncontrolled rioting. As this illustration shows, federal troops finally put down the rioting in a series of battles around the city. An unknown number of people were killed and injured. *Collection of Picture Research Consultants & Archives.*

required to earn an exemption was lowered to fifteen. Nevertheless, resentment continued to smolder.

Confederate conscription laws also ran afoul of states' rights advocates, who feared that too much power was centered in Richmond. Southerners developed several forms of passive resistance to the draft laws. Thousands of draftees simply never showed up, and local officials, jealously guarding their political autonomy, made little effort to enforce the draft.

Wartime Economy in the North and South

In his 1864 message to Congress, Abraham Lincoln stated that the war had not depleted northern resources. Although the president exaggerated a bit, the statement contained some truth. Northern industry and population did grow during the Civil War. Operating in cooperation with government, manufacturing experienced a boom. Manufacturers of war supplies benefited from government contracts. Textiles and shoemaking boomed as new labor-saving devices improved efficiency and increased production. Congress stimulated economic growth by means of subsidies and land grants to support a transcontinental railroad, higher tariffs to aid manufacturing, and land grants

that states could use to finance higher education. In 1862 Congress passed the **Homestead Act** to make land available to more farmers. The law granted 160 acres of the public domain in the West to any citizen or would-be citizen who lived on, and improved, the land for five years.

Of course the economic picture was not entirely positive. The Union found itself resorting to financial tricks to keep the economy afloat. Facing a cash-flow emergency in 1862, Congress passed the Legal Tender Act, authorizing Treasury Secretary Salmon Chase to issue $431 million in paper money, known as **greenbacks,** that was backed not by specie but only by the government's commitment to redeem the bills. Financial support also came through selling bonds. In the fall of 1862, Philadelphia banker Jay Cooke started a bond drive. More than $2 billion worth of government bonds were sold, and most of them were paid for in

> **Homestead Act**   Law passed by Congress in 1862 that promised ownership of 160 acres of public land to any citizen or would-be citizen who lived on and cultivated the land for five years.
>
> **greenbacks**   Paper money issued by the Union; it was not backed by gold.

greenbacks. These emergency measures helped the Union survive the financial pressures created by the war, but the combination of bond issues and paper money not backed by gold or silver set up a highly unstable situation that came back to haunt Republicans after the war.

The South, an agrarian society, began the war without an industrial base. In addition to lacking transportation, raw materials, and machines, the South lacked managers and skilled industrial workers. The Confederate government intervened more directly in the economy than did its Union counterpart, offering generous loans to new or existing companies that would produce war materials and agree to sell at least two-thirds of their production to the government. Josiah Gorgas started government-owned production plants in Alabama, Georgia, and South Carolina. These innovative programs, however, could not compensate for inadequate prewar industrialization.

The supply of money was also a severe problem in the South. Like the North, the South tried to ease cash-flow problems by printing paper money, eventually issuing more than $1 billion in unbacked currency. The outcome was runaway inflation. By the time the war ended, southerners were paying more than $400 for a barrel of flour and $10 a pound for bacon.

Southern industrial shortcomings severely handicapped the army. During Lee's Maryland campaign, many Confederate soldiers were barefoot because shoes were in such short supply. Ordnance was always in demand. Northern plants could produce more than five thousand muskets a day; Confederate production never exceeded three hundred. The most serious shortage, however, was food. Although the South was an agricultural region, most of its productive acreage was devoted to cotton, tobacco, and other crops that were essential to its overall economy but not suitable to eat. Corn and rice were the primary food products, but supplies were continually reduced by military campaigns and Union occupation of farmlands. Hog production suffered from the same disruptions as rice and corn growing, and while Southern cattle were abundant, most were range stock grown for hides and tallow rather than for food. Hunger became a miserable part of daily life for the Confederate armies.

Civilians in the South suffered from the same shortages as the army. Because of prewar shipping patterns, the few rail lines that crossed the Confederacy ran north and south. Distribution of goods became almost impossible as invading Union forces cut rail lines and disrupted production. The flow of cattle, horses, and food from the West diminished when Union forces gained control of the Mississippi. Imported goods had to evade the Union naval blockade. Southern society, cut off from the outside world, consumed its existing resources and found no way to obtain more.

Women in Two Nations at War

Because the South had fewer men than the North to send to war, a larger proportion of southern families were left in the care of women. Some women worked farms, herded livestock, and supported their families. Others found themselves homeless, living in complete poverty, as the ravages of war destroyed the countryside. One woman wrote to the Confederacy's secretary of war, pleading that he "discharge" her husband so that "he might do his children some good" rather than leaving them "to suffer." Some tried to persuade their husbands to desert, to come home to family and safety. One woman shouted to her husband, who was being drafted for the second time, "Desert again, Jake." The vast majority, however, fully supported the war effort despite the hardships at home and at the front.

Women became responsible for much of the South's agricultural and industrial production, overseeing the raising of crops, working in factories, managing estates, and running businesses. As one southern soldier wrote, women bore "the greatest burden of this horrid war." Indeed, the burden of a woman was great—working the fields, running the household, and waiting for news from loved ones at the front or for the dreaded message that she was now a widow or had lost a child.

Women in the North served in much the same capacity as their southern counterparts. They maintained families and homes alone, working to provide income and raise children. Although they did not face the shortages and ravages of battle that made life so hard for southern women, they did work in factories, run family businesses, teach school, and supply soldiers. Many served in managerial capacities or as writers and civil servants. Even before the war ended, northern women were going south to educate former slaves and help them find a place in American society. Women thus assumed new roles that helped prepare them to become more involved in social and political life after the war.

Women from both South and North actively participated in the war itself. Many women on both sides served as scouts, couriers, and spies, and more than four hundred disguised themselves as men and served as active soldiers until they were discovered. General William S. Rosecrans expressed dismay when one of

As Mary Ashton Rice Livermore pointed out, many women served in many different capacities during the Civil War. An unknown number of them actually dressed as men to join the fighting. Frances Clayton was one of the few documented cases of such Civil War gender-bending. *Left and right: Boston Public Library/Rare Books Department—Courtesy of the Trustees.*

his sergeants was delivered of "a bouncing baby boy," which was, the general complained, "in violation of all military regulations." Army camps frequently included officers' wives, female employees, camp followers, and women who came to help in whatever way they could. One black woman served the 33rd U.S. Colored Troops for four years and three months without pay, teaching the men to read and write and binding up their wounds.

Free Blacks, Slaves, and War

The changes the Civil War brought for African Americans, both free and slave, were radical and not always for the better. At first, many free blacks attempted to enlist in the Union army but were turned away. In 1861 General Benjamin F. Butler began using runaway slaves, called contrabands, as laborers. Several other northern commanders quickly adopted the practice. As the number of contrabands increased, however, the Union grappled with problems of housing and feeding them.

In the summer of 1862, Congress authorized the acceptance of "persons of African descent" into the armed forces, but enlistment remained low. After the Emancipation Proclamation, Union officials actively recruited former slaves, raising troops from among the freedmen and forming them into regiments known as the U.S. Colored Troops. Some northern state governments sought free blacks to fill state draft quotas; agents offered generous bonuses to those who signed up. By the end of the war, about 180,000 African Americans had enlisted in northern armies.

Army officials discriminated against African American soldiers in a variety of ways. Units were segregated, and until 1864, blacks were paid less than whites. All black regiments had white commanders; the government refused to allow blacks to lead blacks. Only one hundred were commissioned as officers, and no African American soldier ever received a commission higher than major.

At first, African American regiments were used as laborers or kept in the rear rather than being allowed to fight. But several black regiments, when finally allowed into battle, performed so well that they won grudging respect. These men fought in 449 battles in every theater of the war and had a casualty rate 35 percent higher than white soldiers. Still, acceptance by white troops was slow, and discrimination was the rule, not the exception.

As the war progressed, the number of African Americans in the Union army increased dramatically. By

Eager to fill constantly depleting army ranks, Union officials appealed to African Americans to volunteer for military service. This recruiting poster, which bore the legend "Come Join Us, Brothers," presents a highly glorified vision of what conditions were like for black units. One accurate detail is that the only officer in the scene is white; in fact, hardly any African Americans were permitted to command troops during the Civil War. *Chicago Historical Society.*

1865, almost two-thirds of Union troops in the Mississippi Valley were black. Some southerners violently resented the Union's use of these troops, and African American soldiers suffered atrocities because some Confederate leaders refused to take black prisoners. At Fort Pillow, Tennessee, for example, Confederate soldiers massacred more than a hundred African American soldiers who were trying to surrender.

About sixty-eight thousand black Union soldiers were killed or wounded in battle, and twenty-one were awarded the Congressional Medal of Honor. Probably no unit acquitted itself better in the field than the **54th Massachusetts.** On July 18, 1863, it led a frontal assault on Confederate defenses at Charleston Harbor. Despite sustaining grievous casualties, the African American troops captured the fort's front wall and held it for nearly an hour before being forced to retreat. Their conduct in battle had a large impact on changing attitudes toward black soldiers and emancipation.

The war effort in the South relied heavily on the slave population, mostly as producers of food and as military laborers. Slaves constituted more than half of the work force in armament plants and military hospitals. Though crucial to the southern war effort, slaves suffered more than other southerners in the face of food shortages and other privations. And after Lincoln issued the Emancipation Proclamation, fears of slave revolts prompted whites to institute harsh security procedures. Hungry and even less free than usual, slaves became the greatest unsung casualties of the war.

Life and Death at the Front

Many volunteers on both sides in the Civil War had romantic notions about military service. Most were disappointed. Life as a common soldier was anything but glorious. Letters and diaries written by soldiers most frequently tell of long periods of boredom in overcrowded camps punctuated by furious spells of dangerous action.

Though life in camp was tedious, it could be nearly as dangerous as time spent on the battlefield. Problems with supplying safe drinking water and disposing of waste constantly plagued military leaders faced with providing basic services for large numbers of people, often on short notice. Diseases such as dysentery and **typhoid fever** frequently swept

54th Massachusetts   Regiment of African American troops from Massachusetts commanded by abolitionist Colonel Robert Gould Shaw; it led an assault on Fort Wagner at Charleston Harbor.

typhoid fever   An infectious disease transmitted through contact with contaminated water, milk, or food; causes severe intestinal distress and high fever.

While the carnage on Civil War battlefields was almost unimaginable, conditions in field hospitals were more unimaginable still. Medicine and bandages were in short supply and the medical expertise of attending nurses and physicians was often lacking. As shown here, crowded and unsanitary conditions were the rule. Infection often proved more deadly than bayonets and bullets. *Library of Congress.*

through unsanitary camps. And in the overcrowded conditions that often prevailed, smallpox and other contagious diseases passed rapidly from person to person. At times, as many as a quarter of the uninjured people in camps were disabled by one or another of these ailments.

Lacking in resources, organization, and expertise, the South did little to upgrade camp conditions. In the North, however, women drew on the organizational skills they had gained as antebellum reformers and created voluntary organizations to address the problem. At the local level, women like Mary Livermore and Jane Hoge created small relief societies designed to aid soldiers and their families. Gradually these merged into regional organizations that would take the lead in raising money and implementing large-scale public health efforts, both in the army camps and at home. Mental health advocate and reformer Dorothea Dix (see page 342) was also one of these crusaders. In June 1861, President Lincoln responded to their concerns by creating the **United States Sanitary Commission,** a government agency responsible for advising the military on public health issues and investigating sanitary problems. Gradually enfolding many of the local and regional societies into its structure, "The Sanitary," as it was called, put hundreds of nurses into the field, providing much-needed relief for overburdened military doctors. Even with this official organization in place, many women continued to labor as volunteer nurses in the camps and in hospitals behind the lines.

Nurses on both sides showed bravery and devotion. Often working under fire at the front and with almost no medical supplies, these volunteers nursed sick and wounded soldiers, watched as they died not only from their wounds but also from infection and disease, and offered as much comfort and help as they could. **Clara Barton,** a famous northern nurse known as the "Angel of the Battlefield," recalled "speaking to and feeding with my own hands each soldier" as she attempted to nurse them back to health. Hospitals were unsanitary, overflowing, and underfunded.

The numbers of wounded who filled the hospital tents was unprecedented, largely because of technological innovations that had taken place during the antebellum period. New **rifled** muskets had many times the range of the old smooth-bore weapons used during earlier wars—the effective range of the Springfield

United States Sanitary Commission Government commission established by Abraham Lincoln to improve public health conditions in military camps and hospitals.

Clara Barton Organizer of a volunteer service to aid sick and wounded Civil War soldiers; she later founded the American branch of the Red Cross.

rifled Having a series of spiral grooves inside the barrel of a gun that cause the projectile to spin, giving it greater range and accuracy.

rifle used by many Union soldiers was 400 yards, and a stray bullet could still kill a man at 1,000 yards. Waterproof cartridges, perfected by gunsmith Samuel Colt, made these weapons much less prone to misfire and much easier to reload. And at closer range, the revolver, also perfected by Colt, could fire six shots without any reloading. Rifled artillery also added to the casualty count, as did exploding artillery shells, which sent deadly shrapnel ripping through lines of men.

Many surgeons at the front lines could do little more than amputate limbs to save lives. Hospitals, understaffed and lacking supplies and medicines, frequently became breeding grounds for disease. The war exacted a tremendous emotional toll on everyone, even on those who escaped physical injury. As one veteran put it, soldiers had seen "so many new forms of death" and "so many frightful and novel kinds of mutilation."

Conditions were even worse in prison camps. Throughout much of the war, an agreement provided for prisoner exchanges, but that did not prevent overcrowding and unsanitary conditions. And as the war dragged on, the exchange system stopped working effectively. In part the program collapsed because of the enormity of the task: moving and accounting for the large numbers of prisoners presented a serious organizational problem. Another contributing factor, though, was the refusal by Confederate officials to exchange African American prisoners of war—those who were not slaughtered like the men at Fort Pillow were enslaved. Also, late in the war, Union commanders suspended all prisoner exchanges in hopes of depriving the South of much-needed replacement soldiers.

The most notorious of the Civil War prison camps was **Andersonville,** in northern Georgia, where thousands of Union captives languished in an open stockade with only a small creek for water and virtually no sanitary facilities. Without enough food to feed its own armies and civilian population, the Confederacy could allocate little food for its overcrowded prison camps. Designed to house 10,000 men, Andersonville held more than 33,000 prisoners during the summer of 1864. As many as 100 men died of disease and malnutrition within its walls each day; estimates put the death toll at that one prison at nearly 14,000 over the course of the war.

Even death itself came to be redefined, as 8 percent of the white male population in the United States between the ages of 13 and 43 died in such a short time and in such grisly ways. People at the front reported being numbed by the horror. One army surgeon reported, "I pass over the putrefying bodies of the dead . . . and feel as . . . unconcerned as though they were two hundred pigs." Nor was distance any insu-

lation from the horrors of death. The new art of photography brought graphic images of the gruesome carnage directly into the nation's parlors. "Death does not seem half so terrible as it did long ago," one Texas woman reported. "We have grown used to it."

Waging Total War

→ *What factors contributed to the Union's adoption of a total war strategy after 1863?*

→ *Was total war a justifiable option in light of the human and property damage it inflicted and the overall consequences it achieved? Why or why not?*

As northerners anticipated the presidential election of 1864, Lincoln faced severe challenges on several fronts. The losses to Lee and Jackson in Virginia and the failure to catch Lee at Antietam had eroded public support. Many northerners resented the war, conscription, and abolitionism. Others feared Lincoln's powerful central government.

Northern Democrats advocated a peace platform and turned to George B. McClellan, Lincoln's ousted general, as a potential presidential candidate. Lincoln also faced a challenge from within his own party. Radical Republicans, who felt he was too soft on the South and unfit to run the war, began planning a campaign to win power. They championed the candidacy of John C. Frémont (see pages 358–359), who had become an ardent advocate of the complete abolition of slavery.

Lincoln's Generals and Southern Successes

The surest way for Lincoln to stop his political opponents was through military success. Lincoln had replaced McClellan with Burnside, but the results had been disastrous. Lincoln tried again, demoting Burnside and elevating General Joseph Hooker. Despite Hooker's reputation for bravery in battle—his nickname was "Fighting Joe"—Lee soundly defeated his forces at **Chancellorsville** in May 1863 (see Map 14.3

Andersonville Confederate prisoner-of-war camp in northern Georgia where some fourteen thousand Union prisoners died of disease and malnutrition.

Chancellorsville Site in Virginia where in May 1863 Confederate troops led by Lee defeated a much larger Union force.

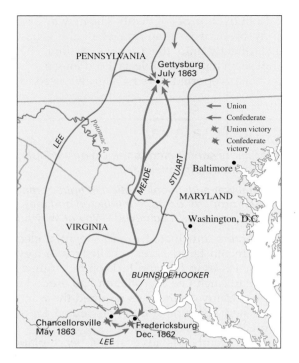

MAP 14.3   Fredericksburg, Chancellorsville, and Gettysburg   This map shows the campaigns that took place during the winter of 1862 and spring of 1863, culminating in the Battle of Gettysburg (July 1863). General Meade's victory at Gettysburg may have been the critical turning point of the war.

and Table 14.4). After Hooker had maneuvered Lee into a corner, Stonewall Jackson unleashed a vicious attack, and Fighting Joe simply "lost his nerve," according to one of his subordinates. Hooker resigned, and Lincoln replaced him with General George E. Meade.

Chancellorsville was a devastating loss for the North, but it was perhaps more devastating for the Confederates. They lost Stonewall Jackson. After he led the charge that unnerved Hooker, Jackson's own men mistakenly shot him as he rode back toward his camp in the darkness. Doctors amputated Jackson's arm in an attempt to save his life. "He has lost his left arm," moaned Lee, "but I have lost my right." Eight days later, Jackson died of pneumonia.

In the West too, Union forces seemed mired during the first half of 1863. General Rosecrans was bogged down in a costly and unsuccessful campaign to take the vital rail center at Chattanooga, Tennessee. Grant had settled in for a long siege at Vicksburg (see Map 14.2). Nowhere did there seem to be a prospect for the dramatic victory Lincoln needed.

The summer of 1863, however, turned out to be a major turning point in the war. Facing superior northern resources and rising inflation, Confederate leaders met in Richmond to consider their options. Lee proposed another major invasion of the North, arguing that such a maneuver would allow the Confederates to gather supplies and might encourage the northern peace movement, revitalize the prospects of foreign recognition, and perhaps capture the Union capital. Confederate leaders agreed and approved Lee's plan.

Lee's advance met only weak opposition as the Army of Northern Virginia crossed the Potomac River and marched into Union territory (see Map 14.3). In Maryland and Pennsylvania the troops seized livestock, supplies, food, clothing, and shoes. Union forces had been converging on the area of **Gettysburg,** Pennsylvania, since early June, anticipating Lee's move but unsure of his exact intention. Learning that the Federals were waiting and believing them to be weaker than they were, on June 29 Lee moved to engage the Union forces. Meade, who had been trailing Lee's army as it marched north from Chancellorsville, immediately dispatched a detachment to reinforce Gettysburg. On the following day, the two armies began a furious three-day battle.

Arriving in force on July 1, Meade took up an almost impregnable defensive position on the hills along Cemetery Ridge. The Confederates hammered both ends of the Union line but could gain no ground. On the third day, Lee ordered a major assault on the middle of the Union position. Eleven brigades, more than thirteen thousand men, led by fresh troops under Major General George E. Pickett, tried to cross open ground and take the hills held by Meade while Major J. E. B. "Jeb" Stuart's cavalry attacked from the east. Lee made few strategic mistakes during the war, but Pickett's charge was foolhardy. Meade's forces drove off the attack. The whole field was "dotted with our soldiers," wrote one Confederate officer. Lee met his retreating troops with the words "It's all my fault, my fault." Losses on both sides were high (see Table 14.5), but Confederate casualties exceeded twenty-eight thousand men, more than half of Lee's army. Lee retreated, his invasion of the North a failure.

On the heels of this major victory for the North came news from Mississippi that Vicksburg had fallen

Gettysburg   Site in Pennsylvania where in July 1863 Union forces under General George Meade defeated Lee's Confederate forces, turning back Lee's invasion of the North.

Battle of Chancellorsville, May 1–4, 1863

	Union Army	Confederate Army
Commanders	Joseph Hooker	Robert E. Lee
Troop strength	75,000	50,000
Losses		
Killed	1,606	1,665
Wounded	9,762	9,081
Captured, missing	5,919	2,018
Total Losses	17,287	12,764

Source: Data from *Battles and Leaders of the Civil War* (1884–1888; reprinted ed., 1956).

Battle of Gettysburg, July 1–3, 1863

	Union Army	Confederate Army
Commanders	George E. Meade	Robert E. Lee
Troop strength	75,000	50,000
Losses		
Killed	3,155	3,903
Wounded	14,529	18,735
Captured, missing	5,365	5,425
Total Losses	23,049	28,063

Source: Data from *Battles and Leaders of the Civil War* (1884–1888; reprinted ed., 1956).

to Grant's siege on July 4. Sherman had been beating back Confederate forces in central Mississippi, and Union guns had been shelling the city continuously for nearly seven weeks, driving residents into caves and barricaded shelters. But it was starvation and disease that finally subdued the defenders. Then on July 9, after receiving news of Vicksburg's fate, **Port Hudson,** the last Confederate garrison on the Mississippi River, also surrendered. The Mississippi River was totally under Union control. The "Father of Waters," said Lincoln, "again goes unvexed to the sea."

Despite jubilation over the recent victories, Lincoln and the North remained frustrated. Northern newspapers proclaiming Gettysburg to be the last gasp of the South had anticipated an immediate southern surrender, but Meade, like McClellan, acted with extreme caution and failed to pursue Lee and his retreating troops. Back in Washington, Lincoln waited for word of Lee's capture, believing it would signal the end of the rebellion. When he learned of Lee's escape, the president said in disbelief, "Our Army held the war in the hollow of their hand and they would not close it."

Disappointment in Tennessee also soon marred the celebration over Gettysburg and Vicksburg. Rosecrans had taken Chattanooga, but on September 18, Bragg's forces attacked Rosecrans at Chickamauga Creek. Rosecrans scurried in retreat to take refuge back in Chattanooga, leaving part of his troops in place to cover his retreat. This force, under the command of George H. Thomas, delayed the Confederate offensive and, in the words of one veteran, "saved the

Port Hudson   Confederate garrison in Louisiana that surrendered to Union forces in July 1863, thus giving the Union unrestricted control of the Mississippi River.

At Gettysburg, a series of battles like the one shown here—this one on the first day of the fighting—cost Confederate General Robert E. Lee more than half of his entire army, and he was forced to retreat into Virginia. President Lincoln hoped that the Union army would pursue the fleeing Confederates and destroy the remnants of Lee's force, but he was disappointed when he learned that Lee had escaped. "Our Army held the war in the hollow of their hand," Lincoln complained, "and they would not close it." *West Point Art Museum, United States Military Academy, West Point, NY.*

army from defeat and rout." Bragg nonetheless was able to follow and laid siege to Chattanooga from the heights of Missionary Ridge and Lookout Mountain, overlooking the city.

With Lee and his army intact and Rosecrans pinned down in Tennessee, the war, which in July had appeared to be so nearly over, was, in Lincoln's words, "prolonged indefinitely." Lincoln needed a new kind of general.

Grant, Sherman, and the Invention of Total War

Among the available choices, Grant had shown the kind of persistence and boldness Lincoln thought necessary. Lincoln placed him in charge of all Union forces in the West on October 16. Grant immediately replaced Rosecrans with the more intrepid and decisive Thomas. Sherman's troops joined Thomas under Grant's command on November 14. This united force rid the mountains above Chattanooga of Confederate strongholds and drove Bragg's forces out of southern Tennessee. Confederate forces also with-

drew from Knoxville in December, leaving the state under Union control.

While fighting raged in Tennessee, Lincoln took a break from his duties in the White House to participate in the dedication of a national cemetery at the site where, just months before, the Battle of Gettysburg had taken the lives of thousands. In the speech he delivered on November 19, 1863, Lincoln dedicated not only the cemetery but the war effort itself to the fallen soldiers, and also to a principle. "Fourscore and seven years ago," Lincoln said, "our fathers brought forth on this continent a new nation, conceived in liberty and dedicated to the proposition that all men are created equal." Though delivered in a low voice that most of the crowd could not hear, the **Gettysburg Address** was circulated in the media and gal-

---

Gettysburg Address   A speech given by Abraham Lincoln on November 19, 1863, dedicating a national cemetery in Gettysburg, Pennsylvania; it expressed Lincoln's maturing view of the war and its purpose.

vanized many Americans who had come to doubt the war's purpose.

The president was delighted with Grant's successes in Tennessee. Lincoln promoted him again on March 10, 1864, this time to general in chief. Grant immediately left his command in the West to prepare an all-out attack on Lee and Virginia, authorizing Sherman to pursue a campaign into Georgia.

In Grant and Sherman, Lincoln had found what he needed. On the surface, neither seemed a likely candidate for a major role in the Union army. Both were West Point graduates but left the army after the War with Mexico to seek their fortunes. Neither had succeeded in civilian life: Grant was a binge drinker who had accomplished little, and Sherman had failed as a banker and a lawyer. Both were "political generals," owing their Civil War commissions to the influence of friends or relatives. Despite their checkered pasts, these two men invented a new type of warfare that eventually brought the South to its knees. Grant and Sherman were willing to wage **total war** in order to destroy the South's will to continue the struggle.

Preparing for the new sort of war he was about to inaugurate, Grant suspended prisoner-of-war exchanges. Realizing that the Confederates needed soldiers badly, he understood that one outcome of this policy would be slow death by starvation for Union prisoners. Cruel though his policy was, Grant reasoned that victory was his primary goal and that suffering and death were unavoidable in war. Throughout the remainder of the war, this single-mindedness pushed Grant to make decisions that cost tens of thousands of lives on both sides.

On May 4, Grant and Meade moved toward Richmond and Robert E. Lee. The next day, Union and Confederate armies collided in a tangle of woods called **The Wilderness,** near Chancellorsville (see Map 14.4). Two days of bloody fighting followed, broken by a night during which hundreds of the wounded burned to death in brushfires that raged between the two lines. Grant decided to skirt Lee's troops and head for Richmond, but Lee anticipated the maneuver and blocked Grant's route at Spotsylvania. Twelve days of fighting ensued. Grant again attempted to move around Lee, and again Lee anticipated him. On June 1, the two armies met at **Cold Harbor,** Virginia. After each side had consolidated its position, Grant ordered a series of frontal attacks against the entrenched Confederates on June 3. Lee's veteran troops waited patiently in perhaps the best position they had ever defended, while Union soldiers expecting to die marched toward them. The assault failed amid unspeakable slaughter.

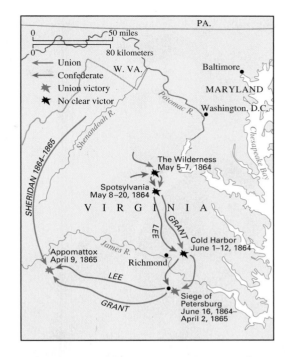

MAP 14.4   **Grant's Campaign Against Lee**   This map shows the series of battles during the late spring of 1864 in which Grant's army suffered staggering casualties but finally drove Lee into retreat. After holding up for months behind heavy fortifications in Petersburg, Lee made a daring attempt to escape in April 1865 but was headed off by General Philip Sheridan's troops. Grant quickly closed in on the greatly weakened Confederate army, forcing Lee's surrender.

One southerner described Grant's assaults as "inexplicable and incredible butchery." The wounded were left to die between the lines while the living fell back exhausted into their trenches. Many of the young federal attackers at Cold Harbor had pinned their names on their shirts in the hope that their shattered

total war   War waged with little regard for the welfare of troops on either side or for enemy civilians; the objective is to destroy both the human and the economic resources of the enemy.

The Wilderness   Densely wooded region of Virginia that was the site in May 1864 of a devastating but inconclusive battle between Union forces under Grant and Confederates under Lee.

Cold Harbor   Area of Virginia, about 10 miles from Richmond, where Grant made an unsuccessful attempt to drive his forces through Lee's center.

Disliked by most of his fellow officers because of his coarse behavior and binge drinking, Ulysses S. Grant had the right combination of daring, unconventionality, and ruthlessness to wear down Robert E. Lee's forces in Virginia and finally defeat the Confederate army. *National Archives.*

bodies might be identified after the battle. Casualties on both sides at Spotsylvania and Cold Harbor were staggering, but Union losses were unimaginably horrible. As one Confederate officer put it, "We have met a man, this time, who either does not know when he is whipped, or who cares not if he loses his whole army." During the three encounters, Grant lost a total of sixty thousand troops, more than Lee's entire army. Said Lee, "This is not war, this is murder." But Grant's seeming wantonness was calculated, for the Confederates lost more than twenty-five thousand troops. And Grant knew, as did Lee, that the Union could afford the losses but the Confederacy could not.

After Cold Harbor, Grant guessed that Lee would expect him to try to assault nearby Richmond next. This time, though, he steered the Union army south of Richmond for Petersburg to try to take the vital rail center and cut off the southern capital. Once again, Lee reacted quickly: he rapidly shifted the **vanguard** of his troops, beat back Grant's advance, and occupied Petersburg. Grant bitterly regretted this failure, feeling that he could have ended the war. Instead, the cam-

paign settled into a siege that neither side wanted. Lee and the Confederates could ill afford a siege that ate up supplies and munitions. And elections were rapidly approaching in the Union.

The Election of 1864 and Sherman's March to the Sea

Lincoln was under fire from two directions. On May 31, 1864, the Republicans met in Cleveland and dumped him from the ticket, officially nominating John C. Frémont as their presidential candidate. Lincoln supporters, who began calling themselves the Union Party, held its nominating convention in June and renominated Lincoln. To attract Democrats who still favored fighting for a clear victory, Union Party delegates dumped Republican Hannibal Hamlin and chose **Andrew Johnson,** a southern Democrat, as Lincoln's running mate. Then, in August, the Democratic National Convention met at Chicago. The Democrats pulled together many **Copperheads** and other northerners who were so upset by the heavy casualties that they were determined to stop the war, even at the cost of allowing slavery to continue. The Democrats selected McClellan as their presidential candidate and included a peace plank in their platform. Thus Lincoln sat squarely in the middle between one group that castigated him for pursuing the war and another group that rebuked him for failing to punish the South vigorously enough.

Confederate president Jefferson Davis did not face an election in 1864, but he too had plenty of political problems. As deprivation and military losses mounted, some factions began to resist the war effort. The Confederate congress called for a new draft, but several states refused to comply. Governors in Georgia, North Carolina, and South Carolina, who controlled their state's militia, kept troops at home and defied Davis to enforce conscription.

Eager to solve their problems, Lincoln and Confederate vice president Alexander H. Stephens had

vanguard The foremost position in any army advancing into battle.

Andrew Johnson Tennessee senator who became Lincoln's running mate in 1864 and who succeeded to the presidency after Lincoln's assassination.

Copperheads Derogatory term (the name of a poisonous snake) applied to northerners who supported the South during the Civil War.

THE GETTYSBURG ADDRESS

When the Civil War began, Lincoln made it clear that defending the Constitution was his only objective. But when he spoke on the Gettysburg battlefield two years later, commemorating the deaths of the thousands who fell there, he gave voice to a broader vision and a more noble goal. In that speech, Lincoln referenced the Declaration of Independence, *not* the Constitution, transforming Thomas Jefferson's stirring announcement of Enlightenment principle that "all men are created equal" into the central element in the great American struggle. We seldom take political speeches very seriously these days, but this one changed the conception of the Constitution itself. After Lincoln's death, Congress enacted the Fourteenth Amendment, transforming Jefferson's—and Lincoln's—statement of principle into the law of the land. To this day—well more than "fourscore and seven years" since Lincoln's famous speech—"we hold this truth to be self-evident" in principle and in law through the Constitution Lincoln envisioned in that speech.

- What does the Gettysburg Address reflect about popular attitudes toward the war following the Battle of Gettysburg? Given what you know about the era, what do you think explains the speech's impact?
- In what significant ways did the principles stated by Lincoln at Gettysburg modify the nation's understanding of the Constitution? How has this understanding manifested itself in legislation and landmark legal cases in recent years?

conversations about negotiating a settlement. Lincoln stated his terms: reunion, abolition, and amnesty for Confederates. Southern officials balked, pointing out that "amnesty" applied to criminals and that the South had "committed no crime." The only possible outcomes of the war for the South, they concluded, were independence or extermination, even if it meant enduring the sight of "every Southern plantation sacked and every Southern city in flames." The words proved prophetic.

Grant had instructed Sherman "to get into the interior of the enemy's country as far as you can, inflicting all the damage you can against their war resources." Sherman responded with a vengeance. Slowly and skillfully his army advanced southward from Tennessee toward Atlanta, one of the South's few remaining industrial centers, against Confederate armies under the command of General Joseph E. Johnston (see Map 14.5). Only Johnston's skillful retreats kept Sherman from annihilating his army. President Davis then replaced Johnston with John Bell Hood, who vowed to take the offensive. Hood attacked, but Sherman inflicted such serious casualties that Hood had to retreat to Atlanta.

For days Sherman shelled Atlanta and wrought havoc in the surrounding countryside. When a last-ditch southern attack failed, Hood evacuated the city on September 1. The victorious Union troops moved in and occupied Atlanta on the following day. Sherman's victory caused tremendous despair among Confederates but gave great momentum to Lincoln's reelection campaign.

Also boosting Lincoln's reelection efforts was General Philip Sheridan's campaign in the Shenandoah Valley, an important source of food for Lee's army. Adopting the same sort of devastating tactics that Sherman used so successfully, Sheridan's men lived off the land and destroyed both military and civilian supplies whenever possible. Accepting high casualties, Sheridan drove Confederate forces from the region in October, laying waste to much of Lee's food supply in the process.

These victories proved the decisive factor in the election of 1864. Sherman's and Sheridan's successes defused McClellan's argument that Lincoln was not competent to direct the Union's military fortunes and quelled much antiwar sentiment in the North. Equally discredited, the Radical Republican platform and the Frémont candidacy disappeared before election day. As late as August, Lincoln had been expecting to lose the election in November, but the victory in Atlanta gave him some hope. When the votes were counted, Lincoln learned that he had defeated McClellan—by half a million popular votes and by a landslide margin of 212 to 21 in the Electoral College.

The southern peace movement had viewed a Democratic victory as the last chance to reach a settlement. Without it, all hope of negotiation appeared lost. Amid the bleak prospects, animosity toward Jefferson Davis increased in the South. But Lee's forces still remained in Petersburg, as did Hood's in Georgia. Southern hopes were dimmed but not extinguished.

Sherman soon grew bored with the occupation of Atlanta and posed a bold plan to Grant. He wanted to ignore Hood, leave the battered Confederates loose

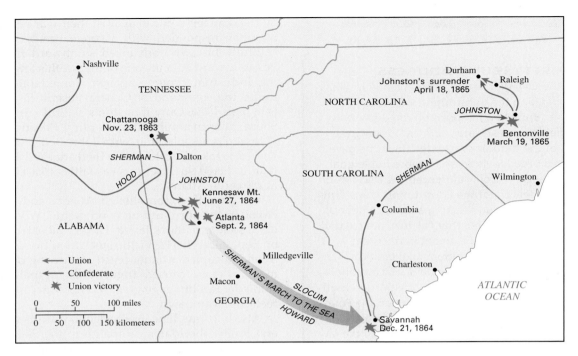

MAP 14.5 **Sherman's Campaign in the South** This map shows how William Tecumseh Sherman's troops slashed through the South, destroying both civilian and military targets and reducing the South's will to continue the war.

at his rear, go on the offensive, and "cut a swath through to the sea." "I can make Georgia howl," he promised. Despite some misgivings, Grant agreed and convinced Lincoln.

A week after the election, Sherman began preparing for his 300-mile **March to the Sea** (see Map 14.5). His intentions were clear. "We are not only fighting hostile armies, but a hostile people," he stated. By devastating the countryside and destroying the South's ability to conduct war, he intended to break down southerners' will to resist. "We cannot change the hearts of those people of the South," he concluded, but we can "make them so sick of war that generations would pass away before they would again appeal to it." With that, he burned most of Atlanta and then set out on his march to Savannah, on the coast. His troops plundered and looted farms and towns on the way, foraging for food and supplies and destroying everything in their path.

While Sherman headed toward Savannah, Confederate general Hood turned north and attacked General George Thomas's Union forces at Franklin, Tennessee, on November 30. Hood lost convincingly in a bloody battle. The Confederate Army of Tennes-

see fragmented, and all opposition to Sherman's onslaught dissolved. Sherman entered Savannah unopposed on December 21.

The March to the Sea completed, Sherman turned north. In South Carolina, the first state to secede and fire shots, Sherman's troops took special delight in ravaging the countryside. When they reached Columbia, flames engulfed the city. Whether Sherman's men or retreating Confederates started the blaze was not clear, but African American regiments in Sherman's command helped to put out the fires after Sherman occupied the South Carolina capital on February 17, 1865.

With the capital in flames, Confederate forces abandoned their posts in South Carolina, moving north to join with Joseph E. Johnston's army in an effort to stop Sherman from crossing North Carolina and joining

> **March to the Sea** Sherman's march through Georgia from Atlanta to Savannah from November 15 to December 21, 1864, during which Union soldiers carried out orders to destroy everything in their path.

Determined to "make Georgia howl," William Tecumseh Sherman and his band of "bummers" slashed their way through the South during the winter of 1864, destroying military and civilian property along the way. Having abandoned traditional lines of supply, Sherman's men raided farms for pork, grain, and other necessities, leaving ruin in their wake. *The New York Public Library/Art Resource, NY.*

Grant in Virginia. Union forces quickly moved into abandoned southern strongholds, including Charleston, where Major Robert Anderson, who had commanded Fort Sumter in April 1861, returned to raise the Union flag over the fort that he had surrendered four years earlier.

The End of Lee and Lincoln

Under increasing pressure from Sherman, the Confederacy's military situation was deteriorating rapidly. In a last-ditch effort to keep the Confederacy alive, Lee advised Davis to evacuate Richmond—the army intended to abandon the capital, moving west as rapidly as possible toward Lynchburg (see Map 14.4). From there Lee hoped to use surviving rail lines to move his troops south to join with Johnston's force in North Carolina. The unified armies might then halt Sherman's advance and wheel around to deal with Grant.

Suffering none of his predecessors' indecisiveness, Grant ordered an immediate assault as Lee's forces retreated from Petersburg. Lee had little ammunition, almost no food, and only thirty-five thousand men. As they retreated westward, under constant pressure from harassing attacks, hundreds of southern soldiers collapsed from hunger and exhaustion. By April 9, Union forces had surrounded Lee's broken army. Saying, "There is nothing left for me to do but go and see General Grant," Lee sent a note offering surrender.

The two generals met at a private home in the little village of Appomattox Courthouse, Virginia. Grant offered generous terms, allowing Confederate officers and men to go home "so long as they observe their paroles and the laws in force where they reside." This guaranteed them immunity from prosecution for treason and became the model for surrender. Grant sent the starving Confederates rations and let them keep their horses.

On the following day, Lincoln addressed a crowd outside the White House about his hopes and plans for rebuilding the nation. He talked about the need for flexibility in pulling the nation back together after the

The nation's mood shifted from celebration to shock when it learned that President Lincoln had fallen to an assassin's bullet. His funeral provided an occasion for the entire country to mourn, not only his death but also the deaths of hundreds of thousands of Americans who had fallen in the Civil War. A rail car pulled by an armored military locomotive carried the president's body on a route that retraced his 1860 campaign throughout the North. In large cities, Lincoln's body was paraded through the streets in mourning processionals. Throughout the countryside, however, people lined the tracks at all hours of the day and night waiting for the train to pass so they could pay tribute to their fallen leader. *Left and right: Picture History.*

long and bitter conflict. He had already taken steps to bring southerners back into the Union. In December 1863, he had issued a Proclamation of Amnesty and Reconstruction offering pardons to any Confederates who would take a loyalty oath. After his reelection in 1864, Lincoln had begun to plan for the Confederacy's eventual surrender, and he pushed for a constitutional ban on slavery, which passed on January 31, 1865.

With victory at hand and a peace plan in place, on April 14 after an exhausting day in conference with his cabinet and with General Grant, Lincoln chose to relax by attending a play at Ford's Theater in Washington. At about ten o'clock, **John Wilkes Booth,** an actor and a southern sympathizer, entered the president's box and shot him behind the ear. Meanwhile, one of Booth's accomplices entered the home of Secretary of State Seward, who was bedridden as a result of a carriage accident, and stabbed him several times before being driven out by Seward's son and a male

nurse. Another accomplice was supposed to assassinate Vice President Johnson but apparently lost his nerve. Although the conspiracy had failed, one of its main objectives succeeded: the following morning, Lincoln died of his wound.

Even though Lincoln was dead and Lee had fallen, the war continued. Joseph E. Johnston, whose forces succeeded in preventing Sherman from joining Grant, did not surrender until April 18. And although most of his forces had been defeated, Jefferson Davis remained in hiding and called for guerrilla warfare and continued resistance. But one by one, the Confederate

John Wilkes Booth Actor and southern sympathizer who on April 14, 1865, five days after Lee's surrender, fatally shot President Lincoln at Ford's Theater in Washington.

officers surrendered to their Union opponents. On May 10, Davis and the Confederate postmaster general were captured near Irwinville, Georgia, and placed in prison. Andrew Johnson, who had assumed the presidency upon Lincoln's death, issued a statement to the American people that armed rebellion against legitimate authority could be considered "virtually at an end." The last Confederate general to lay down his arms was Cherokee leader Stand Watie, who surrendered on June 23, 1865.

The price of victory was high for both the winner and the loser. More than 350,000 Union soldiers had been killed in action. No exact figures exist for the Confederacy, but southern casualties probably equaled or exceeded those of the Union. The war had wrecked the economy of the South, for most of the fighting had occurred there. Union military campaigns had wiped out most southern rail lines, destroyed the South's manufacturing capacity, and severely reduced agricultural productivity. Both sides had faced rising inflation during the war, but the Confederacy's actions to supply troops and keep the war effort going had bled the South of most of its resources and money. Secession had been defeated, but reunion remained a distant and difficult objective.

✔ Individual Voices

Susie King Taylor

(1) *In Taylor's mind, what conditions did the end of the Spanish-American War leave unresolved? What does this say about her perceptions concerning her role in the Civil War?*

(2) *In 1886, Taylor was one of the co-founders of the Women's Relief Corp, an organization devoted to aiding Civil War veterans and furthering recognition for American soldiers. She was the president of the Massachusetts auxiliary in 1898, leading the organization to send aid to soldiers in the Spanish-American War.*

(3) *What is Taylor suggesting here about the way in which the contributions of African American Civil War veterans were regarded? What does this suggest about her motivations for writing about her experiences in that war?*

Like all African Americans, Susie King Taylor had a deep personal investment in the outcome of the American Civil War. A slave herself, she ran away to the Union lines seeking asylum and, like many other "contrabands," joined the Union cause. Unlike most others, however, Taylor recorded her experiences during the war, giving her contemporaries and modern historians a unique insight into the accomplishments and disillusionments that came with fighting for the freedom and equality that the war seemed to promise.

With the close of the Spanish war, and on the entrance of the Americans into Cuba, the same conditions confront us as the war of 1861 left. The Cubans are free, but it is a limited freedom, for prejudice, deep-rooted, has been brought to them and a separation made between the white and black Cubans, a thing that had never existed between them before; but to-day there is the same intense hatred toward the negro in Cuba that there is in some parts of this country. (1)
I helped to furnish and pack boxes to be sent to the soldiers and hospitals during the first part of the Spanish war; (2) *there were black soldiers there too. At the battle of San Juan Hill, they were in the front, just as brave, loyal, and true as those other black men who fought for freedom and the right; and yet their bravery and faithfulness were reluctantly acknowledged, and praise grudgingly given.* (3) *All we ask for is "equal justice," the same that is accorded to all other races who come to this country, of their free will (not forced to, as we were), and are allowed to enjoy every privilege, unrestricted, while we are denied what is rightfully our own in a country which the labor of our forefathers helped to make what it is.*

SUMMARY

Both the Union and the Confederacy entered the war in 1861 with glowing hopes. Jefferson Davis pursued a defensive strategy, certain that northerners would soon tire of war and let the South withdraw from the Union. Abraham Lincoln countered by using the superior human, economic, and natural resources of the North to strangle the South into submission. But both leaders became increasingly frustrated during the first year of the war.

For Lincoln, the greatest frustration was military leadership. Beginning with the first Battle of Bull Run, Union forces seemed unable to win any major battles despite their numerical superiority. Although Union forces under Ulysses S. Grant's command scored victories in the Mississippi Valley, the Federals were stalemated. Robert E. Lee and Thomas "Stonewall" Jackson seemed able to defeat any Union general that Lincoln sent to oppose them.

The war's nature and direction changed after the fall of 1862, however. Lee invaded Maryland and was defeated at Antietam. Despite this crushing loss, Union generals still failed to capture Lee or to subdue Confederate forces in Virginia. Still angered by military blundering, political attacks, and popular unrest, Lincoln issued the Emancipation Proclamation in an effort to undermine southern efforts and unify northern ones. After the proclamation, the only option for either side was total victory or total defeat.

After further reversals in the spring of 1863, Union forces turned the tide in the war by defeating Lee's army at Gettysburg and taking Vicksburg to gain full control of the Mississippi. With an election drawing near, Lincoln spurred his generals to deal the death blow to the Confederacy, and two in particular rose to the occasion. During the last half of 1864, William Tecumseh Sherman wreaked havoc, making Georgia "howl." And Grant, in a wanton display of disregard for human life, drove Lee into a defensive corner. In November, buoyed by Sherman's victories in Georgia, Lincoln was reelected.

Suffering was not confined to those at the front. Governments in both the North and the South had to dig deep into depleting economic resources to keep the war effort going. Inflation plagued both nations, and common people faced hunger, disease, and insufficient police protection. Riots broke out in major cities, including New York. But throughout the country many people responded heroically to their own privations and to suffering at the front. Women such as Mary Livermore and others faced up to epidemics, enemy gunfire, and gender bias to institute public health standards and bring solace to suffering civilians and soldiers alike.

As hope dwindled for the South in the spring of 1865, Lee made a final desperate effort to keep the flagging Confederacy alive, racing to unify the last surviving remnants of the once-proud southern army. But Grant closed a net of steel around Lee's troops, forcing surrender. Lincoln immediately promoted a gentle policy for reunion, but his assassination ended this effort. The saintly American hero was gone, leaving a southern Democrat—Andrew Johnson—as president and a nation reeling in shock. The war was over, but the issues were still unresolved. Both the North and the South were beset with uncertainty about what would follow four years of suffering and sacrifice.

IN THE WIDER WORLD

1860
Lincoln elected

Battle of Bull Run

1863
Emancipation Proclamation

Battle of Gettysburg

Gettysburg Address

1864
Sherman's March to the Sea

Grant invades Virginia

1865
Lee surrenders

Lincoln assassinated

| 1860 | 1861 | 1862 | 1863 | 1864 | 1865 |

1861
Russia abolishes serfdom

Pasteur proves germ theory of disease

1862
France invades Mexico

1863
World's first subway opens in London

Baha'i faith founded in Iran

1864
Red Cross founded in Geneva

Russia conquers Central Asia

1865
Alice in Wonderland published

Salvation Army founded in London

In the United States

War Between the States

1861 Lincoln takes office and runs Union by executive authority until July

Fort Sumter falls

Battle of Bull Run

McClellan organizes the Union army

Union naval blockade begins

1862 Grant's victories in Mississippi Valley

Battle of Shiloh

U.S. Navy captures New Orleans

Peninsular Campaign

Battle of Antietam

African Americans permitted in Union army

1863 Emancipation Proclamation takes effect

Union enacts conscription

Battle of Chancellorsville and death of Stonewall Jackson

Union victories at Gettysburg and Vicksburg

Draft riots in New York City

1864 Grant invades Virginia

Sherman captures Atlanta

Lincoln reelected

Sherman's March to the Sea

Congress passes the Thirteenth Amendment

1865 Sherman's march through the Carolinas

Lee abandons Petersburg and Richmond

Lee surrenders at Appomattox Courthouse

Lincoln proposes a gentle reconstruction policy

Lincoln is assassinated

Reconstruction: High Hopes and Shattered Dreams, 1865–1877

A NOTE FROM THE AUTHOR

For four long, bloody years of civil war, the armies of the North and South slogged through battle after battle. Toward the end of the war, Union armies smashed across the South, leaving wreckage in their wake: shelled buildings, ravaged farms, twisted railroad tracks. Slavery—the dominant economic and social institution in many parts of the South—collapsed.

The end of the war brought many questions. What would be the future status of African Americans? How would the South be reintegrated into the federal union? What would happen to those who had supported the Confederacy? Thousands of voices across the nation proposed very different answers.

Historians use the term *Reconstruction* to describe the years after the Civil War, from 1865 to 1877. In evaluating the meaning and significance of **Reconstruction,** historians focus on several central changes:

- The restoration of the federal union;
- Significant changes in the relationship between the federal government and the states, and in the relative power of the president and Congress;
- The end of slavery and the experience of African Americans, most of them former slaves;
- The restructuring of race relations, especially in the South; and
- Major changes in the politics, economy, and social structure of the South.

The Civil War and Reconstruction, like the American Revolution, form a dividing point in American history, a time when Americans made important and long-lasting choices about their future. Such dividing points attract historians, who seek to understand the momentous decisions that were being made. Historians of Reconstruction have largely agreed that the most ambitious efforts for restructuring race relations and southern politics ended in failure, but they have disagreed on the reasons for failure. As you read this chapter, think about these questions and about the long-term effects of Reconstruction on all Americans.

Reconstruction Term applied by historians to the years 1865–1877, when the Union was restored from the Civil War; important changes were made to the federal Constitution; and social, economic, and political relations between the races were transformed in the South.

✔ Individual Choices

Andy Anderson

Andy Anderson was born into slavery in East Texas in 1843. In 1937, when he was 94 years old, he told an interviewer about the day when he made the decision to be free. The interview was one of more than two thousand conversations with former slaves that the Federal Writers Project collected between 1936 and 1938. Interviewers were instructed to record the interviews exactly, word for word.

Anderson explained that he had been born on the plantation of Jack Haley. Anderson remembered Haley as "kind to his cullud folks" and "kind to ever'body." Haley rarely whipped his slaves, Anderson recalled, and he had been "reasonable" when he did apply the lash. Anderson remembered that Haley treated his slaves so well that neighboring whites called them "petted." With the coming of the Civil War, however, conditions changed. Haley sold Anderson to W. T. House, whom Anderson remembered as a man that "hell am too good fo'," and who whipped Anderson for a minor accident with a wagon.

> De overseer ties me to de stake an' ever' ha'f hour, fo' four hours, deys lay 10 lashes on my back. Aftah I's stood dat fo' a couple of hours, I's could not feel de pain so much an' w'en dey took me loose, I's jus' ha'f dead. I's could not feel de lash 'cause my body am numb, an' my mind am numb. De last thing I's 'membahs am dat I's wishin' fo' death. I's laid in de de bunk fo' two days gittin' over dat whuppin'. Dat is, gittin' over it in de body but not in de heart. No Sar! I's have dat in de heart 'til dis day.

Soon after the whipping, Anderson was sold again, to House's brother John, who, to Anderson's knowledge, had never struck a slave.

Anderson remembered a day, as the Civil War was winding down to its end, when House called his slaves together and told them that they were free and that the official order would soon be given. He offered any who wished to stay the choice to work for wages or work the land as sharecroppers, and he urged the freed people to "stay with me." Anderson was standing near House and said to himself, not expecting anyone to hear,

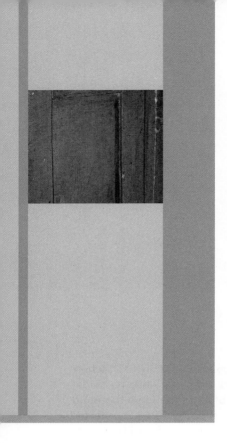

"Lak hell I's will." He meant only that he intended to take his freedom, but House heard him, took it as a challenge, and promised that he would "tend to yous later." Anderson recalled that he was sure to keep his lips closed when he thought, "I's won't be heah."

Anderson left the House plantation for good. He traveled at night to avoid the patrollers, who were on the lookout for African Americans on the road without passes, and hid in the brush during the day. Though he was 21 years old, he'd never been farther from home than a neighbor's house, and he was uncertain of his way. Nonetheless he managed to locate the Haley plantation and to find his father. Haley permitted Anderson to stay on his place until the final proclamation of freedom.

When Sheldon Cauthier of the Federal Writers Project interviewed Andy Anderson, the former slave was living in Fort Worth, Texas. Anderson provided only limited information on his later life. He left Haley's farm soon after emancipation to work on another farm for $2 a month plus clothing and food, and he continued to do farm work until his old age. He married in 1883, when he was about 40, an indication, perhaps, that his labor did not provide enough income to support a family until then. He and his first wife had two children, but both children and his wife died. He married again in 1885, and he and second his wife had six children, of whom four were still living in 1937. His second wife died in 1934, and he married a third time in 1936. He joked with the interviewer that "dere am no chilluns yet f'om my third mai'age." Though we know little of what Anderson experienced during the years of Reconstruction, we do have his dramatic account of how he claimed his freedom.

INTRODUCTION

Andy Anderson was not the only African American who claimed freedom while the war was raging. Anderson's experience was repeated time and time again, with many variations, all across the South. Those decisions were made legal by the Emancipation Proclamation, enforced by the presence of Union armies, and made permanent by the Thirteenth Amendment to the Constitution. The **freed people** now faced a wide range of new decisions—where to live, where to work, how to create their own communities.

The war left many parts of the South in a shambles. Though southerners were dismayed by their ravaged countryside, many white southerners were even more distressed by the **emancipation** of 4 million slaves. In 1861, fears for the future of slavery under Republicans had caused the South to attempt to **secede** from the Union. With the end of the war, fears became reality. The end of slavery forced southerners of both races to develop new social, economic, and political patterns.

The years following the war were a time of physical rebuilding throughout the South, but the term *Reconstruction* refers primarily to the rebuilding of the federal Union and to the political, economic, and social changes that came to the South as it was restored to the nation. Reconstruction involved some of the most momentous questions in American history. How was the defeated South to be treated? What was to be the future of the 4 million former slaves? Should key decisions be made by the federal government or in state capitols and county courthouses throughout the South? Which branch of the government was to establish policies?

As the dominant Republicans turned their attention from waging war to reconstructing the Union, they

---

freed people   Former slaves; *freed people* is the term used by historians to refer to former slaves, whether male or female.

emancipation   The release from slavery.

secede   To withdraw from membership in an organization; in this case, the attempted withdrawal of eleven southern states from the United States in 1860–1861, giving rise to the Civil War.

wrote into law and the Constitution new definitions of the Union itself. They also defined the rights of the former slaves and the terms on which the South might rejoin the Union. And they permanently changed the definition of American citizenship.

Most white southerners disliked the new rules emerging from the federal government, and some resisted. Disagreement over the future of the South and the status of the former slaves led to conflict between the president and Congress. A temporary result of this conflict was a more powerful Congress and a less powerful executive. A lasting outcome of these events was a significant increase in the power of the federal government and new limits on local and state governments.

Reconstruction significantly changed many aspects of southern life. In the end, however, Reconstruction failed to fulfill many African Americans' hopes for their lives as free people.

Presidential Reconstruction

→ *What did Presidents Lincoln and Johnson seek to accomplish through their Reconstruction policies? How did their purposes differ? In what ways were their policies similar?*

→ *How did white southerners respond to the Reconstruction efforts of Lincoln and Johnson? What does this suggest about the expectations of white southerners?*

On New Year's Day 1863, the Emancipation Proclamation took effect. More than four years earlier, Abraham Lincoln had insisted that "this government cannot endure permanently half slave and half free. . . . It will become all one thing, or all the other." With the Emancipation Proclamation, President Lincoln began the legal process by which the nation became all free. At the time, however, the Proclamation did not affect any slave because it abolished slavery only in territory under Confederate control, where it was unenforceable. But every advance of a Union army after January 1, 1863, brought the law of the land—and emancipation—to the Confederacy.

Republican War Aims

For Lincoln and the Republican Party, freedom for the slaves became a central concern partly because **abolitionists** were an influential group within the party. The Republican Party had promised only to prohibit slavery in the territories during their 1860 electoral campaign, and Lincoln initially defined the war as one to maintain the Union. Some leading Republicans, however, favored abolition of slavery everywhere in the Union. As Union troops moved into the South, some slaves took matters into their hands by walking away from their owners and seeking safety with the advancing army. Former slaves soon became an important part of the Union army. Abolitionists throughout the North—including Frederick Douglass, an escaped slave and an important leader of the abolition movement—began to argue that emancipation would be meaningless unless the government guaranteed the civil and political rights of the former slaves. Thus some Republicans expanded their definition of war objectives to include not just preserving the Union but also abolishing slavery, extending citizenship for the former slaves, and guaranteeing the equality of all citizens before the law. At the time, these were extreme views on abolition and equal rights, and the people who held them were called **Radical Republicans,** or simply Radicals.

Thaddeus Stevens, 73 years old in 1865, was perhaps the leading Radical in the House of Representatives. He had made a successful career as a Pennsylvania lawyer and iron manufacturer before he won election to Congress in 1858. Born with a clubfoot, he seemed always to identify with those outside the social mainstream. He became a compelling spokesman for abolition and an uncompromising advocate of equal rights for African Americans. A masterful parliamentarian, he was known for his honesty and his sarcastic wit. From the beginning of the war, Stevens urged that the slaves be not only freed but also armed, to fight the Confederacy. By the end of the war, some 180,000 African Americans, the great majority of them freedmen, had served in the Union army and a few thousand in the Union navy. Many more worked for the army as laborers.

Charles Sumner of Massachusetts, a prominent Radical in the Senate, had argued for **racial integration** of Massachusetts schools in 1849 and won election to the U.S. Senate in 1851. Immediately establishing himself

---

abolitionist   An individual who condemns slavery as morally wrong and seeks to abolish (eliminate) slavery.

Radical Republicans   A group within the Republican Party during the Civil War and Reconstruction who advocated abolition of slavery, citizenship for the former slaves, and sweeping alteration of the South.

racial integration   Equal opportunities to participate in a society or organization by people of different racial groups; the absence of race-based barriers to full and equal participation.

Thaddeus Stevens, seen here when he was at the height of his power, was the leader of the Radical Republicans in the House of Representatives. He died in 1868. At his request, he was buried in a cemetery that did not discriminate on the basis of race. *Library of Congress.*

as the Senate's foremost champion of abolition, he became a martyr to the cause after he suffered a severe beating in 1856 because of an antislavery speech. After emancipation, Sumner, like Stevens, fought for full political and civil rights for the freed people.

Stevens, Sumner, and other Radicals demanded a drastic restructuring not only of the South's political system but also of its economy. They opposed slavery not only on moral grounds but also because they believed free labor was more productive. Slaves worked to escape punishment, they argued, but free workers worked to benefit themselves. Eliminating slavery and instituting a free-labor system in its place, they claimed, would benefit everyone by increasing the nation's productivity. Free labor not only contributed centrally to the dynamism of the North's economy, they argued, but was crucial to democracy itself. "The middling classes who own the soil, and work it with their own hands," Stevens once proclaimed, "are the main support of every free government." For the South to be fully democratic, the Radicals concluded, it had to elevate free labor to a position of honor.

Not all Republicans agreed with the Radicals. All Republicans had objected to slavery, but not all Republicans were abolitionists. Similarly, not all Republicans wanted to extend full citizenship rights to the former slaves. Some favored rapid restoration of the South to the Union so that the federal government could concentrate on stimulating the nation's economy and developing the West. Republicans who did not immediately endorse severe punishment for the South or citizenship for the freed people are usually referred to as **moderates.**

Lincoln's Approach to Reconstruction: "With Malice Toward None"

After the Emancipation Proclamation, President Lincoln and the congressional Radicals agreed that the abolition of slavery had to be a condition for the return of the South to the Union. Major differences soon appeared, however, over other terms for reunion and the roles of the president and Congress in establishing those terms. In his second inaugural address, a month before his death, Lincoln defined the task facing the nation:

> *With malice toward none; with charity for all; with firmness in the right, as God gives us to see the right, let us strive on to finish the work we are in: to bind up the nation's wounds; to care for him who shall have borne the battle, and for his widow and orphan, to do all which may achieve and cherish a just and lasting peace among ourselves, and with all nations.*

Lincoln began to rebuild the Union on the basis of these principles. He hoped to hasten the end of the war by encouraging southerners to renounce the Confederacy and to accept emancipation. As soon as Union armies occupied portions of southern states, he appointed temporary military governors for those regions and tried to restore civil government as quickly as possible.

Drawing on the president's constitutional power to issue **pardons** (Article II, Section 2), Lincoln issued

moderates   People whose views are midway between two more-extreme positions; in this case, Republicans who favored some reforms but not all the Radicals' proposals.

pardon   A governmental directive canceling punishment for a person or people who have committed a crime.

These white southerners are shown taking the oath of allegiance to the United States in 1865, as part of the process of restoring civil government in the South. Union soldiers and officers are administering the oath. *Library of Congress.*

a Proclamation of **Amnesty** and Reconstruction in December 1863. Often called the "Ten Percent Plan," it promised a full pardon and restoration of rights to those who swore their loyalty to the Union and accepted the abolition of slavery. Only high-ranking Confederate leaders were not eligible. Once those who had taken the oath in a state amounted to 10 percent of the number of votes cast by that state in the 1860 presidential election, the pardoned voters were to write a new state constitution that abolished slavery, elect state officials, and resume self-government. Some congressional Radicals disagreed with Lincoln's lenient approach. When they tried to set more stringent standards, however, Lincoln blocked them, fearing their plan would slow the restoration of civil government and perhaps even lengthen the war.

Under Lincoln's Ten Percent Plan, new state governments were established in Arkansas, Louisiana, and Tennessee during 1864 and early 1865. In Louisiana, the new government denied voting rights to men who were one-quarter or more black. Radicals complained, but Lincoln urged patience, suggesting the reconstructed government in Louisiana was "as the egg to the fowl, and we shall sooner have the fowl by hatching the egg than by smashing it." Events in Louisiana

and elsewhere convinced Radicals that freed people were unlikely to receive equitable treatment from state governments formed under the Ten Percent Plan. Some moderates agreed and moved toward the Radicals' position that only **suffrage** could protect the freedmen's rights and that only federal action could secure black suffrage.

Abolishing Slavery Forever: The Thirteenth Amendment

Amid questions about the rights of freed people, congressional Republicans prepared the final destruction of slavery. The Emancipation Proclamation had been a wartime measure, justified partly by military necessity. It never applied in Union states. State legislatures or conventions abolished slavery in West Virginia, Maryland, Missouri, and the reconstructed state of

amnesty A general pardon granted by a government, especially for political offenses.
suffrage The right to vote.

TABLE 15.1 — Abolition of Slavery Around the World

1772 Slavery abolished in England	**1865** Thirteenth Amendment abolishes slavery everywhere in the United States
1807 British navy begins operations to end the international slave trade	**1888** Slavery abolished in Brazil
1808 United States prohibits the importation of slaves	**1926** Thirty-five nations sign a Convention to Suppress the Slave Trade and Slavery
1820s Slavery abolished in most Spanish-speaking Latin American nations	**1948** United Nations adopts the Universal Declaration of Human Rights, which includes a call for the abolition of slavery and the slave trade
1833 Slavery abolished within the British Empire	**1962** Abolition of slavery in Saudi Arabia
1848 Slavery abolished within the French Empire	
1861 Abolition of serfdom in Russia	**2004** International Year to Commemorate the Struggle against Slavery and its Abolition, proclaimed by the United Nations General Assembly
1863 Emancipation Proclamation (United States); abolition of slavery within the Dutch Empire	

Tennessee. In early 1865, however, slavery remained legal in Delaware and Kentucky, and old, prewar state laws—which might or might not be valid—still permitted slavery in the states that had seceded. To destroy slavery forever, Congress in January 1865 approved the **Thirteenth Amendment,** which read simply, "Neither slavery nor involuntary servitude, except as a punishment for crime whereof the party shall have been duly convicted, shall exist within the United States, or any place subject to their jurisdiction."

The Constitution requires any amendment to be ratified by three-fourths of the states—then 27 of 36. By December 1865, only 19 of the 25 Union states had ratified the amendment. The measure passed, however, when 8 of the reconstructed southern states approved it. In the end, therefore, the abolition of slavery hinged on action by reconstructed state governments in the South.

By abolishing slavery, the United States followed the lead of most of the nations of Europe and Latin America. Table 15.1 summarizes information on the abolition of slavery elsewhere in the world. Though illegal throughout the world, **chattel slavery** still exists in some parts of Africa, notably Mauritania and Sudan, and in some parts of Asia, especially the Middle East.

In other places throughout the world, people are still forced to work in conditions approaching that of slavery, through forced prostitution, debt bondage, and forced-labor camps.

Andrew Johnson and Reconstruction

After the assassination of Lincoln in April 1865, Vice President Andrew Johnson became president. Born in North Carolina, he never had the opportunity to attend school and spent his early life in a continual struggle against poverty. As a young man in Tennessee, he worked as a tailor and then turned to politics. His wife, Eliza McCardle Johnson, tutored him in reading, writing, and arithmetic. A Democrat, Johnson

Thirteenth Amendment Constitutional amendment, ratified in 1865, that abolished slavery in the United States and its territories.

chattel slavery The situation where one person is legally defined as the personal property of another person.

relied on his oratorical skills to win several terms in the Tennessee legislature. He was elected to Congress and later was governor before winning election to the U.S. Senate in 1857. His political support came primarily from small-scale farmers and working people. The state's elite of plantation owners usually opposed him. Johnson, in turn, resented their wealth and power, and blamed them for secession and the Civil War.

Johnson was the only southern senator who rejected the Confederacy. Early in the war, Union forces captured Nashville, the capital of Tennessee, and Lincoln appointed Johnson as military governor. Johnson dealt harshly with Tennessee secessionists, especially wealthy planters. Radical Republicans approved, arguing that Johnson's severe treatment of former Confederates was exactly what the South needed. Johnson was elected vice president in 1864, receiving the nomination in part because Lincoln wanted to appeal to Democrats and Unionists in border states.

When Johnson became president, Radicals hoped he would join their efforts to transform the South. Johnson, however, soon made clear that he was strongly committed to **states' rights** and opposed the Radicals' objective of a powerful federal government. "White men alone must manage the South," Johnson told one visitor, although he recommended limited political roles for the freedmen. Self-righteous and uncompromising, Johnson saw the major task of Reconstruction as **empowering** the region's white middle class and excluding wealthy planters from power.

Johnson's approach to Reconstruction differed little from Lincoln's. Like Lincoln, he relied on the president's constitutional power to grant pardons. His desire for a quick restoration of the southern states to the Union apparently overcame his bitterness toward the southern elite, and he granted amnesty to most former Confederates who pledged loyalty to the Union and support for emancipation. In one of his last actions as president, he granted full pardon and amnesty to all southern rebels, although after 1868 the Fourteenth Amendment prevented him from restoring their right to hold office.

Johnson appointed **provisional** civilian governors for the southern states not already reconstructed. He instructed them to reconstitute functioning state administrations and to call constitutional conventions of delegates elected by pardoned voters. Some provisional governors, however, appointed former Confederates to state and local offices, outraging those who expected Reconstruction to bring to power loyal Unionists committed to a new southern society.

The Southern Response: Minimal Compliance

Johnson expected the state constitutional conventions to abolish slavery within each state, ratify the Thirteenth Amendment, renounce secession, and **repudiate** the states' war debts. The states were then to hold elections and resume their places in the Union. State conventions during the summer of 1865 usually complied with these requirements, though some did so grudgingly. Johnson had specified nothing about the rights of the freed people, and every state rejected black suffrage.

By April 1866, a year after the close of the war, all the southern states had fulfilled Johnson's requirements for rejoining the Union and had elected legislators, governors, and members of Congress. Their choices troubled Johnson. He had hoped for the emergence of new political leaders in the South and was dismayed at the number of rich planters and former Confederate officials who won state contests.

Most white southerners, however, viewed Johnson as their protector, standing between them and the Radicals. His support for states' rights and his opposition to federal determination of voting rights led white southerners to expect that they would shape the transition from slavery to freedom—that they, and not Congress, would define the status of the former slaves.

Freedom and the Legacy of Slavery

→ *How did the freed people respond to freedom? What seem to have been the leading objectives among freed people as they explored their new opportunities?*

→ *How did southern whites respond to the end of slavery?*

states' rights A political position favoring limitation of the federal government's power and the greatest possible self-government by the individual states.

empower To increase the power or authority of some person or group.

provisional Temporary.

repudiate The act of rejecting the validity or authority of something; to refuse to pay.

Before Emancipation, slaves typically made their own simple clothing or they received the used outfits of their owners and over-seers. With Emancipation, those freed people who had an income could afford to dress more fashion-ably. The Harry Stephens family probably put on their best clothes for a visit to the photographer G. Gable in 1866. *The Metropolitan Museum of Art, Gilman Collection, Purchase, The Horace W. Goldsmith Foundation Gift, 2005 (2005.100.277).*

→ *How do the differing responses of freed people and southern whites show different understandings of the significance of emancipation?*

As state conventions wrote new constitutions and politicians argued in Washington, African Americans throughout the South set about creating new, free lives for themselves. In the antebellum South, all slaves and most free African Americans had led lives tightly constrained by law and custom. They were permitted few social organizations of their own. Recent historians have largely agreed that the central theme of the black response to emancipation was a desire for freedom from white control, for **autonomy** as individuals and as a community. The prospect of autonomy touched every aspect of life—family, churches, schools, newspapers, and a host of other social institutions. From this ferment of freedom came new, independent black institutions that provided the basis for southern African American communities. At the same time, the economic life of the South had been shattered by the Civil War and was being transformed by emancipation. Thus white southerners also faced drastic economic and social change.

Defining the Meaning of Freedom

At the most basic level, freedom came every time an individual slave stopped working for a master and claimed the right to be free. Thus freedom did not come to all slaves at the same time or in the same way. For some, freedom came before the Emancipation Proclamation, when they walked away from their owners, crossed into Union-held territory, and asserted their liberty. Toward the end of the war, as civil authority broke down throughout much of the South, many slaves declared their freedom and left the lands they had worked when they were in bondage. Some left for good, but many remained nearby, though with a new understanding of their relationship to their former masters. For some, freedom did not come until ratification of the Thirteenth Amendment.

Across the South, the approach of Yankee troops set off a joyous celebration—called a Jubilee—among those who knew that their enslavement was ending. As one Virginia woman remembered, "Such rejoicing and shouting you never heard in your life." A man recalled that, with the appearance of the Union soldiers, "We was all walking on golden clouds. Hallelujah!" Once the celebrating was over, however, the freed people had to decide how best to use their freedom.

The freed people expressed their new status in many ways. Some chose new names to symbolize their new beginning. Andy Anderson (see page 435), for exam-

---

autonomy   Control of one's own affairs.

This engraving appeared in Frank Leslie's *Illustrated Newspaper* of August 5, 1876. The sculpture by Francesco Pezzicar, titled "The Abolition of Slavery in the United States" but often called "The Freed Slave," was exhibited at the Centennial Exposition in Philadelphia in 1876. It is now in the Revoltella Museum in Trieste, Italy. Unlike many depictions of freed slaves at the time, this sculpture shows a strong black man boldly claiming his political and spiritual independence. The engraver has shown the sculpture surrounded by well-dressed African Americans. Both the depiction of the emancipated slave and the portrayal of the black people viewing the sculpture challenged stereotypes of the day. © *Bettmann/CORBIS.*

ple, had been called Andy Haley, after the last name of his owner. On claiming his freedom, he changed his name to Anderson, the last name of his father. Many freed people changed their style of dress, discarding the cheap clothing provided to slaves. Some acquired guns. A significant benefit of freedom was the ability to travel without a pass and without being checked by the **patrollers** who had enforced the **pass system.**

Many freed people took advantage of this new opportunity to travel. Indeed, some felt they had to leave the site of their enslavement to experience full freedom. Andy Anderson refused to work for his last owner, not because he had anything against him but because he wanted "to take my freedom." One freed woman said, "If I stay here I'll never know I'm free." Most traveled only short distances, to find work or land to farm, to seek family members separated from them by slavery, or for other well-defined reasons.

The towns and cities of the South attracted some freed people. The presence of Union troops and federal officials promised protection from the random violence against freed people that occurred in many rural ar-

eas. In March 1865, Congress created the **Freedmen's Bureau** to assist the freed people in their transition to freedom. In cities and towns, this program offered assistance with finding work and necessities. Cities and towns also offered black churches, newly established schools, and other social institutions, some begun by free blacks before the war. Some African Americans came to towns and cities looking for work. Little housing was available, however, so freed people often crowded into hastily built shanties. Sanitation was poor and disease a common scourge. In September 1866, for example, more than a hundred people died of **cholera** in Vicksburg, Mississippi. Such conditions improved only very slowly.

Creating Communities

During Reconstruction, African Americans created their own communities with their own social institutions, beginning with family ties. Joyful families were sometimes reunited after years of separation caused by the sale of a spouse or children. Some people spent years searching for lost family members.

The new freedom to conduct religious services without white supervision was especially important. Churches quickly became the most prominent social organizations in African American communities. Churches were, in fact, among the very first social institutions that African Americans fully controlled. During Reconstruction, black denominations, including the African Methodist Episcopal, African Methodist Episcopal Zion, and several Baptist groups (all founded well before the Civil War), grew rapidly in the South. Black ministers helped to lead congregation members as they adjusted to the changes that freedom brought, and ministers often became key leaders within developing African American communities.

Throughout the cities and towns of the South, African Americans—especially ministers and church

patrollers During the era of slavery, white guards who made the rounds of rural roads to make certain that slaves were not moving about the countryside without written permission from their masters.

pass system Laws that forbade slaves from traveling without written authorization from their owners.

Freedmen's Bureau Agency established in 1865 to aid former slaves in their transition to freedom, especially by administering relief and sponsoring education.

cholera Infectious and often fatal disease associated with poor sanitation.

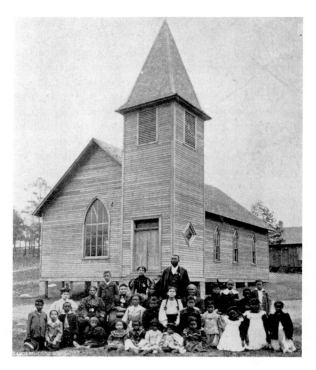

Churches were the first institutions in America to be completely controlled by African Americans, and ministers were highly influential figures in the African American communities that emerged during Reconstruction, both in towns and cities and in rural areas. This photograph of the Colored Methodist Episcopal mission church in Hot Springs, Arkansas, was first published in 1898 in *The History of the Colored Methodist Episcopal Church in America* by Charles H. Phillips, a bishop of that denomination. *Schomburg Center/ Art Resource, NY.*

members—worked to create schools. Setting up a school, said one, was "the first proof" of independence. Many new schools were for both children and adults, whose literacy and learning had been restricted by state laws prohibiting education for slaves. The desire to learn was widespread and intense. One freedman in Georgia wrote to a friend: "The Lord has sent books and teachers. We must not hesitate a moment, but go on and learn all we can."

Before the war, free public education had been limited in much of the South, and was absent in many places. When African Americans set up schools, they faced severe shortages of teachers, books, and schoolrooms—everything but students. As abolitionists and northern reformers tried to assist the transition from slavery to freedom, many of them focused first on education.

The Freedmen's Bureau played an important role in organizing and equipping schools. Freedmen's Aid Societies also sprang up in most northern cities and, along with northern churches, collected funds and supplies for the freed people. Teachers—mostly white women, often from New England, and often acting on religious impulses—came from the North. Northern aid societies and church organizations, together with the Freedmen's Bureau, established schools to train black teachers. Some of those schools evolved into black colleges. By 1870, the Freedmen's Bureau supervised more than 4,000 schools, with more than 9,000 teachers and 247,000 students. Still, in 1870, only one-tenth of school-age black children were in school.

African Americans created other social institutions, in addition to churches and schools, including **fraternal orders, benevolent societies,** and newspapers. By 1866, the South had ten black newspapers, led by the *New Orleans Tribune,* and black newspapers played important roles in shaping African American communities.

In politics, African Americans' first objective was recognition of their equal rights as citizens. Frederick Douglass insisted, "Slavery is not abolished until the black man has the ballot." Political conventions of African Americans attracted hundreds of leaders of the emerging black communities. They called for equality and voting rights and pointed to black contributions in the American Revolution and the Civil War as evidence of patriotism and devotion. They also appealed to the nation's republican traditions, in particular the Declaration of Independence and its dictum that "all men are created equal."

Land and Labor

Former slave owners reacted to emancipation in many ways. Some tried to keep their slaves from learning of their freedom. A very few white southerners welcomed the end of slavery—Mary Chesnut, for example, a plantation mistress from South Carolina, believed that the power of male slaveholders over female slaves led to sexual coercion and adultery, and she was glad

fraternal order An organization of men, often with a ceremonial initiation, that typically provided rudimentary life insurance; many fraternal orders also had auxiliaries for the female relatives of members.

benevolent society An organization of people dedicated to some charitable purpose.

During Reconstruction, the freed people gave a high priority to the establishment of schools, often with the assistance of the Freedmen's Bureau and northern missionary societies. This teacher and her barefoot pupils were photographed in the 1870s, in Petersburg, Virginia. In a school like this, one teacher typically taught grades 1–8. Daylight is coming through the shutter behind the teacher's right shoulder. Note, too, the gaps in the floorboards and the benches for the students which seem to have been constructed from logs. *Clayton Lewis, William L. Clements Library, University of Michigan.*

to see the end of slavery. Few former slave owners provided any compensation to assist their former slaves. One freedman later recalled, "I do know some of dem old slave owners to be nice enough to start der slaves off in freedom wid somethin' to live on . . . but dey wasn't in droves, I tell you."

Many freed people looked to Union troops for assistance. When General William T. Sherman led his victorious army through Georgia in the closing months of the war, thousands of African American men, women, and children claimed their freedom and followed in the Yankees' wake. Their leaders told Sherman that what they wanted most was to "reap the fruit of our own labor." In January 1865, Sherman issued Special Field Order No. 15, setting aside the Sea Islands and land along the South Carolina coast for freed families. Each family, he specified, was to receive 40 acres and the loan of an army mule. By June, the area had filled with forty thousand freed people settled on 400,000 acres of "Sherman land."

Sherman's action encouraged many African Americans to expect that the federal government would redistribute land throughout the South. "Forty acres and a mule" became a rallying cry. Only land, Thaddeus Stevens proclaimed, would give the freed people control of their own labor. "If we do not furnish them with homesteads," Stevens said, "we had better left them in bondage."

By the end of the war, the Freedmen's Bureau controlled some 850,000 acres of land abandoned by former owners or confiscated from Confederate leaders. In July 1865, General Oliver O. Howard, head of the bureau, directed that this land be divided into 40-acre plots to be given to freed people. However, President Johnson ordered Howard to halt **land redistribution** and to reclaim land already handed over and return it to its former owners. Johnson's order displaced thousands of African Americans who had already taken their 40 acres. They and others who had hoped for land felt disappointed and betrayed. One later recalled that they had expected "a heap from freedom dey didn't git."

The congressional act that created the Freedmen's Bureau authorized it to assist white refugees. In a few places, white recipients of aid outnumbered the freed blacks. A large majority of southern whites had never owned slaves, and some had opposed secession. The outcome of the war, however, meant that some lost their livelihood, and many feared that they would now have to compete with the freed people for farmland or wage labor. Like the freed people, many southern whites lacked the means to farm on their own. When the Confederate government collapsed, Confederate money—badly devalued by rampant inflation—

land redistribution The division of land held by large landowners into smaller plots that are turned over to people without property.

became worthless. This sudden reduction in the amount of money in circulation, together with the failure of southern banks and the devastation of the southern economy, meant that the entire region was short of **capital**.

Sharecropping slowly emerged across much of the South as an alternative both to land redistribution and to wage labor on the plantations. Sharecropping derived directly from the central realities of southern agriculture. Much of the land was in large holdings, but the landowners had no one to work it. Capital was scarce. Many whites with large landholdings lacked the cash to hire farm workers. Many families, both black and white, wanted to raise their own crops with their own labor but had no land, no supplies, and no money. Under sharecropping, an individual—usually a family head—signed a contract with a landowner to rent land as home and farm. The tenant—the sharecropper—was to pay, as rent, a share of the harvest. The share might amount to half or more of the crop if the landlord provided mules, tools, seed, and fertilizer as well as land. Many landowners thought that sharecropping encouraged tenants to be productive, to get as much value as possible from their shares of the crop. The rental contract often allowed the landlord to specify what crop would be planted, and most landlords chose cotton so that their tenants would not hold back any of the harvest for personal consumption. Thus sharecropping may have increased the dependency of the South on cotton.

Southern farmers—black or white, sharecroppers or owners of small plots—often found themselves in debt to a local merchant who advanced supplies on credit. In return for credit, the merchant required a lien (a legal claim) on the growing crop. Many landlords ran stores that they required their tenants to patronize. Often the share paid as rent and the debt owed the store exceeded the value of the entire harvest. Furthermore, many rental contracts and **crop liens** were automatically renewed if all debts were not paid at the end of a year. Thus, in spite of their efforts to achieve greater control over their lives and labor, many southern farm families, black and white alike, found themselves trapped by sharecropping and debt. Still, sharecropping gave freed people more control over their daily lives than had slavery.

Landlords could exercise political as well as economic power over their tenants. Until the 1890s, casting a ballot on election day was an open process, and any observer could see how an individual voted (see page 452). Thus, when a landlord or merchant advocated a particular candidate, the unspoken message was often an implicit threat to cut off credit at the

Sharecropping gave African Americans more control over their labor than did labor contracts. But sharecropping also contributed to the South's dependence on one-crop agriculture and helped to perpetuate widespread rural poverty. This family of sharecroppers near Aiken, South Carolina, was photographed picking cotton around 1870. © *Collection of the New-York Historical Society.*

store or to evict a sharecropper if he did not vote accordingly. Such forms of economic **coercion** had the potential to undercut voting rights.

The White South: Confronting Change

The Civil War and the end of slavery transformed the lives of white southerners as well as black southerners. For some, the changes were nearly as profound as for the freed people. Savings vanished. Some homes and

---

capital Money, especially the money invested in a commercial enterprise.

sharecropping A system for renting farmland in which tenant farmers give landlords a share of their crops, rather than cash, as rent.

crop lien A legal claim to a farmer's crop, similar to a mortgage, based on the use of crops as collateral for extension of credit by a merchant.

coercion Use of threats or force to compel action.

other buildings were destroyed. Thousands left the South.

Before the war, few white southerners had owned slaves, and very few owned large numbers. Distrust or even hostility had always existed between the privileged planter families and the many whites who farmed small plots by themselves. Some regions populated by small-scale farmers had resisted secession, and some of them welcomed the Union victory and supported the Republicans during Reconstruction. Some southerners also welcomed the prospect of the economic transformation that northern capital might bring.

Most white southerners, however, shared what one North Carolinian described in 1866 as "the bitterest hatred toward the North." Even people with no attachment to slavery detested the Yankees who so profoundly changed their lives. For many white southerners, the "lost cause" of the Confederacy came to symbolize their defense of their prewar lives, not an attempt to break up the nation or protect slavery. During the early phases of Reconstruction, most white southerners apparently expected that, except for slavery, things would soon be put back much as they had been before the war.

As civil governments began to function in late 1865 and 1866, state legislatures passed **black codes** defining the new legal status of African Americans. These regulations varied from state to state, but every state placed significant restraints on black people. Various black codes required African Americans to have an annual employment contract, limited them to agricultural work, forbade them from moving about the countryside without permission, restricted their ownership of land, and provided for forced labor by those found guilty of **vagrancy**—which usually meant anyone without a job. Some codes originated in prewar restrictions on slaves and free blacks. Some reflected efforts to ensure that farm workers would be on hand for planting, cultivating, and harvesting. Taken together, however, the black codes represented an effort by white southerners to define a legally subordinate place for African Americans and to put significant restrictions on their newly found freedom.

Some white southerners used violence to coerce freed people into accepting a subordinate status within the new southern society. Clara Barton, who had organized women as nurses for the Union army, visited the South from 1866 to 1870 and observed "a condition of lawlessness toward the blacks" and "a disposition . . . to injure or kill them on slight or no provocation."

Violence and terror became closely associated with the **Ku Klux Klan,** a secret organization formed in

In this picture, the artist has portrayed a Republican leader, John Campbell, pleading for mercy from a group of bizarrely dressed Klansmen in Moore County, North Carolina, on August 10, 1871. Campbell was a white grocery store owner who was active in the local Republican Party; the Klansmen flogged him before releasing him. Those responsible were captured and photographed in their Klan costumes, providing the basis for this drawing. Curiously, the artist has depicted Campbell as an African American. *The Granger Collection, New York.*

1866 and led by a former Confederate general. The turn to terror suggests that Klan members felt themselves largely powerless through normal politics, and

---

black codes   Laws passed by the southern states after the Civil War restricting activities of freed people; in general, the black codes restricted the civil rights of the freed people and defined their status as subordinate to whites.

vagrancy   The legal condition of having no fixed place of residence or means of support.

Ku Klux Klan   A secret society organized in the South after the Civil War to restore white supremacy by means of violence and intimidation.

used terror to create a climate of fear among their opponents. Most Klan members were small-scale farmers and workers, but the leaders were often prominent within their own communities. As one Freedmen's Bureau agent observed about the Klan, "The most respectable citizens are engaged in it." Klan groups existed throughout the South, but operated with little central control. Their major goals were to restore **white supremacy** and to destroy the Republican Party. Other, similar organizations also formed and adopted similar tactics.

Klan members were called ghouls. Officers included cyclops, night-hawks, and grand dragons, and the national leader was called the grand wizard. Klan members covered their faces with hoods, wore white robes, and rode horses draped in white as they set out to intimidate black Republicans and their Radical white allies. Klan members also attacked less politically prominent people, whipping African Americans accused of not showing sufficient deference to whites. Nightriders also burned black churches and schools. By such tactics, the Klan devastated Republican organizations in many communities.

In 1866 two events dramatized the violence that some white southerners were inflicting on African Americans. In early May, in Memphis, Tennessee, black veterans of the Union army came to the assistance of a black man being arrested by white police, setting off a three-day riot in which whites, including police, indiscriminately attacked African Americans. Forty-five blacks and three whites died. In late July, in New Orleans, some forty people died, most of them African Americans, in an altercation between police and a largely black prosuffrage group. General Philip Sheridan, the military commander of the district, called it "an absolute massacre by the police." Memphis and New Orleans were unusual only in the numbers of casualties. Local authorities often seemed uninterested in stopping such violence, and federal troops were not always available when they were needed.

Congressional Reconstruction

→ *Why did congressional Republicans take control over Reconstruction policy? What did they seek to accomplish? How successful were they?*

→ *How did the Fourteenth and Fifteenth Amendments change the nature of the federal Union?*

The black codes, violence against freed people, and the failure of southern authorities to stem the violence

turned northern opinion against President Johnson's lenient approach to Reconstruction. Increasing numbers of moderate Republicans accepted the Radicals' arguments that the freed people required greater federal protection, and congressional Republicans moved to take control of Reconstruction. When stubborn and uncompromising Andrew Johnson ran up against the equally stubborn and uncompromising Thaddeus Stevens, the nation faced a constitutional crisis.

Challenging Presidential Reconstruction

In December 1865, the Thirty-ninth Congress (elected in 1864) met for the first time. Republicans outnumbered Democrats by more than three to one. President Johnson proclaimed Reconstruction complete and the Union restored, but few Republicans agreed. Events in the South had convinced most moderate Republicans of the need to protect free labor in the South and to establish basic rights for the freed people. Most also agreed that Congress could withhold representation from the South until reconstructed state governments met these conditions.

On the first day of the Thirty-ninth Congress, moderate Republicans joined Radicals to exclude newly elected congressmen from the South. Citing Article I, Section 5, of the Constitution (which makes each house of Congress the judge of the qualifications of its members), Republicans set up a Joint Committee on Reconstruction to evaluate the qualifications of the excluded southerners and to determine whether the southern states were entitled to representation. Some committee members wanted to launch an investigation of presidential Reconstruction. In the meantime, the former Confederate states had no representation in Congress.

Congressional Republicans also moved to provide more assistance to the freed people. Moderates and Radicals approved a bill extending the Freedmen's Bureau and giving it more authority against racial discrimination. When Johnson vetoed it, Congress drafted a slightly revised version. Similar Republican unity produced a **civil rights** bill, a far-reaching meas-

---

white supremacy The racist belief that whites are inherently superior to all other races and are therefore entitled to rule over them.

civil rights The rights, privileges, and protections that are a part of citizenship.

ure that extended citizenship to African Americans and defined some of the rights guaranteed to all citizens. Johnson vetoed both the civil rights bill and the revised Freedmen's Bureau bill, but Congress passed both over his veto. With creation of the Joint Committee on Reconstruction and passage of the Civil Rights and Freedmen's Bureau Acts, Congress took control of Reconstruction.

The Civil Rights Act of 1866

The Civil Rights Act of 1866 defined all persons born in the United States (except Indians not taxed) as citizens. It also listed certain rights of all citizens, including the right to testify in court, own property, make contracts, bring lawsuits, and enjoy "full and equal benefit of all laws and proceedings for the security of person and property." This was the first effort to define in law some of the rights of American citizenship. It placed significant restrictions on state actions on the grounds that the rights of national citizenship took precedence over the powers of state governments. The law expanded the power of the federal government in unprecedented ways and challenged traditional concepts of states' rights. Though the law applied to all citizens, its most immediate consequence was to benefit African Americans.

Much of the debate in Congress over the measure focused on the situation of the freed people. Some supporters saw the Civil Rights Act as a way to secure freed people's basic rights. Some northern Republicans hoped the law would encourage freed people to stay in the South. For other Republicans, the bill carried broader implications because it empowered the federal government to force states to abide by the principle of equality before the law. They applauded its redefinition of federal-state relations. Senator Lot Morrill of Maine described it as "absolutely revolutionary" but added, "Are we not in the midst of a revolution?"

When President Johnson vetoed the bill, he argued that it violated states' rights. By defending states' rights and confronting the Radicals, Johnson may have hoped to generate enough political support to elect a conservative Congress in 1866 and to win the presidency in 1868. He probably expected the veto to appeal to voters and to turn them against the Radicals. Instead, the veto led most moderate Republicans to abandon hope of cooperating with him. In April 1866, when Congress passed the Civil Rights Act over Johnson's veto, it was the first time ever that Congress had overridden a presidential veto of major legislation.

Defining Citizenship: The Fourteenth Amendment

Leading Republicans, though pleased that the Civil Rights Act was now law, worried that it could be amended or repealed by a later Congress or declared unconstitutional by the Supreme Court. Only a constitutional amendment, they concluded, could permanently safeguard the freed people's rights as citizens.

The **Fourteenth Amendment** began as a proposal made by Radicals seeking a constitutional guarantee of equality before the law. But the final wording—the longest of any amendment—resulted from many compromises. Section 1 of the amendment defined American citizenship in much the same way as the Civil Rights Act of 1866, then specified that

No State shall make or enforce any law which shall abridge the privileges or immunities of citizens of the United States; nor shall any State deprive any person of life, liberty, or property, without due process of law; nor deny to any person within its jurisdiction the equal protection of the laws.

The Constitution and Bill of Rights prohibit federal interference with basic civil rights. The Fourteenth Amendment extends this protection against action by state governments.

The amendment was vague on some points. For example, it penalized states that did not **enfranchise** African Americans by reducing their congressional and electoral representation, but it did not specifically guarantee to African Americans the right to vote.

Some provisions of the amendment stemmed from Republicans' fears that a restored South, allied with northern Democrats, might try to undo the outcome of the war. One section barred from public office anyone who had sworn to uphold the federal Constitution and then "engaged in insurrection or rebellion against the same." Only Congress could override this provision. (In 1872 Congress did pardon nearly all former Confederates.) The amendment also prohibited federal or state governments from assuming any of the

Fourteenth Amendment Constitutional amendment, ratified in 1868, defining American citizenship and placing restrictions on former Confederates.

enfranchise To grant the right to vote to an individual or group.

IT MATTERS TODAY

THE FOURTEENTH AMENDMENT

The Fourteenth Amendment is one of the most important sources of Americans' civil rights, next to the Bill of Rights (the first ten amendments). One key provision in the Fourteenth Amendment is the definition of American citizenship. Previously, the Constitution did not address that question. The Fourteenth Amendment cleared up any confusion about who was, and who was not, a citizen.

The amendment also specifies that no state could abridge the liberties of a citizen "without due process of law." Until this time, the Constitution and the Bill of Rights restricted action by the *federal* government to restrict individual liberties. The Supreme Court has interpreted the Fourteenth Amendment to mean that the restrictions placed on the federal government by the First Amendment also limit state governments—that no *state* government may abridge freedom of speech, press, assembly, and religion.

The Supreme Court continues to interpret the Fourteenth Amendment when it is presented with new cases involving state restrictions on the rights of citizens. For example, the Supreme Court cited the Fourteenth Amendment to conclude that states may not prevent residents from buying contraceptives, and cited the due process clause among other provisions of the Constitution, in *Roe v. Wade*, to conclude that state laws may not prevent women from having abortions.

- Look up the Fourteenth Amendment in the back of this book. How does the Fourteenth Amendment define citizenship? Using an online newspaper, can you find recent proposals to change the definition of American citizenship? Can you find examples of other nations that have more restrictive definitions of citizenship?
- What current political issues may lead to court cases in which the Fourteenth Amendment is likely to be invoked?

cepted a penalty in congressional representation. Stevens wanted to bar former Confederates not just from holding office but also from voting. Woman suffrage advocates, led by **Elizabeth Cady Stanton** and **Susan B. Anthony,** complained that the amendment, for the first time, introduced the word *male* into the Constitution in connection with voting rights.

Despite such concerns, Congress approved the Fourteenth Amendment by a straight party vote in June 1866 and sent it to the states for ratification. Johnson protested that Congress should not propose constitutional amendments until all representatives of the southern states had taken their seats. Tennessee promptly ratified the amendment, became the first reconstructed state government to be recognized by Congress, and was exempted from most later Reconstruction legislation.

Although Congress adjourned in the summer of 1866, the nation's attention remained fixed on Reconstruction. In May and July, the bloody riots in Memphis and New Orleans turned more moderates against Johnson's Reconstruction policies. Some interpreted the congressional elections that fall as a referendum on Reconstruction and the Fourteenth Amendment, pitting Johnson against the Radicals. Johnson undertook a speaking tour to promote his views, but one of his own supporters calculated that Johnson's reckless tirades alienated a million voters. Republicans swept the 1866 elections, outnumbering Democrats 143 to 49 in the new House of Representatives, and 42 to 11 in the Senate. Lyman Trumbull, senator from Illinois and a leading moderate, voiced the consensus of congressional Republicans: Congress should now "hurl from power the disloyal element" in the South.

Radicals in Control

As congressional Radicals struggled with President Johnson over control of Reconstruction, it became clear that the Fourteenth Amendment might fall short of ratification. Rejection by ten states could prevent its acceptance. By March 1867, the amendment had been rejected by twelve states—Delaware, Kentucky, and all the former Confederate states except Tennessee. Moderate Republicans who had expected the Fourteenth

Confederate debt or from paying any claim arising from emancipation.

Not everyone approved of the final wording. Charles Sumner condemned the provision that permitted a state to deny suffrage to male citizens if it ac-

Elizabeth Cady Stanton   A founder and leader of the American woman suffrage movement from 1848 (date of the Seneca Falls Conference) until her death in 1902.

Susan B. Anthony   Tireless campaigner for woman suffrage and close associate of Elizabeth Cady Stanton.

Amendment to be the final Reconstruction measure now became receptive to other proposals that the Radicals put forth.

On March 2, 1867, Congress overrode Johnson's veto of the Military Reconstruction Act, which divided the Confederate states (except Tennessee) into five military districts. Each district was to be governed by a military commander authorized by Congress to use military force to protect life and property. These ten states were to hold constitutional conventions, and all adult male citizens were to vote, except former Confederates barred from office under the proposed Fourteenth Amendment. The constitutional conventions were then to create new state governments that permitted black suffrage, and the new governments were to ratify the Fourteenth Amendment. Congress would then evaluate whether those state governments were ready to regain representation in Congress.

Congress had wrested a major degree of control over Reconstruction from the president, but it was not finished. Also on March 2, Congress further limited Johnson's powers. The Command of the Army Act specified that the president could issue military orders only through the General of the Army, then Ulysses S. Grant, who was considered an ally of Congress. It also specified that the General of the Army could not be removed without Senate permission. Congress thereby blocked Johnson from direct communication with military commanders in the South. The Tenure of Office Act specified that officials appointed with the Senate's consent were to remain in office until the Senate approved a successor, thereby preventing Johnson from removing federal officials who opposed his policies. Johnson understood both measures as invasions of presidential authority.

Early in 1867, some Radicals began to consider impeaching President Johnson. The Constitution (Article I, Sections 2 and 3) gives the House of Representatives exclusive power to **impeach** the president—that is, to charge the chief executive with misconduct. The Constitution specifies that the Senate shall hold trial on those charges, with the chief justice of the Supreme Court presiding. If found guilty by a two-thirds vote of the Senate, the president is removed from office.

In January 1867, the House Judiciary Committee considered charges against Johnson but found no convincing evidence of misconduct. Johnson, however, directly challenged Congress over the Tenure of Office Act by removing Edwin Stanton as secretary of war. This gave Johnson's opponents something resembling a violation of law by the president. Still, an effort to secure impeachment through the House Judiciary Committee failed. The Joint Committee on Reconstruction,

Tickets such as these were in high demand, for they permitted the holder to watch the historic proceedings as the Radical leaders presented their evidence to justify removing Andrew Johnson from the presidency. *Collection of Janice L. and David J. Frent.*

led by Thaddeus Stevens, then took over and developed charges against Johnson. On February 24, 1868, the House adopted eleven articles, or charges, nearly all based on the Stanton affair. The actual reasons the Radicals wanted Johnson removed were clear to all: they disliked him and his actions.

To convict Johnson and remove him from the presidency required a two-thirds vote by the Senate. Johnson's defenders argued that he had done nothing to warrant impeachment. The Radicals' legal case was weak, but they urged senators to vote on whether they wished Johnson to remain as president. Republican unity unraveled when some moderates, fearing the precedent of removing a president for such flimsy reasons, joined with Democrats to defeat the Radicals. The vote, on May 16 and 26, 1868, was 35 in favor of conviction and 19 against, one vote short of the required two-thirds. By this tiny margin, Congress endorsed the principle that it should not remove the president from office simply because members of Congress disagree with or dislike the president.

Political Terrorism and the Election of 1868

The Radicals' failure to unseat Johnson left him with less than a year remaining in office. As the election approached, the Republicans nominated Ulysses S.

impeach   To charge a public official with improper, usually criminal, conduct.

Grant for president. A war hero, popular throughout the North, Grant had fully supported Lincoln and Congress in implementing emancipation. By 1868, he had committed himself to the congressional view of Reconstruction. The Democrats nominated Horatio Seymour, a former governor of New York, and focused their efforts on denouncing Reconstruction.

In the South, the campaign stirred up fierce activity by the Ku Klux Klan and similar groups. **Terrorists** assassinated an Arkansas congressman, three members of the South Carolina legislature, and several other Republican leaders. Throughout the South, mobs attacked Republican offices and meetings, and sometimes attacked any black person they could find. Such coercion had its intended effect at the ballot box. For example, as many as two hundred blacks were killed in St. Landry Parish, Louisiana, where the Republicans previously had a thousand-vote majority. On election day, not a single Republican vote was recorded from that parish.

Despite such violence, many Americans may have been anticipating a calmer political future. In June 1868 Congress had readmitted seven southern states that met the requirements of congressional Reconstruction. In July, the secretary of state declared the Fourteenth Amendment ratified. In November, Grant easily won the presidency, carrying twenty-six of the thirty-four states and 53 percent of the vote.

Voting Rights and Civil Rights

With Grant in the White House, Radical Republicans now moved to secure voting rights for all African Americans. In 1867 Congress had removed racial barriers to voting in the District of Columbia and in the territories, but elsewhere the states still defined voting rights. Congress had required southern states to enfranchise black males as the price of readmission to the Union, but only seven northern states had taken that step by 1869. Further, any state that had enfranchised African Americans could change its law at any time. In addition to the principled arguments of Douglass and other Radicals, many Republicans concluded that they needed to guarantee black suffrage in the South if they were to continue to win presidential elections and enjoy majorities in Congress.

To secure suffrage rights for all African Americans, Congress approved the **Fifteenth Amendment** in February 1869. Widely considered to be the final step in Reconstruction, the amendment prohibited both federal and state governments from restricting a person's right to vote because of "race, color, or previous condition of servitude." Like the Fourteenth Amendment,

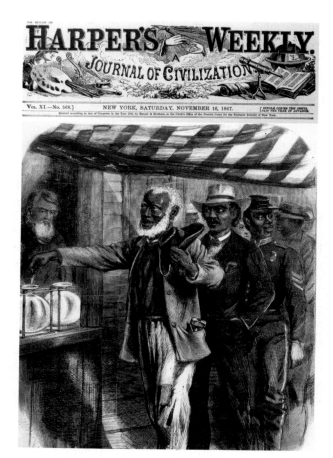

This engraving appeared on the cover of *Harper's Weekly* in November 1867. It shows black men lined up to cast their ballots in that fall's elections. Note that the artist has shown first an older workingman, with his tools in his pocket; and next a well-dressed, younger man, probably a city-dweller and perhaps a leader in the emerging black community; and next a Union soldier. Note, too, the open process of voting. Voters received a ballot (a "party ticket") from a party campaigner and deposited that ballot in a ballot box, in full sight of all. Voting was not secret until much later. *Harper's Weekly, Nov. 16, 1867. The Granger Collection, New York.*

the Fifteenth marked a compromise between moderates and Radicals. Some African American leaders argued for language guaranteeing voting rights to all male citizens, because prohibiting some grounds for

Terrorists   Those who use threats and violence to achieve ideological or political goals.

Fifteenth Amendment   Constitutional amendment, ratified in 1870, that prohibited states from denying the right to vote because of a person's race or because a person had been a slave.

disfranchisement might imply the legitimacy of other grounds. Some Radicals tried, unsuccessfully, to add "**nativity,** property, education, or religious beliefs" to the prohibited grounds. Democrats condemned the Fifteenth Amendment as a "revolutionary" attack on states' authority to define voting rights.

Elizabeth Cady Stanton, Susan B. Anthony, and other advocates of woman suffrage opposed the amendment because it ignored restrictions based on sex. For nearly twenty years, the cause of women's rights and the cause of black rights had marched together. Once black male suffrage came under discussion, however, this alliance began to fracture. When one veteran abolitionist declared it to be "the Negro's hour" and called for black male suffrage, Anthony responded that she "would sooner cut off my right hand than ask the ballot for the black man and not for woman." The break between the women's movement and the black movement was eventually papered over, but the wounds never completely healed.

Despite such opposition, within thirteen months the proposed amendment received the approval of enough states to take effect. Success came in part because Republicans, who might otherwise have been reluctant to impose black suffrage in the North, concluded that the future success of their party required black suffrage in the South.

The Fifteenth Amendment did nothing to reduce the violence—especially at election time—that had become almost routine in the South after 1865. When Klan activity escalated in the elections of 1870, southern Republicans looked to Washington for support. In 1870 and 1871, Congress adopted several Enforcement Acts—often called the Ku Klux Klan Acts—to enforce the Fourteenth and Fifteenth Amendments.

Despite a limited budget and many obstacles, the prosecution of Klansmen began in 1871. Across the South many hundreds were indicted, and many were convicted. In South Carolina, President Grant declared martial law. By 1872, federal intervention had broken much of the strength of the Klan. (The Klan that appeared in the 1920s was a new organization that borrowed the regalia and tactics of the earlier organization; see pages 447–448.)

Congress eventually passed one final Reconstruction measure. Charles Sumner introduced a bill prohibiting **discrimination** in 1870 and in each subsequent session of Congress until his death in 1874. On his deathbed, Sumner urged his visitors to "take care of the civil-rights bill," begging them, "Don't let it fail." Approved after Sumner's death, the **Civil Rights Act of 1875** prohibited racial discrimination in the selection of juries and in public transportation and **public accommodations.**

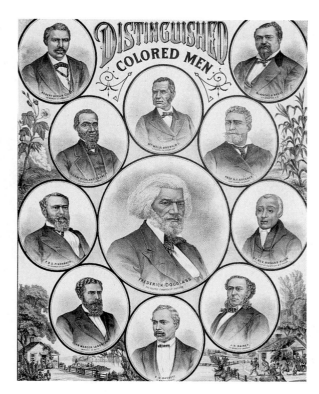

This lithograph from 1883 depicts prominent African American men, most of whom had leading roles in Black Reconstruction. Among those featured, Frederick Douglass is in the center. Left of him is Louisiana Governor P.B.S. Pinchback. In the upper right is U.S. Senator Blanche K. Bruce. *Library of Congress.*

Black Reconstruction

→ *What major groups made up the Republican Party in the South during Reconstruction? Compare their reasons for being Republicans, their relative size, and their objectives.*

disfranchisement   The taking away of an individual's or group's right to vote.

nativity   Place of birth.

discrimination   Denial of equal treatment based on prejudice or bias.

Civil Rights Act of 1875   Law passed by Congress in 1875 prohibiting racial discrimination in selection of juries and in transportation and other businesses open to the general public.

public accommodations   Hotels, bars and restaurants, theaters, and other places set up to do business with anyone who can pay the price of admission.

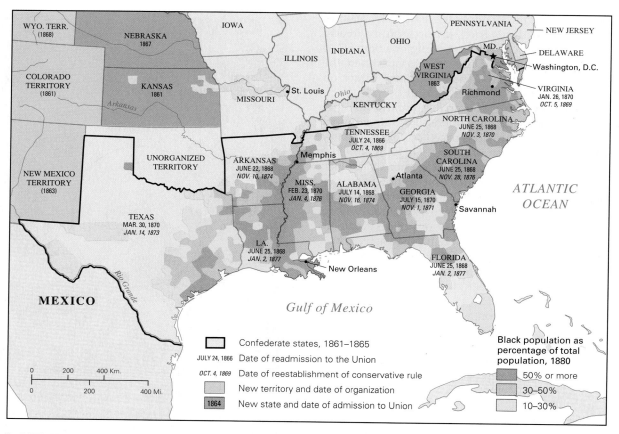

MAP 15.1 **African American Population and the Duration of Reconstruction** This map shows the proportion of African Americans in the South, and also includes the dates when each of the former Confederate states was under a Reconstruction state government. Does the map suggest any relationship between the proportion of a state's population that was African American and the amount of time that the state spent under a Reconstruction state government?

→ *What were the most lasting results of the Republican state administrations?*

Congressional Reconstruction set the stage for new developments at state and local levels throughout the South, as newly enfranchised black men organized for political action. African Americans never completely controlled any state government, but they did form a significant element in the governments of several states. The period when African Americans participated prominently in state and local politics is usually called **Black Reconstruction.** It began with efforts by African Americans to take part in politics as early as 1865 and lasted for more than a decade. A few African Americans continued to hold elective office in the South long after 1877, but by then they could do little to bring about significant political change. Map 15.1 indicates the proportion of African Americans in each

of the southern states, and also the years when each state was under a Reconstruction state government.

The Republican Party in the South

Not surprisingly, nearly all African Americans who participated actively in politics did so as Republicans. African Americans formed the large majority of those who supported the Republican Party in the South. Nearly all black Republicans were new to politics, and they often braved considerable personal danger by

---

Black Reconstruction The period of Reconstruction when African Americans took an active role in state and local government.

participating in a party that many white southerners equated with the conquering Yankees. In the South, the Republican Party also included some southern whites along with a smaller number of transplanted northerners—both black and white.

Suffrage made politics a centrally important activity for African American communities. The state constitutional conventions that met in 1868 included 265 black delegates. Only in Louisiana and South Carolina were half or more of the delegates black. With suffrage established, southern Republicans began to elect African Americans to public office. Between 1869 and 1877, fourteen black men served in the national House of Representatives, and Mississippi sent two African Americans to the U.S. Senate: Hiram R. Revels and Blanche K. Bruce.

Across the South, six African Americans served as lieutenant governors, and one of them, P. B. S. Pinchback, succeeded to the governorship of Louisiana for forty-three days. More than six hundred black men served in southern state legislatures during Reconstruction, but only in South Carolina did African Americans have a majority in the state legislature. Elsewhere they formed part of a Republican majority but rarely held key legislative positions. Only in South Carolina and Mississippi did legislatures elect black presiding officers.

Although politically inexperienced, most African Americans who held office during Reconstruction had some education. Of the eighteen who served in state-wide offices, all but three are known to have been born free. P. B. S. Pinchback, for example, was educated in Ohio and served in the army as a captain before entering politics in Louisiana. Most black politicians first achieved prominence through service with the army, the Freedmen's Bureau, the new schools, or the religious and civic organizations of black communities.

Throughout the South, Republicans gained power only by securing some support from white voters. These white Republicans are usually remembered by the names fastened on them by their political opponents: "carpetbaggers" and "scalawags." Both groups included idealists who hoped to create a new southern society, but both also included opportunists expecting to exploit politics for personal gain.

Southern Democrats applied the term **carpetbagger** to northern Republicans who came to the South after the war, regarding them as second-rate schemers—outsiders with their belongings packed in a cheap carpet bag. In fact, most northerners who came south were well-educated men and women from middle-class backgrounds. Most men had served in the Union army and moved south before blacks could vote. Some

Bags made of carpeting, like this one, were inexpensive luggage for traveling. Southern opponents of Reconstruction fastened the label "carpetbaggers" on northerners who came south to participate in Reconstruction, suggesting that they were cheap opportunists. *Collection of Picture Research Consultants & Archives.*

were lawyers, businessmen, or newspaper editors. Whether as investors in agricultural land, teachers in the new schools, or agents of the Freedmen's Bureau, most hoped to transform the South by creating new institutions based on northern models, especially free labor and free public schools. Few in number, transplanted northerners nonetheless took leading roles in state constitutional conventions and state legislatures. Some were also prominent advocates of economic modernization.

Southern Democrats reserved their greatest contempt for those they called **scalawags**, slang for someone completely unscrupulous and worthless. Scalawags were white southerners who became Republicans. They included many southern Unionists, who had opposed secession, and others who thought the Republicans offered the best hope for economic recovery. Scalawags included merchants, artisans, and professionals

carpetbagger Derogatory term for the northerners who came to the South after the Civil War to take part in Reconstruction.

scalawag Derogatory term for white southerners who aligned themselves with the Republican Party during Reconstruction.

The Hampton Normal and Agricultural Institute was founded in 1868 with financial assistance from the Freedmen's Bureau and the American Missionary Association. Its purpose was to provide education for African Americans to prepare males for jobs in agriculture or industry, and to prepare women as homemakers. As a normal school, it also trained teachers. One of Hampton's most prominent graduates was Booker T. Washington (see pp. 581–582), who attended shortly after this picture was taken around 1870.
Archival and Museum Collection, Hampton University Archives.

who favored a modernized South. Others were small-scale farmers who saw Reconstruction as a way to end political domination by the plantation owners.

The freedmen, carpetbaggers, and scalawags who made up the Republican Party in the South hoped to inject new ideas into that region. They tried to modernize state and local governments and make the postwar South more like the North. They repealed outdated laws and established or expanded schools, hospitals, orphanages, and penitentiaries.

Creating an Educational System and Fighting Discrimination

Free public education was perhaps the most permanent legacy of Black Reconstruction. Reconstruction constitutions throughout the South required tax-supported public schools. Implementation, however, was expensive and proceeded slowly. By the mid-1870s, only half of southern children attended public schools.

In creating public schools, Reconstruction state governments faced a central question: would white and black children attend the same schools? Many African Americans favored racially integrated schools. On the other hand, southern white leaders, including many southern white Republicans, argued that integration would destroy the fledgling public school system by driving whites away. In consequence, no state required school integration. Similarly, southern states set up separate black normal schools (to train schoolteachers) and colleges.

On balance, most blacks probably agreed with Frederick Douglass that separate schools were "infinitely superior" to no public education at all. Some found other reasons to accept segregated schools—

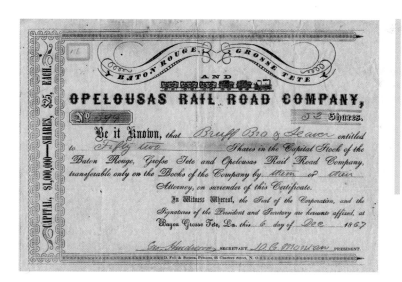

This stock certificate was issued in 1867, to underwrite operation of the the Baton Rouge, Grosse Tete, and Opelousas Railroad. Despite its name, it only connected Anchorage, a town across the river from Baton Rouge, with Grosse Tete, about fifteen miles away, and was apparently never extended to Opelousas, another thirty or forty miles distant. This railroad was constructed before the Civil War, partly with governmental funds. During Reconstruction, however, bonds for this railroad mysteriously disappeared from the state's custody and the railroad collapsed. *James O. Fuqua Papers, Louisiana and Lower Mississippi Valley Collections, LSU Libraries, Baton Rouge, La.*

separate black schools gave a larger role to black parents, and they hired black teachers.

Funding for the new schools was rarely adequate. Creating and operating two educational systems, one white and one black, was costly. The division of limited funds posed an additional problem, and black schools almost always received fewer dollars per student than white schools. Despite their accomplishments, the segregated schools institutionalized discrimination.

Reconstruction state governments moved toward protection of equal rights in areas other than education. As Republicans gained control in the South, they often wrote into the new state constitutions prohibitions against discrimination and protections for civil rights. Some Reconstruction state governments enacted laws guaranteeing **equal access** to public transportation and public accommodations. Elsewhere efforts to pass equal access laws foundered on the opposition of southern white Republicans, who often joined Democrats to favor **segregation.** Such conflicts pointed up the internal divisions within the southern Republican Party. Even when equal access laws were passed, they were often not enforced.

Railroad Development and Corruption

Across the nation, Republicans sought to use the power of government to encourage economic growth and development. Efforts to promote economic development—North, South, and West—often focused on encouraging railroad construction. In the South, as elsewhere in the nation, some state governments granted state lands to railroads, or lent them money, or committed the state's credit to **underwrite** bonds for construction. Sometimes they promoted railroads without adequate planning or determining whether companies were financially sound. Some efforts to promote railroad construction failed as companies squandered funds without building rail lines. During the 1870s, only 7,000 miles of new track were laid in the South, compared with 45,000 miles elsewhere in the nation. Even that was a considerable accomplishment for the South, given its dismal economic situation.

Railroad companies sometimes sought favorable treatment by bribing public officials. All too many officeholders—South, North, and West—accepted their offers. Given the excessive favoritism that most public officials showed to railroads, revelations and allegations of corruption became common from New York City to Mississippi to California.

equal access The right of any person to a public facility, such as streetcars, as freely as any other person.

segregation Separation on account of race or class from the rest of society, such as the separation of blacks from whites in most southern school systems.

underwrite To assume financial responsibility for; in this case, to guarantee the purchase of bonds so that a project can go forward.

Southern politics proved especially ripe for corruption as government responsibilities expanded rapidly and created new opportunities for scoundrels. Many Reconstruction officials—white and black—had only modest holdings of their own and wanted more. One South Carolina legislator bluntly described his attitude toward electing a U.S. senator: "I was pretty hard up, and I did not care who the candidate was if I got two hundred dollars." Corruption was usually nonpartisan, but it seemed more prominent among Republicans because they held the most important offices. One Louisiana Republican claimed, "Corruption is the fashion." Charges of corruption became common everywhere in the nation as politicians sought to discredit their opponents.

The End of Reconstruction

→ *What major factors brought about the end of Reconstruction? Evaluate their relative significance.*

→ *Many historians began to reevaluate their understanding of Reconstruction during the 1950s and 1960s. Why do you suppose that happened?*

From the beginning, most white southerners resisted the new order that the conquering Yankees imposed on them. Initially, resistance took the form of black codes and the Klan. Later, some southern opponents of Reconstruction developed new strategies, but terror remained an important instrument of resistance.

The "New Departure"

By 1869, some leading southern Democrats had abandoned their last-ditch resistance to change, deciding instead to accept some Reconstruction measures and African American suffrage. At the same time, they also tried to secure restoration of political rights for former Confederates. Behind this **New Departure** for southern Democrats lay the belief that continued resistance would only cause more regional turmoil and prolong federal intervention.

Sometimes southern Democrats supported conservative Republicans for state and local offices instead of members of their own party, hoping to defuse concern in Washington and dilute Radical influence in state government. This strategy was tried first in Virginia, the last southern state to hold an election under its new constitution. There William Mahone, a former Confederate general, railroad promoter, and leading Democrat, forged a broad political **coalition** that ac-

cepted black suffrage. In 1869 Mahone's organization elected as governor a northern-born banker and moderate Republican. In this way, Mahone got state support for his railroad plans, and Virginia successfully avoided Radical Republican rule.

Coalitions of Democrats and moderate Republicans won in Tennessee in 1869 and in Missouri in 1870. Elsewhere leading Democrats endorsed the New Departure and accepted black suffrage but attacked Republicans for raising taxes and increasing state spending. And Democrats usually charged Republicans with corruption. Such campaigns brought a positive response from many taxpayers because southern tax rates had risen significantly to support the new educational systems, railroad subsidies, and other modernizing programs. In 1870 Democrats won the governorship in Alabama and Georgia. For Georgia, it meant the end of Reconstruction.

The victories of so-called **Redeemers** and New Departure Democrats in the early 1870s coincided with renewed terrorist activity aimed at Republicans. The worst single incident occurred in 1873. A group of armed freedmen fortified the town of Colfax, Louisiana, to hold off Democrats who were planning to seize the county government. After a three-week siege, well-armed whites overcame the black defenders and killed 280 African Americans. Leading Democrats rarely endorsed such bloodshed, but they reaped political advantages from it.

The 1872 Presidential Election

The New Departure movement, at its peak in 1872, coincided with a division within the Republican Party in the North. The Liberal Republican movement grew out of several elements within the Republican Party. Some were moderates, concerned that the Radicals had gone too far, especially with the Enforcement Acts, and had endangered federalism. Others opposed Grant on issues unrelated to Reconstruction. All were appalled

New Departure   Strategy of cooperation with some Reconstruction measures adopted by some leading southern Democrats in the hope of winning compromises favorable to their party.

coalition   An alliance, especially a temporary one of different people or groups.

Redeemers   Southern Democrats who hoped to bring the Democratic Party back into power and to suppress Black Reconstruction.

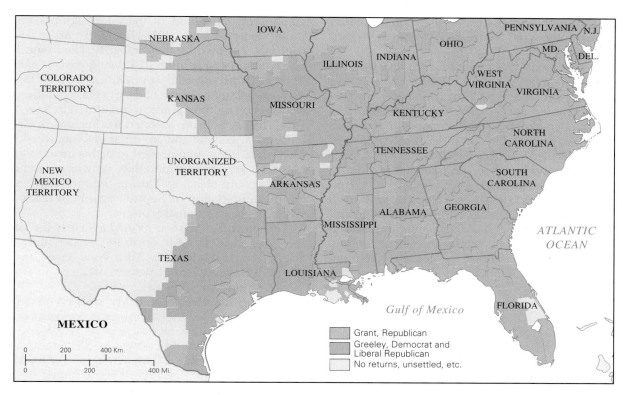

MAP 15.2 **Popular Vote for President in the South, 1872** This map shows which candidate carried each county in the southeastern United States in 1872. Looking at both this map and Map 15.1 (page 454), you can see the relation between Republican voting and African American population in some areas, as well as where the southern Republican Party drew support from white voters.

by growing evidence of corruption in the Grant administration. Liberal Republicans found allies among Democrats by arguing against further Reconstruction measures.

Horace Greeley, editor of the *New York Daily Tribune,* won the Liberal nomination for president. An opponent of slavery before the Civil War, Greeley had given strong support to the Fourteenth and Fifteenth Amendments. But he had sometimes taken puzzling positions, including a willingness to let the South secede. His unkempt appearance and whining voice conveyed little of a presidential image. One political observer described him as "honest, but . . . conceited, fussy, and foolish."

Greeley had long ripped the Democrats in his newspaper columns. Even so, the Democrats nominated him in an effort to defeat Grant. Many saw the Democrats' action as desperate opportunism, and Greeley

alienated many northern Democrats by favoring restrictions on the sale of alcohol. Grant won convincingly, carrying 56 percent of the vote and winning every northern state and ten of the sixteen southern and border states (see Map 15.2).

The Politics of Terror: The "Mississippi Plan"

By the 1872 presidential race, nearly all southern whites had abandoned the Republicans, and Black Reconstruction had ended in several states. African Americans, however, maintained their Republican loyalties. As Democrats worked to unite all southern whites behind their banner of white supremacy, the South polarized politically along racial lines. Elections in 1874 proved disastrous for Republicans: Democrats won more than two-thirds of the South's seats in the House of Representatives and "redeemed" Alabama, Arkansas, and Texas.

Terrorism against black Republicans and their remaining white allies played a role in some victories by Democrats in 1874. Where the Klan had worn disguises and ridden at night, by 1874 in many places Democrats openly formed rifle companies, put on red-flannel shirts, and marched and drilled in public. In some areas, armed whites prevented African Americans from voting or terrorized prominent Republicans, especially African American Republicans.

Republican candidates in 1874 also lost support in the North because of scandals within the Grant administration and because a major economic **depression** that had begun in 1873 was producing high unemployment. Before the 1874 elections, the House of Representatives included 194 Republicans and 92 Democrats. After those elections, Democrats outnumbered Republicans by 169 to 109. Now southern Republicans could no longer look to Congress for assistance. Even though Republicans still controlled the Senate, the Democratic majority in the House of Representatives could block any new Reconstruction legislation.

During 1875 in Mississippi, political violence reached such levels that the use of terror to overthrow Reconstruction became known as the **Mississippi Plan.** Democratic rifle clubs broke up Republican meetings and attacked Republican leaders in broad daylight. One black Mississippian described the election of 1875 as "the most violent time we have ever seen." When Mississippi's carpetbagger governor, Adelbert Ames, requested federal help, President Grant declined, fearful that the southern Reconstruction governments had become so discredited that further federal military intervention might endanger the election prospects of Republican candidates in the North.

The Democrats swept the Mississippi elections, winning four-fifths of the state legislature. When the legislature convened, it impeached and removed from office Alexander Davis, the black Republican lieutenant governor, on grounds no more serious than those brought against Andrew Johnson. The legislature then brought similar impeachment charges against Governor Ames, who resigned and left the state. Ames had foreseen the result during the campaign when he wrote, "A revolution has taken place—by force of arms."

The Compromise of 1877

In 1876, on the centennial of American independence, the nation stumbled through a deeply troubled—and potentially dangerous—presidential election. As rev-

elations of corruption in the Grant administration multiplied (see pages 491–492), both parties sought candidates known for their integrity. The Democratic Party nominated Samuel J. Tilden, governor of New York, as its presidential candidate. A wealthy lawyer and businessman, Tilden had earned a reputation as a reformer by fighting political corruption in New York City. The Republicans selected **Rutherford B. Hayes,** a Civil War general and governor of Ohio, whose unblemished reputation proved to be his greatest asset. Not well known outside Ohio, he was a candidate nobody could object to. During the campaign in the South, intimidation of Republicans, both black and white, continued in many places.

First election reports indicated a victory for Tilden (see Map 15.3). In addition to the border states and South, he also carried New York, New Jersey, and Indiana. Tilden received 51 percent of the popular vote versus 48 percent for Hayes.

Leading Republicans quickly realized that their party still controlled the counting and reporting of ballots in South Carolina, Florida, and Louisiana, and that those three states could change the Electoral College majority from Tilden to Hayes. Charging **voting fraud,** Republican election boards in those states rejected enough ballots so that the official count gave Hayes narrow majorities and thus a one-vote margin of victory in the Electoral College. Crying fraud in return, Democratic officials in all three states submitted their own versions of the vote count. Angry Democrats vowed to see Tilden inaugurated, by force if necessary. Some Democratic newspapers ran headlines that read "Tilden or War."

For the first time, Congress faced the problem of disputed electoral votes that could decide the outcome of an election. To resolve the challenges, Congress created a commission: five senators, chosen by the Senate, which had a Republican majority; five representatives, chosen by the House, which had a

---

depression A period of economic contraction, characterized by decreasing business activity, falling prices, and high unemployment.

Mississippi Plan Use of threats, violence, and lynching by Mississippi Democrats in 1875 to intimidate Republicans and bring the Democratic Party to power.

Rutherford B. Hayes Ohio governor and former Union general who won the Republican nomination in 1876 and became president of the United States in 1877.

voting fraud Altering election results by illegal measures to bring about the victory of a particular candidate.

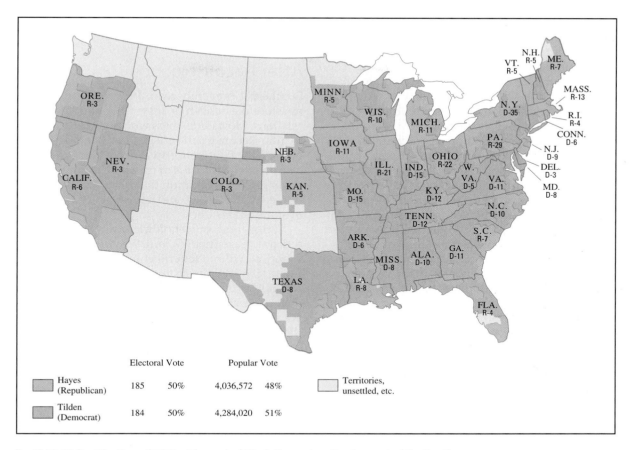

MAP 15.3 **Election of 1876** The end of Black Reconstruction in most of the South combined with Democratic gains in the North to give a popular majority to Samuel Tilden, the Democratic candidate. The electoral vote was disputed, however, and was ultimately resolved in favor of Rutherford B. Hayes, the Republican.

Democratic majority; and five Supreme Court justices, chosen by the justices. Initially, the balance was seven Republicans, seven Democrats, and one independent from the Supreme Court. The independent withdrew, however, and the remaining justices (all but one of whom had been appointed by Republican presidents) chose a Republican to replace him. The Republicans now had a one-vote majority on the commission.

This body needed to make its decision before the constitutionally mandated deadline of March 4. Some Democrats and Republicans worried over the potential for violence. However, as commission hearings droned on through January and into February 1877, informal discussions took place among leading Republicans and Democrats. The result has often been called the **Compromise of 1877.**

Southern Democrats demanded an end to federal intervention in southern politics but insisted on fed-

eral subsidies for railroad construction and waterways in the South. And they wanted one of their own as postmaster general because that office held the key to most federal patronage. In return, southern Democrats seemed willing to abandon Tilden's claim to the White House.

Although the Compromise of 1877 was never set down in one place or agreed to by all parties, most of its conditions were met. By a straight party vote, the commission confirmed the election of Hayes. Soon after his peaceful inauguration, the new president

---

Compromise of 1877 Name applied by historians to the resolution of the disputed presidential election of 1876; it gave the presidency to the Republicans and made concessions to southern Democrats.

ordered the last of the federal troops withdrawn from occupation duties in the South. The Radical era of a powerful federal government pledged to protect "equality before the law" for all citizens was over. The last three Republican state governments fell in 1877. The Democrats, the self-described party of white supremacy, now held sway in every southern state. One Radical journal bitterly concluded that African Americans had been forced "to relinquish the artificial right to vote for the natural right to live." In parts of the South thereafter, election fraud and violence became routine. One Mississippi judge acknowledged in 1890 that "since 1875 . . . we have been preserving the ascendancy of the white people by . . . stuffing ballot boxes, committing perjury and here and there in the state carrying the elections by fraud and violence."

The Compromise of 1877 marked the end of Reconstruction. The Civil War was more than ten years in the past. Many moderate Republicans had hoped that the Fourteenth and Fifteenth Amendments and the Civil Rights Act would guarantee black rights without a continuing federal presence in the South. Southern Democrats tried hard to persuade northerners—on paltry evidence—that carpetbaggers and scalawags were all corrupt and self-serving, that they manipulated black voters to keep themselves in power, that African American officeholders were ignorant and illiterate and could not participate in politics without guidance by whites, and that southern Democrats wanted only to establish honest self-government. The truth of the situation made little difference.

Northern Democrats had always opposed Reconstruction and readily adopted the southern Democrats' version of reality. Such portrayals found growing acceptance among other northerners too, for many had shown their own racial bias when they resisted black suffrage and kept their public schools segregated. In 1875, when Grant refused to use federal troops to protect black rights, he declared that "the whole public are tired out with these . . . outbreaks in the South." He was quoted widely and with approval throughout the North.

In addition, a major depression in the mid-1870s, unemployment and labor disputes, the growth of industry, the emergence of big business, and the development of the West focused the attention of many Americans, including many members of Congress, on economic issues.

Some Republicans, to be certain, kept the faith of their abolitionist and Radical forebears and hoped the federal government might again protect black rights. After 1877, however, though Republicans routinely condemned violations of black rights, few Republicans showed much interest in using federal power to prevent such outrages.

After Reconstruction

Southern Democrats read the events of 1877 as permission to establish new systems of politics and race relations. Most Redeemers worked to reduce taxes, dismantle Reconstruction legislation and agencies, and grab political influence away from black citizens. They also began the process of turning the South into a one-party region, a situation that reached its fullest development around 1900 and persisted until the 1950s and in some areas later.

Voting and officeholding by African Americans did not cease in 1877, but the context changed profoundly. Without federal enforcement of black rights, the threat of violence and the potential for economic retaliation by landlords and merchants sharply reduced meaningful political involvement by African Americans. Black political leaders soon understood that efforts to mobilize black voters posed dangers to candidates and voters, and they concluded that their political survival depended on favors from influential white Republicans or even from Democratic leaders. The public schools survived, segregated and underfunded, but presenting an important opportunity. Many Reconstruction-era laws remained on the books. Through much of the 1880s, many theaters, bars, restaurants, hotels, streetcars, and railroads continued to serve African Americans without discrimination.

Not until the 1890s did black disfranchisement and thoroughgoing racial segregation become widely embedded in southern law. African Americans continued to exercise some constitutional rights. White supremacy had been established by force of arms, however, and blacks exercised their rights at the sufferance of the dominant whites. Such a situation bore the seeds of future conflict.

After 1877, Reconstruction was held up as a failure. Although far from accurate, the southern whites' version of Reconstruction—that conniving carpetbaggers and scalawags had manipulated ignorant freedmen—appealed to many white Americans throughout the nation, and it gained widespread acceptance among many novelists, journalists, and historians. William A. Dunning, for example, endorsed that interpretation in his history of Reconstruction, published in 1907. Thomas Dixon's popular novel *The Clansman* (1905) inspired the highly influential film *The Birth of a Nation* (1915). Historically inaccurate and luridly racist, the book and the movie portrayed Ku Klux Klan members as heroes who rescued the white South, and especially white southern women, from domination and debauchery at the hands of depraved freedmen and carpetbaggers.

Against this pattern stood some of the first black historians, notably George Washington Williams, a Union army veteran whose two-volume history of African Americans appeared in 1882. *Black Reconstruction in America,* by W. E. B. Du Bois, appeared in 1935. Both presented fully the role of African Americans in Reconstruction and pointed to the accomplishments of the Reconstruction state governments and black leaders. Not until the 1950s and 1960s, however, did large numbers of American historians begin to reconsider their interpretations of Reconstruction. Historians to-

day recognize that Reconstruction was not the failure that had earlier been claimed. The creation of public schools was the most important of the changes in southern life produced by the Reconstruction state governments. At a federal level, the Fourteenth and Fifteenth Amendments eventually provided the constitutional leverage to restore the principle of equality before the law that so concerned the Radicals. Historians also recognize that Reconstruction collapsed partly because of internal flaws, partly because of divisions within the Republican Party, and partly because of the political terrorism unleashed in the South and the refusal of the North to commit the force required to protect the constitutional rights of African Americans.

Examining a Primary Source

✔ Individual Voices

A Freedman Offers His Former Master a Proposition

This letter appeared in the *New York Daily Tribune* on August 22, 1865, with the notation that it was a "genuine document," reprinted from the *Cincinnati Commercial.* At that time, all newspapers had strong connections to political parties, and both of these papers were allied to the Republicans. By then, battle lines were being drawn between President Andrew Johnson and Republicans in Congress over the legal and political status of the freed people.

① *How does the author indicate that the lives of these freed people have changed by leaving Tennessee for Ohio?*

② *Anderson's monthly wages of $25 in 1865 would be equivalent to about $2,280 today. The amount he asks for as compensation for his slave labor, $11,680, in 1865 would be equivalent to more than $130,000 today.*

DAYTON, Ohio, August 7, 1865
To my Old Master, Col. P. H. Anderson, Big Spring, Tennessee
Sir: I got your letter and was glad to find that you had not forgotten Jordan, and that you wanted me to come back and live with you again, promising to do better for me than anybody else can. . . .

I want to know particularly what the good chance is you propose to give me. I am doing tolerably well here; I get $25 a month, with victuals and clothing; have a comfortable home for Mandy (the folks here call her Mrs. Anderson), and the children, Milly[,] Jane and Grundy, go to school and are learning well. . . . Now, if you will write and say what wages you will give me, I will be better able to decide whether it would be to my advantage to move back again. **①**

As to my freedom, which you say I can have, there is nothing to be gained on that score, as I got my free-papers in 1864 from the Provost-Marshal-General of the Department at Nashville. Mandy says she would be afraid to go back without some proof that you are sincerely disposed to treat us justly and kindly—and we have concluded to test your sincerity by asking you to send us our wages for the time we served you. This will make us forget and forgive old sores, and rely on your justice and friendship in the future. I served you faithfully for thirty-two years, and Mandy twenty years, at $25 a month for me and $2 a week for Mandy. Our earnings would amount to $11,680. **②** Add to this the interest for the time our wages has been kept back and deduct what you paid for our clothing and

③ *How does the author use this letter to raise a wide range of issues about the nature of slavery and about the uneasiness of freed people about life in the South in 1865?*

④ *Evaluate the likelihood that this letter was actually written by a former slave. What are the other possibilities? Why do you think this letter appeared in newspapers in August of 1865?*

three doctor's visits to me, and pulling a tooth for Mandy, and the balance will show what we are in justice entitled to. . . . If you fail to pay us for faithful labors in the past we can have little faith in your promises in the future. We trust the good Maker has opened your eyes to the wrongs which you and your fathers have done to me and my fathers, in making us toil for you for generations without recompense. . . .

In answering this letter please state if there would be any safety for my Milly and Jane, who are now grown up and both good looking girls. You know how it was with poor Matilda and Catherine. I would rather stay here and starve and die if it had to come to that than have my girls brought to shame by the violence and wickedness of their young masters. You will also please state if there has been any schools opened for the colored children in your neighborhood, the great desire of my life now is to give my children an education, and have them form virtuous habits. ③

From your old servant, JOURDAN ANDERSON. ④

P.S.— Say howdy to George Carter, and thank him for taking the pistol from you when you were shooting at me.

SUMMARY

At the end of the Civil War, the nation faced difficult choices regarding the restoration of the defeated South and the future of the freed people. Committed to ending slavery, President Lincoln nevertheless chose a lenient approach to restoring states to the Union, partly to persuade southerners to abandon the Confederacy and accept emancipation. When Johnson became president, he continued Lincoln's approach.

The end of slavery brought new opportunities for African Americans, whether or not they had been slaves. Taking advantage of the opportunities that freedom opened, they tried to create independent lives for themselves, and they developed social institutions that helped to define black communities. Because few were able to acquire land of their own, most became either sharecroppers or wage laborers. White southerners also experienced economic dislocation, and many also became sharecroppers. Most white southerners expected to keep African Americans in a subordinate role and initially used black codes and violence toward that end.

In reaction against the black codes and violence, Congress took control of Reconstruction away from President Johnson and passed the Civil Rights Act of 1866, the Fourteenth Amendment, and the Reconstruction Acts of 1867. An attempt to remove Johnson from the presidency was unsuccessful. Additional federal Reconstruction measures included the Fifteenth Amendment, laws against the Ku Klux Klan, and the Civil Rights Act of 1875. Several of these measures strengthened the federal government at the expense of the states.

Enfranchised freedmen, white and black northerners who moved to the South, and some southern whites created a southern Republican Party that governed most southern states for a time. The most lasting contribution of these state governments was the creation of public school systems. Like government officials elsewhere in the nation, however, some southern politicians fell prey to corruption.

In the late 1860s, many southern Democrats chose a "New Departure": they grudgingly accepted some features of Reconstruction and sought to recapture control of state governments. By the mid-1870s, however, southern politics turned almost solely on race. The 1876 presidential election was very close and hotly disputed. Key Republicans and Democrats developed a compromise: Hayes took office and ended the final stages of Reconstruction. Without federal protection for their civil rights, African Americans faced terrorism, violence, and even death if they challenged their subordinate role. With the end of Reconstruction, the South entered an era of white supremacy in politics and government, the economy, and social relations.

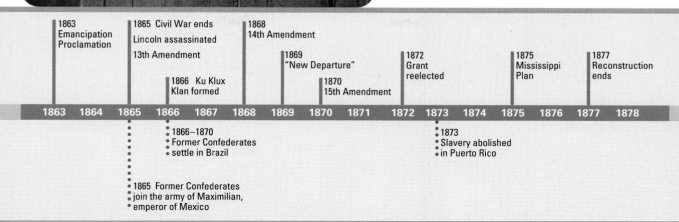

IN THE WIDER WORLD

1863			1865 Civil War ends			1868				1872			1875	1877

1863 Emancipation Proclamation

1865 Civil War ends
Lincoln assassinated
13th Amendment

1866 Ku Klux Klan formed

1868 14th Amendment

1869 "New Departure"

1870 15th Amendment

1872 Grant reelected

1875 Mississippi Plan

1877 Reconstruction ends

1863 1864 1865 1866 1867 1868 1869 1870 1871 1872 1873 1874 1875 1876 1877 1878

1866–1870 Former Confederates settle in Brazil

1873 Slavery abolished in Puerto Rico

1865 Former Confederates join the army of Maximilian, emperor of Mexico

In the United States

Reconstruction

1863 Emancipation Proclamation

The Ten Percent Plan

1864 Abraham Lincoln reelected

1865 Freedmen's Bureau created

Civil War ends

Lincoln assassinated

Andrew Johnson becomes president

Thirteenth Amendment (abolishing slavery) ratified

1866 Ku Klux Klan formed

Congress begins to assert control over Reconstruction

Civil Rights Act of 1866

Riots by whites in Memphis and New Orleans

1867 Military Reconstruction Act

Command of the Army Act

Tenure of Office Act

1868 Impeachment of President Johnson

Fourteenth Amendment (defining citizenship) ratified

Ulysses S. Grant elected president

1869–1870 Victories of "New Departure" Democrats in some southern states

1870 Fifteenth Amendment (guaranteeing voting rights) ratified

1870–1871 Ku Klux Klan Acts

1872 Grant reelected

1875 Civil Rights Act of 1875

Mississippi Plan ends Reconstruction in Mississippi

1876 Disputed presidential election: Hayes versus Tilden

1877 Compromise of 1877

Rutherford B. Hayes becomes president

End of Reconstruction

✔ Suggested Readings

CHAPTER 1   Making a "New" World, to 1588

Marvin B. Becker. *Civility and Society in Western Europe, 1300–1600* (1988).
   A brief but comprehensive look at social conditions in Europe during the period leading up to and out of the exploration of the New World.
Alfred W. Crosby. *The Columbian Exchange: Biological and Cultural Consequences of 1492* (1972).
   The landmark book that brought the Columbian impact into focus for the first time. Parts of the book are technical, but the explanations are clear and exciting.
Alvin M. Josephy. *America in 1492: The World of the Indian Peoples before the Arrival of Columbus* (1992).
   An overview of American civilizations prior to Columbus's and subsequent European intrusions. Nicely written, comprehensive, and engaging.
Roland Oliver and J. D. Fage. *A Short History of Africa* (1988).
   The most concise and understandably written comprehensive history of Africa available.

CHAPTER 2   A Continent on the Move, 1400–1725

Peter N. Moogk. *La Nouvelle France: The Making of French Canada—A Cultural History* (2000).
   An excellent overview of French activities in Canada during the colonial era.
Oliver A. Rink. *Holland on the Hudson: An Economic and Social History of Dutch New York* (1986).
   A comprehensive overview of Dutch colonial activities in New Netherland with an emphasis on both the activities of the Dutch West India Company and private traders in creating the culture of Dutch New York.
Daniel H. Usner, Jr. *Indians, Settlers, and Slaves in a Frontier Exchange Economy: The Lower Mississippi Valley before 1783* (1992).
   A highly acclaimed study of the complex world of colonial Louisiana.
David Weber. *The Spanish Frontier in North America* (1992).
   A broad synthesis of the history of New Spain by the foremost scholar in the field.

CHAPTER 3   Founding the English Colonies in the Eighteenth Century, 1585–1732

Philip Barbour. *Pocahontas and Her World* (1970).
   A factual account of the life of an American Indian princess celebrated in folklore.
David Cressy. *Coming Over: Migration and Communication between England and New England in the Seventeenth Century* (1987).
   An excellent introduction to the transatlantic community of England and the colonial world.
John Demos. *A Little Commonwealth: Family Life in Plymouth Colony* (1970).
   A beautifully written and very engaging portrait of family and community life in Plymouth Plantations.
James Horn. *Adapting to a New World: English Society in the Seventeenth Century Chesapeake* (1996).
   An examination of the mix of traditional and innovative characteristics of this early colonial society.

Mary Beth Norton. *In the Devil's Snare* (2003).
   This book places the events of 1692 in the context of European imperial rivalries, especially the intense struggles between England and France for control of North America.

CHAPTER 4   The English Colonies in the Eighteenth Century, 1689–1763

Bernard Bailyn. *Voyagers to the West: A Passage in the Peopling of America on the Eve of the Revolution* (1986).
   A survey of the character of, and motives for, emigration from the British Isles to America during the eighteenth century.
Ira Berlin. *Generations of Captivity: A History of African American Slaves* (2004).
   An examination of the variety and complexities of slavery as an experience and as a legal and economic institution.
Patricia Bonomi. *Under the Cope of Heaven: Religion, Society, and Politics in Colonial America* (1986).
   Bonomi examines the role of religion in colonial society, with special emphasis on the Great Awakening.
Richard Hofstadter. *America at 1750: A Social Portrait* (1971).
   This highly accessible work includes chapters on indentured servitude, the slave trade, the middle-class world of the colonies, the Great Awakening, and population growth and immigration pattern.
Jane T. Merritt. *At the Crossroads: Indians and Empires on a Mid-Atlantic Frontier, 1700–1763* (2003).
   Merritt takes a close look at the interaction between Indians and colonists in the backcountry of Pennsylvania and narrates the growing tensions between settlers and Native Americans.
Betty Wood. *The Origins of American Slavery* (1998).
   This is a brief but excellent look at the use of enslaved labor in the West Indies and in the English mainland colonies and at the laws that arose to institutionalize slavery.

CHAPTER 5   Deciding Where Loyalties Lie, 1763–1776

Carol Berkin. *Revolutionary Mothers: Women in the Struggle for America's Independence* (2005).
   This book recounts the role of colonial women—European, African American, and Indian—in the years before and during the American Revolution.
Colin G. Calloway. *The American Revolution in Indian Country: Crisis and Diversity in Native American Communities* (1995).
   A well-written account of the variety of Indian experiences during the American revolutionary era.
Edward Countryman. *The American Revolution* (1985).
   An excellent narrative of the causes and consequences of the Revolutionary War.
David Hackett Fischer. *Paul Revere's Ride* (1994).
   This lively account details the circumstances and background of the efforts to rouse the countryside in response to the march of British troops toward Lexington.
Woody Holton. *Forced Founders: Indians, Debtors, Slaves and the Making of the American Revolution in Virginia* (1999).
   Holton provides a new interpretation of the factors that went into transforming wealthy planters into revolutionaries.
Liberty! PBS series on the American Revolution.

Using the actual words of revolutionaries, loyalists, and British political leaders, this six-hour series follows events from the Stamp Act to the Constitution.

Pauline Maier. *American Scripture: Making the Declaration of Independence* (1998).

This path-breaking book points out that the ideas expressed in the Declaration of Independence were widely accepted by Americans, and proclaimed in state declarations of independence before Jefferson set them down in July 1776.

Edmund Morgan. *Benjamin Franklin* (2002).

A distinguished historian of colonial America draws a compelling portrait of Benjamin Franklin, following the printer-writer-scientist-diplomat through major crises and turning points in his life and the life of his country.

CHAPTER 6   Recreating America: Independence and a New Nation, 1775–1783

Sylvia Frey. *Water From a Rock: Black Resistance in a Revolutionary Age* (1991).

This scholar of African American religion and culture examines the experiences of African Americans during the Revolution and the repression that followed in the Southern states that continued to rely on slave labor.

Joseph Plumb Martin. *Ordinary Courage: The Revolutionary War Adventures of Joseph Plumb Martin*, ed. James Kirby Martin (1993).

The military experiences of a Massachusetts soldier who served with the Continental Army during the American Revolution.

Charles Royster. *A Revolutionary People at War: The Continental Army and American Character, 1775–1783* (1996).

Royster's in-depth account of military life during the Revolution provides insights into both the American character and the changing understanding of the political ideals of the war among the common soldiers.

Alfred Young. *The Shoemaker and the Tea Party: Memory and the American Revolution* (2000).

Young looks at the memories of an aging shoemaker who witnessed the Boston Tea Party. These memories reveal the meaning of the Revolution to ordinary Americans.

CHAPTER 7   Competing Visions of the Virtuous Republic, 1770–1796

Carol Berkin. *A Brilliant Solution: Inventing the American Constitution* (2002).

A highly readable account of the crises that led to the constitutional convention and the men who created a new national government.

Lyman Butterfield, et al., eds. *The Book of Abigail and John: Selected Letters of the Adams Family, 1762–1784* (1975).

The editors of the Adams Papers have collected part of the extensive correspondence between John and Abigail Adams during the critical decades of the independence movement.

Saul Cornell. *The Other Founders: Anti-Federalism and the Dissenting Tradition in America, 1788-1828* (1999).

A perceptive analysis of the ideology of dissent and its legacy in American political life.

Joseph Ellis. *Founding Brothers: The Revolutionary Generation* (2002).

An award-winning study of the most notable leaders of the American Revolution, and an examination of their political ideas and actions.

Thomas P. Slaughter. *The Whiskey Rebellion* (1986).

A vivid account of the major challenge to the Washington government.

Gordon Wood. *The Creation of the American Republic, 1776-1787* (1998)

An award winning examination of the ideals and political principles that form the basis of the American republic.

CHAPTER 8   The Early Republic, 1796–1804

Stephen E. Ambrose. *Undaunted Courage: Meriwether Lewis, Thomas Jefferson, and the Opening of the American West* (1996).

A critically acclaimed and highly readable narrative exploring the relationship between Jefferson and Lewis and their efforts to acquire and explore Louisiana.

Alexander DeConde. *This Affair of Louisiana* (1976).

Dated, but still the best overview of the diplomacy surrounding the Louisiana Purchase.

Joseph J. Ellis. *American Sphinx: The Character of Thomas Jefferson* (1996).

Winner of the National Book Award, this biography focuses on Jefferson's personality seeking to expose his inner character; highly readable.

Joanne B. Freeman. *Affairs of Honor: National Politics in the New Republic* (2001).

Jeffrey L. Pasley. *"The Tyranny of Printers": Newspaper Politics in the Early American Republic* (2001).

Taken together, these two groundbreaking studies of political culture in the Early Republic bring a whole set of new perspectives to the topic. Freeman concentrates on honor as a political force, while Pasley illustrates the power of an increasingly self-conscious press in shaping the political landscape.

David McCullough. *John Adams* (2001).

A highly acclaimed and extremely readable biography of one of America's true founding fathers.

James Ronda. *Lewis and Clark Among the Indians* (1984).

A bold retelling of the expedition's story, showcasing the Indian role in both Lewis and Clark's and the nation's successful expansion into the Louisiana Territory and beyond.

CHAPTER 9   Increasing Conflict and War, 1805–1815

Gregory E. Dowd. *A Spirited Resistance: The North American Indian Struggle for Unity, 1745–1815* (1992).

Hailed by many as one of the best works on Native American history, this well-written study covers the efforts by Indians to unite in defense of their lands and heritages, culminating in the struggles during the War of 1812.

R. David Edmunds. *The Shawnee Prophet* (1983); *Tecumseh and the Quest for Indian Leadership* (1984).

Each of these biographies is a masterpiece, but taken together, they present the most complete recounting of the lives and accomplishments of these two fascinating Shawnee brothers and their historical world.

John Denis Haeger. *John Jacob Astor: Business and Finance in the Early Republic* (1991).

William E. Foley and C. David Rice. *The First Chouteaus: River Barons of Early St. Louis* (1983).

Taken together, these two books provide a comprehensive overview of the fur trade during its early years, showcasing the importance of business tycoons like Astor and the Chouteaus and demystifying this huge business enterprise.

Donald Hickey. *The War of 1812: A Forgotten Conflict* (1989).

Arguably the best single-volume history of the war, encyclopedic in content, but so colorfully written that it will hold anyone's attention.

Robert A. Rutland. *Madison's Alternatives: The Jeffersonian Republicans and the Coming of War, 1805–1812* (1975).

An interesting review of the events leading up to the outbreak of war in 1812 and the various alternatives Jefferson and Madison had to choose from in facing the evolving diplomatic and political crises.

CHAPTER 10   The Rise of a New Nation, 1815–1836

George Dangerfield. *The Era of Good Feelings* (1952).
An older book, but so well written and informative that it deserves its status as a classic. All students will enjoy this grand overview.

Angie Debo. *And Still the Waters Run: The Betrayal of the Five Civilized Tribes* (1940; reprint, 1972).
A classic work by one of America's most talented and sensitive historical writers, a truly engaging history of this tragic sequence of events.

Richard E. Ellis. *The Union at Risk: Jacksonian Democracy, States' Rights, and the Nullification Crisis* (1987).
An invigorating reconsideration of the Nullification Crisis set in context with the other problems that beset the Jackson administration, suggesting how close the nation came to civil war in the 1830s.

Charles G. Sellers. *The Market Revolution: Jacksonian America, 1815–1846* (1991).
A far-reaching reassessment of economics and politics during this period focusing on the rise of the market economy and the responses, both positive and negative, that led to the rise of Jacksonian democracy.

George Rogers Taylor. *The Transportation Revolution, 1815–1860* (1951).
The only comprehensive treatment of changes in transportation during the antebellum period and their economic impact. Nicely written.

John William Ward. *Andrew Jackson: Symbol for an Age* (1955).
More a study of American culture during the age of Jackson than a biography of the man himself, Ward seeks to explain Old Hickory's status as a living myth during his own time and as a continuing monument in American history.

CHAPTER 11   The Great Transformation: Growth and Expansion, 1828–1848

Ira Berlin. *Slaves Without Masters* (1975).
A masterful study of a forgotten population: free African Americans in the Old South. Lively and informative.

Ray Allen Billington. *America's Frontier Heritage* (1966).
Patricia Nelson Limerick. *The Legacy of Conquest* (1988).
Two classics in the field of American western history; Billington represents the classic Turnerian perspective while Limerick gives voice to the anti-Turnerian "New Western History."

Stuart M. Blumin. *The Emergence of the Middle Class: Social Experience in the American City, 1760-1900* (1989).
Considered by many to be the most comprehensive overview of the emergence of the middle class in America during the nineteenth century.

Bill Cecil-Fronsman. *Common Whites: Class and Culture in Antebellum North Carolina* (1992).
A pioneering effort to describe the culture, lifestyle, and political economy shared by the antebellum South's majority population: nonslaveholding whites. Though confined in geographical scope, the study is suggestive of conditions that may have prevailed throughout the region.

Thomas Dublin. *Women at Work: The Transformation of Work and Community in Lowell, Massachusetts, 1826–1860* (1979).
An interesting look at the way in which the nature of work changed and the sorts of changes that were brought to one manufacturing community.

Elizabeth Fox-Genovese. *Within the Plantation Household* (1988).
A look at the lives of black and white women in the antebellum South. This study is quite long, but is well written and very informative.

Isabel Lehuu. *Carnival on the Page: Popular Print Media in Antebellum America* (2000).
An overview of the explosion in print media during the early nineteenth century and its role in shaping national culture.

Donald W. Meinig. *Imperial Texas* (1969).
A fascinating look at Texas history by a leading historical geographer.

Christopher L. Miller. *Prophetic Worlds* (2003).
This new edition includes commentary that helps to define the debates that this book has sparked about the history of the Pacific Northwest during the pioneer era.

Kenneth N. Owens, ed. *Riches for All: The California Gold Rush and the World* (2002).
A collection of essays by leading scholars about the California Gold Rush and its impact on both national and international life.

Wallace E. Stegner. *The Gathering of Zion* (1964).
A masterfully written history of the Mormon Trail by one of the West's leading literary figures.

John David Unruh. *The Plains Across* (1979).
Arguably the best one-volume account of the overland passage to Oregon. The many pages melt as the author captures the reader in the adventure of the Oregon Trail.

CHAPTER 12   Responses to the Great Transformation, 1828–1848

Eugene D. Genovese. *From Rebellion to Revolution: Afro-American Slave Revolts in the Making of the Modern World* (1979).
Although it focuses somewhat narrowly on confrontation, as opposed to more subtle forms of resistance, this study traces the emergence of African American political organization from its roots in antebellum slave revolts.

Karen Haltunen. *Confidence Men and Painted Women: A Study of Middle-Class Culture in America, 1830–1870* (1982).
A wonderfully well-researched study of an emerging class defining and shaping itself in the evolving world of early nineteenth-century urban space.

Thomas R. Hietala. *Manifest Design* (1985).
An interesting and well-written interpretation of the Mexican War and the events leading up to it.

Edward Pessen. *Most Uncommon Jacksonians: The Radical Leaders of the Early Labor Movement* (1967).
A look at early labor movements and reform by one of America's leading radical scholars.

Ronald G. Walters. *American Reformers, 1815–1860* (1978).
The best overview of the reform movements and key personalities who guided them during this difficult period in American history.

Susan Zaeske. *Signatures of Citizenship: Petitioning, Antislavery, and Women's Political Identity* (2003).
A fascinating study of how participation in reform campaigns helped lead early nineteenth-century women into a new sense of political identity.

CHAPTER 13   Sectional Conflict and Shattered Union, 1848–1860

Don E. Fehrenbacher. *Prelude to Greatness* (1962).
A well-written and interesting account of Lincoln's early career.

Don E. Fehrenbacher. *Slavery, Law, and Politics: The Dred Scott Case in Historical Perspective* (1981).
An excellent interpretive account of this landmark antebellum legal decision, placing it firmly into historical context.

William E. Gienapp, et al. *Essays in American Antebellum Politics, 1840–1860* (1982).
> A collection of essays by the rising generation of new political scholars. Exciting and challenging reading.

Michael F. Holt. *The Political Crisis of the 1850s* (1978).
> Arguably the best single-volume discussion of the political problems besetting the nation during this critical decade.

Stephen B. Oates. *To Purge This Land with Blood* (1984).
> The best biography to date on John Brown, focusing on his role in the emerging sectional crisis during the 1850s.

David Potter. *The Impending Crisis, 1848–1861* (1976).
> An extremely long and detailed work but beautifully written and informative.

James Rawley. *Race and Politics: "Bleeding Kansas" and the Coming of the Civil War* (1969).
> An interesting look at the conflicts in Kansas, centering upon racial attitudes in the West. Insightful and captivating reading.

Harriet Beecher Stowe. *Uncle Tom's Cabin* (1852; reprint, 1982).
> This edition includes notes and chronology by noted social historian Kathryn Kish Sklar, making it especially informative.

CHAPTER 14   A Violent Choice: Civil War, 1861–1865

Bruce Catton. *This Hallowed Ground: The Story of the Union Side of the Civil War* (1956).
> Catton is probably the best in the huge company of popular writers on the Civil War. This is his most comprehensive single-volume work. More detailed but still very interesting titles by Catton include *Glory Road: The Bloody Route from Fredericksburg to Gettysburg* (1952), *Mr. Lincoln's Army* (1962), *A Stillness at Appomattox* (1953), and *Grant Moves South* (1960).

Paul D. Escott. *After Secession: Jefferson Davis and the Failure of Confederate Nationalism* (1978).
> An excellent overview of internal political problems in the Confederacy by a leading Civil War historian.

Ann Giesberg. *Civil War Sisterhood: The U.S. Sanitary Commission and Women's Politics in Transition* (2000).
> A study of how women's activism in forming the sanitary movement during the Civil War recast their view of themselves as political figures and helped shape an emerging women's movement.

Alvin M. Josephy. *The Civil War in the American West* (1991).
> A former editor for *American Heritage,* Josephy writes an interesting and readable story about this little-known chapter in Civil War history.

William Marvel. *The* Alabama *& the* Kearsarge: *The Sailor's Civil War* (1996).
> Military and social historians have compared this new study favorably with *The Life of Billy Yank* (1952) and *The Life of Johnny Reb* (1943), Bell Irvin Willey's classic studies of life for the common soldier, calling it an insightful narrative of the Civil War experience for the common sailor.

James McPherson. *Battle Cry of Freedom: The Civil War Era* (1988).
> Hailed by many as the best single-volume history of the Civil War era; comprehensive and very well written.

Emory M. Thomas. *The Confederate Nation* (1979).
> A classic history of the Confederacy by an excellent southern historian.

Garry Wills. *Lincoln at Gettysburg: The Words That Remade America* (1992).
> A prize-winning look at Lincoln's rhetoric and the ways in which his speeches, especially his Gettysburg Address, recast American ideas about equality, freedom, and democracy. Exquisitely written by a master biographer.

CHAPTER 15   Reconstruction: High Hopes and Shattered Dreams, 1865–1877

W. E. B. Du Bois. *Black Reconstruction in America: An Essay Toward a History of the Part Which Black Folk Played in the Attempt to Reconstruct Democracy in America, 1860–1880* (1935; reprint edns., 1998, 2007).
> Written more than seventy years ago, Du Bois's classic book is still useful for information and insights. Recent editions usually include useful introductions that place Du Bois's work into the context of work by subsequent historians.

Carol Faulkner. *Women's Radical Reconstruction: The Freedmen's Aid Movement* (2004).
> A new study of the role of women in the Freedmen's Bureau and in federal Reconstruction policy more generally.

Eric Foner. *Reconstruction: America's Unfinished Revolution, 1863–1877* (1988; reprint, 2002).
> A thorough treatment, incorporating insights from many historians who have written on the subject during the fifty years preceding its publication.

Leon F. Litwack. *Been in the Storm So Long: The Aftermath of Slavery* (1979).
> Litwack focuses on the experience of the freed people.

William S. McFeely. *Frederick Douglass* (1991).
> A highly readable biography of the most prominent black political leader of the nineteenth century.

Michael Perman. *Emancipation and Reconstruction*, 2nd ed. (2003).
> A good, short and well written introduction to the topic.

Hans L. Trefousse. *Thaddeus Stevens: Nineteenth-Century Egalitarian* (1997).
> A recent study of perhaps the most important leader of the Radical Republicans.

C. Vann Woodward. *Reunion and Reaction: The Compromise of 1877 and the End of Reconstruction*, rev. ed. (1956; reprint, 2001).
> The classic account of the Compromise of 1877 with an afterward by William S. McFeely.

CHAPTER 16   An Industrial Order Emerges, 1865–1880

Edward L. Ayers. *The Promise of the New South: Life After Reconstruction* (1992, 2007).
> A comprehensive survey of developments in the South.

Robert V. Bruce. *1877: Year of Violence* (1959, 1989).
> The classic account of the 1877 railroad strike.

Alfred D. Chandler, Jr., with Takashi Hikino. *Scale and Scope: The Dynamics of Industrial Capitalism* (1990, 2004).
> Alfred Chandler's writings changed historians' thinking about the emergence of industrial capitalism in the United States; this is one of his key works.

Melvyn Dubofsky. *Industrialism and the American Worker, 1865–1920*, 3rd ed. (1996).
> A brief introduction to the topic, organized chronologically.

Ari Hoogenboom. *Rutherford B. Hayes: Warrior and President* (1995).
> An excellent biography that also includes important information on the politics of the era.

William S. McFeely. *Grant: A Biography* (1981, 2002).
> The standard biography of Grant, including his troubled presidency.

David Montgomery. *Workers' Control in America: Studies in the History of Work, Technology, and Labor Struggles* (1979).
> A classic work for understanding craft unions and labor more generally.

David Nasaw. *Andrew Carnegie* (2006).
> A recent and highly readable reconsideration of Carnegie's career.

Glenn Porter. *The Rise of Big Business, 1860–1910*, 3rd ed. (2006).

A brief and well-written introduction, surveying the role of the railroads, vertical and horizontal integration, and the merger movement.

Frank Roney. *Frank Roney: Irish Rebel and California Labor Leader, an Autobiography*, edited by Ira B. Cross (1931).

Roney's life as an iron molder and labor leader, in his own words.

CHAPTER 17 Becoming an Urban Industrial Society, 1880–1890

Ron Chernow. *The House of Morgan: An American Banking Dynasty and the Rise of Modern Finance* (1990, 2001).

An award-winning account of Morgan's bank and Morgan's role in the emergence of finance capitalism.

_____. *Titan: The Life of John D. Rockefeller, Sr.* (1998, 2004).

Well written and engaging, based on extensive research in Rockefeller family papers.

Robert W. Cherny. *American Politics in the Gilded Age, 1868–1900* (1997).

A brief survey of the politics of this period.

Leon Fink. *Workingmen's Democracy: The Knights of Labor and American Politics* (1983).

One of the best overall treatments of the Knights of Labor.

John Higham. *Strangers in the Land: Patterns of American Nativism, 1860–1925* (1965, 1983).

This classic book first defined the contours of American nativism and still provides an excellent introduction to the subject.

Jill Jonnes. *Empires of Light: Edison, Tesla, Westinghouse, and the Race to Electrify the World* (2003).

A recent and popular account of the battles over DC and AC current, and of the larger corporate and financial economy within which the key figures worked.

Alan M. Kraut. *The Huddled Masses: The Immigrant in American Society, 1880–1921*, 2nd ed. (2001).

A helpful introduction to immigration, especially the so-called new immigration.

Rebecca J. Mead. *How the Vote Was Won: Woman Suffrage in the Western United States, 1868-1914* (2004).

A recent study of the woman suffrage movement in the West.

Raymond A. Mohl. *The New City: Urban America in the Industrial Age, 1860–1920* (1985).

An excellent introduction to nearly all aspects of the growth of the cities.

Mark Wahlgren Summers. *Party Games: Getting, Keeping, and Using Power in Gilded Age Politics* (2004).

A fascinating account of political parties during the late 19th century.

CHAPTER 18 Conflict and Change in the West, 1865–1902

Yong Chen. *Chinese San Francisco, 1850-1943: A Trans-Pacific Community* (2000).

A well-researched study of the largest Chinatown and its relations with China.

Juan Gómez-Quiñones. *Roots of Chicano Politics, 1600–1940* (1994).

The political history of Mexican Americans from the first Spanish settlements in the Southwest up to the eve of World War II.

Norris Hundley, Jr. *The Great Thirst: Californians and Water, 1770s–1990s* (1992).

Among the best of recent studies surveying the role of water in the West.

Patricia Nelson Limerick. *The Legacy of Conquest: The Unbroken Past of the American West* (1987).

A major criticism of the Turner thesis, posing an alternative framework for viewing western history.

Glenda Riley. *A Place to Grow: Women in the American West* (1992).

A short and well-written survey of the subject, by the leading historian on the topic.

Philip Weeks. *Farewell, My Nation: The American Indian and the United States in the Nineteenth Century*, 2nd ed. (2000).

An excellent overview of the experience of Native Americans when they confronted the expansion of U.S. settlement west of the Missouri River.

Richard White. *"It's Your Misfortune and None of My Own": A History of the American West* (1991).

Like Limerick, White seeks to reconsider the history of the West, from the first European contact to the late 1980s.

CHAPTER 19 Economic Crash and Political Upheaval, 1890–1900

Jane Addams. *Twenty Years at Hull House* (1910, reprint, 1999, 2006).

Nothing conveys the complex world of Hull House and the striking personality of Jane Addams as well as her own account. It is available online. The recent editions have useful introductions by current historians who help to establish the context. The original is available online.

Robert L. Beisner. *From the Old Diplomacy to the New, 1865–1900*, 2nd ed. (1986).

A concise introduction to American foreign relations in this period, challenging some of LaFeber's conclusions.

Robert W. Cherny. *A Righteous Cause: The Life of William Jennings Bryan* (1985, 1994).

Includes a survey of the politics of the 1890s, especially the election of 1896.

Lewis Gould. *The Presidency of William McKinley* (1980).

A major contribution to historians' understanding of McKinley's presidency, including the war with Spain and the acquisition of the Philippines.

Louis R. Harlan. *Booker T. Washington: The Making of a Black Leader, 1856–1901* (1975).

The standard biography of Washington, which includes a good account of the racial situation in the South in the 1890s.

Walter LaFeber. *The New Empire: An Interpretation of American Expansion, 1860–1898* (1963).

A classic account, the first to emphasize the notion of a commercial empire.

Robert C. McMath, Jr. *American Populism: A Social History, 1877–1898* (1993).

A good, succinct introduction to Populism.

David Silbey. *A War of Frontier and Empire: The Philippine-American War, 1899-1902* (2007).

The most recent treatment of the U.S. conquest of the Philippines.

Kathryn Kish Sklar. *Florence Kelley and the Nation's Work: The Rise of Women's Political Culture, 1830-1900* (1995).

Much more than the biography of Florence Kelley, who for a time worked at Hull House, this book explores the larger topic of women and politics in the late nineteenth century.

CHAPTER 20 The Progressive Era, 1900–1917

Kathleen Dalton. *Theodore Roosevelt: A Strenuous Life* (2002).

Probably the best one-volume biography of the dominant figure of the age, who continues to fascinate both historians and the public more generally.

K. Austin Kerr. *Organized for Prohibition: A New History of the Anti-Saloon League* (1985).

A well-written treatment of the organization that formed the prototype for many organized interest groups.

Lester D. Langley. *The Banana Wars: United States' Intervention in the Caribbean, 1898–1934*, 2nd ed. (2001).
  A sprightly and succinct account of the role of the United States in the Caribbean and Central America.

David Levering Lewis. *W. E. B. Du Bois: Biography of a Race, 1868–1919* (1993).
  A powerful biography of Du Bois that delivers on its promise to present the "biography of a race" during the Progressive Era.

David G. McCullough. *The Path between the Seas: The Creation of the Panama Canal, 1870–1914* (1977).
  Perhaps the most lively and engrossing coverage of this subject.

Theodore Roosevelt. *An Autobiography* (1913; abridged ed. reprint, 1958).
  Roosevelt's account of his actions sometimes needs to be taken with a grain of salt but nevertheless provides insight into Roosevelt the person. Available online.

Upton Sinclair. *The Jungle: The Uncensored Original Edition*, ed. by Kathleen De Grave and Earl Lee (1905, 2003).
  This socialist novel about workers in Chicago's packing-houses is a classic example of muckraking; this edition includes the full, unexpurgated version that was originally published in serial form in a muckraking journal. The shorter version is available online in several places.

Shelton Stromquist. *Reinventing "The People": The Progressive Movement, the Class Problem, and the Origins of Modern Liberalism* (2006).
  A leading historian provides an interpretation of progressivism with a focus on labor history.

CHAPTER 21   The United States in a World at War, 1913–1920

Kendrick A. Clements, Eric A. Cheezum. *Woodrow Wilson* (2003).
  The best current one-volume treatment of Wilson's presidency.

Alfred W. Crosby. *America's Forgotten Pandemic: The Influenza of 1918* (2003).
  A thorough study of the great flu epidemic of 1918 that killed 600,000 Americans.

David P. Kilroy. *For Race and Country: The Life and Career of Colonel Charles Young* (2003).
  A carefully researched and well-written biography of Young, putting his struggles for racial equality into the context of the times.

Sinclair Lewis. *Main Street* (1920; reprint, 1999, 2003).
  An absorbing novel about a woman's dissatisfaction with her life and her decision to work in Washington during the war. The recent reprints include useful introductions that help to understand the context. The original is available online.

Erich Maria Remarque. *All Quiet on the Western Front*, trans. A. W. Wheen (1930; reprint, 2005).
  The classic and moving novel about World War I, seen through German eyes. Recent reprints include an introduction that helps to understand the context.

Richard Slotkin. *Lost Battalions: The Great War and the Crisis of American Naitonality* (2005).
  The wartime experiences of two New York state units, one of African Americans and the other largely of European immigrants.

Barbara W. Tuchman. *The Guns of August* (1962; reprint, 2004).
  A popular and engaging account of the outbreak of the war, focusing on events in Europe.

Robert Zieger. *America's Great War: World War I and the American Experience* (2001).

An excellent and recent overview of the U.S. during World War I.

CHAPTER 22   Prosperity Decade, 1920–1928

Frederick Lewis Allen. *Only Yesterday: An Informal History of the 1920s* (1931, 2000).
  An anecdote-filled account that brings the decade to life.

Kareem Abdul-Jabbar with Raymond Obstfeld. *On the Shoulders of Giants: My Journey through the Harlem Renaissance* (2007).
  The former basketball superstar considers the long-term influence of the Harlem Renaissance, including its influence on his life and on basketball.

Lynn Dumenil. *The Modern Temper: American Culture and Society in the 1920s* (1995).
  A good examination of changing social and cultural patterns in the 1920s.

Robert H. Ferrell. *The Presidency of Calvin Coolidge* (1998).
  Ferrell brings to life the national politics of the 1920s.

F. Scott Fitzgerald. *The Great Gatsby* (1925).
  The most famous fictional portrayal of the fast cars, pleasure seeking, and empty lives of the wealthy in the early 1920s. Available online.

The Smithsonian Collection of Classic Jazz. Five compact disks (1987).
  An outstanding collection that reflects the development of American jazz, with annotations and biographies of performers.

David Stenn. *Clara Bow: Runnin' Wild* (1990).
  The best and most carefully researched of the biographies of Bow.

Jules Tygiel. *The Great Los Angeles Swindle: Oil, Stocks, and Scandal During the Roaring Twenties* (1996).
  An engagingly written account of Los Angeles in the 1920s.

CHAPTER 23   The Great Depression and the New Deal, 1929–1939

Michael A. Bernstein. *The Great Depression* (1987).
  A detailed economic examination of the causes and effects of the Depression, with American manufacturing as a primary focus.

Julia Kirk Blackwelder. *Women of the Depression: Caste and Culture in San Antonio, 1929–1939* (1984).
  A tightly focused study on Mexican American, African American, and Anglo women in the world of San Antonio during the Depression.

Lizabeth Cohen. *Making a New Deal: Industrial Workers in Chicago, 1919–1939* (1990).
  A detailed examination of the inclusion of African American and immigrant workers in the CIO and in New Deal politics.

David Kennedy. *Freedom from Fear: The American People in Depression and War, 1929–1945* (1999).
  A well-written and researched comprehensive examination of a period that shaped recent American history.

Maury Klein. *Rainbow's End: The Crash of 1929* (2001).
  A compelling account of the stock market crash set within the framework of the many social, political, cultural, and economic events that surrounded it.

Robert McElvaine. *The Great Depression: America, 1929–1941* (1984).
  An excellent overview of the origins of and responses to the Depression.

George McJimsey. *The Presidency of Franklin Delano Roosevelt* (2000).
  A brief and positive account of Roosevelt's struggles to combat the Depression and the Second World War, contains a well-presented annotated bibliography.

Amity Shaes, *The Forgotten Man: A New History of the Great Depression* (2007)
>Develops the view that governmental actions contributed to the severity and length of the Great Depression.

Patricia Sullivan. *Days of Hope: Race and Democracy in the New Deal Era* (1996)
>A positive view on the ways in which New Deal actions led to the shift in the African American vote from the Republican to the Democratic Party.

Studs Terkel. *Hard Times: An Oral History of the Great Depression* (1970).
>A classic example of how oral histories can provide the human dimension to history.

Susan Ware. *Holding Their Own: American Women in the 1930s* (1982).
>An examination of the impact of the Depression on the lives and lifestyles of women.

Joan Hoff Wilson. *Herbert Hoover: Forgotten Progressive* (1970).
>A positive evaluation of the life of Herbert Hoover that stresses his accomplishments as well as his limitations.

CHAPTER 24   America's Rise to World Leadership, 1929–1945

Robert Dallek. *Franklin D. Roosevelt and American Foreign Policy, 1932–1945* (1979).
>An excellent, balanced study of Franklin Roosevelt's foreign policy.

Justus D. Doenecke. *Storm on the Horizon: The Challenge to American Intervention, 1939–1941* (2001).
>Well-documented and -written examination of American isolationists prior to Pearl Harbor that shows the complexity of the movement and the issues.

Sherna B. Gluck. *Rosie the Riveter Revisited: Women, the War, and Social Change* (1987).
>An important work examining the changes that took place among women in society during the war.

John Keegan. *The Second World War* (1990).
>An excellent one-volume work that summarizes the military and diplomatic aspects of World War II.

William O'Neill. *A Democracy at War: America's Fight at Home and Abroad in World War II* (1993).
>A good introduction to American society and politics during the war as well as an excellent view of the military campaigns against the Axis powers.

Ronald Spector. *Eagle Against the Sun* (1988).
>One of the best-written general accounts of the war in the Pacific.

Ronald Takiaki. *Double Victory* (2002).
>A wide-ranging look at American minorities' contribution to the war effort at home and abroad. Clearly demonstrates how these efforts set the foundation for the civil rights movements that followed.

David Wyman. *The Abandonment of the Jews* (1985).
>A balanced account of the Holocaust.

CHAPTER 25   Truman and Cold War America, 1945–1952

Paul Boyer. *By the Bomb's Early Light: American Thought and Culture at the Dawn of the Atomic Age* (1985).
>A useful analysis of the impact of atomic energy and the atomic bomb on American society, from advertising to mock "atomic air bomb drills."

Jim Cullen. *The American Dream: A Short History of an Idea that Shaped a Nation* (2003)
>An introductory view of the multi-nature of the American Dream from colonial America with an emphasis on the postwar period.

John Gaddis: *The Cold War: A New History* (2005)
>A concise, thoughtful analysis of the events, ideology, and people that characterized the Cold War from1945 to 1991.

Max Hastings. *The Korean War* (1987).
>A short, well-written study of the military dimension of the Korean War.

Marc Trachtenberg. *A Constructed Peace: The Making of the European Settlements, 1945–1963* (1999).
>A well-researched study of the politics and issues that surrounded the origins of the Cold War from a multinational perspective.

David McCullough. *Truman* (1992).
>A highly acclaimed biography of Truman.

Ted Morgan. *Reds: McCarthyism in the Twentieth-century America* (2003)
>An overview of the anti-communism in the United States that places McCarthy as part of a wide-spread movement based of growing fears of Soviet Communism and an uncertainty about the postwar world.

James Patterson. *Grand Expectations: The United States, 1945–1974* (1996).
>A general, readable view of American society and politics in the postwar period.

Jules Tygiel. *Baseball's Great Experiment: Jackie Robinson and His Legacy* (1983).
>Reflections on the life experiences and decisions that brought Jackie Robinson to break the color barrier in professional baseball.

Stephen J. Whitfield. *The Culture of the Cold War* (1991).
>A critical account of the impact of the Cold War on the United States that argues that a consensus that equated "Americanism" with militant anticommunism dominated American life.

CHAPTER 26   Quest for Consensus, 1952–1960

Stephen E. Ambrose. *Eisenhower: The President* (1984).
>A generally positive and well-balanced biography of Eisenhower as president by one of the most respected historians of the Eisenhower period.

Michael Bertrand. *Race, Rock, and Elvis* (2000).
>Provides a view of how Elvis and his music not only shaped American music but altered views about class, race, and gender.

Taylor Branch. *Parting the Waters: America in the King Years, 1954–1963* (1988).
>An interesting and useful description of the development of the civil rights movement that focuses on the role of Martin Luther King Jr.

Elizabeth Cohen. *A Consumer's Republic: The Politics of Mass Consumption in Postwar America* (2003).
>An important study of the connections between business, politics, and culture that have shaped American society following World War II to the mid-1960s.

Robert A. Devine. *Eisenhower and the Cold War* (1981).
>A solid and brief account of Eisenhower's foreign policy, especially toward the Soviet Union.

David Halberstam. *The Fifties* (1993).
>A positive interpretive view of the 1950s by a well-known journalist and author, especially recommended for its description of famous and not-so-famous people.

Peter Hahn. *Caught in the Middle East: U.S. Policy Toward the Arab-Israeli Conflict, 1945-1961* (2006).
>An excellent examination of the United States special relationship with Israel and the differences in approaches between Truman and Eisenhower.

Eugenia Kaledin. *Mothers and More: American Women in the 1950s* (1984).

A thoughtful look at the role of American women in society during the 1950s.

Joanne J. Meyerowitz, ed. *Not June Cleaver: Women and Gender in Postwar America, 1945–1960* (1994).

An excellent collection of essays that explore the variety of views on women's roles in American culture, society, and politics.

Mark Newman. *The Civil Rights Movement* (2004)

A concise introduction to the civil rights movement with an emphasis on the activities of local communities and women.

James Patterson. *Brown v. Board of Education: A Civil Rights Milestone and Its Troubled Legacy* (2001).

A timely study of the events and decisions that led to the *Brown* case as well as an examination of the role the *Brown* decision has had on American politics, society, and race relations.

CHAPTER 27 Great Promises, Bitter Disappointments, 1960–1968

Peter Braunstein and Michael Doyle, eds. *Imagine Nation: The American Counterculture of the 1960s and 1970s* (2001).

A wide range of essays that provide useful evaluations on the many aspects of the counterculture.

Irving Bernstein. *Promises Kept: John F. Kennedy's New Frontier* (1991).

A brief and balanced account of Kennedy's presidency that presents a favorable report of the accomplishments and legacy of the New Frontier.

Michael Beschloss. *The Crisis Years: Kennedy and Khrushchev, 1960–1963* (1991).

A strong narrative account of the Cold War during the Kennedy administration and the personal duel between the leaders of the two superpowers.

Clayborne Carson. *In Struggle: SNCC and the Black Awakening of the 1960s* (1981).

A useful study that uses the development of SNCC to examine the changing patterns of the civil rights movement and the emergence of black nationalism.

Margaret Cruikshank. *The Gay and Lesbian Liberation Movement* (1992).

Provides a good introduction and insight into the gay and lesbian movement.

Robert Dallek. *Flawed Giant: Lyndon B. Johnson, 1960–1973* (1998).

An important biography that focuses on politics and foreign policy.

Sidney M. Milkis and Jerome M. Mileur. *The Great Society and the High Tide of Liberalism* (2005).

An excellent series of essays that examines Great Society liberalism and legislation.

David Horowitz. *Betty Friedan and the Making of the Feminist Movement* (1998).

Uses the central figure of the women's movement to examine the beginnings and development of the movement.

Michael Kazin and Maurice Isserman. *America Divided: The Civil War of the 1960s* (2000).

The social and cultural currents of the 1960s are skillfully woven into an overall picture of American society.

Jeffrey Ogbar. *Black Power: Radical Politics and African American Identity.* (2005)

A well-written study of the varieties of the Black Power movement and the development of an American consciousness.

CHAPTER 28 America Under Stress, 1967–1976

Stephen Ambrose. *Nixon: The Triumph of a Politician, 1962–1972* (1989).

An excellent examination of Nixon and his politics—the second volume of Ambrose's three-volume biography.

Larry Berman. *No Peace, No Honor: Nixon, Kissinger, and Betrayal in Vietnam* (2001).

A critical view of Vietnamization and the politics of ending the American presence in Vietnam.

Edward Berkowitz. *Something Happened: A Political and Cultural Overview of the Seventies* (2006)

An introduction to the seventies that shows that it was a period of activism with significant debate over the limits of the economy, culture, and foreign policy.

Philip Caputo. *Rumor of War* (1986).

The author's account of his own changing perspectives on the war in Vietnam. Caputo served as a young marine officer in Vietnam and later covered the final days in Saigon as a journalist. His views frequently reflected those of the American public.

Ian F. Haney Lopez. *Racism on Trial: The Chicano Fight for Justice* (2003).

An interesting use of two trials to examine the development of Chicano identity and the idea of race and violence.

Burton Kaufman. *The Presidency of James Earl Carter, Jr.* (1993).

A well-balanced account and analysis of Carter's presidency and the changing political values of the 1970s.

Stanley Kutler. *The Wars of Watergate* (1990) and *Abuse of Power: The New Nixon Tapes* (1997).

The former work details the events surrounding the Watergate break-in and the hearings that led to Nixon's resignation. The latter provides transcripts of selected Nixon tapes.

Joanne Nagel. *American Indian Ethnic Revival: Red Power and the Resurgence of Identity and Culture* (1996).

A thorough analysis of the Red Power movement and how it helped to shape cultural and political change.

David F. Schmitz. *The Tet Offensive: Politics, War, and Public Opinion* (2005)

An outstanding examination of the Tet offense and its ramifications on American policymakers and politics.

Marylin Young. *The Vietnam Wars, 1945–1990* (1991).

A brief, well-written and a carefully documented history of Vietnam's struggle for nationhood with a focus on American policy toward Vietnam since near the end of WWII.

CHAPTER 29 Facing Limits, 1976–1992

A. J. Bacevich, et al. *The Gulf Conflict of 1991 Reconsidered* (2003).

A collection of essays that provide both insight and an excellent overview of the Gulf War.

Douglas Brinkley. *The Reagan Diaries* (2007)

An interesting personal view of Reagan's view of the events that shaped his administration and world affairs.

Roger Daniels. *Coming to America* (1990).

A solid analysis of the new immigrants seeking a place in American society; especially effective on Asian immigration.

Michael Duffy and Don Goodgame. *Marching in Place: The Status Quo Presidency of George Bush* (1992).

An insightful but critical analysis of the Bush presidency.

John L. Gaddis. *The United States and the End of the Cold War* (1992).

An excellent narrative of events in the Soviet Union and the United States that led to the end of the Cold War, as well as a useful analysis of the problems facing the United States in the post–Cold War world.

David J. Garrow. *Liberty and Sexuality: The Right to Privacy and the Making of* Roe v. Wade (1994).

An in-depth and scholarly account of the origins and impact of *Roe v. Wade* and the legal and political issues dealing with privacy, gender, and abortion.

Lisa McGirr. *Suburban Warriors: The Origins of the New American Right* (2001).

A study of how the ideology and issues of the New Right found fertile soil within the American middle suburban class.

Michael Schaller. *Reckoning with Reagan* (1992).

A brief but scholarly analysis of the Reagan administration and the society and values that supported the Reagan revolution.

Bruce Schulman. *The Seventies: The Great Shift in American Culture, Society, and Politics* (2001).

A readable and comprehensive overview of the central issues that defined the decade.

Studs Terkel. *The Great Divide* (1988).

An interesting and informative collection of oral interviews that provide a personal glimpse of changes recently taking place in American society.

CHAPTER 30   Entering a New Century, 1992–2007

Michael Bernstein and David A. Adler, eds. *Understanding American Economic Decline* (1994).

A collection of essays by economists and knowledgeable observers who analyze the slowing down of the American economy and its impact.

Douglas Brinkley. *The Great Deluge: Hurricane Katrina, New Orleans and the Mississippi Gulf Coast* (2007).

A narrative account of one of the greatest natural disasters to occur in the United States.

Zbigniew Brzenzinski. *The Choice: Global Domination or Global Leadership* (2004).

A penetrating analysis of American post-911 foreign policies by an ex-insider.

Congressional Quarterly's Research Reports.

A valuable monthly resource for information and views on issues facing the United States and the world.

Anthony Gidden. *Runaway World: How Globalization is Reshaping Our World* (2002).

A readable and positive appraisal of globalization and its effects on a world society and its people.

David Halberstam. *War in Time of Peace: Bush, Clinton, and the Generals* (2001).

An understandable account of American foreign policy and policymakers coming to dealing with a post–Cold War world where the major issues are terrorism, genocide, and nation-building.

Ernest May. ed. *The 9/11 Commission Report with Related Documents* (2007)

Provides a usable background to the events preceding and after the 9/11 terrorist attacks that provides useable documents to examine the issues.

James MacGregor Burns and Georgia J. Sorenson. *Dead Center: Clinton-Gore Leadership and the Perils of Moderation* (1999).

An interesting and readable view of the politics of the Clinton revival of the Democratic Party and the Clinton administrations.

Randy Shilts. *And the Band Played On: Politics, People and the AIDS Epidemic* (1987).

A compelling book on the AIDS epidemic and the early lack of action by society; written by a victim of AIDS.

Strobe Talbott and Nayan Chanda, eds. *The Age of Terror: America and the World After September 11* (2001).

An informative collection of essays that place the attacks of September 11 in historical and political context.

Andrea K. Talentino. *Military Intervention after the Cold War: The Evolution of Theory and Practice* (2005)

An interesting view that connects post–Cold War interventions to globalization that utilizes examples of interventions in Somalia, Haiti, and Kosovo.

Bob Woodward. *Plan of Attack* (2004).

Based on interviews, an account of the internal decisions the Bush administration made that led to the decision to go to war with Iraq.

✔ Documents

Declaration of Independence in Congress, July 4, 1776

When, in the course of human events, it becomes necessary for one people to dissolve the political bonds which have connected them with another, and to assume, among the powers of the earth, the separate and equal station to which the laws of nature and of nature's God entitle them, a decent respect to the opinions of mankind requires that they should declare the causes which impel them to the separation.

We hold these truths to be self-evident: That all men are created equal; that they are endowed by their Creator with certain unalienable rights; that among these are life, liberty, and the pursuit of happiness; that, to secure these rights, governments are instituted among men, deriving their just powers from the consent of the governed; that whenever any form of government becomes destructive of these ends, it is the right of the people to alter or to abolish it, and to institute new government, laying its foundation on such principles, and organizing its powers in such form, as to them shall seem most likely to effect their safety and happiness. Prudence, indeed, will dictate that governments long established should not be changed for light and transient causes; and accordingly all experience hath shown that mankind are more disposed to suffer, while evils are sufferable, than to right themselves by abolishing the forms to which they are accustomed. But when a long train of abuses and usurpations, pursuing invariably the same object, evinces a design to reduce them under absolute despotism, it is their right, it is their duty, to throw off such government, and to provide new guards for their future security. Such has been the patient sufferance of these colonies; and such is now the necessity which constrains them to alter their former systems of government. The history of the present King of Great Britain is a history of repeated injuries and usurpations, all having in direct object the establishment of an absolute tyranny over these states. To prove this, let facts be submitted to a candid world.

He has refused his assent to laws, the most wholesome and necessary for the public good.

He has forbidden his governors to pass laws of immediate and pressing importance, unless suspended in their operation till his assent should be obtained; and, when so suspended, he has utterly neglected to attend to them.

He has refused to pass other laws for the accommodation of large districts of people, unless those people would relinquish the right of representation in the legislature, a right inestimable to them, and formidable to tyrants only.

He has called together legislative bodies at places unusual, uncomfortable, and distant from the depository of their public records, for the sole purpose of fatiguing them into compliance with his measures.

He has dissolved representative houses repeatedly, for opposing, with manly firmness, his invasions on the rights of the people.

He has refused for a long time, after such dissolutions, to cause others to be elected; whereby the legislative powers, incapable of annihilation, have returned to the people at large for their exercise; the state remaining, in the mean time, exposed to all the dangers of invasions from without and convulsions within.

He has endeavored to prevent the population of these states; for that purpose obstructing the laws for naturalization of foreigners; refusing to pass others to encourage their migration hither, and raising the conditions of new appropriations of lands.

He has obstructed the administration of justice, by refusing his assent to laws for establishing judiciary powers.

He has made judges dependent on his will alone, for the tenure of their offices, and the amount and payment of their salaries.

He has erected a multitude of new offices, and sent hither swarms of officers to harass our people and eat out their substance.

He has kept among us, in times of peace, standing armies, without the consent of our legislatures.

He has affected to render the military independent of, and superior to, the civil power.

He has combined with others to subject us to a jurisdiction foreign to our constitution, and unacknowledged by our laws, giving his assent to their acts of pretended legislation:

For quartering large bodies of armed troops among us;

For protecting them, by a mock trial, from punishment for any murders which they should commit on the inhabitants of these states;

For cutting off our trade with all parts of the world;

For imposing taxes on us without our consent;

For depriving us, in many cases, of the benefits of trial by jury;

For transporting us beyond seas, to be tried for pretended offenses;

For abolishing the free system of English laws in a neighboring province, establishing therein an arbitrary government, and enlarging its boundaries, so as to render it at once an example and fit instrument for introducing the same absolute rule into these colonies;

For taking away our charters, abolishing our most valuable laws, and altering fundamentally the forms of our governments;

For suspending our own legislatures, and declaring themselves invested with power to legislate for us in all cases whatsoever.

He has abdicated government here, by declaring us out of his protection and waging war against us.

He has plundered our seas, ravaged our coasts, burned our towns, and destroyed the lives of our people.

He is at this time transporting large armies of foreign mercenaries to complete the works of death, desolation, and tyranny already begun with circumstances of cruelty and perfidy scarcely paralleled in the most barbarous ages, and totally unworthy the head of a civilized nation.

He has constrained our fellow-citizens, taken captive on the high seas, to bear arms against their country, to become the executioners of their friends and brethren, or to fall themselves by their hands.

He has excited domestic insurrection among us, and has endeavored to bring on the inhabitants of our frontiers the merciless Indian savages, whose known rule of warfare is an undistinguished destruction of all ages, sexes, and conditions.

In every stage of these oppressions we have petitioned for redress in the most humble terms; our repeated petitions have been answered only by repeated injury.

A prince, whose character is thus marked by every act which may define a tyrant, is unfit to be the ruler of a free people.

Nor have we been wanting in our attentions to our British brethren. We have warned them, from time to time, of attempts by their legislature to extend an unwarrantable jurisdiction over us. We have reminded them of the circumstances of our emigration and settlement here. We have appealed to their native justice and magnanimity; and we have conjured them, by the ties of our common kindred, to disavow these usurpations, which would inevitably interrupt our connections and correspondence. They, too, have been deaf to the voice of justice and of consanguinity. We must, therefore, acquiesce in the necessity which denounces our separation, and hold them, as we hold the rest of mankind, enemies in war, in peace friends.

We, therefore, the representatives of the United States of America, in General Congress assembled, appealing to the Supreme Judge of the world for the rectitude of our intentions, do, in the name and by the authority of the good people of these colonies, solemnly publish and declare, that these United Colonies are, and of right ought to be, FREE AND INDEPENDENT STATES; that they are absolved from all allegiance to the British crown, and that all political connection between them and the state of Great Britain is, and ought to be, totally dissolved; and that, as free and independent states, they have full power to levy war, conclude peace, contract alliances, establish commerce, and do all other acts and things which independent states may of right do. And for the support of this declaration, with a firm reliance on the protection of Divine Providence, we mutually pledge to each other our lives, our fortunes, and our sacred honor.

JOHN HANCOCK
and fifty-five others

Constitution of the United States of America and Amendments*

Preamble

We the people of the United States, in order to form a more perfect union, establish justice, insure domestic tranquillity, provide for the common defense, promote the general welfare, and secure the blessings of liberty to ourselves and our posterity, do ordain and establish this Constitution for the United States of America.

Article I

Section 1 All legislative powers herein granted shall be vested in a Congress of the United States, which shall consist of a Senate and a House of Representatives.

Section 2 The House of Representatives shall be composed of members chosen every second year by the people of the several States, and the electors in each State shall have the qualifications requisite for electors of the most numerous branch of the State Legislature.

No person shall be a Representative who shall not have attained to the age of twenty-five years, and been seven years a citizen of the United States, and who shall not, when elected, be an inhabitant of that State in which he shall be chosen.

Representatives and direct taxes shall be apportioned among the several States which may be included within this Union, according to their re-spective numbers, *which shall be determined by adding to the whole number of free persons, including those bound to service for a term of years and excluding Indians not taxed, three-fifths of all other persons.* The actual enumeration shall be made within three years after the first meeting of the Congress of the United States, and within every subsequent term of ten years, in such manner as they shall by law direct. The number of Representatives shall not exceed one for every thirty thousand, but each State shall have at least one Representative; *and until such enumeration shall be made, the State of New Hampshire shall be entitled to choose three, Massachusetts eight, Rhode Island and Providence Plantations one, Connecticut five, New York six, New Jersey four, Pennsylvania eight, Delaware one, Maryland six, Virginia ten, North Carolina five, South Carolina five, and Georgia three.*

When vacancies happen in the representation from any State, the Executive authority thereof shall issue writs of election to fill such vacancies.

The House of Representatives shall choose their Speaker and other officers; and shall have the sole power of impeachment.

Section 3 The Senate of the United States shall be composed of two Senators from each State, *chosen by the legislature thereof,* for six years; and each Senator shall have one vote.

Immediately after they shall be assembled in consequence of the first election, they shall be divided as equally as may be into three classes. The seats of the Senators of the first class shall be vacated at the expiration of the second year, of the second class at the expiration of the fourth year, and of the third class at the expiration of the sixth year, so that one-third may be chosen every second year; *and if vacancies happen by resignation or otherwise, during the recess of the legislature of any State, the Executive thereof may make temporary appointments until the next meeting of the legislature, which shall then fill such vacancies.*

No person shall be a Senator who shall not have attained to the age of thirty years, and been nine years a citizen of the United States, and who shall not, when elected, be an inhabitant of that State for which he shall be chosen.

The Vice-President of the United States shall be President of the Senate, but shall have no vote, unless they be equally divided.

The Senate shall choose their other officers, and also a President *pro tempore,* in the absence of the Vice-President, or when he shall exercise the office of President of the United States.

The Senate shall have the sole power to try all impeachments. When sitting for that purpose, they shall be on oath or affirmation. When the President of the United States is tried, the Chief Justice shall preside: and no person shall be convicted with-out the concurrence of two-thirds of the members present.

Judgment in cases of impeachment shall not extend further than to removal from the office, and disqualification to hold and enjoy any office of honor, trust or profit under the United States: but the party convicted shall nevertheless be liable and subject to indictment, trial, judgment and punishment, according to law.

Section 4 The times, places and manner of holding elections for Senators and Representatives shall be prescribed in each State by the legislature thereof; but the Congress may at any time by law make or alter such regulations, except as to the places of choosing Senators.

The Congress shall assemble at least once in every year, and such meeting *shall be on the first Monday in December, unless they shall by law appoint a different day.*

Section 5 Each house shall be the judge of the elections, returns and qualifications of its own members, and a majority of each shall constitute a quorum to do business; but a smaller number may adjourn from day to day, and may be authorized to compel the attendance of

---

* Passages no longer in effect are printed in italic type.

absent members, in such manner, and under such penalties, as each house may provide.

Each house may determine the rules of its proceedings, punish its members for disorderly behavior, and with the concurrence of two-thirds, expel a member.

Each house shall keep a journal of its proceedings, and from time to time publish the same, excepting such parts as may in their judgment require secrecy; and the yeas and nays of the members of either house on any question shall, at the desire of one-fifth of those present, be entered on the journal.

Neither house, during the session of Congress, shall, without the consent of the other, adjourn for more than three days, nor to any other place than that in which the two houses shall be sitting.

Section 6   The Senators and Representatives shall receive a compensation for their services, to be ascertained by law and paid out of the treasury of the United States. They shall in all cases except treason, felony and breach of the peace, be privileged from arrest during their attendance at the session of their respective houses, and in going to and returning from the same; and for any speech or debate in either house, they shall not be questioned in any other place.

No Senator or Representative shall, during the time for which he was elected, be appointed to any civil office under the authority of the United States, which shall have been created, or the emoluments whereof shall have been increased, during such time; and no person holding any office under the United States shall be a member of either house during his continuance in office.

Section 7   All bills for raising revenue shall originate in the House of Representatives; but the Senate may propose or concur with amendments as on other bills.

Every bill which shall have passed the House of Representatives and the Senate, shall, before it become a law, be presented to the President of the United States; if he approve he shall sign it, but if not he shall return it with objections to that house in which it originated, who shall enter the objections at large on their journal, and proceed to reconsider it. If after such reconsideration two-thirds of that house shall agree to pass the bill, it shall be sent, together with the objections, to the other house, by which it shall likewise be reconsidered, and, if approved by two-thirds of that house, it shall become a law. But in all such cases the votes of both houses shall be determined by yeas and nays, and the names of the persons voting for and against the bill shall be entered on the journal of each house respectively. If any bill shall not be returned by the President within ten days (Sundays excepted) after it shall have been presented to him, the same shall be a law, in like manner as if he had signed it, unless the Congress by their adjournment prevent its return, in which case it shall not be a law.

Every order, resolution, or vote to which the concurrence of the Senate and House of Representatives may be necessary (except on a question of adjournment) shall be presented to the President of the United States; and before the same shall take effect, shall be approved by him, or being disapproved by him, shall be repassed by two-thirds of the Senate and House of Representatives, according to the rules and limitations prescribed in the case of a bill.

Section 8   The Congress shall have power

To lay and collect taxes, duties, imposts, and excises, to pay the debts and provide for the common defense and general welfare of the United States; but all duties, imposts and excises shall be uniform throughout the United States;

To borrow money on the credit of the United States;

To regulate commerce with foreign nations, and among the several States, and with the Indian tribes;

To establish an uniform rule of naturalization, and uniform laws on the subject of bankruptcies throughout the United States;

To coin money, regulate the value thereof, and of foreign coin, and fix the standard of weights and measures;

To provide for the punishment of counterfeiting the securities and current coin of the United States;

To establish post offices and post roads;

To promote the progress of science and useful arts by securing for limited times to authors and inventors the exclusive right to their respective writings and discoveries;

To constitute tribunals inferior to the Supreme Court;

To define and punish piracies and felonies committed on the high seas and offenses against the law of nations;

To declare war, grant letters of marque and reprisal, and make rules concerning captures on land and water;

To raise and support armies, but no appropriation of money to that use shall be for a longer term than two years;

To provide and maintain a navy;

To make rules for the government and regulation of the land and naval forces;

To provide for calling forth the militia to execute the laws of the Union, suppress insurrections, and repel invasions;

To provide for organizing, arming, and disciplining the militia, and for governing such part of them as may be employed in the service of the United States, reserving to the States respectively the appointment of the officers, and the authority of training the militia according to the discipline prescribed by Congress;

To exercise exclusive legislation in all cases whatsoever, over such district (not exceeding ten miles square) as may, by cession of particular States, and the acceptance of Congress, become the seat of government of the United States, and to exercise like authority over all places purchased by the consent of the legislature of the State, in which the same shall be, for erection of forts, magazines, arsenals, dockyards, and other needful buildings; — and

To make all laws which shall be necessary and proper for carrying into execution the foregoing powers, and all other powers vested by this Constitution in the government of the United States, or in any department or officer thereof.

Section 9   The migration or importation of such persons as any of the States now existing shall think proper to admit shall not be prohibited by the Congress prior to the year 1808; but a tax or duty may be imposed on such importation, not exceeding $10 for each person.

The privilege of the writ of habeas corpus shall not be suspended, unless when in cases of rebellion or invasion the public safety may require it.

No bill of attainder or ex post facto law shall be passed.

No capitation, or other direct, tax shall be laid, unless in proportion to the census or enumeration herein before directed to be taken.

No tax or duty shall be laid on articles exported from any State.

No preference shall be given by any regulation of commerce or revenue to the ports of one State over those of another; nor shall vessels bound to, or from, one State, be obliged to enter, clear, or pay duties in another.

No money shall be drawn from the treasury, but in consequence of appropriations made by law; and a regular statement and account of the receipts and expenditures of all public money shall be published from time to time.

No title of nobility shall be granted by the United States: and no person holding any office of profit or trust under them, shall, without the consent of the Congress, accept of any present, emolument, office, or title, of any kind whatever, from any king, prince, or foreign state.

Section 10   No State shall enter into any treaty, alliance, or confederation; grant letters of marque and reprisal; coin money; emit bills of credit; make anything but gold and silver coin a tender in payment of debts; pass any bill of attainder, ex post facto law, or law impairing the obligation of contracts, or grant any title of nobility.

No State shall, without the consent of Congress, lay any imposts or duties on imports or exports, except what may be absolutely necessary for executing its inspection laws: and the net produce of all duties and imposts, laid by any State on imports or exports, shall be for the use of the treasury of the United States; and all such laws shall be subject to the revision and control of the Congress.

No State shall, without the consent of Congress, lay any duty of tonnage, keep troops or ships of war in time of peace, enter into any agreement or compact with another State, or with a foreign power, or engage in war, unless actually invaded, or in such imminent danger as will not admit of delay.

Article II

Section 1   The executive power shall be vested in a President of the United States of America. He shall hold his office during the term of four years, and, together with the Vice-President, chosen for the same term, be elected as follows:

Each State shall appoint, in such manner as the legislature thereof may direct, a number of electors, equal to the whole number of Senators and Representatives to which the State may be entitled in the Congress; but no Senator or Representative, or person holding an office of trust or profit under the United States, shall be appointed an elector.

The electors shall meet in their respective States, and vote by ballot for two persons, of whom one at least shall not be an inhabitant of the same State with themselves. And they shall make a list of all the persons voted for, and of the number of votes for each; which list they shall sign and certify, and transmit sealed to the seat of government of the United States, directed to the President of the Senate. The President of the Senate shall, in the presence of the Senate and House of Representatives, open all the certificates, and the votes shall then be counted. The person having the greatest number of votes shall be the President, if such number be a majority of the whole number of electors appointed; and if there be more than one who have such majority, and have an equal number of votes, then the House of Representatives shall immediately choose by ballot one of them for President; and if no person have a majority, then from the five highest on the list said house shall in like manner choose the President. But in choosing the President the votes shall be taken by States, the representation from each State having one vote; a quorum for this purpose shall consist of a member or members from two-thirds of the States, and a majority of all the States shall be necessary to a choice. In every case, after the choice of the President, the person having the greatest number of votes of the electors shall be the Vice-President. But if there should remain two or more who have equal votes, the Senate shall choose from them by ballot the Vice-President.

The Congress may determine the time of choosing the electors and the day on which they shall give their votes; which day shall be the same throughout the United States.

No person except a natural-born citizen, *or a citizen of the United States at the time of the adoption of this Constitution,* shall be eligible to the office of President; neither shall any person be eligible to that office who shall not have attained to the age of thirty-five years, and been fourteen years a resident within the United States.

In cases of the removal of the President from office or of his death, resignation, or inability to discharge the powers and duties of the said office, the same shall devolve on the Vice-President, and the Congress may by law provide for the case of removal, death, resignation, or inability, both of the President and Vice-President, declaring what officer shall then act as President, and such officer shall act accordingly, until the disability be removed, or a President shall be elected.

The President shall, at stated times, receive for his services a compensation, which shall neither be increased nor diminished during the period for which he shall have been elected, and he shall not receive within that period any other emolument from the United States, or any of them.

Before he enter on the execution of his office, he shall take the following oath or affirmation:—"I do solemnly swear (or affirm) that I will faithfully execute the office of the President of the United States, and will to the best of my ability preserve, protect and defend the Constitution of the United States."

Section 2   The President shall be commander in chief of the army and navy of the United States, and of the militia of the several States, when called into the actual service of the United States; he may require the opinion, in writing, of the principal officer in each of the executive departments, upon any subject relating to the duties of their respective offices, and he shall have power to grant reprieves and pardons for offenses against the United States, except in cases of impeachment.

He shall have power, by and with the advice and consent of the Senate, to make treaties, provided two-thirds of the Senators present concur; and he shall nominate, and by and with the advice and consent of the Senate, shall appoint ambassadors, other public ministers and consuls, judges of the Supreme Court, and all other officers of the United States, whose appointments are not herein otherwise provided for, and which shall be established by law: but Congress may by law vest the appointment of such inferior officers, as they think proper, in the President alone, in the courts of law, or in the heads of departments.

The President shall have power to fill up all vacancies that may happen during the recess of the Senate, by granting commissions which shall expire at the end of their next session.

Section 3   He shall from time to time give to the Congress information of the state of the Union, and recommend to their consideration such measures as he shall judge necessary and expedient; he may, on extraordinary occasions, convene both houses, or either of them, and in case of disagreement between them, with respect to the time of adjournment, he may adjourn them to such time as he shall think proper; he shall receive ambassadors and other public ministers; he shall take care that the laws be faithfully executed, and shall commission all the officers of the United States.

Section 4   The President, Vice-President and all civil officers of the United States shall be removed from office on impeachment for, and on conviction of, treason, bribery, or other high crimes and misdemeanors.

Article III

Section 1   The judicial power of the United States shall be vested in one Supreme Court, and in such inferior courts as the Congress may from time to time ordain and establish. The judges, both of the Supreme and inferior courts, shall hold their offices during good behavior, and shall, at stated times, receive for their services a compensation which shall not be diminished during their continuance in office.

Section 2   The judicial power shall extend to all cases, in law and equity, arising under this Constitution, the laws of the United States, and treaties made, or which shall be made, under their authority;—to all cases affecting ambassadors, other public ministers and consuls;—to all cases of admiralty and maritime jurisdiction;—to controversies to which the United States shall be a party;—to controversies between two or more States;—*between a State and citizens of another State;*—between citizens of different States;—between citizens of the same State claiming lands under grants of different States, and between a State, or the citizens thereof, and foreign states, citizens or subjects.

In all cases affecting ambassadors, other public ministers and consuls, and those in which a State shall be party, the Supreme Court shall have original jurisdiction. In all the other cases before mentioned, the Supreme Court shall have appellate jurisdiction, both as to law and fact, with such exceptions, and under such regulations, as the Congress shall make.

The trial of all crimes, except in cases of impeachment, shall be by jury; and such trial shall be held in the

State where said crimes shall have been committed; but when not committed within any State, the trial shall be at such place or places as the Congress may by law have directed.

Section 3 Treason against the United States shall consist only in levying war against them, or in adhering to their enemies, giving them aid and comfort. No person shall be convicted of treason unless on the testimony of two witnesses to the same overt act, or on confession in open court.

The Congress shall have power to declare the punishment of treason, but no attainder of treason shall work corruption of blood, or forfeiture except during the life of the person attainted.

Article IV

Section 1 Full faith and credit shall be given in each State to the public acts, records, and judicial proceedings of every other State. And the Congress may by general laws prescribe the manner in which such acts, records, and proceedings shall be proved, and the effect thereof.

Section 2 The citizens of each State shall be entitled to all privileges and immunities of citizens in the several States.

A person charged in any State with treason, felony, or other crime, who shall flee from justice, and be found in another State, shall on demand of the executive authority of the State from which he fled, be delivered up, to be removed to the State having jurisdiction of the crime.

No person held to service or labor in one State, under the laws thereof, escaping into another, shall, in consequence of any law or regulation therein, be discharged from such service or labor, but shall be delivered up on claim of the party to whom such service or labor may be due.

Section 3 New States may be admitted by the Congress into this Union; but no new State shall be formed or erected within the jurisdiction of any other State; nor any State be formed by the junction of two or more States, or parts of States, without the consent of the legislatures of the States concerned as well as of the Congress.

The Congress shall have power to dispose of and make all needful rules and regulations respecting the territory or other property belonging to the United States; and nothing in this Constitution shall be so construed as to prejudice any claims of the United States, or of any particular State.

Section 4 The United States shall guarantee to every State in this Union a republican form of government, and shall protect each of them against invasion; and on application of the legislature, or of the executive (when the legislature cannot be convened), against domestic violence.

Article V

The Congress, whenever two-thirds of both houses shall deem it necessary, shall propose amendments to this Constitution, or, on the application of the legislatures of two-thirds of the several States, shall call a convention for proposing amendments, which, in either case, shall be valid to all intents and purposes, as part of this Constitution, when ratified by the legislatures of three-fourths of the several States, or by conventions in three-fourths thereof, as the one or the other mode of ratification may be proposed by the Congress; provided *that no amendments which may be made prior to the year one thousand eight hundred and eight shall in any manner affect the first and fourth clauses in the ninth section of the first article;* and that no State, without its consent, shall be deprived of its equal suffrage in the Senate.

Article VI

All debts contracted and engagements entered into, before the adoption of this Constitution, shall be as valid against the United States under this Constitution, as under the Confederation.

This Constitution, and the laws of the United States which shall be made in pursuance thereof; and all treaties made, or which shall be made, under the authority of the United States, shall be the supreme law of the land; and the judges in every State shall be bound thereby, anything in the Constitution or laws of any State to the contrary notwithstanding.

The Senators and Representatives before mentioned, and the members of the several State legislatures, and all executive and judicial officers, both of the United States and of the several States, shall be bound by oath or affirmation to support this Constitution; but no religious test shall ever be required as a qualification to any office or public trust under the United States.

Article VII

The ratification of the conventions of nine States shall be sufficient for the establishment of this Constitution between the States so ratifying the same.

Done in Convention by the unanimous consent of the States present, the seventeenth day of September in the year of our Lord one thousand seven hundred and eighty-seven and of the Independence of the United States of America the twelfth. In witness whereof we have hereunto subscribed our names.

GEORGE WASHINGTON
and thirty-seven others

Amendments to the Constitution[*]

Amendment I

Congress shall make no law respecting an establishment of religion, or prohibiting the free exercise thereof; or abridging the freedom of speech, or of the press; or the right of the people peaceably to assemble, and to petition the government for a redress of grievances.

Amendment II

A well-regulated militia being necessary to the security of a free State, the right of the people to keep and bear arms shall not be infringed.

Amendment III

No soldier shall, in time of peace, be quartered in any house without the consent of the owner, nor in time of war, but in a manner to be prescribed by law.

Amendment IV

The right of the people to be secure in their persons, houses, papers, and effects, against unreasonable searches and seizures, shall not be violated, and no warrants shall issue but upon probable cause, supported by oath or affirmation, and particularly describing the place to be searched, and the persons or things to be seized.

Amendment V

No person shall be held to answer for a capital, or otherwise infamous crime, unless on a presentment or indictment of a grand jury, except in cases arising in the land or naval forces, or in the militia, when in actual service in time of war or public danger; nor shall any person be subject for the same offense to be twice put in jeopardy of life or limb; nor shall be compelled in any criminal case to be a witness against himself, nor be deprived of life, liberty, or property, without due process of law; nor shall private property be taken for public use without just compensation.

Amendment VI

In all criminal prosecutions, the accused shall enjoy the right to a speedy and public trial, by an impartial jury of the State and district wherein the crime shall have been committed, which district shall have been previously ascertained by law, and to be informed of the nature and cause of the accusation; to be confronted with the witnesses against him; to have compulsory process for obtaining witnesses in his favor, and to have the assistance of counsel for his defense.

[*] The first ten Amendments (the Bill of Rights) were adopted in 1791.

Amendment VII

In suits at common law, where the value in controversy shall exceed twenty dollars, the right of trial by jury shall be preserved, and no fact tried by a jury shall be otherwise reexamined in any court of the United States, than according to the rules of the common law.

Amendment VIII

Excessive bail shall not be required, nor excessive fines imposed, nor cruel and unusual punishments inflicted.

Amendment IX

The enumeration in the Constitution, of certain rights, shall not be construed to deny or disparage others retained by the people.

Amendment X

The powers not delegated to the United States by the Constitution, nor prohibited by it to the States, are reserved to the States respectively, or to the people.

Amendment XI
[Adopted 1798]

The judicial power of the United States shall not be construed to extend to any suit in law or equity, commenced or prosecuted against one of the United States by citizens of another State, or by citizens or subjects of any foreign state.

Amendment XII
[Adopted 1804]

The electors shall meet in their respective States, and vote by ballot for President and Vice-President, one of whom, at least, shall not be an inhabitant of the same State with themselves; they shall name in their ballots the person voted for as President, and in distinct ballots the person voted for as Vice-President, and they shall make distinct lists of all persons voted for as President, and of all persons voted for as Vice-President, and of the number of votes for each, which lists they shall sign and certify, and transmit sealed to the seat of government of the United States, directed to the President of the Senate;—the President of the Senate shall, in the presence of the Senate and House of Representatives, open all the certificates and the votes shall then be counted;—the person having the greatest number of votes for President shall be the President, if such number be a majority of the whole number of electors appointed; and if no person have such majority, then from the persons having the highest numbers not exceeding three on the list of those voted for as President, the House of Representatives shall choose immediately, by ballot, the President. But in choosing the President, the votes shall be taken by States, the representation from each State having one vote; a quorum for this purpose shall consist of a member or members from two-thirds of the States, and a majority of all the States shall be necessary to a choice. And if the House of Representatives shall not choose a President whenever the right of choice shall devolve upon them, before the fourth day of March next following, then the Vice-President shall act as President, as in the case of the death or other constitutional disability of the President.

The person having the greatest number of votes as Vice-President shall be the Vice-President, if such number be a majority of the whole number of electors appointed; and if no person have a majority, then from the two highest numbers on the list the Senate shall choose the Vice-President; a quorum for the purpose shall consist of two-thirds of the whole number of Senators, and a majority of the whole number shall be necessary to a choice. But no person constitutionally ineligible to the office of President shall be eligible to that of Vice-President of the United States.

Amendment XIII

[Adopted 1865]

Section 1 Neither slavery nor involuntary servitude, except as a punishment for crime whereof the party shall have been duly convicted, shall exist within the United States, or any place subject to their jurisdiction.

Section 2 Congress shall have power to enforce this article by appropriate legislation.

Amendment XIV

[Adopted 1868]

Section 1 All persons born or naturalized in the United States, and subject to the jurisdiction thereof, are citizens of the United States and of the State wherein they reside. No State shall make or enforce any law which shall abridge the privileges or immunities of citizens of the United States; nor shall any State deprive any person of life, liberty, or property, without due process of law; nor deny to any person within its jurisdiction the equal protection of the laws.

Section 2 Representatives shall be apportioned among the several States according to their respective numbers, counting the whole number of persons in each State, excluding Indians not taxed. But when the right to vote at any election for the choice of Electors for President and Vice-President of the United States, Representatives in Congress, the executive and judicial officers of a State, or the members of the legislature thereof, is denied to any of the male inhabitants of such State, being twenty-one years of age and citizens of the United States, or in any way abridged, except for participation in rebellion, or other crime, the basis of representation therein shall be reduced in the proportion which the number of such male citizens shall bear to the whole number of male citizens twenty-one years of age in such State.

Section 3 No person shall be a Senator or Representative in Congress, or Elector of President and Vice-President, or hold any office, civil or military, under the United States, or under any State, who, having previously taken an oath, as a member of Congress, or as an officer of the United States, or as a member of any State legislature, or as an executive or judicial officer of any State, to support the Constitution of the United States, shall have engaged in insurrection or rebellion against the same, or given aid or comfort to the enemies thereof. Congress may, by a vote of two-thirds of each house, remove such disability.

Section 4 The validity of the public debt of the United States, authorized by law, including debts incurred for payment of pensions and bounties for services in suppressing insurrection or rebellion, shall not be questioned. But neither the United States nor any State shall assume or pay any debt or obligation incurred in aid of insurrection or rebellion against the United States, or any claim for the loss or emancipation of any slave; but all such debts, obligations, and claims shall be held illegal and void.

Section 5 The Congress shall have power to enforce, by appropriate legislation, the provisions of this article.

Amendment XV

[Adopted 1870]

Section 1 The right of citizens of the United States to vote shall not be denied or abridged by the United States or by any State on account of race, color, or previous condition of servitude.

Section 2 The Congress shall have power to enforce this article by appropriate legislation.

Amendment XVI

[Adopted 1913]

The Congress shall have power to lay and collect taxes on incomes, from whatever source derived, without apportionment among the several States, and without regard to any census or enumeration.

Amendment XVII

[Adopted 1913]

Section 1 The Senate of the United States shall be composed of two Senators from each State, elected by the people thereof, for six years; and each Senator shall have one vote. The electors in each State shall have the qualifications requisite for electors of [voters for] the most numerous branch of the State legislatures.

Section 2 When vacancies happen in the representation of any State in the Senate, the executive authority of such State shall issue writs of election to fill such vacancies: Provided, that the Legislature of any State may empower the executive thereof to make temporary appointments until the people fill the vacancies by election as the Legislature may direct.

Section 3 This amendment shall not be so construed as to affect the election or term of any Senator chosen before it becomes valid as part of the Constitution.

Amendment XVIII
[Adopted 1919; Repealed 1933]

Section 1 After one year from the ratification of this article the manufacture, sale, or transportation of intoxicating liquors within, the importation thereof into, or the exportation thereof from the United States and all territory subject to the jurisdiction thereof, for beverage purposes, is hereby prohibited.

Section 2 The Congress and the several States shall have concurrent power to enforce this article by appropriate legislation.

Section 3 This article shall be inoperative unless it shall have been ratified as an amendment to the Constitution by the legislatures of the several States, as provided by the Constitution, within seven years from the date of the submission thereof to the States by the Congress.

Amendment XIX
[Adopted 1920]

Section 1 The right of citizens of the United States to vote shall not be denied or abridged by the United States or by any State on account of sex.

Section 2 The Congress shall have power to enforce this article by appropriate legislation.

Amendment XX
[Adopted 1933]

Section 1 The terms of the President and Vice-President shall end at noon on the 20th day of January, and the terms of Senators and Representatives at noon on the 3rd day of January, of the years in which such terms would have ended if this article had not been ratified; and the terms of their successors shall then begin.

Section 2 The Congress shall assemble at least once in every year, and such meeting shall begin at noon on the 3d day of January, unless they shall by law appoint a different day.

Section 3 If, at the time fixed for the beginning of the term of the President, the President-elect shall have died, the Vice-President-elect shall become President. If

a President shall not have been chosen before the time fixed for the beginning of his term, or if the President-elect shall have failed to qualify, then the Vice-President-elect shall act as President until a President shall have qualified; and the Congress may by law provide for the case wherein neither a President-elect nor a Vice-President-elect shall have qualified, declaring who shall then act as President, or the manner in which one who is to act shall be selected, and such persons shall act accordingly until a President or Vice-President shall have qualified.

Section 4 The Congress may by law provide for the case of the death of any of the persons from whom the House of Representatives may choose a President whenever the right of choice shall have devolved upon them, and for the case of the death of any of the persons from whom the Senate may choose a Vice-President whenever the right of choice shall have devolved upon them.

Section 5 Sections 1 and 2 shall take effect on the 15th day of October following the ratification of this article.

Section 6 This article shall be inoperative unless it shall have been ratified as an amendment to the Constitution by the Legislatures of three-fourths of the several States within seven years from the date of its submission.

Amendment XXI
[Adopted 1933]

Section 1 The eighteenth article of amendment to the Constitution of the United States is hereby repealed.

Section 2 The transportation or importation into any State, Territory, or Possession of the United States for delivery or use therein of intoxicating liquors, in violation of the laws thereof, is hereby prohibited.

Section 3 This article shall be inoperative unless it shall have been ratified as an amendment to the Constitution by conventions in the several States, as provided in the Constitution, within seven years from the date of submission thereof to the States by the Congress.

Amendment XXII
[Adopted 1951]

Section 1 No person shall be elected to the office of President more than twice, and no person who has held the office of President, or acted as President, for more than two years of a term to which some other person was elected President shall be elected to the office of President more than once. But this article shall not apply to any person holding the office of President when this article was proposed by the Congress, and shall not prevent any person who may be holding the office of President, or acting as President, during the term within which this article becomes operative from holding the office of President or acting as President during the remainder of such term.

Section 2 This article shall be inoperative unless it shall have been ratified as an amendment to the Constitution by the legislatures of three-fourths of the several States within seven years from the date of its submission to the States by the Congress.

Amendment XXIII

[Adopted 1961]

Section 1 The District constituting the seat of Government of the United States shall appoint in such manner as the Congress may direct:

A number of electors of President and Vice-President equal to the whole number of Senators and Representatives in Congress to which the District would be entitled if it were a State, but in no event more than the least populous State; they shall be in addition to those appointed by the States, but they shall be considered for the purposes of the election of President and Vice-President, to be electors appointed by a State; and they shall meet in the District and perform such duties as provided by the twelfth article of amendment.

Section 2 The Congress shall have the power to enforce this article by appropriate legislation.

Amendment XXIV

[Adopted 1964]

Section 1 The right of citizens of the United States to vote in any primary or other election for President or Vice-President, for electors for President or Vice-President, or for Senator or Representative in Congress, shall not be denied or abridged by the United States or any State by reason of failure to pay any poll tax or other tax.

Section 2 The Congress shall have the power to enforce this article by appropriate legislation.

Amendment XXV

[Adopted 1967]

Section 1 In case of the removal of the President from office or of his death or resignation, the Vice-President shall become President.

Section 2 Whenever there is a vacancy in the office of the Vice-President, the President shall nominate a Vice-President who shall take office upon confirmation by a majority vote of both Houses of Congress.

Section 3 Whenever the President transmits to the President pro tempore of the Senate and the Speaker of the House of Representatives his written declaration that he is unable to discharge the powers and duties of his office, and until he transmits to them a written declaration to the contrary, such powers and duties shall be discharged by the Vice-President as Acting President.

Section 4 Whenever the Vice-President and a majority of either the principal officers of the executive departments or of such other body as Congress may by law provide, transmit to the President pro tempore of the Senate and the Speaker of the House of Representatives their written declaration that the President is unable to discharge the powers and duties of his office, the Vice-President shall immediately assume the powers and duties of the office as Acting President.

Thereafter, when the President transmits to the President pro tempore of the Senate and the Speaker of the House of Representatives his written declaration that no inability exists, he shall resume the powers and duties of his office unless the Vice-President and a majority of either the principal officers of the executive department[s] or of such other body as Congress may by law provide, transmit within four days to the President pro tempore of the Senate and the Speaker of the House of Representatives their written declaration that the President is unable to discharge the powers and duties of his office. Thereupon Congress shall decide the issue, assembling within forty-eight hours for that purpose if not in session. If the Congress, within twenty-one days after receipt of the latter written declaration, or, if Congress is not in session, within twenty-one days after Congress is required to assemble, determines by two-thirds vote of both Houses that the President is unable to discharge the powers and duties of his office, the Vice-President shall continue to discharge the same as Acting President; otherwise, the President shall resume the powers and duties of his office.

Amendment XXVI

[Adopted 1971]

Section 1 The right of citizens of the United States, who are eighteen years of age or older, to vote shall not be denied or abridged by the United States or by any State on account of age.

Section 2 The Congress shall have power to enforce this article by appropriate legislation.

Amendment XXVII

[Adopted 1992]

No law, varying the compensation for the services of the Senators and Representatives, shall take effect, until an election of Representatives shall have intervened.

Presidential Elections

Year	Number of States	Candidates	Parties	Popular Vote	% of Popular Vote	Electoral Vote	% Voter Participation[a]
1789	11	**George Washington**	No party			69	
		John Adams	designations			34	
		Other candidates				35	
1792	15	**George Washington**	No party			132	
		John Adams	designations			77	
		George Clinton				50	
		Other candidates				5	
1796	16	**John Adams**	Federalist			71	
		Thomas Jefferson	Democratic-Republican			68	
		Thomas Pinckney	Federalist			59	
		Aaron Burr	Democratic-Republican			30	
		Other candidates				48	
1800	16	**Thomas Jefferson**	Democratic-Republican			73	
		Aaron Burr	Democratic-Republican			73	
		John Adams	Federalist			65	
		Charles C. Pinckney	Federalist			64	
		John Jay	Federalist			1	
1804	17	**Thomas Jefferson**	Democratic-Republican			162	
		Charles C. Pinckney	Federalist			14	
1808	17	**James Madison**	Democratic-Republican			122	
		Charles C. Pinckney	Federalist			47	
		George Clinton	Democratic-Republican			6	
1812	18	**James Madison**	Democratic-Republican			128	
		DeWitt Clinton	Federalist			89	
1816	19	**James Monroe**	Democratic-Republican			183	
		Rufus King	Federalist			34	
1820	24	**James Monroe**	Democratic-Republican			231	
		John Quincy Adams	Independent-Republican			1	
1824	24	**John Quincy Adams**	Democratic-Republican	108,740	30.5	84	26.9

Year	Number of States	Candidates	Parties	Popular Vote	% of Popular Vote	Elec-toral Vote	% Voter Partici-pation[a]
		Andrew Jackson	Democratic-Republican	153,544	43.1	99	
		Henry Clay	Democratic-Republican	47,136	13.2	37	
		William H. Crawford	Democratic-Republican	46,618	13.1	41	
1828	24	**Andrew Jackson**	Democratic	647,286	56.0	178	57.6
		John Quincy Adams	National Republican	508,064	44.0	83	
1832	24	**Andrew Jackson**	Democratic	688,242	54.5	219	55.4
		Henry Clay	National Republican	473,462	37.5	49	
		William Wirt	Anti-Masonic	101,051	8.0	7	
		John Floyd	Democratic			11	
1836	26	**Martin Van Buren**	Democratic	765,483	50.9	170	57.8
		William H. Harrison	Whig			73	
		Hugh L. White	Whig			26	
		Daniel Webster	Whig	739,795	49.1	14	
		W. P. Mangum	Whig			11	
1840	26	**William H. Harrison**	Whig	1,274,624	53.1	234	80.2
		Martin Van Buren	Democratic	1,127,781	46.9	60	
1844	26	**James K. Polk**	Democratic	1,338,464	49.6	170	78.9
		Henry Clay	Whig	1,300,097	48.1	105	
		James G. Birney	Liberty	62,300	2.3		
1848	30	**Zachary Taylor**	Whig	1,360,967	47.4	163	72.7
		Lewis Cass	Democratic	1,222,342	42.5	127	
		Martin Van Buren	Free-Soil	291,263	10.1		
1852	31	**Franklin Pierce**	Democratic	1,601,117	50.9	254	69.6
		Winfield Scott	Whig	1,385,453	44.1	42	
		John P. Hale	Free-Soil	155,825	5.0		
1856	31	**James Buchanan**	Democratic	1,832,955	45.3	174	78.9
		John C. Frémont	Republican	1,339,932	33.1	114	
		Millard Fillmore	American	871,731	21.6	8	
1860	33	**Abraham Lincoln**	Republican	1,865,593	39.8	180	81.2
		Stephen A. Douglas	Democratic	1,382,713	29.5	12	
		John C. Breckinridge	Democratic	848,356	18.1	72	
		John Bell	Constitutional Union	592,906	12.6	39	
1864	36	**Abraham Lincoln**	Republican	2,206,938	55.0	212	73.8
		George B. McClellan	Democratic	1,803,787	45.0	21	
1868	37	**Ulysses S. Grant**	Republican	3,013,421	52.7	214	78.1
		Horatio Seymour	Democratic	2,706,829	47.3	80	
1872	37	**Ulysses S. Grant**	Republican	3,596,745	55.6	286 [b]	71.3
		Horace Greeley	Democratic	2,843,446	43.9		
1876	38	**Rutherford B. Hayes**	Republican	4,036,572	48.0	185	81.8
		Samuel J. Tilden	Democratic	4,284,020	51.0	184	

Year	Number of States	Candidates	Parties	Popular Vote	% of Popular Vote	Electoral Vote	% Voter Participation[a]
1880	38	**James A. Garfield**	Republican	4,453,295	48.5	214	79.4
		Winfield S. Hancock	Democratic	4,414,082	48.1	155	
		James B. Weaver	Greenback-Labor	308,578	3.4		
1884	38	**Grover Cleveland**	Democratic	4,879,507	48.5	219	77.5
		James G. Blaine	Republican	4,850,293	48.2	182	
		Benjamin F. Butler	Greenback-Labor	175,370	1.8		
		John P. St. John	Prohibition	150,369	1.5		
1888	38	**Benjamin Harrison**	Republican	5,477,129	47.9	233	79.3
		Grover Cleveland	Democratic	5,537,857	48.6	168	
		Clinton B. Fisk	Prohibition	249,506	2.2		
		Anson J. Streeter	Union Labor	146,935	1.3		
1892	44	**Grover Cleveland**	Democratic	5,555,426	46.1	277	74.7
		Benjamin Harrison	Republican	5,182,690	43.0	145	
		James B. Weaver	People's	1,029,846	8.5	22	
		John Bidwell	Prohibition	264,133	2.2		
1896	45	**William McKinley**	Republican	7,102,246	51.1	271	79.3
		William J. Bryan	Democratic	6,492,559	47.7	176	
1900	45	**William McKinley**	Republican	7,218,491	51.7	292	73.2
		William J. Bryan	Democratic; Populist	6,356,734	45.5	155	
		John C. Wooley	Prohibition	208,914	1.5		
1904	45	**Theodore Roosevelt**	Republican	7,628,461	57.4	336	65.2
		Alton B. Parker	Democratic	5,084,223	37.6	140	
		Eugene V. Debs	Socialist	402,283	3.0		
		Silas C. Swallow	Prohibition	258,536	1.9		
1908	46	**William H. Taft**	Republican	7,675,320	51.6	321	65.4
		William J. Bryan	Democratic	6,412,294	43.1	162	
		Eugene V. Debs	Socialist	420,793	2.8		
		Eugene W. Chafin	Prohibition	253,840	1.7		
1912	48	**Woodrow Wilson**	Democratic	6,296,547	41.9	435	58.8
		Theodore Roosevelt	Progressive	4,118,571	27.4	88	
		William H. Taft	Republican	3,486,720	23.2	8	
		Eugene V. Debs	Socialist	900,672	6.0		
		Eugene W. Chafin	Prohibition	206,275	1.4		
1916	48	**Woodrow Wilson**	Democratic	9,127,695	49.4	277	61.6
		Charles E. Hughes	Republican	8,533,507	46.2	254	
		A. L. Benson	Socialist	585,113	3.2		
		J. Frank Hanly	Prohibition	220,506	1.2		
1920	48	**Warren G. Harding**	Republican	16,143,407	60.4	404	49.2
		James M. Cox	Democratic	9,130,328	34.2	127	
		Eugene V. Debs	Socialist	919,799	3.4		
		P. P. Christensen	Farmer-Labor	265,411	1.0		
1924	48	**Calvin Coolidge**	Republican	15,718,211	54.0	382	48.9
		John W. Davis	Democratic	8,385,283	28.8	136	

Year	Number of States	Candidates	Parties	Popular Vote	% of Popular Vote	Electoral Vote	% Voter Participation[a]
		Robert M. La Follette	Progressive	4,831,289	16.6	13	
1928	48	**Herbert C. Hoover**	Republican	21,391,993	58.2	444	56.9
		Alfred E. Smith	Democratic	15,016,169	40.9	87	
1932	48	**Franklin D. Roosevelt**	Democratic	22,809,638	57.4	472	56.9
		Herbert C. Hoover	Republican	15,758,901	39.7	59	
		Norman Thomas	Socialist	881,951	2.2		
1936	48	**Franklin D. Roosevelt**	Democratic	27,752,869	60.8	523	61.0
		Alfred M. Landon	Republican	16,674,665	36.5	8	
		William Lemke	Union	882,479	1.9		
1940	48	**Franklin D. Roosevelt**	Democratic	27,307,819	54.8	449	62.5
		Wendell L. Wilkie	Republican	22,321,018	44.8	82	
1944	48	**Franklin D. Roosevelt**	Democratic	25,606,585	53.5	432	55.9
		Thomas E. Dewey	Republican	22,014,745	46.0	99	
1948	48	**Harry S Truman**	Democratic	24,179,345	49.6	303	53.0
		Thomas E. Dewey	Republican	21,991,291	45.1	189	
		J. Strom Thurmond	States' Rights	1,176,125	2.4	39	
		Henry A. Wallace	Progressive	1,157,326	2.4		
1952	48	**Dwight D. Eisenhower**	Republican	33,936,234	55.1	442	63.3
		Adlai E. Stevenson	Democratic	27,314,992	44.4	89	
1956	48	**Dwight D. Eisenhower**	Republican	35,590,472	57.6	457	60.6
		Adlai E. Stevenson	Democratic	26,022,752	42.1	73	
1960	50	**John F. Kennedy**	Democratic	34,226,731	49.7	303	62.8
		Richard M. Nixon	Republican	34,108,157	49.5	219	
1964	50	**Lyndon B. Johnson**	Democratic	43,129,566	61.1	486	61.7
		Barry M. Goldwater	Republican	27,178,188	38.5	52	
1968	50	**Richard M. Nixon**	Republican	31,785,480	43.4	301	60.6
		Hubert H. Humphrey	Democratic	31,275,166	42.7	191	
		George C. Wallace	American Independent	9,906,473	13.5	46	
1972	50	**Richard M. Nixon**	Republican	47,169,911	60.7	520	55.2
		George S. McGovern	Democratic	29,170,383	37.5	17	
		John G. Schmitz	American	1,099,482	1.4		
1976	50	**Jimmy Carter**	Democratic	40,830,763	50.1	297	53.5
		Gerald R. Ford	Republican	39,147,793	48.0	240	
1980	50	**Ronald Reagan**	Republican	43,899,248	50.8	489	52.6
		Jimmy Carter	Democratic	35,481,432	41.0	49	
		John B. Anderson	Independent	5,719,437	6.6	0	
		Ed Clark	Libertarian	920,859	1.1	0	
1984	50	**Ronald Reagan**	Republican	54,455,075	58.8	525	53.1
		Walter Mondale	Democratic	37,577,185	40.6	13	
1988	50	**George Bush**	Republican	48,901,046	53.4	426	50.2
		Michael Dukakis	Democratic	41,809,030	45.6	111[c]	
1992	50	**Bill Clinton**	Democratic	44,908,233	43.0	370	55.0
		George Bush	Republican	39,102,282	37.4	168	
		Ross Perot	Independent	19,741,048	18.9	0	

Year	Number of States	Candidates	Parties	Popular Vote	% of Popular Vote	Electoral Vote	% Voter Participation[a]
1996	50	**Bill Clinton**	Democratic	47,401,054	49.2	379	49.0
		Robert Dole	Republican	39,197,350	40.7	159	
		Ross Perot	Independent	8,085,285	8.4	0	
		Ralph Nader	Green	684,871	0.7	0	
2000	50	**George W. Bush**	Republican	50,456,169	47.88	271	50.7
		Albert Gore, Jr.	Democratic	50,996,116	48.39	267	
		Ralph Nader	Green	2,783,728	2.72	0	
2004	50	George W. Bush	Republican	62,040,610	51	286	60.7
		John F. Kerry	Democratic	59,028,109	48	252	
		Ralph Nader	Independent	463,653	1	0	

Candidates receiving less than 1 percent of the popular vote have been omitted. Thus the percentage of popular vote given for any election year may not total 100 percent.

Before the passage of the Twelfth Amendment in 1804, the Electoral College voted for two presidential candidates; the runner-up became vice president.

Before 1824, most presidential electors were chosen by state legislatures, not by popular vote.

[a]Percent of voting-age population casting ballots (eligible voters).

[b]Greeley died shortly after the election; the electors supporting him then divided their votes among minor candidates.

[c]One elector from West Virginia cast her Electoral College presidential ballot for Lloyd Bentsen, the Democratic Party's vice-presidential candidate.

✔ Index

Abenaki Indians, 46

Abolitionist: Douglass and, 367 and illus., 368; Dred Scott decision and, 382; Harpers Ferry and, 384; movement, 369, 437; Republican Party and, **437**; riots and, 413; Slave Power and, 359; Slave Power conspiracy and, 376; slavery and, **345**

Absentee planters, 88

Absolute monarch, 25

Acadia, 108, 111, 112

Acculturation, 231, 289

Ácoma pueblo, 43

Acquired immunity, 22

Activists and activism: Great Awakening and, 102

Adams, Abigail, 142, 177, 186, 211

Adams, Charles Francis, 404, 411

Adams, John: American Revolution and, 166; Articles of Confederation and, 180; *Common Sense* and, 140; as Congregationalist, 228; Declaration of Independence and, 141; Declaration of Rights and Grievances, 135; drafting the declaration and, 140; election of 1800 and, 216 and map; factions and, 198; France and, 212, 215; George Logan and, 210; Great Britain and, 185; Hamilton and, 211, 215; Jonathan Sewall and, 129; Mercy Otis Warren and, 177; military occupation and, 130; Paris peace talks and, 165; partisan politics and, 212 and illus.; Pinckney and, 211; as representative, 188; Republican press and, 215; resumption of trade and, 140; split administration of, 212; Sugar Act and, 123; as vice president, 211; as vice-president, 194; voting rights and, 179; Washington's cabinet and, 212

Adams, John Quincy: Calhoun and, 267; characterizations of, 284, 285; 1824 election, 280 and map; election of 1828, 284 (illus.); Florida and, 275; national expansion and, 356; policies of, 281; presidential election of 1824 and, 279; as secretary of state, 274; Treaty of Indian Springs and, 289

Adams, Samuel: American Revolution and, 143; Articles of Confederation and, 180; boycotts and, 129; 134, 135 and illus.; Constitution Convention and, 188;

inciter of hatred, 130; Mery Otis Warren and, 205; new Constitution and, 191; as rebellious leader, 136; redcoats and, 137; Sons of Liberty, **124**; Townshend Acts and, 128

Adams-Onís Treaty, 275

Ad hoc, 105

Adoration of the Magi (Master of Viseu), 21

The Adulateur (Mercy Otis Warren), 177

Advertisements and advertising: broadside as, 124

Africa: Columbian Exchange and, 24; culture of Islam and, 18; diseases and, 23; France and trade in, 112; French Louisiana and, 51; imperial wars and, 109; increase of slaves from, 66; Islam and, 4, 5; kinships systems in, 15, 16, 17; Sahara Desert and, 4, 15, 16 (map), 17; slave trade, 93, 93 and illus., 94 (illus.); slave trade and, 24 and illus.; trade with, 23

African Americans: abolition and equal rights of, 437; as abolitionists, 369; 1877 and rights of, 462; Benjamin Banneker, 230; black codes and, 447; Civil Rights Act of 1866 and, 449; civil rights and, 141; during Civil War, 416, 417 and illus.; Columbia, South Carolina and, 426; culture of, 336; discrimination by Union Army, 416, 417; draft riots and, 413; Dred Scott and, 383; education and, 444; election of 1872 and, 459 (map); equal rights of, 444; Fourteenth Amendment and, 452, 453; as freed people, 443, 444; free in the south, 304; impact of the Revolution on, 171, 172; integrated education and, 456, 457; Jackson and, 254; Lincoln's solution and, 383; political slavery and, 142; (1880) population of, 454 and map; Radical Republicans and, 452; religion and, 443, 444; Republicans and terrorists, 460; restrictions on free, 348; ridicule of, 171 (illus.); "the Negro's hour" and, 453; Underground Railroad and, 373; 1866 violent riots and, 448; voting and, 282

African Methodist Episcopal Church, 230, 231, 443

African Methodist Episcopal Zion Church, 443

A Glance at New York in 1848 (Benjamin Baker), 336

Agrarian capitalism, 375

Agriculture: of Africans, 15; of American

Indians, 8, 13, 48; commercial society and, 197; exports to England, 89, 90; labor force of southern, 92; of Mississippi Valley, 320; northern seaports and, 132 (map); patroonships and, 40; revolution, 8; rice, 79; sharecropping and, 446; Squanto and colonists, 68; tobacco and, 63

Alabama: secession of, 388

Alamo, 355

Albany, New York, 39, 109

Albany Plan of Union, 109

Albemarle Sound, 79

Albright, Madeleine, 170

Alcohol and alcohol industry: Greeley and, 459; perception of, 343; prohibition of, 371; as threat to morality, 370

Alcott, Bronson, 315

Alexander Hamilton (Charles Wilson Peale), 183 (illus.)

Algonquin Indians, 20, 46

Algonquin language, 48, 62

Alien and Sedition Acts, 214, 217, 218

Allegory, 334

Allen, Ethan, 151, 156

Allen, Richard, 230, 231

Almshouse, 167

Amendments: to Articles of Confederation, 181; Bill of Rights as, 196, 197; reversing racism, 383; Tenth, 214; unrepealable, 388. *See also* Constitution, U.S.

Amenities, 219

America: allies of, 150; differences betweens England and, 118; geology of, 5, 6; imperial wars and, 110; pre-Columbian, 13; recognition of, 156; war effort advantages of, 150

American and Foreign Anti-Slavery Society, 369

American Anti-Slavery Society, 344, 345, 369

American Bible Society, 314, 326, 363

American Board of Commissioners for Foreign Missions, 314, 353

American Colonization Society, 344

"American Eden," 36

American Indians: alliance choices by, 118; alliance system of, 46, 47; American Revolution and the, 142; Battle of Horseshoe Bend and, 254; California and, 321, 322; Caribbean slavery and, 79; Cherokees' bicameral government, 289; class system of, 45; colonies and colonization by, 34; colonists and